LITERATURE & THE LEARNER

Frances S. Goforth

University of South Florida

Wadsworth Publishing Company
I(T)P® An International Thomson Publishing Company

Belmont, CA • Albany, NY • Bonn • Boston • Cincinnati • Detroit • Johannesburg • London • Madrid
Melbourne • Mexico City • New York • Paris • Singapore • Tokyo • Toronto • Washington

Dedication for

My parents, Nannie and Frank Sprott,
who gave me the confidence to try, the curiosity to learn,
and introduced me to the joy of literature.

My children, Gene, Gary, Steven, and Susan,
who share their zest for living, their honest reactions to books,
and encourage my endeavors.

Their spouses, Tonya, Karen, and Steve,
who share their inquisitive spirits, offer support, and
provide a reading environment in their homes.

My grandchildren, Kelly, Geoffrey, Ashley, Kristen, Lauren,
Steven, Jr., Michael, Christopher, and Matthew,
who by sharing their "Mam-Maw" time
introduce other children to the delight of exploring literature.

My husband, Gene,
who waits patiently, cooks wonderful meals,
and gives affection and assurance at the right time.
It's time to travel again!

Education Editor: *Joan Gill*
Editorial Assistant: *Valerie Morrison*
Project Editor: *Angela Mann*
Marketing Manager: *Jay Hu*
Text Designer: *Maureen McCutcheon*
Cover Designer: *Stephen Rapley*
Print Buyer: *Barbara Britton*

Copy Editor: *Pat Lewis*
Permissions Editor: *Veronica Oliva*
Art Editor: *Roberta Broyer*
Photo Researcher: *Kathy Ringrose*
Illustrators: *John and Judy Waller, Laura Seeley*
Compositor: *Carlisle Communications*
Printer: *World Color Book Services, Taunton*

COPYRIGHT © 1998 by Wadsworth Publishing Company
A Division of International Thomson Publishing Inc.
I(T)P® The ITP logo is a registered trademark under license.

Printed in the United States of America
1 2 3 4 5 6 7 8 9 10

Cover art credits: Illustration at middle left by Floyd Cooper reprinted by permission of Philomel Books from *Coming Home: From the Life of Langston Hughes,* copyright © 1994 by Floyd Cooper. Illustration at middle right by Floyd Cooper reprinted by permission of Philomel Books from *The Girl Who Loved Caterpillars,* adapted by Jean Merrill, illustrations copyright © 1992 by Floyd Cooper. **Cover photo credit:** Tom & Dee Ann McCarthy/The Stock Market. **Inside credits:** See pages 623–624.

For more information, contact Wadsworth Publishing Company, 10 Davis Drive, Belmont, CA 94002, or electronically at http://www.thomson.com/wadsworth.html

Library of Congress Cataloging-in-Publication Data
Goforth, Frances S.
    Literature and the learner/Frances S. Goforth.
        p.   cm.
    Includes bibliographical references and index.
    ISBN 0-314-20413-X
    1. Children's literature—Study and teaching. 2. Children's
literature—History and criticism.
PN1008.8.G64 1997
809'.89282—dc21   97-13263

Contents in Brief

Contents

Part One

LEARNING & LITERATURE: AN INTRODUCTION

Part Two

LITERARY GENRES: FICTION

Part Three

LITERARY GENRES: NONFICTION & OTHER LITERARY TYPES

Chapter 6
Biography & Information Books:
The Knowledge of Society

Chapter 7
Poetry: The Emotions, Thoughts,
Images of a Society

Part Four

LITERATURE IN THE CLASSROOM

Chapter 10
Oral & Visual Presentations of Literature

Chapter 11
Approaches to Literary Study

Chapter 12
Principles for Designing a Literature Curriculum

Preface

This is the diamond age of juvenile literature. Today many talented authors and artists create literature especially for young people. They authentically portray past, present, and future worlds. They do not shield children from the realities of life nor do they sensationalize topics to exploit children's naive perspective of life. Improved publishing techniques allow contemporary artists to experiment with innovative visual creations that were not possible a few years ago.

This is also the diamond age of literary study. Because literature motivates students to learn, educators recognize the importance of using it as a vital instructional component for all discipline areas. As teachers continuously expose learners to literature, boys and girls acquire and apply personal listening, speaking, reading, writing, viewing, and thinking abilities. In contemporary literature young people gain valuable historical, scientific, sociological, and technological information that enhance their cognitive abilities. By encountering familiar experiences in literature, children understand themselves better, recognize their responsibilities to others and their environment, and begin to clarify their future goals. When young people explore diverse traditions, beliefs, and cultures in literature, they gain respect for other people and strive to exist in harmony in this global society.

This book highlights the *literature, intended audience*, and *teaching techniques* educators use to help children develop a lifelong habit of reading literature for pleasurable and for informational purposes—the ultimate goal of literary study. The purpose of the book is to introduce adults to a variety of quality juvenile literature, to help them realize the natural literary preferences of young people, and to guide them to recognize the abundant opportunities available to use literature as an integral part of the entire school day.

The primary goals of *Literature and the Learner* include:

1. Giving the reader a succinct, comprehensive coverage of the distinctive characteristics of the various prose, poetry, and dramatic structures and components of fiction and nonfiction literature;

2. Identifying and emphasizing the literary preferences and general responses to literature of children ages 4 through 16;

3. Providing a variety of instructional approaches and strategies to use when guiding children's literary awareness and strengthening their oral, visual, verbal, cognitive, and social development.

4. Introducing the reader to a variety of quality literary selections and the pleasures derived from reading, listening to, and viewing literature for pleasurable and informational purposes.

ORGANIZATION

To accomplish these goals the book is divided into four parts. Part One introduces the reader to the *learner* and the *literature*. This section highlights major learning and developmental theories, young people's literary preferences, the structures, forms, and elements of quality literature, and effective instructional techniques to present literature to learners. The first chapter gives the reader an overview of the forms and structures of literature and the literary characteristics of the various literary genres. The chapter also introduces book selection sources, book awards, and publishing trends. The last part of the chapter highlights the learner, focusing on the relationship between children's language,

psychological, educational, and reader-response theories, writings, and research findings.

Part Two includes a three-chapter discussion of fictional literature and presents the distinctive characteristics of folk, fantasy, and realistic fiction. Each genre chapter includes the distinctive characteristic of the literary genre and the distinguishing characteristics of the subgenres. Notable authors, artists, and their contributions give the reader an overview of the historical development of literature and the genres. Each genre chapter provides information about the benefits individuals gain from exploring the literature, appropriate selection criteria, and techniques children and adults use to choose literature to view, hear, or read. The instructional strategies give educators ideas about presenting the genre

cognitive and social development, and their literary preferences and interests. Other chapters identify individual titles and additional information about learners, their reactions, and possible responses to literature. Chapter 2 suggests *teaching techniques* successful literature teachers use when presenting literature to young people. The chapter describes a literature-rich environment, the influence of pertinent learning and development theories on literary study, and various verbal and visual responses children produce when reacting and responding to literature. The chapter also describes the *aesthetic* and *efferent* instructional focuses teachers will adopt to present literature. Finally, the chapter proposes an instructional routine, the Literary Transaction Process, to guide the adult's presentation of individual books and literature collections. Throughout the process the learner makes connections to the text, constructs meanings of the text, and often creates responses to the literature. The Literary Transaction Process applies major

in the classroom. The chapters also suggest a variety of visual and verbal responses learners create to represent their reactions and responses to the literature they explore.

Part Three describes nonfiction literature and other literary types. This four-chapter division discusses nonfiction literature (including biographies and information books), poetry, books with pictures, and literature reflecting parallel cultures. The poetry chapter offers poems that represent the various poetic types, forms, and elements. Because books with pictures appear in all

Part Four contains three chapters that offer techniques and strategies for teachers and learners to use when presenting individual literary selections and thematic collections of literature in the classroom. Chapter 10 describes oral, visual, and audiovisual presentations of literature. Chapters 11 and 12 emphasize the value of designing and implementing an organized approach to literary study. Chapter 11 describes three approaches to literary study—the pure literature approach, the literature-based language arts approach, and the using literature across the curriculum approach. Teachers use the three approaches independently or simultaneously throughout the day. This chapter identifies various literary theories that serve as the foundation for literary study. In addition, the chapter identifies the goals, instructional procedures, and effective instructional techniques teachers use to implement each approach. The chapter stresses the importance of developing a support group with the media specialists,

literary genres, the chapter explains the styles, media, and elements artists use to create books with pictures. The chapter that highlights literature reflecting parallel cultures focuses on the traditions, values, and historical and contemporary lifestyles of multi-ethnic, African-American, Asian-American, Hispanic, and Native American groups. Each chapter in this section describes the literary characteristics of the genres and types, identifies notable creators, gives information about learners' literary preferences, and suggests techniques for presenting the literature.

parents, or guardians, and discusses the various evaluative techniques teachers and students use to determine an individual's literary maturity and growth. Finally, this chapter proposes reflection guides for teachers to use to assess the success of a literary approach. Chapter 12 identifies five principles teachers consider when designing a literature curriculum. These principles include the relationship between language and literature, the selection and presentation of quality literature, the organization of literature, various groupings of students, and suggestions for assessing individual learners and the curricular approaches.

The objectives of a juvenile literature course will vary according to the academic area teaching the course. Therefore, each chapter in *Literature and the Learner* is an independent component of the total subject. While related topics are cross-referenced in each chapter, the order of presenting the chapters is flexible. Because Chapter 1 gives the reader an overview of the learner and literature, this is an appropriate introductory chapter. The seven genre chapters can be presented as preferred. Chapter 2 and the three instructional chapters in Part Four are suitable to discuss before, during, or after the genre chapters.

SPECIAL FEATURES

Literature and the Learner presents a comprehensive coverage of the literary genres, discusses literary preferences and responses of learners, identifies and briefly describes outstanding juvenile fiction and nonfiction literature, and suggests instructional strategies and techniques to use when presenting literature to learners. While several literary theories have evolved throughout the years, this book supports reader response literary theories. All reader response theories recognize the reciprocal interchange (transaction) that takes place between the reader and the author's text to construct an interpretation or meaning of the literary selection. Louise Rosenblatt, who developed the transactional theory of the literary work, reminds us that individuals adopt a predominately aesthetic ("lived through") stance and/or an efferent ("take away" information) stance toward the literature they read, listen to, or view. Therefore, a teacher who accepts reader response theories adopts a predominately aesthetic instructional focus or an efferent instructional focus when presenting literature to learners. Teachers who design and implement effective reader response literary studies must have a general knowledge of the various components of literature, be aware of factors influencing a learner's preferences and responses to literature, and recognize compatible instructional practices. Other writers and researchers, notably Alan Purves and Judith Larger, provide valuable information about response-based literary studies. Leading theories of learning and development propose instructional paradigms that support reader response and response-based instructional practices. This book describes the leading literary, psychological, and educational theories, proposes compatible instructional practices, and suggests additional readings to guide the reader's understanding of the components of successful literature approaches and curriculum.

The text contains the following special features to help the reader organize, synthesize, and develop techniques to share literature with learners:

Chapter Reflections This feature, written in question format, gives the reader an overview of the important information discussed in the chapter. The questions also serve as a chapter review.

Did You Know About Boxes
Readers like to know more about the people who create the literature they enjoy exploring. Each genre chapter features two people, or a husband-and-wife team, or a family who create literature for the genre. The informal discussion contains interesting facts about the person's life, information about the way the person creates visual or verbal narrative, and a photo. Appendix G suggests sources to obtain information about creators.

Did You Know About
THE PINKNEY DYNASTY?

*M*eet Jerry, the patriarch, Gloria Jean, the matriarch, Brian, their son, and Andrea, their daughter-in-law—the successful illustrators and authors of the Pinkney dynasty. In 1964 Jerry's talent was recognized when his illustrations for *The Adventures of Spider: West African Folk Tales* were published. Since then, his artwork has received three Caldecott honor awards, many Boston Globe–Horn Book Awards, three Coretta Scott King Awards, and two honor awards. Almost every day, Jerry receives a request to illustrate a new manuscript. How does he decide which manuscripts to illustrate? He says a well-written manuscript must reach him on an emotional level and say something that is important to him. When planning the illustrations for a selected manuscript, he thinks about the story, jots down notes as ideas come, draws a few rough thumbnail sketches, and, in his desire to realistically portray the verbal narrative, does a lot of research on the topic. He builds a set for the characters similar to a scene in the theater. He uses live models (often members of his family) and photographs. When he uses children models, he reads the manuscript to them, and together they act out the story. Then the hard work begins; he must select the right colors for his trademark watercolor and pencil drawings. The settings, clothing, and all of the details must be right for his realistic style. As he sketches the pictures on the paper, the magic begins for him—the pictures in his head seem to come to life. According to Pinkney, many times the "pictures take off on their own." Just look at his pictures in *Mirandy and Brother Wind* or the books he illustrated for Julius Lester, including the *Uncle Remus Series* and especially

Above: Gloria Jean Pinkney; Below: Jerry Pinkney

their acclaimed *John Henry*. The pictures achieve perfect union between verbal and visual narrative. Thanks to Jerry Pinkney, John Henry has become that powerful man who is stronger than a steam hammer!

Two books written by Gloria Jean, his wife and partner of thirty-five years, received his high seal of approval and have become popular picture storybooks—*Back Home* and *The Sunday Outing*. While the elder Pinkneys deserve the honors bestowed on them, so does their son Brian, a drummer and artist who has made a name in the art world! Brian, who began using watercolors like his father, soon discovered that scratchboard and oil paints were his medium. He used them in Robert San Souci's *Sukey and the Mermaid*, which won an ALA Notable Award and was named a Coretta Scott King Honor Book. Brian also used scratchboard and oil to illustrate William Hooks's *The Ballad of Belle Dorcas* and Lynn Joseph's *A Wave in Her Pocket: Stories from Trinidad*. Brian received a Caldecott honor book for *The Faithful Friend* by Robert San Souci (1996). In 1991 Brian married Andrea Davis, a writer and editor. Together they created *Alvin Ailey, Seven Candles for Kwanzaa,* and *Dear Benjamin Banneker.* Andrea also wrote a novel about her childhood, *Hold Fast to Dreams.* It isn't surprising to learn that Jerry and Gloria Jean's other three children, Troy, Scott, and Myles, are also involved in art therapy, design, and photography! Myles's book *Raining Laughter* will be published in 1997.

What is the secret of this artistic dynasty's success? The answer is talent, hard work, love, high standards, and "sharing" of ideas (this last statement was added by Andrea).

Literary Response Modes for Fantasy Literature

Students may want to express further reactions to the genre or narratives by producing *Literary Response Modes (LRMs)*. (See Chapter 2 and Appendix B for additional information about LRMs.) An individual or group production of an LRM promotes students' honest responses to a fantasy narrative. In addition to the LRMs suggested for each such genre, students may choose to produce responses such as the following:

Select a favorite incident and read it to another.

Give a book talk to entice another to read the selection.

Discuss personal reactions to a selection with someone familiar with a narrative.

Write personal reflections evoked by the selection in a journal.

Fold a piece of paper in quarters or sixths and label each section with the following headings: se[t], characters, conflicts, language, questions ab[out] narrative, or other concerns. While reading [of] the selection, students will write one- or two- [re-] actions to each element. Later, use the react[ions for] discussion and comparison.

Teachers can use fantasy literature in vario[us con-]tent areas. Have groups of students create v[isual] products that are authentic to the topic and [may] be found in literature selections. The follo[wing are] possibilities:

Sketch several favorite incidents.

Prepare a game board with questions that [are docu-]mented in content materials.

- **Literary Links** A literary link is a resource or link the teacher uses when presenting a literary selection in the classroom. Model literary links appear in Chapters 2, 3, 8, 11, and in Appendix E. The links use the connect, construct, and create components of the literary transaction process. Each model link is slightly different to show the flexibility of the teacher resource.

- **Literary Response Modes** As students read, listen to, or view literature they reflect, react, and respond to the selection. Frequently, teachers encourage learners to create visual or verbal literary responses modes (LRMs) that reflect these feelings to an individual literary selection or a thematic collection of books. Chapter 2 introduces LRMs. Each chapter suggests LRMs for individual books, collections, or the genre, and Appendix B describes the various verbal and visual LRMs children and teachers can produce.

Abbreviated Literary Link

"ALADDIN AND THE WONDERFUL LAMP" FROM *THE ARABIAN NIGHTS*.

RECOMMENDED FOR FOURTH GRADE AND ABOVE

SUMMARY

A cunning African magician tricked Aladdin, an idle son of a poor tailor, into a cave where Aladdin found many treasures and a wonderful lamp. The sorcerer demanded the lamp, which he knew would make him a powerful person. Aladdin refused to give him the lamp, and the magician sealed up the cave with Aladdin in it. After several days in the cave, Aladdin accidentally realized the value of the lamp and the ring the magician had given him earlier. Aladdin fell deeply in love with a sultan's daughter and managed to marry her with the help of his mother and the genie in the lamp. Aladdin and his wife were very happy living in the palace built by the genie. One day his wife, who did not know the value of the old lamp, traded it to the African sorcerer for a new one. Troubles began when Aladdin's wife and the palace disappeared. With the help of the ring, the genie, and the lamp, clever Aladdin rescued his wife and palace, and they lived happily ever after.

CONNECT

- Create a *word wall* displaying unique language, such as "piteously, Persia, lamenting, a hideous genie, chink, idle dream, scimitar, thither, pious, roc egg, wretch."

- Give a *book talk* such as the following: I went to a flea market over the weekend. I was stopped by a strange-looking man who told me that he wanted to give me a ring and a lamp. He told me that if I rubbed the ring and lamp at the same time, I would discover a secret. He told me that he couldn't give them to just anyone because if they fell into the wrong hands, the world would be in trouble. Since I had an honest face, he felt that he could trust me. I was skeptical at first, but he insisted that I take them. I put the ring and lamp away, intending to bring them to school and make my discovery here. You know how impatient I am; late Sunday night, I just had to rub them and say, "Oh ring and lamp reveal your secret to me." As I was rubbing the lamp, I turned it over, and there inside the lamp, I found a book and a note. The note said, "Open the book to find out about Sinbad the Sailor, Ali Baba and the forty thieves, and especially about Aladdin who used the ring and lamp to help him reach his goal. These stories were originally told by a young girl named Scherazade to the king of Persia for 1,001 nights, and the stories saved her life. They were passed from one generation to another in coffeehouses and marketplaces. Then they were written in this book." I opened the book and found that it was a first edition, written in 1709 by Antoine Galland.

Here in the classroom today are a ring, a lamp, and a collection of stories.

- Read the title, "Aladdin and the Wonderful Lamp." Organize students in *buddy teams*. Distribute copies of the tale to each group. After the students have read the tale, ask those who have seen the movie to compare the tale to the movie.

- Students will write comparisons or reactions to novelle in their *LitLogs*.

CONSTRUCT

- Ask students what they would wish for if they had a magic ring or lamp. *Chart* their wishes. Group wishes into categories, such as wealth, happiness, and benefits for others.

- Place an old piece of carpet on the floor. Ask a student to sit on the *Flying Carpet*. This person assumes the *role* of Aladdin and makes comments about the wishes expressed by class members. The comments will be based on the student's knowledge of Aladdin's personality.

- *Interview* Aladdin. Different students will assume the role of Aladdin to answer questions such as the following: Did you act cleverly when the stranger visited you and your mother? Why was your mother afraid of the lamp? Tell us about the sultan and the vizier and their plan. Where did the genie come from? Did you really think the genie would deliver so much? Were you amazed to find out how the people helped you? How did you know who the false Fatima really was? How did you change during the story?

CREATE

- *Illustrate with paint* some wishes requested earlier.

- *Write a rationale* why the wish should be granted.

- Prepare a *readers theatre script* for the story and present a dramatic reading of the script to another class.

- Prepare *sketches or illustrations* for various incidents in the story. Use these sketches as a background for the *bulletin board or hall wall* to advertise the tale (or various stories from the *Arabian Nights*.)

- Write a *news report* from the vizier's point of view reporting Aladdin's trickery to wed the princess. "Anonymous reporters" could write other reports from *inside* Aladdin's palace.

- Students will write *annotations* for different selections from *The Arabian Nights*. Share annotations and compare individual stories in terms of characters, problems, conflicts, and solutions.

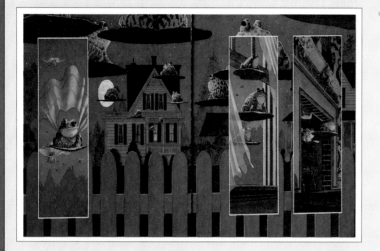

• **Pictures from Children's Books**
Each chapter contains pictures from children's books that reflect the various artistic elements, styles, media, and book design discussed in Chapter 8. Many picture captions include questions that you may one day use in your own classroom.

The original paintings for the part and chapter openers enhance the seasonal motif used throughout the book. Photographs showing teachers, learners, and literature enrich and help interpret the verbal narrative of the book.

• **Visual Graphics** Various types of visual graphics appear in all chapters of the book. Each genre chapter contains several visual webs that provide detailed information about the literary characteristics of quality literature representing the genre or subgenres. Throughout the book different visual graphics highlight important information about literature, the learner's development and literary preferences, and techniques for presenting instructional techniques and strategies.

FIGURE 5.2 Characteristics of Literary Categories of Realistic Fiction

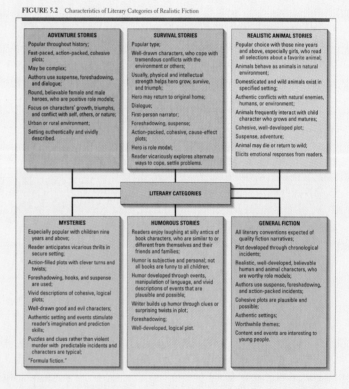

CHAPTER 2

CHILDREN'S BOOKS MENTIONED IN THE CHAPTER

Ahlberg, J. & A. Ahlberg. 1986. *The Jolly Postman or Other People's Letters.* Boston: Heinemann. 5–11 yrs.

Fleischman, P. 1988. *Rondo in C.* Illus. Janet Wentworth. New York: Harper & Row. 9–12 yrs.

Newberry, C. T. 1993. *April's Kittens.* New York: Harper & Row. 5–9 yrs.

Prelutsky, J. (Ed.) 1983. *The Random House Book of Poetry.* Illus. Arnold Lobel. New York: Random. 4–14 yrs.

Rathman, P. 1995. *Officer Buckle and Gloria.* New York: Putnam. 5–10 yrs.

Silverstein, S. 1974. *A Light in the Attic.* New York: HarperCollins. 6–14 yrs.

White, E. B. 1952. *Charlotte's Web.* Illus. Garth Williams. New York: HarperCollins. 8–12 yrs.

Yolen, J. 1987. *Owl Moon.* Illus. John Schoenherr. New York: Philomel. 6–10 yrs.

LIT SET

"Old Stormalong, the Deep-Water Sailman" in B. A. Botkin (Ed.). 1949. *The Treasury of American Folklore* (pp. 185–192). New York: Crown.

"Stormalong" in C. Carmer (Compiler). 1949. *America Sings* (pp. 30–34). New York: Knopf.

Felton, H. 1986. *True Tall Tales of Stormalong: Sail of the Seven Seas.* Englewood Cliffs, N.J.: Prentice-Hall.

Malcolmsson, A. & D. J. McCormick. 1952. *Mr. Stormalong.* Boston: Houghton Mifflin.

"Stormalong" in M. P. Osborne. 1991. *American Tall Tales* (pp. 37–44). Engravings by M. McCurdy. New York: Knopf.

Shay, F. 1930. *Here's Audacity! American Legendary Heroes* (pp. 17–31). New York: Macaulay.

- **Bibliography** Three types of bibliographies appear in the back of the book, beginning on page 504. Approximately 10,000 individual titles are included in the chapter bibliographies. Each genre chapter contains a listing of notable creators and their contributions. This bibliography gives the reader a historical perspective of the genre and juvenile literature. The lists of children's books mentioned in the chapter give the reader complete bibliographic information about the representative titles included in the narrative, and thematic bibliographies appear for most chapters.

  The bibliographies suggest literature published in the late 1980s and 1990s to give the reader a contemporary listing of books available in the particular designation. Therefore, the reader has a comprehensive listing of quality historical and contemporary juvenile literature.

  The literary selections include an approximate age designation that gives the reader a general idea about the literature children at a particular age like to read, listen to, or view. These age designations were determined primarily by the content included in the book or unique stylistic elements appearing in a selection or particular genre. To determine the suitability of a particular literature selection accurately, a teacher observes the reactions of the young people who are exploring it.

Literary Vocabulary

Allegory Fiction in which the action and characters represent truths about human conduct or experiences.

Alliteration The repetition of stressed, initial sounds of words. The repeated sound is generally made by a consonant and the words are usually consecutive words or words very close to one another within a sentence; e.g., "funny, furry, fox."

Allusion A figurative or symbolic reference to a well-known event or character in life or in literature.

Annotation A brief, descriptive summary of the major events in the plot. When applicable, information about the setting, theme, major characters' names, and an indication of the literary genre are included.

Antagonist The major character(s) who creates the most conflict and actively opposes the protagonist.

Anthology A book containing several selected stories, poems, plays, or songs. The selections may be written by one person or a number of people.

Assonance The repetition of a vowel in stressed syllables without the repetition of consonants. An assonance is used as a substitute for a rhyme; e.g., "Slap" and "dash;" "fate" and "make;" "time" and "mind."

Bibliographic information A listing of the author(s), date of publication, title of the work, name of the illustrator, place of publication, and publishing company.

Canon Meritorious literature that has been sanctioned by literary authorities.

Cliffhanger Unresolved suspense at the conclusion of a chapter.

Climax The high point of the story where the reader does not know the outcome. At this point the conflict begins to be resolved.

Conflict Tension or struggle between two opposing forces.

Connotation Feelings and emotional associations surrounding a word or phrase.

Consonance The recurrence or repetition of identical or similar consonants; e.g., "'Twas a bit of a bun and a ben. . . ."

Conventions Widely accepted or generally agreed upon stylistic devices used in literature; e.g., cliffhangers.

Creator The author, artist, or poet who created a particular piece of literature.

Critic A person who evaluates the quality of a literary selection.

Denotation The explicit or dictionary meaning of a word.

Denouement The outcome and resolution of the plot.

Didactic Teaching a religious or moralistic lesson through literature. Pleasure or entertainment is a secondary purpose.

Excerpt A passage or selection removed from a longer piece of literature.

Figurative language The use of words and phrases in a nonliteral way to give new and/or unusual meanings to the language.

Flashback Moving out of chronological order and looking at a previous event.

Foil A character who is opposite or different from the protagonist. The foil emphasizes the protagonist's traits; events or settings may also be used as foils.

Hyperbole A deliberate exaggeration that could not be meant literally; e.g., "She was hungry enough to eat a horse."

Idiom An expression that is peculiar to a language, and whose meaning is not meant to be taken literally; e.g., "with a grain of salt."

Imagery The use of vivid descriptions (words or phrases) that appeal to the senses and stimulate the imagination of the audience.

Internal rhyme Rhyming words appearing inside a line of verse.

Irony An event or outcome of an event that is different from what the reader expects or anticipates while reading.

Literary elements The literary conventions of fiction, i.e., the theme, plot, characterization, setting, style, point-of-view, and format.

- **Appendices** The Appendices give the reader additional reference information. Separate appendices present the definitions of selected literary vocabulary, describe visual and verbal literary response modes, offer techniques for making books, and identify the major awards given to juvenile literature. These appendices include a model literary link; a discussion of censorship of literature; selection tools and teacher references to consult when obtaining information about juvenile literature, the learner, creators, and instructional techniques; and the current addresses of major publishing companies.

ACKNOWLEDGMENTS

A book such as this requires the helpful assistance of many people. The creative staff at Wadsworth Publishing Company deserves my gratitude for the visually attractive pages and the eye-catching cover. To the children, teachers, and Mr. Holder, the Principal at Harbour View Elementary School, in Summerfield, Florida, thank you for the photographs taken at your school. I also want to thank Laura Seeley, who created the original paintings for the part and chapter openers of the book. Her paintings enrich the text and add to the visual impact of the book.

I appreciate the significant contribution made by two friends who wrote original essays for this book. Thank you Judith Kase-Polisini, a recognized expert in drama, for writing "Using Drama with Literature." Melanie Fernandez's essay on "Censorship of Literature" presents an insightful discussion of a topic of concern to educators and parents.

I am grateful to the staff at Wadsworth Publishing Company for their invaluable assistance and their ability to facilitate the publication of the book. First to Joan Gill, my acquisitions editor. Thank you for giving me the confidence to start this project six years ago and for patiently helping me finish it. A special thank you to Angela Barnhart who firmly guided me through the manuscript stage and coordinated the review process. I also appreciate Valerie Morrison taking care of the minute details during the final stage.

The project editor is a vital link in the successful publication of a book and I had the good fortune of working with two expert editors. Thank you Barb Fuller for helping me in the initial production stages. I am especially grateful to Angela Mann, who skillfully guided me through the complexities of publishing a book. Thank you Angela for giving me a gentle nudge when a deadline approached and for solving those insurmountable problems with such tact, speed, and perfection. And thanks also to Cathy Linberg, who filled in during Angela's maternity leave and pulled together the last loose ends of the book's production.

Thank you to Veronica Oliva for obtaining the necessary permissions for the excerpts from children's literature. Kathy Ringrose, the photo researcher, deserves my thanks for working diligently to acquire permissions to use the selected pictures from children's books and to find the historical photographs. A very special thank you is given to Pat Lewis, my copy editor. Thank you Pat for meticulously editing several draft manuscripts, for removing my "creative" errors, and for making many helpful suggestions that turned the revisions into a readable book.

Conscientious reviewers give authors many valuable insights about the concepts, content, and style of a book. I appreciate the time reviewers spent critiquing the long, rough drafts of the original manuscripts for this book. They include: Richard F. Abrahamson, *University of Houston*; Norma H. Bagnell, *Missouri Western State College*; Jane Bingham, *Oakland University*; Deborah L. Brotcke, *Aurora University*; Cullen Burns, *Western Michigan University*; James W. Carlsen, *Texas A&M—Corpus Christi*; Winter Chauvin, *Stephen F. Austin State University*; Francine L. DeFrance, *Cerritos College*; Bruce A. Goebel, *Montana State University*; Aleta Hannah, *Delaware State University*; C. Gordon Hitchings, *Edinboro University of PA*; Donna L. Jacobs, *Essex Community College*; Helene Lang, *University of Vermont*; J. Lickteig, *University of Nebraska at Omaha*; Marsha C. Markman, *California Lutheran University*; Janelle B. Mathis, *University of Arizona*; Alice Menzor, *New Mexico Highlands University*; Dianne L. Monson, *University of Minnesota, Minneapolis*; Kay Moore, *California State University—Sacramento*; Emilie Warner Paille, *Georgia State University*; Lenore Parker, *Lesley College, MA*; Earleen De La Perriere, *SUNY—Brockport*; Norma Jean Prater, *Auburn University at Montgomery*; Muriel Radebaugh, *University of*

Eastern Washington; Barbara Ramirez, *Clemson University*; Angelle G. Ruppert, *Delgado Community College*; Dale L. Sakrison, *Bemidji State University*; Linda Shadiow, *Northern Arizona University*; Mary-Agnes Taylor, *Southwest Texas State University*; Nancy Todd, *University of Wisconsin—Whitewater*; Mary Ellen Varble, *Eastern Illinois University*; and Lewis H. Walker, *Shorter College*. Their candor and constructive comments helped me improve the quality of the finished product.

Thank you to the thousands of students at the University of South Florida and classroom teachers who taught me so much about juvenile literature, children, and teaching. Your candid reactions to the literary selections and your insightful questions about presenting literature to young people helped me develop the philosophy of literature instruction proposed in this book. I am especially thankful for my special friends and family who gave me confidence to continue this project and understood when I did not have time for a chat, a cup of coffee, or a meal.

Frances S. Goforth
Tampa, Florida

Part One

LEARNING & LITERATURE AN INTRODUCTION

The Literature & the Learner

... *A* children's story is the best art-form for something you have to say ...
a children's story which is enjoyed only by children is a bad children's story.

—C. S. Lewis

*W*hen did you first realize the unique experiences associated with reading, listening to, or looking at books?

Were you cuddling in some wonderful person's lap or listening to your fifth grade teacher read *The Secret Garden?*

Were you listening while a friend enthusiastically shared a new book?

Were you exploring a visual narrative or absorbing a poet's word pictures?

Were you tingling from the suspense a mystery writer had created?

Were you imagining the world described by a storyteller or being transported to another time and place by an author's re-creation of a past era?

Fortunately, someone, at some time, helped you discover the wonder of literature—the ability of words and images to give you a clearer vision of your personal concerns and an understanding of scientific, historical, and social information that helps you interact effectively with your surroundings. This book is dedicated to the reader's personal exploration of literature and avenues for sharing literary experiences with young people.

THE LITERATURE

Literature read, listened to, and viewed by babies through fourteen years is highlighted in this book. Information about the age of the intended audience is given for individual books or genres only as a benchmark for adults to consider when presenting literature in the classroom. When selecting or suggesting the most appropriate literature for individual or group experiences, it is best to observe the topics that appeal to the young people, note their general literary preferences, and consider their language, cognitive, and social development.

We know as children's experiences, knowledge, and feelings change, they frequently read with pleasure books they rejected earlier. The wise adult will introduce young people to a variety of literary selections with appealing subjects and give them time to sample, reject, or enjoy the selected stories or poems.

This chapter introduces the forms, structures, elements, and genres of literature explored by young people and describes how a child's language, cognitive, and social development influences her or his literary interests and preferences. Specific information related to individual literary genres and strategies for presenting the literature are discussed in each genre chapter. The last section of the book incorporates this information in a discussion of how literature can be used in the classroom and ways to give young people a broad exposure to literature.

A DEFINITION OF CHILDREN'S LITERATURE

Some people classify everything written as *literature,* including newspapers, magazines, and instructional materials containing a controlled vocabulary, syntax, and prescribed content. As the following definition indicates, however, newspapers and textbooks are not considered "literature." For purposes of this book, *children's literature* includes fiction and nonfiction compositions that

authentically and imaginatively express the thoughts, emotions, experiences, and information about the human condition,

offer insights and/or intellectual stimulation,

relate to the experiences, developmental levels, and literary preferences of the intended audience.[1]

With more than 60,000 individual books available for babies to young people aged fourteen, it is also necessary to separate *mediocre* literature from *quality* literature. Quality children's literature meets the criteria listed above *and,* because it effectively includes the literary conventions expected of all fiction and nonfiction, is also considered of high literary merit.

This definition of *children's literature* respects the audience and recognizes the necessity of presenting literature of high literary merit to young people. The definition reaffirms Lukens's statement that children's literature should have the same literary merit expected of adult literature.

Because children's experiences, knowledge, and interests are limited, their literature differs from adult literature but only in "degree . . . not in kind."[2]

Some authors of children's literature claim they write for themselves and do not consider the child reader. Nevertheless, Avi, the author of *Nothing but the Truth: A Documentary Novel* (1991), *Poppy* (1995), and numerous other books for young people, says that he and other writers "represent children in our books as we adults perceive them."[3] Many successful juvenile books are autobiographical and draw on important thoughts and crucial incidents from the author's own childhood. Some authors find inspiration for their stories and poems in oral comments or written documents. Whatever the initial source, however, authors always write for children from an adult perspective.

Authenticity is a hallmark of effective writing for young people. The author must present historical, social, and scientific information accurately, so that children can understand and perhaps apply it to their lives. When depicting a particular time in history, the author authentically portrays the concerns, conflicts, and values of the people. Therefore, authors of juvenile literature may include violence, "adult" language, or questionable behavior if it is appropriate for the setting and the characterization. Children's literature, like all literature, reflects the society that creates it.

ORGANIZATION: LITERARY FORMS AND STRUCTURES

Literary compositions are organized according to form and structure. When designing a literary composition, the author uses a suitable literary form to express the chosen literary structure. Authors use the following *literary forms*:

- *Prose.* The ordinary written or spoken language that is used to give information, relate events, express ideas, or present opinions; a literary medium that corresponds closely to everyday speech patterns and is used to provide detailed descriptions of ideas, objects, or situations.

- *Poetry.* A unique form of expression using rhythm, sound, and imaginative language to create an emotional response to an experience, feelings, or fact.

- *Drama.* A literary composition presented in dialogue and intended for a theatrical presentation.

Authors arrange literary compositions in a *structure*, which can be either of the following:

- *Fiction.* An imaginary oral, written, or visual narrative invented by the artist, teller, or author.

- *Nonfiction.* Information that may be expressed in expository or narrative form to convey facts, theories, generalizations, or concepts about a particular topic.

CLASSIFICATION: LITERARY GENRES

Literature is also classified according to *literary genre*, that is, a distinctive category of literary compositions characterized by a particular style, form, or content. Each literary genre found in children's literature has distinctive characteristics we can objectively judge to determine the literary merit of the visual and verbal texts. Literary compositions (essays, short stories, novels, plays, sonnets, and the like) are placed in one of the following literary genres:

Folk literature. Fictionalized oral and written tales, songs, and poems meant to entertain and assimilate the beliefs, values, and mores of a society. Poetry subgenres include Mother Goose and nursery rhymes, ballads, and epics. Prose subgenres include myths, legends, tall tales, folk tales, fairy tales, novelle, jest, anecdotes, pourquoi, trickster tales, and fables. An example is Jakob and Wilhelm Grimm's *German Popular Tales* (1822).

Fantasy literature. Imaginary verbal and visual narratives that evoke wonder and magic impossible in the real world. Literary Fairy Tales, Low Fantasy, High Fantasy, and Science Fiction are the four subgenres of fantasy. An example of Low Fantasy is Margery Williams's *The Velveteen Rabbit: Or How Toys Become Real* (1922).

Realistic fiction. Authentic stories that could happen, but may not be documented. Authors portray fictional humans and/or animals in prose or poetry. The times, place, and people portrayed distinguish the two subgenres, historical fiction (example: Laura I. Wilder's *Little House on the Prairie* [1953]) and contemporary realistic fiction (example: Judith Viorst's *Alexander and the Terrible, Horrible, No Good, Very Bad Day* [1972]).

Nonfiction literature. The factual telling of stories and information, usually written in expository discourse. The subgenres are biographies (example: Alice Provensen's *My Fellow Americans: A Family Album* [1995]), autobiographies (example: Eve Bunting, *Once Upon a Time* [1995]), and information books (example: Philip Isaacson's *A Short Walk around the Pyramids and through the World of Art* [1993]). Several "new" subgenres such as photo-essays and informational storybooks are emerging; they tell stories about factual people, places, and events (example of a photo-essay: Sarah Lovett's *Extremely Weird Snakes* [1993];

example of an informational storybook: Joanna Cole's *The Magic School Bus Inside the Human Body* [1989]).

Poetic compositions. A poet's subjective response to experiences, feelings, thoughts, and ideas. The poet uses rhythm, sound, imagery, and repetitive language in rhyming patterns or unrhymed poems to create narrative, humorous, nonsense, or lyric poems and verses. An example is Jack Prelutsky's *The Random House Book of Poetry* (1983).

Another classification of juvenile literature is found in all literary genres:

Books with pictures. Both fiction and nonfiction literature are found in wordless books, picture books, picture storybooks, concept books, photo-essays, and illustrated books. An example is Anne Isaacs's *Swamp Angel* (1994) illustrated by Paul D. Zelinsky. (See Isaacs color plate.) *Swamp Angel* describes the escapades of a pioneer woman who eventually defeats a

marauding bear and is transformed into Swamp Angel. The amusing tale is interpreted through the flawless blend of verbal and visual narratives.

Additional information about each genre is given in the appropriate chapters of the book. Figure 1.1 on page 6 presents the structure, forms, literary genres, and types of books found in children's literature.

LITERARY CONVENTIONS FOUND IN QUALITY LITERATURE

All fiction and nonfiction literature contain distinctive literary conventions or elements. When properly developed, the literary conventions give curious readers information, bring them to tears, or incite gales of laughter. Quality literature for children contains the same elements as adult literature and must achieve the same high literary merit expected of adult literature. Because the literature relates to

The second-biggest pine tree in Tennessee landed smack beside them. At the top of that tree was a beehive the size of a hill, oozing rivers of honey. After five days without food, Tarnation couldn't resist.

He rolled over in his sleep and sank his jaws into the sweet syrupy torrent. As he guzzled and slurped, Swamp Angel snored down one last tree.

Paul O. Zelinsky's places his primitive oil paintings on cherry, maple, and birch veneers. He also uses the wood for borders. His paintings are filled with action and show the strength and determination of Swamp Angel to overcome Tarnation, the bear, in Anne Isaacs's original tall tale, Swamp Angel.

FIGURE 1.1   The Forms, Structures, and Genres of Juvenile Literature

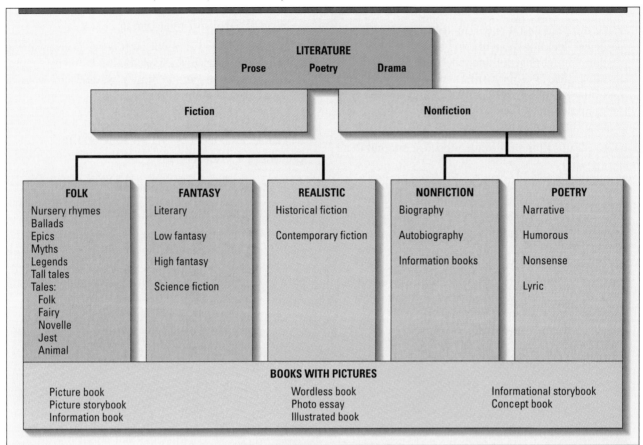

the background, developmental characteristics, literary preferences, and interests of the audience, the content and sophistication of language differ in adult and juvenile literature. The author's ability to develop these literary elements determines the literary merit of a particular literary selection.

By successfully combining the elements into a cohesive whole, the author influences the reader's conscious or unconscious reactions and interpretation of the verbal narrative. For example, while reading or rereading your favorite book, did you unconsciously become a character? Did you predict the character's behavior, give her or him advice, or feel proud or disappointed about his or her behavior? If you cared about the character, the author successfully developed the characters. Did your favorite book contain believable events that were filled with suspense, surprises, and foreshadowing? Did you continue reading until you found out "what happened next"? If so, the author served as your guide and designed an effective plot. While reading your favorite book, did you see pictures in your head showing the setting or the physical attributes of the characters or the information described? Did

you feel an emotional connection to the book or feel sad when you finished the last page? If so, you absorbed the author's style of writing, became an active participant in the world of the book, and gave the book high ratings.[4] If you stopped to ponder the personal meaning or information gained from the book, then you considered the author's purpose or theme. When these elements connect and meet the literary expectations, the author has effectively designed or created a book of high literary merit or quality literature.

Obviously, many fictional conventions are different from nonfiction elements, yet four conventions are expected of both structures. First, the author must create a well-written book by carefully choosing powerful language and structure. Second, the author must consider his or her purpose for writing the book and satisfy the audience by adequately covering the subject. Third, while imaginary events, characters, or settings may be used in fictional writings, the elements should be consistent and authentic to the world designed by the author. Likewise, quality nonfiction literature should contain accurate and current information. Finally, to help the reader enjoy and understand the subject, fictional writers should devise a logical plot structure, and nonfiction writers should use an appropriate text structure. In this way, authors of quality fiction and nonfiction literature interest the audience by presenting an authentic, credible coverage of the subject that is organized appropriately in a well-written narrative.

LITERARY ELEMENTS IN FICTION LITERATURE

Fictional writings are imaginary compositions found in folk literature, fantasy, realistic fiction, fictionalized biographies, informational storybooks, and some photo-essays. E. B. White's *Charlotte's Web* (1952) is a flawless example of fictional writing. The novel, popular with readers from 6 to 66 years old, describes the adventures of Charlotte, a spider, and her barnyard friends, especially Wilbur the pig. White incorporates all components expected in a high-quality fictional narrative. For example, in fictional writing the connected narrative focuses on a succession of events that present the characters' conflicts. The writer connects the incidents to a central theme or to multiple secondary themes. Early in the narrative, the author describes or ignores the setting and introduces the characters and their major conflicts. In the body of the prose, poetry, or dramatic narrative, the believable actions of the characters are described in a series of connected events. At the conclusion of the narrative, the problems are either resolved or left unresolved. The author's style is reflected in his or her ability to use language and to consistently weave the various elements together.

Thus, the literary elements inherent in all quality fictional writing are a *worthwhile theme*, a *logical plot, multifaceted characters*, an *appropriate setting*, an *effective style of writing*, and a narrator who presents a clear *point of view*. Together, these elements provide a definition of fictional writing. In some literary genres, variations are acceptable. For example, in folk literature the characters are generally stereotyped. Acceptable literary elements are described in each genre chapter. The characteristics of the various literary elements are presented in Figure 1.2 on page 8.[5] An outline of the various elements appears at the end of the chapter.

ELEMENTS IN NONFICTION LITERATURE

Nonfiction literature informs and instructs the audience and introduces readers to past, present, and future worlds. Writers of nonfiction literature objectively describe people, places, and things in prose and poetry in autobiogra-

phies, biographies, and information books. Writers engage in research, examining journals, diaries, letters, and other source materials, to give the audience an authentic coverage of the topic. While biographies are typically written in a narrative structure, they must contain authentic, factual content. Therefore, they serve as a link between fiction and information books. Although authors of information books frequently use expository text structures, an increasing number of informational picture storybooks are appearing and are usually written in a story format. Photo-essays containing photographs and a narrative or expository verbal text are also a popular form of biography and information book. Because accuracy and authenticity are primary concerns, nonfiction writers generally include such resources as an appendix, glossary, index, bibliography of sources used, or list of additional readings about the subject. Other organizational structures such as a table of contents, chapter headings, and subheadings frequently appear in the books. Biographers usually organize their books around events in the subject's life, while writers of information books carefully arrange the factual material so that readers can easily find specific information. Nonfiction writers carefully select photographs, maps, graphs, charts, or time lines to enhance, interpret, or replace the verbal text.

Nonfiction elements include an appropriate tone and style of writing, authentic information, suitable details and scope of content, an organizational structure appropriate to the content and reader, and appropriate visuals and format. These criteria are presented in outline form at the end of the chapter and are discussed in Chapter 6. Figure 1.3 on page 9 presents nonfiction elements expected of quality biographies, autobiographies, and information books.

GENERAL GUIDELINES FOR SELECTING QUALITY LITERATURE

Although each literary genre has distinctive characteristics that separate it from other genres, certain general criteria are used when choosing all quality literature. These criteria are based on the literary elements for quality fiction and nonfiction literature just described. Specific criteria for selecting each type of literature are discussed in the genre chapters.

Depending on the purpose for using the literature, both children and adults may be involved in the selection process. If the selection criteria are discussed informally with the children while they are choosing literature, it is usually not necessary to teach formal lessons about the differences between genres and the expected conventions. For example, while the teacher and children are selecting a picture storybook to use for a dramatic script, they can talk about the characters'

FIGURE 1.2 Literary Elements in Fictional Writings

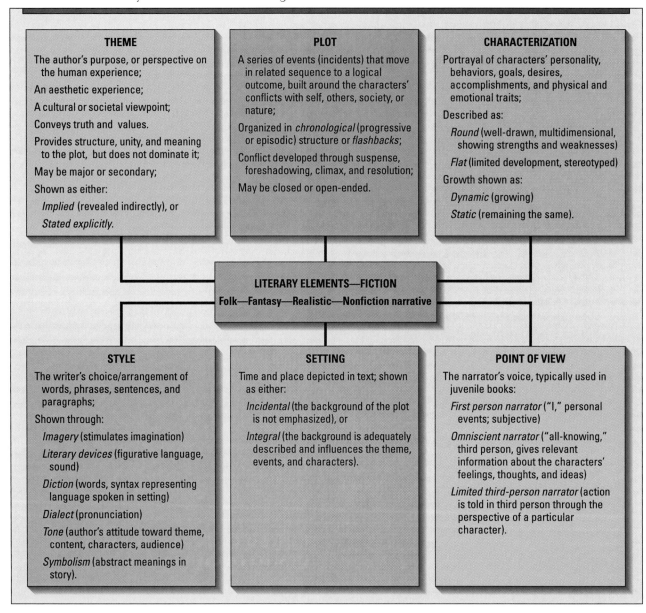

THEME

The author's purpose, or perspective on the human experience;

An aesthetic experience;

A cultural or societal viewpoint;

Conveys truth and values.

Provides structure, unity, and meaning to the plot, but does not dominate it;

May be major or secondary;

Shown as either:

Implied (revealed indirectly), or

Stated explicitly.

PLOT

A series of events (incidents) that move in related sequence to a logical outcome, built around the characters' conflicts with self, others, society, or nature;

Organized in *chronological* (progressive or episodic) structure or *flashbacks*;

Conflict developed through suspense, foreshadowing, climax, and resolution;

May be closed or open-ended.

CHARACTERIZATION

Portrayal of characters' personality, behaviors, goals, desires, accomplishments, and physical and emotional traits;

Described as:

Round (well-drawn, multidimensional, showing strengths and weaknesses)

Flat (limited development, stereotyped)

Growth shown as:

Dynamic (growing)

Static (remaining the same).

LITERARY ELEMENTS—FICTION
Folk—Fantasy—Realistic—Nonfiction narrative

STYLE

The writer's choice/arrangement of words, phrases, sentences, and paragraphs;

Shown through:

Imagery (stimulates imagination)

Literary devices (figurative language, sound)

Diction (words, syntax representing language spoken in setting)

Dialect (pronunciation)

Tone (author's attitude toward theme, content, characters, audience)

Symbolism (abstract meanings in story).

SETTING

Time and place depicted in text; shown as either:

Incidental (the background of the plot is not emphasized), or

Integral (the background is adequately described and influences the theme, events, and characters).

POINT OF VIEW

The narrator's voice, typically used in juvenile books:

First person narrator ("I," personal events; subjective)

Omniscient narrator ("all-knowing," third person, gives relevant information about the characters' feelings, thoughts, and ideas)

Limited third-person narrator (action is told in third person through the perspective of a particular character).

development and whether the author has included sufficient descriptions and events for a complete script. This instructional strategy helps the children become familiar with the plot structure, the characters, and the author's style of writing. Several researchers investigated children's awareness of the structures of literature and their ability to recognize literary conventions.[6] Frequently, older children can identify certain conventions. Most researchers agree that children who informally explore a variety of literary selections develop an understanding of the literary components and express a pos-

itive attitude toward literature. Throughout this book various instructional strategies are suggested to help children become more sophisticated selectors of the books they read, listen to, view, and interpret.

Table 1.1 on page 11 lists a variety of questions that can be considered when selecting quality fiction. Selectors are reminded to use only questions that are applicable to the literature being reviewed. Additional criteria addressing the distinctive characteristics of a particular genre are discussed in the genre chapters.

FIGURE 1.3   Elements in Nonfiction Literature

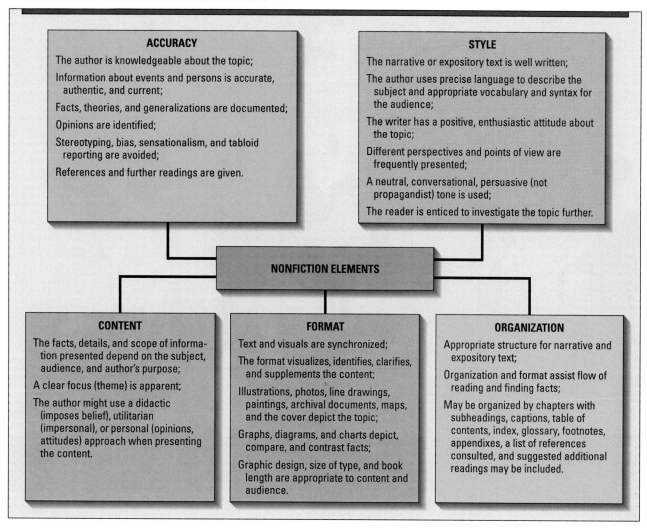

SOURCES FOR BOOK SELECTIONS

Various sources are available in school and public libraries to help adults select quality literature. Three different types of sources are available:

Selection tools are books and pamphlets published monthly, bimonthly, quarterly, or annually. They list new and reissued juvenile books and may include annotations and a rating scale to indicate the quality of the books. They are organized by genre, subject, or some other method. Two popular selection tools are *Adventuring with Books*, now in its eleventh edition, published by the National Council of Teachers of English and *The Horn Book Guide*, published twice a year by the *Horn Book Magazine*.

Review sources are magazines or pamphlets, published periodically, that list paperback and hardback books published over a specified period of time. Some sources use a rating scale to indicate the quality of the books. All sources use classifications, such as alphabetical listing by subject areas, genre classifications, or thematic units. Some review sources include articles about using literature with children. Two excellent sources are *The Bulletin of the Center for Children's Books*, published by the University of Illinois Press, and *Book Links*, a bimonthly magazine published by the American Library Association.

Professional journals are published periodically by professional organizations. The journals review juvenile books in each issue and frequently contain articles

The children's faces show their delight listening to an interesting book.

about using literature. Two outstanding journals are *Language Arts*, published eight times a year, September through April, by the National Council of Teachers of English, and *The Reading Teacher*, published eight times a year by the International Reading Association.

Other journals annually list outstanding books in their respective subject areas; *Social Education* (published by the National Council of Social Studies Teachers), *The Science Journal*, and *Science and Children* (published by the Council of Science Teachers) are examples. Popular sources, addresses, and additional information appear in Appendix G.

BOOK AWARDS

Since 1922 when the Newbery Medal, the first award for American children's literature was initiated, the number of awards for juvenile books and creators has increased to more than a hundred different awards and prizes. The awards add prestige to the field of children's literature and

are given by professional organizations, private foundations, and publishing companies.

The coveted awards are given for different purposes. For example, the *Newbery Medal* is given annually to the author of the most outstanding juvenile book published in the United States the previous year. The 1997 Newbery Medal was given to E. L. Konigsburg for her realistic novel, *The View from Saturday* (1996). The *Caldecott Medal*, which is also given annually, is awarded to the artist who created the most outstanding picture book published in the United States the previous year. David Wisniewski received the 1997 Caldecott Medal for his picture storybook version of the legendary Jewish creature *Golem* (1996).

Some awards are given to an outstanding creator in recognition of the person's entire contribution to children's literature. Such an award is the *Hans Christian Andersen Award*. This international award is given biennially to one author and one illustrator. In 1996 Uri Orlev, an Israeli writer, won the author award, and Klaus Ensikat, a German illustrator, won the award for illustration. The

TABLE 1.1 Selection Criteria for Quality Fiction Literature

Theme

Is the theme appropriate and worthwhile for the intended audience?

Is the theme stated? Is it too obvious?

Does the theme overpower the plot?

Is the theme implied or clearly developed?

Is a secondary theme included?

What is the significance of the title?

Plot

Is the plot developed through a chronological structure? Are flashbacks included?

Is the plot original? Is it credible?

Is the plot interesting? Is it suitable for the intended audience?

Is the plot predictable? If so, does the predictability destroy the reader's interest?

Is the plot consistent or authentic to the world developed by the author?

Is the plot logically developed? Is it properly paced?

In a chronological plot, does the introduction present the problems?

Does the plot exploit violence or dwell on sensational details?

Does the plot adequately develop the theme(s)?

Characterization

Do the characters grow and change during the narrative?

If anthropomorphism is used, is it used appropriately?

Are the actions of the characters appropriate for their age and background?

Are the behavior and accomplishments of the characters convincing?

Are the characters well drawn, showing strengths and weaknesses?

Are the characters free of stereotypical actions and reactions?

Do the characters interact appropriately?

Style of Writing

Does the author have an interesting style of writing, such as, unusual vocabulary, descriptive language, various images, humor, figurative language, symbolism, rhythm, sound, and repetition?

Does the language stimulate the reader's imagination?

Does the author use language that is authentic to the setting and the characters?

Does the author use a consistent style that is appropriate for the book's subject?

Is the language suitable for the intended audience?

If dialect is used, is it authentic and does it help develop the characterization?

Does the author help the reader develop empathy for the characters and events?

Does the author create a suitable mood for the narrative?

Setting

Is the setting authentic to the time and the geographic location?

Is the setting accurate to the plot?

Is the setting incidental or integral to the verbal and visual narratives?

Does the author bring the historical or contemporary period to life?

Point of View

Does the narrator use an appropriate point of view for the narrative?

Does the narrator use an appropriate point of view for the genre?

Other Criteria

Is the content of the book suitable for the developmental level of the audience?

Do the illustrations accurately visualize the setting, characters, and events?

Do the illustrations realistically expand, enhance, supplement, or replace the verbal narrative?

NCTE Excellence in Poetry for Children is given every three years to a poet living in the United States, who has made a major contribution to juvenile poetry. Barbara Esbensen received the award for her poetry in 1994. In 1995 Virginia Hamilton received the Laura Ingalls Wilder Award. This award is given every three years to a U.S. author or illustrator who has made a substantial and lasting contribution to children's literature.

The *International Reading Association Children's Book Award* is given annually to new authors of promise. In 1996 Marie Bradby and Chris K. Soentpiet received the award for their picture book *More Than Anything Else*; Elizabeth

Adler received the award for her novel *The King's Shadow*; and Susan E. Quinlan received an award for *The Case of the Mummified Pigs*. Other awards recognize authors or artists from a particular ethnic group. For example, the *Coretta Scott King Award* is given annually to an African-American author and illustrator for an outstanding book, published in the United States the previous year, that is educational and inspirational to young people. Walter Dean Myers received the 1997 award for his text in *Slam!* (1996). Jerry Pinkney received the 1997 award for his illustrations in Alan Schroeder's book *Minty: A Story of Young Harriet Tubman* (1996). Some awards are presented to books from a particular literary genre, such as the *Orbis Pictus Award for Outstanding Nonfiction for Children.* This award is given annually for outstanding nonfiction children's books published the preceding year in the United States. Jim Murphy received the award in 1996 for his photo-essay *The Great Fire.*

The winners of all the awards discussed so far are selected by adults. In addition, each year children in forty-one states select a favorite book from a master list compiled by librarians, educators, and children. A description of the most popular awards and a complete listing of recipients and honor books appear in Appendix C.

PUBLISHING TRENDS

Throughout history three trends have influenced the books published for children: popular child-raising philosophies, educational practices, and publishing techniques. Juvenile literature published in the 1990s reflects these trends. The first trend is obvious when we compare what is accepted behavior for children today with the behavior depicted in historical fiction. Another aspect of current attitudes toward children is the value adults place on book ownership. The number of commercial bookstores has multiplied in the last decade, and juvenile sections have expanded. Large retail stores carry mass market paperback juvenile books. Many popular, older books have been reissued; these trigger fond memories in adults' minds and entice them to buy the books for a favorite child. Parents, guardians, and friends can easily find books to give boys and girls for special occasions.

Educational practices influence the type and number of juvenile books published each year. As teachers use more trade books (a generic term for books other than textbooks) in the classroom for pleasure and instruction, the number and types of juvenile books have multiplied. Consequently, easy-to-read nonfiction and fiction books of various types are readily available. Because contemporary children are introduced to a variety of books, they are familiar with more literature than in previous years.

The effects of trends in publishing are reflected in various ways. For example, the cost of hardback books has skyrocketed, but softcover (paperback) books are readily available and reasonable in price. Publishers now use sophisticated marketing techniques to impress adult buyers. Dolls, stuffed toys, book bags, and T-shirts accompany many books, and eye-catching displays in bookstores advertise various series. The close relationship between books and other media is reflected in the number of books that inspire television programs or movies. Consider the popularity of Chris Van Allsburg's *Jumanji* (1981). Media moguls spend lavishly on television, newspaper, and billboard advertisements. Saturday morning cartoons frequently feature animated book characters, and after-school specials are based on popular juvenile books. Fortunately, technological advances allow artists to experiment with a variety of media and designs. Many books with pictures contain full-color, camera-separated reproductions, photographs, historical documents, or computer-generated graphics. Susan Jeffers's illustrations for Reve Lindberg's *The Midnight Farm* (1987) are an example of the high-quality artwork found in juvenile books with pictures. (See Lindberg color plate on page 13.) Paper-engineered "toy" books, such as Keith Faulkner's *Wide Mouth Frog* (1996) created by Jonathan Lambert are popular. Many sturdy, attractive board books, pop-up books, scratch n'sniff books, and books with pictures that pull out to be three feet long are available.

Publishing companies are restructuring and conglomerates are thriving; thus, fewer companies now control the market. Since the 1970s the juvenile market has represented 7 to 10 percent of total book sales in the United States. The number of juvenile titles published annually has increased dramatically in the twentieth century rising from 270 in 1880 to 993 in 1930. By 1970 approximately 2,000 new juvenile titles were being published each year. By 1982 the number had grown to 2,566. In less than a decade, the number doubled, rising to almost 5,000 new individual titles for juveniles in 1990. In 1993 American publishers produced 5,469 juvenile hardback and paperback books. Output declined slightly in 1994, however, to 5,321 books, and preliminary figures for 1995 indicate an additional decline to 4,489 new titles. These numbers represent a substantial decline in the production of mass market paperback books and may support "a general assumption that children's book publishing has entered a period of slowdown." Nevertheless, juvenile books continue to represent approximately 11 percent of the total books produced in the United States.[7] Altogether, approximately 60,000 individual titles are available in juvenile literature.

Not only has the quantity of juvenile books increased over the last decades, but the quality of books and the stature of children's literature have escalated as well. Today, children's books reflect people from all cultural, religious, and social groups. Authors represent both genders fairly and show the contemporary roles assumed by males and females. Varied content, all literary genres, outstanding writing, and breathtaking art are found in books for young people. Today, talented writers and authors are willing to devote a lifetime to creating appealing children's books.

This is indeed a glorious time for children's literature. All trends are positive: parents value sharing and purchasing books, educators recognize the power of using trade books for all curricular areas, and publishing companies are producing more outstanding books than ever for young people.

Here is the dark of the midnight farm,
Safe and still and full and warm,

Deep in the dark and free from harm
In the dark of the midnight farm.

Susan Jeffers uses pen with ink, dyes, and gouache over pencil in her detailed realistic illustrations for Reve Lindberg's The Midnight Farm. *The hidden animals in the illustrations extend Lindberg's narrative to reveal many friends a child thinks about while going to sleep. Do you see her friends?*

LEARNERS AND THEIR LITERATURE

> Children's literature has become one of the important ways the adult world defines childhood. Avi[8]

Most people, young and old alike, read, listen to, and view literature for the pleasure derived from the experience. As Louise Rosenblatt, a noted literary theorist, explains, when we read, we either assume a predominantly *aesthetic* stance (or purpose) or a predominantly *efferent* stance toward the visual and verbal narratives.[9] By exploring literature from an *aesthetic* stance, we concentrate on the *"lived-through experience"* and absorb the author's word or the artist's images that are flowing into our thoughts. When assuming a predominantly *efferent* stance toward the text, we focus on the information we *"take away from the reading."*

While assuming the aesthetic and/or efferent stance, we simultaneously connect the images evoked by the text to our previous experiences and knowledge (*schema*).

This stirs our imagination and helps us construct meanings from the visual and verbal narratives. These meanings introduce us to the beauty of the language, to the author and perhaps the artist's expressions of emotions, thoughts, or information. As we experiment or manipulate the language, we become aware of the potential power of language to express our feelings and impressions to others. Through our vicarious experiences with the verbal and visual images presented in the literature, we may be transformed into the character(s), which helps us understand human motives. As we attempt to predict the events in the text, we expand our critical thinking skills. Our curiosity is nurtured as we read the literature and gain scientific, historical, social, and cultural information about ourselves and others. This information is found in both fiction and nonfiction prose, poetry, and drama. While exploring the text, we might move freely back and forth between the *aesthetic* and *efferent* stances.

This young reader seems lost in the images and ideas found in his book.

DEVELOPMENTAL CHARACTERISTICS THAT INFLUENCE LITERARY PREFERENCES AND INTERESTS

When some children enter a preschool or a kindergarten classroom, they have already spent many hours using language and visual modalities to explore topics in literature. These children have also developed a schema for story or a "sense of story."[10] By recognizing the elements of the literary forms, children can anticipate, predict, and interpret the narrative clues and become discriminating in the selection of quality literature. Other children might enter the same classroom with limited experiences with literature. Clearly, the children have different expectations and knowledge about reacting to, interacting with, and valuing literature. (See photo above.) Children who have positive experiences with literature exhibit an interest in learning, reading, writing, listening, and speaking and in literature itself. Furthermore, children who have explored literature have developed book-sharing

skills: they will sit with another, focus on specific parts of a text or page, turn the pages, and react with others about the information stimulated by the verbal and visual narratives. Thus, a child's previous literary experiences, combined with his or her language, cognitive, and social development, will affect that child's attitude toward literature.

Adults who interact with young people and their literature must become knowledgeable about the general developmental characteristics of children at various ages and understand how these factors influence children's literary preferences and interests. Fortunately, researchers have identified general characteristics of language, cognitive, and social development and have made general statements about the literary preferences and interests of children at particular ages. A teacher can combine this information with literature discussions and observations of children's reactions to individual literary selections when choosing suitable literature to meet the children's needs, development, literary preferences, and interests.

General Characteristics of Language Development
A baby's first attempts at verbal and nonverbal language come early in life.[11] Children quickly learn that if they make funny sounds, a big person will pick them up, jiggle and hug them, or give them a prize—food. As children grow, they become aware of the patterns of sounds and ways to put those sounds together to evoke positive responses from the important people in their lives. From the early repetition of sounds to the formation of words and sentences, children are aware of the importance of making their desires and feelings known to others through verbal and nonverbal language. Through language children explore and discover their world and the environment beyond. They enjoy experimenting with and manipulating language to discover new words and to make up new words that express their feelings. While chanting repetitive words and patterns, they find words and phrases that rhyme and begin to understand the wonder and power of language.

Language acquisition is a lifelong process. Usually, children understand language and its structure before they can use it effectively. Literature introduces young people to the endless possibilities of using language to inform, express opinions and feelings, and attempt to persuade others. Additional information about the functions of language, the need to acquire language in a holistic process, and various ways to stimulate and develop language are discussed in Chapter 12.

General Characteristics of Cognitive Development
A child who smiles at an adult and says "kitty" while rubbing a kitten is reflecting her background knowledge about a kitten. This knowledge is obvious to the adult who re-

members that several days earlier the child screamed with terror and hid behind the adult when the kitten came into the room. With modeling and encouragement from the adult, the kitten became a wonderful new discovery for the child, and her knowledge became apparent.

While exploring language and communicating with others, some children are intrinsically motivated to understand their world better. They extend their knowledge by experimenting and monitoring their environment. Lev Vygotsky, a noted Russian psychologist, felt thinking and speaking are interrelated and that children master their surroundings through speech.[12] This theory addresses the child's acquisition of knowledge and interaction of speech and relates to the importance of socialization.

Jean Piaget, a noted Swiss psychologist, identified four stages of development through which children progress before reaching intellectual maturity. Educators have found Piaget's developmental stages helpful when attempting to understand children's cognitive growth.

Piaget's stages are as follows:

Sensorimotor stage. Children from birth to approximately two years of age use their senses and motor activities to investigate the world.

Preoperational stage. Children approximately two to seven years focus on their personal world; they can use symbols, but cannot perform mental operations, such as reversibility. They do not understand logical concepts, such as conservation.

Concrete operational stage. Children from age seven to about eleven or twelve have a literal interpretation of the world and use concrete, tangible thinking, mental operations, and simple logic to solve problems.

Formal operational stage. Young people approximately eleven years and above can reason logically, understand abstract information and theoretical propositions, formulate and test hypotheses, and deal with social interactions.[13]

Further descriptors of the stages are identified in the tables at the end of this section.

Literary experiences stimulate and help develop the cognitive processes. As children reflect on visual and verbal narratives, they discuss their reactions with others. By personally reacting to literature, they are acquiring and refining their thinking skills.

General Characteristics of Social Development

Humans are social creatures. The need to acquire language and communicate facilitates that social need. As we socialize with others, we acquire the beliefs valued by our family and the standards of behavior recognized as the acceptable way to function within various social, cultural, and religious groups.

While acquiring language and becoming knowledgeable about the world, the child is also maturing socially. The desire to interact socially with others is a strong innate instinct in most humans. In the 1960s Erik Erikson developed the psychosocial development theory, which holds that the personality develops according to predetermined steps. Because society provides a series of psychosocial challenges, the child develops various aspects of positive and negative personality traits while moving unevenly through the various stages.[14] Erikson's social stages for children are as follows:

Trust versus Mistrust. Babies to approximately two years of age begin to develop a sense of trust in others or a sense of suspicion.

Autonomy versus Shame or Doubt. At approximately two to three years, children develop a sense of independence or doubt about their own abilities.

Initiative versus Guilt. At approximately four through seven years, children develop a positive view toward their desires and actions or guilt over their actions.

Industry versus Inferiority. While developing academic skills, children between seven and eleven years of age develop a sense of confidence in their accomplishments or may develop a sense of inadequacy.

Identity versus Role Diffusion. During the adolescent years, young people develop a sense of identity or a sense of purpose.

Exploring literature helps young people recognize and eventually understand the different roles played by people in their society. For example, while exploring fiction and nonfiction literature, children are exposed to different views held by people regarding acceptable behavior, beliefs, standards, and motives. (See photo on p. 16.) The authentic content found in nonfiction literature and an awareness of theme, plot, and characterization in fiction help children develop these socialization skills. As learners encounter fictional or biographical writings with well-developed plots, convincing characters, and thought-provoking themes, they learn to care about the characters and empathize with them. Through these experiences, they also encounter positive ways to express emotions and develop a feeling of self-worth and esteem. Individual stories and poems that highlight children interacting with others and developing socially are identified in several chapter bibliographies.

Children remember information about historical events as they work together to create a response to books they have read.

General Characteristics of Literary Preferences and Interests

A *literary preference* is determined by asking a person to choose a particular literary structure, form, convention, or genre over another. Preferences are forced choices in that the person expressing the preference must choose among items selected by another person. Frequently, literary preferences are determined by asking a question such as, Do you prefer hearing your teacher read a fantasy book, a folktale, or an information book? If an information book is selected, the teacher realizes the child prefers to listen to information books rather than fantasy books or folktales. An *interest* is a person's personal choice and implies freedom of choice. To determine a child's interest, an adult frequently observes the topic discussed by the child or the genre chosen for independent reading. Literary preferences give teachers general ideas about the literature children enjoy exploring, while interests motivate young people to explore various subjects or forms of literature.

Experience with language, life, and literature affects the child's literary preferences and interests. Preferences and interests are dynamic and are subject to change based on the person's feelings, experiences, emotional and physical needs, stages of development, and familiarity with literature. Teachers use the information about literary preferences and interests to introduce children to various literary selections representing their preferences and interest. Teachers also present other literary genres and books by different authors and artists to help children discover the diversity of literature. By exploring a variety of literary forms, structures, and genres, young people can become discriminating in selecting quality literature for various purposes. For example, Laura Ingalls Wilder's *Little House Series* is popular with children eight years and older. (See Wilder color plate.) This historical fiction series introduces children to a family living in the western United States during the last century. After enjoying the series, young people will select information books and biographies to find out more about pioneers.

Garth Williams's realistic black and white charcoal drawings enhance and enrich Mrs. Wilder's Little House Series. *The drawings for the* Little House in the Big Woods *are filled with action and reveal the personality of the characters.*

TABLE 1.2 General Statements about Young People's Literary Preferences and Interests

> Young people select and reread books by recognized authors and series books.
>
> Young people personally select books or poems from a particular "favorite" genre.
>
> The literary preferences of girls and boys change significantly at around eight or nine years of age.
>
> Girls and boys express the largest number of differences in literary preferences between the ages of ten through fourteen.
>
> Boys ten years and older prefer a male protagonist; girls like female characters, but they also like male characters.
>
> Young people of all ages like humorous stories and poems. Because there are developmental levels of humor ranging from slapstick to symbolism, the type of humor preferred varies according to the developmental level of the child.
>
> Children prefer prose and poetry narratives with a reasonable number of characters, whose names are not too difficult to remember.
>
> Literature with multiple abstract themes or complex plot structures may be rejected by preschool through middle grade children.
>
> Young people prefer conversation rather than long descriptive passages.
>
> Children's interest in reading peaks around fifth grade.
>
> The topic of the book must satisfy the young person's curiosity and personal concerns and stimulate his or her imagination.
>
> A child's achievement level does not seem to influence her or his literary preferences.
>
> The location of a child's residence (inner city, suburban, rural) does not seem to influence his or her literary preferences.
>
> A child's race does not seem to influence her or his literary preferences.
>
> Conflicting evidence exists regarding the influence of social class on a child's literary preferences.
>
> Young people nine years and older like paperback books.
>
> Children seven years and above prefer "formula" paperbacks rather than challenging hardbacks.
>
> Children frequently select books they have seen on television, movies, or commercial tapes.

General Statements about Young People's Literary Preferences and Interests

Since the late 1800s, researchers have attempted to discover the literary preferences of children at various chronological ages.[15] The studies had varied purposes including discovering the type of books children selected in the library, their attitudes about books, and gender-related issues. Some early studies were based on group data, yet the researcher made generalizations about individual children at a particular age group. Drawing general conclusions from the findings were difficult because a variety of techniques were used to obtain the responses, including interviews, questionnaires, checkout lists from libraries, fictitious titles and synopses, records kept by students, and case studies. In some studies children listened to stories or poems and were asked to choose a favorite selection from the literature read aloud. Whether forced-choice or open-ended questions were used, the children frequently did not or could not answer the questions truthfully. Despite these and other problems, the findings of compatible studies could be correlated, and general statements about young people's literary preferences and interests emerged. Table 1.2 lists the statements regarding young people's literary preferences and interests.

TABLE 1.3 Language, Cognitive, and Social Development and Literary Preferences and Interests of Babies to Toddlers

LANGUAGE DEVELOPMENT	COGNITIVE DEVELOPMENT	SOCIAL DEVELOPMENT	LITERARY PREFERENCES
Babies	**Babies**	**Babies**	**Babies**
Acquire language by hearing oral language of others.	Children are in Piaget's *sensorimotor stage*.	Children are in Erikson's *Trust versus Mistrust stage*.	Listen to stories, poems, and jingles told by adults or older children.
Use simple words to label objects.	Learn through the senses.	Need to feel loved and accepted.	Enjoy durable cloth, board books with simple, uncluttered, clear pictures, limited subject matter.
Respond through body movements to the rhythm, inflections, and tones of language.	Touching and verbalizing are necessary for normal development.	Parental interaction (hugging, rocking, play, speaking) is vital to development.	The books may become a toy.
Make coos and babbles resembling adult speech sounds.	Respond to stimuli through body movements and facial expressions.	Socialization is learned through the senses.	Enjoy rhymes with short verses and rhythmic language.
Squeal with delight to get attention.	Invite parental responses with movements and vocalizations.	Respond to attention through body movements, facial expressions, and vocalization.	Look at simple concept books to name and label familiar objects.
First oral language usually contains beginning consonant and vowel sounds.	Sights and sounds make impressions.	React to familiar people and other stimuli.	Enjoy lullabies and songbooks that are sung or told.
Parents' reactions encourage and reinforce the child's attempts at vocalization.	Learn through play with objects and as an active partner with others.		Enjoy finger rhymes, games, and interactive books that encourage active physical movements and interactions with others.
	Recognize familiar objects and acquire names for them.		Prefer literature that stimulates sensory awareness.
			Like short, simple stories about familiar world.
			Need many "two-lap" reading experiences.
			Enjoy turning pages while looking at books with others.
Toddlers (2–3 Years Old)	**Toddlers (2–3 Years Old)**	**Toddlers (2–3 Years Old)**	**Toddlers (2–3 Years Old)**
Language develops rapidly.	May move into Piaget's *preoperational stage*.	Begin to develop independence ("me do"), begin to dress and care for personal needs.	In addition to the materials above, older toddlers like fiction, picture storybooks with little mysteries or characters searching for someone or something.
Identify objects and familiar experiences in pictures.	Use subjective judgment.	Begin to identify and hold on to personal belongings.	Like stories with child-parent relationships.
Name large and small body parts.	Can classify familiar objects.	May be argumentative about personal objects ("mine").	Enjoy stories and concept books about familiar animals, pets, and objects.
Repeat rhyming, repetitive words and phrases and play with language.	Can remember two or three items in a list.	Still need to feel secure.	Prefer books with a simple story line and real and fanciful humans/animals.
By two years many are using 50–200 words and 2–3 word sentences.	Do not distinguish between fact and fantasy.	Sibling rivalry begins.	Enjoy literature with familiar sounds from surroundings, nature, animals.
Use "telegraphic" speech (only basic words necessary to communicate, e.g., "Mary go").		Imitate observed behaviors.	Respond to books with patterned sounds of naming and action words and phrases.
		Transform objects into make-believe objects, e.g., a rock becomes an animal.	Enjoy simple, rhythmic nursery rhymes.
		Begin to be aware of differences between boys and girls.	

CHARACTERISTICS OF CHILDREN'S LANGUAGE, COGNITIVE, AND SOCIAL DEVELOPMENT, LITERARY PREFERENCES, AND INTERESTS

The characteristics associated with children's language, cognitive, and social development and the statements about their literary preferences and interests can be used as guidelines for selecting suitable literature for children of various ages. As is typical of all generalizations about children's development and preferences and interests, some children may prefer visual or verbal narratives enjoyed by older or younger girls or boys. Characteristics of the language, cognitive, and social development of babies through young people aged fourteen, as well as their literary preferences and interests, are listed in Tables 1.3 through 1.8.[16]

TABLE 1.4 Language, Cognitive, and Social Development and Literary Preferences and Interests of Children Three and Four Years Old

LANGUAGE DEVELOPMENT	COGNITIVE DEVELOPMENT	SOCIAL DEVELOPMENT	LITERARY PREFERENCES
At three years use up to 900 words and 3–4-word sentences.	Some are in Piaget's *preoperational stage.*	Some are in Erikson's *Initiative versus Guilt stage.*	Prefer realistic picture storybooks about everyday experiences, immediate environment, interacting with family members, extended family and friends.
At four years use up to 1,500 words and 5–5 ½-word sentences.	Behavior is based on subjective judgment.	Are egocentric; feel they are the center of the universe.	Enjoy books with favorite TV characters.
Enjoy manipulating the sounds and rhythms of language, nonsense words.	Can observe an act and imitate it later.	Are developing a concept of self and are aware of personal feelings.	Enjoy simple Low Fantasy with imaginary friends, animals, personified toys.
Can articulate most consonant sounds.	Until later cannot place objects in different groupings by color, size, shape, or use.	Require a caring, safe environment.	Many are afraid of scary books with strange animals, strangers, or frightening situations.
Understand some rules of language and may use past tense; may overgeneralize "ed" and "s."	Many judge an object on the basis of appearance; cannot understand quantities remain the same despite changes in appearance.	Cannot sit still for long periods of time.	Have a natural affinity for animals; prefer books with pets.
Ask many "why" or "how" questions.	Attend to only one dimension at a time.	May withdraw from an unhappy situation; often suggest the problem does not exist.	Like simple concept books about immediate environment, occupations, some wild animals, seasons.
Speech is becoming more complex; are comfortable using adjectives, adverbs, pronouns, and prepositions.	Cannot begin at the end of an operation and work back to the start.	May blame others for their mistakes.	At four years enjoy absurd situations and foolish, silly behavior.
Most interpret language literally.	Cannot understand someone else's point of view.	Are beginning to be aware of cultural background.	Develop an awareness of "story schema" and book-sharing skills.
Most can use language to express needs, feelings.	Many are stubborn and resist ordinary routines.	Judge the feelings of others by observing their nonverbal language.	Prefer simple, fast-moving, sequenced plots with suspense and quick, happy endings.
Can tell a simple story, but not necessarily in the proper sequence.	Many cannot distinguish between fact and fantasy; believe inanimate objects are alive.	Enjoy playing with other children and developing friendships; some develop imaginary friends.	Enjoy reading about human or animal childlike characters who have similar experiences and succeed.
	Believe natural phenomena are caused by human beings.	Develop independence for personal care; resist adult help.	Continued interest in rhythmic sounds, repetition of phrases.
		At four years begin to move from "mine" to "ours."	Enjoy playing with silly words, upside-down situations, preposterous incongruities.
		Enjoy "parallel" play.	
		Have short attention spans and move quickly from one activity to another, often without completing a task.	
		Jealousy and sibling rivalry expected.	

TABLE 1.5 Language, Cognitive, and Social Development and Literary Preferences and Interests of Kindergarten Children

LANGUAGE DEVELOPMENT	COGNITIVE DEVELOPMENT	SOCIAL DEVELOPMENT	LITERARY PREFERENCES
At five years use up to 2,200 words and longer sentences averaging 6 words.	Most are in Piaget's *preoperational stage.*	Most are in Erikson's *Initiative versus Guilt stage.*	Enjoy stories with conflicts and characters who must take responsibility for their actions.
Language is more complicated; use clauses.	Many can remember and complete several directions.	Usually are outgoing, sociable, and friendly.	Like to hear longer stories and poems.
Most produce grammatically correct sentences.	Most can classify objects according to distinguishing features, such as size, shape, color, and use.	Are still egocentric.	Big books are popular.
Understand and use many prepositions.	May pretend to tell time, but have a limited understanding of the concept of past or future time.	Most can handle their emotions better, but may lose control in a new, unusual, or frightening situation.	Are aware of story structure and patterns of rhyming verses.
Ask many questions searching for information and meaning of words.	Are beginning to separate reality and fantasy.	Many respond to intrinsic motivation.	Prefer realistic stories, but Low Fantasy (animals, personified objects) bordering on fantasy is also popular.
Enjoy retelling a short story if it is organized in a logical sequence.		A caring, secure environment is still needed.	Enjoy concept books explaining simple, familiar objects and topics of personal interest.
Begin to learn to read and write their names and label objects; some are beginning to write simple sentences.		Are more cooperative, but tend to be aggressive in some situations; may blame others for mistakes.	Like to browse through books alone.
Enjoy participating in simple dramatic presentations, skits, puppet shows, etc.		Are beginning to understand consequences and rewards of personal behavior.	Enjoy looking at picture books with friends.
Memorize favorite stories and poems; "pretend" read the visual and verbal narratives.		May exhibit unacceptable behavior when seeking attention.	Prefer literature with structured plot, fast action, suspense, simple story line, and a happy ending.
		Enjoy playing with others, but like to work alone.	Like simple, illustrated folktales.
		Enjoy role-playing family interactions, occupations, gender-related roles.	Enjoy humorous, predictable prose and poetry.
		Are aware of cultural background.	Appreciate new and unique language when shared with an adult or older child.
		Loud noises, strange places, or different animals might frighten them.	Enjoy zany stories and poems.
			Wordless books, concept books, (counting, alphabet with a story) picture storybooks, and narrative, humorous poems are favorites.

TABLE 1.6 Language, Cognitive, and Social Development and Literary Preferences and Interests of Children Six and Seven Years Old

LANGUAGE DEVELOPMENT	COGNITIVE DEVELOPMENT	SOCIAL DEVELOPMENT	LITERARY PREFERENCES
At six years use 2,500 words and 7-word sentences.	Children are in Piaget's *pre-operational stage.*	May be in Erickson's *Initiative versus Guilt stage.*	Enjoy simple folktales, trickster tales, Mother Goose rhymes.
Most use more complex sentences.	Mature children move into Piaget's *concrete operational stage.*	Many are developing emotional stability and confidence in others, but in stressful situations might strike out against adults and other children.	Enjoy realistic books and poems about immediate family, extended family, intergenerational characters, personal concerns and interactions between characters; and environment.
Many use correct pronouns and verbs and understand approximately 6,000 words.	Many can reason logically.		
Enjoy telling stories, reciting favorite poems, using language for dramatic play, such as reader's theatre, puppet shows, simple plays.	Most can engage in flexible and reversible mental operations.	Many are becoming independent from adults.	Like real and fantasy adventures.
	Most can classify objects according to a particular attribute such as size, shape, or order.	Most are dependable and helpful to parents and teachers; still need a caring, secure environment.	Familiar with structures of stories and poems.
Enjoy playing with multiple meanings of words; manipulate language.	Most can count to ten and identify ten objects; many can count higher and have a basic understanding of simple number concepts, such as "greater than" and "less than."	Sibling rivalry is apparent, but most protect younger siblings and other children.	Aware of nonfiction text structure.
Enjoy rereading a favorite book many times and talking about the book with peers and adults.		Respond to praise; take pride in their accomplishments at home and school.	Enjoy more complex plot, several problems, foreshadowing, surprise endings; expect justice in story line.
Most are capable of communicating with others.	Most identify and use primary colors.	Many are very anxious about the unknown.	Like to hear stories and poems they may not be able to read independently.
Children are expanding their reading and writing abilities.	Many can focus on several aspects of an event simultaneously.	Value friendships and playing with friends, but want to be first.	Enjoy illustrated information books about topics of interest, such as hobbies, travels.
	They still have a vague concept of the passing of time, but many can tell time.	Enjoy playing outside with favorite toys.	Like Low Fantasy, anthropomorphic animals, objects.
	Most can distinguish between reality and fantasy.	Many sit and listen to appealing stories, poems, and instructions from adults.	Can identify and empathize with characters.
	Many can deal with abstract ideas and statements not tied to something observable or imaginable.	Have definite ideas about right and wrong; may be inflexible in their opinions.	Enjoy hearing and repeating new, unique words, phrases, verses, repetitive language.
	Short-term memory improves with age; a five-year-old can recall four or five numbers; a ten-year-old can recall six or seven.	Enjoy visiting familiar and new places with trusted persons.	Enjoy slapstick humor.
		Are aware that humans and animals suffer pain, death, and sorrow, as well as happiness.	Enjoy picture storybooks, wordless books, easy-to-read, beginning readers, concept books, short chapter books.
		Are aware of cultural background.	Enjoy books written or illustrated by a favorite person.
			Enjoy reading series books.
			Like to choose literature.

TABLE 1.7 Language, Cognitive, and Social Development and Literary Preferences and Interests of Children Eight to Ten Years Old

LANGUAGE DEVELOPMENT	COGNITIVE DEVELOPMENT	SOCIAL DEVELOPMENT	LITERARY PREFERENCES
Oral, written, and reading abilities are improving rapidly; variations in abilities are apparent.	Most are in Piaget's *concrete operational stage.*	Most are in Erikson's *Industry versus Inferiority stage.*	Enjoy realistic prose and poetry showing peer and parent interactions and suitable resolutions.
Enjoy demonstrating reading, writing, and oral abilities.	Begin to use basic logic and problem-solving techniques.	Are determined to master tasks set for them.	Like information books about personal and curricular topics.
Use language for imaginative, affective, informative, persuasive, and ritualistic purposes.	Understand time and spatial relationships.	Constantly measure themselves against their peers.	Enjoy knowing about past events and like historical fiction.
Vocabulary is expanding.	Memory improves as many can focus on certain stimuli and ignore others.	Frequently feel inferior if they cannot prove abilities.	Prefer biographies of historical and contemporary subjects they admire.
Most use longer, more complex sentence structures, elaborate phrases, past tense.		Are becoming independent from adults and strongly influenced by peers.	Can understand flashback plot structure; enjoy episodes, foreshadowing, more complex plot structure.
Understand figurative language, multiple meanings of words and phrases.		Still seek adult recognition and support.	Traditional literature, High Fantasy, and Science Fiction are selected.
Enjoy playing with language, telling jokes, and scripted and informal drama.		Cooperative with peers, but may not be dependable and complete tasks.	Choose humorous stories and poems with characters who are the same age or slightly older and question societal rules.
Most apply acceptable rules of language, understand root words, and enjoy history of words and languages.		Feel confident in familiar environment.	Like longer, more complex chapter books, mysteries, photo-essays, series books, and favorite authors.
		Express fears about remote, unknown, fanciful situations with ghosts, witches, unusual or wild animals.	Girls generally prefer personal and social problems, realistic animal stories, and Low Fantasy.
		More flexible in concepts of right and wrong; begin to understand reasons for people's behavior.	Boys generally prefer nonfiction, books with action, adventures, and sports stories, and poems.
		Understand different points of views.	Like books with characters or information reflecting specific cultural and social backgrounds.
		Boy-girl "romantic" interests are beginning by age ten.	Choose books with international settings that depict typical concerns and have acceptable resolution of conflicts.
		Feel others should agree with their reasoning and solutions to problems.	Like strange but true content.
			Enjoy hearing and discussing literature that they might not be able to read independently.

TABLE 1.8 Language, Cognitive, and Social Development and Literary Preferences and Interests of Young People Eleven to Fourteen Years Old

LANGUAGE DEVELOPMENT	COGNITIVE DEVELOPMENT	SOCIAL DEVELOPMENT	LITERARY PREFERENCES
Most use oral and written language effectively.	Many are moving into Piaget's *formal operational stage.*	Many are in Erikson's *Identity versus Role Diffusion stage,* but their social skills are not consistent.	Diverse reading tastes, often gender related: boys like adventure, special interest (sports, hobbies), nonfiction, Science Fiction; girls like interpersonal relationships.
Enjoy discussing readings and personal writings with others.	Can apply formal logic, reasoning, and problem solving.	Are anxious to be independent from adult society; assume personal responsibilities, yet desire security and limited constraints.	Like to explore values, morals, cultural identity, personal identity, and identity as a member of a social group.
Many use complex sentence structures to express information, ideas, feelings, opinions.	Most can apply abstract thinking to problems; limited use of concrete experiences.	Conflicts between conformity and acceptance by peer group and family expectations may lead to rebellion and free exchange of opinions held by group.	Prefer longer books with believable characters who deal realistically with personal and familiar conflicts.
Most understand themes, character development, and motives.	Understand chronological ordering of past events, the passing of time.	From moment to moment, they change from moody, irritable, rebellious, and hyperactive youngsters to self-confident, happy, care-free young people.	At eleven years prefer happy endings, light, funny explorations, murder mysteries, High Fantasy, adventure; girls like romance books and poems.
Can use and understand satire, metaphors, similes, and symbolism.	Comprehend the viewpoints of others.	Because of uneven, rapid physical growth and changes, they may be critical, self-conscious, or preoccupied with appearance.	Most like books that address the reader's doubts, fears, and anxieties.
Adopt the special language of their peer group.	Able to reflect and monitor personal mental processes.	Develop a social consciousness; are aware of racial, gender, class, and cultural bias and stereotyping; develop strong feelings about groups.	Many topics may not be appropriate for elevens: inner-city gang wars, racial prejudice, premarital sex, social and political corruption; books often present a negative tone.
	Can form hypotheses and use scientific logic.	Have a sense of justice and are quick to judge and reject imperfections of adults.	Older students prefer realistic books addressing the five D's: drinking, drugs, divorce, depression, and death.
		May feel inferior and inadequate if they do not measure up to personal expectations.	Enjoy historical fiction and biography, myths, legends, tall tales, epics, ballads, novelle, High Fantasy, and Science Fiction.
		Strive to complete a job and do it properly; will diligently practice a chosen interest, such as sports, music, art; frequently get involved in too many activities.	Horror novels are very popular, especially those written by a favorite author.
		Strong influences felt from peer group; may challenge parental and social controls and rules.	Enjoy comparing contrasting points of view found in several books on the same topic.
		Develop strong expectations and attraction to members of the opposite sex; want to be accepted by members of the opposite and same sex.	Enjoy reading more complex information books, and reference books about topics of personal and curricular interest.
		Social behavior is erratic as they experiment with various ways to interact suitably with peers and in society; this may lead to confusion of roles and rejection by others.	

BOOKS OF FICTION

THEME

The theme is the author's main purpose (reason) for writing the literary selection. Typically, it presents a worthwhile truth about life to give the reader a better perspective on the human experience. Themes found in books for young readers include establishing relationships with others, searching for moral values, acceptance of self and others, respect for authority, the ability to cope with situations, and growing up.

- The theme provides unity and meaning to the plot. It can be either of the following:
  1. *Implied.* Revealed indirectly through the unfolding of the incidents; e.g., a philosophical statement.
  2. *Stated directly.* Announced explicitly. In folk literature, it may be stated at the conclusion of the tale as a moral.

PLOT

The plot is what happens in the text; it is the series of events (incidents) that moves in a related sequence to a logical outcome.

- A well-developed plot is built around the characters' conflicts with self, others, society in general, and nature. The author develops this conflict by using the following techniques:
  1. *Suspense.* The emotional reaction to the plot that arouses the reader's interest.
  2. *Cliffhanger.* A hook, the exciting ending of an incident that makes it difficult to stop reading.
  3. *Foreshadowing.* Clues about the outcome that stimulate interest without destroying the suspense.
  4. *Climax.* The peak or turning point of the conflict or the point when the reader knows the outcome of the incident or text.
  5. *Resolution.* The denouement, the final action after the climax.
  6. *Inevitability.* The feeling that the conclusion was necessary and inescapable.
  7. *Closed ending.* A conclusion leaving no unanswered questions.
  8. *Open ending.* The final outcome of the conflict is unknown.
  9. *Sensationalism is not acceptable.* Sensationalism includes unrelieved suspense focusing on the thrilling or startling rather than well-developed characters, worthwhile ideas, or content.

Typically, the plot is *organized* in one of the following patterns:

1. *Narrative.* A chronology of events.
2. *Flashback.* Events that happened earlier are injected into the chronological sequence of events.

Typically, the plot is *structured* in one of the following sequences:

1. *Progressive.* A problem (conflict) is presented; then the action of each event builds to a climax (rising action), followed by the denouement or resolution (the falling action) and conclusion.
2. *Episodic.* One incident (short episode) is portrayed to a conclusion, followed by other episodes. The incidents use the same central characters or a unified theme.

CHARACTERIZATION

Characterization is the development (portrayal) of the character's personality, behaviors, goals, desires, accomplishments, and the like.

Characterization is either:

1. *Round.* Characters are multidimensional and well drawn and show strengths and weaknesses.
2. *Flat.* Characters have limited personality or are stereotyped.

The GROWTH of the characters is either:

1. *Dynamic.* Growing, ever changing.
2. *Static.* Remaining the same.

SETTING

The setting, or the time and place described in the literary work, is either of the following:

1. *Incidental.* A backdrop to the plot development and characterization.
2. *Integral.* Essential to the theme, action, events, and those characters influenced by time and place.

STYLE

Style is the writer's choice and arrangement of words, phrases, sentences, and paragraphs. Style is shown through the following:

1. *Imagery.* The choice of words that appeal to the reader's imagination.
2. *Choice of literary devices.* The use of figurative language, sound, and diction (see Appendix A, Literary Vocabulary).

3. *Diction.* The choice and arrangement of words, phrases, and sentences in regard to the spoken language in a literary work.
4. *Tone (mood).* The author's attitude toward the theme, content, and characters of the literary work and its intended audience.

POINT OF VIEW

The point of view is the position from which the story is told. Authors of books for children typically use one of the following:

1. *First-person narrator.* "I," the person to whom the events happened describes the feelings and actions of others; a purely subjective point of view.
2. *Omniscient narrator.* An all-knowing third person, who tells all the relevant information about the characters' feelings, ideas, and thoughts.
3. *Limited third-person narrator.* Action is shown through the eyes of one person.

NONFICTION ELEMENTS
(Biography, Autobiography, Information Books)

SUBGENRE OR APPROACH
Biographical approaches include authentic biography, fictionalized biography, and biographical fiction. *Information books* include survey books, concept books, and experiment books, journals, and encyclopedias and almanacs.

ACCURACY, AUTHENTICITY, CURRENCY
The content and visuals in nonfiction books are expected to present *accurate, authentic, current* information about the persons, places, times, events, and content included.

- Nonfiction books contain *facts, theories,* and/or *generalizations.* The reader must recognize whether the information is presented as fact, theory, or generalization.
- *Stereotyping* should be omitted and diversity revealed. An adequate amount of information will be presented, and when applicable, *diverse viewpoints* are anticipated.
- Occasionally, sources used or recommended will be cited for future reference.

STYLE
For biography, the language and diction must be appropriate to the content, characterization, and audience. All expectations for narrative texts are anticipated for a biography. The book should be interesting and clearly written.

- Information books may be written in narrative or expository discourse. If a narrative text is used, the criteria identified for fiction are expected.
- If expository (factual) discourse is used, one or more of the following text structures will be used: simple listing, sequence, comparison and contrast, cause and effect, and problem and solution.

- For all nonfiction, a suitable amount of information about the topic is expected, whether narrative or expository text structure is used. The text and visuals must be appropriate to the intended audience.
- New, unusual, or specialized vocabulary will be defined or clarified in the text and visuals. A glossary or pronunciation guide may be included. The mood of the text is expected to be suitable to the content and audience.

WRITER'S CREDENTIALS
Occasionally, information books are written by professional writers in consultation with an expert in the area. When the credentials of the author are given, the qualifications support the accuracy and authenticity of the book.

ORGANIZATION STRUCTURE
One or more of the following organizational features are used, especially in information books: table of contents, index, glossary, pronunciation guide, chapter headings, and subheadings.

VISUALS
Captions, legends, labels, maps, graphs, and illustrations may be used in nonfiction literature to help clarify, enhance, and supplement the text.

CHARACTERIZATION
In biography, autobiography, and narrative information books, the author is expected to:

- Provide accurate information about the character's life, including strengths and weaknesses.
- Portray the cultural, emotional, and/or intellectual life of the person.
- Objectively portray the subject's life and times.

Summary

The focus in this book is on the *literature* and *the learner* (babies to young people fourteen years of age). Children's literature includes fiction and nonfiction compositions that authentically and imaginatively express thoughts, emotions, experiences, and information about the human condition. The compositions relate to the experiences, developmental characteristics, literary preferences, and interests of children at various ages. They offer the audience insights and/or intellectual stimulation. Authors use prose, poetry, and dramatic forms to present fiction and nonfiction literature. The literature is classified according to the following literary genres: folk literature, fantasy literature, historical and contemporary realistic fiction, biographies and information books, and poetry. Books with pictures are found in all literary genres. Quality literature for young people should adhere to the literary conventions expected of fiction and nonfiction literature. Whether a fictional narrative will have high literary merit depends on the author's ability to achieve a worthwhile theme, a logical plot, multifaceted characters, an appropriate setting, an effective style of writing, and a narrator who presents a clear point of view. Nonfiction writers frequently present the facts in an expository format, but narrative compositions are becoming popular. All nonfiction literature must be well written in an appropriate style. Accurate content with suitable details and coverage, an organizational structure appropriate to the content and reader, and visuals are also important.

With approximately 60,000 individual titles available in children's literature today, some general guidelines can help adults select quality fiction and nonfiction literature. Fortunately, a variety of sources for book selection are available to guide the selector; they include selection tools, review sources, professional journals and book awards. Approximately 5,000 individual juvenile books have been published each year since 1990. The books reflect the trends that have always influenced children's literature — child-raising philosophies, educational practices, and publishing techniques.

Based on research studies, certain statements can be made about the literary preferences and interests of children at various ages. Correlating these statements with information about a child's language, cognitive, and social development provides adults with information about the literature that is appealing to most children at certain ages. These general characteristics can only provide guidance, however. An individual child's background knowledge, experiences, physical and emotional development and needs, and prior literary experience also influence the literature he or she will choose to read, listen to, or view at a particular time.

This is a glorious time for children's literature. Parents value book ownership, teachers use literature extensively in all areas of the curriculum, and talented authors and artists are creating many outstanding books for children. Hence one can truly say, "Welcome to the world of children's literature!"

NOTES

The opening quotation is from Lewis, C. S. 1963. On three ways of writing for children. *The Horn Book Magazine.* 39(5). October. 459–69, at 460, 462.

1. This definition was developed during personal conversations between Goforth, F. S. and Houston, G. 1985.
2. Lukens, R. 1995. *A Critical Handbook of Children's Literature.* (5th Ed.). New York: HarperCollins. 7.
3. Avi. 1993. The child in children's literature. *The Horn Book Magazine.* 69(1). January/February. 40–50. The reader is encouraged to read this entire essay to grasp the author's philosophy about writing for children and the reasons for children's literature.
4. Wallace, I. 1989. The emotional link. *The New Advocate.* 2(2). Spring. 75–82.
5. For additional information about literary elements and nonfiction standards, see sources such as Dietrich, R. F., & Sundell, R. H. 1978.

The Art of Fiction (3d Ed.). New York: Holt, Rinehart & Winston. 45–47, 79–81, 127–30, 175–80, 217–22, 271–72; James, H. 1948. *The Art of Fiction and Other Essays.* New York: Oxford University Press. 3–23; Lukens, R. 1995. 11–198; Zinsser, W. (Ed.). 1990. *Worlds of Childhood: The Art and Craft of Writing For Children.* Boston: Houghton Mifflin.

6. The following studies report findings about children's understanding of literary conventions and cite pertinent sources in the field: Emery, D. 1992. Children's understanding of story characters. *Reading Improvement.* 29(1). Spring. 2–9; Lehr, S. S. 1991. *The Child's Developing Sense of Theme: Responses to Literature.* New York: Teachers College Press.
Additional articles containing instructional activities to stimulate children's awareness of the conventions are cited in the following sources: Cook, J. 1993. What characters! *Teaching Pre*

K–8. 23(5). February. 32–33; Manning, M. & G. 1993. Strategy: Genre studies. *Teaching Pre K–8.* 24(7). April. 84–85; Monson, D. L. Realistic fiction and the real world. In Cullinan, B. (Ed.). 1992. *Invitation to Read.* Newark, Del.: International Reading Association. 25–39; Norton, D. E. 1993. Modeling inferencing of characterization. *The Reading Teacher.* 46(1). September. 64–67; Norton, D. E. 1992. Understanding plot structures. *The Reading Teacher.* 46(3). November. 254–58; Richards, J. C., & Gipe, J. P. 1993. Getting to know story characters: A strategy for young and at-risk readers. *The Reading Teacher.* 47(1). September. 78–79; Watson, J. J. 1991. An integral setting tells more than when and where. *The Reading Teacher.* 44(9). May. 638–46.

7. Statistics reported by Gary Ink, Research Librarian, *Publishers Weekly.* Book title output and average prices: 1994 final and 1995 pre-

liminary figures. In *The Bowker Annual: Library and Book Trade Almanac.* 1996. (11th Ed.). New Providence, N.J.: R. R. Bowker. 542–45.

8. Avi. 1993. 45.
9. Rosenblatt, L. 1994. *The Reader, the Text, the Poem: The Transactional Theory of the Literary Work.* (2d Ed.). Carbondale, Ill.: Southern Illinois University Press. 22–47.
10. See the following for additional information about story schema: Applebee, A. N. 1978. *The Child's Concept of Story.* Chicago: University of Chicago Press; Brown, D. L., & Briggs, L. D. 1992. What teachers should know about young children's story awareness. *Reading Improvement.* 29(2). Summer. 140–43.
11. For additional information about language development, see sources such as Applebee, A. N. 1978; Britton, J. 1970. *Language and Learning.* New York: Penguin Books; Brown, R. 1973. *A First Language/the Early Stages.* Cambridge, Mass.: Harvard University Press; Loban, W. 1976. *Language Development: Kindergarten through Grade Twelve.* Urbana, Ill.: National Council of Teachers of English; Piaget, J. 1955. *The Language and Thought of the Child.* New York: Meridian; Slodbin, D. I. 1981. Children and language: They learn the same way all around the world. In Heterington, E. M., & Parke, R. D. (Eds.). *Contemporary Readings in Child Psychology.* (2d Ed.), New York: McGraw-Hill. 122–26; Wells, G. 1986. *The Meaning Makers: Children Learning Language and Using Language to Learn.* Portsmouth, N.H.: Heinemann.

12. Vygotsky, L. S. 1978. *Mind in Society: The Development of Higher Psychological Processes.* Cambridge, Mass.: Harvard University Press. 25. Also, Vygotsky. 1962. *Thought and Language.* Cambridge, Mass.: MIT Press.
13. Piaget, J. 1954. *The Construction of Reality in the Child.* New York: Basic Books.
14. Erikson, E. 1963. *Childhood and Society.* New York: Norton; Erikson, E. 1968. *Identity: Youth and Crisis.* New York: Norton.
15. For additional information about children's literary preferences, see sources such as Monson, D. L., & Sebesta, S. 1991. Reading preferences. 664–73. In Flood, J., Jensen, J. M., Lapp, D., & Squire, J. R. (Eds.). *Handbook of Research on Teaching the English Language Arts.* New York: Macmillan. Short, K. G. (Ed.). 1995. *Research and Professional Resources in Children's Literature: Piecing a Patchwork Quilt.* Newark, Del.: International Reading Association. 65–74, 116–22.
16. For additional information about children and adolescents' cognitive, social, and moral development, see sources such as Elkind, D. 1970. *Children and Adolescents.* New York: Oxford University Press; Gardner, H. 1983. *Frames of Mind.* New York: Basic Books; Kaplan, P. S. 1991. *A Child's Odyssey: Child and Adolescent Development.* (2d Ed.). St. Paul, Minn.: West; Kelly, G. A. 1963. *A Theory of Personality.* New York: Norton; Kohlberg, L. 1964. Development of moral character and moral ideology. In Hoffman, M. L., & Hoffman, L. W. (Eds.). *Review of Child Development Research.* New York: Russell Sage Foundation; Marlow, A. H. 1970. *Motivation and Personality.* New York: Harper & Row; Mussen, P. H., Conger, J. J., & Kagan, J. 1979. *Child Development and Personality.* New York: Harper & Row.

Connect, Construct, Create
with Literature

$\mathcal{W}$hen we connect to the author or artists' ideas—construct meanings from the thoughts stimulated by the visual and verbal narratives—create responses to the literature, we are transacting with literature and developing a life-long habit of using literature for entertainment and informational purposes.

How do you create a literature-rich environment in the classroom?

What is an instructional focus and how is it designed and implemented?

What is a Literary Response Mode and what is its purpose?

What is the Literary Transaction Process?

What is a Literary Link and how is it designed and implemented?

How do you determine a child's literary preferences and growth?

When we value something, we talk about it with others, we display it in a prominent place in our immediate environment, and we constantly add new examples to our collection. Those of us who value literature line our walls with bookcases, fill them with books, and prominently display literature in our home, office, or school. We share new and old literary selections with everyone in our environment—colleagues, friends, family, and especially children. We have an insatiable desire for books, both new books and old favorites.

Think for a moment:

Do you put aside the cares of the day to curl up with a good book?

Do you rush to the encyclopedia or another information book to find an answer to a question or problem?

Do you prefer reading books from a particular genre? Do you occasionally read a book from another genre if it is highly recommended by a friend or a respectable book reviewer?

Do you discuss books with friends, colleagues, or even strangers?

If you answered "yes" to most of these questions, you realize the power of literature. You are *connected* to the ideas presented by an author or artist. You *construct* meanings from the ideas stimulated by the visual and verbal narratives. You *create* pictures of the events in your head. Throughout this process you are actively visualizing yesterday's world, seeking a better understanding of today's world, and envisioning the world of tomorrow!

As we reflect on the place of literature in our lives, we naturally want to share our treasure with others. Fortunately, many literary experiences can be duplicated in the classroom. We can entice, motivate, and help children experience the rewards of savoring an author's words and phrases and enjoying the thoughts stimulated by an artist or poet. We can turn young people on to literature.

Certain factors, such as the role assumed by adults, the learner's expectations, the environment, and instructional strategies, can help young people *connect* to fiction and nonfiction literature, *construct* meanings from the ideas suggested by verbal and visual narratives, and *create* responses to prose, poetry, and drama. The first part of this chapter highlights the successful literature teacher, the variables influencing learner's literary experiences, the components of a literature-rich environment, the influence of various learning and development theories on the presentation of literature, suggestions for designing instructional focuses based on *aesthetic* ("lived through") and *efferent* ("taking information away from the reading") stances assumed while exploring literature, and visual and verbal modes of responding to literature. Next the chapter discusses the Literary Transaction Process, a model for incorporating *connection, construction, creation* components when exploring literature with young people. Suggestions are then given for designing a Literary Link, a resource for teachers to use when presenting individual literature to children. Finally, strategies to assess the student's literary maturity and elicit the literary preferences of individual children are presented.

A SUCCESSFUL LITERATURE TEACHER

A successful literature teacher is enthusiastic about literature and shares that delight with others. Enthusiasm is contagious; young people who are around teachers who share a love and respect for prose, poetry, and drama catch their teacher's delight and express positive reactions toward literary experiences. In such an environment, learners view themselves as readers, freely select literature for personal and group activities, and respond naturally to the selections.[1]

Successful literature teachers consider the maturity, preferences, and prior experiences of the boys and girls and expand their literary preferences by introducing them to a variety of quality classical and contemporary literature. Enthusiastic teachers model appropriate strategies and effectively present various oral, visual, and written techniques for students to use when reflecting, reacting, and responding to prose, poetry, and drama. Successful literature teachers discover their students read more books and enjoy discussing them with others.[2]

Realizing the importance of becoming familiar with a variety of quality literary selections, teachers may form Teachers as Readers groups. Teachers from a particular grade level, from all grade levels, or from several schools within a district meet at a regular time to discuss literature in informal sessions. The participants express their personal feelings about the prose, poetry, and drama they have read, and they share successful instructional techniques they have used with individual titles or thematic units. While sharing the books with colleagues, they can model various strategies used in the classroom, such as "literary conversations" (informal discussions) and visuals (transparencies, webs, and charts, described in Chapter 10), and compare students' visual or verbal responses to individual books (literary responses are discussed later in this chapter). The groups give teachers an opportunity to become familiar with a wide variety of books, enable them to share appropriate strategies to use with the literature, and encourage them to design classrooms that use literature for instructional and pleasurable experiences. Administrators who value literature-based approaches encourage teacher participation and schedule time for faculty to plan grade-level and schoolwide literature programs. Several sources describe the membership, organization, and values of forming Teachers as Readers clubs.[3]

In summary, a successful literature teacher:

Is aware of a variety of quality fiction and nonfiction literature.

Considers students' cultural background, experiences in life and with literature, and developmental abilities when presenting literature.

Uses appropriate strategies to help individuals *connect, construct, and create* interpretations of the literature they encounter.

Facilitates appropriate instruction based on the literature, learners, and curricular goals.

Arranges the classroom environment to enhance individual and group exploration and experiences with quality literature.

Invites students to collaborate with others in literature classrooms.

Involves learners in decision making, such as choosing literature for personal and group experiences and devising techniques for presenting literature and personal responses to others.

Thus, a successful teacher assumes a variety of roles. He or she is a *reflective* person, an *informed* professional who *models* and *designs* an appropriate instructional environ-ment, a person who *respects* learners and their interpretations of literary selections, and a person who *encourages* others to reach their potential. Figure 2.1 summarizes the roles assumed by successful teachers.

 ## A LEARNER'S EXPECTATIONS

Literature gives young people insights into their personal behavior and positive experiences beyond their personal environment. Through these experiences, they develop a greater respect for others. Through literature, boys and girls are introduced to the beauty, power, and flexibility of language. They acquire language models to use when expressing ideas, information, and feelings in oral and written communication. Because of these benefits, learners have the right to expect teachers to provide opportunities to use literature. Figure 2.2 on page 32 presents the various opportunities young people expect in a literature-rich classroom.

 ## FACTORS THAT INFLUENCE THE LITERATURE SELECTED BY YOUNG PEOPLE

Avid readers usually come from homes where parents, siblings, grandparents, or caregivers take them to the library, encourage them to read, discuss books with them, and surround them with a variety of reading materials.[4] The research is clear: learners who are given the opportunity to select, read, and react with others about literature develop a habit of reading literature for entertainment and information.[5] Jane Yolen's picture story book *Owl Moon* (1987), with John Schoenherr's expressive illustrations, contains features that entice children to explore literature. (See Yolen color plate on page 32.)

Ask children what factors influence the literature they choose to explore, and they will freely answer. Factors typically cited by children are listed in Table 2.1.[6]

 ## A LITERATURE-RICH ENVIRONMENT

A literature-rich classroom might contain an old easy chair, some carpet squares, pillows on the floor by a bookcase filled with appealing books, pictures of children reading, a poster advertising favorite books, perhaps stuffed animals, a large tree trunk covered with paper leaves containing young people's written reactions to books, or an eye-catching banner about books. (See photo on p. 34.) Such a room celebrates reading literature, listening to literature, writing about literature, and discussing literature

FIGURE 2.1   Roles Assumed by a Successful Literature Teacher

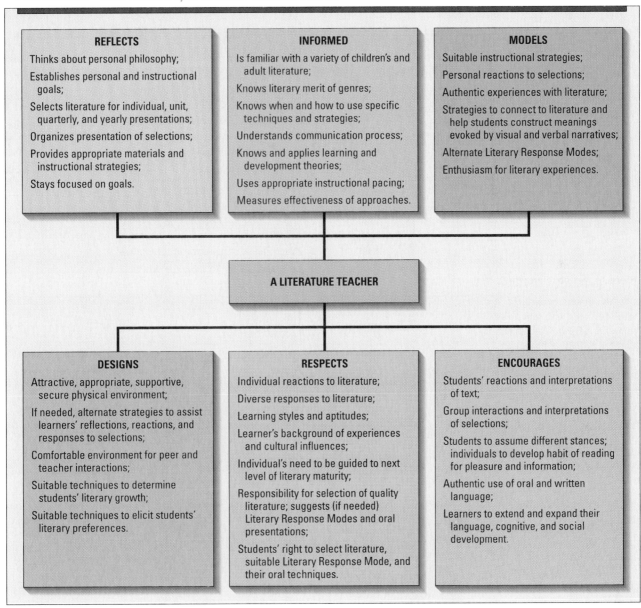

REFLECTS

Thinks about personal philosophy;

Establishes personal and instructional goals;

Selects literature for individual, unit, quarterly, and yearly presentations;

Organizes presentation of selections;

Provides appropriate materials and instructional strategies;

Stays focused on goals.

INFORMED

Is familiar with a variety of children's and adult literature;

Knows literary merit of genres;

Knows when and how to use specific techniques and strategies;

Understands communication process;

Knows and applies learning and development theories;

Uses appropriate instructional pacing;

Measures effectiveness of approaches.

MODELS

Suitable instructional strategies;

Personal reactions to selections;

Authentic experiences with literature;

Strategies to connect to literature and help students construct meanings evoked by visual and verbal narratives;

Alternate Literary Response Modes;

Enthusiasm for literary experiences.

A LITERATURE TEACHER

DESIGNS

Attractive, appropriate, supportive, secure physical environment;

If needed, alternate strategies to assist learners' reflections, reactions, and responses to selections;

Comfortable environment for peer and teacher interactions;

Suitable techniques to determine students' literary growth;

Suitable techniques to elicit students' literary preferences.

RESPECTS

Individual reactions to literature;

Diverse responses to literature;

Learning styles and aptitudes;

Learner's background of experiences and cultural influences;

Individual's need to be guided to next level of literary maturity;

Responsibility for selection of quality literature; suggests (if needed) Literary Response Modes and oral presentations;

Students' right to select literature, suitable Literary Response Mode, and their oral techniques.

ENCOURAGES

Students' reactions and interpretations of text;

Group interactions and interpretations of selections;

Students to assume different stances; individuals to develop habit of reading for pleasure and information;

Authentic use of oral and written language;

Learners to extend and expand their language, cognitive, and social development.

and signals that *reading, writing, talking, listening, thinking, and learning are taking place in this room!*

In a literature-rich environment, students are surrounded by print and audiovisual materials. Children are saturated with strategies to elicit and stimulate personal *reactions, reflections,* and *responses* to literature. In such an environment, the teacher considers students' expectations and attitudes to create a trusting atmosphere where literacy and learning develop and thrive. Teachers who consider each student's capabilities and interests encourage

them to reach their potential as learners. In an environment filled with literature, students and teachers select literature, discuss individual interpretations of literature, and build a consensus about the selection to become a "community of learners." Students in such an environment discover the pleasures and rewards of literature.[7] The atmosphere and physical arrangement of the classroom reflect not only the teacher's expectations about students but also the teacher's personality, instructional focus, and style of teaching.

FIGURE 2.2 Opportunities Learners Expect in a Literature-Rich Classroom

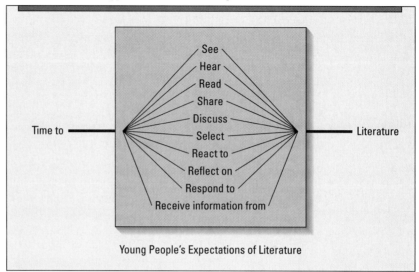

Young People's Expectations of Literature

John Schoenherr's watercolor paintings blend with Jane Yolen's verbal narrative in Owl Moon *to show the stillness of the open spaces while a child and Pa walk through the woods on a cold winter's eve to go owling. Do you see the rabbit?*

TWO LITERATURE-RICH CLASSROOMS

A visit to two literature-based classrooms in the same school reveals some of these valued characteristics:

Pat has hundreds of books, scattered all over her second grade room. Her children read and browse through them throughout the day. To the left of the entrance is a writing center with paper, pencils, pens, and markers. Books written by the children for several years about Max the cat, a class mascot, line a table next to the center. Behind the large writing table is a bulletin board containing the children's fin-

ished writings and visuals representing the literature currently being read in the class. A computer and printer occupy the rest of the wall. Bookcases lining the north wall under the windows contain Pat's personal library and books her students selected from home, school, or the public library. Included in the collection are award-winning works of fiction and nonfiction, other books with interesting content, and books the children are comfortable reading. Pat also includes several classics for her children to explore. She displays visual and written Literary Response Modes recently completed by the children on a small rope stretched across the room. In the west corner, Pat displays original wordless

TABLE 2.1 Factors That Influence the Literature Young People Choose to Explore

Previous experiences with literature (consistently mentioned by children):

    Books previously presented by the teacher or librarian.

    Books seen on television, movies, audio and videotapes, filmstrips, computer programs or other technology, i.e., hypertext.

    A book from a series, because they felt secure selecting it.

    A book by a favorite author or artist.

    A book containing an interesting topic.

Social interactions with literature:

    Children like books suggested by friends and adults.

    Children value interacting with others about the books they are reading, hearing, viewing, and discussing.

    They want to be involved in selecting the literature they read independently, with a partner, in a small group, and with the entire class.

    Young people are enticed to read books if commercial, district, school, or classroom incentives are offered.

Availability of books:

    Classroom libraries, which are imperative.

    Classrooms that advertise literature (through displays, strategies).

    Personal libraries, gifts, bookstore, book club.

    Opportunities to borrow books from a bookmobile or school and public libraries.

Features of a book that are important to children:

    An interesting book that keeps their attention.

    A book that reminds them of other another book.

    Characters who are believable.

    A logical plot that is filled with suspense and action.

    Events that depict interactions with others or the environment.

Favorite techniques adults use to entice the children to explore a book:

    Introduce a variety of books using oral presentations such as reading aloud, book talks, book discussions, and appropriate visuals.

    Several days after a student begins reading a book, have a short (1 minute) discussion eliciting the child's reaction to the book.

    With the student's assistance, keep a record of "favorite books" on the chart or in a database.

    Frequently encourage students to recommend and share favorite prose and poetry selections with others.

    Display students' visual and written responses to books.

    Discuss literature presented in movies, videos, and television programs.

texts published by the children. Information books containing social studies and science topics the students are studying are in a case by the wordless texts. On the east side of the front board are math papers the children recently completed. A science project is in production and nonfiction books related to the topic are located by the science center.

The children's furniture is arranged in clusters and moved often for various group activities. When you first enter Pat's class, you are overwhelmed by the number of books and original writing displayed in the room. One might wonder how the children and Pat can work in such a crowded room. You soon discover, however, that the children are busy reading, discussing books, writing stories and expository papers, and completing subject area assignments. Learning is happening in this classroom.

Tom's fifth grade classroom occupies a portable building. There you find desks arranged in clusters for cooperative grouping. Bookcases are on the north and east walls of the room. Information books relating to the various topics under discussion in math, science, and social studies are found in the cases. Single and multiple copies of fiction and nonfiction books are prominently displayed and readily accessible to the students. A movable display board is in a conspicuous place near the entrance to the room. Posted on the display are students' papers related to the various subject areas. A large chalkboard at the front of the classroom is used for large group instruction. Displayed on the west wall is information about literary groups, responses to books read independently and in literary groups, book recommendations, a science project, and social studies assignments. Hanging from the ceiling over the desks are various stages of responses to the different novels the groups are reading. Some students are working in pairs or literacy groups, while others are reading independently. The floor, chairs, and tables are covered with

These young writers are excited about writing original stories and sharing them with others. The question they are probably asking themselves is, will my friends like my story?

students and their current reading, writing, and talking projects. The teacher is participating in an active literature discussion with a small group of students. The room is filled with writings about math, economics, science, authors, poets, and artists. The students are actively involved in learning.

Each teacher clearly has respect for students. Each uses literature for various purposes throughout the day. Each has designed a literature-rich classroom by prominently displaying many fiction and nonfiction selections, as well as the products developed by the students while reading literature. In both classrooms the books are accessible to all children, who use them extensively. Each room has several centers. One room uses cooperative learning groups extensively, and the furniture is arranged to accommodate these groups. Although the teachers use literature for instruction in all curricular areas, they also know that, in literature-based instruction, all types of appropriate materials are used to meet the students' needs. An integrated approach is used for most instruction. In both rooms the students have literature books in their desks and read often.

In this school at least two teachers at each grade level are using literature-based approaches. Many children in those classrooms choose to take their literature books with them throughout the school. They talk about books with other students and adults. The Media Specialist reports the children use the media center extensively. Frequently, they know the title of the book they want to check out of the library; if not, they ask the Media Specialist for help in finding other books by a particular author, poet, or artist, or they request books from a certain literary genre.

PHYSICAL ARRANGEMENT OF A CLASSROOM

Teaching and learning are enhanced by an appropriate physical environment.[8] Teachers realize that students who are involved in various groupings need to be able to move around the classroom. To accommodate these activities, the furniture arrangement must be flexible and easily changed. While the size of the classroom remains constant, the furniture is rearranged to meet the needs of the instructional grouping. Learners are no longer confined to sitting quietly at their desks, completing worksheets. Rather, they are actively involved in peer, group, and individual activities that require open spaces, clusters of tables and chairs, and a variety of related books and audiovisual materials. In some classrooms children read under the table; in others they read in large beanbag chairs. When cooperative literary groups are used, desks or tables are moved to give children the space they need. Whole class instruction requires a different arrangement. Teachers must plan easy movement between the furniture and classroom centers.

Teachers in literature-rich classrooms experiment with the space by rearranging the classroom furniture for various activities. Plastic files for students' papers are set up in strategic places. Records and personal supplies are kept in a locked file cabinet. Large group instruction is still a vital part of the instructional period, but rarely do teachers arrange desks in rows that take up all the classroom space. Some teachers place their desk in a corner of the room or remove it entirely. If so, they use a small adult table when completing paperwork. Many teachers use their desks for student-teacher and peer conferences. Therefore, the desktop must be kept clean![9]

For particular instructional activities, teachers use a cart to move books and supplies from one group to another. Small quiet spaces, needed for pairs or small groups of students, are arranged by using movable dividers, such as large, decorated appliance cartons. Plastic file boxes and mobile bulletin boards are used for special centers. Teachers collaborate and share unused spaces near their rooms to convene temporary, small groups.[10]

Classroom Centers

A classroom center is a small space in the classroom reserved for a particular activity involving individual students or small groups. Centers give students an opportunity to be responsible for their own learning and behavior. In the past, preschool and primary teachers used centers extensively. Now as older learners are involved in more independent activities and grouped in pairs and teams, other teachers are discovering the value of centers.

The arrangement of the center usually depends on its purpose and the space available in the classroom or adjoining area. Some centers are simply large open spaces where students read alone or with a friend while sitting on comfortable chairs, carpet squares, or large pillows. Others include suitable-sized, large or small, round or square tables and chairs. Books, paper, writing instruments, appropriate materials, and directions for instructional activities should be readily accessible to students.

Centers designed for specific instructional activities are changed when the tasks are completed. Other centers, such as the literature center, remain in the same place, but are refurbished regularly with different materials. The centers must be attractive to entice the children to use them.[11]

The number of centers in a classroom depends on the size and layout of the room, the teacher's instructional goals, and the age and maturity of the students. For an ideal literature-rich classroom, teachers at all grade levels will have one or more of the following centers:

A *literature center* filled with a variety of fiction and nonfiction materials.

A *writing center* with a table and chairs for two to six students and a supply of writing, illustrating, and book-making materials.

A *message center*[12] including LitBits (questions about literature books); scavenger hunt clues intended to lead students to new books; a letter from a character in one book to a character in another book; a petition from the class to the Media Specialist to purchase a book; and a list of books recommended by a member of the class with a short message explaining why others should read the books.

A *discussion area*, a large group area with puppets, felt boards, and the like, to be used for quiet conversations and dramatic presentations.

A *listening center* with suitable records, tapes, videos, related books, and audiovisual materials.

Flexible learning centers containing specific activities to be completed in a short time and replaced with other instructional materials.[13]

Although having all centers is desirable, students must not be overwhelmed with too many materials and centers. Therefore, many teachers begin with one to three centers, preferably the literature, listening, and writing centers, and add other centers gradually. When the writing and listening centers are placed next to the literature center, students will read, listen, and view fiction and nonfiction literature while writing about related topics.[14] Combining centers is also possible; literature can be integrated into various centers by including picture books in the art center, for example, or adding information books to the learning center.

When a center is introduced, the teacher discusses its purpose, explains how to use the materials and equipment in the center, and gives students an opportunity to role-play desirable behavior. All children use a center before another is added.

After students become accustomed to using centers, elicit their help in modifying existing centers. Then, depending on the students' age and abilities, they can gradually assume responsibility for designing, arranging, and managing centers. In this way, students feel they own and are responsible for their learning environment.

The Literature Center

The purpose of the literature center is to give students an opportunity to explore, read, or view books, magazines, and other reading materials. Students use the center during assigned reading times and free time. When students are using the center for independent or group reading, the teacher can observe individual student's reading habits, desire to participate, ability to select and read literature for personal reading, and willingness to discuss literature with other students and the teacher.

The center consists of one or more bookcases and a quiet area. (See photo on the right.) Children in classrooms with literature centers read 50 percent more books than children in classrooms without them.[15] Young people of all ability levels are attracted to a literature center and will select literature from the center if it is visually appealing and contains books of interest to the students organized in an appropriate way. The literature center should convey the message "Come look me over and read!"

The placement of the center is the first consideration. The center should be large enough for several students to sit comfortably and should be easily accessible. Bookcases should be in a prominent place with a quiet area behind or to the side. Students like to spend time browsing to find a book for independent reading. They will read quietly if they have the privilege of using a quiet area. However, students lose interest in reading a book if they must hastily pull it from the shelf and climb over other children sitting around the bookcase. Table 2.2 lists the components and materials suggested for a literature center.

The Classroom Library Students and teachers should give book talks (discussed in Chapter 10) several times a week about books in the classroom library. The talks feature books students are not reading or literature recently added to the library. Place the featured books in a special place and highlight them with various "book advertisements." Change the books periodically and involve the students in the selection of featured books. Next to the book collection display *Book Recording Devices* (a visual record of books the children read, see Appendix B).

Some children need help selecting books for independent reading. Teachers can demonstrate strategies for selecting books. For example, the teacher can talk to the children about how she or he chooses books. First, look for a book a friend, newspaper, or book review source has

A classroom library is a special, comfortable place to explore books and other reading materials.

suggested. Read advertisements for new books, look for books by a favorite author, or ask the librarian for the names of popular books others are reading. Select several books, read the jackets and several pages and look at the pictures. From this brief review, we select one or two books to check out.

After the girls and boys are comfortable using the center, designate certain students to help monitor and rearrange books and related materials.[16] Table 2.3 lists information about selecting books for the collection, ideas for organizing and arranging the library, and procedures for the use and care of the collection.

The Listening Center

Individuals or small groups of students sit at the listening center to listen to, view, and read literature. Students can follow the story in a book while listening to an audio recording of the narrative. They can listen to books they

TABLE 2.2 Components of a Literature Center

Bookcases

Display books with the titles showing in an open bookcase.

Cover old bookcases with a fresh coat of paint or adhesive materials to coordinate with the color scheme of the room.

Finished boards placed across cement blocks or bricks make good shelving.

Plastic files, milk crates placed on their side, baskets of various sizes, and barrels are suitable for use.

When available, revolving racks are the best way to display paperback books.

Display racks showing the entire book are especially suitable for picture books.

Be sure the cases are accessible to the children and are visually attractive.

Quiet area

Students need a "special" quiet area to read books.

Depending on their age and behavior, one to four students can read quietly at the area.

Separate the quiet area from the bookcase with movable furniture or partitions.

Consider the size available for the area. On the floor behind the partition, prepare comfortable sitting areas for the children to read; use big pillows, beanbag chairs, a soft rug, large squares of carpet, and the like.

Some teachers encourage students to bring stuffed animals from home to hold while reading.

Browse box

The purpose of this box is to give children a variety of materials to review.

Barrels, baskets, and boxes covered with adhesive paper are appropriate containers.

The box contains appropriate magazines, newspapers, brochures, original books, plays, and riddle and puzzle books.

The suitability of the materials and the interests of individual students are considered when selecting materials.

Teachers place atlases, dictionaries, a thesaurus, and other reference books near the center.

Artifacts, pictures, models, posters, props, and other visuals related to selected books are displayed in or near the literature center.

Also display materials produced by students representing the literature found in the classroom.

can read independently or to books above their reading level. Several students can listen to the same literary selection at the same time. The components of a listening center are listed in Table 2.4 on page 39.

Reserve a place in the classroom for a special chair called the "author's chair." A child sits in the chair while reading original writing or a published book. Other children sit around the chair while the "author" is reading. This experience gives the child author and illustrator an opportunity to share creations and to practice oral reading. Schedule this activity several times a week. Place the chair between the listening and writing centers.

The Writing Center

A writing center is a special place where students gather to write. At a writing center, even preschool students can dictate stories to an adult. All types of writing materials from colorful paper and pens to a computer should be available in the center. Table 2.5 on page 39 lists the components of a writing center.

The Bulletin Board

Place a visually attractive, well-designed *bulletin board* near the centers. Use the board to advertise students' writings, content-related projects, and visual responses to books. Use the boards to introduce literature and curricular topics. Visuals celebrating the use of literature in the classroom and materials related to curricular topics are also displayed. The literature, curricular themes, holidays, and special events provide suitable topics for the board. At the beginning of the year, the teacher prepares the board, but quickly encourages different groups of students to design and decorate it. Remind the students of a few rules for preparing a board, including the following:

Use appropriate background material and borders on the board.

The lettering must be legible and large enough for all to see.

Some colors do not show up at a distance.

Change the board often to keep it visually attractive.

TABLE 2.3 Designing the Classroom Library

Book selection

An adequate classroom library consists of five to eight hardcover or paperback books per student. Some books will be part of the permanent collection; others are temporary selections.

The 100 to 150 books should represent quality prose and poetry, fiction and nonfiction selections.

The books should represent the children's literary preferences, background, and knowledge and be developmentally appropriate for their language, cognitive, and social maturity and abilities.

Include several copies of popular books.

Include books that accurately portray all cultural and ethnic groups. The books should depict authentic cultural values, lifestyles, and history.

Generally, books with racist, sexist, or controversial language or content are not placed in the library.

Include a variety of suitable, familiar and unfamiliar books, e.g., books read by the teacher, new ones introduced in book talks by adults or children, or original books written by members of the class.

Choose books that will elicit students' personal reactions, discussions, and divergent reactions.

Include books that stretch individual preferences and reading abilities.

Select books containing exemplary models of the English language, e.g., well-written descriptive passages, metaphorical language, and rhythmic, cadenced language.

Include some classics children will enjoy reading. These classics should represent the diverse literary heritage of America.

Include tried-and-true favorites such as *Charlotte's Web, A Light in the Attic,* and *The Random House Book of Poetry.*

Select fiction and nonfiction books that are related to topics to be highlighted later in subject areas.

Hardcover books are best for a classroom library, but children like softcover books. Paperbacks last a year or two in a classroom library, especially if the cover is laminated.

Involve students in the selection process as much as possible. They enjoy the task and gain experience choosing books for personal reading.

As various genres are discussed, help students identify distinctive characteristics of each genre. Encourage them to use these criteria when choosing books. (See the genre chapters for selection criteria and distinctive characteristics.)

Obtaining books for the library

Obtain books from your personal library, the children's personal libraries, the school media center, and the public library.

Go to garage sales in affluent communities and school media sales, and ask friends and family for old books in good condition.

Book warehouses and children's book clubs are also good sources.

Some school and public libraries allow teachers to check out large numbers of books. If this service is used, check out several books from the same genre, books with related content or special interests, such as mysteries, animal stories, and humorous books.

Write a grant for money to purchase books.

If feasible, ask parents to donate books to the library in honor of their child's birthday or a special occasion.

Request to use textbook funds to purchase books for the classroom library.

Organizing and arranging the book collection

Keep the center attractive and organized.

Organize books for easy access: alphabetize the books according to author or title, arrange them by genre or content. Use the numbering system used in the school media center. Color-code the permanent collection.

Display books so students can see the titles.

Display the cover of a "special book" temporarily on top of the bookcase.

Student librarians can check books in and out, repair them, return them to the bookcases, and select special books to display each week. Students develop a sense of responsibility and ownership of the books and care of the library.

At the beginning of a new theme, quarter, holiday, or other logical time, replace books that are not read by students, add fiction and nonfiction selections to fit a new theme, the holiday, or season of the year.

Procedures for using the center

The teacher and students plan, arrange, and monitor the center.

At the beginning of the year, teachers and students might formulate a checkout policy: how many books a child can take from the collection, the books students can take from the classroom, check-out time and the like.

State the rules positively, such as, "At the bookcase we browse and select books to read," "We read in a quiet center!"

Plan a checkout system for books to be read in the classroom and another for those taken from the classroom.

If grade-level teachers share books, arrange procedures and policies for sharing before school begins.

TABLE 2.4 Components of a Listening Center

Equipment for the center ranges from expensive commercial listening centers with multiple earphones to simple audio recorders, preferably with earphones.

Place the books and tapes together in reclosable plastic bags.

The teacher can produce tapes by taping reading-aloud sessions.

Record students telling or reading a favorite book, poem, or wordless text. Place tapes and material in the center for others to enjoy.

Most students enjoy listening to books, chants, jokes, riddles, tongue twisters, or rhymes. They like to hear a friend reading original stories. Also include the literature in the center with the tape.

After listening to parents read to the children, ask those who read clearly to make tapes of designated books.

Ask older children to make tapes reading stories for younger children or ask students from one class to make tapes about literature they like for another class. Place the literature with tapes in the center.

Buddies enjoy presenting a dramatic reading of a story, poem, or play on tape.

TABLE 2.5 Components of a Writing Center

Writing materials including the following:

    Stacks of paper of various sizes, shapes, colors, and textures, lined and unlined paper.

    Colored pens, pencils, markers, and crayons.

    A computer, printer, and supplies.

    Bookmaking supplies, such as cardboard, cereal boxes, glue, and dental floss.

    Rubber stamps.

    Notebook, rings, and fasteners.

A large writing table.

Various containers such as boxes and baskets to hold materials.

Labels, magazines for words, and greeting cards.

Individual folders for students' completed and ongoing writing are filed in boxes within reach of the center.

Completed written responses to books are prominently displayed near the center.

At the listening center these students listen to a book while looking at the pictures and reading the verbal narrative. One young reader was so interested in the story that she had to peep at the next page to find out what happened next.

An appealing bulletin board can advertise good books for young people to read independently.

Ideas for bulletin boards can be found in professional magazines and books.

Place students' responses to books on bulletin boards in the school hallway. Other appropriate places are a designated place in the school media center, the administrative center, or the lunchroom. (See photo above.)

AVENUES FOR EXPLORING AND EXTENDING THE POWER OF LITERATURE

The literature teacher plans and implements appropriate strategies that give students an opportunity to react personally, reflect, and respond to literature. The rest of this chapter will explore the many possibilities learners have to *connect, construct,* and *create* responses to the literature they encounter.

As teachers select literature and design instructional techniques to use with children while exploring it, they must also consider each student's learning process, their personal educational beliefs, and their teaching style. These factors influence the predominant teaching stance or instructional focus they use when presenting literature to children.

THEORIES OF LEARNING AND DEVELOPMENT

The instructional model a teacher uses in a classroom will be influenced by one or more theories of learning and development.[17] Teachers who rely entirely on textbooks for literacy instruction are influenced by learning and development theories represented by Cognitive Information Processing Theories and literature approaches suggested by author-driven theories. Cognitive Information Processing Theories are based on the assumption that discrete skills can be identified and that learners must master those skills before proceeding to the next higher level. Author-driven literary theories suggest that meaning in a book is static and thus is found solely in the text. Students are expected to "find the author's meaning." Additional information about author-driven theories is presented in Chapter 11.

Another literature approach, influenced by reader-response theories, ascribes to the belief that the author evokes the reader's interpretation of the text, but the reader constructs meaning depending on his or her personal background "schema." Reader-response theories are discussed further in Chapter 11 and provide the literature foundation for literature-based instruction and whole language instruction. Two learning and development theories, the Piagetian/Naturalist Theories and the Social-Constructivist Theories, serve as the basis for reader-response theories. The Piagetian/Naturalist perspective of learning focuses on a person's innate cognitive structures and the role of the environment in allowing language and general cognitive structures to unfold naturally. Piagetian stages are consistent with this theory. The Social-Constructivist Theory, based on the work of Lev Vygotsky, holds that knowledge is based on consensually formed social interactions.

All three of the broad theories of development and learning are used in developing a literature study. The wise teacher understands each theory and uses suitable implications from each to design successful literature-based strategies. Table 2.6 summarizes the instructional implications, the role of the learner, and the classroom environment suggested by each theory. This information is based on the writing of McCarthey and Raphael.[18]

INSTRUCTIONAL FOCUSES USED WITH LITERATURE

Many teachers are now a part of the decision-making process. They decide which materials, instructional sequence, strategies, and techniques they will use. In choosing the instructional focus for stance toward presenting literature, the teachers consider the needs of the students and the instructional goals. People who are involved in selecting strategies, techniques, and materials to accomplish their personal and professional goals usually work harder and more efficiently. Typically, teachers who are empowered to make curricular decisions also give students opportunities to make decisions about their learning.

TABLE 2.6 Instructional Implications for the Three Theories of Learning and Development

COGNITIVE-INFORMATION PROCESSING THEORIES	PIAGETIAN/NATURALIST THEORIES	SOCIAL-CONSTRUCTIVIST THEORIES
Instructional Implications	**Instructional Implications**	**Instructional Implications**
Teachers use direct instruction; hierarchical skills build on one another.	Instruction is based on natural wholeness of language.	Instruction similar to *Piagetian/Naturalist.*
Skills are taught in isolation in structured, artificially created materials, e.g., workbooks.	Broad objectives used.	Instruction *more* teacher directed than *Piagetian/Naturalist,* but *less* controlled than a cognitive information classroom. Lecture not employed, but if needed, the teacher introduces information within natural context, such as a mini-lesson.
Students learn letter sounds, words, and skills automatically.	Instruction exists in natural, recurring print environment.	
Actual reading and writing neglected until student has mastered skill areas.	Literature used for instructional purposes.	Students work independently or with peers and teacher.
	Focus is student centered, e.g., interesting topics and materials.	Clear, specific objectives developed around needs of students, then the content.
	Instructional focus on students' acquisition of strategies and skills in natural interactions with printed text.	Many activities encourage peer interaction and exploration.
	Instruction in class, small group, team, peer grouping, and individualized.	Teacher models strategies and supports students; assistance is gradually removed.
	The teacher is a facilitator, who encourages students to explore areas of interest.	The teacher is a facilitator, who encourages students to explore areas of interest.
	Students experiment with language and use it in functional, natural modalities. Teacher and students explore language and literacy.	Students experiment with language and its use in functional, natural modalities. Teacher and students explore language and literacy.
	Teachers use open-ended questions and promote opportunities to share responses, writing, and thoughts with peers and teacher.	
	Independent reading and writing are encouraged.	

(Continued)

COGNITIVE-INFORMATION PROCESSING THEORIES	PIAGETIAN/NATURALIST THEORIES	SOCIAL-CONSTRUCTIVIST THEORIES
Role of the Learner	**Role of the Learner**	**Role of the Learner**
Teacher assumes active role for instruction and learning.	Student is active discovering and constructing meaning.	Similar to *Piagetian/Naturalist.*
Student relatively passive, following teacher's lead in learning specific skills.	Learners interact with natural environment.	Teacher and student are actively involved in constructing knowledge together.
	Student's background schema considered for instruction.	Instruction begins with student's actual development, attempts to extend child to higher level of understanding (e.g.,"zone of proximal development").
	Teacher provides opportunities and models strategies for students to use when acquiring knowledge.	Learners enjoy manipulating language for communication.
	Teacher provides opportunities for students to learn to make decisions for themselves.	Students are decision makers and select literature.
	Children explore language and experiment with it in ways interesting to them.	Students actively participate as they develop literary strategies in a meaningful context and work toward specific literacy goals.
Classroom Environment	**Classroom Environment**	**Classroom Environment**
Pleasant, comfortable environment, but not vital for instruction.	Print-rich environment.	Similar to *Piagetian/Naturalist* with print-rich environments, range of books, opportunities for natural, functional writing, reading, and listening.
	Many books and other reading materials.	Instruction highlights the use of dialogue between teacher and student and among peers.
	Many opportunities to use and integrate language, for functional purposes.	Teacher not merely a facilitator, but formative in the development of students' thinking about literacy.
	Students select topics, books, and language activities.	Classroom is social because the audience is considered in reading and writing experiences and students assist one another.
	Students free to experiment with language without ridicule.	*Author's Chair:* Students share writings with others and develop oral language.
	Classroom is social because the audience is considered in reading and writing experiences and students assist one another.	*Dialogue Journals, LitLogs,* or literature journals are used to write reactions to a selection.
	Author's Chair: Students share writings with others and develop oral language.	
	Dialogue Journals, LitLogs, or literature journals are used to write reactions to a selection.	

The way teachers present literature is influenced by their personal philosophy about teaching literature, their teaching style, their personality, and their knowledge about the students' learning process. Teachers who believe that meaning is found "in" the text support author-driven literary theories. Teachers who believe meaning occurs during the "transaction" between the text and the reader support reader-response literary theories.[19]

Teachers who are influenced by author-driven theories think students will find the author's intention ("meaning") by reading the text. The meaning may be based on the instructor's educated interpretation. Usually, the teacher's instructional focus supports the Cognitive Information Processing Theories of learning and development. These teachers involve students in such instructional techniques as analyzing literary elements, explaining themes, and identifying specified facts to support the meaning implied by the author. To accomplish their instructional goals, the teachers expect students to answer literal comprehension questions, write summaries, and paraphrase the meaning residing in the text. Frequently, they adopt the instructional focus prescribed by content area textbooks. Most teachers use the teaching strategies suggested in the teacher's edition of the students' textbook, although they may modify the techniques somewhat.

In contrast, teachers who adopt reader-response theories generally design instructional strategies that are compatible with the Piagetian/Naturalist and Social-Constructivist theories of learning and development. Many teachers agree with Louise Rosenblatt that the reader and the text ("a set of signs capable of being interpreted as verbal symbols")[20] act on each other to evoke possible meanings suggested by the author's words. Therefore, teachers use appropriate instructional strategies, techniques, and materials that will elicit students' natural response to a literary selection.

Transactional Instructional Focuses

During the last decade, reader-response literary theories have become popular as a suitable theoretical base for the instructional focus of literature teachers. One reader-response theory, the Transactional Theory, offers valuable direction for teachers who use literature throughout the curriculum for pleasure and informational purposes. Three principles are important in Transactional Theory and are incorporated into a transactional instructional focus. First, the theory asserts that a reciprocal interchange takes place between the reader and the text, and through this experience a transaction is evoked to create a person's interpretation of the author's text. Second, during a reading and writing experience, a person assumes a predominantly *aesthetic* or a predominantly *efferent* stance (attitude) toward a text. This stance influences the reader's reactions, reflections, and responses to the literary selection. Third, because of personal background, various external and internal clues in the book, and the purpose for reading, a person may move freely back and forth on an aesthetic-efferent continuum while making personal interpretations. Teachers who endorse a transactional instructional focus implement a predominant *aesthetic instructional focus* (highlighting the *"lived-through"* experience or pleasure) and a predominant *efferent instructional focus* (highlighting instruction based on the *information students take from the text*).[21]

An *aesthetic instructional focus* encourages the individual to assume an aesthetic ("lived-through") transaction with prose or poetry compositions. Research findings suggest that, when young people are given a choice, they prefer to adopt a predominantly aesthetic stance toward the literature they read. When responding aesthetically to a selection, individuals describe their visualizations, wonder why certain things happened, and predict what might happen if they changed the plot. They also describe intertextual connections with other selections or express personal associations with the characters and events portrayed in the visual and verbal poem or story.[22] People who assume a predominantly aesthetic stance are involved with the text; the text taps a connection within the person and makes the narrative personal. It is this personal connection that helps turn a reader into a person who enjoys literature and searches for other experiences with literary selections. This experience alone is a powerful reason for introducing students to literature and helping them develop a lifelong habit of reading for pleasure.

The *efferent instructional focus* encourages the learner to assume an efferent (to "take away" information) transaction with the text. Efferent experiences give people an opportunity to move outside their environment, to begin to search for answers about important issues affecting others, and to value the universe around them. This focus highlights literary experiences that help satisfy a person's curiosity and might guide the reader to become more compassionate and concerned about others. While reading and responding to a text, students may ask questions about the content or literary elements in the text. To help students gain a broader knowledge about the subject or literary elements, the questions are addressed effectively in an efferent instructional setting. The efferent instructional focus guides young people to develop a lifelong habit of turning to literature for informational purposes.

According to the transactional viewpoint, adults share literary selections with children for different purposes at different times. Just as individuals move between aesthetic and efferent stances when experiencing literature, teachers may also move between suitable instructional focuses as necessary. Young people who are encouraged to adopt different stances with literature realize the purposes for each stance and are more likely to assume a suitable stance as they transact with a literary selection. Through instructional experiences that are compatible with reader-response theories, children learn to assume appropriate stances in future reading, writing, and speaking situations.[23]

Guidelines for Implementing Transactional Instructional Focuses   Certain external clues, such as the book cover or title, and clues within the text, such as, "Once upon a time," the book's format, or its literary genre, may influence the stance a reader assumes toward a text. The instructional focus also influences the predominant stance (or mind-set) the learner adopts toward the literature. Therefore, teachers must be aware of the predominant stance a person might naturally assume toward a text and use suitable techniques and strategies to help students make connections to the text. If necessary, teachers use appropriate questions to help students construct meanings and transact with the literature. While spontaneous, natural responses to the literature are valued, occasionally the

TABLE 2.7 Guidelines for Implementing a Transactional Instructional Focus

Frequently, teachers initially encourage students to assume a predominantly aesthetic stance toward the literature. Emphasis is placed on a person's private reactions, reflections, memories, images, sensations, and emotions evoked by the ideas and attitudes stimulated by the author's text.

Learners are involved in the selection of literature. They have time to read, reflect on the text, and react to transactions evoked by the text. This experience leads to personal involvement with the characters and events, and the literature becomes personalized.

Teachers show respect for the learner's spontaneous reactions and responses. These expressions may be used to stimulate further discussion.

Students select oral and written responses that reflect their personal interpretations as evoked by the text.

Students are involved in independent and collaborative experiences with literature.

The teacher's presentation and language influence the predominant stance the learner assumes toward a selection. For example, before reading Peggy Rathman's *Officer Buckle and Gloria* (1995), a casual comment such as "Gloria was a good friend to Officer Buckle" sets the stage for an aesthetic reading of the story; in contrast, saying "After I finish reading this story, I want you to tell me why Officer Buckle talked to the schoolchildren" sets the stage for an efferent reading. Generally, open-ended questions elicit aesthetic responses, and literal or critical questions elicit an efferent stance.

If a teacher observes that the students need assistance understanding factual materials, literary elements, or acquiring reading, writing, listening, or speaking skills, she or he moves to an efferent instructional focus. Occasionally, a mini-lesson (described next) is included in the instructional focus. This instructional focus could highlight the following:

 Discussing the text, such as the author's language, the features and structure of the text, the content presented in the narrative, and the theme.

 Recalling the content, plot, and characters' behavior.

 Using literature and relevant materials when analyzing, summarizing, and categorizing information to help students gain information, clarify issues, analyze, synthesize, and draw conclusions.

SOURCE: Rosenblatt, L. M. 1980. What facts does this poem teach you? *Language Arts.* 57. 386–94.

teacher will encourage students to create responses to the selection. Table 2.7 presents general guidelines for implementing transactional instructional focuses.

Mini-lessons   Occasionally, after students have participated in a discussion or shared their reactions to a book, the teacher might conduct a mini-lesson. A mini-lesson is a brief lesson lasting five to fifteen minutes that is designed to focus specifically on literature or content-related topics. A teacher conducts a mini-lesson if he or she observes that students need assistance understanding the content or literary elements of the selection or need additional reading, writing, speaking, listening, or content related instruction. Additional information about the purpose and procedures for implementing a mini-lesson appears in Table 2.8 on page 45.[24]

 RESPONSES TO LITERATURE

Think about the last book you read. Was there something in the book you *wanted to share* with someone? That was a *response.*

Think about the *mental pictures* you formed while reading the book. You were *visualizing*—a type of *response.*

Think about your *anticipation* of the events or characters' behavior as you read. You read faster to confirm, modify, or change your *predictions*—a type of *response.*

Think about the final *response* you shared with someone: "This is a great book!" "That was a dumb book! Why did I waste my time?" "Why did the author . . . ?"

Obviously, responding to literature is a natural aspect of immersing oneself in the literature. It gives us a chance to reflect, relive, or reread some or all of the selection. Human beings are social animals, and we have a natural desire to express our feelings and ideas about a poem, play, or story to other people. Responding to literature is a vital component of the literary experience—one we want to share with our students.

The responses at the beginning of this section are spontaneous responses that would be expected of mature readers. They are active, subjective, and usually emotional. Frequently, a reader pauses and reflects on the meanings emerging from the images evoked by the text. At this time the person attempts to clarify ideas, relationships, and attitudes sensed while transacting with the text. A response may or may not be observed by others. It may be overt and immediate or belated and surface long after a person reacts to a text. In his book *Rondo in C* (1988), Paul Fleischman writes about how listening to a girl play music evokes memories in members of

TABLE 2.8 Implementing a Mini-Lesson in a Literature Classroom

Teachers use mini-lessons to give students specific information about the following:

    Fiction and nonfiction elements used by the creator to stimulate reflections, reactions, and responses to a selection.

    Genres of literature.

    Linguistic skills or strategies they need to know and use.

    Content-related information needed to understand topics in a literary selection.

Teachers conduct mini-lessons with an individual, a small group, or the total class.

Immediately after the lesson, students apply the information gained from the session to the selection. For example, as students reread the text, they may use literary models for personal writing or convert a long, descriptive narrative to a conversation between experts discussing the passage.

Mini-lessons provide:

    An efficient way to introduce, review, and reteach skills and strategies.

    An opportunity for students to practice skills and strategies immediately.

Teachers are urged not to distort fiction and nonfiction elements or the linguistic devices used by the creator to teach a grammar, social science, science, math, art, or music lesson.

Running downhill till you can't stop yourself

Janet Wentworth uses pastel paintings for Paul Fleischman's Rondo in C. *The artist portrays the memories evoked by the pianist playing Beethoven's "Rondo in C." This young man remembers the freedom of playing at the beach on a sunny summer day. Other members of the audience think of special events, especially a young woman who remembers saying goodbye to a friend at the train station.*

the audience. (See Fleischman color plate.) Janet Wentworth provides a visual interpretation of the memories. This book depicts the power of the arts (music, art, and literature) to evoke ideas and feelings. This evocation causes a transaction between the person and the artistic medium and creates a response by the person to the artistic medium.

While many individuals respond spontaneously to literature, others do not choose to respond naturally. To guide children toward a response-centered experience with literature, teachers plan opportunities for them to engage in the beauty of the language, discuss their reactions with others, experiment with the writer's craft, or realize the vast amount of information they gain from literature selections. Students express their responses to literature by using a visual or verbal *Literary Response Mode.*

LITERARY RESPONSE MODES

A **Literary Response Mode (LRM)** is a visual or verbal mode produced by an individual to express her or his response to a selection. Many individuals spontaneously select and produce an LRM to represent their response to a selection. Occasionally, another person, usually a teacher, will need to suggest several LRMs an individual might produce to express an authentic response. The student chooses the LRM that most nearly expresses his or her response to the literary selection. Often teachers use a mini-lesson to give specific directions for future LRMs. For example, after reading the Ahlbergs' *The Jolly Postman or Other People's Letters* (1986), the teacher may complete a letter-writing session and then suggest the students write a letter to a favorite folktale character. Children could learn how to produce collages before the teacher suggests they create a personality collage representing their understanding of a book character's behavior. Students produce LRMs before, during, or after reading, viewing, or listening to literature and other media.

We classify LRMs as Visual or Verbal Response Modes. *Visual Response Modes* are divided into two classifications: *Artistic/Visual Modes* and *Manipulative (movable) Modes*. *Verbal Response Modes* are also divided into two classifications: *Oral/Aural Modes* and *Written Modes*. Table 2.9 on page 47 presents examples of Visual and Verbal Response Modes.

LRMs *focus* on the text and direct the person's attention to the content, illustrations, or outstanding elements in the literary selection. LRMs also *extend* the selection or present ideas about what "could" happen after the book is finished. LRMs might help students make predictions about future events or give them an opportunity to apply ideas presented in the book to other areas of interest. For example, an individual *focuses* on a text when writing a script for a readers theatre based on incidents from a selection. The selection is *extended* if the learner researches a historical period portrayed in a book and writes or presents an interview of a person who lived during the period. Whether focusing the response on the text or pictures or extending it, students' responses must remain connected to their personal meanings and interpretations resulting from their experience with a literary selection.

LRMs highlight the *outstanding literary elements* (the plot, point of view, content, characters, and the like) in fictional literature and the *nonfiction elements* (accuracy, style, content, format, organization) in nonfiction literature. By highlighting these elements, a person responds to the literary conventions the writer or artist incorporates in the narrative or reacts and critiques the creator's ability to use the elements effectively. Role-playing an incident from

Clare Newberry's black-and-white charcoal drawings for her book April's Kittens *are so real viewers cannot resist stroking the kittens while exploring this picture storybook. Newberry uses lines to show the shapes, charcoal shading for the kitten's fur, and red paint to highlight April and her kitttens.*

a character's life helps a learner understand the motives of the character and the author's ability to portray the character credibly. Experimenting with various media or artistic styles used by an artist gives an individual a better understanding of the artist's craft and abilities. Writing a conversation between characters from different books gives students an opportunity to focus on stylistic devices used by various authors or poets. The production of visual and verbal modalities gives children experience manipulating stylistic devices used by artists or authors. Through these experiences, the students understand the features and structures of visual and verbal language. After presenting Clare Newberry's book *April's Kittens* (1940, 1993) and discussing the realistic art used by Newberry, the art teacher could explain techniques for using charcoal and sketching kittens. While sketching kittens in charcoal, the boys and girls will recognize Newberry's incredible ability to make her kittens appear lifelike. (See Newberry color plate above.) After completing an LRM such as this, learners become discriminating in selecting literature and media. Other benefits individuals gain from producing LRMs are listed in Table 2.10 on page 48.

TABLE 2.9 Examples of Literary Response Modes

VISUAL RESPONSE MODES

ARTISTIC	MANIPULATIVE
1. Mural, poster, collage, mosaics	1. Board games representing literary elements
2. Travel brochure	2. Oral/written trivia questions/riddles
3. Woodcut/scratchboard techniques	3. Crossword, search and find/jigsaw puzzles
4. Thumbprint	4. Felt/magnetic/felt, magnetic, or hoop-n-loop objects/board
5. Illustrations for original books	5. Puppets
6. Character/country mask	6. Marionettes
7. Comic strip stories	7. Models (wood, soap, clay)
8. Artistic media	8. Cooking suggested in book
9. Peep show, diorama, mobile	9. Book quilts/literary wall hanging
10. Regalia, display/doll	10. Cross-stitch/embroidery suggested by literature
11. Pennant, banner	11. Scrapbook
12. Time line	12. Book binding
13. Lapel pin, campaign button	13. Wood construction
14. Flip book, big book	14. ID bag
15. Bookmark	15. Character clues
16. Book jacket	16. Wordless book
17. Bumper sticker	17. Personality pop-ups
18. Story in a can	18. Book cube
19. Advertising story board	19. Roller movie
20. Book scene on plastic tray	20. Slides/transparencies from book

VERBAL RESPONSE MODES

ORAL	WRITTEN
1. Shadow/finger play	1. Prose/poetry literary models
2. Chalk talk	2. Script: Interview the author/character
3. Charades, pantomime	3. Original song lyrics about text
4. Awards presentation	4. Publisher's blurbs to sell book
5. Panel discussion	5. Fan letter to creator
6. Auction book/poem/character	6. Original "fake lore"/literary fairy tale/book
7. Interview: author/character	7. Advertisement for title/character/author/series
8. Debate or mock trial	8. Diary/journal
9. Role-play	9. Script: Original play, reader's theater, radio, TV
10. Improvisation, creative drama	10. Literary newspaper (for genre, setting, etc.)
11. Reader's theater	11. Enticing book review for school paper
12. Formal drama	12. Write-on (letter to a favorite character and reply)
13. Radio/TV/video book talk	13. Letter/dialogue between characters
14. Puppet show	14. Rewrite story for younger child
15. Acceptance speech for award	15. Letter to friend/editor/adult recommending book
16. My-Candidate-for-Election	16. "What if . . ." letter/poem/prose
17. This-Is-Your-Life (character/creator)	17. Predict creator/character's future
18. Demonstrate topic in title	18. Rewrite with different characters/point of view
19. Cast dinner party for characters	19. Write reflections while reading
20. Commercial or advertisement for book	20. Compare titles written by a creator or genre/type
21. Recommend character	21. Literary preference survey
22. Sing original lyrics	22. Write "legal brief" defending character
23. Sing ballads, songs	23. Glossary/thesaurus/quotations from book
24. Story mapping (also written)	24. Biographical sketch of author/poet/artist

LRMs are "artifacts" to be shared, displayed, or placed in a student's portfolio. They are not graded, unless the student chooses one for alternative assessment, as discussed later in the chapter. Descriptions of LRMs are found in Appendix B.

THE LITERARY TRANSACTION PROCESS

Several years ago in response to the question, How do I present literature to my students? I searched the professional literature and to my surprise could not find a model for presenting literature that I felt was suitable. I wanted a model that reflected my philosophy of learning and development, incorporated a child-centered approach, represented the reader-response theories, and included information about the structure and elements of literary genres. I wanted a model that could be used with all approaches of literary study, including the Pure Literature Approach (which focuses on an aesthetic reading), the Literature-Based Language Arts Approach (which uses literature for language arts instruction), and the Literature Across the Curriculum Approach (which features literature-based instruction). These approaches are discussed in Chapter 11.

With these expectations in mind, I began to reflect on my previous experiences presenting literature. I knew that the audience wanted an enticing introduction and that they might need additional information about the content, characters, or pertinent information given in the book. I expected individuals to make associations to a selection based on their unique experiences and understandings of life and literature. Thus, *connecting* students to the selection and helping them continue these connections throughout the literary experience became one component of the model.

By accepting the tenets of Piagetian/Naturalist and Social-Constructivist Theories of learning and the reader-response theories, I knew students needed to be actively involved with the author's text. They needed time to think about, or reflect on, the literature they were hearing, reading, or viewing. Because of the influence of the Whole Language Movement and the Social-Constructivist Theory of learning, the idea that students are "meaning-makers" was intriguing and applicable. The concept *construct* became another major component in the model.

The integrated approach to language production and content areas is an effective strategy. When a complete literature selection is used, we expose young people to a cohesive plot structure, well-developed characters, comprehensive themes, varied settings, and a variety of linguistic choices writers use to express their thoughts, ideas, and emotions. Through this exposure and practice, learn-

TABLE 2.10 Benefits Individuals Gain When Producing Literary Response Modes

Individuals who produce **Visual LRMs:**

Are introduced to a variety of visual styles, media, and techniques.

Develop a knowledge of the artist's craft.

Appreciate the abilities of individual artists.

Use various media, styles, and techniques to enhance their personal artistic skills.

Use their imaginations as they express themselves artistically.

Have their efforts recognized when their products are displayed.

Recognize the importance of understanding the action and plot sequence when they write suitable questions for games.

Individuals who produce **Verbal LRMs:**

Explore, in written or oral form, their personal feelings about a selection and contemplate the reasons for their reactions.

Have an opportunity to explore the writer's craft, the use of language, and the sequence and structure of books, poems, and plays.

Use literary models to produce similar written or oral models.

Experience the excitement and rewards of creating original prose, poetry, songs, or expository texts.

Organize a topic, use an oral or written modality, and present it to others.

Enhance their personal oral and written abilities.

Have an opportunity to practice communicating with others.

ers can express their personal reactions and responses to literature using all visual and verbal modalities. Thus, the concept *create* was a logical component to include in the model.

Connect, Construct, Create became the components of the **Literary Transaction Process,** the model of literary study proposed in this book. Additional information about the process and suggested applications of the model can be found in Goforth and Spillman, *Using Folk Literature in the Classroom: Encouraging Children to Read and Write.*[25]

Individuals *connect* their prior background knowledge or experiences with the concepts stimulated by the author's text. These connections allow them to make associations with other texts and personal experiences, that is, to make intertextual ties. The connections stimulate predictions and expectations about the events and characters and elicit a continued interest in the selection. When individuals read, view, or listen to literature, they reflect on the ideas, images, and associations evoked by the text to *construct* meanings evoked by a "transaction" with the text. They react to their interpretations or understandings gained from the transaction to *create* responses to the selection.

Each component of the Literary Transaction Process—connect, construct, create—can be used alone. The process is fluid and recursive; that is, the components do not occur in a prescribed, linear fashion, but can recur at any time. One component does not necessarily precede another, except that individuals usually connect their personal knowledge with the text early in the process. Typically, the components blend into one another. For example, connections help the learner construct meanings from the ideas, information, and ideas stimulated by the author's text, while simultaneously, the learner creates reactions, interpretations, and responses to the meaning evoked during the transaction with the text.

Literature is not presented in a static, routine manner. Yet literature study, like all language arts and content area instruction, is carefully planned and presented. Direct instruction might be needed as in mini-lessons, or the teacher might need to serve as a group facilitator, a member of a literary conversation, or a participant in a literary group discussion. The Literary Transaction Process encourages optional roles and responsibilities for teachers and learners. The process must remain fluid.

Figure 2.3 shows the Literary Transaction Process in visual form. The overlapping circles represent the relationships among the reader's use of the three phases, connect, construct, create. The shaded portion of the figure represents the actual transaction between the reader and the text and reflects the dynamic nature of the nonlinear, recursive process.

FIGURE 2.3 The Literary Transaction Process

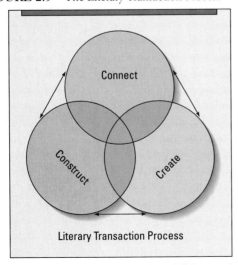

Literary Transaction Process

SOURCE: Goforth, F. S. and Spillman, C. 1994. *Using Folk Literature in the Classroom.* Phoenix, AZ: Oryx Press, p. 10. Used by permission.

IMPLEMENTING THE LITERARY TRANSACTION PROCESS

The instructional stance the teacher adopts reflects his or her purpose for presenting a literary selection. When planning the presentation of literature, the teacher selects the most appropriate grouping pattern. Whether a whole class, buddy reading, individual reading, small literary groups, or other grouping pattern is selected depends on the materials used: a whole class reads a novel, literary groups read different books, individuals read independently, and paired, buddy teams read the same book. Other criteria to consider are the needs and interests of the learners, the impact of the selection if read individually or in small or large groups, and the teacher's instructional goals. Picture storybooks or short novels may be presented through shared reading techniques or by the teacher reading aloud while the class listens or follows in a book. Grouping decisions for novels may vary from one reading session to another, as discussed in Chapter 12.

Because the focus and goals of the literary approaches (as discussed in Chapter 11) are different, appropriate strategies and techniques must be selected for each approach. To further clarify the connect, construct, create components of the Literary Transaction Process and to help the teacher select applicable strategies and techniques when presenting literature, Tables 2.11, 2.12, and 2.13 present implications about learners and implications for teachers. Many implications about learners *and* teachers are applicable to all three components. The components are not necessarily used in the same order each time. The order of presentation depends on the literature, the students, and the teacher's instructional focus and goals.

CONNECT COMPONENT

Schema Theory influences the *connect* component of the Literary Transaction Process. A connection to the text depends on the individual's "schemata," or the knowledge a person acquires regarding a concept or subject, that is hierarchically stored in his or her brain.[26] Schemata guide the individual's understanding of the content and the relationships suggested by the emerging literary work. Table 2.11 lists additional implications about a person's need to connect to a text and how teachers help the connection.[27]

CONSTRUCT COMPONENT

The *construct* component focuses attention on the reader and the text. It is based on Transactional Theory and the Piagetian/Naturalist and Social-Constructivist Theories of

TABLE 2.11 Connect: Implications about Learners and Teachers

IMPLICATIONS ABOUT LEARNERS	IMPLICATIONS FOR TEACHERS

The individual is influenced by:
 	
    Background knowledge.
 	
    Cultural influences and values.
 	
    Social experiences.
 	
    Prior experiences with literature.
 	
"Literary schema" is developed through exposure and experiences with the structures of various genres.
 	
Connection is also influenced by an individual's:
 	
    Linguistic and cognitive abilities.
 	
    Expectations for literary experience.
 	
    Interest at the time.
 	
    Literary preferences.
 	
    Stance assumed to literature.
 	
Individual preferences and past and present experiences with literature and life are more influential to the learner than the difficulty level of the material.
	Use the following, as applicable, to assist the learner's connection to a text:
	
	Use an instructional focus that assumes the following:
	
	    An enticing introduction is presented.
	
	    Natural probes, prompts, and questions are used to activate schemata and elicit personal and intertextual associations.
	
	Present additional information about content, structure, and elements found in a selection.
	
	Encourage the learner's curiosity, anticipation, and imagination.
	
	Use book talks, reading aloud, storytelling, visuals, and LRMs.
	
	Use suitable related books, stories, poetry, plays, nonfiction books, media, appropriate basal stories, visuals, and music.
	
	Display suitable visuals in the literature center and on the bulletin board.
	
	Place information books and materials related to the content of the selection in a prominent place in the classroom.
	
	Present relevant information at the appropriate time, before, during, and after reading the selection.
	
	Encourage learners to find additional information about the topic and share with class.
	
	Feature content in literature and in learners' LRMs in the literature center.
	
	Conduct oral discussion that focuses on the prediction of literary elements shown on cover, title, end papers, acknowledgments, dedication, and chapter titles.
	
	If not inferred from the context of the text, discuss unknown, unusual, or figurative language that might confuse the learners.
	
	Use various strategies, such as webbing, clustering, or other visuals (as described in Chapter 10), to elicit information about the story grammar or text structure to give students clues about the content and literary elements included in the selection.

learning and development. Its implications about learners and implications for teachers are listed in Table 2.12 on page 51.[28]

Reflect on a Literary Selection

While constructing meaning or transacting with a text, individuals need a period of quiet time to think about and reflect on the ideas, associations, content, language, or questions evoked by the text and illustrations. If an individual cannot construct meanings, it is a good idea to encourage him or her to use a strategy mature readers use: *reread* the portion of the text that is not clear.

Another strategy to guide the construction process is *retelling* a part or all of the selection. When we retell a story, we reconstruct the sequence of events and think about the major characters. This individual strategy allows reflection, reconstruction, and refinement of oral communication.[29]

Rereading and retelling are effective techniques to help learners clarify their understandings and interpretations of the author's text. These strategies give teachers an opportunity to observe the student's interpretation of the ideas, thoughts, and associations formed while transacting with the text. They replace the traditional practice of the teacher using many literal questions to test the learner's comprehension of the text. Rereading and retelling strategies can be used by an individual before interacting with others, or they can be used in a group setting. The strategies are particularly effective when young people are attempting to "verify" or search for interpretations and reactions about a selection and to reach an educated consensus.

TABLE 2.12 Construct: Implications about Learners and Teachers

IMPLICATIONS ABOUT LEARNERS	IMPLICATIONS FOR TEACHERS
Individuals construct intellectual insights and understandings from the author's literary work.	Because of the social and cultural aspects of language and the need to construct meanings, learners need many opportunities to share their original reactions to literature with peers and teachers. This sharing helps individuals choose to modify or reinforce their original meanings.
Learners combine the related knowledge that is evoked by the images and language patterns of the text to develop reactions and interpretations.	Students have the potential to develop beyond their particular level of independent functioning and a knowledgeable other (teacher or peer) can help them expand and make additional connections.
Communication is a social and cultural process. The "sense" (meaning) of a word is acquired from the context in which it appears. The meaning of a word changes as it appears in different contexts.	To assist construction:
Learners make meanings as they focus on images, feelings, and ideas suggested by the verbal symbols ("the text").	A teacher models reading, writing, and thinking and personal strategies used to construct meanings.
They gain insights from the associations made by connecting to the author's ideas, attitudes, and information while constructing these meanings.	Reciprocal techniques are used. The teacher models, then gradually relinquishes to the learner the responsibility for personal constructions. (See Chapter 12.)
	When applicable, the teacher models and uses probes, prompts, and literal questions to help the learner make connections.
	Literary discussion groups provide interactions with peers and teachers.
	Visuals such as story mapping, KWL, Attribute Charts, and Venn Diagrams, are used to encourage students to cluster and organize their thoughts and information. (See Chapter 10.)

They elicit holistic experiences with literature and are natural strategies mature readers use as part of the construction process.

Individual Reflections   Professional writers keep journals of ideas and events to help them remember their experiences and/or clarify their thoughts. Young people who use a **Literary Log** (**LitLog**) to record their personal reflections to literature also clarify their thoughts and may use the logs later for personal writings.[30]

After writing in LitLogs, students usually express a more sophisticated reaction to a selection. Some children use their logs to express personal understandings and ideas suggested by the text that they do not feel comfortable sharing in an oral session.

In a LitLog, a writer:

Expresses images, feelings, and emotions felt while experiencing a text.

Reflects on previous experiences stimulated by the narrative.

Reflects on the content presented in the literature.

Reacts to the writer or artist's style of effectively expressing emotions, ideas, and information.

Questions the artist or author's language, facts, events depicted, authentic setting, or character development.

Clarifies the theme or authenticity of the setting, events, and actions of the characters.

Makes intertextual connections between events in the book and other books, characters, or media.

Constructs meanings from the author's text.

The versatility of the log and the opportunity it gives students to privately express personal reflections stimulated by the literature make this a worthwhile technique to use with literature. A student's attitude toward writing, the instructional focus, and the teacher's attitude toward personal journals frequently determine the success of LitLogs.

Instructional Procedures for Using LitLogs   In transaction terminology, the focus of a LitLog is aesthetic; it elicits a "lived-through" reflection. If the teacher requests specific information found in the text, the LitLog is used for efferent purposes. The teacher who assumes an aesthetic instructional focus might elicit personal reflections to a particular portion of a text or encourage students to make intertextual connections to personal events or other books. In such a risk-free environment, students ask questions about language or content they do not understand.

When LitLogs are introduced, the teacher discusses their purpose and answers students' questions about the activity. During the initial discussion, students and teacher develop guidelines for keeping a log, such as the following:

Write legibly so you can read your entry later.

Write a word the way it sounds in your log.

Your thoughts are private.

Later, if necessary, other guidelines could be added, but too many may overwhelm students and cause them to limit their written reflections. Since reflections are private, adults do not read LitLog entries without the student's permission. Litlogs are not graded.

LitLogs are used in group discussions or in literary conversations with the teacher. During a discussion, the participants might ask for elaboration of short, incomplete replies. Writers are then encouraged to write complete thoughts in future reflections. Young people write complete reflections if they feel the teacher values honest opinions and thoughts. When adults write in LitLogs and share their reflections with girls and boys, they show the significance of writing personal reflections. Their students usually express a positive attitude toward writing and frequently choose to share their LitLog with the teacher.

Teachers may use probes or prompts to help students clarify their reflections. Occasionally, young people need help understanding language, content, or literary elements. Prompts elicit additional personal associations, determine the accuracy of the content depicted in the text, or make predictions about future events. Probes and prompts are discussed in Chapter 10.

After students are comfortable using LitLogs, they can change the format to a dialogue journal. In this technique peers and adults write reflections and dialogue about the narrative. While the LitLog is a successful written reflection, Written Literary Responses can provide other ways of combining writing and literature. Other ideas for writing in the literature classroom are suggested in the various genre chapters and in Chapter 12, such as writing responses to literature, using the structures and forms of literature as models for writing, and writing to convey information obtained from literature.

React to a Literary Selection

When young people enjoy expressing their interpretations, connections, and ideas about a book, they are reacting to it. Individuals clarify, modify, and perhaps confirm their thoughts about a narrative when they discuss their reactions with one or two people. Then, when they discuss their reactions with a larger group, they feel confident and may express more sophisticated reactions to the selection.

Students eagerly share reactions to literature when teachers schedule regular sessions to talk about books. Teachers who value the experience will schedule ten to fifteen minutes several times a week for small group sharing. (A suggested weekly schedule is presented in Chapter 12.) They hold the sessions after the children read a book, early in the morning, at the conclusion of the day, or at some other appropriate time. Pairs or triads meet informally, sitting on the floor or in chairs. It is not absolutely necessary for all group members to finish reading a book before reacting to it. Students discuss their reactions to a book they are reading, and if applicable, their questions are answered. Every person does not react during each session, but all participants are encouraged to express their reactions often.

At this time, a teacher can have a book conference with an individual child. Students initiate the content to be discussed in the conversation. If they are hesitant, the teacher asks a probe, such as "What would you like to tell me about the book?" (Other ideas for probes and prompts are given in Chapter 10, and additional information about book conference appears in Chapter 12.)

Literary Discussion Groups Language is a social process that matures as individuals express their ideas and information with others. The literary discussion group is a natural way to help students understand and use the various functions of language. Literary discussion groups also provide a forum for friends to share their interpretations of a selection. Through the discussion, participants explore and compare their reactions, which helps them express a mature response to the literature. Discussion groups, described in Chapters 10 and 12, are an integral part of the Literary Transaction Process.

Group Reactions Buddy conversations elicit oral dialogues, a natural component of reading. Many boys and girls who are quiet in large group discussions will talk about literature with one or two people. Frequently, in larger groups all participants do not have the opportunity to express personal reactions or fear that they may be judged by the other members if they express personal thoughts. In an informal buddy conversation, participants feel they are taking fewer risks.

A buddy conversation involves two or three children and an adult. The two-way communication between speaker and listener requires participants to observe the etiquette of conducting a conversation. Periodically, the etiquette guidelines need to be modeled and discussed:

Take turns talking.

Use a soft voice. Only the members of your small group need to hear your comments.

Think about what you are going to say before saying it.

Listen to others and respond to their comments.

CREATE COMPONENT

Although the *create* component is discussed last, learners could create a response to a book's general content before they connect to the text and construct meanings. Learners use oral or written modalities to create responses or interpretations of a literary work. The creating phase gives young people an opportunity to share their personal reflections or understandings of a selection with others. Learners and teachers use Literary Response Modes (LRMs) to create responses to literature.

This phase of the process replaces traditional book reports in which students literally retell the plot and analyze or critique literary elements, but may not include their personal reactions and responses. (See photo below.) Frequently, teachers use book reports to find out if students have read a book. Traditional book reports are based on an author-driven approach to literature study. Proponents of this approach believe that meaning is found

only "in" the text and that the learner is responsible for interpreting the author's intentions. The goal is accomplished when the student finds the author's "meaning" in the text, as the teacher understands it. The student then evaluates the quality of the text and the author's style of writing. This philosophy does not consider the reciprocal nature of the event between the reader and the text. The traditional book report is not compatible with the Literary Transaction Process.

Learners need many opportunities to use all language modalities (reading, writing, thinking, speaking, viewing, and listening) in a natural way when responding personally to the literature, thinking critically about the literature, and creatively reacting to the ideas stimulated by the literature. In other words, they need opportunities to create. Table 2.13 on page 54 lists additional implications about the learners and implications for teachers who encourage students to create reactions and responses to literature.[31]

Look where books are taking us. Read a book and join us!

TABLE 2.13 Create: Implications About Learners and Teachers

IMPLICATIONS ABOUT LEARNERS	IMPLICATIONS FOR TEACHERS
Learners need many opportunities to plan and create oral or written responses to the literature read, viewed, or heard. The instructional focus, the learner's stance, the particular selection, and the learner's needs and background determine the visual or verbal creation he or she chooses to produce.	Individuals do not produce a visual or verbal response every time they read, hear, or see a book. Creations are valued and respected. Creations are produced by individuals or a group. Learners are encouraged to share their creations with others. Ideas for creations must not trivialize the selection and the learner's reflections, reactions, and responses to a selection. The creation process must not overpower the student's personal response to the literary work. Note particular creations produced by students and encourage them to try different modalities. Prepare visual and verbal LRMs, artistic and manipulative modes, and oral and written modes.

 ## A MODEL LITERARY LINK REPRESENTING THE LITERARY TRANSACTION PROCESS

The **Literary Link** is the teacher's link to a literary selection. A Literary Link is a resource guide for a teacher to use with a particular piece of literature. The link contains information about the selection, such as fiction or nonfiction elements, information about the writer or artist, grouping of students, organizational procedures, other strategies and techniques to use with the selection, and related materials.

A large cottage industry has sprung up to produce teacher's guides for literature-based instruction. The guides, priced from five to twenty dollars each, are available for many popular children's books. These guides are written for a universal population, not individual students or classes, however. Usually, they are filled with many comprehension, irrelevant, literal questions. The workbook pages frequently include multiple-choice or essay tests for accountability purposes, but have no activities that require students to tap into their personal reflections, reactions, or responses to the literature. The guides may contain many excellent ideas, but because they usually use an author-driven approach and a basal format, critics claim the instruction procedures lead to the "basalization" of literature.[32]

During this transitional period, many writers and practitioners, realizing the instructional focus needs to change, have suggested a variety of procedures teachers can use to present literature in the classroom.[33] Fortunately, many outstanding professional materials are available that suggest various reader-response techniques for teachers to use in presenting literature. The books suggest thematic organizations of books and guides for individual books.[34]

As with all models of instruction, teachers need an instructional routine to use when presenting literature. The routine must represent the desired instructional goals and instructional focus, highlight important features of the literature, and consider individual students. The routine's framework should be consistent, yet flexible. Because each literary selection contains unique features, teachers need a variety of instructional strategies and techniques to elicit students' individual transactions with the text.

After reviewing the professional materials and experimenting with a variety of instructional routines, a Literary Link representing the Literary Transaction Process evolved. The instructional routine contains the three recursive components teachers can use to organize appropriate instructional goals and strategies to help students *connect*, *construct*, *create* with a particular literary selection. Procedures for designing a Literary Link are presented in the next section.

PREPARING A LITERARY LINK

To prepare a Literary Link, you need a *paperback book*, a *highlight marker*, and a *pen*. A paperback edition is recommended, because many of us were taught not to write in expensive hardback books. If a paperback edition is not available or you do not own the hardback book, you can use adhesive notepads.

Ideally, you should read the book aesthetically—to enjoy it—before beginning the Literary Link. The first step in preparing the link itself is to list information about the characters, plot development, setting, theme, style, and language of the book, along with its strengths and weaknesses, on the front pages of the book (put this information in the same place for each link). Next, read the comments on the front and back covers; this information might be used in a book talk. Also, note the dedication, information about the writer, and other information given about the book. Then, in the margins of the pages or on the notepaper, jot down your personal reflections, reactions, and questions you anticipate children might have about the literary elements or content (some people can do this while reading the book initially). When you encounter unique language, descriptions, or other stylistic devices you feel would be interesting to discuss with the students, highlight the passage with a marker.

Decide which pages can be "blocked" together to create a segment suitable for students to read in one session. Make sure each block includes complete incidents or enough information about an event or characters so readers can understand what is happening. This information should give the students an idea about what might happen next in the narrative. Authors frequently use "foreshadowing," especially at the end of a chapter. This is a good place to stop and use probes or prompts to elicit predictions and develop students' anticipation about what will happen next. Write probes (on the page or notepaper) to encourage discussion about the clues that support students' predictions. Later, students will confirm or change their predictions. It is a good idea to briefly annotate each block and place probes, prompts, LRMs, and log notations with the annotation. (For a model of the suggested format, see the Literary Link for *Snow Treasure*, an old, but popular and relevant book, in Appendix E.)

While reading, write additional probes and prompts as they come to mind. Write ideas for LRMs that seem to flow naturally from the pages. Note outstanding features of the book. Perhaps the characters are well-drawn, the plot is filled with suspense or adventure, or the setting is unusual or very familiar. Depending on the maturity of the students, you might also want to note weaknesses, such as inaccurate portrayal of a time period or inconsistent behavior of a character, to discuss at the conclusion of the reading. Be sure you change the LRMs from book to book. Making a crayon resist is fun the first or second time, but then it becomes a boring task.

Review the probes, prompts, LRMs, and log notations, and cull those that seem trivial or irrelevant. After identifying other elements of the Literary Link, select appropriate instructional goals that naturally evolve from the selec-

tion. Choose goals that fit the text and your students and represent school or district objectives. When chosen in this way the goals will naturally evolve from the text and be pertinent to your students. This procedure prevents books from being used to *teach* predetermined reading, language, or content skills. The Literary Transaction Process provides many opportunities for students to acquire and develop language and content. The process focuses on learners' applying the *connect, construct, create* strategies as they *read, reflect, react* to the books they explore. The Literary Link must include strategies and techniques to reach these goals.

Throughout the year, collect materials related to the book, such as newspaper and magazine articles about the book's content, visuals, model LRMs, bibliographies of related materials, and additional information about the creator. Store the materials together in a large expandable container, notebook, or hanging files in a plastic file box.

Initially, preparing a Literary Link may seem overwhelming, but it becomes easier with practice. Reading a book this way usually takes about an hour longer than normal, and completing the instructional goals and strategies takes several hours. The benefits of having a link readily available outweigh the time spent. In the heat of a discussion, it is helpful to have a handy reference of suggested probes, prompts, character information, and order of events to support ideas and stimulate further discussion. Once you have prepared a link, you can review it several years later and remember the details of the book and suggested instructional strategies.

A link is flexible and can be modified to meet the students' needs and interests. While reading and designing the link, think about the content in the book and how it will affect your students. Also, think about appropriate strategies to achieve your instructional goals. Presenting books in this way encourages students to explore the books they read and to honestly express the feelings and ideas they have experienced to *connect, construct, create* transactions with a literary work.

A model Literary Link for "Captain Stormalong: Five Fathoms Tall" appears at the end of this chapter. Procedures for collecting background information before presenting literature to students are found in Table 2.14 on page 56.

ASSESSING THE LEARNER'S LITERARY GROWTH

Assessment is most effective if it is part of instruction and focuses on the goals of the curriculum. When different types of instruments and methods are used, assessment is ongoing and continuous. If a variety of language modalities,

TABLE 2.14   Background Information to Collect Before Presenting Literature

1. Read the book aesthetically the first time. Then consider the following and write the information in the front of the book or on adhesive notepads:

   Highlight *outstanding literary elements* found in the text.

   Determine *grouping technique* to be used.

   Highlight *unique language* or outstanding *literary style* used by the author, poet, or artist.

   Identify *setting, characters, important content, artistic style,* and *media.*

   Write *probes* and *prompts* in book (or on adhesive notepads) by related text. Select those representing instructional goals, such as:

      Literal probes (encourage story grammar, recall, clarification of text).

      Inferential probes (focus on text and help the reader interpret the selection).

      Involvement prompts (relate to the reader's schemata to help the reader connect ideas, make associations, retain information, and stimulate emotions).

      Evaluative probes (encourage students to critique fiction or nonfiction elements).

      Extension prompts (allow a reader to explore beyond the author's text).

2. Block a suitable number of pages for students to read at one session, e.g., according to "foreshadowing," "hooks," a chapter.

3. Identify alternative Literary Response Modes that naturally evolve from the readers' responses to the selection *and* the instructional goals:

   Schedule time students will need to produce LRMs.

   Collect supplies for LRMs.

4. Annotate literary selection. If applicable, write a book talk.

5. Develop materials to connect to text:

   Select *literary genre/type* information to be discussed.

   Organize *bibliographic information* to discuss about the author, poet, or artist.

   Decide *award information* or *unusual features of the text* to highlight.

6. Select probes and prompts to help construction of meaning, if needed.

7. Collect related materials:

   Other books, poetry, media, or visuals.

   Instructional materials and supplies.

8. Identify instructional goals to be emphasized.

9. Estimate total class time needed to present entire book, i.e., reading, strategies, production of LRMs.

10. Collect materials for the literature center:

    If applicable, select Book Response Devices to be used.

    Design, organize, and construct a bulletin board.

11. If applicable, select assessment instruments to be used to identify the student's literary growth:

    If applicable, design a *student portfolio.*

    Organize a schedule for evaluation.

produced in authentic contexts, are used and the evaluative criteria are appropriate to the learner's developmental and cultural backgrounds, assessment is appropriate.[35]

Observations, checklists, and other informal measures are appropriate to use in a literature classroom to assess children's literary growth. Paper and pencil essays, formal book reports, multiple-choice tests, and standardized instruments are not suitable for the literature classroom. Unfortunately, in the name of accountability, the results of standardized, formal measures often determine the con-

tent to be taught in classrooms. Most proponents of standardized measures believe that if a subject area, such as art or literature, cannot be measured objectively, it is a "frill" and should not remain in the curriculum. Fortunately, many educators today realize the folly of this thinking and are designing alternative assessments, such as Portfolio Assessment.

Portfolio Assessment is a valuable technique for a literature teacher to use. The term *portfolio* was borrowed from artists. In the classroom, a portfolio is a large file, folder, or box used by the learner to store all or selected "artifacts" produced for each subject. *Artifacts* include LRMs, original writings, and papers written for each content area. Samples of students' productions are kept for each report period or longer. Portfolios give learners, teachers, parents, and guardians an overview of the productions started and completed by an individual during a specified period. A student's background and aptitude are considered when the portfolio is reviewed. Through various strategies, a literature teacher observes students using all language modalities in authentic settings.[36]

Portfolios are intended to supplement and, in some schools, replace standardized tests. Since the learners' language growth is measured by their ability to use language effectively, they must speak, write, read, and listen to others. Much has been written and research conducted on the use of portfolios in the classroom.[37]

The LRMs produced by a student provide an example of alternative assessment.[38] Students select the LRM to be used. The student, teacher, or peers might assess the student's literary growth using ideas such as the following:

1. The student can give a book talk, tell a story, read a book, or the like. The criteria discussed in Chapter 10 can be used to evaluate the student's oral communication skills. Several oral presentations can be evaluated throughout the year to measure growth and maturity.

2. A letter written from a character in a book to a friend in the class can be used for assessment. The student and teacher can use criteria suggested in the language arts textbook to evaluate the letter.

3. An essay can be evaluated using holistic grading techniques.

4. Written LRMs produced over a period of time can be collected and compared using criteria highlighted during literature or language arts classes. For example:

   Is the writer:

   Using more descriptive language? fewer clichés? figurative language appropriately? language encountered in the literature?

   Experimenting with a variety of sentence patterns?

   Developing characters? themes?

   Using dialogue between characters? Writing from a different point of view?

   Developing a logical plot structure?

   Portraying authentic settings?

   Using different text structures in expository writing?

To the writer:

What do you like about your story? your essay?

How is your writing improving?

Did you use phrases or words that didn't quite say what you wanted to say? What is a better way to express your ideas?

What do you do when you have trouble expressing yourself?

Read your favorite part.

5. Visual LRMs can be evaluated based on criteria presented in Chapter 8.

Literature teachers observe students' communication behavior, their reactions and responses to a literary work, and the LRMs they produce. A teacher uses criteria such as those in Table 2.15 at different times for different purposes to determine the learner's literary growth. Teachers

TABLE 2.15 Criteria to Assess Learner's Literary Growth

Consider the learner's:

Willingness to listen attentively to the literary selection being read aloud.

Contribution to the discussion of a literary selection.

Interest in rereading literature previously heard, seen, or read.

Request to adults to read literature selections.

Desire to read literature independently.

Response to a range of literary genres.

Desire to express an interpretative response to literature read, heard, or seen.

Ability to select and begin LRMs promptly.

Ability to complete LRMs accurately and on time.

Appropriate use of the classroom literature center.

Ability to express personal involvement with the literary selection.

Desire to express insights for personal behavior and knowledge gained from experiences with literature.

Suitable knowledge about fiction or nonfiction elements and literary genres.

Ability to apply literary knowledge, compare literary works, and identify literary heritage of various groups.

Ability to use literature in all discipline areas.

Willingness to voluntarily read literature within all discipline areas.

Desire to read a variety of literary selections that demand various cognitive abilities and thought.

Interest in literature and willingness to read for pleasure, aesthetic satisfaction, and information.

Willingness to select books from various literary genres.

select *only* those criteria appropriate to the student's age, maturity, and literary goals.

Based on the works cited earlier and experience using portfolios and other alternative assessment tools in the literature classroom, the following steps are recommended for assessing a learner's literary growth and maturity:

1. In the front of each student's portfolio, include a page for the student to list Books I Have Read and another page for Books I Want to Read. Leave room for the student to add the author, title, and short comments for each book. The first page is used when an individual or group completes a book. The second page is used when a peer or teacher recommends books the student wants to read. Both lists are ongoing and may be kept in the learner's portfolio during the year or collected periodically and filed in the student's portfolio kept by the teacher.

2. Graph the number of books read each month and the yearly cumulative record.[39]

3. List (and date) LRMs *produced* and *attempted*. Students will select the LRMs to be retained in their portfolio.

4. The learner keeps a Self-Evaluation Checklist representing his or her growth. See Table 2.16 on page 59 for an example.

5. During each report period, the teacher will observe all students and complete a teacher checklist such as in Table 2.17 on page 59 to decide a student's literary growth. It is discussed with the child and kept in the teacher's portfolio.

 ## TECHNIQUES FOR DETERMINING AN INDIVIDUAL LEARNER'S LITERARY PREFERENCES AND ATTITUDES

It is a good idea to determine the specific literary preferences of individual learners. Over a period of time, the teacher can observe how individuals and groups of children react and respond to individual books and literary genres. Literature discussion sessions are an ideal time to conduct an interview about the types of literature the children enjoy reading. Occasionally, ask the children to write in their LitLog about their literary preferences. The results of the observations, interviews, and questionnaires can be compared to published preferences to establish descriptors for a particular school (see Chapter 1).

Many of the instructional techniques discussed in this chapter and in Chapters 10, 11, and 12 are helpful in determining young people's preferences and attitudes toward literature. Particularly useful are the checklist for observing children's literary growth, artifacts placed in the child's literature portfolio, children's spontaneous reflections, their written and oral reactions, and their personal responses to specific literary titles or genres.

When eliciting learners' reactions to literature, it is helpful to introduce them to a variety of books, give them time to skim or read the books, and then ask about their personal literary preferences. Table 2.18 on page 60 lists a variety of options teachers can use to elicit learners' literary preferences.[40]

TABLE 2.16 Criteria for a Self-Evaluation Checklist

I am reading more literature this period than last period. Yes or No? _____

How do I know? _____

I select literature for personal reading from the following sources:

_____

_____

I enjoy reading _____ kinds of literature.

Last year I enjoyed reading _____. kinds of literature.

I had _____ teacher conferences about the literature I am reading.

I wrote in my LitLog _____ times each week.

I rate my participation in the Cooperative Literary Group as _____

Explain your rating: _____

I started _____ LRMs this period.

I completed _____ LRMs this period.

I learned more about _____

because I read: _____

I would like to find out more about _____

TABLE 2.17 Criteria for a Teacher Checklist

DOES	(STUDENT'S NAME:)	YES	SOMETIMES	NEVER
Participate in the discussion?				
Read silently (or listen) when others are reading?				
Participate appropriately in:				
Whole class reading?				
Cooperative Literature Groups?				
Buddy reading?				
Independent reading?				
Ask probes and prompts?				
Use context clues to read unknown vocabulary?				
Find examples of _____ (fiction or nonfiction elements) in other literature?				
Always search for books with a particular topic?				
Always read from one literary genre?				
Respond positively to literature?				
Make entries often in a LitLog?				
Reread literature heard, seen, or read?				
Respond to a variety of literary genre/types?				
Begin and finish LRMs promptly, accurately, and on time?				
If appropriate, did the learner:				
Complete a Book Recording Device?				
Apply insights gained from literature to personal life?				
Apply suitable knowledge of fiction and nonfiction elements and literary genres?				
Progress to more complex literature throughout the year?				
Read and write in content area classes?				

TABLE 2.18 Options for Eliciting Learners' Literary Preferences

Begin a database (bibliographic listing, brief annotation) of literature the teacher introduces to the class.

Help the learners prepare a database of literature titles they recommend.

Help children categorize recommendations according to literary genre, content, or other classifications.

Talk about the classifications and how they relate to the learners' literary preferences.

Periodically review the list and have children select the Top Five (Ten) Books.

Compare Top Ten lists and discuss literary preferences.

Elicit the help of parents or guardians by sending home a simple questionnaire, such as the following:

Check the statements that apply to your child's reading at home:

☐ My child suggests books for me to read to him/her.

☐ The title of the last book we read together was _____.

☐ My child reads to me or another member of the family.

When my child checks out a book, he/she selects it because:

    ☐ We have read it at home.

    ☐ The teacher/librarian has read it aloud at school.

    ☐ A friend suggested the book.

    ☐ The teacher/librarian suggested the book.

    ☐ The book was in a television program, movie, or videotape.

    ☐ I suggest books for her/him to read.

    ☐ A brother/sister/grandparent suggests books for her/him to read. (Circle the appropriate person)

    ☐ _____ suggests books for her/him to read.

    ☐ My child likes to read all of the books written by a favorite author/artist.

☐ The name of the author or artist my child has mentioned is _____.

☐ My child likes to read books about _____.

Give a similar questionnaire to the child in class. Have her or him help tally or graph the results and then compare them.

Use open-ended questions such as those suggested in the Self-Evaluation Checklist in Table 2.16.

Have small groups of children compare information from the Self-Evaluation Checklist to determine literary preferences of the members of the class.

Use applicable information obtained from the Teacher Checklist in Table 2.17.

Help learners recognize their literary preferences by reviewing their visual or verbal responses to a literature selection.

Periodically, use short oral or written questionnaires. Before distributing them, discuss the differences between literary genres, clarify content, and the like.

Select appropriate questions from the following:

    What was the name of your favorite book I read in class? _____

    What book did you read that I introduced in a book talk? _____

    Give the titles of two books you selected from the library that you would recommend to a friend: _____

    _____

    Lately, you selected the following *kinds* of books to read

    _____   _____

    _____   _____

    (*Or you can have the children check an appropriate box*)

    ☐ Myths   ☐ Mysteries

    ☐ Historical fiction   ☐ Humorous poetry

    Note: All genre discussed in class are listed.

    When I read a magazine, I usually select an article about _____

Note: Questions such as these could be added to the Self-Evaluation Checklist (Table 2.16) to determine the learner's literary growth.

Summary

Literature is a vital part of our lives. Students need to experience the process of selecting books for individual and group reading. They need many opportunities to browse and check out books from the school media center, the public library, or local bookstores.

Literature teachers are entrepreneurs, who advertise, share, and sell books! Children whose classroom is filled with books and audiovisual materials react to the environment and discover the excitement of making literature a worthwhile part of their lives. Techniques for planning and designing classrooms and suitable strategies were discussed in the chapter.

The *aesthetic* and *efferent* instructional focuses were also described. The instructional focus adopted by the teacher influences the stance a girl or boy assumes when reading, reflecting, and reacting to a literary selection. *Literary Response Modes (LRMs)*, visual and verbal modalities individuals use to create responses to literature, were identified and discussed. A model for presenting literature in the classroom, the *Literary Transaction Process*, was also introduced. The three strategies incorporated in the model—*connect, construct, create*—were described, and a variety of instructional strategies and techniques literature teachers use to implement the process were highlighted. The process is compatible with the three approaches to literary study.

The rationale and description of a *Literary Link*, a teacher's link to literature, were discussed. The link contains suggested probes and prompts, instructional goals, strategies, assessment of students' literary maturity, and related resources the teacher could use with a particular literary selection. Suggested procedures for planning and producing a link were presented. A model Literary Link appears at the end of the chapter. Techniques for identifying young people's literary growth were suggested, as were procedures for eliciting individual students' literary preferences.

Young people are more likely to exhibit a positive attitude toward literature when they are in a classroom that is conducive to reading, relating, and responding to prose, poetry, and drama. This experience will inspire them to develop a lifelong habit of reading literature for information and pleasure, the ultimate goal of exploring literature with young people.

Literary Link

"CAPTAIN STORMALONG: FIVE FATHOMS TALL"

FROM STOUTENBURG, A. 1960. *AMERICAN TALL TALES.* NEW YORK: VIKING. 37–50.

RECOMMENDED FOR 4TH–6TH GRADES.

GENRE: Folk literature: Tall tale

SETTING: The ocean

THEME: Humorous exaggeration

GROUPING: Teacher read-aloud
Literary discussion group
Paired reading

INSTRUCTIONAL GOALS:

- Become familiar with tall tales.
- Understand hyperbole and exaggeration.
- Evaluate characterization.
- Become familiar with whaling industry and tall sailing ships.
- Recognize geographical places in tale.
- Expand writing and discussion.
- Read for pleasure and humor.

SUMMARY

The storks brought Alfred Bulltop Stormalong (or he brought the storks who dropped him off) to the New England shore during a storm. He was so big that his parents used a whale boat for a cradle and anchored it just offshore because there wasn't any other place large enough for it. When they wanted to wake up the freckled-faced, curly-haired boy (who could walk at birth and had a full set of teeth), they blew a foghorn. For breakfast the baby would eat large quantities of whale milk, clam chowder, johnnycake, maple syrup, fish, lobster, salt pork, and baked beans and brown bread. As Stormalong grew older, he helped his parents on their farm, but his heart

(Continued)

was at sea. They tell many tales about this **A**ble **B**odied Sailor, as he sailed on the *Silver Maid.* Finally, he had his own clipper ship, the *Courser*, whose wheel was so large that it took thirty-three regular sailors to whirl it, though Stormy could move it with one finger. The mast was high enough to scrape the sun and graze the moon. His adventures took him from the North Sea to the Caribbean and finally to rest, perhaps at Cape Cod.

CONNECT
- Before presenting the tale display one *banner* each day on the literature center bulletin board. For example, Who fought a kraken? What was the biggest clipper ship ever built? Who built it? Who was a successful potato farmer? Why are the Cliffs of Dover white? Why did a clipper ship captain run a race with a steamship? Entice the students with the banners, but do not tell the tale. Encourage them to find out what the banners mean.

- If the students are familiar with other tall tales, *brainstorm* what they know about the subgenre.

- Record their responses on a *literary ladder*. This ladder should be tall and wide. (See Chapter 10.)

- Ask the students, If you were going to tell a tall tale about what you ate for breakfast, what would you say? At this point let the students prepare a menu for a *tall tale breakfast*.

- Wear a nautical costume and give a *book talk* using a tall tale exaggeration (see summary for ideas). Who does he remind you of? Can you do what he did? Of course, you can, because you can tell a tall tale!

- Place "seafaring language" on the *word wall* arranged in the shape of a tall ship: for example, frigate; brigantine; sloop; keel; fathoms; seafaring; schooner; mast; mizzenmast; bowsprit; cleaver; figure-of-eight knot; rigging.

CONSTRUCT
Read the story either through a teacher read-aloud or by grouping students to read in pairs and literary discussion groups.

- Divide the class into *literary discussion groups*. Give each group one "block" of text to read and discuss. This is a long story that naturally divides into two "blocks." Encourage groups to generate probes. Each group will present assigned portions of the tale to the rest of the class. They will prepare probes for discussion.

- To extend the discussion, you might use *probes* such as: Describe your most vivid memory of the story. What advice would you give Stormalong about his adventures?

- These questions may also be used as starters for writing in the *LitLog* for those students who need suggestions.

- This is an opportune time to integrate literature and social studies, especially with lessons on the American Revolution,

John Paul Jones and the *Bon Homme Richard*, and the whaling industry.

CREATE
- Write a *What If? Incident* and insert other tall tale adventures.

- Share incidents, illustrate them, and then place them in a *bound book*.

- *Discuss* Stormalong's movements. Pinpoint (with a colored marker) on a map the locations mentioned in the tale.

- *Draw a sketch* of the *Courser* (using the proper dimensions). Draw a sketch of the *Liverpool Packet*. Place both drawings on the board and compare the two ships.

- Display pictures of today's ships. *Discuss* the differences. For example, Was the *Courser* as big as a battleship? How would it compare to an aircraft carrier?

- Present a *chain-the-tale* with one or more tall tales.

- Several variations of "Stormalong" have sea chanteys. (See page 34 in Carmer, *America Sings*, for a Stormalong song.) Elicit the assistance of the music teacher, sing songs, and write original chanteys.

- Find other tall tales. Place information and sketches of each character on appropriately shaped paper, such as an axe for Paul Bunyan or a keelboat for Mike Fink. Display in the classroom or school media center.

- Prepare a *tall tale map*. Use a large map of the United States and identify the places the characters lived and traveled. Trace each character's travels using different colored markers or yarn. Add tall tale character information from above to the maps. Display in the media center with books about the characters.

LitSet: RELATED BOOKS AND TALES
- "Old Stormalong, the Deep-Water Sailman." In Botkin, B. A. (Ed.). 1949. *The Treasury of American Folklore.* New York: Crown. 185–92.

- "Stormalong." In Carmer, C. (Collector). 1949. *America Sings.* New York: Knopf. 30–34.

- Felton, H. (1986). *True Tall Tales of Stormalong: Sail of the Seven Seas.* Englewood Cliffs, N.J.: Prentice-Hall.

- Malcolmson, A., & McCormick, D. J. 1952. *Mr. Stormalong.* Boston: Houghton Mifflin.

- "Stormalong." In Osborne, M. P. 1991. *American Tall Tales.* (Engravings M. McCurdy). New York: Knopf. 37–44.

- Shay, F. 1930. *Here's Audacity! American Legendary Heroes.* New York: Macaulay. 17–31.

Note: See Chapter 3 for additional information about tall tales.

This Literary Link is adapted from *Using Folk Literature in the Classroom*, 1994, by Frances S. Goforth and Carolyn Spillman.
Used with permission of The Oryx Press, 4041 N. Central Ave., Suite 700, Phoenix, AZ 85012. (800) 279-6799.

NOTES

The introductory statement is paraphrased from the chapter.

1. Hickman, J. 1981. A new perspective on response to literature: Research in an elementary school setting. *Research in the Teaching of English.* 15(4). 353–54; Pablo, E. R. 1986. Factors that promote the development of permanent interest in reading. In Cott, E. G. (Ed.). *Proceedings of the Annual Symposium on Reading.* Guam: International Reading Association. 41–55; Shapiro, J., & White, W. 1991. Reading attitudes and perception in traditional and nontraditional reading programs. *Reading Research and Instruction.* 30(4). 52–66.

2. Hepler, S., & Hickman, J. 1982. The book was okay, I love you—Social aspects of response to literature. *Theory into Practice.* 21. 278–83; Johnson, R. L. 1990. Making the transition from basals to literature-based reading. *The Society for Developmental Education.* 197–99; Schell, L. 1991. *How to Create an Independent Reading Program.* New York: Scholastic. 19–20.

3. Cardarelli, A. F. 1991. Teachers under cover: Promoting the personal reading of teachers. *The Reading Teacher.* 45(9). 664–68; Flood, J., & Lapp, D. 1994. Teacher book clubs: Establishing literature discussion groups for teachers. *The Reading Teacher.* April. 574–76; Micklos, J. 1991. Teachers as readers groups: Reviving the love of literature. *Reading Today.* June/July. 20–21; Parish, A. S. 1995. Having a LARC. *The Reading Teacher.* 49(3). November. 270–72.

4. Durkin, D. 1966. *Children Who Read Early.* New York: Teachers College Press; Foertsch, M. A. 1992. Reading in and out of school. *Educational Testing Service.* National Center for Education Statistics (A variety of research studies conducted in the area are discussed in this report.); Heibert, E. H. 1981. Developmental patterns and interrelationships of preschool children's print awareness. *Reading Research Quarterly.* 16. 236–60; Holdaway, D. 1979. *The Foundations of Literacy.* Sydney: Ashton Scholastic.

5. Galda, L., & Cullinan, B. E. 1991. Literature for literacy: What research says about the benefits of using trade books in the classroom. In Flood, J., Jensen, J. M., Lapp, D., & Squire, J. (Eds.). *Handbook of Research on Teaching the English Language Arts.* New York: Macmillan. 529–35.

6. For additional information, see sources such as Palmer, B. M., Codling, R. M., & Gambrell, L. B. 1994. In their own words: What elementary students have to say about motivation to read. *The Reading Teacher.* 48(2). October. 176–78; Fielding, L., & Roller, C. 1992. Making difficult books accessible and easy books acceptable. *The Reading Teacher.* 45(9). May. 678–85; Fresch, M. J. 1995. Self-selection of early literacy learners. *The Reading Teacher.* 49(3). November. 220–27; Reed, A. J. S. 1988. *Comics to Classics: A Parent's Guide to Books for Teens and Preteens.* Newark, Del.: International Reading Association. 13–18; Saccardi, M. 1993/1994. Children speak: Our students' reactions to books can tell us what to teach. *The Reading Teacher.* 47(4). December/January. 318–24.

7. For additional information about the literature environment, see sources such as Galda, L., & Cullinan, B. 1991. 532; Manning, M. & G. 1993. How comfortable is your classroom? *Teaching Pre K–8.* 24(2). October. 127; Manning, M. & G. 1993. Creating a good psychological environment. *Teaching Pre K–8.* 24(3). November/December. 102–3; Tway, E. 1991. The elementary school classroom. In Flood, J., Jensen, J. M., Lapp, D., & Squire, J. (Eds.). 425–37.

8. For additional information about research on the topic, see Morrow, L. M. 1991. Promoting voluntary reading. In Flood, J., Jensen, J. M., Lapp, D., & Squire, J. (Eds.). 686–89.

9. Hart-Hewins, L., & Wells, J. 1990. *Real Books for Reading: Learning to Read with Children's Literature.* Markham, Ontario: Pembroke. 62–63; Rivlin, L., & Weinstein, C. 1984. Educational issues, school settings, and environmental psychology. *Journal of Environmental Psychology.* 4. 347–64; Routman, R. 1994. *Invitations.* Portsmouth, N.H.: Heinemann. 423–26, Wiseman, D. L. 1992. *Learning to Read with Literature.* Boston: Allyn & Bacon. 59–61.

10. For ideas and sketches about arranging primary and intermediate classrooms, see sources such as Cox, C., & Zarrillo, J. 1993. *Teaching Reading with Children's Literature.* New York: Macmillan. 22, 37, 154; Reutzel, D. R., & Cooter, R. B. 1992. *Teaching Children to Read: From Basals to Books.* New York: Merrill. 251, 255, 259, 267, 270; Routman, R. 1994. 424–25; Salinger, T. 1993. *Models of Literacy Instruction.* New York: Merrill. 24–25; Tompkins, G. E., & Hoskisson, K. 1995. *Language Arts: Content and Teaching Strategies.* (3d Ed.). New York: Merrill. 40–41.

11. Morrow, L. M. 1992. The impact of a literature-based program on literacy achievement, use of literature, and attitudes of children from minority backgrounds. *Reading Research Quarterly.* 27. 250–75.

12. Harste, J. C., & Short, K. G., with Burke, C. 1988. *Creating Classrooms for Authors.* Portsmouth, N.H.: Heinemann. 309–12.

13. Macon, J. M., Bewell, D., & Vogt, M. E. 1991. *Responses to Literature.* Newark, Del.: International Reading Association. 27.

14. For additional information about centers, see sources such as Loughlin, C. E., & Martin, M. D. 1987. *Supporting Literacy: Developing Effective Learning Environments.* New York: Teachers College Press; Staab, C. 1991. Classroom organization: Thematic centers revisited. *Language Arts.* 68(2). February. 108–13.

15. Bissett, D. 1970. The usefulness of children's books in the reading program. 79. In Catterson, J. H. (Ed.). *Children and Literature.* Newark, Del.: International Reading Association. 73–80; Morrow, L. M., & Weinstein, C. S. 1986. Encouraging voluntary reading: The impact of a literature program on children's use of library centers. *Reading Research Quarterly.* 21: 330–46.

16. For additional information about a classroom library, see sources such as Fractor, J. S., Woodruff, M. C., Martinez, M. G., & Teale, W. 1993. Let's not miss opportunities to promote voluntary reading: Classroom libraries in the elementary school. *The Reading Teacher.* 46(6). 476–84; Morrow, L. 1991. 687; Routman, R. 1994. 428; Salinger, T. 1993. 121.

    For additional information about obtaining books for a classroom library, see sources such as Cairney, T. H. 1991. *Other Worlds: The Endless Possibilities of Literature.* Portsmouth, N.H.: Heinemann. 42–43; Chayet, B. 1994. 20 Penny-pinching ways to double your classroom library. *Instructor.* 104(1) July/August. 51–53; Galda, L. 1988. 99; Salinger, T. 1993. 25; Schell, L. 1991. 14–16; Strickland, D. S., Walmsley, S. A., Bronk, G., & Weiss, K. J. 1994. Making the most of book clubs. *Instructor.* 103(9). May/June. 44–47.

17. Farrell, E. J. 1991. Instructional models for English language arts, K–12. In Flood, J., Jensen, J., Lapp, D., & Squire, J. (Eds.). 63–84; Pace, G. 1991. When teachers use literature for literacy instruction: Ways that constrain, ways that free. *Language Arts.* 68(1). January. 12–25.

18. McCarthey, S. J., & Raphael, T. E. 1992. Alternative research perspectives. In Irwin, J., & Doyle, M. A. (Eds.). *Reading/Writing Connections: Learning from Research.* Newark, Del.: International Reading Association. 2–30.

19. For additional information about various literary theories and literary approaches, see Chapter 11. See also Langer, J. A. 1992. Rethinking literature instruction. In Langer, J. A. (Ed.). *Literature Instruction: A Focus on Student Response.* Urbana, Ill.: National Council of Teachers of English. 35–53; Rosenblatt, L. M. 1991. Literary theory. In Flood, J., Jensen, J. M., Lapp, D., & Squire, J. R. 57–62.

20. Rosenblatt, L. M. 1994 (2d Ed. 1978). *The Reader, the Text, the Poem: The Transactional Theory of a Literary Work.* Carbondale, Ill.: Southern Illinois University Press. 12. See also Rosenblatt, L. M. 1983. *Literature as Exploration.* (4th Ed.). New York: Modern Language Association.

21. For additional information about a transactional instructional focus, see sources such as McGee, L. M. 1992. Focus on research: Exploring the literature-based reading revolution. *Language Arts.* 69(7). November. 529–37; Zarrillo, J. 1991. Theory becomes practice: Aesthetic teaching with literature. *The New Advocate.* 4(4). Fall. 221–34; Zarrillo, J. J., & Cox, C. 1992. Efferent and aesthetic teaching. In Many, J., & Cox, J. (Eds.). *Stance and Literary Understanding: Exploring the Theories, Research, and Practice.* Norwood, N.J.: Ablex. 239–45.

22. For additional research information about aesthetic reading and responses, see sources such as Cox, C., & Many, J. 1992. Toward an understanding of the aesthetic response to literature. *Language Arts.* 69(1). January. 28–33; Cox, C., & Zarrillo, J. 1993. *Teaching Reading with Children's Literature.* New York: Merrill; Many, J. 1992. Living through literacy experiences versus literacy analysis: Examining stance in children's response to literature. *Reading Horizons.* 32(3). 169–83.

    For additional information about intertextuality (the association of one text to another to help individuals make associations and connections and construct meanings about the texts they encounter), see Cairney, T. H. 1992. Fostering and building students' intertextual histories. *Language Arts.* 69(7). November. 502–7.

23. Rosenblatt, L. M. 1988. Writing and reading: The transactional theory. Office of Educational Research and Improvement. Washington, D.C.: Technical Report 416.

(ERIC Document. Reproduction Services No. ED 292 062. p. 6.); Rosenblatt, L. M. 1991. Literature–S.O.S.! *Language Arts.* 68(6). October, 444–48; Rosenblatt, L. M. 1994. The transactional theory of reading and writing. In Ruddell, R. B., Ruddell, M. R., & Singer, H. (Eds.). *Theoretical Models and Processes of Reading.* (4th Ed.). Newark, Del.: International Reading Association. 1057–92.

24. The mini-lesson concept was initiated for writing workshops by Calkins, L. M. 1986. *The Art of Teaching Writing.* Portsmouth, N.H.: Heinemann. The strategy was further elaborated by Atwell, N. 1987. *In the Middle.* Portsmouth, N.H.: Heinemann. See also Salinger, T. 1993. 29–31.

25. Goforth, F. S., & Spillman, C. V. 1994. *Using Folk Literature in the Classroom: Encouraging Children to Read and Write.* Phoenix, Ariz.: Oryx. 9–16.

26. Anderson, R. C. 1994. Role of reader's schema in comprehension, learning, and memory. In Ruddell, R. B., Ruddell, M. R., & Singer, H. (Eds.). *Theoretical Models and Processes of Reading.* (4th Ed.). Newark, Del.: International Reading Association. 469–82; Bransford, J. D. 1994. Schema activations and schema acquisition: Comments on Richard C. Anderson's remarks. In Ruddell, R. B., Ruddell, M. R., & Singer, H. 483–95.

27. For additional information about the Connect component, see sources such as Applebee, A. M. 1977. A sense of story. *Theory into Practice.* 16. 342–48; Lehr, S. 1991. *The Child's Developing Sense of Theme: Responses to Literature.* New York: Teachers College Press. 5–10, 20–21; Rosenblatt, L. M. 1994. 20; Rubin, A. 1985. How useful are readability formulas? In Osborn, J., Wilson, P., & Anderson, R. C. (Eds.). *Reading Education: Foundations for a Literature America.* Lexington, Mass.: D. C. Heath. 61–78.

28. For additional information about the Construct component, see sources such as Heibert, E. H. (Ed.) 1991. *Literacy for the Diverse Society.* New York: Teachers College Press. 295; Vygotsky, L. 1986. *Thought and Language.* Cambridge, Mass.: MIT Press. xxxvii. L. S. Vygotsky, a Russian psychologist, proposed the concept of the "zone of proximate development" in the mid-1920s and published it later in the United States in *Thought and Language.* It reflects the Social-Constructivist's assertion that learners can reach their approximate level of development in a supportive environment, accompanied by planned instruction from teachers or knowledgeable others.

29. Morrow, L. M. 1992. 253.

30. For additional information about the LitLog, see sources such as Fulps, J. S., & Young, T.

1991. The what, why, when and how of reading response journals. *Reading Horizons.* 32(2). 109–16; Hancock, M. R. 1993. Exploring and extending personal response through literature journals. *The Reading Teacher.* 46(6). 466–74; Parsons, L. 1990. *Response Journals.* Portsmouth, N.H.: Heinemann.

31. For additional information about the Create component, see sources discussing responses to literature and sources such as Squire, J. R. 1994. Research in reader response, naturally interdisciplinary. 644. In Ruddell, R. B., Ruddell, M. R., & Singer, H. (Eds.). *Theoretical Models and Processes of Reading.* (4th Ed.). Newark, Del.: International Reading Association. 637–52.

32. Goodman, K. 1988. Look what they've done to Judy Blume!: The "basalization" of children's literature. *The New Advocate.* 1(2). 29–41; Hade, D. D. 1994. Aiding and abetting the basalization of children's literature. *The New Advocate.* 7(1). Winter. 29–44.

33. For additional information about designing teacher's guides, see sources such as Eeds, M., & Peterson, R. 1991. Teacher as curator: Learning to talk about literature. *The Reading Teacher.* 45(2). October 118–26; Larrick, N. 1991. Give us books! . . . but also . . . give us wings! *The New Advocate.* 4(2). Spring. 77–83; Hepler, S. 1988. A guide for the teacher guides: Doing it yourself. *The New Advocate.* 1(3). Summer. 186–95; Hopkins, L. B. 1991. The ultimate teacher's guide to whole language in the whole wide world. *The New Advocate.* 4(2). Spring. 85–88.; Wertheim, J. 1988. Teaching guides for novels. *The Reading Teacher.* 42(3). 262.

34. See professional materials such as Danielson, K. E., & LaConty, J. 1994. *Integrating Reading and Writing through Children's Literature.* Needham Heights, Mass.: Allyn & Bacon; Goforth, F. S., & Spillman, C. V. 1994; Moss, J. F. 1984. *Focus Units in Literature: A Handbook for Elementary School Teachers.* Urbana, Ill.: National Council of Teachers of English; McClure, A. A., & Kristo, J. V. (Eds.). 1994. *Inviting Children's Responses to Literature.* Urbana, Ill.: National Council of Teachers of English. The three books by Raines, S. C., & Canady, R. J. 1989. *Story Stretchers: Activities to Expand Children's Favorite Books.* Mt. Rainier, Md.: Gryphon; 1991. *More Story Stretchers: More Activities to Expand Children's Favorite Books.* Mt. Rainier, Md.: Gryphon; 1992. *Story Stretchers for the Primary Grades.* Mt. Rainier, Md.: Gryphon; Raines, S. 1994. *450 More Story Stretchers for the Primary Grades.* Mt. Rainier, Md.: Gryphon; Roberts, P. L. 1993. *A Green Dinosaur Day: A Guide for Developing*

Thematic Units in Literature-Based Instruction, K–6. White Plains, N.Y.: Longwood; Somers, A. B., & Worthington, J. E. 1979. *Response Guides for Teaching Children's Books.* Urbana, Ill.: National Council of Teachers of English; Soresen, M., & Lehman, B. (Eds.) 1995. *Teaching with Children's Books: Paths to Literature-Based Instruction.* Urbana, Ill.: National Council of Teachers of English.

35. For additional information about assessing learners' literary growth, see sources such as Crofton, L. K. (Ed.). 1994. Inquiry-based evaluation. *Primary Voices K–6.* National Council of Teachers of English. 2(2). April; Teale, W. H., Hiebert, E. H. & Chittenden, E. A. 1987. Assessing young children's literacy development. *The Reading Teacher.* 40(8). April. 772–77.

36. For additional information about the rationale, organization, format, and collection of a portfolio, see sources such as Cambourne, B., & Turbill, J. Assessment in whole language classrooms: Theory into practice. *The Elementary School Journal.* 90(3). 337–50; Crofton, 1994; Farr, R. 1992. Putting it all together: Solving the reading assessment puzzle. *The Reading Teacher.* 46(1). September. 26–36; Hansen, J. 1992. Literacy portfolios emerge. *The Reading Teacher.* 45(8). April. 604–7; Heibert, E. A. 1992. Portfolios invite reflection from students and staff. *Educational Leadership.* 49(8). 58–61; Lamme, L. L., & Hysmith, C. 1991. One school's adventure into portfolio assessment. *Language Arts.* 68(8). December. 629–40; Valencia, S. 1990. A portfolio approach to classroom reading assessment: The whys, whats, and hows. *The Reading Teacher.* 43(4). January. 38–40.

37. Books such as the following are helpful when implementing portfolio assessment: Goodman, K., Goodman, Y., & Hood, J. W. (Eds.). 1989. *The Whole Language Evaluation Book.* Portsmouth, N.H.: Heinemann; Harp, B. (Ed.). 1993. *Assessment and Evaluation in Whole Language Programs.* Norwood, Mass.: Christopher-Gordon; Tierney, R. J. and others. 1991. *Portfolio Assessment in the Reading-Writing Classroom.* Norwood, Mass.: Christopher-Gordon.

38. Winograd, P. 1994. Developing alternative assessments: Six problems worth solving. *The Reading Teacher.* 47(5). February. 420–23.

39. Flood, J., & Lapp, D. 1989. Reporting reading progress: A comparison portfolio for parents. *The Reading Teacher.* 42(7). March. 508–14.

40. For additional information about determining children's literary preferences, see sources such as Schell, L. 1991. 26–30; The questionnaire is a modification of the idea presented by Timion, C. S. 1992. In Irwin, J. W., & Doyle, M. A. (Eds.). 211.

Part Two

LITERARY GENRES
FICTION

3

Folk Literature

The Roots and Wings of Society

The values and the dreams of society are reflected in the old tales and verses.

From leprechauns to talking yams and mighty heroes, a host of characters, some fanciful and some real, inhabit the world of folk literature. In tales, songs, and verses, the fanciful feats of the characters have amused, terrified, frightened, or satisfied audiences from earliest times.

Originally, anonymous storytellers and balladeers told or sung folk literature to entertain the people and present the mores, beliefs, and traditions of a primitive society. The tellers attempted to explain natural phenomena, an understanding of self, relationships with others, and their environment. As time passed, the cultural heritage of the society was preserved through the selections. Some selections, like *Tales from the Arabian Nights*, were originally written. Many tales, however, such as "Sleeping Beauty," began as oral renditions and changed through time depending on the audience's interests and the teller's whim. Through folk literature, people and their culture come alive! The values and the dreams of a society are reflected in the old tales and verses; thus, folk literature truly represents the roots and wings of society.

WHAT IS FOLK LITERATURE?

Folk literature is the literary category within the broader classification of **folklore**. Folklore encompasses the rituals, customs, superstitions, and manners of a particular group that are passed orally or in writing from one generation to the next.[1] Folklore includes not only literature, but also traditional dances, holidays, tools, symbols, and rituals. As one commentator has said, "Folk Literature, a branch of folklore, is the window through which children in today's world may view cultures of long ago."[2]

Folk literature includes both prose and poetry narratives, which can be classified into thirteen subgenres consisting of tales, verses, and songs. These subgenres are discussed later in the chapter.

THE BEGINNINGS OF FOLK LITERATURE

All scholars agree that the literature of the "folk" must be considered within the context of a culture. Some feel illiterate people transmitted the literature orally. Others contend that although peasants contributed to the oral telling of the literature, the literates of a society wrote prose and poetry narratives containing forms similar to those found in oral renditions.[3]

Folk literature evolved through stages compatible with human understanding and maturity. For example, tellers attempted to allay early humans' fear of natural phenomena, such as earthquakes and thunder, by relating creation stories that explained why these events occurred. These early stories often included anthropomorphic objects and animals because primitive people believed objects or animals had feelings, emotions, and desires similar to their own. It is possible that the irrational, violent behavior portrayed in much folk literature represented acceptable behavior in early times. Religious beliefs and social rituals of early societies are still found in folk literature.[4]

THE TRANSMISSION OF FOLK LITERATURE

For years those who study folk literature have asked several questions:

Before the invention of advanced technology and transportation, why did similar tales, poems, and songs appear all over the earth?

Why do similar versions (variants) of particular narratives exist?

Are the literary (written) narratives also classified as "folk" literature?

In an attempt to answer these and related questions, interested scholars from anthropology, education, ethnomusicology, linguistics, psychology, and sociology have collected, categorized, and analyzed folk literature selections through the years. Because they approached the questions from different perspectives and used different research procedures, they frequently did not reach the same conclusions. For example, all folklorists do not agree about how the narratives were transmitted, which literature should be classified as "folk," which labels and definitions should be used to classify subgenres, and where specific stories should be placed within subgenres. Some of this controversy is due to the fluid, dynamic nature of the individual selections. For example, classifying a story might be difficult because some of the protagonists and events were changed when the story was transferred from written prose to oral poetry and vice versa. Determining the original format and place of creation in myths and some epics is difficult because the tales existed long before the advent of writing.

Theories of Transmission

As scholars studied the theories of transmitting folk literature, two major theories, the *diffusion theory* and the *polygenesis theory* emerged.

According to the **diffusion theory,** as people migrated through wars, religious missions, or explorations, they shared their cultural stories with others, exchanged the narratives, and modified the original ones by varying the setting, characters, and adventures. Similar motifs (the smallest recognizable unit of independent meaning), stylistic devices, and story structures emerged to form the foundation of folk literature selections. This may explain why there are many variants of popular tales such as "Little Red Cap" and "Goldilocks and the Three Bears" and why there are nine hundred written variations of the "Cinderella" tale.[5]

Folklorists who support the diffusion theory also maintain that all tales emerged from a central diffusion center. According to this argument, because ancient humans initially inhabited only a small portion of the earth, all folk literature selections must have originated at that center. As people gradually migrated from the center, they encountered groups who had migrated earlier, told stories, listened to other narratives, and adapted their tales to incorporate new elements. Though many scholars discount the central diffusion center idea, other respected folklorists recognize the feasibility of such a center.[6]

Scholars supporting the **polygenesis theory** (meaning "many beginnings") claim that all humans have similar psychological concerns and needs, such as the explanation of natural phenomena, the understanding of self, individual relationships with others, and the environment. According to this theory, early people in various regions created similar tales to meet their personal concerns. Though popular with early scholars, this theory is no longer as widely accepted by contemporary folklorists as it was earlier.

LINGUISTIC ORIGINS OF FOLK LITERATURE

Some folklorists claim that *only* narratives disseminated through the oral tradition or by word of mouth are legitimate folk literature selections. With the invention of the printing press, some stories appeared in written modes, were spread orally, and later returned in written variation. This circular process continued until it became difficult to identify the linguistic origin of some tales, songs, and poems.

Jason (1991) clarified the oral versus written controversy by pointing out that different tellers used four linguistic methods:

1. Folk and fairy tales, simple epics, legends, jests, proverbs, and riddles were *produced and performed orally* by nonprofessional and semiprofessional storytellers.

2. Myths, hymns, and national epics, classified as oral high/learned literature (written), were *performed orally* by semiprofessional and professional storytellers and religious leaders.

3. Chapbooks, folk almanacs, and sermons first occurred in *written* form, produced by semiprofessionals and professionals.

4. High/classic narratives and poems were *written* in the traditional format and style of recognized authors, such as Sophocles, Dante, and Cervantes.[7]

By becoming aware of the origins and transmission of tales, we begin to understand why variants of familiar tales are found in most societies and why other tales are unique to a specific group. After listening to storytellers and oral histories, Virginia Hamilton compiled an unusual collection of traditional and true tales about African-American females in *Her Stories: African American Folk Tales, Fairy Tales, and True Tales* (1995). (See Hamilton color plate on page 69.) The mystical and sometimes eerie tales are enhanced by Leo and Diane Dillon's illustrations. This is the third collection the Dillons have illustrated for Hamilton. See Did You Know on page 70 for more information about Leo and Diane Dillon.

BENEFITS GAINED FROM EXPOSURE TO FOLK LITERATURE

Not only did the old tales influence the development of past societies, but these same tales can also influence individuals living in contemporary society. The benefits individuals gain from a continuous exposure to folk literature selections are listed in Table 3.1 on page 69.[8]

✻ SUBGENRES OF FOLK LITERATURE

A careful analysis of the classification of folk literature is revealing and frustrating. Folklorists have different purposes for studying selections, and their interpretations of the selections differ. Therefore, they do not necessarily agree on labels, definitions, or representative examples for each subgenre. When the traditional compositions were transmitted through tellers and time, the plot structure might remain constant, but the distinctions between the forms were often lost. Because of the dynamic nature of folk literature selec-

Leo and Diane Dillon use dark hues of blue, black, and green for Virginia Hamilton's Her Stories: African-American Folktales, Fairy Tales, and True Tales. *The full-page realistic paintings are drawn on illustrator board. The pictures enrich the storyline and are arranged to achieve perfect balance with the verbal narrative.*

TABLE 3.1 Benefits Individuals Gain from a Continuous Exposure to Folk Literature

Tales, verses, and songs embody a child's conception of the world.

Individuals are aware of the potential of the human imagination to explain history, philosophy, and psychology, as depicted in the tales they encounter.

Young people enjoy hearing and producing the language in folk literature.

Folk literature gives individuals an opportunity to experience fantasy worlds and simultaneously to reflect on realistic human conditions.

Through experiences with folk literature, young people can observe the consequences of acceptable and unacceptable behavior, the failures and successes of characters, and their determination to reach their goals.

Individuals encounter historical and folk heroes of particular groups.

Young people can compare and contrast motifs or universal truths valued by various cultures, such as the importance of families or caring for others.

Exposure to folk literature increases literary options available to young people.

tions, a tale could change from fairy tale to myth or from animal tale to local legend. Thus, any rigid classification is almost impossible.[9] Adding to the ambiguity between subgenres is the lack of concern early printers and collectors showed for literary classifications. By the early nineteenth century, a particular narrative might be included in both a fairy tale collection and a folktale anthology.

This book presents thirteen subgenres of folk literature acceptable to many folklorists.[10] The subgenres give adults a way to organize the thousands of tales, verses, and songs. The adult may choose to introduce students to the classifications, but the most important reason for using folk literature selections with children is enjoyment.

The following sections present the historical development, distinguishing characteristics, and representative examples of each subgenre, and suggest ways for using each subgenre in the classroom. Figure 3.1 on page 71 indicates the original linguistic modality of each subgenre of folk literature.

✿ FOLK LITERATURE TRANSMITTED PRIMARILY IN POETRY FORMAT

Figure 3.2 on page 72 presents a summary of information about folk literature transmitted primarily in the poetry format. This section will examine the three major subgenres: Mother Goose, ballads, and epics.

MOTHER GOOSE

Very young children squeal with delight when they physically "Knock on the door . . . peep in . . . pull the latch and walk in." Infants go to sleep listening to the gentle rocking motion of a lullaby. They move and jump with the definite rhyme of "Jack be nimble, Jack be quick. Jack jumped over the candle stick." Young children are not concerned that the content is nonsense in "Mistress Mary quite contrary how does your garden grow?" All children screech with joy when their friends have trouble reciting very fast "Peter Piper picked a peck of pickled peppers. . . ." Pickled Peppers?

From an early age, children seem to naturally delight in the rhythm, predictable rhymes, riddles, and fanciful content found in **Mother Goose** rhymes (called Nursery Rhymes in England and "folk" rhymes in parts of Europe and Scandinavia). They physically move to the skip rope rhymes, bounce their balls, count objects, quickly speak tongue twisters, sing lullabies, and recite the charms, fragments of

Did You Know About
THE DILLONS?

As a child, Leo always knew he wanted to be an artist, and his parents encouraged him. As a child, Diane always knew she wanted to be an artist, and her parents encouraged her. Leo and Diane, who were born just eleven days apart, met at Parsons School of Design. Though they were competitors, they fell in love and eventually married.

These talented artists are a respected artistic team. They illustrate the same manuscript, and each contributes to every illustration. Thus, the illustrations give the appearance of the work of one artist. By working together as one artist, they create a third artist, which they believe makes them more successful than they would be individually. Their success is based on teamwork, cooperation, and respect for the other person's talents, abilities, and ideas. For years they shared the same studio, but because they have different work habits—Leo likes to listen to the same music over and over again while working, but Diane likes different music—they now have separate studios in their home in Brooklyn, New York. They like to illustrate fantasy because they feel they have more creative freedom with this genre. After they accept a manuscript to illustrate, they look for details to highlight in the illustrations, consider the setting, and share ideas about the finished product.

The Dillons are especially well known for the illustrations they have created for folk literature or culture-specific texts. In 1976 they won their first Caldecott Medal for the illustrations in Verna Aardema's African tale, *Why Mosquitos Buzz in People's Ears* (1975). They used an expressionistic folk art style with a combination of ink and watercolor applied with an air brush and splatter techniques. They also applied pastels to the art and used vellum and

frisket masks in some illustrations. The following year they won the Caldecott Medal for Margret Musgrove's information book, *Ashanti to Zulu: African Traditions* (1976). Obviously, the time they spend researching the art of the culture is worthwhile, because their artwork enhances, supplements, and unifies the verbal narrative. They have illustrated several books by Aardema based on African folktales. They used a Japanese art form and a combination of pastel, watercolor, and ink in Katherine Paterson's Japanese tale, *The Tale of the Mandarin Ducks*. Their artwork has enriched three of Virginia Hamilton's African-American collections. In 1996 the Dillons received an Honor Award from the Coretta Scott King Award for Hamilton's *Her Stories*.

Leo and Diane's son Lee is an artist who paints, sculpts, and makes jewelry. The three Dillons cooperated on the artwork for Nancy Willard's *Pish Posh, said Hieronymus Bosch*. Lee sculpted the ornate silver frame that surrounds the paintings in the book (see Chapter 7).

The Dillons like to experiment with media and enjoy watching the scenes and characters take form on paper. They see this process as the magic of art. They are perfectionists who delight in including nuances, visual comments, and details in their pictures. Sometimes the viewer must look at the picture several times before discovering all the details. For example, the Dillons included a little red bird in each illustration in *Why Mosquitos Buzz in People's Ears* even though the text does not mention the bird. The apparent joy the Dillons feel for the adventure of creating visual narratives for others is appreciated by the children and adults who are lucky enough to explore the visual images produced by this gifted pair of artists.

FIGURE 3.1   Folk Literature Subgenres Transmitted Primarily in Prose and Poetry Format

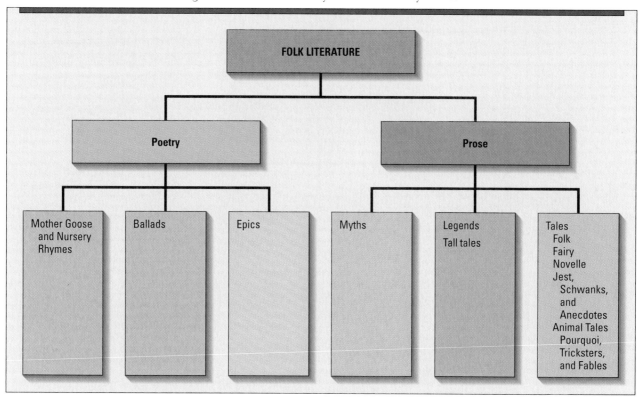

ballads, and prayers included in Nursery Rhymes. A collection of Mother Goose rhymes could include some seven hundred simple, nonsense, humorous verses.

William and Ceil Baring-Gould, writing in the *Annotated Mother Goose*, showed that the early rhymes, which were not meant for the nursery, also contained adult earthiness, ribaldry, vulgarity, political satire, religious themes, and popular street songs that make some contemporary adults question whether they should be used with young children.[11] Figure 3.3 on page 73 summarizes the distinguishing characteristics of Mother Goose Rhymes.[12]

Historical Development of Mother Goose Rhymes
In their authoritative collection, *The Oxford Dictionary of Nursery Rhymes*,[13] the Opies trace the origin of many rhymes back to Roman times. They report that one out of four rhymes was current in Shakespeare's youth.

Who Was "Mother Goose"? Perhaps Mother Goose was the mother of King Charlemagne who was called "Queen Goose-Foot" because of the size or shape of her feet. Or perhaps Mother Goose was another French queen—"Goose-Footed Bertha," so called because she married a close relative, Robert the Pious, and later, sup-

posedly gave birth to a monstrous child with the head of a goose. The French legend depicts "Goose-Footed Bertha" surrounded by children, spinning her wheel and telling stories to all around her, as "Mother Goose."

Charles Perrault used the term "Mother Goose, teller of tales" in 1697 in his *Histoires ou contes du temps passe, avec des moralités* (Histories or tales of long ago, with morals). Also included in the title was the phrase *"Contes de ma Mere l'Oye"* (Tales of Mother Goose). Perrault, a distinguished member of the French Academy, compiled a collection of eight tales to entertain the court and published them under the name of his son, Perrault d'Armancouthis. In 1729 J. Pote published the collection in England as *Mother Goose's Fairy Tales*. The tales are discussed later in the Fairy Tales section.

Bostonians claim that Mother Goose was an American. Thomas Fleet, a New England printer, published a broadside in 1719, titled *Songs for the Nursery*, or *Mother Goose's Melodies*. It contained the lullabies sung to his children by his mother-in-law, Elizabeth Goose. To this day, Bostonians enjoy taking visitors to the Old Granary Burying Ground where reputedly Mother Goose was buried, without a headstone, around the mid-1750s. Other tracts with the name "Mother Goose (or Nursery) Rhymes" were published in

FIGURE 3.2   Folk Literature Subgenres Transmitted Primarily in Poetry Format

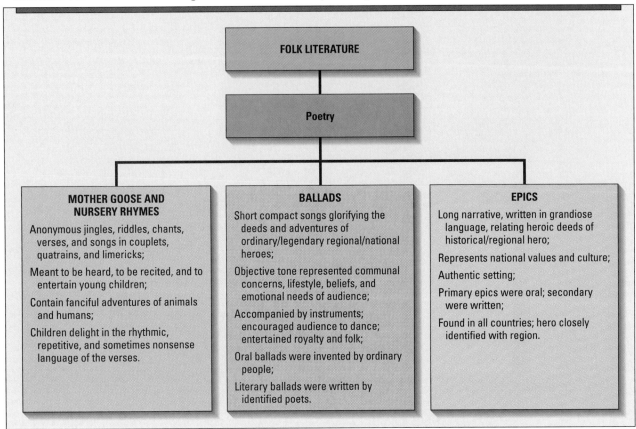

the New World during this period, but unfortunately none of these publications exists today.

In 1771 rhymes were again linked to an English "Mother Goose" when the stepson of John Newbery, the English entrepreneur and printer, published *Mother Goose Melody.* Isaiah Thomas reprinted Newbery's book in the United States in 1785. This collection, titled *Mother Goose Melody: or Sonnets for the Cradle,* included many well-known rhymes, such as "Tom Tucker," "Hey, Diddle, Diddle," and "Jack and Jill."

Whether the origin of Mother Goose was French or English, the poet Walter de la Mare says that Mother Goose Rhymes charm children's ears with rhyming language that tumbles from the tongue to vividly portray little scenes with fanciful objects and living creatures. However fanciful or nonsensical the rhymes are to adults, de la Mare concludes that they lead children directly into poetry and their natural fascination with the rhythmic patterns of language.[14]

Mother Goose and Nursery Rhymes with Children

Babies and toddlers become aware of games they can play with others when they physically dramatize rhymes about parts of the body, such as "This little piggy. . . ." Four- and five-year-olds enjoy many natural experiences manipulating the language when they hear books such as Blanche Fisher Wright's classic *The Real Mother Goose* (1916). Preschool children enjoy the fantastic events such as the cow jumping over the moon! The natural rhythms of the narratives invite children to sing and move to the imaginative rhymes.

Eight- to ten-year-old children enjoy tricking their peers with nursery rhyme riddles. They spend hours bouncing balls and chanting jump rope and sidewalk rhymes and verses found in collections such as Yolen's *Street Rhymes around the World* (1992). Children at this age enjoy collecting, comparing, and contrasting rhymes found in different collections such as Iona Opie's *Tail Feathers from Mother Goose: The Opie Rhyme Book* (1988), illustrated by Maurice Sendak. Ten- to twelve-year-olds are intrigued with the history of Mother Goose and like to investigate the cultural and political history connected to certain rhymes. The best source for this information is William and Ceil Baring-Gould's *The Annotated Mother Goose* (1962). Though the collections include adult themes and content, such as murders, starvation, dishonesty, trickery, and prejudice, children understand they should not interpret the narratives literally.

FIGURE 3.3 Distinguishing Characteristics of Mother Goose (Nursery, Childhood) Rhymes

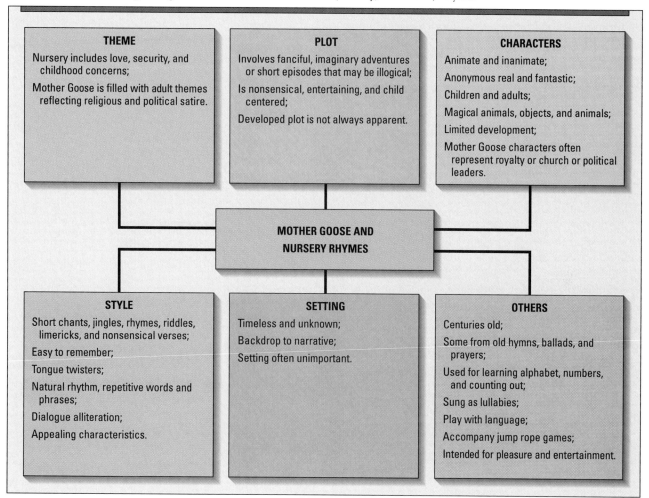

THEME
Nursery includes love, security, and childhood concerns;

Mother Goose is filled with adult themes reflecting religious and political satire.

PLOT
Involves fanciful, imaginary adventures or short episodes that may be illogical;

Is nonsensical, entertaining, and child centered;

Developed plot is not always apparent.

CHARACTERS
Animate and inanimate;

Anonymous real and fantastic;

Children and adults;

Magical animals, objects, and animals;

Limited development;

Mother Goose characters often represent royalty or church or political leaders.

MOTHER GOOSE AND NURSERY RHYMES

STYLE
Short chants, jingles, rhymes, riddles, limericks, and nonsensical verses;

Easy to remember;

Tongue twisters;

Natural rhythm, repetitive words and phrases;

Dialogue alliteration;

Appealing characteristics.

SETTING
Timeless and unknown;

Backdrop to narrative;

Setting often unimportant.

OTHERS
Centuries old;

Some from old hymns, ballads, and prayers;

Used for learning alphabet, numbers, and counting out;

Sung as lullabies;

Play with language;

Accompany jump rope games;

Intended for pleasure and entertainment.

Recognized artists have produced many collections with both contemporary and traditional illustrations. Children and adults still appreciate Kate Greenaway's children playing in a tranquil English countryside in *Mother Goose, or the Old Nursery Rhymes* (1881). They are charmed by the Victorian children portrayed by Marguerite de Angeli in her collection, *The Book of Nursery and Mother Goose Rhymes* (1954), and by Tasha Tudor's decorated collection, *Mother Goose* (1944). Many contemporary collections illustrate the traditional rhymes with bold splashes of color, as in *Mother Goose Treasury* by Raymond Briggs (1966) and *Tomie de Paola's Mother Goose* (1985). Humorous, stylized illustrations are found in collections such as *The Random House Book of Mother Goose* by Arnold Lobel (1986) and *James Marshall's Mother Goose* (1979). *Brian Wildsmith's Mother Goose* contains his trademark—colorful harlequin designs. Very young children like Eric Hill's *The Nursery Rhyme Peek-a-*

Book (1982). Beatrix Potter's *Beatrix Potter's Nursery Rhyme Book* (1995) includes new and previously published verses and illustrations. Two collections with outstanding authentic illustrations and a variety of rhymes from around the world for children and adults are Floella Benjamin's *Skip Across the Ocean: Nursery Rhymes from Around the World* (1995), illustrated by Sheila Moxley, and Judy Sierra's *Nursery Tales Around the World* (1996), illustrated by Stefano Vitale. Other notable artists who have adapted and illustrated collections or single rhyme books include Paul Galdone, Susan Jeffers, Alice and Martin Provensen, Rodney Peppe, and Janet Stevens.

After the girls and boys enjoy the pictures accompanying a collection, have a pair of children select a favorite rhyme. Then, using media suitable for the rhyme, have the partners draw the major incidents from the rhyme on a long strip of paper. Display the pictures on a bulletin board or fold the paper as an accordion book. Read or dramatize the rhyme. A team can make masks or puppets for the various characters in a rhyme and dramatize it. Older children can read or dramatize a rhyme for younger children and share their artistic creations.

BALLADS

Short narrative songs dramatically glorifying the adventures and feats of legendary or ordinary heroes are called *ballads* (from the Italian *ballare*, meaning to dance). Frequently, the ballads were sung to the accompaniment of musical instruments by balladeers, bards, troubadours, or skalds who encouraged their audience to dance during the performance.

Ballads are simple narrative poems that dramatically tell a single incident in the hero's life. They reflect the community life, cultural beliefs, and emotional needs of the audience. Many ballads have religious or political overtones, but most deal with communal concerns, local and national history, romance, and the legends of the people.[15]

Historical Development of Ballads

Ballads emerged in Europe around the eleventh or twelfth century and continue to thrive in most countries today. The songs developed during the Middle Ages, as minstrels traveled from castle to castle, village to village, and country to country entertaining the nobility, wealthy townspeople, higher clergy, and peasants with adventures of folk heroes and the news of the day. The earliest English ballad is "Judas," which dates to the late thirteenth century. Many of the early ballads were transmitted from singer to singer by word of mouth. Over the next centuries, they became a popular literary form. The old ballads were brought to America by the early settlers. As they moved across the country, they carried the traditional ballads with them and modified the ballads to reflect their own interests. Although the American pioneers created many original ballads, a third of the older ballads survived and are still sung today.

During the late nineteenth century, Francis Child identified 305 ballads, which he published in *The English and Scottish Popular Ballads*. Child divided the ballads into categories including ballads of magic, romantic and tragic ballads, medieval minstrely, ballads of historical and semi-historical events, local and minor historical ballads, and comic songs.[16]

Ballads evolved from two sources, *traditional folk ballads* and *literary ballads*. All ballads have distinguishing characteristics, which are presented in Figure 3.4 on page 75.

Traditional Folk Ballads These songs were transmitted orally by anonymous, semiliterate singers and poets. The folk claimed the songs, sometimes modified them, and made them their own. Many ballads were tales of adventure or episodes in war. Others told romantic stories, while some were tragic tales ending in death. Frequently, they included the supernatural. Popular ballads about Robin Hood first appeared in the fourteenth century. Numerous ballads about this legendary hero and his men of Lincoln Green were developed through the seventeenth century. Maid Marian did not appear until the later stories.

By the sixteenth century, many folk ballads began to be printed on single sheets of paper known as "broadsides," which were decorated with crude woodcuts. Familiar tunes to be used with the song would be suggested. Broadside ballads were sold for one penny by chapmen who traveled around the countryside. Though not as literate as traditional ballads, broadside ballads were accessible and popular among the ordinary folk and often were used to spread the local news. Familiar folk songs such as "Down in the Valley" emerged from the traditional folk ballad.

Literary Ballads The literary or written ballad is associated with the person who created it. From the sixteenth through the nineteenth century, ballads were a popular form, and prominent authors such as William Shakespeare, William Wordsworth, Sir Walter Scott, Robert Burns, John Keats, Lewis Carroll, Alfred Noyes, and Rudyard Kipling created new literary ballads. American poets such as Henry Wadsworth Longfellow, John Greenleaf Whittier, Stephen Vincent Benét, and Robert Frost also wrote original ballads. These talented writers refined the literary format and developed literary ballads that remain popular with contemporary audiences.

Ballads in the Classroom

Since ballads were originally intended to amuse and entertain adults, they frequently involve violence, horrible deaths, tragedies, and other behaviors that are inappropriate to present to children. Therefore, ballads must be chosen wisely, considering the age and maturity of the individual students in a class. Children of all ages enjoy the music of the ballads, but they may not understand the words. Usually, students nine years and older enjoy the verbal narratives. Several books with pictures contain ballads such as Amy Cohn's collection *From Sea to Shining Sea* (1993). This collection of American tales, songs, and poems is illustrated by fourteen Caldecott winners. A notable single tale book with pictures is Julius Lester's *John Henry* (1994), the ballad of a man who beat the steam drill with his sledgehammer. Jerry Pinkney's superb illustrations capture Lester's contemporary retelling of the ballad. After reading and viewing this book, students can compare it to other versions of the ballad, such as Ezra J. Keat's *John Henry* (1987). The comparison will lead naturally to fur-

FIGURE 3.4 Distinguishing Characteristics of Ballads

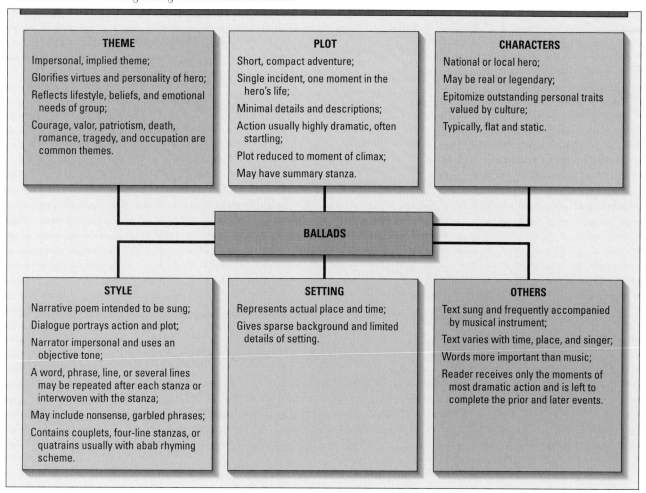

ther discussion of the hero's physical attributes and American history and will give students a better understanding of ballads. After reading about John Henry, students can write ballads about local heroes.

Ballads are also an ideal introduction to the study of a culture and its people. A study of the westward expansion of the United States, for example, is enhanced by singing ballads such as "The Streets of Laredo," "The Old Chisholm Trail," "Get Along Little Dogies," "Billy the Kid," "Sweet Betsy of Pike," and "Frankie and Johnny." The following are some familiar ballads with their topics:

"She's a Grand Old Flag"—patriotism.

"Casey Jones"—occupations.

"Frankie and Johnny"—romantic tragedies.

"Jesse James"—bad men.

"The Great Silkie of Sule Skerry"—the supernatural.

"On Top of Old Smoky"—crime and punishment.

"Robin Hood"—folk heroes.

"Revolutionary Tea"—wartime.

"Bonnie and Clyde"—outlaws.

"Happy Birthday"—celebration.

Stephen Foster's songs—regional ballads.

EPICS

The word *epic* comes from the Greek word *epos*, meaning a saying or an oracle. In folk literature an *epic* is often a long narrative poem, written in grandiose language, portraying the heroic deeds of a historical or traditional hero as he or she undertakes a series of adventures. The poem typically includes events related to the historical development of a nation or a culture. Popular epics include the Sumerian *Gilgamesh*, Homer's *Iliad* and *Odyssey*, and the Anglo-Saxon *Beowulf*. The term *epic* is also used to describe a novel or a movie of grandiose proportions, such as Tolstoy's *War and Peace* and Cecil B. DeMille's *The Ten Commandments.*

By relating the deeds of a national hero, the epic celebrates the virtues and feats valued by that society. The hero is endowed with physical and emotional characteristics deemed important by the society, such as virtue, patience, fortitude, and wisdom. Typically, an epic is imbued with a sense of the supernatural. Usually, the hero is buffeted by the gods and achieves a godlike stature by undergoing the cycle of adventures. Figure 3.5 provides an overview of the literary characteristics of epics.

Historical Development of Epics

Epics have appeared all over the world. A society would use them to stir the martial spirit of its warriors. The epics praised the exploits of heroic ancestors and supplied mod-

els of ideal heroic behavior to the national warriors. The heroic songs were sung before a battle or in the banquet halls to celebrate national victories. Over time the songs were adopted and enhanced by the people.

These long narrative poems are classified as *folk* epics or as *literary* epics. *Folk epics* are primitive oral compositions that were originally sung or recited and passed on in the oral tradition. *Literary epics* are long, narrative poems that were originally written by a particular person. Literary epics have a sophisticated structure and literary expressions and were disseminated in a written format.[17]

Examples of folk epics include *Gilgamesh*, a Sumerian epic from c. 3000 B.C.; Homer's *Iliad* and *Odyssey*, ancient Greek epics related to the Trojan War; and *Beowulf*, the oldest English poem. *Gilgamesh*, which is perhaps the oldest extant work in the oral tradition, is a five-poem cycle in twelve books. It tells the story of King Gilgamesh, who was

FIGURE 3.5 Distinguishing Literary Characteristics of Epics

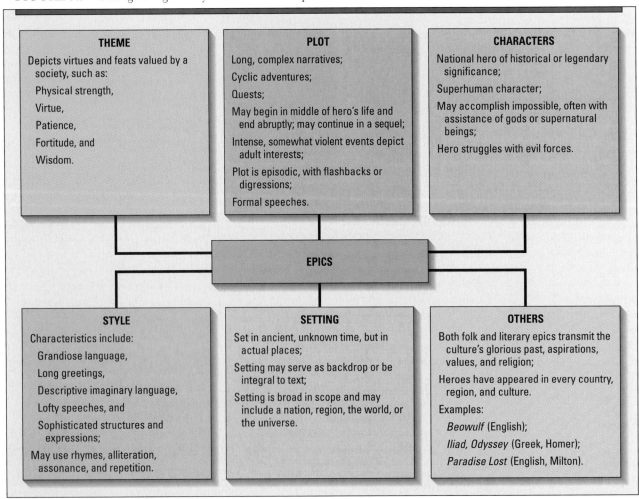

part human and part god and encountered many adventures as he sought immortality. Several hundred years after the great Trojan War, which scholars believe occurred around 1200 B.C., the Greek poet Homer is credited with recording *The Iliad*, which tells the story of the Trojan War, and *The Odyssey*, which relates the adventures Odysseus (Ulysses) encountered as he returned to his home in Ithaca after the war. People had sung about the events of the war before Homer shaped the oral traditions into an epic around the eighth century B.C. *Beowulf*, which was recorded around A.D. 1000, relates the adventures of a legendary Geatish hero who kills two demonic monsters, Grendel and Grendel's mother, who have been devastating the kingdom of Hrothgar, a Danish king. Later Beowulf meets a dragon and kills it with the help of Wiglaf, his young follower, but dies of his wounds.

Several examples of literary epics include Virgil's *Aeneid* (c. 30–20 B.C.), an extension of Homer's poems and a celebration of the founding of Rome; the *Chanson de Roland*, a medieval French epic from c. 1100; the *Cantar de Mio Cid*, a medieval Spanish epic from the early twelfth century; and *The Divine Comedy*, Dante's personal epic, which was written in Italian in the early fourteenth century. English epics include Edmund Spenser's *Faerie Queene*, a mixture of epic and romance that was written in the sixteenth century and is considered by some to be the greatest narrative poem in English literature. In 1677 John Milton wrote *Paradise Lost*, the greatest of all postclassical epics. The most notable American epics are Henry Wadsworth Longfellow's Native American epic, *The Song of Hiawatha* (1855), and Walt Whitman's *Leaves of Grass* (1855), considered the autobiography of a generic American.[18]

Epic Poetry in the Classroom

The strong national and cultural philosophy revealed by the characters and events makes epics ideal folk literature to use when studying a region or culture. Young people eleven years and older enjoy epics. The narrative poems help students gain insight into cultural values, heroes, and ideals. They can identify and compare these values to current ideals or goals in the United States. Before reading the poetry, students must understand the historical events depicted, the goals of the heroes, and the formal, stylized language used in epics.

Recently, several books with pictures have appeared to introduce elementary-age students to the exciting adventures of epics. Paul Fleishman's *Dateline: Troy* (1996) is a unique introduction to the Trojan War, and Barbara Picard's retellings of Homer in *The Iliad of Homer* (1960) and *The Odyssey of Homer* (1952) give fourth graders and above an enjoyable introduction to these epics. These

books are helpful when students read Rosemary Sutcliff's *Black Ships before Troy: The Story of the Iliad* (1995) and her *Wanderings of Odysseus: The Story of the Odyssey* (1996). Sutcliff's books are appealing to middle-grade students and present a well-written, descriptive account of the epics. The *Gilgamesh* epic is introduced to upper elementary-age students through Ludmila Zeman's readable trilogy *Gilgamesh the King* (1992), *The Revenge of Ishtar* (1993), and *The Last Quest of Gilgamesh* (1995). Susan Jeffers's *Hiawatha* (1983) presents a visual account of Longfellow's epic poem that fourth grade and older students will enjoy before exploring the original epic.

Other hero tales, classified as *legends* (another subgenre of folk literature), are presented in prose. Epic characters such as Robin Hood may also be the subject of prose narratives. (See Wyeth's painting of Robin Hood and Maid Marian on page 78.) These books are exciting reading for middle-grade students and are discussed later under the legend subgenre.

❋ FOLK LITERATURE SUBGENRES TRANSMITTED PRIMARILY IN PROSE FORMAT

The Standard Dictionary of Folklore, Mythology, and Legend classifies all traditional prose narratives as either *myths*, *legends*, or *tales*.[19] All regional, cultural, and ethnic groups have prose folk literature. Some scholars arrange the narratives in broad categories around literary or character elements. The following are the most notable classifications with an example of each:

Cumulative tales—"This Is the House That Jack Built."

Talking-beast tales—"Puss in Boots."

Droll or humorous tales—"Clever Elsie."

Pourquoi stories or creation myths—"Why the Bear Has a Stumpy Tail."

Realistic tales—"Zaleth the Goat."

Wonder tales—"Cinderella."

Stith Thompson, the co-editor of the *Aarne-Thompson Type-Index* and the author of *Motif-Index of Folk-Literature* says, however, that whether transmitted in oral or written format, in English the term *folktale* has come to mean all forms of prose narrative handed down through the generations.[20] Therefore, each prose subgenre must be identified, and the distinguishing characteristics of each must be delineated. Figure 3.6 on page 79 summarizes the folk literature subgenres transmitted in prose format.

N. C. Wyeth used bright colors in his realistic oil painting for Paul Creswick's 1917 edition of Robin Hood. *In this painting Robin Hood meets Maid Marian.*

MYTHS

As we read myths, many questions come to mind. For example:

How would the world be different if Pandora had not opened the box?

How did King Midas's daughter feel when she couldn't hug her father?

How would our lives be different if Persephone had not eaten the four pomegranate seeds?

In fact, myths generate more questions in the reader's mind than they answer.

Myths are cultural beliefs framed in symbolic stories. They began before modern history, deal with encounters between gods and mortals, and are set in a period beyond time. The quests and adventures are presented as truths without a historical background, but supported by cultural beliefs. Myths represent scientific thinking of a prescientific period when people depended on supernatural explanations for various phenomena. They reflect human understanding of how people, animals, and particular places came to be the way they are; why natural phenomena occur; and why various peoples have their own unique characteristics. All groups have myths to explain their religious beliefs, traditions, rituals, and customs.

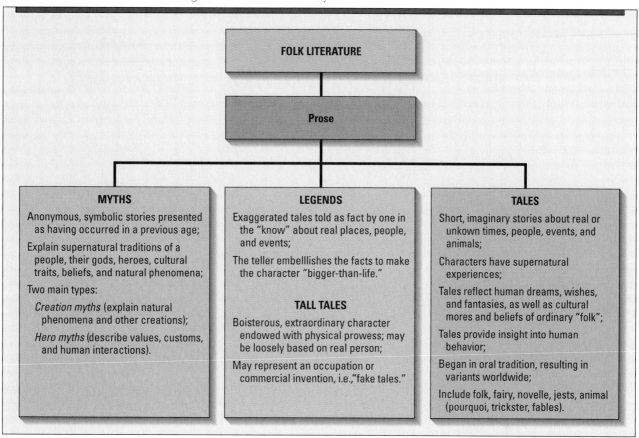

Myths are the product of a cultural group, not the creation of an individual. The stories focus on the adventures of sacred or semidivine heroes, but the major characters also include deities, who have supernatural powers. A particular cycle of stories will feature various gods from the society's pantheon. Figure 3.7 on page 80 presents the distinguishing characteristics of myths.

Historical Development of Myths

The term *myth* comes from the Greek word *mythos* meaning a tale, speech, or story. Myths emerged in ancient times when prehistoric people were asking questions about the universe and their place in it. To answer these questions, they invented explanations for the existence of humans and the rest of their environment. These explanations were disseminated in story format and represented the accepted values, mores, and beliefs of the group. As people began to question their relationships with one another and with the universe, they invented stories with characters who represented human personalities. The characters were idealized and took the form of deities—superhuman beings, animals, or plants. The deities were related to one another and

appeared over a cycle of stories. The themes symbolized abstract moral qualities revered by the society, such as love and fortitude.

Ancient Greek, Roman, Norse, and Native American myths are most familiar in English-speaking countries today, but myths from African Americans, South America, Africa, China, and elsewhere are now available. Although they come from different cultures, all myths have common universal themes, in that they attempt to explain creation, divinity, religion, and natural phenomena. They also provide exemplary models of human behavior. Although each culture has unique gods, the gods' positions in the supernatural world, their virtues, and the human characteristics they represent are similar in myths from most cultures.

Types of Myths

Myths overlap to some degree with folktales, legends, and epics. Many myths contain themes and motifs common to legends and other folktales; similarly, many folktales contain fragments or remnants of myths. Myths can be distinguished from these other subgenres, however, in that they always feature deities. Myths are broadly classed as *creation*

FIGURE 3.7 Distinguishing Literary Characteristics of Myths

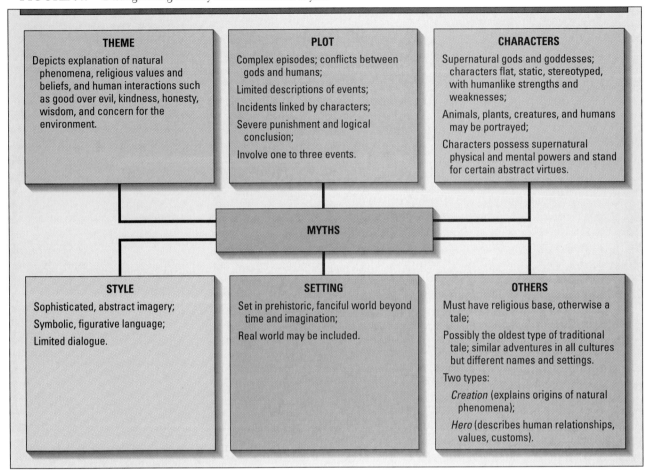

myths, as seen in Lynn Moroney's *Moontellers: Myths of the Moon from Around the World* (1995), and *hero myths*, as in Neil Philip's *The Illustrated Book of Myths: Tales and Legends of the World* (1995). Yet, as Virginia Hamilton, a notable author and collector of African-American tales, reminds us, some myths appear in more than one type and may "defy typecasting."[21]

Creation Myths Creation myths were early humans' prescientific explanations for the existence of people, animals, and objects. This classification includes *pourquoi* (or "why" and "how") tales. These simple tales often give humorous explanations for the characteristics of humans and animals. Some representative examples from various countries are the African tale "Why Wisdom Is Found Everywhere," the Zuni tale "How the Coyote Danced with the Blackbirds," and the Kiowa tale "Why the Ant Is Almost Cut in Two." These amusing tales stimulate the imagination and resemble extended fables. They are discussed in more detail later in the chapter.

Other creation stories were invented to explain the origin of the universe and its inhabitants. Creation myths help people everywhere verbalize personal interpretations about why, how, and where all things in their environment came into existence. Virginia Hamilton's *In the Beginning: Creation Stories from Around the World* (1988) is an outstanding collection of myths from around the world, explaining early humans' beliefs about the origin of the earth and its beings. Barry Moser's expressive watercolor illustrations help interpret the authentic stories. Familiar stories included in the collection are "Cyclops," "Prometheus," and "Pandora."

Hero Myths Hero myths focus on the gods' relationships with other gods and with supernatural beings and creatures. Unlike creation myths, these stories highlight, but do not explain, the attributes possessed by the hero—the god. The hero accepts difficult tasks and may be transformed while attempting to accomplish them, as portrayed in Shirley Climo's *Atalanta's Race: A Greek Myth* (1995).

Alexander Koshkin's illustrations dramatically interpret the story. Hero myths helped early people understand the values held by their society, as in Lois Duncan's Navajo tale *The Magic of Spider Woman* (1996), accompanied by almost surrealistic illustrations by Shonto Begay. Complex myths portray the gods' interactions with other gods. These stories are adult in content and are frequently interpreted differently by different folklorists.[22]

Myths in the Classroom

The simple *creation* myths are easy for children aged five to nine to understand. These stories portray human qualities relevant to young children. Although most stories have a complex structure, primary-age children can understand hero tales such as the story of King Midas's greed. Frequently, myths contain unusual names for settings and individual gods, sophisticated language, and abstract symbolism with religious connotations. Therefore, children need introductory information, which can be found in several collections of myths, such as Ann Pilling's *Realms of God: Myths and Legends from Around the World* (1993), whose text is enhanced by Kady Denton's illustrations. Also highly recommended for the elementary classroom are the d'Aulaires' *Book of Greek Myths* (1962) and their *Norse Gods and Giants* (1967). The chapter bibliography lists several highly recommended collections of myths from around the world.

Every day young people encounter allusions to myths. Consider the planets, the U.S. space program, and the various commercial products bearing the names of mythological deities such as Apollo, Gemini, Mercury, and Atlas. After reading a variety of myths, learners can prepare a collage of commercial products named after mythological characters and display the collage with representative books.

Initially, myths are presented aesthetically or for pleasure. Students enjoy pronouncing the names of the gods and learning their positions in the fanciful world of ancient myths. Instructional techniques such as comparison charts (described in Chapter 10) elicit comparisons of names and responsibilities of gods between cultures. A presentation of myths from various countries gives students a broader knowledge of people around the world. After encountering these myths, learners could prepare an advertisement for a product or company named for a god. When selecting a name, the child will consider the character's attributes. For example, a publishing company could be named Anansi, because he regarded himself as the wisest creature in the universe.

Mythology lends itself to dramatic presentations and artistic expressions. Oral presentations allow listeners to hear the storyteller's language and experience the adventure and intrigue in the stories. Oral discussions provide an opportunity to discuss why ancient people used the story format to present the truths held by a society; how variants of the stories have lived throughout the world through time; and how humans used their imaginations to explain the universe and their place in it several millennia ago.

LEGENDS

Most people have pondered the feats and accomplishments of a regional hero. Stories about a neighborhood haunted house are believed and passed on to others. Some people believe aliens have visited them. When such prose narratives dealing with real people, places, or events, are set at another time, mingled with superstitions, and told as fact, we classify them as **legends.**

Legends enhance and expand historical information about wars, migrations, and heroes. The prose narratives may be either secular or sacred; they explain the creation of places and natural phenomena, human and animal transformations, or heroic deeds. Similar legends are found throughout the world. Legends are closely related to myths, ballads, epics, folktales, and tall tales, but unlike myths, legends do not contain supernatural deities. The same story may exist as both a prose legend and a poetic ballad or epic such as "Robin Hood" and "El Cid." The storyteller may exaggerate the adventures of a historical person to the point that the legend becomes a tall tale. Legends and tall tales exist about Davy Crockett and John Chapman, the legendary model for Johnny Appleseed.[23] Figure 3.8 on page 82 summarizes the distinguishing characteristics of legends.

Historical Development of Legends

Wherever two or more people are together, they will eventually invent legends and tell them as truth! Perhaps, humans have a natural desire to modify, expand, and stretch a tale until it becomes a new legend. Throughout time, people have invented legends in both oral and written format. Sometimes the tales were based on historical fragments or documentation and used to explain why certain places, animals, and vegetation exist.

In early days professional and semiprofessional tellers of tales recited and sang legends through the countryside. Fragments of tales, such as the stories of the legendary King Arthur, spread orally before Sir Thomas Malory recorded the legend in his book *Morte d'Arthur*. William Caxton published the Arthurian legend in the late fifteenth century. The Arthurian legends and the adventures of Robin Hood continue to inspire contemporary authors; the chapter bibliography lists a number of new books that retell these tales such as Hudson Talbott's *King Arthur and the Round Table* (1995) and Robert Leeson's *The Story of Robin Hood* (1994).

FIGURE 3.8   Distinguishing Characteristics of Legends

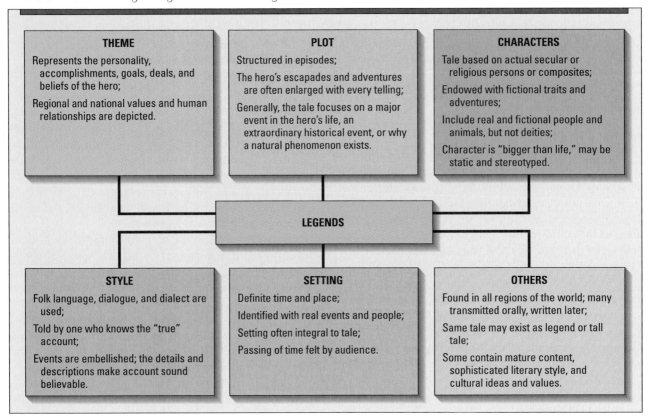

Types of Legends

Three types of legends are found in folk literature: *hero legends*, *local legends* (also called *sage*), and *explanatory legends*. Though the forms overlap, each has enough distinguishing characteristics to warrant separate discussion.

Hero Legends   Because people are curious about popular folk heroes, saints, activists, and warriors, legends develop about them. A legend grows out of the teller's imagination and frequently attributes accomplishments to the protagonist that are improbable, though not impossible. This process was particularly common before historical records were meticulously kept. The Egyptian queen Cleopatra, the French saint Joan of Arc, and the Swiss hero William Tell are examples of people who inspired legends. Leonard Fisher presents a refreshing retelling of an old legend in his book *William Tell* (1996). (See Fisher color plate on page 83.) Two Americans who have inspired hero legends are Daniel Boone and Jesse James.

Hero legends also include saint heroes. Saint legends were originally read in church and accepted as truth. These tales about religious leaders were originally literary, but entered the oral tradition and became a part of folktale collections. Legends about St. Nicholas, St. Valentine, and St. Patrick are especially popular. In 1993 Margaret Hodges retold the story of the popular Irish saint in her book *Saint Patrick and the Peddler*. Paul Brett Johnson brings the Irish countryside to life in his pictures that accompany the legend.

Local Legends (or Sage)   Local legends describe extraordinary events that the teller and audience believe. A local legend attaches itself to a particular setting, although sometimes the same legend is told in several places. Local legends tell about humans' "true" encounters with marvelous creatures, such as revenants (spirits who return), fairies, the devil, and water spirits; sightings of the Loch Ness monster in Scotland or the Bigfoot monster in heavily wooded areas all over the world are also the subjects of local legends. Stories about buried treasures in the southwestern United States are the basis of many pioneer legends, and tales about unidentified flying objects and aliens are found in contemporary legends. Local legends also recount the escapades of historical people, such as Icabod Crane and the Pied Piper of Hamelin. Middle school students and older will enjoy C. J. Taylor's verbal and visual narratives from eight Native American tribes in *The Monster from the Swamp: Native Legends of Monsters, Demons, and Other Creatures* (1995).

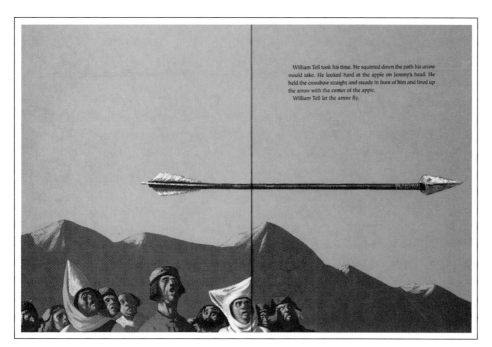

Leonard Everett Fisher effectively uses a variety of brilliant colors in the expressionistic drawings for his William Tell. *The background and unique faces add to the excitement and drama of this retelling of a popular legend. Did the arrow hit the mark?*

William Tell took his time. He squinted down the path his arrow would take. He looked hard at the apple on Jemmy's head. He held the crossbow straight and steady in front of him and lined up the arrow with the center of the apple.
William Tell let the arrow fly.

Explanatory Legends   Explanatory legends are also local and explain the origin of certain landmarks, such as a lover's leap, or why various animals, natural phenomena, or plants exist. Though explanatory legends are similar to myths without deities, the local flavor makes the tale more believable than the lost worlds of myths. Tomie de Paola created three explanatory legends about flowers: *The Legend of the Poinsettia* (1994), *The Legend of the Bluebonnet: A Tale of Old Texas* (1983), and *The Legend of the Indian Paintbrush* (1988).

Legends in the Classroom

Historical events, people, and important places in the immediate environment are intriguing to young people. In particular, the "truthful" reporting of facts in legends encourages children to invent original "truthful reports" about school and other events.

Because of the "folk" language used in legends, the stories are ideal to read aloud and tell. Young people can take a simple legend, embellish it, and tell it as fact so that their audience will believe it. After reading and enjoying many legends, a student or groups of students can write original legends about local events, places, or people. Use the same activity with historical persons of a particular ethnic or cultural group. Students' linguistic abilities are enhanced as they write, tell, and read legends.

Many simple legends entertain young audiences, but the stories must be chosen carefully because they may contain mature content and themes. Most legends are appropriate for students in fourth grade and above. Fortunately, excellent books are available with legends from various countries that entertain and give historical and cultural information about the region; Ed Young's *Cat and Rat: The Legend of the Chinese Zodiac* (1995) and Nancy Van Laan's *In a Circle Long Ago: A Treasury of Native Lore from North America* (1995) are examples. Van Laan introduces the lifestyles of different Native American tribes through legends, poems, and appropriate illustrations by Lisa Desimini. Chapter bibliographies also suggest picture story books dealing with single events in the hero's life, such as Robert San Souci's *Young Guinevere* (1993), illustrated by Jamichael Henterly.

TALL TALES

> Did Capt'n Stormalong *really* make the Cliffs of Dover white?
>
> Did Babe and Paul *really* dig the Great Lakes?
>
> Did Davy Crockett *really* kill a bear at age three?

These and many other questions tumble from children's lips when they hear tales about the Capt'n, Paul, and Daniel. Such tales are classified as tall tales.

Tall tales are exaggerated, humorous tales about historical or imaginary humans and animals, who accomplish the "impossible" in rugged environments. The tales are intended for amusement and pleasure only. They can be considered either a type of legend or a separate subgenre of folk literature. In this book we describe tall tales as a separate subgenre of folk literature because the stories are closely woven into the American "folk" culture. Figure 3.9 summarizes the characteristics of tall tales.

Historical Development of Tall Tales

During America's western expansion, when the pioneers camped at night beside a fire or river, they relaxed by recounting humorous anecdotes. Sometimes they told tales from their native country, but sometimes they related embellished stories about contemporary folk heroes. Both the teller and the audience knew that the tales were grandiose and were designed to see who could tell the biggest fib. After all, the pioneers were traveling in a big country, and the tales seem to express the philosophy that "everything is bigger and better in the new world." The teller was free to invent new characters and events. From such beginnings, the tall tale, with its exaggerated characters and ridiculous events, emerged as America's major contribution to folk literature. Though some immigrants, especially from Ireland, brought cultural tall tales with them, the characters and settings changed to fit the environment and the people, and only the structure of the tall tale remained.

In the early twentieth century a commercial writer was hired to advertise the lumber industry. He selected traditional legendary folk heroes, invented others, and borrowed the tall tale format. He wrote exaggerated stories about a lumberman's life and glorified the occupation. These tales were successful, and other businesses began to use tall tales in advertising. Eventually, folklorists called these written commercial tall tales *fakelore*, while the traditional oral tales remained tall tales.[24] Many popular tall tale characters were invented by advertising agencies. For example, Paul Bunyan and Babe the Blue Ox represented the lumber industry and the northern part of the country; the cowboy Pecos Bill, and his horse Widowmaker represented the Southwest; John Henry and his twenty-pound hammer represented the power of the railroad in the West; Mike Fink, the riverboat keelman, sailed primarily on the Mississippi River; Joe Mazark, the steel man, represented the steel mills of Pennsylvania and the Midwest; and Captain Stormalong, the great sea captain, represented the New England coast.[25]

FIGURE 3.9 Distinguishing Characteristics of Tall Tales

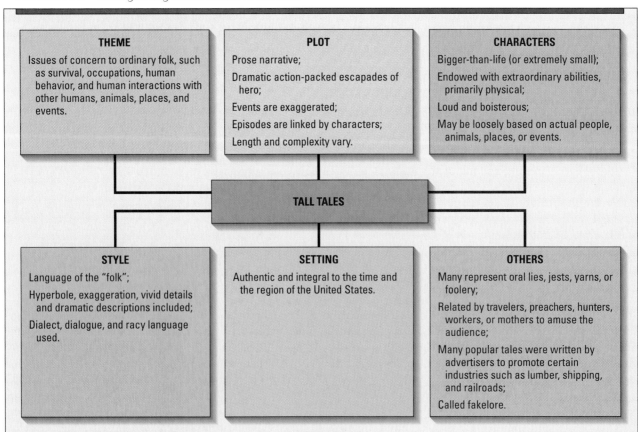

Tall Tales in the Classroom

Children seven years and over enjoy tall tales, if they are willing to suspend belief in reality and let their minds soar with "wings" to accept the exaggerated characters who effortlessly achieve superhuman feats.

Some tales highlight people's inhumanity to others, violence, killings, and use racy language; these tales, are not meant for elementary school. Fortunately, many suitable selections are available in books with pictures such as Steven Kellogg's series of picture books about Pecos Bill, Paul Bunyan, Mike Fink, Johnny Appleseed, Sally Ann Thunder Ann Whirlwind Crockett, and Carol Purdy's *Iva Dunnit and the Big Wind*, which Kellogg illustrated. Various familiar and unknown tall tale characters are included in several excellent collections for second grade and above. Adrian Stoutenberg presents familiar tales in her classic collection *American Tall Tales* (1976). Patrick McManus introduces new characters in his entertaining collection *Never Cry "Arp!" and Other Great Adventures* (1996). Mary Pope Osborne's amusing retellings of seven tales in *American Tall Tales* (1991) are enhanced by Michael McCurdy's humorous, folk art illustrations. (See Osborne color plate at right.)

After exploring these and other tales listed in the bibliography, children can ponder why the tales are called "The Windies." By singing published songs about the bigger-than-life characters and exaggerated events, young people experience the full potential of tall tales. Children enjoy the challenge of reading or telling published or original tales. The idea of writing a "big lie" is appealing to most children. Even though the characters and their actions are exaggerated, the settings and geographical information are historically accurate. Therefore, tall tales enrich the study of American history.

FOLKTALES

Folktales are short fictionalized prose narratives that are not historically accurate, but authentically represent the culture, region, or ethnic group that created them. The dreams, wishes, and fantasies of the folk are depicted in the adventures of the human and animal characters. In folktales all issues are clear. The conflict is stated initially, and the characters move quickly to attempt to resolve it. The characters are purposely stereotyped. They are either all good or all bad. Brave deeds are rewarded. Evil actions are punished. Therefore, the audience know immediately with whom to place their sympathies. The stories frequently use conversations, repetitive language, refrains, and a general economy of language. Many tales were developed through repeated storytelling, while others were written originally.

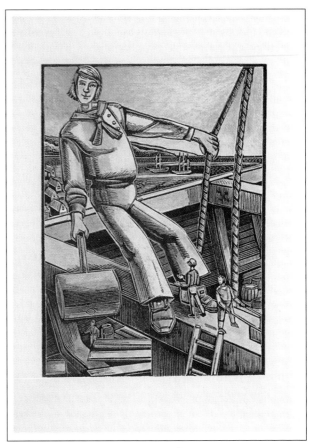

Michael McCurdy's colored wood engravings show Alfred Bulltop Stormalong's size, power, and courage in Mary Pope Osborne's book, American Tall Tales. *The artist used single blocks of end-grain maple for each engraving and added watercolor to the final print. McCurdy is recognized for his outstanding wood engravings.*

Folktales developed in all regions of the world and in all societies. Wherever they developed, they reflect the beliefs, mores, and traditions valued by the group.

Stith Thompson adapted the work of A. Aarne and classified folktales into five categories, each having a corresponding number in the *Aarne-Thompson Type-Index*. Based upon their identifiable motifs (the smallest recognizable elements existing independently in a story), Thompson classified the tales as animal tales (numbers (1–299); ordinary folktales (300–1199); anecdotes, stories about clever, stupid, lucky folk, and lying tales (1200–1999); formula tales (2000–2399); or unclassified tales (2400–2499).[26]

During the 1980s, Margaret MacDonald and D. L. Ashliman modified Thompson's index and added categories not in the original list.[27] These books are extremely helpful in selecting suitable folktales for the classroom.

MacDonald's reference also organizes the tales according to ethnic groups and provides an excellent bibliography of collections and single-tale books published before 1982. Ashliman annotated each motif and listed all variants related to the motif. The distinguishing characteristics of folktales are summarized in Figure 3.10.

Historical Development of Folktales

From the earliest times, all societies have had folktales, or stories about their lives and their environment. The historical development of folktales is closely intertwined with all folk literature. Discussing the history of Mother Goose or fairy tales or legends without talking about folktales is impossible. Therefore, the historical development of folktales is discussed throughout this chapter.

When early collectors compiled old tales from a country, they were not interested in subgenre designations; thus, folktales and fairy tales were published in the same collection. Furthermore, a tale from one region might have the characteristics of a folktale, while a variant from another region might have fairy tale characteristics. While each subgenre has distinguishing characteristics, the major focus should be on the fact that many of the old tales were told by anonymous tellers throughout the world and that the tales were preserved when the movable printing press was invented.

Although other collectors preceded Die Brüder Grimm (The Brothers Grimm), their collections won particular renown. Jakob and Wilhelm Grimm published *Kinder- und Hausmärchen* (Folk Tales for Children and the Home) in 1812. The first edition contained eighty-six old German folk and fairy tales, and the second edition, which was published in 1815, added seventy more tales. Folklorists working around the world have found recognizable variants of all of the Grimms' tales. Today, the tales have been translated into seventy languages and remain the most influential and widely known collection of folk and fairy tales in the literate world. See Did You Know on page 87 to discover more about the Grimm brothers.

FIGURE 3.10 Distinguishing Characteristics of Folktales

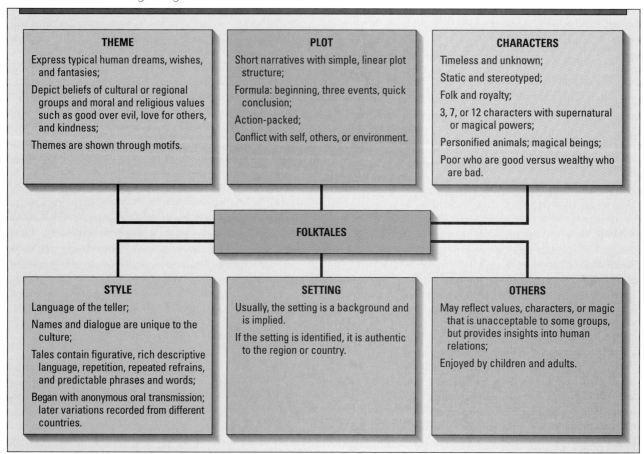

Did You Know About
DIE BRÜDER GRIMM?

Jakob and Wilhelm Grimm were born one year apart, Jakob in 1785 and Wilhelm in 1786, in Hanau, Germany. They were inseparable—they shared the same books, had the same interests, and lived their entire lives under the same roof. Wilhelm married Dortchen Wild in 1825 and they had three children. They invited Jakob to live with them, and he became a permanent member of the family. After Wilhelm died in 1859, Dortchen cared for Jakob until his death in 1863.

Their father, who died when the brothers were young, was a lawyer. Their mother and her six children were very poor, but thanks to the generosity of an uncle, Jakob and Wilhelm attended law school in Marburg. They intended to become lawyers, but while at the university Jakob encountered a professor who changed their plans. Jakob, the more scholarly of the brothers, became interested in studying the structure and history of the German language. He wrote an influential German grammar and began compiling a German dictionary. Wilhelm, the brother with an artistic flair and a popular storyteller, suggested that the old folktales, myths, legends, and sayings would provide authentic sources for the language. Realizing that the rich traditional German language was in danger of being lost, the brothers believed that by recording the folk materials, they would also learn about old customs and superstitions, which would provide a link to ancient societies. They began searching for folk storytellers and listened to stories told by Wilhelm's wife and family, other family members,

and neighbors. The largest number of stories came from a peddlar, Frau Viehmann. For years scholars believed Frau Viehmann was a peasant, but old records revealed that she was from a middle-class Huguenot family and that French was her first language. Clearly, she knew Perrault and contributed his stories to the collection. Although the brothers retained the content and manner of the teller's renditions, scholars now believe that they took some liberties in rewriting, altering, and elaborating the tales. Nevertheless, the stories are a great scholarly work of art.

The thousand copies of the first edition sold out, but the tales did not impress the critics. They did, however, touch the imagination and emotions of the people, who enthusiastically endorsed them. In 1815 the second edition was published, and the book was translated into seventeen languages. In 1822 Sir Edgar Taylor, a London lawyer and scholar, translated and published the English edition of the tales as *German Popular Tales*. George Cruikshank used woodcuts to illustrate the tales. With the popularity of the new editions and the translations, the Grimm brothers enjoyed publishing success. In 1840 they were appointed to the faculty at the University of Berlin by the king of Prussia and continued their research and writing. Hans Christian Andersen visited the Grimms in 1843, and Jakob traveled to Copenhagen to visit Andersen the next year. Jakob also traveled to Italy, Switzerland, and Austria. The brothers lived comfortably in Berlin until their deaths.

Folktales in the Classroom

Folktales have always been a favorite genre for storytellers and artists, but today the library shelves are filled with profusely illustrated folktales from every corner of the world. Children's initial encounter with folktales should be pleasant. Since the storyteller's voice is retained in the tales, they need to be heard. Thus, a wise adult will tell the stories, read them aloud, or play recordings of them. Young people enjoy reading or telling favorite stories to younger children or their peers, especially at storytelling festivals. Folktales contain dialogue, repetitive phrases, alliteration, and other figurative language that comes to life when presented in plays, puppet shows, and reader's theatres (a scripted narration read by different members of the group).

John Steptoe's attention to detail and his use of cool greens and blues brings the Zimbabwe region to contemporary children in his original fable, Mufaro's Beautiful Daughters. *The pictures contain detailed drawings that show contrasting textures. Steptoe uses gouache to portray perhaps the most beautiful African women in juvenile literature. The creator achieves a perfect balance between the visual and verbal narratives to successfully tell this exciting tale inspired by a late nineteenth-century Zimbabwe folk tale.*

Folktales are excellent models for rewriting or original writing. Naturally, they are most appropriate to use in a social studies class when introducing and studying a cultural, ethnic, regional, or religious group.

The bibliography presents a variety of outstanding folktale collections representing diverse groups. The selector is encouraged to look at the source notes to determine the cultural authenticity of the book. Fortunately, many new collections and books with pictures now include these sources. Popular collections include Virginia Hamilton's *The People Could Fly* (1988), *Many Thousand Gone* (1992), and *Her Stories: African American Folktales, Fairy Tales, and True Tales* (1995), all illustrated by Leo and Diane Dillon; and Hamilton's *When Birds Could Talk and Bats Could Sing: The Adventures of Bruh Sparrow, Sis Wren, and Their Friends* (1996), illustrated by Barry Moser. Other collections include tales, songs, and verses from all groups. Some examples are Jane Yolen's *Favorite Folktales from Around the World* (1986); Michael Rosen's *South and North and East and West* (1992), illustrated by various English artists; and Eric Kimmel's collection of tales about a Jewish folk hero, *The Adventures of Hershel of Ostropol* (1995), accompanied by black and white drawings by Trina Schart Hyman. As the chapter bibliography indicates, numerous single-story picture books with representative folk art illustrations are also available. Some examples include the Mexican tale *Mediopollito I Half-Chicken* (1995) by Alma Ada (translated by Rosalma Zubizarreta), with illustrations by Kim Howard that enhance the old tale; an Inca tale, *Miro in the Kingdom of the Sun* (1996), retold by Jane Kurtz and illustrated with

tinted woodcuts by David Frampton; and John Steptoe's last and most exquisite book, *Mufaro's Beautiful Daughters* (1987). (See Steptoe color plate.) This African tale exemplifies the perfect unity that is possible between the visual and verbal narratives.

After the boys and girls view these and other books with pictures, talk about the medium and style used by the artist and the suitability of the illustrations to the text; encourage students to illustrate original writings. Have the children prepare a diorama of their favorite scene. Have the students create a personal response to a folktale by selecting a visual Literary Response Mode suggested in Chapter 2 or Appendix B.

FAIRY TALES (MÄRCHEN)

Fairy tales are imaginary "wonder tales" that include enchantments and supernatural or marvelous elements and occurrences. Magic charms, disguises, and spells are frequently used by supernatural characters to protect or help the human or animal characters. The prose narratives may be of some length and show how people behave in a magical world. Many stories portray people in their daily lives, interacting with imaginary characters or creatures who may give the protagonist magical powers. More than any other folk literature, fairy tales represent pure fantasy. This subgenre represents folk literature in its purest form. Many narratives originated with the peasants, perhaps in the east in the Middle Ages.[28] Though closely related to folktales, fairy tales have distinguishing characteristics, which are summarized in Figure 3.11 on page 89.

FIGURE 3.11 Distinguishing Characteristics of Fairy Tales (Märchen)

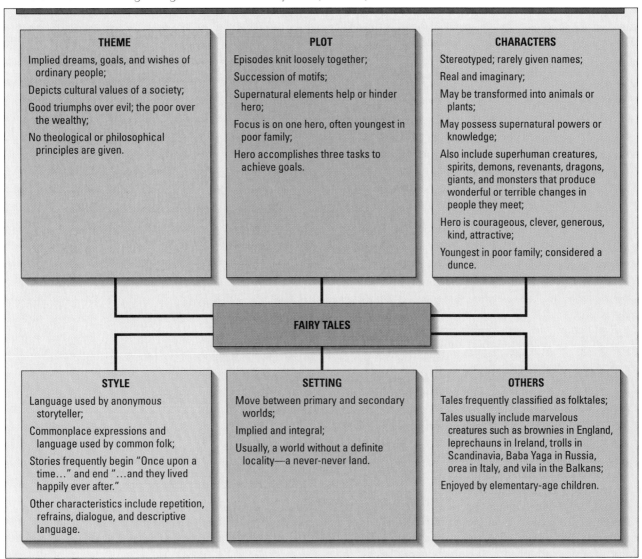

THEME
Implied dreams, goals, and wishes of ordinary people;
Depicts cultural values of a society;
Good triumphs over evil; the poor over the wealthy;
No theological or philosophical principles are given.

PLOT
Episodes knit loosely together;
Succession of motifs;
Supernatural elements help or hinder hero;
Focus is on one hero, often youngest in poor family;
Hero accomplishes three tasks to achieve goals.

CHARACTERS
Stereotyped; rarely given names;
Real and imaginary;
May be transformed into animals or plants;
May possess supernatural powers or knowledge;
Also include superhuman creatures, spirits, demons, revenants, dragons, giants, and monsters that produce wonderful or terrible changes in people they meet;
Hero is courageous, clever, generous, kind, attractive;
Youngest in poor family; considered a dunce.

FAIRY TALES

STYLE
Language used by anonymous storyteller;
Commonplace expressions and language used by common folk;
Stories frequently begin "Once upon a time..." and end "...and they lived happily ever after."
Other characteristics include repetition, refrains, dialogue, and descriptive language.

SETTING
Move between primary and secondary worlds;
Implied and integral;
Usually, a world without a definite locality—a never-never land.

OTHERS
Tales frequently classified as folktales;
Tales usually include marvelous creatures such as brownies in England, leprechauns in Ireland, trolls in Scandinavia, Baba Yaga in Russia, orea in Italy, and vila in the Balkans;
Enjoyed by elementary-age children.

Historical Development of Fairy Tales

Märchen is the diminutive form of the Old German *mar*, meaning a short story. When the Grimms' tales were published in English as *German Popular Tales*, no comparable term existed in English for the German *märchen*. Therefore, the translators used the term *fairy tales* (from the Old French *faerie*, meaning the supernatural creatures who inhabited Old France). Fairy tale is actually a confusing designation for this body of folk literature because only a few stories contain fairies. Nevertheless, the term has become universally accepted for the subgenre.

The most important contributions to folktales overall and to fairy tales in particular are the collections published by *Charles Perrault, Jakob and Wilhelm Grimm*, and *Hans*

Christian Andersen. As mentioned earlier in the Mother Goose section, in 1697 Charles Perrault published a collection of eight old tales: "The Sleeping Beauty," "Little Red Riding Hood," "Blue Beard," "Puss in Boots," "Diamonds and Toads," "Cinderella or the Little Glass Slipper," "Riquet with the Tuft," and "Little Thumb." The book was called *Contes de Ma Mère l'Oye* (Tales of Mother Goose). The tales, which were translated into English in 1729, were simple, yet sophisticated, and spoke directly to children. Whether Perrault published his son's stories or listened to his son's nurse tell the stories, his eight tales were filled with humor, lively dialogue, and dramatic events. The popularity of the tales encouraged Madame d'Aulnoy, a governess to the wife of King Louis XIV, to publish a retelling of several old

French tales in 1700. Her intent was to amuse the court, and her long, complex, dull narratives featured double meanings, sexual overtones, and elaborate language. In 1757 Madame Beaumont published a retelling of "Beauty and the Beast," a version that is still popular today.

Among the eighty-six folk and fairy tales translated by Sir Edgar Taylor for the English edition of the Grimms' tales were ten fairy tales that are still enjoyed by contemporary children: "Jorinda and Jorindel," "The Golden Bird," "Rumpelstilts-kin," "The Elves and the Shoemaker," "Twelve Dancing Princesses," "Seven Ravens," "The Water of Life," "Snow White and the Seven Dwarfs," "Faithful John," and, of course, "Ashpiettel ("Cinderella")." (See Crane's illustration of Snow White and the evil Queen.)

Hans Christian Andersen published a collection of Danish tales in 1835. Included in the collection were such favorite tales as "What the Good-Man Does Is Sure to Be Right!" "Hans Clodhopper," "Great Claus and Little Claus," and "The Wild Swans." Andersen retained the original plots, but added embellishments and some characterizations to the old tales. While his retellings were fresh and enjoyable, Andersen's major contribution to literature was the refinement of the *Literary Fairy Tale*, an original tale written in the style and structure of folk literature. His tales are considered a bridge between folk literature and fantasy (Andersen and Literary Fairy Tales are discussed in the next chapter).

Folk literature collections were popular from the seventeenth through the nineteenth century. Nannies entertained their young charges with oral renditions of the old tales and verses. As folktales were relegated to the nursery, they became a major part of children's literature.[29] This period was called the "Golden Age of Folk Literature," because tales from many countries were published. In the mid-nineteenth century, Peter Christian Asbjornsen and Jorgen E. Moe published *East o' the Sun and West o' the Moon*, a collection of Scandinavian folktales. The collection is still popular, especially the title tale and "The Three Billy-Goats Gruff." Joseph Jacobs and Andrew Lang were particularly influential in developing collections of fairy tales. Both men chose wisely and meticulously adapted the tales for the enjoyment of English children, not adults. Jacobs published *English Fairy Tales*, two volumes (1890–1894); *Celtic Fairy Tales*, two volumes (1892–1894); and *Indian Fairy Tales* (1892). Two tales from these collections, "Three Little Pigs" and "The Little Red Hen," are still popular today. Andrew Lang began publishing his series of "colored" fairy tale collections in 1889 with *Blue Fairy Book*, followed by *Red Fairy Book* (1890), *Green Fairy Book* (1892), *Pink Fairy Book*, and *Yellow Fairy Book* (1894). These collections are still enjoyed by young people, and new editions are published periodically.

Walter Crane's hallmark decorative border and meticulous details are seen in his illustration for the 1889 edition of Grimm's Household Tales *published in London, England by Routledge. This illustration for "Snow White" shows the evil Queen in disguise offering Snow White the poisoned apple. Crane frequently hand-printed the text. His detailed, decorative illustrations are in complete harmony with the verbal narrative that Lucy Crane translated.*

Fairy Tales in the Classroom

Fairy tales represent the typical youngster's perception of the world—pure idealism and faith in goodness. This fantasy land filled with awesome creatures is a pleasure for children aged seven to twelve. By the time they leave elementary school, most children have lost interest in this subgenre. Because these wonder tales are intended to provide pleasure and to stimulate the imagination, the wise teacher will use an aesthetic focus with the tales.

After reading aloud or telling the stories, engage the children in informal discussions, eliciting personal, spontaneous responses. Encourage the students to express these responses through verbal and visual Literary Response Modes that represent their personal reactions. Have students retell a tale to younger children. Prepare a recording of the retelling and place the tape in the literature center with a copy of the tale illustrated by the teller.

Ask students to collect samples of the language found in the stories, such as repetitive phrases and names of people, places, and animals, and place the samples on a word wall. Students can locate variants of a tale by exploring collections with stories from various countries. Books such as Sarah Hayes's *The Candlewick Book of Fairy Tales* (1993), with integral illustrations by P. J. Lynch, and Rose Impey's *Read Me a Fairy Tale: A Child's Book of Classic Fairy Tales* (1993), with Ian Beck's suitable illustrations, are excellent sources. Students could extend a tale by writing about another event that could happen at the conclusion of the tale, or they could write a contemporary version of an old tale.

Heather Forest's *Wonder Tales from Around the World* (1995), with illustrations by David Boston and an audiotape of suitable music, could be used to develop a folk festival. Students will also collect other folk songs, tales, and poems from a particular region. Groups of students will prepare simple costumes and present a dramatic reading of a tale and poem. Between the readings, members of the class will sing the songs. Videotape the production and show it to other groups of children.

Ask children to find various collections of fairy tales from a region. After they read the collections, have students identify and compare the marvelous creatures, language, typical motifs, and folk art found in the various collections. Neil Philip's *American Fairy Tales: From Rip Van Winkle to the Rootabaga Stories* (1996), with complementary black and white wood engravings by Michael McCurdy, is an excellent book to serve as the focal book for American fairy tales. Joseph Bruchac's *The Boy Who Lived with the Bears: And Other Iroquois Stories* (1995), which is illustrated with appropriate folk art, would be a good beginning collection for Native American tales.

The chapter bibliography is filled with outstanding retellings of favorite tales from collectors such as Perrault, Lang, Asbjornsen and Moe, Jacobs, and the Brothers Grimm. Feature a collector each month. Discuss the person's life and books. Read, discuss, and create several suitable responses to the collector's books. To introduce the collector, use books such as Anthea Bell's translation of the Grimms' *The Six Servants* (1996), with portraits by Sergei Goloshapoz, or Byron Barton's retelling of Jacobs' *The Three Bears* (1991).

Outstanding books with pictures inspire children to create artistic responses such as a mural of pictures from a favorite tale. Students can also prepare a three-dimensional display of a never-never land, with creatures and scenery made from clay and various natural materials. Students can write a travel brochure about the setting. Use a book such as Jean Merrill's *The Girl Who Loved Caterpillars* (1992), with authentic paintings by Floyd Cooper, to explore Asian folk art. (See Merrill color plate.)

Floyd Cooper uses oil wash painting to realistically portray Jean Merrill's adaptation of The Girl Who Loved Caterpillars: A Twelfth-Century Tale from Japan. *The arrangement of the verbal text and paintings add to the drama of the story. Through his use of color, texture, and attention to detail, Cooper authentically portrays the culture and environment of the period.*

FIGURE 3.12 Distinguishing Characteristics of Novelle

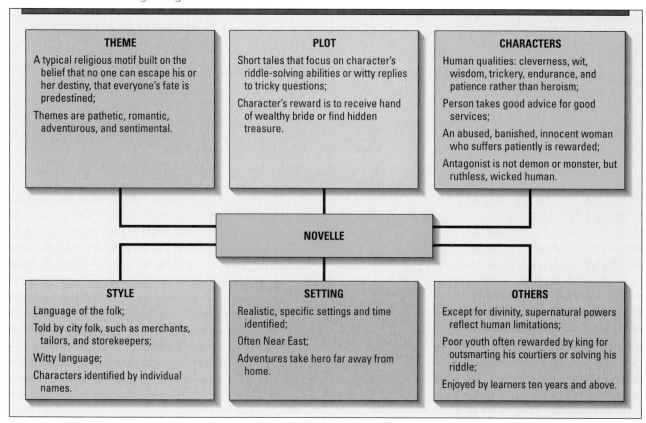

NOVELLE

Another prose subgenre is the **novella** (plural *novelle*). The novella is closely related to the märchen in structure, and sometimes a clear distinction is not always evident. In some cultures a story will possess all of the characteristics of a novella, while in another region the same story, such as "Cap o' Rushes," will appear as a marchen. The narrative usually features real settings and characters, while folktale motifs and marvelous or supernatural events are used to a lesser degree. Novelle are classified as *romantic tales*. Figure 3.12 identifies the distinguishing characteristics of novelle.

Historical Development of Novelle

Novelle originated in classical antiquity (second century B.C.). The written, literary form appeared in Indic, Persian, and Arabic collections, in Greco-Roman collections, and in medieval romance literature. Hence, novelle draw elements from a number of cultures and reflect the philosophy and religious ideals of Buddhism, Islam, Judaism, and Christianity. The most famous novella focuses on Scheherazade, a vizier's daughter who held off

her own execution by telling the sultan enchanting stories. After 1,001 nights had passed and an equal number of stories, she had borne the sultan three children. The tyrant made the storyteller his queen and ordered his chroniclers to write down all the tales she had told him, which became the *Tales from the Arabian Nights*. This selection includes such famous tales as "Ali Baba and the Forty Thieves," "Sinbad the Sailor," and "Aladdin and the Wonderful Lamp." (An abbreviated *Literary Link* for the latter story appears at the conclusion of this chapter.) The stories were transmitted orally for many generations, and the composite work developed over several centuries. The first reference to the *Arabian Nights* is in a ninth-century fragment. Between 1704 and 1712, Antoine Galland published the first European translation of the *Arabian Nights*.[30]

Novelle in the Classroom

Novelle naturally appeal to children above ten years of age. Learners at this age are fascinated by the adventures, the settings, the witty replies, and the riddles solved by the characters. The light treatment given to romance in the stories might also appeal to young people.

The teacher or students could read or tell a short original "tale a day" for 1,001 or 101 days. Readers theatre, role-playing, and informal drama naturally emerge from the tales. Individuals or groups could write a novella using a contemporary setting.

The teacher may need to give information about the setting or religious philosophies before sharing the stories with the children. The stories will lead to informal discussions. Consideration of the themes could lead to a study of Arabic or Persian culture or to a comparative study of Buddhism, Islam, Judaism, and Christianity.

Since the novelle are filled with riddles, have the students write riddles that can be answered after reading a tale. For example, "I left salt off the meat to help my father realize how much I loved him. Who am I?" (from "Cap o' Rushes"); "I took the one thing I liked best in my husband's house to my home. Who am I? What did I take?" (from "Clever Manka," who took her husband); "I shouted 'Open, Sesame!' to a rock and a special place opened up to me. Who am I?" (from "Ali Baba and the Forty Thieves").

The most popular novelle are the *Tales from the Arabian Nights*. Kate Wiggin and Nora Smith's 1901 edition of *The Arabian Nights: Their Best-Known Tales* was reissued in 1993. In 1994 Neil Philip published *The Arabian Nights*, illustrated by Sheila Moxley. Two versions were published in 1995: Brian Alderson's *The Arabian Nights: Or Tales Told by Sheherezade during a Thousand Nights and One Night*, with vivid illustrations by Michael Foreman, and Deborah Lattimore's *Arabian Nights: Three Tales*, with original retellings and dramatic illustrations. Recently, several books with pictures have been published from the old tales, namely, Carol Carrick's *Aladdin and the Wonderful Lamp* (1989), with illustrations by Donald Carrick, and Eric Kimmel's *The Tale of Aladdin and the Wonderful Lamp: A Story of the Arabian Nights* (1992), with Ju-Hong Chen's paintings highlighting the Islamic setting. Other familiar novelle are "Cap o' Rushes," "Clever Manka," and "Rapunzel." Two Rapunzel tales appeared in 1995: Diane Stanley's spirited retelling *Petrosinella: A Neapolitan Rapunzel* (originally published in 1981) and Alix Berenzy's *Rapunzel* (1995), a fresh retelling of the story with realistic illustrations that enhance the old tale. (See Berenzy color plate.)

Jests, Schwanks, and Anecdotes

Short tales told for a laugh are called *jests*, *schwanks*, *humorous anecdotes*, or *merry tales*. The single-incident tales describe absurd acts of foolish people or contrast clever and foolish behavior. The tales may include deception, are often satirical, and may be ribald. *Noodlehead* or *numskull* tales are humorous anecdotes that depict foolish or clever behavior and are attached to a particular person or groups of people. The object of the joke may change, but the ridicule, or practical joke, remains the same, and the tales are repeated from one generation to the next. Figure 3.13 on page 94 summarizes the distinguishing characteristics of this subgenre.

Alix Berenzy uses both language and images to retell the popular tale Rapunzel. *Berenzy shows the contrasts of the tale through her colored pencils and gouache paintings. On some pages the artist presents stark, dark, eerie paintings and on other pages the romantic elements of the story are shown through soft, light paintings. Some pages are entirely filled with details, while other pages contain a single figure shown on a contrasting white background. The charm of the story is reflected in this picture of Rapunzel, with her golden hair shimmering by the firelight, sitting by the window waiting for her Prince Charming to come and rescue her.*

FIGURE 3.13 Distinguishing Characteristics of Jests, Schwanks, and Anecdotes

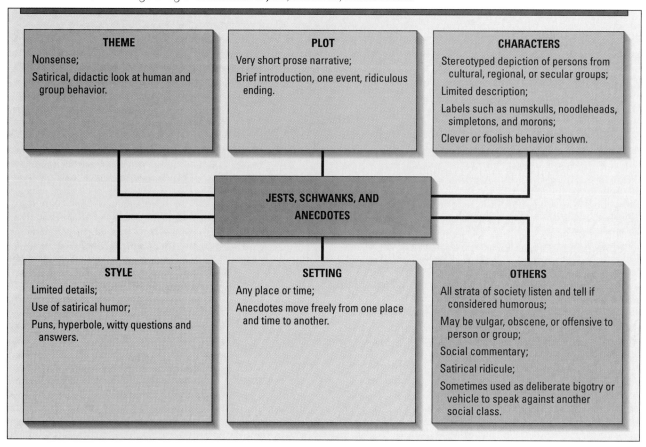

Historical Development of Jests, Schwanks, and Anecdotes

Many anecdotes told as contemporary jokes are in fact three or four thousand years old. The same story patterns were told or sung during medieval times and recorded in jest books. Today, the simple narratives are translated into tales about a mother-in-law, a rival college or social group, a miser, or a numskull. The anecdotes may also deliberately slur or ridicule people from an ethnic, racial, regional, or religious group. Usually, the narrator is not a member of the group being ridiculed. Occasionally, people use jokes as a vehicle to speak up against those in power, as in political and social satire. The jests and humorous anecdotes are easy to remember and move freely from one place to another.[31]

Jests, Schwanks, and Anecdotes in the Classroom

Children enjoy chuckling at topics that are a part of their immediate environment. These jokes are humorous to the children depending on their age and cognitive level. It is important to monitor the anecdotes so that individuals or groups are not offended by the content. While traditional jests may be used in the classroom, personalizing the joke to an individual student or a particular social or racial group is not recommended.

A "joke for the day" is a good way to keep up class spirits. Many contemporary joke books are available for children and are a good source for teacher or student sharing.

ANIMAL TALES

Animal tales are popular with children and adults. Most people have a special affinity for animals and can see themselves and others in the antics of literary animals. Three types of animal tales are found in folk literature: *pourquoi (explanatory) tales, trickster tales,* and *fables.* Many animal tales overlap with myths, legends, and folktales. Yet each type of animal tale has distinguishing characteristics unique to that particular subgenre.

In each classification the tales show the cleverness of one animal and the naïveté or gullibility of another. The tales are appealing to young people because the deception is humorous and the absurd situations are easy to identify.

Children see themselves and others in the animals who are thinly disguised humans.

Historical Development of Animal Tales

Animal tales in folk literature stem from four major sources: collections of literary fables from India; *Aesop's Fables* from ancient Greece; literary animal tales from medieval and Renaissance Europe, which are represented in the cycle of Reynard the Fox; and oral tales that developed in Russia and the Baltic states. The literary fables from India include the Buddhist tales known as the *Jataka* whose origin is unknown, though the stories were in existence in the fifth century B.C. and the illustrations are from the second or third century B.C. Also from India comes *The Panchatantra*, a collection of tales composed in Kashmir about 200 B.C. Perhaps the most famous literary collection of animal tales, *Aesop's Fables*, originated in ancient Greece. Some of the tales traveled to Africa and from there were carried to the New World.

Types of Animal Stories

Pourquoi (Explanatory) Tales   As noted during the discussion of creation myths, pourquoi tales are fictional stories that provide logical explanations for the origin and physical characteristics of certain animals. The tales are intended only for entertainment and are not meant to be believed. Representative examples appear in African tales, such as "Why the Monkeys Live in Trees," and Muskogee (Creek) Native American tales, such as "Why Grandmother Spider Stole the Sun." Figure 3.14 summarizes the distinguishing characteristics of pourquoi tales.

Trickster Tales   In trickster tales a shrewd, wise, or cunning protagonist humorously outwits another animal. An example is the *Uncle Remus Tales*, which migrated from India through Africa and Europe before arriving in North and South America. Popular characters in trickster tales include Anansi, a spider of African origin; Zomo, a hare from Africa; the coyote and raven from Native American tales; Rabbit from Korea; Mahi from Hawaii; and Reynard, the well-known European fox. Figure 3.15 on page 96 identifies the distinguishing characteristics of trickster tales.

Fables   Fables are short animal tales intended to teach a lesson. Generally, the moral (or lesson) is stated at the end of the story. One animal clearly depicts good traits while another exhibits bad characteristics. Fables originated in both India and Western Europe.

The tales of the *Jataka* from India, which are written in prose and poetry, deal with the rebirths of Buddha who was reincarnated in the form of different animals until he became the last Buddha. The tales depict humans living as animals and learning ethical lessons while interacting with other animals. The morals and didactic verses are removed from many English translations. The *Panchatantra*, a collection of five books, including *The Fables of Bidpai*, is the oldest collection of Indian fables. The longer tales have

FIGURE 3.14   Distinguishing Characteristics of Pourquoi

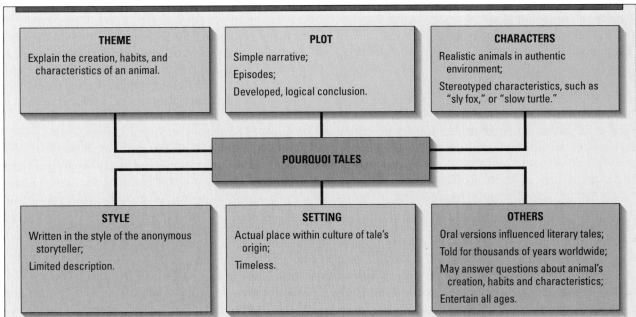

THEME
Explain the creation, habits, and characteristics of an animal.

PLOT
Simple narrative;
Episodes;
Developed, logical conclusion.

CHARACTERS
Realistic animals in authentic environment;
Stereotyped characteristics, such as "sly fox," or "slow turtle."

POURQUOI TALES

STYLE
Written in the style of the anonymous storyteller;
Limited description.

SETTING
Actual place within culture of tale's origin;
Timeless.

OTHERS
Oral versions influenced literary tales;
Told for thousands of years worldwide;
May answer questions about animal's creation, habits and characteristics;
Entertain all ages.

FIGURE 3.15 Distinguishing Characteristics of Trickster Tales

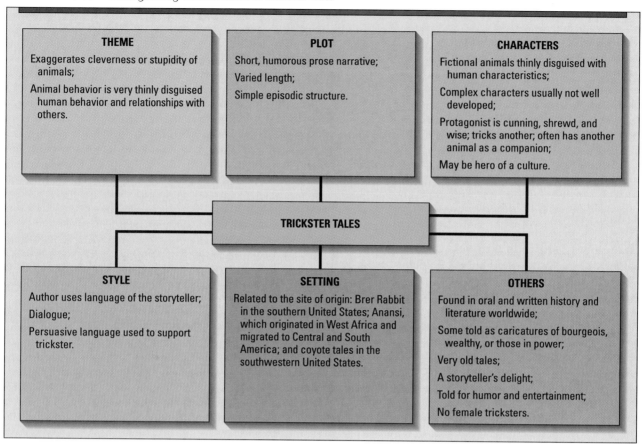

THEME
Exaggerates cleverness or stupidity of animals;

Animal behavior is very thinly disguised human behavior and relationships with others.

PLOT
Short, humorous prose narrative;

Varied length;

Simple episodic structure.

CHARACTERS
Fictional animals thinly disguised with human characteristics;

Complex characters usually not well developed;

Protagonist is cunning, shrewd, and wise; tricks another; often has another animal as a companion;

May be hero of a culture.

TRICKSTER TALES

STYLE
Author uses language of the storyteller;

Dialogue;

Persuasive language used to support trickster.

SETTING
Related to the site of origin: Brer Rabbit in the southern United States; Anansi, which originated in West Africa and migrated to Central and South America; and coyote tales in the southwestern United States.

OTHERS
Found in oral and written history and literature worldwide;

Some told as caricatures of bourgeois, wealthy, or those in power;

Very old tales;

A storyteller's delight;

Told for humor and entertainment;

No female tricksters.

moralistic verses interspersed. The tales were intended to instruct nobility from India.

The best-known collection of fables bears the name of Aesop, a Samian slave who reportedly lived in Greece between 620 and 560 B.C. We do not know whether Aesop himself created the tales or whether his name was simply attached to the form. *Aesop's Fables* were translated into Latin in the first and third centuries A.D. William Caxton, the first English printer, published an English translation of *Aesop's Fables* in 1484. During the seventeenth century, the French poet Jean La Fontaine used sources such as the Latin version of *Aesop's Fables* and *The Fables of Bidpai* to publish a collection of fables bearing his name. The simple verses with animal characters and moral overtones are closer to Aesop's than to the tales from India. Some folklorists theorize that folk materials were used for fable plots, but that the highly structured fable format must have been the product of a literate, sophisticated culture.[32] Figure 3.16 on page 97 summarizes the distinguishing characteristics of fables.

Pourquoi Animal Tales in the Classroom

A pourquoi animal tale stimulates a child's imagination. As boys and girls discuss the fictional tales, they question the storyteller's explanations for the animal's creation, physical traits, or mental abilities. After enjoying the old tales, young people can create new pourquoi tales about favorite animals. During storytelling or reading aloud sessions, a child can sit in the author's chair and share his or her pourquoi. The short tales naturally lead to dramatization and puppet shows. Children can illustrate original tales with torn-paper collages and then place the tale in a bound book.

Julius Lester's *How Many Spots Does a Leopard Have? And Other Tales* (1989), with expressive paintings by David Shannon, is an outstanding collection of twelve tales with African and Jewish roots. The author's source notes give the reader additional information about the subgenre and explain how he rewrote the tales. This information is beneficial to share before children write original tales. Encourage the students to look for source notes when ex-

FIGURE 3.16 Distinguishing Characteristics of Fables

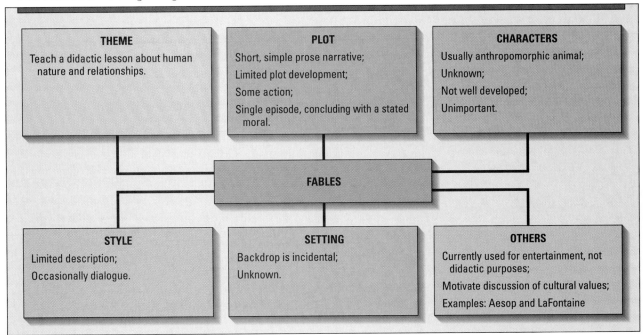

THEME
Teach a didactic lesson about human nature and relationships.

PLOT
Short, simple prose narrative;
Limited plot development;
Some action;
Single episode, concluding with a stated moral.

CHARACTERS
Usually anthropomorphic animal;
Unknown;
Not well developed;
Unimportant.

FABLES

STYLE
Limited description;
Occasionally dialogue.

SETTING
Backdrop is incidental;
Unknown.

OTHERS
Currently used for entertainment, not didactic purposes;
Motivate discussion of cultural values;
Examples: Aesop and LaFontaine

ploring pourquoi books with pictures such as Mary-Joan Gerson's adaptation of *Why the Sky Is Far Away: A Nigerian Folktale* (1992), with Carla Golembe's authentic illustrations; Eric Maddern's *Rainbow Bird: An Aboriginal Folktale from Northern Australia* (1993), with vivid paintings by Adrienne Kennaway; Angela McAllister's *When the Ark Was Full* (1990), with Michaela Bloomfield's illustrations that enhance this humorous tale; Verna Aardema's *How the Ostrich Got Its Long Neck: A Tale from the Akamba of Kenya* (1995), with Marcia Brown's authentic illustrations.

Trickster Tales in the Classroom

We can summarize the use of trickster tales in three words: fun, fun, fun! All of us see our dreams and ambitions in the trickster tales. Sometimes we think, "Wouldn't it be great, if I could outwit someone, just one time?" People of all ages seem to relish the antics of the small animal characters who use their wits to save the day! The animal becomes a hero and succeeds where the larger characters cannot. Trickster characters and children live in similar worlds: both live in a world where bigger "characters" are in control.

Trickster tales are meant to be heard. Thus, storytelling and reading aloud are the most effective way to present the tales. An audiotape of children in a particular grade level telling or reading a tale could be prepared and given to the media center with illustrated copies of the tales.

Because certain characters are identified with a particular country or region, have the children identify and label the character's place of origin on a world map. Attach a ribbon to the character and fasten a sheet of paper to the other end of the ribbon. Then, when the children discover tales about the character, have them write the name of the tale on the paper, add a short description of the character's traits or adventures, and post the information on a bulletin board around the map.

Compare the personality traits, physical attributes, and tricks of characters from different countries. Chart the characteristics and adventures on a large graphic visual, as described in Chapter 10 and Appendix B. A good way to begin this activity is to share tales from Josepha Sherman's *Trickster Tales: Forty Folk Stories from Around the World* (1996), with line drawings by David Boston. After identifying the various creatures and their locations, a team of students could select one animal, read several tales, and prepare the chart for that particular trickster. The group can read or tell a favorite story to the class. Then the children can make a book cube, as described in Chapter 10, or a personality collage for each trickster.

Children can laugh and vicariously fulfill their dreams of being in charge of their world through aesthetic experiences with various tales. Recommended collections about a particular trickster include Harold Courlander and George Herzog's *The Cow-Tail Switch and Other West African Stories* (1947), with Madye Lee Chastain's illustrations; Joel

Chandler Harris's tales adapted by Van Dyke Parks in *Jump! The Adventures of Brer Rabbit* (1986), with realistic illustrations by Barry Moser; Julius Lester's retelling of *The Tales of Uncle Remus* (1987), with Jerry Pinkney's realistic illustrations (three other books are in the series); Maria Brusca and Tona Wilson's *Pedro Fools the Gringo: And Other Tales of a Latin American Trickster* (1995), with Maria Brusca's illustrations that enhance the tales; and Tom Pohrt's *Coyote Goes Walking* (1995). The chapter bibliography lists several single-story picture storybooks, but those created by Gerald McDermott are especially appealing: *Raven: A Trickster Tale from the Pacific Northwest* (1993) and *Zomo the Rabbit: A Trickster Tale from West Africa* (1992). (See McDermott color plate.) These and other tales created by McDermott are filled with interesting language and vivid illustrations that interact to tell a humorous tale.

Fables in the Classroom

Children aged five to twelve enjoy the ridiculous behavior of the characters when fables are presented as funny, short animal adventures. Students like to guess the moral of the story and then discuss it. Although fables were originally intended to teach a lesson, boys and girls will enjoy them if they are presented in a fun, not didactic, manner. Students enjoy making up a moral, then writing an original fable to fit the moral. The teacher could also suggest a moral to the class and then have groups of students write

an original tale. They can illustrate and read the fable to the class. Later, display the various fables with the moral on a Fable of the Month bulletin board.

Have the children select a fable and dramatize it. Use collections such as Anne Rockwell's *The Acorn Tree and Other Folktales* (1995) and David Kherdian's *Feathers and Tails: Animal Fables from Around the World* (1992), with Nonny Hogrogian's authentic illustrations. Many other collections and single-story books with pictures are listed in the chapter bibliography. The 1989 collection of *Aesop's Fables* by Lisbeth Zwerger, a Hans Christian Andersen winner, is especially appealing, because the author-artist presents a new interpretation of several old fables. (See Zwerger color plate on page 99.) Contemporary literary fables such as James Thurber's *Fables of Our Time* (1940) and Arnold Lobel's 1981 Caldecott winner, *Fables* (1980) give young people a humorous, unique view of animals.

❋ FOLK LITERATURE IN THE CLASSROOM

Five hundred years after William Caxton published *Aesop's Fables*, adapters and artists have published thousands of single-tale picture books and folk literature collections throughout the world. The uninitiated may be shocked to open *Perrault's Fairy Tales* to the story "Little

Gerald McDermott's stylized illustrations are recognized for his use of color, line, and shape. His gouache paintings for Zomo the Rabbit: A Trickster Tale from West Africa *reflect these features. He uses brilliant hues of yellow, red, green, blue, and brown to reflect the art of the culture. Through simple, bold lines the shapes are carefully arranged to show the movement of the story and the power of the characters over the environment. He combines his verbal narrative with the images to become a part of the visual composition.*

Lisabeth Zwerger's expressionistic drawings for Aesop's Fables *show the artist's ability to use colored ink and soft water color wash to portray the fable "The Tortoise and the Hare." Zwerger's simple lines and use of space with limited background effectively reflect the economy of text found in fables and her drawings enhance the storyline.*

TABLE 3.2 Guidelines for Selecting Folk Literature

Select prose and poetry that reflects the interests and developmental levels of the individuals who will listen to, view, and read the selections.

Choose selections with suspenseful, action-packed events and stereotyped characters who arouse emotional reactions from the audience.

Select tales, verses, and songs that contain the natural language of storytellers or singers, such as repetitive phrases, alliteration, unusual names and places, and dialogue.

Choose prose and poetry selections that contain enough details for the audience to understand the theme, the goals and actions of the characters, and the plot development.

Determine the cultural authenticity of the book by looking at the source notes or other resources used to ensure the accuracy of the text. Consider the credentials of the author-artist, the type of research conducted, and whether source notes or references are included.

Select prose and poetry that is culturally authentic and contains universal truths valued by various ethnic, regional, cultural, or religious groups and by society in general.

Choose worthwhile narratives with limited violence and acceptable content.

Select literature with illustrations that are authentic to the group portrayed and enhance, supplement, replace, or give an appropriate interpretation of the verbal narrative.

Red Cap" ("Little Red Riding Hood") and find that the wolf was not after Little Red Cap's basket of food. The discovery of the "grimm" reality of life as portrayed in the Grimms' *German Popular Tales* may be a similar surprise. Objections to using individual selections with children have been raised by various groups but for quite different reasons. Some religious groups object to the supernatural elements found in most folk literature selections. Meanwhile witches and warlocks complain that the tales portray their lifestyles and traditions negatively.

Using folk literature successfully in the classroom depends primarily on making appropriate selections and implementing instructional techniques to whet students' interest in reading, hearing, and viewing the genre. Selection criteria and appropriate instructional approaches are described in the next section.

CRITERIA FOR CHOOSING FOLK LITERATURE SELECTIONS

Since folk literature was originally intended to amuse and instruct adults, some selections contain adult themes and violence that might frighten one child, while another child of the same age might concentrate on the humor in the tale and overlook the violence entirely. The same is true of

children's reactions to the various subgenres. The information provided here about children's natural reactions to the subgenres represents typical reactions of children at a particular age. Some young children might enjoy part of an epic, and some older students enjoy the riddles found in Mother Goose rhymes. Thus, when selecting a tale, verse, or song, note the content and whether it has the potential to negatively affect the students.

The distinguishing characteristics of each subgenre provide representative patterns we can expect to find when choosing exemplary literature. Table 3.2 cites guidelines for selecting folk literature tales, songs, and verses.

It is a good idea to involve students in the selection of folk literature. After selections are introduced and discussed, encourage students to identify the distinctive characteristics they observe. With their assistance, record guidelines for selection on a chart and display it in the literature center. Encourage students to use the visual when selecting, writing, and presenting folk literature in the classroom.

INSTRUCTIONAL FOCUSES

Ideally, students' initial exposure to folk literature should be an aesthetic reading that will elicit personal, spontaneous reactions and interpretations of the tale. To achieve this goal, teachers assume an aesthetic instructional focus. Folk literature is best introduced, explored, and enjoyed in a comfortable environment. Strategies such as the following will assure an aesthetic experience with literature:

Place many collections of tales and verses and single-story picture books in the classroom library. Change the books periodically. Return favorites. Encourage students to bring collections and picture books from home or the public libraries and add to the book collection.

Display visuals of the characters or settings mentioned in the tales before, during, and after introducing them.

Use a variety of oral techniques with the selections, such as reading aloud, storytelling, book talks, and various audiovisuals.

When reading or discussing a selection, encourage the students to anticipate, predict, confirm, and clarify the narrative; for example, use suitable probes and prompts, prediction visuals, and written reflections.

Model your delight with the characters and events by talking about your personal reactions and interpretations.

Personally read folk literature selections.

Besides the students' personal, spontaneous reactions and interpretations of the tales, groups or individuals enjoy producing Literary Response Modes (LRMs) reflecting their interpretations of the selection. (Chapter 2 discusses LRMs in more detail, and Appendix B contains descriptions of selected LRMs.) Several writers have suggested numerous techniques to use with folk literature selections.[33] Table 3.3 on page 101 suggests some LRMs that teachers and students can use to respond to folk literature.

Summary

We naturally enjoy telling stories about our lives, our struggles, our dreams, and our fears. In doing so we are sharing with others our folk literature, the "cement of society" that includes the traditional wisdom, rituals, superstitions, and values of a social, ethnic, or religious group.[34] Even today the myths, legends, and tales influence individuals and society.

Traditional poetry and prose selections have been shared for thousands of years and continue to be popular with contemporary children and adults. People passed the prose and poetry from one generation to the next in oral or written format. The tellers and singers used the literature to entertain their audience and to inculcate the cultural mores and beliefs valued by a group. Adventurous travelers, soldiers, and missionaries transmitted the stories and verses. The literature changed from one telling to the next and continues to change today.

All people need stories for enjoyment and enlightenment. Simple Mother Goose rhymes, ballads and epics, myths, legends, tall tales, folktales, fairy tales, novelle, anecdotes, pourquoi, trickster tales, and fables all meet humans' universal need to share with others their stories and traditions—their "roots." At the same time, folk literature gives individuals the freedom to allow their imaginations to soar to unknown worlds and interact with fanciful and real creatures. In doing so, the tales and verses give us "wings." Thus, folk literature will ever remain the roots and wings of society!

TABLE 3.3 Suggested LRMs to Use with Folk Literature

Write a script for a tale and present a radio or television program.

Present a storytelling festival. Students will select favorite stories and tell them.

Use the distinguishing characteristics of the various subgenres to prepare a Literary Ladder (see Chapter 10). Write an original tale, poem, or song.

Retell or rewrite a transformation tale. Set it in contemporary times.

Retell or rewrite a tale from the villain's point of view.

Cook with Snow White. Prepare the foods she would cook for the seven dwarfs.

List Cinderella's household tips for keeping a castle. Publish and distribute tips.

Write a Folktale Newspaper from Around the World (a newspaper with articles about the tales from various cultures).

Group students and have them collect folk literature from a particular country. Have them share their favorite tales and compare characters, events, and creatures.

Use various media to illustrate tales from a particular cultural, ethnic, or regional group. Use the artistic style represented by the group.

Select a tale and make visuals for felt, magnetic, hook 'n loop boards, or puppets.

Tell the tale using the board, visuals, or puppets.

Play charades using titles of favorite tales.

Play "LitBit," a game using questions and riddles from various tales.

Use tales from a culture to introduce the culture in social studies. Make a quilt.

Give book talks about tales recommended for reading. Use Wanted Posters.

Write an original local legend using real places or people in the community.

Write a ballad about a historical hero and sing it to others. Make a personality collage of the ballad hero.

Collect unusual vocabulary, names, and settings, and write imaginary and real definitions of the terms.

Interview an elderly family member or neighbor about the old days. Write a story based on the information from the interview.

Construct a diorama depicting a setting from a tale, such as the witches' woods, the giant's home, or a water fairy's castle.

Groups will collect favorite tales. Copy the tales on special paper. Illustrate using appropriate style and media. Place the tales and illustrations in a book made by the group.

Write, tell, and dramatize tales about a visit from Paul Bunyan (Pecos Bill and Slewfoot Sue or Johnny Appleseed) to your school, town, or home. (Remember the bigger the lie, the better.) See the Literary Link for *Captain Stormalong* at the end of Chapter 2.

Find as many variants of a particular tale as possible. Compare and contrast the events, characters, theme, setting, and style. Record information on visuals such as a Venn diagram or a feature attribute chart. Read or tell each variant. Let the class select their favorite variant. (MacDonald and Ashlim's books are helpful resources for this LRM.)

Discuss: Why do collectors of tales include source notes? Compare the notes included with different variants of the same tale.

Survey friends to ascertain their beliefs about supernatural creatures.

"ALADDIN AND THE WONDERFUL LAMP" FROM *THE ARABIAN NIGHTS.*

RECOMMENDED FOR FOURTH GRADE AND ABOVE

SUMMARY

A cunning African magician tricked Aladdin, an idle son of a poor tailor, into a cave where Aladdin found many treasures and a wonderful lamp. The sorcerer demanded the lamp, which he knew would make him a powerful person. Aladdin refused to give him the lamp, and the magician sealed up the cave with Aladdin in it. After several days in the cave, Aladdin accidentally realized the value of the lamp and the ring the magician had given him earlier. Aladdin fell deeply in love with a sultan's daughter and managed to marry her with the help of his mother and the genie in the lamp. Aladdin and his wife were very happy living in the palace built by the genie. One day his wife, who did not know the value of the old lamp, traded it to the African sorcerer for a new one. Troubles began when Aladdin's wife and the palace disappeared. With the help of the ring, the genie, and the lamp, clever Aladdin rescued his wife and palace, and they lived happily ever after.

CONNECT

* Create a *word wall* displaying unique language, such as "piteously, Persia, lamenting, a hideous genie, chink, idle dream, scimitar, thither, pious, roc egg, wretch."

* Give a *book talk* such as the following: I went to a flea market over the weekend. I was stopped by a strange-looking man who told me that he wanted to give me a ring and a lamp. He told me that if I rubbed the ring and lamp at the same time, I would discover a secret. He told me that he couldn't give them to just anyone because if they fell into the wrong hands, the world would be in trouble. Since I had an honest face, he felt that he could trust me. I was skeptical at first, but he insisted that I take them. I put the ring and lamp away, intending to bring them to school and make my discovery here. You know how impatient I am; late Sunday night, I just had to rub them and say, "Oh ring and lamp reveal your secret to me." As I was rubbing the lamp, I turned it over, and there inside the lamp, I found a book and a note. The note said, "Open the book to find out about Sinbad the Sailor, Ali Baba and the forty thieves, and especially about Aladdin who used the ring and lamp to help him reach his goal. These stories were originally told by a young girl named Scherazade to the king of Persia for 1,001 nights, and the stories saved her life. They were passed from one generation to another in coffeehouses and marketplaces. Then they were written in this book." I opened the book and found that it was a first edition, written in 1709 by Antoine Galland.

Here in the classroom today are a ring, a lamp, and a collection of stories.

* Read the title, "Aladdin and the Wonderful Lamp." Organize students in *buddy teams*. Distribute copies of the tale to each group. After the students have read the tale, ask those who have seen the movie to compare the tale to the movie.

* Students will write comparisons or reactions to novelle in their *LitLogs*.

CONSTRUCT

* Ask students what they would wish for if they had a magic ring or lamp. *Chart* their wishes. Group wishes into categories, such as wealth, happiness, and benefits for others.

* Place an old piece of carpet on the floor. Ask a student to sit on the *Flying Carpet*. This person assumes the *role* of Aladdin and makes comments about the wishes expressed by class members. The comments will be based on the student's knowledge of Aladdin's personality.

* *Interview* Aladdin. Different students will assume the role of Aladdin to answer questions such as the following: Did you act cleverly when the stranger visited you and your mother? Why was your mother afraid of the lamp? Tell us about the sultan and the vizier and their plan. Where did the genie come from? Did you really think the genie would deliver so much? Were you amazed to find out how the people helped you? How did you know who the false Fatima really was? How did you change during the story?

CREATE

* *Illustrate with paint* some wishes requested earlier.

* *Write a rationale* why the wish should be granted.

* Prepare a *readers theatre script* for the story and present a dramatic reading of the script to another class.

* Prepare *sketches or illustrations* for various incidents in the story. Use these sketches as a background for the *bulletin board* or *hall wall* to advertise the tale (or various stories from the *Arabian Nights.*)

* Write a *news report* from the vizier's point of view reporting Aladdin's trickery to wed the princess. "Anonymous reporters" could write other reports from *inside* Aladdin's palace.

* Students will write *annotations* for different selections from *The Arabian Nights*. Share annotations and compare individual stories in terms of characters, problems, conflicts, and solutions.

- Record information from above on a *plot and character chart*.

- Identify the attributes of novelle and record them on a *literary ladder*. Cut the chart into the shape of the magic lamp, a genie, or other content typical of the tale.

- *Write letters* to the media specialist, public librarians, and school administration requesting additional copies of the novella for their respective libraries. Justify the request.

- *Write letters* to the School Curriculum Committee (or appropriate personnel) stating why all fifth and sixth grade students should read stories from *The Arabian Nights*.

- *Brainstorm* the meaning of "roc egg." Draw *sketches* of it. Prepare a *story mobile* with the "roc egg" as the initial object. Make papier-mâché "roc eggs." Make a "roc egg" tree.

- Ask students how they would present this novelle to other students.

- Students will prepare a *storytelling festival* using a variety of tales from *The Arabian Nights*.

- Write biweekly *book links* about literature read and publish them in the local newspaper.

SOURCES FOR THE TALE

- Carrick, C. 1989. *Aladdin and the Wonderful Lamp*. Illus. D. Carrick. New York: Scholastic.

- Cole, J. 1982. *Best-Loved Folktales of the World*. Illus. J. K. Schwarz. Garden City, N.Y.: Doubleday. 467–77.

- Lang, A. 1991 (reissue). *Reader's Digest Arabian Nights*. Pleasantville, N.Y: Readers Digest. 199–214.

- Philip, N. (Ad.) 1994. *The Arabian Nights*. Illus. Sheila Moxley. New York: Orchard.

- Sutherland, Z., & M. C. Livingston. 1984. "Aladdin and the Wonderful Lamp." In *The Scott, Foresman Anthology of Children's Literature*. Glenview, Ill.: Scott, Foresman. 295–301.

This Literary Link is adapted from *Using Folk Literature in the Classroom* by Frances S. Goforth and Carolyn Spillman. Used with permission of The Oryx Press, 4041 N. Central Ave., Suite 700, Phoenix, AZ 85012. (800) 279-6799.

NOTES

1. Dundes, A. 1965. *The Study of Folklore*. Englewood Cliffs, N.J.: Prentice-Hall. 4.

2. Goforth, F. S., & Spillman, C. J. 1994. *Using Folk Literature in the Classroom: Encouraging Children to Read and Write*. Phoenix, Ariz.: Oryx Press.

3. Bluestein, G. 1972. *The Voice of the Folk*. Amherst, Mass.: University of Massachusetts Press; Fine, G. A. 1987. Joseph Jacobs: A sociological folklorist. *Folklore* 98; Yearsley, M. 1924. *The Folklore of Fairy Tale*. London: Watts & Co.

4. Leach, M., & Fried, J. (Eds.). 1972 (1949). *Standard Dictionary of Folklore, Mythology, and Legend*. New York: Funk & Wagnalls. 398–404; Yearsley, M. 1924. 24.

5. Rooth, A. B. 1951. *The Cinderella Cycle*. Lund, Sweden: Glurup.

6. For additional information about the evolution of folklore, see sources such as Brunvand, J. H. 1968. *The Study of American Folklore: An Introduction*. New York: Norton, 83–86; Dundes, A. 1965; Fine, G. A. 1987. 186–87.

7. Jason, H. 1991. Marginalia to P. Bogatyren & R. Jakobson's essay "Die fololore als eine besondere form des schaffens." *Folklore*. 102. i.

8. For additional information about benefits individuals gain from folk literature, see sources such as Bettelheim, B. 1976. *The Uses of Enchantment*. New York: Knopf; Favat, F. A. 1977. *The Child and Tale*. Urbana, Ill.: National Council of Teachers of English. 54; Messner, R. 1989. Children and fairy tales—what unites them and what divides them. *Western European Education*. 21(2). 6–28.

9. Thompson, S. 1946. *The Folktale*. New York: Dryden Press. 10.

10. Several sources were consulted such as Brunvand, J. H. 1968; Dorson, R. (Ed.) 1972. *Folklore and Folklife*. Chicago: University of Chicago Press; Leach, M., & Fried, J. (Eds.). 1972 (1949); Gomme, G. L. 1967. *The Handbook of Folk-lore*. Nendelin, Liechtenstein: Kraus Reprint; Krappe, A. H. 1964. *The Science of Folklore*. New York: Norton. See also sources cited with specific subgenres.

11. Baring-Gould, W. S., & Baring-Gould, C. 1962. *The Annotated Mother Goose*. New York: Bramhall House. 12–13.

12. For additional information about Mother Goose, nursery, and childhood rhymes see sources such as Barchilon, J., & Pettit, H. 1960. *The Authentic Mother Goose Fairy Tales and Nursery Rhymes*. Swallow Press; Baring-Gould, W. C., & C. 1962. 16–19; Leach, M., & Fried, J. 1972. 751–52; Green, P. B. 1899. *Nursery Rhymes and Tales*. London: Methuen & Co. (Reissue 1968. Detroit: Singing Tree Press).

13. Opie, I. & P. 1952. *The Oxford Dictionary of Nursery Rhymes*. New York: Oxford University Press.

14. de la Mare, W. 1956. *Nursery Rhymes for Certain Times*. London: Faber & Faber.

15. For additional information about ballads, see sources such as Coffin, T. P. 1962. The folk ballad and the literary ballad: An essay in classification. In Beck, H. P. (Ed.) *Folklore in Action*. Philadelphia: American Folklore Society. 58–70; Cuddon, J. A. 1977. A *Dictionary of Literary Terms*. Garden City, N.Y.: Doubleday. 68; Krappe, A. H. 1964. 173–88; Richmond, W. E. 1972. Narrative folk poetry. In Dorson, R. M. 1972. *Folklore and Folklife*. Chicago: University of Chicago Press. 85–98; Shipley, J. T. (Ed.). 1976. *Dictionary of World Literary Terms*. New York: Philosophical Library. 63–64.

16. Child, F. J. 1882–98. *The English and Scottish Popular Ballads*. (5 vols.). New York: Houghton Mifflin. (Reprint 1965. Dover).

17. For additional information about the epic, see sources such as Ben-Amos, D. (Ed.). 1976. *Folklore Genres*. Austin, Tex.: University of Texas Press. 48; Guerber, H. A. 1966. *The Book of the Epic*. New York: Bible & Tannen. 5; Holman, C. H. 1972. *A Handbook to Literature*. Indianapolis: Bobbs-Merrill. 194; Oinas, F. J. 1972. Folk epic. In Dorson, R. 1972. 99–115.

18. Cuddon, J. A. 1977. 223–25.

19. Leach, M., & Fried, J. (Eds.). 1972. 1140–42.

20. Thompson, S. 1955–1958. *Motif-Index of Folk-Literature*, 6 vols. Bloomington: Indiana University Press; Aarne, A., & Thompson, S. 1961. *The Types of the Folk-Tale: A Classification and Bibliography*. Folklore Fellows Communications, no. 184. Helsinki: Suomalainen Tiedeakatemia.

21. Hamilton, V. 1988. *In the Beginning: Creation Stories from Around the World*. New York: Harcourt Brace Jovanovich. 156.

22. For additional information about myths, see sources such as Bullfinch, T. 1970 (New Ed.).

Bullfinch's Mythology. New York: Crowell. author's preface; Leach, M., & Fried, J. (Eds). 1972. 778; Thompson, S. 1946. 9.

23. For additional information about legends, see sources such as Bascom, W. 1965. The forms of folklore: Prose narratives. *Journal of American Folklore*. 78. January/March. 3–20; Brunvand, J. H. 1968. 87–100; Dorson, R. 1972. 159–179; Egoff, S. 1981. *Thursday's Child*. Chicago: American Library Association. 214–17.

24. Dorson, R. 1959. *American Folklore*. Chicago: University of Chicago Press. 4.

25. Battle, K. P. (Compiler) 1986. *Great American Folklore*. New York: Simon & Schuster. xvi–xxiv.

26. Aarne, A. & Thompson, S. 1961. 30–35.

27. Ashliman, D. L. 1987. *A Guide to Folktales in the English Language*. Westport, Conn.: Greenwood Press; MacDonald, M. R. 1982. *The Storyteller's Sourcebook: A Subject, Title, and Motif Index to Folklore Collections for Children*. Detroit: Neal-Schuman.

28. For additional information about folk and fairy tales, see Thompson, S. 1946. Ireland to India: Peoples and lands. In *The Folktale*. New York: Dryden Press. 13–187; Travers, P. L. 1967. Only connect. In Egoff, C., Stubbs, G. T. & Ashley, L. F. (Eds.). 1980. *Only Connect: Readings on Children's Literature*. (2d ed.). Toronto: Oxford University Press. 183–206.

29. Tolkien, J. R. R. 1947. "On Fairy-Stories." In *Essays Presented to Charles Williams*. Oxford: Oxford University Press. 34–36.

30. For additional information about novella, see: Degh, L. 1972. Folk narrative. In Dorson, R. 1972. 67–68; Thompson, S. 1946. 8.

31. Thompson, S. 1946. 10. 188–217.

32. For additional information about animal tales, see sources such as Del Negro, J. M. 1996. Trickster tales. *Book Links*. 5(4). 43–47; Leach, M., & Fried, J. 1949. 61–62; Leach, M., & Fried, J. 1972. 361; Thompson, S. 1946. 217–28, 319–28.

33. For additional information and ideas about using folk literature in the elementary classroom, see sources such as Bearse, C. I. 1992. The fairy tale connection in children's stories: Cinderella meets Sleeping Beauty. *The Reading Teacher*. 45(9). 688–95; Bosma, B. 1992. *Fairy Tales, Fables, Legends, and Myths*. (2d Ed.). New York: Teacher's College Press; Goforth, F. S., & Spillman, C. V. 1994. (This book suggests ideas for Connect, Construct, Create strategies for 54 individual stories, songs, and verses for kindergarten through sixth grade organized according to themes); Sipe, L. R. 1993. Using transformations of traditional stories: Making the reading-writing connection. *The Reading Teacher*. 47(1). September. 18–26; Spritzer, D. R. 1988. Integrating the language arts in the elementary classroom using fairy tales, fables, and traditional literature. *Oregon English*. 11(1). 23–26; Young, T. A., & Ferguson, P. M. 1995. From Anansi to Zomo: Trickster tales in the classroom. *The Reading Teacher*. 48(6). March. 490–503.

34. Sutherland, Z., & Arbuthnot, M. H. 1991. *Children and Books*. (8th Ed.). New York: HarperCollins. 182.

4

Fantasy

The Mirror of the Mind

Come with me, readers," said the creator, "together we will explore unknown worlds, unusual creatures, and fanciful objects. Come with me, readers, I will be at your side.

Chapter Reflections

✶

What is fantasy literature?

What are the distinctive characteristics of the genre?

What are the appealing and objectional aspects of the genre?

What are the distinguishing characteristics of the four subgenres of fantasy literature?

How is fantasy literature used in the classroom?

The reader's willingness to respond positively to the writer-creator is vital to the success of all literature, but it is imperative to the success of fantasy literature. (See Flora White's illustration of Peter Pan.) The English poet William Coleridge, discussing the stance assumed by the reader when encountering the supernatural in his poem *The Rime of the Ancient Mariner*, spoke of the importance of the "... shadows of imagination that willing suspension of disbelief for the moment, which constitutes poetic faith."[1] The phrase "willing suspension of disbelief" became an accepted creed of literature of the fantastic, until 1947 when J. R. R. Tolkien, the author of the saga of Middle-earth, questioned Coleridge's idea.[2] Tolkien suggested that "suspension of *disbelief*" represented an adult perception of the value of reading fantasy. Tolkien contended that readers who like a fantasy selection will believe it—not suspend disbelief. He affirmed the reader's capacity for literary belief by stating that the "sub-creator" (his term for the writer-creator) must artistically produce a "Secondary World" that the reader enters and, while inside, believes that it is "true." Tolkien explained that the enthusiastic reader is in an enchanted state of "secondary belief." Readers who believe the sub-creator's fanciful adventures want to sense the wonder portrayed by the author and to see the creation in their "mind's eye." They sustain this belief as long as the story-maker credibly portrays this other world. Once disbelief in the Secondary World occurs, Tolkien explains, the reader will immediately return to the primary world and look at the abortive Secondary World from the outside. The spell will be broken and the art has failed.

One of Lewis Carroll's fanciful creatures described successful fantasy when it said:

> "Well, now that we have seen each other," said the unicorn, "If you'll believe in me, I'll believe in you, is that a bargain?"[3]

Never-never land is portrayed here in an early edition of Sir James M. Barrie's Peter Pan *through Flora White's expressionistic watercolor paintings. In this painting the mermaids come up in extraordinary numbers to play with their bubbles.*

✶ WHAT IS FANTASY LITERATURE?

This book uses the term *fantasy* to refer to a literary form, but the art of fantasy also includes painting, music, and film.[4] Whether artists, musicians, filmmakers, or writers, fantasists usually break barriers and suspend the rules of everyday life.

Fantasy writers, critics, and theorists describe fantasy literature in a variety of ways, although some common elements can be discerned.[5] Robert Heinlein, a noted writer of Science Fiction, described fantasy as "a story that is imaginary-and-not-possible."[6] To Lloyd Alexander, the creator of the Prydain series, fantasy is "reality pretending to be a dream."[7] Theorist W. R. Irwin described fantasy as "a story based on and controlled by an overt violation of what is generally accepted as possibility; it is the narrative result of transforming the condition contrary to fact into 'fact' itself."[8] Eric Rabkin emphasizes the importance of reality in fantastic narratives: "... the fantastic is reality turned precisely 180° around, but this is reality nonetheless, a fantastic narrative reality that speaks the truth of the human heart."[9] Rudolph Schmerl clarifies the writer's "deliberate presentation of improbabilities . . . through . . . the use of unverifiable time, place, characters, or devices—to a typical reader within a culture whose level of sophistication will enable that reader to recognize the improbabilities."[10] C. N. Manlove also alludes to the reader when defining fanciful literature: "A fiction evoking wonder and containing a substantial and irreducible element of supernatural or impossible worlds, beings or objects with which the mortal characters in the story or the reader become on at least partly familiar terms."[11] Wolfe concluded that the most widely acceptable definition of literary fantasy is "a fictional narrative describing events that the reader believes to be impossible."[12]

These representative definitions of literary fantasy highlight the importance of the imagination, the process of transforming the impossible to the possible, the inclusion of the supernatural, the need to portray other worlds rooted in "fact," and the appearance of "magic" in the real world. The narratives evoke wonder and contain marvels, inexplicable times, places, and characters. Today many, though not all, emphasize the importance of the reader's response. Woolsey[13] reminds us that effective fantasy literature brings together the strange and the familiar, the magical and the commonplace; it may be unreal, but it is true. Fantasy keeps the human sense of wonder—imagination—alive.

THE DISTINCTIVE CHARACTERISTICS OF FANTASY LITERATURE

Four distinct elements appear in most definitions of fantasy literature. First, fantasy literature is a *narrative* published in a picture book, in a chapter book, or as a collection of short stories. Second, *all literary elements of fiction* are portrayed in fantasy literature. Third, fantasists *manipulate time, place, characters,* and *objects* to evoke *wonder* and *turn reality around precisely 180 degrees.* Finally, through the fantasist's creation, the reader recognizes the improbable elements and *believes the impossible.* When Max moves from the real world to a Secondary World *Where the Wild Things Are* (1963), Maurice Sendak accomplishes these four distinct elements. Through limited text and detailed illustrations, he successfully convinces his audience to believe the impossible while reading this favorite picture book. (See Sendak color plate.)

Fantasists have a natural love of the genre and a desire to tell stories. They believe what they write and have a childlike curiosity that enables them to stretch the fantastic while remaining consistent with their inventions. Consciously or unconsciously, effective fantasists draw from their inner strength and convictions. Some writers, such as Patricia McKillip in *The Forgotten Beasts of Eld* (1974), use medieval folk literature as the basis of their narratives. Other authors use simple and direct fantasy, as the Scottish writer Mollie Hunter did in *The Mermaid Summer* (1988). Describing her approach, Hunter says, "True fantasy is always firmly rooted in fact or in some instantly recognizable circumstance acceptable to the reader."[14]

Tolkien acknowledged the special "kind of elvish craft" used by fantasy sub-creators, because the genre is a "sudden glimpse of the underlying reality or truth."[15] He insisted that fantasy was more difficult to produce than realistic fiction. This led him to conclude that some fantasy selections are merely "fanciful" and others are underdeveloped, while in some selections fantasy is used frivolously, as decoration.[16]

Early authors, such as Geoffrey Chaucer in *The Canterbury Tales* (1387), Jonathan Swift in *Gulliver's*

Maurice Sendak uses tempera and ink in his expressionistic paintings of Max and the Wild Things in his book, Where the Wild Things Are. *He achieves texture and shading by using line. The detailed line drawings and the green, blue, and purple tempera add drama to the verbal narrative and provide details about the personality of the Wild Things and their environment.*

FIGURE 4.1 Distinctive Literary Characteristics of Fantasy Literature

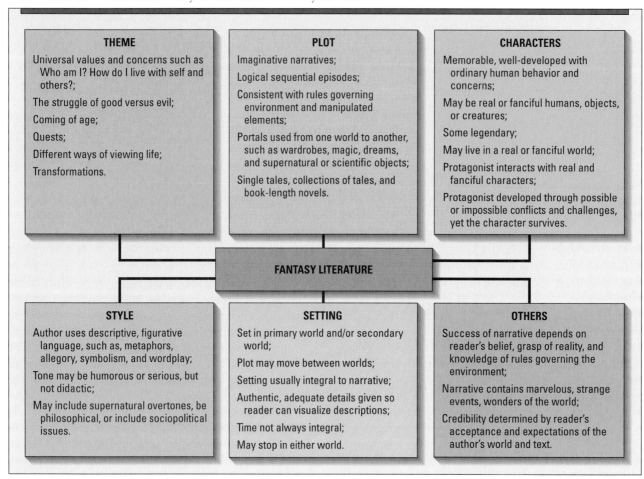

THEME

Universal values and concerns such as Who am I? How do I live with self and others?;

The struggle of good versus evil;

Coming of age;

Quests;

Different ways of viewing life;

Transformations.

PLOT

Imaginative narratives;

Logical sequential episodes;

Consistent with rules governing environment and manipulated elements;

Portals used from one world to another, such as wardrobes, magic, dreams, and supernatural or scientific objects;

Single tales, collections of tales, and book-length novels.

CHARACTERS

Memorable, well-developed with ordinary human behavior and concerns;

May be real or fanciful humans, objects, or creatures;

Some legendary;

May live in a real or fanciful world;

Protagonist interacts with real and fanciful characters;

Protagonist developed through possible or impossible conflicts and challenges, yet the character survives.

FANTASY LITERATURE

STYLE

Author uses descriptive, figurative language, such as, metaphors, allegory, symbolism, and wordplay;

Tone may be humorous or serious, but not didactic;

May include supernatural overtones, be philosophical, or include sociopolitical issues.

SETTING

Set in primary world and/or secondary world;

Plot may move between worlds;

Setting usually integral to narrative;

Authentic, adequate details given so reader can visualize descriptions;

Time not always integral;

May stop in either world.

OTHERS

Success of narrative depends on reader's belief, grasp of reality, and knowledge of rules governing the environment;

Narrative contains marvelous, strange events, wonders of the world;

Credibility determined by reader's acceptance and expectations of the author's world and text.

Travels (1726), and Daniel Defoe in *Robinson Crusoe* (1716), used fantasy elements in their books, as did William Thackeray and Charles Dickens in the nineteenth century. The first modern adult English fantasy was George MacDonald's *Phantastes*, published in 1858.[17] Children who had access to the books intended for adults read, reread, and enjoyed them as much as the adult readers did. Indeed, young people and adults enjoy fantasy equally, which supports C. S. Lewis's declaration that adults enjoy a good juvenile book as much as children do.[18] After an extensive review of the history of children's literature, Egoff found that most children's classics are fantasies. She concluded that one reason for this is that fantasy does not depend on the immediacy of time and surroundings expected in other fictive literature.[19] Susan Cooper, the author of *The Dark Is Rising* (1973), believes fantasy is a metaphor through which we can discover ourselves.[20] Many fantasists emphasize universal truths and basic humanity, making exploration of the literature an essential and delightful experience for all ages.

Because young people may read adult fantasy, such as Stephen King's horror novels, we need to identify the differences between juvenile and adult fantasies. In juvenile fantasies, the supernatural beings and other content are not as violent as they may be in adult books. Similarly, the author's tone is not as frightening or somber in juvenile fantasy, most human protagonists are young, juvenile fantasies are shorter, the print is larger, and they are usually illustrated. Natalie Babbitt, the author of *Tuck Everlasting* (1975), summarizes the differences as follows: juvenile fantasy literature generally expresses joy, has a happy or satisfying ending, and gives the reader more hope than is found in fantasy intended for an adult audience.[21]

Quality fantasy literature contains the literary conventions expected of all books of fiction. In addition, the fantasist must help the reader believe the fantasy elements by retaining an *internal consistency* throughout the book. In *The Lion, the Witch, and the Wardrobe* (1950) and the other six books in the series, C. S. Lewis carefully describes the imaginary world of Narnia. Throughout the Chronicles of

Narnia, Lewis consistently retains the distinct features of each world. His fanciful creatures and human characters are believable and behave appropriately for the individual settings. Because Lewis retains internal consistency, his readers are willing to accept the events portrayed and eagerly continue reading the books. Successful fantasists present an original idea or twist in the plot or characterization and give the audience an entirely new perspective. For example, Pauline Clarke read that the Brontës played with toy soldiers as children. She took this fact, considered what might happen if a contemporary boy found the toy soldiers, and wrote an original, highly successful fantasy, *The Return of the Twelve* (1964). Internal consistency, originality, and other distinctive characteristics expected of quality fantasy literature are presented in Figure 4.1 on page 108.[22] The distinguishing characteristics of the four subgenres of fantasy literature are presented later in the chapter.

✳ THE FOUR SUBGENRES OF FANTASY LITERATURE

Fantasy literature is difficult to classify; indeed, scholars have identified more than twenty classifications of fantasy stories. Depending on the focus of the individual selector, fantasy literature is organized according to categories such as the following:

Content. For example, Animal Fantasies or Ghost Stories.

Literary elements. For example, themes, good versus evil, allegory, or time-slip fantasy.

Degrees of seriousness. For example, Light Fantasy or Dark Fantasy.

Degrees of fantasy or magic. For example, Past Time Fantasy, Stories of Magic, or Enchanted Realism.

Sex of the author. For example, feminist perspective.

Setting of the narrative. For example, High Fantasy, Low Fantasy, Curious Worlds, or Utopia.

Fantasy stories. For example, Fanciful Creatures or Fanciful Adventures.[23]

Some of the categories overlap; others are too broad, have characteristics found in several subgenres, or do not exhibit distinct characteristics. Still other categories are so specific that they result in too many overlapping subgenres. The actual classification of specific selections into a subgenre can be difficult. Madeleine L'Engle's *A Wrinkle in Time* (1962), for example, is classified as fantasy–science fiction because it is hard to decide whether fantasy or science fiction is the more powerful element in the narrative.

Tolkien, Tymn, Zahorski, Boyer, and other theorists have concluded that the most efficient way to subdivide fantasy stories is according to the setting appearing most often in the narrative. *Low Fantasy* narratives are set primarily in the real world and contain mostly realistic elements with some fantasy. *High Fantasy* narratives are set primarily in a "Secondary World" and contain many fanciful elements influenced by folk literature.[24]

Classifying by setting is easier and quicker than many other forms of classification. Some narratives, however, move freely from one world to another. Therefore, the final factors used to classify a story into a subgenre are the length of the narrative, the amount of time the characters spend in a particular world, and the influence of folk literature on the narrative.

Woolsey reacted to this free movement of characters in time and space by suggesting another subgenre for fantasy stories—*Combination Low and High*. Lukens, however, questions the need for so many subgenre distinctions because the free movement between worlds found in certain narratives creates a tremendous overlap between subgenres.[25]

Based on an extensive review of the theoretical and professional writing concerning literary fantasy, this book will use four subgenres of fantasy literature: *Literary Fairy Tales*, *Low Fantasy*, *High Fantasy*, and *Science Fiction*.

This chapter discusses the distinguishing characteristics of each subgenre, indicates notable selections of the subgenre, and suggests instructional techniques to use with fantasy literature in the classroom.[26] As with all genres, teachers need to be able to identify, classify, and evaluate selections to be presented to students. When students become familiar with literature, they like to discuss the structure of selections and to classify stories in the various subgenres. Occasionally, teachers may help young people classify and compare selections using a genre approach, but in general, genre information is intended to provide background for the teacher and to help in making curriculum decisions. Chapter bibliographies are organized according to subgenre designations and thematic classifications to assist in curricular development.[27]

LITERARY FAIRY TALES

Literary Fairy Tales are original tales that imitate the format of folk literature and contain similar content. These imaginary narratives are the bridge between folk literature and fantasy. They are similar to folk literature in three ways. First, they are tales, not book-length narratives. Second, their motifs and content, including magic, fairies, brownies, and other creatures, are typical of those found in folk literature. Third, the authors use the literary structures of oral folk literature to write the tales. Fantasy tales differ from folktales, however, in that fantasy tales originate in a written format rather than the oral tradition of some folk literature. An identified author, not an anonymous person, writes fantasy literature. Hence, the stories reflect the individual's time, personal philosophy, and personality. The stories are therefore classified as **Literary** (meaning originally written) **Fairy Tales** (containing content and style of writing similar to folk literature selections). Some authorities prefer the term *Literary Folk Tales*. An original pourquoi tale by Amy MacDonald, *The Spider Who Created the World* (1996), is an example of this subgenre. (See MacDonald color plate.) The bold illustrations by G. Brian Karas enhance this well-developed Literary Fairy Tale.

Distinguishing Literary Characteristics of Literary Fairy Tales

Writers of Literary Fairy Tales choose this subgenre because they want to use the structure of oral folk and fairy tales and, in a limited space, invent action-packed adventures with memorable characters. The real and fanciful characters may be empowered with magic. The tales deal with universal themes and the concerns of the creator. The variety of these tales is evident when we consider that Ethel Pochocki's *The Mushroom Man* (1993) tells of an unusual friendship, *The Magic Hare* (1993) by Lynne Reid Banks presents a series of trickster tales, and Susan Meddaugh's *Hog-Eye* (1995) offers a young female pig's humorous explanation for missing school. Literary Fairy (Folk) Tales contain the distinguishing literary characteristics listed in Figure 4.2 on page 111.

Notable Literary Fairy Tales

Hans Christian Andersen, the Danish folklorist and fantasist, is credited with writing the first Literary Fairy Tales. In 1846 his first collection, *Wonderful Stories for Children*, was published in English. The collection included his most famous traditional Danish tales and some of his original Literary Fairy Tales, such as "The Little Mermaid," "The Tinder-Box," and "The Tin-Soldier." These and other tales can be found in Neil Philip's *Fairy Tales of Hans Christian Andersen* (1995). Isabelle Brent's illustrations enhance the old tales. (For additional information about Andersen, see Did You Know? on page 112.) As Andersen's popularity spread, other talented writers, who had a strong love and knowledge of the old oral tales, began writing original tales using the folk literature format, and the subgenre identified as Literary Fairy Tales developed.

Since the mid-1800s, both young people and adults have received the tales enthusiastically. Companies continue to publish popular Literary Fairy Tales in single-tale picture books and reissue old collections, such as Philip's collection described above. They also publish new fanciful tales in individual books or collections.

Table 4.1 on page 113 lists notable authors of Literary Fairy Tales and summarizes their contribution to the historical development of the subgenre. Other outstanding Literary Fairy Tales are included in the chapter bibliographies. The classroom use of fantasy literature, including Literary Fairy Tales, will be discussed in detail in the last section of this chapter, but here it is appropriate to suggest some Literary Response Modes (LRMs) that can be used with this subgenre (see Table 4.2 on page 115).

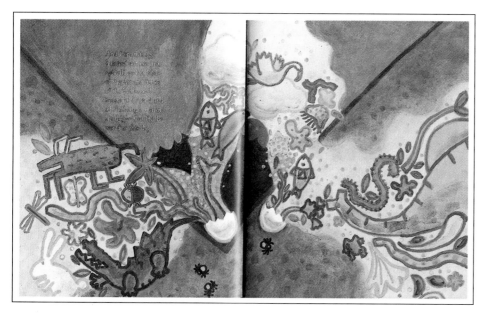

G. Brian Karas uses acrylic and gouache expressive illustrations to enhance Amy MacDonald's The Spider Who Created the World. *The artist uses bold lines and backgrounds filled with color to portray the fanciful creatures.*

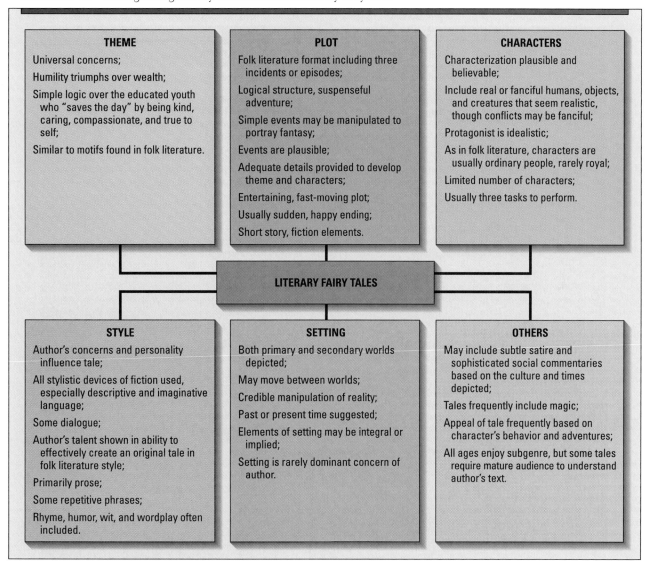

LOW FANTASY

The subgenre **Low Fantasy** is characterized by book-length fanciful narratives set primarily in the real, primary world, but including characters or events with plausible fantasy elements. The term *Low Fantasy* refers to the setting—the primary world—and is not an indication of the importance assigned to the subgenre, nor is it used as an evaluative term.[28]

Distinguishing Literary Characteristics of Low Fantasy
Authors achieve fantasy in this subgenre by manipulating a few elements, while the rest of the elements are realistic. The real and fanciful characters may be involved in activities influenced by supernatural and magical events. Some

of the imaginary incidents and characters cannot necessarily be explained rationally or scientifically, yet writers of Low Fantasy selections strive to maintain internal consistency in their narratives. *Tooth Fairy* (1995) by Peter Collington is a good example of internal consistency. (See Collington color plate on page 115.) Throughout this wordless book, the viewer sees the nighttime work of the tooth fairy as she moves from the Secondary World to the real world of the little girl who has lost her tooth.

Although Low Fantasy narratives are realistic in most details, they are imaginary. Their success depends largely on the audience's willingness to assume "secondary belief" in the fantasy portrayed in the primary world. Figure 4.3 on page 116 lists distinguishing literary characteristics of Low Fantasy.

Did You Know About
HANS CHRISTIAN ANDERSEN?

Hans Christian Andersen grew up in Odense, Denmark (a small town fourteen miles from Copenhagen), in the early 1800s. He lived with an insane grandfather, a grandmother who was a pathological liar, an alcoholic mother, and an illiterate cobbler father. He helped his grandmother care for the garden in the local asylum for the mentally ill. There he chatted with the patients, observed their behaviors, and visited with the attendants. By the time Andersen was fourteen, his father had died. The young man himself had managed to acquire a basic education and had worked for a short time in a cloth factory. After reading a bad translation of Shakespeare, he decided to move to Copenhagen to study for the theater—the passion of his life—and become famous!

In Copenhagen he attempted acting, singing, and dancing, but after receiving additional education, he discovered his talent for writing and his desire for travel. His plays, novels, poems, and travel books were mildly successful. When he received a small yearly pension from King Frederick VI, Andersen became financially independent. He continued to travel in Europe and in 1835 published the first *Wonder Stories for Children*. In his unique style, Andersen retold old Danish folktales such as "The Tinder-Box," "Little Claus and Big Claus," and "The Princess on the Pea," which had been told to him by his mother, grandmother, and poor old women in their spinning room. He also included original stories, such as "Little Ida's Flowers." An English translation entitled *Wonderful Stories for Children* was published in 1846. The book did not receive critical acclaim, but Andersen continued to write original tales using a folk literature format. He began publishing a new collection at Christmas time, and soon an Andersen collection could be found beneath all respectable Christmas trees. By 1862–63 his complete collection contained 168 traditional and original tales, such as "The Emperor's New Clothes" (based on a skit by Cervantes). Literary Fairy Tales included "The Ugly Duckling," "The Snow Queen," "The Nightingale," "The Red Shoes," "The Little Fir Tree," "The Little Match Girl," and "The Constant Tin Soldier." Many of his original tales contained unusual happenings and weird events that reflected his early experiences as a young, impressionable boy in Odense. Some tales reflected his insecurity, his romantic ideas, and his pessimistic view of human nature. After years of ridicule and rejection, Andersen finally received the critical recognition he deserved. Before he died, he was wealthy and included royalty and literary celebrities among his friends. Although his writing career flourished, he lamented the fact that he was ugly. He fell in love several times, but did not marry. He remained a lonely "ugly duckling" all of his life.

Today, a statue of Andersen stands in the center of Copenhagen. A small statue of "The Little Mermaid" (his most popular Literary Fairy Tale) sits by the seashore to honor this Danish fantasist, who created the Literary Fairy Tale. His tales have been translated into 100 languages and appear in many new picture storybooks each year. Denmark is proud of its native son who became famous because he wrote wonder stories for children!

Notable Low Fantasy

Low Fantasy includes classifications such as Animal Fantasies (Richard and Florence Atwater's *Mr. Popper's Penguins* [1938]), Beast Tales (Richard Adams's *Watership Down* [1974]), Enchanted Realism (Lucy Boston's Green Knowe Series), Stories of Magic (Edith Nesbit's *Enchanted Castle* [1968/1992]), Ghost Stories (Walter de la Mare's *Broomsticks and Other Tales* [1925]), and Light Fantasy

TABLE 4.1 Notable Literary Fairy Tales

DATE	AUTHOR, TITLE	COMMENTS
1835	H. C. Andersen, *Wonder Stories for Children*	First collection of traditional tales and Literary Fairy Tales published by the Danish fantasist.
1846	English translation, *Wonderful Stories for Children*	First English translation of Andersen's *Wonder Stories.*
1851	J. Ruskin, *The King of Golden River*	First English Literary Fairy Tale; well-written, humorous, irony influenced by Grimms and Andersen.
1855	W. Thackeray, *The Rose and the Ring*	This humorous original tale includes all the ingredients of a true fairy tale: a good fairy godmother, a hero/heroine, talismans, a little misfortune, and a happily-ever-after ending. Thackeray was encouraged to publish after Andersen's success.
1857	F. Browne, *Granny's Wonderful Chair*	Pleasurable tales to instill goodness.
1870	F. Stockton, *Ting-A-Ling*	An American Literary Fairy Tale. A minute fairy who rides an insect chariot with the first friendly giant in children's literature saves princesses and a prince. Details society's laughable decorum; carefully written with an acceptable solution. Stockton's tall tales influenced the subgenre.
1871	G. MacDonald, *At the Back of the North Wind*	The stories of this Scottish author presented the basic tenets of Christianity in a childlike manner without being didactic. This book tells the story of Diamond, a poor stableboy who lives in two worlds: the poverty of Victorian London and his dream world where the goddess-like figure of North Wind guides him.
1872	*The Princess and the Goblin*	This simple, fast-paced story is set in a Secondary World split between the good mountainside where Princess Irene and Curdie, the miner's son and his family live, and the evil world of the goblins. As the good children struggle against the evil goblins, they have many adventures. MacDonald influenced later writers and this tale is still popular.
1887	H. Pyle, *The Wonder Clock: or, Four & Twenty Marvelous Tales*	A collection of twenty-four tales from a popular English writer; includes "One Good Turn Deserves Another" and "King Stork."
1888	O. Wilde, *The Happy Prince and Other Tales*	"The Happy Prince" and "The Selfish Giant," the best-known tales, represent a higher state of spirituality; through experience and sacrifice, the characters experience the final ecstasy of death.
1889 1893	A. Lang, *Prince Prigio* *Prince Ricardo*	A mischievous fairy godmother endows Prince Prigio and his son, Prince Ricardo, with many magic gifts that they must learn to use appropriately. Lang, who is best known for his "color" fairy tale books, was an expert on fairies and oral folk literature.
1899	E. Nesbit, *The Complete Book of Dragons*	Nine stories of magic about children who can tame dragons that adults cannot tame.
1902	R. Kipling, *Just So Stories*	Best example in juvenile literature of mythic, humorous, stylistic tales.
1905	L. Housman, *A Doorway in Fairyland*	One of four collections of elegant, yet humorous variations on oral tales.
1921	E. Farjeon, *Martin Pippin in the Apple Orchard*	Like the author's later collections written in 1937 and 1955, these stories reflect that period's conception of children—innocent, sweet, perfect.
1922 1923 1930	C. Sandburg, *Rootabaga Stories* *Rootabaga Pigeons* *Potato Face*	Original American literature for children dealing with Rootabaga Country. Humorous, unique characters and plots by a master at creating word pictures.
1927	W. de la Mare, *Told Again*	In these tales based on folk literature, the youthful protagonists seem fragile. They might succeed through craftiness (not magic), but they were motivated by love and selflessness. The poet was the first to write ghost stories for children.
1930	E. Coatsworth, *The Cat Who Went to Heaven*	A poor Japanese artist includes his white cat in a picture for Buddha, and the cat is allowed into heaven. This popular Newbery winner depicts human love for an animal.
1938	K. Grahame, *The Reluctant Dragon*	A humorous tale of a boy who saves a peace-loving dragon forced to fight Saint George.
1943	A. de Saint-Exupery, *The Little Prince*	A popular allegory depicting an alien boy's encounter with the author, who tells of his travels throughout the universe.

(Continued)

TABLE 4.1   Notable Literary Fairy Tales *(Continued)*

DATE	AUTHOR, TITLE	COMMENTS
1943	J. Thurber, *Many Moons*	A wise court jester finds a way to cure Princess Lenore by giving her the moon. Strong folk literature influence.
1966	I. B. Singer, *Zlath the Goat and Other Tales*	Popular Newbery honor book containing seven stories about the foolish people of Chelm, the devil, and an allegory about a young boy and his goat.
1967 1974 1989	J. Yolen, *The Girl Who Cried Flowers and Other Tales* *The Emperor and the Kite* *The Faery Flag: Stories and Poems of Fantasy and the Supernatural*	Collections of tales by a talented American writer that reflect her ability to write original tales with strong folk literature influence. The characters have traditional traits.
1976	J. Williams, *Everyone Knows What a Dragon Looks Like*	A young gate sweeper is polite to a small fat man with a long white beard and gives him food and drink. As a result, the old man takes the form of a dragon and rescues the city.
1980	R. Munsch, *The Paper Bag Princess*	A unique tale about a princess who saves her prince, but with a surprise ending.
1982	P. Fleischman, *Graven Images: Three Stories*	A Newbery honor book containing a humorous tale and two ghost stories; detailed descriptions by a master storyteller.
1992	U. K. Le Guin, *A Ride on the Red Mare's Back*	A boy who has been kidnapped by the trolls is rescued by his young sister with the help of a magical toy horse that becomes a real horse when needed.
1992	L. Alexander, *The Fortune-Tellers*	A poor young carpenter receives a fortune in a surprising way.
1992	C. Van Allsburg, *The Widow's Broom*	A tale by an outstanding author-illustrator about a widow who tricks her neighbor with a broom left by a witch.
1992	K. Paterson, *The King's Equal*	A beautiful, wise, good shepherdess outwits an arrogant prince.
1993	R. Sutcliff, *The Minstrel and the Dragon Pup*	A minstrel rescues his gentle dragon pup. In the process he restores the young prince's health.
1993	A. Ehrlich, *Parents in the Pigpen, Pigs in the Tub*	The barnyard animals decide it would be nicer to live in the farmhouse, so the farmer's family moves to the barn where there are no more chores to do. This hilarious original tall tale is enhanced by Steven Kellogg's illustrations.
1995	H. C. Andersen, *The Swineherd*	Anthea Bell provides a fresh translation of Andersen's story about a princess who loses a kingdom and a prince bridegroom. Lisbeth Zwerger's expressive illustrations supplement the tale.

(Roald Dahl's *Charlie and the Chocolate Factory* [1972]).[29] Some people organize the subgenre according to content, such as Personified Toys and Other Inanimate Objects (Margery Williams's *The Velveteen Rabbit* [1922/1970]), Tales of Pure Imagination (Ruth Gannett's *My Father's Dragon* [1986]), and Curious Worlds (William Mayne's *Earthfasts* [1966]).

Elementary-age students are interested in literature in these categories. Among their favorite selections are Animal Fantasies (personified animals and talking beasts) and those with humor or wit, as found in Light Fantasy. Young people enjoy stories with weird events, Ghost Stories, tales of terror and horror, and those with supernatural characters and events. They enjoy reading and hearing Stories of Magic that contrast ordinary events and fabulous occurrences. Eric Nones effectively moves from realistic events to fabulous occurrences by giving wings to the protagonist in *Angela's Wings* (1995). (See Nones color plate on page 116.) Through the verbal and visual narratives, the reader accepts Angela's problem—achieving self-esteem—and the way she solves it.

Enchanted Realism gives young people time to daydream and explore the dreamlike elements of reality. Tales of Pure Imagination and Curious Worlds allow the child's imagination to soar. All children enjoy imagining what they would do if their toys or dolls could play with them; narratives classified as Personified Toys and Other Inanimate Objects give them an opportunity to explore these thoughts. A classic example is Carlo Collodi's *Adventures of Pinocchio* (original Italian publication, 1882; English translation, 1944). This tale of a personified puppet continues to delight children and adults alike. Roberto

TABLE 4.2 Suggested LRMs for Literary Fairy Tales

These short tales are read or heard in one session. The content, characters, and structure are similar to folk literature. After reading or listening to several Literary Fairy Tales, students will produce LRMs that reflect personal responses to the tales. For example:

Students will read several tales and compare and contrast such aspects as the setting, characters, themes, style of writing, and illustrations.

They will record the similarities and differences on a visual graphic, such as a Venn diagram.

Groups of students will list on a chart the motifs (themes) found in several traditional fairy tales and several Literary Fairy Tales. They will compare, contrast, and record their responses on a comparison chart.

One set of partners will write a letter to an advice columnist about problems a character encountered in the tale (or a problem the character might encounter). Another set of partners will answer the question by suggesting actions different from those depicted in the tale.

Individuals will prepare a shadowbox representing an incident from a favorite tale.

Select a collection of tales written by Hans Christian Andersen (or another fantasist). Students will compare the traditional tales with the original tales created by Andersen and will also compare the illustrations accompanying each type of tale. Chart the similarities and differences, and display the chart in the media center. Use a Character Continuum (described in Appendix B) to chart character traits. Ask students to select a favorite tale from the collection, and include a copy of the tale with the chart.

Students will prepare a wordless book to accompany a favorite tale.

Students will prepare puppets and a script of a tale and present a puppet show to several groups of students.

Individuals or groups will write a contemporary version of a favorite tale.

Students will pretend to be a miniature (or giant) creature and write a description of the classroom from the perspective of the fanciful creature. After writing the descriptions, the students will discuss them. Later, individuals or groups can write and illustrate a story about a visit from the creature.

Partners will select a favorite tale and prepare an ID Bag containing artifacts that relate to the characters, settings, and plot of the tale. Students will retell the story displaying the artifacts at the appropriate places in the story. (See Appendix B for additional information about an ID Bag.)

A group of students will select a favorite tale and prepare the objects for a felt board. The students will arrange the story into a readers theatre script. One person will place the objects on the board while the other students read the script.

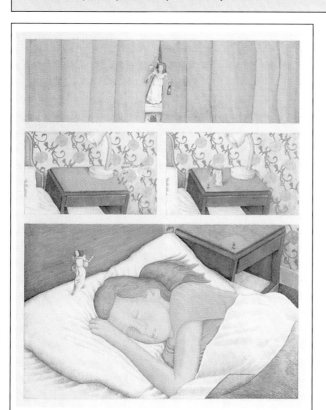

Innocenti's illustrations for the 1988 edition bring the nineteenth-century Italian countryside to life.

Indeed, it is not surprising that many Low Fantasy narratives are popular with children and with many adults. Low Fantasy narratives have received many major awards, attesting to their literary merit. (For information on Margaret Mahy, a leading writer of fantasy, see Did You Know? on page 117.)

Placing a selection on a notable list suggests that authorities recognize either the historical importance of the book or the influence it has exerted on the development of that particular subgenre. Selecting a reasonable number of books for the notable Low Fantasy list in Table 4.3 on page 118 was especially difficult, because many authors have influenced the

Peter Collington uses shades of gold, blue, and pink watercolor to show the life of a tooth fairy in his wordless book, Tooth Fairy. The artist's detailed, realistic illustrations show a sleeping child and a busy tooth fairy. Collington uses colored pencils to achieve the texture and shading. The colors highlight and dramatize the character's activities. The artist develops the plot structure by arranging the different size pictures in a logical sequence.

FIGURE 4.3   Distinguishing Literary Characteristics of Low Fantasy

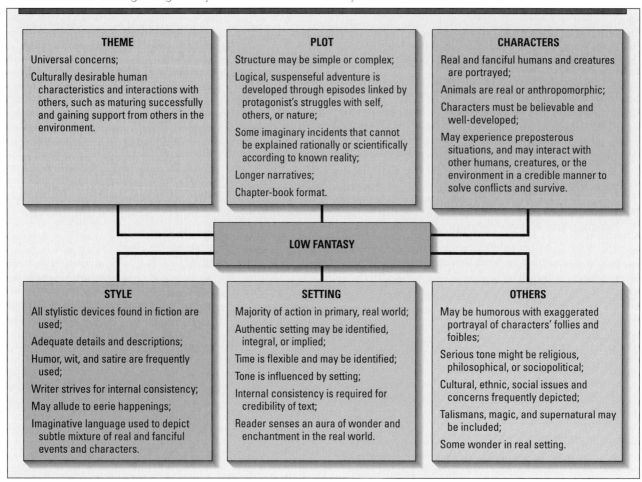

THEME

Universal concerns;

Culturally desirable human characteristics and interactions with others, such as maturing successfully and gaining support from others in the environment.

PLOT

Structure may be simple or complex;

Logical, suspenseful adventure is developed through episodes linked by protagonist's struggles with self, others, or nature;

Some imaginary incidents that cannot be explained rationally or scientifically according to known reality;

Longer narratives;

Chapter-book format.

CHARACTERS

Real and fanciful humans and creatures are portrayed;

Animals are real or anthropomorphic;

Characters must be believable and well-developed;

May experience preposterous situations, and may interact with other humans, creatures, or the environment in a credible manner to solve conflicts and survive.

LOW FANTASY

STYLE

All stylistic devices found in fiction are used;

Adequate details and descriptions;

Humor, wit, and satire are frequently used;

Writer strives for internal consistency;

May allude to eerie happenings;

Imaginative language used to depict subtle mixture of real and fanciful events and characters.

SETTING

Majority of action in primary, real world;

Authentic setting may be identified, integral, or implied;

Time is flexible and may be identified;

Tone is influenced by setting;

Internal consistency is required for credibility of text;

Reader senses an aura of wonder and enchantment in the real world.

OTHERS

May be humorous with exaggerated portrayal of characters' follies and foibles;

Serious tone might be religious, philosophical, or sociopolitical;

Cultural, ethnic, social issues and concerns frequently depicted;

Talismans, magic, and supernatural may be included;

Some wonder in real setting.

And as the months flew by, Angela's life had gone back to normal. Well, sort of. People still did notice her.

Throughout Eric Jon Nones's Angela's Wings *the artist successfully portrays various perspectives in his water color illustrations. The artist uses lines and space to show movement and effectively portrays the characters and the details of the multiethnic neighborhood. The visual and verbal narratives harmoniously combine to present the fanciful storyline.*

Did You Know About
MARGARET MAHY?

$\mathscr{F}$ind Whakatane, New Zealand, on the map and you will discover Margaret Mahy's hometown, a place where she grew up with twenty-six cousins. Today she lives in the shell of an old volcano in the South Island of New Zealand with her dog, Cello, and an assortment of cats who like to sleep on her fax machine, photocopier, and laser printer. Like many writers, Mahy sees pictures in her head while reading and writing, but she has another aid as well—she also hears a voice telling her a story. Could this be the reason her stories come to life when we read them aloud?

Mahy has always seen herself as a writer and at seven wrote her first story about a boy who followed a golden pheasant to the house of a witch. She liked to play with language and write poetry, which she submitted to the children's section of a local newspaper; at eight, she was a published poet! Her teachers were not impressed with her work, however, because she was messy and liked to chat with her friends! Since writing was not emphasized in the schools, in high school she formed a writing club with two friends. They wrote and shared their writings after school. Later, her friends stopped writing, but Mahy persevered and

in 1969 published her first book, *A Lion in the Meadow*. Between the mid-1970s and 1991, she published numerous picture books, novels, and short stories. Though best known for her fantasy writing, Mahy has also written realistic fiction for young people. In 1994, she wrote a short autobiography explaining why she chooses to write for juveniles.

A versatile writer such as Mahy enjoys manipulating the words and structures of the language. She has a vivid imagination that enables her to turn the ordinary into the extraordinary. Before she starts to write a story, she plans the beginning, knows more or less how it will end, but is not sure about the middle. She takes long walks about the volcano with her dog and tells him the story, and her fanciful stories come to life.

Mahy likes to travel and talk to other adults and children about writing. She develops her stories to end well for the good characters because such stories entertain and strengthen us. She feels that folktales help people make sense of their own lives. Obviously, Margaret Mahy gives us strength and opens our imaginations, while entertaining us. Wonder if we could visit her volcano and listen to her tell stories?

development of juvenile literature. Other outstanding Low Fantasy narratives are included in the chapter bibliography. Table 4.4 on page 120 suggests LRMs that can be used with Low Fantasy selections.

HIGH FANTASY

The subgenre **High Fantasy** is characterized by imaginary book-length narratives set primarily in a "Secondary World"; the narratives are rooted in folk literature and epic in proportion. These fantasies are created from the fantasist's vision and imagination. The real and fanciful humans, animals, and creatures become involved in magical or supernatural experiences that defy reality. Writers must portray all of the elements consistently and convincingly to help the audience accept and believe the impossible while in the Secondary World.

Distinguishing Literary Characteristics of High Fantasy
As we have noted, fantasies classified as High Fantasy are set primarily in the Secondary World. The characters may visit or encounter inhabitants of the real world, but the invented world is an integral element of the narrative. Often these chapter books have the aura of medieval times and the mood of folk literature. The legendary, well-drawn hero may move into the Secondary World because of a talisman or may be in the Secondary World from the beginning.

TABLE 4.3 Notable Low Fantasy

DATE	AUTHOR, TITLE	COMMENTS
1863	C. Kingsley, *The Water-Babies*	Popular, multilevel fantasy; genuine storytelling about a contemporary child placed in an imaginary world.
1881	C. Collodi, *The Adventures of Pinocchio*	A popular Italian classic about the adventures of a mischievous, personified puppet.
1894	R. Kipling, *The Jungle Book*	Mowgli is taught the "laws of nature" by anthropomorphic animals. The superiority of humankind is clearly depicted by the master storyteller.
1902	B. Potter, *The Tale of Peter Rabbit*	First of twenty-eight descriptive Animal Fantasies created by the author-artist. The "little" picture books have a didactic tone, but reflect her ability and love of nature and animals.
1902 1907	E. Nesbit, *The Five Children and It* *Enchanted Castle*	Two of the author's twelve books written for children. Nesbit, a trendsetter in the genre, combined the ordinary with fantasy. She wrote solely for children's pleasure and set the rules for the use of magic in children's literature. There was no didacticism in her work.
1908	K. Grahame, *The Wind in the Willows*	The adventures of Rat, Mole, Toad, and Badger on the Riverbank make up the most complex of all Edwardian fantasies. The personified animals were effectively described by a master storyteller.
1920	W. de la Mare, *Broomsticks and Other Tales*	The first author to include Ghost Stories in his collection. His specters were rarely transformed into tangible figures, but he did address the existence of spiritual beings in our world.
1920	H. Lofting, *The Story of Dr. Dolittle*	The first of thirteen books about the animal doctor who could communicate with and care for animals. The books had simple themes and plots. Lofting's later books contained racist remarks, a reflection of his time.
1922	M. Williams, *The Velveteen Rabbit*	The earliest, popular toy animal in fantasy literature. The story of a rabbit who became "real" because of a child's love. The book contains more emotion and depth than are typically found in picture books for young children.
1926	A. A. Milne, *Winnie-the-Pooh*	Short little episodes centered around Christopher Robin and his toy animals who came to life. The author expresses the delights of childhood. This is a favorite story told with subtle humor and understood differently by all ages.
1934	P. L. Travers, *Mary Poppins*	The first of five books about the "perfect" Victorian nanny who brings magic and chaos to the lives of ordinary "poor little rich" children; popular, humorous adventures.
1938	R. and F. Atwater, *Mr. Popper's Penguins*	This Newbery Honor Book describes the adventures of a paperhanger who creatively solves the problems of keeping twelve penguins; a popular, humorous narrative.
1938	Dr. Seuss, *The 500 Hats of Bartholomew Cubbins*	The second, and perhaps the best, of the many humorous, fanciful, rhyming picture books created by T. Geisel. Bartholomew was unable to remove his hat in the presence of the king.
1939	R. Lawson, *Ben and Me*	Amos the mouse tells the "true" facts about the life and inventions of Benjamin Franklin. Some events and characters are imaginary; a humorous fanciful biography.
1944 1948 1954	*Rabbit Hill* *Robbut: A Tale of Tails* *The Tough Winter*	Well-developed fantasies about the adventures of talking animals in their environment. Human characters interact realistically with the fanciful animals. *Rabbit Hill* was a Newbery winner.
1945	A. Lindgren, *Pippi Longstocking*	The first of Pippi's adventures. Pippi is the strongest girl in the world. She lives with a monkey and a horse and enlivens the lives of her friends Annika and Tommy. The book is imaginative, with an exaggerated, tall-tale character.
1947	R. Godden, *The Doll House*	In this miniature dramatic novel, the writer uses the conversation between the characters to carry the plot, a technique not used again until the 1960s. Other authors have rarely duplicated her ability to sensitively use dolls to probe children's emotions.
1952 1945 1970	E. B. White, *Charlotte's Web* *Stuart Little* *The Trumpet of the Swan*	The author uses the reality of the barn and its inhabitants to portray eternal friendship in the "perfect," most popular Animal Fantasy of the twentieth century. The other books are also outstanding Animal Fantasies.
1954	L. M. Boston, *The Children of Green Knowe*	The first of six books about Green Knowe and Tolly who bridges time to communicate with three children who died in Green Knowe in 1666. As Tolly's grandmother tells him about the children, they become his companions. The setting is strong and the characters are well developed.

(Continued)

TABLE 4.3 Notable Low Fantasy (*Continued*)

DATE	AUTHOR, TITLE	COMMENTS
1958	P. Pearce, *Tom's Midnight Garden*	On the stroke of thirteen, Tom enters an old-fashioned garden, where he meets Hatty, a homeless girl. As they play together, he soon realizes that she is aging, while he has controlled time. The garden disappears, but he meets Hatty again. Pearce's style and ability to portray emotions are outstanding.
1960 1981	G. Selden, *The Cricket in Times Square* *Chester Cricket's Pigeon Ride*	A series about Chester Cricket, Tucks, a streetwise mouse, and Harry the Cat. In the first book, they use Chester's musical ability to help the owners of a newsstand in Times Square. Based on the town mouse and the country mouse theme, otherwise the talking animals are true to their species.
1961 1964 1988	R. Dahl, *James and the Giant Peach* *Charlie and the Chocolate Factory* *Matilda*	Three of many books by a favorite fantasist who entertains children with cautionary but humorous folktale–animal stories. The first book, a tall tale, describes an orphan boy's adventures with a giant peach; it features strange characters and a happy ending. Though controversial, the author's books are enjoyed by readers who assume a childlike stance.
1962– 1963	P. Clarke, *The Return of the Twelves*	When Max's family moves to an old house, he finds a box of wooden soldiers who come to life around him. He must return them to their original owners before the wrong people get them. An exciting adventure with well-drawn characters.
1966	W. Mayne, *Earthfasts*	The lives of two friends, Keith and David, are endangered when they encounter Nellie Jack John, an eighteenth-century drummer boy who has a candle with a cold flame that has the power to reverse time and bring King Arthur and his men back to life. The title means "earth bound" and "fixed in the ground." Supernatural creatures live in the real world, and time is suspended in the past. Mayne's competent use of the language and dialogue and his interest in science are apparent.
1971 1986 1990	R. O'Brien, *Mrs. Frisby and the Rats of NIMH* *Rasco and the Rats of NIMH* *R-T, Margaret, and the Rats of NIMH*	This fantasy and Science Fiction book won the Newbery Medal. In the first book, the protagonist helps laboratory rats escape; the rats establish a utopian society away from humans. Two other fantasies featuring the rats of NIMH were written by the late author's daughter, Jane Conly.
1974	R. Adams, *Watership Down*	Published first as an adult novel, this book portrays rabbits in their own environment with the ability to communicate with one another. They are determined to keep their freedom in this complex, contemporary adventure.
1975	N. Babbitt, *Tuck Everlasting*	The dream of eternal life is explored through Winnie Foster and her relationship with the ever young Tuck family. An outstanding example of the genre in every aspect; some controversial material.
1980 1986 1989 1993	L. R. Banks, *The Indian in the Cupboard* *The Return of the Indian* *The Secret of the Indian* *The Mystery of the Cupboard*	A popular fantasy series with children, featuring Omri whose plastic toy Indian comes to life when removed from a magic cupboard. When additional plastic toys are placed in the cupboard with Little Bear, troubles begin. The characters and their adventures override the stereotypical language and behavior, which some consider controversial.
1982 1985 1990	D. King-Smith, *Pigs Might Fly* *Babe: The Gallant Pig* *Ace: The Very Important Pig*	A popular fantasist depicts the English countryside in a series of books about pigs who communicate with other animals in their own environment; they are friendly, capable, and lovable—similar to Wilbur, the pig in E. B. White's *Charlotte's Web*.
1983	M. Mahy, *The Haunting*	A master storyteller depicts Barney who becomes a companion and apprentice magician to his uncle. He discovers a secret power possessed by men in his family, until his older sister becomes the magician; the supernatural is portrayed as an ordinary part of life.
1990	N. Willard, *The High Rise Glorious Skittle Skat Roarious Sky Pie Angel Food Cake*	A young girl searches for a recipe to cook her mother a birthday cake and finds angels and a cake.
1992	S. Meddaugh, *Martha Speaks*	An Animal Fantasy by a talented author-artist about an ordinary pig who eats alphabet soup and begins to talk. Her family encounters troubles until she saves the day.
1993	M. Mahy, *The Three-Legged Cat*	A hilarious story about Tom, a large, three-legged cat, who longs to see the world. His mistress's brother Danny, a drifter, replaces his hat with a new model, Tom, who departs on top of Danny's bald head.

(Continued)

TABLE 4.3 Notable Low Fantasy (*Continued*)

DATE	AUTHOR, TITLE	COMMENTS
1994	S. Waugh, *The Mennyms*	A family of intelligent, life-size living dolls are made by an elderly woman. For years after her death, they live undisturbed in an old house in London, until their security is threatened by the new landlord who writes a letter stating his intention to visit them. Also see the sequels *Mennyms in the Wilderness* (1995) and *Mennyms Under Siege* (1996).
1995	Avi, *Poppy*	Poppy, a brave, persistent deer mouse, attempts to find a new home for her family away from the evil Mr. Ocax, a great horned owl.
1995	R. Kipling, *The Jungle Book: The Mowgli Stories*	An appealing reissue of Kipling's popular Mowgli stories. Jerry Pinkney's illustrations complement and interpret the verbal narrative.

TABLE 4.4 Suggested LRMs for Low Fantasy

Low Fantasy includes fanciful elements. The setting is usually in the primary world. LRMs such as the following highlight the distinctive characteristics of the subgenre:

Rewrite an incident without fantastic elements. Compare the two versions. Students will decide which version they prefer and justify their choice.

Select a book without pictures of a fanciful creature. Individually or in pairs, students will make a model of the creature from clay, papier-mâché, or a combination of materials. Display the creatures and the book in the classroom or school media center.

Using a Low Fantasy containing a miniature world, such as Mary Norton's *The Borrowers,* prepare a diorama of a room described in the book.

Use thumbprints to draw a picture of a miniature animal.

Place students in groups. Each group will select a particular writer, read several tales written by the person, and prepare a Creator Cluster. Students will identify the literary elements used often by the author. Cluster the information and discuss it with others.

A group will present a dramatic presentation of an incident written by the author. Display the author's books. Entice the audience to read them.

A group will challenge other groups to find additional books written by the person, especially those classified in another genre; for example, Jane Yolen has written selections for all fantasy subgenres, realistic fiction, and poetry. Compare and discuss the author's style. Perhaps a prize (free time to read) can be given to students who find other books written by the person.

A Creator Comparison Chart will be prepared after the previous LRM is completed. List the creator's names down the left side of the chart, and write the literary elements at the top of the chart. Write comparison information in the appropriate blocks.

In High Fantasy the Secondary World must be internally consistent. We expect the writer to give enough information about the history, language, occupations, dress, housing, and lifestyle of the people to be convincing. If the narrative is carefully crafted, the reader is transported to "another time and place." For a short time, the audience experiences the wonder and enchantment of the setting, only to return to the real world, refreshed and ready to take on its challenges. This Secondary World of wonder and enchantment is vividly depicted in Margaret Hodges's *Saint George and the Dragon* (1984), a picture storybook based on a story from Edmund Spenser's *Faerie Queene*, which was written in 1590. (See Hodges color plate on page 121.) The epic adventure, characters, and fierce dragon come to life in Trina Schart Hyman's remarkable illustrations.

Lloyd Alexander, the creator of the Prydain series and other books of fantasy, claims High Fantasy has the ability to "quicken the heart," refresh and delight, make us laugh and cry, and give us new visions of the possibilities of life.[30] The distinguishing literary characteristics of High Fantasy are summarized in Figure 4.4 on page 122.

Notable High Fantasy

Creators of High Fantasy frequently write a series of books to develop their Secondary Worlds and its inhabitants in depth. Brian Jacques's *Redwall series*, Patricia McKillip's *Hed series*, and Diana Wayne Jones's *Delmark series* are examples. Writing several books gives the creator an opportunity to develop the characterization, continue the plot through various events and through time, provide details about the Secondary World, and help the reader become familiar with the large cast of characters. Between 1900 and 1919 L. Frank Baum wrote fourteen Oz books, but the first, *The Wonderful Wizard of Oz*, remains popular with children almost a century after it was published. (See the

Trina Schart Hyman has captured a medieval setting for Margaret Hodges' adaptation of Saint George and the Dragon. *Hyman accomplishes this effect through brush and ink, colored pencils, crayon, and acrylic washes. Decorative borders surround the pictures and contain detailed pictures of flowers. The borders give the appearance of looking through a window at the action of the story. The artist uses lines to define the detailed shapes, show texture, and shading. The colors highlight the characters and drama of the story.*

color plate on page 123.) These and other series are cited in the Imaginary World bibliography.

Perhaps the most popular High Fantasy books among young people are C. S. Lewis's tales of Narnia, a Secondary World initially reached by Edmund and Lucy through a door in a wardrobe, and J. R. R. Tolkien's *The Hobbit*, which describes Bilbo Baggins's adventures. Young people frequently progress to Tolkien's three-volume *Lord of the Rings*. Not only are these books the touchstone of fantasy literature, but the authors were influential in delineating the theory of fantasy literature. Young people and adults who begin their exploration of the genre by reading or hearing Lewis's *The Magician's Nephew*, followed by *The Lion, the Witch, and the Wardrobe*, or Tolkien's *The Hobbit* usually become addicted to the genre.[31]

High Fantasy selections often ask more questions than they answer. Many feature older protagonists and appeal to children above ten years of age. Few narratives are available in picture book format. Table 4.5 on page 124 lists some notable selections, and other outstanding selections are listed in the bibliography at the end of the chapter. Some LRMs for use with High Fantasy are suggested in Table 4.6 on page 125.

SCIENCE FICTION

Isaac Asimov described **Science Fiction** as an imaginative narrative that "deals with the reaction of human responses to changes in the level of science and technology."[32] Hugo Gernsback, who used the term *Scientifiction* in 1929 to describe his magazine, *Amazing Stories*, defined it as "a charming romance intermingled with scientific fact and prophetic vision."[33] Other definitions have emphasized the literary elements expected in the narratives or highlighted the reader's response. The relationship of the subgenre to other genres is the focus of some definitions while others proclaim Science Fiction to be the philosophical underpinning of the universe. To Norman Spinrad, "Science fiction is anything published as science fiction."[34]

Wolfe lists thirty-three different definitions for this subgenre. He observes that this subset of fantasy has been defined so frequently that there is little critical consensus as to the elements to be included or excluded. Definitions of this subgenre frequently mention scientific content, social extrapolation, and a cognitive link to the "real world."

While the line between some High Fantasy selections and Science Fiction selections is sometimes difficult to discern, Science Fiction requires scientific plausibility, whereas internal consistency rules fantasy stories. Both subgenres succeed or fail based on the reader's willingness to accept the author's perspective. The reader will accept this perspective, though it differs from real life, if the world invented by the writer is plausible and consistent. The reader will accept the author's creation if given a reason to

FIGURE 4.4   Distinguishing Literary Characteristics of High Fantasy

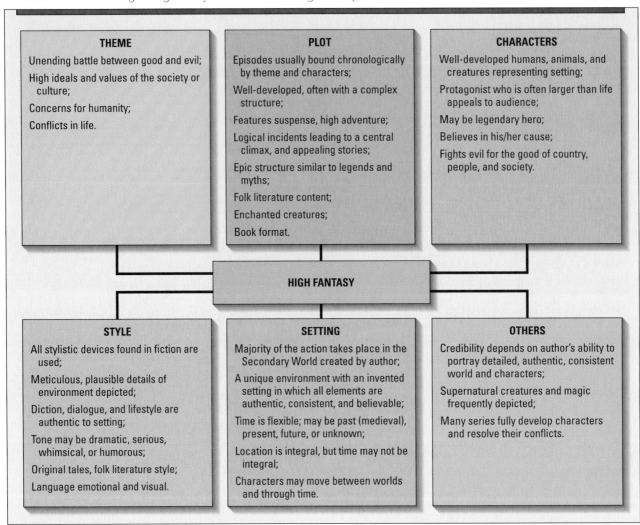

believe what might have been, what could have been, or what will be in the future.[35]

Benefits Gained from Experiences with Science Fiction

Ben Bova, a Science Fiction author, has identified several values children gain from exploring Science Fiction.[36] First, writers prepare children for scientific and technological changes they may encounter as adults. Second, young readers vicariously experience what might happen if societal values change. Third, writers warn children of the dangers of an unchecked society. Fourth, Science Fiction provides an excellent opportunity for readers to live in another time and place, to experience a new environment guided by the writer. This look to the future brings a new perspective of life to the reader. Fifth, Science Fiction encourages students in science classes to consider scientific possibilities and to stretch their creative problem-solving abilities and prediction skills.

Distinguishing Literary Characteristics of Science Fiction

Two additional points need to be remembered when reviewing the distinguishing characteristics of Science Fiction in Figure 4.5 on page 126.[37] First, Science Fiction is about science and the future. Second, Science Fiction "isn't about reality; it is about sharpening our understanding of reality."[38]

Notable Science Fiction

Both Edgar Allan Poe and Jules Verne influenced the development of Science Fiction. Although Poe's time travel writings were published before Verne's writings, Verne is recognized as the "Father of Science Fiction."[39] In the early 1900s, pulp and fan magazines and Hollywood movie

"You ought to be ashamed of yourself!"

producers controlled the subgenre. By the 1940s, Science Fiction had become a commercial, though not a literary success. It was not until after World War II that scholarly study of Science Fiction began.[40]

In 1947 Robert Heinlein wrote *Rocket Ship Galileo*, considered to be the first American juvenile Science Fiction to merit serious attention.[41] Ninety-nine juvenile titles were published by 1976. By 1987 the number had increased to 180.[42] By 1995 the number had increased to a total of 287 juvenile Science Fiction books.[43]

Young people, aged ten years or older, may express an interest in Science Fiction. Several factors influence the popularity of the subgenre. First, children are more likely to enjoy Science Fiction if they discover books written by recognized authors who have strengthened the literary merit of the subgenre, such as Robert Heinlein, Isaac Asimov, Ray Bradbury, John Christopher, Madeleine L'Engle, Robert O'Brien, H. M. Hoover, William Sleator, Pamela Service, Pamela Sargent, and Annabel and Edgar Johnson.

(text continues on page 128)

TABLE 4.5 Notable High Fantasy

DATE	AUTHOR, TITLE	COMMENTS
1865	L. Carroll, *Alice's Adventures in Wonderland*	Perfect example of a nonsensical fantasy adventure; intended to entertain Alice Liddell and her sisters. The first dream fantasy in children's literature, it is filled with puns, imaginary creatures, and adventures.
1871	L. Carroll, *Through the Looking-Glass and What Alice Found There*	Sophisticated entry to a reverse world; a tightly controlled game of chess with unforgettable characters, tricks, and gadgets.
1900	L. F. Baum, *The Wizard of Oz*	Fresh and inventive, the first fully created imaginative world. The quest story features Dorothy who is blown from Kansas by a cyclone to the land of Oz where she meets many memorable characters. Dorothy is courageous, caring, and determined to succeed—the ultimate American child of the Western frontier. This is the first of fourteen Oz books by Baum. The first two books are the best in his series. Other people wrote twenty-seven other books, which are questionable and inconsistent.
1904	J. M. Barrie, *Peter and Wendy* (retitled *Peter Pan,* 1911)	First appearing as an adult novelette, then as a play, and finally as a book, it tells the adventures of Peter Pan, the half-fairy boy, ruler of Never-land, who lures the Darling children by promising them an opportunity to fly to his land. Playful childlike characters and adventures mixed with social commentary.
1937	J. R. R. Tolkien, *The Hobbit* "Lord of the Ring" trilogy:	The first book is an adventure set in a perfectly believable secondary world. It tells of the unassuming hobbit, Bilbo Baggins, who is forced into an exciting, yet dangerous quest to help thirteen dwarfs recover their gold. Incidents are loosely joined to develop Bilbo's character. The trilogy contains complex moral overtones and memorable characters representing distinctive characteristics of fantasy.
1954	*The Fellowship of the Ring*	
1955	*The Two Towers*	
1956	*The Return of the King*	
1951	C. S. Lewis, Chronicles of Narnia:	Seven books of Narnia portray desirable elements of fantasy literature. The narrations are based on folk literature. Narnia is believable; the secondary world is clearly described and internal consistency is achieved. The large number of characters are recognizable from one book to another. Lewis's philosophy is evident in these books written for children. The tone is not didactic; the well-drawn children move easily from home to Narnia, and then back home; the characters do not possess magical powers, yet fantastic events occur. Lewis influenced future fantasy literature. Read *The Magician's Nephew* first, then *The Lion, the Witch, and the Wardrobe* (the most popular title).
1951	*The Lion, the Witch, and the Wardrobe*	
1951	*Prince Caspian: The Return to Narnia*	
1952	*The Voyage of the "Dawn Treader"*	
1953	*The Silver Chair*	
1954	*The Horse and His Boy*	
1955	*The Magician's Nephew*	
1956	*The Last Battle*	
1952	M. Norton, *The Borrowers* series:	Five books about a miniature world and its inhabitants. The borrowers are little people six inches high; they live on the "borrowings" of big people and do not want to be seen by them. Arrietty is seen by the boy, learns from him, and saves her people. Dramatic tension in believable narratives.
1955	*The Borrowers Afield*	
1959	*The Borrowers Afloat*	
1961	*The Borrowers Aloft*	
1982	*The Borrowers Avenged*	
1964	L. Alexander, *The Prydain* series:	An American fantasist has created a popular series, loosely based on a Welsh legend, set in a credible, medieval Prydain. The characters experience plausible magic. Through the descriptive series, Taran searches for his identity and maturity. See also Alexander's other fantasy adventures such as *Westmark* (1981), *The Kestral* (1982), and *The Beggar Queen* (1984).
1964	*The Book of Three*	
1965	*The Black Cauldron*	
1966	*The Castle of Lyr*	
1967	*Taran Wanderer*	
1968	*The High King*	
1968	U. Le Guin, *A Wizard of Earthsea*	The first of the Earthsea trilogy explores the search for maturity and the battle between good and evil. Earthsea, a credible Secondary World, contains magic controlled by the wizards. This book is less abstract than later books in the trilogy. The theme and the protagonist, Ged, are well-developed. Le Guin, a noted wordsmith, incorporates Asian philosophy and religion, especially Zen and Taoism, in her books, which are popular adult reading.
1969	P. Dickinson, *The Weathermonger*	Combining technology and legend, this first book in the Changes trilogy describes a contemporary England that has been changed to a preindustrial era. Geoffrey must find out why England has changed. Fast-paced narratives.
1969	*Heartsease*	
1970	*The Devil's Children* (last two classified as Science Fiction)	

TABLE 4.5 Notable High Fantasy (*Continued*)

DATE	CREATOR, TITLE	COMMENTS
1973	S. Cooper, *The Dark Is Rising*	A popular quest series, focusing on love, high and wild magic, and conflicts and battles
1965	*Over Sea, Under Stone*	between good and evil. Well-drawn characters engage in fantasy adventures set in the
1975	*The Grey King*	British Isles and other worlds. This master storyteller is influenced by Arthurian tales.
1974	*Greenwitch*	
1977	*Silver on the Tree*	
1985	R. McKinley, *The Hero and the Crown*	Dragonslayer, Lady Aerin, realizes she must overcome many adversaries to win her crown, return to her people, and rule them wisely. Includes dragons, spells, enchantments,
1982	*The Blue Sword*	witches, and magicians; excellent characterizations.
1982	M. A. Pierce, *The Darkangel*	A young woman is kidnapped to be the bride of a "vampyre." Her servant Aeriel is cap-
1984	*The Gathering of Gargoyles*	tured while attempting to save her mistress. Aeriel discovers the vampyre's secret and is
1989	*The Pearl of the Soul of the World*	the only one who can save the world. In this imaginative, fantasy romance, set in future time on the moon, the forces of good and evil battle. Outstanding High Fantasy.
1987	B. Jacques, *Redwall*	In this popular series, a band of good animals inhabit the land around Redwall Abbey and
1988	*Mossflower*	through a series of adventures protect themselves and their land against evil enemies.
1990	*Mattimeo*	The books are filled with many battles, complicated perils, despicable enemies, brave
1992	*Mariel of Redwall*	warriors, desperate rescues, unexpected allies, deeply mourned deaths, grand celebra-
1993	*Salamandastron*	tions, hearty feasts, humorous characters, suspense, and clever tactics.
1994	*Martin the Warrior*	
1995	*The Bellmaker*	

TABLE 4.6 Suggested LRMs for High Fantasy

This subgenre is set primarily in the Secondary World. The narratives are epic in scope and contain legendary heroes (objects/events) who may receive help from supernatural or magic creatures. While reading or listening to High Fantasy selections, students could react to the book by creating LRMs such as the following:

Each student will write an original history of his or her last name. Place information books on etymology in the literature center. Students will draw a coat of arms on a shield, representing information about their name. The written history and coat of arms will be placed on a banner. Hang the banners in a prominent place in the school.

Using various media, individuals or groups will draw scenes of the secondary world portrayed in a narrative.

Students will prepare a travel brochure to entice others to visit the land by reading the book.

Individuals will write a diary entry for a week (or longer) for a fanciful character. In the diary describe the character's feelings and behavior.

Young people will debate an issue presented in the selection, such as why Aerin in Robin McKinley's *The Hero and the Crown* should slay the dragon and if her actions were appropriate to regain the crown. Alternatively, debate the writer's ability to help the reader believe the fanciful elements included in the book.

Students will find a comic book or cartoon set in another world, such as "Prince Valiant." They will analyze and discuss the text and visuals used by the artist. In groups students will write another incident for a High Fantasy selection or rewrite a favorite incident. They will then reproduce an incident using language, visuals, and a format similar to that used by the cartoonist.

Learners will prepare a story map of an incident. At the top of a large sheet of paper, draw a large box; in the middle of the paper, draw a large sketch of an object representing the narrative; at the bottom of the page, draw another box. Use arrows to join the boxes and outline. In the top box, list the major characters and three words representing their personalities. In the middle box, sketch write major events in chronological order. In the bottom box, write the conclusion of the incident. For narratives with portals, sketch an outline of the portal in the middle box and list the events. Decorate the story map with sketches of content in the narrative. Discuss and then display the story maps.

Students will list the distinguishing criteria of High Fantasy on a large visual shaped like a castle, a shield, or another object representing the subgenre.

FIGURE 4.5   Distinguishing Literary Characteristics of Science Fiction

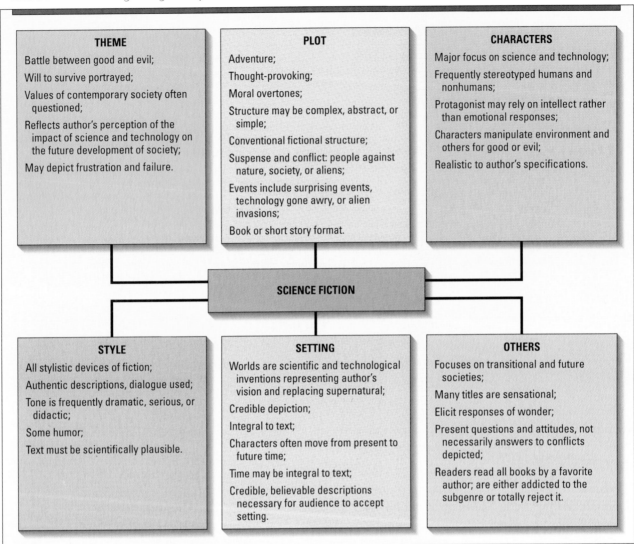

THEME

Battle between good and evil;

Will to survive portrayed;

Values of contemporary society often questioned;

Reflects author's perception of the impact of science and technology on the future development of society;

May depict frustration and failure.

PLOT

Adventure;

Thought-provoking;

Moral overtones;

Structure may be complex, abstract, or simple;

Conventional fictional structure;

Suspense and conflict: people against nature, society, or aliens;

Events include surprising events, technology gone awry, or alien invasions;

Book or short story format.

CHARACTERS

Major focus on science and technology;

Frequently stereotyped humans and nonhumans;

Protagonist may rely on intellect rather than emotional responses;

Characters manipulate environment and others for good or evil;

Realistic to author's specifications.

SCIENCE FICTION

STYLE

All stylistic devices of fiction;

Authentic descriptions, dialogue used;

Tone is frequently dramatic, serious, or didactic;

Some humor;

Text must be scientifically plausible.

SETTING

Worlds are scientific and technological inventions representing author's vision and replacing supernatural;

Credible depiction;

Integral to text;

Characters often move from present to future time;

Time may be integral to text;

Credible, believable descriptions necessary for audience to accept setting.

OTHERS

Focuses on transitional and future societies;

Many titles are sensational;

Elicit responses of wonder;

Present questions and attitudes, not necessarily answers to conflicts depicted;

Readers read all books by a favorite author; are either addicted to the subgenre or totally reject it.

TABLE 4.7   Notable Science Fiction

DATE	CREATOR, TITLE	COMMENTS
1863	J. Verne, *Five Weeks in a Balloon*	First romance of the future; adventure story motivated science discussion and invention; combined science and fancy.
1869–1871	*Twenty Thousand Leagues under the Sea*	Verne's best-known Science Fiction. Captain Nemo, an idealist and outlaw, wanted to harness the laws of nature in his romantic quest for vengeance. Verne's credible prediction of the future is impressive.
1876	L. P. Senarens, *The Steam Man of the Prairie*	First of a popular adventure series. Frank Reade, later Frank Reade, Jr., explored airships, submarines, armored cars, and other wonders around the world in search of buried treasures and islands haunted by the ghosts of shipwrecked sailors. Concerned with scientific, technological, and societal advancement.
1901	L. F. Baum, *The Master Key: An Electrical Fairy Tale*	Rob Joslyn accidentally summoned the Demon of Electricity who gave the boy various electrical and mechanical devices. After many adventures around the world with the devices, Rob returned them to the Demon because people were not wise enough to handle advanced technology. A pioneering attempt to adapt science to fantasy to create an American fairy tale.

TABLE 4.7 Notable Science Fiction (*Continued*)

DATE	CREATOR, TITLE	COMMENTS
1906	E. Nesbit, *The Story of the Amulet*	The first time travel fantasy written with contemporary children as characters.
1906	R. Rockwood, *Through the Air to the North Pole; or, The Wonderful Cruise of the Electric Monarch*	First of eight Great Marvel books. These Verne-like adventures surpassed Tom Swift in literary quality and imagination, but were not as popular.
1911	V. Appleton, *Tom Swift and His Electric Rifle*	First of 38 volumes dealing with young, inventive genius Tom Swift. Did not deal with space travel or other common topics of subgenre. These books of adventure were popular despite their predictable plots and stereotyped characters. The series reflected national values.
1933	N. Hunter, *The Incredible Adventures of Professor Branestawn*	One of eight books depicting the madcap professor; combined Science Fiction and fantasy; popular in Great Britain; included whimsy and spoofing of culture.
1947	W. P. du Bois, *The Twenty-One Balloons*	Newbery Medal winner. Professor Sherman makes a balloon tour over the Pacific and is forced down near Krakatoa, where he is invited to join a utopian group. He escapes after the eruption of the volcano. Humorous; well-written; imaginative.
1952	A. Norton, *Star Man's Son*	Author's first and best Science Fiction. Fors, a mutant, proves himself as Star Man, an explorer; set in postholocaust world.
1954	L. del Rey, C. Matschatt, and C. Carmer (Eds.), *The Year after Tomorrow: An Anthology of Science Fiction Stories*	First collection of Science Fiction stories written for youth.
1955	R. Heinlein, *Tunnel in the Sky*	Rod Walker and 49 classmates are sent to an unknown world for survival. They band together to form a new society and are forced back into teen roles. Contains stereotyped, sexist characters.
1962	M. L'Engle, *A Wrinkle in Time*	Newbery Medal winner. Fantasy–Science Fiction deals with struggles between good and evil. Meg's love saves her father. The book is well-written with developed characters and worthwhile themes.
1967	J. Christopher, *The White Mountain*	First volume in the Tripod trilogy. Tripods successfully invade Earth, but humans eventually triumph. Convincing future life in England; exciting, suspenseful journey.
1973	L. Yep, *Sweetwater*	Tyree is torn between a music career and obeying his father, the captain of the Silkies (descendants of starship crews from Earth), who attempt to survive on the water-bound planet Harmony. Descriptive, credible, narrative adventure that raises issues of ecology and a boy's rite of passage.
1983	P. Sargent, *Earthseed*	The narrator and her shipmates were born of genetic material and nurtured by their spaceship, Ship. They are sent to colonize a new world, but cannot survive without Ship's protection.
1988 1990	W. Sleator, *The Duplicate Strange Attractors*	David duplicates himself, and trouble begins when David A duplicates David B, leading to a fatal conclusion. The story continues in the next book.
1990	H. M. Hoover, *Away Is a Strange Place to Be*	In the 24th century, Abby and Bryan, a spoiled, self-centered boy, are kidnapped and forced to build a new habitat. They survive and escape together. A fast-paced story that emphasizes characterization and cooperation.
1988 1991 1995	G. Rubinstein, *Space Demons Skymaze Galax-Arena: A Novel*	A series of books about the adventures of a brother and sister with Skymaze, an ingenious computer game. In the last book, the siblings are kidnapped and forced to perform as gymnasts for the insectlike inhabitants of the planet Vexa.
1990 1991 1991	T. Pratchett, *Truckers Diggers Wings*	The Bromeliad Trilogy is a science fantasy about the adventures of "nomes," small four-inch-high replicas of humans. The nomes have lived hidden from humans for years while searching for a safe home. In the last book, they search for a spaceship waiting to receive nomes who live on earth. A popular, humorous, well-written series.
1993	L. Lowry, *The Giver*	This Newbery winner depicts a future society without poverty, inequality, and unemployment. From The Giver, Jonas acquires a conscience, emotions, color, and memory. He realizes he must change the society. Well-drawn characters and fearful events from a master storyteller.
1994	N. Farmer, *The Ear, the Eye, and the Arm: A Novel*	In the year 2194, parents hire detectives with unusual paranormal abilities and investigative techniques to search for kidnapped children who escape and are captured and recaptured several times. A suspense-filled story.

TABLE 4.8   Suggested LRMs for Science Fiction

The credibility of Science Fiction is based on the writer's ability to portray future worlds based on plausible scientific knowledge. The narratives often contain social commentary that examines the effects of technological progress. The protagonist struggles with technology gone wild or with alien forces. LRMs such as the following will highlight the distinctive characteristics of Science Fiction:

In groups students will read books about robots, such as Slote's *My Robot Buddy*. They will then construct a robot from boxes, cartons, Styrofoam balls, foil, pipe cleaners, and the like. They will name the robot and write an essay describing the robot's interaction with creatures from other Science Fiction materials. Students will give an oral presentation to another class.

Individuals will write "A Week in the Life of _____ (the robot), in the Year 2030." The events described in the robot's life must be authentic and plausible.

Students will research occupations available in the future and write a description for a job they would like to perform.

Students will predict and list their grandchildren's occupations, hobbies, lifestyles, clothes, and transportation.

Different groups will role-play what would happen if aliens invaded their hometown, home, or school. A class member will assume the role of an alien. Other students will interview the alien about hobbies, occupations, and lifestyles. The information used in the interview must be accurate information presented in a narrative. Use the information to introduce the alien to the principal, relatives, or friends.

The class will prepare a computer-generated newsletter reporting information about events and fanciful creatures in a selection or the information from the interviews. Include appropriate computer graphics in the newsletter. Distribute the newsletter to interested persons.

In triads, students will assume the role of a music director for a movie to be made of their favorite Science Fiction book. They will choose music for the filming of the book. Other students will assume the role of the costume director for the movie. They will research clothes worn by characters in the book. Use a montage technique to prepare the costumes for the movie.

The class will plan a 2020 Party in Space. Individual students will select a favorite character from a Science Fiction book. One group will design the appropriate background for the party, another will select the menu, another group will plan games to be played at the party, and another will find music the characters would enjoy hearing. Students will make these decisions based on information from selections. Students will make a mask representing their selected character. The class will have the party and invite other classes or administrators. At the party, individuals will tell about their characters, their lifestyle, and why the food, setting, games, and music were selected. Display artifacts and books in the media center.

Second, children who encounter popular Science Fiction movies and comic books may look for literary Science Fiction. Third, young people who are interested in societal, scientific, or technological changes and advances frequently enjoy Science Fiction. Authors often include topics, such as political abuses and mind control, theological speculations, sexism, the evils of racism, ecology, the demands of society, and individual freedoms.[44] Finally, young people who are interested in the exploration of space turn to Science Fiction for a different view of scientific speculations. Notable juvenile Science Fiction is listed in Table 4.7 on page 126.[45] Table 4.8 suggests LRMs for use with Science Fiction selections.

✺ FANTASY LITERATURE IN THE CLASSROOM

"Animals don't talk, teacher," announced a five-year-old boy to his teacher who was reading aloud from Kevin Henkes's *Owen*.

When young people encounter fantasy selections, they frequently ask, "Is that true?" Some children ask the question to confirm the literary genre and unconsciously assume an appropriate mind-set or stance to the selection. Some children know the narrative is fantasy, but want to be sure, for example, that a monster such as the one in Mercer Mayer's *There's a Nightmare in My Closet* (1968) will not invade their home. Others ask the question because they have not had a balanced exposure to all literary genres and do not know the differences between fantasy, realistic fiction, and nonfiction literature.

The age of the reader does not determine whether the person will accept or reject a fantasy selection. C. S. Lewis said that the division of books by age fits the needs of publishers but does not necessarily reflect a child's reading habits or abilities.[46] Children usually react to fanciful selections on an emotional level, whereas adults typically react on an analytical level. Fantasy literature is appealing to individuals if they can differentiate between real and make-believe and if they accept the fanciful images described by the author. The literary merit, the format of the book or short story, and the way the narrative is presented also influence the person's acceptance of the fantasy.

Since the 1970s distinguished authorities have expressed some hesitation about using fantasy literature with young people. Generally, the concerns focus on the belief that fantasy literature encourages the reader to escape from reality and turn to magical events and creatures for guidance. By looking at both sides of the issues, as presented in the next section, a knowledgeable adult can select appropriate techniques and strategies to use when presenting fantasy literature in the classroom.

CONCERNS ABOUT USING FANTASY LITERATURE

Interest in literary genres frequently reflects the conditions in society at large. For example, when people are experiencing major changes in their personal lifestyles, they may question social institutions, such as religion or government, and turn to stories about the wisdom of life or myths and enchantment for answers. Unfortunately, as Joseph Campbell laments, we live in a demythologized world without the guidelines or rituals of a society that is aware of established patterns of behavior, which can lead to destructive behavior.[47] Fantasy literature deals with the substance of myth: the protagonist searches for a particular ideal or object and eventually, after various unsuccessful and successful experiences, achieves the goal and returns home a wiser person. Fortunately, both writers and society at large recognize the need for stories about the wisdom of life and have shown a renewed interest in fantasy literature since the 1980s.

Most critics of fantasy literature dismiss it as an attempt to escape from the realities of everyday life. They feel that children who are encouraged to use their imaginations and explore created worlds with fanciful creatures will not be ready to face the problems they may encounter in the real world. According to this view, children should be encouraged to read about realistic situations that will prepare them for the real world. C. S. Lewis responded to this idea by pointing out that the typical realistic story revolves around immediate wish fulfillment, such as the desire for wealth, a fancy car, or eternal love. In contrast, fantasy narratives give young people ideals and goals to attain later in life and alternative ways to cope with problems. Through these vicarious experiences, the reader gains a new perspective on the real world.[48] Psychologists Bruno Bettelheim and Rollo May caution that children who do not have an opportunity to explore magical lands and vicariously experience ways to solve difficult problems in fantasy literature frequently escape reality through drug-induced dreams or other hallucinatory experiences. Then, when faced with the harsh reality they may encounter as teenagers and adults, they are not adequately prepared to solve their problems successfully.[49]

Another concern, expressed by some notable scholars, is that the supernatural creatures and magical events portrayed in some fantasy narratives will frighten children and cause them to react in violent ways. Obviously, children react differently to the magical elements in the literature. However, children who have prior experiences with literature feel safe when they encounter witches and ogres because they know the creatures are in the world of the book and do not inhabit the children's world. Several studies have shown that children with rich fantasy experiences reacted to play activities and confrontations in a creative, verbal manner rather than in a physically aggressive way. Children with little experience with fantasy displayed little thought and had a tendency to react in a more physical manner.[50]

In addition to these general concerns, certain groups object to specific content of fantasy literature. Many books of fantasy have come under attack, but the criticisms leveled at two very popular fantasists, Roald Dahl and R. L. Stine, are typical. (Additional information about criticism of all literary genres is presented in Appendix G.) Dahl has been criticized for making racial slurs in *Charlie and the Chocolate Factory* (1964); using sexist, stereotyped images; fostering sadism, especially in *Matilda* (1988); including too much violence; ridiculing society (especially adults); and his tendency to annihilate adults as seen in the first page of his book *James and the Giant Peach* (1961). Dahl's books are linked to folk literature and should be analyzed as such. He contended that as a fantasist, he portrayed stereotyped characters who exhibit obvious good or bad traits and behavior. As a result of decisions made by the characters, justice prevails—the good characters receive rewards and the bad characters get the punishment they deserve. Dahl felt his books showed how good and bad people behave and helped children develop moral judgment. Dahl had confidence in his readers and felt they would understand that the violence was not real and was reserved to the book.

Recently, preteens and teenagers have discovered R. L. Stine. They are rushing to the bookstore to find his latest books and to the mall for book bags, costumes, and other merchandise covered with Goosebumps. Stine developed his ghost stories to entice boys to read and he has achieved his goal! He has now published more than two hundred juvenile horror novels similar to the works of Stephen King. With more than thirty Goosebump Books such as *Welcome to Dead House* (1992), written for eight to twelve year olds, and more than forty Fear Street Books such as *The House of Evil: The First Horror* (1994), for twelve to fifteen year olds, Stine has flooded the market with "scary" books. Stine feels that the real world is much scarier to children than the world he writes about. He wants his books to entertain children, not frighten them. Some adults are concerned that receiving a steady diet of violence from the books could numb children's compassion and encourage them to emulate the violent behavior. For this reason, horror novels could present a problem. Obviously, as long as the books are popular and financially successful, recognized authors will create

Molly Bang moves from realistic art, as seen in this picture, to surrealistic art and returns to realistic images in her book, The Grey Lady and the Strawberry Snatcher. *Through mixed media collage and full color paintings, Bang shows the interaction between the Grey Lady and the Strawberry Snatcher. Her full-color, realistic paintings show the details of the environment, while her surrealistic art shows large areas of empty spaces, with objects that are almost hidden. What do you think is under the Snatcher's feet?*

them, and publishers will continue to issue them. To avoid problems, teachers should sample the books their children are reading and present a variety of other appealing fantasy selections.[51]

Another issue of concern is the way females are portrayed in literature in general, but especially in fantasy literature. Beginning in the late 1970s, two major questions emerged: What common themes, content, and concerns are shared by female writers but not expressed by male writers? How many female protagonists reflect diverse cultural values rather than the stereotypical female behavior and attitudes expected in traditional societies? Concerned individuals are analyzing all literature to answer these questions.[52]

Perhaps more than other groups of writers, individual fantasists write in professional journals. In these articles they discuss reasons for writing fantasy, repudiate critics of the genre, and suggest inherent reasons for exploring fantasy literature. These essays help clarify various aspects of fanciful literature and provide insights into the thinking of the writers. This information can help adults understand children's reactions to the genre and guide our presentation of fantasy literature.

To use fantasy literature effectively, teachers need to be knowledgeable about the genre, understand the benefits students gain from exploring fantasy literature, be familiar with guidelines for selecting quality fantasy literature, and be able to select a suitable instructional focus and strategies to use with fantasy selections. The rest of the chapter focuses on these aspects of planning and presenting fantasy literature in the classroom.

BENEFITS GAINED FROM EXPLORING FANTASY LITERATURE

Pure delight and entertainment are the foremost purposes for exploring fantasy literature. *The Grey Lady and the Strawberry Snatcher* (1980), a wordless book created by Molly Bang, is an ideal book of fantasy to use with children aged six through eleven years. (See Bang color plate.) Through the visual narrative, the viewer is amazed by the ability of the Grey Lady to trick the Strawberry Snatcher. The illustrations move from a real world setting to an imaginary world and back to the real world and a satisfying ending. Bang guides the viewer to form mental images to link

TABLE 4.9 Benefits Gained from Exploring Fantasy Literature

Exploring fantasy literature is a pleasurable and entertaining experience.

Children typically invent and tell fantasy stories; thus, fantasy is a natural literature for children.

Individuals use their imagination to visualize the ideas and wonder presented in fantasy literature.

Children who have rich experiences with fantasy literature invent more creative and structured stories than those with limited exposure to fantasy.

As individuals explore conflicts and sorrow through fantasy literature, they gain hope and the capacity to believe.

Fantasy literature stimulates divergent thinking such as "what if?" which is essential for scientific inquiry, creative problem solving, and original thinking.

The language fantasists use, such as metaphors, similes, irony, and symbolism, stimulates the mind and enhances language development. Generally, children with rich fantasy experiences have a larger expressive vocabulary and use a variety of language patterns to express their thoughts.

When young people explore fantasy literature, they are introduced to various options that help them select appropriate ways to react to situations they encounter in the real world.

Fantasy literature is an effective way to explore answers to cultural, social, and philosophical issues, such as good versus evil and caring for others. Generally, individuals use this information when they interact with others.

Children with rich fantasy experiences react verbally rather than physically to situations they encounter.

TABLE 4.10 Guidelines for Selecting Fantasy Literature

Distinctive Characteristics of the Genre/Subgenres

As is expected of all books of fiction, quality fantasy literature contains a worthwhile theme; an action-packed, suspense-filled plot with a suitable introduction, logical events, and a satisfactory conclusion; believable characters; an interesting, appealing story; language that evokes images; and an identifiable setting. In addition, distinctive literary criteria unique to the genre such as the following are considered:

Does the author create a credible environment that naturally encourages the audience to suspend belief in the real world and continue to accept the author's creation throughout the book? For example, does the writer establish behaviors, lifestyles, and traditions that remain consistent throughout the Secondary World?

Does the author clearly describe the setting?

Do the characters behave and interact in a believable manner within the primary world or the Secondary World?

Is the quest, survival, or conflict possible in the world created by the author? Are the events dramatic, exciting, and suspenseful?

In Science Fiction, does the author extrapolate scientific facts to develop the plot and the characters' actions? Are the events scientifically plausible? Are questions about the future scientifically plausible?

Are the interactions among the real, fanciful, and scientific elements possible and plausible?

Are the plot and theme original? Are the fanciful elements used in a unique manner?

Do the illustrations enhance, supplement, interpret, or replace the verbal narrative?

Age-Appropriate Content

Will the audience understand and question the characters' motivation?

Will the audience be able to distinguish fanciful elements, hypothetical propositions, and reality?

If applicable, will the audience recognize the movement of the characters from one world to another?

Will the book evoke wonder?

Will the fanciful or supernatural elements frighten young people unnecessarily?

If violence is included, is it anticipated and acceptable within the context of the story?

Will the book naturally evoke aesthetic reactions?

---

with her visual images, a process that leads the viewer to feel a sense of wonder.

Without using a didactic tone, successful fantasists evoke a sense of wonder in the reader, make the impossible seem possible, and shed light on the hidden realities of the human mind and heart. These images exercise the mind and stimulate the reader's imagination. Jane Langston reminds us that "fantasy gives us a dream back to keep . . . it feeds a hunger we didn't know we had."[53] Langston achieves these goals in *The Diamond in the Window* (1962) and *The Fledgling* (1980), which tell the story of the Hall family and their mystical adventures.

In this literary genre, fanciful creatures may exist in another world, yet universal concerns and truths existing in all worlds are authentically portrayed within the parameters created by the fantasist. Fantasy gives an individual the freedom to explore a range of topics, such as love, courage, justice, and survival, outside the constraints of personal reality. Table 4.9 lists some benefits individuals gain from exploring fantasy literature.[54]

GUIDELINES FOR SELECTING FANTASY LITERATURE

When selecting quality fantasy literature, the teacher considers several factors, such as the distinctive characteristics of fantasy literature, the distinguishing characteristics of each subgenre, and the suitability of the content to the students' age. Selection criteria are written in question form in Table

4.10 on page 131. To aid in the selection, a variety of questions are suggested for each category, but it is unlikely that all questions will be used when choosing a fantasy selection.

INSTRUCTIONAL FOCUSES, TECHNIQUES, AND STRATEGIES

Researchers have found that the ability to fantasize is a personality characteristic that becomes part of a person's cognitive lifestyle. By the time a child is five years old, this trait is almost formed. Nevertheless, we can help children further develop their ability to fantasize and use their imaginations through creative play, dramatic activities, writing original stories, retelling stories or excerpts, positive adult models, audio and visual experiences, and various fantasy literature. Thus, by presenting fantasy literature, we are helping young people become divergent, flexible thinkers and creative problem solvers.[55]

Fantasy literature is the "literature of the mind."[56] As we know, fantasy literature is successful if the reader accepts the writer's creation and is willing to believe the writer throughout the book or story. The reader assumes a predominantly aesthetic stance toward the selection, reacting spontaneously to the "lived-through" experience evoked by the visual and verbal narratives. When reacting to a story or book, children might use verbal or nonverbal expressions: For example, a sense of *wonder* might elicit "Wow!" *Delight* might be expressed as "I like the way. . . ." *Disbelief* might elicit "Do you really think that could happen that way? I don't!" Finally, the children might remain *silent* while reflecting on the ideas presented in the text.

Spontaneous reactions and responses thrive in a classroom where the teacher assumes an *aesthetic instructional focus* (see Chapter 2). When we use this instructional focus, we respect individuals' natural, emotional, and subjective responses to literature. Young people enjoy reading, listening to, and viewing fantasy literature if the selection is interesting, the content is appealing, and the narrative is appropriate to the children's cognitive development.[57] Techniques such as the following elicit an aesthetic focus and can be used effectively when presenting fantasy literature in the classroom:

Read aloud fantasy selections. This technique helps students develop a positive attitude toward the genre and introduces them to selections they might not choose to read independently. Young, less mature students enjoy hearing and viewing stories and poems that border on fantasy. Older, more mature students enjoy sophisticated narratives that slightly frighten and evoke reflections and natural reactions.

Give *book talks* about selected fantasy literature and the genre.

Encourage peer and teacher interactions by discussing personal interpretations of a selection.

While students are reading, viewing, or discussing the selection, if applicable, *clarify* the narrative and *stimulate* the students' anticipation, prediction, and confirmation of events. Use techniques such as prompts, prediction visuals, and writing reflections, and compare the illustrations used for the same tale or subgenre.

Choose fantasy literature for your *personal classroom reading.*

Include appropriate fantasy literature in *thematic units,* LitSets.

Display pictures and regalia that represent fanciful creatures or content portrayed in the fantasy literature shared with students.

Provide *information books* related to the topic for reference. For example, Eve Bunting's *The Night of the Gargoyles* (1994) tells about the nighttime adventures of stone gargoyles that embellish a museum's facade. The gargoyles come to life, gossip, lounge in the fountain, frighten a watchman, and generally enjoy life during the night. David Wiesner's gray illustrations help interpret Bunting's humorous, yet slightly frightening verbal narrative. (See Bunting color plate on page 133.) Because many children do not know what gargoyles are or how they are used, it might be helpful to have information books about gargoyles when presenting this book.

Other techniques such as the following are compatible with an aesthetic instructional focus. These techniques help the learners understand the fantasy genre and evoke belief in a narrative:

Slowly direct students through a *visualization activity.* Begin by saying to the students, "Close your eyes. Think about the most beautiful place you have seen or would like to see." (You may need to describe a place.) "Try to relax and concentrate on the scene. Smell the odors, and feel the wind on your face. Look ahead, something is approaching. What is it?" (At this point describe the appearance of a fanciful creature or an event similar to one in the book. Guide students through an interaction with the event or creature.) Students will open their eyes and talk about the experience: "Were you able to visualize the creature (or event)? Why? Did you touch it? How did it feel? What could you do with it? What did it smell like in the other world?"

till night comes.

David Wiesner uses gray and white water color to create the realistic stone gargoyles for Eve Bunting's Night of the Gargoyles. *The artist uses shape and color to effectively enhance the verbal narrative.*

Explain that fantasists usually imagine "in their mind's eye" and design an environment where the fanciful elements can authentically exist. For example, if a narrative is set in the Secondary World, the geography, the characters, their behavior, and even their dress must be consistent with the rules governing this world. If the writer does not retain "internal consistency," the reader will not believe the writer and will not accept the fantasy elements.

Use techniques such as "Thinking Aloud" to model your belief in fanciful elements. This role modeling demonstrates how you accept the fanciful elements and are willing to believe in the narrative. The technique gives the students permission to believe in the impossible. It also shows them how to assume a "secondary belief" in the fantasy selections.

Be prepared to facilitate students' questions and reactions to help them believe in fantasy elements by using *probes* similar to the following: "Are you glad a creature such as this doesn't live in our town? How did you feel when you heard or read about _____ (fanciful setting, creatures, a fanciful element)? Do you think _____ (the protagonist) behaved properly in this situation? How did _____ (the protagonist) know how to outwit _____ (the antagonist)?"

After the previous discussion, help students interact personally with the characters, by asking *prompts*, such as the following: "How would your life change if a dinosaur lived in your neighborhood?" "What would you do if you had magical powers? Why?" "What if others behaved differently, such as . . . ?" "If _____ (the protagonist) asked your opinion about outwitting _____ (the antagonist), what would you tell him or her?"

TABLE 4.11   Suggested Integrated LRMs for Fantasy Literature

---

The two LRMs suggested here represent the integrated use of visual and verbal modalities.

1. Organize the class into groups. Each group will design a world. This world may be similar to one or several encountered in fantasy literature. To design the world, the groups will:

    Write a description of the world, include the geographic setting, climate and seasons, occupations of the people, the government, hobbies, games played by the children, and the like.

    Prepare a mural or other large visual of the world.

    Read their description and display the mural. The class will select several worlds to complete:

    Prepare a tableaux showing the main setting for the world.

    Dress dolls in the typical dress of the people.

    Display the people in their occupations, hobbies, or schools.

    Invent a written alphabet; write a short narrative in the language.

    After completing the world, display the tableaux, related books, and a description of the world, and share with other classes. Display later in the media center.

2. Watch a television program, cartoon, or movie that includes fantasy elements. Record information about the following:

    Is the information plausible?

    Is the plot logical? Plausible? Consistent?

    How do the sound and visual effects influence the story?

    Why do you believe the fantasy? If not, why?

    If the media production is based on a book learners have read, discuss the similarities and differences. Do you prefer the media production or the book? Why?

    Analyze and discuss with a group who watched the same production.

    Write a Critic's Review of the media production. (See Chapter 10 for information about critiquing audiovisual media.)

    Critique the plot, characters, actors, setting, and other fanciful elements.

    Suggest books to read on a similar topic. Rate the production.

    Organize Critics' Reviews in a fanciful movie or TV newsletter.

    Distribute related books in the media center.

    Present a daily review on the school TV program.

Literary Response Modes for Fantasy Literature

Students may want to express further reactions to the genre or narratives by producing *Literary Response Modes (LRMs)*. (See Chapter 2 and Appendix B for additional information about LRMs.) An individual or group production of an LRM promotes students' honest responses to a fantasy narrative. In addition to the LRMs suggested for each such genre, students may choose to produce responses such as the following:

Select a favorite incident and read it to another.

Give a book talk to entice another to read the selection.

Discuss personal reactions to a selection with someone familiar with a narrative.

Write personal reflections evoked by the selection in a journal.

Fold a piece of paper in quarters or sixths and label each section with the following headings: setting, characters, conflicts, language, questions about the narrative, or other concerns. While reading or hearing the selection, students will write one- or two-word reactions to each element. Later, use the reactions for discussion and comparison.

Teachers can use fantasy literature in various content areas. Have groups of students create visual products that are authentic to the topic and might be found in literature selections. The following are possibilities:

Sketch several favorite incidents.

Prepare a game board with questions that are documented in content materials.

Construct a village, castle, or other environment from the selection.

Prepare a Character Attribute Chart to identify personalities. Based on information from content area materials, decide if the characterization is influenced by fantasy or reality. Note: Major events (lifestyle) can be listed and designated as fact or fantasy. Rate the author's ability to be internally consistent or scientifically plausible throughout the book.

Draw the setting or other fanciful elements using crayon resist, watercolor, or media suggesting fantasy. Compare fanciful elements to realistic drawings or photos of similar settings or persons.[58]

Table 4.11 on page 134 presents two more LRMs that can be used while exploring fantasy literature. Modify the LRMs based on the students' anticipated reactions to a selection, the instructional goals, and responses naturally generated by a selection.

Summary

Imaginary narratives containing marvels that evoke wonder are classified as fantasy literature. The success of the fantasy narrative depends on the author's ability to consistently manipulate the setting, time, characters, and objects and to turn reality around precisely 180°, so that the audience, based on their understanding of reality, will willingly assume a belief in the impossible and become absorbed in the creation.

Literary Fairy Tales, a subgenre of fantasy literature, are the bridge between folk literature and fantasy literature. These short original tales are the creations of writers who use the creatures, content, and literary structure of traditional oral literature to produce Literary Fairy Tales. The tales are published in picture books and short story collections.

Short stories and book-length fanciful stories are classified as either *Low Fantasy* or *High Fantasy*. This designation refers *only* to the setting of the narratives. Fantasy stories set primarily in the real world are classified as Low Fantasy. Fantasy stories set primarily in another Secondary World are classified as High Fantasy.

The setting is a major element of the stories, and writers must retain internal consistency in their narratives. Each subgenre also has other distinctive characteristics, however. For example, writers of Low Fantasy must portray the interaction between real and fanciful elements to help the reader accept their existence in the real world. Authors of High Fantasy are free to design an entirely new world that may contain legendary heroes and become epic in scope. The characters, creatures, and events, as well as the movement and portals between worlds and time, are limited to the parameters delineated by the writer. All fanciful stories must be internally consistent; that is, they must always authentically represent the primary or secondary setting. The fanciful elements must be credible to the reader, who, for the moment, accepts the impossible as possible.

The fourth subgenre, *Science Fiction*, includes narratives expressing the author's concerns about the potential power and influence of science and technology on future known and unexplored worlds. Science Fiction writers must authentically portray scientific, technological, and sociological issues so that the audience perceives their inventions as acceptable and plausible.

Fantasy literature can become a vital part of the classroom if the teacher is knowledgeable about selecting quality fantasy literature, understands the relationship between the learner and the literary genre, and knows appropriate instructional stances and suitable techniques to highlight the genre. This chapter has presented information about the distinctive characteristics of the four subgenres of fantasy literature, notable literature available for classroom use, and instructional focuses, techniques, strategies, and LRMs to strengthen the interaction between young people and fantasy literature.

Fantasy literature reflects the author's vision. If the narrative is successful, it captures the imagination of the audience, who willingly moves, for a while, into an environment containing fantasy elements invented through the mind of the writer. By exploring fantasy literature together, the creator/author and the audience reveal *the mirror of the mind.*

NOTES

Introductory dialogue written by Frances S. Goforth.

1. Coleridge, W. T. 1817. (1975 printing). *Biographia Literaria*. London: J. M. Dent. 168–69.

2. Tolkien, J. R. R. 1947. On fairy-stories. This seminal essay originally appeared in *Essays Presented to Charles Williams*. Oxford: Oxford University Press. The essay was included in Tolkien's *Tree and Leaf*. 1964. London: Unwin. In 1966 the essay was published in *The Tolkien Reader*. 1966. New York: Ballantine. 36. The theoretical discussion represents Tolkien's philosophy about fairy-stories or fantasy. The essay is quoted extensively and is highly recommended for persons interested in fantasy literature.

3. Carroll, L. (Introduction and notes by M. Gardner). 1960. *The Annotated Alice*. Illus. J. Tenniel. New York: Clarkston N. Potter. 287.

4. Rabkin, E. S. 1976. *The Fantastic in Literature*. Princeton, N.J.: Princeton University Press. 189.

5. Wolfe, G. 1986. *Critical Terms for Science Fiction and Fantasy*. New York: Greenwood Press. 38–40. Wolfe presents twenty-three definitions of fantasy literature.

6. Heinlein, R. A. 1959. Science fiction: Its nature, faults, and virtues. 23. In Davenport, B., Heinlein, R. A., Kornbluth, C. M., Bester, A., & Bloch, R. *The Science Fiction Novel: Imagination and Social Criticism*. Chicago: Advent Publishers.

7. Alexander, L. 1968. Wishful thinking—or hopeful dreaming? *The Horn Book Magazine*. 44(4). August. 383–90.

8. Irwin, W. R. 1976. *The Game of the Impossible: The Rhetoric of Fantasy*. Urbana, Ill.: University of Illinois Press. 4.

9. Rabkin, E. S. 1976. 28.

10. Schmerl, R. 1961. Reason's dream: Anti-totalitarian themes and techniques of fantasy. *Dissertation Abstracts*. 21. 2298.

11. Manlove, C. N. 1986. The elusiveness of fantasy. In *The Shape of the Fantastic*. Westport, Conn.: Greenwood Press. 54. This definition originally appeared in his book, *Modern Fantasy: Five Studies*. Cambridge: Cambridge University Press. 1975. Each component of the definition is discussed in the 1986 publication.

12. Wolfe, G. 1986. 38.

13. Woolsey, D. 1989. Dreams and wishes: Fantasy literature for children. In Hickman, J., & Cullinan, B. (Eds.). *Children's Literature in the Classroom: Weaving Charlotte's Web*. Needham Heights, Mass.: Christopher-Gordon. 109–19.

14. Hunter, M. 1975. *Talent Is Not Enough*. New York: Harper & Row. 59.

15. Tolkien, J. R. R. 1966. 71.

16. Tolkien, J. R. R. 1966. 48–49.

17. Wolfe, G. 1986. Introduction, xviii.

18. Lewis, C. S. 1963. On three ways of writing for children. *The Horn Book Magazine*. 39(5). October. 462. This essay is often quoted and is highly recommended for adults interested in fantasy literature.

19. Egoff, S. 1981. *Thursday's Child*. Chicago: American Library Association. 83.

20. Cooper, S. 1981. Escaping into ourselves. In Hearne, B., & Kaye, B. (Eds.). *Celebrating Children's Books*. New York: Lothrop. 22.

21. Babbitt, N. 1970. Happy endings? Of course, and also joy. *The New York Times Book Review*. November 8. 1, 50.

22. For additional information about the distinctive characteristics of fantasy literature, see sources such as Cook, E. 1969. *The Ordinary and the Fabulous*. Cambridge: Cambridge University Press; Egoff, S. 1967. *The Republic of Childhood*. Toronto: Oxford University Press. 133, 134; Le Guin, U. K. 1979. *The Language of the Night: Essays on Fantasy and Science Fiction*. Edited by S. Wood. New York: Putnam; Molson, F. J. 1989. *Children's Fantasy*. Mercer Island, Wash.: Starmont House; Yolen, J. 1981. *Touch Magic: Fantasy, Faerie and Folklore in the Literature of Childhood*. New York: Philomel Books.

23. For additional information about the various classifications of fantasy literature, see sources such as Aquino, J. 1977. *Fantasy in Literature*. Washington, D.C.: National Education Association. 24–26; Cameron, E. 1969. *The Green and Burning Tree*. Boston: Atlantic/Little, Brown. 3–134; Egoff, S. 1988. *Worlds Within: Children's Fantasy from the Middle Ages to Today*. Chicago: American Library Association. 5–14; Lukens, R. 1995. A *Critical Handbook of Children's Literature*. (5th Ed.). 20–23. New York: HarperCollins. See also sources cited in specific subgenres.

24. The following sources support two subdivisions of fantasy stories: Eyre, F. 1971. *British Children's Books in the Twentieth Century*. New York: Dutton. 116–17; Klingberg, G. 1976. The fantastic and the mythical as reading for modern children and young people. In *How Can Children's Literature Meet the Needs of Modern Children*. 15th IBBY Conference. 32; Waggonner, D. 1978. *The Hills of Faraway: A Guide to Fantasy*. New York: Atheneum; Tolkien, J. R. R. 1966. 37; Tymn, M. B., Zahorski, K. J., & Boyer, R. H. 1979. *Fantasy Literature: A Core Collection and Reference Guide*. New York: R. R. Bowker.

25. Lukens, R. 1995. 19–20; Woolsey, D. 1989.

26. For additional information about notable juvenile fantasy books, see sources such as Egoff, S. 1988; Lynn, R. H. 1995. *Fantasy Literature for Children and Young Adults*. New York: R. R. Bowker. xxxvii–xlvii; May, J. 1978. The American literary fairy tale and its classroom uses. *Journal of Reading*. November. 153–59; Molson, F. J. 1989; Townsend, J. R. 1996. *Written for Children: An Outline of English-Language Children's Literature*. Lanham, Md.: Scarecrow Press.

27. Sources such as the following have recommended fantasy literature: *The Bulletin of the Center for Children's Books*. Champaign, Ill.: University of Illinois. 1990–present; Egoff, S. 1988; *Horn Book Guide*. Boston: Horn Book Magazine. 1989–present; Jensen, J. M., & Rosen, N. L. (Eds.). 1993. *Adventuring with Books: A Booklist for Pre-K–Grade 6*. Urbana, Ill.: National Council of Teachers of English; various professional journals cited in Appendix G: author's reactions.

28. Zahorski, K. J., & Boyer, R. H. 1982. The secondary worlds of high fantasy. In Schlobin, R. C. (Ed.). *The Aesthetics of Fantasy Literature and Art*. Notre Dame, Ind.: University of Notre Dame Press and Harvester Press. 56–81.

29. Egoff, S. 1988. 9–14.

30. Alexander, L. 1975. High fantasy and heroic romance. In Heins, P. (Ed.). 1977. *Crosscurrents of Criticism*. Boston: Horn Book. 170–77.

31. Adults who want to know more about fantasy literature are encouraged to read Lewis's essay "On Three Ways of Writing for Children" (see note 18) and Tolkien's essay "On Fairy-Stories" in *The Tree and the Leaf* and *The Tolkien Reader* (see note 2).

32. Asimov, I. 1981. *Asimov on Science Fiction*. Garden City, N.Y.: Doubleday.

33. Gernsback, H. 1926. Cited in Scholes, R., & Rabkin, E. S. 1977. *Science Fiction: History, Science, Vision*. New York: Oxford University Press. 39.

34. Spinrad, N. 1974. *Modern Science Fiction*. Garden City, N.Y.: Anchor. Introduction.

35. Wolfe, G. 1986. 108.

36. Bova, B. 1975. *Through Eyes of Wonder: Science Fiction and Science*. New York: Addison Wesley. Cited in Jerauld, J. 1992. Out of this world. *Book Links*. 2(2). 29–31.

37. For additional information about the distinguishing characteristics of Science Fiction, see sources such as Aldiss, B. W. 1986. What should a science fiction novel be about? In Saciuk, O. H. (Ed.). *The Shape of the Fantastic*. Westport, Conn.: Greenwood Press. 235–47; Bova, B. 1981. *Notes to a Science Fiction Writer*. (2d Ed.). Boston: Houghton Mifflin; Daugherty, L. 1986. The response of wonder: Science fiction and literary theory. In Saciuk, O. H. (Ed.). 236–40; Egoff, S. 1969. Science fiction. In Egoff, S., Stubbs, G. T., & Ashley, L. F. (Eds.). *Only Connect*. Toronto: Oxford University Press. 384–98; Engdahl, S. L. 1971. The changing role of science fiction in children's literature. *Horn Book Magazine*. 47(5). October. 449–55; Heinlein, R. A. 1959. 17–63.

38. Aldiss, B. W. 1986. 247.

39. Pierce, J. J. 1987. In the beginning, also Verne and the Verneans. In *Foundations of Science Fiction*. Westport, Conn.: Greenwood Press. 27–39.

40. Aldiss, B. W. 1986. 221–22.

41. Molson, F. J. 1987. Children's and young adult science fiction. In Barron, N. (Ed.). *Anatomy of Wonder*. New York: R. R. Bowker. 329.

42. Barron, N. (Ed.). 1987. *Anatomy of Wonder*. New York: R. R. Bowker. vii.

43. See *Horn Book Guides*. June 1989 through December 1995.

44. Molson, F. J. 1987. 329–74. This chapter reviews the history and development of juvenile Science Fiction and gives an excellent selected annotated bibliography of 180 Science Fiction books for readers aged six through fifteen. Of this number, 56 titles were selected for a core list with 44 titles receiving the highest acclaim. 778–80.

45. For additional information about notable juvenile Science Fiction books, see sources such as Egoff, S. 1969. 384–98; Molson, F. J. 1987. 329–74; Lynn, R. H. 1995. xxxvii–xlvii; Pierce, J. J. 1987. 27, 33–37.

46. Lewis, C. S. 1963. 465.

47. Agena, K. 1983. Return of enchantment. *New York Times Magazine*. November 27. 80; Campbell, J., with B. Moyers. 1988. *The Power of Myth*. New York: Doubleday; Campbell, J. 1968. *Hero with a Thousand Faces*. (2d Ed.). Princeton, N.J.: Princeton University Press.

48. Lewis, C. S. 1963. 466.
49. Bettelheim, B. 1977. *The Uses of Enchantment: The Meaning and Importance of Fairy Tales.* New York: Vintage. 51; May, R. 1991. *The Cry for Myth.* New York: Delta. 15.
50. For a comprehensive discussion of objections to fantasy literature, see Tunnell, M. O. 1994. The double-edged sword: Fantasy and censorship. *Language Arts.* 71(8). December. 606–12. See also Biblow, E. 1973. Imaginative play and the control of aggressive behavior. In Singer, J. L. (Ed.). *The Child's World of Make-Believe.* New York: Academic Press. 104–28; Pulaski, M. A. 1974. The rich rewards of make believe. *Psychology Today.* 7(8). January. 70–72; Singer, J. L. 1968. The importance of daydreaming. *Psychology Today.* 2(11). April.
51. Campbell, P. 1994. The sand in the oyster. *The Horn Book Magazine.* 70(2). March/April.

234–38; Culley, J. 1991. Roald Dahl—"It's about children and it's for children"—but is it suitable? *Children's Literature in Education.* 22(1). 59–73.
52. For additional information about the issue, see sources such as Cranny-Francis, A. 1990. *Feminist Fiction: Feminist Uses of Generic Fiction.* New York: St. Martin's Press; Hatfield, L. 1993. From master to brother: Shifting the balance of authority in Ursula K. Le Guin's *Farthest Shore* and *Tehaun.* In *Children's Literature.* New Haven, Conn.: Yale University Press. 21, 43–65; Helson, R. 1970. Fantasy and self discovery. *The Horn Book Magazine.* 46(2). April. 121–24; Lynn, R. H. 1995. xxxv; Wolfe, G. 1986. 40.
53. Langston, J. 1973. The weak place in the cloth: A study of fantasy for children. *The Horn Book Magazine.* 49(5). October. 433–41; 49(6). December. 570–78, quotation at 577.

54. For additional information about benefits individuals gain from exploring fantasy literature, see Aquino. 1977. 19; Langston. 1973. 191; Cooper, S. 1990. Fantasy in the real world. *The Horn Book Magazine.* 66(3). May/June. 304–15; Egoff, S. 1988. 17–20; Fisher, M. 1961. *Intent Upon Reading.* New York: Watts. 149–50; Lynn, R. H. 1995. xxxi–xxxii; Pulaski, M. A. 1974. 70–72; Singer, J. L. 1968; Woolsey, D. 1989. 114.
55. Pulaski, M. A. 1974. 70–72.
56. Aquino, J. 1977.
57. Elleman, B. 1982. Chosen by children. *Booklist.* 79. December. 507–9; Lukens, R. 1995. 22.
58. Some ideas for LRMs were modified from Yopp, R. H. & H. K. 1992. *Literature-Based Reading Activities.* Boston: Allyn & Bacon. Some visual activities were modified from Borton, T. 1973. Fantasy in the classroom. *Learning.* 1(3). January. 20–29.

5

Realistic Fiction

A Reflection of the Society It Creates

◆ ◆ ◆ *O*ne of the best ways of teaching them [children] about the world they live in, about how other people think and feel, is through a good story.

—Nina Bawden

*R*ealistic fiction is an authentic story that reflects *yesterday's memories* (Patricia Hermes's *On Winter's Wind: A Novel*, 1995), *today's reality* (Patricia MacLachlan's *Baby*, 1993), and *tomorrow's dreams* (Rachel Isadora's *Lili on Stage*, 1995). C. S. Lewis, the renowned author, reminds us that realistic fiction must contain "truth to life." Identifying "truth" can be confusing however, because it can represent something that usually happens, or something that often happens, or something that happens only once.[1] We must remember that "truth," or reality, changes with the time, the place, and the people. Therefore, we expect the "truth" in realistic fiction to be "a reflection of the society it creates."

WHAT IS REALISTIC FICTION?

Realistic fiction depicts situations that could happen, but are not necessarily documented. It consists of realistic narratives, written in prose, poetry, or drama, and presented in picture book or chapter book format. The books portray fictional human or animal characters interacting in the primary world. Henry James, a recognized nineteenth-century author and critic, declared, "The only reason for the existence of a novel is that it does attempt to represent life."[2] Thus, the juvenile novels depict plausible events, are set in historical or contemporary surroundings, and include the authentic concerns, values, and lifestyle of people or animals living in a particular time and place.

Successful realistic fiction tells "authentic stories" that are plausible accounts of what might have happened in a particular time and place. The stories portray the genuine feelings, experiences, desires, and concerns of characters who might have lived at that time and place. Master story-tellers involve the reader with the times and plight of the characters, and the authentic story becomes important to the reader.

THE DISTINCTIVE CHARACTERISTICS OF REALISTIC FICTION

Like all literary genres, quality realistic fiction narratives have distinctive literary characteristics. By identifying the literary elements of a selection, we can classify it by genre and determine its literary merit. Whether written in prose or poetry, realistic fiction deals with characters and events that are fictional but nevertheless plausible and possible. Writers are responsible for accurately depicting the times, geography, lifestyles, cultural values, and language of the selected setting. We expect certain literary conventions in historical and contemporary realistic fiction selections. Figure 5.1 on page 140 summarizes the distinctive elements of realistic fiction.[3]

THE WRITER'S RESPONSIBILITIES

Authors of realistic fiction write personal or family memoirs, report regional stories, or invent narratives that realistically portray a historical period, place, and people. They are encouraged to trust children's innate ability to grasp the subtle nuances suggested in the narrative and to resist using didactic overtones in their writings.[4]

Because our world contains diverse groups, authors of realistic fiction depict many societal experiences. Some literary critics assert that only members of a specific group can write about that group. This issue has arisen particularly in regard to the portrayal of "parallel cultures" in multicultural literature.[5] We expect writers to present the authentic values, lifestyles, and history of a group. Rewriting history and using stereotypes are unacceptable practices.

Katherine Paterson, a two-time winner of the Newbery Medal and a popular writer of both historical and contemporary fiction, says that authors are responsible for learning enough about a setting so that they can bring the characters to life through a well-written story that authentically depicts the time, place, and people. Paterson also acknowledges, though, that despite her sensitivity and attempts to be objective, she too brings a certain bias to her writing (for more about Paterson, see Did You Know?). Thelma Seto, a Japanese-American writer, compliments Paterson's integrity when writing books set in Japan. According to Seto, writing is a moral issue that requires the author to be honest and reflect integrity.[6] Most authors acknowledge their personal background of experiences and try hard to make a particular period, place, and people

FIGURE 5.1 Distinctive Literary Characteristics of Realistic Fiction

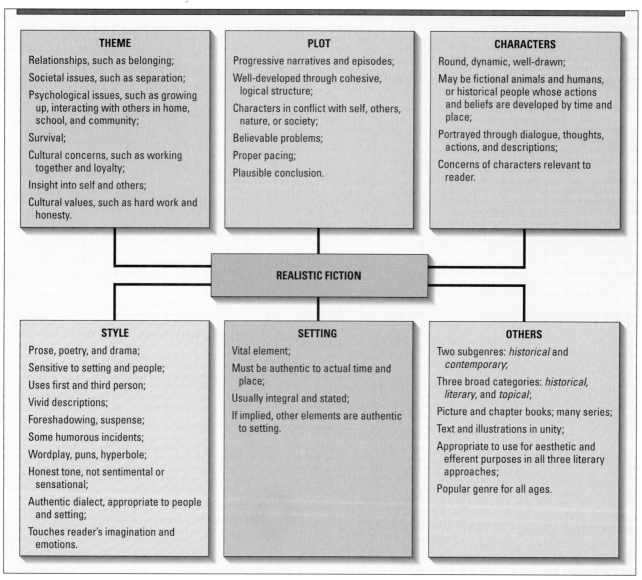

come to life. Jane Yolen, the author of almost two hundred books for children, including *Before the Storm* (1995), warns of a trend toward the "Balkanization" of literature. She fears that insisting that authors tell only their own stories will result in rigid borders being drawn across the world of stories. Yolen reminds us that a master storyteller will "re-invigorate, re-create, and re-vision" the literature of different groups through the "cross-cultural fertilization" of ideas and images. All thinking people are influenced by the thoughts and experiences of others. If writers are limited to writing only stories from their immediate environment, will innovative, careful authors be overly restricted? If a particular society does not happen to produce a gifted

writer, will its culture be lost because no one else can write about it?[7]

We could look at this issue another way by asking the following questions:

Should male authors include female characters in their books?

Should human writers include realistic animals in their books?

These questions may seem ridiculous, but they highlight the necessity for authors, whatever their ethnic, cultural, gender, religious, or societal background, to carefully research the setting and honestly portray people, places, and

Did You Know About
KATHERINE PATERSON?

Imagine being born to American missionary parents in China before World War II and spending your first seven years in places where you looked and talked differently than the other children. Think about fleeing with your parents, not once, but twice, to protect your life. How would it feel to attend thirteen different schools in your first eighteen years and live in thirty different homes in three different countries? How would you feel if children in your native country thought you were different just because you were born in another country? Katherine Paterson knows those feelings. How did she handle them? While teaching in a rural Virginia school, she completed a master's degree in Christian Education and wanted to go back to China as a missionary. Because that country was closed to American missionaries, she traveled in Japan and fell in love with the country and the people. She learned the language and became an assistant to rural pastors. Later, she returned to the United States, met the man of her dreams, John Paterson, and became a pastor's wife, a mother of four, and a writer. One of her children came from Hong Kong, and her youngest came from an Apache reservation in Arizona.

At age seven while living in Shanghai, Paterson published her first story. During graduate school, professors encouraged her to write, but her early stories were not very successful. Fortunately, a publisher's reader discovered her unsolicited manuscript, and *The Sign of the Chrysanthemum* was published in 1973, followed in consecutive years by *Of Nightingales That Weep* and *The Master Puppeteer*. The time she had spent living in Japan, first by herself and

later with her husband as a missionary, and hours of research gave her the background to write these acclaimed novels of feudal Japan. In addition to her childhood in Asia, Paterson also draws on contemporary experiences for her books. After her oldest son's friend died at age seven, she published her first Newbery Medal winner, *Bridge to Terabithia*. The experiences of keeping two foster children from Cambodia led to the publication of *The Great Gilly Hopkins*. A collection of nine stories about Christmas resulted in *Angels and Other Strangers*. She explored the eternal problems of sibling rivalry in her second Newbery Medal winner, *Jacob Have I Loved*. She combined childhood memories of singing on a radio show with her musical family and her discomfort as an adult at being treated as a celebrity in *Come Sing, Jimmy Jo*. In recent years while writing about issues such as the early days of child labor in *Lyddie*, she also returned to her early experiences in Asia to publish *Rebels of the Heavenly Kingdom* and *The Tale of the Mandarin Ducks.*

Paterson believes an author releases the reader's imagination, stretches the reader's world, and gives humor and hope. When the author gives the child something worthwhile to read, the child makes connections, and the story becomes important to his or her life. Through literature, she reminds us, we are given "language for life" and "experience the spectrum of human emotion." Literature doesn't teach us virtue and morality; rather it helps us become "more compassionate, wiser human beings" (from a speech given at the 1995 Annual Convention of the National Council of Teachers of English).

events. Just as we want books to stimulate children's growth and vision, we must be careful not to restrict conscientious writers and silence their voices in the name of cultural purity.

THE APPEAL OF REALISTIC FICTION

Realistic fiction appeals to males and females of all ages. Children and adults enjoy the believable characters who have exciting adventures in real settings. The events and characters frequently remind the reader of personal situations with family members, friends, or acquaintances. Does Ramona in Beverly Cleary's *Ramona Quimby, Age 8* (1981) remind you of a friend? Do you have a brother like Fudge in Judy Blume's *Fudge-a-Mania* (1990)? Perhaps you have a sister like Tomie de Paola in *The Baby Sister* (1996). (See the de Paola color plate.) If not, at least you can share their experiences in realistic fiction.

Tomie de Paola uses simple ink line drawings and watercolor in his stylized illustrations for Baby Sister. *The artist carefully arranges his illustrations to depict a little boy's feelings when a new sister is brought home for the first time. Did this happen to you?*

Conflicts depicted in the narratives may be similar to the audience's experiences, or they may be different. By encountering a different perspective on life, children frequently gain a new outlook on the world. Even when realistic settings and incidents are familiar to the reader, the genre gives young people an opportunity to temporarily escape from their real-world concerns. As young people observe the characters making choices and living with the consequences, they gain valuable information about dealing with personal conflicts encountered in daily life. Realistic fiction frequently evokes a strong emotional response such as joy, happiness, grief, or fear and encourages readers to explore their personal reactions to a particular situation.

Realistic narratives expose boys and girls to the feelings, attitudes, rituals, and beliefs of various countries, regions, cultures, and ethnic and religious groups. This exposure acquaints young people with the similarities and differences between people. Realistic fiction has the potential to help individuals understand their personal behavior and the actions of others in real-life situations.[8]

✾ SUBGENRES OF REALISTIC FICTION

Realistic fiction, which must be *believable* (to the reader), contains authentic narratives about people who could have lived at a particular time and actual place. We classify realistic narratives as either *historical fiction* or *contemporary fiction*. The time in which a selection is set determines whether it is considered historical or contemporary fiction. Distinguishing between the subgenres in this way presents some difficulties, however. While historical fiction is clearly set in the past, when does the past begin? Some authorities would classify any realistic narrative set prior to the birth of the reader as historical fiction. Others classify a book as historical fiction if the setting is two generations before the present.[9] Some realistic fiction such as Sheila Burnford's *The Incredible Journey* (1961) deals with universal issues that are important to several generations of readers. In such a book, the actual date is usually not integral to the story line. We classify a book as contemporary fiction if the author does not affix an actual date to the events, the theme, the characters' behavior, or their lifestyle and if the content is universal and deals with issues pertinent to contemporary children.

For the purposes of this book, we recognize the equal influence of *the reader*, *the writer*, and *the text* and use the following classifications:

Historical fiction highlights a period before the reader's life began.

Contemporary fiction highlights a period during the reader's lifetime or addresses universal issues that are not restricted to a particular historical date.

This system is easier to use than the others suggested, although it does mean that the classification will vary with the reader. Thus, the same realistic narrative classified as historical fiction by a six-year-old might be considered contemporary fiction by a thirty-six-year-old. All elementary-age children classify their teacher's contemporary fiction as historical fiction. That is why they say to us, "Teacher, tell us about the old days, when you were a child—you know, before television, microwaves, video games, and computers."

THE DISTINGUISHING CHARACTERISTICS OF HISTORICAL FICTION

Stina, in Lena Anderson's *Stina* (1989) and *Stina's Visit* (1991), echoes a universal request of grandchildren throughout the centuries when she says to her grandfather, "Tell me another story." History becomes alive when passed in a story from one generation to the next. Generally, history buffs listened to many stories about their own people or others who had adventures in faraway places. Historical information is always easier to remember if it is associated with people. By reading Birdy's often humorous journal entries in Karen Cushman's *Catherine, Called Birdy* (1994), young people become aware of the differences between childhood in the Middle Ages and contemporary times. They also respect Birdy's determination and courage in attempting to change the system. Many students want to learn more about the Puritans' treatment of witches after reading Elizabeth George

Speare's *The Witch of Blackbird Pond* (1953) and Patricia Clapp's *Witches' Children: A Story of Salem* (1982) with its description of the "spell-bound" Puritan girls. Recent fictional narratives such as Jane Yolen's *Encounter* (1992) give contemporary children different insights into the eventual destruction of the Taino civilization in the Caribbean after the Spanish exploration. (See the Yolen color plate.) David Shannon's illustrations in *Encounter* help interpret Yolen's text describing what might have happened during that first encounter. (See Chapter 9 and "The World in 1492" in the bibliography for different points of view about this historical event.)

The setting and most events depicted in historical fiction are based on actual happenings, but many details and characters may be fiction, as in the popular historical narrative, *Johnny Tremain* (1943). In her 1944 Newbery Medal acceptance speech, Esther Forbes acknowledged that Johnny, a fictional apprentice to Paul Revere, evolved while she was writing her adult biography, *Paul Revere and the World He Lived In* (winner of the 1942 Pulitzer Prize). Johnny, who became disabled, and his friends of liberty had various fictional, yet possible, experiences as they helped America's pre-revolutionary leaders. As in all quality historical fiction, these fictional characters authentically reflect the concerns and lifestyle of the people who lived at that time and place.

Historical fiction is also produced by contemporary authors to highlight a particular historical setting, as Patricia MacLachlan did in *Sarah, Plain and Tall* (1985). Through visual and verbal narratives, picture storybooks bring a place and time to life, as in David Williams's *Grandma Essie's*

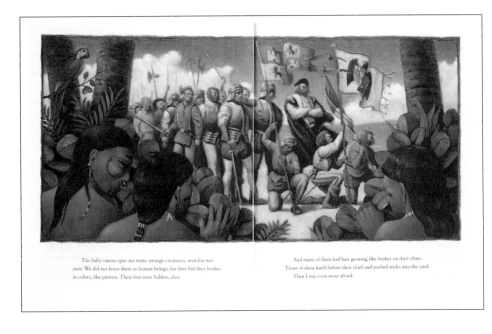

David Shannon uses acrylic paints and earth tone colors in his paintings for Jane Yolen's book, Encounter. *The artist uses his imagination to create single-page paintings and double-page spreads that realistically portray Yolen's fictional account of the encounter between Columbus, his men, and the Taino people.*

Covered Wagon (1993). Wiktor Sadowski's illustrations recreate the scenes Grandma Essie saw as a girl when she migrated through Missouri, Kansas, and Oklahoma. With the passage of time, a realistic book that highlights a contemporary setting and issues becomes historical realistic fiction; this has happened to Louisa May Alcott's *Jo's Boys* (1886).

Some contemporary authors of historical fiction, such as Gloria Houston, weave family or regional stories into their fictionalized narratives. Houston used an old family story for *The Year of the Perfect Christmas Tree* (1988). The book is dedicated to her mother Ruth. Barbara Cooney visited Houston's home in Spruce Pine, North Carolina, before illustrating the book. (See the Houston color plate.) The blending of the visual and verbal narratives gives the reader information about the area during World War I, its Christmas traditions, and the concern of people in the community for Ruthie and her mother. Table 5.1 on page 145 offers ideas for studying a regional author.

Whether the story idea is original or based on a family tale, all writers spend time researching the historical details. If possible, they interview people who know about the time and place. They listen for the cultural or ethnic perspectives prevalent in the community. They search for the unique qualities of the people involved and ask questions such as the following:

What tools and household goods did the people use?

What were the typical occupations of adults at the time and place?

How did children help their parents?

How were the homes constructed?

Did people live in cities or in rural settings?

What government or educational system did the people use at this time and place?

What religious or cultural beliefs did the people value?

What were the people's major concerns and what problems did they encounter?

A successful writer is aware that too many unusual names or historical details can overpower a story, but also realizes that enough details must be included in the narrative to keep the attention of the audience.[10] When a designated setting is authentic, students can compare the past and the present to gain information from a historical story. For this reason, quality historical fiction is used effectively in social studies lessons.

THE DISTINGUISHING CHARACTERISTICS OF CONTEMPORARY FICTION

Contemporary fiction is set in the present time in places that exist somewhere in this world. It contains human or animal characters, who act as people or animals behave in that particular setting. The incidents are possible for the setting, but they may not have actually happened. Teachers and media specialists often place these books on award lists or use them for book talks because most children of all ages enjoy them.

Children like to read contemporary fiction containing enough detail to help them visualize the setting, such as Will Hobbs's *Bearstone* (1989) and *Beardance* (1993). Books such as Avi's *Who Was That Masked Man, Anyway?* (1992) satisfy young people's desire for adventure and suspense. Foreshadowing is a favorite stylistic device to advance the plot. Betsy Byars uses this technique along with realistic conversations in *The Not-Just-Anybody Family* (1986) and the other Blossom family books. Young people enjoy books portraying children who react as they would like to behave, as in Robert Newton Peck's *Soup* series. Children also like to read about characters, such as Ellen Conford's Jenny Archer, who talk and dress the way they do and want similar things. Also popular are books like

Barbara Cooney's stylized acrylic paintings capture the spirit of a mountain tradition in Gloria Houston's The Year of the Perfect Christmas Tree. *In this picture Cooney shows the beautiful dress that Mama made for Ruthie, the heavenly angel. The artist uses various colors and different visual arrangements to enrich Houston's verbal narrative.*

TABLE 5.1 Suggested LRM: A Study of a Regional Author

This LRM has been prepared as a study of Gloria Houston, but it can easily be adapted for other regional authors. Houston's picture books are *The Year of the Perfect Christmas Tree* (1988), *My Great Aunt Arizona* (1992), *But No Candy* (1992), and *Littlejim's Gift* (1994). The teacher or students will read Houston's novels *Littlejim* (1990) and *Mountain Valor* (1994) aloud to the class. The following activities can be used:

Collect Houston's books or those of another regional author.

Group the children in literature discussion groups. Give each group copies of one of Houston's books.

Ask each group to prepare a KWL (described in Chapter 10) listing the following:

1. What I know about the Appalachian Mountain region.
2. What I want to know about lifestyles before the mid-twentieth century. (See the interview questions suggested in "The Distinguishing Characteristics of Historical Fiction.")
3. What I would like to know about the people in Houston's book.

After reading the book by Houston, the group will complete the KWL by charting "What I found out about the setting while reading the book."

Each group will identify information about the setting in their book. The group will list the information on a visual graphic such as a circle for a Venn diagram (see Chapter 10). The circles will be joined, and a circle that intersects all the other circles will be placed in the center. Facts found in all the books will be listed in the center circle (the intersecting circle).

Students will prepare a diorama or table exhibit of an Appalachian town similar to Spruce Pine, North Carolina.

Additional LRMs to be used with the books:

Students exchange the picture books and, if suitable, add additional information about the setting and people to the diagram.

Students tell their parents, grandparents, other relatives, or friends one story. They will then interview the adult to find out a special story about a favorite relative. The interview information will be used to write an original book: *The Year of Our Perfect Christmas Tree, My Great Aunt* _____ *, Courage at the Beach,* and the like.

The following are other realistic books set in Appalachia that could be read and discussed by individuals or groups of students:

Dionetti, M., & Riggio, A. 1991. *Coal Mine Peaches.* 6–10 yrs.

Hendershot, J. 1987. *In Coal Country.* 6–10 yrs.

Lowry, L. 1987. *Rabble Starkey.* 10–14 yrs.

Naylor, P. 1991. *Shilo.* 10–13 yrs.

Mills, L. 1991. *Rag Coat.* 9–12 yrs.

Paterson, K. 1985. *Come Sing, Jimmy Jo.* 10–13 yrs.

Rappaport, D. 1987. *Trouble at the Mines.* 10–13 yrs.

Reeder, C. 1993. *Moonshiner's Son.* 11–15 yrs.

Rylant, C. 1991. *Appalachia: Voices of the Sleeping Birds.* 6–12 yrs.

White, R. 1988. *Sweet Creek Holler.* 12–15 yrs.

See the Chapter Bibliography for additional books set in Appalachia.

Students could compare the information about the region and characters, continue the KWL, the clustering technique, complete a comparison chart, or complete a Venn diagram. (See Chapter 10.)

Students will research in information books, the lifestyle, music, art, crafts, and traditions of the people who live in the region. Groups will present the information to others using various LRMs and appealing visuals as suggested in Chapter 2 and in Appendix B.

Students will select a favorite author or illustrator of realistic fiction and prepare a Did You Know about the person. They should speculate as to why the writer sets her or his books in a particular geographic region and time.

Select an "Appalachian Author" of the year. Prepare speeches, present them to the class, conduct elections, and select an author. Write to the author, describe the procedure used for the selection, and explain why he or she was chosen for the honor.

Marion Dane Bauer's *On My Honor* (1986), which portray children who struggle with difficult problems. The escapades of contemporary characters who live in unfamiliar places, such as South Africa, the setting for Rachel Isadora's *At the Crossroads* (1991), fascinate young people. Believable characters who struggle with situations similar or different from those experienced by the reader, such as Gary Soto's Latino children in *Baseball in April* (1991) and *The Skirt* (1992), are enjoyed equally by girls and boys. Learners vicariously experience the consequences of the characters' actions and decide if their decisions were correct and worthy of emulation.

Whereas authors of historical fiction must carefully research the setting of their books, authors of contemporary fiction must have a broad understanding of the children who read their books. They attempt to portray characters who react and behave as contemporary children might. Authors select themes and events that reflect the concerns of today's children. Through the actions of believable characters, their problems are solved in an acceptable manner. Young people expect authors of contemporary fiction to resolve conflicts honestly, as Katherine Paterson does in *Flip-Flop Girl* (1994).

✳ CATEGORIES OF REALISTIC FICTION

Historical fiction and contemporary realistic fiction written in prose and poetry narratives appear in books with pictures, chapter books, and novels. Well-written narratives are enjoyed and selected by people of all ages, if the style of writing is developmentally appropriate and the content is appealing to the individual (see Chapter 1). These narratives can be categorized according to historical period, literary type, and theme:

Historical categories designate the particular time and place.

Literary categories include adventure stories, survival stories, animal stories, mysteries, humorous stories, and general fiction.

Thematic categories include topics such as family living, personal relationships, interactions in school, societal concerns, cultural lifestyles, and international literature.

These classifications are flexible. Books are placed in a particular category depending on the literary *conventions* included in the narrative (such as the setting, themes, characterization, and plot) and the *content.* Many books may be placed in all three categories. For example, in Miriam Nerlove's *Flowers on the Wall* (1996), which deals with the experiences of a Jewish family during World War II, the narrative focuses on the time and place (*setting*), the behavior of the characters (*characterization*), the will to survive (*plot*), and the treatment of the people (*content*). Therefore, the book could be assigned to a historical category, a literary category (a survival story), or a thematic category (family living, personal responsibility, and societal issues). Or consider Virginia Hamilton's *The House of Dies Drear* (1984), in which African-American children in contemporary Ohio encounter a "ghost" from pre–Civil War days. We classify *The House of Dies Drear* as a mystery (a literary category), as a family story (a thematic category), and, because the children discover the house was a stop on the Underground Railroad, as a historical category. The actual assignment of a book to a specific category depends on the learner's purpose for viewing, listening to, or reading the book and the teacher's instructional goals.

Whatever the category, well-written, appealing realistic stories are effective to use for reading aloud, independent

Ted Lewin presents New York City at the turn of the twentieth century in his detailed illustrations for Elisa Bartone's Peppe the Lamplighter. *The artist highlights the importance of a lamplighter in his detailed pictures that include contrasting light and dark watercolor washes in shades of blue, gold, pink, and white. Have you read a book by lamplight?*

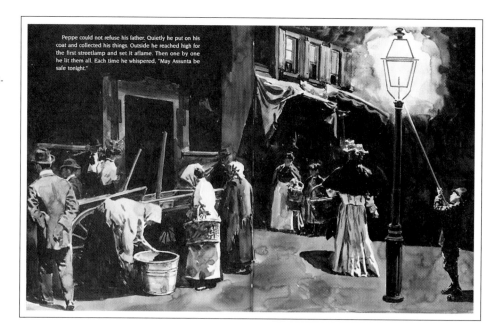

reading, small group sessions, or literature-based language arts and content area classes. Young people gain a broader historical perspective and a better understanding of the literary characteristics of a category if they explore several books in the same category. Children select a book for independent reading if the story is interesting and the content appealing. Teachers highlight the literary classification when presenting realistic fiction in a literature class and emphasize the selection's content in classes using literature-based instruction. Therefore, the designations must remain flexible to meet the needs of the students and the teacher's instructional approach.

The bibliography lists outstanding examples of realistic fiction organized according to historical settings, literary classifications, and themes. The range of ages that might enjoy each book is also suggested.[11]

HISTORICAL CATEGORIES

All realistic selections authentically depict a particular place and time and important events in the history of a country or a group of people. Selections about a particular historical period must accurately portray the interests, concerns, attitudes, and lifestyles of people or animals who could have lived in a particular place during the specified time. Rosemary Wells achieves those goals in *Waiting for the Evening Star* (1993), which depicts life in a small Vermont farming community at the beginning of the twentieth century. The story is enhanced by Susan Jeffers's illustrations. Elisa Bartone's *Peppe the Lamplighter* (1993) is also set at the turn of the century. Ted Lewin's illustrations enrich the story of an immigrant Italian family in New York City and help the setting come to life. (See the Bartone color plate on page 146.) The visual and verbal narratives created for both historical picture storybooks authentically portray the same period in history and clearly show how the place where people lived affected their lifestyle.

Other outstanding examples of realistic fiction organized according to historical periods from antiquity to the 1900s are presented later in the chapter in the notable selections in Tables 5.5 through 5.10 and in the bibliography. The literary merit of a historical selection is determined by the distinctive literary characteristics expected of all realistic fiction (see Figure 5.1). Table 5.2 suggests Literary Response Modes (LRMs) to use with historical fiction.

LITERARY CATEGORIES

Outstanding examples of realistic fiction are found in many literary categories: *adventure stories*, such as Karen Ackerman's *Bingleman's Midway* (1995); *survival stories*

TABLE 5.2 Suggested LRMs: Historical Fiction

Compare the description of the setting, time, and place in several books. Chart the descriptions. Check their accuracy by consulting nonfiction books or pictures or by interviewing people who lived at that time or in that place. Then determine if the descriptions of the setting presented in the books are consistent with the information obtained.

Select a historical period. Read several books set in the period that contain similar conflicts; for example, Alice Dalgliesch's *The Courage of Sarah Noble* (1954), Sally Keehn's *I Am Regina* (1991), and Elizabeth Speare's *Sign of the Beaver* (1983). Identify the characters' conflicts, and explain how the characters resolve their problems. Have children assume the role of a character; invite book characters (students) to tell the class about themselves. Other students will interview the book characters. The characters will give a book talk to advertise the book and attempt to entice others to read more about their adventures.

Alternative idea: Select books with similar conflicts but different settings, and repeat this LRM.

After reading fiction and nonfiction books about U.S. history, prepare a time line representing America's development during some period, such as the colonial period, revolutionary era, western expansion, or the early twentieth century. The class will select major events of the period and identify the various groups of people and individuals important to the events. Students will research individual events and people. Then they will assume the role of a person representing the event, wear a simple costume representing the period, and discuss the importance of their event and person. They will cite sources used for information (encyclopedias are not acceptable sources). The living time line will be taped to show to other classes, to display and discuss in a parent meeting, or to show on the school television channel.

NOTE: When presenting a historical period, include all groups involved in important events. For example, include literature about both Native Americans and the pioneers when studying the western expansion (see Chapter 9).

about the city, such as Carolyn Coman's *What Jamie Saw* (1995), or about the wilderness, such as Jennifer Armstrong's *Black-Eyed Susan* (1995); *realistic animal stories*, such as C. S. Adler's *Courtyard Cat* (1995); *mysteries*, such as Betsy Byars's Herculeah Jones series, *Tarot Says Beware* (1995); *humorous stories*, such as Louis Sachar's *Marvin Redpost: Alone in His Teacher's House* (1994); and *general fiction*, such as Barbara Nichol's *Beethoven Lives Upstairs* (1994). Preference surveys and observations indicate that people of all ages enjoy quality realistic fiction found in literary categories, if the content is appealing and the style of writing is developmentally appropriate. Today, authors and artists are experimenting with the verbal and visual narratives to create original formats. Graeme Base presents an unusual mystery in *The Eleventh Hour: A Curious Mystery* (1988). The clues to solve the mystery are discreetly hidden in the details of the visual and verbal text. Anyone who cannot solve the mystery after reading and looking at the narratives can turn to the conclusion of the book where the clues are identified and the mystery is explained. Readers ten years and older are fascinated by the challenge of locating the clues hidden in the details of the narratives and finally solving the mystery. (See the Base color plate.)

Figure 5.2 on page 149 lists the distinguishing characteristics of each type of story included in the literary categories. Examples of outstanding realistic narratives in the first five literary categories are included in the bibliography at the end of the chapter. General fiction selections were arbitrarily placed in historical or thematic categories.[12] Table 5.3 on page 150 suggests LRMs for use with mystery series.

Graeme Base is noted for his use of brilliant colors and his ability to combine realistic and imaginary elements in his visual and verbal narratives. His book The Eleventh Hour: A Curious Mystery *reflects those elements. The viewer must carefully search his gouache paintings for hidden clues to the mystery. While his detailed backgrounds and borders provide additional clues and information to ponder, his paintings do not overwhelm the viewer. Did you find the hidden clues in this picture of a magnificent cat?*

THEMATIC CATEGORIES

Realistic fiction in thematic categories encourages young people to explore content that is of interest and to delve into psychological and sociological issues of concern to historical and contemporary people. As explained earlier, these authentic stories are classified according to themes such as *family living* (as in Jane Conly's *Trout Summer,* 1995); *personal relationships* (as in Frances and Aileen Arrington's *Stella's Bull,* 1994); *interactions in school* (as in Anne Fine's *Flour Babies,* 1994); *societal issues* (as in Chap Reaver's *Bill,* 1994); *cultural lifestyles* (as in Rudolfo Anaya's *The Farolitos of Christmas,* 1995); and *international literature* (as in the Australian creator Alison Lester's *My Farm,* 1994).

The literary merit of a fictionalized narrative is determined by the quality of the literary conventions included in the realistic story. Figure 5.3 on page 151 identifies the distinctive characteristics of each broad theme. Table 5.4 on page 150 suggests LRMs for use with school stories. Outstanding selections are listed in the bibliography. Since many themes represent contemporary concerns, most of the books selected for this category are set in the period from 1989 to the present.

✳ HISTORICAL DEVELOPMENT OF REALISTIC FICTION

From the earliest times, realistic stories have included historical events and the concerns of people at a particular time and place. The books reflect the society's perception of children and the prevalent child-raising techniques. During the seventeenth century, for example, the Puritans were intent on saving the souls of the young and began to write didactic narratives especially for children. These stories reflected the Puritan belief that children were born evil and that adults should direct them away from the fires of hell. The narratives presented a clear message: children at very young ages were responsible for the consequences of their behavior. In the process of publishing these moralizing stories, the Puritans created the first fictionalized literature written especially for children—realistic fiction.[13]

Children also enjoyed the old traditional tales and other books of social and moral instruction that were not as intense as the Puritans' "good godly books." In 1744 an English entrepreneur, John Newbery, published *A Little Pretty Pocketbook,* which was intended for the amusement and instruction of Little Master Tommy and Pretty Miss Polly. Newbery published some thirty realistic books with religious, social, and instructional lessons, but he always intended them for children's "amusement and pleasure." Newbery's books were popular into the nineteenth century

FIGURE 5.2 Characteristics of Literary Categories of Realistic Fiction

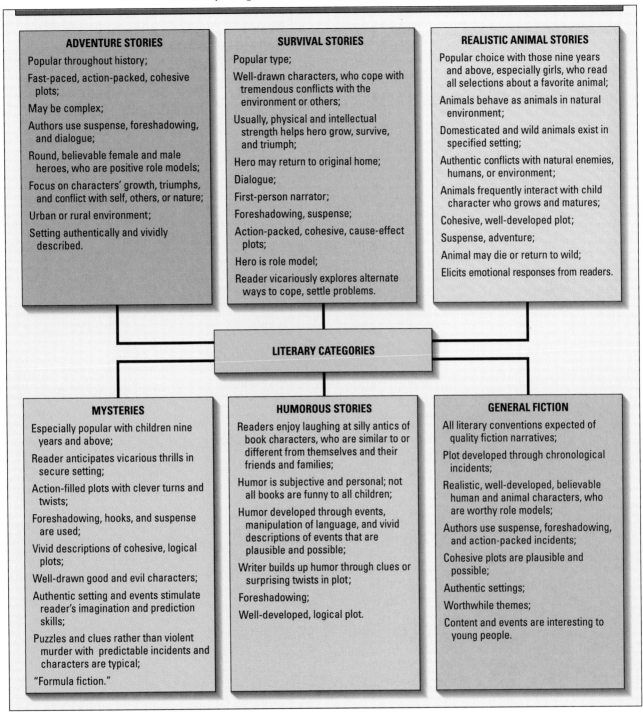

ADVENTURE STORIES

Popular throughout history;

Fast-paced, action-packed, cohesive plots;

May be complex;

Authors use suspense, foreshadowing, and dialogue;

Round, believable female and male heroes, who are positive role models;

Focus on characters' growth, triumphs, and conflict with self, others, or nature;

Urban or rural environment;

Setting authentically and vividly described.

SURVIVAL STORIES

Popular type;

Well-drawn characters, who cope with tremendous conflicts with the environment or others;

Usually, physical and intellectual strength helps hero grow, survive, and triumph;

Hero may return to original home;

Dialogue;

First-person narrator;

Foreshadowing, suspense;

Action-packed, cohesive, cause-effect plots;

Hero is role model;

Reader vicariously explores alternate ways to cope, settle problems.

REALISTIC ANIMAL STORIES

Popular choice with those nine years and above, especially girls, who read all selections about a favorite animal;

Animals behave as animals in natural environment;

Domesticated and wild animals exist in specified setting;

Authentic conflicts with natural enemies, humans, or environment;

Animals frequently interact with child character who grows and matures;

Cohesive, well-developed plot;

Suspense, adventure;

Animal may die or return to wild;

Elicits emotional responses from readers.

LITERARY CATEGORIES

MYSTERIES

Especially popular with children nine years and above;

Reader anticipates vicarious thrills in secure setting;

Action-filled plots with clever turns and twists;

Foreshadowing, hooks, and suspense are used;

Vivid descriptions of cohesive, logical plots;

Well-drawn good and evil characters;

Authentic setting and events stimulate reader's imagination and prediction skills;

Puzzles and clues rather than violent murder with predictable incidents and characters are typical;

"Formula fiction."

HUMOROUS STORIES

Readers enjoy laughing at silly antics of book characters, who are similar to or different from themselves and their friends and families;

Humor is subjective and personal; not all books are funny to all children;

Humor developed through events, manipulation of language, and vivid descriptions of events that are plausible and possible;

Writer builds up humor through clues or surprising twists in plot;

Foreshadowing;

Well-developed, logical plot.

GENERAL FICTION

All literary conventions expected of quality fiction narratives;

Plot developed through chronological incidents;

Realistic, well-developed, believable human and animal characters, who are worthy role models;

Authors use suspense, foreshadowing, and action-packed incidents;

Cohesive plots are plausible and possible;

Authentic settings;

Worthwhile themes;

Content and events are interesting to young people.

and influenced the literature published in the United States and other countries around the world.

Many books published for children were intended for instruction until 1839 when Catherine Sinclair published *Holiday House.* Moral lessons were limited in her book,

and many believe it represents the true beginning of children's literature.[14]

During the early nineteenth century, folk literature collections, fantasy stories, nonsense poetry, and poetry written for and about children were published. By the 1860s,

TABLE 5.3 Suggested LRMs: Mystery Series

The teacher or media specialist will give a book talk to introduce several *mystery series* that focus on a mystery and another topic, such as sports or ecology, a character, or a particular setting. (See the series by George, Howe, Greenberg, Otfinosky, and Naylor in the mystery section of the bibliography.)

Group students according to personal interests. A group will read several books in the same series and identify similarities among the books.

The group will prepare a prescription for writing a story that combines a mystery and another issue. They will discuss and compare prescriptions written by other groups.

Later, pairs of students will use the prescription to write a mini-mystery.

Pairs of students could brainstorm and prepare an original mini-mystery to tell to a younger group of students. The younger students could draw illustrations for the mystery and give them to the older students. If desired, the older students could write the mystery. Then the written text and illustrations could be placed in a bound book and presented to the media center.

TABLE 5.4 Suggested LRMs: Look at School Stories

Select a variety of school stories written by different authors (see the bibliography for suggestions).

Distribute the books to pairs or groups. Have the children read and discuss the books, focusing on the characters and their behavior. Ask the students to present an oral discussion of the following:

Compare and contrast the school in the book and their own school.

Consider whether the characters are friends. Do the characters act as though they are friends when they are in school?

Describe what they would do if a character was their schoolmate.

Discuss whether the principal, media specialist, or a guidance counselor would like to have the character be a student in this school.

The students will prepare a travel brochure of their hometown and the surrounding area and send the brochure and an invitation to a book character to visit their school for a week. The students will plan an itinerary for the visit, including activities the character would enjoy.

Students will role-play introducing the character to the school principal, media specialist, guidance counselor, or parents. The actor who plays the character must behave as the character would in a similar situation. After the role-playing situation, the class will decide if the adults would like to have the character in their school.

noted authors such as Louisa May Alcott, Samuel Clemens, Mary Mapes Dodge, Anna Sewell, Joanna Spyri, and Frances Burnett were publishing realistic stories that reflected lifestyles of families around the world. (See the color plate of Louisa May Alcott's *Little Women* on page 152.) In 1873, *The St. Nicholas Magazine*, the first literary magazine for children, began publication. During this Golden Age of Children's Literature, authors had the freedom to include humor, sadness, and realism in literature written especially for the amusement of young people. Children's literature thrived. Simultaneously, the American public library system developed, making books easily accessible to the ordinary child.

By the early twentieth century, adults had begun to regard childhood as a time of "secure escape." More children were released from the demands of adulthood, yet they lived in a secure environment provided by caring adults. By this time, many authors felt they should write juvenile realistic fiction for children's pleasure. Didactic tales were no longer popular. Now the protagonists were believable children who interacted with others and experimented with their environment. Parents were not necessarily well-developed characters, but remained in the background providing the safety net and security if needed.

During the 1930s, series books such as Nancy Drew and the Hardy Boys were popular juvenile reading. Several people were hired by the Stratemeyer Syndicate to write books for the mystery series. The patterned plots were highly predictable, and the characters were not developed, so the books were not necessarily of high literary merit.[15]

During World War II, U.S. publishers continued publishing juvenile books. Many were realistic picture storybooks, chapter books, and novels that depicted the world during wartime and reflected adults' perception of children and childhood. After the war, the number of juvenile realistic narratives increased dramatically. The authors conscientiously portrayed the historical period and accurately addressed the major concerns of society. Nevertheless, most of the books depicted middle-class white Americans of European ancestry.

By the late 1960s, adults' ideas about childhood and child-raising techniques had changed dramatically. Adults no longer felt children needed to be hidden from the realities of life. In the United States, a new realistic fiction emerged—the "problem novels." These novels, published primarily for young people aged eleven years and above, reflected changing societal and psychological attitudes and no longer sheltered young people from contemporary issues. The books dealt with divorce (such as Peggy Mann's *My Dad Lives in a Downtown Hotel*, 1973), child abuse (such as Irene Hunt's *The Lottery Rose*, 1978), and sexual

FIGURE 5.3   Characteristics of Thematic Categories of Realistic Fiction

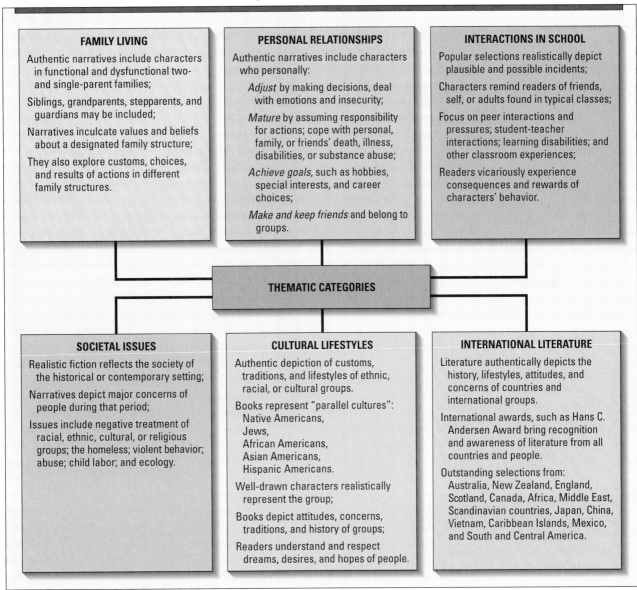

FAMILY LIVING

Authentic narratives include characters in functional and dysfunctional two- and single-parent families;

Siblings, grandparents, stepparents, and guardians may be included;

Narratives inculcate values and beliefs about a designated family structure;

They also explore customs, choices, and results of actions in different family structures.

PERSONAL RELATIONSHIPS

Authentic narratives include characters who personally:

Adjust by making decisions, deal with emotions and insecurity;

Mature by assuming responsibility for actions; cope with personal, family, or friends' death, illness, disabilities, or substance abuse;

Achieve goals, such as hobbies, special interests, and career choices;

Make and keep friends and belong to groups.

INTERACTIONS IN SCHOOL

Popular selections realistically depict plausible and possible incidents;

Characters remind readers of friends, self, or adults found in typical classes;

Focus on peer interactions and pressures; student-teacher interactions; learning disabilities; and other classroom experiences;

Readers vicariously experience consequences and rewards of characters' behavior.

THEMATIC CATEGORIES

SOCIETAL ISSUES

Realistic fiction reflects the society of the historical or contemporary setting;

Narratives depict major concerns of people during that period;

Issues include negative treatment of racial, ethnic, cultural, or religious groups; the homeless; violent behavior; abuse; child labor; and ecology.

CULTURAL LIFESTYLES

Authentic depiction of customs, traditions, and lifestyles of ethnic, racial, or cultural groups.

Books represent "parallel cultures": Native Americans, Jews, African Americans, Asian Americans, Hispanic Americans.

Well-drawn characters realistically represent the group;

Books depict attitudes, concerns, traditions, and history of groups;

Readers understand and respect dreams, desires, and hopes of people.

INTERNATIONAL LITERATURE

Literature authentically depicts the history, lifestyles, attitudes, and concerns of countries and international groups.

International awards, such as Hans C. Andersen Award bring recognition and awareness of literature from all countries and people.

Outstanding selections from: Australia, New Zealand, England, Scotland, Canada, Africa, Middle East, Scandinavian countries, Japan, China, Vietnam, Caribbean Islands, Mexico, and South and Central America.

escapades (such as Judy Blume's *Forever*, 1975). The last two books were intended for older children. These realistic narratives featured multiple conflicts experienced by children and adults in urban and rural settings. (See the cover of Mary Mapes Dodge's *Hans Brinker, or The Silver Skates* on page 152.) Most problem novels included a wise teacher, caretaker, or caring parent who gave the reader advice about coping with these conflicts. The characters were stereotyped, though, and had more problems than they could solve realistically. Some books contained excessive sensationalism and didactic tones. Therefore, crit-

ics did not judge them to be quality fiction. Problem novels published in the 1990s encountered similar criticisms.[16]

Another trend that began in the 1960s was the interest in realistic stories reflecting the lifestyle of people from "parallel cultures." Virginia Hamilton, John Steptoe, Taro Yashima, and other outstanding authors from diverse backgrounds began writing such books.

In the 1980s, some adults expressed concern about the negative depiction of social issues in television, movies, and MTV. Parents wanted children to experience the "secure

Meg, Jo, Beth, and Amy are shown in one of the full-color oil paintings by Jessie Wilcox Smith for Louisa May Alcott's popular 1915 edition of Little Women.

Clara M. Burd illustrated the cover for Mary Mapes Dodge's Hans Brinker, or The Silver Skates. *The Dutch people acclaimed this popular historical fiction as the best example of family life in Holland in the 1860s. Hilda Van Stockum also created realistic illustrations to enhance the realistic verbal narrative.*

escape" they had known and encouraged them to read realistic books with universal themes, such as Jane Yolen's *Owl Moon* (1987). Though problem novels were still published, many authors gave young readers a respite from the realities of life in the 1980s and published successful sequels to earlier books. Two notable examples are the sequels written by Cynthia Voigt and Mildred Taylor.

Realistic series have always been popular with upper elementary and middle school readers; witness the success of *The Babysitter's Club*, *Sweet Valley High*, and the new *Nancy Drew* books. Young people enjoy series books because they encounter old friends and can predict the outcome of the plot. Unfortunately, these elements frequently diminish the literary merit of individual books and the entire series, although some series such as those of Voigt and Taylor are of high literary merit.

Today, children's literature reflects the variety of philosophies of childhood and child-raising techniques held by adults. Because realistic novels always reflect the society, some writers of juvenile contemporary fiction are exploring societal issues such as the impact of dysfunctional families, violence, drugs, and AIDS on young children. Meanwhile other writers are producing books with traditional families, who interact with grandparents, friends, and other adults. Humor, mischievous children,

and realistic consequences for one's behavior are frequently found in contemporary fiction written for children in the 1990s. Children will enjoy laughing again at Alexander's antics in Judith Viorst's *Alexander, Who Is Not (Do You Hear Me?) Going (I Mean It!) to Move* (1995). Viorst, a talented writer and poet, gives her books intriguing titles that capture the reader's attention. Then, using childlike dialogue, she turns a familiar family event into a hilarious story. The black and white drawings by Robin P. Glasser are reminiscent of those drawn by Ray Cruz for Viorst's very popular *Alexander and the Terrible, Horrible, No Good, Very Bad Day* (1972). (See the Viorst plate on page 154.)

Many parents want their children to explore books depicting familiar cultural and religious experiences. Others plead for more diverse family structures. Writers of realistic fiction are sensitive to these concerns and frequently in-

Did You Know About
GARY PAULSEN?

*W*ho is that guy wearing overalls and a cowboy hat or baseball hat? "He is a writer," you say. "No," is the reply, "I heard he was a teacher, field engineer, editor, soldier, actor, director, farmer, rancher, truck driver, trapper, professional archer, singer, sailor, and a musher who ran the Iditarod twice." Gary Paulsen has done all of these things. Now he spends eighteen hours a day, seven days a week, writing novels about his experiences. He has published approximately 150 books for juvenile and adult audiences. A turning point for Paulsen came in 1983 when he published *Dancing Carl*. Since then he has written several dozen novels for young adults that have won him the critical and popular recognition he deserves. *Dogsong, The Winter Room,* and *Hatchet* were Newbery Honor books, and many of his novels have appeared on the American Library Association's list of Best Books for Young Adults, as well as a number of other honor lists. *Hatchet* was followed by two sequels, *The River* and *Brian's Winter*, which offered an alternative ending. It will be interesting to see how *Hatchet*'s fans respond to these books.

Paulsen frequently sets his books in the outdoors, and his protagonists are males with strong survival instincts. For example, in *Nightjohn*, a pre–Civil War slave risks his life to teach others to read. In *Dogsong*, an Eskimo boy is on a quest to prove his manhood. Gary wrote this book because he ran the Iditarod. We see the hardships and joys of growing up on a farm in Minnesota in *The Winter Room*. In *Cookcamp*, a young boy lives in the woods with his grandmother. A charlatan, an itinerant preacher, and his son steal from the poor, until the son begins to question their life in *The Tent*.

Paulsen fills his books with adventures that reflect his first-hand experiences. Insecurity, persistence, and stubborn courage are common traits found in his characters and in his own life.

Paulsen uses clear, efficient language effectively. His male protagonists are among the strongest found in juvenile books. He expresses his love of nature and his disdain for those who destroy it. Like most writers, Paulsen encourages children to read everything they are told to read and everything they are told not to read. From reading emerges writing. He feels that reading books saved his life. Add to that a curious nature and you have Gary Paulsen, a "chronicler" of life.

---

clude children interacting in various family structures and neighborhoods. Because various groups are highly critical of books they feel include objectionable content, censorship of juvenile realistic books has increased since the 1980s. Additional information about the censorship of children's books is found in Appendix D.

Many groups are vocal about the use of male-dominated, Western European literature in schools. Fortunately, quality fiction that realistically portrays the experiences of people from diverse populations has increased, as discussed in Chapter 9. Well-drawn, believable female protagonists are flourishing in children's literature. At the same time, well-drawn, believable male protagonists such as Brian in Gary Paulsen's *Hatchet* (1987) and Jamal in Walter Dean Myers's *Scorpions* (1988) are on the decline. (For more information on Gary Paulsen see "Did You Know?") Girls and boys need positive role models in their literature; therefore, we need a balance of well-drawn contemporary female and male protagonists in quality realistic fiction.

It is exciting to read the new visual and verbal narratives published by today's creators and to imagine the creative and innovative books that they will publish in the twenty-first century!

Robin Preiss Glasser's black-and-white realistic drawings compliment Judith Viorst's book, Alexander, Who Is Not (Do You Hear Me?) Going (I Mean It!) to Move. *The artist uses cross-hatching, shading, and outlines in her detailed pen-and-ink drawings to support the humorous text about a familiar family crisis—moving to another city.*

✳ NOTABLE SELECTIONS OF REALISTIC FICTION

Acknowledging that realistic fiction includes both historical and contemporary settings, the notable selections in Tables 5.5 through 5.10 on pages 155–158 are organized according to the *historical period portrayed in the book.* By organizing the notable selections according to the setting, the books are automatically arranged by subgenres: *historical fiction,* which is set at a period before the reader's birthday, and *contemporary fiction,* which is set during the lifetime of the reader or reflects universal issues and concerns.

Each table lists books published during a particular period or set during that period, but published at another time. The date of publication is given in the first column. The middle column gives the author's name, title of the book, and setting (place and date), and the last column offers comments about the literary conventions and content of the book. Each notable book authentically depicts the lifestyles, societal concerns, and attitudes of people living during the designated period. They influenced the development of children's literature and are appealing to children.[17]

✳ REALISTIC FICTION IN THE CLASSROOM

Realistic fiction is the favorite literary genre of many children and adults. Individuals' background knowledge, experiences, and curiosity about a time, place, or people influ-

Books take us to other times and places and give us experiences with friends we could not meet in our lifetime.

TABLE 5.5 Notable Realistic Fiction Set from Antiquity Until 1800

PUBLICATION DATE	AUTHOR, TITLE (SETTING)	COMMENTS
1963	H. Behn, *The Faraway Lurs* (Northern Europe, 3500 B.C.)	A Romeo and Juliet love story featuring teenagers who live in the Stone Age.
1978	R. Sutcliff, *Sun Horse, Moon Horse* (British Isles, A.D. 50)	To save his people from imprisonment, Lubrin, the son of an early chieftain, agrees to draw a huge horse on the chalk downs of England for his captors.
1961	E. G. Speare, *The Bronze Bow* (Jerusalem, A.D. 30)	After his father is crucified by the harsh Romans and his mother dies, Daniel vows to avenge their deaths. After meeting Jesus, he realizes the importance of the healing power of love.
1949	M. de Angeli, *The Door in the Wall* (England, 1300)	Robin, the crippled son of a nobleman, becomes ill and is taken to a monastery. After saving the king's castle he learns the true meaning of the saying, "There are many doors in the wall." Newbery Medal winner.
1928	E. Kelly, *The Trumpeter of Krakow* (Poland, 1461)	A complex adventure story about the quest for the Tarnov Crystal and the courageous vow of Joseph (the Krakow trumpeter) to break a two-hundred-year-old oath and save his people. Newbery Medal winner.
1992	J. Yolen, *Encounter* (Caribbean island, 1492)	This story depicts a possible encounter between Columbus and the Taino people. Through the eyes of a Taino boy, the reader sees the destruction brought by Columbus and his men.
1671	J. Janeway, *A Token for Children, Being an Exact Account of the Conversion, Holy and Exemplary Lives, and Joyful Deaths of Several Young Children* (England and U.S., 1671)	A Puritan writer vividly describes saintly children who died young in the rapture of prayer and evil children who experienced prolonged, painful deaths. This book remained popular for over a century and influenced later literature written for children.
1983	E. G. Speare, *The Sign of the Beaver* (Maine frontier, 1700s)	Young Matt is left to care for a Maine cabin while his father returns to Massachusetts for the rest of the family. He is befriended by Attean, grandson of a chief of the Beaver clan. Matt's maturity and the cooperation between Europeans and Native Americans are explored.
1765	J. Newbery (publisher), *The Renowned History of Little Goody Two Shoes, Otherwise Called Mrs. Margery Two Shoes* (England, 1765)	Considered the first juvenile novel written especially for children. Oliver Goldsmith was probably the author. The book describes the life of Margery Meanwell, a young woman who could do no wrong and always achieved her goals. The book is filled with sociological issues of the day, but is lighter in tone than other books published during this time.
1943	E. Forbes, *Johnny Tremain* (U.S., 1776)	Fictional account of a boy who is apprenticed to Paul Revere. After the boy is involved in an accident, he and his friends help Revere and the heroes of the American Revolution. Newbery Medal winner.

ence their enjoyment of realistic selections. While exploring realistic fiction, individuals learn about the past, vicariously experience a variety of strategies to use when interacting with others, or learn to survive in different environments. They can then apply this information to future experiences. Because more stories and poems are available in historical and contemporary fiction than in any other literary genre except folk literature and information books, choosing quality realistic narratives can be an overwhelming task.

Several factors are discussed in this section of the chapter to help teachers effectively present realistic literature in the classroom. First, the benefits individuals gain from exploring the genre are identified. Guidelines for selecting quality realistic fiction are suggested. Finally, appropriate instruc-

tional focuses and LRMs to use with various categories of realistic literature are described. Additional ideas to use with realistic fiction are presented in the Literary Link for John Gardiner's *Stone Fox* (1980) that appears at the end of Chapter 11, and a Literary Link for Marie McSwigan's *Snow Treasure* (1942) is presented in Appendix E.

BENEFITS INDIVIDUALS GAIN FROM EXPERIENCES WITH REALISTIC FICTION

People who have stories have memories. These memories give a society historical roots to use as a measure of the successes or failures of particular groups and individuals.

TABLE 5.6 Notable Realistic Fiction Set in the Nineteenth Century

PUBLICATION DATE	AUTHOR, TITLE (SETTING)	COMMENTS
1839	C. Sinclair, *Holiday House* (England, early 1800s)	Realistic portrayal of family life with active, mischievous, curious children. Represents true beginning of children's literature. Popular for 100 years.
1991	K. Paterson, *Lyddie* (Lowell, Mass., 1840s)	A farm girl describes her experiences working in a textile mill. The book realistically depicts the working conditions, frequency of tuberculosis, life in the dormitories, 13-hour days, and mistreatment of young women.
1960	S. O'Dell, *Island of the Blue Dolphins* (Pacific island, mid-1800s)	A fictionalized account, based on the story of Karana, a Native American girl, who lived alone for 18 years on an island off the coast of California. Newbery Medal winner.
1865	M. M. Dodge, *Hans Brinker, or The Silver Skates* (Holland, 1865)	A realistic story about a Dutch family's life, including illness, poverty, scorn, and finally a skating race. The book highlights the children's reactions to tragedy. Many exciting events.
1868	L. M. Alcott, *Little Women* (U.S., 1860s)	A realistic view of a Victorian family of strong-willed, independent daughters. The genteel family experienced both joy and sadness as they waited for their father to return from the Civil War. Still read and enjoyed by young people.
1873	*St. Nicholas Magazine*, M. M. Dodge, editor	First American literary magazine for children; included poetry, articles, and excerpts from children's literature. Very popular and influential for the time.
1876	M. Twain, *The Adventures of Mark Twain* (U.S., early 1870s)	The adventure-filled escapades of fun-loving, free-spirited individuals who lived on the Mississippi River. The characters and plot are well developed.
1883	R. L. Stevenson, *Treasure Island* (England and the sea, 1880s)	A model adventure story of the sea, filled with excitement, suspense, and well-drawn characters, including heroes and pirates. Written for children; still read and enjoyed by all ages.
1884	J. Spyri, *Heidi* (Switzerland, mid-1880s)	The author vividly describes the setting while portraying a young girl who moves to her grandfather's home. Young people still enjoy this book.
1932	L. I. Wilder, *Little House in the Big Woods* (Wisconsin, late 1880s)	The first in the series of books about the Ingalls family who survive the hardships of nature and poverty, but always with support, love, and Pa's fiddle.
1986	P. MacLachlan, *Sarah, Plain and Tall* (Western U.S., 1880s)	The lives of the members of a motherless family, surviving on the prairie, are changed when Sarah answers the father's advertisement for a wife. Sarah comes temporarily until she and the family can decide if she is a suitable wife and mother. The family's love for each other is conveyed through the well-developed characters of the children and Sarah. Newbery Medal winner.

TABLE 5.7 Notable Realistic Fiction Set Between 1900 and 1945

PUBLICATION DATE	AUTHOR, TITLE (SETTING)	COMMENTS
1908	L. M. Montgomery, *Anne of Green Gables* (Canada, 1908)	The first of eight books about a lively, curious, free-spirited orphan who lived on Prince Edward Island in Canada. The other books follow her life as she grows up and has a family.
1909	F. H. Burnett, *The Secret Garden* (England, early 1900s)	A spoiled, young, orphan girl who grows up in her uncle's house learns the true meaning of love, beauty, and acceptance of those who are different.
1943	R. McCloskey, *Homer Price* (U.S., early 1900s)	The idyllic life of a curious, sometimes mischievous, midwestern boy who is involved in many humorous situations, inventions, and other "business" endeavors.
1969	W. Armstrong, *Sounder* (Rural South, early 1900s)	The author vividly describes the life of an African-American sharecropper, his family, and his dog. The harsh events are realistically plausible and possible. The boy, his mother, and Sounder, the dog, are well developed. Newbery Medal winner.

(Continued)

TABLE 5.7   Notable Realistic Fiction Set Between 1900 and 1945 *(Continued)*

PUBLICATION DATE	AUTHOR, TITLE (SETTING)	COMMENTS
1969	B. and V. Cleaver, *Where the Lilies Bloom* (Appalachia, 1930s)	Mary Call Luther keeps her father's death a secret so she can keep her family together. The strong protagonist is realistically portrayed as are the conflicts she overcomes.
1975	V. Hamilton, *M. C. Higgins, the Great* (Rural U.S., 1930s)	M. C., a dreamer, looks at the world from the top of a 40-foot pole located at his Ohio home. A hitchhiker who enters his life helps him see that if he is to succeed, he must take hold of his life. The African-American characters are realistically portrayed. Newbery Medal winner.
1976	M. Taylor, *Roll of Thunder, Hear My Cry* (Rural U.S., 1930s)	Realistic portrayal of a loving, supportive African-American family and their experiences in rural Mississippi before and during the civil rights movement. Newbery Medal winner.
1942	V. L. Burton, *The Little House* (Urban U.S., 1940s)	Describes the changes that happen to a little house when the city expands and shows how a house can be transformed with love.
1944	E. Estes, *The Hundred Dresses* (U.S., 1940s)	Wanda, a poor Polish girl who wears the same dress to school every day, is teased when she tells the fifth grade "snobs" that she has 100 dresses at home. When her family moves, the girls find out she did indeed have the dresses. Newbery honor book.
1946	M. de Angeli, *Bright April* (U.S., 1940s)	One of the first children's books to deal with a middle-class African-American girl. She moves and finds a solution to overcoming prejudiced members of her Brownie troop.

TABLE 5.8   Notable Realistic Fiction Set Between 1946 and 1980

PUBLICATION DATE	AUTHOR, TITLE (SETTING)	COMMENTS
1956	M. DeJong, *The House of Sixty Fathers* (China, after WW II)	A Chinese boy is befriended by 60 American soldiers who help him find his mother.
1961	S. Burnford, *The Incredible Journey* (Canada)	The adventures of two dogs and a cat who survive against almost unsurmountable odds. The author's ability to visualize the animals' conflicts with their environment makes this a favorite animal book.
1964	L. Fitzhugh, *Harriet the Spy* (U.S., 1960s)	Lonely 11-year-old Harriet records the actions of those she observes in her journal. Trouble begins when her journal is discovered.
1969	J. Steptoe, *Stevie* (U.S., 1960s)	Robert is tired of Stevie following him everywhere he goes until Stevie's mother takes him home. Strong realistic plot, well-developed African-American boys.
1967	E. Konigsburg, *From the Mixed-Up Files of Mrs. Basil E. Frankweiler* (New York City, mid-1960s)	Claudia and her brother run away to live in the Metropolitan Museum of Art. Their adventure involves the mystery of the little angel statue and leads them to Mrs. Frankweiler who helps them return home in a different way. Newbery Medal winner.
1970	B. Byars, *The Summer of the Swan* (U.S., late 1960s)	Sara protects her mentally retarded brother from the teasing of older boys. When he is lost, she discovers the importance of helpful friends. Newbery Medal winner.
1967	S. E. Hinton, *The Outsiders* (U.S.)	The young writer vividly describes the operations of gangs on city streets. The teenager's reasons for belonging to a gang give older readers insight into the interaction of gang members.
1970	J. Blume, *Are You There God? It's Me, Margaret* (U.S.)	Margaret asks questions about social, sexual, and religious values.
1976	K. Paterson, *The Bridge to Terabithia* (Rural Virginia)	A realistic portrayal of the adventures, happiness, and sorrows of Jess and his fifth grade friend, Leslie. A popular realistic novel with well-developed themes, characterization, and plot and an outstanding writing style. Newbery Medal winner.
1977	B. Byars, *The Pinballs* (U.S.)	Three foster children survive countless obstacles. The carefully crafted themes, characters, and incidents are plausible and possible.

TABLE 5.9 Notable Realistic Fiction Set in the 1980s

PUBLICATION DATE	AUTHOR, TITLE (SETTING)	COMMENTS
1979 1982 1983	D. & J. Howe, *Bunnicula* *Howliday Inn* *The Celery Stalks at Midnight* (U.S.)	A popular series of light mysteries featuring the adventures of the Monroe family pets, Harold the dog and Chester the cat. In the first book, the amateur dog and cat detectives attempt to solve the mystery of the vampire bunny. Other books depict equally amusing, fun-filled adventures with the animals.
1981 1982	C. Voigt, *Homecoming* *Dicey's Song* (U.S.)	After being abandoned by their parents, Dicey Tillerman and her three siblings journey across the eastern seaboard to an unknown grandmother. The two books depict their plight and gradual acceptance of life. *Dicey's Song* was a Newbery Medal winner. See also *A Solitary Blue* (1983) and *Sons from Afar* (1987).
1983	B. Cleary, *Dear Mr. Henshaw* (U.S.)	Through letters and journal entries, the reader learns of Leigh's parents' divorce, his mother's struggles, the love of his dog, and his father's neglect. The author believably portrays with humor the mysteries of life and adult relationships. Newbery Medal winner. See also the sequel, *Strider* (1991).
1987	G. Paulsen, *Hatchet* (Canadian wilderness)	When 13-year-old Brian successfully lands a small plane in the wilderness, his troubles begin. Hurt by his parents' divorce, Brian learns to survive in the wilderness and in life. An exciting adventure story with strong characters. Newbery Honor Book.
1988	W. D. Myers, *Scorpions* (Urban sidewalks)	Gangs, guns, and murder in the inner city are vividly and realistically depicted. Jamal, a 12-year-old boy, must make difficult decisions. Believable interracial characters and events. Newbery Honor Book.
1988	J. Yolen, *The Devil's Arithmetic* (U.S., 1980s–Poland, 1940)	A time-travel novel depicting the Holocaust and Jewish traditions. A girl attempts to change history. Some classify the book as fantasy, but strong authentic features override the fantasy elements.
1989	W. Hobbs, *Bearstone* (Utah Canyon)	Questioning his life and his culture, Cloyd, a homeless, 14-year-old troublemaker, discovers the strength of his Native American lifestyle through Walter's love and sharing of their common traditions.

TABLE 5.10 Notable Realistic Fiction Set in the 1990s

PUBLICATION DATE	AUTHOR, TITLE (SETTING)	COMMENTS
1990 1995	D. Macaulay, *Black and White* *Shortcut* (U.S.)	The innovative author/artist visually depicts four stories in one in *Black and White,* the 1991 Caldecott winner. The reader must follow clues to find the story line. In *Shortcut,* Macaulay combines nine very short events that conclude with happy endings for the characters.
1991 1994	E. Bunting, *Fly Away Home* *Smoky Night* (Urban U.S.)	Bunting presents issues of concern to contemporary society. The first book takes a unique look at the homeless. In the second book, two cats help unfriendly, interracial neighbors become friends, as they cope on the night of the Los Angeles riots. David Diaz's primitive collages enhance and add to the excitement of the narrative. Caldecott winner.
1992	V. Alcock, *A Kind of Thief* (U.S.)	Elinor's father is arrested for embezzling. She retrieves his locked briefcase from storage and is certain it contains the money. Deciding what to do with the briefcase is a difficult decision for the 13-year-old girl.
1994	J. Hickman, *Jericho* (U.S.)	The book alternates between two plot lines: the life of 12-year-old Angela and that of her great-grandmother, Min. The reader sees the parallels in the two characters' lives and the strong bond of family.
1995	H. McKay, *Dog Friday* (U.S.)	Robin and his mother's bed-and-breakfast business and their lives are invigorated and enlivened when the Robinson family moves next door. The four unusual, enthusiastic Robinson children and their old dog help Robin overcome his fear of dogs and cope with a bully.

Historical fiction gives young people these memories and knowledge. Stories record individuals' behavior and the consequences of their decisions. Wise people learn from their ancestors. They repeat their ancestors' successes and avoid their mistakes. Contemporary girls and boys can use the events in historical fiction as guides for their personal actions. Typically, historical fiction is fascinating to children eight years and above. Children of this age understand the passing of time and are curious about events and people who lived before their lifetime. Five year olds, as well as their grandparents, however, will be attracted to a book such as Roy Gerrard's *Wagons West!* (1996). Through a unique verbal narrative and original illustrations, Gerrard introduces interesting characters and captures the pioneers' spirit in this humorous picture storybook about the "wild west." (See the Gerrard color plate.)

As young people explore contemporary fiction, they are amazed to find places, problems, and people they encounter or could encounter every day. Thus, by experiencing contemporary fiction, children aged four and above discover positive role models and suitable alternative solutions to personal concerns. Table 5.11 on page 160 identifies benefits individuals may gain from exploring realistic fiction.[18]

THE SELECTION OF QUALITY REALISTIC FICTION

Three factors are considered when selecting all realistic fiction: (1) the literary merit of the realistic narrative, (2) whether the content is appropriate for the age, and (3) the teacher's instructional goals. Table 5.12 on page 161 lists questions to consider when selecting quality literature. A variety of questions are suggested to help the selector determine the suitability of a realistic narrative. The selector will rarely use all the questions when choosing an individual book.[19] The bibliography will also assist in selecting quality realistic fiction.

INSTRUCTIONAL FOCUSES

"That reminds me of the time . . . ."

"My grandfather told me about the time he did something like that."

"I have a friend just like . . . ."

"I wish I could do what she did."

"Did you know my family came from . . . ?"

"I wanted to shout with joy when . . . ."

Roy Gerrard's compressed, little people are shown in full color in his book, Wagons West! *Through a rhyming verbal text and stylized watercolor and line drawings, the author-artist describes the adventures of pioneer families who traveled on the Oregon trail. Have you ever seen people like those drawn by Gerrard?*

TABLE 5.11   Benefits Individuals Gain from Exploring Realistic Fiction

---

When individuals explore historical fiction:

They experience historical events through stories and learn about political affairs, society, science, attitudes, beliefs, hardships, and the environment during a particular historical period. This helps them understand the similarities and differences of people throughout time.

They become aware of the circumstances influencing past events and human behavior. They realize past and present decisions influence future generations and begin to understand how a leader's decisions can influence the future of a country.

They encounter their personal historical heritage and develop a positive feeling of national, ethnic, cultural, or racial pride.

They can interpret the past to develop a broader understanding of universal human truths applicable to all ages, such as the importance of truth in human relationships and governmental affairs.

They realize historical people were real and that individual or group decisions and efforts led to successful or unsuccessful endeavors. People learn from history.

They are more likely to be enthusiastic about studying the social sciences, including history, sociology, anthropology, and geography.

When individuals explore contemporary fiction:

They vicariously explore the world. These experiences expand children's interests and knowledge.

They are introduced to various human relationships. Quality narratives provide successful techniques to use when interacting with family, peers, and others in their environment.

They vicariously experience situations similar to those found in their immediate environment or situations they have not personally experienced, such as conflicts, fears, anger, grief, and competition. The narratives portray alternative techniques for young people to use to deal positively with others and achieve realistic goals.

They encounter realistic portrayals of lifestyles, traditions, and concerns of people from parallel cultures. Young people recognize the similarities and differences of diverse groups. This recognition heightens their sensitivity to the beliefs and values held by various groups. When they understand others, young people usually attempt to form genuine friendships with people of various groups.

As the preceding reactions illustrate, successful realistic fiction naturally elicits personal, emotional, and aesthetic responses from individuals. Initially, teachers elicit a predominantly aesthetic instructional focus, but because realistic fiction includes a variety of topics, it may be used later for an efferent instructional focus. A realistic narrative is chosen according to its literary merit, its potential to enhance the learner's life or to provide information, and the learner's interest in the topic. Children's interests change so surveys should be administered periodically throughout the year to learn their current interests (as suggested in Chapter 2). We can combine children's interests with instructional goals when making curricular decisions. For example, we consider students' interests when selecting thematic topics, when choosing literature for content area instruction, and when suggesting stories for independent or group language arts experiences.

When realistic selections are presented for pleasure, the subjects included in the literature should be appealing to the children and should be age appropriate. If a selection is used for literature-based instruction, the topic of the literature and the language and cognitive abilities of the individual or group are considered. The potential of a narrative to evoke children's emotional responses is also important when choosing a realistic narrative in a classroom. Children or teachers can read the selection to the class, give a book talk, tell the stories, or use various dramatic, visual or media techniques as suggested in Chapter 10 to present the selected realistic narratives.

Throughout this chapter, several LRMs have been suggested for use with realistic fiction. The following section suggests more visual and verbal LRMs for use with historical and contemporary fiction.

TABLE 5.12 Guidelines for Selecting Quality Realistic Fiction

Literary Merit of the Book

All realistic fiction must meet the guidelines for quality fiction: a worthwhile theme; an action-packed, suspense-filled, logical plot; credible characters; an interesting, appealing story with descriptive, flowing language; and an identifiable setting. In addition, consider literary criteria unique to realistic fiction, such as the following:

Does the author authentically portray the people, period, and place? Are the events based on typical experiences of the group? Does the author realistically portray the setting and events without using sensationalism?

Are the beliefs valued by the people appropriately portrayed in the book?

Are factual details integrated into the narrative?

Do the theme and plot deal with concerns and conflicts typical of the setting?

Were the characters' actions and accomplishments possible at this time and place? Do the believable characters provide suitable role models? Does the narrative give young people hope that they can achieve their goals and dreams?

Is the language authentic to the setting? If dialect is used, is it authentic and does it help develop the characterization?

Age-Appropriate Content and Presentation

Are worthwhile topics portrayed in the narrative?

Does the content appeal to the social, emotional, and cognitive maturity of the girls and boys?

Will the youngsters understand and question the characters' motivation?

Will learners be able to determine whether the author consistently depicts authentic events in the fictionalized narrative?

Does the writer evoke emotional and cognitive responses from the audience?

If violence is included, is it anticipated and acceptable to the audience within the context of the story?

What benefits will young people gain from exploring this book?

Purposes for Using the Literature

What aesthetic reactions might this book stimulate?

What efferent experiences naturally evolve from this book?

Will this book be compatible with other books used in a thematic unit of study?

How does this book enhance, supplement, or replace other instructional materials?

LITERARY RESPONSE MODES TO HIGHLIGHT THE GENRE

Learners select suitable LRMs when responding naturally and spontaneously to the authentic stories. If appropriate, the teacher might suggest LRMs for the learners to create to achieve instructional goals or to help the children make connections to the literature or construct meanings of the author's text. Literary Response Modes elicit students' natural reactions and responses to a particular selection or collection of books. While children react aesthetically to realistic narratives, the teacher and students will informally discuss the theme(s), the setting, the characters, and the reasons for their behavior(s). Then they can discuss the author's ability to realistically portray people in various situations during a particular time. Figure 5.4 on page 162 suggests verbal and visual LRMs to use with historical and contemporary realistic literature. Table 5.13 on page 163 suggests LRMs for books set during wartime. Table 5.14 on page 163 suggests several LRMs for current issues in realistic fiction, and Table 5.15 on page 164 suggests LRMs to be used with books organized in thematic categories or LitSets.

FIGURE 5.4 Suggested LRMs to Use with Realistic Fiction

SUGGESTED LRMs FOR REALISTIC FICTION SELECTIONS

VISUAL LRMs

With students' assistance, prepare picture files of photographs representing content in selected books. Display photos before students read books. Laminate and organize pictures. Make files available to students to advertise books.

Prepare a personality collage using the hidden picture format. Place pictures or sketches on poster board. Do not include the title of the book on the collage until other students write their guesses of the title on slips of paper. After several students have correctly identified the title, add it to the collage.

Prepare a "Where Am I?" Prepare a story (character) cube (see Chapter 10). Place clues or riddles on sides of the cube. Have other students guess the setting or something about the characters. Write students' guesses on a sheet of paper. When several students have correctly identified the information, add the title of the book to the cube.

Prepare a mural representing the setting of the book. First sketch the setting, and add details each day until the setting is complete.

Select books from different centuries and geographic locations. Prepare a visual information chart showing the cultural values, lifestyles, family structure, government, and the like. Compare similarities and differences.

Select several characters from a book or the protagonists from several books. Chart conflicts, actions, and resolutions. In another color of ink, write alternate solutions.

VERBAL LRMs

Write a "Choose Your Own Adventure." The class will write about an actual school event. Select a place to stop. Brainstorm alternate endings. Partners will select an idea and complete it. Groups will edit each ending to make it consistent with the beginning. Compile endings. Place them in an appropriate format to create a book. Add illustrations and photographs from magazines to the book. Laminate the book, and have students read it to their classmates. Later, place the book in the school media center.

Dramatize an exciting incident from the book.

Videotape students performing individual adventures. Place the tape in the media center. Teachers can borrow the tape to advertise a book.

Select a book written in the third person. Rewrite an excerpt or paragraph using the first person (or vice versa). Discuss why the author chose this point of view. Decide whether it was a good choice. Why?

Select a favorite episode. Rewrite it and present it as a readers theatre. Use simple costumes to represent the characters' personalities.

Students will tell their favorite incident in a book and invent an original incident to follow it. (The original incident must be consistent with the published one.)

Groups will assume the roles of several characters. Each student will discuss or write about how the character whose role he or she has assumed felt at a particular time in the book and why other characters behaved as they did.

TABLE 5.13 Suggested LRMs: Compare Literature Set During Wartime

When discussing a war in social studies:

Select several books depicting a wartime period (see the bibliography).

Individuals or groups will select a book to read. The book is first read aesthetically; then students will do the following:

Focus on the characters, discuss their actions, and speculate as to why they behaved as they did. Record the speculations.

Focus on the setting, and record major facts learned about the events, places, and period of history.

Focus on the war, list reasons why the war began, describe the treatment of soldiers on both sides, indicate how the enemies were treated, describe how the war concluded, and explain what was accomplished by the war.

Join with one or two other persons or groups reading about another wartime period. Share the information gathered from the first book with others. Chart this information on a visual graphic (described in Chapter 10). List the book and setting in the left column, and place information about the characters, setting, and events across the top of the page.

Students can interview a veteran about the war and ask questions about information obtained in the books. Invite the veteran to speak to the class about his or her wartime experiences.

Encourage students to read other realistic fiction or nonfiction books about the period. Share information with other members of the class. Read about other wars, and compile the information on a similar chart.

After students read other fiction and nonfiction books, hold group or class discussions about ways the war could have been prevented.

TABLE 5.14 Suggested LRMs: Current Issues in Literature

Have students, individually or in pairs, select a current issue of concern to members of the class. Find information books about the topic. Read one or more books of realistic fiction about the issue.

Compare the depiction of the issue in the fiction and information books. Decide whether the authors were honest and authentic in their portrayal.

Have students survey the attitudes of peers about the issue, graph the findings, and report them to the class.

Have students prepare a scrapbook of newspaper and magazine articles discussing the issue or reporting an actual event related to it.

Group students in pairs and have them select one or two news reports and rewrite the report as an interesting, *authentic* story. Students will use the facts from the event, but will add fictional incidents and peers as characters. This experience gives students a better idea of the author's responsibility when writing realistic fiction.

Have students prepare a newspaper. The actual report of the event will appear in a column called *Real News,* and the authentic story will appear in a column to the right, called *Narrative News.*

The Real and Narrative News columns will be placed in a *flip book.* The book will contain two columns, one for the Real News and one for the Narrative News. When preparing the layout for the publication, place the Real News on the left side of the paper. Place the Narrative News on the right. Be sure to place the Real News and the Narrative News on the same page. Add a title and illustrations to the book. Bind it with plastic bindings or rings.

Ask several students to present a *radio show* to the class. One student will read the real news. Other students will read in a dramatic manner the narrative news. Read the news on the school television station.

TABLE 5.15 Suggested LRMs: Books Organized in Thematic Categories (LitSets)

Consult the bibliography to find books (LitSets) suggested for the following LRMs:

Read books about *child labor* or about children who worked for their *family's survival* (in migrant families or during the Great Depression). List the characters' occupations. Outline the treatment of the character(s). Collect articles about teenagers working. Compare earlier employment to contemporary teenagers working. Discuss: Why did the children work? Talk about child-labor laws and migrant workers' children.

Research demographics of *family structure* and *lifestyles* in contemporary America (or other countries). Ask students to describe their family. Draw a family tree with two or more generations. Group students from similar family backgrounds. Students will read and discuss several books representing their group's family structure. Analyze the accuracy with which the books portray two-parent, single-parent, and extended families; grandparents; and foster children. Chart the books; rate them according to accuracy and justify the ratings. Share information with the class. Give a book talk on a favorite book.

Select *different disabilities*. Read several books with characters with disabilities. (Also see the bibliography on school interaction.) Interview special education teachers; ask about the characteristics of disability and different ways to work with children in a classroom. Read several fictional books or stories about disabilities. Consider how the character compensated for the disability. Discuss stereotypes, misconceptions, and prejudices about people with disabilities. Determine the accuracy of the disability portrayed in the book: Does the author solve the character's problems unrealistically? Prepare a bibliography. Rank the authenticity of selected books. Note the number of books on different disabilities. Are some disabilities such as autism omitted? Give this information to the media specialist. Ask students to update the bibliography.

After reading about the *elderly,* adopt an elderly person who lives at home or in a nursing home. If the person has an audio-recorder, make an audiotape, telling about yourself, your family, and your school. Ask the person to tell a story (on the tape) about something that happened to them when they were young. Write letters to the elderly person. Visit the person several times during the year. Elicit the assistance of the art teacher. Make a wall hanging, wreath, or simple gift to take on the visit. Try to write to the person each month and send pictures or a tape. The elderly look forward to the communication. After a visit, share information learned from the elderly person.

Select a theme from the *Personal Relationship Bibliography*. Prepare a bulletin board with large, different-colored circles for the following subthemes: Adjusting, Maturing, Coping, Achieving. Students will read books listed under each subtheme in the bibliography. After reading a book, students will complete a Book Recording Visual (in a shape that indicates the character's gender). Include the author, title, problem, and the way the character adjusted, matured, coped, or achieved on the boy or girl visual. Cluster the visuals around the subtheme.

Incorporate fiction books into science classes. Focus on the climate, natural phenomena, how people interact with the environment, how the climate influences their lifestyle, how people leave an impact on the natural landscape, and similar topics. Compare information in fiction, textbooks, and encyclopedias. Compare people's behavior in earlier periods to the way they act today in terms of the following: use of land, migration, immigration, and reactions after hurricanes, flooding, fires, or other disasters. List alternate ways to react to the situation.

Summary

Realistic narratives, written in prose, poetry, or drama, presented in picture book or chapter book format, portray believable fictional human or animal characters. Realistic fiction depicts situations that *could happen*, but are not necessarily documented. The plausible events, set in historical or contemporary surroundings, portray authentic concerns, values, and lifestyles of people of that particular time and place. Successful realistic fiction tells "authentic stories" about the feelings, experiences, desires, and concerns of characters who are important to the reader.

We classify realistic narratives as either *historical fiction* (realistic selections set before the reader's life began) or *contemporary fiction* (realistic selections set during the reader's lifetime). We classify selections in *historical categories* (designated according to historical period), *literary categories* (adventure stories, survival stories, realistic animal stories, mysteries, humorous stories, general fiction), and *thematic categories* (including family living, personal relationships, interactions in school, societal issues, cultural lifestyles, and international literature).

By exploring this popular genre, young people vicariously experience the choices of the characters and the consequences of their actions and thereby find alternative ways to deal with personal conflicts encountered in daily life. People express strong emotional responses to the narratives if they empathize with the characters. The realistic stories give young people a temporary escape from their real-world concerns. Realistic literature exposes young people to feelings, attitudes, rituals, and beliefs of different countries, regions, cultures, and ethnic or religious groups. These experiences help them become aware of the similarities and differences between people. Realistic fiction has the potential of helping individuals understand their personal behavior and the actions of others. Realistic fiction that "attempts to represent life" by containing "truth to life" can help the reader accomplish these goals, for it will be "a reflection of the society it creates."

NOTES

The opening quotation is from Nina Bawden. 1980. Emotional realism in books for young people. *The Horn Book Magazine.* 56(1). 17.

1. Lewis, C. S. 1961. *An Experiment in Criticism.* London: Cambridge University Press. 60–61. See entire essay, On Realisms. 57–73.

2. James, H. 1948. *The Art of Fiction and Other Essays.* New York: Oxford University Press. 5. See entire essay. 3–22.

3. For additional information about the distinctive literary characteristics of realistic fiction, see Booth, W. C. 1961. *The Rhetoric of Fiction.* Chicago: University of Chicago Press; Dietrich, R. F., & Sundell, R. H. 1978. *The Art of Fiction.* (3d Ed.). New York: Holt, Rinehart & Winston. 1–6, 45–46, 79–81, 127–30, 175–80, 217–22, 271–72; Forester, E. M. 1954. *Aspects of the Novel.* New York: Harcourt, Brace & World. 44–154; Otten, C. F., & Schmidt, G. D. (Eds.). 1989. *The Voice of the Narrator in Children's Literature: Insights from Writers and Critics.* New York: Greenwood Press. 161–205; Walsh, J. P. 1981. The art of realism. In Hearne, B., & Kaye, M. (Eds.). *Celebrating Children's Books.* New York: Lothrop, Lee & Shepard. 35–44.

4. Susan Sharpe, a contemporary writer of juvenile realistic fiction, addresses this issue in the following article: 1992. Why didacticism endures. *The Horn Book Magazine.* 68(6). November/ December. 694–96.

5. The term *parallel cultures* was suggested by Virginia Hamilton, winner of the Hans Christian Andersen, Newbery, and Laura Ingalls Wilder awards, to describe "people of color," "minority groups," and "multicultural" groups. She argues that all peoples stand side by side as equals. See Hamilton, V. 1992. Planting seeds. *The Horn Book Magazine.* 68(6). November/December. 647–80. For additional discussion of the terms and who can write about a culture, see Bishop, R. S. 1993. Books from parallel cultures: What's happening? *The Horn Book Magazine.* 70(1). January/February. 105–9; Silvey, A. (Editorial). 1993. Varied carols. *The Horn Book Magazine.* 69(2). March/April. 132–33; See also the letters from M. Aronson, an editor, and B. B. Murphy, an author. 1993. Letter to the editors. *The Horn Book Magazine.* 69(4). July/August. 390–91. For additional information about the topic, see Chapter 9.

6. Paterson, K. 1994. Cultural politics from a writer's point of view. *The New Advocate.* 7(2). Spring. 85–91; Seto, T. 1995. Multiculturalism is not Halloween. *The Horn Book Magazine.* 71(2). March/April. 169–74.

7. Yolen, J. 1994. An empress of thieves. *The Horn Book Magazine.* 70(6). November/December. 702–5.

8. For insightful essays on young people's reactions to fiction, see Bawden, N. 1980. Emotional realism in books for young people. *The Horn Book Magazine.* 56(1). February. 17–33; Mackey, M.

1990. Filling the gaps: *The Baby-Sitters Club*, the series book, and the learning reader. *Language Arts.* 67(1). September. 484–89.

9. Cai, M. 1993. Variables and values in historical fiction for children. *The New Advocate.* 5(4). 278–91.

10. Adamson, L. G. 1994. *Recreating the Past: A Guide to American and World Historical Fiction for Children and Young Adults.* Westport, Conn.: Greenwood Press. Introduction.

11. Books included in the selected bibliographies were recommended by at least two of the following sources: *The Bulletin of the Center for Children's Books*, published monthly by the Graduate School of Library and Information Science, Champaign, Ill.: University of Illinois Press; Carroll, F. L., & Meacham, M. (Ed.). 1992. *More Exciting, Funny, Scary, Short, Different, and Sad Books Kids Like about Animals, Science, Sports, Families, Songs, and Other Things.* Chicago: American Library Association; Estes, S. (Ed.) 1992. *Popular Reading for Children III.* Chicago: American Library Association; *The Horn Book Guide to Children's and Young Adult Books*, published since 1989 in March and September by *The Horn Book Magazine*; Jensen, J. M., & Roser, N. L. (Ed.) 1993. *Adventuring with Books.* (10th Ed.). Urbana, Ill.: National Council of Teachers of English; Rudman, M. K. 1995. *Children's Literature: An Issues Approach.* (3d Ed.). White Plains, N.Y.: Longman; and the author of this book.

12. For additional information about the categories of realistic fiction, see Baskin, B. H., & Harris, K. H. 1984. *More Notes from a Different Drummer: A Guide to Juvenile Fiction Portraying the Disabled.* New York: R. R. Bowker; Cleary, B. 1982. The laughter of children. *The Horn Book Magazine.* 58(5). 555–64; Fakih, K. O. 1993. *The Literature of Delight: A Critical Guide to Humorous Books for Children.* New Providence, N.J.: R. R. Bowker; George, J. C. 1973. Newbery acceptance speech. *The Horn Book Magazine.* 49(4). August. 337–47; Howe, J. 1990. Writing mysteries for children. *The Horn Book Magazine.* 66(2). 178–83; Hunter, M. 1990. *Talent Is Not Enough.* New York: Harper & Row; Shirley, J. T. (Ed.). 1943. *Dictionary of World Literature.* New York: Philosophical Library. 407–8; Spinelli, J. 1991. *Mania Magee: Homer on George Street. The Horn Book Magazine.* 67(1). 39–42.

13. Egoff, S. A. 1981. *Thursday's Child: Trends and Patterns in Contemporary Children's Literature.* Chicago: American Library Association. 31.

14. Egoff, S. A. 1988. *Worlds Within.* Chicago: American Library Association. 35.

15. Soderbergh, P. A. 1980. The Stratemeyer strain: Educators and the juvenile series book, 1900–1980. In Egoff, S., Stubbs, G. T., & Ashley, L. F. (Eds.) *Only Connect: Readings on*

Children's Literature. (2d Ed.). Toronto: Oxford University Press. 63–73.

16. For additional information about problem novels, see sources such as Chaston, J. D. 1991. American Children's fiction of the eighties: Continuity and innovation. *Children's Literature in Education.* 22(4). 223–32; Egoff, S. 1980. The problem novel. In Egoff, S., Stubbs, G. T., & Ashley, L. F. 356–69; Sutton, R. 1994. *The Big Picture: Living in Secret* by Cristina Salat. *Bulletin of the Center for Children's Books.* Champaign, Ill.: University of Illinois Graduate School of Library and Information Science. 46(7). 203–4.

17. For additional information about notable realistic fictions, see sources such as Egoff, S. A. 1981. 31–79; Egoff, S. A. 1988. 34–39, 68–69, 173–76; Gillespie, M. C. 1970. *Literature for Children: History and Trends.* Dubuque, Iowa: Wm. C. Brown. 75–94; Megs, C., Eaton, A. T., Nesbitt, E., & Viguers, R. H. 1953. *A Critical History of Children's Literature.* New York: Macmillan; Smith, D. V. 1963. *Fifty Years of Children's Books 1910–1960: Trends, Backgrounds, Influences.* Champaign, Ill.: National Council of Teachers of English; Smith, E. S. (Revised by M. Hodges & S. Steinfirst). 1980. *The History of Children's Literature.* Chicago: American Library Association; Yolen, J. 1993. How children's literature has evolved. In Rudman, M. K. (Ed.). *Children's Literature: Resource for the Classroom.* (2d Ed.). Norwood, Mass.: Christopher-Gordon. 3–18.

18. For additional information about the benefits gained by exploring realistic fiction, see sources such as Cormier, R. 1981. Forever pedaling on the road to realism. In Hearne, B., & Kaye, M. (Eds.). *Celebrating Children's Books.* New York: Lothrop, Lee & Shepard. 45–61; Fox, P. 1988. Unquestioned answers. In Hearne, B. (Ed.). 1993. *The Zena Sutherland Lectures: 1983–1992.* New York: Clarion. 115–37; Garfield, L. 1988. Historical fiction for our global times. *The Horn Book Magazine.* 64(6). 736–42; Levstik, L. S. 1993. Making the past come to life. In Cullinan, B. (Ed.). *Fact and Fiction: Literature Across the Curriculum.* Newark, Del.: International Reading Association. 8–10; Paterson, K. 1989. Peace and the imagination. *The Spying Heart: More Thoughts on Reading and Writing Books for Children.* New York: Lodestar Books. 151–71; Steele, M. Q. 1971. Realism, truth, and honesty. *The Horn Book Magazine.* 46(1). February. 17–27.

19. In addition to the sources cited in note 3, see sources such as the following for additional information about selection criteria: Levstik, L. S. 1993. 10–12; Root, S. L. 1977. The new realism—some personal reflections. *Language Arts.* 54(1). January. 19–24.

Part Three

LITERARY GENRES NONFICTION & OTHER LITERARY TYPES

Biography & Information Books

The Knowledge of Society

*B*ooks make their greatest mark when they reach readers in their growing years. The young look everywhere for that ground of truth on which they can stand before they commit the power of their body and mind to the world as it is, or as they might wish to remake it.

— Milton Meltzer

The need to know characterizes the average person living in the last decade of the twentieth century—the Information Age. Now, more than ever, because of technological advances, information has exploded. With the flick of a switch, live coverage of world news comes into our homes, our schools, and our businesses. Very early in life, children see live pictures of starving children from around the world. We hear government officials attempting to sway our opinion by speaking to us live from a historical monument. Occasionally, we see our friends or family members on news programs. So much information can be overwhelming, however, especially when we lack the knowledge to put it in perspective. Authentic nonfiction literature gives girls and boys the background they need to understand the facts they are receiving. With information, individuals can make appropriate choices later

in life. Patricia Lauber, a distinguished author of information books, says she wants to help the reader understand the workings of the earth, to instill a "sense of wonder" and respect for the land, and to lead young people to understand that successful science books "touch the mind, the heart, the imagination."[1] Russell Freedman, who is responsible for shaping the current high standards of factual photo-essays, says that the purpose of nonfiction literature is to inform, instruct, and enlighten. Nonfiction literature provides pleasure for the reader while telling a compelling, truthful story about past, present, and future worlds. Freedman feels that a nonfiction writer looks for a story in nearly every subject.[2] Among the numerous photo-essays created by Freedman is *Buffalo Hunt* (1988). This book describes the importance of buffalo to the Indians of the Great Plains and explains why the animals almost became extinct. Freedman's text is enhanced by the paintings and drawings of artists who traveled to the West in the 1800s and recorded the Native Americans' lifestyle. (See the Freedman color plate.)

A record number of quality nonfiction books are published annually on topics ranging from AIDS to zoo keeping. Through this literature, girls and boys can pursue current interests such as the environment in Joan Anderson's *Earth Keepers* (1993), delve into new and unusual topics through books such as Jim Brandenburg's *To the Top of the World: Adventures with Arctic Wolves* (1993), or learn about the development of machines in David Macaulay's *The Way Things Work* (1988). Exciting, factual biographies and autobiographies, such as Russ Kendall's *Russian Girl: Life in an Old Russian Town* (1994), give life to men and

Alfred Jacob Miller painted this picture, "Hunting Buffalo" around 1858. The artist shows the Native American style of hunting—notice the clever way they captured the animals.

women from various regions and groups. (See Chapter 9 for a discussion of the treatment of *parallel cultures* in literature.) As literature is used extensively for pleasure and for instructional purposes in the classroom, nonfiction literature has taken a prominent place on the library shelves along with fictional literature. Currently, two-thirds to three-fourths of the literature in most school libraries is nonfiction.[3]

This chapter describes the distinctive characteristics of nonfiction literature, identifies unique characteristics of nonfiction's two subgenres, biography (autobiography) and information books, and provides a historical perspective of each subgenre. Successful instructional techniques to use with the literature are included throughout the chapter. The bibliography lists recommended biographies and information books published primarily since 1988. Books included in the bibliography were recommended by several reputable review sources and are arranged according to historical periods, topics of interest to young people, and curricular topics.[4] Choosing quality nonfiction literature can be an overwhelming task, considering that approximately 2,000 new juvenile nonfiction titles are published annually in the United States and other countries.[5]

WHAT IS NONFICTION LITERATURE?

Carter and Abrahamson have defined nonfiction as "any book that is not a novel or a short story."[6] Many people do not like the term *nonfiction* as the name of the category however. Seymour Simon, a renowned author of juvenile science books such as *The Heart: Our Circulatory System* (1996), argues that "non" has a negative connotation and suggests that something does not exist, as in nonreaders. He prefers the term *true* or *real books* to distinguish nonfiction selections from works of fiction, which he calls *not true* or *not real books.*[7] Although Simon's terminology might be appropriate for nonfiction selections, one could argue that fantasy and realistic fiction contain authentic settings, realistic characterizations, and believable events. Therefore, we cannot describe fiction as *not true.*

Jean Fritz, an outstanding biographer, also objects to calling the genre *nonfiction* because both fiction and nonfiction have a common ancestor in story. She reminds us, "The art of fiction is making up facts; the art of nonfiction is using facts to make up a form."[8]

Despite such objections, the genre is likely to continue to be called *nonfiction.* Some of the confusion about the distinction between nonfiction and fiction has developed because of the way books are classified in the Dewey Decimal system, which is used in many libraries.

Originally, all works were grouped into ten major subject divisions: generalities, philosophy, religion, social sciences, language, pure science, applied sciences, the arts, literature, and geography and history. The literature section included poetry, drama, novels, and short stories. The works were also classified by the language in which they were written. As the number of novels and short stories increased, they were removed from the literature section and shelved separately by the last name of the author in a section designated *fiction.* Meanwhile, under the Dewey Decimal system, folktales, poetry, plays, comic books, jokes, riddles, and superstitions remained in the literature classification. Therefore, literature and other books classified under the nine other subject designations are *not fiction* or *nonfiction.*[9]

THE DISTINCTIVE CHARACTERISTICS OF NONFICTION LITERATURE

Authors of nonfiction literature may become passionate and obsessed with their subject because they spend years researching it. Milton Meltzer, a master storyteller of more than 80 juvenile books such as *Hold Your Horses!: A Feedbag Full of Fact and Fable* (1995), believes writers cannot remain neutral: "If they were, they would not be human; they'd be dead souls. Writers need to be honest, to spit the truth out, to tell what they know, what they think." Meltzer's books are filled with accurate facts, but he also wants to "raise questions in the minds of young readers," to challenge them "to examine the past as they move into their future," and to give young people "vision, hope, energy."[10]

After collecting many facts about a topic, the writer selects the most important information to highlight in the book. In this process, the author considers the maturity and interests of the intended audience, the purposes for writing the book, and the information currently available on the subject. The author then uses the most appropriate style of writing to present the selected information. A narrative text is typically used for biographies and informational storybooks. Authors generally use an expository text for other information books. Description, sequence, cause/effect, comparison/contrast, and problem/solution structures are used for expository text. Suitable pictures, illustrations, graphs, documents, and other visuals are included in nonfiction literature to enhance, supplement, enrich, or replace the information presented in the verbal narrative.

Leonard Everett Fisher, a prolific author and illustrator of nonfiction books, realizes that nonfiction writers, like fiction writers, must give the reader memorable and exciting materials. As seen in his book *Gandhi* (1995), Fisher

Leonard Everett Fisher uses gray acrylic paint with highlights of white for Gandhi. *The artist's realistic illustrations show the protagonist's power and peaceful existence in his images.*

carefully selects an appropriate visual and verbal style when presenting the information in his books.[11] (See the Fisher color plate.)

Quality nonfiction literature deals with interesting topics that are appealing to the audience. It is well-written and presents accurate facts and adequate details. Authors consider the audience, highlight the selected information, organize it appropriately, use a suitable format, and include appealing visuals. (See Chapter 1 for additional information about each nonfiction element.) The subgenres of nonfiction literature—biographies and information books—have additional distinguishing characteristics that are discussed later in this chapter.

⬩ THE SUBGENRES OF NONFICTION LITERATURE

From preschool through high school, young people choose to read nonfiction literature for pleasure and informational reasons. Indeed, boys and girls regard nonfiction literature as an exciting way to explore topics related to their immediate interests, future aspirations, and current research projects. The books stimulate thinking and imagination and also help satisfy the reader's curiosity about the world and its inhabitants.

Nonfiction literature, which is written in narrative or expository discourse, is classified as one of the following subgenres:

Biography is a narrative focusing on the life and times of a particular person. Beth Brust's *The Amazing Paper*

Cuttings of Hans Christian Andersen (1994) is an example.

> **Autobiography,** a first-person narrative focusing on events in the author's life, is also included in this subgenre. Jane Bayer's *A Writer's Story: From Life to Fiction* (1995) is an example.

Information books are factual books presenting documented information about a particular topic. Richard and Jonah Sobol's *Seal Journey* (1993) is an example.

⬩ BIOGRAPHY (AUTOBIOGRAPHY)

Biographies are a link between fiction and information books. Although biographers cannot invent facts, Jean Fritz feels they must "understand and know how to use fiction."[12] The writer is expected to portray the strengths and frailties of a person while telling an interesting and exciting story. Biographies may be written in a narrative, story form, but the description of the events in the person's life is based upon documented evidence. Therefore, biography is a subgenre of nonfiction rather than fiction. Note that for purposes of this discussion, we will consider autobiography simultaneously with biography.

THE DISTINGUISHING CHARACTERISTICS OF BIOGRAPHY

Biographers give others a glimpse into the life of a person who interests them. To accomplish this goal, they enthusiastically search for material and people who can give them information about their subject. Writers may become enthralled by their subject as they research her or his life, but they must portray the subject impartially in their book. A master storyteller realizes the audience enjoys a narrative with suspense, tension, surprises, action, and a logical conclusion. Readers will be fascinated by a biography if it reveals the author's compassion for the subject and knowledge about the period.

Like all nonfiction literature, biographies and autobiographies must accurately present documented facts about the subject's life and times. These books, which are written in a fictional narrative, are expected to have a worthwhile subject, a relevant theme, an appropriate chronological order, well-developed, realistic characters, and an interesting style of writing. Contemporary juvenile biographies and autobiographies contain photographs, pictures, archival documents, and drawings. For example, through illustrations and verbal narrative, Alan Say tells about several generations of his family in the picture storybook biography *Grandfather's Journey* (1993). This biography received the

Caldecott Award for its realistic art. Through the simple, straightforward verbal text, the reader is introduced to Say's Japanese grandfather, his adventures in the United States, his life in his native land, and his desire to visit America again. Say's visual and verbal narratives also reveal his love and respect for his grandfather and his desire to live in both his native land and his adopted country. (See the Say color plate.) The distinguishing characteristics of quality biographies are presented in Figure 6.1 on page 173.

APPROACHES TO JUVENILE BIOGRAPHY

Authenticity is the hallmark of all nonfiction literature. With the advent of computerized research techniques and the accessibility of multiple sources of documentation, it has become easier for biographers to present an accurate—not distorted—view of the subject's life and times. Adult and juvenile biographies differ mainly in the amount of documentation and details they include. Adult biographies frequently present a comprehensive examination of

So they returned to the village where they had been children. But my grandfather never kept another songbird.

The last time I saw him, my grandfather said that he longed to see California one more time. He never did.

Allen Say's watercolor paintings for Grandfather's Journey *give the appearance of photographs. Each realistic painting contains suitable soft colors and is framed with simple black lines and a white border. The artist places the simple text at the bottom of the paintings as a caption.*

FIGURE 6.1 Distinguishing Characteristics of Quality Biographies

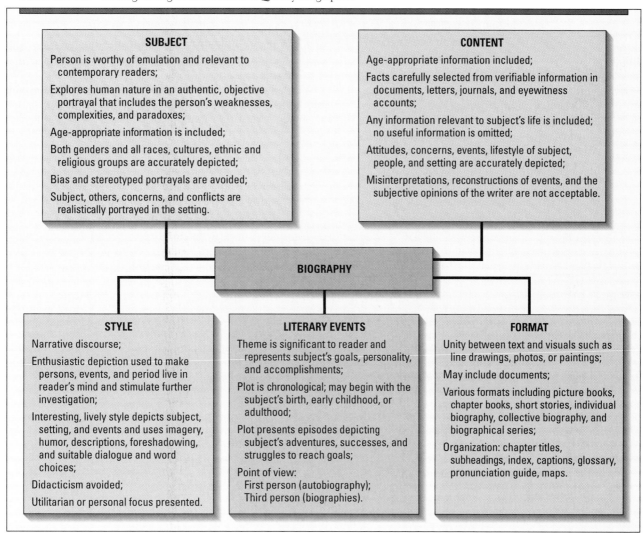

the subject's life and carefully document all information included. Juvenile biographies often highlight only the portion of the subject's life that is appropriate to the maturity and interests of the audience. Contemporary juvenile biographies list the writer's sources and may include a bibliography of additional readings, but they generally include less documentation than adult biographies. Russell Freedman challenges his colleagues to show respect, not reverence, for the subject and at the same time to show respect for the reader when selecting the specific content to include in juvenile biographies.[13]

Juvenile biographies and autobiographies are classified into three categories: *authentic biographies, fictionalized biographies*, and *biographical fiction. Authentic biographies*, the largest category of juvenile biographies, are developed entirely from documented evidence. *Fictionalized*

biographies are based on documented evidence and authentically depict the societal concerns and values of the time. At the same time, however, the biographer includes fictional conversations and may dramatize events to capture the attention of the audience. *Biographical fiction*, the category containing the smallest number of juvenile biographies, presents historical information in a slightly distorted, dramatic manner.

Authentic biographies rely primarily on documented evidence, eyewitness reports, letters, diaries, collected papers, and audio- and videotapes for information about the subject's life and times. Although these sources are informative, they rarely include actual conversations or reveal the thoughts and motives of the subject. Another potential problem is that people may see the same event differently, so relying on a single eyewitness account may lead to a biased portrayal. Most juvenile biographies are authentic in that they are based on verifiable evidence. Sometimes, however, without using direct quotations, the author will include invented conversations, based on documented evidence, to reveal the subject's strengths and frailties. A biographer may also speculate or draw inferences about the subject's thoughts and motives when interpreting his or her actions.[14]

Biographers present their subjects realistically but with compassion. We expect the protagonist to be a person worthy of emulation and deserving of recognition. Different biographers often focus on different aspects of a particular subject's life, however. Therefore, by reading several biographies about the same person, learners can gain special insights into his or her life and times.

Early reputable biographers produced juvenile biographies with authentic texts but paid little attention to authentic, attractive visuals. Many early juvenile biographies contained inferior illustrations or black and white silhouettes that did not enhance, enrich, or supplement the verbal narrative. In the late 1970s Russell Freedman began to expand the photo-essay format by combining selected paintings, archival documents, paintings, and drawings with the verbal narrative. Photo-essays and other suitable artwork are now used extensively in juvenile biographies and information books and give the verbal narrative credibility. Freedman has won wide recognition for his photo-essays including his Newbery winner, *Lincoln: A Photobiography* (1987), and his Newbery Honor book, *Eleanor Roosevelt: A Life of Discovery* (1993). (For more information about Freedman, see "Did You Know?" on page 175.) Another critically acclaimed biographer, Jim Murphy, has continued the development of photo-essays in his authentic biographies, such as his account of Robert Louis Stevenson's adventures in *Across America on an Emigrant Train* (1994). Murphy uses period engravings to trace the experiences of Joseph Plumb Martin in *A Young Patriot: The American Revolution as Experienced by One Boy* (1996). Contemporary biographers include bibliographies, author's notes, and other source materials in biographies intended for young readers seven years and above.

Fictionalized biographies, which present a free interpretation of available facts, also appear in juvenile literature. Writers use all available historical records including journals, letters, and accounts by those who knew the subject, but sometimes this documentation fails to provide many details about the subjects. In this case, writers of juvenile biographies occasionally fictionalize their works by inventing conversations and dramatizing events. By fictionalizing the text, an author can supply enough plausible details to evoke a reader's interest in the historical period and its people.[15] Fictionalized elements must not overpower the historical evidence, however. Recently, several authors have written successful fictionalized biographies. For example, Mary Christian depicts the adventures of an unknown frontiersman who traveled with Lewis and Clark in her acclaimed biography, *Who'd Believe John Colter?* (1993). Anne Neimark, working from limited documentation, gives her readers insight into the life of a talented artist in her fictionalized biography, *Diego Rivera: Artist of the People* (1992). Susan Roth depicts a lifelike, plausible character in *Marco Polo: His Notebook* (1991). In *Shaker Boy* (1994), Mary Lyn Ray uses authentic information in her fictionalized account of the lifestyle of the Shakers. Such writers mark a change from earlier biographers who freely fictionalized the subject's life without admitting this to the reader. Today, authors announce the fictionalized elements of their biographies and challenge readers to find inconsistencies and inaccuracies in their portrayal of historical and contemporary people, places, and events. Jean Little, who chronicled her mother's childhood in Taiwan as the child of missionaries through her early days as a medical student in *His Banner over Me* (1995), is typical of these authors. So is Laurie Lawlor, who wove together historical details and vignettes to depict the life of John Chapman in *The Real Johnny Appleseed* (1995). Lawlor also pointed out the differences between Chapman's journey planting apple trees from the East Coast to Iowa and the legends attributed to him in the popular tall tale.

Several other fictionalized biographies besides those just mentioned remain popular with young people. Ingri and Edgar d'Aulaire's *Abraham Lincoln* (1939), Jean Lee Latham's Newbery winner, *Carry On, Mr. Bowditch* (1955), and Virginia Hamilton's *Anthony Burns: The Defeat and Triumph of a Fugitive Slave* (1988) are favorites. F. N. Monjo uses a child narrator to present biographical information of interest to youngsters and then lists the invented events at the conclusion of his fictionalized biographies; for example, see *The One Bad Thing about Father* (1970), *The Vicksburg Veteran* (1971), *Me and Willie and Pa: The Story of Abraham Lincoln and His Son Tad* (1973), *Poor Richard in France* (1973), *Grand Papa and Ellen Aroon* (1974), *King George's Head Was Made of Lead* (1974), and *Letters to Horseface* (1975).

Biographical fiction is loosely based on historical facts and usually includes imaginary events and conversations. The most successful examples of this approach are Robert Lawson's hilarious biographies *Ben and Me* (1939), *Mr. Revere & I* (1953), and *Captain Kidd's Cat* (1956), featuring a mouse narrator, a horse narrator, and a cat narrator, respectively. Contemporary books including as much fiction as Lawson's biographies are categorized as historical fiction.

Did You Know About
RUSSELL FREEDMAN?

*L*ife is filled with true and fascinating stories, and a keen observer of human behavior will use these stories in books. Russell Freedman is such a person. Early in his career, he worked as a reporter and editor for the Associated Press and wrote publicity statements for television programs. When Freedman heard about a teenager who had invented a Braille typewriter, he began to wonder how many other teenagers had made significant contributions. In 1961, after carefully researching the question, Freedman published his first book, *Famous Teenagers Who Made History*. The book was followed by biographies about people such as Jules Verne and Thomas Alva Edison. Beginning in 1969, he wrote *How Animals Learn* and twenty-three other nonfiction books on animals. At this time he decided to use informative photographs rather than illustrations in his books. He spends many hours searching through photo archives around the country looking for the right photos to enhance his writings. Since 1961 Freedman has published at least one biography or information book each year.

Whether he chooses a topic or finds photographs first, we do not know, but one thing is apparent, the photographs and the verbal narrative mesh perfectly. Freedman was a man before his time. His *Immigrant Kids* (1980), developed from a photography exhibit at the New York Historical Society, received excellent re-

views, but photographs in information books were not well received at the time. Fortunately, Freedman continued to publish photo-essays. With his 1983 publication *The Children of the Wild West*, Freedman's technique and books won the recognition they deserved. He won the prestigious Western Heritage Award from the National Cowboy Hall of Fame for this book. Finally, in 1988 his *Lincoln: A Photobiography* received the Newbery Medal—the first time in thirty-two years that a nonfiction book had received the award. It would have been impossible for the committee to overlook his thorough, interesting style of writing that blends with the large collection of photographs about Lincoln's world. Many nonfiction writers consider Russell Freedman to be one of the top four writers of nonfiction materials and list him among those who have made significant changes in the genre.

Although information books are usually used just to find bits of information, readers eagerly read Freedman's books from the first word to the last. We know we can trust his books. The facts are accurate, the photos are intriguing, and best of all, the books are entertaining to read. By combining pleasurable reading with information and high-quality photographs, Freedman has challenged future nonfiction authors to create accurate, interesting, well-written nonfiction literature that is visually attractive.

FORMS OF BIOGRAPHIES

Whether they are authentic biographies, fictionalized biographies, or biographical fiction, biographies are also classified as individual biographies, collected biographies, or biographical series. The biographical form selected depends on the author's purpose and the intended audience.

Individual biographies depict the life of one person. They may take either of the following forms:

Complete biographies deal with the person's entire life from birth to the grave. Some authors simply describe the main events of the person's life. David Adler's easy-to-read picture book biographies, such as *A Picture Book of Jesse Owens* (1992), are examples. Other writers deal comprehensively with many aspects of the subject's life. An example is Beverly Ghermon's *E. B. White: Some Writer!* (1992). Authors report that this popular form is difficult to write, because many important details may not be related to the selected events. Too many details make a book tedious to read, yet enough details must be included to make the person's life a cohesive story.

Partial biographies highlight the major events of the subject's life or a particular period that influenced his or her accomplishments or development. Many partial biographies begin in the person's childhood and conclude with the subject's first major accomplishment; for example, see Bill Peet's *Bill Peet: An Autobiography* (1989). Other partial biographies concentrate on a particular period in the person's life; an example is Zlata Filipovic's *Zlata's Diary: A Child's Life in Sarajevo* (1994).

A **collective biography** includes several brief biographies or accounts of incidents in the lives of people who have common interests, backgrounds, or achievements. Individuals selected for collective biographies have successfully accomplished the major theme of the collection. In *Is There a Woman in the House . . . or Senate?* (1994), Bryna Fireside describes the accomplishments of ten women who are members of Congress. *Take a Walk in Their Shoes* (1989) by Glennette Turner is about fourteen outstanding African Americans.

Collective biographies introduce young people to successful people who can become positive role models. Girls and boys often become curious about individuals portrayed in collective biographies and read complete or partial biographies to find out more about them. Alice Provensen's *My Fellow Americans: A Family Album* (1995) is a collective biography that includes Americans from diverse categories such as patriots, entertainers, naturalists, and politicians. Provensen's distinctive illustrations enrich her "observations and reflections" to give a historical perspective on the events and people discussed in the oversized volume. (See the Provensen color plate.)

Biographical series are multiple volumes of individual biographies published by a company under a series name, such as Rizzoli's *Weekend With Series*. Many publishing companies produce biographic series focusing on a particular career, such as Owen's *Meet the Author Collection* and Abrams's *First Impressions Series*, or a theme, such as Millbrook's *Gateway Greens Biography*. A literary type may be incorporated in a series, as in David Adler's *Picture Book Series*. When young people discover an appealing series, they will attempt to read every title in the series.

Nonfiction series, both biographies and information books, serve as a useful introduction to a topic or person. Reading them may lead the child to undertake a further investigation of the topic and explore books presenting a comprehensive coverage of the subject. While individual books in a series are useful for independent reading or cur-

Alice Provensen uses a unique format for her collective biography My Fellow Americans: A Family Album. *In a limited space she uses ink and oil paints to realistically portray Americans who made outstanding contributions to the development of various areas of American life. Do you know the contributions made by the people in this illustration?*

ricular goals, overall a series may present several problems. For one thing, a company usually instructs the various authors of individual books to follow a specified formula or pattern. Thus, each book in the series may contain the same number of pages and be written about the same period in a subject's life. This rigid format may prevent authors from presenting a unique perspective about the subject and frequently leads to stilted writing or misleading information. Some series mismatch the content and the intended audience. They may limit their coverage so severely that they omit vital information, or they may present so much information that it overwhelms the audience. Despite these problems, the number of nonfiction series is multiplying. Therefore, the quality of individual titles must be determined before suggesting them for individual reading or classroom purposes.

BIOGRAPHIES AND AUTOBIOGRAPHIES IN THE CLASSROOM

We select biographies and autobiographies with high literary merit and subjects worthy of emulation for classroom activities. Adults making curricular decisions about using biographies in class settings consider the benefits students gain from experiences with the subgenre, guidelines for selecting quality biographies, and instructional goals and techniques to encourage students' responses to the selected literature.

Learners' Preferences and Benefits Individuals Gain from Experiences with Biographies

People constantly search for heroes and are curious about the lives of people they admire. Biographies provide information about potential heroes and their times. While reading biographies, young people learn about human nature, about people who perform good deeds, and how people cope in difficult times. Often young people become emotionally involved with the subject and come to admire people who triumph over adversity. Children develop a positive sense of identity as they read biographies about people whose gender or cultural, religious, or racial group is the same as or different from their own. Boys and girls also like biographies about people who have hobbies or special interests similar to their own.

One factor that influences the biographer's selection of content is the developmental stage of the intended audience. For example, preschool to eight year olds are in the "Me, Myself, & I" stage of development. They are attempting to understand themselves and their environment. Therefore, short picture book biographies such as David Adler's *A Picture Book of Patrick Henry* (1995) capture their attention. The pictures and the simple, straightforward stories fascinate most children more than the biographical information. By the time children reach eight or nine years, they understand the passage of time and are curious about people who lived in other times and places. They are searching for positive role models. Biographies supply these models by describing interesting people who have succeeded in their chosen field. This is the reason many well-written contemporary biographies are available about people in various careers, from architects to sports figures to creators of children's books, such as Sid Fleischman's autobiography *The Abracadabra Kid* (1996). By fourth grade many girls and boys become biography buffs. As time passes, they will read other genres, but still enjoy returning to biographies of favorite heroes. At this time the peer group is a strong influence in their lives. They like to challenge their friends to read all of the biographies about a particular person, all of the books in a series, or all of the books written by a particular biographer. Adolescents prefer biographies about people who fought for a cause and were victorious.[16]

Fortunately, successful, contemporary biographies representing diverse groups are now available for young people of all ages. Because young people's interests are varied,

TABLE 6.1 Benefits Gained from Experiences with Biographies and Autobiographies

Students gain insights and information about the concerns, conflicts, and accomplishments of a person and a time in a pleasurable narrative.

The information from a biography gives students background knowledge about people and historical settings.

Biographies authentically present the events in a person's life and the spirit of the times.

Historical events and people are brought to life when encountered in a biography.

Successful biographical narratives stimulate the reader's imagination.

A character's behavior gives students information about human relationships that might guide their actions with others.

This subgenre serves as a model for students' personal writing.

People portrayed in quality biographies and autobiographies provide positive role models for young people.

outstanding biographies enjoyed by five to sixteen year olds are presented in the bibliographies. The biographies are combined with information books to provide a comprehensive coverage of a particular topic. Benefits young people gain from experiences with biographies and autobiographies are listed in Table 6.1.

Guidelines for Selecting High-Quality Juvenile Biographies

Because juvenile biographies describe events in the life of a person, the subgenre should include accurate content, coherent organization, *and* the literary conventions expected in fiction, such as credible characters, worthwhile themes, an appropriate style of writing, and a logical, cohesive plot. To authentically portray the person and the times, contemporary biographers use many realistic photographs, illustrations, and archival documents. Therefore, the format of the book is also a major consideration. Table 6.2 on page 178 lists various criteria to use when selecting quality juvenile biographies and autobiographies.[17] Considering whether the book appropriately incorporates fiction and nonfiction components helps the selector determine its literary merit. The various guidelines are stated as questions to give the selector a comprehensive view of each component. Each question will not be considered for an individual book.

Instructional Focuses

Biographies and autobiographies focus on personalities and behaviors of individuals and can therefore serve as positive role models for young people. To appreciate this

TABLE 6.2 Guidelines for Selecting Quality Biographies and Autobiographies

---

Accuracy and Authenticity

Is the information presented in the book current and accurate?

Does the author cite the sources consulted and other readings?

Do the text and visuals portray the subject accurately?

Content

Did the author select suitable information about the subject and the times?

Did the author cover the subject's life adequately and accurately?

Does the biography authentically portray the attitudes, concerns, and conflicts typical of the period?

Style

Is the subject presented clearly and in an interesting writing style?

Does the author use suitable language, adequate descriptions, humor, foreshadowing, and an appropriate point of view?

Does the author use a utilitarian or personal focus when depicting the person and the times?

If the author includes invented conversations, are they believable? Is the language suitable for the time and place?

Are the biases and stereotypes of the person and society eliminated?

Characterization of Subject(s)

Is the subject worthy of emulation?

Are the strengths, frailties, and complexities of the subject portrayed authentically?

Is the subject portrayed as a believable person? A mortal or a superhero?

Do the characters elicit positive and negative emotional reactions from the reader?

Theme

Does the theme represent the subject's goals, personality, and accomplishments?

Is the theme(s) worthwhile?

Plot

Does the author begin and conclude the book at the most appropriate time in the subject's life?

Is the person's life developed logically?

Does the book include enough details to deal comprehensively with the subject and setting?

Format and Illustrations

Are the most appropriate visuals used to depict the person and times?

Do the illustrations enhance the content?

---

primary purpose for exploring the subgenre, use an aesthetic instructional focus to highlight the successes and foibles of the protagonists. To achieve the aesthetic focus, initially read the book aloud or have students read it individually or in group sessions. Students will react spontaneously to the subject and the events in her or his life.

After students react to the content and literary characteristics of the book, instructional strategies emphasizing an efferent approach are used if they are applicable to the teacher's curricular goals. An efferent approach highlights the information given in the book and encourages students to learn facts about the person, setting, or group values and interactions. (See Chapter 2 for additional information about instructional focuses.)

Literary Response Modes

The instructional strategies and Literary Response Modes (LRMs) highlight personal relationships and give information about the subject's environment. After the initial discussion, students can prepare visual or verbal LRMs that reflect their personal responses to the subject and the book. Table 6.3 on page 179 lists LRMs that can be used with quality biographies and autobiographies to highlight the subject's life and times and achieve the desired instructional objectives. The bibliography lists outstanding biographies recommended for classroom activities. The books are categorized according to historical periods and various topics.

HISTORICAL PERSPECTIVE OF THE SUBGENRE

In the primitive hero stories found in oral folk literature, we have the beginnings of biography. Early juvenile biographies were used to inculcate the moral convictions of a society. Typically, the biographer included imaginary events and conversations, along with some basic facts. Reverend Mason Locke Weems's *Life of George Washington* was an example of this practice. He published the first edition in 1800, but it was not until the fifth edition was published in 1806 that he made up the story about the cherry tree. Generally, juvenile biographies published before the late twentieth century portrayed the subject as a perfect person without a blemish. Controversial subjects or historical events were frequently omitted. Adults felt that children needed idealized characters to emulate and believed that these dramatized biographies would entice youngsters to history. For some children, the books accomplished their goals, but others saw the heroes as stereotyped, legendary figures, similar to the characters in tall tales.

As biographies became popular reading, publishing companies began producing biographical series. In 1932, for example, Bobbs-Merrill published the first biography in its

TABLE 6.3   Suggested LRMs for Biographies and Autobiographies

To decide the accuracy of the content, setting, and events of a subject's life, the students, individually or in groups, will read the following:

Diane Stanley & Peter Vennema, *Cleopatra*

Geraldine Harris, *Ancient Egypt*

Judith Rosher, *Ancient Egypt*

Rosalie David, *Growing Up in Ancient Egypt*

Antony Mason, *The Children's Atlas of Civilizations*

After reading the books, they will prepare an *Attribute Chart* listing facts about Cleopatra and her times. See the example below.

In the left column of the chart, list major facts about Cleopatra and her times.

In the second column, list facts about Cleopatra mentioned in the biography.

In the third column, list facts found in information books.

In the last column, evaluate the authenticity of the biography considering questions such as the following: Does the biography give accurate information? Does the author include an adequate amount of information? Does the book contain too many details about the person and times?

Facts about Cleopatra	Facts about Cleopatra from the Biography	Facts about Cleopatra from Information Books	Authenticity of the Biography
Her reign as queen			
Her political ambitions			
The world in her lifetime			

Talk about the illustrations in the books, especially the Egyptian-style illustrations Diane Stanley and Peter Vennema used in *Cleopatra*. Using mosaic tiles that were popular during Cleopatra's lifetime, the artists authentically depict the setting and dress in the illustrations to expand the verbal narrative. (See the Stanley color plate on page 181.)

To highlight character development and the depiction of the theme, brainstorm and record the characteristics "heroes" are expected to possess. Partners or triads of students will select and read together a biography about a hero from history, government, science, sports, or another topic of interest. After reading, the students will list the subject's personal attributes described in the book that helped make the person a "hero," such as personality traits, leadership ability in times of strife, and ability to overcome physical, mental, emotional, and environmental obstacles. From the list the students could do the following:

Prepare a *personality cube* with words or sketches of each attribute identified in the text. Include the number of the page describing the attribute.

Partners could prepare a written application or present a nomination speech recommending the subject's entrance into the *Literary Heroes Hall of Fame*.

Construct (in the media center) a *Hero's Walk to Fame*. Partners will place a large (12″ × 12″) star on shiny gold paper. The hero's name is written (in a visually attractive manner) in the center of the star. The title of the biography and the author's name are placed at the bottom of the star. Place the stars in conspicuous places. Begin at the door of the media center and continue to the biography section of the library. (Several classes could join to prepare a display on a hall bulletin board leading to the media center.)

Partners will select an event in the text that proves the subject is a "hero." Write a script based on the event for a radio show "*Hallmarks of Heroism.*" Partners will present the script, using different voices for each character and sound effects or appropriate music in the background. Representative visuals are prepared with the author's name, title of the biography, and call number of the book. Use the tape and visuals for a book talk with other students.

To highlight the author's style of writing, students will read a biography about a favorite historical person. Individually or in triads, students will write an article about the author's writing style. Publish the article in a class book titled, *Biographies Written for Children in (school name) Elementary School.*

Students will write the article as if they are the author. To write the article, they will do the following: (1) If biographical information about the author is available, students should incorporate it into the article. (2) The students will collect excerpts from the biography that represent the author's style. (3) If information is available, they will explain why the author chose the subject, the process used by the author to write the biography, and the characteristics of the author's style (include excerpts from the book to document the author's craft). (4) Include several ideas about writing biographies or writing in general. The articles will be placed in the class book.

The class will discuss the various biographers' writing styles and list the characteristics of the styles on a chart titled *The Biographer's Craft*. The chart will be placed in the writing center to help the students when they are writing.

(Continued)

TABLE 6.3   Suggested LRMs for Biographies and Autobiographies (*Continued*)

Students will discuss the suggestions for writing.

The school administration, media specialist, and each member of the class will receive a copy of the book.

Teachers in other classes will be encouraged to invite a panel of students (representing the biographers) into their room to discuss the books.

To highlight the quality and impact of illustrations, photographs, and archival documents used in biographies, students will review biographies written before 1980. The purpose of the review is to look at the illustrations, photographs, documents, and other visuals used in the books. Students will give the name of the biography, the author, and the illustrator and will list the types of visuals used. Students will react to the visuals. Then students will review and list visuals used by writers such as Russell Freedman, David Adler, and other contemporary biographers. They will compare the style of writing and the visuals used by writers at different times. Later, the students will write a short letter to the biographer and illustrator describing their personal reactions to the books.

The children will select the biography with the most effective visuals. A *Certificate of Excellence in Illustrations* signed by the members of the class will be prepared for the winning biographer-illustrator. If the biographer-illustrator is alive, they will mail the letter, the certificate, and another letter describing the award to the person. If the biographer is not alive, the letters and certificate could be mailed to the editor of biographies at the publishing company. Mail another letter to the media specialist and professor of children's literature at a neighboring college or university. Mail only one letter to each person and anticipate a reply.

To highlight the literary structure of this nonfiction subgenre, the class will *read* and *discuss* several diaries or journals, such as the following:

Jane Boulton, *Only Opal: The Diary of a Young Girl*

Zlata Filipovic, *Zlata's Diary: A Child's Life in Sarajevo*

Anne Frank, *The Diary of a Young Girl*

Karen Hesse, *Letters from Rifka*

Amelia Stewart Knight, *The Way West: Journal of a Pioneer Woman*

K. L. Mahon, *Just One Tear*

Rafik Schami, *A Hand Full of Stars*

UNICEF, *I Dream of Peace*

The students will identify and place on a semantic map *distinguishing features* of the subgenre such as the following: dated, short entries are written; the text is written from a first person point of view; the conflicts and solutions are presented in a subjective manner; and the writer expresses personal thoughts, feelings, and emotions at the time of the entry.

In cooperative groups, the students will complete an LRM such as the following:

Place distinguishing features on a *Literary Ladder* (as described in Chapter 10) titled *Diaries and Journals*. The ladder is displayed in the classroom, hung as a mobile in the media center, or placed on a hall bulletin board.

Partners will make a bound book (see Appendix B). They will then select a favorite biography and write in the book diary entries the character might have written during a particularly exciting event in his or her life.

Small groups of students will compare the conflicts a subject encountered and described in a diary or journal with current events in their own lives. They will prepare a comparison chart such as the following:

Topics	Subject's Life	My Life
Family members		
Home life		
Location		
Food		
Entertainment		
Tradition		
School		
Etc.		
Events (conflicts, problems, etc)		

Students will decorate the charts with pictures representing the subject and their own lives. The groups will display and discuss the comparisons.

Prepare a time line representing the period covered in the diary. Write a narrative from the entry about major points in the subject's life. Illustrate the narrative. Place illustrations on the time line *or* illustrate the major events listed on the time line.

Cleopatra VII was eighteen years old when she became Queen of Egypt in the year 51 B.C. As was the custom, she ruled together with her brother, Ptolemy XIII, who was only ten. As was also the custom, Ptolemy became her husband. This was only a formality, though, since he was still a child.

The young king was guided by three important advisers. Since the male was traditionally the chief ruler, these three men expected to rule the country in Ptolemy's name.

But Cleopatra was strong-willed and ambitious. She longed to return her country to the glory of its earlier years. Perhaps Egypt could even regain the empire it had once had under the warlike Pharaoh Thutmose III, fourteen hundred years before. Cleopatra wanted to accomplish this herself, but Ptolemy's advisers were stronger than the young queen. By the time Cleopatra was twenty, they had driven her out of Egypt.

Diane Stanley captures the times in her book, Cleopatra. *By using various colors of gouache paints she presents her impressions of the famous queen, her companions, and their adventures. Do you wonder how Stanley painted the colorful mosaic tiles that were frequently used during Cleopatra's lifetime?*

Famous Childhood Series. Over the years the company published more than two hundred biographies about significant figures in American history. Different people wrote the biographies, but they used similar literary techniques, such as imaginary dialogue and overdramatized events. The black and white line drawings or black silhouettes were not realistic. Nevertheless, the biographies were popular with children because the stories focused on the childhood of the subject.

By the 1970s, juvenile biographies had begun to change for several reasons. First, critics began to question the literary techniques used in previous biographies. Dramatization, idealization, and omissions were no longer acceptable. Second, ideas about childhood were changing. Many felt biographers had a responsibility to present a subject's weaknesses as well as his or her strengths. Doing this also required a full disclosure of historical events. Finally, the celebration of two important anniversaries led to an increase in biographies of the persons involved in the events.

First, in 1975, during the Bicentennial celebration of the origins of the United States, many biographies were published about participants in the American Revolution. Then, in the early 1990s, the Quincentenary of Columbus's journey to the Americas was celebrated. At this time many questions emerged about the adventures of Columbus and his men. Some biographers included the traditional perspective of his explorations, while others presented new interpretations. "The World in the 1490s" bibliography lists outstanding nonfiction books addressing the various viewpoints about Columbus and his men. This issue is still discussed, especially in light of the emergence of multicultural concerns.

By the 1980s, biographers were including many sports and entertainment celebrities in partial and collective biographical series. Although children enjoy reading short stories about favorite commercial heroes, the series format does not allow complete coverage of the person's life. Typically, the biographer sensationalizes events or omits the subject's frailties or unwise decisions. Although the biographies are about popular subjects and are entertaining, many are poorly written and contain no pictures or only inferior ones.

During the last two decades, the number of biographies of women and people from diverse racial, cultural, and ethnic groups has increased. Before that time in the United States, most biographies dealt with Western European or American males, usually political leaders. It is interesting to note that of the fifty-nine books receiving the Caldecott Award, three were biographies; two biographies were recognized as honor books. Of the seventy-five books receiving the Newbery Awards, five were biographies, and twenty other biographies were recognized as honor books.

As mentioned earlier, contemporary juvenile biographies are photo-essays or contain illustrations. This is quite a departure from the sketches and silhouettes included in biographies published earlier in the twentieth century. Table 6.4 on page 183 lists notable juvenile biographies and autobiographies.[18] In summary, we can say:

A good story + an authentic portrayal of a worthwhile subject = a successful biography

INFORMATION BOOKS

Information books—books of facts—open readers' minds to the world beyond themselves. By providing information about all facets of life, these books stimulate readers' natural curiosity about the world. Through information books we find out about ourselves, our neighbors, and the animals and vegetation that inhabit the world with us. We learn about those who lived before us and search for answers to questions about our existence—the same questions people have pondered since the beginning of the universe. In the process, we may discover answers to questions we did not know enough to ask. One sign of an educated person is the realization that we have much to learn about life before we existed, life while we exist, and life after we exist. Through authentically crafted information books, learners can come to understand the results of their actions and the reasons for others' behavior. They can look to history to find explanations of the daily decisions made by people and society. Through information books learners can take responsibility for protecting nature and caring for animals. By reading a variety of information books relating to diverse topics, learners receive necessary guidance to deal with the reality of society.

THE DISTINGUISHING CHARACTERISTICS OF INFORMATION BOOKS

Quality factual literature about history, psychology, religion, science, art, music, technology, life skills, careers, and other special interests is currently available to people of all ages. Depending on the topic and intended audience, authors frequently use expository discourse to present the selected facts. Whereas biographers know the person and her or his times, authors of information books must be knowledgeable in their field.

Information books are frequently joint projects between a professional children's literature author and a specialist in the subject area. The professional writer may lack the specialist's detailed knowledge of the field, while the specialist may not know how to write for children. Sometimes the two will coauthor the book, or sometimes the specialist will be asked by the author or publishing company to review the final draft of the manuscript for accuracy and currency. Nevertheless, the author is ultimately responsible for writing an authentic information book that young people will enjoy reading.[19] Knowing the reputation and credentials of an author gives the reader confidence in the accuracy and currency of the data presented in a book.

Initially, young people select an information book because of the content. While readers may not anticipate an entertaining story, they do expect adequate details and a clear error-free explanation of the topic. Readers who are familiar with nonfiction literature may not expect fictionalized characters, but they do appreciate descriptive language, a logical organization, an enthusiasm for the topic, and a respect for the reader's intelligence. Bruce Brooks accomplishes these literary goals in his information books, such as *Making Sense: Animal Perception and Communication* (1993).

Contemporary information books include illustrations, photographs, and graphic aids, such as maps, charts, graphs, and diagrams that help readers understand the topic. Richard Platt provided the text for *Stephen Biesty's Incredible Cross-Sections*. The illustrator, Stephen Biesty, created cutaway drawings for eighteen objects or structures, ranging from a galleon and a tank to the Empire State Building. Three-foot-long, fold-out pictures provide minute details about an ocean liner and a steam train. The text and illustrations include many unusual and obscure details, which give the reader many hours of enjoyment. (See the Platt color plate on page 184.)

Individuals choose to read information books for different reasons. Some people select an information book because they are fascinated by the topic. Others use information books for references. The purpose determines the way the person reads the book. A person fascinated by a topic usually reads the book from cover to cover, whereas someone searching for specific information will read only the section containing that information. To help readers find specific material, information book authors frequently include reference aids such as a table of contents, chapters with subheadings, an index, and a glossary.

TABLE 6.4 Notable Juvenile Biographies and Autobiographies

DATE	AUTHOR, TITLE	COMMENTS
1934	C. Meigs, *Invincible Louisa*	First biography to win the Newbery Medal. The story of Louisa May Alcott.
1939	I. and E. d'Aulaire, *Abraham Lincoln*	First biography to win the Caldecott Award. A partial biography, ending with the end of the Civil War. Interesting bits of information about Lincoln's life are included.
1939	J. Daugherty, *Daniel Boone*	Second biography to win the Newbery Medal. Authentic depiction of the American adventurer's life and times.
1944	G. Foster, *Abraham Lincoln's World*	This Newbery honor book depicts the major events and important people living during Lincoln's lifetime.
1950	C. I. Judson, *Abraham Lincoln, Friend of the People*	Newbery honor book, authentically based on careful research. Unlike other biographers, Judson felt Lincoln's life was no more poverty-stricken than that of others at the time. Lincoln and his loving, supporting family are realistically portrayed.
1951	E. Yates, *Amos Fortune, Free Man*	Third biography to win the Newbery Medal. This complete biography told of a man who was born free in Africa and sold as a slave, but later purchased his freedom and that of several others.
1956	J. L. Latham, *Carry On, Mr. Bowditch*	Fourth biography to win the Newbery Medal. This fictionalized biography portrays the life and accomplishments of a mathematician who wrote a textbook used by ship navigators for over 100 years.
1965	Aliki, *A Weed Is a Flower: The Life of George Washington Carver*	The first of four easy-to-read picture books. It tells the story of a man who was born a slave and became a famous American research scientist.
1967	A. Frank, *Anne Frank: The Diary of a Young Girl*	The tragedy of a young Jewish girl and her family who attempted to survive in Holland during World War II.
1973	J. Lester, *To Be a Slave*	The author of this Newbery honor book meticulously edited the transcripts of a black who escaped from a southern plantation. The book contains first person narration.
1973	J. Fritz, *And Then What Happened, Paul Revere?*	The first of 10 entertaining authentic biographies, with intriguing titles, about famous Americans. The foibles and accomplishments of the subject are portrayed in this short book. As is typical of Fritz's other books, humorous incidents are included.
1987	R. Freedman, *Lincoln: A Photobiography*	The fifth nonfiction winner of a Newbery Medal. This authentic, well-written book set the standard for authentic biographies with a photo-essay format.
1988 1995	B. Cleary, *A Girl from Yamhill My Own Two Feet: A Memoir*	Two autobiographies of a famous author of children's books. The first book, which begins with her early life in Yamhill, Oregon, shows the uneasy relationship between the author and her mother. The second book continues through her college days, her early married years, and the publication of her first book. Avid fans will recognize similarities between Ramona and Cleary's life.
1993	A. Say, *Grandfather's Journey*	A picture book biography loosely based on the life of the grandfather of this author-artist. This Caldecott winner shows the protagonist's love for his homeland and the United States.
1993	J. Murphy, *Across America on an Emigrant Train*	A photo-essay biography describing Robert Louis Stevenson's trip across America in 1879.
1993	A. Pinkney, *Alvin Ailey*	A picture book biography about the founder of the Alvin Ailey American Dance Theater. Ailey's cultural pride and his work with young people are shown. Brian Pinkney's illustrations convey Ailey's ability as a dancer.
1994	Z. Filipovic, *Zlata's Diary: A Child's Life in Sarajevo*	A diary account of a child's life in Sarajevo from September 1991 to October 1993. The problems of war, bombing, and surviving are effectively described.
1994	D. Stanley & P. Vennema, *Cleopatra*	A fictionalized, complex picture book about the famous Egyptian queen. From the limited information available, the writers have reconstructed a story about this controversial and powerful woman. Stanley used Egyptian folk art for the illustrations.
1995	D. Stanley, *Leonardo da Vinci*	Stanley portrays the culture of Renaissance Florence as well as Leonardo's life and achievements. The outstanding illustrations do not attempt to imitate the work of Leonardo or other artists of Renaissance Italy, but instead stand as a dramatic counterpoint to it.

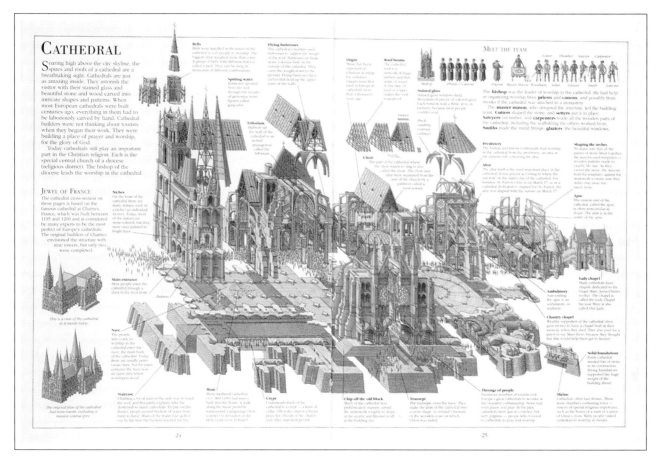

Stephen Biesty's detailed line drawings enhance and supplement Richard Platt's text for Stephen Biesty's Incredible Cross-Sections. *The author-artist team provides detailed information without overwhelming the viewer. Each topic is presented on a separate double page. Biesty uses gouache paint in appropriate colors to highlight his realistic pen-and-ink drawings. When returning to a page, viewers are surprised to discover new facts and images they did not see the first time. The three-foot pages for the* Ocean Liner *and* Steam Train *are special treats for young and old alike.*

We identify certain creators with particular topics; the artist Aliki, authors Millicent Selsam and Vicki Cobb, and photographer Bruce McMillan create nature books. Leonard Everett Fisher writes books about historical crafts and trades and illustrates them with bold engravings. Milton Meltzer writes outstanding books about the lifestyles of various cultural, racial, and social groups and about unusual topics such as the potato and gold. David Macaulay's books are recognized by their detailed graphics, occasional fictionalized characters, and informative facts about architecture and technology. James Cross Giblin chooses topics such as skyscrapers, windows, and chairs. We recognize Seymour Simon for his beautiful colored photographs and diverse subjects ranging from snakes to the solar system. Lynne Cherry, Laurence Pringle, and Brent Ashabranner choose a variety of topics for their books. Gail Gibbons combines her artistic abilities and curiosity about the world to create visually exciting and informative books especially for the youngest child. For additional information about this talented creator of informational picture books, see "Did You Know About Gail Gibbons?"

Besides the nonfiction elements expected of all informative literature, quality information books are expected to meet specific standards applied to the subgenre. Figure 6.2 on page 186 presents the nonfiction elements included in quality information books.

TEXT STRUCTURES USED IN INFORMATION BOOKS

Selecting the appropriate organizational structure is a vital consideration for authors of information books. Some authors choose expository discourse, while others select a nar-

Did You Know About
GAIL GIBBONS?

"Why?" "How does it work?" These are the questions young children constantly ask. These questions are also the basis of Gail Gibbons's books. The author-artist looks at insects, animals, the planets, or caves and caverns and asks questions to find out more about the topic. She consults books and talks to experts. She asks the questions young people would ask, and her information picture books, more than forty of them, give young children just the right amount of information about a subject.

Gibbons enhances and supplements her straightforward verbal narrative with simple, bold, colorful illustrations. Look at her illustrations. They extend the text and enable children to use their visual skills to learn more about a topic.

Gibbons like to create picture information books because she feels they are like a puzzle. When you have a question, you ask people, search through books, and find the answers. She investigates a topic and adds informational clues to the visual and verbal narratives. When she answers her questions, the puzzle pieces fit together, and she creates a book.

Topics young children are curious about are the subjects of her books. In *Recycle*, Gibbons tells

children how we conserve energy and reduce pollution when we recycle objects. Gibbons explains the basic steps in recycling and also recommends ways children can recycle objects. Young children who want to know more about weather can look at Gibbons's *Weather Forecasting* and *Weather Words and What They Mean*. She succinctly defines words commonly used in weather forecasting and includes pictures to clarify the topic.

Gibbons typically writes about scientific topics, but she has also written *Say Woof: The Day of a Country Veterinarian, Deadline! From News to Newspaper*, and *Check it Out!*

Gail Gibbons is curious about the world. She has the ability to view the world from a child's perspective. Children recognize the childlike curiosity in her books and enjoy looking for the answers to their questions in her informational picture books. Wise preschool and early primary grade teachers have a collection of Gibbons's books in their classroom library. Who knows, an adult might learn something from her books too!

---

rative text structure, and others combine narrative and expository discourse. The intended audience, the subject, the author's preference, and the purpose of the book influence the selection.

An author who presents information in a narrative structure includes an authentic setting and believable characters. The characters are involved in events that identify, describe, or explain the topic. While authentic, accurate content is the major focus of a narrative information book, the author must use a suitable style of writing and appropriate literary devices such as imagery, suspense, and foreshadowing. Various formats such as informational storybooks, short stories, and novels are used to produce an appealing, well-written story. Whereas short stories and

novels usually include illustrations, informational storybooks use illustrations to enhance, interpret, supplement, or replace the verbal narrative. In her 1996 informational storybook *Where Once There Was a Wood*, Denise Fleming uses a simple repetitive poem to tell a story about the destruction of wildlife. Her bright collages enhance and provide many details of the story. (See the Fleming color plate on page 187.)

Since informational storybooks, short stories, and novels use a familiar fictional literary pattern, young people of all ages enjoy listening to, reading, viewing, and discussing the books.[20] Another contemporary author-artist, Lynne Cherry, uses the informational storybook format effectively in *The Armadillo from Amarillo* (1994). Cherry's believable

FIGURE 6.2   Distinguishing Characteristics of Information Books

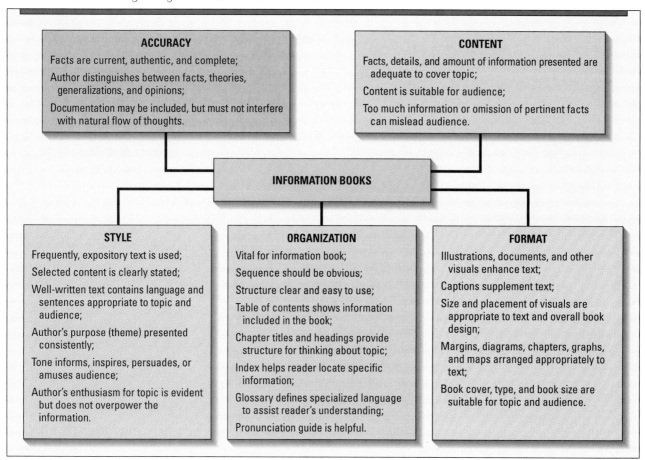

protagonist, Sasparillo, an armadillo from Amarillo, explores the world on an eagle's back and introduces the reader to various geographical regions. She conveys the information through an interesting text and full-color paintings. In the following text Sasparillo meets the eagle and asks for a ride:

> One day he asked the golden eagle
> as she came breezing by,
> "What can I do for a bird's-eye view
> from up in the big blue sky?"
>
> "Hop on my back," said the eagle,
> "I'll fly you wide and far.
> And then you'll see, eventually,
> where in the world we are."[21]

Recently, writers of information books for older readers have used narrative techniques with the expository structure. This format allows the author to bring the people and historical events to life in the mind of the reader. Jerry Stanley dramatizes a period of American history in *Children of the Dust Bowl* (1992) by including personal memories of people who lived during the time. Notice how the living conditions come to life in the following excerpt:

> Every morning the house had to be cleaned. Everett Buckland of Waynocka said, "If you didn't sweep the dust out right quick between the storms, you'd end up scooping it out with a shovel." And every morning someone had to go check the animals. The fierce gales buried chickens, pigs, dogs, and occasionally cattle. Children were assigned the task of cleaning the nostrils of cows two or three times a day.[22]

R. D. Lawrence effectively combines narrative and expository text in *Wolves* (1990). Before discussing the wolves' lifestyle, Lawrence describes his first encounter with a pack of wolves:

> Eight timber wolves surrounded me, howling eerily. I was convinced that they meant to kill and eat me. Fear made my mouth go dry.[23]

Notice the way Lawrence captures the attention of his audience with this suspenseful first-person narrative. After in-

where once
the ferns unfurled
and purple violets grew

Denise Fleming is known for her handmade paper and unique collages as seen in her book Where Once There Was a Wood. *The author-artist uses a simple poetic text and many brilliant colors to encourage people to protect the environment. Notice her hand-written text and the way she arranges the language and images to present a visually attractive composition.*

troducing the topic, he uses an expository style to give information about the wolves:

> No two wolves look exactly alike. Some wolves are all black except for a white mark on their chests. Arctic wolves are all white. Others may be a combination of gray, white, fawn, black, and brown. People who study wolves soon learn to identify each animal by the markings on its fur, which are unique. (p. 14)

The narrative and expository text present an interesting description of the topic. Maps, illustrations, and colored photographs are used to enhance and supplement the verbal text.

Narrative information books build on young people's familiarity with the narrative structure and have the potential to guide them toward factual literature. More writers are choosing a narrative text for their information books. Perhaps the *Magic School Bus Series* written by Joanna Cole and illustrated by Bruce Degan has recently influenced the popularity of narrative information books. This series, intended for five to nine year olds and enjoyed by older readers as well, shows the ability of a narrative text to present information. In all books in the series Cole uses a conversational style and displays class essays on each page to present facts about a selected topic. Degan's humorous cartoons supplement and enrich the information.

Authors of information storybooks frequently present facts about a subject by showing the realistic interactions of animals or human characters in their natural environment and using a narrator to add additional information about the subject. Most information storybooks are books with pictures and include illustrations to supplement, enrich, and clarify the topic. As seen in the following excerpt, Jonathan London uses a narrative text to briefly describe the life of a mother grizzly bear and her cub in his information storybook *Honey Paw and Lightfoot* (1995):

> Finally, in the heart of winter
> Lightfoot was born.
> Helpless, almost hairless, blind,
> no bigger than a hamster.
> He nursed in the deep dark warmth
> of his mother's den.
>
> Come spring, two moons later,
> Honey Paw and Lightfoot awoke.
> Lightfoot bumbled out . . .
> He followed
> as his mother hunted and grazed
> and dug for roots,
> showing her cub good foods to eat.[24]

In this simple text London presents information about the cub at birth and the food the grizzly bears eat. Through the factual narrative style the author uses descriptive language to vividly portray the bear's adventures and habitat, making the bears special to the reader. The realistic watercolor paintings by Jon Van Zyle help interpret and expand the facts presented in the verbal narrative. At the conclusion of the book London includes a note from the author to give the reader additional information about grizzly bears and kodiak bears. A bibliography of other informational storybooks appears at the end of this book.

Expository discourse conveys, explains, describes, interprets, or defines particular information. This is the most popular text structure used by writers of information books. Patrick Moore, a noted astronomer, discusses the hot planets and, after briefly describing Mercury, describes Venus:

> The next planet, Venus, is nearly as big as the Earth. It can be very bright, and you can often see it in the west after sunset or in the east before the sun rises. It has very thick air, which we could not breathe, and it is so hot that any water there would boil away. It will be a long time before anyone can go to Venus for a visit.[25]

Writers of juvenile information books frequently personalize the factual expository text by including "you" in the verbal narrative. Seymour Simon effectively uses the expository text structure in his photo-essays. He concludes his book *Galaxies* (1988) with the following paragraph:

> How many galaxies are there in the universe? Does the universe have an end? No one knows. This map plots the locations of one million galaxies. But for every galaxy pictured here, there may be ten thousand more galaxies yet unknown. Scientists think that there may be one hundred billion galaxies in our expanding universe. The universe itself is without a boundary, so that one can travel at the speed of light forever without reaching an edge.[26]

Simon's readable text fascinates readers eight years and older. They like the questions that encourage them to wonder about the topic. He clearly states what scientists know about the galaxies and what they believe to be true. He presents distances in the Galaxy in an understandable way and uses clear, bold photographs to help the reader interpret his expository text.

The typical structures of expository texts are *description, sequence, cause/effect, comparison/contrast,* and *problem/ solution.* These structures are not unique to expository texts and may also be found in narrative discourse.[27] Writers use understandable language and present the information, ideas, or attitudes in a logical structure. They present the information in chronological order or begin with simple facts and add more complex concepts. Authors may use more than one structure in a single book. In the United

Nations book *Rescue Mission: Planet Earth* (1994), for example, the editors use prose, poetry, and illustrations to describe various worldwide problems such as pollution, poverty, malnutrition, and disease (description structure). They also present the factors creating the problems (cause/effect structure) and discuss actions people have taken to solve the problems (problem/solution structure).

Young people understand a subject if they are aware of the text structures used by the author. Table 6.5 on page 189 identifies the various structures and suggests instructional strategies for presenting the structures, format cues, verbal signals, visual representatives, and selected books to help students understand each structure.

TYPES OF INFORMATION BOOKS

Information books are classified into four types: *survey books; concept books; experiment, activity, and question-answer books;* and *encyclopedias and almanacs. Survey books* give readers of all ages an overview of a topic or an in-depth coverage of a particular aspect of a topic. *Concept books,* intended primarily for young children, present specific information about numerals, letters, colors, sizes, shapes, and simple concepts of interest to the children. *Experiment, activity,* and *question-answer books* give readers of all ages specific information about history, math, science, art, music, language, and social development. The books are organized according to topic and encourage experiments and other interactive activities. *Encyclopedias* and *almanacs* are intended for all ages and present documented information according to topic or subtopic.

Appropriate illustrations, photographs, graphs, maps, time lines, and other visuals supplement, enhance, or replace verbal text. Therefore, authentic illustrations, photographs, and visuals must be placed appropriately on the page with the verbal text. The artist or photographer decides the most appropriate medium to use to clearly reveal the details of the topic and to give the viewers a realistic portrayal of the subject. All information books must be current, accurate, and presented in the most appropriate format for the content and the intended audience. Figure 6.3 on page 191 describes the four types of information books and suggests representative literature. In the next section additional information is presented about three specialized categories of concept books.

Concept Books

Concept books identify and discuss a particular topic that is of interest to children two years and older. The books are typically arranged according to a category or a theme. The following sections discuss the distinguishing characteristics of *alphabet books, counting books,* and *single concept books* and suggest strategies for presenting them in

TABLE 6.5 Suggested Instructional Strategies to Use with Each Expository Text Structure

Instructional Guidelines for All Text Structures

Define each structure and identify them in an information book.

Discuss format clues, verbal signals, and appropriate visual representations.

Identify clues and signals used in selected books.

Chart segments from the selected text on appropriate visuals.

Have learners write expository texts after identifying suitable information and charting it on appropriate visual representations.

Simple Listing

Simple listing defines or describes an object, an event, and/or a concept. The author lists characteristics, features, and examples of the subject. Lists frequently begin with simple information and progress to increasingly complex information about the subject.

Format cues: Identify heading, subtopics, and familiar formats.

Verbal signals: "For example," "characteristics are . . . ."

Visual representatives: Semantic mapping, clustering.

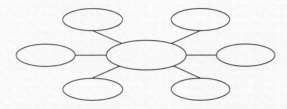

Selected Books

Atelsek, J. 1993. *All about Computers;* Macdonald, F. 1991. *A Medieval Cathedral;* Martinet, J. 1993. *The Year You Were Born, 1983, 1984, 1986, 1987;* Merbrew, W. C., & Riley, L. C. *Television: What's Behind What You See;* Pollock, S. 1995. *The Atlas of Endangered Resources.*

Sequence

Sequence items or events are listed in numerical, chronological, or logical order. This structure is similar to simple listing.

Format cues: Identify headings, subtopics, and appropriate sequence.

Verbal signals: "First, second, third . . ."; "next," "then," "finally," "before," "when," "on (date)," "not long after."

Visual representatives:

Selected Books

Aliki. 1989. *My 5 Senses;* Millard, A. 1996. *Pyramids;* Simon, S. 1996. *Wildfires;* Ward, G. C., & Burns, K. with P. R. Walker. 1994. *Baseball the American Epic: Who Invented the Game?*

Comparison/Contrast

Comparison/contrast information about a subject is presented from different perspectives. The author discusses differences and similarities or pros and cons of two or more objects, approaches, concepts, or points of view.

Format cues: Identify the facts to be compared or contrasted.

Verbal signals: "Different," "to contrast," "alike," "the same as," "however," "either . . . or . . . ."

Visual representatives: Comparison or features charts, Venn diagrams.

(Continued)

Selected Books

Ridington, R. & J. 1992. *People of the Trail: How Northern Forest Indians Lived;* Kindersly, B. & A. 1995. *Children Just Like Me.*

Cause/Effect

The **cause/effect** structure describes an event or problem and explains the consequences of the action. The author describes one or more problems and explains how they lead to the actions, effects, or conclusion assumed.

Format cues: Identify what happened and the actions taken to cause it to happen.

Verbal signals: "The reasons why," "if . . . then . . . ," "as a result," "therefore," "because."

Visual representative:

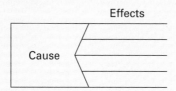

Selected Books

Lauber, P. 1995. *Who Eats What? Food Chains and Food Webs;* Gates, P. 1995. *Nature Got There First.*

Problem/Solution

The **problem/solution** structure states the problem(s), describes the action, and suggests solutions. The question/answer format is a variation of this structure.

Format cues: Identify the problem, actions taken to solve it, and solutions.

Verbal signals: "The problem is . . ."; "the puzzle is solved . . . ."

Visual representatives:

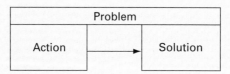

Selected Books

Few, R. 1993. *Macmillan Children's Guide to Endangered Animals;* Johnson, N. 1989. *The Battle of Gettysburg.*

the classroom. The bibliography presents recommended books representing various classifications of concept books. Concept books are a category of books with pictures and are also discussed in Chapter 8.

Alphabet Books   *Alphabet books* introduce children to the sounds and forms of letters and words. They help youngsters recognize the standard alphabetical nature of the language. Through the visual and verbal narratives, children become aware of the phoneme-grapheme (sound-letter) relationships of the language.[28]

Books for preschool-age children, such as Nona Hatay's *Charlie's ABC* (1993), present the upper- and lowercase versions of a single letter on a page. Clear, large type with adequate space around the letters, words, and other text is preferable for this age. The key words, related objects, and content must be developmentally appropriate for the intended audience. For example, to help young children identify a particular letter and the sound(s) associated with it, only one or two objects whose name begins with the featured letter and represents the same sound are shown on a page. The letters appear in standard alphabetic order. Kindergarten and older children who have some background knowledge about letters and sounds enjoy books with incidental background information and ideas, such as Shelley Rotner's *Action Alphabet* (1996), which uses col-

FIGURE 6.3 Four Types of Information Books

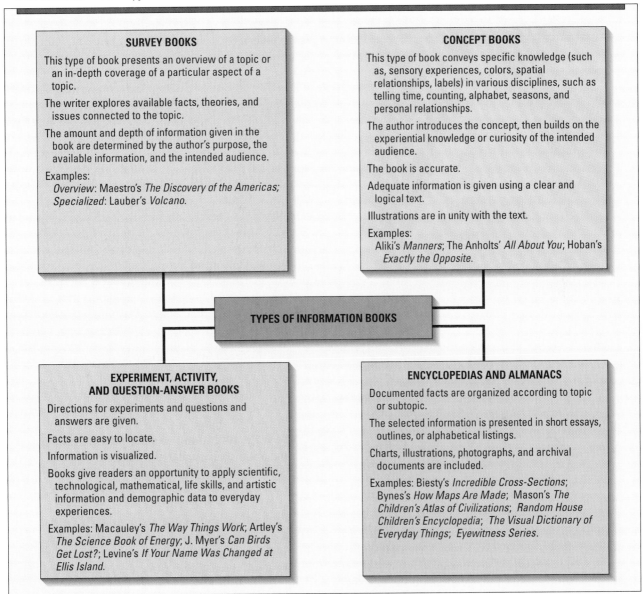

SURVEY BOOKS

This type of book presents an overview of a topic or an in-depth coverage of a particular aspect of a topic.

The writer explores available facts, theories, and issues connected to the topic.

The amount and depth of information given in the book are determined by the author's purpose, the available information, and the intended audience.

Examples:
Overview: Maestro's *The Discovery of the Americas*; *Specialized*: Lauber's *Volcano*.

CONCEPT BOOKS

This type of book conveys specific knowledge (such as, sensory experiences, colors, spatial relationships, labels) in various disciplines, such as telling time, counting, alphabet, seasons, and personal relationships.

The author introduces the concept, then builds on the experiential knowledge or curiosity of the intended audience.

The book is accurate.

Adequate information is given using a clear and logical text.

Illustrations are in unity with the text.

Examples:
Aliki's *Manners*; The Anholts' *All About You*; Hoban's *Exactly the Opposite*.

TYPES OF INFORMATION BOOKS

EXPERIMENT, ACTIVITY, AND QUESTION-ANSWER BOOKS

Directions for experiments and questions and answers are given.

Facts are easy to locate.

Information is visualized.

Books give readers an opportunity to apply scientific, technological, mathematical, life skills, and artistic information and demographic data to everyday experiences.

Examples: Macauley's *The Way Things Work*; Artley's *The Science Book of Energy*; J. Myer's *Can Birds Get Lost?*; Levine's *If Your Name Was Changed at Ellis Island*.

ENCYCLOPEDIAS AND ALMANACS

Documented facts are organized according to topic or subtopic.

The selected information is presented in short essays, outlines, or alphabetical listings.

Charts, illustrations, photographs, and archival documents are included.

Examples: Biesty's *Incredible Cross-Sections*; Bynes's *How Maps Are Made*; Mason's *The Children's Atlas of Civilizations*; *Random House Children's Encyclopedia*; *The Visual Dictionary of Everyday Things*; *Eyewitness Series*.

---

ored photographs of children engaged in outdoor activities to represent each letter of the alphabet. Another innovative alphabet book is Stephen Johnson's *Alphabet City* (1995). Johnson photographed objects in the city that show the shape of each letter in the alphabet. (See the Johnson color plate on page 192.)

The illustrations and verbal text should be compatible and consistent with the theme, mood, and setting of the book. As the bibliography indicates, many talented artists are creating alphabet books for children of all ages. Books for older children may have innovative designs, as in Graeme Base's *Animalia* (1987), or unusual content, as in Doug Cushman's *The ABC Mystery* (1993).

Presenting Alphabet Books in the Classroom While learning the forms of the letters and the sounds associated with them, preschool children enjoy arranging the letters in alphabetical order and combining them in simple words. Young children can use a book such as Nikki Grimes's *C Is for City* (1995) to identify the names of objects beginning with a particular letter. Pat Cummings's brightly colored illustrations enhance Grimes's rhyming text, which identifies objects found in the city whose names begin with the featured letter. Simple picture dictionaries and thesauri are also helpful for this age.

A copy of the alphabet should be placed at the children's eye level in kindergarten and primary classes. It is a good

Stephen Johnson's paintings for Alphabet City *give the appearance of colored photographs. The artist uses pastels, water color, gouache, and charcoal on hot-pressed water color paper to bring the city to life. Johnson shows each letter of the alphabet in an object typically found in an urban environment. Notice the letters in your environment.*

idea to display, read aloud, and discuss alphabet books throughout the year in preschool and lower primary classes. Later, the class can use an alphabet book such as Bruce Whatley and Rosie Smith's *Whatley's Quest* (1995) as a model for telling, writing, or illustrating an original story. Whatley and Smith identify animals with names beginning with a specified letter. Hidden objects on each page also represent the featured letter. Through experience with such visual and verbal narratives, young children come to recognize the standard form of letters and understand how we combine letters to form words. Older primary children enjoy discussing Eve Sanders's *What's Your Name?: From Ariel to Zoe* (1995). Later, they can follow the format of the book, share the meaning of their name, and make up a story explaining why the name fits or does not fit their personality.

After comparing alphabet books that use different artistic styles and media, individuals or groups may create an illustrated alphabet book that contains information from a particular curricular area. For example, alphabet books such as Consie Powell's *A Bold Carnivore: An Alphabet of Predators* (1995) can be used in a science lesson when discussing the survival of animals and the food chain. Jo Bannatyne-Cugnet's *A Prairie Alphabet* (1992) could be used as an introduction to a study of Canada. With Eve

Merriam's *Goodnight to Annie: An Alphabet Lullaby* (1992) as a model, first or second grade children can use alliteration, assonance, or onomatopoeia to write an original alphabet book about the sounds heard around school. After hearing John Updike's poems accompanying each letter of the alphabet in *A Helpful Alphabet of Friendly Objects* (1995), older children can write a rhyming alphabet book. They can then select appropriate music and create a musical alphabet book. The students can sing their musical alphabet book to younger children and give the book to the class. Older readers can find alphabet books intended for their age, such as Andrea Helman's *O Is for Orca: A Pacific Northwest Alphabet Book* (1995), Patricia Mullins's *V for Vanishing: An Alphabet of Endangered Animals* (1994), and Judith Viorst's *The Alphabet from Z to A (With Much Confusion on the Way)* (1994). After reading and discussing the books, they can compare them to alphabet books intended for young children and identify the features that make the books appropriate for older students.

Counting Books   *Counting books* introduce children to the patterns and meanings of numbers. Simple counting books, such as *Number Pops* (1995), are written for babies to preschool children. These books show written numerals and how they can be arranged. Kindergarten and primary-age children enjoy stories with counting rhymes, such as Tedd Arnold's *Five Ugly Monsters* (1995), and books that present a story about numbers, such as Sandy Nightingale's *Pink Pigs Aplenty* (1992). Most counting books have compatible illustrations that give children concrete, visual experiences to help them understand numerals and mathematical concepts. Debbie MacKinnon uses colored photographs of toddlers and familiar objects in *How Many?* (1993), Arthur Geisert uses black and white drawings in *Pigs from 1 to 10* (1992), Denise Fleming uses brilliant colored illustrations in *Count* (1992), and Charles Sullivan combines contemporary fine art and photography in *Numbers at Play: A Counting Book* (1992). Books for children seven years and older explain how numerals are manipulated through addition, subtraction, multiplication, and division; Loreen Leedy's *2 × 2 = Boo!: A Set of Spooky Multiplication Stories* (1995) is an example. Books intended for older children present more complex mathematical concepts or pose mathematical puzzles, as in Mitsumasa Anno's *Anno's Counting House* (1986) and Tom and Muriel Feelings's *Moja Means One* (1975). The topic, the mathematics curriculum, and the complexity of the verbal narrative determine the suitability of the book for students.

Counting books may include numerals from 1 to 10 or continue to 100 or higher, as in Pam Munoz Ryan's *One Hundred Is a Family* (1994). The numerals may be presented from lowest to highest or highest to lowest, as Philemon Sturges shows in *Ten Flashing Fireflies* (1995).

The numeral must be the focal point on the page so that children can identify and count it. Therefore, the artist highlights the numeral, leaving adequate space between it and any objects or verbal narrative that might also be on the page. In a book intended for the youngest children, only one picture representing a numeral should appear on a double-page spread. Books for older children usually include several visible and hidden objects.

Presenting Counting Books in the Classroom Counting books are fun to read aloud to preschool and lower primary grades. Youngsters enjoy chanting and reciting with the teacher the narrative of books such as Nick Sharratt's *Rocket Countdown* (1995). By chanting and reciting the verbal text, children learn number concepts in a natural, enjoyable way. Early readers like to read books such as Pamela Paparone's *Five Little Ducks: An Old Rhyme* (1995), because the text is predictable and they can "read" it the first time they hear it. Counting books are a vital part of the preschool and early primary mathematics class. Children in upper primary grades enjoy hearing and reading humorous books such as Max Grover's *Amazing and Incredible Counting Stories!: A Number of Tall Tales* (1995). This book would be an excellent springboard to entice students to write or tell original tall tales involving the manipulation of numbers. Counting books such as S. T. Garne's *One White Sail: A Caribbean Counting Book* (1992), Amanda Wallwork's *No Dodos: A Counting Book of Endangered Animals* (1993), and Mary Beth Owens's *Counting Cranes* (1993) can supplement and enhance a social studies or science lesson. Children could be encouraged to write and illustrate original counting books describing topics studied in various subject areas.

Counting books with a story, such as Martha Weston's *Bea's Four Bears* (1992), are displayed in the classroom and used during read aloud sessions. Sophisticated verbal narratives that focus on number concepts, such as Eve Merriam's *Twelve Ways to Get to Eleven* (1993) and Jon Scieszka's *Math Curse* (1995), must be shared with others and later enjoyed as a favorite independent reading book. Older children could make costumes representing various animals and pose for photographs wearing the costumes in groups representing numerals from 1 to 10. Place the photographs in a bound book. Leave space on each page for a younger child to write a narrative. Then display the book in the media center. Use *The Lifesize Animal Counting Book* (1994) as a model for this activity.

Single Concept Books *Single concept books* are written primarily for two to eight year olds. The books introduce children to basic information about a particular topic, which can be any subject of interest to the intended audience, such as colors, textures, geometric shapes, sizes, time, seasons, transportation, nature, animals, physical development, or interacting with others. Sandra Jenkins explores such concepts as

color, shapes, and patterns in her paper engineering book *Flip-Flap* (1995). Margaret Miller's clear, expressive photographs show the excitement of a new pet in Joanna Cole's *My New Kitten* (1995). This single concept book is an example of how the visual and verbal narratives can work together to present information. (See the Cole color plate.)

In *My World of Words* (1995), Debbie MacKinnon presents colors, numbers, shapes, opposites, and sound words. Geoff Dann's colorful photographs enhance her verbal text. This book explains a concept in one or several words or sentences, a typical format for a concept book meant for young children. The verbal narrative presents information the intended audience can grasp, rather than a storyline. Artists use suitable media to create simple, clear pictures that authentically supplement, enhance, or extend the concepts or mood of the verbal text. The simple verbal narrative and realistic illustrations are placed together on the same or adjacent pages to give the child visual and verbal information about the subject.

Presenting Single Concept Books in the Classroom Single concept books are factual books that can be used successfully throughout the day for aesthetic or efferent purposes. Young children enjoy interacting with a book, such as Craig Brown's *City Sounds* (1992). The children can make the sounds the farmer hears while driving into the city. Children will enjoy producing a visual or verbal response to Woodleigh Hubbard's *The Friendship Book* (1992), Julie Paschkis's *So Happy/So Sad* (1995), or Jeanne Modesitt's *Sometimes I Feel like a Mouse: A Book about*

Margaret Miller's colored photographs are a perfect complement to Joanna Cole's My New Kitten. *The book is intended for very young children. The clear photographs give children visual information about the topic.*

Feelings (1992). After listening to Marjorie Weinman Sharmat's *The 329th Friend* (1992), the children can plan a party for characters from favorite books. They will use Sharmat's model and list the needs of each character. Books such as Lucy Micklethwait's *I Spy: An Alphabet in Art* (1992) and Bodel Rikys's *Red Bear* (1992) introduce art appreciation and color. Sara Fanelli's *My Map Book* (1995) presents twelve maps of spaces, concepts, and time. The nearly wordless book naturally elicits discussion and leads children to write a narrative for each map. A single concept book can be used in a subject area to give children a variety of experiences with the topic. For example, Loreen Leedy's *The Monster Money Book* (1992) would help children understand the various ways to use money.

While reading a single concept book aloud, the teacher can add details needed by a specific group of children. The illustrations often clarify or expand the topic. Young children can write and illustrate a single concept book about shapes, sizes, or other topics discussed in content area classes. Older students enjoy writing simple concept books to instruct young children about a particular topic. They can read the book to younger children and discuss the topic with them. Through the writing process, young people discover the importance of using just the right words or images to explain a concept to another person. Concept books are ideal to use when helping children understand the subjects presented in the literature they are reading. These books are also valuable resources for literature-based instruction. The chapter bibliography presents outstanding concept books related to child development, science, social science, and history.

INFORMATION BOOKS IN THE CLASSROOM

Today teachers have many high-quality information books to use with learners of all ages. As they present various types of information books throughout the curriculum, teachers recognize the benefits associated with using literature as a supplement or replacement for content area textbooks. The teacher's goals, the content area, and the needs and abilities of individual learners are considerations when selecting the most appropriate instructional focus. This section discusses the benefits gained from experiences with information books, guidelines for selecting high-quality information books, and suitable instructional focuses to use when including information books in the classroom.

Benefits Individuals Gain from Experiences with Information Books

Investigating a subject is as exciting as following clues of a mystery or vicariously experiencing others' adventures. A book's content is the major factor to consider when select-

ing an information book. Fortunately, information books are available on all topics. Teachers may select a familiar topic to verify learners' prior knowledge or provide additional information about the subject. Students also enjoy expanding their horizons by reading books on unfamiliar subjects. Readers of all ages like information books.[29] Table 6.6 summarizes the benefits individuals gain when they explore the subgenre.

Guidelines for Selecting High-Quality Information Books

When literature is used widely throughout the curriculum, teachers and children become actively involved in selecting information books to read for pleasure and informational purposes. Consequently, clear criteria are needed to help in the selection process. Teachers must review information books periodically to assess their accuracy and currency. Publishing companies do not continue publishing outdated books. Librarians typically remove them from the library shelves and place them in a special "historical section" for adult reference only. The quality of factual literature has increased tremendously. Now quality books in both softcover and hardcover are available on subjects pursued for pleasure and information.

In the last decade, information books have changed radically in several ways. First, authors use more varied language, as in fictional literature. They strive to make the fac-

TABLE 6.6 Benefits Gained from Exploring Quality Information Books

Quality information books stimulate young people's natural curiosity.

The books give individuals authentic, in-depth, and current information about various subject areas.

Quality information books stimulate questions, predictions, and further inquiry about different topics.

As learners encounter new information and different points of view in the books, they can connect old and new information to construct meanings about a topic.

Experiences with quality nonfiction literature give girls and boys a better understanding of the process scientists pursue when searching for facts, developing theories, and applying relevant information.

When exploring quality books, young people become aware of the various structures and forms used to communicate facts, theories, generalizations, and opinions.

Well-written information books provide models for students to use when discussing, writing, and reading facts about a particular topic.

Young people have the opportunity to aesthetically explore factual materials presented in information books.

tual text not only understandable, but interesting to read. Second, photographs, illustrations, archival documents, and other visuals supplement the text and are appealing to explore. The photo-essay format may give the appearance of a simple picture book, but some contain content that is suitable for a mature audience. Third, complicated subjects, previously reserved for older students, are simplified and presented in appropriate formats for younger children's limited experience and short attention span. Fourth, authors include bibliographies, appendixes, and notes documenting sources consulted. Fifth, survey books presenting either an overview or specialized information have become popular. Previously, information books contained long formulaic texts describing an entire topic. Finally, three-dimensional, movable books with pop-ups, pull-tabs, and lift-flaps are gaining popularity in factual literature.

As Table 6.7 shows, when selecting books for a particular age, the content, the language, and the writer's focus

TABLE 6.7 Guidelines for Selecting Quality Information Books

Content of the Book

Does the author provide important details about the subject that are suitable for the audience?

Does the author present an adequate amount of information about the topic?

Is the author's focus (purpose for writing the book) clear and manageable?

Accuracy and Currency of Information

Does the author include accurate details and information about the topic?

Does the information reflect current information about the subject?

Does the author distinguish between facts, theories, generalizations, and opinions?

Does the author's professional background qualify him or her to write about the selected topics?

Do the text and illustrations avoid stereotyping, bias, or sensationalized presentation of information?

Are anthropomorphism (attributing human traits to nonhuman subjects), teleology (defining natural phenomena in terms of purpose), and stereotyping of groups avoided?

If documentation is included in the text, does it interfere with the flow of reading?

Style of Writing

Does the book have the potential to stimulate the reader's imagination and curiosity about the topic?

Is the language suitable for and appealing to the intended audience?

Are the tone and mood appropriate for the audience?

Is the author objective in presenting the authentic information?

If applicable, is appropriate terminology used and defined?

Is the book interesting to read?

Organization of the Book

Is the information organized logically, e.g., from general to specific, from simple to complex, from familiar to unfamiliar, or chronologically?

Does the book include organizational aids such as a table of contents or chapter subheadings?

Does the book include suitable reference aids such as focus questions, a glossary, an index, a bibliography, or additional readings?

Is specific information easy to find?

Format of the Book

Do the illustrations, photographs, and archival documents accurately visualize, and enhance the text?

Are the illustrations and text arranged appropriately on the page?

Are captions, maps, charts, diagrams, and other graphics used? Do they supplement the information?

Are the visuals, typeface, and size of the book suitable for the subject and the audience?

Does the cover establish the mood of the book?

Is the binding sturdy?

must be considered.[30] As noted earlier, the content, the accuracy and currency of information, the author's writing style, and the organization and format are specific selection criteria for quality information books. Questions are suggested to give the selector a comprehensive view of each component, but all questions will not be considered for each book. To qualify as an information book of high literary merit, however, a book must receive a positive rating on each component of the selection guide.

Instructional Focuses

Information books are suitable to use with various aesthetic experiences, such as reading aloud and discussing content included in books of fiction. Nonfiction books are also frequently used as part of Literature-Based Instruction, where literature is used for instructional purposes in various content areas. In these classrooms, literature supplements or replaces subject area textbooks for several reasons:

We achieve individualization of instruction when we use a variety of literature books.

Nonfiction literature contains interesting content and is visually appealing.

Literature frequently provides more information about particular topics.

Nonfiction literature is organized logically and is easy to understand.

Quality nonfiction literature includes current facts and theories about a particular topic.[31]

Quality informational literature intended for all ages is readily available for use in all curricular areas. Reading Lloyd Moss's *Zin! Zin! Zin! A Violin* (1995), for example, enriches a music or literature class. The colorful illustrations by Marjorie Priceman capture the alliterative verses that introduce the sounds of ten orchestral instruments and

That lazy clown, the big BASSOON!
He plays low down, we're laughing soon.
Here, Grumpy, get your place in line,
And give us a NONET—that's NINE.

Marjorie Priceman's humorous gouache illustrations realistically portray Lloyd Moss's text for Zin Zin a Violin. The text is placed in the illustrations with the cartoon-like characters to present a rollicking, rhythmic story. Can the orchestra members play the instruments that way? A bassoon is fun to play. Ask your music teacher about the funny, low sounds made on a bassoon.

show how they are grouped within an orchestra to achieve a balanced, effective performance. (See the Moss color plate on page 196.) Chapters 11 and 12 present additional suggestions about using literature in various content areas.

Students' interests should be considered when selecting appropriate literature for instructional purposes. The findings from studies surveying students' interest in information books suggest the following:

Children of all ages select information books to read, but older children are more likely to select information books.

Young people of all ability levels are interested in the subgenre. For example, disabled readers frequently express an interest in information books so they can learn about "things."

Beginning around eight years, more boys than girls chose information books for pleasurable reading.

The information books chosen by young people do not necessarily relate to the topics studied in school.

Individual students choose a variety of topics in selected information books.[32]

Teachers who implement an integrated curriculum select appropriate disciplinary content and teach those identified skills and strategies throughout the day. Teachers need a variety of current, authentic factual materials for an integrated curriculum. Quality nonfiction literature is the logical choice to accomplish this instructional approach.

The bibliography, which is organized by both historical periods and by topics and includes biographies and information books, will aid in selecting quality nonfiction. Biographies and information books are grouped together by period or topic, which should help adults implementing a literature-based program.

Literary Response Modes

Table 6.8 on page 198 contains a variety of Literary Response Modes (LRMs) students could produce when responding to the information books used in various discipline areas throughout the day. Literary Response Modes are suitable instructional strategies to achieve the instructional objectives of Literature-Based Instruction. The suggested LRMs can be modified to suit the content in available books. Young people and adults choose LRMs to elicit students' natural reactions to the content found in the books. The LRMs in the table highlight the distinctive literary characteristics expected in quality information books: coverage of the content, accurate and current information, writing style, organization of the book, and its format.

HISTORICAL PERSPECTIVE OF INFORMATION BOOKS

In 1658 Johan Amos Comenius, a Bavarian priest and educator, wrote and illustrated the *Orbis sensualium pictus (The Visible World in Pictures)*, the first picture book intended to instruct children. Comenius believed children learned best through first-hand experiences. Since these experiences would not be possible for all areas, he described

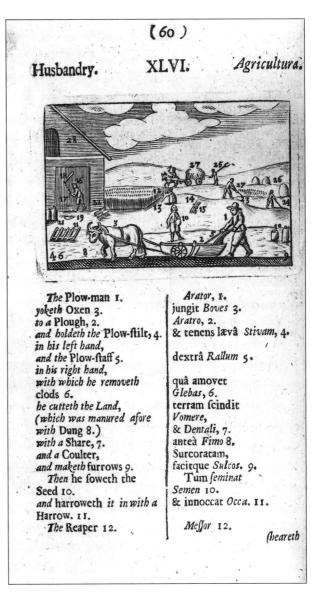

This picture from Orbis sensualium pictus *shows Comenius's attention to detail in his wood cut, intended to help children relate words to pictures. Can you write a narrative for numbers 13 through 28?*

TABLE 6.8 Suggested LRMs for Information Books

Highlighting the Content

Pair students with partners or place in small groups. Give each group a different book on the same topic. Have students prepare a visual graphic (as described in Chapter 10). They will record the major facts found in the book on the graphic.

The group will display their visual and compare the information given in the different books. The students will identify inconsistencies and omissions in particular books. Volunteers will consult other informational sources for accurate facts about the subject. The class will review each book to find out if the author omitted important facts or included too many details. The class will decide if they need the facts to fully understand the subject. Based on the class discussion, each group will write a critique about their book. The critiques will be displayed in the *Critic's Corner*. Copies of the critiques will be given to the media specialist and mailed to the local newspaper with a request that they be published on the children's page.

Highlighting the Accuracy and Currency of Information

Students will select their favorite nonfiction authors after reading several information books written by different authors. The class will decide what they would like to know about a writer, such as biographical information (including professional education); why the person writes information books; why the individual writes for children; and how the author selects a subject for a book, researches the subject, and chooses the format for presenting the content.

A group of students will select a favorite author and prepare an *Author Study* that provides the information requested by the class. The students will also attempt to find resources and references cited by the author for further study of the subject.

Each group will present pertinent facts given by the writer on an attractive visual, such as a banner or booklet.

Students will find books written by the author and give enticing book talks about the books. Visuals with objects representing the topics the author writes about will be used with the book talks.

Each group will prepare a dramatic script including interesting information about the author and his or her books. The groups will read their scripts to other class members or grade level classes.

Display the visuals and selected books by the author in the media center or show and discuss the author on the school's *Show Case of Favorite Authors.*

Highlighting the Author's Writing Style

Two or three students will select a topic and collect information about it. (The teacher could suggest specific topics, such as facts discussed in future content areas.)

Share information books using appealing language or formats that stimulate the reader's imagination and curiosity; examples include Diane Siebert's *Mojave* and *Heartland;* Bert Kitchen's *Somewhere Today* (figurative, repetitive language); Bruce Brooks's *Making Sense: Animal Perception and Communication* (flowing, descriptive language); Barbara Rogasky's *Smoke and Ashes: The Story of the Holocaust* (descriptive, appealing language and syntax); Ron Hirschi's *Discover My World Desert* (narrative questions and descriptive illustrations); and Michael Chinery's *Questions and Answers about Seashore Animals* (succinct answers, unique format, illustrations to enhance the text). Discuss the author's and illustrator's craft, such as language, syntax (sentence structure), organization, and appropriate visuals.

The students will write an information book for younger students using a style similar to that of a favorite author and illustrator.

The books will be published as "pop-up" books or accordion books (See Appendix B).

Determining Whether the Content Is Organized Appropriately (Can You Find the Facts?)

Students will discuss the attributes, features, and traits of the subject. They will prepare a comparison chart as described in Chapter 10. Individuals or small groups will select specific "nuggets of information" cited in a content area textbook (e.g., the geography, population, or other demographic information about the home state, or facts about a cultural or international group). Students will choose at least three nonfiction books containing the information. Students will list the facts in individual columns on the left side of the chart. The author and title of the information book will be listed at the top in individual columns. On the far right side of the chart, add two other columns, "Omitted" and "Too Many Facts." Then the student will look for the individual facts.

Indicate the convenience of finding specific information in the book by identifying the structure, organizational aids, and reference aids used in the book. In the appropriate columns, list the books that omitted facts or gave too many facts.

Display the charts and books. After students report their findings, the class will compare the organization, structure, and reference aids in each book. The students will decide the structure, organization, and reference aids that help in finding specific information.

Highlighting the Format of the Book

Individuals or groups of students will choose two or three information books illustrated by a particular person. The students will identify the illustrations, photographs, archival documents, maps, and other graphic aids used by the illustrator. They will analyze the format (see the format component in Table 6.7).

TABLE 6.8 Suggested LRMs for Information Books (*Continued*)

The students will become the illustrator's publicist. Students will organize a marketing campaign to sell and advertise the illustrator's books. The class will discuss persuasive communication. Written, oral, and visual products will be prepared to convince peers, media specialists, administrators, and parents (at a school parents meeting) that the illustrator's books should be included in all classroom libraries. Various forms of written advertisements will emphasize the outstanding format features used by the illustrator. Students will include in the visual the media and techniques used by the artists. The written and visual materials will include labels, charts, and other graphics.

The campaign will be videotaped and shown in other classes and to the individuals mentioned above.

At the end of the production, lead the children in a discussion of the questions suggested in Table 6.7. Have students identify the outstanding format features that help them comprehend the subject.

Using Photo-Essays in the Classroom

Photo-essays are especially useful in subject area classrooms. They give students a realistic portrayal of a topic. By exploring several photo-essays about the same subject, students see different perspectives and gain a broader introduction to the topic.

Photo-essays are suitable for independent or class reading and discussion. Reading aloud a book with photographs can be a challenge because the photographs are essential to understanding the topic. Viewers need time to look at the details of a photograph.

The teacher will write a grant to purchase several inexpensive cameras so students can take photographs. Invite a professional photographer to offer helpful hints about taking photographs.

When the class members go on a field trip, have them take photographs and then create a large mural of the photographs. Children can label the photographs describing information learned on the trip. Class members can use the photographs to present an interesting oral presentation—"Ask the Experts"—about the trip to students who did not attend. Show the photographs.

Groups of students will prepare a photo-essay about information learned in a subject area class.

Teams of students will take photographs of special events during the year. They will write a fiction or nonfiction text for the photographs about the event. They will combine the various essays and photographs to create a photo-essay "A Year in Ms. Brown's Fourth Grade Class." They will copy the photo-essay for each member of the class. A laminated bound copy of the book will be prepared for the teacher and media center.

Students might be encouraged to bring pictures from home that could be used for a class photo-essay or a family book. Walter Dean Myers's *Brown Angels: An Album of Pictures and Verse* (1993) would be a useful model for such a project.

objects found in nature. He also drew crude woodcuts to accompany his text, which was written in Latin and the native language of the country where the book was published. As seen in the photograph, the numbers of the woodcuts corresponded to numbers in the text to help the reader connect text and illustrations. The book, with its interesting and informative format, remained popular for more than a hundred years.[33] In 1990, in its honor, the National Council of Teachers of English inaugurated the Orbis Pictus Award for nonfiction books. Jean Fritz received the first award for her biography, *The Great Little Madison* (1989).

For many centuries, adults thought children's books were primarily for instruction. Most books of fiction written from the sixteenth through the mid-nineteenth century were meant for instructional purposes. Didactic information books, such as *The New England Primer*, provided moralistic education while teaching children to read (see Chapter 11). Finally, in the twentieth century, information books began to be written especially for young people. Since then, numerous books of facts have introduced children to the beauty of the world, the wonder of art and music, and the joy of investigating all subjects in the universe.

In the nineteenth and early twentieth centuries, however, the writers were not very meticulous about the authenticity of their information, especially when writing for the youngest children. It was felt that young children could better understand information if it was presented in a fictionalized format.

Information books are now an important part of children's literature. In 1921 an information book, Hendrik Willem Van Loon's *The Story of Mankind*, received the first Newbery Medal. Dorothy P. Lathrop received the first Caldecott Medal in 1938 for Helen Fish's *Animals of the Bible*. Several artists have won the Caldecott Medal for information books. They include Roger Duvoisin for Alvin Tresselt's *White Snow, Bright Snow* in 1948, Marc Simont for Janice Udry's *A Tree Is Nice* in 1957, Robert McCloskey's *Time of Wonder* in 1958, and Leo and Diane Dillon for Margaret Musgrove's *Ashanti to Zulu: African Traditions* in 1977. In the 1980s two poetry collections, classified in the Dewey decimal system as nonfiction, won the Newbery Medal: Nancy Willard's *A Visit to William*

Blake's Inn: Poems for Innocent and Experienced Travelers (1981) and Paul Fleischman's *Joyful Noise: Poems for Two Voices* (1988). Outstanding information books recognized as Newbery honor books include Kathryn Lasky's *Sugaring Time* (1983) and Patricia Lauber's *Volcano: The Eruption and Healing of Mount St. Helens* (1986).

By the latter part of the twentieth century, outstanding information books with colorful photographs or paintings were available for young people.[34] Notable information books are listed in Table 6.9.

GENERAL INSTRUCTIONAL STRATEGIES TO USE WITH NONFICTION LITERATURE

All nonfiction literature—biographies, autobiographies, and information books—can be presented in the classroom using instructional strategies such as the following:

Read aloud nonfiction literature throughout the day and school year.

Prepare a bibliography of literature for parents to share with their children. The bibliography should include appropriate nonfiction literature that will supplement the content being taught during the year.

Prepare a game board. Children will prepare questions for the game as they read various nonfiction selections.

Discuss books in small groups or the entire class. To encourage aesthetic reactions to the literature, use probes and prompts such as the following: "What thoughts entered your mind while you were reading (hearing) the book?" "What were the important ideas you remember from the text?"

Prepare and wear (throughout the school) a badge advertising a nonfiction selection. Title the badge, "Ask Me About . . . (*title of the book*)." Add a small picture to the badge that represents the selection.

Take photographs around the school. Small groups of students will write a book using Diane Siebert's *Heartland* as a model. Publish the books and display in the school media center or in the administrative suite.

Write an authentic biography about a family member. Use information books for background knowledge; interview the subject or people who knew the person; request photographs and artifacts belonging to the subject. Publish the book, with photocopied documents, and display artifacts with the book. The students will read their books on a school television program and tell why they selected the particular person to be the subject of the book.[35]

TABLE 6.9 Notable Information Books

DATE	AUTHOR, TITLE	COMMENTS
1921	A. W. Van Loon, *The Story of Mankind*	This history of the world was the first recipient of the Newbery Medal.
1925	M. Bauer & E. R. Peyser, *How Music Grew from Prehistoric Times to the Present Day*	This book is the most important and comprehensive history of music available for young people. In 1939 the authors revised the book to include American and early twentieth-century music.
1925	E. La Prade, *Alice in Orchestralia*	A description of orchestral instruments that is set in fantasy and includes whimsical plays on words.
1930	W. M. Reed, *The Earth for Sam*	With photographs and amusing sketches, the author describes the earth's changes through geological periods.
1933	M. & M. Petersham, *The Story Book of Things We Use*	The first picture book in a series by the author/illustrators about things in a child's immediate environment.
1933	V. M. Hillyer & E. G. Huey, *A Child's History of Art*	Stories and pictures of paintings, sculpture, and architecture are included in this book.
1934	L. Lenski, *The Little Auto*	Simple descriptions and black and white drawings of the workings of an auto are included in this picture book, which is a part of a series.
1935	C. L. Fenton, *Along the Hill*	This book, for beginning geologists, contains an introduction to the study of rocks and the formation of the earth's surface.
1937	H. D. Fish, *Animals of the Bible*, illus. D. P. Lathrop	First winner of the Caldecott Medal describes through visual and verbal text the flora, fauna, and animals mentioned in the Bible.
1944	F. M. Fitch, *One God: The Ways We Worship Him*	The rituals of worship, religious festivals, and observances of Jews, Catholics, and Protestants are clearly described with beautiful photographs in this book.

TABLE 6.9 Notable Information Books (*Continued*)

DATE	AUTHOR, TITLE	COMMENTS
1947	R. & A. Linton, *Man's Way from Cave to Skyscraper*	Distinguished anthropologists trace culture in all parts of the world from prehistoric times to the 1940s.
1947	A. Tresselt, *White Snow, Bright Snow,* illus. Roger Duvoisin	The Caldecott winner describes events during a snowfall.
1956	J. Udry, *A Tree Is Nice,* illus. Marc Simont	The author describes the pleasures of trees.
1957	Robert McCloskey, *Time of Wonder*	The adventures of people living on the coast of New England.
1960	F. Branley, *Let's-Read-and-Find-Out Series*	Science concepts are presented in this picture book series for young people.
1964–1967	M. Meltzer, *In Their Own Words: A History of the American Negro,* vols. 1–3	This is a three-volume survey of African-Americans' history in America. It is based on authentic documentation from letters, diaries, journals, autobiographies, speeches, resolutions, newspapers, and pamphlets.
1966	M. E. Selsam, *Benny's Animals, and How He Put Them in Order,* illus. A. Lobel	The classifications of animals are described for beginning readers with large print and appropriate illustrations.
1970	H. S. Zim & S. Bleeker, *Life and Death*	An excellent book discussing life expectancy, aging, the clinical definition of death, and rituals and legal procedures following death.
1971	J. C. George, *All Upon a Stone*	This book is an unusual and explicit description of ecology for young people by a reputable fiction and nonfiction author.
1976	M. Musgrove, *Ashanti to Zulu: African Traditions,* illus. L. & D. Dillon	A Caldecott winner describing the lifestyle and traditions of 27 African tribes. The brilliant illustrations are authentic to the tribe.
1983	K. Lasky, *Sugaring Time*	A Newbery honor book describing the collection and processing of maple syrup.
1986	P. Lauber, *Volcano: The Eruption and Healing of Mount St. Helens*	A Newbery honor book containing photographs and text that accurately describe the eruption of Mount St. Helens and its aftermath.
1986	J. Cole, *The Magic School Bus at the Waterworks*	The first book in a popular series describes, in a humorous narrative, Ms. Frizzle and her children's adventures at the waterworks while riding on a magic school bus.
1988	D. Macaulay, *The Way Things Work*	The author/artist has written a visual guide to the world of machines from levers to lasers, cars to computers. A detailed survey book.
1991 1991	B. Brooks, *Predator!* *Nature by Design*	The first photo-essay in the series looks at the relationships between predator and prey and the ways animals attract or hunt their food. The second photo-essay discusses how animals build their homes. The author-photographer has written many outstanding information books about animals and nature.
1992	S. Simon, *Snakes*	Another photo-essay about nature by this prolific author. The effective text and photographs (by various people) describe the physical characteristics, habits, and environment of various species of snakes.
1993	J. Brandenburg, *To the Top of the World: Adventures with Arctic Wolves*	This wildlife photographer created a photo-essay about his experiences living with a pack of wolves in the Arctic.
1995	J. Murphy, *The Great Fire*	Using accounts from survivors, the author authentically describes the fire that burned much of Chicago in October 1871. The interesting text is supplemented with photographs. The 1996 winner of the NCTE Orbis Pictus Award for Outstanding Nonfiction.
1995	K. Kenna, *A People Apart*	This book presents a respectful insight into a profoundly devout culture, the Old Order Mennonites. Rare photographs were given to the author and photographer, Andrew Stawicki, who created this outstanding photo-essay.
1995	P. Lauber, *Hurricanes: Earth's Mightiest Storms*	Another book by this outstanding science author. Lauber explains why, where, and how hurricanes form on coastal areas and profiles major hurricanes. Maps, diagrams, and historical and contemporary photos are included. The book describes weather instruments, explains how storms are named, and examines the effect of the monster storms on the people who live in fragile coastal areas.

Have students present a conversation between people who might have lived during the setting of a biography. The students will discuss relevant issues of the time and place. They will consult information books for suitable additional facts about the issues and the lifestyle of the people. These facts will be included in the conversation.

Prepare a question box. Encourage students to place questions about people or subjects in the box. Students will volunteer to become experts on a particular subject or person. The experts will form a panel to answer questions placed in the box or debate controversial issues from different perspectives.

After reading several biographies and information books about a particular subject, such as personal relationships, family life, or diverse lifestyles, the students will select a subject and write a poem related to the topic. A suitable poetic form must be selected to express their emotional response to an experience. A bio-poem would be suitable for a biography or personal memories; a limerick is suitable for a humorous situation; an oriental poem is appropriate for nature or animals; a narrative poem would suit an experience at the zoo; the 5W poem is suitable for people or content; the acrostic poem for a person or subject (see Chapter 7 for various poetic forms).

Write a personal or business letter to inform or communicate information to interested or potentially interested persons. Students can also write letters between characters of different books; letters to request information from experts; and letters to inform others about the quality of a book and the need to purchase it for all students.

Prepare a travel guide through a region, an orchestra, the ocean floor, a bear's cave, or other locations.

Prepare a current event visual about topics in a book. Visuals may include cartoons, book jackets, a slide-tape journey through a geographic region, collage cubes, or a bulletin board.

Play appropriate music during a book talk or when the class discusses a particular book or subject.

Share poems related to the subjects of a nonfiction book.

Write and ask riddles about persons and subjects in nonfiction literature.

Prepare a list of terms used in information books, such as Civil War terms or mathematical terms, and place on a word wall. Students will have an opportunity to research the terms. Then students will take turns telling an oral story using the terms. Give a term to a team of students. They will find the definition and pantomime the meaning of the word to others who will guess the term.

LRMs To Use with Nonfiction Literature

Since nonfiction literature uses informative, persuasive, expressive, and ritualistic language to communicate facts, ideas, and attitudes, the following oral and written LRMs give students an opportunity to gather, organize, synthesize, and respond to the genre in a similar manner. Students will select a topic listed in the bibliography, such as architecture, economics, adventurers, or a historical period. They will read a biography and an information book about a specific subject. Then, individually or in teams, students will produce one or several of the following LRMs:

Write a news report or release for a newspaper/magazine or radio/television program. The article or script should be authentic and objective. Students will state the primary event, fact, or problem succinctly and clearly. They will then present evidence relating to the issue. The actions reported should be supported by eyewitness accounts. The information must be accurate and presented clearly and succinctly in an appropriate sequential, logical, or chronological order. The last paragraph of the article or script restates the issue and directs the audience to future reading or reporting.

Interview a person who lived at a particular time or is an expert about a specific topic. The interviewer uses preselected questions to ask for clarification of a person's actions, learn about events, or gain information about an event or topic. The interviewer then reports on the interview in writing or orally. The report should be accurate and presented clearly, logically, and succinctly. The interviewer does not make personal comments or make personal interpretations about the information given in the interview.

Advertise an artifact from the historical period of a nonfiction book or an artifact related to a book's subject. The oral or written ad is based on authentic and current research or personal experience or research. The short descriptive narrative follows this sequence: "What is the product? Who needs it? What will happen if persons purchase (or do not purchase) the product?" Students will discuss advertising techniques such as bandwagon, celebrity testimony, transfer, plain folks, glittering generalities, name calling, and/or snob appeal. The seller will focus on the beauty, power, and strength of the product and its appeal to others. The facts must be plausible/believable to the audience. Evoke a positive response from the audience by using emotional words. Visuals, photographs, models, films, and display posters may accompany the advertisement.

Write a job description based on information from a biography and information books related to a particular career. Discuss professional job descriptions. Talk about format. The information must be accurate, and the description should cover topics such as educational requirements, duties and responsibilities, working hours, vacation time, working conditions, location, and advantages and disadvantages connected to the job.

Write a news editorial or memo to present an issue in a logical, succinct, and chronological structure. Clearly state adequate information about the issue. Provide supporting statements to verify the writer's position or clarify the issue. Indicate actions or solutions to be taken to solve the issue. The initial information is presented objectively, while the conclusion may be subjective and persuasive. The editorial is presented in news or magazine articles or radio/television programs.

Prepare journals/diaries that relate to events, actions, or information in the nonfiction literature. The entries should be plausible and presented chronologically in episodes and flashbacks. The entries should be written in the first person to reflect the perspective of a person involved in an event or of an expert commenting on the event; the entries may also reveal the writer's personal reactions to a subject. Subjective entries are based on authentic, plausible reactions of the person writing in the journal/diary.

Write books or narratives using the structure and format found in a biography or nonfiction literature and then orally share the books with others. The writer will objectively present accurate historical, scientific, or psychological information about a person, event, object, or animal. The facts are arranged from simple to complex, from known to unknown, or in chronological, alphabetical, or numerical order. If the audience does not understand the vocabulary and terms, they should be defined. The information should be current. The writer will vary the language and sentences to keep the attention of the audience. The writer should include suitable details, avoid generalizations, and identify facts and theories. Visuals, photographs, organizational aids, reference aids, subheadings, captions, maps, charts, diagrams, and other graphics are included.

Present directions, recipes, and experiments orally or in writing to explain, inform, or describe how to do something. The communication must be presented clearly and accurately in sequential order. Give precise descriptions. Use standard forms for abbreviations and punctuation. The information must be presented in a suitable sequence. Write the text or script in the second or third person.

Table 6.10 presents some suggested LRMs for specific topics.

TABLE 6.10 Suggested LRMs for Specific Topics

See appropriate books listed in the bibliography to produce the LRMs.

Social Concerns

Read nonfiction and fiction books dealing with *homeless* children and adults. (See Societal Concern heading in the bibliography.) The learners will become familiar with the problems homeless people encounter. (*Note:* The teacher must be aware of homeless children in the class or school to determine if this is an appropriate topic to investigate. A period in history, such as the Great Depression, could be an alternate topic.)

After reading several books individually or in small groups, the learners will discuss and compare the information about homeless people in the fiction and nonfiction books. In groups they will discuss questions such as the following: Why are people homeless? Where do they get food? Clothes? Where do they sleep and take a bath? This information will be recorded on a visual graphic (see Chapter 10).

Learners will collect newspaper and magazine articles about homeless people in the community, state, and nation. They will interview parents and other adults about the problems homeless people have in the local community. If possible, they will find out how governmental and private organizations help homeless people.

This information will be recorded on the visual graphic. Small groups will write questions about the lifestyle of homeless people and their treatment such as the following: Why are people homeless? How do they live? How do various organizations help them?

The teacher will invite a social worker or the school counselor to talk to the class about the questions. The learners will take notes during the discussion. With the guest, they will identify ways they can help homeless people. After the visit, the learners will compare the information given in the books, in articles, and by the visitor. Chart the information.

Learners will evaluate the authenticity of the books read based on the information gained from the study.

Learners will share the information orally with other classes.

(Continued)

TABLE 6.10 Suggested LRMs for Specific Topics *(Continued)*

Conservation, Ecology, and the Rain Forest

After reading a selection of biographies and information books recommended in the bibliography, assume the role of a naturalist touring your community. Take the children on a field trip to a body of water, forest, or other location to see the relationships between plants and animals. The students will prepare a journal describing the field trip. Later journal entries will discuss the community, state, or national efforts to preserve the location; and action recommended to ensure a balance in the eco-system.

Newspaper and magazine articles relating to the topic should be collected. Students will write local agencies requesting information about conservation actions in the community or state. The students will write a magazine article outlining a conservation problem, describing actions already taken, and suggesting future actions. The article will be based on information from an article, information received from the agencies, and information from a nonfiction book. The published article, the students' article, related information from the agency, and a list of other sources to consult will be placed in a class *Conservation Scrapbook.*

Information from the scrapbook and from various nonfiction books will serve as the basis of a class play describing appropriate actions the children, school, and other governmental agencies should take to improve the situation.

Immigration

Select books from the Twentieth Century Bibliography related to immigration to the United States and other countries. Read books such as Russell Freedman's *Immigrant Kids,* Ellen Levine's . . . *If Your Names Was Changed at Ellis Island,* and Lila Perl's *The Great Ancestor Hunt: The Fun of Finding Out Who You Are.* Also select books from the Realistic Fiction: Twentieth Century Bibliography related to the topic, such as Maxinne Leighton's *An Ellis Island Christmas.*

Discuss the hardships the immigrants endured to come to the New World. Prepare a comparison chart (see Chapter 10) recording the differences between the immigrants' lifestyle as described in a book and the lifestyle of contemporary children.

Invite a member of a genealogical society to visit the classroom to talk about "searching for your ancestors." Have the students interview elderly members of the family. Students will complete a genealogical chart as shown in Perl's *The Great Ancestor Hunt.*

Learners will also collect information about their ancestors and write a short book about them. They will write the book from the point of view of a child who lived at the time. Maps tracing the family's journey to the present community and other authentic visuals of interest should be incorporated into the text. They could also include a fictional coat of arms in the book.

If elderly family members are not available, students will interview local historians to learn local legends and stories about the town. Students will write a short book about early pioneers in the community. They should tell the story from the perspective of a person who was there. Time lines and photographs could be included in the book. Dioramas and murals could be placed with the books.

The books could be the beginning of a Genealogical Society of the elementary school.

Summary

People constantly search for heroes. They are concerned about personal relationships. They are naturally curious about their environment and the other humans and creatures who inhabit the world. Nonfiction literature provides the information and insights needed to help answer these questions and concerns. The popularity of the genre reflects the benefits individuals gain from exploring factual materials.

Nonfiction literature informs, instructs, and introduces the reader to the past, the present, and the future. We expect certain elements in quality nonfiction literature: adequate coverage of content, accuracy and currency of information, objectivity of the author, an adequate writing style, and an appropriate organization, format, and visuals.

We categorize nonfiction literature into two subgenres: *biographies/autobiographies* and *information books*. Biographies and autobiographies are narratives focusing on the life and times of a particular person. Many biographies are *authentic* (accurately report the person's life and times). Some biographies are *fictionalized* (based on documented evidence with invented conversations or dramatized events); others are *biographical fiction* (fictionalized narratives loosely based on documented evidence). Biographies are presented as individual biographies (giving complete or partial coverage of the subject's life and times), collective biographies (a collection of brief biographies or stories about events in the lives of people who have common interests, backgrounds, or accomplishments), and biographical series (multiple volumes of individual biographies published by a particular company under the series name).

Information books are factual books presenting documented information about a particular topic. The books are written in narratives or expository discourse. The information is presented in an appropriate structure depending on the intended audience, the content, the author's preference, and the purpose of the book. The subgenre contains four types of books: survey books; concept books; experiment, activity, and question-answer books; and encyclopedias and almanacs.

The characteristics, types, specific evaluative criteria, historical perspective, and notable selections of both subgenres of nonfiction literature are discussed in this chapter. Instructional strategies and Literary Response Modes are suggested to give young people an opportunity to react to nonfiction literature. The bibliography at the end of the book includes recommended biographies, autobiographies, and information books organized according to historical periods and specific topics.

NOTES

The opening quotation is from Milton Meltzer. *Nonfiction for the Classroom.* New York: Teachers College Press. 21.

1. Luber, P. 1992. The evolution of a science writer. In Freeman, E. B., & Person, D. G. (Eds.). 1992. *Using Nonfiction Trade Books in the Elementary Classroom.* Urbana, Ill.: National Council of Teachers of English. 11–16.
2. Freedman, R. 1992. Fact or fiction? In Freeman, E. B., & Person, D. G. (Eds.). 2–10.
3. Carter, B., & Abrahamson, R. F. 1990. *Nonfiction for Young Adults: From Delight to Wisdom.* Phoenix, Ariz.: Oryx. x.
4. Books included in the bibliography were recommended by at least two of the following sources: *The Bulletin of the Center for Children's Books.* University of Illinois. 1991–present; *The Horn Book Guide.* The Horn Book Magazine. 1989–present; Jensen, J. M., & Roser, N. L. (Eds.). 1993. *Adventuring with Books: A Booklist for Pre-K–Grade 6.* (10th Ed.). Urbana, Ill.: National Council of Teachers of English; Kobrin, B. 1988. *Eyeopeners!* New York: Viking; Kobrin, B. 1995. *Eyeopeners II.* New York: Scholastic.
5. *The Horn Book Guide to Children's and Young Adult Books.* Boston: The Horn Book, Inc. Issues from 1990 to 1995.
6. Carter, B., & Abrahamson, R. F. 1990. xii.
7. *Reading Today.* 1990. Facts can be fun: An interview with author Seymour Simon. February/March. 32.
8. Fritz, J. 1988. Biography: Readability plus responsibility. *The Horn Book Magazine.* 64(6): 759–60.
9. Carter, B., & Abrahamson, R. F. 1990. x–xii.
10. Meltzer, M. 1994. Seeding passion, energy, and hope: Writing and social responsibility. In Saul, W. (Ed.). *Nonfiction for the Classroom.* New York: Teachers College Press. 20–22. This book contains essays reconfigured from more than 150 original speeches and papers presented by Meltzer. This essay presents his philosophy of writing nonfiction literature based on his more than thirty-five years of creating outstanding books. He provides many refreshing insights about people of historical importance and offers ideas for using nonfiction literature in the classroom.
11. Fisher, L. E. 1988. On the fiction of nonfiction. *The Five Owls.* 3(1). September/October. 1–3.
12. Fritz, J. 1990. The known and the unknown: An exploration into nonfiction. 181. In Hearne, B. (Ed.). *The Zena Sutherland Lectures: 1983–1992.* New York: Clarion Books. 164–82.
13. Freedman, R. 1992. 5.
14. Girard, L. W. 1988. The truth with some stretchers. *The Horn Book Magazine.* 64(4). 464–69.
15. Zarnowski, M. 1990. *Learning about Biographies: A Reading-and-Writing Approach for Children.* Urbana, Ill.: National Council of Teachers of English. 44–52.
16. For additional information about children's interest in biographies, see sources such as Herman, G. B. 1977. Footprints on the sands of time: Biographies for children. *Children's Literature in Education.* 9. Summer, 85–94; Zarnowski, M. 1990. 3–6.
17. For additional information about selecting biographies and autobiographies, see sources such as Bowen, C. D. 1968. *Biography: The Craft and the Calling.* Boston: Little, Brown; Carr, J. 1982. What do we do about bad biographies? *Beyond Fact: Nonfiction for Children and Young People.* Chicago: American Library Association. 119–29; Kendall, P. M. 1985. *The Art of Biography.* New York: Norton; Wilms, D. M. 1978. An evaluation of biography. *Booklist.* 75. September 15. 218–20.
18. For additional information about notable biographies, see sources such as Giblin, J. C. 1988. The rise and fall and rise of juvenile nonfiction, 1961–1988. *School Library Journal.* 35. October. 27–31; Meigs, C., Eaton, A. T., Nesbitt, E., & Viguers, R. H. 1966. *A Critical History of Children's Literature.* New York: Macmillan. 571–79; Smith, D. V. 1963. *Fifty Years of Children's Books.* Champaign, Ill.: National Council of Teachers of English; Sutherland, Z., & Arbuthnot, M. H. 1991. *Children and Books.* (8th Ed.) New York: HarperCollins. 503–19.
19. Lutz, D. 1996. Science is what scientists do, or wetenschap is wat wetenschappers doen. *The Horn Book Magazine.* 73(2). March/April. 166–73; McMillan, B. 1993. Accuracy in books for young readers: From first to last check. *The New Advocate.* 6(2). 98.
20. Leal, D. J. 1993. The power of literary peer group discussions: How children collaboratively negotiate meaning. *The Reading Teacher.* 47(2). 114–20. Leal found that nonfiction books that combine a narrative and expository text had the greatest potential to enhance student discussion.
21. Cherry, L. 1994. *The Armadillo from Amarillo.* San Diego: A Gulliver Green Book. 11.
22. Stanley, J. 1992. *Children of the Dust Bowl: The True Story of the School at Weedpatch Camp.* Photos. New York: Crown. 7.
23. Lawrence, R. D. 1990. *Wolves.* Illustrations by D. Siemens and colored photos. San Francisco: Sierra Club Books/Little Brown. 6.
24. London, J. 1995. *Honey Paw and Lightfoot.* Illustrations by Jon Van Zyle. San Francisco, Calif.: Chronicle Books. 11–14.
25. Moore, P. 1994. *The Starry Sky.* Illustrations by P. Doherty. Brookfield, Conn.: Copper Beech Books. 42.
26. Simon, S. 1988. *Galaxies.* Colored photos. New York: Mulberry. 28.
27. For additional information about the structure of expository texts, see sources such as Beck, I. L., & McKeown, M. G. Research directions. Social studies texts are hard to understand: Mediating some of the difficulties. *Language Arts.* 68(6). 482–90; Mason, J. M., & Au, K. H. 1986. *Reading Instruction for Today.* Chicago: Scott, Foresman. 217–18; Meyer, B. J. F. 1975. *The Organization of Prose and Its Effects on Memory.* Amsterdam: North-Holland.
28. For additional information about alphabet books, see sources such as Chaney, J. 1993. Alphabet books: Resources for learning. *The Reading Teacher.* 47(2). October. 96–104; Roberts, P. L. 1990. Alphabet books: Activities from A to Z. *The Reading Teacher.* 44(1). September. 84–85; Smolkin, L. B., & Yaden, D. B., Jr. 1992. O is for mouse; First encounters with the alphabet book. *Language Arts.* 69(1). October. 432–41; Thompson, D. L. 1992. The alphabet book as a content area resource. *The Reading Teacher.* 46(3). November. 266–67.
29. For additional information about benefits, see sources such as Fisher, M. 1972. *Matters of Fact: Aspects of Non-Fiction for Children.* Leicester, England: Brockhampton Press. 9–17; Kobrin, B. 1995. 4–9; Moss, B. 1991. Children's nonfiction trade books: A complement to content area texts. *The Reading Teacher.* 45(1). 26–32.
30. For additional information about selecting information books, see sources such as Dowd, F. S. Trends and evaluative criteria of informational books for children. In Freeman, E. B., & Person, D. G. 1992. *Using Nonfiction Trade Books in the Elementary Classroom: From Ants to Zeppelins.* Urbana, Ill.: National Council of Teachers of English. 34–43; Kobrin, B. 1995. 45–55; Sudol, P., & King, C. M. 1996. A checklist for choosing nonfiction trade books. *The Reading Teacher.* 49(5). February. 422–24.
31. Moss, B. 1991. 28.
32. For a summary of research findings see Carter, B., & Abrahamson, R. F. 1990. 1–15; Carter, B., & Abrahamson, R. F. 1993. Factual history: Nonfiction in the social studies program. In Cullinan, B. E. (Ed.). *Fact and Fiction: Literature Across the Curriculum.* Newark, Del.: International Reading Association. 34 (see also the entire essay: 31–56).
33. Hodges, M., & Steinfirst, S. 1980. *Elva S. Smith's The History of Children's Literature.* Chicago: American Library Association. 40, 231.
34. For additional information about notable information books, see sources such as Giblin, J. C. 1988; Meigs, C., Eaton, A. T., Nesbitt, E., & Viguers, R. H. 1966; Smith, D. V. 1963; Vardell, S. 1991. A new "picture of the world": The NCTE Orbis Pictus Award for Outstanding Nonfiction for Children. *Language Arts.* 68(6). 474–79.
35. For additional information about students writing biographies, see Graves, D. H. 1989. *Investigate Nonfiction.* Portsmouth, N.H.: Heinemann; Zarnowski, M. 1990. Also, Freeman, E. B., & Person, D. G. (Eds.) 1992. Parts II and III.

Poetry

The Emotions, Thoughts, Images of a Society

Go with the poem.
Hang glide
above new landscape
into other weather.

Sail the poem.
Lift.
Drift over treetops
and towers.

Loop with the poem.
Swoop, dip.
Land.
Where?
Trust the poem.

—Lilian Moore, "Go with the Poem"

*W*hat language motivates babies to react with gurgles and laughter? . . .

> repetitive syllables, "mama," "papa"

What language helps young children when they are learning to read? . . .

> rhyming words

What language do children use when they play with language? . . .

> rhyming, cadenced, repetitive language

As young children spontaneously explore the sounds, rhythm, and rhyme of language, they are naturally drawn to poetry and the power of verse to express ideas and feelings and convey information. Throughout the ages, children have sung, chanted and recited jingles, verses, and rhymes and bounced, clapped, and played to their cadences. As early as 1908 Huey reminded adults that poetry naturally leads children to a love of language, a way to learn language, and a link to express thoughts, feelings, and ideas.[1]

WHAT IS POETRY?

What is Poetry? Who knows?
Not a rose, but the scent of the rose;
Not the sky, but the light in the sky;
Not the fly, but the gleam of the fly;
Not the sea, but the sound of the sea;
Not myself, but what makes me
See, hear, and feel something that prose
Cannot: and what it is, who knows?

(Eleanor Farjeon, "Poetry")

Poets use rhythm, sound, and fascinating language to excite "beautiful, imaginative, or elevated thoughts."[2] A poet intends every word to stimulate an emotional reaction in the reader. Rarely does anyone react neutrally to the images and music of a poem. Individuals usually respond with delight or reject a poem altogether. Quality poetry is emotionally satisfying to the audience. A personal relationship and sense of trust develop between the poet and the individual who fully savors and experiences the poem.

People describe poetry's appeal in various ways. The poet Mary O'Neill felt poetry that "sings, or carries a musical beat is most appealing to children, as it was to me when I was a little girl."[3] Karla Kuskin gives a recipe for a poem: "word sounds, rhythm, description, feeling, memory, rhymes and imagination . . . can be put together a thousand different ways. . . ." Different people write differently about the same situation: "as differently as we are from each other . . . it is those differences that make our poems interesting."[4]

Poetry is the poet's subjective response to his or her world. Poems describe memories and feelings. "Many memories are memories of feelings."[5] Poetry "presents ideas and truths concisely and imaginatively."[6] Perhaps no single definition can encompass all of poetry's aspects because poetry is a subjective, emotional response to words, a situation, a feeling, or a thought and means different things to different people.

The poet Eve Merriam knew that she could express the inexpressible through poetry. While it may not answer all questions, poetry "helps make us kin by sharing questions" about life. Poetry does not "solve problems, but it can air them in a more directly emotional way than any other form of writing. It can lead to discussion of feelings. . . ." It can "bring bruises into sunlight so they can heal . . . and there is laughter as well as pain."[7]

Because poetry demands precise word choices, it requires a balance between the intellect and the senses. Quality juvenile poetry entails the same literary expectations as adult poetry. "Many poems are descriptions of places, moods, things. . . . A good description doesn't tell you everything . . . but it uses a few special details arranged with care. It is these details and their special arrangement that make a particular picture. . . . Another kind of description is a list of many details. The list is held together with word sounds and rhythm."[8] Successful poets select words and phrases that express the familiar in unusual ways; they put an idea into words that the audience can understand and experience personally. Finally, successful poets artistically share their feelings to evoke spirited responses from their audience.[9] Ten-year-old Daniel described poetry this way: "It's a way to let people know how you feel and at the same time a way to entertain them."[10]

Jane Dyer uses clear watercolors to complement her poetry anthology, Animal Crackers. *The artist uses a variety of styles representing folk art (as in this painting); quaint, old-fashioned art; contemporary art; and realistic style. She creates a variety of pleasing borders and arranges the art and poems in compatible visual compositions.*

Poetry with its concise, emotional language and patterned format, encompasses certain elements, types, and forms that are not typical of prose or drama. Young people who are saturated with a wide variety of poetry discover these unique structures and use that knowledge when selecting poems for personal enjoyment. They also choose books of poetry with appealing pictures that help them interpret the poet's language and thoughts. Jane Dyer uses eye-catching illustrations and an innovative book design to enhance the poetry of such eminent poets as William Carlos Williams, Alfred Lord Tennyson, and Eugene Fields, in her anthology *Animal Crackers: A Delectable Collection of Pictures, Poems, and Lullabies for the Very Young* (1996). (See the Dyer color plate.) The distinctive characteristics of poetry, notable juvenile poets and their contributions, and various ways poetry can be presented in the classroom are discussed in this chapter.

💧 THE DISTINCTIVE CHARACTERISTICS OF POETRY

A poem is a magical boat to ride
in a sea of words with a rhyming tide.
It takes us from some hum-drum shore
to places we never have been before—
shimmering islands of sensation
captured by imagination.
New lands wait for us to sight,
so climb aboard! The wind is right.
Rocking rhythms will take us along
to the rising crest of a noteless song.

(Bobbi Katz, "Poems")

Katz's "Poems" highlights the language, imagery, rhyme, sensations, rhythm, and form writers use to express their thoughts and feelings through poetry. Although many of these linguistic elements are also used in prose, poets depend on certain elements such as sounds, rhythm, exact word choices, and perhaps rhyme to imaginatively and succinctly express their reflections, escapades, and intellectual insights in narrative, lyric, nonsense, or humorous poetry in rhymed or unrhymed poetic forms. Thus, poetry is distinguished from prose by the writer's use of various *poetic elements, types,* and *forms.* While the elements, types, and forms are interrelated, poets wisely select the most appropriate components of each to effectively portray the subject. The distinguishing characteristics of poetic types, elements, and forms are explored in the next section of this chapter.[11]

TYPES OF POETRY

Narrative, lyric, nonsense, and *humorous* verses and poems are frequently found in juvenile poetry. These types are not as clearly delineated as the various rhymed and unrhymed forms, but each is distinct and needs to be considered separately.

Narrative poetry tells a story. The poet uses various forms, rhyming schemes and rhythms to present a story involving one or more characters and events. Children find this type particularly appealing because the poem presents a complete vignette, as in John Ciardi's poem about an event that children of all ages may have experienced:

Daddy fixed the breakfast.
He made us each a waffle.
It looked like gravel pudding.
It tasted something awful.

"Ha, ha," he said, "I'll try again.
This time I'll get it right."
But what *I* got was in between
Bituminous and anthracite.

"A little too well done? Oh well,
I'll have to start all over."
That time what landed on my plate
Looked like a manhole cover.

I tried to cut it with a fork:
The fork gave off a spark.
I tried a knife and twisted it
Into a question mark.

I tried it with a hack-saw.
I tried it with a torch.
It didn't even make a dent.
It didn't even scorch.

The next time Dad gets breakfast
When Mummy's sleeping late,
I think I'll skip the waffles.
I'd sooner eat the plate!

(John Ciardi, "Mummy Slept
Late and Daddy Fixed Breakfast")

Lyric poetry is usually quiet and describes a mood or feeling. The poems may be written as songs, sonnets, or odes of praise or celebration. Although rhyming schemes and patterns differ, these short poems always elicit strong feelings about the subject. In the following lyric poem, David McCord describes a special place all children cherish when life becomes hectic:

This is my rock,
And here I run
To steal the secret of the sun;

This is my rock,
And here come I
Before the night has swept the sky;

This is my rock,
This is the place
I meet the evening face to face.

(David McCord, "This Is My Rock")

Nonsense poetry is a playful distortion of a particular situation, place, or character. The poet may use meaningless, nonsense words, strong rhythms, and various rhyming schemes and play with the sounds of the language to present absurd situations that require the audience to suspend belief in reality and move into the poet's world. Frequently, the poems evoke laughter as in the following limerick:

I raised a great hullabaloo
When I found a large mouse in my stew,
    Said the waiter, "Don't shout
    And wave it about,
Or the rest will be wanting one, too!"

(Author unknown)

Humorous poems present a funny, believable, and perhaps slightly distorted view of a situation. In this type of poetry, the poet frequently uses a regular rhythm and rhyming scheme and plays with the sounds of the language. Children of all ages like to laugh at the real or imaginary characters and pretend to be part of the situation. Bruce Lansky's *Kids Pick the Funniest Poems* (1991) is a collection of humorous poems enjoyed by children.

Narrative and lyric poetry are identified by the poet's purpose for writing the poem, while nonsense and humorous poems are identified by the content and the poet's word choices. In juvenile poetry, poets often combine types of poetry. They may write a nonsense or humorous poem using the story format or insert a humorous twist into a lyric poem as Gwendolyn Brooks does in her description of Keziah's special place:

I have a secret place to go.
Not anyone may know.

And sometimes when the wind is rough
I cannot get there fast enough.

And sometimes when my mother
Is scolding my big brother,

My secret place, it seems to me,
Is quite the only place to be.

(Gwendolyn Brooks, "Keziah")

Outstanding examples of all four types of poems appear throughout the chapter. Figure 7.1 on page 211 presents general information about the four types of poems typically found in juvenile poetry.

POETIC ELEMENTS

Individuals hear the sound of a poem, feel its rhythm or rhyme, and visualize the ideas it conveys. Poetry is a sensory experience that depends on the poet's ability to use the poetic elements effectively. Poets imaginatively project the *content* through carefully *selected language* expressed through *rhythm, sounds, word patterns*, and perhaps *rhyme*. Although each poetic element can be described independently, all of the elements enhance and support the others to create a poem we will remember.

Poets may remember even the most mundane events and later re-create them in poems. Their personal feelings and ideas are expressed in the content of narrative, lyric, humorous, and even nonsense verses and poems.

Poets have an incredible ability to recognize and use the sounds of the language to eloquently express their insights and observations. Some sounds are short and brittle, while others are liquid and flowing. Sounds may be soft or loud,

FIGURE 7.1 Types of Poetry

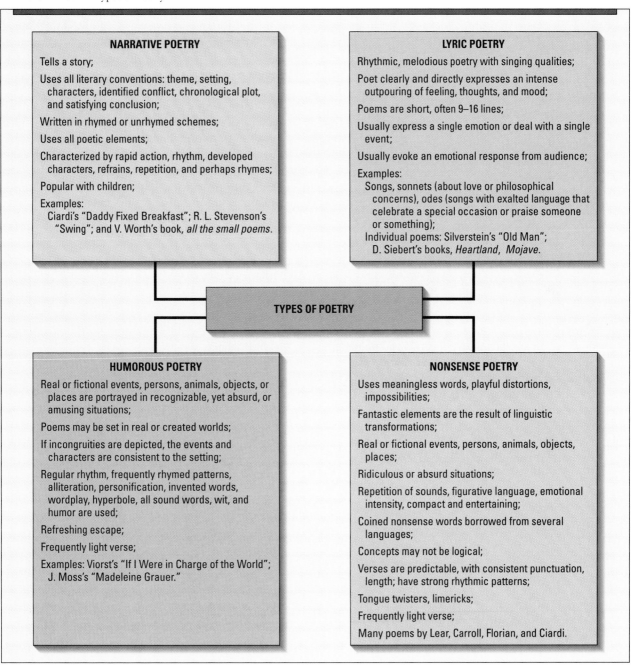

NARRATIVE POETRY

Tells a story;

Uses all literary conventions: theme, setting, characters, identified conflict, chronological plot, and satisfying conclusion;

Written in rhymed or unrhymed schemes;

Uses all poetic elements;

Characterized by rapid action, rhythm, developed characters, refrains, repetition, and perhaps rhymes;

Popular with children;

Examples:
  Ciardi's "Daddy Fixed Breakfast"; R. L. Stevenson's "Swing"; and V. Worth's book, *all the small poems*.

LYRIC POETRY

Rhythmic, melodious poetry with singing qualities;

Poet clearly and directly expresses an intense outpouring of feeling, thoughts, and mood;

Poems are short, often 9–16 lines;

Usually express a single emotion or deal with a single event;

Usually evoke an emotional response from audience;

Examples:
  Songs, sonnets (about love or philosophical concerns), odes (songs with exalted language that celebrate a special occasion or praise someone or something);
  Individual poems: Silverstein's "Old Man"; D. Siebert's books, *Heartland, Mojave*.

TYPES OF POETRY

HUMOROUS POETRY

Real or fictional events, persons, animals, objects, or places are portrayed in recognizable, yet absurd, or amusing situations;

Poems may be set in real or created worlds;

If incongruities are depicted, the events and characters are consistent to the setting;

Regular rhythm, frequently rhymed patterns, alliteration, personification, invented words, wordplay, hyperbole, all sound words, wit, and humor are used;

Refreshing escape;

Frequently light verse;

Examples: Viorst's "If I Were in Charge of the World"; J. Moss's "Madeleine Grauer."

NONSENSE POETRY

Uses meaningless words, playful distortions, impossibilities;

Fantastic elements are the result of linguistic transformations;

Real or fictional events, persons, animals, objects, places;

Ridiculous or absurd situations;

Repetition of sounds, figurative language, emotional intensity, compact and entertaining;

Coined nonsense words borrowed from several languages;

Concepts may not be logical;

Verses are predictable, with consistent punctuation, length; have strong rhythmic patterns;

Tongue twisters, limericks;

Frequently light verse;

Many poems by Lear, Carroll, Florian, and Ciardi.

but the poet's ability to use just the right sound in the proper place frequently determines the popularity of a poem. Skillful poets use alliteration, assonance, consonance, and onomatopoeia. *Alliteration* is the repetition of stressed initial consonant sounds in consecutive words in a line of verse or stanza to achieve a flowing or singing effect; for example, "Similar syllables sing the song." *Assonance* is the repetition of a vowel in stressed syllables without the repetition of consonants. An assonance is used as a substitute for a rhyme; for example, "Slap" and "dash;" "fate" and "make;" "time" and "mind." *Consonance* is the recurrence of identical or similar consonant syllables within a line with vowel sounds interspersed; for example, "Beat! Beat! Drums!—Blow! Bugles! Blow!" *Onomatopoeia* is the use of words that represent or imitate the sound made; for example, "Swish, whack, zap, buzz." Poets also repeat sounds, rhymes, words, or phrases to highlight or enrich phrases, lines, or refrains.

Writers achieve *rhythm* through the regular arrangement of stressed and unstressed syllables in a line of poetry. A poem's rhythm or cadence highlights the mood and subject. It also enhances the sounds and adds to the dramatic effect. The natural pauses suggested by the language give the audience a feel for the rhythm and may encourage the audience to move physically. Poets achieve rhythm through *meter*, the arrangement of the stressed, or accented, syllables in a particular pattern. The most popular meters are *iambic*, which consists of two syllables, the first unstressed, the second stressed; *trochaic*, which consists of two syllables, the first stressed, the second unstressed; *anapestic*, which consists of three syllables, the first two syllables unstressed, the last stressed; and *dactylic*, which consists of three syllables, the first stressed, the last two unstressed. The number of *feet*, or metrical units, in a line also contributes to rhythm. *Tetrameter*, which has four feet per line, and *pentameter*, which has five feet per line, are the most popular arrangements. The most common meter/feet combination in juvenile poetry is the *iambic tetrameter*, that is, an eight-syllable line, stressed on every second beat, as in "The dog and cat went down to town." These technical terms are taught indirectly to students when discussing the rhythm of a poem. They can be compared to the musician's use of half-notes and quarter-notes to achieve rhythm in music.

Given poetry's compact nature, writers must carefully select words and vivid phrases that clearly express their feelings and ideas. Mary O'Neill highlights the ability of words to express different ideas:

Some words clink
As ice in drink.
Some move with grace
A dance, a lace.
Some sound thin:
Wail, scream and pin.
Some words are squat:
A mug, a pot,
And some are plump,
Fat, round and dump.
Some words are light:
Drift, lift and bright.
A few are small:
A, is and all.
And some are thick,
Glue, paste and brick.

. . . .

Some words are hot:
Fire, flame and shot.
Some words are sharp,
Sword, point and carp.
And some alert:
Glint, glance and flirt.
Some words are lazy:
Saunter, hazy.

. . . .

Some words can fly—
There's wind, there's high:
And some words cry:
"Goodbye . . .
Goodbye. . . ."

(Mary O'Neill, "Feelings about Words")

The success of a poem frequently depends on the poet's use of imagery and figurative language. *Imagery* is the use of words or phrases to evoke the senses and stimulate the imagination of the audience. *Figurative language* is the use of words and phrases in a nonliteral way that gives new and unusual meaning to the language. When poets describe a feeling or object, they frequently use similes or metaphors to compare one object to another. A *simile* compares two things that are different; the comparison often begins with words such as *like*, *as*, or *similar*; for example, "His smile is as bright as the sun." A *metaphor* compares two unlike things to suggest a resemblance; for example, "Her eyes were stars." Poets also use *personification*, which gives human characteristics to nonhuman things, as in "The water smiles," and *hyperbole*, which is an exaggeration or overstatement, as in "He split his sides open laughing." Jane Yolen uses imagery and figurative language to describe the woodpecker in the following poem:

His swift
ratatatatat
is
as casual as a jackhammer
on a city street,
as thorough as an oil drill
on an Oklahoma wellsite,
as fine as a needle
in a record groove,
as cleansing as a dentist's probe
in a mouthful of cavities,
as final as a park attendant's stick
on a lawn of litter.

Ratatatatatatat.
He finishes his work
on the maple tree,
then wings off again
to the pine,
leaving his punctuation
along the woody line.

(Jane Yolen, "Woodpecker")

Rhyme is the regular recurrence of similar sounding words. A poet manipulates the language to develop a rhyming scheme. Not all poems are rhymed. The differences between rhymed and unrhymed poems are discussed in the next section. Figure 7.2 on page 213 describes the elements of poetry. Additional information can be found in Appendix A.

FORMS OF POETRY

Before writing, poets make several decisions, such as:

Will I use a rhymed or unrhymed poetic form?

Will I use stanzas and refrains in my poem?

Will I visualize my thoughts in the shape of the content of the poem?

FIGURE 7.2   Elements of Poetry

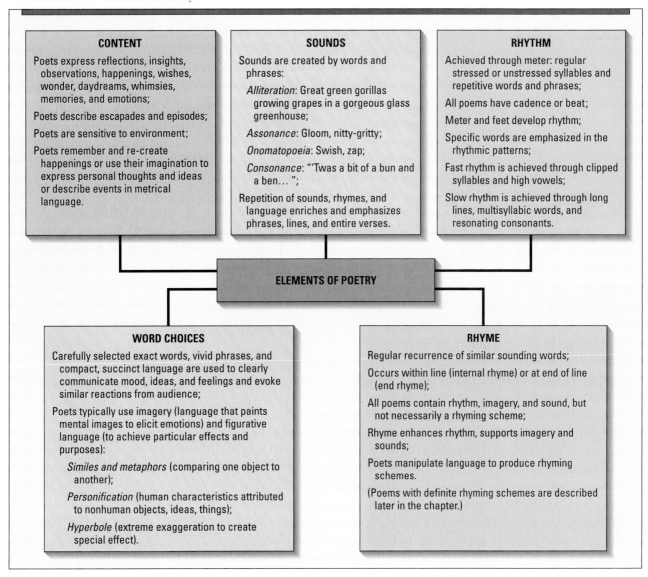

CONTENT

Poets express reflections, insights, observations, happenings, wishes, wonder, daydreams, whimsies, memories, and emotions;

Poets describe escapades and episodes;

Poets are sensitive to environment;

Poets remember and re-create happenings or use their imagination to express personal thoughts and ideas or describe events in metrical language.

SOUNDS

Sounds are created by words and phrases:

Alliteration: Great green gorillas growing grapes in a gorgeous glass greenhouse;

Assonance: Gloom, nitty-gritty;

Onomatopoeia: Swish, zap;

Consonance: "'Twas a bit of a bun and a ben… ";

Repetition of sounds, rhymes, and language enriches and emphasizes phrases, lines, and entire verses.

RHYTHM

Achieved through meter: regular stressed or unstressed syllables and repetitive words and phrases;

All poems have cadence or beat;

Meter and feet develop rhythm;

Specific words are emphasized in the rhythmic patterns;

Fast rhythm is achieved through clipped syllables and high vowels;

Slow rhythm is achieved through long lines, multisyllabic words, and resonating consonants.

ELEMENTS OF POETRY

WORD CHOICES

Carefully selected exact words, vivid phrases, and compact, succinct language are used to clearly communicate mood, ideas, and feelings and evoke similar reactions from audience;

Poets typically use imagery (language that paints mental images to elicit emotions) and figurative language (to achieve particular effects and purposes):

Similes and metaphors (comparing one object to another);

Personification (human characteristics attributed to nonhuman objects, ideas, things);

Hyperbole (extreme exaggeration to create special effect).

RHYME

Regular recurrence of similar sounding words;

Occurs within line (internal rhyme) or at end of line (end rhyme);

All poems contain rhythm, imagery, and sound, but not necessarily a rhyming scheme;

Rhyme enhances rhythm, supports imagery and sounds;

Poets manipulate language to produce rhyming schemes.

(Poems with definite rhyming schemes are described later in the chapter.)

Will I use conventional punctuation or be creative in my mechanics?

These questions are all answered by the form the poet chooses to use.

This section will examine various forms used with rhymed and unrhymed poetry and verse. Visual forms are also used in juvenile poetry and are described later in this section.

Poets arrange poetry in *stanzas*, or *verses*. A *stanza* is a group of two or more lines of poetry written in a definite form and spaced apart from each other. Some poems also include a refrain. A *refrain* is the repetition of one or more words or phrases at the end of a stanza or at regular inter-vals in the poem. In David Bouchard's book *If You're Not From the Prairie* (1995), a repetitive refrain, stanza, and repetitive refrain appear on each double-page spread. Henry Ripplinger's paintings appear on the adjoining page. This arrangement highlights the poet's love of his land and strengthens the emotional impact of the lyric poem. (See the Bouchard color plate on page 214.)

Rhymed Forms

In rhymed forms of poetry, similar sounding syllables or words recur regularly throughout the poem. The similar sounding words may occur at the end of the line (end rhyme) or within the same line (internal rhyme). Listen to

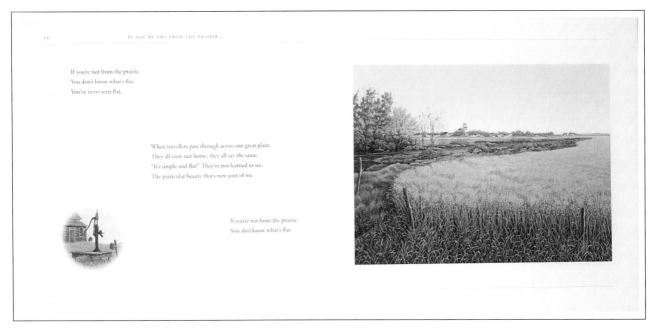

If you're not from the prairie,
You don't know what's flat.
You've *never* seen flat.

When travellers pass through across our great plain,
They all view our home, they all say the same:
"It's simple and flat!" They've not learned to see,
The particular beauty that's now part of me.

If you're not from the prairie,
You *don't* know what's flat.

Henry Ripplinger created realistic images to enrich Bouchard's lyric poetry If You're Not from the Prairie. *The artist uses white space effectively to highlight the detailed acrylic paintings and emphasize the repetitive verses.*

the internal rhyme and ending rhyme used by Karla Kuskin as she describes an experience in the wintertime:

We'll play in the snow
And stray in the snow
And stay in the snow
In a snow-white park.
We'll clown in the snow
And frown in the snow
Fall down in the snow
Till it's after dark.
We'll cook snow pies
In a big snow pan.
We'll make snow eyes
In a round snow man.
We'll sing snow songs
And chant snow chants
And roll in the snow
In our fat snow pants.
And when it's time to go home to eat
We'll have snow toes
On our frosted feet.

(Karla Kuskin, "Snow")

Poets use the various meters discussed previously with rhymed poetry. The following are the main forms of rhymed poetry:

Couplets consist of two consecutive, rhymed lines of poetry, usually an *aa* rhyming scheme. In a *closed cou-*plet, a thought or image is presented in two lines. In an *open couplet,* the second line flows into the next couplet. Brooks's "Keziah" is written in the couplet form. N. H. Bodecker's *"Let's Marry Said the Cherry and Other Nonsense Poems"* is a collection of couplets. Ted Hughes also used the form in poems such as "Roger the Dog" and "My Brother Bert."

Triplets or *tercets* are stanzas with three lines that usually rhyme. Though not as popular as couplets or quatrains, triplets have been used by several poets. David McCord's "This is My Rock" is an example of the use of triplets. Jack Prelutsky also used triplets for several poems including "Auk in Flight" and "Don't Ever Seize a Weasel by the Tail." Also, see Theodore Roethke's "The Sloth." *The Random House Book of Poetry* (1983), edited by Prelutsky, includes these and other triplets and couplets.

Quatrains are four-line stanzas characterized by a single rhyming scheme. Possible rhyming schemes include *abcd* rhyme; *a* and *b*, *c* and *d* rhyme; *a* and *d*, *b* and *c* rhyme; and *a* and *c*, *b* and *d* rhyme. Many juvenile poems are written in this form. Ciardi used the quatrain form in "Mummy Slept Late and Daddy Fixed Breakfast," and Robert Louis Stevenson used it in "The Swing." In the following lyric poem, written in the quatrain form, Jeff Moss uses the *abcb* rhyming scheme:

On the other side of the door
I can be a different me,
As smart and as brave and as funny or strong
As a person could want to be.
There's nothing too hard for me to do,
There's no place I can't explore
Because everything can happen
On the other side of the door.

On the other side of the door
I don't have to go alone.
If you come, too, we can sail tall ships
And fly where the wind has flown.
And wherever we go, it is almost sure
We'll find what we're looking for
Because everything can happen
On the other side of the door.

(Jeff Moss, "The Other Side of the Door")

Ballads are short narrative poems, written in the language of the ordinary people to describe a dramatic situation. The poet-singer used couplets, tercets, or quatrains, often rhyming the second and fourth lines. Typically, the ballad includes a refrain. The ballad tells of an incident in the life of a real or fanciful subject. It is written in a sad, humorous, historical, tragic, weird, or sensational manner. Dialogue, action verbs, limited descriptions, and repetitive language are used to highlight the escapades of the hero or villain. "Robin Hood," "John Henry," "The Old Chisholm Trail," "On Top of Old Smoky," and "Yankee Doodle" are all examples of familiar ballads. (See Chapter 3 for additional information.)

Clerihews (KLER-i-hyoos) are light verse frequently written as quatrains using the *aabb* rhyming scheme. Many lines may be unequal in length. Usually, a clerihew tells something humorous about the character. Poets use the following line pattern:

Line 1. The character's name.
Line 2. Tell something about the character (end with a word that rhymes with line 1).
Line 3. Tell something else about the person (does not rhyme with the first two lines).
Line 4. Tell more about the person (end with a word that rhymes with line 3).

For example:

There once was a boy named Bobby.
He didn't have a hobby.
He had to eat burnt rice,
But he was still very nice.

This clerihew was written about characters in Laurence Yep's *Star Fisher* by five students, Jennifer

G., Tricia, Kathy, Kristen, and Jennifer (1994). The history of clerihews, writing techniques, and several clerihews can be found in Paul Janeczko's *Poetry from A to Z* (1994). Michael Rosen includes several clerihews by Edmund Clerihew Bentley (who invented the poetic form) in his anthology *The Kingfisher Book of Children's Poetry* (1993).

Folk rhymes ("sidewalk chants," "jump-rope chants," and "raps") come from the ordinary folk and depend on the rhythm and sounds of the language to describe the subject. The rhymes may be couplets or repeated lines of repetitive phrases or words with new language patterns added to each line. Poets develop the strong beat of the humorous or nonsense verse through all elements, especially sound. Internal or ending rhymes are frequently used. Folk rhymes encourage physical responses. For examples of familiar hand-clapping, ball-bouncing, counting-out, just-for-fun teases, and comeback rhymes, see Joanna Cole's *Anna Banana: 101 Jump-Rope Rhymes* (1989) and Cole and Stephanie Calmenson's *Miss Mary Mack and Other Children's Street Rhymes* (1990). Rhymes from seven countries are included in Jane Yolen's anthology *Street Rhymes around the World* (1992).

Limericks are humorous five-line verses, characterized by an *aabba* rhyming scheme. The character, setting, and conflict are identified in the first and second lines. Lines one, two, and five have three beats, while lines three and four have two beats. Lines three and four are shorter than the other three. By using subtle humor (unusual spelling, oddities, and humorous twists), the verse finishes with a surprise. Edward Lear did not invent the limerick form, but he popularized it with his collection *Book of Nonsense* (1846). Two examples of Lear's limericks follow:

There was an Old Man of Dumbree
Who taught little owls to drink tea;
    For he said, "To eat mice
    Is not proper or nice,"
That amiable Man of Dumbree.

There was an Old Man who, when little,
Fell casually into a kettle;
    But growing too stout
    He could never get out—
So he passed all his life in that kettle!

(Edward Lear)

Contemporary anthologies contain limericks for contemporary audiences. See also Ciardi's *The Hopeful Trout and Other Limericks* (1989).

Jingles are easy-to-remember rhyming verse highlighting sound rather than sense. Jingles contain a succession of sounds or repeated phrases. Saved for special occasions such as holidays or birthdays or for times when a person needs a laugh or wants to spoof someone, jingles are a play with language. Nursery rhymes, words with games, Mother Goose riddles, and street chants are examples of jingles.

Riddles are puzzles that must be solved or answered before they can be understood. Verbal play and the manipulation of language characterize riddles. Excellent riddles are found in Adler's *The Carsick Zebra and Other Animal Riddles* (1983).

Unrhymed Forms

Poetry and verse using an unrhymed scheme does not have an end rhyme, but it usually has an internal cadence and rhythm. Free verse and blank verse are the most popular unrhymed forms.

Free verse is unrhymed verse with no restrictions on length, on the number of syllables in each line, or on rhythmic patterns. Free verse uses emotional language and has the appearance of prose, but is typically more rhythmic. Many poets enjoy the freedom of creating their own rules of rhythm and rhyme. As in prose, the rhythm of free verse depends on a cadence rather than metrical feet. Related words are placed together to develop the natural rhythm and meaning of the verses, eliminating the need for arbitrary or similar arrangement of lines. Because the verses frequently are short, the writer must carefully select a few words that vividly express the desired images. Poets often employ alliteration, assonance, onomatopoeia, and other combinations of sound. Free verse is less predictable than rhymed verse. As in prose, meanings change according to the phrases used and the arrangement of the verse.

Young people enjoy writing free verse, but they often find it difficult to understand when hearing or reading it. Three award-winning poets, Arnold Adoff, Barbara Juster Esbensen, and Valerie Worth, have mastered the form, as seen in Adoff's *Sports Pages* (1986), Esbensen's *Words with Wrinkled Knees* (1986), and Worth's *all the small poems* (1987). One poem from Adoff's collection represents the form and highlights the format:

Sometimes   we leap and land.

Sometimes   we leap and fall.

Sometimes   we catch the other team   before they score.

Sometimes   we jump too soon   and get faked out of our
socks.

Or   We can be sharp on the pick-off play at third.

we can have rocks in our heads and miss that
softly batted ball,
And miss that
One
sweet chance to
save
the
day.

I lose. I win. We lose. We win.

The team finishes   in last place.

The team is

in the play-offs at last

and past defeats fade

fast.

We have our moments.

(Arnold Adoff, "We Have Our Moments")
from *Sports Pages*

Blank verse is a verse form with a regular meter, but without an end rhyme. The lines contain eight to ten syllables. Poets use an iambic pentameter meter, which has five feet, or stressed syllables, with an unstressed and a stressed pattern in each line. Blank verse is frequently used in narrative poems, drama and storytelling. William Shakespeare, William Wordsworth, and Robert Frost all used the form. It is rarely found in juvenile poetry, however.

Poetry with a Definite Form   This section presents unrhymed forms of poetry that follow a definite form. Students enjoy using these forms when they write poetry.

Acrostic. An acrostic is an unrhymed form that describes a person or topic. The topic or person's name is written vertically on the left. Then a word or phrase that relates to the subject and begins with the appropriate letter is placed to the right of each letter. For example:

Absurd,
Nasty,
Grumpy,
Rude,
Yesterday I was!

(Marguerite L., age 11)

Chant. This unrhymed form has no fixed form. A musical beat is created by repeating words or phrases relating to the topic. Early humans used chants to protect themselves from animals and nature. Rap and contemporary music use the chant form.

Cinquain (SING-cane). This unrhymed form contains twenty-two syllables, distributed in five lines as follows:

    Line 1. Two syllables or one word giving the title

    Line 2. Four syllables or two words of description

    Line 3. Six syllables or three words expressing an action

    Line 4. Eight syllables or four words expressing a feeling

    Line 5. Two syllables or another word for the title

For example:

Boys
How awful
They're teasers, too
Dirty, rough, tough, sweaty
Pew!

                          (Jimmy D., age 12)

Terquain. A simplified form of the cinquain, this unrhymed form contains three lines with the following pattern:

    Line 1. One word announcing the subject

    Line 2. Two or three words describing the subject

    Line 3. One word expressing a feeling about or a synonym for the subject

For example:

Terquains
Easy to write
Fantastic!

                            (Kelly, age 12)

Lanterne. This unrhymed form has five lines, each of which has a fixed number of syllables as follows:

    Line 1. One syllable

    Line 2. Two syllables

    Line 3. Three syllables

    Line 4. Four syllables

    Line 5. One syllable

For example:

Poem
with sound,
metaphors,
rhythm, cadence
Fun!

                        (Kristen, age 11)

With their tree shape, lanternes are especially useful at Christmas time.

Diamante (dee-ah-mahn-TAY). A diamante is an unrhymed form written in the shape of a diamond. The verse contains contrasting thoughts in seven lines. It is best to use this form with fifth grade and above. The form is developed as follows:

    Line 1. One noun indicating the subject (title)

    Line 2. Two adjectives describing the subject in line 1.

    Line 3. Three participles relating to the subject in line 1 (-ing or -ed words)

    Line 4. Four nouns related to the subject in line 1.

    Line 5. Three participles related to the subject in line 7 (-ing or -ed words)

    Line 6. Two adjectives describing the subject in line 7

    Line 7. One noun (the opposite of the subject in line 1)

For example:

Child
Young, energetic
Playing, laughing, tumbling
Growth, change, knowledge, development
Working, achieving, succeeding
Older, wiser
Adult

                        (Author unknown)

Ten-year-old Susan, the only girl in a family, modified the form with this verse:

Sisters
Gabby, nosey.
Shopping, eating, buying.
Happy, funny, active, feminine.
I should have three of them!
Girls!

Haiku (HI-ku). This Japanese poetry form contains seventeen syllables organized in three unrhymed lines of 5, 7, and 5 syllables. In a haiku, the line ending does not break the cadence or distort the language. Haiku does not contain internal or end rhymes. Traditionally, haiku dealt with the seasons or nature and aimed at capturing a precise moment in verse. Modern haiku has a broader range of subjects, but still follows the strict syllable count. Perhaps the best collection of Japanese haiku for juveniles is Harry Behn's *Cricket Songs* (1964).

Several selections from Behn's collection illustrate this form:

Snow fell until dawn.
Now every twig in the grove
glitters in sunlight.

(Rokwa)

Well! Hello down there,
friend snail! When did you arrive
in such a hurry?

(Issa)

When my canary
flew away, that was the end
of spring in my house.

(Shiki)

Haikon. This form has the same arrangement of three lines with 5, 7, and 5 syllables as haiku but the syllables are written around a picture describing the content of the poem.

Tonka. Tonka is another unrhymed form originating in Japan. As in haiku, the traditional subjects were nature and the seasons. For contemporary children, use nature, the seasons, or subjects of personal interest. The verse contains thirty-one syllables divided into five lines as follows:

Line 1. 5 syllables

Line 2. 7 syllables

Line 3. 5 syllables

Line 4. 7 syllables

Line 5. 7 syllables

For example:

Where is my puppy?
It's time for him to be home.
I will look for him,
Over at my best friend's house
My cute puppy isn't there!

(Sonya W., age 11)

Parallel Poems. This unrhymed form uses repetitive words or phrases to express an idea. Terms such as the following are used:

Fear is. . . .
Love is. . . .
You might think I . . . , but really I. . . .
I used to think . . . , but now I know that. . . .

Repeat-a-word. In this unrhymed form, words or phrases are repeated at the beginning, middle, or end of a line. The repetition catches the reader's attention,

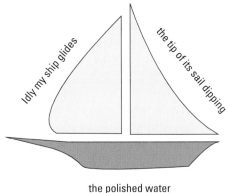

the polished water

Otsuji

A sample haikon

emphasizes a point or an event, and may become humorous. For example:

Red is the color of bloodshot eyes,
Red is the color of sunburned thighs,
Red is the color of a bloody nose,
Red is the color of stepped-on toes.

(Clifford F., age 9, "Red")

5-W poem. Each line of this unrhymed form answers a W question. For example:

Who is the subject ?	A little boy
What is the subject doing?	Eating a midnight snack
When does the action take place?	Late at night
Where does the action take place?	At his kitchen table
Why does the action take place?	To feed his hunger.

(David B., age 11, "Midnight Snack")

Biopoem. A biopoem is an unrhymed form that deals with a familiar real or fictional character. There are eleven lines, which are not written in complete sentences. Words such as *I, me,* and *my,* are not used. Each line begins with certain words or traits and presents specified information as follows:[12]

Line 1. First name of subject.

Line 2. Four traits that describe the subject.

Line 3. Tell who is a relative of the subject.

Line 4. Tell what the subject cares about (3 items).

Line 5. Tell what the subject is feeling (3 items).

Line 6. Tell about things the subject needs (3 items).

Line 7. Tell what the subject fears (3 items).

Line 8. Tell what the subject gives (3 items).

Line 9. Tell what the subject would like to see (3 items).

Line 10. Tell where the subject lived.

Line 11. Last name.

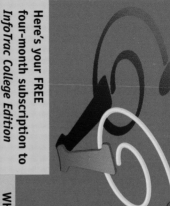

INFOTRAC

COLLEGE EDITION

THE ONLINE LIBRARY ®

Here's Your Four Month Subscription Account ID Number!

Anytime, anywhere access. That's InfoTrac College Edition. To begin accessing all the articles now available to you, point your web browser to: **http://www.infotrac-college.com/wadsworth**

And type in your account ID number: **PPQNPSJ73x**

For tech support, e-mail: wp-support@infotrac-college.com

For example:

Abraham
Poor, hardworking, woodsman, tall
Son of Thomas
Educated by borrowing books, went to school "by little's," storyteller.
Mother died when 9 years old, loving stepmother, liked folks
Wrestler, enjoyed debating, longed for more education
Worked 15 years to repay business debt, elected state representative, studied law
Left home to see the world, studied law to become successful, became a politician because he enjoyed being with people
Early life was in a one room cabin
Lincoln.

(Katherine Laframboise, "Lincoln's Young Life," based on information in Russell Freedman's *Lincoln: A Photobiography*)

Character poetry. This unrhymed form focuses on things of interest to a character from a book or the writer. To write the verse form, use some or all of the following lines:

Line 1. Three things I enjoy doing are. . . .
Line 2. Three foods I love to eat are. . . .
Line 3. Three things that bug me are. . . .
Line 4. Three places I want to visit are. . . .
Line 5. Three people I admire are . . . because. . . .
Line 6. Three fears I have are. . . .
Line 7. Three treasures I own are. . . .
Line 8. Three wishes I have are. . . .

For example:

JOAN likes tea with Miss May, picnics, and school.
JOAN loves to eat good apple pie, tea, and cookies.
JOAN is bothered by her mother, prejudice, some classmates.
JOAN wants to visit China.
JOAN admires Miss May, Papa, Bernice.
JOAN fears poverty.
JOAN treasures the Starfisher legend.
JOAN wishes to belong, and her mother's understanding.
JOAN is smart and good-hearted.

(Marta, Tracey, Angela, Rebekah, Mary, and Deborah [1994], based on information from Laurence Yep's *Star Fisher*)

ABE likes to read, learn, debate.
ABE loves maple syrup, flap jacks, biscuits.
ABE is bothered by slavery, fighting.
ABE wants to visit Europe, Washington, D.C.
ABE admires Grant, his wife and sons.
ABE fears death, supernatural.
ABE treasures his wallet, his hat.

ABE wishes for freedom, equality.
ABE was self taught and honest.

(Laura, Donna, Cathy, Andrea, Keri, and Angela P. [1994], based on Freedman's *Lincoln: A Photobiography*)

I am poetry. This unrhymed form presents an autobiography or biography of a book character. The following pattern is used:

Stanza One

I am (two special characteristics you have)
I wonder (something you are curious about)
I hear (an imaginary sound)
I see (an imaginary sight)
I want (an actual desire)
I am (the first line of the poem repeated)

Stanza Two

I pretend (something you pretend to do)
I feel (a feeling about something imaginary)
I touch (an imaginary touch)
I worry (something that really bothers you)
I cry (something that makes you very sad)
I am (the first line of the poem repeated)

Stanza Three

I understand (something you know is true)
I say (something you believe in)
I dream (something you dream about)
I try (something you really try to accomplish)
I hope (something you hope for)
I am (repeat the first line of the poem)

For example:

I am a Native American boy.
I wonder what I will see at the top of the mountain.
I hear voices of the past.
I see visions of my ancestors.
I want to keep those visions alive.
I am a Native American boy.

(Tonya, Sacha, Marti, Julie, Lorie, and Laura, "Cloyd" [1994], motivated by Will Hobb's *Bearstone*)

I am kind and helpful
I wonder if Joan's mother likes me.
I hear the washing of clothes.
I see a huge garden.
I want to have a family
I am kind and helpful.
I understand how Joan feels.
I say all people are equal.
I dream about having lots of friends.
I try to get along with the Lee family.
I hope the Lees will be successful.

(Rory, Jacki, Valerie, Amy, and Guerline, "Miss Lucy" [1994], motivated by Yep's *Star Fisher*)

Visual Poetry

Some poetic forms highlight the visual impact of the poem. Concrete poetry and creative poetry are two examples of visual poetry.

Concrete Poetry In *concrete poetry*, the poem is arranged in a visual shape. In this ancient verse form, the subject of the poem dictates the shape, while space, sound, descriptive language, and punctuation complete the visual. Early poets experimented with "shaped poems" by using various sizes of letters, different typefaces, colors, and symbols to visually present their message. Joan Bransfield Graham used visual poetry in her 1994 collection *Splish Splash*. Since this is a different way of looking at words, they "bump into each other in a new way. Writing a concrete poem is like making a sculpture with words."[13] Graham's poem "Popsicle" is a good example of this form:

```
          P o p s i c l e
          P o p s i c l e
          t i c k l e
          t o n g u e   f u n
          l i c k s i c l e
          s t i c k s i c l e
          p l e a s e
          d o n ' t   r u n
          d r i p s i c l e
          s l i p s i c l e
          m e l t ,   m e l t
          t r i c k y
          s t o p s i c l e
          p l o p s i c l e
          h a n d   a l l
                    s
                    t
                    i
                    c
                    k
                    y
```

(Joan B. Graham, "Popsicle")

Creative Poetry In *creative poetry*, poets experiment with punctuation marks to express their individuality. Through creative use of punctuation marks, the rhythm, rhyme, humor, or verbal images of the poem can be reinforced. e. e. cummings is the best-known poet who has used creative punctuation. Reading his *in Just-spring* or *hist wist* (1989) is a challenge. Deborah Kogan Ray's artistic interpretations help the reader understand the poet's message.

ORGANIZATION OF JUVENILE POETRY

Depending on the type of poetry, the subject, and the length of the poem or verse, writers and anthologists arrange juvenile poetry in individual books, individual collections, general anthologies, and thematic anthologies.

When a book is devoted to an *individual poem*, it is usually beautifully illustrated according to the artist's interpretation of the poem. The poet and the artist may be the same or they may be different people. Since 1871 when Edward Lear first published *The Owl and the Pussy Cat*, many artists have interpreted the poem in a single book. Seven contemporary artists have created different artistic interpretations of the poem: Lorinda Bryan Cauley (1986), Paul Galdone (1987), Claire Littlejohn (1987), Jan Brett (1991), Helen Cooper (1991), Louise Voce (1991), and Nicki Palin (1993). In the 1990s a variety of narrative poems have been published in individual books. David Frampton used bold woodcuts to depict the activities of fifteen farm children in Jim Aylesworth's *My Son John* (1994). In 1992 both Steven Kellogg and Posy Simmonds artistically interpreted Hilaire Belloc's humorous Victorian satire *Matilda, Who Told Lies and Was Burned to Death*. Leo and Diane Dillon dramatically depict a young narrator, her animal friends, and the Alaskan countryside in Nancy Carlstrom's narrative poem *Northern Lullaby* (1992). Eugene Field's poem *The Gingham Dog and the Calico Cat* (1990) was reissued and given a new interpretation by Janet Street. Robert Frost's blank verse poem *Birches* was illustrated by the award-winning illustrator Ed Young. In 1974 Susan Jeffers illustrated Frost's *Stopping By Woods on a Snowy Evening*. Henry Wadsworth Longfellow's *Paul Revere's Ride* was reissued and illustrated by Nancy Winslow Parker in 1985 and by Ted Rand in 1990. Nancy Willard published *Pish, Posh, Said Hieronymus Bosch* in 1991. Leo and Diane Dillon created the acrylic illustrations for Willard's poem. Each illustration is placed in a sculptured frame made by their son Lee. (See the Willard color plate on page 221.)

Individual collections are poetry books containing poems and verses by one poet. Some examples include Shel Silverstein's *Where the Sidewalk Ends* (1974), *A Light in the Attic* (1981), and *Falling Up* (1996); Dennis Lee's *Garbage Delight* (1978) and *Jelly Belly* (1983); J. P. Lewis's *Hippopotamusn't and Other Animal Verses* (1990), *Two-Legged, Four-Legged, No Legged Rhymes* (1991), *Earth Verse and Water Rhymes* (1991), and *Ridicholas Nicholas: More Animal Poems* (1995); and Douglas Florian's collections of everyday activities *Beast Feast* (1994) and *Bing Bang Boing* (1994). Award-winning poet Arnold Adoff

Leo and Diane Dillon created elaborate acrylic and oil paintings for Nancy Willard's humorous vignettes in Pish Posh, Said Hieronymus Bosch. *The artist team used dark hues in a variety of colors for their paintings. Lee, their son, sculptured an elaborate frame in silver, bronze, and brass with gold overlays and assembled on wood. Each illustration was photographed in the frame and placed on a white background that highlights the unique features of the picture.*

published a dozen collections between 1975 and 1995, and Eve Merriam also published a dozen collections between 1964 and 1994. Jack Prelutsky published *The New Kid on the Block* (1984), *Something Big Has Been Here* (1990), and *A Pizza the Size of the Sun* (1996). The title poem from Prelutsky's first collection is an example of the humorous poetry we expect from this prolific poet:

> There's a new kid on the block,
> and boy, that kid is tough,
> that new kid punches hard,
> that new kid plays real rough,
> that new kid's big and strong,
> with muscles everywhere,
> that new kid tweaked my arm,
> that new kid pulled my hair.
>
> That new kid likes to fight,
> and picks on all the guys,
> that new kid scares me some,
> (that new kid's twice my size),

that new kid stomped my toes,
that new kid swiped my ball,
that new kid's really bad,
I don't care for her at all.

(Jack Prelutsky, "The New Kid on the Block")

(For more information about Prelutsky, see Did You Know?) Many other individual collections are listed in the bibliography.

General anthologies are books of poetry assembled by an anthologist. They include poems by different poets on a variety of topics and themes. A representative volume is X. J. and Dorothy Kennedy's *Talking like the Rain* (1992), which contains 120 poems on subjects ranging from "Families" to "Calendars and Clocks." The poets include both traditional writers such as Edward Lear and Robert Louis Stevenson and contemporary poets such as Nikki Giovanni and Judith Viorst. A popular general anthology collected by Jack Prelutsky and illustrated by Arnold Lobel is *The Random House Book of Poetry* (1983). This anthology contains 572 poems written by 163 poets and arranged in fourteen units. An original poem by Prelutsky introduces each unit. Four-color or sepia illustrations by Lobel appear on each page. From 1970 to 1995, Lee Bennet Hopkins compiled thirty-two anthologies. Nancy Larrick edited eight collections since 1965. Since 1982, the award-winning poet Myra Cohn Livingston edited fifteen anthologies in addition to publishing twenty-seven collections of her own work. Other anthologies are listed in the bibliography.

Thematic anthologies are devoted to poems with a specific theme or subject matter. A thematic anthology may be a collection by a single poet or an anthology with poems by a variety of poets. Many subjects of interest to juveniles are found in these specialized anthologies. Examples include humorous poems in William Cole's *Poem Stew* (1981) and nature poems in Aileen Fisher's *Cricket in a Thicket* (1963) and *Out in the Dark and Daylight* (1980). Dilys Evans's *Monster Soup and Other Spooky Poems* (1992) is a Halloween anthology. Celebration poems are included in Livingston's *Birthday Poems* (1989). In the 1960s Mary O'Neill wrote several thematic collections: *Hailstones and Halibut Bones* (1961) about the feelings of colors, *Take a Number* (1968) about numbers, and *Words, Words, Words* (1966) and *What Is That Sound?* (1966) about the English language. Many thematic anthologies deal with animals. Beverly McLoughland's *The Hippo's a Heap: And Other Animal Poems* and Jane Yolen's collection about fourteen species of birds, *Bird Watch: A Book of Poetry* (1990), are examples. Laura Whipple compiled an anthology of animal

Did You Know About
JACK PRELUTSKY?

Could a boy who was bored whenever teachers read poetry possibly grow up to become a poet who gets children to laugh at their friend and his slightly skewed perspective of life? Jack Prelutsky was that boy. Something happened along the way—perhaps the time he spent singing in summer opera companies or his experiences as an actor, photographer, day laborer, carpenter, clerk, bookseller, taxi driver, moving man, waiter, dishwasher, lecturer, and door-to-door salesman helped Prelutsky to see poetry differently. Perhaps the words, phrases, and ideas he collected in his more than fifty journals help him write poetry differently. Perhaps his thoughts about poetry changed when he began to write about outlandish animals, creatures, and situations. Whatever happened, Jack Prelutsky has helped take poetry from the boring to the farcical, from the ordinary to the extraordinary. Before Prelutsky entered our lives, who had heard of a Baby Ugg or a ferocious dragon "with claws like silver sabers"? What is a "Zoosher" or a "Flotz" and what do they do? Would you like for Bulgy Bumme or Jilliky Jolliky Jelliky Jee to live in your hometown? I know I'm really afraid of the new kid on the block, how about you? His nightmare poems really scare me!

Over the last twenty years, this master poet has created more than forty works aimed at making poetry fun, not boring. Prelutsky is a master manipulator of the language; he is a magical rhyme maker—he does what comes naturally to children. Can you imagine writing a book of poetry about *My Parents Think I'm Sleeping?* Prelutsky thinks like a child—they squeal with delight when they hear his poems. Children can picture in their heads the peculiar people he invents.

Prelutsky collects pottery, photographs, frog paraphernalia, and crazy art and performs in operas, musicals, and choruses. He likes to travel, sculpt, do collage, take walks, and ride a bicycle. Somehow we know those interests will find their way into his poetry. His work is influenced by Lewis Carroll, Dylan Thomas, Edgar Allan Poe, William Butler Yeats, William Shakespeare, John Donne, Gilbert and Sullivan's operettas, and American folk songs. He reads his poetry aloud or sings it with his guitar, which he feels keeps his meter straight.

Prelutsky may visit a school and read unpublished poetry to get his critics' opinions. Children know he is honest and open with them. He may be silly or scary, and they like that treatment. He uses language they understand, even when it has many syllables. Because Prelutsky believes poetry must be heard, he is moving into audiovisual media presentations.

His poems reflect his belief that poetry is communication and should be for everyone. With poets like Jack Prelutsky, children will never again think that poetry is boring!

poems in *Animals, Animals* (1989), illustrated by Eric Carle. Whipple and Carle also created a companion anthology about dragons, *Eric Carle's Dragons and Other Creatures That Never Were* (1991). Several thematic anthologies have been published about food and eating, such as Nadine Westcott's *Never Take a Pig to Lunch: And Other Poems about the Fun of Eating* (1994). Traditional Chinese poems are found in *Demi's Dragons and Fantastic Creatures* (1993), and classical Japanese poems about the seasons and animals are included in Demi's *In the Eyes of the Cat: Japanese Poetry for All Seasons* (1992). Recently, several collections of Native American poetry have been published, such as Shonto Begay's *Navajo: Visions and Voices across the Mesa* (1995). This excerpt from the free verse in this anthology reflects the Navajo's love and respect for nature:

GRANDMOTHER
▽ ▽ ▽

Grandmother was strong, like a distant mesa.
From her sprang many stories of days long ago.
From her gentle manners
lessons were learned
not easily forgotten.
She told us time and again
that the earth is our mother,
our holy mother.

"Always greet the coming day
by greeting your grandparents.
Yá' át' ééh Shi cheii (Hello, My Grandfather)
to the young juniper tree.
Yá' át' ééh Shi másání (Hello, My Grandmother)
to the young piñon tree."

The lines in her face were marks of honor,
countless winters gazing into the blizzard,
many summers in the hot cornfield.
Her strong brown hands, once smooth,
carried many generations,
gestured many stories,
wiped away many tears.
The whiteness of her windblown hair,
a halo against the setting sun.

My grandmother was called Asdzán Áłts'íísí,
Small Woman, Wife of Little Hat,
mother of generations of Bitter Water Clan,
she lived 113 years.

14

Begay's acrylic paintings help interpret his poetry collection, Navajo: Visions and Voices across the Mesa. *Notice the series of brush strokes the artist uses to create his full-color painting.*

In the early spring, the snowfall is light
upon the mesa.
It does not stick to the ground very long.
I walk through this patchwork of snow and earth,
watching the ground for early signs.
Signs of growth. Signs of rebirth.

Larkspur and wild onions are still
within the warmth of the earth.
I hear cries of crows off in the distance.
A rabbit bounds off into the sagebrush flat.
A shadow of a hawk disturbs the landscape momentarily.
It sees food and life abundant below that I cannot see.
The cycle of life continues.

(Shonto Begay, excerpt from "Early Spring")

Throughout the book, Begay presents detailed paintings to enhance the verses and give the reader a clearer view of the Navajo's perspective and experiences. (See the Begay color plate.)

The thematic bibliographies at the end of the book list poetry books that are appealing to young people and can be used as part of various curricular areas.

NOTABLE JUVENILE POETS AND THEIR MAJOR CONTRIBUTIONS

In the early days, young people and adults were expected to react positively to the same epics, ballads, jingles, and rhymes.[14] Juvenile poetry began with nursery rhymes and didactic poems about children and how they should behave.

Nursery rhymes developed from the oral tradition of folk literature. Mothers and nannies recited and sang these light, nonsense verses to amuse their children. An early collection, *Tommy Thumb's Pretty Song Book* (1744), was published by John Newbery. From the Middle Ages to the middle of the nineteenth century, poems recited by children reflected the religious and social mores of the time. Two popular moralistic, didactic collections were John Bunyan's *A Book for Boys & Girls or Country Rhymes for Children* (1686) and Isaac Watts's *Divine and Moral Songs* (1715, 1866). Bunyan's collection contained Puritan allegorical poems that were milder than his famous prose *Pilgrim's Progress.* The poems included in Watts's collection were based on the belief that they could control children's behavior through the fear of death and punishment.

"Come on in—try it!" is Karla Kuskin's invitation to children to hear, feel, and taste the "wonderful words, rhythmic language and wonderful sounds." Her curiosity about life leads her to search for topics that will appeal to the observant ear and eye of young children who enjoy her poetry.

In her poetry collection *Near the Window Tree: Poems and Notes*, Kuskin attempts to answer the question children frequently ask writers of poetry and prose: "Where do you get your ideas?" In several of her books, such as *The Rose on My Cake*, Kuskin talks to the reader about the formula (elements) for creating a poem. It involves establishing the rhythm, finding the right words, expressing feelings and memories, finding rhymes, and using imagination.

For an assignment in a graphic arts course, Kuskin was required to write, design, illustrate, print, and bind a book. From that assignment came her first published book, *Roar and More*. Kuskin is the writer and illustrator of more than forty books for young people; some were written in prose, others in poetry. It is her poetry that most people recognize. In 1979 she received the National Council of Teachers of English Award for Poetry for Children. This award is

given for a poet's body of work. Kuskin has also received numerous other awards, and her poems are included in many anthologies for children.

Kuskin writes from childhood memories and imagination; she writes about the things that make her laugh and about what she loves to read. She feels young people will naturally turn to poetry because they enjoy the rhythm and sounds of words. This pleasure with poetry is stifled if a teacher imposes too many rules and unfamiliar subject matter on children. Children enjoy familiar speech and humor. Kuskin's poems reflect the type of poetry a child enjoys. Kuskin frequently replaces rhyme with rhythm—and it works. Her subjects are important to children, and her simple line drawings are a perfect companion to her poems.

Kuskin describes her writing this way—splash thoughts on a page, rewrite, whittle, rewrite, use the most precise words, use original thoughts, rewrite, spark the reader's imagination, play with the language, play with the rhythm, rewrite until it sounds right. Throughout the process, read and listen to the expressions. Perhaps if we followed Kuskin's lead, we too could communicate through poetry.

Few original poems were written about children during the latter half of the eighteenth century. William Blake's *Songs of Innocence* (1789, 1966) and *Songs of Experience* (1793) were exceptions. These joyful, lyrical poems celebrated childhood, and young people quickly adopted them. See Nancy Willard's *A Visit to William Blake's Inn* (1981) for an imaginary visit to the inn run by Blake, and enjoy Willard's poems inspired by Blake.

In the early nineteenth century, Ann and Jane Taylor published *Original Poems for Infant Minds by Several Young*

Persons (1804, 1977), a collection that interpreted a child's world in simple, playful verses. Contemporary children still recite and enjoy the poem from the collection that begins "Twinkle, twinkle little star." William Mulready artistically interpreted William Roscoe's fanciful verse in *The Butterfly's Ball* (1807). Also in the early nineteenth century, another American, Clement Moore, brought the Dutch legendary patron of Christmas to American children in the narrative poem, "A Visit from St. Nicholas" (1823, 1971). Children still love this ballad today as "Twas the Night before Christmas."

By the middle of the nineteenth century, poems highlighting the beauty of nature and typical childhood experiences had replaced the moralistic, didactic verses. Now, humorous, nonsense, lyrical, and thought-provoking poems were available for children. Poets such as Edward Lear, Lewis Carroll, and Robert Louis Stevenson looked at the world from a child's perspective. Children today still enjoy many poems published in the last half of the nineteenth century, such as Stevenson's "The Swing":

> How do you like to go up in a swing,
> Up in the air so blue?
> Oh, I do think it the pleasantest thing
> Ever a child can do!
>
> Up in the air and over the wall,
> Till I can see so wide,
> Rivers and trees and cattle and all
> Over the countryside—
>
> Till I look down on the garden green,
> Down on the roof so brown—
> Up in the air I go flying again,
> Up in the air and down!

(Robert Louis Stevenson, "The Swing")

Imaginative poetry was flourishing by the 1920s. Poets such as Walter de la Mare and A. A. Milne set the standards for quality poetry for children. The number of poetry books written for children increased during the twentieth century. In the late 1960s and 1970s, juvenile poetry reflected the new realism in children's literature. Diverse content, such as protest poems, poetry about diverse cultural and racial groups, and humorous verse about human foibles, appeared. Currently, many talented poets are specializing in juvenile poetry. Poets are experimenting with various poetic forms and types that appeal to youth; more humorous verses, new forms of free verse, and poetry children can understand are being written. Contemporary poets are also becoming more diverse and include persons from both genders and all cultural, ethnic, and religious groups. Thus, contemporary juvenile poetry realistically portrays the experiences of these groups.

Talented illustrators now recognize the value of interpreting, supplementing, and enhancing the poetry with suitable illustrations. Currently, most poetry books for children contain appropriate illustrations ranging from black and white drawings to four-color illustrations.

In 1977 the National Council of Teachers of English established an award for Excellence in Poetry for Children. The council gives the award for the poet's total contribution to children's literature. David McCord, Aileen Fisher, Karla Kuskin, Myra Cohn Livingston, Eve Merriam, John Ciardi, Lilian Moore, Arnold Adoff, Valerie Worth, and Barbara Juster Esbensen have received the award (for more information about Karla Kuskin, see Did You Know? on page 224). The American Library Association has awarded two Newbery Medals to poetry books: Nancy Willard's *A Visit to William Blake's Inn* in 1981 and Paul Fleischman's *Joyful Noise: Poems for Two Voices* in 1988. Finally, in 1993 the Lee Bennett Hopkins Poetry Award was established by the Children's Literature Council in Pennsylvania. This award recognizes the influence of the anthologist in juvenile poetry. The council gives the award to an American poet or compiler for a volume published during the preceding year. Such awards will continue to improve the quality of poetry published for young people.

As the twenty-first century dawns, people are showing a resounding interest in juvenile poetry. Children and adults alike are intrigued by contemporary poets' ability to use varied poetic forms, types, and elements in original and fascinating ways. Thus, contemporary poetry is becoming more appealing, understandable, and enjoyable to the listener, the reader, and the oral interpreter. Myra Cohn Livingston's free verse typifies poetry that captures an important contemporary event:

> Some of the time
> I get on the bus
> with mother
>
> (just the two of us)
>
> and we go to the place
> where she works all day.
>
> We take some games
> so I can play,
>
> and some of the time
> I help a lot
> with work that mother
>
> just forgot—
> (or couldn't finish—
> or did all wrong—)
>
> It's good
> she needs me
> to come along.

(Myra Cohn Livingston, "Working with Mother")

Many notable poets have influenced the development of juvenile poetry. Selecting a few outstanding poets was difficult, but Tables 7.1 through 7.8 list those cited in several sources as the most outstanding juvenile poets. The notable poets and their poetry are arranged chronologically to show the historical development of juvenile poetry.

TABLE 7.1   Notable Juvenile Poets and Poetry: Eighteenth and Nineteenth Centuries

DATE	POET, TITLE OF BOOK	COMMENTS
1686	J. Bunyan, *A Book for Boys & Girls or Country Rhymes for Children*	Puritan allegorical poems for children; milder than Bunyan's prose; include some humor.
1715	I. Watts, *Divine and Moral Songs*	Poems about children and God's love were included, as were many familiar hymns still sung today.
1744	*Tommy Thumb's Pretty Song Book*	Earliest published collection of nursery rhymes still surviving from John Newbery's press.
1789 1793	W. Blake, *Songs of Innocence* *Songs of Experience*	Portrayed innocence and wonder of youth; celebrated childhood rather than admonishing children.
1804	A. and J. Taylor, *Original Poems for Infant Minds*	Fresh poems about pastoral, everyday experiences; included "Twinkle, Twinkle Little Star" and "I Love Little Pussy."
1806	W. Roscoe, *The Butterfly's Ball*	Beginning of modern picture book. The happy, rhythmic verses portrayed and personified mischievous creatures in pleasurable activities.
1823	C. Moore, *A Visit from St. Nicholas*	A beloved American Christmas ballad.
1842	R. Browning, *The Pied Piper of Hamelin*	An imaginary ballad that popularized narrative poetry.
1846	E. Lear, *The Complete Book of Nonsense*	Absurd limericks and nonsense verses with appropriate illustrations; written to amuse and entertain without condescension or sentimentality.
1864	L. Carroll, *Jabberwocky*	Nonsense verse from *Through the Looking Glass*.
Late Nineteenth Century		
1871	E. Lear, *The Owl and the Pussy-Cat*	Popular narrative nonsense poem.
1872	C. Rossetti, *Sing Song*	Songs, verse, and limericks about events of interest to children.
1885	R. L. Stevenson, *A Child's Garden of Verses*	Describes personal memories of everyday childhood experiences. The simple style, imaginative structures, and musical rhythm of the verses influenced later writers of juvenile poetry.
1887	W. Allingham, *Rhymes for Young Folks*	Irish songs and adventures of fairies and wee folk.
1888	E. Thayer, *Casey at the Bat*	Famous baseball ballad.
1890	L. E. Richards, *In My Nursery*	Poems about hilarious events with wordplay and strong rhythm.
1891	J. W. Riley, *Rhymes of Childhood*	Rhythmic poems, written in American dialect, about people and adventures.
1896	E. Field, *Poems of Childhood*	Beloved toys and childhood dreams come to life in these childlike, narrative poems that are still enjoyed today.
1897	E. V. Lucas, *A Book of Verses for Children*	Many moralistic verses, but also many verses of interest to children; includes humorous verse and "story" poems.
1899	W. B. Rands, *Lilliput Lyrics*	Poems and verse about the beautiful, wonderful world; filled with humorous alliterations describing adventures all children would like to experience.

TABLE 7.2 Notable Juvenile Poets and Poetry: 1900–1920s

DATE	POET, TITLE OF BOOK	COMMENTS
1902	W. de la Mare, *Songs of Childhood*	The first of several collections of musical, imaginative, lyrical, humorous, and mysterious poetry.
1903	K. D. Wiggin and N. A. Smith, *Golden Numbers* and *The Posy Ring*	Two popular juvenile anthologies, with quality narratives and few familiar poets; challenging reading, intended for adults to read aloud.
1920	H. Conklin, *Poems by a Little Girl*	Published when the poet was 10 years old; short, descriptive, free verse about animals and objects observed in her childhood.
1920	R. Fyleman, *Fairies and Chimneys*	Imaginative poems about fairies.
1922	E. M. Roberts, *Under the Tree*	Simple, perfect word choices are used in these rhyming poems written from a child's perspective about the wonders of nature and the experiences of childhood.
1924	A. A. Milne, *When We Were Very Young*	Two collections of rhyming verse with unique language, giving Christopher Robin's private view of childhood. Both collections influenced future juvenile poets and helped children see the pleasure of poetry.
1927	*Now We Are Six*	
1925	D. Aldis, *All Together*	First American poet to celebrate childhood experiences using simple rhyme and singsong meter.
1925	B. Thompson, *Silver Pennies*	An anthology of imaginative, modern poetry focusing on the everyday experiences of children.
1926	R. Field, *Taxis and Toadstools*	Poems about the city and the country through children's eyes.
1927	J. S. Tippett, *I Live in a City*	Children's curiosity about their city environment and experiences is revealed through these simple verses.

TABLE 7.3 Notable Juvenile Poets and Poetry: 1930–1940s

DATE	POET, TITLE OF BOOK	COMMENTS
1930	C. Sandburg, *Early Moon*	Free verse about nature, people, the seasons, the sea, and the stars by this popular American writer.
1930	S. Teasdale, *Stars To-night: Verses Old and New for Boys and Girls*	Lyrical, rhymed verses about nature, stars, night, and the sea are sensitively illustrated with pen-and-ink drawings.
1930	T. S. Eliot, *Old Possum's Book of Practical Cats*	This well-known collection of lyrical poems about cats was recently set to music in the show, *Cats*.
1932	L. Hughes, *The Dream Keeper and Other Poems*	First juvenile poetry collection to portray an African-American experience.
1933	R. and S. V. Benét, *A Book of Americans*	A humorous view of notable persons in American history.
1935	Association for Childhood Education International Committee, *Sung under the Silver Umbrella*	A popular anthology containing diverse poems selected to appeal to young children.
1935	L. Untermeyer, *Rainbow in the Sky*	A favorite anthology of favorite traditional and modern poems.
1937	J. E. Brewton, *Under the Tent of the Sky*	An anthology focusing on animals.
1942	O. Nash, *Good Intentions*	Familiar nonsense verses with outrageous surprises.
1945	M. and M. Petersham, *The Rooster Crows*	The 1946 Caldecott winner containing a collection of rhymes, games, and jingles.
1945	B. P. Geismer and A. B. Suter, *Very Young Verse*	An anthology of simple verse about the everyday interests of preschoolers.
1948	G. Adshead, *An Inheritance of Poetry*	An anthology containing works by distinguished American and English poets.

TABLE 7.4 Notable Juvenile Poets and Poetry: 1950s

DATE	POET, TITLE OF BOOK	COMMENTS
1951	M. H. Arbuthnot, and S. Root, *Time for Poetry* (revised, 1959)	A comprehensive anthology of traditional and modern poets.
1952	D. McCord, *Far and Few: Rhymes of the Never Was and Always Is*	A collection of rhythmic, repetitive refrains about animals and other childhood events.
1954	K. Lines, *Lavender's Blue*	A collection of unconventional Mother Goose and folk rhymes.
1955	W. J. Smith, *Laughing Time*	A collection of hilarious nonsense verses.
1955	H. Plotz, *Imagination's Other Place*	An anthology about science and mathematics.
1955	W. Cole, *Humorous Poetry for Children*	An anthology of nonsense verses.
1956	H. Read, *This Way, Delight*	An anthology of traditional verse for mature, older children.
1956	G. Brooks, *Bronzeville Boys and Girls*	A collection presenting a realistic view of African-American children who live in a crowded urban area.
1956	K. Kuskin, *Roar and More*	Kuskin's first book combined verse and pictures to depict noises made by various animals.
1957	H. Plotz, *Untune the Sky*	An anthology about music and art.
1957	H. Ferris, *Favorite Poems, Old and New*	A large anthology of traditional and modern poems and verses on a variety of subjects.
1958	B. S. de Regniers, *Something Special*	A collection of hilarious, imaginative verses.
1958	M. C. Livingston, *Whispers and Other Poems*	A collection of poems on sensory experiences and the wonders of childhood.
1959	J. Ciardi, *The Reason for the Pelican*	Nonsense verse and imaginative poems.
1959	M. A. Hoberman, *Hello and Good-by*	Lively, rhythmic verse about events important to young children.
1959	R. Frost, *You Come Too: Favorite Poems of Robert Frost for Young Readers*	Nature poems, with multiple meanings depending on the reader's maturity.

TABLE 7.5 Notable Juvenile Poets and Poetry: 1960s

DATE	POET, TITLE OF BOOK	COMMENTS
1960	K. Starbird, *Speaking of Cows*	In a conversational, questioning style, everyday experiences are presented from a child's perspective.
1960	A. Fisher, *Going Barefoot*	Melodic, free verse narratives include the seasons, pets, and nature as children might encounter them.
1961	T. Roethke, *I Am!—Says the Lamb*	A nonsense collection.
1961	M. O'Neill, *Hailstones and Halibut Bones*	Various colors stimulate a collection of thoughts, moods, and ideas.
1962	E. Merriam, *There Is No Rhyme for Silver*	A collection of free verse about subjects interesting to children.
1964	W. Cole, *Beastly Boys and Ghastly Girls*	An anthology containing poems about humorous and mischievous children and events.
1965	B. J. Esbensen, *Swing Around the Sun*	Free verse collection about childhood experiences.
1967	L. Moore, *I Feel the Same Way*	The poet experiments with poetic elements and format while presenting childlike thoughts.
1967	J. Prelutsky, *A Gopher in the Garden and Other Animal Poems*	Humorous, rhyming verses about animals.

TABLE 7.6 Notable Juvenile Poets and Poetry: 1970s

DATE	POET, TITLE OF BOOK	COMMENTS
1970	F. Holman, *At the Top of My Voice and Other Poems*	Repetition, rhyme, cadence, and conversational style are used to think about childhood experiences.
1970	L. Clifton, *Some of the Days of Everett Anderson*	One of seven picture books, written in verse about a young protagonist growing up and coping with urban life.
1971	N. Giovanni, *Spin a Soft Black Song*	Collection of free verse depicting African-American lifestyle and relationships.
1971	C. Watson, *Father Fox's Pennyrhymes*	Original rhymes and jingles reminiscent of traditional folk literature verses.
1971	V. Worth, *Small Poems*	First of four "Small" poetry collections. The simple, free verses depict everyday objects and events of interest to children.
1972	J. Houston, *Songs of the Dream People*	An anthology of Eskimo and other Native American poems.
1973	A. Adoff, *Black Is Brown Is Tan*	First collection to depict an interracial family.
1974	S. Silverstein, *Where the Sidewalk Ends*	A popular collection of poems and verse about topics of interest to children; includes all poetic types and forms, and both humorous and serious content.
1974	N. M. Bodecker, *Let's Marry Said the Cherry and Other Nonsense Poems*	Popular collection of nonsense verse written in couplets about imaginary topics.
1975	X. J. Kennedy, *One Winter Night in August and Other Nonsense Jingles*	A collection of humorous verses with weird content and delightful language.
1978	E. Greenfield, *Honey, I Love and Other Love Poems*	Using rhythmic language, the poet's first book to depict an African-American child's experiences and observations.

TABLE 7.7 Notable Juvenile Poets and Poetry: 1980s

DATE	POET, TITLE OF BOOK	COMMENTS
1980	J. Yolen, *How Beastly! A Menagerie of Nonsense Poems*	A collection of original beasts portrayed in Learish fashion.
1980	K. Kuskin, *Dogs & Dragons, Trees & Dreams*	The poet discusses and models various poetic types, forms, and elements.
1981	N. Willard, *A Visit to William Blake's Inn. Poems for Innocent and Experienced Travelers*	Original poems describing a fictional visit to an imaginary inn run by William Blake. This was the first poetry book to win the Newbery Medal; also selected as a Caldecott honor book.
1983	J. Prelutsky, *The Random House Book of Poetry for Children*	An outstanding anthology of traditional and contemporary poets; contains diverse poetic forms and types and a range of topics; organized thematically.
1984	J. Prelutsky, *The New Kid on the Block*	A popular collection of poems and verses using various poetic forms and types to depict the wonders of living.
1988	P. Fleischman, *Joyful Noise: Poems for Two Voices*	The characteristics of various insects are humorously depicted in an original format that directs two voices to speak the poetry. This was the second poetry collection to win the Newbery Medal.
1988	B. S. de Regniers et al., *Sing a Song of Popcorn*	An anthology of quality traditional and contemporary poems, artistically interpreted by Caldecott winners.
1989	V. D. H. Sneve, *Dancing Teepees: Poems of American Indian Youth*	An anthology of 19 poems from the oral tradition of Native Americans.
1989	M. Singer, *Turtle in July*	Poems arranged according to the months, depicting activities of animals from their perspective.

TABLE 7.8 Notable Juvenile Poets and Poetry: 1990s

DATE	POET, TITLE OF BOOK	COMMENTS
1990	J. P. Lewis, *A Hippopotamusn't and Other Animal Verses*	Through wordplay, varied tone, and meter, the poet presents a humorous view of animals.
1990	D. Chandra, *Balloons and Other Poems*	The poet uses free verse and varied poetic forms to depict vivid images of the environment and adventures of contemporary children.
1990	J. Lynn, *Coconut Kind of Day: Island Poems*	The adventures of a young Caribbean girl are rhythmically portrayed and artistically interpreted.
1990	G. Soto, *A Fire in My Hands: A Book of Poems*	A collection of free verses celebrating life and experiences in a Hispanic neighborhood.
1991	E. Greenfield, *Night on Neighborhood Street*	A collection of urban poems about family and everyday experiences from an African-American child's perspective.
1991	M. A. Hoberman, *Fathers, Mothers, Sisters, Brothers*	An anthology of poems about traditional and nontraditional family life.
1992	B. McLoughland, *Through Our Eyes*	An anthology of poems about nontraditional families and contemporary issues and concerns of children.
1992	A. Bryan, *Sing to the Sun*	A collection of free verse detailing the African-American poet-artist's perspective of life.
1992	A. Hirshfelder and B. Singer (selectors), *Rising Voices: Writings of Young Native Americans*	An anthology of poems by Native American youths.
1992	Huang, Tze-si (translator), *In the Eyes of the Cat: Japanese Poetry for All Seasons*, Illus. Demi	An anthology of classic Japanese poems arranged by season, animals, and their activities and interpreted by appropriate illustrations.
1994	C. Levy, *A Tree Place and Other Poems*	Forty poems giving insights into nature, such as the anger a volcano stores up before erupting and how a flower feels when a butterfly touches it. Simple language with appealing cadences.
1995	J. Viorst, *Sad Underwear and Other Complications: More Poems for Children and Their Parents*	A variety of poems by a favorite poet and writer about topics of interest to children. Many humorous, some serious.

POETRY IN THE CLASSROOM

Don't be polite.
Bite in.
Pick it up with your fingers and lick the juice that
    may run down your chin.
It is ready and ripe now, whenever you are.

You do not need a knife or fork or spoon
or plate or napkin or tablecloth.

For there is no core
or stem
or rind
or pit
or seed
or skin
to throw away.

(Eve Merriam, "How to Eat a Poem")

Perhaps, while writing this poem, Eve Merriam was thinking about the audience exploring poetry. She leaves the impression that poetry is intended for pleasure, that it is "OK" to pick up a poem and enjoy the language and the feelings and ideas expressed by the poet. She leaves the impression that poetry can be explored anytime during the day without a formal instructional presentation. Finally, she leaves the impression that a person has the right to react and respond personally to the poem without analyzing the poet's meanings. At least those were my impressions—do you agree?

In this section we will consider various ways poetry can be used in the classroom and strategies that can make the classroom an environment that encourages pleasurable experiences with poetry as Merriam suggests. For an overview, see Figure 7.3 on page 231.

Paul Janeczko, the poet and anthologist, reports that children frequently ask him if he loved poetry when he was

FIGURE 7.3 Poetry in the Classroom

CLASSROOM ENVIRONMENT

Provide a relaxed, informal, accepting atmosphere.

Share a variety of poems representing various poetic forms, types, elements, and content.

Share several poems each day.

Have a special Poetry Place in the room to show you value poetry.

Display many illustrated collections and anthologies around the room.

Encourage children to browse through the books and copy favorite poems in a Class Anthology.

Place a listening center at the Poetry Place. Include tapes of poets, children, and adults reading popular poems.

Encourage students to make additional recordings.

TEACHER'S ROLE

Be enthusiastic about poetry.

Become familiar with a variety of poems with different content, elements, forms, and types.

Present quality poetry that will appeal to the students. Avoid sentimental or abstract poems with unfamiliar content.

Avoid a didactic approach to poetry.

Use suitable poems and appropriate strategies when sharing poems in all discipline areas.

Personally choose to read poetry during independent reading time.

Write poetry when students are writing.

Share personal reactions to independent reading with students.

Share original poems with students.

Respect students' personal reactions to selected poems.

SPECIFIC TECHNIQUES

Poetry is meant to be heard. Read a poem several times to highlight the sounds, rhythm, and rhyme.

Encourage aesthetic reading and reactions.

Encourage students to react to the feelings and thoughts elicited by a poem.

Use poetry to enhance and supplement all discipline areas.

Light verse is a good introduction to poetry.

Gradually add serious poems with abstract language or complex ideas.

Introduce many poets and their writings.

Compare the poets' styles and presentation of content. Invite local poets to class to discuss writing poetry.

Remember, children who hear a favorite poem several times may later memorize and recite it.

POETRY IN THE CLASSROOM

EXPERIENCES WITH POETIC LANGUAGE

Elicit aesthetic reactions to poetic language.

If necessary, at the initial aesthetic reading, discuss unique language, unfamiliar content, or abstract concepts.

Encourage sensory awareness and emotional reactions to the poems.

Stimulate imaginative reactions to the poetic language.

Give students time to savor, explore, and discuss language used by poets.

Encourage learners to use suitable poetic language in personal communication.

WRITING EXPERIENCES

Stimulate and motivate students to write; but do not force them to use a particular form.

Use published poems as models to stimulate personal writing.

Provide alternative ideas and visuals to motivate writing.

Have oral discussions before actual writing.

Encourage children to experiment with various poetic forms, types, and language.

Remember, unrhymed verse is easy for most children to write.

Never evaluate ideas; react to the form and elements used.

Be honest and fair; never overpraise.

Have students keep a journal with notes on personal poetry, pictures, lists of interesting vocabulary, and favorite poems.

ORAL AND VISUAL EXPERIENCES

Have students present poems using various oral and dramatic techniques, such as reading to a peer, readers theatre, puppets, pantomime, shadow-plays, and role-playing.

Play appropriate music while sharing poetry.

Display visuals related to poems presented in class in the Poetry Place.

Encourage students to copy favorite poems on a banner; prepare a mural with poetry from a popular poet.

Have students illustrate poems in the Class Anthology with drawings, collages, photographs, and various media.

Display students' poems and visual responses on the bulletin board in the Poetry Place.

Place "Did You Know...?" biographical sketches about poets at the Poetry Place. Encourage students to add sketches about other poets.

a boy and they are surprised when he says "no!" He tells them that poetry was no more important to him than "Washington's wooden teeth." In school he didn't enjoy reading poetry. He remembers memorizing and reciting verses that would "edify, enlighten, and illuminate."[15]

Janeczko's experiences are not unusual. For years I have asked college students to write down their "instant reaction" to the word *poetry*, especially in terms of their experiences with poems in the elementary years. Many college students do not remember encountering poetry in elementary school. The reactions of students who do have memories about poetry are divided equally between strong negative and strong positive responses. Typical negative reactions include the following: "I was forced to memorize poetry." "My teacher expected me to write poems with a particular rhyming scheme." "All we did in poetry classes was analyze poems, and I could never guess the meaning of the poem." "It never occurred to me that the teacher's interpretation might not be right!" "I never did like the poems my teachers made us read and learn; they were so dumb—so sentimental and romantic. I thought all poems were like the ones the teacher chose, so I rejected all poetry."

Typical positive reactions include the following: "My teacher liked the poems I wrote." "My teacher read lots of poems to us. I remember she cried and laughed when we did. She loved poetry and so did we!" After hearing responses from hundreds of adults, I am convinced that the poems the teacher shares and the way the teacher presents poetry influence the child's reaction to the genre. The following are some strategies that should *not* be used when presenting poetry in the classroom. To destroy children's natural love of poetry:

Force them to become critics who must always analyze the poet's meaning and craft.

Require them to memorize poems studied in class.

Present poems that they cannot understand.

Present poems with content that is not important to them.

Neglect poetry; present it only at a holiday season or once a month.[16]

Use poems only to teach morals, virtues, or safety.

Present only traditional poems by poets such as Shakespeare, Emily Dickinson, Robert Frost, and Carl Sandburg. Chow Loy Tom conducted a study in 1969 and found that teachers most frequently used "Paul Revere's Ride," "The Daffodils," and "Fog." Of the 41 poems typically shared in the elementary classes, 37 poems were written before 1928.[17] Today many teachers present only Silverstein and Prelutsky.

Require all children to recite the same poetry, primarily on Friday afternoons.

Use poetry in unrelated assignments, such as for handwriting, spelling lists, or "creative" activities, such as competitions for Dental Health Month or seasonal activities.

Require them to complete worksheets about poetry elements, types, and forms, or give them formal tests to assess their knowledge about poetry.

Do not give them opportunities to express a personal opinion about a poem.

Do not let them reject your favorite poem or enjoy a poem you do not like.

Use the same poetic types, forms, and poets throughout the year.

Force them to copy lines of poetry as a form of punishment.

Use only your own favorite sentimental, romantic, and nostalgic poems.

Instead of using such methods, the wise teacher will use techniques that tap into the feelings and senses evoked by poetry. Teachers who consider children's natural poetry preferences will begin the year with humorous narrative poems and nonsense verse. Gradually, they will share serious lyric poetry. Students will be encouraged to browse through poetry books and to share them orally with others. In this way, children begin to realize poems are available for all occasions. Perhaps, this will lead them to search for poems throughout their lives and to express their personal thoughts about poetry. Young people need to hear teachers, other children, media specialists, and parents read poetry. A guaranteed way to turn children away from poetry is to ask them to read a poem silently the first time they encounter it.

When the classroom is informal and relaxed, children will naturally share poetry with friends. An environment such as this encourages learners to enjoy the rhythm, flow, repetition, and images expressed in the poet's language. In this environment, children become aware of poetic language and forms. To fully savor the poet's ideas and words, students need to hear a poem several times. Allowing time for children to respond to a poem heightens their understanding and appreciation of the verse.

Poetry need not be limited to the literature class. There are poems to fit any occasion that may arise within the classroom. In her poem "Today," Kaye Starbird describes weather. J. Patrick Lewis gives information about camels in "How to Tell a Camel." Karla Kuskin describes a special happening in "The Rose on My Cake," and Eve Merriam discusses a special memory in "Association," her poem about sports. Marci Ridlon wonders about the importance of a family member in "My Brother," and Mary O'Neill describes a teacher in "Miss Norma Jean Pugh." A teacher who knows and loves poetry will find opportunities to enhance learning through poems and verses.[18] When a poem such as Maria Pratt's "A Mortifying Mistake" is used, the children might pay more attention to learning multiplication tables:

> I studied my tables over and over, backward and forward,
>   too.
> But I couldn't remember six times nine, and I didn't
>   know what to do,
> Till my sister told me to play with my doll, and not to
>   bother my head.
> "If you call her 'Fifty-four' for awhile, you'll learn it by
>   heart," she said.
>
> So I took my favorite, Mary Ann (though I thought 'twas
>   a dreadful shame
> To give such a perfectly lovely child such a perfectly hor-
>   rid name).
> And I called her my dear little "Fifty-four" a hundred
>   times, till I knew
> The answer of six times nine as well as the answer of two
>   times two.
>
> Next day, Elizabeth Wiggleworth, who always acts so
>   proud,
> Said, "Six times nine is fifty-two," and I nearly laughed
>   aloud!
> But I wished I hadn't when teacher said, "Now Dorothy,
>   tell if you can,"
> For I thought of my doll—and sakes alive!—I answered,
>   "Mary Ann!"
>
> (Maria Pratt, "A Mortifying Mistake")

The teacher's role in the poetry curriculum might be summed up as follows:

> Teachers who love poetry encourage children to love poetry!
> If you share poetry enthusiastically, your children will
>   share your enthusiasm.
> If you search for poetry, your children will search for poetry.
> If you share poetry throughout the day, your children will
>   find poems for all subjects.
> If you respond to the emotions of the poems, your chil-
>   dren will respond emotionally.
> If you read aloud quality poems, your children will enjoy
>   reading quality poetry.
> If you read poetry with expression, your children will
>   read with expression.
> If you model personal reflections about poetry, your chil-
>   dren will feel comfortable sharing their reflections with
>   others.
> If you collect poetry, your children will collect poetry.
> If you display poetry, your children will add to the display.
> If you write poetry, your children will write poetry.

> If you present poetry in different ways, your children will
>   respond positively to poetry.
> Teachers who love poetry develop poetry lovers!

BENEFITS YOUNG PEOPLE RECEIVE FROM EXPERIENCES WITH POETRY

Poetry gives young people an opportunity to laugh, to sigh, and to feel a sense of wonder. The ideas and visions of others express many of our personal feelings. Poetry frequently gives us a better perspective about our own world. It also provides insights into others' desires and attitudes and gives us encouragement as in the following poem by Langston Hughes:

> Hold fast to dreams
> For if dreams die
> Life is a broken-winged bird
> That cannot fly.
>
> Hold fast to dreams
> For when dreams go
> Life is a barren field
> Frozen with snow.
>
> (Langston Hughes, "Dreams")

After discussing Hughes's poetry, read to the class Floyd Cooper's biography, *Coming Home from the Life of Langston Hughes* (1994). Through his verbal and visual narratives, Cooper gives his readers insight into the situations in Hughes's life that influenced his later poetry. (See the Cooper color plate on page 234.) Exploring such poetry can be a pleasurable experience that gives young people the many rewards identified in Table 7.9 on page 235.

SELECTING POETRY FOR YOUNG PEOPLE

> Only be willing to search for poetry and there will be
>   poetry. . . .
>   (Yuan Mei, "Only Be Willing to Search for Poetry")[19]

Since a poem may evoke emotional and intellectual responses from those who explore it, children need many experiences with various types and forms of poetry at different times. Sometimes a light poem will tickle a child's fancy. At another time, a serious lyrical poem may give the child new insight into a personal situation. While laughter is good medicine, sometimes we need to grieve, to sulk, to remember, to ponder. Poetry can evoke all those responses. It can also give us thoughts to ponder later. Myra Cohn Livingston's essay "Poetry and Self" contains a valuable discussion about poetry's relationship to our lives. She highlights the various emotions children feel as they grow up and

Other times Langston's ma would come to Lawrence. Once it wasn't the best of times for her. Money was scarce. She snapped at Langston and it hurt.

Later that evening they went to St. Luke's Church where Langston's ma was giving a performance. She told him that she had a wonderful surprise for him. That he was going to be on the stage with her. That he was going to be a star, just like she was going to be.

Langston didn't like the surprise. That evening he was the one with the surprise. As his ma introduced him, behind her back Langston made faces: He crossed his eyes, stretched his mouth, and imitated her. Everyone burst out laughing. The more people laughed, the more faces he made.

Embarrassed, his mother rushed off stage.

Floyd Cooper's brown, gold, and sepia illustrations enhance this biography Coming Home: From the Life of Langston Hughes. *Cooper's realistic oil wash illustrations were painted on board. Wonder what happened to Langston when he came off the stage?*

the decisions they make in life. Both children and adults will benefit from hearing and reading the seventy poems by twenty-nine poets included in the essay. Many of the poems capture a feeling at a particular moment in a person's life.[20]

Learners' Poetry Preferences

Children's poetry preferences have remained constant throughout the last fifty years.[21] Whatever their scores on standardized measures, most girls and boys aged six to fifteen enjoy one or more of the following poetic structures:

Narrative poetry

Humorous poetry

Poems using simple imagery and metaphoric language

Amusing poems that are not sentimental or didactic in tone

Poems with familiar, contemporary settings, conflicts, and content

Poems describing the actions and lives of humans or animals

Poems containing rhythm, rhyme, sounds, and contemporary language

Young children do not naturally prefer lyric poetry, free verse, haiku, or poems with complex, metaphorical language. Vachel Lindsay's narrative poem incorporates many of the features enjoyed by preschoolers to seven year olds:

There was a little turtle.
He lived in a box.
He swam in a puddle.
He climbed on the rocks.

He snapped at a mosquito.
He snapped at a flea.
He snapped at a minnow.
And he snapped at me.

TABLE 7.9 Benefits Individuals Gain by Exploring Poetry

Poetry encourages people to dream and to reflect on the wonders of the universe.

Poetry stimulates an individual's imagination, senses, and emotions.

Poetry encourages young people to be sensitive to the feelings of others and to respect their personal attitudes.

While exploring poetry, young people gain a different perspective and broader understanding of the world.

Through experiences with poetry, young people learn to appreciate the power of language to inform, persuade, and encourage others.

Exploring poetry gives students insights into the intricacies and nuances of the language.

Poetry introduces students to words and phrases they might not encounter otherwise.

When young people interact with poetry, they experience the delight of manipulating and using language in different ways.

By exploring a variety of poems and verses, young people become aware of various poets and enjoy searching for other poetry written by the poets.

Exploring a variety of poems expands young people's interest in a topic and inspires them to find other poems related to the subject.

He caught the mosquito.
He caught the flea.
He caught the minnow.
But he didn't catch me.

(Vachel Lindsay, "The Little Turtle")

In 1993 Kutiper and Wilson analyzed the library circulation figures in three schools to determine the poetry preferences of 2,500 children.[22] The researchers found the most popular poets were Jack Prelutsky, Shel Silverstein, and Judith Viorst. Children frequently checked out narrative and humorous poetry that had rhythm, rhymes, easy-to-understand language and appealing content. These findings are consistent with previous studies. When young people read the popular Judith Viorst's humorous poem "Mother Doesn't Want a Dog," they like the content, the strong rhyme, and the surprise at the end:

Mother doesn't want a dog.
Mother says they smell,
And never sit when you say sit,
Or even when you yell.
And when you come home late at night
And there is ice and snow,
You have to go back out because
The dumb dog has to go.

Mother doesn't want a dog.
Mother says they shed,
And always let the strangers in
And bark at friends instead,
And do disgraceful things on rugs,
And track mud on the floor,
And flop upon your bed at night
And snore their doggy snore.

Mother doesn't want a dog.
She's making a mistake.
Because, more than a dog, I think
She will not want this snake.

(Judith Viorst, "Mother Doesn't Want a Dog")

Teachers are encouraged to expand their students' poetry horizons by beginning with popular poets, then gradually adding poetry written by other contemporary and traditional authors. After children feel comfortable with poetry, poems requiring higher-level thinking can be added. Unfortunately, some award-winning poets and traditional poets are not popular with children. Many of these poets use poetic forms, elements, and content that are difficult to understand or are not appealing to contemporary children. Many award-winning poets, for example, write lyrical poetry in free verse with complex imagery and metaphorical language.

While we should respect students' natural poetry preferences, we also know the poems they encounter will help them become discriminating in selecting poetry. Children exposed to a variety of quality poetry written by various poets will, through exploration, develop a taste for all types of poetic structures. Fortunately, there are many poetry collections and anthologies available for children to listen to, read, share, and recite.

Children become bored with a steady diet of humorous, slapstick verse. Those who love poetry have probably explored both free verse and poems filled with figurative language. Perhaps they have discovered poems about eating or poems about sports and verses that rhyme and those that don't. Poems with strong rhythm or those with a slight cadence evoke dreams or memories. Poetry lovers have discovered poems written many years ago and those written yesterday. In poetry, they explore questions about life and read poems that deal with social issues or poetry that opens new avenues in the mind. In her lyric poem "When All the World's Asleep," Anita Posey asks a question that puzzles many children:

Where do insects go at night,
When all the world's asleep?
Where do bugs and butterflies
And caterpillars creep?
Turtles sleep inside their shells;

The robin has her nest.
Rabbits and the sly old fox
Have holes where they can rest.
Bears can crawl inside a cave;
The lion has his den.
Cows can sleep inside the barn,
And pigs can use their pen.
But where do bugs and butterflies
And caterpillars creep,
When everything is dark outside
And all the world's asleep?

(Anita E. Posey, "When All the World's Asleep")

Young people who enjoy poetry will enthusiastically share it with others and find poems to use for celebrations. Students can cultivate an interest in free verse and lyric poetry, as well as humorous, nonsense, and narrative verse. Young people naturally gravitate to favorite poets, but when they are introduced to the poetry created by different poets, they will develop a deeper appreciation and understanding of a variety of poetic writings. Fortunately, many new poetry collections created by diverse groups are now available for young people. An example is Neil Philip's *Songs Are Thoughts: Poems of the Inuit* (1995). The poems were collected in the 1920s and are meant to be sung, rather than read. (See the Philip color plate.)

Although certain poets may be popular with you and your students, introduce other traditional and contemporary poets. The notable poets listed earlier in this chapter and the bibliographies of recommended collections, anthologies, and individual poetry books should provide assistance in selecting poetry.

When choosing poetry books for personal or classroom use, the merit and appeal of the poems, the poets, and the overall quality of the book are considered. Table 7.10 on page 237 presents various questions to be considered when selecting individual poems and poetry books.

Maryclare Foa's folk art paintings help interpret the Inuit poems collected by Neil Philip in his book, Songs Are Thoughts: Poems of the Inuit. *The vivid colors representing the Native American group give the viewers additional information about the culture. Wonder what poem this painting accompanies?*

Collecting Poetry for the Classroom

Beatrice Schenk de Regniers was talking to teachers and children when she advised "Keep a poem in your pocket":

Keep a poem in your pocket
and a picture in your head
and you'll never feel lonely
at night when you're in bed.

The little poem will sing to you
the little picture bring to you

a dozen dreams to dance to you
at night when you're in bed.

So—
Keep a picture in your pocket
and a poem in your head
and you'll never feel lonely
at night when you're in bed.

(Beatrice Schenk de Regniers,
"Keep a Poem in Your Pocket")

TABLE 7.10 Guidelines for Selecting Poems and Poetry Books

Selection Criteria for an Individual Poem

Determine the quality of the poem by considering questions such as these:

  Does the poem have the potential to evoke sensory images?

  Does the poem have a cadence, a beat, a definite rhythm?

  If the poem is written in a rhyming format, are the rhymes natural?

  Are the sounds of the poem appealing?

  Does the poet use language in unique, impressive ways to succinctly present ideas, descriptions, and emotions?

  Does the poet present fresh, imaginative ideas and feeling?

  Reject a poem written in a condescending, didactic way.

Determine the appeal of the poem by considering questions such as these:

  Does the poet use poetic types and forms that are naturally appealing to young people and retain their attention?

  Are familiar childhood experiences or interesting topics presented in the poem?

  Does the poem extend and enrich a person's insight or knowledge?

  Will the poem's language be understood by the audience, yet expand their linguistic abilities?

  Does the poem stimulate the emotions and imagination of the intended audience?

Selection Criteria For Poetry Books

Determine the overall quality of a book by considering questions such as these:

  Are the poems consistent in quality throughout the book?

  Are both familiar and new poets included in the book?

  Are the poems compatible with and appear to reinforce the purpose of the book?

  Do the poems stimulate a variety of thoughts and emotions?

  Are poems representing various moods ranging from happy to serious included in the book?

  Are the poems too sentimental?

Review the poets included in the book by considering questions such as these:

  Is the book a collection written by one poet?

  If the book is an anthology, does it include a variety of traditional and contemporary poets?

  Are exemplary creations of notable poets included in the book?

  Are exemplary creations of unknown poets included in the book?

  Are the selected poems included in other poetry books?

Review the layout of the book by considering questions such as these:

  Are the poems arranged according to a particular theme?

  Are appropriate illustrations or visuals used to enhance and supplement the poetry?

  Are the poems and illustrations arranged in a suitable visual design?

  Does the book include a table of contents, index, or topical headings to help the audience find individual poems?

To paraphrase de Regniers's words:

> Teachers, keep a poem in your pocket
> and a poem in your head
> and you'll always find the time to share it
> just mark what I've said.

Variety is the spice of life and adds to the excitement of exploring poetry. Help your students discover various poems by placing thick poetry anthologies, slim collections, and thematic poetry books on various topics in your classroom. Beautifully illustrated books by one or several traditional and contemporary poets will capture the students' attention. Include verses that are easy to read or understand, but also add some that are more complex and will stimulate discussion and challenge the students' thinking. Poems that enhance class themes, verses about special days, poems about the weather, scary poems, poems to sing, and those that invite participation are appropriate additions. Story poems, those describing an experience, quiet and noisy poems, nature poems, silly verses, fantasy poetry,

and those describing family members and friends are appealing to children. Poems for choral speaking entice students to present an oral interpretation. Poetry representing diverse groups and regions of the country is suitable to include in the collection. Change the poems periodically.

A pleasant way to celebrate a birthday is to give a poetry book to the class. Teachers who invite children to find poems in magazines, books, and newspapers are thrilled when a child proudly announces, "I found this poem or anthology and thought about our class!"[23] Share a poem from Joseph Bruchac and Jonathan London's book *Thirteen Moons on Turtle's Back: A Native American Year of Moons* (1992). The paintings by Thomas Locker enhance the story and will stimulate varied reactions. "Baby Bear Moon" by the Potawatomi is an example of how stunning imagery can stir the imagination without rhythm or rhyme:

> Long ago a small child
> was lost in the snow.
> We thought she had frozen,

Thomas Locker's oil paintings cover one and a half pages in Joseph Bruchac's The Earth Under Sky Bear's Feet: Native American Poems of the Land. *The folk art paintings capture the nighttime portrayed in the twelve narrative poems from native people in this thematic collection.*

but when spring came again,
she was seen with a mother bear
and her small cubs.

She had slept
all through the winter
with them, and from then on
the bears were her family
and her friends.

When we walk by on our snowshoes
we will not bother a bear
or her babies. Instead
we think how those small bears
are like our children.
We let them dream together.

(Potawatomi, "Baby Bear Moon")

In 1995, Bruchac published a companion volume, *The Earth Under Sky Bear's Feet: Native American Poems of the Land.* (See the Bruchac color plate on page 238.)

APPROPRIATE INSTRUCTIONAL STRATEGIES TO USE WITH POETRY

Many instructional strategies enhance students' emotional reactions to poems and verses. Instructional techniques such as forced memorization of an irrelevant poem, overanalyzing a poet's perceived meaning, and clapping the meters of a poem often overshadow the poem's emotional impact. Children deserve to enjoy poetry aesthetically before using other activities. Poetry should not be reserved for a special "poetry time." Poetry time is every moment of the day. Some poems contain language that evokes memories or images, some poems may supplement a social studies or math class, and others enhance a science lesson. Since poetry is music, poems attract students to both music and art.

Poetry also expands a child's vocabulary. The sound and rhythm of poems make them easy to chant and imitate for personal writing. Exposing young people to a variety of poems on various subjects satisfies their diverse interests. Poetry is inexpensive to use in the classroom because most poems are short enough to copy on charts or transparencies.

Reading poetry for pleasure, naturally reacting to its sounds and melody, drawing pictures evoked by a poem, and copying a favorite poem are all appropriate instructional strategies to use with poetry. Other successful strategies to help students develop a positive attitude toward poetry include designing a Word Wall containing unique language from a poem, rereading a favorite poem and savoring its images and language, re-creating a poem in an innovative way by changing or manipulating the phrases or rhyming words, and writing original verses.

Saturate children with a variety of poems representing various poetic forms, types, and elements. Identify different poetic forms, types, and elements. Examine the similarities and differences between the poetic structures. Discuss the ways different poets use various elements to stimulate emotions, arouse the senses, and inform their audience. Discussing the differences between prose and poetry enhances this discussion. Students can rewrite poetry as prose or vice versa and then compare the versions to see which has the greater emotional impact or gives the reader a better understanding of the topic. Poetic structures can be presented during the study of a poet or anthologist. During a discussion of a poem, use literal or critical questions sparingly. Probes such as the following focus on the child's sense or schema: "What picture comes to your mind as you hear this poem?" Table 7.17 later in the chapter suggests a variety of instructional strategies to help learners focus on different poetic structures.

Children naturally react physically to the rhythm, rhyme, repetition, and sound of poetry. Frequently, they interact with the poem by clapping, swaying, or moving to the beat. Free verse, blank verse, and lyric poetry also have a cadence that encourages interaction. Lillian Morrison's poem written in the shape of a skateboard is an example:

Skimming
an asphalt sea
I swerve, I curve, I
sway; I speed to whirring
sound an inch above the
ground; I'm the sailor
and the sail, I'm the
driver and the wheel.
I'm the one and only
single engine
human auto
mobile.

(Lillian Morrison, "The Sidewalk Racer or On the Skateboard")

While physical interaction is fun and natural, overemphasizing the rhythm may focus children's attention on the rhythmic patterns, so that they misunderstand the poet's ideas, feelings, and language. In addition to reciting and chanting rhyming poems, young people need to encounter free verse to help them understand that poets do not always use a rhyming scheme. It is also a good idea to present serious poems that require students to reflect on the poet's thoughts.

Organizing a Poetry Place in the Classroom

Teachers who value poetry prominently display poems and poetry books around the room and have a special Poetry Place. In the Poetry Place, children and teachers can copy poems on banners and murals, display them in frames, or fasten them on the bulletin board.

Poetry written by other children and exemplary models of poetry motivate young people to write original poems and verses. The Poetry Place should have colored and shaped paper, markers, pictures, and stamps, so children can copy favorite poems and original poetry for a *Personal Poetry Anthology*. Students will use drawings, collages, photographs, and other visual media to illustrate the poems in the anthology.

Reading Poetry

Reading poetry is a pleasurable activity. Children who have had many poetry experiences naturally join the reader at repetitive phrases or refrains, at rhyming words, at conversations, or at the answer during question-and-answer poems. Frequently, students will stop the adult reader and insist on reading their favorite poems to the class. Amazingly, some who volunteer to read poetry will be the same students who "cannot read prose in reading classes." Knowing when to stop a child from reading can be difficult, so plan a time for volunteers to share poetry with others.

Oral readers must pronounce and articulate the poet's language appropriately. The reader's tonal qualities, timing, and intonation levels influence the listener's interpretation of a poem. A natural, conversational, enthusiastic reading is recommended rather than a dramatic reading that might overshadow the poem. Typically, readers practice reading poems orally before sharing them with others. While practicing the poem, the reader experiments with proper vocal qualities, natural pauses in the poem, suitable volume, timing, intonation levels, and other oral expressions. If a copy of the poem is placed on a transparency or chart, students can join the oral reading. Poems about the daily weather, chants, jump-rope rhymes, and other popular and familiar verses successfully elicit vocalization and natural movements.

Aural experiences help young people cultivate a positive attitude toward poetry. Initially, the adult serves as the model for children's oral reading, but eventually, girls and boys feel comfortable reading poetry orally to their peers. Each reader may interpret the same poem differently, but when suitable vocal and nonverbal techniques such as those in Table 7.11 on page 241 are used, these variations reward both the listeners and the readers.

Reading poetry with a friend is an enjoyable activity, especially when our friends listen to us.

Practice reading A. A. Milne's "Vespers" using the techniques suggested in the table:

Little Boy kneels at the foot of the bed,
Droops on the little hands little gold head.
Hush! Hush! Whisper who dares!
Christopher Robin is saying his prayers.

God bless Mummy. I know that's right.
Wasn't it fun in the bath to-night?
The cold's so cold, and the hot's so hot.
Oh! God bless Daddy—I quite forgot.

If I open my fingers a little bit more,
I can see Nanny's dressing-gown on the door.
It's a beautiful blue, but it hasn't a hood.
Oh! God bless Nanny and make her good.

Mine has a hood, and I lie in bed,
And pull the hood right over my head,
And I shut my eyes, and I curl up small,
And nobody knows that I'm there at all.

Oh! Thank you, God, for a lovely day.
And what was the other I had to say?
I said "Bless Daddy," so what can it be?
Oh! Now I remember it. God bless Me.

Little Boy kneels at the foot of the bed,
Droops on the little hands little gold head.
Hush! Hush! Whisper who dares!
Christopher Robin is saying his prayers.

(A. A. Milne, "Vespers")

TABLE 7.11 Effective Oral Presentation of Poetry

DESIRABLE VERBAL AND NONVERBAL QUALITIES	POINTS TO CONSIDER WHEN ORALLY READING POETRY
The reader naturally enunciates and pronounces the poet's language clearly, distinctly, and smoothly.	The voice is used to express the poet's mood and ideas, show the beauty and power of language, and express the emotional impact of the poem.
The reader is aware of proper rhythm, phrasing, punctuation, and diction.	Listen to tapes by professional actors to refine oral reading abilities.
Gestures are limited and distracting mannerisms are eliminated.	Follow the natural rhythm of the poem.
The reader varies the reading speed and the pitch and volume of the voice to fit the mood, language, and cadence of the poem.	Use the punctuation marks to achieve appropriate intonation: a comma requires a short pause; an exclamation mark requires a forceful reading; a question mark requires the voice to remain in the middle intonation level; a period requires the reader to stop and then speak in the lowest intonation level.
Suitable vocal techniques stimulate an interest in poetry.	If the poet does not use punctuation marks, use the natural intonation level.
Appropriate facial and body movements enhance and highlight the reader's interpretation of a poem.	When practicing the poem, look for the poet's movement, moods, and meanings; note unusual vocabulary, unfamiliar phrases, unique pauses, and definite rhythmic patterns.
	Continue practicing until the language flows and the presentation is natural and comfortable.
	Prepare a tape and critique your overall presentation.
	Each poem is unique and requires a different presentation: for example, read Milne's "Hippity" in a lively, bouncy voice to interpret the language and content of the poem, but read his "Vespers" first slowly and quietly, and then enthusiastically, to show the tender, changing moods of the narrator.
	A reader is more confident about a presentation when she or he is familiar with or has memorized the first line or verse of a poem.
	Listening to a tape of a poet reading his or her poetry gives students additional insights into the poet's life and craft.
	Illustrations enhance and supplement a poem, but they may make children dependent on another's visual interpretation of a poem and stifle their personal imagination.

Note: See Chapter 10 for additional information about the oral interpretation of literature.

Use a soft voice for the lines and phrases in italic type and a louder, more enthusiastic voice for the rest. As an experiment, read the poem again using the same volume throughout, and see how much harder it is to understand.

Choral Speaking

During choral speaking, two or more voices speak as one. This oral interpretation technique gives young people a perfect opportunity to explore personal interpretations of a poem, interact and cooperate with others, and enhance personal oral and reading abilities.

Poetry comes to life when speakers interpret the poet's language through choral speaking. The following components are highlighted when several voices speak poetry simultaneously:

Sound is achieved through the rising and falling inflection within a phrase.

Stress is achieved when soft and loud voices emphasize various syllables or words to create the mood of the narrative.

Duration is the time required for speakers to say long/short syllables and influence the tempo and rhythm of the poem.

Pitch is the use of high and low sounds of the voice to interpret the poet's thoughts, information, and attitude.

TABLE 7.12   Benefits Gained from Experiences with Choral Speaking

Speakers have an opportunity to experiment with the sounds and feelings evoked by the poem.

Speakers and listeners experience the aural pleasure of poetry.

Speakers use three language modalities, listening, speaking, and reading.

Choral speaking helps students develop various vocal qualities, such as articulation, enunciation, intonation, pronunciation, and pauses, and also helps them with nonverbal communication.

Choral speaking helps students recognize the value of using appropriate oral skills when reading, speaking, and listening to others.

This group endeavor may help individuals overcome their fear of public speaking. The group support leads to a sense of unity among class members.

Students can transfer the oral techniques they learn to other oral presentations, such as drama, storytelling, and reading aloud.

Through choral speaking, students learn the purpose for using punctuation marks in written texts and are likely to use this knowledge in personal writing.

Although choral speaking is not limited to poetry, poems and verses are considered a good source to begin the activity. When poetry is spoken, students become aware of the melody, mood, and sounds of the language. Besides the aural exploration of poetry, choral speaking gives young people the other valuable benefits listed in Table 7.12.[24] Although these benefits are important, the ultimate purposes for using choral speaking are to introduce quality poetry, to challenge young people to search for poetry, and to give them a variety of pleasurable experiences with poetry.

Choral speaking is a successful classroom strategy if suitable original and published poetry is selected. When using original poetry, the child-poet is involved in arranging the activity and can become the director. Guidlelines for selecting poetry for choral speaking are listed in Table 7.13.

Choral speaking thrives in a low-anxiety classroom, where students feel free to take risks. Encourage the students to experiment with vocal qualities and interpret poetic language. Table 7.14 on page 243 lists guidelines for directing choral speaking. Using these guidelines, try arranging Mary Ann Hoberman's "Yellow Butter" for choral speaking:

Yellow butter purple jelly red jam black bread

Spread it thick
Say it quick

Yellow butter purple jelly red jam black bread

Spread it thicker
Say it quicker

Yellow butter purple jelly red jam black bread

TABLE 7.13   Guidelines for Selecting Suitable Poetry for Choral Speaking

Select poems students have heard and express an interest in learning. Most children enjoy simple, humorous, rhythmic verses. Also consider the age, reading, and speaking abilities of individual students.

Select poems that are worth the time required for practice.

Select simple, short, entertaining poems at first. As children begin to experiment with various choral arrangements, add more complex, lyrical poems to the students' repertoire. Avoid poems that are sentimental, didactic, or contain controversial or sensitive content.

Whatever the simplicity or complexity of the poem, a flowing cadence, melodic sounds, and definite rhyming pattern are required for successful choral speaking. Overemphasizing the meter may overpower the content and presentation.

Poems representing a particular mood, poems with contrasting sounds, and poems with action that elicits movement or manipulation of vocal qualities are ideal selections for choral speaking.

Now repeat it
While you eat it

Yellow butter purple jelly red jam black bread

Don't talk
With your mouth full!

(Mary Ann Hoberman, "Yellow Butter")

Table 7.15 on page 244 provides general information about directing, voicing, and selecting poetry for five arrangements of choral speaking.

Using Poetry throughout the Day

Use poetry throughout the day as a primary *instructional focus*, with a particular book or a thematic collection of books, and in all *curricular areas*. Poetry dealing with thematic or discipline subjects enhances, supplements, or provides additional information about selected topics included in literary and instructional materials. Figure 7.3 earlier in the chapter provides general information about presenting poetry in the classroom. Initially, give students aesthetic experiences with poems and verses. Instructional techniques, such as choral speaking, original writing, drama, and visual and musical responses, can highlight poetry. These techniques connect students to the topic, help them personally interpret the poem, and invite natural creations and reactions to the poetry.

Poetry as the Instructional Focus Enjoy and study poetry in a variety of ways, such as the following:

Read and enjoy individual poems discussed previously.

Use an anthology or collection; highlight the purpose of the book, the poets included in the book, and the poetic types, forms, or elements.

Select poems relating to a theme, such as friendship or caring for others.

Choose quality poetry representing a particular poetic type, form, or specific poetic element for enjoyment and study.

Combine several areas suggested above: for example, choose poems representing a theme and present them according to a particular form, such as cinquains about food, diamantes about animals, haiku about seasons, limericks about pigs, acrostic poems about music, free verse about scary creatures or events, or humorous poems about school or adults.[25]

Study and enjoy the poetry written by a particular poet.

Poetry with Prose and Thematic Units Suitable poems naturally fit with a single book or a thematic collection of books. Poetry can heighten the emotional appeal of the material. It can provide supplementary information

TABLE 7.14 Guidelines for Directing Choral Speaking

1. Initially, the teacher will select the poems, arrange the choral speaking, and direct the activity. With experience, students enjoy selecting, arranging, and directing the activity.
2. Students need to hear a poem several times before attempting to speak it with others. During this introduction, conduct certain connection activities, such as interpreting the content, describing the melody, or discussing emotions elicited by the poem.
3. Audio- and videotapes of exemplary models of choral speaking arrangements are helpful. Teachers and the media specialist can collect tapes and circulate them throughout the school.
4. Audiotape the students while reading, then encourage them to use the tapes for personal critiques of the presentation. Note unacceptable qualities, such as reading in a singsong rhythm, using a monotone voice, speaking too fast or too slow, speaking too loud or too soft, not pausing, or not reading with others. Students can strive to eliminate undesirable qualities during future sessions.
5. Select students according to their natural speaking voices. Typically, in the primary grades high and low voices are selected. In the intermediate grades, select high, medium, and low voices. Encourage students to experiment with tonal qualities and to vary their voices while interpreting a poem. Do not encourage students to strain their voices by speaking too high or too loud. Place students with similar voices together.
6. Practice group reading first, then solo parts. Do not overemphasize individual words or rhythm. Use spontaneous gestures and movements. The drama of the presentation comes from the blending of voices, the pauses, the emphasis, and the language of the poem. When using scenery, costumes, or sound effects, they should enhance—not overpower—the oral interpretation and the poet's language and emotions.
7. Use a variety of poetic types, forms, and arrangements throughout the year. Poems performed for others require several practice sessions. If students lose interest in a poem, present it immediately or select another to perform. (See Table 7.15 for additional information about the selection of poetry for various choral speaking arrangements.)
8. Begin choral speaking practice with a favorite poem. Recite the old poem, then introduce the new poem and arrangement. Familiar poems require limited practice.
9. Place the poem on a chart or transparency, or give students individual copies of the poem. Some students may choose to memorize the poem.

TABLE 7.15 Choral Speaking Arrangements

Refrain

In this arrangement a child or teacher reads the body of the poem, and the class reads the refrain or chorus in unison. This is the easiest arrangement to model and learn.

1. Initially, the adult reads most lines to establish the rhythm and rhyme for the students.
2. Students speak the repeated lines or refrain.
3. This is an easy arrangement to model and learn; it can be used to introduce the idea of choral speaking.
4. *Alternate method:* Divide the class into two groups seated separately. Each group will read a different stanza or refrain.

Tips for Selecting Poems

The poem must have a recurring chorus or repetitive phrases throughout.

Poems with short refrains that do not disrupt the cadence of the poem are appropriate.

Both rhymed and unrhymed poems are suitable to use.

The cadence and flow of the language must be appropriate for choral speaking.

Examples

J. Prelutsky, "Old Lady," "No, I Won't Turn Orange," "Today Is Very Boring," "The Baby Uggs Are Hatching," "Rolling Harvey down the Hill," "Yak."

M. Sendak, "Pierre: A Cautionary Tale."

M. Child, "Thanksgiving Day."

E. Merriam, "Loose Berry Jam," "Tube Time."

M. A. Hoberman, "Yellow Butter."

V. Lindsay, "The Mysterious Cat."

D. McCord, "The Fisherman."

E. Lear, "The Jumblies."

D. Lee, "I Eat Kids YUM YUM."

Line-A-Person

An individual reads one or more sentences independently.

1. Each person reads a complete sentence or thought, not necessarily one line.
2. The first person can introduce the poem and read the first sentence or thought.
3. Encourage readers to keep the cadence smooth and the poem flowing.
4. The participants can stand in a line before the group to read the poem.
5. The participants can read the last sentence together.
6. This is an easy arrangement to implement and is successful in the primary grades.

Tips for Selecting Poems

Couplets and quatrains are best to use.

The lines, couplets, or quatrains must contain a complete thought.

Use poems with standard punctuation, especially periods and semicolons.

Both unrhymed and rhymed poems are suitable to use.

The poem must be long enough so that each group member has a part to read.

Examples

Unknown, "Five Little Squirrels."

C. Sandburg, "Arithmetic."

Unknown, "Four Seasons."

J. Ciardi, "The Myra Song."

Mother Goose, "One, Two, Buckle My Shoe," "Old Mother Hubbard."

L. Morrison, "The Sidewalk Racer or On the Skateboard."

TABLE 7.15   Choral Speaking Arrangements *(Continued)*

J. Prelutsky, "The Snatchits," "Oh, Teddy Bear," "Spaghetti! Spaghetti!" "Homework! Oh, Homework!"

S. Silverstein, "Oh Have You Heard," "Warning," "Adventures of a Frisbee," "Me and My Giant," "Sick," "Kidnapped!"

R. L. Stevenson, "My Shadow," "Bed in Summer."

B. Bagert, "Mean Teachers."

R. Field, "My Inside-Self."

Antiphonal (Dialogue)

Two or more groups speak alternate stanzas in this arrangement. Voices may be combined to provide a more effective interpretation of the poem.

1. Boys, girls, or groups speak in various vocal pitches.
2. Use this arrangement with intermediate-age students because their voices are naturally high, medium, and low.
3. Antiphonal arrangements require vocal contrasts, such as stronger versus lighter voices or higher versus lower voices.
4. High voices are light and suggest excitement and happiness. Medium voices are intended for continuous narration. Low, deep voices suggest serious, gruff, scary tones.

Tips for Selecting Poems

Select poems participants like because this arrangement requires much practice.

Poems with dialogue or those that ask questions or elicit responses are suitable.

Limericks are good sources.

Use poems that feature contrasts, such as light, medium, and deep tones or bright and dark sound.

Examples

M. Brown, "The Secret Song."

C. Rossetti, "Who Has Seen the Wind?"

A. A. Milne, "Puppy and I," "The Good Little Girl," "Father William."

P. Fleischman's poems in *I Am Phoenix* and *Joyful Noise.*

V. Hobb, "One Day When We Went Walking."

J. Ciardi's poems in *The Hopeful Trout and other Limericks.*

W. Cole's poems in *The Book of Giggles.*

S. Silverstein, "Poor Angus."

W. Blake, "The Piper."

E. Lear, "The Owl and the Pussycat."

R. Fyleman, "What They Said."

Unison

The entire group speaks the poem together.

1. All speakers must simultaneously use the same pauses, parallel inflections, and intonation.
2. Use similar vocal qualities, such as all high/low voices or soft/strong voices.
3. This arrangement is the most difficult to speak and should not be used until students have had much experience with choral speaking and other arrangements.
4. *Alternate method:* One group (person) can pantomime the action of the poem while another group speaks.

Tips for Selecting Poems

Short poems with strong rhythm, cadence, and contrasting moods are appropriate.

Nursery rhymes, limericks, and nonsense verses are good to use.

Examples

S. Silverstein, "Hug O'War," "Merry," "Rock 'N' Roll Band" (with sound effects).

J. Taylor, "The Star."

C. Sandburg, "Fog."

O. Nash, "The Camel."

(Continued)

TABLE 7.15   Choral Speaking Arrangements *(Continued)*

L. Hughes, "Dreams."

C. Zolotow, "People."

S. Milligan, "The Wiggley-Woogley Men."

E. Lear, J. Ciardi, and W. Cole, limericks.

M. Chute, "Dogs."

V. Lindsay, "The Little Turtle."

W. Cole, "Here Comes the Band."

K. Kuskin, "If I Were A. . . ."

R. L. Stevenson, "Rain."

Unknown, "Rain, Rain, Go Away."

W. de la Mare, "Someone."

Nursery Rhyme, "There Was a Crooked Man."

Cumulative

One person/group will read a verse or couplet, another person/group will join the first at the second verse, and other persons/groups will join at the following verses. The entire group will read the last verse together. This arrangement is also called a "crescendo arrangement."

1. Voices are added or subtracted, building up to and moving away from the climax of the poem.
2. Select a poem enjoyed by the children because this arrangement requires practice.
3. Participants must use the same pauses, parallel inflections, and intonation.
4. Similar vocal qualities are recommended, such as all high/low voices or soft/strong voices.
5. *Alternate method:* A person/group joins the reading as described above, except all groups are reading in the middle of the poem. Then one person/group stops speaking at the end of each verse until one person/group reads the final verse. A long, narrative poem is required for this arrangement.

Tips for Selecting Poems

Narrative poems are best for this arrangement.

Both rhymed and unrhymed poems are appropriate.

Poems with flowing language and cadence should be selected.

Examples

E. Lear, "The Owl and the Pussy-Cat."

J. Tippett, "Trains."

J. Ciardi, "Mummy Slept Late and Daddy Fixed Breakfast."

A. Adoff, "The Cabbages Are Chasing the Rabbit."

A. Lobel, "The Rose in My Garden."

Traditional, "Old Mother Hubbard," "There Was a Crooked Man," "This Is the House That Jack Built," "One, Two."

E. Merriam, "Five Little Monsters."

Unknown, "Five Little Chickens."

J. W. Riley, "The Nine Little Goblins."

D. McCord, "Bananas and Cream."

S. Silverstein, "The Little Blue Engine."

J. Prelutsky, "The Bogeyman."

about the setting and clarify information presented in the prose narrative. Identify the content, literary elements, important concepts, or instructional goals to be highlighted while reading the fiction or nonfiction selection. Then select poems that are appealing to the children and relate to the identified areas. Fortunately, thematic poetry collections are available, and the editors of many general anthologies have arranged the poems according to subject. This strategy can be developed as follows:

Verna Aardema's picture storybook *Why Mosquitoes Buzz in People's Ears* is based on a West African cumulative tale. The book, illustrated by Leo and Diane Dillon, describes the problems certain African animals encounter when the iguana plugs his ears. After children aged seven to ten read, hear, and discuss the book, they can make a Poetry Collection of West African Animals. Poems such as the following can be included in the collection: "mosquito" by Valerie Worth; "Five Little Owls," author unknown; "Lion" by William Jay Smith; "When You Talk to a Monkey," by Rowena Bennett; "The Snake" by Emily Dickinson; and "The Crow" by William Canton.

Poetry Used in All Discipline Areas Poetry effectively complements, extends, and provides additional information about the content or topic taught in all discipline areas. Poems generally give students a different viewpoint about a subject. Students can hear a poem that naturally fits the content. After they spontaneously respond to the poem, they can discuss facts presented in the poem that are pertinent to the topic. The media specialist will help you find suitable poetry books such as those in the chapter bibliography. Place Shel Silverstein's poem on a transparency and share it before a spelling lesson:

I'm no good at History,
Science makes no sense to me,
Music is a mystery,
English is no friend to me,
Math is my worst enemy,
Economics tortures me,
Gym takes too much energy,
Reading is a chore to me,
Geography just loses me,
I hate Sociology,
Chemistry confuses me,
I barf in Biology,
Astronomy's just stars to me,
Botany's just flower smelling,
Even Art's too hard for me.
Well, at least I'm good at *Speling!*

(Shel Silverstein, "One in Sixteen")

Writing Original Poetry

Successful poetry teachers realize students write poetry for the intrinsic delight and reward of creating original products. Young poets are constantly searching for new and refreshing ways to express ideas, attitudes, emotions, and information through poetry. Nevertheless, expressing their emotions and thoughts in poetry is easier for some people than for others. Most students need encouragement and praise to write poetry. You will find some boys and girls like to share their poems with others, but some do not. In general, young people enjoy *manipulating* the language, *imitating* poetic types and forms, and *producing* original poetry or prose.

Published poems, written by children and adults, are excellent models to stimulate original writing. When students write original poems, they discover new ways to express their ideas and emotions. They discover more about the art of poetry and develop a stronger feeling for the poet's craft, since they see themselves as poets. Students who write original poetry frequently explore published poems and express a positive attitude toward poetry. As young poets begin writing poems and verses, their main focus is directed to the content, images, memories, descriptions, and feelings they wish to express. Poetic elements will be highlighted through various instructional strategies and minilessons.

A developing poet needs time to explore the various types and forms of poetry. Most immature poets find unrhymed verse easier to write than rhymed forms. Children who practice writing unrhymed verse are less likely to think that all poems must contain ending rhymes. As young poets have aural experiences with verses and poems, they will begin to experiment with the various forms and types and discover the patterns that are comfortable for them to write.

Young poets who work with a Poet-in-Residence are more confident about writing poetry. After working extensively with children in creative writing, Myra Cohn Livingston, an award-winning poet, became convinced that we cannot teach poetry.[26] She believed that as children explore poetry, they come to understand how poets use various poetic elements to achieve the desired effect, conciseness, and imagery. Most young people who explore various poetic elements used in different types and forms of poetry naturally attempt to write original poetry. When they write poems, they experience the delight and intrinsic rewards of creating an original product. Children who write poetry share their *imagination*, *inform* others, *express* their feelings, and offer their opinions in an attempt to *persuade* others. While no magical formula exists to help children write poetry, teachers can constantly share and surround learners with the best examples of quality poetry.[27] Table 7.16 on page 248 suggests general instructional techniques to motivate "budding poets," and Table 7.17 on page 248 suggests more specific instructional strategies to stimulate original writing. As young poets' attention is focused on the various poetic structures, they become sensitive to their personal voice and feelings. Through these experiences young people develop a better understanding of the tools and craft of poetry.[28]

Criteria for Judging Original Poetry Formal grading of original poetry is not recommended. When the poet's endeavor is studied, consider the effective use of poetic elements and the style of writing separately. A checklist such as

TABLE 7.16   General Techniques to Motivate Poetry Writing

1. **Connect** children and poetry. Read poetry every day. Share different types and forms of poetry. Encourage students to "discover" the similarities and differences. Show art in books with pictures or individual art by famous artists to stimulate ideas for original writing. Some poets enjoy listening to soft background music while writing.
2. **Construct** meanings of poetry. While discussing the various types and forms of poetry, prepare a Class Comparison Chart containing the various "poetry patterns" found in poems. Encourage students to find poems written in the various structures. They could copy and identify the structures. Writing a description of the structure might help students fully understand it.
3. When introducing students to a different poetic form or type, have the students write a collaborative class poem. Later, individuals or partners will write original poems.
4. Early in the year discuss general information about writing poetry. Help students understand that poems can be written about every subject; that poems may be serious or silly; that they may or may not rhyme; that poets punctuate poems in different ways; that poems may be written in shapes; that poems follow a specific type or form; and that poets can experiment with different patterns.
5. Create a *Poetry Word Wall* displaying language found in a poem or poetry. Select unfamiliar words and phrases, words with unusual sounds, words that rhyme, imaginative similes, metaphors, and examples of onomatopoeia. Change the wall often. Elicit the students' help in finding new, unique, fresh poetic expressions to display on the wall. Students can draw pictures representing the language.
6. **Create** original poems by using the writing process. Brainstorm ideas, forms, and elements. Select a topic, and write a rough draft using the forms, types, and elements discussed. Meet in peer groups for feedback; revise as desired. Edit the poem. Read it to others. Publish the poet's favorite poem.
7. In peer groups, consider questions such as the following: Is there consistent rhythm in the poem? Do the words flow? Can another person understand the poet's thoughts? Are unnecessary words removed? Are other words needed?
8. Display each poet's choice in the classroom, hallway, and media center. Publish the poems in a class or school anthology. Have a celebration party to introduce the anthology and poets to the school.
9. Find local, state, and national poetry contests. Encourage students to enter them. Organize a local poetry contest. Contact the local newspaper. Ask it to co-sponsor the contest. Publish original poems in books and the newspaper.

TABLE 7.17   Instructional Strategies Focusing on Various Poetic Structures

Ask the children to compare unlike objects making comparisons that are strange, but logical. For example, use "like" or "as" in a sentence: "My dog is like an elephant; he has a big mouth and a long snout."

Ask the children to imagine how it would feel to look into a moth's eyes. Discuss their reactions and ask them to complete the following:

I looked into the eyes of a moth and what do you think I saw?

I saw _____ .

Ask the students to imagine how it would feel to be a favorite insect or object. Talk about the creature's fears; identify its friends and enemies. Cluster the students' responses according to the various categories. Have them select one or two words from the cluster and use them to write a poem from the animal or object's perspective. Students could also select three responses from each cluster and write a tercet. Remember that, initially, the ideas and expressions are more important than writing a "perfect" poem.

William Jay Smith's "The Toaster" and Charles Malam's "The Steam Shovel" are excellent examples of poems using personification. Read a poem, and discuss the poet's use of personification. Then share an information book about a topic, such as musical instruments (Neil Ardley, *Eyewitness Book of Music* [1989]), creatures at the seashore (Michael Chinery, *Questions and Answers about Seashore Animals* [1994]), or other subjects of interest to students. Brainstorm ways to personify topics found in the information books. Then, using the content in the information books, write original verse containing personification.

After reading a nonfiction book, divide students into triads. Each triad will select a topic from the book and write sentences with alliteration. Each sentence must be logical and contain many adjectives or verbs beginning with the same letter as the topic. A dictionary and thesaurus are helpful when writing sentences with alliteration. For example:

Vivid sounds vibrated through the vortex when the visiting virtuoso volunteered to play the violin.

Proud puffins look a bit like penguins as they precariously prance their plump bodies along the precipice.

Encourage students to become *language collectors.* As they read, ask them to listen for and record words that capture their attention and imagination; words that help them visualize an event; words that tickle their fancy; and language that vividly expresses a thought or an emotion.

In a prominent place in the room, prepare a Poet's Picture (a framed portion of the bulletin board where students can write these snippets of language).

Discuss the use of the language in poems. Suggest that students incorporate the "snippets of language" into their personal writing.

Encourage imitation of form. Read and discuss poems and verses representing specific forms of poetry. Invite students to write *Clever Couplets, Terrific Triplets, Queenly Quatrains,* or *Laughable Limericks.* To stimulate writing use a strategy such as the following: After reading and talking about limericks, give students the beginning of a published limerick. Ask them to complete the verse by writing a new ending. Later compare their lines with the original. For example:

There was an old man from Peru

Who dreamed he was eating his shoe:

He woke in a fright

In the middle of the night

And found _____ .

(Author unknown)

(Original ending: It was perfectly true.)

Or

I raised a great hullabaloo

When I found a large mouse in my stew,

Said the waiter, "_____

_____

_____!"

(Author unknown)

(Original ending: "Don't shout

And wave it about,

Or the rest will be wanting one, too!")

Read Judith Viorst's *If I Were in Charge of the World* (1981). Ask the students to brainstorm what they would do if they were in charge of the world. Cluster the responses. Use relevant ideas to write a verse. For example:

If I were in charge of the world,

art and computers would be taught three times a day

and math, music, and hygiene would be discussed once a week.

If I were in charge of the world,

my mom would wash the dishes,

my brother would clean up my room,

and Alice Ann Andrews would move to Alaska!

(Toni, age 11)

Tap into the children's background experiences by asking them to write a one-line wish poem. Combine several lines into one poem. For example:

I wish I were a kite, to Disney World I'd fly,

I'd dance with Mickey, Pooh Bear, and Big Bird,

and then I'd steal a kiss from Snow White and Cinderella, too!

I wish I could go to Epcot,

to visit pavilions from countries near and far,

I'd sample their music, their treasures and food, and dream of visiting

every place some day!

(Gene, age 9)

Read several pages from Mary O'Neill's *Hailstones and Halibut Bones* (1961), such as:

"The sound of black is 'Boom! Boom! Boom!' echoing in an empty room!

Purple is the time just before night . . . a violet opening in spring."

Discuss the importance of color in our world by using prompts such as these:

What is your favorite color?

How does it sound?

What does it feel (taste, smell, look) like?

Does it remind you of a special time? A special person?

In peer groups, discuss responses to various colors; use these thoughts to complete a color poem similar to O'Neill's.

Write a color poem. Select a favorite book character or cultural hero. Then suggest a color that reminds the student of the person. Lois Lowry portrays the importance of color in her Newbery winner, *The Giver*. After reading the book, students might respond as follows:

The Giver is gray. He is white as snow. He is yellow as the bright sun.

Jonas is bright green as the grass. He is red as an apple. He is sunny yellow.

In the beginning of the book, Father was as warm as blue; later he became black as coal.

Ask the students to suggest a color that reminds them of an important person, such as President Clinton, Adolf Hilter, Martin Luther King, Jr., Sitting Bull, or author Virginia Hamilton. For example:

Albert Einstein is bright blue as a cloudless sky and red as the energy of a volcano.

Use a wordless text, such as Molly Bang's *The Strawberry Snatcher*. Organize the students in triads. Ask each triad to talk about the artist's use of color, line, and texture and the media and style the artist used in the book to express the author's thoughts. Discuss the artist's craft, and encourage triads of students to use a specific form and write a collaborative poem about the book. For example:

Strawberries, how red, and rich, and firm.

Escaping the Mushroom-footed Snatcher's thin fingers and green thumb is a challenge.

The blueberry brambles are hard to see, but the berries ease the Snatcher's hunger and pain.

Strawberries, strawberries, so sweet and delicious for my family to eat.

Fran

Explore the sounds and smells found in books, such as Dennis Lee's *Garbage Delight* and Tomie de Paola's *The Popcorn Book*. Write poetry about the topics included in the book. For example, after reading de Paola's book, pop popcorn. Ask students to list words or phrases that describe the sounds, smells, and pleasure of eating popcorn. Use the language to write lines of verse. Combine the lines in a class poem. For example:

Popcorn sounds like a ball bouncing, like thunder roaring.

Popcorn tastes like a dried salty sea, like a crunchy pickled-pepper.

Popcorn smells like a special birthday present.

Popcorn is better than free play period on a sunny day.

Jill Bennet's *Noisy Poems* provides many poetic models: sounds, rhyme, rhythms, meters, and shapes. Have partners choose a familiar environment (in the city, country, or school). Talk about objects, animals, or people who might live in the environment. Then have the partners match the things living in the environment with verbs or rhyming words that describe the environment. The partners will use the sentences to write a rhyming or unrhyming, cohesive verse. For example,

I hear sounds at the farm—

Cows mooing, birds chirping,

Dogs barking, bees buzzing,

These are the sounds I hear at the farm—

Sheep baaing, horses neighing,

Pigs oinking, crows cawing,

These are the sounds I hear at the farm—

Mother calling her family to dinner,

Dad's tractor, children shouting at play,

These are the sounds I hear at the farm.

A poet can arrange an original poem for choral speaking.

the following guides the assessment. It is important for adults to respect, value, and honestly praise all creative efforts.

Young poets may analyze their original writings using the following criteria:

Are you happy with the poem? Have you said what you wanted to express?

Is this a good example of your writing?

Is this an innovative, creative effort?

Did you use poetic elements that evoke imagery? Did you use figurative language? Did you use language that stimulates sounds? Does the language help the audience understand your ideas and emotions?

Did you maintain a constant cadence throughout the poem?

Did you maintain a consistent point of view throughout the poem?

Did you effectively use the elements expected in the selected form and type?

How did you publish and share the poem?

While realizing that all of their poetry may not be of equal merit, students will find that these questions can help them achieve higher-quality poems. These criteria are also helpful for teachers to use when discussing the poems with the poet and measuring the student's linguistic maturity and growth.

Dramatic Experiences with Poetry

Dramatic experiences give young people an opportunity to focus on the emotional aspects of a poem. As part of the dramatic presentation, the boys and girls will discuss the author's purposes and the language chosen, which leads them to a broader understanding of the poem. When a poem has characters, assuming a character's role will give the student a better understanding of the character's feelings and actions. Table 7.18 lists specific dramatic experiences to use with poetry.[29]

Artistic Experiences with Poetry

As mentioned earlier in the chapter, illustrations are frequently used in collections, anthologies, and picture books of individual poems. The illustrations explain a poem, expand an image, supplement the poem, or decorate (borders) the book. Because children may need additional information to help them fully savor the poet's ideas and feelings, illustrations extend young children's pleasure and their appreciation of poetry. Fortunately, publishers recognize the power of illustrations in poetry books and commission award-winning illustrators to interpret the poems. In their interpretations, the illustrators use suitable artistic styles, me-

TABLE 7.18 Dramatic Experiences with Poetry

Have students pantomime the action while they listen to a narrative poem such as Ogden Nash's "Adventures of Isabel," Edward Lear's "The Owl and the Pussy Cat," Eugene Field's "The Duel," Vachel Lindsay's "The Little Turtle," and Michael Rosen's *We're Going on a Bear Hunt* (1989).

Have students explore the setting of a poem, by asking, How do you move in a snowstorm? In tall grass? Have the students describe the setting if it is not mentioned in the poem.

Encourage students to move with the rhythm suggested in the poem. For example, A. A. Milne's "They're Changing the Guard at Buckingham Palace" suggests a march. Have students think of poems that suggest clapping or a dance.

Have students write, then read a script for a Reader's Theater interpretation of a favorite poem.

Have students prepare a dramatic presentation describing what happened after a poem is concluded.

Have students dramatize metaphors or similes, such as "as light as a feather" or "as quiet as a mouse."

Give students the beginning of a comparison statement from a poem and direct them to dramatize the end of the statement. For example:

The building was as high as a _____ .

The sand dune looked like _____ .

Have students present a "kaleidoscope" drama. Divide students into small groups and give each group a different verse of a long narrative poem. Each group will prepare a dramatic interpretation of their verse. Then students will present the verses in the proper sequence.

Have students prepare an audio- or videotape of several events from a particular poem. Use the tapes to advertise and entice others to read the poem.

Have students answer the roll by reciting several lines from a poem. Other students will guess the title and author of the poem.

Have partners read a verse from a familiar poem. Other students will guess the poet and the title of the poem.

Have students make puppets and prepare a puppet show based on a narrative poem.

Have students use sign language to orally present a poem.

After students read a poem with outstanding examples of metaphor, such as Sandburg's "Fog," have them create and dramatize new metaphors. For example: The fog crept in on _____ .

NOTE: See Chapter 10 for general information about dramatization of literature.

dia, and techniques. Some anthologists choose art to accompany poetry. The sepia photographs enhance Walter Dean Myers's poems in *Brown Angels: An Album of Pictures and Verses*. (See the Myers color plate on page 252.) In fact, all of the illustrations shown in this chapter are compatible with the poems and help the reader enjoy the selected poems. Because visuals also serve as an invitation for readers

Friendship

There is a secret thread that makes us friends
Turn away from hard and breakful eyes
Turn away from cold and painful lies
That speaks of other, more important ends
There are two hard yet tender hearts that beat
Take always my hand at special times
Take always my dark and precious rhymes
That sing so brightly when our glad souls meet

Myers selected sepia photographs to enhance his poems in Brown Angels: An Album of Pictures and Verses. *The photographs fit the poems perfectly. The creator arranges early 20th-century photographs differently on each page. Can you find old photographs to accompany your favorite poems?*

to think about the poet's ideas, the illustrations stimulate personal meanings of the poem.[30]

Various techniques can be used to stimulate students' imagination and elicit various visual responses to a poem. For example, while students listen to a poem—perhaps a recording by the poet—ask them to close their eyes and visualize the poet's words in their "mind's eye." When the poem is finished, ask them prompts such as the following:

What pictures came to mind while you listened to the poem?

What sounds did you hear as you heard the poem?

What did you feel while listening to the poet's words?

Record the responses on a chart. Later, use prompts to elicit responses to other poems. Ask students to paint a picture of their visual interpretation of a poem. Students will choose the most appropriate artistic medium or technique to represent the mood or content of the poem. For example, finger paints represent the mood of lyrical poetry, photographs interpret realistic poetry, and the scratch board technique represents the eerie, mysterious content of a Halloween poem. Display the art in a prominent area of the room. Later, place it in a class scrapbook or class anthology. Additional instructional techniques such as those listed in Table 7.19 on page 253 give students exciting opportunities to combine two areas that evoke highly emotional responses—art and poetry.[31] The bibliography includes a section on poetry books with outstanding illustrations.

Musical Experiences with Poetry

We can sing any poem with a regular, strong cadence and a rhyming scheme. Young children quickly discover the poetic elements in nursery rhymes and predictable texts. Primary and middle-grade youngsters who follow the text of a popular song while the music is playing recognize the poetic structures. Students who understand the relationship of music and poetry are more likely to accept and value all poetry. The bibliographies for this chapter and Chapter 3 list songs and music books to use in the classroom.

Talk about the natural pauses, refrains, and other elements composers must consider when writing music for a poem. Compare the way poets achieve rhythm with the way musicians achieve rhythm with various notes and rests. The students and teacher can compose an appropriate melody for a popular poem. Read to the class poems from T. S. Eliot's *Old Possum's Book of Practical Cats*, such as "The Rum Tum Tigger," "The Song of the Jellicles," and "Macavity: The Mystery Cat." Point out that many poems in this collection became the script for the musical show *Cats*. Elicit the assistance of the music teacher and prepare a musical based on poems shared in class.

Talk about the way music makes a person feel when listening to it. Discuss the importance of music in encouraging us to listen, recite, and move to a poem. Why do babies happily move their bodies to music and poetry? Why do people dance to music? Why do we repeat

TABLE 7.19 Artistic Responses with Poetry

When sharing poetry with illustrations, discuss the style, media, and techniques used by the artist.

Discuss whether the illustrations are appropriate for the poem and whether they enhance, supplement, or provide additional information about the poem. Also, consider the suitability of the visual display of the poem and illustrations.

After discussing the artist's interpretation, have the students select a poem, copy it on a large sheet of paper, and choose the most appropriate medium—e.g., paint, collage, woodcutting, scratch board—to illustrate the poem.

As part of a study of a recognized artist or book illustrator, encourage students to select poetry the person might choose to accompany her or his creations. To help the students make poetry selections, talk about poetic structure and artistic elements, such as color, line, texture, shape, space, and visual design. (See Chapter 8 for a discussion of artistic elements.)

Present compatible poetry, art, and music together. Students can select a favorite poem; then, small groups can choose appropriate music and artwork to interpret the poem. Groups will display the art and play the music while rereading the poem to the class. Later, the class will select the most appropriate art and music for the poem.

Present O'Neill's *Hailstones and Halibut Bones* to help children understand the feelings, sounds, and emotions evoked by color in our lives. Display a picture and ask students to find poems that represent the emotions, content, and artistic features portrayed in the picture. Students will decide if the art and poetry are compatible. Change the display using pictures representing various artistic styles, media, and techniques.

Write a riddle about a nonsense character. Place the riddle on a mobile. Use titles, such as "Who Am I?" "Where Am I Found?" "Where Do I Live?" The riddles can also be written on bookmarks titled "Can You Find Me?" Periodically, these bookmarks will "magically" appear in books in the classroom library.

When haiku poetry is shared, elicit the art teacher's assistance, and teach students Sumi-e painting. These paintings can accompany a haiku copied from published writings or original haiku. Place the verses and paintings on rice paper (or paper with a similar texture). Cut the paper in the shape of a scroll, roll the scrolls, and tie gold cords around them. Paintings and verses could be placed on panels, as in Ed Young's *Lon Po Po*. When using Japanese or other East Asian verses, display picture books with art from the same country in the classroom. Discuss the art and consider the compatibility of the verses and the art. If possible, invite a person who can help the students write an original poem in the appropriate East Asian language.

Display and discuss folk art representing a cultural, ethnic, or religious group that produced a poem. Show pictures representing the setting of a poem, a famous person in a poem, or other objects or topics discussed in a poem.

Have students copy a favorite poem on a piece of cloth, and draw a simple picture representing the content or emotions of the poem. Piece the cloth together for a Poetry Quilt. Cut the cloth in the shape of a banner. Display the quilt/banner in a prominent place in the classroom or the school.

Construct a "Poet Tree." Attach a large paper tree to a bulletin board or place a tree limb in a planter. Cut paper in the shape of leaves, flowers, or fruit. Write the poetry of one poet or poems representing a theme on the shaped paper. Attach the poems to the limbs of the tree.

As a class project, prepare a collage of poems. Place the collage on a mural. Display the mural in the classroom, hallway, or media center.

Have students prepare a shadowbox, roller movie, or diorama representing a poem.

Have students bring regalia or objects that represent the content in a poem.

Have students prepare a bumper sticker advertising a poem or poetry book. Display it in the Poetry Place, school media center, lunchroom, or administrative office.

Older students will ask younger children to name, read, and discuss their favorite poem. The older students will copy, illustrate, and publish the poems in a *Big Book of Poetry*. They will write a dedication to the younger students in the book and give it to them.

Have students copy their favorite poem on a bookmark. The children will visit a center for elderly adults, share the poem with the adults, and give them the bookmarks.

Make Poetry Pockets from heavy cloth. Place the pockets in the Poetry Place. Label the pockets according to content, poetic form, or type. A sentence strip chart or an apron with several pockets can also be used for the pockets. Students will copy favorite poems and place them in the pockets. Change the poems periodically. Encourage students to read poems placed in the pockets. Pockets or other attractive containers can be made to store personal poetry collections. This idea was stimulated by Beatrice de Regniers's poem, "Keep a Poem in Your Pocket."

the "catchy" language and repetitive phrases found in songs? Why do teenagers constantly fill their world with music? Why do parents and grandparents enjoy reminiscing about old times when they hear a favorite old song on the radio or television? Why do young people want copies of music produced by their favorite musician? These questions focus on the importance of music in our lives.

Invite the students to talk to adults about songs they remember from their childhood—lullabies, ballads, spirituals, camp songs, singing games and the like. If possible, tape the adult singing the song or invite adults into the class to talk about favorite poems of the past. Obtain recordings of traditional songs. Give the students a copy of the text of the song and have them listen to or sing along with a recording of the song. Talk about the text, the verse, and how the poem and music must fit together.

Have the students find copies of songs, bring them to class, and continue the discussion of poetry and music. Have the students select an instrumental recording that fits a poem. Play it as background music while reading the poem to the class.

A Potpourri of Poetry Ideas

Poetry can be used in many other ways in the classroom. Here are a few more ideas:

Give students an aural-visual experience with poetry by using videos, audiotapes, records, compact discs, interactive computer programs, photographs, other visuals, and transparencies. Develop a listening and viewing center containing representative examples of poetic types, forms, and elements. Have students select compatible art and music for a favorite poem.

Have students select and copy a poem representing the "best" contemporary poetry. Send the poem to an astronaut who is leaving for outer space.

Use Judith Viorst's "Mother Doesn't Want a Dog" or another poem about something a mother would not let a child keep. Ask students to write a story about what would happen if they brought a pet home. Would their mother let them keep it? Would their father help? If they were allowed to keep the pet, would they take care of it? How?

Ask students to invite characters from poems to their birthday party or to visit the class. Ask them what characters they would not like to invite. Have students select a poem that describes their feelings about these characters.

Have students select a poem for a friend or family member who is angry, happy, or sad. Copy it and give it to the person.

Have students select a poem that describes the daily weather.

Ask students to find a poem that describes the way they would like to travel to school (on a yak or newt), read the poem, and draw a picture of a classmate riding on the selected transportation.

Ask students to find an unusual object that they can write on, such as a lamp shade or an odd-shaped bottle. Have them write several thoughts about the object using metaphors, similes, or personification. Write the thoughts on the object, and then write a free verse containing the thoughts on a colored card and place it on the object.

Tape sounds mentioned in a poem and play the sound track while reading the poem.

Have students give their peers directions for making something, using a poem such as Silverstein's "Peanut Butter."

Have students write a news story for the school television telling about the experiences in "Mummy Slept Late and Daddy Fixed Breakfast" or another narrative or nonsense poem.

Have students hold a Poetry Party. Bring food mentioned in a poetry collection, such as Dennis Lee's *Garbage Delight* or William Cole's *Poem Stew*, to school. Have a food sampling party. Prepare copies of recipes in a *Garbage Delight Menu*. Children could attend the party dressed as favorite characters from poetry. (See the bibliography for other possibilities.)

Have students write poetry and illustrate it to send to Poetry Pals in another room or school.

Have students collect, compare, and share poems written on the same subject, such as food, animals, or magical creatures.

Organize a poet's parade for the school or grade level. The children will dress as a poet or characters in a poem. While parading through the school, the students will give other children copies of poems written by the selected poet or a copy of the poem containing the character.

Summary

Poems and verses are created in metrical structure to communicate a poet's thoughts, memories, or feelings or to provide facts. The content, rhythm, rhyme, sounds, and other language used by poets elicit strong emotional responses from young people.

Narrative, lyrical, humorous, and nonsense poetry are created in both rhymed and unrhymed verse and poems. Popular rhymed forms of juvenile poetry include couplets, triplets, quatrains, ballads, clerihews, folk rhymes, limericks, jingles, and riddles. Unrhymed forms of juvenile poetry are arranged in free and blank verse. Poets also create poetry using definite forms, such as haiku, biopoems, diamantes, parallel poems, character poems, and others.

In the early days, traditional nursery rhymes and moralistic poems were used for instructional purposes and to teach children acceptable social values and behavior. By the mid-eighteenth century, poets began writing verses and poems about children's everyday experiences that aimed to entertain young people, rather than instruct them. Children responded positively to the rhymes, rhythms, sounds, and succinct language used by the poets. Like prose, poetry reflects the society that creates it, and today's poets are creating poetry with diverse subject matter and innovative poetic structures and forms. Contemporary books of poetry are beautifully illustrated, bringing the child, the poet, and the artist together.

Poetry gives young people an opportunity to laugh, to sigh, and to feel a sense of wonder about the world around them. Their imaginations, emotions, sensitivity toward others, personal perspectives, and knowledge are enhanced when they have positive experiences with various poets who create poems with diverse poetic structures.

A successful poetry teacher carefully selects and collects poetry and designs a classroom to reinforce students' desire to interact with poems and enhance their positive feelings toward poetry. Teachers select poems to use throughout the day based on their knowledge of students' preferences and their familiarity with the various techniques that are available for use when presenting poetry in a risk-free environment. The first part of this chapter gives background information about poetry for the adult, such as the characteristics, types, and forms of poetry; the organization of poems in books; the benefits young people gain from poetry; and notable poets throughout history. The second part of the chapter focuses on the use of poetry in the classroom. A variety of instructional strategies are suggested. These strategies include hearing, reading, and writing poetry; choral speaking; and visualizing, dramatizing, and singing poems. The strategies help children make personal connections to poetry, help them construct interpretations of poems, and provide opportunities for them to create personal reactions and responses to a variety of appealing verses and poems.

The most highly recommended poetry anthologies, collections of poems, individual poems, and thematic poetry books are listed in the bibliography at the end of the book.

NOTES

The opening poem is from Moore, L. 1979. *Go With the Poem.* New York: Atheneum.

1. Huey, E. B. 1908 (1968 reissue). *The Psychology and Pedagogy of Reading.* Cambridge, Mass.: MIT Press. 332: See also Emans, R. 1978. Children's rhymes and learning to read. *Language Arts.* 55(8). 937–40.
2. *Webster's Encyclopedic Unabridged Dictionary of the English Language.* s.v. "poetry."
3. Personal communication with M. O'Neill, August 2, 1982.
4. Kuskin, K. 1980. *Dogs & Dragons, Trees & Dreams.* New York: HarperCollins. 78.
5. Kuskin, K. 1980. 41.
6. Walter, N. W. 1967. *Let Them Write Poetry.* New York: Holt, Rinehart & Winston. 73.
7. Merriam, E. 1993. The world outside my skin. 51. In Taxel, J. (Ed.). (1993). *Fanfare. The Christopher-Gordon Children's Literature Annual.* 1. Norwood, Mass.: Christopher-Gordon. 49–79.
8. Kuskin, K. 1980. 20, 23.
9. Worth, V. 1992. Capturing objects in words. *The Horn Book Magazine.* 68(5). 568–69.
10. In Goforth, F. S., & Richmond, K. 1985. Unpublished research study. University of South Florida. Tampa, Fla.
11. For additional information about poetic types, elements, and forms, see sources such as Kuskin, K. 1980; Livingston, M. C. 1981. Nonsense verse: The complete escape. In Hearne, B., & Kaye, M. (Ed.). *Celebrating Children's Books.* New York: Lathrop, Lee & Shepard. 122–39; Luken, R. J. 1995. *A Critical Handbook of Children's Literature.* (5th Ed.). New York: HarperCollins. 235–66; Padgett, R. (Ed.). 1987. *The Teachers and Writers Handbook of Poetic Forms.* New York: Teachers & Writers Collaborative; Strouf, J. L. H. 1993. *The Literature Teacher's Book of Lists.* West Nyack, N.Y.: Center for Applied Research in Education.
12. See the discussion of biopoetry in Gere, A. R. 1985. *Roots in the Sawdust: Writing to Learn Across the Disciplines.* Urbana, Ill.: National Council of Teachers of English.
13. Graham, J. B. 1994. It's a shape poem. *Instructor.* 103(4). November/December. 60.
14. For additional information about notable poets, see sources such as Gillespie, M. C. 1970. *Literature for Children: History and Trends.* Dubuque, Iowa: Wm. C. Brown. 57–94; Haviland, V. 1979. *Children and Poetry.* (2d Ed.). Washington, D.C.: Library of Congress;

Hopkins, L. B. 1993. American poetry for children—the twentieth century. In Taxel, J. (Ed.). *Fanfare*. Norwood, Mass.: Christopher-Gordon. 75–82; Smith, D. W. 1963. *Fifty Years of Children's Books 1910–1960*. Urbana, Ill.: National Council of Teachers of English. 13–16, 18–19, 43–44, 59, 78–79.

15. Janeczko, P. B. 1993. Sparks and wonder: Poetry for children in the 90s. 83. In Taxel, J. (Ed.). (1993). 83–96.

16. Terry, C. A. 1974. *Children's Poetry Preferences: A National Survey of Upper Elementary Grades*. Urbana, Ill.: National Council of Teachers of English.

17. Tom, C. L. 1969. What teachers read to pupils in the middle grades. (Doctoral dissertation, Ohio University, 1969.) *Dissertation Abstract International*. 30. (04). 1248-A.

18. For additional information about presenting poetry, see sources such as Fawcett, G. 1995. Poetry and the princess. *Language Arts*. 72(7). 508–11; Galda, L. 1993. Giving the gift of a poet's words: Sharing poetry with older children. 106. In Taxel, J. (Ed.). 105–16; Sloan, G. D. 1991. *The Child as Critic: Teaching Literature in Elementary and Middle Schools*. (3d Ed.). New York: Teacher's College Press. 101–3; Wicklund, L. K. 1989. Shared poetry: A whole language experience adapted for remedial readers. *The Reading Teacher*. 42(7). 478–81.

19. Mei, Y. 1962. "Expression of feelings VII." 69. In Kotewell, R., & Smith, N. L. (Eds. and Trs.). *The Penguin Book of Chinese Verse*. New York: Penguin Books.

20. Livingston, M. C. 1993. Poetry and self. In Taxel, J. (Ed.). (1993). 5–47.

21. For additional information about young people's poetry preferences, see sources such as Jordan, A. M. 1921. Children's interest in reading. *Contributions to Education, No. 107*. New York: Teachers College, Columbia University; Mackintosh, H. K. 1924. A study of children's choices in poetry. *Elementary English*. 1. 85–89; Bridge, E. B. 1966. Using children's choices of and reactions to poetry as determinant in enriching literary experiences in the middle grades. (Doctoral dissertation, Temple University. 1966.) *Dissertation Abstracts International*. 27. (11). 3749A; Purves, A. C., & Beach, R. 1972. *Literature and the Reader*. Urbana, Ill.: National Council of Teachers of English. 78–79; McCall, C. J. 1979. A determination of children's interest in poetry resulting from specific poetry experiences. (Doctoral dissertation, University of Nebraska, 1979.) *Dissertation Abstracts International*. 40. (08). 4401A; Simmons, M. 1980. Intermediate grade children's preferences in poetry. (Doctoral dissertation, University of California, Berkeley. 1981.) *Dissertation Abstracts International*. 41. (08); Terry, C. A. 1974; Fisher, C. J., & Natarella, M. A. 1984. Young children's preferences in poetry: A national survey of first, second and third graders. *Research in the Teaching of English*. 16(4). 339–54; Kutiper, K. S. 1985. A survey of the adolescent poetry preferences of seventh, eighth, and ninth graders. (Doctoral dissertation, University of Houston. 1985.) *Dissertation Abstracts International*. 47. (02). 0451A; Kutiper, K., & Wilson, P. 1993. Updating poetry preferences: A look at the poetry children really like. *The Reading Teacher*. 47(1). September. 28–35.

22. Kutiper, K., & Wilson, P. 1993.

23. Fisher, C. J. 1993. On becoming a collector. In Taxel, J. (Ed.). 133–36.

24. For additional information about choral speaking, see sources such as: Barchers, S. I. 1994. *Teaching Language Arts: An Integrated Approach.*. Minneapolis/St. Paul: West. 91–96; Trousdale, A. M., & Harris, V. J. 1993. Missing links in literary response: Group interpretation of literature. *Children's Literature in Education*. 24(3). 195–207; McCauley, J. K., & McCauley, D. S. 1992. Using choral reading to promote language learning for ESL students. *The Reading Teacher*. 45(7). 526–33: Miccinati, J. L. 1985. Using prosidic cues to teach oral reading fluency. *The Reading Teacher*. 39(3). 206–12; Norton, D. E. 1993. *The Effective Teaching of Language Arts*. (4th Ed.). New York: Merrill/Macmillan; Tierney, R. J., Readence, J. E., & Dishner, E. K. 1990. *Reading Strategies and Practices: A Compendium*. (3d Ed.). Boston: Allyn & Bacon. 424–28.

25. Scofield, P. 1985. Gold coins entice students to read and write poetry. *The Reading Teacher*. 39(3). December. 371–74.

26. Livingston, M. C. 1976. But is it poetry? *The Horn Book Magazine*. 48(1). February. 24–32; also, Livingston, M. C. 1990. *Climb into the Bell Tower: Essays on Poetry*. New York: Harper & Row. This collection of the poet's writings presents her concern about children producing quality poetry and the role and responsibilities of the teacher of poetry.

27. For additional information about motivating young poets, see sources such as Duthie, C., & Zimet, E. K. 1992. Poetry is like directions for your imagination! *The Reading Teacher*. 46(1). 14–24; Tompkins, G. E. 1994. *Teaching Writing: Balancing Process and Product*. (2d Ed.). New York: Macmillan. 251–99; Janeczko, P. B. 1994. *Poetry from A to Z: A Guide for Young Writers*. New York: Bradbury; Wolk, S. 1994. Adolescents, poetry, and trust. *Language Arts*. 71(2). 108–14.

28. For additional strategies, see sources such as Koch, K. 1970. *Wishes, Lies, and Dreams: Teaching Children to Write Poetry*. New York: Chelsea House. 86, 105, 174, 256; Koch, K. 1973. *Rose, Where Did You Get That Red? Teaching Great Poetry to Children*. New York: Random House; Wilson, L. 1993. Positively Poetry. *Teaching Pre K–8*. 23(3). November/December. 54–55.

29. Taylor, A. 1994. "On the pulse": Exploring poetry through drama. *Children's Literature in Education*. 25(1). 17–28.

30. Harms, J. M., & Lettow, L. J. 1994. Illustrations in poetry volumes: Defining and amplifying meaning. *Language Arts*. 71(2). February. 121–25.

31. For additional ideas about artistic responses with poetry, see sources such as Smith, J. 1976. *Creative Teaching of Reading and Literature in the Elementary School*. Boston: Allyn & Bacon. 308–23; Whitehead, R. 1968. *Children's Literature: Strategies of Teaching*. Englewood Cliffs, N.J.: Prentice-Hall. 120; Seifert, P. 1994. A poetry quilt. *Instructor*. 104. 46–47.

Books with Pictures

The Beauty of the World

A picture book really exists only when a child and a book come together, when the stream that formed in the artist's mind and heart flows through the book and into the mind and heart of the child.

—Marcia Brown

Generally, the largest number of children's books in a library or a bookstore are books with pictures. The books represent a variety of artistic styles and media. They may be decorated with large, colorful, shiny illustrations; simple, black and white line drawings; or pictures in colors of varying intensity. Some books consist only of pictures, others have a few pictures and a verbal text, while others feature pictures that interpret, enhance, replace, decorate, or describe the verbal text. The books may be small enough for a little hand or so large that a child can hold them only while sitting in an adult's lap. The books may be fictional or nonfictional narratives with real or imaginary people, animals, creatures, and personified objects.

Books with pictures are found in all genres of literature. Many individual poems and poetry collections are profusely illustrated. The customs, traditions, and values depicted in folk literature may be enhanced by pictures accompanying the verbal text. Fanciful portrayals help readers visualize fantasy narratives. Pictures of actual humans, animals, or objects enhance or describe realistic fiction. Many nonfiction commentaries are documented and supplemented with photographs, colored illustrations, and black and white sketches. Books with pictures encompass every moral, social, historical, and scientific issue. The content may be simple as in board books or complicated as in classical novels illustrated with a few well-chosen pictures. With such a broad range of content and book design, suitable books with pictures can engage the hearts and stimulate the minds of people of all ages.

Books with pictures are a unique category of literature because visual symbols—and frequently verbal symbols as well—provide the content from which readers create meaning from the books. Depending on the subject and the type of book, visual narratives evoke the book's mood, establish the setting, portray the theme, develop the plot, depict the characters, tell the story, or provide information (dispense knowledge). The ultimate purpose of a book with pictures is to give the viewer an aesthetic experience and to stimulate the mind.

The distinctive artistic characteristics of books with pictures, the visual and verbal characteristics and the relationship of the two narratives, and the classification of books with pictures are highlighted in the first part of the chapter. Next, the chapter describes ways of presenting various types of books with pictures and explains how the books are used in the classroom to help young people appreciate, enjoy, and gain information from the visual and verbal texts. Finally, the chapter concludes with a discussion of the historical development of books with pictures.

DISTINCTIVE ARTISTIC CHARACTERISTICS OF BOOKS WITH PICTURES

Perhaps the finest art many children will encounter is found in books with pictures. Young people who have pleasurable experiences with art in books naturally respond to the art and seek avenues for expressing their aesthetic satisfaction. Both artists and authors communicate ideas, feelings, and information by carefully selecting visual or verbal elements and arranging them appropriately within the narrative. Authors select words and arrange them in sentences and paragraphs, while artists select various artistic elements and media and arrange them to communicate their ideas and feelings. The more we learn about the way artists and authors communicate, the more clearly we can express our aesthetic satisfaction for illustrations in books.

Effective visual communication depends on the artist's ability to combine compatible artistic elements, media, style, and composition in a particular visual message. The following sections will describe each of these components separately to provide a comprehensive overview of the distinctive artistic characteristics of books with pictures, but it is important to remember that the components are interrelated and do not exist in isolation. This information is intended primarily for background information for the adult and might be used informally in a classroom session.

ARTISTIC ELEMENTS

An artist uses various combinations of artistic elements—line, shape and form, color, texture, and space—to create an image. These elements can be compared to the vocabulary of verbal narratives. Individual elements are selected, combined, and arranged with a compatible style and media to evoke thought, emotions, and attitudes through the visual message. As readers look from one visual sequence to another, they gain a holistic impression of the text that may guide their interpretation of the visual narrative.

Line is frequently found in illustrations for children. The artist uses thin or thick, wavy or straight, continuous or broken, bold or delicate lines to express ideas, moods, and shapes or patterns. Bonnie and Arthur Geisert's illustrations in *Haystack* (1995) reflect the ability of the artists to tell their story almost entirely through various straight and curved lines. Note the details achieved through various strokes of the lines. (See the Geisert color plate.) Other artists use crosshatching (small x's) or delicate, almost invisible lines to achieve shading or the desired images.

Shape and form are produced when the lines enclose a space. The shape and form may be geometric, shaded, or free-form and may have sharp or soft edges. Through these elements, objects are highlighted. Look at the way Barbara Porte achieves shape and form in the illustrations in her book *Chickens! Chickens!* (1995). (See the Porte color plate, page 262). Obviously, Stephen Johnson uses this visual element effectively in his book *Alphabet City* (1995).

Color is widely used in juvenile books with pictures. Our world is bombarded with color, and artists freely incorporate it in their illustrations. With its various intensities, hues, and tones, color conveys the emotions and the mood of the characters and often moves the action of the visual narrative. Notice the contrast between the black and white illustrations and the color illustrations in A. B.

Curtiss's *Hallelujah, A Cat Comes Back* (1996) and Keith Faulkner's use of color in *Wide Mouth Frog* (1996). (See the Curtiss color plate, page 263).

Texture projects a rough or smooth surface. Visual texture gives the illusion of these surfaces. Artists achieve texture through repeated patterns and the arrangement of lines and shapes. Note the texture Baker achieves in her collage in *The Story of Rosy Dock* (1995). (See the Baker color plate, page 260). Texture is also evident in the pictures in Diane Stanley and Peter Vennema's *Cleopatra* (1994).

Space is the "air" between and around objects in the illustrations. An artist creates the illusion of space through perspective or the way objects relate to each other. Compare the use of space in Demi's *Buddha* (1996) and Denise Fleming's *Where Once There Was a Wood* (1996). (See the Demi and Fleming color plates, pages 260 and 187).

Artists are aware of the unique characteristics of each element and the visual impact achieved by combining the elements. These characteristics are presented in Figure 8.1 on page 261.[1]

PRINCIPLES OF DESIGN

When planning the artwork for a book, the artist strives to achieve visual balance, variety, and patterns.[2] To achieve a suitable arrangement of images, the artist is guided by, though not restricted to, the principles of design: balance, rhythm/movement, proportion, emphasis, pattern, unity, and variety. Because these principles are compatible with beauty in nature and harmonious living with others, they are natural to use in analyzing a visual composition.

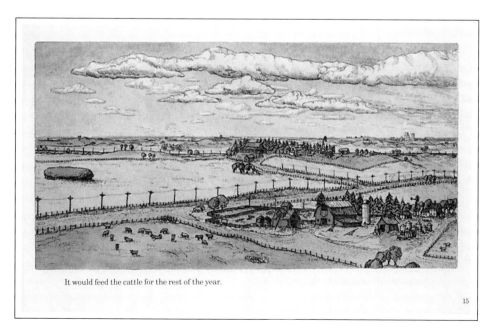

It would feed the cattle for the rest of the year.

15

Arthur Geisert effectively portrays farm life in the early 20th century for Bonnie Geisert's Haystack. *The realistic colored etchings clearly help interpret the author's simple verbal text.*

And then the desert
suddenly blossomed.
Birds and animals appeared.
The air came alive with insects,
and perfumed flowers
grew everywhere.

Jeannie Baker is recognized for her mixed media collage as seen in her book The Story of Rosy Dock. *Her collage landscapes tell the story of the introduction of Rosy Dock to the Australian countryside. What organic materials did she use to construct the photographed realia? How does she achieve that dramatic dimensional effect in her illustrations?*

Demi's Chinese folk art highlights her biography, Buddha. *The artist uses red, green, gold, and blue Chinese paints, ink, and brushes in her paintings. Her large paintings are framed in gold. To achieve movement and balance, she blends small colored sketches into the large paintings. She also arranges the verbal narrative so that it becomes a part of the entire visual composition.*

FIGURE 8.1   Artistic Elements

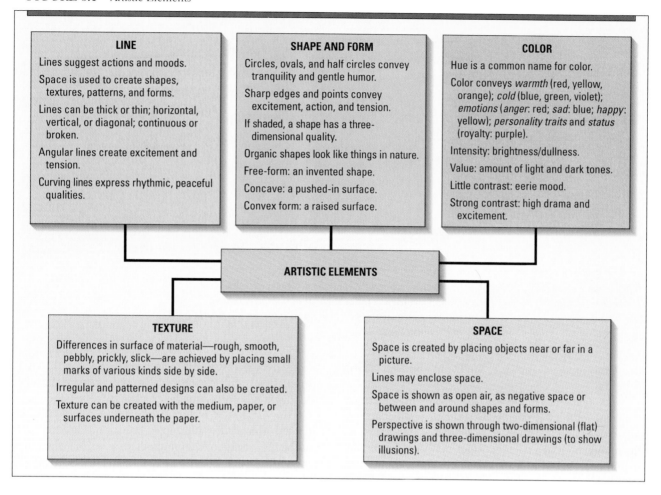

LINE

Lines suggest actions and moods.

Space is used to create shapes, textures, patterns, and forms.

Lines can be thick or thin; horizontal, vertical, or diagonal; continuous or broken.

Angular lines create excitement and tension.

Curving lines express rhythmic, peaceful qualities.

SHAPE AND FORM

Circles, ovals, and half circles convey tranquility and gentle humor.

Sharp edges and points convey excitement, action, and tension.

If shaded, a shape has a three-dimensional quality.

Organic shapes look like things in nature.

Free-form: an invented shape.

Concave: a pushed-in surface.

Convex form: a raised surface.

COLOR

Hue is a common name for color.

Color conveys *warmth* (red, yellow, orange); *cold* (blue, green, violet); *emotions* (*anger*: red; *sad*: blue; *happy*: yellow); *personality traits* and *status* (royalty: purple).

Intensity: brightness/dullness.

Value: amount of light and dark tones.

Little contrast: eerie mood.

Strong contrast: high drama and excitement.

ARTISTIC ELEMENTS

TEXTURE

Differences in surface of material—rough, smooth, pebbly, prickly, slick—are achieved by placing small marks of various kinds side by side.

Irregular and patterned designs can also be created.

Texture can be created with the medium, paper, or surfaces underneath the paper.

SPACE

Space is created by placing objects near or far in a picture.

Lines may enclose space.

Space is shown as open air, as negative space or between and around shapes and forms.

Perspective is shown through two-dimensional (flat) drawings and three-dimensional drawings (to show illusions).

Using the principles of design as a guide, the artist prepares a *visual composition* (the arrangement of details in a picture on a page). The artist uses different types of *balance* to create interest and project the desired impressions. In *symmetrical balance*, both halves of the composition are identical; one is the mirror of the other. Symmetrical balance projects a formal feeling of security and peace, but used too frequently throughout the book, the illustrations may become boring. In *asymmetrical* or *informal balance*, the sides are balanced, but are not identical. Asymmetrical balance expresses action, informality, and variety and is usually more interesting to the viewer than symmetrical balance. In *radial balance*, lines or shapes move away from a central point; radial balance is often symmetrical and projects the same feelings as symmetrical balance, but has a broader visual effect. Notice the way Barbara Porte achieves balance in her illustrations for *Chickens! Chickens!* (1995). (See the Porte color plate, page 262).

Rhythm projects a feeling of movement. Visual patterns, flowing lines, or gradual changes in the spacing of shapes or colors create rhythm or movement. To give a sense of rhythm, the artist uses regular, flowing movements or irregular or alternating movements. These movements are achieved through vertical, horizontal, diagonal, curving lines and shapes. See David Wiesner's *Tuesday* (1993), page 304.

Visual patterns are the repeated arrangements of visual elements. The patterns can be regular or irregular placements or the gradual use of lines, shapes, or colors. Large patterns unify an image. Small patterns are used sparingly to add interest to the visual. A. B. Curtiss's illustrations for *Hallelujah, A Cat Came Back* (1996) are an example of the effective use of patterns in borders. (See the Curtiss color plate, page 263.)

Emphasis is used to capture and hold the viewer's attention and to highlight thoughts and ideas. It is achieved through a dominant feature, a focal point or center of interest. Contrasting sizes, shapes, or colors are

Barbara Porte arranges colored silhouettes of chickens throughout her book Chickens! Chickens! *The shapes reinforce the theme of the book and connect the verbal and visual narratives to help achieve balance in the visual compositions. Porte uses oil-based enamel house paint for her colorful, naive illustrations. What do you notice in the illustrations?*

frequently used for emphasis. See Demi's *Buddha* (1996), page 260.

Proportion refers to the way part of something relates to the whole or the way one object relates to another according to size, amount, number, or degree. When artists use the human body as a reference, they may show it with normal dimensions or as a caricature (exaggerated and distorted). Depending on the content to be portrayed, an artist may depict idealized proportions. Artists may use the expected scale for an object or emphasize its importance by changing the size, scale, or proportion of a particular feature. Dan Yaccarino experiments with proportion, point of view, and space in *If I Had a Robot* (1996).

Unity of design gives the viewer a feeling that all visual components are compatible and work together. Illustrators achieve unity through *repetition* (repeating the visual element), *simplicity* (unifying an image by using one major color, shape, or element), *harmony* (using related colors, textures, or materials), *theme and variation* (showing the subject or topic of a work of art in several ways), *proximity* (clustering parts together), and *continuity* (aligning edges of forms so the eye moves from one part to another in a logical order). Because a totally unified illustration might be dull, artists frequently use a *variety* of contrasting elements to add interest. Variety can be expressed subtly by making changes in texture or color or more obviously by using different materials, colors, or sizes.

The *point of view* is the angle from which the viewer sees an object or scene. In Pat Schories's *Mouse Around*

(1991), for example, the viewer sees the action through a mousehole and obtains a close-up view. In Robert McCloskey's *Make Way for Ducklings* (1969), the viewer has an aerial view of the action and may feel more detached from it. Looking up to the action or object may cause the viewer to feel intimidated, as occurs when looking at the wolf in Ed Young's *Lon Po Po* (1989). Artists may change their point of view from one visual to another to keep the viewer's attention, to show different ways of looking at images, and to stimulate the viewer's imagination.

Various cultural art traditions use different perspectives. In the traditional Western perspective, for example, larger shapes seem closer because they are usually placed in the foreground, and roads appear to narrow as they recede into the distance. In contrast, in Egyptian tomb painting, the figures' feet and faces are shown in profile, and in traditional Chinese landscape painting, a figure coming toward the viewer is tiny, almost lost. Art representing the culture reflected in a book frequently appears in juvenile literature and merits discussion to guide young people's understanding of the visual message. See Chapters 3 and 9.

ARTISTIC STYLE

Have you ever looked at a book and immediately said, "I like this book"? The content, artistic elements, and media may be similar to others, yet something evokes an immediate response. Frequently, the elusive feature of a book that sets it apart from all others is the artist's imprint on the

A. B. Curtiss uses a pen and stylus to create the 19th-century style engravings for his book, Hallelujah, A Cat Comes Back. *His yellow Victorian borders highlight the decorative frame that surrounds each detailed black-and-white drawing. The artist's limited use of color enhances his unique line drawings.*

content—the artist's signature or style. Nodelman defines the artistic style as the "effect of all the aspects of a work considered together, the way in which an illustration or text seems distinct or even unique."[3] The artist's style emerges from the artistic elements, principles of design, medium, and details in the visual text.

Scholars have identified at least fifteen artistic styles, but not all are typically used in juvenile books with pictures. Therefore, this book will consider the three major categories of styles found in juvenile books: Historical Art, Cultural Art, and Original Art:[4]

Historical Art styles are the styles developed during a particular time or place. For example, Renaissance art developed during the fifteenth through seventeenth centuries. It is a realistic style that emphasizes forms, proportioning of space, and dramatic lighting; Paul Zelinsky uses this style for his illustrations of the Grimms' *Rumpelstiltskin* (1986). Twentieth-century art also depicts the intellectual and emotional ideas of the

artists. Twentieth-century styles include Expressionism, which emphasizes emotion and uses intense, shocking colors, as in John Steptoe's *Stevie* (1969); and Surrealism, which mixes realism with bizarre, dislocated imagery, as in Molly Bang's *The Grey Lady and the Strawberry Snatcher* (1980). (See the Bang color plate, page 130.) Kiefer has identified eight other distinct periods of art history.[5]

Cultural Art styles reflect the art prevalent in a culture, especially rural or tribal societies. Some examples include naive art, which uses simple forms, childlike perspective, and bright colors, as in Barbara Cooney's illustrations for Donald Hall's *Ox-Cart Man* (1979); and folk art, which reflects the images typically associated with a particular religion, ethnic group, or geographic region. Asian art is characterized by linear and spatial effects, painting on silk, and fine paper and inks, as in Demi's illustrations for *Buddha*. (See the Demi color plate, page 260.)

Original Art styles are associated with a particular person. It is possible to identify the artist by looking at the art used in a book. Typically, artists feature certain content and artistic elements in their illustrations. Their personality, creative talent, and mastery of the craft influence these selections. Dr. Seuss, for example, is closely associated with humorous content and a cartoon art style; Beatrix Potter used watercolor effectively to realistically portray her fantasy animals; Virginia Burton is noted for the perfect unity she achieved between her visual and verbal texts.

While classifying art styles is important, novice art critics become confused when they try to identify each style available to artists. To add to this frustration, some illustrators use more than one style in a particular book. A review of outstanding juvenile books with pictures reveals that five artistic styles are used most frequently: *realistic art, expressionistic art, impressionistic art, humorous art,* and *folk art.* Art styles such as Cubism, Surrealism, and Pointillism are occasionally used in juvenile books at this time. (For information about Chris Van Allsburg, an artist with a distinctive style, see Did You Know? on page 264.) The distinctive features of the five popular styles are described in Figure 8.2 on page 266. Titles representing each style are listed in the bibliography at the end of the book.

MEDIA AND GRAPHIC TECHNIQUES USED BY ARTISTS

Contemporary artists make many decisions before beginning a series of visual narratives. A major decision is the selection of the materials she or he will use as the medium of

Did You Know About
CHRIS VAN ALLSBURG?

Let's go to the North Pole on the widow's broom, watch the wretched stone, or play Jumanji's game. Maybe you would like to play in Abdul Gasazi's garden or share Ben's dream or solve the mysteries of Harris Burdick. Perhaps the stranger will tell you about the two bad ants or how the Z was zapped. We can visit these places and experience these events with our guide, Chris Van Allsburg.

Two of his first six books won Caldecott medals—*Jumanji* and *The Polar Express*. Van Allsburg planned to get a law degree, but in his sophomore year in college, he decided to enroll in art classes "on a lark." Five years later he had a degree in art, had studied at the Rhode Island School of Design, and had begun a career in sculpture. For relaxation he drew pictures. His wife, Lisa, an elementary teacher, encouraged him to show the drawings to a publisher, and his career as an artist and author of juvenile books began.

Van Allsburg uses folk literature motifs, such as the quest, the journey, and adventures away or within the home. He is noted for

the mysterious and the puzzling. Reality and fantasy are intermingled in his verbal and visual narratives. His natural artistic talent, early training, and experience as a sculptor are apparent in his outstanding artwork. Surrealistic style is his trademark. A little dog appears in his books. Van Allsburg varies his medium from black and white conte pencil to colored conte crayons, to pastel crayon and ink and paints. His verbal narratives are simple with flat characters, yet they have intriguing plots and thought-provoking themes. In some of his books, such as *The Polar Express*, he employs a dreamlike quality. In others, such as *Jumanji*, dreams become reality that the reader must accept. In *The Widow's Broom* (see the Van Allsburg color plate, page 265), he surprises his readers, and in *The Wretched Stone*, he addresses a social problem.

Van Allsburg's books are just as likely to be found on an adult's coffee table as in a kindergarten or senior high classroom. They speak to us on many levels because they make us stop, reflect, and react with vigor!

---

expression. Artists use *media* (materials, processes, and techniques) to express their ideas and information visually.[6] When selecting the medium, the artist ponders questions such as these:

Should I draw the pictures in inks, pastels, crayons, or charcoal to help the viewers interpret the text?

Will the paintings be more stunning if I use watercolor, gouache, tempera, or oil paints?

Would photography, collage, or a graphic reproduction technique, such as woodcuts, stone lithography, or scratchboard, achieve the desired visual statement?

What feelings or information do I want to communicate in the visual expression?

What materials, processes, and techniques do I enjoy using?

What artistic design and style are compatible with the particular medium or technique I have chosen?

By wisely selecting and competently combining all the artistic features, the illustrator can effectively interpret, enhance, replace, and/or embellish the verbal narrative.

Many artists use a particular medium or technique in almost all their books; Leo Lionni, for example, uses collage, as in *Swimmy* (1963), and Emily McCully often uses watercolor, as in her impressionistic art in *The Pirate Queen* (1995). (See the McCully color plate, page 267.) Others like to combine media to express the spirit of the narratives,

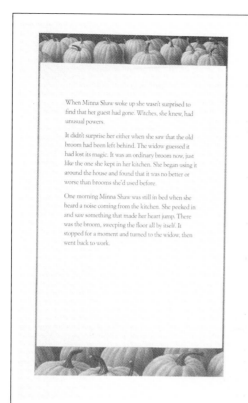

When Minna Shaw woke up she wasn't surprised to find that her guest had gone. Witches, she knew, had unusual powers.

It didn't surprise her either when she saw that the old broom had been left behind. The widow guessed it had lost its magic. It was an ordinary broom now, just like the one she kept in her kitchen. She began using it around the house and found that it was no better or worse than brooms she'd used before.

One morning Minna Shaw was still in bed when she heard a noise coming from the kitchen. She peeked in and saw something that made her heart jump. There was the broom, sweeping the floor all by itself. It stopped for a moment and turned to the widow, then went back to work.

Chris Van Allsburg realistically portrays the setting and the characters in his book The Widow's Broom. *The grainy texture shown in the pictures is a distinguishing feature of the sepia litho pencils used by the artist. Throughout the book, he uses the same technique to frame his verbal narrative. The illustrations are filled with action as seen in this picture with the movement of the broom and the reaction of the widow to the broom. Why does this broom move like that? Can this broom perform other jobs?*

as Jerry Pinkney's pencil and watercolor paintings do in Patricia McKissack's *Mirandy and Brother Wind* (1988).

Figures 8.3 and 8.4 on pages 268 and 269 were developed to help adults identify the materials and graphic techniques used in juvenile books with pictures. When appropriate, the information should be discussed informally with students. Figure 8.3 describes the various art forms and media used in juvenile books with pictures, while Figure 8.4 describes photography, collage, and graphic reproduction techniques. The printing process sometimes blurs or erases the distinguishing features of the medium. The bibliography lists representative books created in a specific medium or technique.[7]

PHYSICAL FEATURES OF A BOOK

Illustrators have a limited space to communicate; therefore, the physical features of a book—the cover, the title page, the size and shape of the book, the endpapers, the typography, and the paper—are chosen carefully to complement and reinforce the artistic and verbal narratives. The aesthetic appeal and overall design of the book emerge when the narratives and physical features are combined.

Designers realize the hard or soft *cover* chosen for the book influences its visual impact. The cover advertises the book and entices the reader to pick it up. An appealing cover, which is often an illustration from the book, will capture a person's attention. It is still true that "a book is judged by its cover."

How many books have you read because you were attracted by the cover? The cover usually includes an enticing visual, the title, and the names of the creators. The visual gives the reader interesting information about the text. Based on our knowledge about the type of book an author writes or the visuals created by the artists, we can predict the genre of the book. By looking at the cover, reading the title, or looking at the picture, we anticipate the subject. By directing young people's attention to the cover, adults can elicit predictions of events and characters and stimulate anticipation of the content. Hardcover books frequently have a *dust cover*, a paper jacket folded over the book with an attractive picture, the title, and the creators' names. Many librarians place a protective cover over the dust cover and attach it to the book. Some book covers are plain, and even adults enjoy looking at an enticing dust cover.

The *endpapers* are attached to the inside of the front and back covers. The paper is usually heavier than the paper used for the pages. Some endpapers are plain; others contain a design. A wise artist uses the endpapers to provide additional information about the book. Virginia Burton

FIGURE 8.2 Artistic Styles in Juvenile Books with Pictures

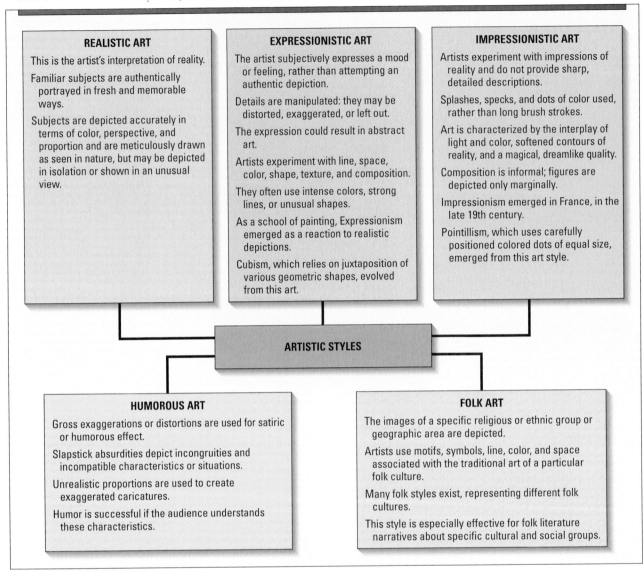

REALISTIC ART

This is the artist's interpretation of reality.

Familiar subjects are authentically portrayed in fresh and memorable ways.

Subjects are depicted accurately in terms of color, perspective, and proportion and are meticulously drawn as seen in nature, but may be depicted in isolation or shown in an unusual view.

EXPRESSIONISTIC ART

The artist subjectively expresses a mood or feeling, rather than attempting an authentic depiction.

Details are manipulated: they may be distorted, exaggerated, or left out.

The expression could result in abstract art.

Artists experiment with line, space, color, shape, texture, and composition.

They often use intense colors, strong lines, or unusual shapes.

As a school of painting, Expressionism emerged as a reaction to realistic depictions.

Cubism, which relies on juxtaposition of various geometric shapes, evolved from this art.

IMPRESSIONISTIC ART

Artists experiment with impressions of reality and do not provide sharp, detailed descriptions.

Splashes, specks, and dots of color used, rather than long brush strokes.

Art is characterized by the interplay of light and color, softened contours of reality, and a magical, dreamlike quality.

Composition is informal; figures are depicted only marginally.

Impressionism emerged in France, in the late 19th century.

Pointillism, which uses carefully positioned colored dots of equal size, emerged from this art style.

ARTISTIC STYLES

HUMOROUS ART

Gross exaggerations or distortions are used for satiric or humorous effect.

Slapstick absurdities depict incongruities and incompatible characteristics or situations.

Unrealistic proportions are used to create exaggerated caricatures.

Humor is successful if the audience understands these characteristics.

FOLK ART

The images of a specific religious or ethnic group or geographic area are depicted.

Artists use motifs, symbols, line, color, and space associated with the traditional art of a particular folk culture.

Many folk styles exist, representing different folk cultures.

This style is especially effective for folk literature narratives about specific cultural and social groups.

drew the development of transportation on the endpapers of *Mike Mulligan and His Steamshovel* (1939). Maurice Sendak's designs on the endpapers of *Where the Wild Things Are* (1963) set the stage for Max's fantasy adventure with the "Wild Things." Both Les Tait for Shulamith Oppenheim's *The White Stone in the Castle Wall* (1995) and Holly Meade for Nancy Van Laan's *Sleep, Sleep, Sleep: A Lullaby for Little Ones Around the World* (1995) included maps on the endpapers of their books. Also see Alice Provensen's endpaper in *My Fellow Americans* (1995) for a lesson in American history.

The weight and quality of *paper* selected by the publisher influence the visual impact of a book. Artists prefer that the publisher use high-quality paper to highlight their visuals, but publishers may use lighter-weight, lower-quality paper to lower the cost of the book. Compare the paper in a softcover book with that in a hardcover version. In addition to the cover, lighter-weight, lower-quality paper is used in paperback editions. Usually, with lighter-weight, lower-quality paper, the pictures and type bleed through from one page to another.

Finally, when a book is bound, the pages are sewn on the side or in the center in one or more sections called *signatures*. A standard signature consists of sixteen pages. The pages of a book are arranged in a particular order; then they are printed on the front and back of a large sheet of paper.

Emily McCully filled her impressionistic watercolor paintings with action to portray the fictionalized history of an Irish pirate in her book, The Pirate Queen. *The artists includes action and movement in some pictures; other pictures show the quiet Irish countryside. How does McCully use artistic elements and principles of design to portray the protagonist's personality?*

After the pages are cut, the signatures are arranged in the appropriate order and bound. (Additional information about book production is included in Appendix B.)

A book's message can be enhanced by its design, which ideally is planned by the artist and/or the publisher's book designer. The design also includes the appropriate placement of the visual sequences within the verbal narrative. To achieve this, the verbal manuscript is separated into individual events or meaning-bearing passages, the visual message portrayed in each visual sequence is considered, and a suitable size for the individual pictures and the arrangement of the pictures on single and/or double-page spreads are determined.

Artists and designers visually communicate with their viewers by the shape of the pictures and the book. Borders are used to highlight details and focus objectively on particular objects. They may provide additional information about the content and suggest the action of the verbal text. The artist

may use various borders to present a different perspective. For example, in her book *Armadillo Rodeo* (1995), Jan Brett frames her double-page illustrations in borders that look like stitched leather used for boots. (See the Brett color plate, page 270.) *Typography* is chosen to highlight certain aspects of the visual or verbal narratives. The artist may use the type to portray part of the visual message or to balance and unify the words and pictures. A legible typeface of appropriate size for the text is used in the visual sequences. The selected typography also provides the desired margins between words and pictures. Unusual and innovative typography was used in Virginia Kroll's *Naomi Knows It's Springtime* (1993) and Sally Noll's *Lucky Morning* (1994).

Jon Scieszka and Lane Smith successfully manipulated all principles of design in their popular book *The Stinky Cheese Man & Other Fairly Stupid Tales* (1992). This amusing, thought-provoking Caldecott honor book does not use the standard format and composition generally found in books with pictures and has considerable visual impact as a result. (See the Scieszka color plate, page 271.)[8]

◊ THE VISUAL AND VERBAL CHARACTERISTICS OF BOOKS WITH PICTURES

The success of a book with pictures depends on the creator's ability to design unique, yet compatible visual and verbal narratives (text). Artists and authors develop their narratives by using *individual language* (words and images), arranged in acceptable *compositions*, and portrayed in an appropriate style. The harmonious narratives evoke emotional and cognitive responses from the reader and lead to a transaction between reader and text.

This section first examines visual and verbal narratives separately and then discusses the relationships between them. How individuals read the visual and verbal narratives is examined next. Finally, the classifications of books with pictures are identified.

VISUAL AND VERBAL NARRATIVES

Books with pictures are created around visual and/or verbal texts or narratives that help the audience understand the story or identify pertinent information. Particular elements (language or images), arrangements (compositions), and styles are used differently in visual and verbal narratives to accomplish this goal.[9]

Visual Narratives
Whether illustrating fiction or nonfiction literature, the artist's interpretations are reflected in the artistic elements,

FIGURE 8.3 Varieties of Art Forms: Media for Paintings and Drawings

VARIETIES OF ART FORMS

PAINTING

Paintings in two-dimensional images have height and width and are flat.

Available in many forms, paint can be applied to wet or dry, shiny or rough surfaces (paper, canvas, wood) with large or small brushes, swabs, palette knives, rollers, sponges, and other tools.

Paint is a mixture of pigment and a binding medium (oil, water, glue, egg, wax, latex); it may be thick or thin, liquid or paste.

Paint is matte or shiny; it may be transparent or translucent (can see through) or opaque (cannot see through).

Colors vary in intensity and brightness depending on how they are diluted and applied.

Watercolor: Powdered color paint mixed with water; applied in tinting, shading, and washes in a light-to-dark sequence on dry or wet paper. Transparent; often surface can be seen beneath, because clear brush strokes are visible within individual pictures. Term also means artwork done with this paint.

Tempera: Water-based paint that is thick and opaque; pigment is mixed with glue, egg yolk (egg tempera), or another binder; covers and mixes like oil paints; softens and mixes with any dry paint underneath. Easy to brush on; dries rapidly to a dull, matte finish. Colors are bright and strong. Poster paint is a type of tempera.

Gouache (gwäsh): Mixture of color pigments with a white filler or with chalk and water. Opaque because of the white pigment and thick layers of color; looks similar to oil paint and tempera when printed.

Oil: Color mixed with linseed oil; thinned with turpentine and mixed with other colors. Thick and opaque, but can be diluted; add to water to create a transparent glaze. Wet paint will not mix with dry paint underneath. Applied from tubes with brush or palette knife on canvas, board, or paper.

Acrylic (a-CRILL-ik): Liquid acrylic plastic is used to bind color pigment; similar to oil, but dissolves in water before it dries. Acrylic paint produces vibrant, almost shocking colors. Oil and acrylic dry slowly; can be manipulated, changed, and covered with varnish or gel.

DRAWING

Flat, two-dimensional images are drawn on paper, wood, or canvas surfaces.

Graphite pencils (lead pencils): Number of pencil indicates line drawn, e.g., 6B (soft, dark), 9H (hard, light). Shading, cross-hatching, and blending can be done with a sharp or dull pencil point. Grainy texture seen in lines. Lines can be removed by rubbing eraser over them.

Colored pencils: Similar to graphite pencils, except with overlaying colors; produce clean unhesitating lines. With a conte pencil, the artist rubs dust from the pencil and then dips the pencil into the dust, using the pencil like a brush to blend the dust and the lines made by the pencil.

Charcoal: A dark-colored form of carbon made from vegetable or animal substances. Available in natural sticks (vine charcoal), compressed sticks, or pencils. Soft charcoal used for dark values, hard charcoal for light values; shades created by blending areas with a cloth or finger; lines removed by a kneaded eraser. Produces black, grainy lines, depending on roughness of paper. Textured papers best.

Pastel crayons (colored chalk): A paste composed of a color ground and compounded with an aqueous binder. Produces a "soft and furry," grainy texture. Can be used on wet or dry paper. Sharp lines made by dipping chalk in water or liquid starch; like charcoal, soft and smears easily. A clear fixative spray protects drawings from smears. Term refers to picture made with pastel crayons; also a tint of color.

Oil pastels: A greasy, sticklike medium. Colors blended on paper or layered. Crayon-pastel and pastel-oil are made of chalky pigments mixed with wax and oil.

Crayon: Stick of colored wax that can be used on the pointed end or on the broadside to show linear design, texture, and surface details. Can be drawn lightly or pressed hard. Etchings, rubbings, and crayon resists are made with crayons.

Pen and ink: A wet medium used for drawings. Many sizes and different kinds of pen points are made from natural materials and flexible or rigid steel points pushed into a handle. Pens, such as ballpoints, felt-tip markers, and fountain pens have their own ink supply. Inks available in many colors. Permanent ink and India ink will not smear.

Wash: Thin ink applied with brush, swab, or sponge to combine lines and shapes.

FIGURE 8.4 Collage, Photography, and Graphic Techniques

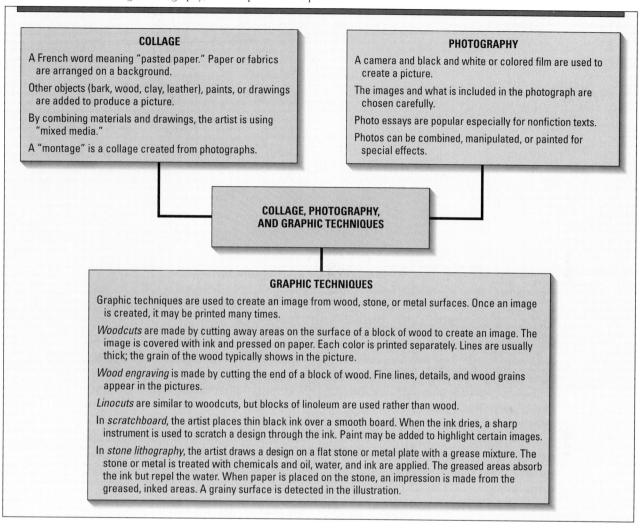

COLLAGE

A French word meaning "pasted paper." Paper or fabrics are arranged on a background.

Other objects (bark, wood, clay, leather), paints, or drawings are added to produce a picture.

By combining materials and drawings, the artist is using "mixed media."

A "montage" is a collage created from photographs.

PHOTOGRAPHY

A camera and black and white or colored film are used to create a picture.

The images and what is included in the photograph are chosen carefully.

Photo essays are popular especially for nonfiction texts.

Photos can be combined, manipulated, or painted for special effects.

COLLAGE, PHOTOGRAPHY, AND GRAPHIC TECHNIQUES

GRAPHIC TECHNIQUES

Graphic techniques are used to create an image from wood, stone, or metal surfaces. Once an image is created, it may be printed many times.

Woodcuts are made by cutting away areas on the surface of a block of wood to create an image. The image is covered with ink and pressed on paper. Each color is printed separately. Lines are usually thick; the grain of the wood typically shows in the picture.

Wood engraving is made by cutting the end of a block of wood. Fine lines, details, and wood grains appear in the pictures.

Linocuts are similar to woodcuts, but blocks of linoleum are used rather than wood.

In *scratchboard*, the artist places thin black ink over a smooth board. When the ink dries, a sharp instrument is used to scratch a design through the ink. Paint may be added to highlight certain images.

In *stone lithography*, the artist draws a design on a flat stone or metal plate with a grease mixture. The stone or metal is treated with chemicals and oil, water, and ink are applied. The greased areas absorb the ink but repel the water. When paper is placed on the stone, an impression is made from the greased, inked areas. A grainy surface is detected in the illustration.

media, style, and principles of design (composition) used to develop the visual narrative.

When pictures accompany or tell a fictional story, they highlight the conventions of theme, plot, characterization, setting, and point of view in the visual text. Through a series of pictures, the artist develops the events of the story by chronologically depicting the characters' actions. Each visual sequence shows a clear progression of movement through carefully paced events filled with suspense and surprises. As is typical of a well-developed verbal narrative, a theme is developed throughout the visual sequences, and all conflicts and details are satisfactorily concluded at the end of the story. Visual narratives portray emotions in overt or subtle ways; for example, the intensity of the colors frequently develops the mood. We see this in David Kirk's colorful and hilarious illustrations in *Miss Spider's Wedding*. (See the Kirk color plate, page 271.) When the artist changes the size and shape of the pictures, a dramatic element is added. While readers feel comfortable with a familiar context, they also enjoy predicting events. If the audience cares about what is happening to the characters, they are interested in following the storyline.

Books with pictures are also found in nonfiction literature. Concept books, such as alphabet, counting, or simple concept books, which are intended primarily for the youngest child, contain one or two words or a limited text and depend primarily on the visual narrative. Other nonfiction literature effectively uses illustrations and photographs to inform, expand, enhance, document, or supplement a verbal narrative. For example, Lloyd Bloom's illustrations highlight the intense emotions depicted by David Adler in *One Yellow Daffodil: A Hanukkah Story* (1995), and Marjory Dressler's photographs show the reactions of children as they listen to the tales of a headless

Jan Brett tells another story by framing the art in the borders of Armadillo Rodeo. *In bright pen and watercolor paintings, the artist highlights bluebonnets, scenes from Texas, and the red boots that are important to the rodeo girl and the armadillo. Can you "read" the pictures and follow both stories?*

horseman in Kate Waters's *The Mysterious Horseman: An Adventure in Prairietown, 1836* (1994). The living museum at Conner Prairie, Indiana, is the setting for Waters's photo-essay. Dressler's photographs and Waters's narrative also bring to life the lifestyle of pioneers living in a frontier village. The bibliography presents outstanding examples of informational storybooks and photo-essays. Whether the visual text replaces or enhances the verbal narrative, the visual details must represent authentic facts and accurately portray the setting, subject, and content presented in the book. Frequently, the books include legends, graphs, maps, or photographs to document the accuracy of the information. Except for informational storybooks and some photo-essays, nonfiction books with pictures do not adhere to fictional story conventions.

Before creating illustrations for a book, the artist considers the intended audience and the content of the book. Then he or she selects artistic elements, style, media, and compositions that will appropriately depict the verbal narrative. The reader's ability to understand the information portrayed is an indication of the success of a visual narrative.

Verbal Narratives

Verbal narratives depend on the author's choice and arrangement of words, phrases, sentences, and paragraphs. Fiction writers focus on story conventions such as the theme, plot, characterization, setting, style, and point of view. Except in illustrated books, plot and character development may be limited in books with pictures. Typically, the author uses a narrative style of writing and logical se-

quence of time and reaches a satisfactory conclusion through linear movement of the text. Many books with pictures contain only thirty-two pages (or two signatures); therefore, the author must select the language carefully. Because of the length restrictions, the narratives are short and may be a bit choppy. If the author describes the setting, it is usually integral to the text. To highlight the sounds of the language, authors use various stylistic devices, such as repetition or rhyme. Selected images and languages evoke the imagination and emotions and draw the person into the spirit of the text.

Information books give the audience adequate coverage of a selected topic. Frequently, the author uses an expository style of writing to accurately present the specific content. The author may describe the subject in a few words or in simple sentences. Occasionally, in information books with pictures, the author uses a narrative style, and the illustrations enhance, interpret, or supplement the verbal narrative. Whether the author uses a narrative or an expository style, the narrative must be interesting to the intended audience. (Additional information about expository text structure appears in Chapter 6.)

The Relationship between the Visual and Verbal Narratives

When a book depends equally on visual and verbal narratives to tell a story or provide adequate information, the two texts must present a sense of "unity" and cooperation. When the visual and verbal texts are combined, two languages come together. Each language cooperates with,

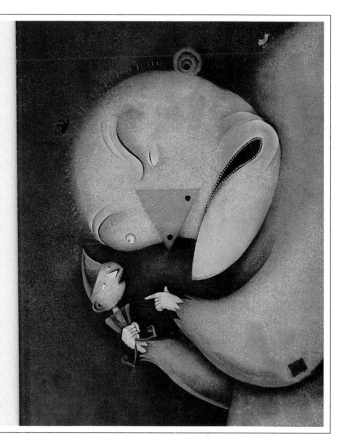

JACK'S STORY

Once upon a time **there was a Giant. The Giant squeezed Jack** and said, "TELL ME A BETTER STORY OR I WILL GRIND YOUR BONES TO MAKE MY BREAD. AND WHEN YOUR STORY IS FINISHED, I WILL GRIND YOUR BONES TO MAKE MY BREAD ANYWAY! HO, HO, HO." The Giant laughed an ugly laugh. Jack thought, "He'll kill me if I do. He'll kill me if I don't. There's only one way to get out of this." Jack cleared his throat, and then began his story.

Once upon a time there was a Giant. The Giant squeezed Jack and said, "TELL ME A BETTER STORY OR I WILL GRIND YOUR BONES TO MAKE MY BREAD. AND WHEN YOUR STORY IS FINISHED, I WILL GRIND YOUR BONES TO MAKE MY BREAD ANYWAY! HO, HO, HO." The Giant laughed an ugly laugh. Jack thought, "He'll kill me if I do. He'll kill me if I don't. There's only one way to get out of this." Jack cleared his throat, and then began his story. Once upon a time there was a Giant. The Giant squeezed Jack and said, "TELL ME A BETTER STORY OR I WILL GRIND YOUR BONES TO MAKE MY BREAD. AND WHEN YOUR STORY IS FINISHED, I WILL GRIND YOUR BONES TO MAKE MY BREAD ANYWAY! HO, HO, HO." The Giant laughed an ugly laugh. Jack thought, "He'll kill me if I do. He'll kill me if I don't. There's only one way to get out of this." Jack cleared his throat, and then began his story.

Lane Smith's abstract pictures for Jon Scieszka's The Stinky Cheese Man and Other Fairly Stupid Tales *were "rendered in oil and vinegar." Smith's mixed media collage is compatible with the verbal narrative. The book contains rearranged format, strange type, a confused story and weird pictures. "Grind your bones to make my bread?" How do you render a picture with oil and vinegar?*

David Kirk's bright green, yellow, red, and blue oil paintings enhance the verbal narrative of his book, Miss Spider's Wedding. *Kirk fills the stylized paintings with details and a witty verse printed in a unique format. Wonder why Holley calls Miss Spider the "fairest creature in all the world?"*

elaborates on, expands, and perhaps interferes with the other. When we read the book, we take the individual clues, combine them, and develop a comprehensive interpretation of the entire narrative.

Visual texts clarify or explain details not given in the verbal text, such as a character's physical appearance or behavior.[10] By providing details about the setting, for example, the visual text helps the reader understand the terrain the character must overcome. Visual texts can also deviate from the verbal text to expand on ideas or information that is only suggested in the verbal text.

The artist and author blend the two languages to produce the most powerful impact on the audience. First, they decide the content of their respective texts. Then, they select compatible styles that will express the joint message. Finally, the separate narratives are laid out together page by page to make the subject meaningful to the audience. The proper arrangement of words and pictures strengthens and supports each text; indeed, the proper placement of the visual sequence within the verbal text distinguishes an outstanding book from a mediocre one. When the artist and author are different people, frequently the author writes the verbal text before the illustrations are created. Then the artist reads the verbal narrative, selects the content to include in the illustrations, and determines what artistic style, media, and composition will highlight the verbal text. Generally, an artist would not use abstract art, for example, to illustrate a narrative about a historical event.

People react differently to visual and verbal texts. Some find the visual text more interesting, while others prefer the verbal text. For this reason, young people need to encounter both texts and develop verbal and visual literacy. (Suitable strategies to enhance students' visual literacy are presented later in this chapter.)

READING VERBAL AND VISUAL NARRATIVES

Readers (viewers, listeners) use different procedures to "read" verbal and visual narratives. As we read the words and pictures, we search for different clues to expand and refine the information gained from each text. We expect the texts to be compatible and to help us arrive at an intelligent interpretation of the whole book. Our schema (prior experiences and knowledges) strengthens the personal interpretations we construct from the narratives. A truly outstanding book with pictures evokes emotional reactions, which stimulate aesthetic responses, a vital reason for reading a book.

Recently, scholars in various academic areas have focused on the process of reading verbal and visual narratives.[11] They generally assume that when we "read" the visual narrative, we receive the content in a holistic, surface impression. As our eyes move from left-to-right, up-and-down the pictures, we simultaneously begin to focus on certain visual elements (clues) such as color, line, shape, texture, space, and composition. As our eyes move in random fashion from the whole picture to specific clues, we detect the movement of objects within the picture; when we return to the picture as a whole, we combine those details, perceive the contents, and comprehend the visual text.[12] As we proceed through the book, we repeat this process and constantly move from one narrative to the other, searching for additional clues that help us make adequate connections and impressions. At the same time, our eyes move through the verbal narrative in a linear progression. As we identify and combine verbal clues, such as words, sentences, paragraphs, and written mechanics, we formulate a cohesive message. To these verbal clues, we connect our previous knowledge, make predictions, add to the communication, and construct meaning from the narrative.

Even when reading a book alone, we frequently scan the pictures before reading the verbal text. After reading the verbal text, our eyes often return to the pictures before moving to the next page. In English books with pictures, the words are frequently placed on the left-hand side of the page; then, suitable pictures are arranged with the text. When a picture and text are placed across two pages (a double-page spread), usually the picture begins on the left page and continues across to the right page. This arrangement allows the reader to look briefly at the picture, read the text, and then return to the picture before continuing the narrative. When more than one picture appears on a page, the reader spends more time reading the pages of the book. In some cases, the visual narrative interferes with the natural flow of the verbal text, creating comprehension problems. In general, though, we have no difficulty moving from one text to another.[13]

Remarkably, young children can weave together the visual and verbal narratives and eagerly request books with pictures. A person's schema and purposes for reading influence what he or she chooses to recognize in the narratives. This selection affects the way the individual reacts to a book and the process by which he or she draws meaning from it.

◊ CLASSIFYING BOOKS WITH PICTURES

Books with pictures contain diverse subject matter, which determines the visual medium and style used by the artist and the verbal text structure used by the author. We classify books with pictures in two general ways. First, books are classified according to the space given to the visual and verbal narratives, respectively. Second, the content of a book also determines its classification.

Classifying Books with Pictures According to the Visual and Verbal Narratives

The easiest way to classify books with pictures is to consider the space given to the visual and verbal narratives. In this classification, books with pictures are organized in three broad categories. First, some books with pictures are *wordless books*, narrated entirely by pictures; an example is Eric Rohmann's *Time Flies* (1994). The second category consists of *picture books*, which in turn are divided into two types. Picture books of the first type depend primarily on the illustrations to portray a minimal storyline, as in Susan Akass's *Swim, Number Nine Duckling* (1995), illustrated by Alex Ayliffe. This type also includes information books that depend primarily on illustrations to provide facts such as alphabet books, counting books, and simple concept books. Catherine and Laurence Anholt have created several informational picture books, such as *What Makes Me Happy* (1995). Picture books of the second type, called *picture storybooks*, rely equally on visual and verbal narrations to tell a story or provide information about a topic. Anne Isaacs's *Swamp Angel* (1994), illustrated by Paul Zelinksy, is an example of this type.[14] *Illustrated books* form the third category of books with pictures. The verbal narrative is the major focus of this category. The illustrations appear only occasionally to help interpret or embellish the verbal narrative. The 1994 edition of Jack London's *Call of the Wild*, illustrated by Barry Moser, is an example. As Figure 8.5 shows, these books can be placed on a continuum according to the amount of visual or verbal text included in the book.

Classifying Books with Pictures According to the Content

Books with pictures are also classified by content, which influences the verbal and visual narratives used by creators.

Fictional picture books, especially *picture storybooks*, contain stories on various topics ranging from a person's daily life to social issues, such as dysfunctional families. Frequently, these books deal with the antics of real and imaginary animals, creatures, and humans. Since the books rely equally on visual and verbal narratives, illustrations are produced in every medium, graphic technique, and style to complement and interpret the fictional narrative.

Nonfiction books with pictures, such as *information books* and *concept books*, contain factual materials and are written primarily in expository text. This classification includes alphabet books, counting books, and single concept books on mathematical, scientific, social, or historical subjects. Also included in the nonfiction classification are books containing authentic information written in narrative discourse, such as *informational storybooks*. Artists use suitable artistic media, styles, and designs to replace or supplement the verbal narrative. (See Chapter 6 for a discussion of information books with pictures and the bibliography for a list of exemplary books.)

Classifying individual books with pictures in tidy, specific categories is difficult for several reasons. First, the books are found in every genre. For example, a *picture book* may be a book of fiction written in a narrative discourse or a nonfiction book written in an expository text. Second, contemporary artists and authors frequently experiment with innovative techniques and use different visual and verbal styles, which may bridge several literary genres. In the last decade, two new types of books have evolved from this experimentation, the *photo-essay* and the *informational storybook*. A photo-essay combines photographs and verbal text, is written in narrative and/or expository discourse, and describes a person, place, time, or topic. Jim Brandenburg's *An American Safari: Adventures on the North American Prairie* (1995) is an example. Brandenburg's photo-essay combines personal memories and describes, through verbal narrative and outstanding colored photographs, the disappearance of animal and plant life on the North American

FIGURE 8.5 A Continuum of Books with Pictures

VISUAL NARRATIVE ONLY	VISUAL AND VERBAL NARRATIVES	PRIMARILY VERBAL NARRATIVE
Wordless Books	Picture Books	Illustrated Books
	Picture Storybooks	
	Informational Storybooks	
	Photo-Essays	
	Concept Books	
	Information Books	

prairie. Such books include photographs, maps, and other materials that document the authenticity of the book's content. *Informational storybooks* combine the characteristics of both fiction and nonfiction. Authentic information is presented in the picture storybook format. An example of an informational storybook is Jonathan London's *Honey Paw and Lightfoot* (1995). Third, classifying books with pictures is difficult because these books are no longer reserved for young children. Many books contain content, themes, and artistic and verbal styles that evoke responses from people of all ages. An excellent example of this trend is Eve Bunting's 1995 Caldecott winner, *The Smoky Night* (1994). Figure 8.6 summarizes the various categories of books with pictures.

PRESENTING VARIOUS CATEGORIES OF BOOKS WITH PICTURES

As we have just seen, there are various types of books with pictures. This section will present additional information about specific categories of books with pictures. Some books are intended for children of a specific age, such as books for babies, toddlers, or preschoolers. Other books, such as toy books, are distinguished by a special format. This section will also provide additional information and specific techniques for presenting wordless books and picture books. The bibliography includes outstanding books representing the various categories.

PRESENTING CLOTH AND BOARD BOOKS

The first books for babies and toddlers help them develop an interest in art and literature. By sharing many pleasurable experiences with books, adults encourage children to express positive reactions to literature. Many books invite the young child to look, count, identify, touch, make sounds, and play with the objects or materials in the pictures. This manipulation helps expand children's language, helps them identify objects with similar sounds, and introduces them to new objects. Whether the books are large or small, they invite individual explorations. Usually, the "two-lap" books are shared by two people, with the

FIGURE 8.6 Categories of Books with Pictures

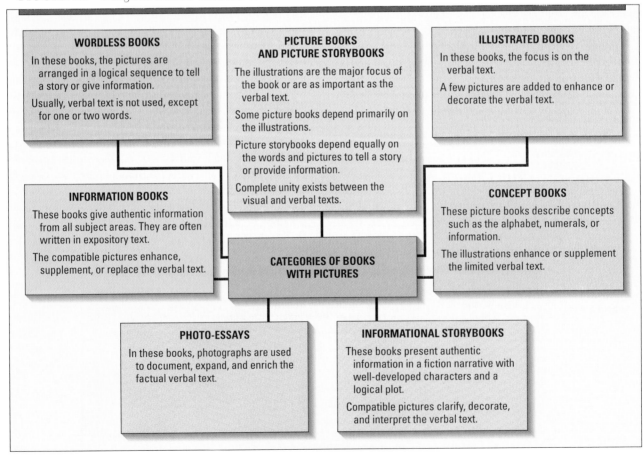

child sitting on an adult's lap. This pleasant experience helps the child develop a positive attitude toward reading books and enjoying literature.

Adults who read books to babies and toddlers agree that their books need to be sturdy and contain a few simple pictures of familiar experiences. The limited text uses everyday language written in clear, bold letters. Young children like simple humor and predictable stories they understand. They enjoy manipulating objects, imitating simple sounds, and chanting the narrative with an older reader. Cloth books and board books are the most popular books to use with this age.

Cloth books are intended for the youngest child. They are constructed of sturdy washable, soft, nontoxic materials or plastics. They are light and just the right size for a youngster to hold, tug, and perhaps taste. Older toddlers enjoy manipulating the zippers, buttons, and laces that are often included in the books. The very simple, colorful, realistic pictures show familiar objects in the child's environment. One or two words or a simple sequence of events may accompany the pictures. An adult reader will initiate a discussion about the pictures with the child.

Board books have a thick cover and pages covered with a durable laminated material. Some books, such as Angela Johnson's *Joshua by the Sea* (1994), have a simple story. Others, such as Bettina Paterson's *In My House* (1992), present a sequence of pictures to use for storytelling. Stories typically feature pets, families, and children involved in everyday experiences as in Lucy Cousins's *Farm Animals* (1991). Other books identify familiar objects, letters, or numerals as in Amanda Leslie's *Play Kitten Play: Ten Animal Fingerwiggles* (1992). Well-designed board books have clear, realistic illustrations with large, simple type. Usually, the artist shows one or two objects on each uncluttered page. Whether the book identifies objects, imitates sounds, or tells a story, children need the best book for the purpose.

Board books are usually small enough for the youngest child to hold. The thick, sturdy pages are easy for a young child to turn. As children practice turning the pages of the book, they develop page-turning and book-holding techniques. Children discover the format of books and learn to recognize the typical placement of letters and pictures on a page. Although young children can hold and handle the books, they prefer sharing them with someone else. These books expand a child's world, stimulate thinking, and help the child develop social skills and adopt a positive attitude toward visual and verbal narratives found in literature.

PRESENTING TOY BOOKS

Toy books are paper-engineered books that contain a special device to attract and involve the participant, as in Chuck Murphy's *Chuck Murphy's One to Ten Pop-Up Surprises!* (1995). The books have movable parts that pop up, pull out, smell, fold out, or form a diorama. They appeal to children and adults of all ages who enjoy looking at the pictures and discovering which object will move, when to move it, and how to move it. In books such as Paul Zelinsky's *The Wheels on the Bus* (1990), the person moves an object to discover the storyline.

Pop-up books are a popular type of movable, paper-engineered book. Some, such as Marc Brown's *Arthur Goes to School* (1995), tell simple stories, while others, such as Eric Carle's *The Honeybee and the Rabbit: A Moving Picture Book* (1995), give information about animals or nature. Other books, such as Kerry Argent's *Happy Birthday, Wombat!* (1991), describe familiar experiences. The artist uses drawings, paintings, or photographs to highlight the verbal text. As the viewer turns the page, a three-dimensional object pops out of it. The pages are made of sturdy paper or synthetic materials that can hold up under the repeated movements. The physical acts of turning the page, looking at the details in the illustration, and perhaps moving objects on the page give the viewers a chance to play with this toy book. While the full effect of Keith Faulkner's *Wide-Mouthed Frog* (1996) cannot be experienced in a photograph, we can see the brilliant colors and the humor. (See the Faulkner color plate, page 276.)

PRESENTING WORDLESS BOOKS

In a *wordless book*, a series of illustrations depicts the story or gives information about the content. Usually, the book contains no verbal text, although the artist may include a few words to supplement the pictures. Some wordless books contain simple stories as in Lena Anderson's *Bunny Fun* (1991). Other artists develop a more complex plot, as Mitsumasa Anno did in *Anno's Journey* (1981). The books are intended for children aged twelve months through adults. Since the books have no verbal narratives, the sequence of illustrations shows the setting, develops the plot, and portrays the characters' actions and feelings. Therefore, the illustrations in wordless books must be of the highest artistic merit. The illustrations provide "complexity and detail, as well as continuity and consistency."[15] In addition to meeting standards suggested for all books with pictures, we expect wordless texts to provide clear details of the plot in the series of illustrations and to accurately depict the information necessary to move the storyline. Notice the movement of the visual sequences in David Wiesner's *Tuesday* (1991), and the details included in his watercolor illustrations.

Jonathan Lambert's bright collages with paint are compatible to the humor of Keith Faulkner's Wide-Mouthed Frog. With colorful water scenes in the background, the audience is delighted when they turn the pages and the various inhabitants of the wetland pop up. On different pages, the frog with the wide mouth asks a bird, mouse, and alligator what they eat. Something special happens when the alligator answers!

Artists who produce wordless books use their visual story-telling skills to encourage the viewer to personally interpret the narrative. Peter Collington is a master artist who extends the reader's visual abilities in his series of books such as *Tooth Fairy* (1995). (See the Collington color plate, page 115.) Indeed, the reader and the artist become active partners in creating the story. Different viewers may interpret the same text differently, and occasionally these interpretations are different from the artist's intentions. The earliest wordless text is believed to have been Lynd Ward's *Madman's Drum*, published in 1930. Since then, artists have created fewer than six hundred titles.[16]

Wordless books stimulate the reader's imagination and creative thinking. Young people acquire cognitive, visual, and linguistic competencies when they respond to the books. While exploring wordless books, a viewer:

"Reads" the illustrations rather than words to interpret the narrative.

Understands how the pictures and objects work together to present sequential action and form a cohesive text.

Acquires the conventions of print, such as the left-to-right sequence of language, and learns how to handle books.

Develops a "sense of story" (the story structure) by focusing on the details of the illustrations to understand the plot structure, characters, themes, setting, or point of view.

Acquires literal, inferential, predictive, and problem-solving strategies.

Uses visual strategies while searching for visual clues to interpret the plot or gain information. This helps the viewer expand visual literacy skills.

Enhances oral and written language competencies while reading and reacting to the book.

Acquires a common background of experiences.

Develops a positive attitude toward communicating with others.[17]

Some artists create a series of wordless books; Mercer Mayer's popular series about *A Boy, a Dog, and a Frog* (1967) is an example. Children enjoy reading all of the books in the series. When exploring some wordless books, such as Pat Schories's *Mouse Around* (1991), the viewer must carefully follow the details of the sequence. Other books, such as David Wiesner's *Free Fall* (1988), require the viewer to have an adequate experiential background to understand the plot and interpret the illustrations. Some artists are noted for unique formats. For example, John Goodall uses detailed watercolor and ink drawings and half pages inserted between the full pages to tell his story, as in *Puss in Boots* (1990). With such variations in designs, it may be necessary for an adult to connect the child to the format and content of the book. Guidance may be needed to help the child construct meanings from the images. Table 8.1 on page 277 lists suggested guidelines for presenting a wordless book. A Literary Link for David Wiesner's *Tuesday* (1991) appears at the end of this chapter, and the chapter bibliography lists outstanding wordless books.

TABLE 8.1   Guidelines for Presenting a Wordless Book

Initially, adults will lead the presentation.

Connect
- Organize students into a small group with a table.
- Introduce the wordless book format.
- Introduce the content of the book.
- Elicit personal background about the topic.
- Identify techniques for "reading" a wordless book:
  - Discuss details in illustrations.
  - Discuss the artistic elements, style, media, and principles of design used by the artist.
  - Discuss the sequence of the illustrations.
- If applicable, give bibliographic information about the artist.
- If applicable, introduce unusual vocabulary.
- Elicit student descriptions of the cover and discuss the title, setting, or characters shown on the cover.
- Elicit predictions about the plot, characters, setting, etc.

Construct
(Focus on Visual Narrative)
- Use questions, probes, and prompts to discuss visual elements:
  - Use literal retelling.
  - Elicit personal interpretations and impressions of events, characters, etc.
  - Consider the visual merit of the illustrations.
- If needed, clarify the language, details, events, or characters' actions.
- Discuss the visual impact of the book.
- Have individuals or groups use information about the artist to retell the story.
- If needed, share personal interpretations by discussing the setting, characters, mood, theme, visual elements, design, and format of the book.
- Discuss the merits of a wordless text.

Create
(Literary Response Modes)
- Encourage spontaneous responses or suggest alternative LRMs, such as the following:
  - Write a verbal narrative.
  - Dramatize the text through a radio program, puppets, or other activities.
  - Produce original artwork about the content by experimenting with the artist's media, style, and design.
  - Assume a different point of view and create another wordless text by using different media, style, design, and book format.

SOURCE: These guidelines were refined by the author and many teachers using wordless books with children.

PRESENTING PICTURE BOOKS

Some *picture books* depend primarily on visual sequences to depict a feeling or impression or provide information. A well-developed storyline is not apparent in this type of picture book. A *picture storybook* tells a story or provides information through visual and verbal narratives. The success of this type of book depends on the compatibility of the visual and verbal narratives.

The two types of picture books share certain features. Both usually contain only one story or topic, and the artist arranges the illustrations to tell, enhance, or supplement the verbal narrative. As discussed earlier, the artwork must be appropriate to the mood or content of the verbal text. Arnold Lobel encourages creators to produce a picture book that re-

mains interesting after repetitive readings and a book that will "rise out of the lives and passions of its creator."[18]

As individuals explore the various images and expressions found in the books, they encounter real or imaginary humans, animals, or objects who engage in universal experiences, such as dreaming, setting goals, and interacting with others. By vicariously experiencing these activities and other challenges of growing up, young people gain a better understanding of their own feelings and behavior. They also receive valuable insights about solving familiar conflicts. In addition, by exploring picture books, children are introduced to the lifestyles of people from diverse groups. This experience helps readers understand and accept the behavior of others. Picture books also enhance visual awareness and verbal and cognitive development.

Picture books may contain mature content; thus, people of all ages, from babies through adults, enjoy reading picture books. The passions and experiences of the members of the Pinkney dynasty are apparent in the books created by this talented family. To find out more about them, see "Did You Know?" on page 279.[19]

◊ USING BOOKS WITH PICTURES IN THE CLASSROOM

People with positive attitudes toward literature are likely to recall sitting on the lap of a beloved grandparent, parent, or older sibling and listening to the person read a story and talk about the pictures. Without a doubt, children's earliest literature experiences focus on the "beautiful" pictures they enjoyed looking at repeatedly. Young children delight in "reading" a book to an adult. Because the artist depicts objects or scenery and portrays the characters or plot, the audience can read the visual and verbal narratives, interpret the story, or identify important information.

THE TEACHER'S ROLE

Although the verbal narrative is important in books with pictures, the visual narrative is the focus of this chapter. When presenting books with pictures, the teacher will encourage the learners to look at and react to the artwork.[20] To accomplish this goal, the teacher will present—through reading aloud, discussion, and book talks—a variety of books with pictures created with various media, styles, and design. While reading or sharing a picture book with children, an informal discussion about the art may focus on the ideas and feelings they experience while viewing the pictures. Through continuous exploration of the art and informational discussions incorporating art-related terminology, students will learn to use appropriate terminology to express their reactions and share the information gained from the illustrations. Knowledge of terms from art history does not influence children's artistic responses. Yet, as young people experiment with various media, styles, and compositions, they develop a broader understanding of the artistic process and the artist's craft and want to know and use the proper artistic terminology.

Listen to a young child "reading" his or her favorite book to another. Obviously, very early in life, children learn to "read" pictures and gain information and meanings from the visual narratives. While they may not be able to "read" the verbal text, they can "read" visual narratives. Unfortunately, in most school settings, verbal literacy is emphasized and reading visuals is often ignored. Visual literacy—the ability to use illustrations to express ideas, emotions, and information—can be refined through continuous experiences with books with pictures.[21]

Pictures are powerful tools all people can use to communicate with others. Pictures do not demand a particular socioeconomic or educational level. They give all people pleasurable experiences and information. By visualizing cultural traditions and information, pictures give the audience an opportunity to learn about others. Books with pictures provide the motivation for all ages to develop artistic and aesthetic awareness.

An adult generally introduces children to books with pictures through oral reading. Specialized techniques for reading aloud are discussed in Chapters 7 and 10, but a few techniques should be highlighted here. All ages want to see the illustration when the reader turns the page, but it should also be shown when it enhances or helps interpret the verbal text. Hold the pictures at the eye level of the audience. When reading aloud, follow the punctuation marks and keep the momentum of the text flowing. Unless the children need additional information about the content presented in the book, do not stop reading until it is finished. Then give the listeners time to react spontaneously to the subject and visual aspects of the book. If appropriate, the teacher will encourage additional responses from the girls and boys.

Teachers who select appropriate books recognize the benefits viewers gain from pictures in books, consider the natural artistic preferences of young people, and choose content that is interesting and suitable for students. Table 8.2 on page 280 summarizes the benefits young people gain from exploring pictures in books.[22] The next sections offer suggestions for selecting books that fit students' preferences and are suitable and appealing.

THE ARTISTIC PREFERENCES OF YOUNG PEOPLE

Because young people are influenced by their background of experiences, they are most comfortable with familiar objects. Naturally, they are drawn to realistic art. Indeed, beauty is in the "eyes of the beholder." Children are attracted to the details in the illustrations that adults may overlook. Learning-disabled children surprised a group of teachers when they observed mushrooms under the Snatcher's feet in Molly Bang's *The Grey Lady and the Strawberry Snatcher* (1980). None of the seventy-five adults had noticed the mushrooms.

For several decades researchers have attempted to identify the artistic preferences of young people. Most early researchers were interested in discovering children's reac-

Did You Know About
THE PINKNEY DYNASTY?

*M*eet Jerry, the patriarch, Gloria Jean, the matriarch, Brian, their son, and Andrea, their daughter-in-law—the successful illustrators and authors of the Pinkney dynasty. In 1964 Jerry's talent was recognized when his illustrations for *The Adventures of Spider: West African Folk Tales* were published. Since then, his artwork has received three Caldecott honor awards, many Boston Globe–Horn Book Awards, three Coretta Scott King Awards, and two honor awards. Almost every day, Jerry receives a request to illustrate a new manuscript. How does he decide which manuscripts to illustrate? He says a well-written manuscript must reach him on an emotional level and say something that is important to him. When planning the illustrations for a selected manuscript, he thinks about the story, jots down notes as ideas come, draws a few rough thumbnail sketches, and, in his desire to realistically portray the verbal narrative, does a lot of research on the topic. He builds a set for the characters similar to a scene in the theater. He uses live models (often members of his family) and photographs. When he uses children models, he reads the manuscript to them, and together they act out the story. Then the hard work begins; he must select the right colors for his trademark watercolor and pencil drawings. The settings, clothing, and all of the details must be right for his realistic style. As he sketches the pictures on the paper, the magic begins for him—the pictures in his head seem to come to life. According to Pinkney, many times the "pictures take off on their own." Just look at his pictures in *Mirandy and Brother Wind* or the books he illustrated for Julius Lester, including the *Uncle Remus Series* and especially

Above: Gloria Jean Pinkney; Below: Jerry Pinkney

their acclaimed *John Henry*. The pictures achieve perfect union between verbal and visual narrative. Thanks to Jerry Pinkney, John Henry has become that powerful man who is stronger than a steam hammer!

Two books written by Gloria Jean, his wife and partner of thirty-five years, received his high seal of approval and have become popular picture storybooks—*Back Home* and *The Sunday Outing*. While the elder Pinkneys deserve the honors bestowed on them, so does their son Brian, a drummer and artist who has made a name in the art world! Brian, who began using watercolors like his father, soon discovered that scratchboard and oil paints were his medium. He used them in Robert San Souci's *Sukey and the Mermaid*, which won an ALA Notable Award and was named a Coretta Scott King Honor Book. Brian also used scratchboard and oil to illustrate William Hooks's *The Ballad of Belle Dorcas* and Lynn Joseph's *A Wave in Her Pocket: Stories from Trinidad*. Brian received a Caldecott honor book for *The Faithful Friend* by Robert San Souci (1996). In 1991 Brian married Andrea Davis, a writer and editor. Together they created *Alvin Ailey, Seven Candles for Kwanzaa*, and *Dear Benjamin Banneker*. Andrea also wrote a novel about her childhood, *Hold Fast to Dreams*. It isn't surprising to learn that Jerry and Gloria Jean's other three children, Troy, Scott, and Myles, are also involved in art therapy, design, and photography! Myles's book *Raining Laughter* will be published in 1997.

What is the secret of this artistic dynasty's success? The answer is talent, hard work, love, high standards, and "sharing" of ideas (this last statement was added by Andrea).

TABLE 8.2 Benefits Viewers Gain from Pictures in Books

Pictures help viewers see the beauty of the universe. From pictures the viewer gains a broader perspective on the world and beyond.

Pictures stimulate a viewer's sensitivity to art and help the person respond with pleasure to the beauty in her or his surroundings.

Pictures with artistic merit introduce the viewer to the unlimited artistic expressions available through different media, styles, and book designs.

Illustrations help viewers form an emotional connection to the characters, theme, and events. This emotional connection frequently stimulates the viewer's imagination.

Well-crafted artistic narratives stimulate the viewer's critical and divergent thinking.

Visual clues within an illustration help the viewer understand ideas or facts suggested in the verbal text. This frequently serves as a springboard for vocabulary and concept development.

Illustrations guide viewers to focus on important aspects of the verbal narrative.

Visual literacy skills are enhanced through continuous experiences with pictures; viewers develop a habit of observing their surroundings and use visuals to communicate and receive ideas, information, and feelings.

Exposure to quality art in books helps a child become discriminating and helps her or him reject visually inferior artwork.

TABLE 8.3 General Artistic Preferences of Young People

Generally, young people prefer realistic illustrations. They like art that is compatible with the verbal text.

Young people accept a variety of artistic elements, styles, media, and book designs if the illustrations and verbal text are compatible.

Younger readers prefer illustrations that show action or tell a story.

Color is no guarantee that children will accept pictures in books. If color is used, however, young people prefer bright, rich, intense primary colors (red, blue, yellow). Young children are strongly attracted to color. Children nine years and above like color, but they are also attracted to black and white pictures. A realistic portrayal of the text is more important to children than the artist's use of color.

If the illustrations are in unity with the verbal narrative, girls and boys enjoy humorous pictures, but not necessarily cartoons.

Children enjoy photographs as much as drawings and paintings, if the photographs describe the subject or present supplementary information about it.

Young people like clear details and bold outlines in illustrations rather than a wash or blurred, indistinguishable objects.

Some boys and girls enjoy detailed, cluttered backgrounds, while others find this type of visual distracting and prefer large central objects.

tions to specific artistic elements, styles, media, and content. The findings were frequently based on a student's reactions to isolated pictures or a series of pictures. These researchers disregarded the child's reactions to pictures that were accompanied by verbal narratives as are found in books with pictures. Generally, the researchers were not concerned with children's prior experiences with art, their emotional reactions to the pictures, and the social or cultural factors that might influence their artistic preferences. In the early studies, children were usually surveyed only once; therefore, the researchers did not explore any changes that might appear after the children had many experiences with art. Contemporary researchers focus on the entire book-sharing experience. They observe children reading and viewing books. Frequently, they conduct personal interviews to find out children's personal responses to the total impact of the visual and verbal narratives.[23]

Despite some inconsistent findings, certain generalizations can be made about children's artistic preferences. These findings, which are summarized in Table 8.3, provide basic knowledge about children's artistic preferences that adults can use when presenting books with pictures in the classroom.[24]

APPEALING CONTENT

A person's interest in the content of a book is a vital factor to consider when selecting a book to share or recommend to young people. We know that preschool and primary-age children enjoy books about their immediate environment, low fantasy, realistic animals, real and personified toys, and slapstick humor. Perhaps this is the reason Peggy Rathmann's humorous watercolor and line pictures in *Officer Buckle and Gloria* (1995) are so appealing to kindergarten to primary-age youngsters. (See the Rathmann color plate, page 281.) Young people nine years and above prefer books focusing on peer relationships, adventure, realistic animals, social issues, and various nonfiction topics. (Additional information about the content preferred by young people is presented in Chapter 1 and in each genre chapter.)

The suitability of the content is also dependent on the length, complexity, and sophistication of the information in the book. Usually, books longer than normal (those with more than thirty-two pages) have more complex plot development and characterization. The longer books may also contain abstract themes, unfamiliar language, a serious, nostalgic tone, and a broader, more in-depth discussion of the topic. Most of the longer, more complex, and more so-

Officer Buckle checked on Gloria again.
"Good dog," he said.
Officer Buckle thought of a safety tip he had
discovered that morning.

Peggy Rathmann uses bright blue and red watercolor drawings to expand the verbal text in Officer Buckle and Gloria. *The cartoon-like drawings tell the funny story about the police officer who takes his dog, Gloria, to school to give the children safety lessons. Rathmann's clear white backgrounds highlight the humorous drawings that add to the verbal narrative. Wonder why Gloria is smiling?*

phisticated books are intended for children nine years and above or those with mature reading abilities. Books with age-appropriate vocabulary, suitable conceptual level, and content without racist, sexist, and other stereotypes are preferred for reading and viewing. Visually engaging books with rich language are expected for all ages.

GUIDELINES FOR SELECTING BOOKS WITH PICTURES

When children select books with pictures, they are influenced by the books adults have read, discussed, and presented to them. While peer recommendations are influential, perhaps a more important factor in the selection of personal reading is their individual interest in the book's subject. Therefore, guidelines for selecting books with pictures are based on the

artistic merit of the artwork, the quality of the book design, the compatibility of the visual and verbal narratives, and the children's interest in the art and content of the book.

Table 8.4 on page 282 presents general criteria for selecting books with pictures.[25] The guidelines are organized according to individual components, such as artistic elements, principles of design, physical features, compatibility of media and style with the content and verbal narrative, and the overall quality of the book. Although each component is considered separately in the table, the components are inseparable. The relationship of all components determines the overall quality and suitability of a book for particular children. Several questions are listed for each component to give the selector an overview of that particular aspect of the book. When selecting a book with pictures, only questions applicable to a particular book or the children should be considered. Books receiving many favorable comments should be selected for the classroom.

YOUNG PEOPLE'S REACTIONS TO ART IN BOOKS WITH PICTURES

Children's reactions to art are idiosyncratic. Most young people respond positively to a variety of book illustrations, but their interests and tastes vary according to the books they encounter. Children's artistic awareness is stimulated by the books they explore and the discussions they have about the artistic merit of the illustrations. As young people experience a variety of well-crafted, beautifully designed art in books, their attitudes, preferences, and aesthetic appreciation will change and develop. By the middle grades, young people who continuously explore quality art recognize an artist's technical skills and have a basic understanding of the meanings conveyed through art. They also realize the emotional power of illustrations and become discriminating connoisseurs of quality art.

Like adults, children enjoy sharing their personal reactions to pictures in informal conversations.[26] Young people often discuss the details they observe in the illustrations, express their personal opinions about the artistic elements, and comment on the ability of the visual and verbal narratives to adequately portray the subject. Teachers who use appropriate artistic terminology when discussing the artistic elements encourage young people to use the language when describing their interpretations of the art and their reactions to the artist's craft.

Initially, when necessary, the teacher may use probes and prompts to elicit students' reactions to the art, the compatibility of the visual and verbal narratives, and the artist's

TABLE 8.4 Guidelines for Selecting Books with Pictures

Artistic Elements

Consider questions such as these:

Line: How are the lines used to enhance the illustrations? (Are the lines continuous, broken, heavy, light, soft, or hard?) Do they convey action or rhythm?

Shape and form: Does the artist effectively portray the shapes and forms? Are the forms separated by sharp or soft, subtle outlines? Are natural or geometric shapes used?

Color: What colors are used? Is color used effectively? What function (purpose) do the colors achieve? Does the color or noncolor convey the mood and emotions of the text? Is the color too bright? Harsh? Pale? Is the color natural? Is the color suitable for the content? If color is not used, is it needed?

Texture: Does the artist use strokes, cross-hatching, blending, or light or dark texture? Is the texture appropriate to the visual effect of the illustrations? Does the texture convey tension or add interest or movement? If texture is not used, is it needed?

Space: Is space used effectively in the illustrations? Is the space flat? Shallow? Deep? Does it give an illusion of depth and volume through linear perspective or through atmospheric perspective?

Principles of Design

Consider questions such as these:

Balance: Are the elements of the illustrations arranged in symmetrical, asymmetrical, or radial balance? Is the major focus placed at the top, center, or bottom of the page or all over it? How has the artist arranged the objects to achieve balance on the page? Across two pages? Is the balance pleasing?

Rhythm and movement: Has the artist created rhythm in the illustration? Is there movement within the illustrations? Is there movement between the visual sequences? Are the rhythms or movements vertical, horizontal or diagonal?

Proportion: Are idealized proportions (size, scale) used? Does the artist depict caricature? Are the proportions suitable for the subject?

Emphasis: Does each picture have a focal point? Where are the dominant visual elements placed? Are smaller visual elements repeated throughout the illustration or book? Does the arrangement of the illustrations on the page provide an appropriate focus and visual design?

Pattern: Are patterns of light, shadow, color, or other visual elements repeated within illustrations or throughout the book? Are small designs (motifs) repeated within an illustration? Do the designs create an overall pattern? Are they placed in parts of the illustration or book? Do the patterns enhance the content?

Unity and variety: Do certain principles unify the illustrations? Are certain principles more important than others? What elements add variety to the artwork? Is there unity or variety in the individual illustrations and the series of illustrations?

Physical Features of a Book

Consider questions such as these:

Is the *overall format* of the book appealing? Unique? Consistent with the verbal and visual narratives?

Is the *type* legible and harmonious with the illustrations? Is it compatible with the mood of the text? Is the type placed appropriately in relation to the pictures?

Does the *book jacket/cover* provide enough information to help the audience anticipate the content, characters, and genre of the book? Is the cover up-to-date and appealing to contemporary youth?

Do the *endpapers* provide information about the content?

Is the *binding* suitable for the intended age?

Do the pages open sufficiently for viewers to look at the pictures?

Is the *paper* of high quality? Do the pictures bleed (show) from one page to another?

(Continued)

craft. The following probes and prompts reflect this process:

How do the illustrations make you feel?

What do you see in the illustrations?

Is there something different about the size of the houses (or the color or the size of the objects, or other aspects of the illustrations)?

What medium did the artist use in the book? Did the artist use the same medium in the last book we read?

Do you think the artist used an appropriate style for the verbal text? Why?

How do the illustrations compare to other illustrations by the artist? How do they compare to illustrations in other books with a similar content or genre?

TABLE 8.4 Guidelines for Selecting Books with Pictures *(Continued)*

Compatibility of Media and Style with the Content and Verbal Narrative

Consider questions such as these:

Are the media and style suitable for the content?

How do the illustrations interpret the content?

    Do they help the viewer anticipate the action and the climax of the story?

    Do they portray the setting authentically?

    Do they convincingly depict the characters?

How do the illustrations evoke emotional responses?

How do the pictures portray the details in the verbal narrative?

Do the illustrations detract from the verbal text?

Do the illustrations visualize the appropriate verbal text?

Is the number of illustrations adequate for the verbal narrative?

Do the illustrations enhance, supplement, or document the information provided in the verbal texts to give the viewer additional information, ideas, or feelings?

If the illustrations are used as decorations, is this treatment appropriate?

Overall Quality of a Book

Consider questions such as these:

Consider the criteria suggested in Chapter 1 regarding the literary merit of the book and Chapters 1 and 6 for nonfiction elements.

If a specific ethnic, racial, social, religious, or regional group is depicted, does the artist portray the group in an authentic, appealing manner?

How is this book different from or similar to other books created by the same person(s)?

How is this book different from or similar to other books in the same genre?

Does the book provide a different viewpoint or present the content in a different or unique way?

What is the overall visual impact of the book?

After discussing the art found in books, many children want to produce original artwork. Therefore, an art center with paper of various colors, paints, brushes, pencils, easels, and other art materials is needed. The center should also include a drying and display area, books about fine art, and techniques for using various media. Young children often use illustrations in books as a springboard for their art, but they make no attempt to reproduce the art in the book. In contrast, older children frequently want to experiment with the media, style, or techniques used by an artist, whose work they have seen.

As children learn more about the artist's craft, they become curious about the life of the artist who produces their favorite books. This interest leads to a study of the artist's entire body of work. The teacher can read aloud biographies of noted artists or give book talks about books related to their work. Students and teachers can present biographical sketches of the artists. Written interviews and commercial videos are also available for use in the classroom. Children are also curious about the decisions artists make before illustrating a book: How do artists select a verbal text to illustrate? How do they choose the style and media? How do they design their books? Exemplary books that use various art styles, media, and designs, biographies about artists, and books explaining procedures for producing artistic techniques are identified in the bibliography.

INSTRUCTIONAL FOCUSES USED WITH BOOKS WITH PICTURES

As young people explore books with pictures, they enjoy using both visual and verbal narratives to find out more about a subject. These pleasurable experiences naturally stimulate an aesthetic reaction to the books. Initially, a teacher assumes a predominantly *aesthetic instructional focus* (to give students an opportunity to personally connect or "live through" the visual and verbal texts). Later, if the book contains information presented in a subject area or content that children want to know more about, the teacher assumes an *efferent instructional focus* (to encourage students to take away information from both narratives). Typically, the teacher moves freely from one focus to the other, depending on the students, the book, and the curricular goals. (See Chapters 2 and 11 for additional information about instructional focuses.)

Since girls and boys enjoy and learn from different types of books with pictures, the wise teacher considers three factors when designing the instructional focus and strategies to use with the books. First, the teacher considers how children naturally react to the books. For example, when children hear and view Barbara Joosse's *I Love You the Purplest* (1996) with Mary Whyte's watercolor illustrations, they relate to the character's desire to find out how much her mother loves her. This book naturally elicits an aesthetic response. Thus, the teacher uses an aesthetic focus, giving the children time to react personally to the book and, if desired, to discuss the feelings evoked by the visual and verbal texts. Second, when planning the instructional focus to use with literature, the teacher considers the expected curricular goals. Stacey Schuett's *Somewhere in the World Right Now* (1995) gives primary-age children information about the things that are happening around the world at the same time. The narrative concept book and the detailed, realistic illustrations help children understand the passage of time and the activities of people around the world. When using the book in a science or social science lesson, the teacher may read the book aloud, encourage oral reactions, then assume an efferent instructional focus and use strategies that highlight the information students "take away" from the book. Instruction will highlight telling time and the activities of people throughout the world at a particular time. This instruction is enhanced and supplemented by the compatible visual and verbal narratives. The third factor to consider when planning an instructional focus to use with a book with pictures is the art found in the book. Tana Hoban's colored photographs in *Colors Everywhere* (1995) introduce children to the beauty of the world. The simple photo-essay highlights the importance of color in our lives and gives visual information about the various subjects found in the photographs. An informal discussion about the objects in the photographs and the beauty of the world naturally elicits both an aesthetic and an efferent focus.

As children respond to the books, they can produce various Literary Response Modes (LRMs). For example, after looking at Hoban's book, children might go on a "color hunt" looking for colors in their environment. After the hunt, they can select the appropriate colored sheets of paper, display them, and cluster the objects in their environment according to their colors. After sharing Schuett's book, the children can find and mark on a world map the various places mentioned in the verbal text. The book leads to a discussion of the various time zones in the United States. As students discuss the effect time zones have on business, television, and personal situations, they can be encouraged to research why there are various time zones in the United

States and where they are located. After listening to Joosse's book, the children can discuss the meaning of the colors. Then they can select a color that reflects their love for a special person, write a statement about that love, illustrate the statement, and place the statements on an appropriate sheet of paper in a bound book. Depending on the children and curricular goals, other books with similar content can be used to give children a broader understanding of a subject.

INSTRUCTIONAL STRATEGIES AND LITERARY RESPONSE MODES THAT HIGHLIGHT THE ART IN BOOKS WITH PICTURES

If illustrations in a book are appealing to children, it is easy to motivate them to express their personal reactions to the illustrations in oral, written, or artistic LRMs. Students can present a drama, write illustrated letters to the characters using artwork similar to the art in the book, or prepare a visual display of their interpretation of a book.

Building on children's natural responses to pictures in books, the curricular goals, and the artwork found in the books, various strategies and LRMs are suggested for use with books with pictures. The ideas can be modified for specific books. The suggested strategies and LRMs highlight the artwork in books with pictures. Obviously, the content or verbal narratives are also considered when completing the LRMs. Remember to suggest strategies and LRMs that naturally emerge from the selected books. Encourage students to select visual and verbal responses that reflect their actual interpretations and reactions to the artwork and the entire book. If needed, teachers can suggest alternate LRMs. The following strategies and LRMs elicit aesthetic and efferent responses to enhance children's linguistic, cognitive, and visual development. Many suggestions involve more than one child to give students experience working with others. This experience refines students' social development. The LRMs are organized according to various aspects of artwork.[27]

Exploring and Reacting to Various Artistic Elements

The following strategies and LRMs encourage students to respond to various artistic elements such as line, shape, color, texture, and space:

> Display a collection of books by an artist who is noted for her or his use of an element; for example, Steven Kellogg is known for his extensive use of lines (see Chapter 3). Read the books over a week. Focus on the verbal text. After reading all of the books, ask the students what they noticed about all of the artist's illustrations. Direct their attention to the artistic element.

Elicit reactions to the artist's pictures: Why do they like (dislike) the pictures? Talk about the benefits of using the element. Children can find other books with outstanding examples of a particular element. Compare the illustrations. Encourage children to use the element in original pictures. Display original pictures with information about the element. Highlight the art of the noted artists.

Talk informally about the predominant artistic elements used by artists while sharing a book with pictures. Children are encouraged to find books focusing on a particular element; for example, texture as used by Chris Van Allsburg in *Jumanji* (1981), John Steptoe in *Mufaro's Beautiful Daughters* (1987), Eveline Ness in *Sam Bangs & Moonshine* (1966), Brian Pinkney in Robert D. San Souci's *Sukey and the Mermaid* (1992), and Leo Lionni in various books, especially *Swimmy* (1963). Direct a discussion about the different techniques artists use to achieve texture and the benefits of using texture in the illustrations. Have children select a favorite poem that would be enhanced by a drawing using the element, and draw the picture(s). Display a copy of the poem and the drawings on the literature bulletin board or in another prominent place in the room or in the hall. Title the display *See How Artists Use (Texture) to Enhance a Poem*.

Explore an artist's use of shape in books such as those created by Lois Ehlert, especially *Color Zoo* (1989); Molly Bang, especially *The Paper Crane* (1985); Eric Carle, especially *The Very Lonely Firefly* (1995); Ann Jonas in *Round Trip* (1983); and Gerald McDermott, especially *Zomo the Rabbit* (1992). Talk about the way the artists arrange the elements of the picture to represent shapes and how the media highlight the shapes. Many suggested books were created through collage. The children will select a favorite story and prepare collage illustrations for a selected verbal text. The illustrations can be bound in a flip book and displayed with the story. (The class can make one book, or several groups can make several stories with collage.)

Exploring and Reacting to Various Principles of Design

These strategies and LRMs help students explore aspects of the visual composition including balance, rhythm, proportion, emphasis, patterns, and unity and variety.

Show a large illustration without a distracting background and ask the students what object they saw first. Talk about why this object is seen first; help them understand composition and the placement of illustrations on a page or throughout the book. Show a large illustration with a distracting background, and again ask what object they see first. Susan Jeffers's *The Three Jovial Huntsmen* is a good example. Talk about the difference in an illustration with and without a distracting background.

Show several examples of pictures that extend across a double-page spread, and some examples of several pictures on one page. Discuss why the artists arranged the pictures as they did. What would happen if the artists rearranged the pictures? Photocopy a book in which each page has several pictures. Divide the class into pairs or small groups. Give each group a different page. Ask them to rearrange the pictures. Glue the new arrangements onto a large sheet of paper. Compare the "new" compositions to the original book. Discuss the entire book design of the new pages.

Pair students, and give each pair a book. Have them look at the placement of the illustrations and consider these questions: Are the illustrations placed appropriately with the verbal text they visualize? Did the artist pick the right detail to illustrate? Have them write out their responses. Share the book and responses with three other pairs that have the same or different books. Record overall reaction to the placement of the illustrations. Share reactions in class. Students must be prepared to defend their reactions.

Group the class. Have each group select a story written by a member of the group or class. The group will decide what types of illustrations are needed for the verbal text and what text will be illustrated. Members of the group will prepare the illustrations. They will cut the verbal text at the appropriate places and decide where the illustrations will be placed to enhance or supplement some of the text. They will design the book and prepare it by arranging the text and illustrations in the proper place on the pages. The cover, endpapers, dedication, and title page will be prepared. The book will be bound.

Exploring and Reacting to the Format of Books

These strategies and LRMs encourage students to examine the type, jacket and cover, endpapers, binding, paper, and other aspects of a book's format:

Look at several of J. De Brunhoff's *Babar* books and other books that were handprinted. Compare the form of the letters in various alphabet books and other reading materials. Have the children debate "Printed books are easier to read than handwritten books or those using unfamiliar fonts." (Include also the pros and cons of using different sizes of type.)

Collect several books with endpapers that set the stage for the story, such as David Kirk's *Miss Spider's Wedding* (1995), Maurice Sendak's *Where the Wild Things Are* (1963), and Virginia Burton's books, especially *Mike Mulligan and His Steam Shovel* (1939). Discuss the merit of using the endpapers in this way (limited space for visual and verbal texts, visuals tell the story, and the like).

After students find several books with elaborate borders, have the students look at the borders and list on a chart the objects found in each border, additional details given in the border, reasons the artist used the border (such as to add additional details or display cultural symbols). Have the children research the meaning of traditional symbols, such as apples, spiders, and mistletoe. Talk about the way the artist added additional information to the verbal text and why background information is needed to understand the reason for including the border. See Nancy Ekholm Burkert's and Trina Schart Hyman's folktales for examples of borders.

Share Jon Scieszka and Lane Smith's *The Stinky Cheese Man and Other Fairly Stupid Tales* (1992). Find a copy of Smith's article in the January/February 1993 *The Horn Book Magazine* (see note 14). Share information from the article with the children. Group the children and have them list all of the inappropriate examples of book design and format found in the book. Also, share other books by the author/artist team. Have groups of children write a parody of a favorite tale and illustrate it using the appropriate media and style for the story.

Exploring and Reacting to the Style Used by Artists

These strategies and LRMs encourage students to consider the artist's style (realistic, expressionistic, impressionistic, humorous, or folk art):

Over several weeks, informally discuss the style used by artists in popular books. When discussing the style, display several books using the same style. Have students identify distinguishing features of a particular style and list them on a chart. After the students look at the same style in several books, group the students in style groups. Have the groups find other books using the style. They can make bookmarks listing the reason each book was chosen to represent the style. Place the books on a table with the chart. Let the other groups look at the books and bookmarks and note in writing whether they agree. On a designated date, the group will be the artists of the book and will be asked to defend their selections. If other classmates disagree with

the group's decisions, they will challenge the choices, using the written comments collected while viewing the display. Books inappropriately categorized are moved to the appropriate style display. The teacher can add nonexamples to the display without the children's knowledge. On the day of the discussion, the groups can move the books to the appropriate display.

Collect picture books, picture storybooks, information books, and traditional tales that authentically portray a particular cultural group. Group students in cultural groups. Have each group identify the art typical of the culture (look at the colors used, symbols, traditions, details of the lifestyles, and the like). List the features. While studying the people in social science, include the art and music and refer to the art in the books. Have the students prepare large murals, banners, masks, and other regalia representing the art of the group, and display in the halls. At the end of the study, have the groups look at the books again and determine if the artist realistically portrayed the folk art of the group.

Display several books containing expressionistic or impressionistic art. Survey students' opinions and preferences for art styles. Record preferences, but do not discuss. Ask probes such as, *Do the illustrations enhance, enrich, and extend the verbal text? Cite additional information gained from the illustrations. How do the illustrations make you feel?* Share information books about the various styles and biographies about artists who used the style. After discussing features of style, have the students look at the books again. Throughout the year, display fine art created in the expressionistic or impressionistic style. Also, read other books with the style. Toward the end of the year, survey students' opinions about the art styles. Compare preferences to those in the earlier survey. If preferences have changed, discuss reasons why.

Review several books with humorous art. Note the style and media used by the artists. Talk about the suitability of the illustrations to the verbal text. Direct students to find a humorous folktale, song, short story, or narrative verse. Have the students make humorous art for the story. The students will use the pictures and tell the story to the class. Video tape the students telling the story.

Exploring and Reacting to Media Used by Artists

These strategies and LRMs ask students to consider the various media used by artists:

Elicit the assistance of the art teacher to give students many opportunities to experiment with the various media used by artists of favorite books.

Assign media groups to find several books using a specific medium. Bring books to class and have them list distinguishing characteristics of the medium when printed in a book. Prepare an attractive banner, using the medium to list the characteristics. Display the books and the visual list in the classroom, the art room, or the media center.

Display books using several media. Throughout a week, give the children an opportunity to identify the media on a media card they will sign and turn in. On a designated date, return the media cards to the students, and talk about the medium used in each book. Give a reward (a paperback book perhaps) to the student(s) who correctly identified the medium in the largest number of books.

Have the children read books about artists to learn more about the medium they used and why. Have children find juvenile books containing the medium used by the artist, and compare the illustrations to fine art pictures. Discuss and list distinguishing features of the medium. Note how some features disappear when the pictures are published in a book. Have one group of children write to an editor at a publishing company and ask about printing books. Report the information learned. Also, share juvenile books discussing commercial publishing.

Determining the Compatibility of Media, Style, and Content or Verbal Narrative

These strategies and LRMs ask students to determine whether the medium and style used by the artist are compatible with the verbal text of a book:

Select a traditional tale, such as *Puss In Boots*, published in several books with different media and styles. Read the story from an anthology without pictures. Group the children, and let them decide the medium and style an artist should use to illustrate the story. Share the responses. Then share the books with pictures. Discuss the similarities and differences of the books. Poll the students to find out their favorite book. Group students according to the book chosen as their favorite. Ask the group to write a letter to the artist (if the person is alive; if not, write to the art teacher) reporting the activity. Tell the artist why his or her version was selected as the favorite. Different artists have illustrated and published many traditional tales and poems. Encourage students to find different books containing the same tales, poems, or stories. Compare the art and select the favorite book. Display the books

together and prepare a bulletin board with written reasons for choosing a particular book. Ask other teachers at the same grade level to conduct the same LRM and compare results.

Read Eve Bunting's *Smoky Night* (1994). After discussing the verbal narrative, talk about the artist's medium and style. Were they suitable to the content? Students will defend their answers. Also see Bunting's *Going Home* (1996) by Diaz and compare the books.

Read several stories or books from fantasy, such as Roald Dahl's *The BFG* (1982), or a fantasy story by Jane Yolen from *The Dream Weaver* (1979). Do not show the illustrations in the books. Ask students to create illustrations for the books and to write a paragraph telling why they selected the particular medium for the book. Collect the pictures and reasons. Later talk about the fantasy genre and the need to accept the writer's world and move into that world. Display pictures made earlier while listening to a book. Compare and contrast the media students selected for the fantasy selection and read why the media were selected. Then show the illustrations created for the published books. Compare to students' illustrations. Talk about the potential of illustrations to help the reader accept the writer's world and how the illustrations help the listener/reader visualize the fantasy elements.

Display biographies with black and white pictures, silhouettes, and outlines and biographies with actual photographs, realistic sketches, or colored realistic illustrations. Compare the information gained from the different types of illustrations. Find out which type of illustration they prefer and why. Take a colored photograph of each child. Pair the children, and ask each child to write a biographical sketch about her or his partner. In the sketch give three interesting facts about the person. Display the photographs and sketch on a bulletin board. Arrange photos and sketches in an attractive class scrapbook. If desired, make copies of the photos and sketches for each child to place in a personal scrapbook. Take an 8-by-10-inch picture of the entire class. Place the picture on the cover of the scrapbook. Write a title page and dedication for the scrapbook. Periodically, throughout the year take photos of important events. At the end of the year give groups different photos, and have them write a story or report about the event and arrange the article and photos on a page. Place in the class scrapbook.

Exploring and Expanding Students' Natural Art Preferences

These strategies and LRMs explore students' art preferences in books with pictures:

In the first month of school, read books that conform to the reported artistic preferences of students and some books that do not. Reintroduce the books and ask the students to focus on the illustrations. Ask them to vote using a scale of 1 to 5 (1 means liked the book; 5 means did not like the book). Chart the results on each book. Ask students to write a brief reason for voting 1 or 5 on two books. Have the class summarize and list their art preferences. Conduct this survey after Christmas! Compare results and differences. Survey the class again in April. Compare results with previous surveys.

Bring several books containing an art style that is not popular with children, such as Abstract, Surrealist, or Cubist art. Read the book, paying little attention to the pictures. Before discussing the unique features of the style, elicit students' personal reaction to the style. Discuss features of the style. Present books about the style and fine art using the style. Give groups of students several pictures to look at and talk about. Again, poll students' reaction to the style. Ask students to select a suitable medium, and draw or paint a simple picture with several objects using the style. Discuss and display the pictures.

Over a week or two, read several books with black and white pictures. Before discussing the art, informally elicit conversation about the pictures and about whether color was needed for the verbal text. Give students a questionnaire about their reaction to color in books. Ask questions such as the following: Do you look at the color of the pictures before you select a book to read? Do you select books with black and white pictures? When do you think illustrations need color? Have the children chart the responses on a graph and discuss. Write a letter to the media specialist sharing the graph and a summary of the results.

Play a portion or all of Beethoven's Rondo in C. Ask students to list all of the ideas that come into their minds while listening to the music. Ask volunteers to share their thoughts while listening to the music. Ask if the music reminded them of people and events and how it made them feel. The next day, play the music again while reading Paul Fleischman's *Rondo in C*. Ask students to compare their thoughts to those listed in the book. Talk about the way verbal texts remind us of events and people. Then discuss the visual narrative by Janet Wentworth; direct students' attention to the artist's use of chalk and the suitability of the medium to the verbal text. Throughout the year while looking at pictures, remind students of the power of art to elicit personal thoughts and emotions.

Exploring the Purpose of Illustrations in Books

These strategies and LRMs ask students to consider how illustrations interpret, expand, enhance, clarify, supplement, decorate, or replace the verbal narrative:

Look at several very different alphabet or counting books. Talk about the purpose of the books and decide if the books achieve their purpose. Older students can select a book with a favorite format and produce a book using that format for younger students. (See Chapter 7 bibliography.)

While studying a particular science or social science topic, have the class construct a KWL (a visual graphic described in Chapter 10). Divide the class into small groups. Have each group select a subtopic that the class wants to learn more about. Each group will research its subtopic and prepare a series of visuals (graphs, photographs, drawings, illustrations) presenting information about the subtopic. Use the visuals with an oral presentation about the subtopic. Display the visuals in the room with appropriate verbal labels. Later, discuss the purpose of using visuals and illustrations to enrich an informational presentation.

Divide the class into small groups. Give each group a different favorite narrative poem. Have the group decide the most appropriate content to illustrate, which media and style to use, and how the illustrations will be arranged with the verse on a large poster board. The students will create the visuals to accompany the poem and display the poster in the room. Give students time to view each visual poem; then ask the group to read the poem and talk about how they decided what visuals to use to illustrate the poem. Have the class determine the purpose of the illustrations for each poem.

Ask the students to help select a variety of books describing a topic to be studied in a curricular area. Be sure different types of books with pictures from various literary genres are represented in the selection. Talk about the different purposes for the illustrations in the books and how to identify the purpose: for example, photographs supplement, replace, and document a verbal text; borders decorate and supplement the text; and a series of illustrations expand, clarify, or replace the verbal text. Divide the books by type and genre. Have a different group of students look at each group of books. Ask the students to determine the purpose of the illustrations in each book. Share results with the class, and chart the purposes of the illustrations and use the information for a math lesson. Reinforce the purposes of illustrations as the students use the books for curricular study.

Exploring Functions of the Visual Narrative

These strategies and LRMs explore the ways a visual narrative evokes a mood, establishes the setting, and helps develop the plot structure or characters:

Select several books the children have not seen that have large illustrations visualizing the mood of the book. Number the books. Give the students slips of paper. Have the students number each slip of paper with the number of a book. Cover the books except for several illustrations that show the mood of the storyline. Have the students write the mood of the book on the appropriate paper. Place predictions in a "Prediction Pitcher." Read the books over the week. Return to students' predictions and compare them to the mood of the book. How did the illustrations help the students make predictions about the book? (Consider, for example, the artist's style, details in the book, color, and the like.) Note: This LRM could also be used with the setting and with character and plot development.

Give the students information about the times and people before reading a simple work of historical fiction, such as Floyd Moore's *I Gave Thomas Edison My Sandwich* (1995). After reading the book, talk about the historical characters and information in the book. Present biographical sketches of the historical personalities in the book. Encourage students to find photographs of the people and the times. Students will present an interesting report about the information and display pictures and historical documents about the person and the time and place she or he lived. This LRM will direct students to photo-essays.

Divide the class into small groups. Let each group select a different picture book. Direct the groups to identify the story structure of the book. Direct each group to prepare a visual story map, creative drama, or puppet show for the book.

Read a picture storybook that evokes strong feelings, such as Robert Coles's *The Story of Ruby Bridges* (1995). Do not have a discussion before, during, or after reading the book. Ask students to write thoughts and associations in their LitLog while or after listening to the book. Some students may want to reread or look at the book again. Encourage them to develop their writing. Volunteers will share their writings in a small group. Then the groups and class will discuss the ver-

bal and visual texts of the book and present additional information about the historical period.

Exploring a Sequence of Illustrations

These strategies and LRMs ask students to consider the way a sequence of illustrations can tell a story or provide information about a topic:

Cover the text of a picture book, a picture storybook, or an information book with pictures. Have the children tell the story by reading the pictures; tape the reading. Then read the book to the class. Compare the children's story to the published text. Discuss why students could successfully tell the story or give the information in some books but were not successful in other books.

Read all but the last two pages of Tedd Arnold's *Green Wilma* (1993) (or a book or poem with a surprise ending). Have the children predict the ending. Then, read the last two pages and talk about the students' predictions. If some students guessed the ending, ask how they knew. What details in the illustrations gave them the answer? Was the class surprised at the ending? Discuss the moral on the last page of the book. Let several students read the book to another class using the same technique. Elicit their predictions. Talk about the impact of the details in the picture. Also use Arthur Yorkins's *Hey, Al* (1986).

Select a wordless book, such as David Wiesner's *Free Fall* (1958) or John Goodall's *Paddy's New Hat* (1980). Discuss the way the artist sequences the illustrations to tell the story. Have small groups of children prepare a text for a wordless book. They will use various media when preparing the sequence of illustrations. The sequence must tell a continuous story. The book will be bound in an Accordion Book (see Appendix B). After preparing the book, discuss problems encountered while creating the wordless text. Display the books in the classroom or the school media center. (Older students could write statements about what they learned while preparing a wordless book and add them to the back of the book.)

Determining the Suitability of a Subject for a Particular Type of Book

These strategies and LRMs help students determine the suitability of a subject for a particular type of book:

Read a book with pictures that is an excerpt of a longer classical novel, such as Margaret Hodges's *Gulliver in Lilliput* (1995). Elicit students' reactions. Display a copy of the entire book and, if available, an illustrated, simple version of the classic. Read the excerpted section from the original book. Talk about the differences between the verbal texts. Elicit students' reactions to the illustrations in the excerpted book. Have older students write an excerpted section from a favorite book. Prepare illustrations for the original book. Bind the book and share with younger children.

Have intermediate-age students read an easy-to-read book and identify the unique characteristics of this type of book (see Chapter 11 "Transitional Learners"). The students will decide if the subject is adequately developed in the text. If not, a group of children will rewrite the text adding the missing details. Ask a teacher of younger children to read the book to his or her class. Then the older children will read their rewritten book to the class. The younger children will illustrate the rewritten story. The book will be bound and placed in the school media center.

After studying a particular topic, have the students find books with pictures containing information about the topic. Have students decide if the book adequately covers the topic by noting especially the depth of information given, the vocabulary and terminology used, and the illustrations used in the book. Decide if the book gives enough information for younger children and is therefore suitable for them. Partners could prepare additional verbal texts for the book and illustrate the new pages.

Prepare a KWL about a particular topic. Then read and discuss a simple concept book about the topic. Select a book that has a limited text, one or two pictures per page, and lots of white space, such as Lois Ehlert's *Color Zoo* (1989) or Donald Crews's *Truck* (1990). Ask students to list additional information given in the book. Ask the students if the book gave them enough information. If not, have them find books that will give them adequate information. Talk about the purpose of each book and the age for which it is intended. Discuss the importance of illustrations in a concept book for the intended age. Discuss the purpose of the book.

Other Strategies and LRMs

Other strategies and LRMs to explore the overall quality of a book include the following (see also Table 8.4 under the heading "Overall Quality of a Book"):

Read several books about a particular cultural, ethnic, or religious group. Have students list information about the lifestyle of the group gained from the illustrations and verbal text. Bring several fine art pictures about the group, and ask students to identify additional information. Have students confirm the information in various reference sources and discuss their findings

in class. Discuss the power of art to supplement information gained from a verbal text.

After reading an illustrated book such as E. B. White's *Charlotte's Web* (1952) or A. A. Milne's *Winnie the Pooh* (1924), divide the class into two groups—the visual group and the auditory group. Have the class select an incident from the book. The visual group will prepare a series of visuals about the incident. The auditory group will present a readers theatre based on the incident. The visual group will display and discuss their pictures, then the class will discuss questions such as the following: What information did you receive by hearing the incident? What did you see in the visual that the author did not tell you? (Direct students' attention to the setting, the characters, the mood projected by the visuals, and the movement of the incident in the visuals.) How do you feel about the book after seeing and hearing the incident?

Talk about marketing techniques to advertise a product. Look at the art used in advertisements. Each student will select a favorite book with pictures, select a visual LRM listed in Appendix B, and prepare an advertisement for the book. The advertisements will be posted in the media center with the book.

At the end of the year give each child a 10-by-10-inch square of white cloth. Ask the student to select his or her "favorite" book with pictures. Ask students to draw a picture representing their personal interpretation of the book. Include the author, title, and the child's name in the picture. Students will use thread or fabric markers to draw the picture on the square of cloth. Elicit the assistance of a parent and sew the squares together. Bind the front with a backing of fabric. If desired, place batting inside the front and back. Machine quilt or quilt with ties. Embroider the teacher's name and the year on the quilt. Display it properly in the classroom or in a prominent place in the school.

Sharing Caldecott Books

Share the books selected as the winner and honor books for the Caldecott Medal for a particular year (see Appendix C). Find the author's acceptance speech in *The Horn Book Magazine* (published in the summer after the award is received). Talk about the award, who receives it, and why. Display several other books published the same year. Have children discuss the art in the books and decide if they agree with the committee. Read or summarize the author's acceptance speech and discuss it. Survey the students to see if the article changes their mind about the award. Have the students write letters to the Caldecott Committee of the American Library Association and politely report their reactions to the winner. Mail one letter selected by the class to represent their reactions. (They could repeat this LRM several times throughout the year, but write only one letter to the American Library Association. Other letters could be addressed to the media specialist.)

Give the students a list of the Caldecott winners and honor books. Have the students find the books and select their favorite example of the specified genre. On a designated date, the students will discuss the books representing a particular genre. Display and discuss the selected example, and report students' reactions to it.

THE HISTORICAL DEVELOPMENT OF BOOKS WITH PICTURES

Books with pictures evolved slowly until the mid-nineteenth century, when pictures became an important part of books as a result of several trends.[28] First, in the late 1860s, talented artists were encouraged to experiment with artistic styles and media and to illustrate books for young people. Second, when adults recognized childhood as a separate stage of development, they realized pictures in books helped stimulate children's aesthetic, social, literary, and cognitive development. Fortunately, in the latter part of the twentieth century, technological advances in publishing methods and refined graphic processes have allowed innovative design techniques that have led to a proliferation of books with pictures. This section will focus on several questions:

Identify the artists who influenced the historical development of pictures in books?

How have publishing techniques contributed to the evolution of books with pictures?

What ideas about childhood and educational practices have influenced the publication of books with pictures?

EARLY INFLUENCES

From the fifth century A.D., early manuscripts, handwritten on parchment and rolled into a scroll, were used to teach spiritual truths and traditional learning primarily to children of the nobility or wealthy townspeople. These early manuscripts contained religious verses, secular tales, and stories from natural history. Eventually, social traditions and manners were also included. When the monks who wrote the manuscripts had artistic ability, they added decorations containing realistic and fabulous creatures. The young scholars were not allowed to touch the valuable manuscripts, but the decorations probably amused them.

In the early 1480s, William Caxton brought a printing press with movable type from Germany to England. The first English printer also brought manuscripts and crude woodcuts with him, and in 1484 he printed an English translation of *Aesop's Fables.* Caxton was not concerned with the artistic merit of the book, but he randomly printed 185 crude woodcuts throughout the fables. The illustrations in this and other early books were poorly reproduced from coarsely cut blocks of wood. The books were printed on cheap paper, which made the text and pictures hard to discern, but nevertheless young people and adults enjoyed viewing the pictures placed within the narrative text.

Except for coarse woodcuts printed in broadsides and chapbooks, publishers did not consider it important to include appropriate illustrations in books until the seventeenth century. In 1657, Johann Amos Comenius, a Bavarian monk and teacher, published *Orbis sensualium pictus* (*The Visible World in Pictures*). Comenius believed children learned through concrete experiences so he included woodcuts that realistically illustrated the content. (See the Comenius color plate, page 197). The pictures were numbered, and the numbers also appeared in the text to enable students to match the pictures with the corresponding text discussion.

At the end of the eighteenth century, Thomas Bewick (1753–1828), an artist, began illustrating books as a profession. Young Bewick was apprenticed to an English engraver in Newcastle who gave him an opportunity to experiment with woodcuts, which were not an important commercial product at the time. Bewick invented a tool that allowed him to engrave woodblocks on the end of the wood. The technique allowed him to achieve delicate details in line and space, thus greatly improving the crude woodcuts of the past. His sensitivity to beauty and ability to realistically portray images in alphabet books, fables, and other books were soon recognized, and his wood-engraving technique became a popular method of illustrating books. Thomas became a partner in the Newcastle company and with John, his younger brother, continued to improve the technique in the books they illustrated. Because of the Bewicks' influence and the hand-colored illustrations William Blake included in his collection of poems *Songs of Innocence* (1789), artists in the nineteenth century began experimenting with woodcuts and engravings in illustrated books. Table 8.5 on page 292 lists notable artists and their contributions before the nineteenth century.

THE NINETEENTH CENTURY

Except for William Mulready (1807), Howard Pyle, and the American magazine artists who illustrated popular children's novels in the 1880s, English artists and publishers were primarily responsible for the pictures in books during the nineteenth century. Fortunately, recognized artists began to turn their attention to fictional books for young people. Artists used various styles ranging

DATE	ARTIST, TITLE	COMMENTS
1484	English edition of *Aesop's Fables* (W. Caxton, printer)	Contained 184 crude woodcuts placed randomly through the text; printed on cheap paper and hard to read, but enjoyed by reader.
1658	J. A. Comenius, *Orbis sensualium pictus*	First illustrated book intended for children. Used for educational purposes, the book contained numbers in the text and with the pictures to give the student visual information about the text.
1690+	Broadsides and chapbooks	Crude engraving for characters in the "Famous Histories," such as Tom Thumb and Dick Whittington.
1771	T. Bewick, *The New Lottery Book of Birds and Beasts*	Using the improved wood-engraving technique he developed, Bewick was the first English artist to make a book with pictures for children. The artist's knowledge and love of nature are seen in his book. He and his brother John were the first to sign their pictures for children.
1779	*A Pretty Book of Pictures for Little Masters and Misses or Tommy Trip's History of Beasts and Birds*	
1784	T. and J. Bewick, *The Select Fables of Aesop and Others*	The pleasures of childhood are shown in the woodcuts.
1789	W. Blake, *Songs of Innocence*	To illustrate his poetry about children, the poet ground and mixed colors with his wife's assistance and then applied the color to 27 three-by-five-inch copper engravings.
1792	J. Bewick, *The Looking Glass for the Mind*	Using wood engraving, Bewick created black and white figures of children and their dress that were popular with youth and adults of the time.

Randolph Caldecott's pictures for The Diverting History of John Gilpin *show the movement, humor, and outdoor scenes typical of his colored woodcuts. This picture was used for the design of the Caldecott Medal. Did you notice the personality Caldecott gave his human and animal characters?*

from realistic to cartoon art and refined the technique of producing black and white etchings and sketches.

In the 1860s, Edmund Evans, an English artist and engraver, perfected colored printing. Fortunately, he influenced several noted artists of the time, including Walter Crane, Randolph Caldecott, and Kate Greenaway, to use his technique. With skill and imagination, they began to use color in their illustrations to make children's books beautiful. Frederick Warne had the courage to publish their books, and colored illustrations in books became popular. Walter Crane was convinced that the verbal and visual text should be designed to present a harmonious whole. He used flat colors and firm black outlines to illustrate thirty-five nursery and folk literature picture books. (See the Crane color plate, page 90.) Randolph Caldecott illustrated picture books with simple line drawings adorned with color. (See the Caldecott color plate, page 292). He had a natural instinct for the type of pictures children enjoyed. Many of his illustrations were set in the outdoors and showed animals that seemed to come to life. His imaginative, detailed illustrations set high technical standards for picture books, which logically led Frederic G. Melcher, the chief editor of *Publisher's Weekly*, and the American Library Association to name the major American award for picture books in his honor. The English award for outstanding picture books was named for Caldecott's contemporary, Kate Greenaway. Greenaway illustrated folk literature, but also created colorful, detailed pictures showing young children playing in English gardens. Not liking the dress of children of the day, she drew her children in clothes reminiscent of the early nineteenth century. Her illustrations became so popular that mothers dressed their children in Greenaway's designs. (See the Greenaway color plate, page 294.)

With such illustrators, colored illustrations in books became popular. Juvenile literature entered the "Golden Age of Children's Books" around 1865 as recognized authors and artists began to devote their professional energies to writing and illustrating books for juveniles. Table 8.6 lists notable nineteenth-century artists and their contributions.

TABLE 8.6 Notable Artists and Their Contributions: Nineteenth Century

DATE	ARTIST, TITLE	COMMENTS
1807	W. Mulready, illus., W. Roscoe's *Butterfly's Ball*	Illustrated humorous poems for children. Achieved unity between words and pictures. Popular style copied by many artists.
1823 1853	G. Cruikshank, illus., Grimms's translated *Fairy Tales* *Fairy Library*	Noted artist illustrated many popular juvenile books. Achieved unity with verbal text in his imaginative, bold pictures. He set the standard for modern ideal illustrations.
1846	E. Lear, *A Book of Nonsense*	Humorist was the first author/illustrator. Used few lines in black and white sketches.
1865	J. Tenniel, illus., L. Carroll's *Alice's Adventures in Wonderland*	Cartoonist worked closely with author to capture fantasy text in black and white sketches.
1865	W. Crane, *The House That Jack Built*	First toy book illustrated by Crane and engraved in color by Evans; small format, bold outline, strong, primary colors, handwritten text. Many pictures covered a page or double pages. Crane illustrated many other toy books throughout 19th century.
1878	R. Caldecott, *The Diverting History of John Gilpin*	An established artist who illustrated 16 books in the 1870s; influenced by Evans's process. This first book and other depicted animals, horses, and children in the British countryside. Illustrations showed action, humor, and a free spirit. Major American award for illustrations is named for him.
1878 1881 1886	K. Greenaway, *Under the Window* *Mother Goose* *A Apple Pie*	An English artist influenced by Evans. Detailed illustrations depicted costumed children playing in English gardens in Victorian Age. Pictures more static and decorative than Caldecott's, lighter and more romantic than Crane's. Popular illustrations changed children's dress of period. Major English award for illustrations is named for her.
1883	H. Pyle, *The Merry Adventures of Robin Hood*	American artist and teacher who created realistic, bold, black and white sketches in unity with verbal narrative.
1885 and 1895	E. W. Kemble, illus., M. Twain's *The Adventures of Huckleberry Finn*; A. B. Frost, illus., J. C. Harris's *Uncle Remus Tales*	American magazine artists who illustrated popular juvenile books in black and white sketches. Both communicated a unique artistic spirit within the verbal narratives.
1899 1900	A. Rackham, illus., C. and M. Lamb's *Tales from Shakespeare* Grimms's *Fairy Tales*	The English artist/cartoonist achieved unity with black and white sketches. Early books were humorous and light in mood.

THE TWENTIETH CENTURY

At the beginning of the twentieth century, English artists, Beatrix Potter, Leslie Brooks, and Helen Bannerman, published verbal and visual narratives that set the standard for picture books and picture storybooks as we know them today. In 1902 Beatrix Potter published her first and perhaps most popular book, *The Tale of Peter Rabbit* (see Potter color plate, below right). In contrast to Potter's tiny pictures, Edmund Dulac, another artist, created large, full-color, bright illustations for children's books (see the Dulac color plate, page 295).

By the 1920s, American publishers, artists, authors, librarians, and educators had recognized the importance of juvenile books. The number of quality juvenile books increased. American publishing companies developed separate children's books departments, public libraries were established throughout the United States, and in 1921

Frederic G. Melcher and the American Library Association gave the first Newbery Award (named for the early English printer John Newbery) for an author's contribution to American books. The Caldecott Award, recognizing the artist's contribution to American books, was first awarded in 1938.

The 1930s were known as the "Golden Thirties" in the history of juvenile books. At this time American publishers greatly improved their production techniques, which attracted many well-known artists and authors from around the world to the United States where they joined American writers and illustrators in creating innovative, diverse books with pictures. Because childhood was now recognized as a separate stage of development, adults wanted children to be entertained and instructed with high-quality visual and verbal narratives.

In the 1970s fewer manuscripts were published, and fewer children's books were sold. Despite the awareness of

In this page from Kate Greenaway's book Under the Window *we see happy English children. Her full color paintings show flowers and other details of an English countryside. This book became an immediate success, making her the best-selling artist of her time. Because of her popularity children began wearing floppy hats and the clothes shown in the pictures.*

Using watercolor and line drawings, Beatrix Potter drew The Tale of Peter Rabbit *in an illustrated letter to a young friend who was sick. She was encouraged to publish the book privately, and later Fredrick Warne Company published this and her other 22 books with animal protagonists in English gardens. Although a picture does not cover an entire page, notice the detailed background she includes. Beatrix was a lonely young girl who spent many hours sketching animals and flowers she saw in her garden. Many of the sketches from her childhood appear in her books.*

social issues that permeated society, white, middle-class, suburban life—mothers in aprons and fathers with brief-cases—dominated the books published for young people. Publishers did reject books containing racial, ethnic, gender, or religious stereotypes, however. In the 1980s, problem stories about dysfunctional families, disabled children, divorce, single-parent families, multicultural characters in their own environment, and working mothers emerged in books with pictures. Tables 8.7 through 8.12 on pages 296–300 list notable artists and their contributions from 1900 through the 1980s.

THE 1990S

Innovative artists and book designers needed improved publishing techniques in the last decades of the twentieth century. Fortunately, lasers and other computer-generated publishing methods have replaced many time-consuming activities such as laborious color separations. Full-color printing and many new materials are now available. Artists are experimenting with innovative techniques such as combining media in different ways, developing new collage techniques, and using bold, new colors and lines. They are presenting their ideas in new ways using fabrics, plasticine, and computer graphics.

Adults are now attempting to surround children with age-appropriate books. Parents value book ownership, and regular visits to juvenile bookstores have become commonplace as they can be found in most communities. Books with various formats and paper engineering are readily available for youngsters of all ages. Fabric board books, pop-up books, and movable books have become popular gift items.

Many books with pictures are no longer intended for the youngest child. In fact, books with pictures dealing with every subject from dreams to social issues are now available for babies through adults. The large "coffee-table" picture

Edmund Dulac created bright watercolors for Nathaniel Hawthorne's Tanglewood Tales for Girls and Boys. *The artist was influenced by Eastern art in this book. Notice his attention to detail and use of color in this painting titled, "They were constantly at war with the Cranes."*

books have become very popular with families. Interactive books with pictures are popular with young people.

As educators recognize the need to enhance, supplement, and replace instructional materials with books with pictures, the number of picture books, picture storybooks, concept books, information books, photo-essays, and informational storybooks has multiplied dramatically. Many books with pictures reflect the diverse cultures, races, and groups of people inhabiting the world. A review of books with pictures reveals that in the early 1990s more female protagonists involved in all types of activities are portrayed in the books.[29]

Books with pictures are now published in every literary genre. The genre chapters are filled with many outstanding examples. Since so many individual titles are available in books with pictures, the wise adult must carefully select qual-ity books that are suitable for young people. Not all books are of the same high quality. Adults feel comfortable selecting reissues of old favorites. Some contain the original art, while others serve as a showcase for the talent of new artists.

Many popular artists from the mid-1900s continue to publish new, original books with pictures. They include Maurice Sendak, William Steig, Eric Carle, Tomie de Paola, Leo Lionni, and Barbara Cooney. Fortunately, popular writers such as Jane Yolen, Bill Martin, and Cynthia Rylant are lending their considerable talents to the books as well. Short story collections and poetry books highlighting one or several artists' work have become popular choices.

Table 8.13 on page 300 lists notable artists of the 1990s. Because many notable artists and authors are creating books with pictures, this listing focuses mainly on people who are enjoying popularity in the field for the first time.

TABLE 8.7 Notable Artists and Their Contributions: 1900–Early 1930s

DATE	ARTIST, TITLE	COMMENTS
1900	A. Rackham, illus., W. Irving's *Rip Van Winkle*	Additional books illustrated by Rackham. These were more mysterious, dark, and eerie than his earlier books.
1906	J. M. Barrie's *Peter Pan in Kensington Garden*	
1931	C. Moore, *The Night Before Christmas*	
1901	B. Potter, *The Tale of Peter Rabbit*	First of 16 fantasy tales of animals by this author/illustrator. Delicate, detailed watercolors depict animals and garden scenes. Potter greatly influenced the development of the modern picture storybook.
1903	L. Brooke, *Johnny Crow's Garden*	The first *Johnny Crow* book published by this author/illustrator. Used robust, humorous style similar to R. Caldecott's.
1924	E. H. Shepard, illus., A. A. Milne's *When We Were Very Young*	Black and white sketches contributed to the popularity of these fantasy books. Perfect unity between verbal narratives and visual sequences.
1933	E. H. Shepard, illus., K. Grahame's *The Wind in the Willows*	
1927	W. Nicholson, *Clever Bill*	This English author/illustrator produced a classic children's picture book.
1928	W. Gag, *Millions of Cats*	This American author/illustrator created a picture storybook using black and white wood-block, rhythmic lines and German folk art. An early example of a repetitive picture story-book.
1930	L. Ward, illus., E. Coatsworth's *The Cat Who Went to Heaven*	The 1931 Newbery winner, *The Cat Who Went to Heaven,* was illustrated with fine brush drawings. In *The Biggest Bear,* the 1953 Caldecott winner, Ward used fine woodcuts. He used various media, especially wood engravings, in more than 100 books.
1952	*The Biggest Bear*	
1932	L. Lenski, *The Little Family*	First American picture book of everyday family life. Lilliputian characters shown in outline and flat colors. Stylized naive art; small size. First of a series by the author/illustrator.
1932	G. Williams, illus., L. I. Wilder's *Little House Series*	Black and white pen sketches realistically enhanced the verbal text; perfect example of an illustrated book.
1933	K. Wiese, illus., M. Flack's *The Story about Ping*	American artist used Asian folk art style. The book relies heavily on the pictures to convey the story; author and artist worked closely together.

TABLE 8.8 Notable Artists and Their Contributions: Mid-1930s–1940s

DATE	ARTIST, TITLE	COMMENTS
1937	B. Artzybasheff, *Seven Simeons*	Russian artist immigrated to the United States; used bright-colored lithographs and big pages, characteristic of children's books in France and England.
1937	Dr. Seuss (T. Geisel), *And to Think That I Saw It on Mulberry Street*	The first of 90+ fanciful picture books by the popular author/illustrator. Humorous, fanciful, rhyming verbal text in unity with a visual text that incorporates original artistic style, primary colors, and unique characters.
1938	Establishment of Caldecott Award	First winner: Dorothy Lathrop, illustrator of *Animals of the Bible* (text adapted by H. D. Fish).
1936	I. and E. d'Aulaire, *George Washington*	Fictionalized biography with black and white and colored stone lithographs. Their *Abraham Lincoln* (1939) received the 1940 Caldecott Medal.
1939	L. Bemelmans, *Madeline*	First book in the series about a French girl. The Austrian author/illustrator immigrated to the United States; used expressionistic black and white line drawings, with some yellow pages. 1940 Caldecott honor book.
1939 1942	V. L. Burton, *Mike Mulligan and His Steam Shovel* *The Little House*	The author/illustrator used watercolor and pen. She is noted for the total harmony of movement, rhythm, and decorations in her visual and verbal narratives. *Little House* won the 1943 Caldecott Medal.
1941	H. A. Rey, *Curious George*	The first of a series about a naughty monkey who lives with the man with the big yellow hat. Perfect example of an anthropomorphic animal. The author/illustrator used black lines and bright yellow colors.
1941 1948 1952	R. McCloskey, *Make Way for Ducklings* *Blueberries for Sal* *One Morning in Maine*	Talented author/illustrator portrayed realistic narratives. In Caldecott winner *Make Way for Ducklings* he used realistic sepia lithographs; in *Blueberries for Sal* McCloskey used blueberry lithographs; and in his Caldecott winner *One Morning in Maine* he used soft watercolors.
1942	F. Rojankovsky, *The Tall Book of Mother Goose*	Another noted Russian artist who immigrated to the United States; used bright-colored lithographs and achieved unity with verbal text. Noted for his picture of Humpty Dumpty that looked like Hitler.
1943 1950	R. Duvoisin, *The Three Sneezes* *Petunia*	Swiss artist who immigrated to the United States. This first book was reproduced in line-blocks; other books used colored lithography and fantasy animals.
1949	L. Politi, *Song of the Swallows*	Early distinguished picture storybook with Spanish-American folk art and story. The author/illustrator won the 1950 Caldecott Medal.

TABLE 8.9 Notable Artists and Their Contributions: 1950s–1970s

DATE	ARTIST, TITLE	COMMENTS
1954 1961 1982	M. Brown, *Cinderella* *Once a Mouse* *Shadow*	The first of three Caldecott Awards won by artist/author (also six Caldecott Honor Awards). Uses a variety of styles and media. *Cinderella,* subtle watercolors. *Once a Mouse,* woodcut; *Shadow,* collage. Has written original stories, but major contribution is retelling single folk tales.
1955	T. Yashima, *Crow Boy*	Japanese-American author/illustrator used Japanese folk art, bright-colored lines and crayon to depict shy Japanese country boy whose talent was recognized by a wise teacher.
1957 1957	M. Sendak, illus., E. Minarik's *Little Bear* Dr. Seuss (T. Geisel), *The Cat in the Hat*	Introduction of easy-to-read books containing appealing content, controlled vocabulary, and pictures.
1958	B. Cooney, *Chanticleer and the Fox*	Old English tale produced in scratchboard, black and white with red; 1959 Caldecott winner.
1979	D. Hall's *The Ox-Cart Man*, illus., B. Cooney	Gouache, native art style; 1980 Caldecott winner about a year in the life of an early 20th-century farmer.

TABLE 8.10 Notable Artists and Their Contributions: 1960s

DATE	ARTIST, TITLE	COMMENTS
1962	E. J. Keats, *The Snowy Day*	The 1963 Caldecott winner. The author/illustrator used collage, French marbled papers, wallpaper, Japanese silk papers, texture, and color with paints to create a simple background for a childlike story about an African-American child's everyday experiences in snow.
1963	M. Sendak, *Where the Wild Things Are*	The 1964 Caldecott winner, considered by many to be the "perfect" picture book. This author/illustrator began the trend of fanciful almost "scary" picture books.
1963	B. Wildsmith, *Brian Wildsmith's Mother Goose*	English author/illustrator produces bright gouache pictures with distinctive Cubist art (harlequin designs) in the details of the pictures.
1963 1966	C. Piatti, *The Happy Owl* *Celestino Piatti's Animal ABC*	This Swiss author/illustrator uses poster paint, simple illustrations with one object per page, limited text, and bright colors/outlines.
1962 1963	L. Lionni, *Inch by Inch* *Swimmy*	This author/illustrator used collage, paper, stamps, watercolor washes, and blotted wet pictures in these simple concept books. Both books were Caldecott honor books.
1964	J. Pinkney, illus., J. Arkhurst's *The Adventures of Spider: West African Folktales*	Pinkney used bright watercolor and pencil for the folk-style illustrations in his first juvenile book. This is a popular collection of West African folktales.
1969 1982	W. Steig, *Sylvester and the Magic Pebble* *Dr. Desoto*	This author/illustrator used detailed watercolor with black ink lines for his popular fantasy animal storybook that won the 1970 Caldecott Medal. His unique style is shown in *Dr. Desoto,* an animal fantasy chapter picture storybook.
1969	E. Carle, *The Very Hungry Caterpillar*	The first of a series of popular participation books. Bright, bold collages portray the caterpillar's feasts through the week.

TABLE 8.11 Notable Artists and Their Contributions: 1970s

DATE	ARTIST, TITLE	COMMENTS
1970s	Picture books published in paperback format	Beginning of affordable picture books.
1970	A. Lobel, *Frog and Toad Are Friends*	First of several easy-to-read "Frog and Toad" books; fantasy animals, realistic drawings. The first book in the series was a Caldecott honor book.
1972	T. Hoban, *Push Pull, Empty Full*	First of many simple concept books and photo-essays created by this photographer.
1973 1975	T. de Paola, *Nanna Upstairs, Nana Downstairs* *Strega Nona*	An early autobiographical book written and illustrated by this prolific author/illustrator. His Italian/Irish heritage appears in his recognizable, yet flexible style. The painter is noted for his folk art.
1974 1974	B. Peet, *The Wump World* *Merle, The High-Flying Squirrel*	The first of several picture storybooks written and illustrated by a former Disney animator. His books are humorous stories about animals, illustrated in charcoal with color added.
1973 1990	D. Macaulay, *Cathedral* *Black and White*	A 1974 Caldecott honor book, *Cathedral* is a nonfiction book tracing the building of a cathedral. The author/illustrator is noted for his nonfiction books using line drawings. In 1991 he won the Caldecott Medal for *Black and White.* Using watercolor, he tells four stories in one book.
1974	G. McDermott, *Arrow to the Sun: A Pueblo Indian Tale*	1975 Caldecott winner; early book with pictures for older readers.
1975 1978	M. Anno, *Anno's Alphabet* *Anno's Journey*	The first of several detailed wordless, concept books by the author/illustrator. His watercolor and pen and ink books are enjoyed by all ages.

TABLE 8.12 Notable Artists and Their Contributions: 1980s

DATE	ARTIST, TITLE	COMMENTS
1979 1981	C. Van Allsburg, *The Garden of Abdul Gasazi* *Jumanji*	*Jumanji* was the 1982 Caldecott winner. The popular author/illustrator used black and white detailed lines in his Surrealist art that interprets his verbal text.
1982 1989	E. Young, illus., L. Ai-Lang's *Yeh-Shen: A Cinderella Story from China* *Lon Po Po: A Red Riding Hood Story from China*	The artist retells and illustrates Asian folk tales using vivid pastels, juxtaposition of patterns, and white paper showing elegant panels. *Lon Po Po* was the 1990 Caldecott winner.
1983 1983 1989	T. S. Hyman, illus., *Little Red Riding Hood* *Saint George and the Dragon* *Hershel and the Hanukkah Goblins*	Hyman illustrates fairy tales, legends, and fantasy using realistic characters, vivid colors, and exquisite borders. *Little Red Riding Hood* was a 1984 Caldecott honor book, and *Saint George and the Dragon* was the 1985 Caldecott winner. Hyman also received the Caldecott honor in 1990 for Eric Kimmel's *Herschel and the Hanukkah Goblins* (1989).
1983	A. Browne, *Gorilla*	Popular animal portrayed by an English author/illustrator who uses detailed lines to portray action in a Surrealist style.
1986	L. E. Fisher, *The Great Wall of China*	A recognized artist used black and white detailed line drawings with double-page spreads full of motion in this outstanding information book with pictures for older readers.
1988	B. S. de Regniers, et al., *Sing a Song of Popcorn*	Outstanding example of a poetry collection illustrated by nine Caldecott-winning artists, including M. Brown, the Dillons, M. Simont, and M. Zemach.
1989	L. Ehlert, *Planting a Rainbow* *Color Zoo*	Author/illustrator uses original cut paper technique with simple shapes and flat, intense, bright colors. The concept book contains repetitive, limited verbal text. Excellent design. *Color Zoo* was a 1990 Caldecott honor book recognizing paper engineering.
1989	D. N. Lattimore, *Why There Is No Arguing in Heaven: A Mayan Myth*	Another retelling illustrated by an artist. This Mayan myth is portrayed in dark, lush colors with Mayan sculptural forms and Mayan folk art; the endpapers supplement the verbal narrative. The artist is noted for retelling folk literature and providing additional cultural information. She has also illustrated historical fiction.

TABLE 8.13 Notable Artists and Their Contributions: 1990s

DATE	ARTIST, TITLE	COMMENTS
1990	Demi, *The Empty Pot*	One of several Asian tales delicately illustrated by the artist. Her illustrations meticulously detail the cultural heritage of the tale.
1991	D. Wiesner, *Tuesday*	Realistic watercolor pictures vividly portray the fanciful adventures of flying frogs. This wordless book won the 1992 Caldecott Medal. The artist has influenced the publication of other wordless books.
1991	J. Baker, *Window*	The artist uses multimedia collage in this wordless book to show through a boy's bedroom window his growth from babyhood to adulthood. At the same time, the view shows a lush Australian bush changing as civilization advances.
1992	L. Smith illus., J. Scieszka's *The Stinky Cheese Man and Other Fairly Stupid Tales*	Through the visual and verbal texts, the author/artist team humorously manipulated familiar traditional tales. The book design amuses children who are familiar with picture books.
1992	B. Pinkney, illus., R. D. San Souci's *Sukey and the Mermaid*	Pinkney has mastered the scratchboard technique with oil pastels in this African tale. Pinkney achieved complete unity with the text as he portrays Sukey, Mama Jo, the black mermaid, and Deman.
1992	F. Cooper, illus., J. Merrill's *The Girl Who Loved Caterpillars*	Using realistic, delicate oil wash on board, Cooper captures the beauty of Izumi, the young Japanese girl who must follow her heart in this adaptation of a 12-century Japanese story. His art represents the folk art of the period. Cooper is noted for his portrayal of parallel cultures.
1993	A. Say, *Grandfather's Journey*	In a sparse text, the 1994 Caldecott winner describes the contrast between life in Japan and America in the early 1900s. The detailed watercolor drawings have the appearance of photographs.
1993	J. Murphy, *Across America on an Emigrant Train*	Using black and white photographs and reproductions Murphy vividly describes Robert Louis Stevenson's exhausting trip from Scotland to California in 1879. Murphy has influenced the popularity of the photo-essays.
1994	P. O. Zelinsky, illus., Anne Isaacs's *Swamp Angel*	Zelinsky uses oil on cherry and maple veneer to bring to life this original tall tale about a pioneer woman who is transformed into Swamp Angel. This book is an example of the perfect harmony between this artist/author team.
1995	P. Rathmann, *Officer Buckle and Gloria*	In her visual and verbal texts, the author/illustrator presents a hilarious contemporary tale about a police officer and his buddy, Gloria the dog. The simple line drawings with color enhance and enrich the storyline and received the 1996 Caldecott Medal.
1996	D. Wisniewski, *Golem*	Jewish legend about creature who, in the late 16th century, protected the Jews in Prague from violence. Wisniewski's dramatic sepia and coral cut-paper illustrations received the 1997 Caldecott Medal.
1996	J. Pinkney, illus., A. Schroeder's *Minty: A Story of Young Harriet Tubman*	In typical watercolor and pencil paintings, Jerry Pinkney enhances this fictionalized biographical sketch of the early life of a slave who became a conductor on the Underground Railroad. The illustrations won the 1997 Coretta Scott King Award.

Summary

Books with pictures are found in every literary genre. More juvenile titles are in books with pictures than any other category. Children of all ages enjoy hearing, reading, and viewing the books. The success of a book with pictures depends on the creators' ability to design unique, yet compatible visual and verbal narratives. Young people enjoy reading both narratives and gain valuable information from the books. Visual narratives interpret, expand, enhance, clarify, supplement, decorate, and/or replace the verbal narrative. Visual narratives evoke the mood of the book, establish the setting, help portray the theme, and help develop the characters.

Effective visual communication depends on the artist wisely selecting and competently combining the artistic features in the book. These artistic features include the artistic elements the artist uses to create an image (line, shape and form, color, textures, and space); the styles used to visualize the verbal text (realistic art, expressionistic art, impressionistic art, humorous art, and folk art); the various paint and drawing media, photography, collage, and graphic techniques; and the principles of design that are considered when composing and arranging the various images (balance, rhythm and movement, proportion, emphasis, pattern, unity, and variety). The final consideration of the art in books with pictures involves the features of book production (the cover, size, shape, endpapers, typography, paper). The chapter also discusses how the visual and verbal narratives work together to tell a story or provide information and the way people read the visual and verbal narratives.

Books with pictures are classified according to their visual and verbal narratives and their content. The three major categories are wordless books, picture books, and illustrated books. Various categories within those classifications include information books, informational storybooks, concept books, and photo-essays.

Techniques for presenting the various categories of books and using the books in the classroom are included in the chapter. Factors to consider when presenting the literature are also discussed, such as young people's natural artistic preferences, benefits gained from exploring pictures, and guidelines for selecting books. Depending on the students, the books, and the curricular goals, the teacher designs and implements appropriate instructional focuses and strategies and suggests LRMs for the learners to produce to respond to the visual and verbal narratives.

The historical development of books with pictures began with Comenius's *Orbis sensualium Pictus* in 1658, but it was not until the 1860s that many artists began illustrating juvenile books with pictures. At the end of the twentieth century, innovative artistic techniques, new media and combinations of media, original book designs, and technological advances have resulted in the creation of original, outstanding books with pictures. As children continuously explore books with pictures, they experience "the beauty of the world."

Literary Link

WORDLESS BOOK

WIESNER, DAVID. 1991. *TUESDAY.* NEW YORK: CLARION. 1992 CALDECOTT WINNER.

GENRE: Wordless book: Low Fantasy.

THEME(S):   Anything is possible; seeing is believing; if only dogs could talk!

SETTING: Somewhere in the United States; Tuesday evening around 9:00.

ILLUSTRATIONS: Realistic, colored watercolor paintings on Arches paper; Buomer type.

CHARACTERS: *Protagonists:* frogs. *Others:* turtle, fish, birds, midnight snacker, dozing grandma, Rusty, news reporters, detectives.

LITERARY FOCUS: Aesthetic. Later, if desired, discuss frogs.
- Enjoy fantasy.
- Stimulate imagination.
- Read a wordless book.

- Understand the role of illustrations in telling a story.
- Learn how illustrations are used to move a story forward by foreshadowing and depicting a sequence of events through panels and double-page spreads.

Notice how detailed lines, color, and texture are used to depict the setting and reveal the characters' thoughts and actions. Observe the use of clocks.

AGE OF STUDENTS:
Six years through thirteen years.

ORGANIZATION OF STUDENTS:
Might display the book and other wordless books in the literature center before sharing it with the class; Use small group presentations and discussions. The teacher leads and the children read the illustrations for the story line.

CURRICULAR AREAS: If applicable.

APPROXIMATE TIME REQUIRED:
Three to six days depending on the age of the students and their responses.

CURRICULAR GOALS:
If desired, use an efferent focus after the aesthetic focus:
- Enhance students' oral and written language competencies.
- Focus on frogs and their habitat.
- Enhance visual literacy.

SUMMARY
Around 9:00 on a Tuesday evening, frogs abruptly awaken as their magical flying lily pads take them on an adventure. As the frogs fly from their pond home into a nearby town, they wreak havoc on the citizens. They surprise a midnight snack, tangle with laundry, enter windows, enjoy television, and have an adventure with Rusty the dog. As dawn breaks, they return to their water homes and leave bewildered citizens wondering what happened. The detective has a problem to solve, "Why are there wet lily pads on the street?" "Why is a man raving about seeing flying frogs in the night?" If only Rusty could talk! Yet, wait until next Tuesday at 7:58 P.M., the town is in for a real treat!

BIOGRAPHICAL INFORMATION
David Wiesner (weez-ner) was born on February 5, 1956, in Bridgewater, New Jersey. From an early age, he knew he would be an artist. In art school he discovered Lynd Ward's wordless book *Madman's Drum* and knew this was the type of art he wanted to create. He liked the idea of communicating with his viewers through a series of illustrations rather than through a single picture. He liked the challenge of telling the story through art. As a child, he was fascinated by science fiction and flying saucers. His senior art project was a wordless book. His first book, *Free Fall* (1988), is an impressionistic wordless book, portraying a boy flying through his books and dreams. The books was a Caldecott honor book in 1989. Wiesner has illustrated more than 15 books for other authors and has written and illustrated two books of his own. *Hurricane* is based on an incident in his life with his brother. *June 29, 1999* is an illustrated science fiction fantasy about amazing vegetables produced by a girl's scientific experiment (or did they result from a mistake by a chef on a starcruiser?).

In 1979, while a senior at the Rhode Island School of Design, Wiesner received his first professional job—to draw the March cover for *Cricket Magazine*, a juvenile literary magazine. The editor gave him the freedom to create a cover of his choice, but told him that the magazine contained stories about St. Patrick's Day and frogs. Before long frogs on flying lily pads appeared in Wiesner's sketches. His love of science fiction movies and books and fantasy is apparent in the cover. A decade later, Wiesner returned to his cover and quickly developed the visual narrative for *Tuesday*.

Wiesner says his primary reason for producing a book is to amuse his audience. However, he is delighted if his viewers find a variety of ways to interpret the visual narratives. He feels the creator of a wordless book stimulates the viewer's imagination and together they invent the story line. David Macaulay, a noted artist and creator of many juvenile books with pictures, is a friend and mentor. *Tuesday* is dedicated to Tom Sgouros, Wiesner's teacher.

Share this information informally after reading the book the first time. It is best to share when students begin to question the artist's style, media, and composition or the format of the book.

NOTE TO THE ADULT PRESENTING THE BOOK
The *connect, construct,* and *create* components of this literary link are presented in tabular form to remind the presenter that the components are interrelated and are used in the presentation as needed to help children construct meaning and respond to the visual narratives. Strategies representing the selected literary focus and curricular goals are suggested in probe and prompt format. The table includes page numbers of images that may guide the viewer's reactions to the suggested probes and prompts. The probes and prompts are used *only* to direct or stimulate the viewers' reactions and interpretations. As children have many experiences exploring and reading wordless books, they will need only limited adult direction. Teachers need to consider the literary goals and purposes for using the book, however.

The viewers' initial experience with the book must be aesthetic and pleasurable. Then, through informal inquiry, the probes and prompts focus students' attention on the visual narrative, in particular, on the aspects of the visual narrative that portray the story line. Finally, the curricular goals are implemented depending on the teacher's purpose, the students' reactions to the book, and the use of the book in curricular areas. The curricular strategies are planned as a natural extension to the story and the viewers' interest in pursuing additional inquiry.

Connect

Before presenting the actual book, do the following:

Display several wordless books, but not *Tuesday.*

After several days, say to the students: "You have had an opportunity to look at the books displayed in the literature center. What is different about the books?" "That's right, the books do not have words. These books are called wordless books, or books that tell a story through the visual narrative. How did you 'read' the book?"

Then the adult continues talking about techniques for reading a series of illustrations: "Because we read the details in the pictures and follow the individual pictures to find the story line, we will read the book in small groups." At this point the teacher arranges to share the book with one group while the other students work on other tasks. The teacher explains the arrangement and presents the book to the groups within one or two days.

When introducing Tuesday, *do the following:*

Discuss the cover; elicit predictions about the content of the book from the pictures; encourage students who have read the book to allow others to make predictions: "I wonder what the clock has to do with the story." "What does the title tell us about the book?" "What is sitting in front of the house?" "What is sitting on the green circles?" "I will give you a clue by reading a poem by Jack Prelutsky."

Read and lead a discussion of "I Am Flying!" (in Jack Prelutsky's *The New Kid on the Block,* p. 90).

"We know the green circles are flying, but what is on the circles? Write on a piece of paper what you think is on the circles. Fold the paper and place it in the Prediction Pitcher."

"How does the title relate to the story?"

Direct attention to intertextual connections, such as the format of the book. Ask "Have you read other books that remind you of this one?" (Prepare frog-shaped visuals and lily pads; students will list titles of wordless books on the visuals. Place the visuals on a bulletin board (suggested title "Flying through Wordless Books").

Direct attention to other intertextual connections, such as the genre or content of a book. Share with students other books about an adventure at night. Have the class prepare a comparison chart about the differences and similarities of the plots and characters in the various books. (See the bibliography for related books.)

Make connections to the artist. Share other books written and illustrated by David Wiesner. Talk about the differences and similarities of the books. See LRMs.

Construct

At the first reading, if needed, do the following:

Early in the reading help children recognize and accept fantasy elements: "I didn't know frogs could fly. Maybe the lily pads are magic." "What do flying frogs tell you about the story?"

After the reading, ask, "Do you believe pigs can fly in David Wiesner's books? I do!" In his poem "If Pigs Could Fly," James Reeves has some ideas about what he would do if they could (Natalie Bober, *Let's Pretend,* p. 33). After reading the poem, show the picture on the cover of the poem book and elicit students' reactions.

Help children follow the sequence of illustrations to interpret the story line. Elicit student observations about the pictures: "Do the frogs like to fly? How do you know?"

Throughout the story focus their attention on the *movement* of the story: "Are the frogs staying over the pond?" "Why would they move over the houses (p. 6)?" "Will the dog eat the frog (p. 17)?" "What is the man telling the television crew?" "Why is the police officer investigating (pp. 24–25)?" "What will happen next Tuesday night around 8:00 (last pages)?"

Focus attention on *foreshadowing.* "Why does the man have a surprised look on his face (p. 8)?" "Why do the frogs go into the house?" "How did the frog turn around? What will happen next (p. 17)?" "What will happen to the flying pigs (last page)?"

Focus attention on the *story sequence:* Remind students to begin at the top of the page or to look at illustrations from left to right. Encourage them to read the story from one illustration to another.

Direct attention to the details in the pictures: "What do you know about the frogs? How do they feel at dawn (p. 23)?" "What thoughts are going through the detective's mind (p. 24)?" "How does Rusty feel about the lily pad (p. 24)?" "How do I know the dog's name (p. 19)?" "Throughout the story, how does the artist tell us the time?" (Note that the artist includes a clock in eight pictures.)

The second time through the book, direct students' attention to the *artistic aspects* used by Wiesner to portray mood, characters, setting, plot, and perspective: "How does Wiesner give us clues about the character's feelings in his pictures (pp. 18–19)?" "What do the frogs like to do?" (Sleep, fly, watch television, chase dogs.) "How did the grandmother feel the next day when she was told about the frogs? Did she know they were watching television with her?"

"What do the pictures tell us about the settings (pp. 2, 11, 23)?" "Is the setting real?"

"How does Wiesner arrange his pictures to help us follow his story?" (Discuss the use of panels and double-page spreads.)

"If we know frogs and pigs can't really fly, why do we believe Wiesner's pictures?" (Viewers like the realistic style with fantasy elements; they like the characters and story; Wiesner convinces us to accept his world.)

"How does the artist give us a frog's-eye view of the adventure?" (Discuss the different perspectives shown in the book from the cover—frogs flying, pigs flying—and discuss how the story would be different if all the pictures were drawn from the earth looking up.)

Create

As appropriate, produce selected LRMs before, during, and after presenting the book:

Find other wordless texts; discuss and list unique characteristics of wordless books. Place titles on visuals shaped like frogs and lily pads. Place visuals on the bulletin board.

Brainstorm what will happen to the flying pigs and create an original wordless book.

Prepare a large mural showing what happens when pigs fly.

Find other books and poems about flying animals.

Prepare a television report interviewing the man who saw the frogs.

After the interview, prepare a reporter's rebuttal, explaining why the man could not have seen flying frogs.

Prepare several large lily pads. Ask students to role-play one of the frogs in the story. Play suitable music while the students dramatize where they would go on the lily pad, what they would do once they were there, and, finally, what they would bring back from the visit.

A group of students will prepare a shadowbox of an incident in the book.

Groups of students will name the frogs and write the adventure from the frog's point of view.

Write a dramatic script of the story. Present the drama to another group of students. Include all of the human characters' reactions to the frogs, even grandmother's perspective. Select appropriate music to accompany the presentation.

Groups of students will select an animal other than frogs and pigs. They will prepare the script and puppets for a puppet show about what happened the Tuesday after the pigs flew. They will present the show.

Use the book to tell the story to younger children.

Collect poems about frogs or pigs. Copy the poems; place them in a bound book with appropriate illustrations. Encourage students to add original poems to the collection. Students will share favorite poems throughout the year. The book will be in the class library. At the end of the year present it to the media specialists to be displayed in the school media center.

Prepare a *Wednesday Party*. Plan a menu that would be appropriate for the book: flying frog frappe; dazed dog donuts; amazed man marble cake; lily pad lasagna, pink pig punch, and the like. If possible, the children will prepare the food and serve it to invited guests. At the party, they will tell the story and show LRMs.

Have students write in their LitLogs questions they would ask David Wiesner if they could interview him. Partners will share the questions and, based on the biographical information presented, will attempt to answer the questions. The questions and answers will be shared with other partners to confirm or verify responses. The students will select the best questions and answers. One letter will be written to Mr. Wiesner. The letter will explain the activity, include the selected questions and answers, and request a reply to the questions. The letter could be decorated with appropriate visuals representing several of his books.

David Wiesner's dark blue, green, and white watercolors show the artist's ability to tell a story and describe characters using only pictures in his book Tuesday. *In his detailed background, the artist shows the viewer what is happening to the frogs. When viewers read the three small pictures from left to right, they find out where the frogs go—and they might be able to predict future events.*

NOTES

The opening quotation is from Marcia Brown's speech accepting the Caldecott Medal for *Cinderella*. Annual conference of the American Library Association in Philadelphia. 1995.

1. For additional information about the artistic elements, see sources such as Chapman, L. H. 1992. *A World of Images*. Worcester, Mass.: Davis; Kiefer, B. Z. 1995. *The Potential of Picturebooks: From Visual Literacy to Aesthetic Understanding*. Englewood Cliffs, N.J.: Merrill. 121–31.

2. For additional information about principles of design, see sources such as Chapman, L. H. 1992. 18, 19, 54–59; Marantz, S. S. 1992. *Picture Books for Looking and Learning*. Phoenix, Ariz.: Oryx. 10–12; Shulevitz, U. 1985. *Writing with Pictures: How to Write and Illustrate Children's Books*. New York: Watson-Guptill.

3. Nodelman, P. 1992. *The Pleasures of Children's Literature*. New York: Longman. 137.

4. For additional information about the various styles of art, see Chapman, L. H. 1992. 20–21; Cianciolo, P. 1990. *Picture Books for Children*. (3d Ed.). Chicago: American Library Association. 34–38; Kiefer, B. Z. 1995. 118–20; Nodelson, P. 1988. *Words about Pictures: The Narrative Art of Children's Picture Books*. Athens, Ga.: University of Georgia. 77–100.

5. Kiefer, B. Z. 1995. 193–96.

6. For additional information about media and graphic techniques used by artists, see sources such as Chapman, L. H. 1992; Marantz, S. S. 1992. 5–10.

7. The following sources were consulted to develop the chapter bibliography: Cianciolo, P. 1990. 41–213; *The Bulletin of the Center for Children's Books*. Urbana, Ill.; University of Illinois; *The Horn Book Guide*. Boston: *The Horn Book Magazine*; Jensen, J. M., & Roser, N. L. (Eds.). 1993. *Adventuring with Books: A Booklist for Pre-K–Grade 6*. (10th Ed.). Urbana, Ill.: National Council of Teachers of English; and the author's reactions.

8. For additional information about the physical features of books, see sources such as Goldenberg, C. 1993. The design and typography of children's books. *The Horn Book Magazine*. 69(5). September/October. 559–67; Smith, L. 1993. The artist at work. *The Horn Book Magazine*. 69(1). January/February.

9. For additional information about narratives in books with pictures, see Nodelson, P. 1988. 242–70; Roxburgh, S. 1983–1984. A picture equals how many words?: Narrative theory and picture books for children. *Lion and the Unicorn*. 7–9. 20–33; Shulevitz, U. 1985. 18–61.

10. Elleman, B. 1995. Illustration as art: Character. *Book Links*. 5(1). September. 34–37.

11. For additional discussion about reading verbal and visual narratives, see sources such as Flood, J., & Lapp, D. 1991. Reading comprehension instruction. 732–42. In Flood, J., Jensen, J. M., Lapp, D., & Squire, J. R. (Eds.). *Handbook of Research on Teaching the English Language Arts*. New York: Macmillan; Fransecky, R. B., & Debes, J. L. 1972. "Visual literacy: A way to learn . . . a way to teach." Association for Educational Communications and Technology. Washington, D.C. (*ERIC Document* No. ED 064-884); Golden, J. M., & Gerber, A. 1990. A semiotic perspective of text:

The picture storybook event. *Journal of Reading Behavior*. 22(3). 203–19.; Gombrich, E. H. 1961. *Art and Illusion: A Study in the Psychology of Pictorial Representation*. New York: Pantheon; Iser, W. 1978. *The Act of Reading: A Theory of Aesthetic Response*. Baltimore: Johns Hopkins University Press; Visual image. 1972. *Scientific American*. 227. September. 82–94.

12. Schwarcaz, J. 1982. Relationships between text and illustration. In *Ways of the Illustrator: Visual Communication in Children's Literature*. Chicago: American Library Association. 9–20.

13. Nodelman, P. 1988. 242–43.

14. Sutherland, Z., & Hearne, B. 1977. In search of the perfect picture book definition. *Wilson Library Bulletin*. 52. October. 158–61.

15. Luken, R. J. 1995. *A Critical Handbook of Children's Literature*. (5th Ed.). New York: HarperCollins. 225.

16. Wiesner, D. 1992. Foreword. In Richey, V. H., & Puckett, K. E. *Wordless/Almost Wordless Picture Books*. Englewood, Colo.: Libraries Unlimited. xvi.

17. See the following sources for information about wordless books: Evan, D. 1992. Wordless picture books—the medium is the message. *Book Links*. 1(4). 46–49; Goforth, F. S. 1991. The wordless text: A teacher's dream and a reader's delight. *Florida Reading Quarterly*. 28(3). March. 5–9; Tuten-Puckett, K., & Richey, V. 1993. *Using Wordless Picture Books: Authors and Activities*. Englewood, Colo.: Teacher Ideas Press; Williams, B. O. 1994. Every picture tells a story: The magic of wordless books. *School Library Journal*. 40(8). 38–39.

18. Lobel, A. 1981. A good picture book should. 74. In Hearne, B., & Kaye, M. *Celebrating Children's Books: Essays on Children's Literature in Honor of Zena Sutherland*. New York: Lothrop, Lee & Shepard. 73–80.

19. Sources for Pinkney Did You Know? Bishop, R. S. 1996. The Pinkney family: In the tradition. *The Horn Book Magazine*. 72(1). 42–49; Kovac, D., & Preller, J. 1991. *Meet the Author and Illustrators: 60 Creators of Favorite Children's Books Talk about Their Work*. New York: Scholastic. 50–51.

20. For additional information about the teacher's role, see sources such as Goldstone, B. P. 1989. Visual interpretation of children's books. *The Reading Teacher*. 42(6). 592–95; Kiefer. 1995. 22–40; 55–64; Weigmann, B. A. 1993. Visual literacy, science process skills, and children's books. In *Art, Science and Visual Literacy: Selected Readings from the Annual Conference of the International Visual Literacy Association*. Pittsburgh. September 30–October 4, 1992. 386–94. (*ERIC Document* No. ED 363 328).

21. See sources such as the following for additional information about instructional ideas to help children acquire and develop visual literacy skills and aesthetic awareness: Debes, J. L. 1969. The loom of visual literacy: An overview. *Audiovisual Instruction*. 14(8). October. 25–27; Clayback, J., Goforth, F., and Spillman, C. 1980. Read, translate, compose, and evaluate: Visual language skills. *Language Arts*. 57(6). September. 628–34; Lacy, L. E. 1986. *Art and Design in Children's Picture Books: An Analysis

of Caldecott Award–Winning Illustrations*. Chicago: American Library Association. 1–2; Murphy, S. J. 1992. Visual learning strategies. *Book Links*. 1(5). May. 15–21; Stewig, J. W. 1992. Reading pictures, reading text: Some similarities. *The New Advocate*. 5(1). Winter. 11–22.

22. For additional information about benefits viewers gain from pictures in books, see Bang, M. 1991. *Picture This: Perception and Composition*. Boston: Bullfinch Press; Cianciolo, P. 1990. 1, 15–25; Kiefer, B. Z. 1988. Picture books as contexts for literary, aesthetic, and real world understandings. *Language Arts*. 65(3). 260–71; Langer, S. 1953. *Feeling and Form*. New York: Scribner's. 397; Mackey, M. 1993. *Picture Books and the Making of Readers: A New Trajectory*. Concept Paper No. 7. Urbana, Ill.: National Council of Teachers of English; Wallace, I. 1989. The emotional link. *The New Advocate*. 2(2). Spring. 75–82.

23. Kiefer, B. Z. 1995. 10–12, 44, 54.

24. See the following sources for additional information about the artistic preferences of young people: Groff, P. 1977. Should picture books and young children be matched? *Language Arts*. 54(4). April. 411–16; Kiefer, B. Z. 1985. Looking beyond picture book preferences. *The Horn Book Magazine*. 62(6). November/December. 705–13; Smerdon, G. 1976. Children's preferences in illustrations. *Children's Literature in Education*. 20. 97–131.

25. For additional information about selecting books with pictures, see Bingham, J. M. 1979. Pictorial treatment of blacks and teaching picture reading skills in order to enrich children's vocabularies. Paper presented at the Fourth Great Lakes IRA Regional Conference, Detroit, Michigan, October 1979; Cianciolo, P. 1990. 29–32; Kiefer, B. Z. 1995. 120–23.

26. Kiefer, B. Z. 1995. 22–40.

27. For additional information about using books with pictures in the classroom, see sources such as Cianciolo, P. J. 1994. There is much to see and think about in book illustrations. In Hickman, J., Hepler, S., & Cullinan, B. E. (Eds.). *Children's Literature in the Classroom: Extending Charlotte's Web*. Norwood, Mass.: Christopher-Gordon. 123–34; Farris, P. J., & Fuhler, C. J. 1994. Developing social studies concepts through picture books. *The Reading Teacher*. 47(5). February. 380–87; Griffiths, R., & Clyne, M. 1988. *Books You Can Count On: Linking Mathematics and Literature*. Portsmouth, N.H.: Heinemann; Mitchell, F. S. 1990. Introducing art history through children's literature. *Language Arts*. 67(8). December. 839–46; Norem, M. B. 1991. Using Caldecott books. *The Reading Teacher*. 44(8). 618–20; Wason-Ellam, L. 1991. *Start with a Story*. Portsmouth, N.H.: Heinemann. 18–25, 81–107.

28. See sources such as the following for information about the historical development of juvenile books with pictures: Alderson, B. 1986. *Sing a Song of Sixpence: The English Picture Book Tradition and Randolph Caldecott*. Cambridge: Cambridge University Press; Bader, B. 1976. *American Picturebooks: From Noah's Ark to the Beast Within*. New York: Macmillan; Bland, D. 1958. *A History of Book Illustration: The Illuminated Manuscript and

the Printed Book. New York: World; Brown, M. 1968. One wonders. In Illustrators of Children's Books: 1957–1966. Boston: The Horn Book; Lima, C. W., & Lima, J. A. 1989. A to Zoo: Subject Access to Children's Picture Books. (3d Ed.). New Providence, N.J.: R. R. Bowker. xiii–xix; Roberts, E. E. M. 1981. The Children's Picture Book. Cincinnati: Writer's Digest Books. 16–19; Ward, L. 1978. The book artist: Ideas and techniques. In Kingman, L. (Ed.). The Illustrator's Notebook. Boston: The Horn Book. 80–83.

The following sources were consulted for information about the 1990s: Elleman, B. 1995. Toward the 21st century—Where are children's books going? The New Advocate. Summer. 8(3). 151–65; Evans, D. 1992. An extraordinary vision: Picture books of the nineties. The Horn Book Magazine. 68(6). November/December. 759–63; Stewig, J. W. 1991. Ten from the Decade: Visually significant picture books and why. Paper presented at the annual meeting of the International Reading Association, Las Vegas, May 6–10, 1991; and the author's observations while developing the chapter bibliographies.

29. This information is based on the author's review of The Horn Book Guide for 1990–1995 (the majority of hardback books published in the United States are reported in this guide) and The Bulletin of the Center for Children's Books for 1990–1995 (the majority of books published in the United States are reported in this bimonthly bulletin).

Literature Reflecting Parallel Cultures

A Celebration of Unique and Universal Perspectives

*I*t seems that, although language and customs are different in various parts of the world, there are no differences at all in our hearts.

—Mitsumasa Anno

Chapter Reflections

What is literature reflecting parallel cultures?

What benefits do young people gain from exploring literature reflecting parallel cultures?

What criteria are used to select quality literature reflecting parallel cultures?

How is the literature organized and presented in the classroom?

What quality literature authentically portrays the historical and contemporary culture and lifestyles of African-American, Asian-American, Hispanic-American, and Native American children and adults?

During the 1970s, people from many professions were vocal in their support of bringing cultural and ethnic groups together in political, social, and educational settings. From America to Australia, most developed countries experienced an increase in the number of immigrants. Fortunately, the immigrants brought many of their prized possessions—their oral histories, personal memories, and cultural traditions. Each group of people had their own customs, lifestyles, and traditions.

Obviously, most contemporary communities are diverse societies. If diverse groups are to coexist successfully, they must recognize and respect the unique beliefs of all individuals. They must also acknowledge and observe the universal values revered by the entire community. In 1989, author Virginia Hamilton coined the term *parallel cultures* to avoid the negative connotation of the term *minority group*, which suggests that a group is unequal or inferior and does not have a unique culture, language, or social institutions. In contrast, parallel culture conveys the idea that all groups "stand as equals side by side."[1] Literature reflecting parallel cultures as defined by Hamilton is found in all literary genres and realistically portrays "people of color," especially African Americans, Asian Americans, Hispanic Americans, and Native Americans. This chapter will discuss literature dealing with these four groups and their biological and cultural heritage and identity.

◊ OVERVIEW

Although Euro-Americans are still the largest group in the U.S. population (73 percent in 1995), the number of people from parallel cultures is increasing rapidly. This shift in the population is having an impact on the schools. In 1995,

26 percent of the school-age population were from parallel cultures. Demographers estimate that by the year 2000 that percentage will have risen to 28 percent. If this trend continues by the year 2050, 47.5 percent of school-age children will be from parallel cultures. The largest single group will be children from Hispanic backgrounds. Hispanics or Latinos include all races and may have a Spanish cultural background, a Latin American background, or a Mexican-American background.[2]

As the population becomes more diverse, quality educational systems should recognize and foster the unique traditions and universal values of the various groups in the community. Educators realize the importance of incorporating into the school curriculum authentic experiences and knowledge from the various individuals and groups within the global society. Each group has its own distinct lifestyle, customs, attitudes, and beliefs. Among other things, the groups may differ in whether they emphasize individual autonomy or dependence on others, in the importance they give to material power versus spiritual power, and in their views about nature. At the same time, most members of the global community accept and share certain universal beliefs and values, such as love, compassion, kindness toward others, a vision of a better future, a desire for equal opportunity, a yearning for achievement, and respect for those who overcome adverse situations and survive.[3] The bibliography presents books that focus both on the unique values and experiences of a group and on the universal beliefs acknowledged by all groups of people. An example is Faith Ringgold's *Tar Beach* (1991). (See the Ringgold color plate on page 309.) Cassie, the African-American protagonist, imagines that she is flying over the tar beach (the rooftop of her apartment building) to overcome the difficulties endured by her family in the past. Her dreams are described in the simple verbal narrative and depicted in the detailed, vivid illustrations that convince the reader that Cassie's life will be different from that of her family. The illustrations are from the first of five story quilts Ringgold created to combine autobiography, fictional narrative, painting, and quilt making in one art form. The book highlights her family's experiences but also illustrates the universal belief in family.

A curriculum that is sensitive to cultural and ethnic diversity has as its goal helping all young people to gain a positive self-image and take pride in their culture. Such a curriculum also highlights the historical, social, and political movements of other ethnic, cultural, and religious groups to help children understand their own heritage and to respect that of others. As part of a total curriculum, teachers highlight the unique traditions, experiences, and beliefs valued by a group and compare these to universal values shared and honored by all groups. Through age-appropri-

Tonight we're going up to Tar Beach. Mommy is roasting peanuts and frying chicken, and Daddy will bring home a watermelon. Mr. and Mrs. Honey will bring the beer and their old green card table.

And then the stars will fall around me, and I will fly to the union building.

Faith Ringgold created original expressionistic paintings for her book Tar Beach. *The artist used bright acrylic paints on canvas paper for the paintings. The background material for the verbal narrative is the same canvas paper used in her paintings. Reproductions of the original story quilt are shown in the border at the bottom of each page. At the end of the book the artist-author includes a picture of the original story quilt and information about creating the verbal and visual narratives.*

ate instructional strategies and carefully selected literature reflecting all cultural groups, school-age children will learn to coexist with others and will be prepared to meet the changes and challenges they may encounter in the global society of the future.

Largely through the pioneering work of Augusta Baker, Rudine Sims Bishop, and the Council on Interracial Books for Children, selection criteria are available to help adults and children intelligently choose literature that authentically portrays diverse societies.[4] High-quality literature presents a clear, comprehensive, and compassionate perspective on the unique and universal values of diverse societies in a special way that is not achieved in other materials.[5] This is apparent, for example, when we read a description of the internment of Japanese Americans during World War II in a history textbook and then read Sheila Hamanaka's account in *The Journey: Japanese Americans, Racism, and Renewal* (1990).

DEFINITION OF TERMS

Experts use various terms to refer to major concepts in this area, so some brief definitions of terminology may be useful. The term *multicultural literature* is used to refer to all literary genres that authentically depict the diversity of society by realistically portraying the unique lifestyles and heritage of all social, cultural, and ethnic groups. Such literature takes into account ethnic, cultural, linguistic, socioeconomic, gender, and religious differences. Some commentators suggest that the term *multicultural literature* should be restricted to narratives depicting only ethnic minorities. They believe that presenting ethnic literature can help correct the maladies of racism and social inequity. This narrow view of multicultural literature may lead to the exclusion of other groups, however. Joseph Bruchac, a notable author of many books about Native Americans, urges us to accept the Native American definition of *multiculturalism.*

To the first Americans, the term means "all our relations"—all people, not just some people. Bruchac feels this approach helps us better understand and accept others.[6] The universal concern for others is a theme of Bruchac's *Gluskabe and the Four Wishes* (1995). This picture book describes the journey of four Abenaki men to see Gluskabe, a great hero. Each man asks Gluskabe to fulfill a wish. Only one man remembers the community and is granted his wise wish. Christine Myburg Shrader's illustrations enhance this Abenaki teaching tale. The chapter bibliography includes examples of multiethnic literature portraying various groups successfully interacting with others. Other literature dealing with multicultural groups is presented in the various genre chapters.

Culture is a system of values, beliefs, and standards shared by a group of people. The cultural system directs the attitudes, ideas, and behavior of individuals within the group. The culture may include language, folklore, artistic expressions, patterns of thinking, and social and interpersonal relationships. Culture is a dynamic process that we learn, share, and adapt as constantly changes. Members of a particular culture accept certain "truths" and expectations. They express these beliefs in subtle nuances, allusions, and humor in the group's oral and written literature.

Ethnicity refers to the national origin of one's ancestors. Members of an ethnic group share history, values, and behavior. Frequently, groups are classified according to religion, class, region, nation, or language, as well as by ethnicity.[7]

BENEFITS YOUNG PEOPLE GAIN FROM EXPLORING LITERATURE REFLECTING PARALLEL CULTURES

Enthralling stories and poems can break down barriers, dispel prejudice, and help young people recognize the similarities and differences between people.[8] Quality fiction and nonfiction literature helps children from various cultural backgrounds build a sense of community. Quality literature helps transmit the values, attitudes, mores, concerns, and worldviews of diverse societies. Literature expands children's horizons and helps them explore this complex, puzzling world through the eyes of positive role models. Books convey emotions and information about people. They invite children to empathize with the characters and their conflicts and encourage the reader to adopt new perspectives about self and others. Literature reflecting parallel cultures can be found in all literary genres. Through folk literature, children discover the values and beliefs of a primitive society. Realistic fiction gives children an authentic view of all societies. Nonfiction literature provides accurate information about the history,

lifestyles, traditions, and concerns of diverse societies. Through poetic expression, children gain insight into the dreams, ideas, and thoughts of various groups. Through the visual images, the child's interpretation of a people is enhanced and enriched.

Literature provides girls and boys with a magic *mirror* that reflects the past as well as the present and enables them to view not only their own dreams, hopes, and ambitions but also those of their ancestors. Literature portraying diverse groups gives children a *window* through which to see the traditions, visions, and contributions of individuals they might not otherwise encounter. Through these literary mirrors and windows, young people discover people with similar or different cultural experiences and customs and thereby gain unique perspectives about life. Literature reflecting parallel cultures also identifies the universal values and beliefs shared by all people. By exploring fiction, nonfiction, prose, and poetry that examines these universal beliefs as well as

When families read literature together they explore the mirrors of their lives and through literary windows discover the aspirations, traditions, and contributions of other people.

TABLE 9.1 Benefits Individuals Gain from Exploring Literature Reflecting Parallel Cultures

Benefits from Literature that Mirrors Life

A child's self-esteem is enhanced when literature depicts members of his or her ethnic group. This recognition gives them a positive feeling about their worth as an individual and as a productive member of their society.

Children take pride in their culture when they explore the social, historical, and linguistic heritage transmitted in the literature.

Literature helps children discover their "roots" and understand the contributions their people have made to world history.

Literature helps raise children's aspirations and goals.

As children encounter the stories of others in their group, they discover and begin to understand the expectations of the group.

Benefits from Literature that Opens a Window on Others' Lives

By exploring the rich social, historical, and cultural diversity of other people, children's personal view of others is widened, and their worldview is expanded.

Children are curious about others' lives. Literature is a way to discover and promote an appreciation for the traditions and heritage of others. This helps a young person become tolerant of others.

When children explore diverse groups through literature, they recognize the similarities and differences among humans in all times and places. This helps children develop a sense of belonging to a global community.

Young people develop an appreciation for the common experiences that connect people from varied ethnic and cultural groups and produce a richer society.

Through literature young people realize other people have comparable feelings, emotions, and needs.

Literature helps children recognize, appreciate, accept, and celebrate the similarities and differences between people.

General Benefits Gained from Exploring Literature Reflecting Parallel Cultures

Through literature, young people recognize the imaginative, creative, political, and social contributions of individuals in specific fields of endeavor.

Children stop thinking in stereotypes when they encounter other people in authentic literature.

Through literature, children realize the dynamic nature of culture. They recognize the conflicts that occur when old and new ways merge. This gives them a broader perspective and encourages them to look at the past to learn about the present and make predictions about the future.

Through literary experiences, children gain a broader understanding of national history and geography.

Literature gives children a sense of world problems and a more responsible attitude toward society.

---

the unique beliefs of various groups, youngsters will better understand, respect, and coexist with people from various classes, races, and cultural groups. Table 9.1 lists benefits individuals gain from literature that mirrors their own lives, literature that opens a window to the lives of others, and general benefits gained from exploring literature that reflects parallel cultures.

STRIVING FOR CULTURAL AUTHENTICITY

Young people have the right to expect the literature they explore to give them a better sense of themselves and of others. Therefore, it is vital that the literature reflecting parallel cultures authentically present facts about a group and represent the heart of the society. Rudine Bishop tells us that cultural authenticity is essential when portraying family relationships, beliefs, and customs valued by a group. To assure cultural authenticity, the creator must recognize the nuances of the daily life of a cultural group and not distort or misrepresent the characters.[9]

Cultural authenticity is directly related to a major controversy surrounding multicultural literature: Who should write or illustrate literature reflecting parallel cultures? Thelma Seto, a poet and fiction writer, emphatically states: "Multiculturalism is not Halloween. You cannot put on one mask and 'become' Asian."[10] She reminds Euro-American writers that they cannot imagine or understand the traumas passed from one generation to another in Asian-American families. She eloquently argues that only an insider, a person who is a member of a group, can truthfully and respectfully portray the group. Marc Aronson, an editor, disagrees. Observing that musicians freely cross boundaries when interpreting music, he asks why creators of children's literature are restricted from crossing cultural boundaries. If authors and artists prepare adequately, Aronson says, why can't they produce any type of book they desire?[11] Yet August Wilson, an award-winning African-American dramatist, contends that an outside creator, even with years of research, cannot understand or portray the different ways people respond to the world. Since people have different ideas about religion, manners, and language and do not share the specifics of a culture, he believes an outside writer cannot write authentically about another culture.[12] Certainly, most authors and artists do acknowledge that their experiences and family teachings influence the narratives they produce. This subjective presentation may result in a narrow or distorted interpretation of the lifestyle or beliefs of a culture, or it may give a reader valuable insight into the values and traditions honored by the culture.

As the debate continues, both sides are presenting persuasive arguments.[13] Nevertheless, two underlying issues remain. First, many insider writers feel they are culture-bound and must write only about the cultural or social group of their birth. Second, many authentic stories may not be published because the writer is not a member of the group portrayed in the story. We must ask, "Should we reject quality literature because of the birth credentials of the creator?" Hazel Rochman, the respected co-editor of the American Library Association's *Booklist*, urges adults to recognize the issue. She encourages us to resist the extremes and refuse to lock writers "into smaller and tighter boxes."[14]

Every thinking person would agree that the writer must authentically portray the subtleties of the group, their history, their traditions, and, if applicable, their contemporary life. All people would also agree that a book must express the spirit and heart of the group. Finally, all people would acknowledge that the literary quality of the book is of primary concern. Accordingly, outside writers are encouraged to be rigorous in their research, sensitive to the complexity of the culture, and willing to recognize the limitations of their personal perspective. Many writers describe their background and document the oral and written sources they used to obtain cultural, historical, and social information about the group. At the same time, members of the group have the responsibility to point out mistakes and omissions made by outside writers in their verbal and visual narratives. This information gives selectors outside the group valuable information about specific literature.

On the day of the wedding, Clement looked more handsome than ever and Pauline was a vision in a white satin gown sewn with diamonds, diamond-studded satin slippers, and a veil of antique French lace that had belonged to Clement's mother. The house and gardens were filled with guests who had come from miles around.

Brian Pinkney uses a scratchboard technique to enhance Robert San Souci's book, The Faithful Friend. *He adds color with oil pastels. Pinkney has refined the technique to show movement and uses texture to give a dimensional effect to the paintings.*

A creator who feels responsible for presenting authentic literature will imaginatively share the head and the heart of a group. A sincere creator will refuse to perpetuate stereotypical distortions and will honestly portray the experiences and traditions of a cultural group. The ultimate goal of all creators, whatever their birth credentials, is to produce a book that reflects cultural authenticity and is of the highest literary and artistic merit. These goals are reflected in Robert San Souci's *The Faithful Friend* (1995). This heartwarming story about friendship is set in a Caribbean culture. The culture and setting are authentically depicted in Brian Pinkney's visual narrative. (See the San Souci color plate on page 312.)

CRITERIA TO CONSIDER WHEN SELECTING QUALITY LITERATURE REFLECTING PARALLEL CULTURES

Young people are enthusiastic about exploring literature with characters who have believable experiences or experiences similar to their own. They quickly become immersed in literature about their cultural heritage, and they enjoy reading about important people from their ethnic, regional, or racial group. Young people who are curious about the world want to know more about other people, their traditions, their historical and contemporary lifestyles, and their customs and traditions. As learners explore literature about other people, they empathize with the characters and develop an appreciation and respect for unfamiliar groups. Quality fiction and nonfiction literature reflecting parallel cultures meet these expectations.

People outside a culture can determine cultural authenticity by reading information books about the culture, discussing unique aspects of the culture with people inside the culture, asking insiders to suggest authors and artists who consistently portray the appropriate spirit of the group, and consulting professional sources such as those listed in the chapter notes and the bibliography. When selecting appropriate prose, poetry, and drama portraying parallel cultures, three major criteria are considered. First, the book must meet the standards expected of all good fiction and nonfiction literature. Second, the literature should give readers insight into and perspective on the depicted group and its members' experiences. Third, the book must be historically and culturally accurate. It must reflect authentic cultural consciousness. Table 9.2 on page 314 lists specific questions related to these three criteria. When selecting quality literature reflecting parallel cultures, the selector should choose applicable questions from each criterion.[15]

THE ORGANIZATION OF LITERATURE

Although students may select an individual book for independent reading, frequently a variety of selections reflecting parallel cultures are chosen and organized in a literature collection for small and/or large group classroom experiences. A collection of literary selections widens the students' horizon and helps them develop an appreciation of and respect for people from different backgrounds. When exploring several books about the same topic, young people gain a broader understanding of the subject.

Literature collections reflecting parallel cultures may be culture specific or thematic. A *culture-specific* collection of books highlights a particular cultural or ethnic group, for example, Asian-American literature. Such collections give students valuable information about a group's mores, traditions, heroes, and standards. Young people also become familiar with the individual titles written about a group and the people who create the literature.

A *thematic collection* highlights a particular theme. The collection includes suitable literature reflecting various cultural or ethnic groups. By exploring a theme, students approach a topic from several social and cultural perspectives. Culture-related themes reflect universal concerns such as the following:

The Family Structure; Roles Assumed by Members of the Family

The Stages of Life and Coming-of-Age

Acceptable Communication and Interactions with Others

Religious Beliefs and Instruction

Health and Hygiene Practices

Food Preparation and Eating Manners

Holidays and Celebrations

The Values and Attributes Expected of Individuals and the Group

Educational Practices of the Group

Work and Play Valued by Society

Beliefs and Taboos Associated with Natural Phenomena

Animals and Their Care

Folk Art, Music, and Dance

Expectations and Aspirations of the People

Cultural Values and Occupations Passed from one Generation to the Next

TABLE 9.2 Guidelines for Selecting Quality Literature Reflecting Parallel Cultures

Does the Book Meet the Criteria for Literary Merit or Nonfiction Standards?

Does the author have an interesting writing style?

Is the subject appealing to the audience?

Is the content appropriate to the psychological, cognitive, and developmental level of the audience?

Does the content exploit violence or dwell on sensational details?

Do the illustrations realistically expand, enhance, or replace the verbal text?

If the book is *fiction,* are the characters unique and well developed?

   Is the theme worthwhile?

   Is the setting authentic?

   Is the plot developed logically, with realistic conflicts, tension, and suspense?

   Does the narrator express an appropriate point of view?

   Does the book stimulate the reader's imagination?

   Does the author help the reader develop empathy for the characters and events?

If the book is *nonfiction,* does the author present accurate and current facts, generalizations, or theory?

   Is adequate information provided?

   Is the information presented clearly for the intended audience?

   Are several points of view presented?

   Is the organization logical?

   In a biography, are the strengths and weakness of the character depicted?

Does the Book Help the Reader Gain Insight into the Experiences of the Parallel Culture?

Does the book help the reader develop a sense of pride in her or his ethnic group?

Does the book give the reader a different perspective on and additional information about the depicted group?

Are the characters and their behavior depicted in a nonjudgmental manner?

Are authentic culture-specific values included in the book?

Are universal concerns accurately portrayed in the book?

Does the Book Present an Authentic Historical Perspective and an Authentic Cultural Consciousness?

Does the author sensitively portray the unique patterns of behavior, personal interactions, emotions, attitudes, and styles of communication shared by the group depicted in the literature? Is the protagonist's behavior consistent with the acceptable reactions and experiences of the group?

Are historical events accurately and objectively depicted?

Are the cultural details consistent with the group's experiences and beliefs? Are additional details needed to provide adequate information about the group's lifestyle and traditions?

Do the visual and verbal texts avoid stereotypical images and caricatures?

Does the author recognize the diversity within groups by identifying the setting and specific group membership? For example, are Native American people from one group depicted wearing the clothing of another tribe? Are all members of the ethnic group portrayed as having had the same experiences even though they may have had different experiences and may have been in conflict through the years?

Are the characters supported by authority figures within the group? Are conflicts solved by the protagonist or by benevolent characters outside the group?

Do the illustrations authentically reflect, enhance, expand, or replace the verbal text? Are subtle messages included? Do the illustrations portray the diversity within a group?

Is the language natural and authentic to the historical setting? Do the characters use language appropriate to their educational and social background or situation? If dialect is used, is it authentic? Does the language interfere with the flow of the verbal text? Is sexist, demeaning, offensive, or condescending language used? (For example, "forefathers," "savages," "conniving," "lazy," "treacherous," "backward," and the like.)

If applicable, does the book authentically portray cultural changes reflected in contemporary lifestyles, attitudes, beliefs, or information? (For example, if appropriate, does the book reflect the changing role of females by dressing the characters in contemporary clothing and having them use contemporary customs?)

When introducing a theme such as Living within a Family, Barbara Joosse's *Mama, Do You Love Me?* (1991) could be used with children five to seven years old. Using repetitive, simple language, the book depicts the activities of a family living in the Arctic. The setting and the family's lifestyle are shown in vivid, watercolor illustrations. (See the Joosse color plate on page 316.)

To help teachers and students decide the best way to arrange and explore the literature, Table 9.3 on page 315 presents the advantages of organizing literature in culture-specific and thematic arrangements and also notes some potential problems to be overcome.[16] Additional information about thematic units is presented in Chapter 12.

◊ USING LITERATURE REFLECTING PARALLEL CULTURES IN THE CLASSROOM

Various literary experiences help children understand they are capable, unique individuals who are worthy of respect. When they observe the similarities and differences among

TABLE 9.3 Advantages and Potential Problems Associated with Organizing Literature in Culture-Specific and Thematic Arrangements

CULTURE-SPECIFIC ARRANGEMENT	THEMATIC ARRANGEMENT
ADVANTAGES	
A group's accepted patterns of responding and communicating and its history, values, and other discrete elements such as food, dress, lifestyles, art, and artifacts are the focus of study, making them easy for students to identify and understand.	A topic is presented from several ethnic and cultural perspectives, providing comprehensive coverage.
The diversity within groups is apparent.	Literature presents a different perspective of individuals and groups than textbooks do.
The historical events and people who shaped the culture of a group receive broad coverage.	All groups are presented in a variety of realistic roles and situations.
The books can help students celebrate a group's holidays and unique cultural events.	An ethnic group can be selected for literary study when other subject areas deal with issues, historical events, or themes important to that group. Thus, selections about people from European, African, Native American, Hispanic, and Asian backgrounds who contributed to American history could be studied at appropriate times.
Children from the group will see themselves in the literature and develop a positive, liberating attitude toward school and learning.	Students gain a broader understanding of the interactions of various groups and view themselves from a cross-cultural perspective.
By learning about a specific group, students come to accept and respect that specific culture.	Educators can include all discipline areas, e.g., art, music, history, other social sciences, science, and mathematics.
This is the easiest way to highlight a group.	
POTENTIAL PROBLEMS	
Students study the group in isolation from other groups on a special day, week, or month designated to celebrate an ethnic event. Frequently, the group is not considered before or after the designated time.	The study becomes unmanageable if every cultural group is included in every theme.
Information about the group is presented without comparison or contrast to other groups. Students may not gain a global view of the roles and contributions of diverse groups to local, regional, and national history and society.	Teachers may not be knowledgeable about each group's history and social values.
Students may study ethnic heroes apart from the social and political context of their lives and therefore gain only a partial understanding of their role in society, the reasons for their struggles, and the significance of their success.	This organization may require more class time than more traditional organizations.
The success stories of mainstream ethnic heroes become the focus while more radical and less conforming individuals who are heroes to the ethnic community may be neglected.	Time is required for selecting appropriate literature, planning, and presenting the literature across all content areas.
Issues related to victimization, oppression, struggles against racism, poverty, and empowerment may be ignored.	Teachers may present literature and concepts that may be controversial with parents, school, or school boards; for example, studying the arrival of Columbus from various cultural perspectives or reading a biography about Malcom X.
The focus is on the strange and exotic characteristics of the group—their traditional lifestyles—rather than social and political issues. This helps keep members of the group powerless and marginalized.	This organization is difficult to implement appropriately without assistance from school administrators and continuous district staff development.

people, as shown in literature, students realize people from different cultural backgrounds deserve that same respect. Table 9.4 on page 316 lists specific goals for using literature reflecting parallel cultures in the classroom.

PRESENTING THE LITERATURE IN THE CLASSROOM

The teacher's goals, the selected literature, and the students' background, interests, and developmental level determine the way the literature is presented. In the *pure literature approach*, the presentation and reaction focus on the students' and teacher's appreciation of and pleasure in the literature. In *literature-based language arts instruction*, initially an aesthetic focus toward the literature is assumed. Later an efferent focus is assumed as the literature is used for language arts instruction. When *literature is used across the curriculum*, the literature is used primarily for instructional purposes within all discipline areas (see Chapter 11 for further discussion of these three approaches). Both culture-specific and thematic

How long?

I'll love you until
the umiak flies
into the darkness,
till the stars turn
to fish in the sky,
and the puffin howls at the moon.

Barbara Lavallee uses images of life in Alaska for Barbara Joosse's Mamma Do You Love Me? *The artist fills the bright, expressionistic watercolor paintings with shapes and various forms. Her characters move and show emotions. Lavallee achieves texture through lines and wash. She arranges the verbal narrative in the paintings to form a pleasing visual composition. Notice the traditional Inuit ceremonial masks placed throughout the book. What do the symbols mean?*

TABLE 9.4   Goals for Using Literature Reflecting Parallel Cultures in the Classroom

Individuals will develop pride in their cultural heritage.

Young people will become familiar with the history, values, and behavior of individuals from diverse groups.

Girls and boys will explore various points of view to help them understand historical and contemporary events.

Young people will realize the contributions made by individuals from various groups to the local, regional, and national society and culture.

Children will understand the actions of others and develop a respect for individuals and various cultural and ethnic groups.

Boys and girls will learn to interact with others as they compare and contrast the values, beliefs, and attitudes expressed by people from diverse backgrounds.

collections can be used for all three approaches to literary study. However, certain books in both collections are better for reading aloud in a pure literary study than others. Arthur Dorros's *Isla* is such a book; Elisa Kleven's illustrations show Isla's delight with life. (See the Dorros color plate on page 317.) Linguistic patterns such as repetitive phrases are helpful for literature-based language arts instruction. Obviously, some books give specific information that is needed when literature is used across the curriculum. For example, information books give specific facts about historical periods, while a book of fiction might give students a better understanding of an issue by helping them see it through the eyes of the people involved. Therefore, teachers can pull specific books from culture-specific collections and thematic collections that will best meet the needs of the students and their instructional purposes.

As noted earlier, the bibliography has a thematic section and a culture-specific section. Books in the culture-specific section are arranged according to specific ethnic groups, literary genre, and topic. The nonfiction literature gives students and teachers background information about the various ethnic groups. A flexible organization such as this makes teachers and librarians aware of the variety of literature that is available to use with young people of all ages to meet the curricular goals and instructional purposes of a literature-based culture-specific or thematic literary study.

INSTRUCTIONAL FOCUSES AND STRATEGIES THAT ARE USED TO PRESENT THE SELECTED LITERATURE

After selecting literature that is developmentally appropriate and suitable for the curricular goals, the teacher assumes an *aesthetic instructional focus* to highlight the pleasure—the "lived-through" experiences—students gain from the literature. A teacher might implement this focus by using instructional strategies such as reading a book aloud to the class, then eliciting an informal conversation about the book, and finally encouraging the students to create a visual or verbal Literary Response Mode (LRM) based on their spontaneous reaction to the book. If the literature is used to gain specific information about a culture or several cultures, an *efferent instructional focus* is adopted. One way a teacher could implement this instructional focus is to divide the class into research groups. Then each group selects a topic already introduced or suggested in the literature and locates additional information about the subject. Finally, each group presents the information to the class and places it on a comparison chart. The information might be used later for instructional purposes.

Elisa Kleven multi-media collages enrich Arthur Dorros's Isla. The artist is noted for her bright textured paint and collage creations. She uses various media to fill the background of the expressionistic paintings. How does the photograph introduce the topic? What do you see behind Abuela?

Instructional Focuses Naturally Elicited by Various Literary Genres

Nonfiction literature presents information about the history, values, and heroes of a group and introduces students to people who made significant contributions to society. An aesthetic instructional focus is elicited when biographies or information books are read aloud to the class and informally discussed. Later, when the students are ready to "receive information" from the visual and verbal text, the teacher adopts an *efferent instructional focus* and uses suitable instructional strategies to help children learn specific information about the people or the group. By experiencing both instructional focuses, students gain pleasure and information from the literature.

Through the stories, poetry, and songs of folk literature, children gain an insight into the concerns, values, and customs of primitive people. Books with pictures, traditional literature, and information books highlight the art, music, and literature of the people. Usually, the teacher uses an aesthetic instructional focus and strategies and elicits suitable LRMs based on the students' natural responses to the arts of the people.

Fantasy, historical fiction, and contemporary fiction give students different views of events and issues that are important to a particular group. A variety of fictional stories present different points of view about a group's lifestyle and customs or conflicts encountered by individuals or the group. Although the imaginary stories are authentic and widen the child's perspective about a specific group, they do not replace informational materials. Thus, to provide a comprehensive coverage of a parallel culture, young people should be introduced to both fiction and nonfiction literature.

Instructional Strategies to Present the Literature

When designing appropriate instructional strategies to present the literature, the teacher selects strategies that help children connect to the content, enhance their personal experiences and knowledge, and are compatible with the students' styles of learning. A child's style of learning is influenced by methods of communicating acquired at home. For example, because of previous linguistic and cognitive experiences, many inner-city African-American and Asian-American students benefit from clearly defined directions and direct instruction. Asian-American students may enjoy working in small, same-sex groups. Native American and Hispanic children are accustomed to small group interactions at home and may be hesitant to respond to teacher-directed, large-group instruction. Generally, these children thrive with small, cooperative peer groups and reciprocal teaching.[17] Thus, to accommodate children's

various learning styles, teachers must use a variety of instructional strategies. Figure 9.1 on page 319 presents general information about instructional strategies to use when presenting literature reflecting parallel cultures. Additional information about instructional focuses and instructional strategies is presented in Chapters 2 and 11.

PRESENTING SELECTIONS AND COLLECTIONS

Whether presenting individual titles or an entire literature collection, a teacher can use the Literary Transaction Process described in Chapter 2. Here the teacher *connects* the children to the content, helps them *construct* meanings of the visual and verbal texts, and, if appropriate, encourages them to react to the literature and *create* LRMs. Connections provide background information about the subject of the literary selection. Thus, placing a variety of biographies and information books reflecting parallel cultures in the literature center can help the students make intertextual connections to other literature and provide background information.

The teacher might give a book talk to introduce a title or a collection to the children and include information for a Culture Treasure Hunt. Students then form teams and receive different clues to find in the books. The teams can place the clues and answers on transparencies and orally share them with the class. As the students read and discuss the literature in small or large groups, they can use the transparencies to help them *connect* to the topic and *construct* interpretations of the visual and verbal narratives. LitLogs also help students construct interpretations. Throughout the presentation of the literature, the students can *create* LRMs that naturally reflect their responses to the books. Use the *connect, construct, create* components simultaneously. This will help students gain personal satisfaction from the literature and enhance their understanding and respect for other people. This instructional process is applicable to all literature and all approaches to literary study.

SUGGESTED LITERARY RESPONSE MODES TO USE WITH THE LITERATURE

Alternative LRMs naturally emerge from individual books. While reading the individual books or collection, the students and teacher will react and respond to the literature. Encourage students to *create* LRMs that represent their personal interpretations of the visual and verbal texts. Table 9.5 on page 320 lists general visual and verbal LRMs for literature reflecting a parallel culture. Students can *create* LRMs with individual books and collections from the

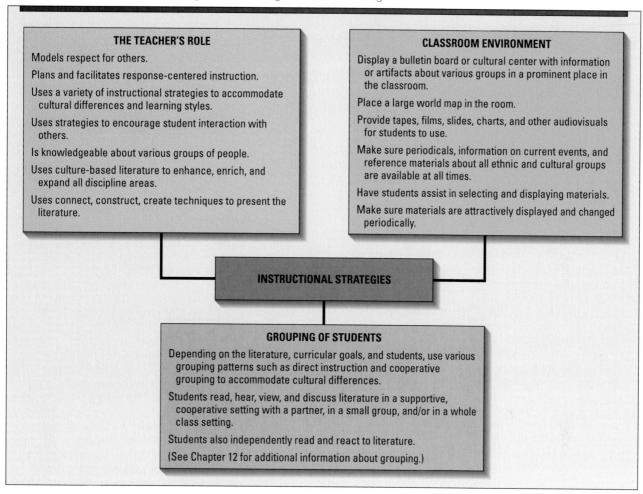

bibliography. Appendix B describes visual and verbal LRMs in more detail.[18]

🜔 THE HISTORICAL DEVELOPMENT OF LITERATURE REFLECTING PARALLEL CULTURES

Before the 1970s, a description of the literature reflecting parallel cultures would have used such words as "distortions," "condescending," "ridicule," "stereotype," "caricature," "exotic," "omission," and "invisible." In the late nineteenth century, several classics included stereotypical characters from parallel cultures, such as Mark Twain's *Adventures of Huckleberry Finn*. Miller-Lachmann reminds us that Twain's books, which are still read and enjoyed today, reflected the attitude of the "empowered" society, the isola-

tionist philosophy of many Americans, and the dominance of white males in the writing and publishing professions.[19]

LITERATURE PUBLISHED BEFORE 1960

Between the mid-nineteenth century and the early twentieth century, two significant books with multicultural characters appeared: Joel Chandler Harris's *Uncle Remus and His Friends* (1892) and Helen Bannerman's *The Story of Little Black Sambo* (1899). Harris recorded old African tales in the dialect spoken by former slaves. Some critics felt the language had a negative connotation because it was associated with slavery. Other critics made derogatory remarks about the language and associated it with ignorant, illiterate speakers. Harris's books continued to be published, but by the mid-1960s they were rarely used in the

TABLE 9.5   Suggested Visual and Verbal LRMs for Use with Literature Reflecting Parallel Cultures

VISUAL LRMs	VERBAL LRMs
Use folk art to prepare a mural depicting cultural information.	Interview persons from the culture.
Prepare a time line showing contributions made by members of a group.	Present a cross-cultural festival; prepare art, dance, music, and food representing various groups.
Prepare a world map showing the native lands of various groups.	Hold a mock election to select ethnic heroes for a Cultural Hall of Fame. Students will write and present a nominating speech supporting a candidate. Conduct debates. Place a picture of the selected hero and a copy of the speech in the Hall of Fame.
Prepare a cultural collage.	
Prepare a chart with interesting words in various languages; decorate with folk art.	
Identify English words borrowed from other countries. Prepare an attractive banner listing the native word and the English word. Cover the English word with a tab. Encourage students to write the words, guess the English word, and confirm by lifting the tab. Have students draw meanings of nouns and verbs.	Have students select a word borrowed from another language and pantomime the meaning.
	Write a magazine feature based on an incident from a book. Place articles in a bound class cultural magazine.
Prepare a tableau using the setting described in a book. Dress dolls in authentic dress. Include native animals in the tableau.	Publish a newsletter about groups.
	Present a radio/television program about a group or theme.
Have individual students decorate an original "I Am Poem" using folk art from their ancestors. Display poems on a bulletin board titled "I Am. . . ."	Establish a pen pal or video exchange with students from another country.
Have students write haiku, haikon, and tonka poetry, decorate it appropriately, display it, and then bind in a book to be presented to the school media center.	Have several students prepare an oral conversation about the rituals of communication accepted by a group. The students will use appropriate nonverbal language and behavior in the presentation.
Prepare a generic game board. Using literature books, teams of students will prepare sets of questions about an ethnic or cultural group or another country.	Have teams of students write poems about an incident in an ethnic hero's life using the "Biopoem" or "Character Poetry" format.
Have each student select an author or artist and prepare an original book cover for the student's favorite book. Display the covers on a creator's bulletin board. Obtain a photograph of the creator and place it on the board with biographical information.	If possible, contact an author, artist, or editor on the Internet. Interview the person. Prepare a computer-generated newsletter about the creator and E-mail it to another school. Request a reply.
Request photographs from cultural families. Take pictures of children in native and/or contemporary dress. Mount the pictures appropriately and display in the hallway or auditorium picture gallery.	Ask students to use prose or poetry to complete the statement, "If I could be anyone in the world, I would be. . . ." Request several reasons for the selection.
Prepare a cultural game book. Use illustrations to describe or give directions for the game. Children will play the game.	Have teams of students prepare a video documentary discussing a cultural theme. The documentary will be written in first person. Each team will prepare a background representing the settings from the book. The students will create and use cultural artifacts or facsimiles in the documentary.
Have individual students prepare a web showing traits, experiences, and interests influenced by their personal background. Partners will prepare a Venn diagram representing their similarities and differences.	
Have students compare the lifestyle and values of diverse parallel cultures. Students will form small groups, in which each person represents a different culture. Groups will complete a cultural feature analysis chart, showing desirable behavior, family relationships, food, religion, and the like.	Have students write to foreign consulates, tourist bureaus, and ethnic organizations for information and pictures about contemporary life in a specific group. The information will be presented in a panel discussion conducted by students who assume the role of contemporary children living in the country or group.
	Have students introduce their partner using the cultural web prepared in the visual LRM.
Identify the text structure used in an information book. Select information from the book and present it on a suitable graphic as described in Chapter 6.	Have teams of students select and present poetry from various groups using a suitable choral speaking arrangement.
Illustrate a story based on another's memory. Prepare a decorated thank you card for the person interviewed. Enclose the story with the card and take it to the person with homemade cookies or other food.	Have partners select a tale or song from a group's folk literature and use the selection as a model to write an original literary folk tale or song with a theme and content related to the group.
Have partners represent a particular country and write and illustrate a description of a typical event that could happen "In One Day" to a child. Bind the descriptions in a book and present them on the school television.	Have students interview elderly persons who came from another country. Students will elicit favorite memories about the country, record the information, and use it to write an imaginative first-person story. They will compare notes and then finish the stories. Then they will discuss a writer's responsibility to authentically portray another person's memories.
Make an artifact such as a corn doll or story cloth representing an ethnic or cultural group.	Tape-record ethnic music. Ask the music teacher to teach children ethnic music. Students will perform the music for other classes. If possible, find adults who will perform ethnic music in class or on a tape recording. Tape ethnic music from radio, TV, or movies. Share the music with the class.

classroom. Recently, Julius Lester, an African-American writer, published a series of books retelling the Uncle Remus tales. Lester retained the storyteller's voice, but modified the language in the original tales. He also included contemporary references in the four collections about Brer Rabbit and his friends. Two especially well-written collections are *The Tales of Uncle Remus: The Adventures of Brer Rabbit* (1987) and *The Last Tales of Uncle Remus* (1994). Jerry Pinkney, an African-American artist, authentically illustrated Lester's books in his trademark pencil and watercolor. In the 1980s, Van Dyke Parks also published a series of books retelling the tales. As a result of these retellings, these trickster tales are now experiencing renewed popularity.

Helen Bannerman wrote and illustrated *The Story of Little Black Sambo* to amuse her children. Bannerman and her husband, an English doctor, lived in India while their children were in school in England. Her simple text and illustrations created a perfect picture book that depicted the adventures of a young boy living in India and his experiences with tigers. The book was published in England in 1899. Unfortunately, Bannerman did not retain the copyright, and within a few years "pirated" editions of the book appeared. Although most retained the original text, Bannerman's simple watercolor illustrations were transformed into degrading caricatures of black people. Africa, not India, became the implied setting, and the distorted, grotesque pictures left the impression that the story was about a simpleton, a black boy who was the son of slaves. By the 1960s, Bannerman's humorous story about an Indian boy who outwitted some tigers was no longer presented to children. Both Julius Lester and Jerry Pinkney enjoyed the book as children and remembered it as the main book they read with a black character. In an attempt to change the stereotyped images of the book, Lester and Pinkney created *Sam and the Tigers: A New Telling of Little Black Sambo* (1996). Their fantasy is set in Sam-Sam-sa-mera, a land where humans and animals live and work together and everybody is named Sam. The African-American protagonist, Sam, encounters five tigers who demand his fancy new school clothes and perhaps his life. Fred Marcellino's *The Story of Little Babaj* (1996) is also based on the old tale. This book retains Bannerman's original rhythmic, repetitive language. Marcellino's realistic illustrations leave no doubt that the story is set in India. It will be interesting to observe how children and adults receive these new picture storybooks.[20]

In the early 1900s, few books with characters representing parallel cultures were published. Unfortunately, the few characters who were included in the verbal and visual narratives were distorted or reflected a stereotypical image of the culture. An excellent example of this practice was Claire Bishop's picture book *The Five Chinese Brothers* (1938), which was based on a Chinese folktale. Kurt Wiese's yellow and black illustrations for the book show Chinese characters with squinty eyes, buck teeth, and traditional Chinese costumes. The popular tale left Caucasians with the impression that all Chinese looked alike and dressed "funny." In many children's books about Holland, artists showed Dutch children wearing large wooden shoes and traditional dress.

After World War II, various groups attempted to promote better relations among peoples throughout the world. Occasionally, authors included protagonists from various ethnic groups in juvenile books, but overall few authentic stories about diverse groups were published in the United States for the next two decades. In 1947 May Hill Arbuthnot included a few examples of quality books with nonwhite protagonists in her popular textbook for teachers, *Children and Books*. The books she reviewed told a good story and presented a sincere image of the "minority" group. Arbuthnot felt the books achieved their purpose by showing that all people are alike under the skin. The characters were presented as responsible citizens of the United States who wanted to live happily and peaceably side by side with other groups. Arbuthnot's philosophy reflected the "melting pot" theory that was popular at the time. According to this theory, whatever their ethnic or cultural background, all people will merge to become "Americans" with the same values, beliefs, and lifelong goals.[21]

LITERATURE PUBLISHED IN THE 1960s AND 1970s

Although Augusta Baker, Charlemae Rollins, and Virginia Lacey had discussed the absence of "minority" children in literature, the problem did not attract much attention until 1965 when Nancy Larrick published an article in *The Saturday Review* reporting the results of her study, "The All-White World of Children's Books." Larrick sent questionnaires to seventy members of the Children's Book Council, which published trade books for children, asking how many African-American characters appeared in their books. From the sixty-three replies (90 percent returns), she discovered that of the 5,000 children's books published in 1962, 1963, and 1964, only 349, or 6.7 percent of the books, included one or more African-American children. Larrick reminded her readers that although integration was the "law of the land," most readers see only white children in their books and reading materials. She described the "invisible child" when she concluded that "Across the country 6,340,000 nonwhite children are learning to read and to understand the American way of life in books which either omit them entirely or scarcely mention them."[22] In the mid-1970s, Chall and others replicated Larrick's study.[23] They found a 100 percent increase in the number of books that included African-American characters. This meant that 689 or 14.4 percent of the 4,775 books published between 1973 and 1975 included an African-American character in the visual or verbal narrative. The researchers celebrated the increase in the number of African Americans in nonfiction literature, especially biography, but noted that only 28 books (4 percent) dealt with the contemporary scene. Since the studies focused on African-American characters, statistics for Asian-American, Hispanic, and Native American characters were not compiled.

Several social and economic factors may have influenced the increase in characters from parallel cultures in books published during the 1970s. At this time the civil rights movement was active, federal money was available to purchase library books, and publishers were aware of the omissions. They began to publish talented artists and authors from inside various groups, such as Virginia Hamilton (*Zeely*, 1967); Eloise Greenfield (*Me and Neesie*, 1975); Ashley Bryan (*Walk Together Children: Black American Spirituals*, 1974); John Steptoe (*Stevie*, 1969); Mildred Taylor (*Roll of Thunder, Hear My Cry*, 1975); Sharon B. Mathis (*The Hundred Penny Box*, 1975); Yoshiko Uchida (*Journey to Topaz*, 1971); Taro Yashima (*Crow Boy*, 1955); Jamake Highwater (*ANPAO: An American Indian Odyssey*, 1977); and Muriel and Tom Feelings (*Jambo Means Hello: A Swahili Alphabet Book*, 1974, and *Moja Means One: A Swahili Counting Book*, 1975).

LITERATURE PUBLISHED IN THE 1980s

Between 1979 and 1984, approximately 10,000 new juvenile titles were published in the United States, but only 100 books or 1.5 percent featured African Americans. By the late 1980s, the percentage of children's books dealing with African Americans had fallen to 1 percent. Fortunately, during this time outstanding writers and artists such as Patricia and Fredrick McKissack, Walter Dean Myers, Muriel and Tom Feelings, Jerry and Gloria Pinkney, and Leo and Diane Dillon were recognized for their contributions to the field and received major awards. Fewer authors published books with Hispanic, Asian-American, and Native American characters. Exceptions were Nichoasa Mohr, a Hispanic writer, John Bierhorst, a Native American author, and Laurence Yep, an Asian-American writer, who received the recognition they deserved. In 1992 Virginia Hamilton became the fifth American to win the Hans Christian Andersen Award, the most distinguished international award given for a person's entire contribution to literature (for more information about Virginia Hamilton, see Did You Know?). Several authors and artists received the Caldecott and Newbery Awards: Virginia Hamilton received the Newbery Medal for *M. C. Higgins the Great* (1974), and Mildred Taylor received it for *Roll of Thunder, Hear My Cry* (1975). The Dillons received the Caldecott Medal for Verna Aardema's *Why Mosquitoes Buzz in People's Ears* (1975) and another Caldecott Medal for Margaret Musgrove's *Ashanti to Zulu* (1976). Interestingly, few books were published by writers inside parallel cultures, yet many creators received major awards. Obviously, only books of high literary merit were being published.

During the 1970s and 1980s, new, alternative presses owned and operated by people of color began to publish literature reflecting parallel cultures. Even in a period of limited funds, there were approximately fifty independent publishing companies, including Just Us Books, Children's Book Press in San Francisco, Black Butterfly Press in New York and Arte Publico Press in Houston. Many companies published only books from a particular ethnic group or from one or two literary genres. The independent presses provided the needed publishing outlet for both new and established authors and artists.

LITERATURE PUBLISHED IN THE 1990s

Trends in publishing, education, and society have influenced the slow, but steady increase in the number of books reflecting parallel cultures published in the 1990s. With the popularity of literature-based instruction and multicultural curricula, educators are requesting more multicultural literature that represents all of the children in their classrooms. Many adults recognize the importance of children seeing themselves in books and want the literature they purchase for children's pleasure to reflect diverse groups. Finally, most publishers have recognized the need to publish quality multicultural literature and have organized special divisions that publish only literature reflecting parallel cultures. These divisions provide more publishing opportunities for both recognized and new authors and artists from all ethnic groups. Mainstream publishers need more nonwhite editors who can identify books that authentically capture the social, historical, and political experiences of people from parallel cultures.

Two major publishing trends involving literature reflecting parallel cultures are evident in the 1990s. One trend is to show more characters representing diverse groups working together in a contemporary setting. These books deal with universal concerns that influence the lives of many contemporary people. They focus on the similar-

Did You Know About
VIRGINIA HAMILTON?

After reading one or more of the more than 30 books created by Virginia Hamilton, it isn't surprising to learn that she grew up in a family of storytellers. Her mother, aunts, uncles, cousins, grandparents, and even her older siblings told stories. When Virginia, the youngest member of the family, was growing up, she heard and absorbed their stories. Grandpa Levi Perry told his ten children and many grandchildren stories about the underground railroad that came through Hamilton's hometown of Yellow Springs, Ohio. Her father was an accomplished classical mandolinist. He wanted to be the greatest mandolinist of his time, but could not join the musicians' union; instead he played in mandolin clubs all over the country. From her father, a college graduate, former newspaperman, and farmer, Hamilton acquired a love of reading, writing, and singing. While growing up in southern Ohio, where five generations of her family had lived, Hamilton spent a happy childhood exploring her beloved land and absorbing history and language and developing a sense of self. After graduating from high school with honors, she studied writing at Antioch College and spent her summers in New York City. For fifteen years, she lived in New York City, writing, reading, and visiting with other writers and artists. After the success of her first novel, *Zeely*, Hamilton returned to her beloved Yellow Springs. Today she lives in Ohio and New York City with her husband of thirty-five years, the

renowned poet, Arnold Adoff. Their two grown sons are musicians—surprise!

Hamilton has written fiction, mythology, folklore, mystery, fantasy, biography, adventure, a ghost story, and a picture storybook, *Drysolongso*, illustrated by Jerry Pinkney. She feels that nonfiction is the most difficult to write because you must retain the information you acquire from research and write an interesting story.

How does one describe a person who received the Newbery Medal in 1975 for *M. C. Higgins, the Great*, several Newbery Honor Awards, and the 1992 International Hans Christian Andersen Award and the 1995 Laura Ingalls Wilder Award for her body of work? She is a writer who remembers the tales of long ago and, with innovative language, weaves them into stories contemporary children relish. The stories deal with universal themes of supportive families, historical events, and maturing characters. Though Hamilton's characters are African American, they serve as role models for children of all social backgrounds. Her literature helps young people create positive images of themselves and gain insights about the social experiences that influence people's lives. Through her skillfully crafted stories, she depicts her people's history and contemporary experiences. Her readers feel hope and realize they have grown from reading her narratives. For three decades, Virginia Hamilton, a creative, talented storyteller, has influenced the development of juvenile literature and will continue to direct its future.

ities of people's needs, desires, and goals. The conflicts and interactions of all people are portrayed, regardless of their cultural background. Books highlighting universal concerns are most numerous in folk literature, realistic fiction, poetry, and nonfiction literature. W. Nikola-Lisa celebrates the diversity of society in his poetry collection, *Bein' with You This Way* (1994). Eve Bunting and David Diaz show

the importance of people from diverse cultures working together to survive in *The Smoky Night* (1994). Many collections of short stories about growing up in America have been published in the 1990s; Joyce Carol Thomas's *A Gathering of Flowers: Stories about Being Young in America* (1990) is an example. Bruce McMillan's photo-essay *Eating Fractions* (1991) shows an African-American boy, a white boy, and a shaggy dog attempting to understand fractions by dividing food. Loretta Berstein and her multicultural group of friends solve the mystery of the missing cats and learn about the homeless in Jill Pinkwater's *Tails of the Bronx: A Tale of the Bronx* (1991). Other examples of multicultural literature are listed in the universal thematic section of the bibliography at the end of the book.

The second major publishing trend is the increase in culture specific literature, which highlights a particular ethnic or cultural group. For example, in *Soul Looks Back in Wonder* (1993) Tom Feelings's vivid illustrations enrich the thirteen poems by notable African-American poets that reveal the creative spirit found in the lives of African-Americans. (See the Feelings color plate.)

The literature highlights and respects the diversity within groups. The literature created in a particular region also reveals the influence of early settlers. For example, both African and Hispanic cultures clearly influence Caribbean literature.

With the increased attention on global issues and concerns, the entire world has become the "immediate environment" of our society. Authentic literature reflecting the history, traditions, beliefs, and lifestyles of people living in all regions of the world is popular reading. Nevertheless, more information is available about African Americans than about any other group because more recognized authors and artists are producing literature dealing with African Americans.

STEREOTYPING OR CENSORSHIP? A CONTINUING PROBLEM

For obvious reasons, members of a group are distressed when they encounter inaccurate details about their culture in literature. Usually, they attempt to remove the book from the library shelves—to censor it—especially if a person outside the group wrote it. While this is an understandable reaction, we must ask if censorship is the answer. Several prominent books have brought this problem to light. In particular, three popular books have been criticized for their stereotypical, inaccurate portrayals of Native American characters. The popular Little House series written by Laura Ingalls Wilder in the 1930s depict Indians in a negative light. Yet in portraying Laura's fears and the whites' view of Indians as their enemies the books reflect the mainstream feelings of the nineteenth century when families were moving into the Native Americans' territories. Beginning with *The Indian in the Cupboard* (1980), the popular fantasy series by Lynne Reid Banks includes several passages that could be interpreted as distorted or demeaning descriptions of Native Americans.

Africa You Are Beautiful

Has anyone told you
    You are beautiful
Africa?
    Your full body
and sensuous lips
    have kissed my soul
and Africa, I am bound to You
        by the drumbeat of
my heart that pumps the
        blood of my birthright
and You are mine.

    Rashidah Ismaili

Tom Feelings's expressionistic paintings enrich the poetry written by thirteen African-Americans in his book Soul Looks Back in Wonder. *Feelings is noted for his mixed media paintings. He uses colored pencils, various types of paper, stencils, and cut-outs for his distinctive collages. Some poems may not be suitable for young children, but the illustrations will naturally elicit discussion.*

Finally, Susan Jeffers's beautiful book with pictures, *Brother Eagle, Sister Sky: A Message from Chief Seattle* (1991), is filled with visual and verbal inaccuracies. Jeffers's verbal narrative is a fictional interpretation of a speech Chief Seattle gave in 1854. A screenwriter distorted the speech in a 1971 film documentary on pollution. Unfortunately, Jeffers's outstanding realistic illustrations include native dress that Chief Seattle's tribe did not wear. Despite these inaccuracies, which have been pointed out in the popular and academic press, the book remains a favorite picture book with a Native American protagonist. Since all three of these books are popular and readily available, students can use them when discussing the creator's responsibility to authentically depict an ethnic group in the visual and verbal texts. Wilder's book can be discussed in terms of its historical context and the view of Native Americans at that time. Banks's fantasy can be compared to writings in the popular media during the early 1920s to 1960s. After enjoying the theme and visual narrative, young people can use Jeffers's book when discussing the dangers of pollution. Teachers are reminded to use sources cited earlier in the chapter to check the cultural authenticity of books.

During the quincentennial anniversary of Columbus's "discovery" of the Americas, Euro-Americans and people representing parallel cultures began to consider the early treatment of the first Americans in a different way. They raised questions about the early explorers' intentions to "civilize" the "savages" and pointed out that the diseases the missionaries and explorers brought with their Bibles caused entire civilizations to die. Authors have explored these questions and have portrayed the events from the Native American perspective. Juvenile books such as Michael Dorris's *Morning Girl* (1992) and *Guest* (1994) and Jane Yolen's *Encounter* (1992) have asked what might have happened when the first Americans welcomed their foreign guests.

Fortunately, more books are now available about all social, cultural, and ethnic groups. The following section describes African-American, Asian-American, Hispanic, and Native American literature intended for children two months to sixteen years. The focus is on the contributions made by notable authors from each group. (See Appendix D for a discussion of censorship amd literature.)

◊ LITERATURE REFLECTING SPECIFIC ETHNIC GROUPS

AFRICAN-AMERICAN LITERATURE

African Americans are citizens of the United States who have an African biological and cultural heritage and identity. Although most African Americans cannot trace their family history to Africa, historically their roots are in Central and West Africa. The largest ethnic group of color living in the United States, African Americans numbered 31,648,000 people in 1995.

Literature about Africans has been available since colonial times in the United States. Several slave narratives about African Americans were published in the nineteenth century. In the 1930s interviews with ex-slaves were gathered for the Works Progress Administration (WPA) Writers Project. These narratives provide the necessary documentation for contemporary books about this period of African-American history. Milton Meltzer, for example, used these and other historical documents to write *The Black Americans: A History in Their Own Words* (1984).

Literature Published in the Early 1900s
In the early twentieth century, African-American writers published a few books of realistic fiction, such as Arna Bontemps's *Sad-Faced Boy* (1937).[24] The illustrations by Virginia Lee Burton authentically depict the African-American boy. The poetry of Langston Hughes in *Dream Keeper* (1962) and James Weldon Johnson in *The Creation* (1927) began to merge into juvenile literature and, until recently, represented the major poetry expressing the African-American experience.

Jesse Jackson's *Call Me Charley* (1945) was an authentic account of an African-American boy's trials, disappointments, and survival in an all-white school. Unfortunately, at this time many black people were drawn with Caucasian features and a colored face. These pictures were caricatures and evoked laughter from the children.

Literature Published in the 1970s and 1980s
As mentioned earlier, by the 1970s authentic experiences of contemporary African Americans were appearing in the realistic fiction for young people. As the number of African-American illustrators and writers increased, books with pictures portrayed children in rural and urban settings, interacting with others in typical children's activities. In 1970 the American Library established the Coretta Scott King Award to honor a notable African-American artist and author each year (see Appendix C). By the 1980s realistic depictions of gangs and violence in the streets appeared in novels for older young people. While the novels portrayed the harshness of the urban streets, many protagonists gave readers insight into the decisions necessary for survival. Frequently, members of the extended family helped the protagonist make the right decisions. Another common theme in realistic fiction was the difficulties youngsters from a different background face when moving into a new neighborhood.

By the mid-1980s, poetry intended for young children began to appear. Eloise Greenfield's *Honey, I Love and*

Other Love Poems (1986) and Nikki Giovanni's *Spin a Soft Black Song: Poems for Children* (1985) were examples. The Caribbean poetry and prose of Ashley Bryan and Lynn Joseph appeared in the 1980s, and Caribbean literature became a part of African-American literature.

The number of biographies increased dramatically, giving the African-American child a "mirror," a series of positive role models, and a sense of identity. Initially, biographers wrote about major political leaders and sports figures. Perhaps the writers and publishers felt these subjects would interest children, but adults worried that the contributions of scientists, artists, and civil rights leaders were slighted. Information books highlighted traditional celebrations.

Literature Published in the 1990s

Recurring themes in the literature published in the 1990s include the importance of human relationships, the sense of community among African Americans, and their history, heritage, and ability to survive physical and psychological hardships. Books with pictures and realistic novels show contemporary children having authentic, everyday experiences. African-American folk literature, which is being published, such as Patricia Mckissack's *The Dark Thirty: Southern Tales of the Supernatural* (1992). In addition to political leaders and sports figures, male and female scientists are now the subjects of biographies.

According to the Cooperative Children's Book Center, African-American creators produced 2 percent of the juvenile books published in the United States in 1993 and 1994 (74 and 82 books, respectively). Of the approximately 3,500 juvenile books published in the United States in 1994, 5 percent or 166 books included African-American characters or African culture. In 1995, 4 percent or 79 of the 1,886 juvenile books depicted African or African-American culture.[25] The African-American experience is portrayed in all literary genres. Books with pictures, folk literature, and biographies are especially numerous, followed by information books and poetry. As is typical of all ethnic literature, creators have published few books of fantasy.

Particularly noteworthy are the efforts to document African-American history. In 1991 Walter Dean Myers published *Now Is Your Time! (The African-American Struggle for Freedom)*, which documented the major historical events in the development of African-American culture. Myers used oral narratives from the WPA project that described the experience of slavery, slave revolts, the Civil War, and the Reconstruction period. Nonfiction literature and poetry described other stages of African-American history, such as the Harlem Renaissance, the period between 1917 and 1935 when such notable writers as Langston Hughes, Zora Neale Hurston, Countee Cullen, James

Weldon Johnson, and Arna Bontemps were active. Authentic novels, biographies, and information books such as Rosa Parks's *My Story* (1992) have been published in the 1990s to present firsthand accounts of the civil rights movement. Because the biological and historical roots of African Americans are in Africa, novels, folktales, and information about Africa are abundant in juvenile literature. These books give children and adults additional information about the historical and contemporary African-American experience.

Table 9.6 on page 327 lists some notable African-American creators, but many other writers and illustrators working in the late 1980s and 1990s also deserve mention. Elizabeth F. Howard, Dolores Johnson, and Angela Johnson write picture books. Camille Yarborough, Mildred Pitts Walter, and Candy Dawson Boyd publish contemporary and historical realistic fiction. Jacqueline Woodson and Walter Dean Myers write young adult novels dealing with authentic problems and contemporary conflicts. The artistic talents of Floyd Cooper, Pat Cummings, Donald Crews, Jerry Pinkey, Brian Pinkney, and James Ransome are seen in books with pictures. For example, Ransome's paintings enhance Elizabeth Howard's story about the relationships within an extended family in *Aunt Flossie's Hats (and Crab Cakes Later)*. (See the Howard color plate on page 328.) The poetry of Lynn Joseph and Nikki Giovanni shows the range of talent coming from people of African-American background.

While African-American writers and artists created many of the books listed in the bibliography, several outside writers have authentically captured the African-American spirit. They include Mary White Ovington, Milton Meltzer, Arnold Adoff, Robert D. San Souci, Juanita Havill, Ann Cameron, William Loren Katz, Janet Bode, and Pat Costa Vigluccie. The last two writers have published sensitive novels about interracial romances and families.

A sign that African-American creators are being recognized by publishing companies and the public is the fact that African-American artists are now illustrating literature without characters reflecting parallel cultures. However, few African-American authors have written about the experiences of other people.

ASIAN-AMERICAN LITERATURE

Asian Americans are the fastest-growing ethnic group in the United States; their numbers increased 141 percent between 1970 and 1980 to 3.5 million and 154 percent between 1980 and 1995 to 8.9 million. Asian Americans include persons whose biological and cultural heritage comes from China, Japan, India, Korea, the Philippines, Vietnam, Laos, Thailand, Cambodia, Pakistan, Indonesia, or Taiwan.

TABLE 9.6 Notable African-American Writers, Poets, and Artists

DATE	AUTHOR/ARTIST, TITLE	COMMENTS
1967	V. Hamilton, *Zeely*	A young African-American girl imagines the beautiful woman she sees on the road is an African queen. Her dreams lead to many adventures. This is the first of many books by this award-winning author.
1969	J. Steptoe, *Stevie*	The first of many picture books created by this talented author-artist. This book relates the feelings of a young boy who must share his family with another visiting child. The events are authentic, and the characters are well developed. Steptoe's *Mufaro's Beautiful Daughters* (1987) was a Caldecott honor book.
1970	L. Clifton, *Some of the Days of Everett Anderson*	The first of six books about the everyday experiences of a child growing up in a loving family living in a city. His dreams, fears, and needs are expressed in poetic language.
1975	M. Taylor, *Roll of Thunder, Hear My Cry*	The saga of the Logans began in this Newbery Medal winner. A strong sense of family is portrayed through these well-developed characters and their conflicts during the depression in the South.
1975	W. D. Myers, *Sam, Cool Clyde and Stuff*	The first of many realistic, contemporary novels for young adults depicting the life and conflict of teenagers surviving on the streets of Harlem. Myers has also written biographies and information books for young adults.
1975	E. Greenfield, *Me and Nessie*	Greenfield's first volume of poetry about African-American children involved in everyday activities. She has written many picture books, biographies, and board books for the youngest children.
1977	A. Bryan, *The Dancing Granny*	One of several picture books created by this African-American folklorist. His brilliant colors and creative style enhance his poetic text.
1988	P. McKissack, *Mirandy and Brother Wind*	This Caldecott honor book is based loosely on folk literature. It depicts the dreams and desires of a young lady who wanted to win the cake walk. One of 30 books published by the author in 20 years. Patricia often teams with her husband, Fredrick, to write picture books, biographies, information books, and folktales about the African-American experience. Jerry Pinkney illustrated *Mirandy and Brother Wind* and many other books written by the McKissacks.

Each country has its own ethnic identity, language, culture, religion, and traditions, and Asian-American literature reflects this diversity. In addition, some Asian Americans are from families who have been in the United States and Canada for generations, while others just arrived from their native country. Thus, making generalizations about the historical experiences, beliefs, traditions, and social values of Asian Americans as a group is difficult. For this reason, the bibliography includes folk literature and nonfiction literature about persons from many Asian countries. This literature "mirrors" Asian children and gives non-Asian readers a better understanding of the background of Asian Americans. Ed Young has created several books based on Chinese tales, especially *Lon Po Po: A Red-Riding Hood Story from China* (1989). (See the Young color plate on page 328.)

Literature Published before 1980
Until about 1950, many books reflecting Asian cultures were "racist," "sexist," and "elitist."[26] Unfortunately, juvenile books perpetuated misleading visual and verbal stereotypes. Men were depicted with Fu Manchu mustaches,

myopic vision, and cereal-bowl haircuts, and both women and men were habitually garbed in traditional dress.

Before the 1980s, folk literature and information books were the main sources of Asian literature for young people. A committee at the Council for Interracial Books for Children identified 66 books with Asian characters published in the United States between 1945 and 1975. At this time, between 2,000 and 3,000 juvenile books were published each year in the United States. One notable author and artist, Taro Yashima, published a series of fascinating picture books with universal themes and Asian protagonists. His books included *The Village Tree* (1953), *Plenty to Watch* (1954), *Crow Boy* (1955), *Umbrella* (1958), *Momo's Kitten* (1961), *Youngest One* (1962), and *Seashore Story* (1967).

In the 1970s, most juvenile books about Asians were written by non-Asians. Katherine Paterson's feudal novels represent this trend with *The Sign of the Chrysanthemum* (1973), *Of Nightingales That Weep* (1974), and *The Master Puppeteer* (1975). Paterson, whose parents were American missionaries, was born and lived in China in her early years. As an adult she lived in Japan, studied its history and

James Ransome's realistic acrylic paintings expand Elizabeth Howard's book Aunt Flossie's Hats (and Crab Cakes Later). *Ransome achieves texture and a dimensional effect by using layers of acrylic paint. The artist uses bright colors, shadings, and patterns in his detailed paintings. The images and verbal narrative are framed with a simple black line. Notice the placement of the detailed paintings and the verbal narrative. Everyone needs an Aunt Flossie!*

Aunt Flossie closed her eyes.
I think she was seeing long ago.
I wondered about crab cakes.
Did they have crab cakes way back then?
Then Sarah sniffed Aunt Flossie's hat.
"No more smoky smell," she said.
But I thought I could smell some,
just a little.

Then Sarah tried a different hat.
Dark, dark blue, with a red feather.
"This one, Aunt Flossie! This one!"
Aunt Flossie closed her eyes and thought a minute.
"Oh my, yes, my, my. What an exciting day!"

We waited, Sarah and I.
"What happened, Aunt Flossie?" I asked.

The wolf acted surprised. "To visit me? I have not met her along the way. She must have taken a different route."

"Po Po!" Shang said. "How is it that you come so late?"

The wolf answered, "The journey is long, my children, and the day is short."

Ed Young uses traditional Chinese folk art to illustrate Lon Po Po: A Red-Riding Hood Story from China. *The artist selects unusual colors for his watercolor and pastel paintings, which are presented in panels that are reminiscent of traditional Chinese screens. Notice the personality given to the realistic children and the impressionistic wolf.*

culture, and wrote three novels. See Chapter 5, Did You Know, for additional information about the author.

Literature Published in the 1980s

In the 1980s, Asian-American books frequently dealt with the clash between traditional values and customs and American values that occurred when Asian immigrants arrived in the United States. Several Asian-American writers described their personal assimilation experiences as children moving to the United States. In her amusing, realistic novel *In the Year of the Boar and Jackie Robinson* (1984), Betty Bao Lord describes likable Shirley Temple Wong's adventures during her first years in New York City. Shirley's devotion to baseball leads her to an experience all children enjoy.

In *Journey to Topaz* (1971) and *Journey Home* (1978), Yoshiko Uchida documented her Japanese-American family's experiences when they were interned in a camp during World War II. Both books give non-Asian readers a revealing view of life from an American who, because of her ethnic background, was placed in a concentration camp in her own country.

In *Dragonwings* (1975), a Newbery honor book, Laurence Yep tells of the plight of a Chinese boy who immigrated with other male members of his family to the United States in the nineteenth century. They worked on the railroad and saved enough money to bring the other members of the family to America. Yep explored another typical problem of Asian Americans in *Child of the Owl* (1977). The protagonist is Casey, a Chinese American who lived in various places in the United States before moving to San Francisco's Chinatown, where she lived for the first time with other Chinese. Here she grappled with conflicts between two cultures and traditions. Yep continues to be the most prolific Chinese-American writer for young people. His publications range from historical novels such as *Sea Glass* (1979) and *The Star Fisher* (1991) to collections of Asian traditional tales such as *The Rainbow People* (1989). (For more information about Yep, see Did You Know? on page 330.)

Literature Published in the 1990s

Asian-American literature of the 1990s is more culture specific, and stereotypes are rarely included in successful contemporary juvenile literature. (See photo on page 331.) For example, the traditional patriarchal Asian family that demands obedience from children is the theme of Lensey Namioka's series about the Yang family. The family has recently immigrated to San Francisco from Shanghai. In the first book, *Yang the Youngest and His Terrible Ear* (1992), Yingtao, the youngest son, is frustrated because he must study music under his father, a music teacher. Unlike other members of his family, Yingtao is tone-deaf. He does not want to study music because he has found other interests at his new school. Realizing he must obey his father, Yingtao attempts to solve his problem in a humorous, yet creative manner. Namioka also depicts this well-drawn Chinese family in a sequel, *Yang the Third and Her Impossible Family* (1995).

The clash of cultures continues to be a popular theme in books for young adults. Linda Crew, a non-Asian writer, effectively explores this theme in her popular young adult book, *Children of the River* (1989). Sundara, an immigrant Cambodian-American high-school student, struggles to please her extended family and to be accepted by her new friends in a small town in Oregon. The author authentically portrays the conflicts between traditional Asian values and contemporary American values and shows how the conflicts affect the choices the characters make in their new homeland. The tragedies and hardships experienced by this Southeast Asian family before they left their homeland are also revealed throughout the book.

More information books are now available, such as Sheila Hamanaka's *The Journey: Japanese Americans, Racism, and Renewal* (1990). The visual and verbal narratives blend to give older readers a factual account of Japanese Americans' experiences in the United States during the twentieth century. The author-artist places the experiences of Japanese Americans during World War II and the oppression many continue to feel in the context of protecting the civil rights of all citizens. The author's personal remembrances, which are woven throughout the narrative, influence the aesthetic power of the book.

Few novels feature contemporary Asian-American characters. Notable exceptions include Suzy Kine's *Song Lee in Room 2B* (1993) and Marie Lee's novels, *If It Hadn't Been for Yoon Jun* (1993) and *Saying Goodbye* (1994). Interestingly, many books have female protagonists. Fortunately, the popular Alan Say depicted strong male protagonists in his picture books for older children; examples include the two American soldiers who entertained Japanese children after World War II in *The Bicycle Man* (1981) and "Billy" Wong in *El Chino* (1990).

A few biographies have been written about Asian heroes, such as Zheng Zhensun and Alice Low's *A Young Painter: The Life and Paintings of Wang Yani—China's Extraordinary Young Artist* (1991) and Alan Say's Caldecott winner, *Grandfather's Journey* (1993). The autobiography format is more popular, however; Yoshiko Uchida's *The Invisible Thread* (1991) and Yoko Kawashima Watkins's *My Brother, My Sister, and I* (1994) are examples.

Folk literature is readily available from all Asian countries, but contemporary Asian characters are still almost nonexistent in contemporary fiction picture books. Demi,

College students do strange things for money. One young man wrote for a science fiction magazine for one cent per word. Later, a friend heard this story and suggested he write a juvenile science fiction book. *Sweetwater* became the young man's introduction to juvenile literature. In retrospect, the writer, Laurence Yep, realized that the Argans, the first colonists from Earth to inhabit the star Harmony, were like his Chinese ancestors, who also were settlers in a foreign country. Yep, whose father Thomas came from China, then began to research his Chinese background and wrote *Dragonwings*, which became a 1976 Newbery honor book and won the International Reading Association's Children's Book Award. The Chinese experiences in America inspired several other books including *Child of the Owl*, a winner of several awards. Yep also wrote several books of fantasy in the Shimmer series, including *Dragon of the Lost Sea*. Yep uses his family in many of his books. For example, his grandmother, an immigrant from China, talked more about her experiences as the first Chinese family in a West Virginia town than about China itself. Her stories evolved into his novel, *The Star Fisher.*

Yep, a second-generation Chinese American, grew up in San

Francisco. His family lived over the grocery store his father owned in an African-American neighborhood. Yep attended a bilingual Catholic school in San Francisco's Chinatown where he was considered a "dummy" because he did not speak Chinese. Yep's parents were athletes, but he was clumsy. In high school he encountered white American culture and began his search to understand the Chinese assimilation in a foreign country. This research serves as the basis for many of his novels.

Yep has a Ph.D from State University of New York at Buffalo, where he wrote his dissertation on William Faulkner's early novels. He lives in Pacific Grove, California, with his wife, JoAnne Ryder, who is also a writer. Ryder is the friend who encouraged him to write that first juvenile science fiction.

Yep's twenty books include fantasy, historical fiction, collections of Chinese folk literature, and an adult autobiography. His writings reflect his desire to look at ordinary things and bring out their special aspects by using his imagination. He is willing to explore the pain and turmoil of being an outsider with "insight, sensitivity, and humor."[27] Laurence Yep leaves his reader with hope and with respect for the protagonist.

---

using authentic Asian folk art, has illustrated several outstanding picture books based on Chinese folktales, such as *Liang and His Magic Brush* (1980) and *The Stonecutter* (1995). Demi has also illustrated Ann Tompert's *Bamboo Hats and a Rice Cake* (1993), which is based on a Japanese tale; *The Artist and the Architect* (1991), a literary folktale; and the biographies *Chingis Khan* (1991) and *Buddha* (1996). In addition, she illustrated several poetry and short story collections including *Demi's Dragons and Fantastic Creatures* (1993).

Since 1990 only 126 books (less than 1 percent of the juvenile books published in the United States) have portrayed Asian Americans. Although the quantity of literature about Asian Americans is small, many books are of high literary merit and honestly portray the diverse groups of Asian Americans. With the large number of Asians immigrating to North America, perhaps in the future Asian-American authors and artists will publish more fiction and nonfiction literature reflecting Asian-American experiences.

As is typical in Asian-American literature, this grandmother introduces her granddaughter to traditional celebrations.

HISPANIC LITERATURE

Hispanic literature reflects the experiences of people who share a culture, language, and heritage from Spain. In the United States, the term *Latino* tends to be used for these people in California, New York City, and Chicago; *Mexican American* is popular in Texas, New Mexico, and Florida; and other regions and the U.S. Census Bureau tend to use *Hispanic*. *Latino*, which has a longer history than *Hispanic*, refers particularly to people with a Latin American background. (Latin America includes Mexico, Central and South America, and the West Indies. Spanish, Portuguese, and, to a lesser degree, French are the official languages in these areas.) *Hispanic* refers especially to people from a Spanish cultural background. Since some people prefer *Hispanic* and others prefer *Latino*, both terms are used in this section.

In 1990, 22 million documented Hispanic Americans were living in the United States; by 1995 the number had risen to almost 27 million. According to the 1990 census,

61.2 percent of the Hispanic population stemmed ultimately from Mexico (they or their ancestors had immigrated from there), 15.1 percent from South and Central America, 12.1 percent from Puerto Rico, 4.8 percent from Cuba, and 6.8 percent from the Dominican Republic and Spain. Although many have come to the United States in recent decades, a larger number of Latinos trace their ancestry in the United States back almost two centuries. The U.S. Census Bureau projects that by the middle of the twenty-first century more than 128 million Hispanics will call the United States home.

Most Hispanics are of mixed biological heritage, deriving from Africa, Europe, Asia, and the Americas. Whatever their biological heritage, Spanish is the common language of the group. Latinos are also united by certain cultural values such as religion, respect and support for the elderly, and loyalty to the immediate and extended family. Their artistic, architectural, and historical legacy has influenced this hemisphere for five hundred years, and their cuisine has become popular throughout the United States. *The Tortilla Factory* (1995) by Gary Paulsen describes the production of food associated with Mexican Americans. The folk art style used by Ruth Wright Paulsen to illustrate the book captures the setting and the spirit of the people. (See the Paulsen color plate on page 332.)

For the last twenty years, Hispanic Heritage Month has been celebrated from September 15 to October 15. Beginning in the 1980s, the media have recognized the growing importance of Hispanics living in the United States. In 1995, ten magazines were being published for Latino households, especially for women. Recognizing that many Hispanics are second- or third-generation Americans, rather than immigrants, some magazines are published in English as well as Spanish. All major metropolitan centers now have several television stations intended for Spanish-speaking people.

Literature Published before 1990

From the 1960s through the 1980s, few authentic juvenile books representing Hispanic Americans were published.[28] Most Hispanic literature for young people consisted of translations of folk literature and autobiographies. The folktales were primarily retold by people outside the culture. The authentic tales retold by Pura Belpre in *Perez and Martina* (1960) and *The Dance of the Animals* (1965) were exceptions.

Although juvenile information books about specific Hispanic countries were published, Isabel Schon, a noted critic of Latino literature, argued that most of the literature gave non-Latinos inaccurate information about Hispanic cultures. She felt the people were stereotyped as lazy and the countries were described as impoverished and suitable

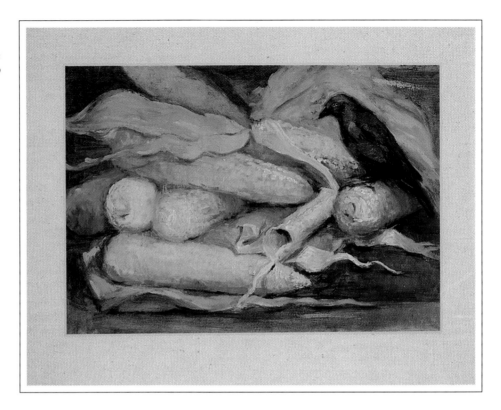

Ruth Wright Paulsen uses oil on linen for her impressionistic paintings for Gary Paulsen's The Tortilla Factory. *The images help interpret the informational text. The artist uses colors associated with nature in her paintings, such as browns, sepia, gold, and green. Do you know how this popular food is produced?*

only as vacation spots. She concluded that the publications gave a one-sided view of the people and their successes. Similarly, Sonia Nieto analyzed juvenile literature written about Puerto Ricans and concluded that of the 56 books published between 1972 and 1982, many were written by outside authors and only 8 could be recommended. She felt 10 others were fairly authentic. She pointed out that most of the books were set in urban areas. Typically, the characters were depicted as helpless, passive caricatures, who caused their own oppression. Social class was highlighted while women and the physical diversity among the people were ignored.

Hispanics at the time were concerned with issues such as the generation gap, overprotective parents, unreasonable rules of conduct for females, first love, and the pain of being rejected in both the United States and their native country. Nicholasa Mohr, one of Puerto Rico's most highly respected authors, realistically confronted these issues in her young adult books, such as *Felita* (1979), *Going Home* (1986), *Nilda* (1986), *El Bronx Remembered* (1986), and *In Nueva York* (1988). Patricia Beatty's *Lupita Mañana* (1981) dealt with the experiences of illegal immigrants from Mexico coming into the United States.

Small presses, established with federal money allocated for bilingual materials, published books in Spanish, English, or a bilingual format. Few of the presses survived the 1980s. The San Francisco–based Children's Book Press is a notable exception and continues to publish books reflecting all parallel cultures.

Literature Published in the 1990s

The number of books published about Hispanic countries and the Hispanic experience in the United States has increased slightly in the 1990s, but is still less than 1 percent of the juvenile books published in the United States. Between mid-1992 and mid-1995, for example, 69 books, less than 0.24 percent of the books published in the United States, were about the Mexican-American experience. Small though this percentage is, it represents a threefold increase in twenty years. More books and reprints about Mexico and South and Central America are also appearing. These books give multifaceted accounts of the regions by including the history, the beauty, and the social, economic, and political realities of the countries. Still, considering the number of Hispanics living in the United States, juvenile literature does not adequately reflect the experiences of Hispanic children.

Publishers have also increased the number of books translated from English into Spanish and Spanish into English. Unfortunately, when many books written originally in Spanish are translated into English, the author's style and the magic of the story are lost.

Obviously these children are sharing a message that connects all cultures—amigos/friends!

Folk literature and information books continue to dominate the slim offerings of Hispanic literature for young people. No Hispanic poetry was published in the United States until the publication of Latin American songs and rhymes in *Arroz con Leche* (1989) and *Las Navidades* (1990). In the 1990s, Gary Soto published two poetry collections about Chicano experiences in *A Fire in My Hands* (1990) and *Neighborhood Odes* (1992). He has also published two short story collections, *Baseball in April and Other Stories* (1990) and *Local News* (1993), with Chicano protagonists who live in contemporary Los Angeles. These four books intended for young adults became popular immediately. Since that time editors have published other collections of poetry and short stories written by young adults. Soto is also noted for his contemporary realistic novels for young adults, such as *Taking Sides* (1991). *The Skirt* (1992), his contemporary novel for upper elementary readers, and *Too Many Tamales* (1993), his picture book for the younger reader, give young people information about the traditions celebrated in Chicano families.

Currently, books reflecting cultural traditions and family practices are appearing. An example is *Family Pictures/Cuadros de familia* (1990), which is illustrated in a naive style by Carmen Lomas Garza, a major Chicana artist. The book contains fourteen pictorial vignettes about her Mexican-American childhood in south Texas. This landmark book serves as a model for Mexican-American literature. New nonfiction literature is appearing, especially from particular series, such as the Hispanic Experience from *Raintree Hispanic Stories Series*, Chelsea House's *The Peoples of North America Series*, and Lerner's *America Books Series*. Chelsea House has also developed a biographical series on Hispanic-American subjects.

NATIVE AMERICAN LITERATURE

Native Americans, also called American Indians, trace their biological and cultural heritage to the original citizens of North America. They are identified by regional designations and membership in a tribe, such as the Seminole, Cherokee, Comanche, Apache, Nez Perce, Aleut, Algonquin, Kickapoo, Navajo, Modoc, and 104 others. In 1980, the U.S. Census Bureau reported 1,326,000 American Indians, Eskimos, and Aleuts living in the United States. By 1990 their numbers had increased to 1,829,000, and by 1995 they totaled 1,924,000. Demographers project that by the middle of the twenty-first century 4,221,000 Native Americans will live in the United States. Although Caucasians have lived side by side with the first Americans for several hundred years, they know very little about the lifestyle and culture of the various tribes. Unfortunately, the earliest history of the Native Americans was not recorded, and considerable misinformation was disseminated in early pioneer days.

Literature Published before the 1980s
Starting in the late nineteenth century, the media, including pulp magazines, newspapers, books, and later movies, presented stereotyped images of Native Americans using terms and phrases such as "savage," "naked red man," "noble

savage," and "the Indians maliciously attacked the 'peaceful' settlers."[29] Most authors led readers to believe that all "Indians" wore the same type of feathers or headdresses; that they were "brutal cowards" who brandished tomahawks to "scalp their victims" (who unfortunately were the readers' ancestors); that all tribes lived in tepees; that women carried their babies on their backs; that the people danced on one leg; and that the tribes were totally dependent on the federal government. The cultural dignity, values, and traditions of the first Americans were seldom presented accurately. Is it any wonder that children are still directed to make and wear Indian headdress and brandish tomahawks as part of an instructional unit on Native Americans? We must remember that Native Americans were the first Americans and that each tribal nation has its own history, traditions, art, dances, ceremonies, and stories. Today, Native Americans are found in every occupation; no longer are they relegated to reservations, though some choose to live there. Quality prose and poetry, fiction and nonfiction Native American literature can give native and nonnative children an authentic perspective on the history, social, political, and cultural diversity of the Native Americans.

From the mid-eighteenth century, Native American folk literature was published for juvenile and adult readers. Many myths and legends, which had been passed on orally within the tribe, were initially written down by non-Native Americans. Before 1980, however, these Native American tales were criticized for being confusing and rambling, lacking a central theme, and having an inappropriate story structure. Apparently, early folklorists were not willing to accept the fact that Native American stories had a circular structure, rather than the linear structure typical of Eurocentric stories. Because the traditional tales and legends were passed orally from one generation to another, Native American storytellers were important members of a tribe. The storyteller told the stories and songs to inculcate, inform, and pass on the tribe's values, mores, and beliefs. The interdependence and connections of members of the tribes were reflected in their tales and rituals. Their folk literature depicted acceptable behavior and helped direct young people through the various stages of life. Entertainment was a secondary purpose for the traditional literature. As folklorists, sociologists, and educators began to understand the structure and purposes of the traditional stories, Native American tales gained respect and their unique qualities were highlighted.

In the 1970s, two writers of note began publishing literature that gave readers authentic insights into the Native American experiences. Jamake Highwater, a cultural anthropologist of Crow and Blackfoot heritage, published *ANPAO: An American Indian Odyssey* (1977). This young adult legend describes the journey of a man who is at-

Imagine what amazing stories this Native American storyteller is telling the children and the teacher.

tempting to achieve maturity. Woven into the text are the history and culture of the Native American peoples. Highwater also provided needed information about American Indian history, art, and culture in *Many Smokes, Many Moons: A Chronology of American Indian History through Indian Art* (1978). In the same decade, John Bierhorst published a well-documented collection of poems, songs, and chants reflecting the Native Americans' sorrows, joys and spirit: *In the Trail of the Wind: American Indian Poems and Ritual Orations* (1971). Bierhorst has also published several collections of Native American mythology and folk literature to give middle grade readers authentic cultural information.

Literature Published in the 1980s

Most of the fiction and nonfiction books written in the early 1980s depicted "Indian" lifestyles of the seventeenth, eighteenth, and nineteenth centuries. Unfortunately, the books were highly inaccurate and perpetuated misconceptions about the traditions, culture, and contemporary lifestyles of Native Americans. Except for Sacagawea and Pocahontas, native women were invisible in the literature.

Several books were written to discredit the misconceptions about American Indians. Jamake Highwater's Ghost Horse trilogy, *Legend Days* (1984), *Ceremony of Innocence* (1985), and *I Wear the Morning Star* (1986), was written from a Native American's perspective. These young adult novels depicted the devastation of Amana's family and community. They showed the pain and suffering experienced by the first Americans in the nineteenth and early twentieth centuries, as the whites encroached on their land and their lives. During the 1980s, several non-Indian writers lived with Native Americans and researched the culture. Margaret Kahn Garaway was a teacher of young Navajo children before writing *The Old Hogan* (1989) and *Askii and His Grandfather* (1989); Paul Pitts also lived and worked on the Navajo reservation before writing *Racing the Sun* (1988), a work of contemporary fiction for middle grade youngsters; and Howard Norman, who speaks the Cree language and translates Cree stories, wrote *Who-Paddled-Backward-with-Trout* (1987), a humorous story about a Cree boy who wants to earn a new name. Finally, Paul Goble, a prolific creator of American Indian folk literature, became an adopted member of the Oglala Sioux and Yakima tribes. Goble spent many hours researching and talking with Native American storytellers before producing his books with pictures, including *The Return of the Buffaloes* (1996).

Traditional Native American literature was enhanced by John Bierhorst's authoritative *Mythology of North America* (1985). Bierhorst continued to publish popular folk literature collections into the 1990s. Russell Freedman used native art reproductions and archival photographs to document the history of nineteenth-century Native Americans in his photo-essays, *Buffalo Hunt* (1988) and *Indian Chiefs* (1987).

Literature Published in the 1990s

Almost 3 percent (543 books) of the juvenile books published in the United States from 1990 to mid-1995 included Native American characters or information about Native Americans' experiences. Folk literature and information books accounted for the largest number of titles. Although more Native American writers such as Richard Littlebear and Luci Tapahonso are producing literature for young people, more contemporary stories are needed. Rarely are Native American youngsters included with other multicultural characters in fiction with universal themes. Other significant trends in the 1990s include the growing number of biographies of Native Americans and an increased emphasis on presenting the Native American perspective in both fiction and nonfiction.

Folk literature still dominates published Native American literature. Native authors use the same cadenced style as an oral storyteller. An example is the story told by Glecia Bear, a noted Cree storyteller, to her niece, Freda Ahenakew, in *Two Little Girls Lost in the Bush: A Cree Story for Children* (1991). Cree artist Jerry Whitehead illustrated the book. Joseph Bruchac III, an Abenaki from Grainfield Center, and Michael J. Caduto have published two collections of Native American tales that retain the authentic story structure: *Keepers of the Earth: Native American Stories and Environmental Activities for Children* (1988) and *Keepers of the Animals: Native American Stories and Wildlife Activities for Children* (1991). As the titles indicate, the books include appropriate activities for children to help them understand the themes. Bruchac has also published several coming-of-age stories, including *The Girl Who Married the Moon* (1994), and a poetry collection, *Thirteen Moons on Turtle's Back: A Native American Year of Moons* (1992). In addition to published authors, storytellers such as Jack Gladstone are appearing all over the country presenting the stories in their original oral form.

More nonfiction literature that reflects the Native American's voice has been published in the 1990s. For example, in *A Boy Becomes a Man at Wounded Knee* (1992) by Ted Wood with Wanbli Numpa Afraid of Hawk, a nine-year-old boy describes the centennial anniversary of the massacre at Wounded Knee. The book also includes information about Lakota culture.

In the 1990s, many information books that highlight historical, cultural, and contemporary information about specific tribes are being published. The books include appropriate graphics, photographs, and tribal art to give children authentic Native American perspectives. For example, Virginia Driving Hawk Sneve, a Lakota author, provides authentic information about various tribes in her nonfiction books published in the *First Americans Series*, such as *The Navajos: A First Americans Book* (1993). The expressive illustrations by Ronald Himler enhance her text. Sneve's poetry collection, *Dancing Teepees: Poems of American Indian Youth* (1989), is a popular collection of poetry written by young Native Americans in their traditional oral style. Native authors and artists show their respect and love for their land in books such as *This Land Is My Land* (1993) by George Littlechild (a member of the Plains Cree nation). Indian children narrated the informational photo-essays *Totem Pole* (1990) and *Apache Rodeo* (1995), published by Diane Hoyt-Goldsmith. Other popular series that usually include folk art are *The New True Books*, published by Children's Press; *Original*

Peoples Series, published by Franklin Watts; and various series published by Chelsea House.

During the 1990s, more authentic biographies about historical and contemporary men and women have appeared in juvenile biographies. Mainstream companies frequently publish individual and collected biographies in series such as Chelsea House's *North American Indians of Achievement Series* (1994 and 1995) and Silver Burdett's *Biography Series of American Indians* (1989).

The Native American perspective is appearing in both fiction and nonfiction literature. Through his lyrical narrative and expressionistic images Barry Ellsworth captures the love and respect for nature expressed by Native Americans in his picture book, *The Little Stream* (1995). (See the Ellsworth color plate.) Ellsworth dedicated the book to the American Indians. Recent books have explored the captivity theme, as in Dolores Johnson's *Seminole Diary: Remembrances of a Slave* (1994), and vision quests, as in James Bennett's *Dakota Dream* (1994), which highlights the protagonist's desire to communicate with the spiritual world. The adventures vary slightly from tribe to tribe, but they usually involve sufferings and hardships. The protagonist may be guided through the quest by a wise

friend, parent, companion, or medicine person. Strong women are beginning to appear in the literature; a good example is Maude in Joann Mazzio's *Leaving Eldorado* (1993). Marcia Keegan's *Pueblo Boy: Growing Up in Two Worlds* (1991) and Russ Kendall's *Eskimo Boy: Life in an Inupiaq Eskimo Village* (1992) deal with children who are growing up in two worlds, learning about traditional tribal beliefs and customs while attending American schools. Three books by non-Indian writers that authentically portray historical and contemporary issues faced by Native Americans are Jean Craighead George's *Julie of the Wolves* (1994), Elizabeth George Speare's *The Sign of the Beaver* (1983), and Scott O'Dell's *Black Star, Bright Dawn* (1988).

Another successful creator who is not Native American is Gerald McDermott, whose humorous books with pictures give younger readers authentic Native American folk literature; see especially his trickster tales *Raven: A Trickster Tale from the Pacific Northwest* (1993) and *Coyote: A Trickster Tale from the American Southwest* (1994). More humorous tales are found in Paul Goble's Plains Indian "noodle head" stories beginning with *Iktomi and the Berries* (1989), and continuing to the fifth book in the series, *Iktomi and the Buzzard* (1994).

Barry Ellsworth's lyrical text and images portray the emotions felt in The Little Stream. *The white background highlights the verbal narrative and becomes a part of the visual impact of each double page. The detailed watercolor paintings appear at the bottom of the page, flow like the stream, and supplement the narrative. The deer and birds connect the language and images to form a perfect visual composition. Note the unusual hand-printed text. What story does the detailed painting tell?*

Summary

Almost 16 percent of the estimated 25,000 juvenile and young adult books published in the United States in the 1990s included African-American, Asian-American, Hispanic, and Native American characters or cultural information.[30] Clearly, the quantity and quality of books reflecting parallel cultures have improved in the last two decades, but much remains to be done. Today, more native creators are producing literature reflecting their cultures. Nancy Larrick, a leading researcher and educator who in 1965 pointed out the "all white world of children's literature," is encouraged by the discussion about multicultural literature in the 1990s, but she laments that so little real progress has been made in the thirty years since her original investigation.[31]

Cultural authenticity is a major consideration when selecting quality fiction and nonfiction literature reflecting parallel cultures. Several techniques to determine cultural authenticity and other general guidelines for selection were discussed in the chapter. A variety of instructional techniques and strategies were suggested for use with quality fiction and nonfiction literature. Historical and contemporary literary offerings and creators were described for the four ethnic groups highlighted in the chapter. The bibliography includes multiethnic literature, African-American literature, Asian-American literature, Hispanic literature, and Native American literature that reflects universal and culture-specific themes.

Young people explore literature for pleasurable experiences. Because high-quality literature emphasizes culture-specific information and concerns, teachers also use it to supplement and enhance all content area instruction. Therefore, outstanding literature "celebrates the unique and universal perspectives" of parallel cultures.

NOTES

The opening quotation is from Mitsumasa Anno in Kovacs, D., & Preller, J. (Eds.). *Meet the Authors and Illustrators.* New York: Scholastic. 13.

1. Hamilton, V. 1989. Acceptance speech for the Boston Globe–Horn Book Award for Nonfiction. *The Horn Book Magazine.* 65(2). 183–85. See also her May Hill Arbuthnot Lecture, April 1993, in Bishop, R. S. 1994. Books from parallel cultures: What's happening? *The Horn Book Magazine.* 70(1). January/February. 105.

2. For additional demographic data about each ethnic group, see sources such as Banks, J. A. & C. A. M. 1993. *Multicultural Education: Issues and Perspectives.* (2d Ed.). Needham Heights, Mass.: Allyn & Bacon. 357–62; Cushner, K., McClelland, A., & Safford, P. 1992. *Human Diversity in Education: An Integrative Approach.* New York: McGraw-Hill; Hodgkinson, H. L. 1985. *All One System: Demographics of Education—Kindergarten through Graduate School.* Washington, D.C.: Institute for Educational Leadership. (ERIC Document Reproduction Services No. ED 261 101); *Statistical Abstract of the United States.* 115th ed. September 1995. Washington, D.C.: U.S. Department of Commerce. 18–21, 160–61.

3. These core, universal values are accepted by the dominant or mainstream culture and by ethnic groups in the United States. They were identified and discussed in sources such as Au, K. H. 1993. *Literacy Instruction in a Multicultural Setting.* San Diego: Harcourt Brace Jovanovich. 5–6; Spindler, G. & L. 1990. *The American Cultural Dialogue and Its Transmission.* London: Falmer Press; Trueba, H. 1990. Mainstream and minority cultures: A Chicano perspective. In Spindler, G. & L. 1990. 122–43.

4. Council on Interracial Books for Children. 1974. *10 Quick Ways to Analyze Children's Books for Racism and Sexism.* (The council was an influential organization founded in 1966 that identified racial stereotypes in children's books and promoted creators, especially those from African-American backgrounds. This pamphlet identified acceptable selection criteria and, through the *Bulletin* and various annotated bibliographies, cited acceptable multicultural literature.); Baker, A. (Ed.). 1971. *The Black Experience in Children's Literature.* New York: New York Public Library. (This annotated bibliography of books with African-American characters is now in its fourth edition, 1989.); Sims, R. 1982. *Shadow and Substance: Afro-American Experience in Contemporary Children's Fiction.* Urbana, Ill.: National Council of Teachers of English. (A useful guide for the selection of suitable literature for and about African Americans. Sims's insightful discussions are helpful to all selecting suitable juvenile literature reflecting parallel cultures.)

5. See sources such as the following for additional information about using multicultural literature: Hansen-Krening, N. 1992. Authors of color: A multicultural perspective. *Journal of Reading.* 36(2). October. 124–29; Harris, V. (Ed.). 1992. *Teaching Multicultural Literature in Grades K-8.* Norwood, Mass.: Christopher-Gordon.

6. Concerns about the politics of multicultural literature are expressed in the following sources: Bruchac, J. 1995. All our relations. *The Horn Book Magazine.* 71(2). March/April, 158–62; Madigan, D. 1993. The politics of multicultural literature for children and adolescents: Combining perspectives and conversations. *Language Arts.* 70(3). March. 168–76. See also *The New Advocate.* 7(2) Spring 1994 and 8(1) Winter 1995.

7. For additional information about the terms, see sources such as Au, K. H. 1993. 1–8;

Bullivant, B. M. 1993. Culture: Its nature and meaning for educators. In Banks, J. A. & C. A. M. (Eds.). 1993. 29–47; Spindler, G. & L. 1990.

8. For additional information about benefits gained from exploring the literature, see sources such as Bieger, E. M. 1996. Promoting multicultural education through a literature-based approach. *The Reading Teacher.* 49(4). December/January. 308–9; Bishop, R. S. 1992. Extending multicultural understanding. In Cullinan, B. (Ed.). *Invitation to Read: More Children's Literature in the Reading Program.* Newark, Del.: International Reading Association. 81–83; Bishop, R. S. 1994. *Kaleidoscope: A Multicultural Booklist for Grades K–8.* Urbana, Ill.: National Council of Teachers of English. xiii–xiv; Salvadore, M. 1995. Making sense of our world. *The Horn Book Magazine.* 71(2). March/April. 229–30; Willett, G. P. 1995. Strong, resilient, capable, and confident. *The Horn Book Magazine.* 71(2). March/April. 175.

9. Bishop, R. S. 1992. Multicultural literature for children: Making informed choices. 40–43. In Harris, V. (Ed.). 1992. 39–53.

10. Seto, T. 1995. Multiculturism is not Halloween. *The Horn Book Magazine.* 71(2). 169–74.

11. Aronson, M. 1995. A mess of stories. *The Horn Book Magazine.* 71(2). 163–68.

12. Wilson, A. 1990. I want a black director. *New York Times.* September 26. p. A15.

13. Consult the following sources for persuasive arguments on all sides of the issue: Cai, M. 1995. Can we fly across cultural gaps on the wings of imagination: Ethnicity, experience, and cultural authenticity. *The New Advocate.* 8(1). Winter. 1–16; Hamanaka, S. 1994. I hope their ears are burning: An author of color talks about racism in children's literature. *The New Advocate.* 7(4). Fall. 227–38; Lasky, K. 1996. To Stingo with love: An author's perspective on writing outside one's culture. *The New Advocate.* 9(1). Winter. 1–7.

14. Rochman, H. 1993. *Against Borders: Promoting Books for a Multicultural World.* Chicago: American Library Association. 18; Rochman, H. 1995. Against borders. *The Horn Book Magazine.* 71(2). March/April. 150.

15. For additional information about selecting literature and bibliographies of outstanding literature, see sources such as the following: Bishop, R. S. (Ed.) 1994. viii–xx; Bishop, R. S. 1992. Multicultural literature for children: Making informed choices. 47–51; Day, F. A. 1994. *Multicultural Voices in Contemporary Literature: A Resource for Teachers.* Portsmouth, N.H.: Heinemann. 5–8; Diamond, B. J., & Moore, M. A. 1995. *Multicultural Literacy: Mirroring the Reality of the Classroom.* White Plains, N.Y.: Longman. 44–46; Miller-Lachmann, L. 1992. *Our Family Our Friends Our World.* New Providence, N.J.: Bowker. 15–21; Rudman, M. K. 1995. *Children's Literature: An Issues Approach.* (3d Ed.). White Plains, N.Y.: Longman. 221–24;

Yokota, J. 1993. Issues in selecting multicultural children's literature. *Language Arts.* 70(3). March. 156–67.

16. For additional information about organizing literature, see sources such as Banks, J. A. & C. A. M. 1993. 198–209; Bieger, E. M. 1996. Promoting multicultural education through a literature-based approach. *The Reading Teacher.* 49(4). December/January. 308–12; Bishop, R. S. 1994. xx–xxii; Meinbach, A. M., Rothlein, L., & Fredericks, A. D. 1995. *The Complete Guide to Thematic Units: Creating the Integrated Curriculum.* Norwood, Mass.: Christopher-Gordon; Pugh, S. L., Garcia, J., & Margalef-Boada, S. 1994. Multicultural tradebooks in the social studies classroom. *The Social Studies.* 85(2). March/April. 62–65.

17. Baruth, L. G., & Manning, M. L. *Multicultural Education of Children and Adolescents.* 29–144.

18. For additional instructional strategies and LRMs, see sources such as Teidt, P., & Teidt, I. 1990. *Multicultural Teaching: A Handbook of Activities, Information, and Resources.* (3d Ed.). Needham Heights, Mass.: Allyn & Bacon. 10–11; Zarrillo, J. 1994. *Multicultural Literature, Multicultural Teaching: Units for the Elementary Grades.* Orlando, Fla.: Harcourt Brace Jovanovich. 4–5.

19. For additional information about the historical development of the literature and general information about the literature from each ethnic group, see sources such as Bishop, R. S. 1994. xiii; Miller-Lachmann, L. 1992. 5–11; Reimer, K. M. 1992. Multiethnic literature: Holding fast to dreams. *Language Arts.* 69(1). January. 4–21.

20. See the following sources for additional information about *Little Black Sambo:* Bader, B. 1996. Sambo, Babaji, and Sam. *The Horn Book Magazine.* September/October. 72(5). 536–47; Lester, J. 1988. The storyteller's voice: Reflections on the rewriting of Uncle Remus. *The New Advocate.* 1(3). Summer. 143–47; Lyon, G. 1996. True pictures: An interview with Jerry and Gloria Pinkney. *Teaching Tolerance.* Fall. 11–15. Also see Van Dyke Parks's retelling of the Uncle Remus tales, especially *Jump Again! More Adventures of Brer Rabbit.* Illus. B. Moser. San Diego: Harcourt Brace Jovanovich.

21. Arbuthnot, M. H. 1947. *Children and Books.* Chicago: Scott, Foresman. 388–89.

22. Larrick, N. 1965. The all-white world of children's books. *The Saturday Review.* September 11. 63–65; 84–85.

23. Chall, J. S., Radwin, E., French, V. W., & Hall, C. R. 1985. Blacks in the world of children's books. In D. MacCann & G. Woodard. (Eds.). *The Black American in Books for Children.* (2d Ed.). Metuchen, N.J.: Scarecrow Press. 211–21.

24. For additional information about African-American literature, see sources such as Sims, R. 1982; Harris, V. J. 1992. Contemporary griots: African-American writers of children's literature. In Harris, V. (Ed.). 55–108; Harris, V. J.

1996. Continuing dilemmas, debates, and delights in multicultural literature. *The New Advocate.* 9(2). Spring. 107–22; Miller-Lachmann, L. 1992. 25–30.

25. Micklos, J. 1996. Multiculturalism and children's literature. *Reading Today.* 13(3). December/January. 1, 8; also *1994* and *1995 Horn Book Guides.*

26. For additional information about Asian-American literature, see sources such as Cai, M. 1994. Images of Chinese and Chinese Americans mirrored in picture books. *Children's Literature in Education.* 25(3). 169–92; Cai, M. 1995. 1–16; Hsu, A. 1995. It's our train. *The Horn Book Magazine.* 71(2). March/April. 241–45; Pang, V. O., Colvin, C., Tran, M., and Barba, R. H. 1992. Beyond chopsticks and dragons: Selecting Asian-American literature for children. *The Reading Teacher.* 46(3). November. 216–24; Reimer, K. M. 1992. 16.

27. Day, F. A. 1994. 206.

28. For additional information about Hispanic-American literature, see sources such as Barrera, R. B., Liguori, O., & Salas, L. 1992. Ideas a literature can grow on: Key insights for enriching and expanding children's literature about the Mexican-American experience. In Harris, V. J. (Ed.) 203–41; Micklos, J. 1996. 8; Nieto, S. 1992. We have stories to tell: A case study of Puerto Ricans in children's books. In Harris, V. J. (Ed.) 171–201; Reimer, K. M. 1992. 16; Schon, I. 1993. Latino books. *Book Links.* 2(4). March. 50–53; Schon, I. 1993. Reading the world: Mexico. *Book Links.* 2(4). March. 45–49.

29. For additional information about Native American literature, see sources such as Barclay, D. A. 1996. Native Americans in books from the past. *The Horn Book Magazine.* 72(5). September/October. 559–65; Bruchac, J. 1995; Dowd, F. S. 1992. Evaluating children's books portraying Native American and Asian cultures. *Childhood Education.* 68(4). 219–24; Gilliland, H. 1980. *Indian Children's Books.* Billings, Mt.: Montana Council for Indian Education; Hirschfelder, A. B. 1993. Native American literature for children and young adults. *Library Trends.* 41(3). 414–36; Johnson, G. 1995. One sings . . . the other doesn't: The role of ritual in stories about Native Americans. *The New Advocate.* 8(2). Spring. 99–107; Noll, E. 1995. Accuracy and authenticity in American Indian children's literature: The social responsibility of authors and illustrators. *The New Advocate.* 8(1). Winter. 29–43; Slapin, B., & Searle, D. (Eds.). 1992. *Through Indian Eyes: The Native Experience in Books for Children.* Philadelphia: New Society.

30. Goforth, F. S. 1995. Content analysis. *The Horn Book Guide, 1990–1995.* This selection tool reviews most of the hard-cover juvenile and young adult books published in the United States.

31. Cited in Micklos, J. 1996. 8.

Part Four

LITERATURE IN THE CLASSROOM

Oral & Visual Presentations of Literature

A book shared is an experience shared, a delight shared. One profits both from the book and from the enriched relationship the reading may have created with someone else.

—Jean Karl

❋ EXPLORING LITERATURE THROUGH ORAL AND VISUAL EXPERIENCES

Jean Karl's statement highlights the importance of sharing literature with others and the aesthetic interactions created by listening to, discussing, dramatizing, and visualizing literature in the classroom. Thus far, throughout this book we have identified and discussed distinctive characteristics of literary genres and exemplary literature and suggested some appropriate instructional focuses and strategies to elicit learners' responses to literature. In addition to independent reading and writing activities, adults and children also use various oral and visual strategies to introduce, share, and react to fiction and nonfiction literature. (See photo below.)

BENEFITS OF AN ORAL PRESENTATION OF LITERATURE

Listening and speaking are a child's earliest form of communication. As children experience and explore oral language, they learn to use language to dispense information, express feelings, interact socially, and persuade others; they also learn to manipulate language for imaginative and cognitive purposes. (See Chapter 12 for additional information about the functions of language.) Oral communication helps instill thinking and problem-solving skills, which lead to intellectual development. Oral communication takes place in a social context. Therefore, when individuals use the modes of oral communication—speaking, listening, and thinking—they also collaborate and negotiate with others. Children use these social interaction skills when they share their reflections, reactions, and responses to literature.

Fortunately, literature is used by many educators to help children develop oral language competency. Through listening and speaking experiences, children expand and enhance their linguistic, intellectual, cognitive, and social competencies. Table 10.1 on page 342 presents benefits individuals gain when they explore literature through oral techniques.[1]

Let me tell you a story. "Once upon a time there was this green gump who..."

TABLE 10.1 Benefits Individuals Gain When Literature Is Presented Through Oral Techniques

---

Through the oral presentation of literature, children hear the cadence of the words and phrases used by authors.

Hearing the descriptive and figurative language used by authors stimulates the listener's imagination.

Young people develop a cohesive spirit as they share the creative ways authors express fanciful and realistic situations, emotions, and content.

The oral presentation of literature gives children and teachers an opportunity to discuss how effectively the author's words, phrases, and sentence structure present information, ideas, and feeling.

Through the oral presentation of literature, children have an opportunity to manipulate and play with repetitive or humorous sounds of the language.

Literature provides alternative language models for children to use when speaking, listening, and writing to others.

Young people become aware of the various art forms, such as pictures, music, and dance, that can be naturally integrated into an oral presentation of literature.

When children present literature through oral techniques, they develop the ability to use oral language for informative, imaginative, expressive, persuasive, or ritualistic purposes.

Through the oral presentation of literature, children and adults identify and discuss various conflicts and behavior and discover alternative ways to solve these problems.

The oral presentation of literature is a natural way to discover and disseminate beliefs, traditions, and the literary heritage of social and cultural groups.

The oral presentation of literature provides a pleasurable, aesthetic way for individuals to share ideas, sensations, events, and personality traits.

The first section of this chapter describes desirable auditory skills children and adults use when they present literature effectively. Verbal expressions and nonverbal elements are discussed separately to provide a reference for the presenters. Next, the benefits, preparation, and presentation of specific oral strategies, such as book talks, book discussions, reading aloud, storytelling, puppets, and drama, are described. Specific visuals, audiovisual media, and multimedia technology that can be used to help children interpret literature are presented in the final section of the chapter. Although the various oral and visual strategies for presenting literature orally are described independently, the strategies are compatible and may be combined for a successful presentation of literature. The strategies discussed in this chapter are intended to be used with all of the fiction and nonfiction prose, poetry, and dramatic literature discussed in the previous chapters.

AUDITORY SKILLS NECESSARY FOR AN EFFECTIVE ORAL PRESENTATION OF LITERATURE

Frequently, we give a book talk, discuss literature, read or tell a story, recite a poem, or use drama to lure children into the fascinating world of children's books. The presentation will be successful if the adult or child uses appropriate, compatible verbal and nonverbal expressions. Just as young children learn to use their voices to communicate with others, inexperienced teachers discover that their voices can be used to entice students to listen, to convince them that a subject is important, and to express joy, sadness, and approval. As teachers develop auditory skills, they learn to use their voices more effectively.

Before entering school, children acquire various regional or cultural verbal and nonverbal expressions.[2] For example, in some cultures children are taught it is disrespectful to look directly into the eyes of an authority figure. In other groups children are taught it is respectful to look directly into the eyes of the speaker. Such a simple difference in oral communication techniques might create major misunderstandings if the adult is not aware of these cultural differences. As we learn more about linguistic variations, we realize that we must recognize and respect cultural differences. At the same time, we must teach learners to adopt an appropriate style of communicating with others in various contexts. If we are to serve as positive role models for young people, we must also identify and refine our personal oral communication skills.[3] The oral presentation of literature provides a natural opportunity for adults and children to refine their verbal and nonverbal expressions.

VERBAL EXPRESSIONS

Think about a person who has an interesting, appealing voice. Why do you like to listen to her? Does she have a pleasant tonal quality? Perhaps she uses proper tone, pitch, and tempo when communicating? Does she articulate sounds and pronounce words clearly so others can understand what she is saying? Does she avoid fillers such as "OK" and "you know" in her conversation? Does she listen and respond to ideas suggested by others and add personal opinions when appropriate?

Desirable vocal expressions individuals use to communicate orally with others are listed in Table 10.2 on page 343.[4] While reading the list, consider how you use your own voice when conversing with others or when presenting literature.

TABLE 10.2 Desirable Verbal Expressions

Use a pleasant, natural tonal quality. Unless you have a naturally deep voice, you may need to breathe deeper and lower the pitch of your voice.

Unless portraying characters, avoid shrill or nasal vocal qualities. Allow the sound to come out of your mouth instead of your nose by exhaling slowly and opening your mouth, allowing half an inch of space between your teeth.

Project your voice so all can hear. Do not scream, but speak at a suitable volume so the entire audience can hear you. Aim or project your words directly to your audience, especially to the people farthest away from you.

Speak at a rate that is comfortable for you. Use a brisk pace that holds the attention of the audience. The average conversational speaking rate is approximately 125–150 words per minute.

Clearly enunciate and articulate syllables and words. Pronounce all words appropriately. Use the accepted pronunciation of educated people in your community.

Eliminate fillers, such as "ah," "like," "you know," and "OK."

Use the appropriate intonation pattern (according to the punctuation of the sentence). Suitable vocal emphasis helps the audience understand the meaning of the text. Remember, the meaning of a sentence changes when different words are emphasized.

Express enthusiasm for the topic.

When presenting literature, show emotions in the text by varying your volume and rate of speaking:

Use a soft, slow tone to build suspense.

Use a loud or fast tone to develop excitement.

Be sensitive to your audience. Modify your volume and speed if necessary to hold their attention.

TABLE 10.3 Desirable Nonverbal Expressions

Use appropriate gestures and facial expressions to:

Convey ideas or emotions.

Emphasize important words or phrases.

Add meaning to a topic.

If you stand, keep your posture erect, but comfortable. Keep your feet pointed at the audience or place one foot behind the other to prevent rocking from one foot to the other.

If you sit, be comfortable and natural. Do not constantly move parts of your body.

Occasionally, you may need to move around the room. If you must move, be discreet, keep the focus on the literature, and if the children are sitting close to you, be careful when moving around them.

Maintain eye contact with members of the audience. Be sensitive to their attention and interest in the story or poem.

Use your hands naturally.

Remember: Distracting, unnecessary movements, such as swinging your leg, twisting your hair, or rattling objects in your pocket, takes attention away from your oral communication!

NONVERBAL EXPRESSIONS

People read our body language while they listen to our words, so it is vital that our nonverbal behavior and verbal message be consistent. Children are particularly sensitive to nonverbal language because it is their first mode of communication.

Observe the gestures, facial expressions, and body movements used by others while speaking. Notice how nonverbal language helps you interpret the person's verbal message. Indeed, nonverbal expressions may convey more meaning than a long oral discourse. Fear, joy, disbelief, disgust, sadness, and other emotions are expressed through the speaker's eyes and face. The listener's nonverbal expressions are also important. Through facial expressions, listeners show their interest in a speaker's message.

Just as pronunciations may vary by region or group, so also does nonverbal language. In some families and cultures, for example, the listener and speaker stand or sit close together and touch frequently. In other groups this behavior would be unacceptable. Teachers must be aware of the nonverbal expressions used by young people.

The oral interpretation of literature gives us an opportunity to model nonverbal language and to discuss and compare cultural variations with students. Suitable nonverbal expressions used in oral communication are listed in Table 10.3.[5] Consider whether you use appropriate nonverbal language when communicating with others.

IMPROVING ORAL COMMUNICATION

To improve oral communication, begin by audio- or videotaping a presentation. Listen to your voice and compare your vocal qualities to the vocal expressions listed in Table 10.2. Your goal is to speak clearly, pronounce the words appropriately, and use a natural flow and cadence in your voice. If you talk too fast, make a conscious effort to talk more slowly. Carefully enunciate the beginning and ending syllables of words; do not slur or clip your words. Listen to national broadcasters and compare your vocal qualities to theirs. Become accustomed to the unique sound of your voice. If necessary, before speaking, lower your volume and tone by pausing for several moments and breathing deeply from the bottom of your feet. Teachers, singers, and other professional speakers must protect their vocal cords and voices. Carol Purdy's *Iva Dunnit and the Big Wind* (1985), with illustrations by Steven Kellogg, gives the oral reader an opportunity to practice suitable pronunciation of dialogue and variations in volume, pacing, and tone. (See the Purdy color plate.)

While preparing your oral presentation, practice standing or sitting before a full-length mirror. Also, observe your nonverbal movements on a videotape. Compare your movements to those suggested in Table 10.3. Make sure your facial expressions are compatible with your message. Some natural body movement is acceptable, but distracting or incompatible movements should be modified.

☀ TECHNIQUES FOR PRESENTING LITERATURE ORALLY

Young people read and interpret verbal narratives and view visual narratives independently or in groups. They also enjoy hearing and discussing stories, expository texts, or poems presented by adults or peers who use various oral techniques, such as book talks, book discussions, reading aloud, storytelling, puppets, and dramatic presentations. This section describes various forms of oral presentations, indicates their benefits, suggests selection criteria, and discusses appropriate procedures for each technique.

BOOK TALKS

Hear ye! Hear ye! In Merry Old England, in days of yore,
Lived a young orphan, Jemmy,
Who had many hair-raising adventures in store.

Jemmy, a homeless street boy, was kidnapped to become the whipping boy for Prince Brat, who could not be punished for his bad deeds. Since the prince was inclined to play dastardly tricks, poor Jemmy was soundly thrashed morning, noon, and night. As Jemmy told the prince, ". . . you get me thrashed so that this hide o'mine feels like the devil run me over with spikes in his shoes" (p. 8). One "moon-glazed" night the prince appeared in Jemmy's chambers and demanded that Jemmy run away with him. Jemmy had no choice, so off they went. Their adventures began when they were captured by Hold-Your-Nose-Billy and his cohort, Cutwater. What would the boys do now? Why did Jemmy write the kidnapper's ransom note, instead of the prince? How did Petunia, the dancing bear from the traveling circus, a bird cage, and some rats help Jemmy and the prince? Did Jemmy escape from the prince? Or did they return alive to the palace? I invite you to read Sid Fleischman's book *The Whipping Boy* (1986) to find out about their adventures and discover how the experiences affected Jemmy and the prince.

Book talks are short, exciting nuggets of information about "special" books or literature related by content, series, genre, author, or illustrator. This oral technique introduces students to literature, advertises the literature, and entices listeners to choose particular books to read. M. K. Chelton says the "hidden agenda" of a book talk is to promote a love of reading.[6] As the book talk for Sid Fleischman's *The Whipping Boy* (1986) illustrates, book talks are not traditional book reviews or literary critiques. The talker presents just enough information about the characters, incidents, setting, and writing style to introduce a book or convince the listeners to hear or

Steven Kellogg interprets Carol Purdy's Iva Dunnit and the Big Wind *with realistic watercolor paintings. The artist uses pen and pencil lines for the detail. Notice the way he uses watercolor to show movement and to portray the wind. Do the children know where their Ma is? Will they help her? Why do they have pillows in their hands?*

read a particular selection. Without realizing it, all people give book talks when they want a friend to read a "good" book and discuss it with them.

Recently, a reading specialist observed that the book talk was the most effective technique she used to help children in her school become active readers. Before presenting a talk, she collects simple props and visuals related to the book. She then visits a classroom, gives a talk, and leaves the book and props in the classroom. The children and teacher enjoy using the visuals when they reread and discuss the book. Teachers and children in her school are reading more books and giving book talks at every opportunity—in their class, in other classes, and on school television programs.[7] Table 10.4 lists various benefits individuals gain from experiences with book talks.

Selecting Literature for Book Talks

All quality fiction and nonfiction literature is appropriate for book talks. Literature that presents appealing content in a suitable manner and works by favorite authors or artists are popular choices. Because book talks are used to introduce students to new topics and creators, only exemplary selections should be presented. Frequently, teachers use book talks to present literature that contains various themes and content that may be discussed in curricular areas. Therefore, outstanding narratives, such as those cited in previous chapters, are chosen to entice students to hear and read literature for individual, group, or class activities.

TABLE 10.4 Benefits Individuals Gain from Book Talks

> Book talks "sell" good literature and leave the audience wanting to know more about the literature or collection of books.
>
> Book talks introduce individuals to quality literature for personal reading.
>
> Book talks give adults opportunities to be enthusiastic about specific books and convey their pleasure in reading literature.
>
> Students and adults develop a positive rapport when experiencing book talks.
>
> Book talks help listeners visualize various settings, people, and cultures.
>
> While hearing a book talk, students become curious about the characters' behavior and decisions.
>
> Book talks stimulate discussion about feelings, ideas, and information suggested by a book.
>
> Book talks guide students to appreciate and understand the creators' craft.
>
> Book talks give students and teachers a common body of knowledge about a particular author, an illustrator, a book's content, a series of books, or a collection of books selected according to a topic.

Presenting a Book Talk

Talkers have discovered that the more complete and better organized their talk is, the more likely they are to persuade others to explore the book. After choosing and reading a book, excerpt, poem, or short story for a book talk, some experienced talkers write a script for the entire talk to be sure they have included all pertinent events and information. Table 10.5 presents suggestions for writing a script. The talker then uses the script to prepare a brief outline with an attention-getting introduction, notes on the major incidents, names of the major characters, and an enticing conclusion. The information is placed on a note card, which can be used during practice and referred to during the talk. Remember, unless trained in the theatre, *do not read a*

TABLE 10.5 Elements of a Book Talk Script

> Begin the talk with an exciting, action-packed incident. Only rarely do you begin at the beginning of the book.
>
> Do *not* retell the entire plot.
>
> Talk about several incidents illustrating the theme, content, or adventures included in the book.
>
> Mention the title and author of the book several times during the talk.
>
> Show the book.
>
> You may want to show representative illustrations during or after the talk.
>
> Use the names of the characters; never say "the boy in the book."
>
> Avoid rambling on about the plot.
>
> Do not give irrelevant details.
>
> Mention the setting and theme of the book.
>
> If applicable, use and define unusual language or technical jargon the audience will need to know to understand the book.
>
> Do not highlight content that is closely related to physical or emotional experiences of the listeners.
>
> Exclude embarrassing content, "taboo" language, or double entendres ("a night to remember").
>
> Conclude the talk by leading into the text. For example, you might say, "In Sid Fleischman's book, *The Whipping Boy*, there are three very important objects: a bird cage, a bear, and some rats." Or you might ask a rhetorical question: "How did a bird cage, a bear, and some rats save Jemmy and Prince Brat? Sid Fleischman tells you in *The Whipping Boy*."
>
> Use the following statement sparingly: "if you would like to find out what happened, read _____ by _____."
>
> If appropriate, give listeners an opportunity to make predictions about the plot or characters.
>
> After the talk, you may want to discuss the cover, title, and other conflicts the characters encounter.
>
> You may want to talk about several books related by content, genre, author, or artist.

TABLE 10.6 Tips for Presenting a Book Talk

> Be enthusiastic!
>
> "Sell" the book in *five minutes* or less!
>
> Use a natural, conversational delivery, present tense, and active voice.
>
> If you can pronounce it properly, use dialect from the book.
>
> Always keep the focus of the talk on the text, not the talker.
>
> If reading from the text, use a few, short passages to show the mood or the author's style.
>
> Don't oversell an inferior piece of literature. The audience can spot a phony talk.
>
> Be prepared for listeners to react and interrupt the talk.
>
> Do not tell the audience how to react to the selection. For example, don't say, "This is my favorite book and you will like it too!"
>
> Show appropriate illustrations and photographs while giving the talk.
>
> If appropriate, use visuals, music, simple costumes, or audiovisuals representing pertinent events or content in the selection.
>
> At the end of the talk, connect the audience to the selection by asking probes and prompts to activate their schema and link the selection to familiar places, persons, or other books.
>
> At the end of the talk, encourage the audience to reflect, react, and respond to the book.
>
> Adults and students can give book talks daily or several times a week.

script when giving a book talk. Use the notes discreetly to give a natural, spontaneous talk. A persuasive book talk encourages others to read the book. Table 10.6 lists tips for presenting a book talk.

Students Who Give Book Talks

Frequently, students want to give book talks after hearing adults give them. (See photo below.) If so, discuss with students the purposes of book talks and explain how to select appropriate literature, prepare a script, and present a talk. Record this information on a chart and display it in the literature center for future reference. After choosing a book, students will prepare an outline of the script. The outline should contain a brief introduction, some information about several incidents, and an enticing conclusion. Encourage students to practice their talks at home. When the students are ready to present the talks, divide them into "peer coaching" groups. One student presents a talk while several other peers listen and use a teacher-student checklist to make notations about it. After the talk, ask peers to discuss the strength of the talk and, if appropriate, make constructive suggestions to improve it. If possible, tape the talks and encourage students to listen to their own talks, reflect on them, and critique the presentation. When the students feel comfortable, they can present their talks to the entire class. Later, the students can give the book talks to another class or present them on the school's radio or television station.

That was a funny book. I want to read it for myself. Notice the Branch Library and the Book Recording Devices on the tree behind the children.

Students may use a visual with the talk to get the audience's attention, help the talker relax, and feel more confident. The names of the author and artist, the title of the book, and a simple sketch or decoration representing the content of the narrative are placed on the visual. The visual may be shaped like an object in the book. For example, a visual shaped like a dog might be used with Beverly Cleary's book *Strider* (1991).

BOOK DISCUSSIONS

A *book discussion* is an informal or structured exchange of opinions, reactions, descriptions, or evaluations of a particular literary selection read by the participants. Book discussions can be conducted in a student-teacher conference, in a small group, or in the full class. A discussion is a "literary conversation," in which group members are free to express their ideas, thoughts, and questions about a selection. Book discussions give participants an opportunity to consider other interpretations.

The discussions help individuals interpret the book's theme, the characters' behavior, the book's content, and the author and artist's style. When teachers participate in the discussion, they share their personal experiences, responses, and insights. They also model appropriate techniques to use when discussing these reactions. Now that teachers are using literature for aesthetic and efferent purposes, they recognize the value of including book discussions in all areas of the curriculum. Table 10.7 lists benefits participants gain from book discussions.[8]

Selecting Literature to Be Discussed

Unabridged literature is more appropriate for a book discussion than an excerpt or an abridged version. When a piece of literature is abridged, the editor usually selects an excerpt of the narrative and may apply a readability formula to the verbal text to determine if the language meets a predetermined age-related reading level. Frequently, to comply with the formula, imaginative, descriptive language is modified or removed from the narrative. Consequently, in abridged literature readers are not exposed to the versatility and richness of the English language. In the shortened version, the theme may not be developed, the setting may not be described, and the plot may not be adequately developed to show the previous events that influenced the characters' behavior. When students read an unabridged version, they usually discuss the author's language, comment on the theme, interpret the major events, and react to the decisions made by the characters. Therefore, it may be impossible for participants to adequately discuss these vital literary elements when an

TABLE 10.7 Benefits Participants Gain from Book Discussions

Participants have an opportunity to express their reactions to books read, heard, or seen.

Participants learn to use oral language to express their ideas about, reactions to, and interpretations of a literary selection.

Participants develop critical thinking skills and use higher-order thinking strategies (associations, comparisons, predictions) when they react to open-ended questions in book discussions. These skills are also developed by comparing and contrasting a book with other familiar literature.

As part of this social interaction, participants have an opportunity to actively acquire language in a meaningful context.

Unfamiliar or unique language used in the book can be discussed; frequently, participants use the language later in personal communications.

Through discussion of literature, participants learn to use appropriate literal and critical questions, inferential probes, involvement prompts, and extension probes and prompts.

Young people become aware of the art of literature when they discuss literary elements, genres, and forms. Later, they recognize the literary structures they encounter and use literary language in their discussions and writings.

Participants have an opportunity to hear other interpretations and to modify or confirm their personal reactions to a selection.

abridged or excerpted version is used. Occasionally, shortened versions of popular literary selections are read by children who have limited reading abilities. When abridged versions are used, the teacher must be aware of the limitations and provide information given previously in the original text.

Ideally, the literature used for oral discussion is of the highest literary merit, such as C. S. Lewis's outstanding fantasy, *The Lion, the Witch, and the Wardrobe* (1961), or it draws on the background experiences of readers and evoke their reactions, such as Louis Sachar's *There's a Boy in the Girls' Bathroom* (1987). Intermediate-age youngsters might need additional background information about Lewis's land of Narnia, but they will need few connections when reading Sachar's novel.

All literature used for book discussions must have a clearly developed, worthwhile theme, well-developed characters, and a logical plot with adequate details. Books with either humorous events or serious incidents are suitable. The humor encourages relaxation and chuckles, while serious topics evoke reflections and clarification of ideas. It is a good idea to discuss the best book created by the author or artist, because this may be the first or only time the child explores the person's literature.

Suitable Content to Emphasize during the Discussion

All literature used for discussion must evoke reactions from the participants and contain content that is worthy of the time spent in discussion. The content that relates to the participants' interests and literary, experiential, and cognitive backgrounds is highlighted in the discussion. New information and content to be presented in content area lessons can also be featured. To select appropriate content for discussion, consider questions such as the following:

What important ideas, issues, and content in the selection do the participants need to understand to help them interpret the text?

What literary elements of fiction, such as characterization, conflicts, mood, theme, plot development, and point of view, or nonfiction elements, such as the accuracy and authenticity of the content, are worthwhile to discuss?

What unique or unusual language can be discussed and highlighted to help the participants interpret the text and recognize an outstanding writing style?

What visual elements can be discussed to help the participants construct meanings from the visual narratives?

The Role of the Discussion Leader

The discussion leader, whether an adult or a student, is a *facilitator* not an *interrogator*, a *guide* not a *taskmaster!*[9] Instead of controlling the discussion, the leader is responsible for involving the participants in the discussion and keeping it flexible. The leader should read the entire selection before conducting the discussion, write appropriate probes and prompts based on the book's content, and model appropriate discussion techniques. Group members may need time to think about the text before expressing their personal reactions. The leader's goal is to guide the discussion without stifling the participants' personal, spontaneous reactions and responses.

Leaders are responsible for interjecting questions or probes to highlight certain concepts, attitudes, ideas, and/or language that participants should consider when interpreting the visual and verbal narratives. The leader might paraphrase or clarify participants' ideas. Frequently, the leader briefly summarizes the important points expressed during the discussion. The leader keeps the focus of the discussion on the narrative until most of the participants have expressed their personal interpretations and made comments about the book. Then the leader uses prompts to elicit the audience's personal interactions with the plot, characters, or content. The leader also invites participants to predict future events or

the actions of the characters. Participants must use appropriate discussion etiquette, such as listening thoughtfully to others, responding at appropriate times, speaking in a suitable volume and tone, and reserving judgments unless requested.

Frequently, the discussion is led by a group member.[10] As a discussion leader or participant, the teacher can observe a student's reactions to the interpretations given by members of the group. In this way, the teacher can gain information about the student's literary and experiential knowledge. By observing the way the students speak and listen to others, the teacher can also assess their ability to communicate. This information can then be used to plan future instruction. For example, presenting a mini-lesson that focuses on verbal or nonverbal expressions might help students communicate more effectively. A mini-lesson highlighting techniques individuals use to interpret literature or ways to respond to a selection can help students react positively to various interpretations of a selection.

In summary, a group leader is a sensitive, intuitive individual who encourages the participants to react honestly to literary selections. The leader balances those responses with suitable probes and prompts. The leader helps participants reach their highest potential as thinkers, learners, and lovers of literature. For additional information about implementing a book discussion group and the role of the participants and the teacher as facilitator-participant, see Chapter 12.

Questioning Techniques and Procedures

When planning questions for book discussions, the teacher should consider the purposes for asking questions and should design questions that elicit appropriate reactions.[11] Researchers have studied all aspects of questioning including types of questions to ask, how and when to ask them, how much time should elapse between a question and the reply, and how to react to answers. J. M. Wedman found that the questioning strategies used by preservice teachers during book discussions enhanced students' reading achievement.[12] He reported that the quality of the text and the reading instruction used influenced the questioning strategies used by the teacher.

W. D. Hammond addressed the number and quality of questions asked before, during, and after a student reads a book and made four recommendations for discussion leaders.[13] First, the leader should ask questions to elicit students' prior knowledge. Second, only important questions should be asked (not just those requesting story details). Third, the questions must motivate students to think about what they are reading. Finally, leaders should ask prompts that involve students personally with the lives of the characters.

J. Zarrillo, speaking from an aesthetic instructional stance, suggests that a leader start a discussion by asking "free response" prompts, such as "What do you want to say about your reading?"[14] The next level of probes and prompts should encourage students to relive the reading experience. He recommends that leaders then elicit personal associations and speculations from participants reflecting their personal interpretations of the literary selection. Finally, Zarrillo reminds the moderator to ask open-ended probes and prompts to elicit the participants' reactions to interesting, puzzling, funny, or sad episodes in the selection.

Students and teachers both ask questions during a book discussion session. Questions motivate participants to respond to the selection and to think critically. When planning and asking questions, the leader considers the materials, the participants, and the purposes for the discussion.

Questions, Probes, and Prompts Leaders need to understand the various types of questions, probes, and prompts that can be used to elicit students' reactions to literature and the appropriate time to ask each type. The participant's background knowledge, the concepts or language to be discussed, the guidance participants require to interpret the texts, and the leader's purposes determine the type of question, probe, and prompt used and when they are asked.

Questions elicit information related to specific details in the narrative and text-based information children are expected to recognize after hearing, reading, or seeing a selection. *Literal questions* are effective for eliciting specific information about details in the text, for retelling the selection, and for some evaluative responses. Tables 10.8 and 10.9 describe two types of questions.

Probes are open-ended questions that focus on the inferential and implied information suggested by the author. They highlight the verbal and visual narratives and help individuals construct meanings. Probes and questions are asked at different times. For example, we might ask a probe initially; then a question might be asked to clarify a concept or a personal interpretation. Table 10.10 describes inferential probes.

Like probes, *prompts* are open-ended statements expressed as questions. They elicit personal interactions with the plot, setting, or characters and their behavior; an example is "Has this happened to you? When?" Since prompts take the focus away from the selection, they are used sparingly and at the right time, which is usually at the end of a discussion. Prompts are described further in Tables 10.11 and 10.12 on page 350.

Probes and prompts help participants become personally involved in the narrative. They elicit a participant's personal associations with the selection and speculations about future actions of the characters. Participants rely on their background knowledge and may need time to reflect

TABLE 10.8 Literal Questions

The leader asks "who," "what," "when," and "where" questions to help students clarify details of literary elements and content. Literal questions have a single answer. They are useful to identify story grammar and evaluate selections. Use them *sparingly* and only to delineate important literary details or information. The following are examples of literal questions:

"Who is telling the story? How do you know?"

"What is the boy's name?"

"What is the setting of the poem?"

TABLE 10.9 Critical Questions

The leader asks participants to judge or critique stylistic devices used by the author, react to the content, compare titles within genres and types, and compare and contrast several works by an author. Students respond according to their knowledge of stylistic devices, genres, or other titles written by the author. Critical questions are closed-ended and demand higher-level thinking. Typically, they are used with mature students. The following are examples of critical questions:

"What is another way the creator could say _____ ?"

"Did you feel the creator took the right amount of time to develop the plot? Explain."

"What information did you need to understand X's behavior?"

"Does this book remind you of another selection? Why? Which one?"

TABLE 10.10 Inferential Probes

The leader asks participants to explore implied and inferred relationships within the text and illustrations. Probes are open-ended and are presented as questions. They help participants focus on the text and construct meanings elicited by the text. Responses are based on participants' background knowledge and new information gained when reacting and reflecting to ideas, information, and images evoked by the selection. Probes should be used *often,* at suitable times, throughout the discussion. The following are examples of inferential probes:

"What did Y mean when she said _____ ?"

"Why do you think X reacted the way he did?"

"What evidence do you have to suggest that Z happened?"

"What do you think will happen next?"

"Let's continue reading to find out if you are right."

TABLE 10.11 Involvement Prompts

The leader encourages participants to connect personal experiences to ideas and information suggested in the literature. Participants draw on personal experiences, interests, and concerns and combine these with ideas and information elicited from the text or illustrations. Prompts are open-ended and are presented as questions. They are usually asked *after* participants have responded to the selection and expressed their interpretations of it. The following are examples of involvement prompts:

"What was your first reaction to the selection?"

"Which character is most interesting to you?"

"Do you know someone who reminds you of this character?"

"What would happen if you behaved as X did?"

"How would you describe this book to a friend?"

"Now that you have heard your friends discuss this book, do you have other thoughts about it?"

TABLE 10.12 Prompts to Extend the Selection

The leader relates content to participants' schemata and explores new areas of thought. The reactions may move in unpredictable directions. *Extension prompts* are presented as questions. They stimulate the participants' imagination and invite them to react authentically to future events not presented by the creator. The following are examples of extension prompts:

"Would your mother want X to be your best friend? How do you know?"

"What do you expect X to find when he arrives in Z?"

"How would you be different if you lived there?"

"What do you think will happen to X in the next five years?"

"If you were to write a sequel to this selection, what events (or characters) would you include or leave out?"

on the material before responding to questions, probes, and prompts.

Participants who have the opportunity to react to higher-order probes and prompts will analyze the selection, make predictions about it, evaluate its quality, and apply personal information; in the process, they make thoughtful responses to the literature. If the teacher models a variety of questions, probes, and prompts, the students will usually apply these same strategies to the topics discussed and are better able to solve future problems satisfactorily. When students use appropriate questions, probes, and prompts, they *connect, construct,* and *create responses* to literary selections. In doing so, the participants clarify and question their personal reactions and interpretations of the literature.

READING ALOUD

A person uses suitable expressions and techniques to *read aloud* an appealing story, poem, or drama to an audience. The reader is successful if the audience is willing to move into the world selected by the reader and become involved in the literature being read and viewed. People of all ages like to listen to a capable person read aloud quality fiction and nonfiction literature. The listeners and reader enjoy a common experience when sharing a Big Book or reading aloud a classic, such as Ann K. Beneduce's retelling of William Shakespeare's *The Tempest* (1996); a wordless book, such as Nancy Tafuri's *Follow Me!* (1990); a collection of folk literature, such as Geraldine McCaughrean's *The Golden Hoard: Myths and Legends of the World* (1996); a fantasy, such as Margaret Mahy's *Tingleberries, Tuckertubs, and Telephones: A Tale of Love and Ice-Cream* (1996); a biography, such as Kate Waters's *Tapenum's Day: A Wampanoag Indian Boy in Pilgrim Times* (1996); or an information book, such as Joan Anderson's *Cowboys: Roundup on an American Ranch* (1996). If unabridged literature of high literary merit is read aloud, the listeners experience the images evoked by the writer and artist, hear the beauty of the language, and see life through the eyes of the creator, reader, and other listeners.[15]

Benefits Individuals Gain from Hearing Literature Read Aloud

From a study of children who read before entering school, D. Durkin concluded that IQ, race, ethnicity, or socioeconomic level did not influence whether a child became an early reader. Instead, early readers had access to printed materials, parents who valued education, and an adult or sibling who was *reading to* them before they entered school.[16] Twenty years later, the authors of *Becoming a Nation of Readers,* an influential document that summarized major research findings concerning the teaching of reading, stated succinctly: "the single most important activity for building the knowledge required for eventual success in reading is reading aloud to children."[17] Reading aloud is a vital activity for school and home. As Table 10.13 on page 351 shows, many listeners gain literary, linguistic, cognitive, and social benefits when they hear another person read literature aloud.[18]

Guidelines for Selecting Suitable Literature to Read Aloud

A reader who chooses a favorite literary selection to present usually projects more enthusiasm and reads with more expression. Unfortunately, some books preferred by adults may not appeal to the girls and boys. Realizing that they should read a book that appeals to the audience, teachers

TABLE 10.13 Benefits Listeners Gain from Hearing Literature Read Aloud

Listeners hear literature they might not choose to read independently at this time.

Students develop an interest in literature and using language when they are exposed to the various structures of literature.

Through this shared experience, listeners develop a positive attitude about books and reading.

Listening to literary selections helps children develop a knowledge of narrative and expository structures.

When children hear literature, their vocabularies and syntax are expanded.

Young people's listening abilities improve when they make predictions, validate their predictions, retell details, or retell stories.

Listeners' reading comprehension improves when they hear literature.

Listening to quality literature enhances and improves students' original writing.

Students who speak nonstandard English or English as a second language benefit from hearing literature.

Hearing and seeing quality literature stimulate the listeners' imagination and creative expressions.

As listeners hear literature, their knowledge of the world increases, and they become aware of events outside their immediate environment. This background knowledge helps them comprehend and interpret literature.

alternate reading a book requested by the children with a personal favorite. Many teachers have a tendency to read exclusively books written by favorite authors that have been popular through the years, such as Eric Carle's *The Very Hungry Caterpillar* (1969); Dr. Seuss's *The Sneetches and Other Stories* (1961); Bill Martin's *Brown Bear, Brown Bear, What Do You See?* (1964, 1992); Roald Dahl's *James and the Giant Peach* (1961); Jon Scieszka's *The True Story of the Three Little Pigs*, illustrated by Lane Smith (1989); Patricia MacLachlan's *Sarah, Plain and Tall* (1985); Katherine Paterson's *The Bridge to Terabithia* (1977); and the perennial favorite, E. B. White's *Charlotte's Web* (1952). All children deserve to hear these books, but there are many more recent, outstanding books that young people will also enjoy hearing, viewing, and reading.

Some adults are hesitant to choose new books because they are uncertain what their listeners prefer. Generally, young people prefer books that have a familiar content or are written by a favorite creator, popular series books, and books with a protagonist who is the same age or slightly older than they are. Chapter 1 presents additional information about children's literary preferences at various ages. Fortunately, several sources are available to help adults select literature enjoyed by young people at various

ages. You should also ask the experts—poll the students to find out their literary and content preferences, as suggested in Chapter 2. Keep a list of these suggestions from one year to the next. School media specialists, public librarians, and employees at children's bookstores are other valuable experts who can recommend books with universal appeal. Teachers can review new literature at the public library or children's bookstore and can consult the selection tools listed in Appendix G, such as *The Horn Book Guide to Children's and Young Adult Books.*

Books with pictures that depend equally upon the verbal and visual narratives to present the story are excellent choices for reading aloud. As the listeners view the illustrations and hear the verbal text, they receive the total impact of the book. Books such as Jane Yolen's *Owl Moon*, illustrated by John Schoenherr (1987), John Steptoe's *Mufaro's Beautiful Daughters: An African Tale* (1987), Maurice Sendak's *Where the Wild Things Are* (1963), and Barbara Cooney's *Miss Rumphius* (1982) achieve complete unity between the visual and verbal narratives and are excellent choices for reading aloud. Many books that achieve this balance are discussed in Chapter 8 and are recommended for oral reading.

A book with an interrelated plot structure or complex characterizations is suitable to read aloud and discuss with others. With such books, learners may benefit from reading a copy of the book silently along with the oral reader. Allan Ahlerg's *The Better Brown Stories* (1996), with its unique format, and Ellen Raskin's *The Westing Game* (1978) are examples of such books. Raskin's fascinating mystery has multiple clues that must be checked and rechecked periodically to help the reader-listener understand the twists in the plot.

Some books include authentic dialect that is vital to the mood and characterization of the story. The reader must read the dialect appropriately so the listeners can hear the cadence and distinctive pronunciations used by a particular cultural or geographic group. Children frequently have difficulty reading such books independently, because the dialect confuses them and they may misunderstand the plot or characters' behavior. Therefore, it is best for learners to initially explore books with dialect such as the following in oral reading sessions: Frances Burdett's *The Secret Garden* (1962) with Yorkshire dialect; Mildred Taylor's *Roll of Thunder, Hear My Cry* (1976) with African-American dialect; and Lois Lenski's *Bayou Suzette* (1943) with Cajun dialect. Later, children will remember the plot and perhaps select the book for independent or group reading.

Although reading aloud books that naturally appeal to children is important, it is also a good idea to expose them to literature from various genres and content. Thus, the oral reader might select a humorous book, such as Betsy

Duffey's *Hey, New Kid!* (1996), after reading a more serious selection, such as Charlotte Sherman's *Eli and the Swamp Man* (1996). Science fiction, such as William Sleator's *Interstellar Pig* (1995), could be followed by popular contemporary fiction, such as Betsy Byars's *The Pinballs* (1977). A historical fiction, such as Mary Hahn's *The Gentleman Outlaw and Me-Eli: A Story of the Old West* (1996), could be read before or after reading nonfiction literature with related content, such as Clinton Cox's biography *The Forgotten Heroes: The Story of the Buffalo Soldiers* (1993) or Judith Alter's information book *Growing Up in the Old West* (1989). Over the course of the year, the oral reader will select literature with protagonists from both genders, various socioeconomic classes, and parallel cultures, such as Virginia Hamilton's *When Birds Could Talk and Bats Could Sing: The Adventures of Bruh Sparrow, Sis Wren, and Their Friends* (1996). (See Chapter 9 for a description of selections reflecting various ethnic groups.) Young people also enjoy hearing nonfiction literature about unusual subjects, such as Aliki's *Wild and Woolly Mammoths* (1996). Several poetry collections, such as Bernice Cullinan's *A Jar of Tiny Stars: Poems by NCTE Award-Winning Poets* (1995), should be easily accessible for oral sharing. Young people who listen to books from various genres and by different creators become aware of the variety of choices that are available for independent and informational reading. Teachers have also discovered that when they read literature written slightly above the listeners' independent reading level, as the reading abilities of the girls and boys mature, they will choose this familiar literature for independent reading. In addition to the books presented in this section, the bibliography lists other outstanding new books to read aloud. Recommended books to read aloud are also listed in each genre chapter. Figure 10.1 presents guidelines for individuals preparing to read literature aloud. Always remember that a good story deserves to be heard, read, and seen several times!

Reading a Selection Aloud

Daily reading aloud should begin early in a child's life. The experience helps children feel special, because they are sharing their personal thoughts and dreams with an important person. A young child sitting in an adult's lap hears the words that are written on the page and talks with the

FIGURE 10.1 Guidelines for Individuals Preparing to Read Aloud

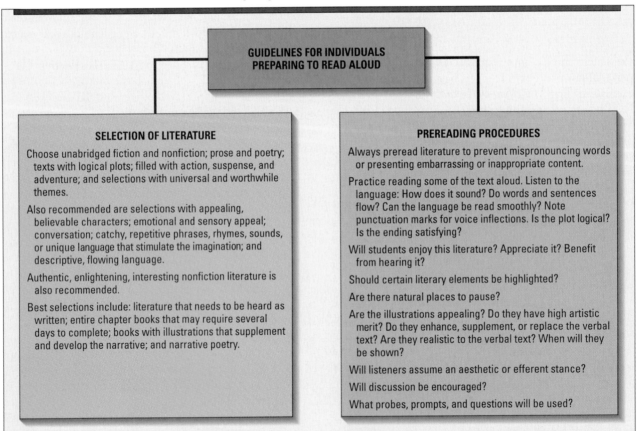

GUIDELINES FOR INDIVIDUALS PREPARING TO READ ALOUD

SELECTION OF LITERATURE

Choose unabridged fiction and nonfiction; prose and poetry; texts with logical plots; filled with action, suspense, and adventure; and selections with universal and worthwhile themes.

Also recommended are selections with appealing, believable characters; emotional and sensory appeal; conversation; catchy, repetitive phrases, rhymes, sounds, or unique language that stimulate the imagination; and descriptive, flowing language.

Authentic, enlightening, interesting nonfiction literature is also recommended.

Best selections include: literature that needs to be heard as written; entire chapter books that may require several days to complete; books with illustrations that supplement and develop the narrative; and narrative poetry.

PREREADING PROCEDURES

Always preread literature to prevent mispronouncing words or presenting embarrassing or inappropriate content.

Practice reading some of the text aloud. Listen to the language: How does it sound? Do words and sentences flow? Can the language be read smoothly? Note punctuation marks for voice inflections. Is the plot logical? Is the ending satisfying?

Will students enjoy this literature? Appreciate it? Benefit from hearing it?

Should certain literary elements be highlighted?

Are there natural places to pause?

Are the illustrations appealing? Do they have high artistic merit? Do they enhance, supplement, or replace the verbal text? Are they realistic to the verbal text? When will they be shown?

Will listeners assume an aesthetic or efferent stance?

Will discussion be encouraged?

What probes, prompts, and questions will be used?

adult about the verbal narrative and the illustrations. As the child turns the page at the appropriate time, she or he learns book-handling skills such as reading from left to right, procedures for turning a page without tearing it, and proper care of books. These reading strategies are further developed in the classroom when the teacher points to the words while reading a Big Book and encourages the children to interact with the text by chanting and completing the rhyming, repetitive words.[19] While reading Martin Waddell's *Owl Babies* (1992), the teacher can give the children an opportunity to interact with the repetitive phrases and expressions used by the various characters. (See the Waddell color plate.)

Audience Considerations   The age of the students, the teacher's purpose, and the instructional program determine the time and schedule for reading aloud sessions. In the elementary classroom, twenty minutes each day generally is the minimum time recommended for a reading aloud session.[20] Appropriate schedules vary with the age of the students:

> Teachers of children from birth through age five read at least *twice* a day—at the beginning of the day, after an active activity, after lunch, or at the end of the day.

> Teachers of children aged six through twelve years read at least *once* a day—after lunch, after an active session, or at the end of the day.

Teachers of students aged thirteen and older read *several* times each week for aesthetic and efferent purposes.

Before reading literature aloud, find out what the listeners know about the content and literary genre. Then *connect* the audience to the selection by introducing and discussing unfamiliar vocabulary or unknown information about the culture, setting, or unique topics they might encounter in the reading. Introduce the title, author, setting, characters, and conflicts. A brief book talk might entice the students to listen.

While reading aloud, be aware of the attention span and mood of the audience. Listeners may be encouraged to join in at repetitive phrases, rhyming words, and refrains. If the listeners are restless and are not interested in the narrative, the reader can cut repetitive phrases, paraphase the text, and quickly finish the selection. When a text is too long to finish in one session, the reader can stop at the end of a chapter or after the writer has used foreshadowing to give the listeners a hint of what might happen next. Teachers of young children usually have a special place where the children sit while listening to literature. Older students are expected to sit quietly in a comfortable place in the room while listening to a literary selection.

After reading, respect the listeners' spontaneous reactions to the selection. Be prepared for an enthusiastic reaction or silence while the listeners think about the text. If the reader wants the audience to react to the text, wait several seconds before asking suitable probes or prompts. Use

Patrick Benson's dark, expressive paintings expand Martin Waddell's Owl Babies. *The artist highlights the characters in the book by using browns, sepia, green, and yellow watercolors on black paper. Benson uses black lines and crosshatching throughout his detailed drawings. The arrangement of verbal narratives within the visual composition presents a harmonious blend of language and images.*

the question "Did you like that?" sparingly. This question verifies the reader's choice of literature or the effectiveness of the reading, but it does not elicit the children's honest and personal reaction to the text. When oral or written reactions are desired, encourage students to select appropriate Literary Response Modes (LRMs) to reflect their personal responses to the selection. Later, the book might be used for instructional purposes. Desirable vocal and nonverbal qualities and techniques for holding books with pictures while reading aloud are presented in Figure 10.2.

Reading Aloud by Students

As students develop confidence in their personal reading abilities, they enjoy reading aloud to peers and younger children. Peer grouping and cross-aged grouping (for example, fourth grade students reading to first grade students) are perfect techniques to use when students read aloud. Before students read aloud, talk to them about choosing appropriate literature, preparing to read a book orally, and techniques for reading aloud. Record the discussion on a chart and display it in the literature center. After students choose a book to read aloud, encourage them to practice reading at home or during "free time" at school. Team students in "peer-coaching" groups, where one student reads to the group while the peers listen. Later, the audience gives the reader constructive comments to improve the oral reading. The class and teacher can develop a simple read aloud checklist from the information at the beginning of this chapter and Figures 10.1 and 10.2. This checklist will be helpful during coaching sessions and

FIGURE 10.2 Guidelines for Reading Aloud Fiction and Nonfiction Literature

GUIDELINES FOR READING ALOUD FICTION AND NONFICTION LITERATURE

DESIRABLE VOCAL AND NONVERBAL QUALITIES

Review Tables 10.2 and 10.3.

Practice reading the verbal text and showing the illustrations.

Remember that a novice reader has a tendency to read too fast.

Speeding up adds to the drama, but when in doubt, slow down.

Read in a natural, interesting voice.

Be prepared to define unusual, unique, or unkown words.

Read according to the punctuation marks: pause at a comma; stop and lower the voice at a period; keep the voice in midintonation level for a question or when turning the page; use a loud, emphatic voice for an exclamation mark.

Vary the voice slightly to show the personality of different characters.

Speak louder and faster to add to the excitement of the text.

Use a slow, soft voice to add suspense or to build up to the climax of a text.

Clearly enunciate words and sentences.

Use the voice for emphasis, but do not read so dramatically as to overshadow the verbal text.

If the language does not flow, paraphrase the text.

Show personal reactions and emotions evoked by the verbal and visual narratives.

Show enjoyment and enthusiasm when reading aloud.

SHOWING PICTURES IN BOOKS

General techniques for showing illustrations:

Sit or stand and hold the book in a comfortable position.

Let the listeners know they will see all of the illustrations.

Hold the book at the audience's eye level.

Hold the book in front of your body or at your side.

Keep eye contact with the audience.

Hold the book so the audience can see your face.

Hold a thick or large book with both hands.

Keep the pages of a large book open with your fingers; do not block portions of the picture with your hand.

Show illustrations on one side of the room first; then move slowly to the other side; next time show the picture on the opposite side of the room first.

When showing books with pictures to young children, show the illustrations at all times.

When showing books with pictures to older children, show the illustrations either when reading the verbal text; or if the illustrations interpret, supplement, or replace the verbal text, show an illustration after reading the verbal text that describes or alludes to the picture.

When showing a picture in a chapter book or novel, show the picture at the appropriate time to add suspense, drama, or excitement to the reading. To keep eye contact, look up at the end of a sentence, paragraph, page, and chapter.

at student-teacher conferences. When confident about reading aloud, the student-reader will read to the class or another group. Audio- or videotaping of the final reading is helpful for self-evaluation and teacher-student evaluation, as well as for the pleasure of other students.

Reading aloud need not be reserved for language arts or literature classes. Appropriate literature can be read aloud to supplement other curricular areas. K. M. Evans presents a strong case for using journal writing and discussion as an integral part of reading aloud to students in the seventh grade.[21] Based on the students' reactions in their journals, Evans found that students expressed positive reactions toward reading and writing and recognized personal growth in reading, writing, speaking, listening, and thinking because of the experience. Students remembered many details of the selection. Evans recommended using an integrated approach such as this with all ages. W. Nikola-Lisa urges teachers to use reading aloud with other techniques such as drama, storytelling, choral reading, and group singing.[22]

STORYTELLING

> "I like to hear my teacher tell stories . . . I see the story in my head!"
>
> "My children listen intently when I tell them a story, especially when I ask them to join in at certain parts of the story."

Storytellers create a story or poem without the assistance of a script. Fortunately, this ancient art has been revitalized today. Storytelling festivals are happening everywhere, and storytellers are in demand at schools and business conferences. People of all ages want to hear stories. Storytelling creates a direct, immediate personal relationship between the teller and the listeners. Many adults use this natural oral technique frequently to relate original stories, family stories, and folk stories.

Teachers who do not tell stories to their students often make comments such as the following:

> "I feel more confident when I hold a book and read aloud."

> "When I tell a story, I do not have the book. I'm afraid I'll forget the story. Then what will I do?"

> "When you are telling a story, the success of the story depends on what you say or do. I'm not an actress—the activity scares me!"

> "I don't have time to memorize a story."

To these comments, we respond, "You're right, it is scary trying to remember a story, when you have only your voice and body to present it. At the same time you must keep the attention of the audience. Still, when you tell a story, you feel a special excitement that doesn't occur with any other literary experience. Besides, telling stories is fun. Try it! Begin with a familiar family story."

Benefits Individuals Gain from Experiences with Storytelling

At one time the storyteller was the most important person in the group. Storytellers had the memories, the "stories of the tribe." They entertained and informed their listeners with stories about the people, animals, and objects in their environment. Without the audience realizing it, the teller transmitted the basic values, mores, and beliefs of the society and interpreted its experiences. Many storytellers became medicine men, priests, or griots. They passed the literary and historical heritage of the society from one generation to the next.[23]

Entertainment, instruction, and the transmission of cultural traditions are the primary benefits listeners gain from storytelling. After hearing a story, children are enticed to read the story for personal enjoyment. Table 10.14 lists additional benefits individuals gain from storytelling experiences.[24]

Suitable Literature for Storytelling

Throughout the centuries folk literature has been the most popular literature used by storytellers to entertain and disseminate the heritage of a cultural group. Folk literature is easy to remember because most tales are organized according

TABLE 10.14 Benefits Individuals Gain from Experiences with Storytelling

Stories introduce listeners to the common heritage of universal truths, such as love, beauty, and courage.

Stories introduce listeners to the traditions, stories, and art of a particular society.

Listeners use their imaginations to visualize the storyteller's world.

Listeners develop a "sense of story," an awareness of the literary elements and structure of a well-written verbal narrative.

By comparing and contrasting stories they hear, listeners become discriminating in their personal selection of literature for independent reading.

Storytellers use higher cognitive skills when they recall narratives.

Storytellers learn to select suitable stories and become aware of the verbal and nonverbal strategies required to tell a story.

Storytellers enhance their oral language abilities.

Listeners who write original stories often use the literary and language patterns heard in storytelling.

Listeners apply information from stories to personal experiences.

Information from all discipline areas comes to life when heard through the storyteller's voice.

to a consistent pattern: an introduction to the characters, the conflict, and the setting; three major incidents; and a logical conclusion. Literary folktales, such as Helen Ketteman's *Luck with Potatoes* (1995), which are the link between folk literature and fantasy, are also favorite selections. As discussed in Chapters 3, 4, and 9, a variety of tales representing all cultural, regional, and national groups are readily available; examples include Neil Philips's *American Fairy Tales: From Rip Van Winkle to the Rootabaga Stories* (1996); Paula Fox's original fables in *The Little Swineherd and Other Tales* (1995); and Pleasant DeSpain's *Eleven Turtle Tales: Adventure Tales from Around the World* (1994).

Not all literature is suitable for novice storytellers. Literature that needs to be presented as written may be told by professional storytellers, but is usually reserved for reading aloud in the classroom. Examples include the stories from A. A. Milne's *Winnie the Pooh* (1926); long narrative poems from a collection, such as Edward Lear's *The Owl and the Pussy-Cat* (1871); and stories or poems with unusual language or dialect, such as Joel Chandler Harris's *Nights with Uncle Remus* (1883). Because this literature must be told as written, it must be memorized and is difficult for novice storytellers to tell spontaneously and naturally. While stories can be easily modified and embellished to suit the audience and the teller's mood, most tellers choose stories with the following literary elements:

A limited number (four to seven) of characters, who are worth emulating and who solve their conflicts in acceptable ways.

A logical, sequential plot with action and suspense.

A worthwhile theme.

Language that stimulates the imagination and is interesting to hear; for example, repetitive or rhythmic words and phrases and refrains.

A quick introduction to the setting, the characters, and their conflicts and perhaps a surprising, yet satisfying conclusion.

Preparing to Tell a Story
Kim Siegelson gives her readers an insider's perspective about the responsibilities of storytellers in her contemporary fiction *The Terrible, Wonderful Tellin' at Hog Hammock* (1996). Jonas, the protagonist, has inherited his grandfather's storytelling talent, but hesitates to take his place when the grandfather dies. Though Jonas has a love and respect for language and stories, he worries that he might not be able to tell the stories as enthusiastically as his grandfather. The reader empathizes with Jonas, who must make the stories live by using only verbal and nonverbal

expressions. By persuading his listeners to accept the stories, he will transmit the island's history to the children.

Professional storytellers have written many books and articles about preparing and presenting a story. Because the teller must practice a story several times to perfect the "art of storytelling," it takes more time to learn a story for storytelling than for other oral presentations.[25] Unfortunately, this requirement may frighten teachers away from an otherwise effective classroom strategy. Still, the benefits for the listeners and storytellers are so great that taking the time to learn a story is worthwhile. Each storyteller develops some personal techniques for learning stories. Table 10.15 lists the procedures many storytellers use when learning a new story.

Presenting the Story
The story is the major focus of the presentation. Some professional storytellers use dramatic techniques, such as simple movements or mime with their stories. Some tellers use backdrops, props, costumes, or music. Use dramatic presentations and visuals if you feel comfortable and natural using them. Do not allow the dramatic effects to overshadow the story.

The most important factors for a successful storytelling experience are the teller's knowledge of the story, the person's enthusiasm for the story, the language chosen, the vocal and nonverbal expressions used, and the teller's sensitivity to the audience.[26] Novice tellers who learn and present stories once or twice a month quickly develop a repertoire of stories and use storytelling extensively in their classrooms.

Audience Considerations   The listeners and the teller develop a special rapport during a storytelling session. This rapport is influenced by the storyteller's ability to bring the story to life, the atmosphere of the classroom, and, often, the seating arrangement of the listeners. Listeners are arranged according to their age and, occasionally, their behavior. Some tellers place the listeners close to them; others encourage students to stay at their places and listen to the story. When telling a somber, scary tale, the storyteller might darken the room and light a "storyteller's candle." When telling a boisterous, rollicking tale, the storyteller might take the listeners outside.

The storyteller should be sensitive to the listeners' reaction to the story. Master storytellers are flexible. They quickly adapt a story to keep the attention and interest of the listeners. If the listeners become restless, the teller might pause, summarize the story, and quickly conclude it. This adaptability is the major strength of storytelling over other oral presentations of literature.

Listeners of all ages enjoy interacting with the teller and the story. Effective storytellers retain the pace of the story

TABLE 10.15 Procedures for Learning a Story to Tell

Unless trained in the theater, *do not memorize* the story. Instead, do the following:

Read the story several times.

Think about the introduction.

Visualize the setting, the characters, the major incidents, and the conclusion.

Prepare a simple outline of the story and list any unusual names of characters.

Next, close the book and try to tell the story. If you forget, do the following:

Open the book, skim the section you forgot, and consider how it connects to the previous section and to the rest of the story; refer to your outline.

Close the book; start at the beginning again, and tell as much as you can.

If you forget again, look at the narrative once more, and repeat the previous suggestions, until you can tell the story all the way through without stopping.

Identify dialogue, repetitive phrases, or unusual names that are necessary for the unique flavor of the story. Tell it again using the selected language.

Timing is important in storytelling. Each story has a particular pace. Tell the story again, paying attention to the way you pace it.

Tape yourself, listen to the tape, and write notes about your telling. If you make a videotape, observe and evaluate your nonverbal expressions—your gestures, the way you use your hands, and your facial expressions.

If you are using an audiotape, tell the story again while standing or sitting in front of a full-length mirror. Observe and evaluate your nonverbal expressions.

By now, you should know the story. Consider:

Do you need to change your voice for certain characters?

Are you familiar with the sequence of the story?

Are you incorporating suitable language?

Are you using a pleasing tonal quality, clear articulation, correct pronunciation, and appropriate rate and volume?

Think about your introduction and conclusion:

How will you connect the audience to the story?

Have you satisfactorily completed the story?

even when they pause for the audience to react with laughter, fear, or wonder. If applicable, the storyteller encourages the listeners to repeat repetitive phrases or react to a character's action by booing, hissing, or jeering.

After completing a story, expert storytellers pause to elicit spontaneous responses from the listeners. They give the audience an opportunity to discuss their reactions to the story. Frequently, the audience remains silent at the end of the story. This indicates they are thinking further about the tale. At other times, listeners may laugh, cry, or begin talking immediately about the story. The content of the story, the instructional goals, and personal reactions determine whether young people create visual or verbal responses to the literature.

The Student Storyteller

After several storytelling sessions, students may express a desire to become storytellers. If so, talk with them about story selection, preparation, and presentation. Prepare a chart listing these elements and display it for students' future reference. Many teachers place students in "buddy" or "peer-coaching" groups. The group will select several short stories, and individual members will practice a story at school and at home. When a teller knows the story, she or he tells it to the small group. Group members can coach the teller using a teacher-student checklist. Audio- or videotaping is also useful for self, peer, and teacher observations. Later, the storyteller shares the story with the entire class or other groups. With the teller's permission, the tape may be placed in the literature center with a written copy of the tale. Other class members can check out the tape for school or home viewing.

Schoolwide storytelling festivals give storytellers an opportunity to share their stories with a wider audience. Many libraries, counties, and states sponsor large festivals. Some people are natural storytellers and enjoy telling stories to large groups, while others enjoy being members of the audience. Storytellers usually expect the audience to participate at certain times during the sessions. Additional information about storytelling is available in recent teacher journals and professional books.[27]

USING DRAMA WITH LITERATURE*

After listening to a story several times, prekindergarten children naturally act it out using simple costumes and props placed in the dramatic play area. Two and three year olds begin pretend play and act out realistic situations to understand life. In dramatic play, the child assumes a role and pretends to be somebody or something else with no training by a teacher or parent. In essence, dramatic play is the child's rehearsal for life.

When drama and literature are combined, aesthetic responses are evoked, and higher-order thinking, problem solving, story schema, and awareness of the diversity of language are enhanced. Through drama young people vicariously experience the events in a character's life, solve the

---

*"Using Drama with Literature" was written by Judith Kase-Polisini, a member of the College of Fellows of the American Theatre and the executive director of the Florida Association of Theatre Education.

character's conflicts, understand another's point of view, become aware of narrative structure, use the unusual and unique language in literary selections, and are actively involved in their learning.[28] For example, primary-age children retain the information included in an informational storybook, such as Jonathan London's *Master Elk and the Mountain Lion* (1995), when they dramatize the encounters between a cougar and a tule elk. Intermediate-age boys and girls become the rag dolls who can speak and think, when they dramatize incidents from Sylvia Waugh's fantasy series *The Mennyms* (1994). Wordless books, such as Quentin Blake's *Clown* (1996), provides adventures to pantomime. The tales and verses in folk literature collections, such as Joseph Bruchac's *Four Ancestors: Stories, Songs, and Poems from Native North America* (1996), give young people prose and poetry narratives to retell through dramatic activities. By using the information in Laurence Yep's autobiography, *The Lost Garden* (1991), ten to twelve year olds can write a script and present a reading or television program based on the major events that influenced Yep's decision to become a writer. Glennette Turner has prepared a miniplay for each biographical sketch in her collected biography *Take a Walk in Their Shoes* (1989). This book can be used as a model for children writing miniplays from nonfiction literature. Whether fantasy, folk literature, realistic fiction, biography, or informational storybook, the prose and poetry must have a clearly developed plot structure, dramatic conflicts, well-developed characters, and dialogue to provide the ideal stimulus for various dramatic activities.

Introducing Dramatic Activities

Literally, a *theatre* is an architectural structure, a building where we go to see plays.[29] Theatre is also a general term for the art of producing and performing plays for audiences. The product of theatre art is a *play* or *drama*, which can be a work of literature or an improvised work with no written script. Plays can be any length from one minute to an hour or more. Thus, you can have drama without theatre, but you cannot have theatre without drama. A theatre experience can be created whenever its essential artistic elements are present: *actors*, or players; the *play*, or idea; and the *stage*, or space to accommodate the actors and the audience.

Students learn from seeing and creating plays. People of all ages enjoy seeing plays in theatres, and some may become motivated to produce their own plays. Beginning groups should start with theatre games and informal, improvised drama before tackling the more complicated process of producing a play with a script. Indeed, many professional plays today are created by bringing together the actors to improvise ideas before setting them down on paper. Table 10.16 on page 359 suggests some beginning dramatic activities.

Teachers find that improvised play making allows children to begin with what they already know how to do: they act out their ideas, make up the dialogue as they go, and share each improvised scene with others in the group. Then, they evaluate the scene and replay it until they are satisfied that it conveys to the audience what they want to say. Members of the group serve as the audience for other members and help form the play during the evaluation. *Informal drama* is widely known as *creative drama*, educational drama, improvisational drama, spontaneous drama, or developmental drama. This method can be used with groups of all ages; I have used it to write three plays that I have produced for children.

One of the main advantages of using creative drama is that all members of the group may take the leading role in a story. In *character and action try-ons*, before a scene is played, all students practice walking like a character and share ideas about how the character walks. Another dramatic technique used effectively with literature is *role-playing*. In this activity, boys and girls assume the role of a selected character and spontaneously present the action and conversation in which the character might engage. Another way to present a character is a *monologue*. In this dramatic technique, the student selects a character, improvises his actions, and writes a speech the character might deliver as if speaking to himself. The student performs the monologue for an audience.

Students work in *unison play* in three ways:

1. Simultaneously performing tasks individually in their own space.

2. Performing the same task in pairs.

3. Performing as members of the same group in a scene (villagers, sailors on a ship, citizens at a community meeting, and the like).

Before creating original plays, it is often helpful to work with a story of interest to the group. Choose a story with a few strong characters and the opportunity to invent others. Avoid stories with lots of characters and too many scenes. For example, to dramatize Aesop's "The Tortoise and the Hare," everyone can try on the two main characters. When it is time to begin the scene, other characters may be invented, such as other animals watching the race, race officials, or even pieces of scenery such as trees, bushes, or the sun. Often the invented characters become more important as students create their own version of the story. Remember also that a story with a few characters and simple action can be played in many styles, such as melodrama, silent movie, western cowboy, or rock musical.

Readers' theatre is a popular dramatic technique used to present fiction and narrative poems orally. The students

TABLE 10.16 Beginning Dramatic Activities

Movement

Wiggle parts of the body or the whole body; then freeze to a sound cue.

Play Simon Says.

In pairs, play mirror. One person is a mirror and directs the action. The other person imitates the action in the mirror. Play with the whole
body or with isolated body parts such as the feet, arms, head, or shoulders.

Move in a random pattern around the room, changing speed, head levels, direction, and the like to sound cues.

Move as though you were moving through bubble gum, honey, outer space, or other substances; move as though you were underwater.

Become as small as possible; grow as big as possible.

Be in an imaginary box, such as a closet with the lights off. Explore the box. Try to move in it. Let it get smaller.

Walk as though you were on spaghetti, ice, bubbles, Jell-O, or thick molasses.

Follow a leader who takes you on an imaginary journey.

Show as many uses as possible for a simple everyday object, such as a spoon, pencil, eraser, brick, or broom.

Take three objects and use them in a scene with the group.

Pantomime

Show how you would eat a banana, ice cream cone, hot dog, or bowl of cereal. Have people guess what you are eating.

Show a person having a problem eating a hamburger.

Show a person walking in bare feet through hot sand, cold snow, slimy glue, or deep mud.

Pretend to wash your face, dress yourself, pick an apple, or other everyday activities.

Pretend you are happy, sad, angry, or frustrated. Have the audience guess your mood.

In pairs, give an imaginary gift to a partner who gives a gift back. Show what you would do with the gift and how you feel about it.

Create an imaginary place for the class to be such as the beach. Everybody acts out what they would do there.

Remain seated, turn to another in random fashion, and say hello without words; then turn to another person and say hello in another way.

Note that some of these scenes include dialogue.

Characterization

Walk or move like a character in character try-ons so that you will feel like the character.

Show how a person acts at different ages.

Show how people in different occupations move, such as a queen or king, a farm worker, ship captain, nurse, or teacher.

Show how animals move; then show how people with animal characteristics move, such as waddling or slithering.

Show a character with feelings. Show a happy puppy, an angry kitten, a frightened cow, and the like.

Talk like a baby, a grandparent, or a teacher.

Voice Improvisation

Interview a character from a book.

Make sounds to go with a simple poem or story. When the narrator says "dog" or "cow," all will bark or "moo," respectively.

Provide sound effects for a story or poem—wind, rain, and the like.

Announce the news of the day.

In pairs, improvise the dialogue between two people in a variety of situations—talking on the phone, arguing, selling something, making an
appointment, buying an object, or contracting for a service.

---

use the verbal text of a literary selection and rewrite it in a
dramatic script format. The script is read by a narrator and
other readers who assume the role of various characters in
the selection. Literature with well-developed characters
and dialogue, such as Judy Blume's *Fudge-A-Mania*

(1990), Peggy Christian's *The Bookstore Mouse* (1995), and
Paul Fleischman's *Joyful Noise: Poems for Two Voices*
(1988), are easy for learners to modify for a dramatic script.

To guide a group in creating and learning through
drama, three points should be remembered. First, because

creative drama is usually a group process, the class should practice working together as an ensemble. Second, group members should be reminded that through dramatic play they have already learned to express their ideas using the language of theatrical improvisation—pantomime and voice improvisation. Third, like any form of physical exercise, "acting out" is a whole body experience, so it is wise to begin with group warm-ups.

Theatre Games

One of the best ways to introduce drama is through theatre games. In these games, the students express an idea dramatically, either verbally or nonverbally. The games are designed to focus the players' attention on solving a specific problem in such a way that they forget to be self-conscious and become comfortable working dramatically with others. Theatre games can be used to warm up the group, develop a sense of ensemble, and remind the group of what they already know about expressing ideas through theatrical improvisation. Thus, the games are valuable in developing a working environment where players trust and respect each other while taking the risks necessary to create and present a play. In *Improvisation for the Theatre*, Viola Spolin explains her unique method of teaching through theatre games and describes many of the games found in other books.[30] Her publisher also provides a Theatre Game File developed for the classroom teacher.

This dramatic activity encourages the development of the three Cs—Cooperation, Concentration, and Creation—in an atmosphere that is both challenging and fun. With each game, and later with each scene from literature, use the following sequence: Plan–Play–Evaluate–Replay–Evaluate–Plan–Play–Evaluate. Build into this sequence active time followed by time for a quiet activity. Give the students the rules of the game, play the game, discuss whether the point or goal of the game was achieved, add a more difficult challenge, replay, and evaluate. This same format is followed when preparing a scene or piece of literature for a dramatic presentation. As the group plays or presents a scene, the leader may side coach, offering suggestions to focus the students' attention on the point of the game or scene.

The fun and challenge come from discovering how to play the game, so the teacher should avoid telling students how to play. Instead, the teacher should structure situations that enable students to learn for themselves how to play the game. In the evaluation period, students will want to share their discoveries about how to play the game, and this should be encouraged. No student should be permitted to become "boss," however. Sometimes the teacher may have to side coach and say, "No fair telling anybody else how to

do it!" This does not prevent the special teacher from helping a disabled student do what he or she wants to do.

Creating Creative Drama from Literature

Once an ensemble is developed, the group plans a scene from a literary selection in terms of the 5 Ws: *Who* are the characters? *Where* are they? *When* does the scene occur (in historical and contemporary time)? *What* are the characters doing? *Why* are they doing it? Then present the play, evaluate, and replay until the group is satisfied with the play.

In creative drama, the play must belong to the group, not the teacher or a director. As a "trigger for the imagination," however, the adult may suggest a story, poem, or situation to be dramatized and then ask the students to discuss the narrative in terms of the 5 Ws. Because the teacher has no preconceived answers for these questions, the answers—and the resulting play—will be the students' creation, not the teacher's.

In the planning period, students will generally volunteer to take roles they think they can handle; often their choices surprise the teacher. In any event, casting roles should be based on volunteers, and not on any preconceived plan of the teacher. Roles should not be owned by specific students because students may wish to switch roles when a scene is replayed. Instead, each student should feel ownership in the play itself.

During the evaluation period after playing, all ideas should be respected. Everyone (including the teacher) must listen carefully to everyone else because one never knows when a truly special idea will emerge. The teacher should encourage the group to begin with the good parts—what they liked, what they remembered, what was special—before talking about ways to improve the scene. Always use the character's name, rather than the name of the player. If a player has trouble with a character, ask the group for suggestions that may help.

Often a group's first scenes will be so chaotic that the teacher will be tempted to stop the performance, but this urge should be resisted. Generally, students themselves will recognize problems and offer valid solutions to prevent future disorder in the replay. By its very nature, creative drama is a cooperative learning venture, and learning from peers is often more valuable than learning from the teacher! A beginning group may need more guidance from the teacher, but as the members become comfortable expressing themselves through improvised drama, the group will take over most responsibility for the creation, becoming actors, directors, designers of simple props or costumes, and critics. Students will self-select their roles according to their knowledge of their own abilities.

Ultimately, the group members will be so proud of their work that they will want to share it with others. Improvised plays may be performed for parents and friends. The play does not need to be written and memorized as long as the members of the audience understand that they are seeing an improvised play or creative drama. In fact, a great deal of dramatic suspense is generated when an audience knows the actors also do not know exactly what will happen next! Table 10.17 presents a variety of strategies for guiding groups in dramatic activities.

TABLE 10.17 Strategies for Guiding Groups in Dramatic Activities

Define the specific space that will be used for the play, and keep students within those perimeters.

The teacher serves as a guide or facilitator of student ideas, never the director.

Begin with activities that help students become more sensitive to themselves, to each other, and to their environment.

Begin with group nonverbal movement or pantomime activities about everyday occurrences.

Begin with activities that give the group practice in working cooperatively.

Never tell students how to perform; instead, structure situations that allow students to figure out how to do things themselves.

Trust the group. Remember, the students already know how to act out scenes.

Repeat the sequence of P–P–E—Plan the play, Play the play, Evaluate the play—many times.

Although the students create the play, the teacher starts and stops all activity.

Provide a standard visual or aural signal, such as a waved scarf, drumbeat, or bell to start or stop the activity.

Encourage students to "try on" voices and actions of characters before playing the whole scene so that the children can walk in other people's shoes to understand how they may feel.

Actors never talk in plays. Only characters talk.

Players cannot know what to say and how to say it until they know who they are, where they are, what they are doing, and why they are doing it when the scene begins.

Drama is physical. To learn how to act out a scene, act out the scene. By repeating this process, analyzing what went right and wrong, and acting it again, a scene is refined. Acting out scenes is a form of researching the subject for the actor.

Use simple costumes representing the historical period or occupation of the character.

Alternate active periods with quiet periods, making the evaluation and planning sessions the quiet periods.

Provide triggers for the imagination. Instead of instructing the group to create a play about "something you care about," suggest a specific event in a book to act out. It is harder to create a character who is a three year old than to create a three-year-old spoiled brat!

Provide new activities each time student interest diminishes, but do not feel you must offer many different activities to maintain attention. Students will learn more from one good theatre game or dramatic activity with many different challenges than from several games or activities played superficially.

All members of the group may perform simultaneously in unison; alternatively, all may perform the same task simultaneously but in their separate spaces; or all may work on the same task in pairs or teams.

Creative drama should involve all members of the group all the time—as players, directors, or audience. Avoid at all costs "taking turns" and solo performances. Ask two or three students to demonstrate simultaneously how they act out a problem while others watch to see if the problem is solved. This avoids a threatening situation when everybody is looking at a single player.

Where physical movement is limited, consider developing a radio play or a readers' theater, or have some students narrate a play while others act it out.

Students with limited strength may provide sound effects and even dialogue for those pantomiming the action.

Some students can narrate while others act out a scene.

Students are motivated to create plays from an interesting story with characters who concern them.

Provide as many concrete examples from literature as necessary to enable students to act out an idea.

If students think they are able to do a scene, let them try it. Let each student determine what he or she can do.

Although the teacher should not direct, the teacher should assist any child who needs help expressing an idea or character.

Students with learning disabilities will work well with short, carefully structured activities at first.

Visuals may facilitate conceptual understanding when working with learning impaired or deaf students.

Use the creative drama process to create puppet plays; create the play after answering the 5 Ws, and add suitable music or rhythms for variety.

Benefits of Informal Classroom Drama

Informal classroom drama offers many benefits. In particular, it helps participants to do the following:

Improve their speaking, listening, reading, and writing abilities and expand their vocabulary.

Recognize the dramatic in literature.

Develop the ability to think analytically and to act decisively and responsibly.

Increase and sustain their ability to concentrate and follow directions.

Strengthen their self-concept by interacting cooperatively with others.

Learn to make commitments and fulfill them.

Learn to deal effectively with intrapersonal and interpersonal situations.

Develop individual and group creativity.[31]

PUPPETS AND LITERATURE

Puppetry, a very old and honored art form, plays a special role in the oral presentation of literature. Stories and poems "come to life" through the voices and actions of the puppets. From the Muppets and other puppet stars of popular television programs, children are familiar with puppets and respond enthusiastically to puppet presentations. Teachers can use puppets to tell stories or poems, explain information, or talk privately with a child. Frequently, teachers use a "special" puppet several times a week to give instructions or talk about social issues that need to be addressed. This "special" puppet does not appear in puppet shows. While one person can present a puppet show, usually two or more people work on the project. Many children are comfortable manipulating puppets and are eager to help the teacher prepare a script, construct the puppets, and present a puppet show.[32] This next section highlights the procedures puppeteers of all ages follow when preparing, constructing, and presenting a show with puppets.

Planning a Puppet Presentation

Use a commercial script, an original script, or an improvised script for the presentation. A successful script contains an introduction, several action-filled events, two to four appealing characters who evoke laughter or jeers from the audience, and a satisfying conclusion. The audience is interested in what the puppet does rather than what it says. Therefore, short speeches, lively dialogue, and physical movement of the characters are the basis of a puppet presentation.

Tales, songs, and poems from folk literature are the easiest to adapt for a puppet show, but almost all fiction and nonfiction literature can be used. Scripts can also be based on a real or fantasy situation, a joke, content from a curricular area, or a social issue. The purpose for presenting the puppet show determines the subject selected for the script. A formal puppet show is entertaining, but spontaneous improvisations are natural for puppets. Table 10.18 summarizes the procedures for presenting a puppet show.

Student Puppet Shows

Young children like to hold the puppets after a show; they want to manipulate the puppets and enjoy giving each

TABLE 10.18 Procedures for Presenting a Puppet Show

After selecting or writing a script, review the plot:

Identify the sequence of events.

Identify the major characters and their personality traits. How do the characters behave in each event? Do the characters change during the presentation? What emotions do they show? How should the characters move? What voices will you give them?

Only two to four puppets should appear on stage at once. Too many puppets can confuse the audience and puppeteers.

Usually, each puppeteer manipulates one or two puppets at a time because the space behind the stage may be crowded.

Select the type of puppet suitable for the script and comfortable for the puppeteer to manipulate. Four types of puppets are available:

Hand puppets include fist puppets, glove puppets, box puppets, papier-mâché puppets, finger puppets, sock puppets, and paper bag puppets.

Stick (or rod) puppets include stick puppets, styrofoam ball puppets, paper plate puppets, object puppets, flat puppets, and shadow puppets.

Body puppets include life-size puppets and board puppets.

String puppets (or marionettes). These are the most difficult to construct and manipulate. See Appendix B for a description of each type of puppet.

After constructing the puppets, practice manipulating them:

Find expressive movement for the puppets.

Give each puppet a voice; remember that puppets speak only "in character."

Use exaggerated, deliberate movements.

Select the place to present the show. A stage is not necessary.

A table, doorway, chair, box, or three-sided apron stage may be used.

Keep the stage and backdrop simple. They must not overpower the puppets. (Descriptions of stages are also included in Appendix B.)

Present the puppet show.

If appropriate, make an audio- or videotape of the show.

Evaluate the presentation.

puppet a voice. Children are spontaneous and natural with puppets. Through puppets young people express ideas, emotions, frustrations, and joy. Puppets give a shy child an outlet for communication, which can become a positive oral experience. Because puppets are ideal creations to represent personal reactions to a literary selection, additional information about constructing various types of puppets is found in Appendix B. A variety of books provide detailed information about constructing puppets and presenting puppet shows.[33]

✳ VISUAL PRESENTATIONS OF LITERATURE

Visuals such as banners, chalk talks, comparison charts, flannel, felt, or magnetic boards, hook 'n loop boards, flip charts, KWLs, literary ladders, mobiles, origami, paper cuttings, pictures, props or realia, roll stories, stories-in-a-can, story cubes, transparencies, visual graphics, visuals with sound, and word walls can all be a successful means of presenting literature to young people.

When choosing a suitable visual presentation, the teacher considers the age and maturity of the children, the suitability of the visual to highlight the content or specific literary elements, and the goals of the presentation. For example, photographs might be appropriate to use with realistic fiction or nonfiction literature, yet inappropriate to use with a folk literature selection. Young children like flannel boards, while older children prefer hook 'n loop boards. Movable visuals such as a flip chart

or a series of transparencies are effective to use with action-filled literature.

Visual presentations of literature benefit young people by doing all of the following:[34]

Help children clarify and visualize the real or fanciful content, objects, or information depicted in a literary selection.

Supplement and enhance students' understanding of the subject and the literary conventions or standards presented by the visual and verbal texts.

Attract and hold students' attention while exploring literature.

Add variety to an oral presentation.

Employ a variety of media to interpret, supplement, or enrich the visual and verbal texts.

Enhance and expand students' visual literacy.

PREPARING AND PRESENTING VISUALS

Several factors should be considered when selecting, preparing, and presenting visuals.[35] For a smooth, effective presentation, use the following techniques:

Select visuals that are appropriate to the selected elements and are large enough for all the audience to see.

If the verbal text is handwritten, use large, legible print. Choose a colored marker that is visible in the back of the room.

Do not place too much information on a page because the audience will read the text and not focus on the presentation. Usually, important words or phrases, rather than complete sentences, are placed on the page.

Organize and number the visuals in order of presentation. Handle them with care. If a visual is constructed from a lightweight material, do not stand before an open window.

Stand to the side of the visual so that the entire audience can see it.

It is more convenient to place the visual on a stand or easel. Place the stand at a 45-degree angle and slightly to one side of the center of the room or the group. Then the speaker can stand in the center of the room and have room to move around the easel.

Remove an object when it is no longer applicable to the oral presentation.

Continue talking while showing the visuals. Talk to the audience, not the visual.

Before the actual presentation, practice using the visual while reading or discussing the literary selection.

Do not violate copyright laws. Educators may not show movies, videos, and television shows without written permission from the holder of the copyright. Discuss the law with your media specialist.

SPECIFIC VISUALS

A variety of visuals are available to use with the oral presentation of literature and content throughout the school day.[36] Visuals can enhance or supplement the content or ideas in a literary selection. They can be presented naturally before, during, or after young people hear, read, or view the literature. In addition, visuals can be used effectively in all curricular areas. This section describes various types of visuals, suggests ways to use them with literature, and offers tips for constructing and presenting them.

Banners
Banners display information or objects depicted in a literary selection. The background of the banner is made from an opened grocery bag, burlap, colored craft paper, or other sturdy material. Attach the visuals to the background banner with glue, tape, pins, or Velcro strips. Tape the top of the background to a dowel rod or a clothes hanger. To display the banner, attach a sturdy string or wire to each end of the rod. Hang the banner in an appropriate place in the classroom.

Chalk Talks
In a *chalk talk*, the presenter tells a story or gives information while drawing major events from the literature selection. (See photo on page 365.) This procedure helps the audience visualize the plot, setting, characters, or content

We make banners in all sizes, shapes, and colors. Why are the girls filling this yellow banner with dresses from Eleanor Estes's book, The Hundred Dresses?

We can make up our own story from the title and funny-looking mice we see in this chalk talk!

found in a literary work. Chalk talks introduce or clarify information in the verbal or visual narratives of the fiction or nonfiction literature.

Colored chalk, markers, or colored pens are used to draw on the chalkboard or on a large piece of paper attached to the wall. Depending on the presenter's artistic ability, drawings can range from realistic art to simple stick figures. The presenter selects the scenes or information to be drawn. While talking about the literary selection, the presenter draws the selected scenes on the background, following a left to right sequence. The presenter should stand to the side of the picture so that the audience can see it while listening to the presenter tell the story or poem. At the conclusion of the presentation, selected scenes representing the entire plot or pertinent information are visually depicted for the audience to view. Watching a narrative or viewing a concrete representation of information can be fascinating for the audience.[37]

Comparison Charts

Comparison charts are used to clarify, expand, and compare the content or literary elements in several literary selections. Students and teachers identify and record specific topics or visual or verbal elements in selected fiction and nonfiction literature. The chart is divided into cells representing elements such as the physical characteristics and personality traits of characters, descriptors of the setting, the themes, the development of the plot structure, and the accuracy and authenticity of geographic, physical, scientific, and historical information. The headings for the columns and rows identify the cells. For example, the headings at the top of the columns could be physical or personality traits of characters (size, feelings for others, whether the characters are static or dynamic, whether they are flat or round). The headings at the left of the chart contain the rows of the characters' names, the book titles, or copies to be compared. The children identify and record the traits in the appropriate cells. After completing the chart, the children compare and contrast the information in the literary selections.

The chart's background is made of paper or other material of various weights and textures. The background color reflects the mood of the topic. Suitable pictures or drawing may be added to the chart. A variety of colored pens are used to record the information. The writing must be legible, and the colors should be visible from a distance.

Flexibility is a major strength of comparison charts. The topics and comparisons are selected according to the students' abilities and interests and the teacher's instructional goals. This informal, interactive visual is popular with students of all ages and can be used in all content area lessons to help young people develop prediction, analysis, comparison, problem-solving, and literary skills. When used in content area lessons, the information given in suitable fiction and nonfiction literature and appropriate textbooks is identified and compared to give young people a broader understanding of the topic. Recording information about the way authors develop characters, plots, and text structures on a chart helps boys and girls understand the writing process. Information about visual narratives from several books with pictures by the same or different artists helps students recognize the artists' ability to interpret, supplement, or replace the verbal narrative. Frequently, students apply this knowledge to their personal writings and original artistic creations.

The chart can be modified and used as a *prediction chart* for example. Label the top columns Event 1, Event 2, and so on and list the characters' names down the left side. Before reading the first event, students predict the actions of the selected characters and record the predictions in the appropriate cells. After reading, they compare their predictions to the actual events, modify their predictions as necessary, and discuss the differences. The process continues until the book is completed.

Flannel, Felt, or Magnetic Boards

Flannel or *felt boards* help children understand the sequence of a story or nonfiction text structure; they also help students visualize the content of the narrative. The visual has two parts—the board and the objects. The presenter places the objects on the board while telling a story or explaining information.

The board can be a project display board or be made of maisonette or plywood. It should be a suitable size for the presenter to handle. The board is covered with an adhesive material, such as felt, flannel, or Pellon (interfacing used by a tailor). The board is placed on an easel, the floor, or the chalkboard tray. Objects are made from sturdy adhesive materials such as felt, flannel, Pellon, or paper. If needed, a suitable adhesive, such as sandpaper or Velcro, is applied to the back of the object. The objects are decorated with paint, paper, or fabric. Different scenes may be drawn on the backing or adhesive material and changed as necessary. Number the objects in the appropriate order for the presentation. Children enjoy using the objects to retell the story or discuss the topic.

While presenting the story or information, place the object being discussed in the appropriate place on the board. After lightly placing the object on the board, attach the object firmly by running your hand over it from top to bottom. Remove the object when it is no longer part of the discussion.

A *magnetic board* shows action of the plot, movement of the characters, or development of the nonfiction text structure. The backing for the board is a sheet of metal, such as a metal (not aluminum) cooking sheet. Various types of paper or fabric are used to construct the visuals. Attach magnetic strips, available at arts and crafts shops, to the back of each visual. Use a large magnet behind the board to move the visuals on the metal backboard. Use the same procedures for this visual as for the felt and flannel boards.

Flip Charts

A *flip chart* is a large writing pad with sturdy front and back covers. The chart is especially useful to show the sequence of the plot, the characters' actions, and the text structure in nonfiction literature. The chart focuses attention on the desired information and helps to expand and enhance the listeners' understanding of the selection. It can also be used in content area lessons.

Patrick's dinosaurs come to life when we see them and move them on a flannel board.

To make a flip chart, use two large poster boards for the front and back covers. On the cover board, put the title, the names of the author and artist, and perhaps a sketch representing the narrative. Sheets of paper slightly smaller than the cover boards are inserted inside. Attach the cover boards and paper together at the top with suitable metal rings, plastic book bindings, or other durable materials that will allow the pages to turn easily when using the chart. Large blank flip charts are also available in teacher supply stores. For fictional literature, the teacher and children record information about the setting, the plot structure, and the characters' behavior on the chart. For nonfiction literature, information about the content, structure, facts, and organization of the selection is recorded. The information is recorded in the proper sequence so that the speaker can turn the pages to show the events in the literary selection in the proper order. If the information is recorded on the pages while the literature is being presented, be sure that the chart has enough blank pages for the information and that sufficient marking pens are available. The recorder should print legibly in large bold letters, using different colors to highlight important information. Key words or phrases, rather than sentences, are recorded so that the pages remain uncluttered and easy to read. Appropriate visuals, pictures, charts, or graphs may be added to illustrate the key points in the verbal text.[38] If possible, place blank sheets of paper between the recorded pages so that the presenter can display only the page containing content being presented. The chart is placed on a sturdy stand so the pages can be turned easily. Although flip charts are usually used with a small group, they can be used with an entire class if the verbal text and visuals are large enough.

Hook 'n Loop Boards

Hook 'n loop boards are similar to felt and flannel boards, but use heavy objects such as stuffed toys for the visuals. The purposes and procedures are identical to those for felt and flannel boards. The surface of the board has a natural finish or is painted. One side of a piece of hook 'n loop (very heavy Velcro) is attached in several places around the board. When an object is mentioned in the narrative the presenter places it on a piece of velcro that is attached to the board. Regular-weight Velcro will not hold the heavy objects, but heavy-weight Velcro may be purchased at arts and crafts shops.

KWL Visual Graphics

The purpose of *KWL visuals* is to show what students *KNOW* about a subject, what they *WANT* to know about a topic, and finally what they have *LEARNED* about the topic after reading fiction or nonfiction literature. These vi-

suals are frequently used to *connect* the reader to a topic, content, or book. Poster paper is used for the background. At the top of the visual, make three columns on the background. Title the columns, from left to right, "What I Know about _____ ," "What I Want to Know," and "What I Learned." Before reading a selection, ask students what they know about the selected topic. On the left side of the paper, record their responses. In the middle column, record what the students want to know about the topic. While reading, students can continue adding to the middle column and begin recording what they have LEARNED in the third column. After reading a section or the entire book, students add more information to the third column. They then review the middle column and circle any information they have not learned. Finding this information could serve as the basis of a research project. Various writing activities could develop from the research project. Individual students or groups can prepare this visual.

Literary Ladders

A *literary ladder* helps students identify the distinctive characteristics of a literary genre, subgenre, character, or plot. The visual consists of several strips of paper attached in a ladder format. Before reading the selection, brainstorm and record what the children know about a genre. While reading the selection or after finishing it, elicit from the children other characteristics they observed about a genre.

Record each characteristic on a separate strip of paper; poster board, card, sentence strip, and other lightweight cardboard. Fasten the strips of paper together with paper clips, pipe cleaners, ribbon, or yarn to form rungs of a ladder. The strips are then attached to a dowel rod or hanger with glue or tape. The strips of paper can be shaped like the content or genre of the selection; for example, the title card of High Fantasy could be shaped like a castle. Figure 10.3 on page 368 developed by Ashley, age 12, shows a literary ladder for Low Fantasy. Hang the ladder in a conspicuous place in the room or in the literature center.

The teacher or students can use the same procedure to create a *vocabulary ladder* with interesting or unusual vocabulary from a piece of literature.

Mobiles

Hang visuals representing various elements of a selection from the base of a *mobile*. Two hangers, dowel rods, or other sturdy materials are attached to form the base of the mobile. Use a variety of materials ranging from paper to netting to make visuals in the shape of objects in a book. Decorate both sides of each visual with pictures or words done with colored pens, markers, or other materials. Attach the visuals to the base using string, yarn, fishing wire, or other thin, yet sturdy cord or thread. Make sure the cord holding the

FIGURE 10.3 A Literary Ladder for Low Fantasy

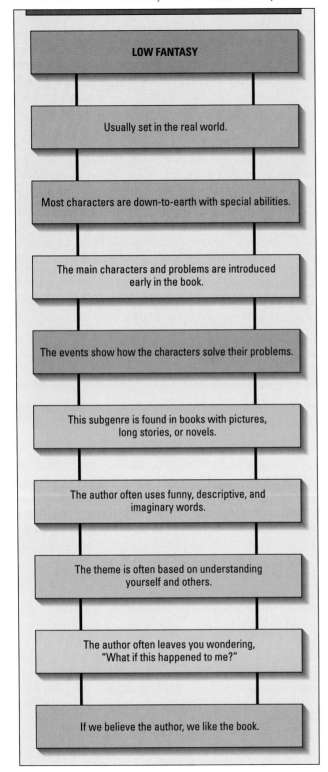

LOW FANTASY

Usually set in the real world.

Most characters are down-to-earth with special abilities.

The main characters and problems are introduced early in the book.

The events show how the characters solve their problems.

This subgenre is found in books with pictures, long stories, or novels.

The author often uses funny, descriptive, and imaginary words.

The theme is often based on understanding yourself and others.

The author often leaves you wondering, "What if this happened to me?"

If we believe the author, we like the book.

visuals does not tangle. Hang mobiles in appropriate places in the classroom, so they can sway in the wind.

Origami

While telling a story, the presenter can use *origami* techniques to fold paper to represent a character or object in the narrative. Many books give directions for origami.[39] This art is easy to master, but must be practiced before using it with a piece of literature. The audience will enjoy the challenge of folding origami objects after the presenter concludes the story.

Paper Cutting

While telling a story or poem, cut paper in the shape of characters or objects from the selection. Before the presentation, fold the paper in half. Draw half of the figure on the paper. While telling the story, cut the figure and open the paper to reveal the object. A string of boys and girls holding hands is a familiar example of *paper cutting*. The paper for this visual must be a proper weight to fold and cut.

Pictures

Mount large, clear photographs and other pictures on colorful, compatible backgrounds. Show the pictures before, during, or after presenting the literature. The pictures authentically represent the narrative since they help the audience visualize scenes, characters, concepts, information, or language from the selection.

Props or Realia

Props are used to inform or enhance the audience's understanding of a selection. They can include such things as fruit, stuffed toys, or historical objects and cultural realia. Display them at appropriate times before, during, or after the narrative is presented. Props and realia are effective visuals because they focus attention on the narrative and help the audience visualize and understand the concepts presented in the selection.

Roll Stories

Roll stories, also called "roller movies," "TVs," or "story boxes," highlight the sequence of a plot and the movements of the characters. Illustrations representing the sequence of the plot are drawn with bright, colorful pens on a long strip of paper. Attach a dowel rod to each end of the paper, and roll the paper smoothly onto one rod (like a scroll). Place the scroll inside a sturdy cardboard or wooden box, which can range in size from a shoe box to a very large detergent box, but must be large enough to display the scroll. Cut a large hole in the front of the box, so the pictures will show through the hole, as on the screen of a television set. Insert the dowel rods vertically into the box. Cut four holes in the box at least half an inch beyond the front hole; these holes should be slightly larger than the rods and should be directly opposite each other with two at the top and two at the bottom. As the story or text is presented, turn the dowel rods to show the pictures in the front hole of the box. The hole should be slightly smaller than the pictures. After the presentation, detach the scroll from the dowel rod. Store the scroll inside the box.

Story Cubes

Story cubes may be purchased or made from sturdy paper, such as a file folder. Figure 10.4 shows a pattern for making a cube; the title and creator's name on one side of the cube and sketches depicting major events in the story or poem on the other sides. Small cubes are used before or after the narrative is presented; large cubes can be used during the presentation as well. Students enjoy making and decorating cubes with their favorite characters or incidents from a selection.

Stories-in-a-Can

A *story-in-a-can* is a type of visual in which a strip of paper with pictures on it is placed in a can and slowly pulled through the can's lid to show the pictures. This visual helps the audience visualize the major events of a story; it can also be used to present a time line of a character's life or depict various content from an information book. While telling a story or poem, the presenter pulls the story strip with pictures of events from the selection through the can's lid.

FIGURE 10.4   A Pattern for a Story Cube

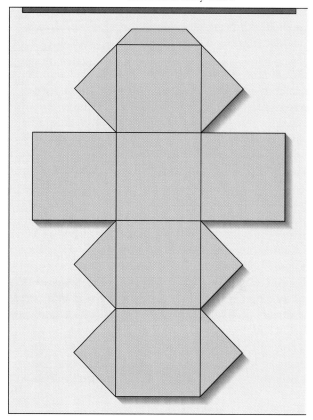

Look at the things I can tell you about The Witches *on my story cube!*

To prepare the visual, select a can with a tight-fitting plastic top. Cover the can with adhesive paper. To make the story strip, cut a strip of paper one-half inch narrower than the diameter of the lid and at least twelve inches long. Divide the story strip into several sections similar to those of a filmstrip; one section will depict the title page, and each of the others will show an incident from the literary selection. Leave a three-inch blank at each end of the strip. Insert the story strip into the can with the conclusion of the story, poem, or essay on the bottom. In the plastic lid, cut a straight, vertical slit slightly wider than the story strip. Carefully pull the strip through the slit until the title page is visible and replace the lid on the can, as in the photo below. Show the appropriate visual sequence while telling the verbal narrative. Use a large can (container) when presenting it to the entire class. Smaller cans can be used when sharing with a small group. Store story strips in the can with a copy of the story or poem. Children enjoy making and using this visual.

It's fun to listen to a storyteller while we see the story-in-a-can.

Transparency Presentations

Transparencies are used with fiction and nonfiction literature to highlight the setting or describe the major events of the plot, the characters' behavior, the text structure, and the content of the selection. Before presenting the literature, the children or teacher draw pictures representing the selected elements on separate acetate sheets. The transparencies are then arranged sequentially, numbered, and displayed at appropriate times. To show the movement of characters and events, draw background scenes on a transparency, and then make separate drawings of the characters or content on another piece of acetate or heavy paper, such as construction paper. Attach a handle made of sturdy acetate to each visual. When telling the narrative, move the individual visuals over the background transparency. To discuss the text structure used in a nonfiction selection, complete the appropriate visual representative as suggested for the various text structures in Table 6.5 (pages 189–190). Simple line drawings can be added to the verbal narrative, but the transparency must be clear and easy to read and should include only an outline of information.

Transparencies with too much verbal text are difficult to read and may confuse the audience. Number the transparencies in order of presentation and place a sheet of paper between individual transparencies. Check the order of the transparencies before beginning a presentation. Place the transparency so that the audience can read it. Stand to the side of the projector, face the audience, and use a pointer or your hand to focus the audience's attention on the content. Place a blank piece of paper over the verbal text that is not relevant to the oral presentation. Keep clear acetate sheets and pens available to prepare additional transparencies as needed. Project a transparency on a wall to serve as scenery for a dramatic presentation.

If the overhead projector has a roll of acetate attached to it, draw sequential scenes or text structure on the strip of acetate. Then display the separate visuals depicting the sequence of the narrative over the different background. Turn off the projector if there is a long time between transparencies. Check the focus and projector before the presentation. Is the fan too loud? Do you have a spare bulb for the projector? Remember to place the overhead projector screen at a 45-degree angle and slightly to one side of the center of the room.

If the students are familiar with a story or text, the transparencies can be presented as a *scrambled story*. The transparencies are scrambled, and the students are challenged to rearrange them in the proper sequence of the plot or text. Then the students use the transparencies to retell the story or give the information.

Visual Graphics

Visual graphics, also called semantic maps, concept maps, story maps, clusters, flow charts, Venn Diagrams, or webs, are used to compare, contrast, and classify information from fiction or nonfiction literature. This popular graphic outline helps the students understand the development of the plot, the characters' actions, the content, or the text structure in fiction or nonfiction stories, essays, or poems. The presenter can establish categories on the visual and record the desired information in the various cells. Background information used to connect students to the text may be recorded on the graphic, as well as information elicited from brainstorming sessions. Information is recorded on the visual before, during, and after the students have listened to or read the literature. Visual graphics are also used to help students compare books, content, or authors and artists. Young people enjoy designing a simple or complex "picture" of information, which helps them become visually literate.

The graphic can be drawn in a variety of ways depending on the purpose for presenting it. To show similarities or differences between content and books, use a Venn diagram that contains two or three intersecting circles. The independent sections of the circles contain information about the individual narratives or topics. The overlapping sections include information about similar aspects of the narratives or topics. Figure 2.2 (on page 32) is a Venn Diagram depicting the Literary Transaction Process. Suggested visual graphics for various nonfiction text structures are shown in Table 6.5 (on pages 189–190). Other visual graphics are used to categorize information to help students activate and organize background knowledge and apply it to new information presented in the book. Throughout this book, the distinctive characteristics of literary genres, distinguishing characteristics of subgenres, and information related to the presentation of literature have been shown on visual graphics.

The popular "story maps" use the flow chart format to help learners identify the plot structure of a book and understand relationships among ideas, characters, solutions, conflicts, and problems. Students and teachers record, in verbal or visual format, the proper sequence of the desired information. Story maps also guide the learners' predictions, generalizations, and conclusions about the narratives. See Table 6.6 for a type of flow chart on page 194.

Writers frequently use a visual graphic when planning and organizing a plot for a new book. The writer identifies major events to be included in the book, then clusters various ideas for the incidents in a visual organization or outline. Students find this to be an exciting way to "visually outline" original books, poems, or plays.[40]

Visuals with Sound

In a *visual with sound*, a commercial or original audio recording is used with a selected visual. Typically, compatible sound effects or instrumental music is used with the visual to highlight the subject of the verbal text or help the audience focus on the visual elements of the selection. The sounds must be carefully synchronized with the visual and the oral presentation.

Word Walls

The purpose of a *word wall* is to visually saturate students with interesting or unusual language used in fiction or nonfiction literature. Write words or phrases from the literature on a card or heavy paper. Select a central location in the room and place the language card on the wall or on a large background shaped to represent content from the selection. Place the title of the selection at the top or in the center of the background. Initially, display a few words from the selection on the wall, and gradually add a few words each day before or after the children listen to or read the text. While discussing the language informally, encourage the students to discover the way the author uses the words in the selection. Encourage them to use the language in original writing or speaking activities. Girls and boys can add other interesting language from the literature to the word wall. The photo on page 372 shows a word wall on *Escape from Fire Mountain* by Gary Paulsen.

STUDENT PREPARATION AND USE OF VISUALS

After the teacher models the use of visuals, students naturally begin using them when rereading or telling a story or poem. Offer students tips for selecting appropriate literature to use with visuals, constructing the visual, and presenting it to an audience. Producing a visual is an appropriate activity for individuals, pairs, triads, or cooperative groups. After students finish constructing the visual, give them time to practice using it while orally presenting the literature. Place individual visuals in resealable plastic bags and store them in the literature center for all class members to use with various pieces of literature.

PRESENTING LITERATURE THROUGH AUDIOVISUAL MEDIA AND TECHNOLOGY

At one time young people were content to receive information and entertainment primarily from print media. Now movies and television and most recently multimedia technologies associated with computers are also becoming

A word wall gives the teacher and child an opportunity to discuss words collected from a book.

popular choices. As these new technologies emerged, many felt that print media would become obsolete and that children would no longer turn to books for pleasure and facts. This has not happened. Educators have discovered that print media and audiovisual technologies stimulate different learning modalities. When both print and non-print media are used in the classroom, children are enthusiastic about learning. Table 10.19 on page 373 lists some benefits of using audiovisual media with literature.[41]

Today, publishers are producing more literature-related materials in a variety of audio and visual media, including movies, sound filmstrips, slides with sound, compact discs (CDs), audiotapes, videotapes, and videocassettes. This section discusses guidelines for selecting nonprint productions, techniques for presenting the productions with literature, and the use of literature, television, and multimedia technologies related to computers.

SELECTING AND PRESENTING AUDIOVISUAL PRODUCTIONS

When selecting suitable productions for use in the classroom, the following criteria should be considered:

The ability of the media to enhance or supplement a narrative.

The instructional purposes and goals.

The appeal of the production to the audience.

The availability of the production.

Fortunately, teachers can rely on the expertise of the school media specialist, public librarians, and selection sources, such as those listed in Appendix G, for recommended audiovisual productions to use in the classroom.[42] After obtaining the audiovisual productions, teachers must preview them to decide if they meet the instructional goals and present the literature in an enticing way. Table 10.20 on page 373 lists suitable criteria for previewing and selecting audiovisual productions to present literature.[43]

Familiarity with the equipment and techniques for presenting a production is essential for a successful audiovisual presentation. Table 10.21 on page 374 lists a variety of techniques that will help ensure a smooth audiovisual presentation of literature.[44]

TELEVISION AND LITERATURE

For the past forty years, researchers have inundated us with statistics about the impact of television on our society. They tell us, for example, that by the time the average American has lived sixty-five years, he or she will have spent *nine years* or more watching television. They warn teachers that children with limited reading abilities spend more time watching television than their counterparts who exhibit mature reading abilities. Educators recognize that television and other media do exert power over children. Multimedia will continue to affect our daily lives, and we must find positive ways to channel this power.

TABLE 10.19 Benefits of Using Audiovisual Media with Literature

Audiovisuals stimulate learners' imagery and strengthen their visual competencies.

Nonprint media introduce students to literature they might not be able to read independently. As their reading abilities mature, they frequently choose for personal reading literature presented through audiovisual productions.

Audiovisuals develop and reinforce students' visual and communication skills.

Students learn how to use audiovisuals and frequently choose to make audiovisual productions for responses to literature.

Students' critical thinking skills are enhanced when they compare audiovisual presentations to the original books.

Through selected audiovisual media, learners hear and see an author or artist reading original literature, explaining why he or she writes for juveniles, or discussing issues related to literature, such as the influence of censorship on the quality and quantity of the literature written for young people.

Some literary selections, such as wordless books and literature with small or detailed illustrations, are difficult to show to an entire class. Audiovisual productions of such literature allow the entire class to see, hear, and view the selection at the same time.

Some literature "comes to life" when individuals hear the sounds of a setting, see actual places, and view live actors presenting the narrative.

Audiovisual productions add variety to the oral presentation of literature.

In quality nonprint media, professionals model exemplary techniques for students and teachers to use when presenting literature.

Learners can hear and see audiovisual programs several times.

Audiovisual productions are effective to use with an entire class when introducing specific books or a thematic collection of literature.

Students can hear the verbal narrative before or while reading the original book.

Background knowledge is expanded and enhanced when students see concrete examples of scientific investigations or reenactments of historical events and social issues.

Suitable background music and sound enhance both fiction and nonfiction literature.

TABLE 10.20 Criteria for Previewing and Selecting Audiovisual Productions to Present Literature

Choose the most suitable production for the audience:

  Consider the potential attention span of the audience and the length of the production.

  An audiotape containing abstract or metaphorical language is not appropriate for younger children, but it may be suitable for older students who are reading the selection while listening to the recording.

Choose an audiovisual presentation that preserves the integrity of the original text and represents authentic, current content. To determine the authenticity of the production, consider the following questions:

  Are the setting, characters, content, and plot similar or identical to the original?

  If the script or pictures are freely adapted from the original text or illustrations, will the adaptations adequately introduce the original narrative?

  Will the adaptation clarify students' questions about the text or confuse the students?

  Have the style and language of the selection been incorporated into the presentation?

Note the technical quality and clarity of the production:

  The voices must be clear and understandable.

  The audio and visual components should be synchronized.

  The visuals must be clear, up-to-date, and easy to see.

  The sound effects or music should help establish the mood but not overpower the production.

  If captions or words are used, they should be legible, clear, and readable.

The audiovisual production must be appropriate for the genre and the verbal and visual narratives; sketches and drawings, for example, are more appropriate for folk literature than photographs of actual animals or persons; whereas photographs are suitable for biographies and information books.

Students of various ages do not prefer any particular medium, so a variety of audiovisual modalities can be used.

Outstanding audiovisual presentations enhance certain books and may encourage students to explore other poems, books, art, and drama.

Select productions that exploit the power of the particular audio and visual media.

TABLE 10.21 Presenting Audiovisual Productions with Literature

Before the Presentation

Practice using the equipment and materials.

Use the visual for the selected purpose and at the appropriate time; do not use the production whenever it arrives in the building or as a filler for Friday afternoon.

Move the students to the viewing center after the equipment and materials are ready for the presentation.

Arrange the students so all can hear and view the presentation.

During the Presentation

Introduce the production before presenting it. Give the students background information about unfamiliar content, the characters' behavior, and other elements to help them understand the selection and production.

Expect all students to respect the rights of others to view and hear the production.

Combine audio and visual media to help clarify or expand students' understanding and enjoyment of a piece of literature; for example, use an audiotape of a poet reading original poetry and pictures showing the setting, content, or ideas expressed by the poet, or use software containing other poems written by the poet. Display poems written by the poet.

Concluding the Presentation

Consider the instructional goals, the literature, and the interests and maturity of the students when planning concluding activities.

Usually, students react spontaneously to worthwhile productions, so schedule time for their reactions. Strategies such as the following might be used:

Hold group discussions to encourage students to express natural reactions and, if needed, to help clarify concepts, language, themes, and other literary elements.

Suggest suitable visual and verbal LRMs reflecting students' natural responses.

Have students compare the original book with the audiovisual production.

In cooperative literary groups, have students list differences between the original narrative and the audiovisual production. Place the differences on a Venn diagram and compare. Select a favorite presentation.

Use video and filmstrips for interactive instruction. Occasionally, stop the production at an appropriate place, ask probes to elicit predictions, and repeat.

Encourage groups of students to research content presented in a literary selection. Have students interview experts about the content. Request that the interview be taped and photographed. Also photograph the person's home, family, or friends. The group will prepare a script for an audiovisual production and include pertinent photographs, segments of the taped interview, and appropriate sound effects. Videotape the production. Place several interviews on the same tape.

After reviewing studies on the relationship of television and literacy, researchers have identified three myths about television: television displaces reading, television viewing negatively affects young readers, and television inhibits language development.[45] Research does not confirm that television displaces reading. Several studies have found that students who watch television more than three hours a day usually do not have mature reading abilities, but watching television rather than reading might be only one of many factors affecting the child's reading ability. We must remember that all of us receive different forms of gratification from viewing television and leisure reading. Researchers have also failed to confirm that television viewing negatively affects young readers. Before this issue can be settled, though, longitudinal studies must be conducted to examine the effects of television on children during each stage of language acquisition from birth to eight years. To date, several studies have suggested that some forms of television programming help children's cognitive development of language. Finally, researchers exploring the third myth have focused on the passive nature of television to determine whether it inhibits language development. They have discovered that many children talk to the television while viewing it. In other words, the children are using language to interact with the television programs. Many children (and adults) react to the actors and discuss their reactions with others while watching a favorite program. How many parents have been amazed when their three-year-old child repeats a television commercial verbatim?

Thus, we might ask, does television actually expand a child's sociolinguistic development? Indeed, television introduces children to a variety of speech forms and dialects. When children talk with others while viewing programs, they are clarifying ideas and developing critical thinking skills. Some evidence suggests children remember information received from television and have a better understanding of some information they receive from the audio and visual components of television. These findings seem to justify the discriminate use of television as one of many instructional tools to enhance children's literary experiences. Note that by recognizing the positive aspects of television does not mean that we should condone unacceptable programming for children. We must continue to encourage guardians to monitor children's television programs carefully, to watch the programs with their children, and discuss the content with the children.

Fortunately, producers, parents, and critics are discussing the positive and negative influences of the medium on children's lives. With the expansion of technology and facilities, more producers are using quality literature for television programs. Research suggests that when children view a televised version of a book, they receive different interpretations of the verbal narrative. Through auditory and visual interpretations, they gain a broader perspective of the literary selection. Children's interpretations of literary selections expand when they have opportunities to hear, view, discuss, and write reactions to televised versions of literature. Older students can compare the print and nonprint versions and evaluate their quality. In this way we can help young people become sophisticated, discriminating consumers of an ever-growing, influential medium.

COMPUTERS AND LITERATURE

Through the computer, various types of media are combined including print, visual, auditory, and video. By combining these powerful media and giving users the ability to interact with them, we are providing a new, uncharted avenue for children to reach their fullest informational potential. According to the National Center for Education Statistics, in 1984, 28.5 percent of students in grades 1 through 12 reported using a computer at school and another 12 percent used a computer at home. By 1993 the numbers had more than doubled; 59 percent of the students said they used a computer at school, and 27.8 percent reported using a computer at home.[46]

Remarkably, many programs can be placed on one thin, silver disc called a CD-ROM. Today, quality CD-ROMs containing quality programs for informational and pleasurable purposes are easy to use and appealing to stu-

dents.[47] In 1991 experts predicted that the amount of CD-ROM hardware available in schools would increase by 260 percent by 1996. Of the 1,000 teachers, media coordinators, and elementary and secondary administrators from around the United States who responded to a survey, which was commissioned by four education associations and Cable in the Classroom:

- 85 percent used computers, laser discs, or CD-ROMs.
- 58 percent used Cable in the Classroom programming (the cable television industry's public service initiative to enrich education).
- 19 percent used Channel One.
- 16 percent used the Internet.
- 13 percent used commercial online services.[48]

Fortunately, software designs and hardware capability for computer-assisted instruction (CAI) have improved tremendously. Designers and educators have a better understanding of individual children's reactions and interactions with the software. They are now incorporating this gender-related knowledge into the programs designed for use in the classroom. With the technological advances of superior voice synthesis, sophisticated graphics, and ease of use, designers are redefining innovative software, such as "hypertext." Hypertext is similar to the "Choose Your Own Adventure" literature format. Using hypertext, authors link information, create paths to related materials, create notes, and present annotations in visual and auditory modalities.[49] In the framework of picture storybooks, hypertext gives children additional knowledge and experiences manipulating verbal and graphic elements. Information is presented in semantic networks that enable meaning to emerge from interrelated concepts and ideas. Thus, through hypertext, children connect to the visual and verbal narratives. CAI programs encourage cooperative techniques that help children learn to cooperate with others. Also, through experiences with CAI, children's motivation to learn is enhanced. With designs and hardware constantly improving, the outlook for literature and language arts software is bright. Educators must continue to choose the very best products that represent fine literature and sound pedagogy.[50]

When all schools are equipped with quality hardware and are connected to the information superhighway and all teachers become computer literate and learn how to use the new software, then technology will have the power to help transform all education. But avid readers agree, technology cannot replace the delight of curling up in a chair and becoming an active part of the book.

Summary

The voice may be the most important instrument a teacher possesses. Therefore, teachers must be concerned about the verbal and nonverbal expressions they use. We know that the oral presentation of literature entices, introduces, and guides students to select literature for personal and informational reasons. Therefore, when orally presenting literature, vocal qualities must be considered. These include a pleasant, natural tonal quality; appropriate projection of the voice; proper pronunciation, enunciation, and articulation of language; suitable intonation patterns; elimination of "fillers"; and the ability to project emotions, knowledge, and enthusiasm for a subject. In addition, proper nonverbal language, including appropriate facial expressions, body language, and eye contact, is necessary for a successful oral presentation of literature and subject matter.

Book talks, book discussions, reading aloud, storytelling, dramatic experiences, and puppet presentations introduce students to specific literature, acquaint students with literature for personal reading, help them visualize the selection's content, and give them an opportunity to communicate (in writing, speaking, listening, and visually) their interpretations and responses to literature. The benefits gained from oral experiences with literature, as well as the selection, preparation, and presentation of literature using oral techniques, were discussed in the chapter.

The chapter also identified and described twenty visual presentations for use when orally presenting literature. Finally, the benefits, selection, and presentation of audiovisuals, television, and multimedia technology with literature were discussed.

NOTES

The opening quotation is from Jean Karl in *From Childhood to Childhood: Children's Books and Their Creators.* 1970. New York: Day. 169.

1. For additional information about developing oral language competencies and the benefits of the oral presentation of literature, see sources such as Allen, R. R., Brown, K. L., & Yatvin, J. 1986. *Learning Language through Communication: A Functional Perspective.* Belmont, Calif.: Wadsworth; Last, E. (Supervisor, English Language Arts). 1986. *A Guide to Curriculum Planning in English Language Arts.* H. J. Grover, State Superintendent. Madison, Wis.: Wisconsin Department of Public Instruction; Sinatra, R. In Cramer, E. H., & Castle, M. (Eds.). 1994. *Fostering the Love of Reading: The Affective Domain in Reading Education.* Newark, Del.: International Reading Association. 104–7; Wells, G. 1986. *The Meaning Makers: Children Learning Language and Using Language to Learn.* Portsmouth, N.H.: Heinemann. 188–91.

2. For additional information about cultural and social differences in oral communication, see Barnes, D., Britton, J., & Torbe, M. 1990. *Language, the Learner, and the School.* Portsmouth, N.H.: Heinemann; Cazden, C. 1988. *Classroom Discourse.* Portsmouth, N.H.: Heinemann; Gallas, K. 1994. *The Languages of Learning: How Children Talk, Write, Dance, Draw, and Sing Their Understanding of the World.* New York: Teachers College Press; Hynds, S., & Rubin, D. L. (Ed.). 1990. *Perspectives on Talk and Learning.* Urbana, Ill.: National Council of Teachers of English; Sulzby, E. 1991. The development of the young child and the emergence of literacy. In Flood, J., Jensen, J. M., Lapp, D., & Squire, J. R. (Eds.). *Handbook of Research on Teaching the English Language Arts.* New York: Macmillan. 273–85.

3. For additional information about oral language in the classroom and the role of the teacher, see sources such as Barchers, S. I. 1994. *Teaching Language Arts: An Integrated Approach.* St. Paul, Minn.: West Publishing Company. 72–77; Gallas, K., Anton-Oldenburg, M., Ballenger, C., Beseler, C., Griffin, S., Pappenheimer, R., & Swaim, J. Focus on research: Talking the talk and walking the walk: Researching oral language in the classroom. *Language Arts.* 73(8). 608–17.

4. For additional information about desirable verbal expressions, see sources such as Griffin, J. 1994. *How to Say It Best.* Englewood Cliffs, N.J.: Prentice-Hall. 315–17; Hasling, J. 1988. *The Message, the Speaker, the Audience.* New York: McGraw-Hill. (4th Ed.). 101–3; Sarnoff, D. 1987. *Speech Can Change Your Life.* New York: Crown.

5. For additional information about nonverbal expressions, see sources such as Cook, J. S. 1989. *The Elements of Speechwriting and Public Speaking.* New York: Collier; Griffin, J. 1994. 285–89; Hasling, J. 1988. 100–101; Mandel, S. 1987. *Effective Presentation Skills.* Los Altos, Calif.: Crisp. 49–53.

6. Chelton, M. K. 1976. Booktalking: You can do it. *School Library Journal.* 18(5). April. 39–43. For additional information about book talks, see also sources such as Betterton, M. H. 1991. Book talks: How to, what for, and why. *Kansas Journal of Reading.* 7. Spring. 19–22; Bodart, J. 1980. *Booktalking with Joni Bodart.* Bronx, N.Y.: H. W. Wilson Video Resource Collection; Rochman, H. 1984. Booktalking them off the shelves. *School Library Journal.* 30(10). August. 38–39.

7. Ryker, S. Pasco Elementary School, Pasco County, Florida.

8. For additional information about book discussions, see sources such as Cullinan, B. E. (Ed.). 1993. *Children's Voices: Talk in the Classroom.* Newark, Del.: International Reading Association; Peterson, R., & Eeds, M. 1990. *Grand Conversations: Literature Groups in Action.* Ontario, Canada: Scholastic; Pierce, K. M., & Billes, C. J. (Eds.). 1993. *Cycles of Meaning: Exploring the Potential of Talk in Learning Communities.* Portsmouth, N.H.: Heinemann.

9. J. Higgins used the term "inquisition," as cited in Eeds, M. A., & Wells, D. 1989. Grand conversations: An exploration of meaning construction in literature study groups. *Research in the Teaching of English.* 23(1). February. 4–29.

10. Cox, C., & Many, J. E. 1992. Stance towards a literary work: Applying the transactional theory to children's responses. *Reading Psychology* 13(11). 37–72.

11. For additional information about the "art of questioning," see sources such as Ash, B. H. 1992. Student-made questions: One way into a literary text. *English Journal.* 81(5). 61–64; Barrett, T. C. 1972. A taxonomy of reading comprehension. *Reading 360 Monograph.* Lexington, Mass.: Ginn; Cassidy, D. J. 1989. Questioning the young child: Process and function. *Childhood Education.* 65(3). Spring. 146–49; Fairbairn, D. M. 1987. The art of

questioning your students. *The Clearing House*. 61. 19–22; Flager, A. M. 1986. How can we improve teacher questioning? A good question. *Reading Improvement*. 23(2). Summer. 145–51; Goodwin, S. S., Sharp, G. W., Cloutier, E. F., Diamond, N. A., & Dalgaard, K. A. 1983. *Effective Classroom Questioning*. Urbana, Ill.: University of Illinois. Office of Instructional and Management Services. (ERIC Document Reproduction Services No. ED 285 497; Wassermann, S. 1991. The art of the question. *Childhood Education*. 67(4). Summer. 257–59; Whitmore, K. F., & Crowell, C. G. 1994. What makes a question good is . . . . *The New Advocate*. 7(1). Winter. 45–57.

12. Wedman, J. M. 1991. The effect of training on the questions preservice teachers ask during literature discussions. *Reading Research and Instruction*. 30(2). 62–70.

13. Hammond, W. D. 1986. Common questions on reading comprehension. *Learning 86*. January. 49–51.

14. Zarrillo, J. 1991. Theory becomes practice: Aesthetic teaching with literature. *The New Advocate*. 4(4). Fall. 221–34.

15. Doiron, R. 1994. Using nonfiction in a read-aloud program: Letting the facts speak for themselves. *The Reading Teacher*. 47(8). May. 616–24; Huck, C. 1992. Literacy and literature. *Language Arts*. 69(7). November. 520–25.

16. Durkin, D. 1966. *Children Who Read Early*. New York: Teachers College Press.

17. Anderson, R. C., Hiebert, E. H., Scott, J., & Wilkinson, I. A. G. 1985. *Becoming a Nation of Readers*. Champaign-Urbana, Ill.: Center for the Study of Reading. 23.

18. For additional information about reading aloud, see sources such as Au, K. H. 1993. *Literacy Instruction in Multicultural Settings*. Ft. Worth, Tex.: Harcourt Brace Jovanovich. 23, 140–41; Brent, R., & Anderson, P. 1993. Developing children's classroom listening strategies. *The Reading Teacher*. 47(2). October. 122–26; Butler, C. 1980. When the pleasurable is measurable: Teachers reading aloud. *Language Arts*. 57. November-December. 882–85; Clay, M. M. 1979. *Young Fluent Readers*. London: Heinemann; Cohen, D. 1968. The effect of literature on vocabulary and reading. *Elementary English*. 45. 209–13; Cosgrove, S. 1987. Reading aloud to children: The effects of listening on the reading comprehension and attitudes of fourth and sixth graders in six communities in Connecticut. Unpublished doctoral dissertation, University of Connecticut; Dressel, J. H. 1990. Effects of listening to and discussing different qualities of children's literature on the narrative writing of fifth graders. *Research in the Teaching of English*. 24(4). 397–414; Elley, W. 1989. Vocabulary acquisition from listening to stories. *Reading Research Quarterly*. 24(2). 174–87; Strickland, D. S. 1971. The effects of a special literature program on the oral language expression of linguistically different, Negro kindergarten children. *Dissertation Abstracts International*. 32. 1406A. (University Microfilm No. 71–28, 560); Taylor, D. 1983. *Family Literacy: Young Children Learning to Read and Write*. Portsmouth, N.H.: Heinemann; Trelease, J. 1989. *The New Read-Aloud Handbook*. (3d Ed.). New York: Penguin.

19. Michner, D. M. 1988. Test your reading aloud IQ. *The Reading Teacher*. 42(2). November. 118–22.

20. Hoffman, J. V., Rosen, N. L., & Bettle, J. 1993. Reading aloud in classrooms: From the modal toward a "model." *The Reading Teacher*. 46(6). March. 496–503.

21. Evans, K. M. 1992. Reading aloud: A bridge to independence. *The New Advocate*. 5(1). Winter. 47–57.

22. Nikola-Lisa, W. 1992. Read aloud, play a lot: Children's spontaneous responses to literature. *The New Advocate*. 5(3). Summer. 199–213.

23. Tooze, R. 1959. *Storytelling*. Englewood Cliffs, N.J.: Prentice-Hall.

24. For additional information about storytelling, see sources such as Briggs, N. E., & Wagner, J. A. 1979. *Children's Literature through Storytelling and Drama*. (2d Ed.). Dubuque, Iowa: W. C. Brown. 10–12; Kempter, S., & Edwards, L. 1986. Children's expression of causality and their construction of narrative. *Topics in Language Disorders*. 7(1). December. 11–20; Roney, R. C. 1989. Back to the basics with storytelling. *The Reading Teacher*. March. 42(7). 520–23; Peck, J. 1989. Using storytelling to promote language and literacy development. *The Reading Teacher*. 43(3). November. 138–41; Morrow, L. 1985. Reading and retelling stories: Strategies for emergent readers. *The Reading Teacher*. 38. 970–75; Livo, N., & Reitz, S. 1986. *Storytelling: Process and Practice*. Littleton, Colo.: Libraries Unlimited.

25. Sawyer, R. 1962. *The Way of the Storyteller*. New York: Viking; Tooze, R. 1959.

26. McCaslin, N. 1996. *Creative Drama in the Classroom and Beyond*. (6th Ed.). New York: Longman. 256.

27. Barton, B. 1986. *Tell Me Another*. Markham, Ontario: Pembroke; Hamilton, M., & Weiss, M. 1991. A teacher's guide to storytelling. *Instructor*. 100(9). May. 27–35; Troeger, V. B. 1990. Student storytelling. *Teaching Pre K–8*. 20(6). March. 41–43.

28. For additional information about using drama and literature in the classroom, see sources such as Fennessey, S. 1995. Living history through drama and literature. *The Reading Teacher*. 49(1). September. 16–19; Hoyt, L. 1992. Many ways of knowing: Using drama, oral interactions, and the visual arts to enhance reading comprehension. *The Reading Teacher*. 45(8). April. 580–84; Young, T. A., & Vardell, S. 1993. Weaving Readers Theatre and nonfiction into the curriculum. *The Reading Teacher*. 46(5). February. 396–406.

29. The following sources are recommended reading for drama: Kase-Polisini, J. 1989. *The Creative Drama Book: Three Approaches*. New Orleans: Anchorage Press; McCaslin, N. 1996; Rosenberg, H. S., & Pinciotti, P. 1986. *Creative Drama and Imagination: Transforming Ideas into Action*. New York: Holt, Rinehart & Winston; Salazar, L. G. 1995. *Teaching Dramatically: Learning Thematically*, Charlottesville, Va.: New Plays; Salisbury, B. 1996. *Theatre Arts in the Elementary Classroom*. (2d Ed.). New Orleans: Anchorage Press; Scher, A., & Varral, C. 1987. *Another 100+ Ideas for Drama*. Portsmouth, N.H.: Heinemann.

30. Spolin, V. *Improvisation for the Theatre*. Evanston, Ill.: Northwestern University Press.

31. Modification of the flyer *Informal Classroom Drama*, a joint publication of the National Council of Teachers of English (Urbana, Ill.) and the Children's Theatre Association of America (Washington, D.C.).

32. McCaslin, N. 1996. 122–56; Paulin, M. 1985. *Creative Uses of Children's Literature*.

Hamden, Conn.: Library Professional Publication. 450–52.

33. Champlin, C. 1980. *Puppetry and Creative Drama in Storytelling*. Austin, Tex.: Nancy Renfro Studios; Cummings, R. 1962. *101 Hand Puppets: A Guide for Puppeteers of All Ages*. New York: McKay; Engler, L., & Fijan, C. 1973. *Making Puppets Come Alive*. New York: Taplinger; Fredricks, M., & Segal, J. 1979. *Creative Puppets in the Classroom*. Rowayton, Conn.: New Play; Luskin, J. 1975. *Easy to Make Puppets*. Boston: Plays; Whittaker, V. 1982. *Give Puppets a Hand*. Grand Rapids, Mich.: Baker Book House.

34. Briggs, N. E., & Wagner, J. A. 1979. 141.

35. For additional information about selecting, preparing, and presenting visuals, see sources such as Bay, G. 1995. *A Treasury of Flannelboard Stories*. Fort Atkinson, Wis.: Alleyside; Chadwick, R. 1995. *Feltboard Storytimes*. Fort Atkinson, Wis.: Alleyside; Gelb, M. J. 1988. *Present Yourself!* Rolling Hills Estates, Calif.: Jalmar Press. 51–55; Griffin, J. 1994. 312–15; Hasling, J. 1988. 88–91; Mallett, J., & Ervin, T. 1995. *Fold and Cut Stories*. Fort Atkinson, Wis.: Alleyside; Mandel, S. 1987. 25–43; Marsh, V. 1995. *Paper-Cutting Stories from A–Z*. Fort Atkinson, Wis.: Alleyside; Marsh, V. 1995. *Mystery-Fold: Stories to Tell, Draw, and Fold*. Fort Atkinson, Wis.: Alleyside.

36. Bauer, C. F. 1977. *Handbook for Storytellers*. Chicago: American Library Association. 183–243.

37. Morrow, L. M. 1979. Exciting children about literature through creative storytelling techniques. *Language Arts*. 56(3). March. 236–41.

38. Norton, D. E. 1993. *The Effective Teaching of Language Arts*. (4th Ed.). New York: Macmillan. 427–30.

39. For additional information about origami, see sources such as Araki, C. 1968. *Origami in the Classroom, Books I and II*. Rutland, Vt.: Tuttle; Murray, W., & Rigney, F. 1961. *Paper Folding for Beginners*. New York: Dover.

40. For additional information about visual graphics, see sources such as Bromley, K. D. 1991. *Webbing with Literature*. Needham Heights, Mass.: Allyn & Bacon; Yopp, R. H. & H. K. *Literature-Based Reading Activities*. Needham Heights, Mass.: Allyn & Bacon. 34–40, 77–82. Also, see commercial materials such as *Breakthroughs: Strategies for Thinking, Graphic Organizers*. Columbus, Ohio: Zaner-Bloser. 1990.

41. For additional information about the benefits of using audiovisual technology and literature, see sources such as Rickelman, R. J., & Henk, W. A. 1992. Technology in the teaching of literature-based reading programs. In Wood, K., & Moss, A. (Eds.) 1992. *Exploring Literature in the Classroom: Content and Methods*. Norwood, Mass.: Christopher-Gordon. 59–83; Rickelman, R. J., & Henk, W. A. 1990. Children's literature and audio/visual technologies. *The Reading Teacher*. 43(9). 682–84; Thron, J. R. 1991. Children's literature: Reading, seeing, watching. *Children's Literature in Education*. 22(1). 51–58.

42. See selection sources, such as Lee, L. K. (Ed.). 1992. *Elementary School Library Collection: A Guide to Books and Other Media*. Williamsport, Pa.: Brodart; Dillon, P. M., & Leonard, D. C. 1995. *Multimedia Technology from A to Z*. Phoenix, Ariz.: Oryx; Witten, R. (Ed.). *Audio Books on the Go: A Listeners' Guide to Books on Cassette*. Portland, Maine: AudioFile.

See also professional journals such as *Media and Methods*, published by the American Society of Education; *Booklist and Book Links*, published by the American Library Association; Sorenson, A. (Ed.). *Children's Book Review*. Brentwood, Tenn.: Grove Communication.
Also, see teacher magazines such as *Instructor*, published by Scholastic, and *Teaching Pre K–8*, published by Highlights for Children.

43. For additional information about previewing and selecting audiovisual productions, see sources such as Bosch, S., Promis, P., & Sugnet, C. 1994. *Guide to Selecting and Acquiring CD-ROMs, Software, and Other Electronic Publications*. Chicago: American Library Association; Rickelman, A. J., & Henk, W. A. 1990; Schindel, M. 1981. Children's literature on film: Through the audiovisual era to the age of telecommunications. *Annual of the Language Association Division on Children's Literature and the Children's Literature Association*. 9.1–13; Slavenas, R. 1981. The effect of audiovisual presentation on interest in books of preschool children. *Dissertation Abstracts International*. 42(4). 1473-A.

44. See the following sources for additional instructional ideas: Barchers, S. I. 1994. 214–54; Berger, M. A. 1994. Seeing and doing science with video. *Instructor*. 103(2). March. 51–53; Lankford, M. D. 1992. *Films for Learning, Thinking & Doing*. Englewood, Colo.: Libraries Unlimited; Rose, D. H., & Meyer, A. 1994. Focus on research: The role of technology in language arts instruction. *Language Arts*. 71(4). April. 290–94; Wright, K. C. 1993. *The Challenge of Technology: Action Strategies for the School Library Media Specialist*. Chicago: American Library Association.

45. Flood, J., & Lapp, D. (Eds.). 1995. Television and reading: Refocusing the debate. *The Reading Teacher*. 49(2). October. 160–64; Neuman, S. 1991. *Literacy in the Television Age: The Myth of the TV Effect*. Norwood, N.J.: Ablex; Singer, J., Singer, D., Desmond, R., Hirsch, B., & Nicol, A. 1988. Family mediation and children's comprehension of television: A longitudinal study. *Journal of Applied Developmental Psychology*. 9. 119–23.

46. Reported in Multimedia in the classroom. 1995. *Instructor*. 104(4). May/June. Special supplement sponsored by Microsoft Corporation; also, Quality Education Data Research of Denver, Colo.

47. Abrams, A. 1996. *Multimedia Magic: Exploring the Power of Multimedia Production*. Needham Heights, Mass.: Longwood; Agnew, P. W., Kellerman, A. S., & Meyer, J. 1996. *Multimedia in the Classroom*. Needham Heights, Mass.: Longwood.

48. Reported in *Reading Today*. 1995. 13(5). 8.

49. Yankovich, N., Meyrowitz, N., & Van Dam, A. 1985. Reading and writing the electronic book. *Computer*. 18. 10.

50. Fernandez, M. 1995. Unpublished manuscript. See also Bender, R., & William, N. 1996. *Computer-Assisted Instruction for Students at Risk: A Teacher's Manual*. Needham Heights, Mass.: Longwood.

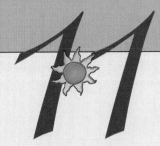

11

Approaches to Literary Study

... *H*ow can we preserve and protect the unique and personal literary experience of each child while at the same time, helping the entire group to grow in an appreciation of and love for literature?

—Kay Vandergrift

Chapter Reflections

What benefits do individuals gain from a continuous exposure to quality literature?

What literary theories and structures of literary study influence the literary approaches used in classrooms?

What are the benefits, suitable literature, and instructional components in a Pure Literature Approach?

What are the benefits, suitable literature, and instructional components in a Literature-Based Approach?

What are the benefits, suitable literature, and instructional components in a Literature Across the Curriculum Approach?

How does the teacher strengthen the professional partnership with the media specialist?

How does the teacher involve parents in the literary approaches?

How do the teacher and administration review and document the effectiveness of the literary approaches?

To meet Vandergrift's challenge, teachers use various approaches to literary study that respect children's natural reactions to literature and help them develop intellectual, imaginative, and critical thinking abilities. Through literature, young people encounter events that help them better understand themselves and others. Because literature introduces them to issues and concerns of other people, students begin to understand the cultural influences that help to shape others' lives. By exploring the visual and verbal models presented in literature, young people come to recognize that language and images can be used in a variety of ways to communicate ideas, attitudes, and information. Thus, literary study gives children many opportunities to react imaginatively to literature, to construct meanings from the verbal and visual narratives, and to create oral and written responses to the literature. This experience helps them communicate more effectively with others. Through literary study, students also learn to recognize the elements of fiction and nonfiction literature and to appreciate the ability of authors and artists to use language and images to create imaginative, cohesive narratives.[1]

At this time, when educators are defining goals and objectives for all areas of the curriculum, Judith Langer urges literature teachers to make intelligent decisions about the inclusion of literature in the classroom.[2] These decisions will be influenced by theories of learning and development, literary theories, and suitable instruction that supports the theories. The first part of the chapter presents a historical overview of early literature used for instructional purposes, literary theories, and instructional structures of literary study. Then, the benefits, literature, and instructional components of the three approaches to literary study for preschool through middle grades are presented. The next section of the chapter discusses the role of the media specialist and parents or guardians in the successful implementation of the literary approaches. Finally, reflection guides for the three approaches to literary study are provided. After the summary, a Literary Link for John Gardiner's *Stone Fox* is proposed.

Throughout history, as literature teachers have selected literature and instructional approaches to use in literary study, they have debated the merits of the different approaches. While the literary approaches may vary, adherents of all approaches agree that young people receive many benefits from a continuous exposure to quality literature. These benefits are presented in Table 11.1 on page 381.[3]

✳ THE HISTORICAL DEVELOPMENT OF LITERARY STUDY

The historical development of literary study is closely intertwined with reading and language instruction. Until the nineteenth century, literature was used to disseminate cultural and scientific knowledge and as the material for teaching reading, language, and ethics. At the beginning of the twentieth century, secondary and higher education literature programs were developed, but literature was not used extensively in the elementary school until the late 1980s. Thus, literary study as we know it today is of relatively recent origin. Nevertheless, its roots extend far into the past.

EARLY LITERATURE USED FOR INSTRUCTIONAL PURPOSES

For centuries only children of noble blood, boys destined for the priesthood, and the children of some upwardly mobile burghers were taught to read. The teacher-priests used expensive religious manuscripts and books of manners and morals, such as *The boke of curtasye, How the good wiff taugte hir dougtir,* and *The schoole of vertue.* After William Caxton brought the printing press from Germany to England around 1477, copies of *Aesop's Fables, Le Morte d'Arthur,* and *The Historye of Reynart the Foxe* became available.

By the sixteenth century, English children read alphabet books, primers, and hornbooks. A hornbook was a

TABLE 11.1 Benefits Individuals Gain from a Continuous Exposure to Quality Literature

Students who experience the diversity of language found in quality literature realize the potential capabilities and extent to which:

> Language describes and expresses all facets of human existence.
>
> They can manipulate words, phrases, and forms of language to express personal desires, feelings, attitudes, and information and communicate with others.

Individuals receive many personal pleasures while exploring familiar and unknown worlds created by authors, poets, and artists.

Learners develop their minds and enhance their thinking abilities as they construct personal meanings from the text and illustrations.

Talented authors and artists stimulate students' imaginative powers when they experience the various creative processes represented in literature.

Through exposure and experience with literature, learners develop an understanding and appreciation of the various literary structures and forms.

By exploring both fiction and nonfiction genres, young people receive a broad knowledge base to help them understand information they will encounter in all areas of study.

Daily exposure to literature provides opportunities for students to assume appropriate aesthetic or efferent stances toward literature.

Literary experiences give individuals an awareness and appreciation of the literary heritage of people from all social, national, ethnic, and racial groups.

Individuals who encounter cultural values portrayed in literature gain insights into the motivations, thoughts, and behavior of self and others.

Literature portrays alternate lifestyles, situations, and behavior young people might not personally experience.

Through literary study, young people explore options to help them set future goals and priorities for their lives.

wooden or metal board shaped like a paddle, to which was attached a piece of parchment with the alphabet, vowel sounds, and the Lord's Prayer. The parchment was covered with a substance called "horn." (See lower photo, page 382.) The alphabet books and primers contained moralistic tales and proverbs and psalms from the Bible. As youngsters learned to read, they also learned the values, mores, and beliefs of their society. When English colonists came to North America, they brought their books and instructional practices with them. Consequently, the history of children's literature in North America was heavily influenced by English practices until the late eighteenth century.

In the North American colonies in the seventeenth century, the single purpose for teaching children to read was to prepare them to read the Bible. By 1674 Massachusetts had established a free reading school. Shortly afterward, most New England communities with a hundred households were required to provide a grammar school for all children. By the 1690s, children were reading first hornbooks and then *The New England Primer*. For more than a hundred years, this primer was the most popular instructional book for teaching children to read. Beginning with "In Adam's fall we sinned all" and ending with "Zaccheus he did climb the tree, his lord to see," it contained verses on religious and later political subjects. (See top photo on page 382.) In addition, various religious tracts written for children by Puritan ministers were available, including John Cotton's *Spiritual Milk for Boston Babes in either England, drawn from the Breasts of Both Testaments for their Souls' Nourishment* (1646). To prepare children for death, Thomas Janeway wrote *The token for the children of New England, or, some examples of children in whom the fear of God was remarkably budding before they died; in several parts of New England; preserved and published for the encouragement of piety in other children.* Originally published in England, it was published in Massachusetts in 1700.

As more ordinary folk learned to read, chapbooks became a popular reading material. These inexpensive tracts containing selections from folk literature and humorous tales were sold by peddlers, or chapmen, to the common folk. By the early eighteenth century, some children enjoyed reading adult novels, such as John Bunyan's *The Pilgrim's Progress* (1678), Daniel Defoe's *Robinson Crusoe* (1719), and Jonathan Swift's *Travels into Several Remote Nations of the World, in four parts, by Lemuel Gulliver* (1726).

In the mid-eighteenth century John Newbery, a London entrepreneur, published stories, ballads, and folktales intended for children's pleasure. American publishers brought pirated reprints of Newbery's books to North America, adapted them, and published them for children. Later, local authors wrote original books with themes similar to those sold by Newbery.[4]

At the beginning of the nineteenth century, many educators believed that children should read only instructional materials that conveyed moral lessons. Many adults thought that all materials written for children should teach, preach, and reprimand, because they viewed children as evil creatures who needed proper discipline by pious and prudent parents. As indicated in the genre chapters, early juvenile realistic books and fantasy popularized this philosophy. In 1836 William McGuffey first published the *McGuffey Eclectic Readers*. These readers, which were intended for specific grades, contained poems, stories, and essays by notable authors such as William Wordsworth and Shakespeare. The stories and verses emphasized patriotism and offered social commentaries on proper behavior. They

Though small in size, this New England Primer, published in 1727, contained verses for each letter of the alphabet. Questions about the people in the Bible and a child's grace were also included on one page. At this time certain words were spelled differently and letters were formed differently, such as f for s. What does the verse for U mean?

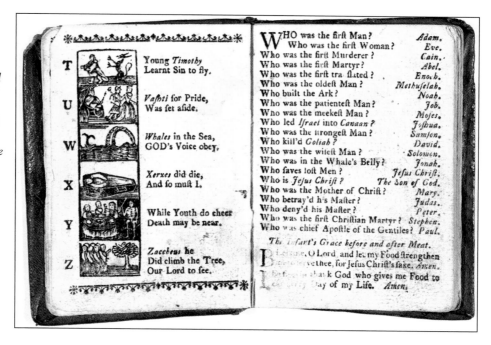

Children used this American colonial hornbook in the eighteenth century for reading instruction. A long cord was attached to the handle so that the children could wear it around their neck like a necklace. Thus, the hornbook was available for the child to read at all times.

were widely used between 1834 and 1900 to teach American children to read.

By the 1920s in the United States, progressive education and the theories of John Dewey had begun to influence adults' perception of childhood and child-raising techniques. Educators now viewed childhood as a stage preceding adulthood. Fortunately, many juvenile books reflected these beliefs. During the Great Depression of the 1930s, anthologies used to teach reading were the primary source of literature available to young people in the United States. At this time the Carnegie Foundation helped communities build public libraries, which made literature available to more children, but few elementary schools had adequate libraries. In 1941 Scott Foresman published *Dick and Jane: New Basic Readers*, which offered a uniform curriculum of carefully selected narratives with age-related, controlled vocabularies. These popular basal readers contained simple stories and poems that focused on the "ideal" middle-class family life. They influenced the development of the basal readers, which became the major instructional material used to teach elementary-age children to read. Standardized measures, used to evaluate the effectiveness of reading instruction, influenced the format and content of the basal readers.

In 1965 the Elementary and Secondary Educational Act provided funding for the purchase of literature books and instructional materials. Now libraries appeared in many public schools. Children made weekly visits to the library. The media specialist gave book talks, read literature to the children, and encouraged children to check out books for independent reading. Teachers developed routines for using literature, such as daily read-aloud sessions and recreational reading periods, also called Silent Sustained Reading. Some teachers experimented with Individualized Reading, which involved the use of literature for reading instruction. By the mid-1980s, with the emergence of an integrated, holistic approach to language arts instruction, literature was being used extensively for reading, writing, and other content area instruction. Today redesigned basal readers include more original literature. In the 1990s, basal readers are being used to some degree in many elementary classrooms to teach young children to read.

LITERARY THEORIES THAT SUPPORT LITERARY APPROACHES

Two major groups of literary theories—the author-driven theories and the reader-response theories—influence contemporary literary approaches. Since the Renaissance, students have read and discussed the *canons*, or "classics," of literature produced by a society. This practice led to the development of the *Imitative Structure* of literary study. Proponents of this literary study believe literature contains the heritage or "great books" of a society and that students who read and imitate the literature will absorb and transmit the beliefs of the society. The knowledge imparted by the author is the focus of this literary study and the study is author-driven. Therefore, students identify the author's intentions or meanings, memorize selected passages, and produce imitations of the literature. Proponents of the contemporary Cultural Literacy approach and the Heritage approach support the Imitative Structure of literary study. Developers of these approaches have selected canons of literature that they believe all educated citizens of the United States should read. Incidentally, many of the chosen books were written by Western European males before the mid-twentieth century.[5]

In the 1930s, a group of literature specialists felt that other literary approaches neglected literature as an art. From this concern *New Criticism* emerged. The New Critics believed that students could objectively study and analyze a text. At the same time, a compatible instructional approach, known as the *Analytical Structure*, emerged. This instructional approach stresses the development of critical thinking and involves students in literary criticism techniques such as categorizing genres and analyzing the text through problem solving, which leads the reader to appropriately interpret and evaluate the text. The Analytical Structure is based on an author-driven theory because it focuses on the reader's ability to search the text and identify the author's meaning as it is reflected in the text.[6] The Cognitive Information Processing Theories of learning and development, discussed in Chapter 2, are compatible with author-driven theories. (See Table 2.6 on page 41.)

In the late 1960s, theorists representing various disciplines, including education, psychology, linguistics, and sociology, began to question the author-driven theories that influenced literature instruction. These theorists focused on the importance of the reader in the reading process. Years earlier, in 1938 Louise Rosenblatt had published *Literature as Exploration*,[7] which articulated her views on the reciprocal contribution made by the reader and the text during the reading event. Forty years later Rosenblatt proposed the *Transactional Theory of the Literary Work* in her book, *The Reader, the Text, the Poem*.[8] According to this theory, the reader focuses attention on certain portions of a text, taps into personal influences (schemata), and *transacts* with the particular text. Proponents of the Transactional Theory believe that meaning is not "in" the text nor the reader. They believe meaning happens during the evocation of a transaction between the reader and the text. Each transaction is different with a different reader, at a different time, in a different context. By the 1980s Rosenblatt's

Transactional Theory and *reader-response theories* had become a leading theoretical basis of literary study.[9]

Various theorists have described the primacy of the reader in the reading event, although they have slightly different views about the influence of the text, the reader, and the reader's response. Among those who encompass reader-response are psychoanalytic theorists, such as N. N. Holland and D. Bleich, who believe the reader is the ultimate source of meaning, and W. Iser, who proposes that the reader "fills in the gap" to make meaning from the text.[10] Rosenblatt supports the reciprocal relationship between reader and text and the resulting transaction. Reader-response literary study is compatible with the *Generative Structure* of literary study, which focuses on the students' experiences with literature and values the students' goals rather than teacher-determined objectives. The Piagetian/ Naturalist Theories and the Social-Constructivist Theories of learning and development, discussed in Chapter 2, support reader-response theories.

Reader-response theories focus on the psychological, cultural, and social issues influencing the reader's transaction with the author's narrative. Author-driven theories highlight the information accumulated from the text. Instruction focuses on the major writers, the geographic or time settings, stylistic devices used by the writers or artists, and the identification and analysis of the structures of genres. Both theories have influenced the literary study approaches used by all literature teachers. Table 11.2 on page 385 summarizes the main elements of the author-driven and reader-response approaches.[11] By understanding the theories that influence literary study, teachers can better design and implement suitable literary approaches in their classrooms.[12]

✳ APPROACHES TO LITERARY STUDY

As we move into the twenty-first century, we need to develop and articulate well-defined approaches to literary study that integrate literature into the entire elementary curriculum. Applicable literary, instructional, and developmental theories support these approaches. Through organized literary approaches, young people develop the habit of reading literature for pleasurable (aesthetic) and informational (efferent) purposes. In addition to literature that appeals to the students and is compatible with their abilities, literature that stretches their literary knowledge and information about various topics should also be used. Students explore a variety of prose, poetry, and dramatic selections that stimulate their imaginations and elicit critical thinking and problem-solving skills. Instructional strategies help students connect, construct, and create responses to their personal reflections on, reactions to, and interpretations of the literature. At the same time, suitable

techniques are used to help young people consider and respect the viewpoints of others. Learners come to recognize the historical, scientific, and social information obtained by exploring literature. To obtain these benefits, children need access to school and public libraries and to an adequate supply of literature books. Media specialists who are knowledgeable about literature and use appropriate instructional techniques with children are vital to the success of literary approaches. Effective literary approaches also elicit the aid of parents or guardians who provide a literary environment in the home and share their personal literature experiences with their children.[13] These support groups are discussed later in the chapter. The last section presents reflection guides to help teachers and administrators review and document the effectiveness of the literary approaches.

While the literary routines used by most elementary teachers are worthwhile (see Table 11.1), young people benefit from continuous, organized literary study. A literary approach is supported by literary theories (presented in Table 11.2), structures of literary study, and the theories of learning and development (presented in Table 2.6 on page 41). The approach includes selected literature, literary goals, and instructional strategies that are suitable for the students and the literature. If the literature is used for aesthetic purposes, the literature is selected first; then the goals that naturally evolve from the selected literature are identified. When literature is used for efferent or instructional purposes, usually the literary and instructional goals are identified first; then literature that elicits those goals is selected.

When designing and implementing classroom or schoolwide literary study, teachers can draw on lists of attributes such as the following for help in identifying applicable literary goals:

The art of literature and literary knowledge is emphasized in the literary study.

The pleasure individuals gain from listening to, viewing, and reading literature is highlighted in the literary approach.

The creator's ability to use language and images to communicate ideas, attitudes, and information is explored in the literary approach.

The beliefs and traditions of diverse cultures are featured in the literary approach.

Scientific, historical, social, and artistic knowledge is identified and taught in the literary approach.

The relationships and interactions between humans and their environment are identified and explored in the literary approach.

TABLE 11.2   The Influence of the Author, Text, Reader, and Instruction in Author-Driven and Reader-Response Theories

INFLUENCE OF	AUTHOR-DRIVEN THEORIES	READER-RESPONSE THEORIES
Author	Writing is influenced by the author's cultural, social, and literary experiences and knowledge. Language is carefully selected to express ideas, attitudes, and knowledge. The author assembles and organizes elements of the plot in a cohesive, logical manner. The central focus of the reading event is to discover the author's intention; that is, the true meaning of the selection is found in the text.	Writing is influenced by the author's cultural, social, and literary experiences and knowledge. Language is carefully selected to express ideas, attitudes and knowledge. The author assembles and organizes elements of the plot in a cohesive, logical manner. Meaning is constructed through the relationship of the audience to the author's text.
Text	The text is an object that has a determinate meaning of its own; that is, it contains the meaning of the selection. The text is detached from social factors and the reader's world.	The text is a set of signs capable of being interpreted as verbal symbols; the signs serve as a blueprint to evoke the reader's transaction with the text. The process is "the evocation of the literary work." Stylistic devices are used to evoke the reader's responses. The theories emphasize the capacity of literature to portray and enliven the human experience for a reader.
Reader	The same meaning can be identified by "educated" readers. The reader is omitted entirely or neglected because the reader is unimportant to the author's intention (meanings). The reader's role is to "discover" correct meaning in an objective, rational, detached manner. When the reader finds the "correct" interpretation of the text, the individual is able to understand what the author is saying and the meaning in the text.	The reader's background experiences with literature and life and aptitude influence the reader's response and transaction with the text. Attention is paid to the reader's responses, thoughts, feelings, and memories. A reader who assumes a predominantly *aesthetic* stance focuses on the images, emotions, and thoughts "lived through" during the reading event. A reader who adopts a predominantly *efferent* stance focuses on information "carried away," extracted, and retained after the reading event. The predominant stance may be selected according to the content suggested in the text, the style of writing, the personal interest of the reader at the time, the individual's purpose for reading a piece of literature, or the instructional focus selected by the teacher.
Instruction	The theories are influenced by *Cognitive Information Processing* theories of learning and development. Instruction is influenced by the Imitative and the Analytical Structure of literary study. The learner is taught *about* skills (conventions, elements) of literature. The instruction focuses on literary content, forms, structures, linguistic relationships as word interactions, metaphorical language, images, symbolism, and the like. The text is analyzed through objective, close reading of its formal structures and techniques to establish the prescribed meaning known by the "educated" reader.	The theories are influenced by *Piagetian/Naturalist Theories* and *Social-Constructivist Theories* of learning and development. Instruction is based on the Generative Structure of literary study and the Process Instructional Model. Students actively share their personal oral and written reactions, responses, and interpretations of the text. The instruction validates answers in the text to achieve a consensus. Biographical, historical, or formal considerations enhance readers' insights into the literature. Instruction is facilitated by the teacher and learners to achieve a "community of readers." Initially, a learner may need teacher or peer assistance to achieve a complete interpretation of the text.

Important issues of past, present, and future societies are recognized and discussed in the literary approach.

Literature is used to teach children to read, write, speak, and think.

This section presents the values and procedures for implementing three approaches to literary study: the *Pure Literature Approach*, the *Literature-Based Language Arts Approach*, and the *Literature Across the Curriculum Approach*. The three approaches are compatible and flexible. They may be used independently or simultaneously in the classroom. Each approach incorporates the characteristics of literary genres, outstanding literary works, and strategies discussed in the previous chapters. Applicable literary theories, structures of literary study, and appropriate theories of learning and development influence the design of an approach. Because readers assume predominantly aesthetic and efferent stances toward literature, reader-response theories strongly influence each approach discussed in this section. To support and elicit these stances, each approach uses suitable *connect, construct,* and *create* components of the *Literary Transaction Process* (described in Chapter 2) and instructional techniques compatible with the *Generative Structure* of literary study. Modified instructional techniques suggested by the *Imitative Structure* of literary study are used to help the learners understand the structure of language, to guide their critiques of the ability of the author and artist to use language and images, and to use literary models when producing original oral and written narratives. Table 11.3 on page 387 describes the three approaches to literary study recommended for prekindergarten through middle-grade classrooms.

PURE LITERATURE APPROACH

The oldest and best-known approach to literary study is the *Pure Literature Approach*. In this approach, the students assume an aesthetic stance toward the literature. The primary focus of the study is the pleasure the students gain from the literary experience. Usually, the teacher reads the literature aloud to the class. If multiple copies of the selection are available, students and partners read along silently during the oral reading. The teacher stops reading at appropriate places to give the learners an opportunity to discuss their reactions to the content and their interpretations of the narrative. After these initial discussions, the teacher may choose to talk informally with the boys and girls about unfamiliar or unique vocabulary used by the writer, exceptional artistic elements or designs used, and particular stylistic devices used by the creator to create a cohesive, well-written narrative. At this point the approach highlights the art of literature—the way the creator uses language and images to present ideas, information, and attitudes.[14]

Benefits and Goals of the Approach

By focusing on the pleasure of experiencing a variety of quality literature, then briefly discussing the art of literature, young people are introduced to various genres and creators. Through this approach they absorb literary knowledge. For example, six- and seven-year-old children listening to Maurice Sendak's *Where the Wild Things Are* (1963) recognize that Max, a real boy, enters (through his dream) a fantasy world inhabited by Wild Things, then returns to reality when he smells his dinner. (See color plate on page 107.) While the children react to the storyline, the teacher talks informally about the different settings and the differences between fantasy and realistic fiction. The children's reactions to the Wild Things give the teacher an opportunity to ask, "What do you know about the Wild Things from looking at this picture? Do you think they are friendly or mean?" Probes such as this elicit a further discussion of the characters. As the teacher uses literary terms such as reality, fantasy, and character, the children become familiar with literary terminology and begin to use it when discussing literature with others.

Similarly, when a teacher reads aloud Scott O'Dell's *The Island of the Blue Dolphins* (1960) to children in fourth through sixth grade, the listeners are intrigued by O'Dell's description of the island where Karana lives and her ability to survive. As the students react, the teacher informally guides them to see O'Dell's ability to use descriptive language, develop suspense, and create exciting adventures. When attention is focused on the literary characteristics, students naturally discuss and offer opinions about the creator's ability to communicate through verbal language and visual images. A discussion of the style, technique, or medium used by the creator gives the young people a broader understanding of the creative process of producing literature. They are encouraged to transfer this knowledge to their personal writings and art. Children who explore a variety of genres and topics and creations by talented authors and artists become discriminating in their selection of literature for recreational and informational purposes.

The quality traditional and contemporary literature used in this approach helps children discern similarities and differences in the lifestyles of people living in different historical periods and helps them understand the issues that have been important to society at different times. Since many young people are not familiar with either their own literary heritage or that of others, this approach gives them an opportunity to explore and appreciate outstanding books that have shaped the literary heritage of all cultural, ethnic, and social groups.

TABLE 11.3   The Three Approaches of Literary Study

PURE LITERATURE APPROACH	LITERATURE-BASED LANGUAGE ARTS APPROACH	LITERATURE ACROSS THE CURRICULUM APPROACH
The major focus of the approach is to give children pleasurable experiences with literature.	Authentic, unabridged literature is used as the major instructional material to teach listening, speaking, reading, writing, visualizing, and thinking.	Appropriate prose, poetry, nonfiction, and fiction literature are used as supplementary and primary instructional materials in all discipline area classes.
Quality classical and contemporary fiction and nonfiction literature are presented.	Initially, the students assume a predominantly aesthetic stance toward the literature; later an efferent focus is assumed for language instruction.	The focus of attention is directed toward the content rather than the literature.
Learners adopt a predominantly aesthetic stance when they listen to, view, and read the literature.	In this approach, the child's attention is directed to the author's language, the artist's images, the function of language, and the development of suitable reading and language strategies.	When the teacher reads a *Focus Book* aloud, the children and teachers assume an aesthetic stance toward the literature. Students may read the book individually, with a partner, or with the entire class.
The teacher uses the *connect* and *construct* components of the *Literary Transaction Process* when presenting the literature. Occasionally, the learners choose to *create* visual and verbal responses to the literature.	The language and characteristics of the literature determine the selections used for instruction of beginning learners, transitional learners, and maturing learners.	A thematic collection of literature highlighting a selected theme or content is organized in a *LitSet.* An efferent instructional focus is implemented when the literature is used for instructional purposes that highlight the selected subject concepts.
The learners explore a variety of literary forms, genres, and elements in the visual and verbal narratives. The literature includes diverse groups, protagonists of both genders, and various topics.	Literature is used for independent reading and large group instruction. The teacher uses the *Literary Transaction Process* when presenting the literature to small groups or the entire class. Mini-lessons are conducted as needed for instruction.	The literature naturally stimulates related inquiry in several discipline areas.
The primary goal of the approach is to inspire students to develop a positive attitude toward literature and a habit of reading and responding to literature for aesthetic satisfaction.	Students are encouraged to read, reflect on, and respond to their interpretations of the literature. They share their oral and written reactions with others.	The teacher uses components of the *Literary Transaction Process* when presenting individual literary selections.
Through informal discussion, the students react and share personal interpretations. They absorb literary knowledge and use suitable literary terminology. They gain information about the genre and how creators use language and images to produce cohesive narratives.	Various instructional components are included in this approach.	In this integrated approach, literature is the link that helps students acquire knowledge and skills, discover the relationships that exist between discipline areas, and transfer the information across disciplines.
		Literature exposes students to authentic situations where they can apply higher-order thinking as they solve problems and engage in scientific inquiry that creates and re-creates knowledge.
		Students use all modalities of language to respond to the information received from the selected literature.

The goals of a Pure Literature Approach are to provide an environment where learners can do the following:

Adopt a predominantly aesthetic stance to the literature they are reading, listening to, viewing, and discussing.

Explore literature of high literary merit that represents all literary genres and includes diverse societies, protagonists of both genres, and various topics.

Recognize various visual and verbal structures, forms, and elements found in quality fiction and nonfiction literature.

Identify outstanding examples of prose, poetry, and drama.

Recognize notable authors, poets, and artists and be familiar with their lives.

Develop a lifelong habit of selecting literature and responding to it for pleasurable purposes.

Literature Used in the Approach

Teachers present only quality, age-appropriate, contemporary and classical literature in this approach. All literary genres are represented in the short stories, novels, poetry, essays, books with pictures, and plays presented. Literature with worthwhile themes, adventure, suspense, well-developed characters, and unusual settings is used throughout the year. The teacher expands the students' horizons by presenting high-quality literature that includes diverse societies, protagonists of both genders, and a variety of appealing topics. Generally, the language in the literature is more complex than in the literature students choose for independent reading. By exploring various topics and well-written prose, poetry, and drama, the learners expand their background knowledge and develop an appreciation for quality literature. In addition, their language and reading abilities mature. Using classical literature also introduces students to language and stylistic devices not typically used by contemporary authors.

In this approach teachers of preschool and primary children enjoy sharing with the children literary selections such as Beatrix Potter's *Peter Rabbit* (1902), Wanda Gag's *Millions of Cats* (1928), Virginia Burton's *Mike Mulligan and His Steam Shovel* (1939), Mary Hoffman's *Boundless Grace* (1995), and many other books described in Chapter 8. Teachers of second grade and above relish the experience of sharing literature such as Margery Williams's *The Velveteen Rabbit* (1922), E. B. White's *Charlotte's Web* (1952), Virginia Hamilton's *Zeely* (1967), Kenneth Grahame's *Wind in the Willows* (1908), A. A. Milne's *Winnie the Pooh* (1926), Natalie Babbitt's *Tuck*

Everlasting (1975), Russell Freedman's *Lincoln: A Photobiography* (1989), Lois Lowry's *The Giver* (1993), and many more books presented in the genre chapters. Nancy Carlstrom and Deborah Kogan Ray's *How Does the Wind Walk?* (1993) combines the verbal and visual narratives to give the reader an ideal aesthetic experience. (See the Carlstrom color plate.) Also see the bibliography of books to read aloud.

Instructional Components of the Approach

Teachers who implement the Pure Literature Approach strive to help students realize the power and delight of language and literature. The teacher and students assume a predominantly aesthetic stance toward the literature. Generally, the teacher reads the selection aloud to the students. An aesthetic instructional focus is assumed as the teacher uses appropriate techniques to *connect* the students to the text and encourages them to *construct* meanings and transact spontaneously with the narrative. Therefore, the *connect* and *construct* components of the Literary Transaction Process are used extensively. Occasionally, the *create* component is used when a child chooses to produce visual or verbal responses to the selection. Instructional techniques used by author-driven theories, such as analyzing the literary structure or attempting to find the author's meaning "in" the text, are not applicable in this literary study. Table 11.4 summarizes the instructional components of the Pure Literature Approach.[15]

Deborah Kogan Ray's expressionistic, acrylic paintings and Nancy White Carlstrom's lyrical verbal narrative answer the question, How Does the Wind Walk? Carlstrom uses figurative language to describe the movement of the wind. Ray uses space, color, and form to highlight the elements presented in the verbal text. How does the artist achieve balance in her painting?

The wind walks with a bounce in her step, playing games as she goes. Taking a hat here, a kite there, then tripping away without a backward glance.

TABLE 11.4 Instructional Components of a Pure Literature Approach

The teacher adopts an aesthetic instructional focus to help learners discover the delight of exploring quality fiction and nonfiction literature.

The teacher uses appropriate literary terminology to direct students' attention to the visual and verbal structures, forms, genres, and elements used in quality literature. As part of sharing the literature, children discover the literary conventions and naturally use appropriate terminology to discuss their impressions. The terminology is not taught directly nor is it tested.

Through aesthetic experiences with literature, learners come to recognize outstanding illustrators and writers. They want to know more about these creators and the reasons they created the students' favorite books.

Throughout the discussion about the people who created the literature, the focus is on the writer's ability to use language effectively and to express ideas, thoughts, and information. In this approach the writer's intentions and motives are not analyzed. The instructional focus remains on an aesthetic reading, the art of literature, and the pleasure derived from experiences with literature.

Depending on the literature and the age of the students, the teacher frequently reads the selection to the class. In this approach students also read independently, with partners, and in small groups.

The *connect* and *construct* components of the Literary Transaction Process are used in the approach. Teachers use book talks, storytelling, and various media to connect the students to the text.

Through informal discussions, students express their personal reactions and interpretations of the literature presented.

Occasionally, students choose to *create* visual or verbal responses to the narratives.

Only informal measures and observational techniques, such as observation of oral responses, written responses in LitLogs, and other oral or written responses, are used to determine the students' literary growth and maturity. Traditional standardized measures, such as multiple-choice tests and essays, are not used, because they do not authentically measure a student's understanding and appreciation of literary works.

LITERATURE-BASED LANGUAGE ARTS APPROACH

Educators who use a Literature-Based Language Arts Approach realize the power of using "authentic" literature as the model and primary material for reading, writing, speaking, listening, viewing, and thinking instruction. In the last decade, due to the influence of psycholinguistics, cognitive psychology, the whole language philosophy of language instruction, and reader-response theories, teachers began designing and implementing Literature-Based Language Arts instruction.[16] This approach uses a variety of complete stories, poems, books with pictures, and novels as natural models to stimulate children's acquisition, development, and production of language. Students are encouraged to construct meanings about the narrative rather than focusing their attention on a subset of skills as prescribed in other instructional materials. The following beliefs support the approach:

All individuals want to communicate effectively with others.

The participants accept and respect all languages and all reactions and responses to the literature.

A variety of unabridged literary selections serve as natural meaning-bearing models to stimulate young people's language acquisition, development, and production.

Learners become effective communicators if they become strategic readers, writers, listeners, and thinkers.

Young people need to express in oral and written language their personal reflections, reactions, and responses to the print and nonprint materials they encounter in the classroom.

With exposure to cohesive (complete, original, "authentic") literature and positive experiences with the literature, students come to recognize the elements, structures, and forms of literature and grasp the potential power of literature in their lives. This leads to a lifelong habit of using literature for pleasurable and intellectual purposes.

Benefits Learners Gain from Experiences with the Approach

Many research studies show that children who use literature for instructional purposes improve in reading achievement and are more enthusiastic about reading, writing, and literature. Children in literature-based approaches express more pride in their linguistic abilities than their counterparts because they see themselves as speakers, readers, and writers.[17]

Because writers of literature combine language patterns in a variety of forms, students who explore various literary genres and creators encounter exemplary models of language and images. These experiences give children many literary options to use when learning and using language modalities. Literature is a successful instructional material because young people feel a natural affinity for the verbal and visual narratives. The literature motivates all to read, listen, write, and talk about the ideas, experiences, and information presented in the familiar literary world or in the strange, unknown literary worlds they may encounter. (See photo on page 390.)

Children who use literature for language arts instruction are enthusiastic about learning to read, write, speak, and listen.

A review of the research in literature-based instruction reveals two universal findings about students in these classrooms. First, they are excited about using "real" books as the major instructional material. Second, they express a positive attitude toward reading, writing, speaking, and literature. A person with a positive attitude is more likely to develop a lifelong habit of reading literature for pleasurable and informational purposes. Teachers who use the literature-based approach are enthusiastic about sharing literature with children and recognize the value of using literature for language arts instruction. Many successful literature-based approaches are designed by teachers who enjoy sharing their successes with other educators. Literature-based teachers may feel that they do not have enough literature and that they need more time to design and implement the approach and to read children's literature. They constantly search for ways to solve these problems and for instructional techniques to help their students become competent communicators. Table 11.5 on page 391 reviews the cognitive, linguistic, and affective benefits individuals gain from experiences with a Literature-Based Language Arts Approach.

Literature Used in the Approach

Authentic, meaning-bearing fiction and nonfiction books, short stories, poems, and plays are used in this approach. The literature contains various language structures necessary for reading and language instruction and production, such as repetitive words and language patterns, predictable plots, and sequential structures. The literature represents various literary genres, contains content that is appealing to the intended age, and includes protagonists from both genders and all cultural, ethnic, and social groups. Literature that will naturally evoke a student's oral or written response is used to reinforce reading, writing, listening, and speaking instruction.

Before the 1930s, literature was used extensively for instructional purposes. During that decade, however, scientific investigations conducted by psychologists and educators led to a demand for a standardized reading and language arts curriculum, which resulted in the development of basal readers and language arts textbooks. Advocates of this instructional program believe that by using materials designed around specific, sequential skill development, they can teach all children to read and write. Although Literature-Based Language Arts Approaches became popular in the 1980s, basal readers and language arts textbooks are still used in many elementary classrooms today.[18]

Today, publishers of basal readers and language arts textbooks are including more original literature written by professional writers and, in many cases, have relaxed readability restrictions. Nevertheless, the original literature included in the new basal has been changed in several ways. Typically, editors remove elements that might be controversial, modify portions of the narrative, and eliminate some or all of the original illustrations. Furthermore, the individuality of the original book is lost when it is included along with other "books" in the basal reader, which resembles a short story anthology. Still, the new basal reader

TABLE 11.5 Benefits Learners Gain from Experiences with a Literature-Based Language Arts Approach

Children who are using literature as the primary language arts instructional material typically have a positive attitude toward reading, writing, and speaking.

Learners who experience the diverse language patterns found in literature realize they too can experiment with language and manipulate it to produce original oral and written narratives and poems. Initially, students use literature as a model for their personal language production.

In this approach, students learn decoding skills and strategies from whole sentences or meaning-bearing phrases, sentences, paragraphs, and cohesive stories and poems. They score equally well or slightly higher than their counterparts in skill-based instruction on reading achievement tests.

Literature provides an authentic context for children to develop an awareness of *semantics* (vocabulary development), *syntax* (sentence structure), and *grapho-phonics* (a sense of word-sound relationships or phonics).

Students involved in this approach view reading, writing, and speaking as natural language-like processes and focus on constructing the meanings evoked by the texts they encounter.

The vocabulary of individuals engaged in this approach is developed and enhanced by the diverse and content-related language in the literature.

Information presented in a literary selection stimulates students' curiosity and desire to know more about a topic.

Students are encouraged to link their personal experiences and knowledge to the content and ideas of a single book or of several books. Therefore they make intratextual connections within a book and between books. They make these same connections between the various creations of a single author or artist and between different authors and artists.

Learners engage in lively, sometimes argumentative discussions about incidents, characters, themes, literary and artistic styles, and authentic portrayals included in the literature they read, listen to, or view.

While acquiring and enhancing language skills and strategies, teachers surround students with literature and encourage them to select literature for personal enjoyment and information. This self-selection process motivates learners to react and interpret the literature they read.

Experiences with literature enhance and enrich the language of language-deficient children. The instructional techniques used in the approach, such as book discussion, oral reading with heterogeneous groups, mini-lessons, and indirect instruction, are also beneficial to the children.

narratives are of higher literary merit than the older readers, and children enjoy reading the stories.[19] We see few changes in new language arts textbooks. Occasionally, teachers use suitable basal selections and language arts textbooks for specific skill instruction in this approach.

Instruction is different for *beginning learners* (children approximately four to seven years), *transitional learners* (children approximately five to eight years), and *maturing learners* (children approximately eight years and above), so the literature used with the three groups is also different. To design the approach, identify the characteristics of language that will be the focus of study. Then choose fiction and nonfiction literature that contains the selected characteristics, and use the selections for language instruction and student production.[20] Representative literature to use with each age is presented in the chapter bibliography. The language characteristics and book design of the literature recommended for each group are identified in Table 11.6 on page 392 (for beginning learners), Table 11.7 on page 393 (for transitional learners), and Table 11.8 on page 394 (for maturing learners).

Instructional Components of the Approach

Literature provides an authentic context for children to explore language, see and hear sound-letter relationships, and recognize the structure of compositions. Through literary experiences children read books in a natural setting, explore language used for a purpose, and actively participate in the reading process. By "reading" and discussing the visual and verbal narratives, children grasp the importance of the relationship between visual and verbal narratives. When discussing the visual and verbal narratives, they have an opportunity to make predictions and confirmations. This literary approach gives teachers an opportunity to model book-reading techniques, use literary terminology during discussion, and, if needed, clarify the vocabulary or content. When responding to the books, children naturally use speaking, listening, writing, viewing, and thinking modalities. (For additional information about language production, see Chapter 12.)

Because a variety of instructional strategies and techniques can be used in the Literature-Based Language Arts Approach, it is a flexible approach. Teachers consider the interests and the linguistic, cognitive, and affective needs of the students before implementing the approach. Students use language modalities in authentic contexts to give them a purpose for communicating with others. The teacher uses oral techniques to present the literature; therefore, the initial introduction is an aesthetic experience. Then, when the literature is used for instructional purposes, an efferent instructional focus is used. The *connect* and *construct* components of the Literary Transaction Process (described in Chapter 2) are used as the instructional routine, and the *create* component elicits oral and written language production that supports additional language instruction. If basal readers or language textbooks are used for instructional purposes, the teacher uses the components of the Literary Transaction Process.[21]

TABLE 11.6 Literature for Beginning Learners

Fiction and nonfiction books with pictures are used with beginning learners. The children prefer literature that contains everyday experiences, action, humor, and animals. Literature with realistic, clear, bright pictures is also popular.

Participation books are picture books that elicit children's involvement with the oral reading of the story, song, poem, or drama. The oral reader encourages children to interact with participation books in the following ways: find a hidden object in an illustration, manipulate the flaps and tabs of a paper-engineered book, recite a repetitive phrase or refrain with the oral reader, count the numerals or sets of objects found on a page, sing songs with the oral reader, move to the rhythm of the language, supply the missing rhyming word at the end of a sentence, and act out the character's action.

Examples: Lorinda Bryan Cauley's *Clap Your Hands* (1992); Marc Brown's paper-engineered *Arthur Goes to School* (1996); Judy Sierra's lullaby *Good Night, Dinosaurs* (1996).

Big Books are enlarged versions of published picture storybooks. Educators designed the books for beginning literacy experiences. They give children the feeling that they are reading a book while sitting in an adult's lap. Suitable books for beginning learners are selected from the enlarged versions. Usually, the books contain repeated words and sentences, simple plots, flowing and rhythmic language, and compatible visual and verbal narratives. Big Books are generally 10 to 16 pages long. Many commercial books are now available.

Books with language play include books that feature odd or distinctive aspects of words and meanings, such as Ruth Heller's *Merry-Go-Round: A Book about Nouns* (1990); riddle books, such as Patrick Lewis's *Riddle-icious* (1996); books that play with literal interpretation of the language, such as Peggy Parish's *Good Driving, Amelia Bedelia* (1995); and books that highlight the sounds of language (alliteration, assonance, consonance, or onomatopoeia) such as Jeffie Gordon's *Six Sleepy Sheep* (1991) and C. M. Millen's *A Symphony for the Sheep* (1996).

Patterned books contain repeated language patterns and predictable words, phrases, and structures. Authors of the books enjoy playing with language. The books have some of the following characteristics:

Limited, interesting language, prose, and poetry.

Repeated, repetitive language patterns, vocabulary, phrases, and refrains.

Cadenced language and rhymes.

Appealing human or animal characters or inanimate objects.

Natural dialogue that is familiar to the children.

A simple, predictable plot that may contain repeated action.

A cumulative plot structure.

A chronological, sequential plot structure.

Questions or a question-and-answer format.

Familiar, interesting subjects.

A visual narrative that enhances, reinforces, or supplements the verbal text.

Examples: Joanna Cole's *Riding Silver Star* (1996); Douglas Forian's poetry collection *On the Wing* (1996); Patricia Lauber's *You're Aboard Spaceship Earth* (1996); Bill Martin's *"Fire! Fire!" Said Mrs. McGuire* (1996); Melanie Walsh's *Do Pigs Have Stripes?* (1996); Sue Williams's *I Went Walking* (1996).

Beginning Learners Interacting with the oral reading of literature, children observe the teacher's reading and naturally develop book-reading strategies. They become familiar with the relationship of spoken and written words, the left-to-right progression of reading, shape of words, spaces between words, punctuation marks, and the arrangement of sentences, paragraphs, pages, and entire books. Through this experience with authentic literature, children develop sight vocabulary, recognize sound-letter relationships, and learn to read with fluency and confidence. Children hear the natural cadence of language and recognize the sounds of language in the repetitive, verbal texts. As the learners' attention is focused on the written text or oral reading, they grasp the relationship between oral language and printed symbols and images. They also recognize the elements and details in the visual narrative, the arrangement of visual sequences, and the artist's use of elements, style, and media. Many primary teachers have achieved remarkable success teaching beginning reading using the literature described in Table 11.6.[22] Maturing learners enjoy writing original patterned books for beginning readers. This activity is helpful to older learners because the books contain basic sentences they can use for language instruction and can modify for original writing. Table 11.9 on page 395 suggests procedures for reading literature with beginning readers.

Transitional Learners Transitional learners use literature to reinforce and enhance beginning reading and

TABLE 11.7 Literature for Transitional Learners

Because children have experiences with quality picture storybooks before selecting this literature for independent reading, they find some books, especially older ones, stilted, contrived, and bland. Fortunately, authors have now mastered the form and are publishing more quality fiction and nonfiction books. Many series are available, but the quality of individual books varies within the series.

Easy-to-read books are picture storybooks designed to reinforce and expand the reader's limited skills and strategies. The language and plot development do not overwhelm the independent reader. Most books have the following characteristics:

The vocabulary is appropriate for the audience and includes some descriptive passages and natural conversations.

Simple sentences are frequently arranged in meaningful chunks.

Books of fiction include believable, realistic and fanciful human and animal characters, and a cohesive plot with few conflicts and incidents.

Information books include simple listing and sequence text structure.

The books have a worthwhile theme.

The content is appealing to the reader and includes topics such as humor, adventure, everyday experiences, mysteries, sports, and other special interests.

Illustrations are placed every two or three pages.

The books usually contain 32 to 48 pages. Very short chapters may be used.

The print is clear and larger than in books for maturing readers. Adequate space is left between the words and lines on each page.

Examples: David Adler's *A Picture Book of Davy Crockett* (1996); Betsy Byars's *The Joy Boys* (1996); Joanna Cole and Stephanie Calmenson's *Give a Dog a Bone: Stories, Poems, Jokes, and Riddles about Dogs* (1996); Bernice Cullinan's *A Jar of Tiny Stars* (1995); Sid Hoff's *Danny and the Dinosaur Go to Camp* (1996); Arnold Lobel's *Frog and Toad Are Friends* (1970); Margaret and Charles Wetterer's *The Snow Walker* (1996).

Transitional books are simple chapter books that bridge the gap between literature for beginning readers and literature for maturing readers. Most of the fiction and nonfiction literature have the following characteristics:

The prose and poetry are appropriate for the intended audience and include descriptive phrases and some figurative language.

The books have a worthwhile theme.

Books of fiction include a well-developed chronological plot, limited conflicts, several incidents, and believable, real and fanciful human and animal characters.

Information books with expository narratives include simple listing, sequence, and cause and effect text structures. Transitional learners also enjoy reading informational storybooks.

The books include appealing topics, such as family interactions, school experiences, sports stories, animal stories, adventures, and simple mysteries.

The print is clear and larger than in books for maturing readers. Adequate space is left between the sentences and lines.

Illustrations and photographs are included about every fourth page.

The books contain 36 to 80 pages and are the size of books for maturing readers.

Examples: Ann Cameron's *Stories Julian Tells* (1981); Dick King-Smith's *Sophie's Lucky* (1996); Robert Newton Peck's *Soup* (1974); Ogden Nash's *Custard the Dragon and the Wicked Knight* (1961); Seymour Simon's *Wildfires* (1996); Donald Sobol's *Encyclopedia Brown Tracks Them Down* (1971).

related language skills and strategies. Usually, the literature is used for independent and partner reading and group instruction. As transitional learners read a complete book, they develop self-confidence about reading. Oral and written Literary Response Modes (LRMs) give them successful experiences using language. Teachers introduce the book by giving a book talk, reading all or portions of the book to the class, or displaying it in the literature center. After completing the book, the child can recommend the book to others by giving an oral LRM. The learner can advertise the book through a visual response and keep a record of books read independently in a Book Recording Device. (See Appendix B).

The books elicit students' aesthetic responses and are especially successful for book discussions in the second through early fourth grade. When presenting a book, the teacher uses the components of the Literary Transaction Process, as described in Chapter 2. Many books contain topics included in various curricular areas and can be used for efferent purposes in subject areas in first through fourth grade.

Maturing Learners Literature is used with maturing learners to develop, enhance, and enrich various language

TABLE 11.8   Literature for Maturing Learners

Novels, short stories, poems, and plays are used to teach and reinforce reading skills and strategies. Well-written contemporary and historical realistic fiction, photo-essays, biographies, information books, traditional literature, and narrative poetry are popular genres to use for instructional purposes. The literature has most of the following characteristics:

The language is vivid, descriptive, and figurative.

Sentence structures are complex.

Books of fiction contain believable, well-developed real and fanciful humans and animal characters. The characters deal with several conflicts.

Books of fiction include well-developed, chronological plot structures with several incidents.

All forms of text structures are used in expository information books.

Books of fiction contain chapters, while information books contain appropriate organizational structures.

Authors include content that is appealing to the intended audience, such as familiar experiences, humor, mystery, survival stories, adventures, animal stories, and information about special interests.

Books of fiction frequently use literary devices, such as suspense, foreshadowing, cliffhangers, imagery, and natural conversations.

Artists include several illustrations in each chapter of the book.

The print is clear and smaller than in transitional books.

The books are the size of books for adults and contain 60 to 150 pages.

Examples: David Adler's *Cam Jansen & the Mystery of the Dinosaur Bones* (1981); Joseph Bruchac's *Children of the Longhouse* (1996); Robert Burch's *Ida Early Comes Over the Mountain* (1980); Barbara Juster Esbensen's *Echoes for the Eye* (1996); Anne Fine's *Step by Wicked Step* (1996); Johanna Hurwitz's *Class President* (1990); Jean George's *Shark Beneath the Reef* (1989); John Gardiner's *Stone Fox* (1980); James and Deborah Howe's *Howliday Inn* (1982); Margaret Mahy's *Tingleberries, Tuckertubs, and Telephones: A Tale of Love and Ice-Cream* (1996); Geraldine McCaughrean's *The Golden Hoard: Myths and Legends of the World* (1996).

Beginning learners become familiar with the spoken and written words and develop book-reading strategies as they read a big book together.

skills and strategies. Teachers and students use book talks, oral reading, and visuals to highlight the language found in the literature. Maturing learners have heard many books read aloud in the Pure Literature Approach and are thus familiar with the narratives. The Literary Transaction Process is used in small and large group sessions. Mini-lessons for skill and strategy development are presented as needed. Chapters 2, 10, and 12 and Appendix B contain additional information about using literature for instructional purposes.

TABLE 11.9 Presenting Literature to Beginning Learners

Connect the students to the book by talking about the content, literary genre, or author. Direct the students' attention to the cover and illustrations. Elicit predictions about story events using details in illustrations as clues. Ask probes such as "What do you think the book is about? Why?" "What does the picture tell you about the book?"

The teacher reads the book aloud and models fluent reading strategies. If appropriate, the teacher focuses the children's attention on the words, the patterns of language, and the verbal details of the sound-letter relationships. The students are encouraged to read with the oral reader.

Then the teacher helps the students *construct* meanings from the author's language and the artist's images. The teacher rereads the book, stops reading at strategic points, and uses techniques such as the following:

Elicit predictions about words or the storyline.

Guide a discussion of verbal and visual elements, such as artistic style, media, and compositions; note vocabulary, the story elements, and the author's style.

Ask students to recall important details, favorite parts, or supporting text for confirmation of predictions.

Use a cloze technique. Cover part of the verbal text and ask the children to repeat the covered text. Discuss the text or predict the covered words or phrases.

Use repeated reading, echo reading, or choral reading.

Group students with a partner, in a triad, or in small groups for collaborative reading. Ask them to choose a passage to read. Occasionally, they can add dialogue or assume the role of a character and read the dialogue.

Students *create* responses to the literature by using strategies such as the following:

Recite, chant, or sing the verbal text.

Prepare a story map showing major incidents in the book.

Brainstorm other incidents that could have happened in the narrative. Elicit descriptive language, new phrases, or sentences. Record on a chart and use later for oral or written responses.

Elicit sequential retelling of the verbal text. Students retell events by placing sentence strips from the narrative in the correct sequence. The teacher could provide a skeleton story outline with connectives such as *Once upon a time . . . One day . . . Then . . . Lastly . . . And then. . . .*

Encourage students to write innovations (or modifications) of the verbal text by discussing the repetitive language and suggesting ways to retain the pattern of the text, while substituting different vocabulary, repetitive phrases, refrains, and rhyming sentences.

Partners can write and illustrate original stories and poems using the patterned structure of the verbal narrative as a model.

Publish the innovations or original stories in books, or hang the sequenced pages on the bulletin board or on a clothesline as a wall story to be reread.

Write and present a play or pantomime the major action of the story.

Prepare an audio- or videotape of a favorite literary selection.

Use flannel objects or a puppet to retell the story.

Become "word detectives." Talk about an unusual word, listen to the sounds of the word and the letters within it, predict its meaning, look up the word in the dictionary, and use it appropriately in an oral or written response.

Display a word wall in the classroom of interesting words from the literature; talk about them and use them in written responses.

Certain instructional components are used with all learners in a Literature-Based Language Arts Approach. Table 11.10 on page 396 lists these instructional components.

LITERATURE ACROSS THE CURRICULUM APPROACH

Jimmy Cook began his article "Literature-Based Anything" by stating, "Want to make a subject come alive? Try a little literature."[23] After listing ways to use specific books in social studies, he concluded that writers are great researchers. Through literature-based instruction, teachers and students learn an overwhelming amount about the topic, and students meet characters who may be the same age, but lived at another time and place.

In the *Literature Across the Curriculum Approach*, literature supplements or replaces content area textbooks. The major focus is on the content, not the literature. A variety of titles, representing all literary genres and types, are used to give learners a broader understanding of each curricular area.

This approach thrived in the 1920s and 1930s, but declined when instruction began to be separated by subject areas.[24] From the 1940s to the 1980s, literature was considered

TABLE 11.10 Instructional Components of a Literature-Based Language Arts Approach

As a part of the *Pure Literature Approach,* the teacher reads aloud quality fiction or nonfiction literature each day.

Students select literature for independent reading and for some small group reading sessions. Students make choices about writing topics and techniques.

Instructional techniques focus on the following:

Constructing meanings from the verbal and visual narratives.

Discussing and using oral and written language within the context of total sentences, paragraphs, and longer syntactic patterns.

Using all language modalities in an integrated approach. For example, students read a literary selection, write a dramatic script, and present it. Simple costumes, scenery, or puppets may be prepared and used with an oral presentation.

Stimulated by the literature, students are actively involved in the production of language to help them become:

Proficient speakers and listeners.

Strategic and appreciative readers.

Effective writers who use both imitative and process writing techniques.

Creative problem solvers.

Visually literate individuals.

Reflective thinkers who choose to respond to literature.

The functional uses of language are incorporated into all instructional techniques; language is used for informative, imaginative, persuasive, expressive, and ritualistic purposes for communicating orally or in writing with others. (See Chapter 12 for additional information about the functions of language.)

Teachers discuss and model personal strategies used when reading, writing, speaking, listening, thinking, and viewing. By becoming aware of the strategies used by mature communicators, students acquire an understanding of mature language production.

Instruction is flexible and is based on the individual needs of students or of the class. It might include many grouping techniques, such as the following:

Mini-lessons as needed for language and cognitive development.

Whole class instruction.

Daily independent reading and writing sessions.

Partner reading, writing, and discussion.

Small cooperative groups for reading, discussing, and creating responses to literature.

Whole class literature discussion groups. (Additional information about grouping is presented in Chapters 2 and 12.)

Depending on the literature and the children, a variety of oral reading techniques are used, including the following:

Choral reading, in which the whole class reads the assigned section.

Shared reading and writing with adults and peers.

Repeated reading, in which the same selection is read several times.

Echo reading, in which the same passage is read immediately after or with another person.

Reading and listening to audiotapes.

Learners use process writing procedures, such as reflecting, drafting, revising, editing, and publishing. Literature naturally elicits the following writing experiences:

Written reactions and responses to the literature.

Written literary models imitating literary structures and forms.

Personal expressions and self-selected writings.

Writing to convey facts. (See Chapter 12 for additional information about using literature to elicit writing experiences.)

Highlight an awareness and understanding of narrative and expository texts through various visual strategies, such as KWL, story mapping, and other visual graphics. (Chapters 1 and 6 discuss text structures; Chapter 10 and Appendix B provide additional information about visuals.)

Students learn to adopt the appropriate stance when exploring a literary selection.

Portfolio assessment techniques are recommended for this approach. Teachers observe the students' literary maturity and participation in all sessions. Observation instruments are used for record keeping. Students are involved in reflective self-evaluation. Language artifacts and LRMs are used for informal assessment measures. Most school districts require standardized tests for comparative data. (Sample checklists and ideas for informal assessments are discussed in Chapter 2.)

a frill to be used as a special treat or if time permitted. Many people limited literature to fiction or fantasy and considered it worthless for use in content areas. These same people believed only expository writing could supply students with the information needed for instructional purposes. In the late 1970s and 1980s, an explosion of information occurred. Teachers realized they needed a different way to organize the discipline areas into cohesive structures and to provide efficient instructional systems to offer the content to students. By this time many new nonfiction literature titles had appeared, and literature was redefined to encompass both fiction and nonfiction. Soon there was a renewed interest in using literature for instructional and pleasurable reasons. Educators agreed that literature is the natural link to join the discipline areas in the curriculum.

Content area teachers teach language arts, and language arts teachers use content information for language arts instruction. Language arts, music, and art are the tools we use to express our thoughts, ideas, information, and emotions. Social studies, science, and math are the content we communicate. In language arts classes, students use content information for oral and written communication. Content area teachers invite students to use language and art modes to convey their understanding of the content. Literature is the perfect vehicle to connect curricular areas. To paraphrase the old Japanese poet:

> Only be willing to search for poetry [literature for instruction], and there will be poetry [literature].

Benefits Learners Gain from Experiences with the Approach

Subject area textbooks cover a broad range of concepts, facts, generalizations, and theories in a limited space. The textbooks must be authentic and should represent differing points of views. Authors use sparse, expository discourse and do not include the emotional and descriptive language that is the hallmark of well-written books of fiction and nonfiction. We expect expository writers to be reporters, stating the facts clearly. Textbook writers are often experts in the field, who can discuss the topic accurately. Sometimes, however, these experts have difficulty explaining basic concepts of their field in simple terms for a younger, naive audience. Therefore, some textbooks are written above the cognitive level of the intended audience, and young people do not understand the information and reject the books.

From their prior experiences reading and responding to fiction, children expect to be able to read expository text in the same way. Unless young people understand the different text structures of expository texts, they may find this type of writing confusing and quickly lose interest. (See Chapter 6 for a discussion of the text structures of nonfic-

tion literature.) Unfortunately, the round robin style of oral reading is frequently used with content area textbooks. Instead of listening to a peer read, young people try to figure out which paragraph they will read and how many "hard" words are in their paragraph. Yet children like to read literature orally. Many teachers recognize that textbooks may give authentic information, include excellent scope and sequence charts, identify suitable topics and instructional goals, but fail to excite students about the content. Frequently, too, the textbooks do not cover the topic comprehensively. Fiction and nonfiction literature, however, are well written and can cover an entire topic, especially if several books are read. As a result, literature is an excellent source to use in a content area classroom to enhance students' understanding of that area. Table 11.11

TABLE 11.11 Benefits Learners Gain from Experiences with a Literature Across the Curriculum Approach

Literature contains authentic, up-to-date information for all content areas. Textbooks become outdated very quickly and are expensive to replace.

Textbook writers have limited space to present many facts, theories, and generalizations. These concepts may be overwhelming to students who may have limited background knowledge. By reading several literary selections that deal with familiar experiences and incorporate prior information, students can link their prior knowledge to these ideas, learn new information, and gain broader insight into a subject.

Literature books are available for children of all cognitive and linguistic abilities to read and explore. Students can select books they can read with comfort and at the same time be exposed to content-related terminology, which expands their vocabulary and gives them vital information about a topic.

Literature with narrative and expository texts are used in discipline areas. Therefore, students experience the differences between these texts and, when applicable, use them in original oral and written communication.

A variety of literature selections can provide comprehensive coverage of topics, ideas, and information for each discipline area. Literature introduces children to different perspectives and a broader understanding of subject areas.

Through literature individuals vicariously experience the adventures, dreams, and thoughts of others. Narratives help students realize that famous scientists, inventors, musicians, artists, and diplomats are human beings who experienced frustrations, joys, successes, or defeats. Readers find out how these people suffered and overcame their problems and left a better world.

Literature used in the content area provides ideas and information to motivate students to use their critical and creative problem-solving abilities.

Students gain deeper insight into historical, sociological, scientific, and psychological issues when they read, hear, and discuss literature.

lists benefits learners gain from the Literature Across the Curriculum Approach.[25]

Literature and Related Materials Used in the Approach
In this approach literature is used as a supplement to and replacement for the subject area textbook. Textbook publishers, aware of past criticisms, are attempting to improve their new editions and are including more literature in their offerings. Currently, if literature is not included in a subject area textbook, the publisher will suggest titles to supplement the textbook. Bibliographies of compatible children's books are frequently found in the teacher's edition of a content area textbook. Many excellent professional materials are available to help teachers implement this approach.[26]

Teachers who are knowledgeable about literary offerings are more comfortable using only literature for instruction. The literature available in the school and community is another factor influencing how much literature is used in curricular areas. Teachers can identify potential thematic units to be used in the classroom and request that the media specialist purchase additional literature for subject area instruction.

Other teachers feel they have more instructional options by combining literature *and* textbooks in content area instruction. Before deciding the role of literature and available textbooks in curricular areas, identify school-mandated instructional goals for each content area. Ask students to suggest topics of personal interest. Combine and cluster the goals; look for natural content links between subjects. Then, review your children's textbooks. Look at the date of publication. Find out if the information is authentic, current, and readable. If so, find specific pages in the textbook that would be suitable to use. Review instructional goals that could be used during the year. Consider the topics, thematic units, instructional strategies, supplementary instructional materials, bibliographies of books, and audiovisual materials included in the text to be used with a literature-based curriculum.

In this approach, literature is organized according to Focus Books and LitSets. A *Focus Book* is an outstanding fiction or nonfiction book that presents the selected theme or related concepts and naturally stimulates related inquiry in several discipline areas. A group or the class reads the book. The book presents topics that naturally stimulate discussion of the selected curricular concepts and leads the students to related topics in various discipline areas. Not all quality literature is suitable for use as a Focus Book. Exemplary Focus Books for primary children include Riki Levinson's *I Go with My Family to Grandma's* (1986) and Jane Yolen's *Encounter* (1992). Outstanding Focus Books for third through sixth grade include John Gardiner's *Stone*

Fox (1980) and Karen Hesse's *Letters from Rifka* (1992). These books highlight the topics selected for the unit study (Levinson's book highlights families; Yolen's book gives another look at Columbus's arrival in the New World; Gardiner's book deals with family survival; and Hesse's book considers the plight of immigrants to the United States). A Literary Link for Gardiner's *Stone Fox* appears at the end of the chapter and shows various ways to use the book throughout the curriculum. A Literary Link for Marie McSwigan's *Snow Treasure* (1942) is presented in Appendix E. This book is an ideal Focus Book for children in third through sixth grade who are studying World War II.

A *LitSet* is a thematic collection of books from various genres that highlight the concepts selected for a unit of study in one or several discipline areas. Much of the bibliography in this book is organized according to topic, theme, or ethnic group. Accordingly, the reader can select compatible literature from the various genres and arrange the books in thematic LitSets. For example, the realistic fiction bibliographies for Chapter 5 are organized according to historical period and theme. Books from these lists can be combined with suitable nonfiction books from the Chapter 6 bibliographies to form a LitSet. Thematic poetry books from the Chapter 7 bibliographies and other appropriate books can then be added to the LitSet. The bibliographies for Chapter 9 are organized according to the various genres reflecting parallel cultures. Teachers can arrange these books in a LitSet for a study of a particular ethnic group. They can also select a topic, such as families or friends, find appropriate literature in Chapter 9, and combine it with compatible fiction and nonfiction literature to design a LitSet. This literature will reflect various groups' perceptions of the selected subject. A LitSet for the Appalachian region is presented in Chapter 5 and a LitSet for the Civil War is presented in the Chapter 6 bibliographies. Additional information about selecting and using Focus Books and LitSets and organizing literature in thematic arrangements is presented in Chapter 12.

Fortunately, professional organizations publish many thematic bibliographies of outstanding literature. A list of "Notable Children's Trade Books in the Field of Social Studies" is published in the April/May issue of *Social Education;* "Outstanding Science Trade Books for Children" are listed in the March issue of *Science and Children;* "Children's Choices" are published in the October issue of *The Reading Teacher;* "Notable Children's Books in the Language Arts (K–8)" are listed in the October issue of *Language Arts.* Each issue of *The Reading Teacher, Language Arts,* and *Book Links* includes thematic bibliographies of literature. Media specialists or public libraries have copies of these journals. Other professional journals, teacher references, and selection tools also publish annotated bibliographies of children's books with content-related topics. (See Appendix G for additional information about the professional materials.) When searching for quality fiction and nonfiction materials for use across the curriculum, review these sources and enlist the assistance of the children and media specialist. Guidelines for selecting literature and related materials to use in various curricular areas are listed in Table 11.12.

Instructional Components of the Approach

The purpose for presenting literature across the curriculum is different from other approaches. For example, in this approach a preschool teacher uses Max Grover's *Circles and Squares Everywhere!* (1996) in a social studies class to highlight a unique view of the urban environment or in a math class to discuss various shapes. (See the Grover color plate on page 400.) To introduce a social studies unit that

TABLE 11.12 Guidelines for Selecting Literature and Related Materials for the Literature Across the Curriculum Approach

---

Use quality fiction, nonfiction, prose, poetry, and drama in the approach.

Include the tools of the subject areas in the study, such as authentic globes and maps, scientific materials for experiments, musical instruments, actual music, charts and diagrams, speeches, diaries, oral history, and all types of media.

Select materials that are interesting and developmentally appropriate for learners.

Select materials that are compatible with the content to be taught. Eric Carl's *The Very Hungry Caterpillar* (1969) is a better choice for a counting lesson than the folktale "The Three Little Pigs," for example.

Choose materials that contain up-to-date information, theories, and generalizations. In subject areas where information is changing rapidly, a book published three years earlier is dated unless it is used to show the historical perspective of the discipline area.

In a LitSet, use a variety of books that reflect different perspectives about selected subjects in a discipline area or in several curricular areas.

Choose materials that are objective and authentic. Subjective, biased materials are not acceptable.

Include a variety of accurate materials that represent diverse populations and indicate the contributions of each group to the field.

Select materials that contain adequate details to stimulate learners' curiosity about a subject and motivate them to investigate related topics in various discipline areas.

Choose nonprint materials, such as visuals, maps, charts, pictures, and other illustrations, that accurately describe the topic and present information in a clear format with appropriate labels. (For additional information about audio and visual productions, see Chapter 10.)

---

highlights the relationship between Native Americans and early pioneers a second-grade teacher reads aloud Angela Medearis's *Dancing with the Indians* (1991), while a fifth-grade teacher reads aloud Elizabeth George Speare's *The Sign of the Beaver* (1983). While reading aloud a Focus Book, the teacher assumes an aesthetic stance to the book. Later, when the teacher returns to the literature and emphasizes the content of the book, an efferent instructional focus is assumed. The teacher directs the learners' attention to the relationships among the characters, the differences between the lifestyles of the groups, and the historical information about the times. When selected concepts are presented in LitSets, literature becomes the primary or supplementary instructional material, and the teacher implements a Literature Across the Curriculum Approach. Throughout the unit of study, the teacher might read aloud thematic literature during the Pure Literature Approach and use other appropriate related materials for the Literature-Based Language Arts Approach. In this integrated approach, literature becomes the link to help students acquire knowledge and skills, discover the relationships that exist between discipline areas, and transfer the information across disciplines.[27]

Literature exposes students to authentic situations where they can apply higher-order thinking as they solve problems and engage in scientific inquiry that creates and re-creates knowledge. Teachers use a cyclical learning process: after reading the literature, students define a problem (conflict), ask probes and questions, find answers from several types of data, reflect on the problem, and develop a solution. By applying the information in different contexts, students can evaluate the results and reach conclusions.[28]

Through appropriate instructional strategies, students are encouraged to construct meanings, gain insights, and acquire new knowledge in authentic, real contexts. Learners use language to respond to the new understandings in natural, functional ways that give them a reason for expressing their ideas and interpretations to others. (See photo on page 401.) Students might need explicit instruction to help them gain some vital information. The *connect, construct,* and *create* components of the Literary Transaction Process, discussed in Chapter 2, are suitable instructional routines to use with literature in content areas. Table 11.13 on page 401 lists instructional components that are frequently found in the Literature Across the Curriculum Approach.[29]

✹ THE SUPPORT TEAM

Without the support of the media specialist and the students' parents or guardians, all literature approaches would be difficult to implement. As we have learned more about

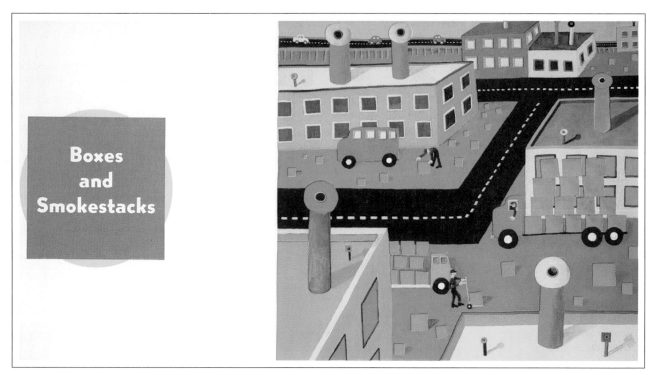

Max Grover uses simple shapes—squares, circles, rectangles—to portray the various objects found in the city in his book, Circles and Squares Everywhere! *Simple words accompany his bright acrylic paintings.*

children's development and learning and use literature differently throughout the curriculum, the roles of the teacher, media specialist, and parents or guardians have changed. This section of the chapter will discuss ways to involve the support team in the development and delivery of successful literature approaches.

THE MEDIA SPECIALIST

When you first join a faculty, you will want to meet several people immediately (not necessarily in this order)—the administration, the administrative staff, the custodian, and the media specialist.[30] The administration and staff will give you the rules of order, the custodian will help keep your room clean, and the media specialist will serve as the liaison between teachers, schools, and the district instructional materials center.

In most schools the media specialist wears many hats simultaneously (reminding us of *The 500 Hats of Bartholomew Cubbins* by Dr. Seuss). The first hat is the media specialist's job to keep the media center—the heart of the school—well stocked and running efficiently. For most people, the job of purchasing, cataloging, processing, sorting, advertising, and circulating thousands of books, media productions, and all the equipment and supplies for

twenty to fifty people or more would be all they could do, but not the media specialist—the superperson of the school!

Another hat most media specialists enjoy wearing is serving as a curriculum consultant. In this job they answer teachers' inquiries about the availability of books, multimedia technologies, and audiovisual productions and related equipment and supplies. To find the most appropriate materials, the media specialist must be knowledgeable about the curriculum. Therefore, he or she should be involved in curricular planning or consulted about suitable materials for possible thematic offerings. Media specialists can give professional advice about curricular decisions if they participate in professional development sessions for new and existing programs. To wear the hat of a curriculum consultant, the media specialist needs teachers and administrators who will review available materials and suggest topics or titles of materials needed for instructional units. Occasionally, a supportive administrator will ask the media specialist to talk at faculty meetings about procedures or issues related to the center, the availability of selection tools, teacher references, indexes, maps, children's and professional magazines, and new literature. The media specialist is a valuable member of the Teacher as Reader Groups.

After reading several books about a historical event, students create replicas of the setting.

TABLE 11.13 Instructional Components of a Literature Across the Curriculum Approach

Teachers schedule large blocks of time to give students time to investigate a topic. Students might read literature with selected subject concepts in language arts class; then, in subject area classes, they can discuss, write about, and respond to the information gained from literature.

Quality fiction and nonfiction literature with selected subject concepts are chosen for use in this approach.

Selected concepts are presented in Focus Books and LitSets.

A variety of materials, such as newspapers, magazines, reference books, atlases, and laboratory equipment, are also utilized in the approach.

Suitable visuals, posters, pictures, games, experiments, recipe books, computer programs, manipulative objects, puppets, and audio and video media are selected for use.

The teacher reads aloud, gives book talks, and employs other oral techniques to introduce the selected literature and share it with the students.

All models of grouping, such as individuals, partners, small cooperative groups, and whole class session, are employed depending on the learners, concepts, and selected literature. (Additional information about grouping is presented in Chapter 12.)

Students obtain knowledge about the topic and share their understandings through oral and written response modes.

Students read, hear, and view the selected materials and respond to important concepts by using various graphic organizers, concept maps, and oral and written techniques.

Written, oral, and visual responses are directly related to the information and interpretations students make from the reading, writing, and discussions.

Students are taught the principles of scientific inquiry and encouraged to conduct research in all the discipline areas.

Students question information and verify and support personal points of view through various oral and written modes, such as role-playing, debates, and other research-based experiences.

Students actively participate in instructional activities that focus on identified goals, major concepts, and knowledge. Information is acquired by using integrated processes, not isolated activities. For example, learners might re-create history by researching a historical person's environment and presenting a conversation between the person's friends. The conversation will include information about the lifestyle of people at that particular period. Also, students could conduct scientific experiments mentioned in a book or interview scientists about their work.

As needed, teachers discuss the different text structures used in expository writings, use appropriate graphic organizers to represent those structures with students, and have the students practice identifying, mapping, and comparing the structures of a text. Students spend time comparing fiction and nonfiction text structures. They identify and compare the facts, generalizations, theories, or fiction found in the literature.

The media specialist's third hat involves working with children. Media specialists teach children how to find, select, and check out print and nonprint materials. Like the teacher, a media specialist's goal is to help children develop a lifelong habit of reading literature and viewing media for recreational and informational purposes. To wear this hat, the specialist needs time to teach children library skills. Mature students are taught checkout procedures and techniques for stocking the library shelves and are used as library assistants. Media specialists like to give book talks, read aloud, and tell students stories and poems. (See the photo below.) They usually spend time with the children in the center or in individual classrooms discussing literature, answering questions about related books and creators, and helping children select books for personal reading. They demonstrate how to use multimedia equipment and encourage students to practice using it to develop programs designed for multimedia technologies. Frequently, media specialists serve as consultants for schoolwide television or radio productions. Obviously, their skills as professional educators and media and literature specialists are used extensively for this very important hat.

The fourth hat is worn when the media specialist organizes author visits, displays LRMs produced by individual students, arranges incentives to read, offers book awards, organizes book fairs, and provides other activities to involve children with literature and media. Book fairs are scheduled events where books are sold. Book vendors, bookstore owners, and other commercial organizations, such as RIF

(Reading Is Fundamental), usually supply the books. The media specialist arranges the center, elicits assistants to sell the books, and organizes the schedule for the fair. The specialist's major concern is the selection of quality books for the fair. Teachers, administrators, children, and parents or guardians can assist the media specialist. Companies supplying the books must be carefully selected. The quality of the literature sends a strong message to the community about the priority the school places on children's programs. A fair consisting of stickers, books with television ties, or commercial pap is not impressive.

Changes and Concerns

Media specialists report that the way teachers use literature greatly influences the type of books children request and the kinds of requests the children make.[31] In schools implementing literature-based approaches, the children use the library more. They ask for specific titles, request books by literary genres, search for fiction and nonfiction literature highlighting a particular topic, and request works by a particular author or artist. Children come to the library to research topics. Most boys and girls know how to use technologies to find specific materials and information. Today more children request more information books, early chapter books, and books for emergent readers, such as predictable books and concept books.

To accommodate these uses of the media center, we must address certain concerns. First, the media center needs to be open all day. To do this, children or parent or

The media specialist is an important part of the instructional team. A favorite hat worn by the specialist is introducing quality literature to children that they may choose for independent reading.

guardian volunteers will be needed. Second, the library collection should be broad enough to offer several fiction and nonfiction books on the same topic and several copies of the popular books. Because the reading abilities and requests of individual children differ, a variety of books and nonprint materials are needed for individual reading. Teachers need multiple copies of Focus Books and media specialists help them obtain the books.

The needs of children and teachers create a dilemma for media specialists—they need time to wear all the hats, time to develop the collection, time to order books, and time to catalog and check them out. Furthermore, media specialists require funds to purchase the needed materials. All faculty members, administrators, parents or guardians, and children can help the media specialist solve these problems, because the available materials affect the quality of the educational programs a school offers.

Professional Partners

Before students visit a library, talk to them about techniques for finding print and nonprint materials and manners in a library. Games such as a "treasure hunt" with clues for finding specific books, materials, references, and literary genres are helpful and appreciated by media specialists.

Kulleseid and Strickland summarize the relationship between the teacher and media specialist by calling them professional partners.[32] This is a partnership between people who "inspire and energize each other," "share expertise and ideas," are "natural allies," and "reach out" and share responsibilities for instruction and the education of children.

INVOLVEMENT OF PARENTS OR GUARDIANS

A partnership of parents or guardians, teacher, and child is crucial to the development of a successful literature approach. Two of the seventeen conclusions drawn from research by the Commission on Reading refer to the role parents (or caregivers) play in classroom programs:

> They help build a "foundation" for their children learning to read, write, speak, and become literate. They are also obligated to support the child's growth as a learner.

The commission suggested that parents or guardians talk about books with their children, read to them, and write with them (as in the photograph below). The commission also recommended that parents or guardians take regular trips with their children to the library (as in the photograph on page 406); encourage reading for pleasure; if possible, purchase children's books; provide time and support for homework; and place reasonable limits on activities such as watching television.[33]

Numerous books have been written about parents or guardians as partners with teachers. Most professional organizations have prepared brochures for teachers to distribute to parents or guardians, and many teacher magazines have monthly articles devoted to the subject.[34] Thus, an abundance of materials is readily available on the subject. Here we will consider ways for teachers to link parents

Sitting in a parent's lap is the best way for a young child to share the pleasure of literature.

or guardians with literature and propose the ABCs for parents or guardians.

Teachers Link Parents or Guardians to Literature
The following suggestions are successful, but check with your administrator before implementing them:

Get to know your students' parents or guardians. Don't wait for an emergency call. Write and invite them to visit school—just for fun. If invited, visit them in the home. By getting to know the parents or guardians, you understand the child.

Communicate individually through letters, dialogue journals, informal conversations, or telephone visits. Celebrate the child's successes, express your concerns, or point out areas needing improvement.

Send biweekly or monthly classroom newsletters home. Include chitchat about what has happened in school and special activities in the future, and list two to five books the parents or guardians might like to share with their children. Ask the children to help write the newsletter and add simple annotations to the book bibliography. If the parents or guardians speak a language other than English, have written communications translated into their native language.

Find ways for all parents or guardians to help at school. Parents or guardians who are at home can help in the traditional ways, such as field trips and socials; working parents or guardians can help their children make crafts or visuals at home for use in instructional activities.

Invite parents or guardians, grandparents, or adult friends who have had unique experiences to come to school and share the experiences. Artifacts are fascinating to the students.

Invite parents or guardians or local celebrities to be "VIP (Very Important Person) readers, storytellers, or artists."

Elicit the Parent-Teacher Group to develop a volunteer citizens group to help with various classroom and library activities. Help the group prepare an attractive bulletin of jobs teachers have requested. Distribute the list throughout the community. Include the name of a person to contact for volunteer work.

Request books in good condition, attractive magazines, and other supplies for the classroom centers. Involve parents or guardians in collecting books for literature thematic units.

Involve children in preparing book packets containing popular softcover books, home activities, and tapes that can be checked out, taken home, enjoyed with parents or guardians, and returned.

Early in the year have a meeting outlining classroom routines, themes, Focus Books, topics to be discussed during the year, goals for the year, and the like. Elicit input from parents or guardians. After the meeting, send out a short written recap of the meeting. Several times during the year conduct Make n'Take workshops for parents or guardians to offer ideas they can use at home with literature.

Ask parents or guardians who have computers or typewriters to type child's original book. Have a parent or guardian publishing committee bind the books. (A grade or schoolwide publishing committee is preferable.)

Ask parents or guardians who have camcorders to videotape special performances.

Always treat each parent or guardian as your very best, new friend. Be available, caring, and encouraging.

Remember that parents or guardians and caregivers are your best allies! Table 11.14 on page 405 presents the ABCs for parents or guardians.

✳ REFLECTION GUIDES FOR THE THREE APPROACHES TO LITERARY STUDY

Teachers need to review and document the effectiveness of a literary study and the total literature curriculum. (See the lower photo on page 406.) To help them accomplish this goal, Tables 11.15, 11.16, and 11.17 on pages 407–412 provide a reflection guide for each literary approach.

USING THE REFLECTION GUIDES

A reflection guide helps teachers think about the selected literature, the related materials, the selected instructional goals, the instruction strategies used during the approach, and their role while presenting the literature. The guides are used as a planning guide, as a description of the components of the total literature curriculum, and as a guide for peer coaching. The following questions help the reviewer identify successes, weakness, omissions, or unnec-

TABLE 11.14 ABCs for Parents or Guardians

Arrange your schedule to share books with each child daily.

Be a reading buddy; encourage other members of the family, especially male members, to join the group. Read a book together, talk about it, and find other books on the same topic or by the same author or illustrator.

Contract with your child to read a certain number of pages of a book or a certain number of books. Reward the child with a new book or some other nonedible treat.

Discuss the books, stories, and poems that were your favorites when you were a child; reminisce about personal experiences sharing books with the child's grandparents, a favorite niece, a friend, or another special person in your early life.

Elicit written dialogue from your child. Write a question, and ask for a written answer.

Fathers make wonderful readers and have great stories to tell! (See the photograph on page 406.)

Give your child a gift certificate from a bookstore for her or his birthday or another special event. Take the child to the bookstore to select the book.

Have an adult book on the end table and let your child see you reading for pleasure.

Invite older siblings and grandparents to read, tell stories, or sing with your child.

Join a children's book club.

Keep a list of favorite books that you remember from your childhood or that are suggested by older siblings, grandparents, friends, or other acquaintances. Check out the books at the library and read them together.

Listen to and respect your child's reactions to a story or poem. Talk informally about the reaction by asking questions such as, "Why did you like the book?" "Did _____ remind you of someone we know?"

Monitor the television programs, videos, and movies your child watches. View them together and talk about the content in the program.

Note the names of juvenile books highly recommended in newspapers, magazines, and other sources.

Open an account for your child to use to purchase one special softcover book or an educational toy once a month or every three months. Take this money from funds for candy or snacks.

Purchase a yearly magazine subscription for your child. Encourage the child to cut out favorite poems, stories, or songs; decorate the selections; and place them in a scrapbook.

Quiz your parents or elderly friends in a nursing home about the books they read as a child, how they learned to read "in the old days," or other reading, school-related experiences. Share the information with the children.

Request recommended books from libraries or bookstores. Read and talk about them with your child. Ask your child to write personal comments about the books. At the same time, write your thoughts about the books, and share them with your child.

Set up a special place for your child to read, write, draw, or sing. Help your child decorate the space to make it special—like literature.

Take your child to a ballet, theater production, or musical based on a popular children's story.

Understand that occasionally your child will not want to talk about the book he or she is reading (or has not finished reading).

Volunteer to participate in classroom and library activities.

Wait patiently while your child chooses a book to check out from the library.

X out any idea that does not work with your child and add two new ones he or she suggests.

Yard sales often have excellent, inexpensive juvenile books.

Zero in on the kinds of books and topics your child likes; then find books to share with her or him about the subject.

essary components of each literary study and the total literature curriculum:

Were the stated goals accomplished?

Were the literature and related materials developmentally appropriate for students, and did they represent quality selections for all literary structures and forms?

Did the instructional focus highlight appropriate aspects of the literature?

Did the instructional strategies consider the needs, interests, and aptitudes of the students?

Did the instructional techniques elicit student responses?

Did the teacher assume the appropriate roles and responsibilities during the study?

Each reflection guide is divided into three sections. The first section requests information about the teacher, class, and selected literature. The second section identifies components included in an approach to literary study. Finally, the third section provides space for additional reflections and suggested modifications of the selected literature, related materials, and instructional components.

What a great way to spend time with Dad—reading a book in the library!

A successful literature curriculum is measured by the children's eagerness to create responses to the literature they have explored.

The checklist in the second section of each guide allows the teacher to determine the achievement of individual components. We suggest the following ratings:

5 = effective achievement.

3–4 = achievement.

2 = some achievement.

1 = unsuccessful.

NA = not applicable.

The comment box is used to clarify ratings or make notations for the future.

The completed reflection guide could be placed with the instructional materials used during a thematic study and reviewed before the study is presented again. Teachers can compare the results of individual thematic studies and decide the overall effectiveness of the literature curriculum.

TABLE 11.15   Reflection Guide: Pure Literature Approach

Teacher's Name			Grade Level		Number of Students			

Literature Presented

CRITERIA	1	2	3	4	5	COMMENTS
Goals A predominantly aesthetic stance is assumed toward the selection. Outstanding literary elements or nonfiction standards are highlighted. A variety of literary genres are presented throughout the year. Various notable writers and artists are discussed. The opportunity for students to select and personally respond to literature is stressed.						
Literature Student preferences were considered. Selection had high literary merit. Poetry, drama, narratives, and expository texts were used to highlight literary conventions (or elements), the author or artist's style, and the content of the selection. Classical and contemporary selections were presented. Throughout the year, selections included diverse cultures, ethnic and racial groups, and both genders. During the year, selections reflected the literary heritage and authentic lifestyles and issues related to various groups. The selections contained interesting topics, appealing conventions, and various genres.						
Instructional Strategies Literary conventions were discussed and explored, not analyzed. The teacher read aloud daily to children. Appropriate terminology was used to discuss conventions and genres. The instructional focus was primarily on an aesthetic stance toward the text. Selected models of grouping were effective. Book talks and storytelling were presented periodically. Language strategies were modeled, discussed, and practiced. Mini-lessons were implemented when needed. Appropriate probes and prompts were modeled, discussed, and practiced. Suitable media were used with literature. Notable writers and artists were discussed.						

(Continued)

TABLE 11.15 *(Continued)*

CRITERIA	1	2	3	4	5	COMMENTS
Student Responses						
Students willingly expressed reflections, reactions, and responses in oral or written modalities.						
Students questioned and discussed issues highlighted in topics, content, and art of literature.						
Students willingly discussed author's craft.						
Students expressed an interest in illustrations and the artistic merit of pictures.						
Students used an appropriate stance toward the text.						
Students participated appropriately in group and independent reading, in writing, and in oral sessions.						
Students expressed an interest in reading for pleasure and information.						
Teacher						
Expressed enthusiastic responses to the text.						
Used a predominantly aesthetic instructional focus.						
Used an efferent stance if needed to clarify interpretations and literary conventions; employed limited analysis of text.						
Was prepared to ask suitable probes and prompts at appropriate times.						
Recognized background of students when connecting students to the text, making intratextual connections, and helping students construct meanings of the text.						
Valued students' personal reactions to the text.						
Identified suitable instructional goals.						
Used instructional techniques that focused on authentic contexts and natural, integrated, authentic oral and written processes.						
Evaluation						
Reflected effectiveness of selected approach.						
Used suitable observation of the student's participation.						
Used suitable informal instruments to assess the student's literary growth and maturity.						

Comments

Identify strengths, areas for improvement, and unnecessary or omitted instructional components:

TABLE 11.16 Reflection Guide: Literature-Based Language Arts Approach

Teacher's Name		Grade Level		Number of Students			

Literature Presented							

CRITERIA	1	2	3	4	5	COMMENTS
Goals						
Approach helps learners acquire and enhance reading, writing, speaking, listening, and thinking skills.						
Approach helps learners become strategic speakers, readers, writers, and thinkers.						
Initially, a predominantly aesthetic stance is assumed toward literature; later an efferent stance might be adopted.						
Various notable writers and artists are discussed.						
Approach helps students develop the habit of selecting and responding to literature.						
Literature						
Quality, meaningful selections were used.						
A variety of literary genres were presented.						
Selections provided exemplary models to be explored by students and to stimulate creative expressions.						
Poetry, drama, narratives, and expository texts were used to stimulate students' reflections, reactions, and responses to topics.						
Classical and contemporary selections containing topics of interest to students were presented.						
During the year, selections included diverse cultures, ethnic and racial groups, and both genders.						
Selections reflecting the literary heritage and authentic issues related to various groups were used.						
Focus Books and LitSets were used.						
Instructional Strategies						
Literary conventions were discussed and explored, not analyzed.						
The teacher read aloud daily to students.						
Appropriate terminology was used to discuss conventions and genres.						
Independent, partner, small group, and whole class models were used.						
Periodically, book talks and storytelling were presented.						
Language strategies were modeled, discussed, and practiced.						
Mini-lessons were implemented to help students become strategic readers, speakers, listeners, writers, and thinkers.						
Appropriate probes and prompts were modeled, discussed, and practiced.						
Suitable media were used with literature.						
Notable writers and artists were discussed.						

(Continued)

TABLE 11.16 *(Continued)*

CRITERIA	1	2	3	4	5	COMMENTS
Student Responses						
Students willingly express reflections, reactions, and responses in oral or written modalities.						
Students questioned and discussed outstanding elements and issues highlighted in the topics and content.						
Students willingly discussed the author's craft.						
Students expressed an interest in illustrations and the artistic merit of pictures.						
Students used appropriate stance toward the text.						
Students participated appropriately in group and independent reading, in writing, and in oral sessions.						
Students expressed an interest in reading for pleasure and information.						
Teacher						
Expressed enthusiastic responses to the text.						
Used an aesthetic instructional focus.						
Used an efferent instructional focus to help students acquire specific language arts skills and strategies.						
Assumed a teacher-participant role in group discussions.						
Was prepared to ask suitable probes and prompts at appropriate times.						
Recognized background of students when connecting students to the text, making intratextual connections, and helping students construct meanings of the text.						
Valued students' personal reactions to the text.						
Used instructional techniques that focused on authentic contexts and natural, integrated oral and written processes.						
Evaluation						
Reflected effectiveness of selected approach.						
Used suitable observation of the student's participation.						
Used suitable informal instruments to assess the student's literary growth and maturity.						

Comments

Identify strengths, areas for improvement, and unnecessary or omitted instructional components:

TABLE 11.17 Reflection Guide: Literature Across the Curriculum Approach

Teacher's Name		Grade Level		Number of Students			

Topic	Subject Areas Included			Literature Presented			

CRITERIA	1	2	3	4	5	COMMENTS
Goals Literature is used for instruction in integrated approach. Both aesthetic and efferent stances are assumed toward the text. Selected goals, topics, and outcomes are identified and accomplished. Major contributors to a field are brought to life through literature. Students have the opportunity to select and respond to literature.						
Literature Contained accurate, compatible information for content. Contained current information, theories, and generalizations. Different perspectives were presented. Reflected diverse populations, their contributions to the discipline area, and authentic issues related to the groups. Poetry, drama, narratives, and expository texts were used to highlight topics portrayed in the book. Selections contained adequate details to stimulate further study. Literature was presented as Focus Books or LitSets.						
Instructional Strategies Instructional strategies focused on selected topics and goals in one or several content areas. Large blocks of time were arranged for several discipline areas to be taught together. Different text structures were introduced and discussed; students used them for oral and written responses. Principles of critical inquiry were discussed and used by students for conducting research. Whole class, independent, partner, and small groupings were used. Periodically, book talks and storytelling were presented. Emphasis was placed on students' recognizing those concepts shared by more than one discipline area. Mini-lessons were used when needed. All language modalities were used to respond to new understandings. Other print and nonprint materials were used. Games, maps and tools of the discipline were used.						

(Continued)

TABLE 11.17 *(Continued)*

CRITERIA	1	2	3	4	5	COMMENTS
Student Responses Students willingly asked questions and sought verification or support for information given. Students were actively involved in solving problems and creating and re-creating knowledge. Oral or written language was used to convey higher-order thinking and transfer concepts across disciplines. Students were involved in identifying, creating, and using various text structures to communicate ideas and information gained from reading and discussing books. Students willingly discussed personal understandings and ideas. Students used an appropriate stance toward the text. Students participated appropriately in group and independent reading, in writing, and in oral sessions. Students expressed an interest in reading for pleasure and information.						
Teacher Enthusiastically used various literary selections for instructional purposes. Identified discipline areas incorporated in the study. Identified subject area goals and incorporated them all equally into the study. Used an aesthetic instructional focus, when applicable. Used an efferent stance to help students acquire information in authentic contexts. Was prepared to ask suitable probes and prompts at appropriate times. Recognized background of students when connecting them to the text, making intratextual connections, and helping them construct meanings and comprehend important content-related theories and generalizations. Valued students' personal understandings of content. Used instructional techniques that focused on authentic contexts and natural, integrated oral and written processes.						
Evaluation Reflected on effectiveness of selected approach. Used suitable observation of the student's participation. Used suitable informal instruments to assess the student's literary maturity.						
Comments Identify strengths, areas for improvement, and unnecessary or omitted instructional components:						

ADMINISTRATIVE AND SCHOOLWIDE ASSESSMENT OF THE LITERATURE CURRICULUM

Teachers can place completed reflection guides in their professional portfolios to document their successes using literature in various curricular areas and to show how literature was used through the year. The reflection guides are especially helpful to use when planning future literary studies in the total literature curriculum. The guides are *not* intended to measure a teacher's ability to teach literature and related areas.[35]

Administrators can use the following questions to measure the effectiveness and quality of a schoolwide literature curriculum:

Is literature presented continuously and effectively in all classrooms?

Do most of the students choose to read literature for recreational and informational purposes?

Are students enthusiastic about sharing reactions, responses, and interpretations of literary selections with peers and school personnel?

Are teachers enthusiastic about reading and sharing books with children?

Do teachers use literature for purposes identified in the various approaches to literary study?

Are the classrooms saturated with print and nonprint materials?

Are instructional decisions influenced by the students' interests, needs, and aptitudes and by the literary merit and content of the selected literature?

Are students actively involved in the selection of literature?

Does the school administration provide adequate facilities and suitable numbers of quality books to meet the instructional needs of the literature curriculum?

Summary

Literature has been a part of the school curriculum since priests used expensive manuscripts to teach some children to read and write. After the invention of the printing press, children were taught to read religious materials and other literature intended primarily for adults. By the mid-eighteenth century John Newbery, an English printer, had begun to publish books to amuse children.

Over the centuries, various instructional techniques have been used to teach children to read and write. This chapter discusses the historical development of literary study and the major theoretical foundations for different instructional programs as represented by the author-driven theories and the reader-response theories.

Three approaches are used independently or simultaneously in today's literature curriculum: the Pure Literature Approach, the Literature-Based Language Arts Approach, and the Literature Across the Curriculum Approach. The benefits individuals gain from each approach, the goals of the literary study, the literature and materials used in each approach, and the instructional components are identified and discussed in the chapter. Reflection guides for determining the effectiveness of each literary study were presented.

To implement the literary approaches successfully, a teacher needs a support team including the media specialist and the students' parents or guardians. The media specialist plays many roles and is involved in an active partnership with the teacher. Parents or guardians can become involved in the literature approaches in many ways. The ABCs for parents or guardians suggest ways parents can support the literary approaches. A Literary Link for John Gardiner's *Stone Fox* appears at the end of the chapter.

GARDINER, J. 1980. *STONE FOX*. (ILLUSTRATOR: MARCIA SEWALL). NEW YORK: HARPER & ROW.

ANNOTATION

Little Willy knew he had to win the National Dogsled Race to make enough money to pay the back taxes on grandfather's farm. He knew Stone Fox had always won the race to make money for his people. Little Willy was hopeful because Searchlight was a strong dog, who had often made the run through the Wyoming snow. Grandfather must get well!

- Genre: Historical fiction
- Theme: "Where there's a will, there's a way!" (stated)
- Setting: Early twentieth century; rural Jackson, Wyoming, on a potato farm (integral)
- Illustrations: Realistic, authentic, black and white drawings

CHARACTERS

- Little Willy: Determined, loving, brave (developed)
- Stone Fox: Strong, determined, fierce competitor (flat)
- Grandfather: Depressed, hopeless, sick, farmer (flat)
- Doc Smith: Wise, observant, caring woman (flat)

READING AND WRITING   The learner will:

- Use context clues for language development.
- Use all language modalities for responses.
- Use foreshadowing and descriptive and figurative language in personal writing and speaking.

IMPLEMENTATION (check grouping used)

- Whole class: _____
- Literature discussion groups: _____
- Independent reading: _____
- Partner reading: _____
- Curricular areas: Language, history, economics, science, math, art (see Table 11.8)
- Approximate time required: Two to three weeks
- Age of students: Nine to eleven years

LITERARY GOALS   The learner will:

- Recognize the use of foreshadowing.
- Identify and respond to characterization.
- Relate the theme to her or his own life.
- Vicariously experience the excitement of the race.
- Identify and relate the sequence of the plot.
- Distinguish characteristics of a legend.

INSTRUCTIONAL OUTCOMES (see Table 11.8 on page 394)

SCIENCE   The learner will:

- Become familiar with life on a farm, including planting, production, and equipment.
- Understand the role of dogs in human occupations and hobbies.

MATHEMATICS   The learner will:

- Become familiar with graphs, measurements, and weights.
- Understand items in a budget.

MUSIC   The learner will identify and sing Native American music.

SOCIAL STUDIES   The learner will:

- Understand taxes and the use of tax money.
- Know about the history, population, and geographic locations of Wyoming.
- Understand the history and lifestyle of Native American tribes on reservations in Wyoming and compare them to the present.
- Understand the equipment and procedures of dogsled racing.

ART   The learner will:

- Experiment with (potato) printing.
- Compare black and white sketches to colored paintings.

CONNECT TO THE TEXT

- *Literature center:* Display Indian artifacts and pictures and figurines of a dog sled and other objects to represent the content of the novel. Examples include a dog, dogsled, potatoes, and pictures of Native Americans. Have information books available for a discussion of Wyoming, historical and contemporary Native Americans in the area, dogsledding, snow sledding, water skiing, farming, potatoes, and training dogs. If possible, have news articles about dogsledding, especially the 1,160-mile Iditarod Trail Sled Dog Race held at the end of March from Anchorage to Nome, Alaska.
- *Genre information:* This book is classified as historical realistic fiction and as an adventure story. (See chapters in this book for additional information about this genre and related literature.) Highlight foreshadowing, characters, theme, setting, and events and content.

- A *model book talk*: "Go Searchlight! Go!" Little Willy loved his big, black dog Searchlight, who was born on his birthday more than ten years ago. Whether Searchlight was pulling a plow or a sled, Willy knew he could depend on his old friend. In the cold Wyoming winter, when the snow was on the ground, Willy hitched Searchlight to the sled for the five-mile trip to school. Often, after school they went to town to sell Grandfather's potatoes or to get supplies for Grandfather. At exactly 6:00 each evening they raced the five miles home. Searchlight knew the way. Little Willy stood on the sled and felt the sting of the cold air on his face. They always made the trip in record time. One evening when they arrived home, a man was waiting for them. Little Willy knew he had to talk to him since Grandfather was sick. Why was the man there? What did he tell Willy that made him realize he would have to save Grandfather's farm? How would he do it? Would he and Searchlight be able to race in the National Dog Race? Could they beat Stone Fox who always won the race? Then he remembered Grandfather's words, "Where there's a will, there's a way!"
- *Word Wall*: The teacher will begin a Word Wall that includes suggested language (in the next section), content-related language, unknown phrases, and sentences from the book. (See Appendix B.) After each chapter, have a different group of students add interesting, unusual, descriptive words to the wall.

CONSTRUCT MEANINGS

Note: In the heading for each segment, the title of the chapter is in quotation marks. First, the type of grouping for the chapter is suggested. The Introduction suggests a way to introduce the chapter. Language suggests words that might be highlighted, and Probes and Prompts suggests possible probes and prompts.

While sharing the book, emphasize the characterization, setting, and the author's use of foreshadowing, theme, and content.

CHAPTER 1: "GRANDFATHER"   Teacher Read Aloud to the whole class.

- *Introduction*: In this chapter we are introduced to the *protagonists* (the main characters) and their problems.
- *Language*: *Harmonica* (musical instrument; a mouth organ); *palomino* (a gold-colored horse with a light mane and tail).
- *Probes and prompts*: What can Little Willy do to help Grandfather feel better? Why doesn't Grandfather want to live?
- Students begin LitLogs.

CHAPTER 2: "LITTLE WILLY"   Partner Reading and Discussion.

- *Introduction*: How can ten-year-old Willy help?
- *Language*: *Mare* (female horse); *strongbox* (secure box for money and important papers); *concerned*

(worried); *harness* (leather straps to be attached to an animal that will pull a *sled*—(look at the illustration on p. 20); *bushel* (a measure for crops).
- *Probes and prompts*: Grandfather is still not well. If his problem is not the crops, what could it be?

CHAPTER 3: "SEARCHLIGHT"   Literature Discussion Groups.

- *Introduction*: This chapter tells more about the characters and their problems. You will also find out more about Little Willy and Searchlight's adventures in the snow. Remember that the story is set in rural Jackson, Wyoming, in the early 1900s. In this chapter you will find out more about winter in Wyoming. Compare winter in Wyoming to winter in your state.
- Begin group *character attribute chart*.
- *Language*: *Purchased* (bought); *deposited* (put something in a safe place such as a bank); *city slickers* (people who live in the city and are not clever about country ways and life).
- *Probes and prompts*: What does the author mean when he says, "The owner of the horse stood on the front porch and watched them, tapping his foot impatiently"? When the author writes this way, what comes to your mind? The author uses a *stylistic device* called *foreshadowing*. The author builds suspense about the plot by giving slight clues to alert the reader to events that might occur later. Gardiner often uses foreshadowing to introduce the chapter, during the chapter, and at the end of the chapter. Does foreshadowing take away from the suspense of the adventure?

CHAPTER 4: "THE REASON"   Partner Reading.

- *Introduction*: Discuss the chapter title and the picture on p. 31.
- *LitLog*: Note the word *derringer* (a small pistol) on p. 30. Write in your log what you think will happen.
- *Language*: *Ricocheting* (skipping motion of an object as it goes along a flat surface); "twang of a ricocheting bullet" refers to screeching, fast-spoken words; *authority* (person in charge). What does *official* mean? What does Snyder mean when he says, "And anyway, it's the law. Plain and simple."
- *Probes and prompts*: Who does Snyder represent? Does he have a right to talk to Little Willy that way? What do you think about Snyder? Why is Grandfather sick? Why didn't he pay the taxes? (Does the author tell us? Where?)

CHAPTER 5: "THE WAY"   Teacher Read Aloud; use "Reciprocal Technique." (See Chapter 12.)

- *Introduction*: Grandfather tells Little Willy, "Where there's a will, there's a way." (Theme) What does this mean?
- *Language*: *Samoyeds* (Siberian huskies; white sled dogs).
- *Probes and prompts*: What are Samoyeds? Will Stone Fox be difficult to beat? Why did Grandfather cry when Little Willy told him about his plan? What does Grandfather know?

CHAPTER 6: "STONE FOX"   Literature Discussion Groups.

- *Introduction:* In this chapter we are finally introduced to Stone Fox. Add more information to your *LitLogs* and the *character attribute chart.*

- *Language: Amateur* (not experienced); *stunned* (shocked; bewildered). What does the author mean when he says, "He felt ten feet tall"? *Legend* (fictional telling of a real or imaginary event); *awesome* (inspiring respective fear); *Arapaho* (Indian tribe found in Wyoming).

- *Probes and prompts:* Will Stone Fox race all five of his Samoyeds? Why wouldn't Stone Fox talk to white men? After meeting Stone Fox, do you think Little Willy has a chance to win the race? From the information the author gives us, why do you think the Native American was given the name "Stone Fox"?

CHAPTER 7: "THE MEETING"   Teacher Read Aloud.

- *Introduction:* Discuss the title of the chapter. Who will meet? Where and how will they meet?

- *Language: Embarrassed* (confused). Why could one say that Doc Smith read Little Willy's mind? ("If you stay a minute, you can have some of that cinnamon cake I've got in the oven.") *Treacherous* (dangerous). What does *investigate* the barking dogs mean? *Massive* (big and heavy; large and solid).

- *Probes and prompts:* Describe Stone Fox's feeling about the Samoyed. How do you feel the night before a big race? Do you think Little Willy had any of those feelings? How did Searchlight feel? (This discussion could also be an entry in the LitLog.)

CHAPTER 8: "THE DAY"   Independent Reading.

- *Introduction:* On p. 63 Little Willy remembers Grandfather saying, "There are some things in this

world worth dying for." Is the author giving us clues about the race? Is the farm worth dying for? Doesn't Grandfather feel that way? Last vote—who do you think will win the race? Both Stone Fox and Little Willy have important reasons to win. Since Little Willy is an amateur, will Stone Fox (the experienced racer) know how to beat him?

- *Language: Abreast* (side by side). What language does the author use to describe Stone Fox? *Clenched* (tightly closed together).

- *Probes and prompts:* Do you believe "Where there's a will, there's a way"? Have you ever felt that way? Did you accomplish your goal? How can Little Willy possibly beat Stone Fox?

CHAPTER 9: "THE RACE"   Literature Discussion Groups or Partner Reading.

- *Introduction:* How should Little Willy begin the race? Is it best to be first at the beginning of a long race? (Have the students ask the coach about racing strategies.)

- *Language: Pursuit* (chasing after another person); *disqualified* (not allowed to do something); *magnificent* (impressive, beautiful, strong).

- *Probes and prompts:* "Stone Fox isn't that far behind." What is the author telling us?

CHAPTER 10: "THE FINISH LINE"   Teacher Read Aloud.

- *Introduction:* Discuss major events of the race before reading the chapter.

- *Language: Forged* (moved forward with difficulty).

- *Probes and prompts:* When Stone Fox spoke, he said a lot. Why did he do what he did? He had the race won. He could have bought back more land for his people. He needed that money. Did he really plan to win? Should the judges declare Little Willy the winner? Why?

Before, during, or after reading a chapter use a suitable strategy or response suggested in Table 11.18. Encourage students to create responses that highlight the content related to various discipline areas.

TABLE 11.18   Suggested Strategies and Responses Related to Various Discipline Areas

Literature and Language

While reading, prepare a story map depicting the plot structure of the text.

Discuss the dedication page and why Gardiner wrote it.

Write letters to creators, asking why they write and illustrate.

Individuals or groups will begin a character attribute chart after reading Chapter 1. Continue the chart while reading the book; as characters are

introduced, add to the characteristics throughout the reading.

Discuss the chapter titles; encourage student to make predictions about chapters before reading. Record replies on a chart; display the chart in the room to discuss later.

Discuss legends. (On p. 51, Gardiner introduces the term. See Chapter 3: Folk Literature.)

Interview an adult, asking about a local legend. If the adult remembers one, audio-

tape it. Bring the tape to school and record. Publish the legend in a book to be checked out by other students.

Find, read, and discuss legends from other regions of the United States and other countries.

Native Americans

Ask students to bring Native American artifacts and pictures.

Discuss: In the early days, sometimes Native Americans were not treated

TABLE 11.18 *(Continued)*

fairly. Discuss the lifestyles on reservations. Compare the past to the present.

Find out about three famous Indian chiefs. Present the information in the "Book of Facts." Illustrate some of the facts. (See Freedman's *Indian Chiefs*.)

Locate an American Indian legend. Compare the legend to a novel.

Make clay replicas of Indian artifacts.

Dogsled Racing

Prepare a KWL. Have each child make three columns on a chart:

What I *Know* about Dogsled Racing; What I Want to *Learn; Where* I Will Find Out. Discuss the student's prior knowledge, and suggest ways to find more information.

Become an expert on dogsled racing. Prepare a news broadcast "Ask the Expert" to tell others about this type of racing.

What does a snow racer look like? What are its size and weight?

Compare riding on a snow sled with riding on water skis.

Students will locate fiction and nonfiction information (prose and poetry) about dogsled racing and racing in general.

Prepare a newspaper item announcing the race in Jackson, Wyoming.

Have the students prepare written information about racing and display it on a literature bulletin board.

Oral and Written Responses

Write a radio script describing the race. Present the script to another group.

Write a letter of commendation from the president of the United States to Stone Fox. Give him a reward. What does he deserve?

Make a medal; role-play the president giving Stone Fox the letter, reward, and medal.

Role-play Stone Fox explaining the race to his people.

Write a prediction about Willy's future. (He is no longer Little Willy.) Did Stone Fox and Willy become friends?

Pretend to be Grandfather; tell friends who did not see the race how Willy saved the farm and how he put into action "Where there's a will, there's a way."

Pretend to be Doc Smith. Write a letter trying to convince the government that Grandfather's taxes should be lowered. Share the letter with others.

Dramatize a conversation between any of the following characters after the race: Miss Williams, Mr. Foster, Lester, or Mr. Snyder.

Economics

Pretend you are Grandfather. Role-play explaining to Little Willy why you did not pay the taxes.

Encourage students to bring in articles about taxes, especially those containing graphs. Discuss and prepare a budget.

Talk about national, state, and local taxes. Find graphs of expenses in newspapers and magazines and cut them out. Discuss various kinds of graphs showing the budget and expenses of different organizations and personal budgets. Prepare a personal, room budget.

After reading p. 39, have the students interview an adult to find out why we pay local, state, and national taxes. What does the adult feel about taxes? Does he or she think they are necessary? Beneficial?

Geography

Identify the book's setting on a national map and a state map.

Find out about the topography of the region. Discuss the information with others.

Draw a map to scale showing Little Willy and Searchlight's race from town to home. Label all of the places mentioned.

In groups students will identify past and present information about Wyoming, such as its weather, population, products, state capital, state song, state flower, state bird, and major sports.

Have students compare information about Wyoming (identified above) to their home state.

Present state information as a travel show, with each group member presenting information about the state.

Prepare a travel brochure advertising the advantages of living or vacationing in Wyoming.

Mathematics

Chart the distance from Wyoming to the students' hometown and other regions of the United States.

Talk about measurements, distances, and map skills.

How many potatoes are in a pound?

Collect potato recipes; cook several at school or at home.

Bring potatoes and a bag to school; place a pound of potatoes in the bag; put a bushel of potatoes in the bag.

Write original word problems using the characters and incidents from the book.

Science

After reading Chapter 2, list facts you found out about potato farming. Have you ever worked in a garden or on a farm? Were you tired after a few minutes? Would it be difficult to work on a potato farm?

Find out more information about farming. Present facts in an oral report.

How much do potato farmers make for a pound of potatoes? A bushel?

Find out more about Samoyeds. What do they look like? How strong are they? Where do they live? Why does Stone Fox use five Samoyeds in the race?

Draw pictures of the dogs and write a "Book of Facts" about Samoyeds. Compare them to other breeds of dogs. Add the information about the Samoyeds to the character attribute chart.

Art

How do you feel when you look at the pictures? The illustrator, Marcia Sewall, has drawn realistic pencil pictures to accompany the text. How do the pictures give clues about the story line? Is color needed? Why?

Draw visual sequences of the plot.

Students will research the author and illustrator and write an autobiography for each of them.

Look at the pictures; note the clothes worn in the early 1900s. Talk about the illustrations. Collect and display pictures of the time.

Make potato prints.

Write a cinquain expressing how Willy or Stone Fox felt during the race. Place the cinquains in a bound book and illustrate them.

BIBLIOGRAPHY: RELATED MATERIALS

Collect fiction and nonfiction books, poetry, media, visuals, and music to help students find out more about the following:

- Dogsled racing (information about sleds, dogs, hardships, and the like).

- Wyoming (information about size, location, geography, history, and the like).

- History of Arapaho Indians (information about living conditions on the reservation, then and now).
  Have students do the following:

- Obtain magazine and newspaper articles about dogsledding, Wyoming, Native Americans and the reservations, budgeting, and various types of graphs.

- Locate information about measuring distances in a math textbook.

- Locate other outstanding examples of foreshadowing. (See Hall, S. 1990. *Using Picture Storybooks to Teach Literary Devices*. Phoenix: Oryx. 56–62.)

See the bibliography for Native Americans and related literature. Also, see books such as the following:

- Nonfiction books:

  Freedman, R. 1987. *Indian Chiefs*. Photos. New York: Holiday. 10–16 yrs. (bibliography).

  Paulsen, G. 1990. *Woodsong*. New York: Puffin. 9–12 yrs.

  Ring, E. 1994. *Sled Dogs: Arctic Athletes*. Brookfield, Conn.: Millbrook. 5–9 yrs. *Good Dogs!* series.

  Wadsworth, G. 1994. *Susan Butcher: Sled Dog Racer*. Minneapolis, Minn. 10–13 yrs. *Achievers series*.

- Fiction books:

  London, J. 1994. *Call of the Wild*. Illus. Barry Moser. New York: Macmillan. 10–14 yrs.

  Whelan, G. 1988. *Silver*. Illus. Stephen Marchesi. New York: Random House. 7–10 yrs. A *Stepping Stone Book*.

  On a bulletin board surround a map of Wyoming with artistic and written LRMs.

NOTES

The introductory question is from Vandergrift, K. E. 1990. *Children's Literature: Theory, Research, and Teaching*. Englewood, Colo.: Libraries Unlimited. 21.

1. For additional information about the goals of literary study, see sources such as Langer, J. 1992. *Literature Instruction: A Focus on Student Response*. Urbana, Ill.: National Council of Teachers of English; Purves, A. C. Toward a reevaluation of reader response and school literature. *Language Arts*. 70(5). September. 348–61.

2. Langer, J. 1992. 35; also see Heald-Taylor, B. G. 1996. Three paradigms for literature instruction in grades 3 to 6. *The Reading Teacher*. 49(6). March. 456–66.

3. For additional information about benefits gained from literature, see sources such as Chambers, A. 1985. The role of literature in children's lives. In *Booktalk: Occasional Writing on Literature and Children*. New York: Harper & Row. 1–13. Whose book is it anyway? 125–38; Cullinan, B. E. 1992. Leading with literature. x–xvi. In Cullinan, B. E. (Ed.). *Invitation to Read: More Children's Literature in the Reading Program*. Newark, Del.: International Reading Association; Huck, C. S. 1992. Literacy and literature. *Language Arts*. 67(7). November. 520–26; Jacobs, L. B. 1966. Give children literature. In Robinson, E. R. (Ed.). *Readings about Children's Literature*. New York: McKay. 3–8; McMillan, M. M., & Gentile, L. M. 1988. Children's literature: Teaching critical thinking and ethics. *The Reading Teacher*. 41(9). 876–860.

4. For additional information about the historical development of literature, see the notable liter-

ature presented in each genre chapter and sources such as Haviland, V. (Ed.). 1973. Before the twentieth century. In *Children and Literature: Views and Reviews*. Glenview, Ill.: Scott, Foresman. 1–36; Of classics and golden ages. 37–97; Hodges, M., & Steinfirst, S. 1980. In E. S. Smith's *The History of Children's Literature*. Chicago: American Library Association. 32, 33, 39, 53–55; Townsend, J. R. 1996. *Written for Children*. (6th Ed.). Lanham, Md.: Scarecrow Press. 3–30.

5. For additional information about the Imitative, Analytic, and Generative Structures for teaching literature, see Purves, A. C., & Monson, D. L. 1984. *Experiencing Children's Literature*. Glenview, Ill.: Scott, Foresman. 181–85.

   For additional information about literary theories, see Rosenblatt, L. M. 1991. Literary theory. In Flood, J., Jensen, J. M., Lapp, D., & Squire, J. R. (Eds.). *Handbook of Research on Teaching the English Language Arts*. New York: Macmillan. 57–62.

   For additional information about canons and cultural literacy, see sources such as Bloom, A. 1987. *The Closing of the American Mind*. New York: Simon & Schuster; Hirsch, E. D. 1987. *Cultural Literacy: What Every American Needs to Know*. Boston: Houghton Mifflin; Hirsch, E. D., & Trefi, J. 1988. *The Dictionary of Cultural Literacy*. Boston: Houghton Mifflin; Spengemann, W. C. 1991. Wanting a national literature. *ADE Bulletin*. 99. Fall. 18–21.

   For additional information about the Heritage Approach to language arts instruction, see Bennett, W. J. 1987. *James Madison*

High School: A Curriculum for American Students. Washington, D.C.: United States Department of Education; Farrell, E. J. 1991. Instructional models for English language arts, K–12. In Flood, J., Jensen, J., Lapp, D., and Squire, J. (Eds.). 1991. 63–84.

6. For additional information about New Criticism, see sources such as Brooks, C., & Warren, R. P. (Eds.). 1938. *Understanding Poetry*. New York: Henry Holt; Wellek, R., & Warren, A. 1949. *Theory of Literature*. New York: Harcourt Brace; Wellek, R. 1986. *American Criticism, 1900–1959*, Vol. 6 of *A History of Modern Criticism*. New Haven, Conn.: Yale University Press; Wimsatt, W. K., & Beardsley, M. 1954. The affective fallacy. In Wimsatt, W. K. (Ed.) *The Verbal Icon: Studies in the Meaning of Poetry*. Lexington: University of Kentucky Press.

   For additional information about other theories, see Crane, R. S. (Ed.). 1952. *Critics and Criticism: Ancient and Modern*. Chicago: University of Chicago Press; Frye, N. 1957. *The Anatomy of Criticism*. Princeton, N.J.: Princeton University Press.

7. Rosenblatt, L. M. 1938. *Literature as Exploration*. New York: Appleton-Century-Crofts.

8. Rosenblatt, L. M. 1994. (1978). *The Reader, the Text, the Poem*. Carbondale, Ill.: Southern Illinois Press.

9. For additional information about the Transactional Theory, see Rosenblatt's books and sources such as Cooper, C. R. (Ed.). 1985. *Researching Response to Literature and the Teaching of Literature: Points of Departure*. Norwood, N.J.: Ablex; Hansson, G. 1992. Reader's responding—and then? *Research in*

the Teaching of English. 26(2). May. 135–48; Holland, N. 1975. *Poems in Persons: An Introduction to the Psychoanalysis of Literature.* New York: Norton; Jacoby, J. 1981. Authority in English 102: Whose text is it anyway? *CEA Critic.* 52(1–2). 2–12; Karolides, N.J. (Ed.). 1992. *Reader Response in the Classroom: Evoking and Interpreting Meaning in Literature.* White Plains, N.Y.: Longman; Purves, A. C., & Beach, R. 1972. *Literature and the Reader: Research in Response to Literature, Reading, Interest, and the Teaching of Literature.* Urbana, Ill.: National Council of Teachers of English.

10. Bleich, D. 1978. *Subjective Criticism.* Baltimore: Johns Hopkins University Press; Holland, N. N. 1975. *5 Readers Reading.* New Haven, Conn.: Yale University Press. Essays by both theorists are also published in Cooper, C. R. (Ed.). 1985. Bleich, 253–72. Holland, 3–21. See also Iser, W. 1978. *The Act of Reading: A Theory of Aesthetic Response.* Baltimore: Johns Hopkins University Press.

11. See Chapter 2 for additional information about Cognitive Information Processing, Piagetian/Naturalist, and Social-Constructivist Theories of learning and development.

    For additional information about Mastery, Heritage, and Process Instructional Models, see Farrell, E. J. 1991. Instructional models for English language arts, K–12. In Flood, J., Jensen, J. M., Lapp, D., and Squire, J. R. (Eds.). 63–84.

    For additional information about the Transactional Theory, see sources such as Rosenblatt, L. M. 1978; Rosenblatt, L. M. 1985. The Transactional Theory of the Literary Work: Implications for research. In Cooper, C. R. (Ed.). 35; Rosenblatt, L. 1977. The Transactional Theory of the Literary Work: Implications for research. Paper presented at the Buffalo Conference on Researching Response to Literature and the Teaching of Literature. Buffalo, N.Y. October. (*ERIC Document* Reproduction Services No. ED 209 667) 8–10.

12. For additional information about the influence of literary theories on curricular decisions, see sources such as Beach, R. 1993. *A Teacher's Introduction to Reader-Response Theories.* Urbana, Ill.: National Council of Teachers of English; Cox, C., & Many, J. E. 1989. Worlds of possibilities in response to literature, film, and life. *Language Arts.* 65(3). 287–94; Feeley, J. T., Strickland, D. S., & Wepner, S. B. (Eds.). 1991. *Process Reading and Writing: A Literature-Based Approach.* New York: Teachers College Press; Kelly, P. 1990. Guiding young students' responses to literature. *The Reading Teacher.* 43(7). 464–70; Probst, R. E. 1992. Five kinds of literary knowing. In Langer, J. *Literature Instruction: Focus on Student Responses.* Urbana, Ill.: National Council of Teachers of English. 54–72; Purves, A., Rogers, T., & Soter, A. 1990. *How Porcupines Make Love II. Teaching a Response-Centered Literature Curriculum.* White Plains, N.Y.: Longman; Vandergrift, K. E. 1990. *Children's Literature: Theory, Research, and Teaching.* Englewood, Colo.: Libraries Unlimited. 1–25.

13. For a review of current literary study, see sources such as Beach, J. D. 1991. New trends in an historical perspective: Literature's place in language arts education. *Language Arts.* 69(7). November. 550–56; Heald-Taylor, B. G. 1996. 456–66; Walmsley, S. A. 1992.

Reflections on the state of elementary literature instruction. *Language Arts.* 69(7). November. 508–14.

14. For additional information about the Pure Literature Approach, see sources such as Jacobs, L. B. 1991. Literary reading. *Teaching Pre K–8.* 21(1). September. 138–39; Nell, V. 1994. The insatiable appetite. From *Lost in a Book: The Psychology of Reading for Pleasure.* In Cramer, E. H., & Castle, M. (Eds.). *Fostering the Love of Reading: The Affective Domain in Reading Education.* 1994. Newark, Del.: International Reading Association. 41–52; Odland, N. 1979. Planning a literature program for the elementary school. *Language Arts.* 56(4). 363–67; Purves, A. C. 1993.

15. For additional information about the instructional components of a Pure Literature Approach, see sources such as Galda, L., & Cullinan, B. E. 1991. Literature for literacy: What research says about the benefits of using trade books in the classroom. In Flood, J., Jensen, J. M., Lapp, D., & Squire, J. R. (Eds.). 529–39; O'Brien, K. L. 1991. A look at one successful literature program. *The New Advocate.* 4(2). Spring. 113–22.

16. For additional information about the Literature-Based Language Arts Approach, see sources such as Cullinan, B. E. 1992. Whole language and children's literature. *Language Arts.* 69. October. 426–30; Fuhler, C. J. 1990. Let's move toward literature-based reading instruction. *The Reading Teacher.* 43(4). 312–15; Huck, C. S. 1996. Literature-based reading programs: A retrospective. *The New Advocate.* 9(1). Winter. 23–33; Theme: Literature-Based Language Arts Programs. 1992. *Language Arts.* 67(7). November; McGee, L. M., & Tompkins, G. E. 1995. Literature-based reading instruction: What's guiding the instruction? *Language Arts.* 72(6). 495–514; Norton, D. E. 1992. *The Impact of Literature-Based Reading.* New York: Merrill. 1–121; Sorenson, M. R., & Lehman, B. A. (Eds.). 1995. *Teaching with Children's Books: Paths to Literature-Based Instruction.* Urbana, Ill.: National Council of Teachers of English.

17. For additional information about the benefits of a Literature-Based Language Arts Approach, see sources such as Flowers, P., & Roos, M. C. 1994. Literature-based reading programs: Elements for success. (*ERIC Document* Reproduction Services No. 373 319); Freppon, P. A. 1991. Children's concepts of the nature and purpose of reading in different instructional settings. *Journal of Reading Behavior.* 23(2). 139–63; DeBoer, J. 1991. The response of fifth grade low achievers to literature-based instruction through whole class and heterogeneous arrangements. Michigan State University. (*ERIC Document* Reproduction Services No. ED 336 736); Robbins, E. L., & Thompson, L. W. 1990. A study of a sixth-grade literature-based reading program. Galveston Public School. (*ERIC Document* Reproduction Services No. ED 325 809); Shapiro, J., & White, W. 1991. Reading attitudes and perceptions in traditional and nontraditional reading programs. *Reading Research and Instruction.* 30(4). 52–66; Short, K. G. (Ed.). 1995. *Research & Professional Resources in Children's Literature: Piecing a Patchwork Quilt.* Newark, Del.: International Reading Association. 90–162.

18. For additional information about using literature for reading and language instruction, see sources such as Harris, S. 1996. Bringing about change in reading instruction. *The Reading Teacher.* 49(8). May. 612–18; Henke, L. 1988. Beyond basal reading: A district's commitment to change. *The New Advocate.* 1(1). 42–51; Huck, C. E. 1992. Books for emergent readers. In Cullinan, B. E. (Ed.). 1991. 2–13; Moustafa, M. 1993. Recoding in whole language reading instruction. *Language Arts.* 70(6). October. 483–87; Trachtenburg, P. 1990. Using children's literature to enhance phonics instruction. *The Reading Teacher.* 43(9). 648–54.

19. For additional information about current basal readers, see sources such as McCarthey, S. J., & Hoffman, J. V. 1995. The new basals: How are they different? *The Reading Teacher.* 49(1). September. 72–75; Reutzel, D. R., & Larsen, N. S. 1995. Look what they've done to real children's books in the new basal readers! *Language Arts.* 72(7). 495–507.

20. See the following sources for additional information about literature for reading and language instruction (some sources include bibliographies): Canavan, D. 1986. *Children's Books That Reinforce Reading Skills.* Oklahoma City, Okla.: Oklahoma State Department of Education; Goforth, F. S. 1989. "And what do you think will happen next?" Predictable materials in the language arts program. *Florida Reading Quarterly.* June. 9–12; Holdaway, D. 1986. *Stability and Change in Literacy Learning.* Portsmouth, N.H.: Heinemann; Rudman, M. K. 1993. Children's literature in the reading program. In Rudman, M. K. (Ed.). *Children's Literature: Resource for the Classroom.* (2d Ed.). Norwood, Mass.: Christopher-Gordon. 171–77, 184–99; Worthy, J. 1996. A matter of interest: Literature that hooks reluctant readers and keeps them reading. *The Reading Teacher.* 50(3). November. 204–12.

21. For additional information about using basal readers in literature-based language arts instruction, see sources such as Flickinger, G. G., & Long, E. S. 1990. Beyond the basal. *Reading Improvement.* 27(2). 149–54; Wiggins, R. A. 1994. Large group lesson/small group follow-up: Flexible grouping in a basal reading program. *The Reading Teacher.* 47(6). 450–60.

22. For additional instructional ideas for beginning learners, see sources such as Combs, M. 1984. Developing concepts about print with patterned sentence stories. *The Reading Teacher.* 38(2). November. 178–81; Holdaway, D. 1979. *The Foundations of Literacy.* Portsmouth, N.H.: Heinemann; Karges-Bone, L. 1992. Bring on the big books. *The Reading Teacher.* May. 45(9). 743–44; Klesius, J. P., & Griffith, P. L. 1996. Interactive storybook reading for at-risk learners. *The Reading Teacher.* 49(7). April. 552–60; McCracken, R. & M. 1986. *Reading Is Only the Tiger's Tail.* Winnipeg, Canada: Peguis; Morrow, L. M. 1989. *Literacy Development in the Early Years: Helping Children Read and Write.* Englewood Cliffs, N.J.: Prentice-Hall; Yopp, H. K. 1995. Read-aloud books for developing phonemic awareness: An annotated bibliography. *The Reading Teacher.* 48(6). March. 538–42.

23. Cook, J. E. 1991. Literature-based anything. *Teaching Pre K–8.* 21(1). August/September. 34–35.

24. For additional information about using Literature Across the Curriculum, see sources such as Guzzetti, B. J., Kowalinski, B. J., & McGowan, T. 1992. Using a literature-based approach to teaching social studies. *Journal of Reading.* 36(2). 114–22; Nordstrom, V. 1992. Reducing the text burden: Using children's literature and trade books in elementary school science education. *Reference Services Review.* 20(1). 57–70; Norton, D. E. 1993. Circa 1492 and the integration of literature, reading, and geography. *The Reading Teacher.* 46(7). 610–14; Towery, R. W. 1991. Integrating literature in social studies instruction: Getting started. *Reading Improvement.* 28(4). 277–82.

25. For additional information about the benefits gained from using Literature Across the Curriculum, see sources such as Armbruster, B. B. 1991. Using literature in the content areas. *The Reading Teacher.* 45(4). 324–25; Beck, I., & McKeown, M. 1991. Research Directions: Social studies texts are hard to understand: Mediating some of the difficulties. *Language Arts.* 68(6). October. 482–90; Butzow, C. M. & J. W. 1989. *Science through Children's Literature.* Englewood, Colo.: Libraries Unlimited. 4–6; Casteel, C. P., & Isom, B. A. 1994. Reciprocal processes in science and literacy learning. *The Reading Teacher.* 47(7). April. 538–45; Johnson, N. M., & Ebert, M. J. 1992. Time travel is possible: Historical fiction and biography—passport to the past. *The Reading Teacher.* 45(7). March. 488–95; Ladd, J. 1993. Global education and children's literature. In Rudman, M. K. (Ed.). 211–38; Lapp, D., & Flood, J. 1993. Literature in the science program. In Cullinan, B. E. (Ed.). *Fact and Fiction: Literature Across the Curriculum.* Newark, Del.: International Reading Association. 68–79; McGowan, T., & Guzzetti, B. 1991. Promoting social studies understanding through literature-based instruction. *The Social Studies.* 82. 16–21; Ross, E. 1994. *Using Children's Literature Across the Curriculum.* Bloomington, Ind.: Phi Delta Kappa Educational Foundation. Fastback #374.

26. An excellent integrated, literature-based social studies curriculum for children is *Graphic Learning: Integrated Social Studies: Grades K–3.* Waterbury, Conn.: 1992.

    Other professional resources available for teachers include Braddon, K. L., Hall, N. J., & Taylor, D. 1993. *Math through Children's Literature: Making the NCTM Standards Come Alive.* Englewood, Colo.: Teacher Ideas Press; Burns, M. 1992. *Math and Literature (K–3).* White Plains, N.Y.: Math Solutions Publications; Doll, C. A. 1990. *Nonfiction Books for Children: Activities for Thinking and Doing.* Englewood, Colo.: Teacher Ideas Press; Fredricks, A. D. 1991. *Social Studies through Children's Literature.* Englewood, Colo.: Teacher Ideas Press; Hefner, C. R., & Lewis, K. R. 1995. *Literature-Based Science.* Phoenix: Oryx; Laughlin, M. K., & Street, T. P. 1992. *Literature-Based Art and Music: Children's Books and Activities to Enrich the K–5 Curriculum.* Phoenix: Oryx; McElmeel, S. 1991. *Adventures with Social Studies through Literature.* Englewood, Colo.: Teacher Ideas

Press; Perez-Stable, M., & Cordier, M. 1994. *Understanding American History through Children's Literature: Instructional Units and Activities for Grades K–8.* Phoenix: Oryx; Saul, W., & Jagusch, E. A. (Eds.). 1991. *Vital Connections: Children, Science, and Books.* Washington, D.C.: Library of Congress; Saul, W., Reardon, J., Schmidt, A., Pearce, C., Blackwood, D., & Bird, M. D. 1993. *Science Workshop: A Whole Language Approach.* Portsmouth, N.H.: Heinemann; Scott, J. (Ed.). 1993. *Science & Language Links: Classroom Implications.* Portsmouth, N.H.: Heinemann; Sheffield, S. 1994. *Math and Literature (K–3).* Portsmouth, N.H.: Heinemann; Tunnell, M. O., & Ammon, R. A. 1993. *The Story of Ourselves: Teaching History through Children's Literature.* Portsmouth, N.H.: Heinemann; Whitin, D. J., & Wilde, S. 1992. *Read Any Good Math Lately? Children's Books for Mathematical Learning, K–6.* Portsmouth, N.H.: Heinemann; Whitin, D. J., & Wilde, S. 1995. *It's the Story That Counts: More Children's Books for Mathematical Learning, K–6.* Portsmouth, N.H.: Heinemann.

27. Lipson, M. Y., Valencia, S. W., Wixson, K. K., & Peters, C. W. 1993. Integration and thematic teaching: Integration to improve teaching and learning. *Language Arts.* 70(4). April. 252–63.

28. Hughes, M. 1991. *Curriculum Integration in the Primary Grades: A Framework for Excellence.* Alexandria, Va.: Association of Supervision and Curriculum Development. 11.125.

29. For additional information about the instructional components of a Literature Across the Curriculum Approach, see sources such as Malloch, J. & I. with Francis, N. 1994. Planning for literature across the curriculum. In Hickman, J., Cullinan, B. E., & Hepler, S. (Eds.). *Children's Literature in the Classroom: Extending Charlotte's Web.* Norwood, Mass.: Christopher-Gordon. 145–51; Manning, M. & G. 1994. *Theme Immersion.* Portsmouth, N.H.: Heinemann; Pardo, L. S., & Raphael, T. E. 1991. Classroom organization for instruction in content area. *The Reading Teacher.* 44(8). April. 556–562; Smith, J. L., & Johnson, H. 1994. Models for implementing literature in content studies. *The Reading Teacher.* 48(3). November. 198–209; Winograd, K., & Higgins, K. M. 1994/1995. Writing, reading, and talking mathematics: One interdisciplinary possibility. *The Reading Teacher.* 48(4). December/January. 310–18; Von Dras, J. 1990. Transitions toward an integrated curriculum. In Short, K. G., & Pierce, K. M. (Eds.) 1990. *Talking about Books: Creating Literate Communities.* Portsmouth, N.H.: Heinemann. 121–33; Thrailkill, C. 1994. Math and literature: A perfect match. *Teaching Pre K–8.* 24(4). January. 64–65.

30. For additional information about the role of the media specialist, see the entire issue of *Language Arts.* 67(5). 1990. September. See especially, Lamme, L. L., & Ledbetter, L. 1990. Libraries: The heart of whole language. *Language Arts.* 67(5). 735–41. See also

Carletti, S., Girard, S., & Willing, K. 1991. *The Library/Classroom Connection.* Portsmouth, N.H.: Heinemann; Goldfarb, L., & Salmon, S. 1993. Enhancing language arts for special populations: Librarians and classroom teachers collaborate. *Language Arts.* 70(7). November. 567–72; Lamme, L. L., & Beckett, C. 1992. Whole language in an elementary school library media center. Office of Educational Research and Improvement (ED), Washington, D.C. (*ERIC Digest* Reproduction Services No. ED 346 874.)

31. For additional information about changes in the use of the school media center, see sources such as Farmer, L. S. 1992. *Creative Partnerships Librarians and Teachers Working Together.* Worthington, Ohio: Linworth H.; Hiebert, E. H., Mervar, K. B., & Person, D. 1990. Research Directions: Children's selection of trade books in libraries and classrooms. *Language Arts.* 67(7). November. 758–63; Hughes, S. M. 1993. The impact of whole language on four elementary school libraries. *Language Arts.* 70(1). September. 393–99.

32. Kulleseid, E. R., & Strickland, D. S. 1989. *Literature, Literacy, and Learning: Classroom Teachers, Library Media Specialists, and the Literature-Based Curriculum.* Chicago: American Library Association. 30–40.

33. Anderson, R. C., Hiebert, E. H., Scott, J., & Wilkinson, I. A. G. 1985. *Becoming a Nation of Readers: The Report of the Commission on Reading.* U.S. Department of Education, Washington, D.C. In collaboration with the National Academy of Education, the National Institute of Education, the Center for the Study of Reading. 117.

34. Suggested books about the involvement of parents or guardians include Bialostok, S. 1992. *Raising Readers: Helping Your Child to Literacy.* Winnipeg, Canada: Peguis; Clay, M. 1988. *Writing Begins at Home: Preparing Children for Writing before They Go to School.* Portsmouth, N.H.: Heinemann; Clay, M., & Butler, D. 1987. *Reading Begins at Home.* Portsmouth, N.H.: Heinemann; McGlip, J., & Michael, M. 1994. *The Home-School Connection: Guidelines for Working with Parents.* Portsmouth, N.H.: Heinemann; Trelease, J. 1989. *The New Read-Aloud Handbook.* New York: Viking Penguin.

    Pamphlets are available from professional organizations, such as the International Reading Association, Reading Is Fundamental, Association for Childhood Education International, National Education Association, and National Parents and Teachers Association.

    Monthly articles are found in *Teaching Pre K–8*, and the U.S. Department of Education, Consumer Information Division has several booklets, such as *Helping Your Child with Homework.* Other materials are available via the Internet.

35. Vogt, M. E. 1991. An observational guide for supervisors and administrators: Moving toward integrated reading/language arts instruction. *The Reading Teacher.* 45(3). November. 206–11.

Principles for Designing
A Literature Curriculum

*L*iterature and the arts in the curriculum can both free the imagination and help people order their worlds.

This function is served by no other part of the curriculum.

—Alan Purves, Theresa Rogers, and Anna Soter

*S*everal years ago when the debate about the use of literature in the elementary classroom was raging, a secondary literature teacher said with profound sympathy, "I might not like the way many of my colleagues teach literature, but at least we have time for literature in the classroom! Apparently, in the elementary school, you do not have time scheduled for literature or an organized literature curriculum!" At the time, she was right, but fortunately, times have changed! Literature is now a vital part of the elementary and middle school curriculum! The literature curriculum encompasses all of the literary routines and approaches used to present literature to young people. A visitor to a literature-based elementary school will observe kindergarten children reacting to the antics of a fly "buzzing" through the alphabet in the Big Book version of Jim Aylesworth's *Old Black Fly* (1992). The visitor will see first graders laughing as they move to the rhythmic language of Libba Gray's *My Mama Had a Dancing Heart* (1995) (see the Gray color plate on page 423) and hear third graders discussing what happened to the gingham dog and the calico cat in Eugene Field's narrative poem "The Duel." Meanwhile the fourth graders are contemplating what might happen to Winnie in Natalie Babbitt's *Tuck Everlasting* (1975) if she drinks the water from the eternal spring, and the sixth graders are transforming their room into King Arthur's court while experiencing Merlin's adventures in Jane Yolen's *Passager* (1996).

A contemporary literature curriculum for all ages is response centered. In this curriculum the focus is not entirely on either the student or the literature, but on the transaction evoked when the reader and text meet. Students in a response-centered curriculum express their personal responses to literary works, respect diverse responses, appreciate the creator's use of language and images, and recognize the value of using literature for personal growth and development. In a response-centered curriculum, girls and boys are encouraged to explore literature for aesthetic and efferent purposes. As in all adventures, the explorers need an experienced guide—the teacher—to help them maneuver through the maze of the new environment—the various genres and numerous selections available to read.

While transacting with complete literary selections, students express personal reflections, display imaginative reactions, and construct thought-provoking interpretations elicited by the author's language and the artist's images. In a response-centered curriculum, teachers use suitable terminology or conduct mini-lessons to help learners discuss the literature intelligently with others and articulate their personal reactions to individual literary works.[1]

An organized literature curriculum has the potential to delight the heart and instruct the mind. Throughout the year literature selections of high literary merit are presented individually or in thematic collections. Teachers involved in an organized program know the literature and the students. They strive to help individuals make connections to a book and to make intertextual associations between books. As students read, react, and respond to literature, they have an authentic context in which to listen to, view, reflect upon, discuss, and write about the literature. They also ask questions and through literature find information that is vital to their daily existence. These literary experiences enhance and refine the students' linguistic and cognitive development.

The design of a successful literature curriculum incorporates one or more literary approaches and adheres to the following principles:

Language and literature are inseparable and are presented holistically in authentic contexts.

Quality fiction and nonfiction literature and related materials are carefully selected and presented in the literature curriculum.

The instructional goals determine the organization of literature presented in the literature curriculum.

In the literature curriculum, students read and write independently, in small groups, and with the entire class.

Teachers and students document each individual's literary growth and maturity; teachers also assess the effectiveness of the entire literature curriculum.

Raúl Colón's watercolor washes, etchings, and colored and litho pencil paintings expand Libba Moore Gray's celebrations in My Mama Had a Dancing Heart. *The artist's realistic paintings capture the rhythm and movement of the verbal text.*

The teacher can implement an effective literature curriculum by incorporating the five principles presented in this chapter with the Literary Transaction Process presented in Chapter 2 and the three literary approaches presented in Chapter 11.

✸ PRINCIPLE ONE: LANGUAGE AND LITERATURE ARE INSEPARABLE AND ARE PRESENTED HOLISTICALLY IN AUTHENTIC CONTEXTS

By using carefully selected images, words, and patterns of language, a talented author or artist can depict an awesome sight or convey a profound philosophical statement. By using the right words, a skilled writer wins the respect of the audience members, entices them to become active participants in an adventure, and encourages them to explore imaginary worlds designed by the creator. Literature and language are inseparable in that the various purposes or functions of language are vividly expressed in literature. Literature provides the avenue for exploring the power and beauty of the language used by brilliant writers. Young people can then experiment with the language found in literature to present personal ideas and thoughts in spoken and written expressions. Thus, literature is a viable model for personal language development. Through a variety of literary experiences, young people discover the conventions of literature to become "readers who write" and "writers who read." Therefore, the first principle to consider when developing a literature curriculum is the relationship between literature and language.

LITERATURE IS A VIABLE MODEL FOR PERSONAL LANGUAGE PRODUCTION

A primary goal of a contemporary language arts curriculum is to help students become proficient listeners, speakers, readers, writers, viewers, and thinkers. Literature contains the finest models of language an individual will encounter. Therefore, young people who discover exemplary fiction and nonfiction stories, poems, and drama enjoy examining the techniques authors use to communicate their ideas to others. This inquiry motivates students to use similar models of language for their personal oral and written productions. Learners need many opportunities to experiment with language and to manipulate it to create original expressions reflecting their feelings, experiences, and information. They also enjoy using language to attempt to persuade others to accept their point of view. Throughout this book many verbal Literary Response Modes (LRMs) have been suggested for use with literature. Appendix B offers additional strategies.

LITERATURE IS A NATURAL MEDIUM FOR EXPLORING AND EXPERIMENTING WITH THE FUNCTIONS OF LANGUAGE

Language is a personal, social process. At an early age, most children internalize and use the basic structures of language used by the adults in their environment. Language is basic to thinking and learning in all disciplines. Indeed, the skillful use of oral and written language may be the single most important means of helping students become informed, thinking citizens. When we communicate with others, we use one or several of the following functions of language:

> We use *informative language* when we say "Let me tell you about. . . ."

> We use *expressive language* when we say "I feel happy when I read. . . ."

> We stimulate the *imagination* when we say "Let's pretend that. . . ."

> We use *persuasive language* when we say "I know you will love this book!"

> We use certain language routines or *ritualistic language* when we write a letter, participate in a debate, or leave a message on an answering machine.[2]

As young people experiment with oral and written language, they need to be aware of these functions and to use each in the proper context. Through literature they can observe the way writers use the various functions of language. Then, as students respond to the literature, they will use similar oral and written language to express their emotions and dreams, convey information, and influence the audience. A description of each function and instructional techniques students can use to explore and produce the functions in authentic contexts are presented in Figure 12.1 on page 425.

YOUNG PEOPLE BECOME "READERS WHO WRITE" AND "WRITERS WHO READ" WHEN THEY ARE AWARE OF THE STRUCTURES, TYPES, FORMS, AND ELEMENTS OF LITERATURE

As the children listen to, view, or read fiction and nonfiction literature, they talk informally about the language and images used by authors and artists. (See photo on page 426.) To encourage learners' responses, discuss the creator's ability to present a concept or emotion clearly. Present biographical sketches, such as "Did You Know About . . . " and emphasize the fact that many creators read extensively while writing. If necessary, conduct mini-lessons about structures, forms, or elements of literature the students do not understand. Encourage the students to express orally or in writing their personal ideas, reactions, wishes, or information to others. Ask peer editing partners to discuss how effectively the communication conveys the author's feelings or information. Create a Word Wall to highlight unusual, unfamiliar, or content-related words and phrases. Discuss, pantomime, and encourage the students to use the language in personal oral and written communication. Display attractive visuals with interesting language, feature a word a day, and highlight repetitive phrases and exciting descriptive sentences. Encourage the students to use oral and written language in various natural experiences each day.

We need to entice some young people to express their reactions to a selection. As we give them many opportunities to express their interpretations with others, they begin to understand the creator's craft and use this information appropriately in their personal oral and written productions. When they begin to read literature through the eyes of a writer and recognize the reactions their written products elicit from others, they become "readers who write and writers who read"!

A PRIMARY GOAL OF THE LITERATURE CURRICULUM IS TO HELP BOYS AND GIRLS BECOME STRATEGIC COMMUNICATORS

Using literature in various subject areas gives students relevant experiences using oral and written language in authentic contexts. When students respond to literature, they practice using the language to learn and to become strategic communicators. A strategic communicator is a person who knows and uses techniques or strategies that foster successful communication with others. A strategy is a selected plan, applied appropriately to reach a goal. A strategic communicator selects the appropriate strategies, such as the following when listening, speaking, reading, and writing:

> Understands and uses the different functions of language.

> Understands and uses oral and written language effectively.

> Assumes an appropriate aesthetic or efferent stance toward the communication.

> Activates personal schemata and integrates them with new information and experiences.

> Listens or looks for important ideas in oral messages and written texts and thinks about them rather than about trivia and useless details.

> Identifies stylistic devices used by a writer or speaker and uses them when communicating through oral or written language.

> Monitors and edits personal communication by rereading, rewriting, questioning, paraphrasing, and perhaps summarizing it.

> Predicts, verifies, and anticipates future events in an oral message or written text. If necessary will modify predictions and generate new ones to construct meanings elicited by the communication.

> Clearly expresses personal reactions, interpretations, or information in oral or written language.[3]

FIGURE 12.1   The Functions of Language

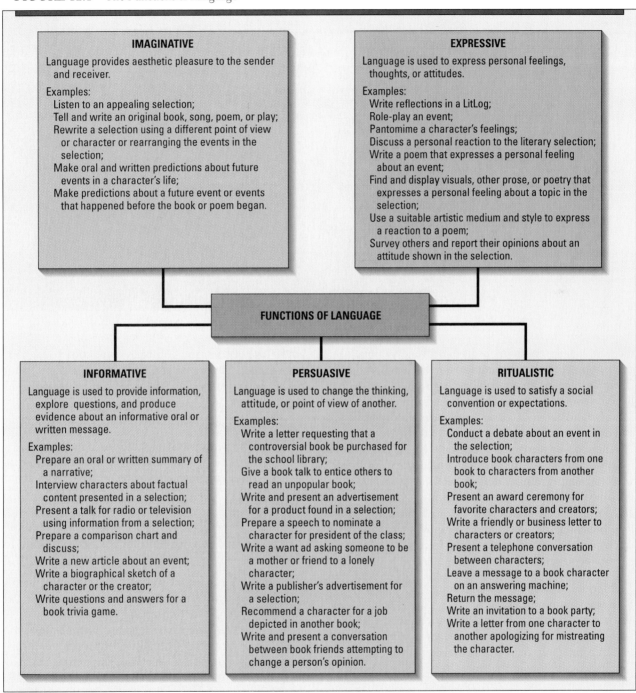

IMAGINATIVE

Language provides aesthetic pleasure to the sender and receiver.

Examples:
 Listen to an appealing selection;
 Tell and write an original book, song, poem, or play;
 Rewrite a selection using a different point of view or character or rearranging the events in the selection;
 Make oral and written predictions about future events in a character's life;
 Make predictions about a future event or events that happened before the book or poem began.

EXPRESSIVE

Language is used to express personal feelings, thoughts, or attitudes.

Examples:
 Write reflections in a LitLog;
 Role-play an event;
 Pantomime a character's feelings;
 Discuss a personal reaction to the literary selection;
 Write a poem that expresses a personal feeling about an event;
 Find and display visuals, other prose, or poetry that expresses a personal feeling about a topic in the selection;
 Use a suitable artistic medium and style to express a reaction to a poem;
 Survey others and report their opinions about an attitude shown in the selection.

FUNCTIONS OF LANGUAGE

INFORMATIVE

Language is used to provide information, explore questions, and produce evidence about an informative oral or written message.

Examples:
 Prepare an oral or written summary of a narrative;
 Interview characters about factual content presented in a selection;
 Present a talk for radio or television using information from a selection;
 Prepare a comparison chart and discuss;
 Write a new article about an event;
 Write a biographical sketch of a character or the creator;
 Write questions and answers for a book trivia game.

PERSUASIVE

Language is used to change the thinking, attitude, or point of view of another.

Examples:
 Write a letter requesting that a controversial book be purchased for the school library;
 Give a book talk to entice others to read an unpopular book;
 Write and present an advertisement for a product found in a selection;
 Prepare a speech to nominate a character for president of the class;
 Write a want ad asking someone to be a mother or friend to a lonely character;
 Write a publisher's advertisement for a selection;
 Recommend a character for a job depicted in another book;
 Write and present a conversation between book friends attempting to change a person's opinion.

RITUALISTIC

Language is used to satisfy a social convention or expectations.

Examples:
 Conduct a debate about an event in the selection;
 Introduce book characters from one book to characters from another book;
 Present an award ceremony for favorite characters and creators;
 Write a friendly or business letter to characters or creators;
 Present a telephone conversation between characters;
 Leave a message to a book character on an answering machine;
 Return the message;
 Write an invitation to a book party;
 Write a letter from one character to another apologizing for mistreating the character.

Students need many opportunities to apply these strategies through the various functions of language. They may also need structured lessons in authentic contexts to become aware of the strategies and become strategic communicators.

In language, we select and apply a strategy to react appropriately to the oral or written stimuli. When we are involved in a particular oral or written communication, we consciously or unconsciously *activate* an appropriate strategy, *apply* it, and *express* our response to the communication or literature. If the selected strategy does not help us receive the appropriate response to the stimuli, we *adjust or modify* the strategy or *select another* one. We then apply

These boys are eager to share the funny and exciting adventures in their books. They are becoming "readers who write" and "writers who read."

the new strategy and monitor its effectiveness so that we can comprehend the communication. The entire process demands selecting appropriate language and modes to deliver the communication. Throughout the process, we are actively thinking, monitoring, and integrating knowledge and experiences.[4]

A person who recognizes the benefits of using the strategies observes others using them and practices using them while reading, writing, listening, viewing, speaking, and thinking. With practice learners begin to understand *why* and *when* particular strategies are used, and eventually they unconsciously select and use appropriate strategies when giving information, expressing ideas and feelings, or attempting to persuade others.

Techniques to Help Students Become Strategic Communicators

In a holistic approach to language instruction, a person selects appropriate modalities of language—reading, writing, speaking, listening, viewing, and thinking—and uses them simultaneously to construct meaning from the narrative and communicate with others. After the teacher and learners discuss the stylistic devices used by writers, usually the child will use similar language, patterns, and structures in personal speaking or writing. For example, after discussing the narrator's point of view, learners experiment with several points of view and select an appropriate one when communicating with others. The speaker or writer constantly monitors, modifies, and corrects the presentation. A

reader uses these same strategies to construct meanings from written and visual narratives. Teachers help young people become strategic communicators by using the following techniques:

Use unabridged versions of meaning-bearing materials.

Model the personal use of strategies to show the learners how to select, apply, and modify them while speaking, writing, and reading.

Explain why and when a strategy should be used.

Provide assistance as children attempt to use the strategy.

Have learners practice using the strategy with different pieces of text.

If applicable, teach the students how to use the three cuing systems of language (the *semantic system*, or word meanings; the *syntactic system*, or the patterns and structures of language; and the *graphophonic system*, or letter-sound relationships). Students apply this knowledge in relevant situations. For example, kindergarten children can suggest rhythmic language to use when writing an innovative version of a Big Book. Fourth graders can write an original Big Book with repetitive patterned language for preschool friends.

Other instructional techniques can also be used with literature to help young people become strategic communicators. Perhaps the *Think Aloud* approach is the most beneficial. When mature readers realize they do not understand a passage, they unconsciously reread it and look for words, phrases, or literary elements to help them understand the narrative. In a Think Aloud session, the teacher verbalizes to the learners the strategies or mental processes she uses to understand a passage. For example, when she is *unsure* of the meaning of the author's text, she thinks "I don't understand"; when she *understands* the text, she thinks, "Oh, now I see"; when she activates her schema and *elaborates* or adds to the text, she thinks, "This reminds me of the time . . . "; when she applies *reasoning* to the text, she thinks, "I know that this will happen if the character does this, therefore, he should. . . . " After the session the teacher discusses how the strategies helped her construct meanings elicited by the narrative and then encourages the students to use appropriate strategies as needed in their personal reading and writing experiences. Certain visuals described in Chapter 10 can also be used to help learners become strategic communicators; these include *Webbing* (a graphic representation of categories and their relationships), *KWL* (individuals list what they *Know*, *Want* to know), and how they will *Learn* about a topic), and *comparison charts.*

Various oral retelling approaches such as *Reciprocal Teaching* and the *ReQuest* approach also give learners suitable practice constructing meanings from the narratives and solving problems suggested by the visual and verbal texts.[5] In Reciprocal Teaching the teacher and learners read a selected narrative. The teacher asks a question related to the narrative, and the students react to the question. Then the teacher and learners take turns leading the discussion and asking the group other probes and prompts. The discussion leader (teacher or student) summarizes various responses and, if necessary, helps the participants reach a consensus about their interpretations of the literary selection. Group members are also encouraged to make predictions about future incidents.

Students especially enjoy the ReQuest strategy. In this approach, the teacher and students read a specified narrative. Then the children ask the teacher questions about the selection. When the students are finished asking the teacher questions, the teacher asks the students questions. This technique gives the teacher an opportunity to model exemplary questions and to praise students who think about the narrative and ask thought-provoking questions. When the students are ready to predict what will happen next in the narrative, they continue reading the text to affirm or modify their predictions. At this time it is a good idea to point out the clues or foreshadowing the author included to help them make suitable predictions. Before using Reciprocal Teaching or ReQuest, the teacher should model exemplary probes and prompts, talk informally

about formulating probes and prompts, and describe the types of replies the questions will elicit. Literal questions are used occasionally. Questioning techniques and examples of various questions, probes, and prompts are presented in Chapter 10.

These techniques give teachers an opportunity to show the purpose of using various communication strategies. The teacher can discuss why certain strategies are chosen, how the strategies can be modified if needed, and when another strategy should be selected for effective communication. After the discussion, students immediately practice selecting and using strategies with others.

THROUGH VARIOUS LITERARY EXPERIENCES, STUDENTS ACQUIRE, ENHANCE, AND DEVELOP WRITING, SPEAKING, AND LISTENING ABILITIES

We naturally use several language modalities, such as reading, writing, speaking, listening, and thinking, when we communicate with others. We listen to a speaker and respond to the thoughts he evokes; we talk about the ideas elicited by a written narrative we read; we use forms and structures of language similar to those used by a speaker to express ourselves in writing. As the LRMs presented in the genre chapters show, all approaches highlight these inseparable relationships. However, the Literature-Based Language Arts Approach emphasizes the unique connection among the modalities, and the selected instructional goals and strategies retain this link. The connection is obvious in LRMs children create in response to literature they read, listen to, or view. For example, after listening to Martin Waddell's *The Pig in the Pond* (1992), first graders enjoy pantomiming what happened when the characters jumped into the pond. Then partners write a sentence predicting what happened after the end of the book. The children can illustrate the sentences, arrange the sentences in a logical order, and place them in a bound book. Finally, using appropriate dramatic actions, the students can read the book to another class. In a fifth grade class, different groups of students can select a favorite event from Betsy Byars's *The Summer of the Swans* (1970). Each group will write a Readers Theatre script for the event and read it to the class. Later the groups can read their scripts to other classes.

Writing Experiences in the Literature Curriculum
When writing, authors move through several stages: reflecting, drafting, revising, editing, and publishing. Research findings suggest that students who select a topic for personal

writing and are aware of their audience produce high-quality written compositions. In the writing process, a student selects a topic, thinks about the incidents or information to include in the narrative, drafts the narrative, shares the draft with peers or the teacher, discusses modifications that might be made, edits the mechanics, and, when satisfied with the narrative, publishes it. By participating in the entire writing process, students come to realize that a draft is not a finished product. Teachers can inform the students that professional writers usually revise and edit their compositions many times before they are published. During the revising and editing stages, teachers frequently conduct mini-lessons related to specific stylistic elements students are not using appropriately. After the lessons, teachers encourage students to use the elements discussed in the lessons in their personal writing.

Writing is a vital component of all approaches to literary study. Students are encouraged to use the writing process in formulating their writings. In the literature curriculum, learners use the most appealing form of prose, poetry, drama, fiction, nonfiction, letters, essays, reports, or short stories when they create the following:

Write a *response* to the literature they have listened to, read, viewed, or discussed.

Use the structure and forms of literature as *models* for writing.

Express in writing personal ideas, attitudes, and thoughts.

Write to *convey facts* gained from reading and discussing a literary selection.

Written Responses to Literature   While exploring a literary selection or after completing it, learners can produce a written reaction or response to the literature. Written verbal LRMs, described in Appendix B, are suggested for this response. For example, younger students can use the words, phrases, content, and illustrations used by Marc Brown in his Arthur Series, such as *Arthur Goes to School* (1996). They will write a letter to Arthur the aardvark, describing their day at school or write to Marc Brown commenting on his style of writing and illustrating. Since letters require a particular format, the teacher might conduct a mini-lesson to discuss the structure of a friendly letter.

Older students can select a partner and write a conversation between two characters from a biography by Diane Stanley such as *Bard of Avon: The Story of William Shakespeare* (1992), *Leonardo da Vinci* (1996), or *Charles Dickens: The Man Who Had Great Expectations* (1993). Alternatively, the conversation could be between characters from two of her books. Before writing the dialogue, the partners will think about the habits, hobbies, and lifestyles of the characters. When the partners write the "authentic" conversations, they will identify and use literary conventions used by Stanley and will also clarify their reactions to the characters. As part of the process, the students also learn how to write conversations. Students also find ideas for written compositions in the reflections, reactions, and interpretations written in their LitLogs, discussed in Chapter 2.

Using the Structures and Forms of Literature as a Model for Writing   All forms and structures of language are found in literature. Teachers help learners observe the stylistic devices used by writers. Later they discuss the ability of the writer to convey ideas, emotions, memories, and information. Then, because most children are intrigued with the different forms and structures found in literary selections, they enjoy manipulating and experimenting with language when creating original compositions. Children can write a narrative for a wordless text. They also like to be reporters and write an article about an incident in a book. It is exciting to write a prediction about the future of a character or to write an article about the person's life in the future. Ideas such as these are found throughout this book and in other books devoted to the teaching of writing.[6]

Personal Written Expressions   The empowerment of teachers and students is a central principle in all literary approaches. A primary component of empowerment is that students should self-select reading materials and choose topics for written or oral productions. Therefore, literature does not stimulate or motivate all written compositions. Students must have the freedom to write about topics that are of interest to them at the time. Furthermore, they must select the way they want to communicate their ideas, such as narrative poems, songs, diary entries, books of experiments, or informational storybooks. Illustrations enhance the original writings.

Writing to Convey Information   Students gain information as they read, listen to, discuss, and think about topics with peers and adults. While sharing facts with others, they clarify, verify, and support their thinking. Learners need time to synthesize, summarize, and reflect on the content they have taken away from the literature. Then they are encouraged to share the content with others through clear, concise, cohesive written statements. Although conveying facts in a narrative format is possible, generally the expository structure is selected for informational writing. Because an expository text is different from a narrative text, writers of expository texts must organize their thoughts in description, sequence, cause-and-effect, compare and contrast and problem-solution structures, as described in Chapter 6. Learners must be aware of the different text structures so they can respond intelligently as listeners, readers, or speakers. Each text structure uses format clues, such as headings or certain words, to signal the type of structure used. A comparison of fictional narrative texts and expository texts is a valuable experience. Then students can use the visual representatives suggested for each structure to plan expository narratives. From the visual the girls and boys can write cohesive paragraphs and essays. As with fictional writing, peer and adult reactions are helpful during the revision, editing, and publication stages of writing factual articles, memos, and photo essays.[7]

Instructional Considerations   Throughout the week in all discipline areas, students can respond to literature, imitate the structures encountered, freely express their thoughts, and convey information obtained from selected literature. The instructional goals, the literature, and the abilities and interests of the children influence the type of writing selected for the literature curriculum. Some children become comfortable using a particular type of writing and need to be encouraged to use other forms. Children need to write daily. In this curriculum, the instructional focus emphasizes linking literature to personal writing experiences.

Writing takes time to plan, draft, revise, edit, and publish. A child might need a week or two to finish a written composition. Occasionally, after writing for several days,

the writer may lose interest in completing the composition. Professional writers tell us they finish some manuscripts quickly while others take longer. If a writer is having difficulty completing the manuscript, perhaps a gentle nudge from an interested person will help her or him complete it. Although we give students time to finish a written product, most teachers request that students publish several writings each report period. Ask students to place finished and unfinished compositions in their writing portfolio. Children who keep a list of Topics I Want to Write in their writing portfolios have a list of topics to complete throughout the year.

Speaking and Listening in the Literature Classroom

Separating speaking and listening from reading and writing is difficult and unnecessary. Students develop and enhance their speaking and listening abilities when they participate in literature discussion groups, oral writing, peer reading and writing, reading aloud, book talks, storytelling, and other oral techniques.

Speaking activities are compatible with the four types of writing: students talk about their responses, they use models from literature for personal presentations, they enjoy expressing their thoughts, and they convey information orally. Since communication is a two-way interaction requiring a sender and a receiver, speakers may expect listeners to use different levels of listening when they are receiving different forms of auditory communication. Listening to literature is a favorite activity for children of all

A literary newspaper gives students an opportunity to write personal responses to the literature they are reading and to convey information presented in the literature to others.

ages. Teachers are confident that the students are listening when appealing literature is read aloud. As they empathize with the characters, laugh at their antics, or imagine the scenery described by the author, the students are listening at an appreciative level. When listeners are receiving information, they listen attentively to the speaker's major points, assimilate them, and remember them. When listening to television advertising or political speeches, for example, listeners will monitor the information to determine if it is fact or opinion.

Chris Van Allsburg's *Bad Day at Riverbend* (1995) is a good book to read aloud. (See the Van Allsburg color plate.) The teacher will emphasize the foreshadowing clues that he includes in the verbal and visual narratives. These clues elicit predictions from children in kindergarten through second grade. The children also enjoy discussing the surprise ending.

Throughout the day the teacher models good listening strategies and encourages the students to listen to others. Individuals need to be aware of rituals of listening, how to listen, and when to respond to auditory messages. Discussing literature with a partner or in small and whole group sessions gives students an opportunity to develop their listening abilities. Chapter 10 discusses verbal and nonverbal expressions and suggests ideas for presenting literature orally. Oral verbal LRMs are suggested in the genre chapters and described in Appendix B.[8] Later in this chapter, independent reading and writing are discussed in the context of grouping students in the literature curriculum.

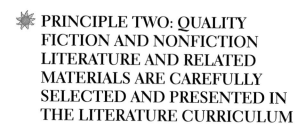

PRINCIPLE TWO: QUALITY FICTION AND NONFICTION LITERATURE AND RELATED MATERIALS ARE CAREFULLY SELECTED AND PRESENTED IN THE LITERATURE CURRICULUM

A major concern of teachers using literature in the classroom is how to choose appropriate literature and related materials for students. Teachers who are not familiar with many literary selections often feel overwhelmed when selecting books and related materials. Professional books and annotated bibliographies such as *Adventuring with Books* can be helpful when choosing books. Many selection sources are organized according to genre, content, or theme and contain a summary of the plot of each book and a critique of its literary merit. Some sources include suggestions for using the books in the classroom. Most media centers and public libraries have copies of selection tools. (Selection sources are described in Appendix G.)

School media specialists and public librarians like to help teachers find suitable fiction and nonfiction literature and related audio and visual materials that are available in the community. As teachers use more literature in the classroom, they purchase books for classroom libraries and enjoy helping the media specialist select books for the school media center. Criteria to consider when selecting literature and related materials are discussed in the next section.

In his book Bad Day at Riverbend, *Chris Van Allsburg develops two stories—one with the black-and-white line drawings, another with greasy slime and red, green, and blue crayon scribbling that appears on the sketches. On the last pages of the book the author–artist gives the reader clues to finish the stories. Wonder who is helping tell the second story?*

But just as they came over the hill, they were frozen in the bright light that suddenly filled the sky.

SELECT LITERATURE THAT CONTAINS HIGH LITERARY MERIT

Children and teachers can become treasure hunters looking for quality literature with content that stimulates individual curiosity and expands intellectual horizons. To determine the quality of a literary selection, classify the book in the appropriate literary genre, identify the distinctive characteristics of the genre, and evaluate the literary merit of the selection. The genre chapters include information about literary characteristics of genres and subgenres and suitable selection criteria.

It is a good idea to discuss book selection techniques with the students and to help them develop a list of selection criteria to use when choosing books for personal and group reading. Have the students prepare a literary ladder, described in Chapter 10, listing the distinctive characteristics to consider when selecting quality literature. With the students' assistance, prepare a list of topics that are of interest to the group. Display book recording devices (described in Appendix B) to highlight books recommended by peers. While discussing a book with students, informally note the outstanding literary elements of the book. Later the students can create an LRM involving the elements. For example, the point of view, characterization, and plot development are highlighted when individual children or partners rewrite an incident from another character's perspective. The writer reads the incident to the class who determines whether the narrative retained the personalities of the characters and the major incidents in the plot. Suitable narratives are tape-recorded for the listening center, and the written narratives are displayed on the bulletin board and eventually placed in the class anthology.

SELECT QUALITY LITERATURE THAT REPRESENTS THE STUDENTS' LITERARY PREFERENCES AND THEIR LINGUISTIC, COGNITIVE, AND SOCIAL DEVELOPMENT

The reader's relationship with the text is of primary consideration when selecting books. Teachers can listen to the children's comments about books, survey their interests, and select fiction and nonfiction literature of high literary merit that represents the students' expressed literary preferences. The teacher also selects well-written books from other genres and topics to enhance the students' literary interests and expand their linguistic, cognitive, and social development. Students enjoy hearing and reading a favorite book many times; they naturally prefer books with lifelike characters who are worthy of emulation. It is interesting to note that boys and girls may reject a book at the beginning of the year and enjoy reading or hearing it later in the year. Teachers also observe that a book that is popular one year may be rejected the next year by children of the same age. (Additional information about students' levels of development and literary

This young man has found a special place to browse through books that are especially interesting to him.

preferences is presented in Chapter 1 and in each genre chapter.)

Although learners may express a desire to read or hear a particular literary genre, a wise teacher will expose them to a variety of prose, poetry, and drama. If students are curious about a historical period, for example, they will enjoy reading both biographies and historical fiction set in that era. Thus, intermediate students who read Russell Freedman's *Lincoln: A Photobiography* (1989) might enjoy Carolyn Reeder's *Shades of Gray* (1989) and Patricia Beatty's *Charley Skedaddle* (1987) when they realize all three books are set during the American Civil War in different regions of the United States. By reading the biography and two books of historical fiction, the students are exposed to different perspectives about the people who lived during that period. Freedman's biography gives the reader a better understanding of Abraham Lincoln's agony as he made difficult decisions about the future of the country. The other books provide insights about the young men who attempted to carry out Lincoln's decisions.

SELECT THE BEST LITERATURE WRITTEN OR ILLUSTRATED BY AN AUTHOR, POET, OR ARTIST

Readers are naturally inclined to try to find out more about the person who created an appealing narrative, poem, or illustration. They wonder what the creator is really like, why she or he wrote or illustrated the selection in that way, and whether the book is autobiographical. When they read other books written or illustrated by that person, they build a friendship with the creator. They feel a sense of security reading books produced by the person because they anticipate his or her style of writing or illustrating.

As readers learn more about creators and their literary offerings, they become more discriminating in their selection of literature. Helping young people become discriminating readers and thinkers is a worthwhile goal of the total literature curriculum. The Literary Link for David Wiesner's *Tuesday* at the end of Chapter 8 provides information about the creator. Each genre chapter features an author and an artist in the "Did You Know About . . . ?" sections. Children can use the books listed in Appendix G to research a favorite creator and write a biographical sketch using the "Did You Know About . . . ?" format. At the end of the year, the sketches prepared during the year are placed in a bound book, given to the media specialist, and displayed in the school library.

SELECT QUALITY LITERATURE PORTRAYING BOTH GENDERS AND VARIOUS ETHNIC, RACIAL, SOCIAL, AND RELIGIOUS GROUPS

The teacher must be aware of the various groups portrayed in the books presented in the classroom throughout the year. Using literature with both male and female protagonists is preferable. Literature featuring various ethnic, racial, social, and religious groups should be presented to students. As young people explore the literary heritage of various groups and encounter realistic portrayals of individuals within the groups, they learn to interact positively with people from diverse societies. They develop a broader understanding of their ancestors' relationships with other groups and discover the personalities, lifestyles, and dreams of persons of various groups. Literature representing parallel cultures is discussed in Chapter 9. An excellent example is Paul Owen Lewis's *Storm Boy* (1995), which uses vivid language and images to describe a boy's adventure on the Northwest Pacific coast. (See the Lewis color plate.)

Totem poles, masks, and other symbols found in the Haida and Tlingit Native American tribes are shown in Paul Lewis's book, Storm Boy. *The artist–author surrounds his vivid black, red, white, and yellow gouache paintings with black frames. The folk art paintings realistically portray the unique story described in the verbal text.*

INTRODUCE STUDENTS TO LITERATURE WITH MORE COMPLEX IDEAS AND LANGUAGE THAN THEY NATURALLY CHOOSE FOR INDEPENDENT READING AND DISCUSSION

The Social-Constructivists believe knowledgeable adults must identify the children's operating level and expand their insights and understanding of concepts. Literature is the perfect medium to use to support this belief. (See Chapters 2 and 11 for additional information about Social-Constructivist Theories.) In addition to presenting literature that is familiar and comfortable to young people, we should also introduce literature with concepts and language they might not understand fully or cannot read without adult assistance. This experience challenges students to explore increasingly complex language and concepts with a more mature reader or adult. By reading challenging materials with students, teachers give them the needed support to think about and expand their language and knowledge. Teachers should select literature and instructional techniques that will enhance students' affective, cognitive, and linguistic development. Instructional support designed to expand the students' background knowledge is also recommended. Students who have positive experiences with literature and are involved in the selection process develop confidence in choosing books for independent reading and discussion.[9]

SELECT UNABRIDGED HARDBACK AND PAPERBACK EDITIONS

When surveyed about their preference for hardbacks versus paperbacks, intermediate-age students prefer reading paperback books. Although the print, paper, and covers in paperback books are of lower quality than those found in hardback books, young people apparently feel comfortable reading paperbacks. Perhaps paperbacks are less intimidating. Inexpensive, soft-covered books can be used in a classroom for one to three years. Some companies place hardback shell covers on paperback books. The paper and print in shell-covered books are the same as in soft-covered books. Shell-covered books do not cost as much as hardback books and usually last about five years in the classroom. The type of book used in the literature curriculum usually depends on how much money is available to purchase individual and multiple copies of books. The media specialist can suggest places to purchase hardback and soft-covered books at reasonable prices. Paperback books are available at a lower price through children's book clubs.

Occasionally, the clubs offer discount prices for multiple copies of individual books.

SATURATE STUDENTS WITH RELATED BOOKS AND AUDIOVISUAL MATERIALS

Sometimes related fiction and nonfiction books, magazines, newspapers, and various audiovisual materials can give children the additional background knowledge they need to understand the content in a book. Since we live in a visual society, tap into your students' visual abilities, and include many audiovisual materials in your presentation of literature. Some students are visual or auditory learners and need additional visual or auditory assistance to fully understand the content, plot development, setting, or characterization of a narrative or poem. Additional information about selecting and presenting films, pictures, videos, newspaper or magazine articles, and other audiovisual productions and multimedia technologies is presented in Chapter 10.

✳ PRINCIPLE THREE: THE INSTRUCTIONAL GOALS DETERMINE THE ORGANIZATION OF LITERATURE PRESENTED IN THE LITERATURE CURRICULUM

The ultimate goal of the literature curriculum is to help students develop a lifelong habit of selecting literature for pleasure and informational purposes. As individuals experience a variety of prose, poetry, and drama, they recognize the beauty and power of language to explore ideas, express feelings and dreams, and convey information. To help students explore the beauty and power of language, teachers provide varied literary experiences by implementing three approaches—the *Pure Literature Approach*, the *Literature-Based Language Arts Approach*, and the *Literature Across the Curriculum Approach*. As Chapter 11 described, these approaches highlight different goals and instructional focuses and are presented independently or simultaneously throughout the day.

In an organized literature curriculum, young people have many experiences with all literary genres, various creators, and a variety of topics. While individual teachers may develop and use literature in their classrooms, typically the grade level, school, or school district is involved in selecting thematic units and recommending instructional goals. When selecting literature for use in the classroom, a major consideration must be the number of available books in the school and county media center.

Administrators realize that when teachers are empowered to select and implement an appropriate literature curriculum, students are more interested in the topics and are motivated to learn; their achievement scores also improve. When individual literary selections and LitSets are used in the classroom, teachers need several copies of the books they use for instructional purposes. The teachers must constantly replace popular books and add new books to update the class and library collections. Thus, administrative support is crucial for the continuing development of a literature curriculum.[10]

When a literature curriculum is developed for an entire school or district, it is a good idea to involve teachers in the process. Teachers representing each grade level meet, review the predetermined schoolwide instructional goals, and identify literature that helps achieve those goals. They select a Schoolwide Core Literature Collection that contains a basic list of books. Usually, they arrange the collection by grade levels so that the same books will not be used in several grades. Then grade-level teachers identify additional fiction and nonfiction literature to expand, enrich, or enhance the grade-level instructional goals. Frequently, the literature selected for the Core Literature Collection is arranged in thematic collections of LitSets. In addition to the thematic collections, teachers also present individual books for pleasurable and instructional purposes.

A LITERATURE CURRICULUM INCLUDES INDIVIDUAL BOOKS

As the reflection guides in Chapter 11 indicated, individual books can be used successfully to meet the goals of each literary approach. In the Pure Literature Approach, individual books are used extensively for pleasure. In this approach the teacher presents classical and contemporary fiction and nonfiction books of high literary merit. The books are not necessarily related to other literature presented in the classroom and are rarely included in the Schoolwide Core Literature Collection.

Individual books are used as Focus Books (or Core Books) to achieve specific goals in both the Literature-Based Language Arts Approach and the Literature Across the Curriculum Approach. A Focus Book contains a topic related to a unit of study. For example, Laura Numeroff's *If You Give A Mouse a Cookie* (1985) enhances children's reading, oral, and writing abilities and may be used in the Literature-Based Language Arts Approach. Marie McSwigan's *Snow Treasure* (1942) helps young people understand human behavior during wartime and may be used in the Literature Across the Curriculum Approach (see the Literary Link in Appendix E). Focus Books also present content related to various discipline areas as seen in the Literary Link for John Gardiner's *Stone Fox* (1980) in Chapter 11.

Individual books are presented to a small group or the entire class through reading aloud, partner reading, or shared reading techniques. When the teacher uses an aesthetic focus to present the book, he or she uses the *connect* and *construct* components and perhaps the *create* component of the Literary Transaction Process. A teacher may use oral techniques to present a Focus Book to different groups of children. Individuals, partners, or small groups also read the books independently. Usually, the teacher uses the book to introduce a unit of study or a topic for study across several curricular areas. For additional instructional strategies, see Chapter 11.

A LITERATURE CURRICULUM INCLUDES THEMATIC COLLECTIONS OF LITERATURE

To achieve the stated instructional goals in the Literature Across the Curriculum Approach and the Literature-Based Language Arts Approach, the teacher also uses thematic collections of literature, or *LitSets*. To create the collections, teachers organize books, poems, short stories, plays, essays, and related audio and visual materials in various categories. Broad categories for LitSets include the content of a literary selection, identified literary structures in specific books, various literary genres, a Focus Book, or the study of a creator. A LitSet supplements, clarifies, supports, or enriches a particular subject area or several related discipline areas.[11]

The teacher should select age-appropriate materials that will achieve the identified instructional goals of the thematic study. When students explore the same central theme in various literary genres, they develop a broader understanding of the topic. By exploring multiple sources, they obtain various perspectives on a particular topic and discover universal concerns of various groups. Thematic organizations help boys and girls make intratextual connections between previous literary experiences and concepts.[12]

Only fiction and nonfiction of high literary merit are selected for a collection. The literature selected over the course of the year should include protagonists of both genders and characters reflecting various groups of people. The teacher should also consider the following when selecting a thematic collection:

Frequently, a particular subject is found naturally in only one or two literary genres. Therefore, to expose students to all genres, the teacher will select a topic found in genres not highlighted in the previous theme.

The selected literature must present the theme and subtopics naturally and authentically.

Students may assist in selecting appropriate materials for the LitSet.

If adequate literary selections are not available for a topic, merge the topic with a broader one or eliminate the topic until adequate literature is available to support it. Teachers can ask the media specialist to purchase selected materials that they need for important themes.

The chapter bibliographies in this book are arranged thematically to assist in selecting materials. Several Literary Links also suggest LitSets to be used with the book. A LitSet is presented in Chapters 5 and 6.

Topics for Thematic Categories of Literature

The instructional goals of the various literary approaches determine the topics selected for LitSets. The topics should be relevant to the teacher's purpose for using literature; the children's interests and development; the instructional goals; the structures, forms, and elements of literature; and the people who create the literature. Each topic must be broad enough to contain subtopics related to various subject areas, but not so broad that the information will overwhelm the children. Generally, literature is organized into five thematic categories: content, genres, elements, Focus Book, and creators.

Thematic organizations provide the vehicle for linking the students' knowledge across contexts and subject areas. The materials arranged in the thematic collections promote this connection. While broad thematic categories are suitable for organizing literature, teachers and students select the individual themes that will accomplish the identified curricular purposes and goals. As noted previously, some schools select themes to be presented throughout the year, but students can have input by suggesting themes and submitting questions about the thematic topic. The teacher uses appropriate suggestions and incorporates relevant questions into the thematic study.[13] The following topics are age appropriate and meet the purposes described above:

Kindergarten through second grade: "Are You My Friend?" "Books to Sing," "Hello Mr. Lobel, Toad, and Frog," and "Dinosaur Time."

Third and fourth grades: "Making Mischief," "I Can Read a Book without Words," "This Is the Cat's Meow," and "A Collection of Weird Friends."

Fifth and sixth grades: "In My Time Machine," "Mysterious Clues," "In the Cupboard with Lynn Reid Banks," and "Fly Away Home."

These topics are suitable for the thematic categories suggested in Figure 12.2 on page 436 for the organization of literature in the curriculum.[14]

Presentation of LitSets and Thematic Instruction

The thematic organization of literature gives students an opportunity to search in various materials for answers to important questions and connect ideas presented in the fiction and nonfiction sources. As learners compare information presented by different writers and question different points of view presented in the selections, they are actively engaged in learning, using techniques of scientific inquiry, and developing the ability to think critically.

Teachers use LitSets with groups of children in one curricular area or in several discipline areas. To do this, they schedule a block of time several times a week for thematic instruction. Teachers who highlight the same topic in all three literary approaches use the LitSets throughout the day. After materials are collected for the LitSet, the teacher will skim the materials, note probes and prompts stimulated by the selections, and identify alternative LRMs the children might create to gain a broader understanding of the topic. The teacher reviews instructional goals and plans instructional strategies that naturally evolve from the literature to help students achieve the goals. The teacher will share one or two books from the LitSet orally with the entire class. Individuals, partners, and small groups will explore the remaining materials in the collection.

The students will use oral techniques such as book talks, storytelling, dramatic activities, written activities, and visuals to entice peers to read the selected literature. For example, students will select a central topic from each book. Small groups will review the topic and select a group member to serve on an Expert Panel. This panel will discuss (or debate) the issue based on the material in the books. Groups can join, compare the coverage of the topic in their particular books, and record the information on a comparison chart. Then they can critique the authenticity, accuracy, and coverage of the topic in each book. Rotate the books between groups, so that all students will have an opportunity to explore most of the books in the LitSet. Another technique is to encourage the students to find suitable poetry for the theme. Have them copy the poems on the computer. At the end of the year, prepare a class poetry anthology. Then copies of the anthology are printed for each class member.

Give the media specialist a list of the themes to be presented during the year, and request appropriate audiovisual materials to use with the LitSet. Reserve a bulletin board for the theme. Have the students display LRMs, visuals, and other related materials, so that the classroom is saturated with information about the topic. Additional instructional strategies, student responses, the role of the teacher, and evaluation procedures for each literary approach are listed in the reflection guides. Other instructional techniques and related books are discussed throughout this book.[15]

FIGURE 12.2 Thematic Categories for the Organization of Literature

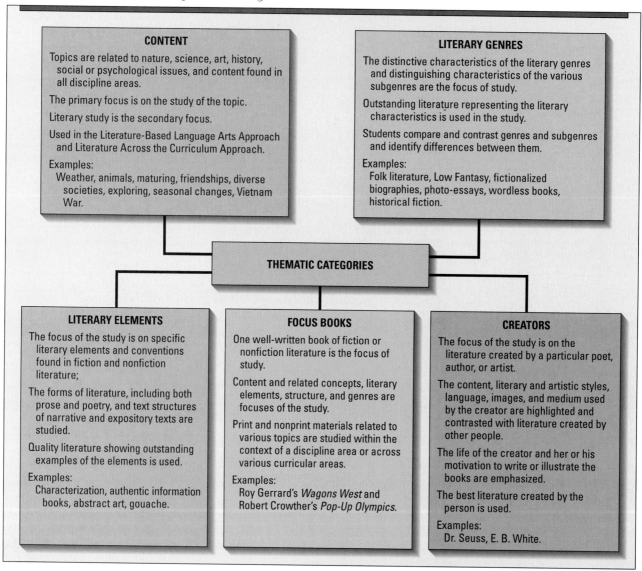

CONTENT

Topics are related to nature, science, art, history, social or psychological issues, and content found in all discipline areas.

The primary focus is on the study of the topic.

Literary study is the secondary focus.

Used in the Literature-Based Language Arts Approach and Literature Across the Curriculum Approach.

Examples:
 Weather, animals, maturing, friendships, diverse societies, exploring, seasonal changes, Vietnam War.

LITERARY GENRES

The distinctive characteristics of the literary genres and distinguishing characteristics of the various subgenres are the focus of study.

Outstanding literature representing the literary characteristics is used in the study.

Students compare and contrast genres and subgenres and identify differences between them.

Examples:
 Folk literature, Low Fantasy, fictionalized biographies, photo-essays, wordless books, historical fiction.

THEMATIC CATEGORIES

LITERARY ELEMENTS

The focus of the study is on specific literary elements and conventions found in fiction and nonfiction literature;

The forms of literature, including both prose and poetry, and text structures of narrative and expository texts are studied.

Quality literature showing outstanding examples of the elements is used.

Examples:
 Characterization, authentic information books, abstract art, gouache.

FOCUS BOOKS

One well-written book of fiction or nonfiction literature is the focus of study.

Content and related concepts, literary elements, structure, and genres are focuses of the study.

Print and nonprint materials related to various topics are studied within the context of a discipline area or across various curricular areas.

Examples:
 Roy Gerrard's *Wagons West* and Robert Crowther's *Pop-Up Olympics*.

CREATORS

The focus of the study is on the literature created by a particular poet, author, or artist.

The content, literary and artistic styles, language, images, and medium used by the creator are highlighted and contrasted with literature created by other people.

The life of the creator and her or his motivation to write or illustrate the books are emphasized.

The best literature created by the person is used.

Examples:
 Dr. Seuss, E. B. White.

✸ PRINCIPLE FOUR: IN THE LITERATURE CURRICULUM, STUDENTS READ AND WRITE INDEPENDENTLY, IN SMALL GROUPS, AND WITH THE ENTIRE CLASS

Students read, react, and respond to literature independently, in small group sessions, and with the entire class. Teachers arrange groups to achieve specific purposes; when the students accomplish the goals, the groups are disbanded. Groups are flexible and are formed in different ways. Some students might work in a group because they want to explore the same literary selection. Students with different abilities might be placed in a group so they can accomplish an instructional goal. Frequently, group membership is determined by the ability of a student to work with others. When students work in groups, they learn to communicate, negotiate, and support others.[16]

TIME IS RESERVED DAILY FOR INDEPENDENT READING AND WRITING

Each day students and teachers spend time alone reading appealing literature and writing self-selected topics. This independent activity releases participants from instructional

It's fun to read books all by yourself—especially ones we select!

TABLE 12.1 Benefits Individuals Gain from Independent Reading and Writing Experiences

The experience gives the reader an opportunity to read self-selected literature and enables the writer to select topics of interest and experiment with various modes to express personal thoughts and feelings.

As students have many experiences reading a variety of literary genres and writing about different topics, they become more discriminating in selecting literature and choosing topics for personal writing.

Individuals become self-confident and realize that they are readers and writers.

While reading independently, learners react spontaneously to visual and verbal narratives in literature. When writing, they feel a sense of freedom from mechanical restraints.

As individuals practice reading and writing, they understand the importance and purposes of communicating effectively in school and throughout life.

Through the experiences young people refine personal strategies related to reading and writing, such as how to draft and edit personal writing, when to skim or scan a text, and how to assume a stance toward a literary selection.

Individuals learn to tune out distractions and increase their power of concentration.

Young people learn to use the resources in the classroom, in school and public libraries, and in bookstores. They develop a habit of using these facilities.

Students better understand the development of a cohesive text and the different text structures found in nonfiction, fiction, and dramatic narratives. Usually, they apply this information to their personal reading, writing, and speaking.

responsibilities and gives them time to read and write for pleasure, which helps them develop a positive attitude toward reading and writing.[17] Research also suggests that children who spend time in independent reading and writing sessions improve in reading achievement, vocabulary growth, language fluency, and the use of oral and written language. Table 12.1 presents other benefits individuals gain from independent reading and writing (also called Sustained Silent Reading, or SSR; Drop Everything and Read and Write, or DEAR; and recreational reading and writing).[18]

Implementing Independent Reading and Writing Sessions

During independent reading and writing sessions, participants read selections recommended by others, explore other materials, and experiment with various types of writing. A classroom filled with all types of reading materials, such as magazines, travel brochures, and hardcover and softcover books, and a variety of paper and instruments to use when writing will motivate students to read and write independently. These materials are placed in a conspicuous place in the room, such as the literature center or a writing center. (See Chapter 2 for additional ideas about designing a literature-rich environment.)[19]

Students need uninterrupted time away from others to read, reflect, and respond to their reading and to write about self-selected topics. Teachers schedule independent reading and writing for the entire class at one time. Students also read or write when they have completed assigned tasks. This activity is successful for all ages. In preschool and kindergarten classes, the children select several books, find a quiet place in the room, and spend time looking at the literature. Teachers initially give the children five to ten minutes to view the books, but by the end of the year, they gradually increase the time to fifteen or twenty minutes each day. In the primary grades, children spend at least twenty minutes each day browsing, viewing, and reading literature and related materials. Intermediate-age students spend at least twenty-five minutes each day in independent reading activities. Students need additional time for independent writing. Primary teachers schedule at least ten additional minutes each day, and intermediate teachers add approximately twenty minutes each day for writing activities.[20]

The teacher introduces independent reading and writing to the students and parents or guardians at the beginning of the school year. The students help develop the routine and procedural guidelines, such as the following:

Everyone in the class reads or writes at the same time.

Only emergency interruptions are allowed.

A reader selects a single piece of reading material for each session.

Teachers announce the time for the session at the beginning of the period. Use a timer to stop the session.

Sharing will be voluntary; students will not be expected to share.

After completing classroom assignments, students can sit quietly in the specified place and read or write. Students must stay on task and not bother other people.

Independent reading and writing are successful and inexpensive activities to implement if many suitable books are available in school and public libraries. This is a good time for teachers to read the literature the children are reading, so that they can discuss it with the children. Teachers can also spend the time reviewing literature that contains controversial words, incidents, or behavior, so that they will be prepared to support the book later, if necessary.

An enthusiastic teacher who provides time for students to read and write personally selected materials is helping them develop a lifelong habit of reading and writing. While many students know what to read and what they want to write about, some students may need help and encouragement selecting books and topics for writing. Teachers use several techniques to help children make these decisions. For example, when teachers or peers recommend books they have read, a student can record the title of interesting books on a list of "Books I Want to Read." The student can keep this list in her or his literature portfolio and refer to it when looking for a book to read. Sometimes the teacher will observe individual students reading books written by the same person or books from the same series or genre. Later the teacher can give book talks to introduce the students to various authors, different series, and all literary genres. To help students select writing topics, teachers can encourage them to keep a LitLog in their portfolios. In this log they will record personal reflections, reactions, or responses to literature they are reading. Students use these thoughts and reactions for further writing. Teachers can suggest various LRMs to stimulate writing ideas. For example, two students who have read the same book will form a partnership. The partners will assume the roles of different characters from the book and write a conversation. The conversations should include comments the characters might make to one another and questions that demand more than a yes or no reply. Usually, partners enjoy the activity for several days or weeks.

Each week the teacher schedules regular time for students to talk about the books they are reading, share personal writing, or show LRMs they have prepared during the independent session. When boys and girls share their responses and read their original writing, they can sit in a chair designated the "author's chair." Teachers do not give assignments during independent reading and writing sessions. Students' products are not evaluated, but teachers may review them informally to help select topics for future mini-lessons.

STUDENTS IN SMALL GROUPS ARE COMFORTABLE SHARING AUTHENTIC PERSONAL INTERPRETATIONS OF A LITERARY SELECTION

Two to six students form a small group to read, discuss, or write about personal interpretations of the same book. Many students like an informal, intimate group because it seems less intimidating than a large group session. In these "risk-free" sessions, students interact with others about their reactions to literature and discuss interesting content in the literature. Through active participation in the group, students will ask questions and support their personal interpretations of the literature.

Girls and boys also learn to clarify their interpretations and express personal opinions about the literary selection. By participating in small groups, young people have an opportunity to practice oral reading skills and share their writing with others who respect their ideas. While using oral and written language for various purposes, learners enhance their linguistic, social, and cognitive abilities.

Before initiating a small group session, the teacher and students will discuss, demonstrate, and practice the roles and responsibilities of participants. With young children and at the beginning of the year with older children, the teacher will announce the group tasks, the pages to read before discussion, and the time schedule. The teacher will introduce the literature to the children through storytelling, dramatic activities, puppets, or other visuals. During the small group sessions, students might participate in activities such as the following:

Learners will form research groups to collect information about a specific topic, author, or genre. Later the group will present the information to the class using enticing, attractive visuals.

Before reading a book, group members will brainstorm or categorize topics related to the selection, make predictions about the characters or the plot, or formulate questions about the topics. After reading the selection, they will modify or confirm their predictions and answer their questions.

After reading several books by a particular author, poet, or illustrator, the group will conduct research about the person's life and style and about topics typically included in his or her literature. The groups will share this information with the class.

STUDENTS PARTICIPATE IN SAME-AGE PARTNERSHIPS AND CROSS-AGE PARTNERSHIPS

When students share literature with others, they may participate in same-age partnerships and cross-age partnerships. In a same-age partnership, students in the same class or grade work together to accomplish a given task. They form a partnership to read and discuss the same text or to react to each other's writing. In a cross-age partnership, a kindergarten or primary child is paired with an older student—a "buddy"—to share literature, writing, viewing, or other instructional topics.

Same-age partnerships are temporary. They are formed according to the literature being read, the students' interests, or their friendships. Usually, students who need addi-

tional assistance with reading or writing are paired with more mature readers and writers. The teacher or the students may form the partnership. Partners sit together in a designated place in the room. They read silently or take turns reading pages chosen by the partners or the teacher. The partners discuss their reactions to the text and help each other with the language and with unfamiliar content or ideas presented in the narrative. The partners also react to original writing.

In cross-age partnerships, the older student is the team leader, and must understand the purpose and goals of each session. Usually, the session lasts fifteen to twenty minutes and is held on a regular schedule. Young children are disappointed if the older student does not attend the sessions as scheduled. Partners and teachers from both classes must support the endeavor.

Cross-age partners share literature and personal writing. (See photo on p. 441.) They also enjoy interacting socially with a student of another age. Frequently, the younger child dictates a personal response to a book to the older student. Then the older student edits the writing and records it, and the younger child illustrates the writing. Cross-age partnerships are also formed for instructional purposes. Not only is the younger child eager to have an older student's instruction, but the older student learns the content by instructing the younger child. Campus spirit is enhanced when younger students see their "hero" on the school grounds. Table 12.2 on page 440 presents guidelines for implementing cross-age partnership sessions.[21]

Same-age partnerships give young people a chance to share topics of interest with a friend. In this partnership the boys are busy confirming their interpretations.

TABLE 12.2 Guidelines for Implementing Cross-Age Partnership Sessions

Students in both classes must understand the routine, procedures, and personal responsibilities for the partnership.

Teachers announce the schedule before the sessions begin.

Before the sessions, teachers arrange places to meet, such as designated hallways, the school media center, the teachers' conference room, or one or both classrooms.

Teachers of older students demonstrate reading aloud techniques, discuss the selection of suitable books for a younger child, suggest suitable writing activities for younger children, and discuss ways to involve the youngsters in the reading and writing activities.

Older students need time to practice reading aloud and to plan related activities. If needed, teachers and peers can offer suggestions for the oral reading or activities.

Teachers talk to the young children about listening and discussing literature, dictating original stories, retelling a narrative, and working cooperatively with the older student.

At the end of each session, older students record the literature read, the activity completed, and each partner's reaction to the experience. They give the information to their respective teachers. Students use criteria such as the following for the reactions:

> Did the partners enjoy the activity?
>
> What did they gain from the experience?
>
> Did the older partner select appropriate literature and activities?
>
> Did the older partner present the materials effectively?
>
> Did the older partner conduct the session appropriately?
>
> Was the session worthwhile?
>
> Should the partners repeat the activity?
>
> If they repeat it, should they modify some portion?

Same-age and cross-age partnerships are a type of peer tutoring that is beneficial for both partners. Both partners use various reading strategies that enhance their reading and writing abilities. The partnership improves each person's self-concept, as the partners learn to interact with others. Partners are enthusiastic about the experience and express a positive attitude toward reading, writing, and other school subjects discussed in the session.

LITERATURE DISCUSSION GROUPS ARE A VITAL COMPONENT OF THE LITERATURE CURRICULUM

Literature discussion groups (also called *literature study groups, literature response groups, book clubs,* or *cooperative literature groups*) consist of five to seven individuals who meet to read, react to, and respond to the same piece of literature. Groups meet several times each week before, during, or after reading, hearing, or viewing the preassigned portion of a book. Members discuss their personal reactions to and interpretations of the selection.

Literature discussion groups are a popular way to give students authentic reasons for talking about, writing about, and thinking about literature they have explored. Many researchers and writers have investigated the use of literature discussion groups and have discovered various benefits individuals gain from the experience; these are presented in Table 12.3 on page 441.[22]

Implementing a Literature Discussion Group

As discussed in Chapter 10, selections for group discussions should include quality contemporary and classical literature with appealing content that represents various genres, features protagonists of both genders, and reflects various groups of people. Students may discuss a Focus Book or an outstanding selection from a LitSet. Suitable nonfiction literature is current, authentic, and well written and contains interesting topics. Suitable fiction is thought provoking, compelling, suspenseful, and filled with vivid, lifelike characters who have exciting adventures.

In some classes several groups read the same book. In other classes each group reads a different book. The students' ability to interact in a group, the number of copies of a book available, and the teacher's confidence in facilitating the groups determines the number of different books used in a classroom at a particular time. Each member of a group or partners will have a copy of the book while reading and discussing it. When several groups are reading different books, the teacher participates with each group two or three times a week. This helps the teacher relinquish control and "empower" the group. When students assume control of the group, they usually will stay on task and ac-

Reading with a "buddy" is a special treat! We have fun reading together and talking about the story.

TABLE 12.3   Benefits Individuals Gain from Participating in Literature Discussion Groups

Through discussion, participants work together to construct meanings of a piece of literature. They clarify, modify, confirm, support, and elaborate personal thoughts and understandings.

In the groups young people discuss personal reactions about a selection without fear of ridicule from peers.

Individuals with limited language and social skills can participate effectively with more mature individuals in the group.

Participants realize literature evokes different reactions and responses from people. In discussion groups they attempt to reach a consensus by listening to, considering, and respecting the opinions of others.

By participating in a supportive environment, students recognize the pleasure of reading and discussing an entire book. This experience motivates learners to choose to read and express personal ideas using different modes of oral and written communication.

Students' writings often reflect concerns and issues discussed in the group.

Young people enjoy talking about the people who create literature. After learning more about the creator, students are likely to comment on the individual's choice of topics, his or her style of writing, or the artistic merit of the visual narratives. Students' original writing and illustrations are influenced and enhanced by this attention to the art of creating literature.

complish the group goals. A projected schedule for the various groups is presented in Table 12.7 on page 446.

When introducing literature discussion groups to a class, the teacher is responsible for selecting the members of the group. As they become comfortable with the activity, students participate in the selection. Some groups consist of several mature readers and one or two less able readers. The teacher ensures that each group includes a responsible person who will keep the group on task and another person who will guide and support other members as needed. Some groups contain students who want to read a particular book. Other groups include students who want to read, write, and discuss a book with special friends.

Literature discussion groups flourish in risk-free, trusting, supportive environments where teachers and peers respect and value all responses. At the beginning of the year and later if necessary, the teacher talks about the purposes and routines of a successful discussion group and describes the role of the leader and the participants. The number of days required for a group to read, discuss, and respond to a book varies depending on the students' abilities, the interactions within the group, the responses the group chooses to create, and the complexity of the literary selection. Students need to spend a minimum of forty-five minutes each day reading, discussing, and writing about their book. Primary children usually spend three or more days reading

TABLE 12.4 A Typical Routine for Reading, Discussing, and Writing about Books

1. The group meets, looks over the book, and talks about the information on the front and back covers. The members might meet with the teacher who gives them information about the text. At the beginning of the year, the teacher suggests the number of pages the group will read before discussion. After experience with discussion groups, the participants make this decision. Some learners prefer to read half or all of a book before discussing it. The age and maturity of the members, their experience responding to literature, and the selected literature help the leader determine the number of pages the group will read.

2. On the same day or the following day, students will read the predetermined pages independently or with a partner.

3. On the same day or the following day, students will discuss their reactions with their partner and write personal reflections, reactions, or questions about the reading.

4. The group meets on one or two days to discuss the reading. Members bring their journal writings and questions to discuss with the group. If appropriate, a group may spend several days preparing a visual or verbal response to the selection. While reading a book, students will periodically prepare a response to advertise the book and share it with the class. This will entice other students to read the selection later. Students may prepare a culminating response after reading, discussing, and responding to the book.

and responding to a book; older students usually spend two or more weeks. Table 12.4 presents a typical routine for a discussion group.

The Role of the Student Participant

All students actively participate in the discussion and spontaneously comment on the literature. Through questions, probes, and prompts, the participants seek to clarify other members' interpretations of the narratives. They also present evidence to support personal responses. Participants practice discussion etiquette while reacting to the literature. They bring to the sessions written questions, personal reflections, and reactions they had while reading independently. Groups work together to construct meanings by rereading a passage, discussing unfamiliar vocabulary, or reviewing nuances that provide clues for interpretation. When group members share personal experiences that influenced their reactions to a book, participants realize that their background understanding and experiences—schemata—influence their personal interpretations. If conflicting interpretations arise in the group, participants attempt to resolve the conflicts.

Initially, participants adopt a predominantly aesthetic stance to the literary selection. This guides them to personally experience the text and reflect on the interesting, pleasing, surprising, frightening, or troubling elements of the verbal and visual narratives. Reflection elicits personal memories that help the students make connections to the text and express reactions and responses to the literary work. To help learners develop literary insights and aesthetic judgments about a piece of literature, the teacher uses literary terminology informally while discussing the elements of the text. For example, the leader will direct the participants' attention to the theme or subthemes, discuss how a biographical character or event in history is authentically portrayed, or highlight the artistic elements or design used by the illustrator to interpret, clarify, or replace the verbal narrative. When participants are aware of literary elements such as these, they recognize the art of literature. Usually, they will use appropriate elements in their original writing or speeches.

The Role of the Teacher Participant-Facilitator

A teacher might be a participant in one group, an observer in another, and a facilitator in another.[23] A teacher participant-facilitator encourages all students to share worthwhile ideas about the literature they are reading, viewing, hearing, and discussing. One way the teacher can do this is by preparing a Literary Link for the literature the children will discuss. (See Chapter 2 and model Literary Links presented throughout the book.) When the students move from one group to another, they will use suitable probes or present personal reflections or reactions to the selection. Students benefit from hearing adult reactions, but the teacher must be cautious not to dominate or control the discussion.

As a participant-facilitator, the teacher empowers the participants to select the books read, lead the discussion, ask questions, express their interpretations of a selection, and select and generate responses representing those interpretations. Initially, many writers and researchers suggested that the teacher should assume a "hands off" approach and be a silent participant who would neither clarify nor add information to the discussions led by students. The problem with this approach, however, is that while some students can discuss their responses, many young people cannot. Often groups without mature leadership become little more than exchanges of surface interpretations of the text.

Experience using literature discussion groups in the classroom has shown that learners need intellectual guidance to reflect and react to the ideas and emotions evoked by the text and the information it presents. Students may also need assistance focusing attention on the important features of the visual and verbal narratives. Therefore, expert teacher participant-facilitators need to consider their vital roles in literature discussion groups. Table 12.5 on page 444 presents a reflection guide for a teacher participant-facilitator to use with literature discussion groups.

Girls and boys like to read a book together and then share their reflections and reactions about the book. Wonder what personal memories this text elicits to help the students clarify their thoughts?

The teacher can answer the questions in the table by analyzing audio- or videotaping sessions or requesting feedback from a peer coaching team.

A Cooperative Group Arrangement Is Suitable for a Literature Discussion Group

A literature discussion group operates more efficiently if the group members use the procedures and routines suggested for a cooperative group arrangement. At the beginning of a cooperative group session, the teacher sets out the purposes of the session, presents specific goals, and defines the roles the participants will assume. Later in the year mature students help specify the purpose, goals, and roles assumed by the group. Research about the cooperative group model suggests students learn group dynamics, express positive attitudes toward learning, and exhibit self-confidence about their academic accomplishments.[24] Participants in cooperative literature discussion groups become interdependent and learn to work together to maximize the learning of all group members. By interacting favorably with other group members, each participant assumes responsibility for helping the group achieve the stated goals.[25]

During the discussion the students assume various roles, such as group leader, recorder, supporter, facilitator, and monitor. After participating in a cooperative group, students review and evaluate the experience, identify the contribution each person made to the accomplishment of group goals, and suggest ways to improve the dynamics of the group. Various procedures and instruments are available for this investigation.[26] The procedures and instructional techniques that teachers use to implement cooperative discussion groups are presented in Table 12.6 on page 444.[27]

TEACHERS USE A KALEIDOSCOPE STRATEGY WITH APPROPRIATE LITERATURE

In the kaleidoscope strategy, a teacher separates a book into distinct incidents. Each group receives a segment, reads it, and prepares an oral presentation of the segment. The teacher then introduces the book, and each group attempts to place its segment in the proper sequence to create a cohesive plot structure. After the segments are arranged in the proper order, each group will orally present its incident. At the end of the presentations, the book will be in the proper sequence.

Not all books are suitable to use with this instructional strategy. The book should be one that the children do not know. The episodes must be well developed and arranged in definite sections. The plot must contain obvious clues or foreshadowing to help the students connect the various incidents. Quality books of fiction with interesting content, well-developed characters, and episodes that include action, suspense, and adventure are suitable. Examples include Sandra Belton's *Ernestine & Amanda* (1996) and Mildred Taylor's *Mississippi Bridge* (1990). Well-written, cohesive nonfiction literature with a sequential structure and segments linking the plot in a logical order is also appropriate. Examples include John Duggleby's *Artist in Overalls: The Life of Grant Wood*

TABLE 12.5 A Reflection Guide for a Teacher Participant-Facilitator

As a participant-facilitator, the teacher will use the following strategies:

Spend less time talking and more time listening to the reactions of student participants.

Respect the learners' interpretations and facilitate individual reactions and responses.

Model open-ended probes and prompts in the group to help learners make personal associations, develop intertextual connections, and construct interpretations elicited by the verbal and visual narratives.

Plan probes and prompts to use, if necessary, to help participants relate to the characters, content, mood, themes, and style of writing; for example, "I wonder . . . ," "Did you feel . . . ?" "If you were . . . ?"

The teacher participant-facilitator will reflect on his or her personal participation by considering the following questions:

Did I wait long enough for participants to react before jumping into the discussion?

Did I introduce the content of the students' discussion, or did I sit quietly and wait for the students to initiate the discussion?

Do I need to reword my probes and prompts to help students gain insights from the literature and apply personal knowledge, feelings, ideas, or attitudes to the visual and verbal elements in the narratives?

Did I miss the "teachable literary moments" by failing to help students connect their impressions to the author's text?

Was I aware of the group dynamics? Did I help facilitate equal participation by all participants?

The teacher participant-facilitator will consider the following factors:

Was the literary selection suitable for the participants? If not, why not?

Did I encourage participants to personally select responses that reflected their natural reflections on and reactions to the content and outstanding literary elements of the selection? If students needed help selecting responses, did I suggest a variety of suitable LRMs?

Would other instructional strategies or techniques encourage interactions from all participants? If so, identify strategies or techniques to use with the next group.

Would other instructional strategies or techniques help participants connect, construct, and create interpretations of the text? If so, identify strategies or techniques to use with the next group.

How did the members benefit from the experience? List the general benefits gained from the experience. Record individual benefits in each child's literature portfolio.

TABLE 12.6 Procedures and Instructional Techniques Used in Cooperative Groups

All group members actively participate in responding to, supporting, and generating interpretations of a text.

The teacher models personal language and response strategies.

Students use problem-solving strategies to react and respond to the literature and support other members of the group.

Participants use appropriate terminology to focus attention on a text's outstanding literary elements and the ability of the author and artist to use these elements effectively in verbal and visual narratives.

Participants use open-ended probes and prompts to discuss the verbal and visual narratives and to elicit personal reactions and responses to the literary selection.

The groups provide a risk-free environment for participants to construct meanings, express reactions, and create literary responses.

The participants use appropriate verbal and nonverbal expressions to communicate ideas, information, and feelings to other group members.

(1996), with its definite chronological structure; Patricia Lauber's *Who Eats What? Food Chains and Food Webs* (1995), with its cause-and-effect structure; Ted Wood's *Iditarod Dream: Dusty and His Sled Dogs Compete in Alaska's Jr. Iditarod* (1996), with its problem-solution structure; and Mike Foley's *Fundamental Hockey* (1996), with its sequence structure.

This strategy introduces children to a book, even though they read only part of the entire book. By focusing on the plot and text structure, the strategy helps children recognize and understand the plot development, text structure, and the importance of a cohesive plot structure. Later, because they are familiar with the entire book, the students usually choose it for independent reading.

IN A LITERATURE CURRICULUM, A CLASS READS A BOOK TOGETHER

In this grouping arrangement, the teacher presents the same book to all students at one time.[28] Participants follow the book discussion procedures presented previously. Students are not arranged in groups for the class reading, but they may join a partner or a small group for future discussion or to create LRMs. The three approaches to literary study use this strategy, but the teacher adopts a different instructional focus for each approach. The teacher or a capable student reads a segment of the narrative to the class. Individual class members or partners have a copy of the book and read silently while the leader reads orally. The teacher directs the students' attention to specific content or elements of the verbal and visual narratives.

This grouping model is used with quality fiction and nonfiction literature, Focus Books, and outstanding selections from LitSets. The teacher designs a Literary Link for the literature, using appropriate *connect*, *construct*, and *create* components. (See Chapter 2 and the Literary Links presented in this book. Note the different patterns for reading individual chapters suggested in the Literary Links.) The teacher reads and discusses a book with a class for a total of approximately forty-five to sixty minutes a day for several weeks. The time scheduled is determined by the learners, the instructional goals, and the literature. During the oral reading and discussion session, the teacher observes the students' reactions to the literature and notes additional instruction students need in various discipline areas, literature classes, and language arts classes. After completing the oral reading, the teacher uses appropriate instructional strategies and may conduct a mini-lesson with a small group or with the entire class. The teacher schedules oral reading with an entire class in literature classes, language arts classes, various discipline area classes, or interdisciplinary sessions that meet in a block of time during several discipline area classes.

THE TEACHER DESIGNS A LONG-RANGE SCHEDULE FOR THE VARIOUS GROUPS

Teachers who use all grouping models find their children react to them differently in different situations. Use several grouping models throughout the day in all discipline areas. Facilitating several groups at one time is an overwhelming task unless the teacher designs a long-range schedule. During the first or second week of the school year, the teacher implements an approach using one group arrangement. Before beginning a group, talk to the students about the procedures to use when participating in the group. Involve the students when planning the group procedures. After the students are comfortable with the first approach and grouping arrangement, add another

approach or grouping arrangement. Continue to gradually add approaches and grouping arrangements, so that by Thanksgiving various approaches and groups are operating successfully.

Typically, teachers schedule language arts classes for approximately 90 to 120 minutes each day and discipline area classes for 45 to 60 minutes each day. When the curriculum is fully implemented, students will participate in several different groups each week. Several groups will meet simultaneously. The teacher schedules independent activities, partner sessions, small groups, and literature discussion groups for 45 minutes or longer. Teachers may conduct mini-lessons for 15 to 25 minutes before or after the independent, small, or whole class sessions. Schedule sessions immediately after the mini-lesson so that students can practice the concepts taught in the lesson. Integrate spelling practice and additional writing times with the groups and use mini-lessons to provide instruction in specific skills, strategies, or information related to topics in the discipline areas.

Table 12.7 on page 446 presents a weekly schedule for all groups that can be modified to fit the school schedule and the needs of the students. Notice that Fridays are flexible. The schedule may have to be changed occasionally, but students need a regular schedule and teachers need to be able to participate in the literature discussion groups a few minutes each time they meet. In addition to the scheduled sessions, teachers hold conferences with students at appropriate times throughout the day.

 PRINCIPLE FIVE: TEACHERS AND STUDENTS DOCUMENT EACH INDIVIDUAL'S LITERARY GROWTH AND MATURITY; TEACHERS ALSO ASSESS THE EFFECTIVENESS OF THE ENTIRE LITERATURE CURRICULUM

A student's literary growth and maturity, as indicated by his or her reactions and responses to and interpretations of literature, is a central concern of teachers who implement a literature curriculum. In the literature curriculum, the teacher emphasizes the child's ability to understand verbal and visual narratives and to produce cohesive original writings and speeches. Another major concern is the information children acquire from the literature they explore for instructional purposes. Therefore, the teacher and students use a variety of informal techniques to document each individual's literary growth and maturity.

TABLE 12.7 Suggested Schedule for Groups

DAY OF THE WEEK	GROUP 1	GROUP 2	GROUP 3	GROUP 4	GROUP 5
Monday	Read silently; if time permits, discuss reading with partner.	Meet with LDG.*	Engage in partner or independent reading and writing.	Meet with LDG.	Engage in partner or independent reading and writing.
Tuesday	Meet with LDG.	Engage in partner or independent reading and writing.	Meet with LDG.	Meet with LDG.	Read silently; if time permits, discuss reading with partner.
Wednesday	Meet with LDG.	Meet with LDG.	Read silently; if time permits, discuss reading with partner.	Engage in partner or independent reading and writing.	Meet with LDG.
Thursday	Engage in partner or independent reading and writing.	Read silently; if time permits, discuss reading with partner.	Meet with LDG.	Read silently; if time permits, discuss reading with partner.	Meet with LDG.
Friday	Prepare LRM or engage in whole group sharing or independent reading.	Prepare LRM or engage in whole group sharing or independent reading.	Prepare LRM or engage in whole group sharing or independent reading.	Prepare LRM or engage in whole group sharing or independent reading.	Prepare LRM or engage in whole group sharing or independent reading.

*LDG = literature discussion group.

THE TEACHER AND STUDENTS USE A VARIETY OF INFORMAL TECHNIQUES TO DOCUMENT INDIVIDUAL LITERARY GROWTH AND MATURITY

In the elementary school at this time, teachers use both informal and standardized instruments to measure students' scholastic growth. Standardized multiple-choice instruments measure students' knowledge of language and related content areas, but do not assess their ability to use language in authentic contexts and to apply content knowledge to appropriate contexts. Therefore, standardized instruments are not applicable to a literature curriculum. Instead, the teacher and students use observational techniques, informal checklists, and literary responses collected throughout the year as evidence of the individual's literary growth and maturity. These instruments and "artifacts" help teachers appraise children's responses to literary selections and their ability to communicate interpretations of literature. The teacher observes each student's strengths and weaknesses in such areas as his or her ability and willingness to use various language modalities, attitude toward literature, language, and content areas, eagerness to check out a new book and finish reading it, use of literature for informational purposes, and participation in small groups and class sessions. The checklists in Chapter 2 provide additional criteria and instruments that teachers and students can use to assess an individual's literary growth and maturity. Teachers also use the book conference, discussed in the next section, to gather additional information about a child's interpretation of literature and ability to articulate his or her responses to literature.

THE TEACHER AND STUDENTS PARTICIPATE IN A BOOK CONFERENCE TO SHARE LITERARY EXPERIENCES

A book conference gives a teacher and a child an opportunity to share feelings, ideas, and the pleasure gained from prose, poetry, and drama.[29] A book conference is different from a book discussion. A book discussion takes place in a small or large group session, and the teacher is not necessarily present. A book conference or conversation emerges from a reader's natural instinct to share personal insights about a literary selection. Readers want to share the excitement they feel when they read about a pack of wolves saving Julie in Jean Craighead George's *Julie of the Wolves* (1972). They want to express their disgust with Cinderella's mean, ugly stepsisters after reading the folktale. When they see John Schoenherr's illustrations for Jane Yolen's *Owl Moon* (1987), they want to talk about walking in the snow looking for owls and how the cold wind felt on their faces. Why should we keep a secret about a book that touches our heart or gives us a different perspective about a person or a historical event? (See photo on page 447.)

What could be nicer than sharing your thoughts about a book with a special adult friend?

Special friendships develop between a student and a teacher when they talk about the feelings or insights evoked by a story, a poem, or a picture. The partners freely express their ideas and opinions as they talk about characters or events they like or dislike. Book conferences give the partners time to question the behavior of a character, view the beautiful setting described through the creator's language and images, and exchange information gained from a literary selection. A book conversation gives the child and teacher five to ten minutes to talk face-to-face about these experiences. The conversation is informal, and the partners talk as they would to respected friends or colleagues. The partners listen thoughtfully, give the other person time to reflect on her or his reactions, and tactfully question her or his response to a book.

A contemporary book conference is different from traditional book conferences. In traditional conferences the teacher checked to see if the child had actually read a book, investigated the child's understanding of the author's meaning, or asked the child to analyze the creator's intent. In contemporary conferences the focus is on the transaction between the reader and the text. In a classroom rich with literary experiences, the teacher is aware of the literature the child is reading and knows how the child relates to literature from the various reactions and responses the child produces.

Both partners initiate the conversation by asking prompts such as "What did you think about the book?" or "What surprised you about . . . ?" Because participants are actively involved in a response-centered curriculum throughout the year, they know how to challenge and question personal interpretations. Partners expect different interpretations and are prepared to provide evidence supporting their personal responses. The children's prior experiences with literature prepare them to ask for clarification or elaboration of a narrative. They are also willing to modify a personal interpretation if the narrative supports the change. During the book conference, a teacher models strategies that she or he uses to construct meanings of the narrative. To help the child think beyond the written word, contemplate why the character reacted as she did, and predict what will happen next, the teacher also uses probes and prompts such as "I wonder . . . ," "And then I thought . . . ," "Do you think that . . . ?" "Will the author . . . ?" and "What clues did the author give us about . . . ?" Conversations stimulate the participants' imagination, evoke personal experiences, and elicit creative problem-solving strategies. Partners use literal questions sparingly. These questions refresh the participants' memory of important details presented in the book, help the partner recall a sequence of events, or help clarify the characters' behavior.[30] Partners use "book language" so they can discuss the literary and artistic elements in the book intelligently. They use proper terminology when they talk about the creator's ability to use language and images effectively. Partners compare and contrast the characters in the same book or in other books. They talk about the similarities and differences among the literary genres or the books written or illustrated by a certain person. In some book conferences, the student reads a selected passage orally or shares a verbal or written response to literature. The student also selects favorite books and creators.

Teachers conduct a book conference in a quiet corner of the room. Participants sit at the same level and face each other. A table is helpful, but not necessary. A teacher usually conducts three or more conferences each day and talks about books with all students each week. At the beginning of the school year, the teacher schedules the conferences; later the students request them. The teacher provides a sign-up sheet to schedule book conferences. The students' names appear in the left column of the sheet; to the right of each student's name, space is provided for the requested time and the title of the literature to be discussed. If a student does not request a time for a conference, the teacher schedules it. At the end of a conference, the student sets goals for reading and LRMs to be completed before the next conference. The student records the goals on a sheet in his or her literature portfolio. The teacher adds comments about the book conference in the portfolio. Teachers choose scheduling techniques that are easy for the children and use simple notations that give them additional information about the child's literary growth and maturity. This informal conference is not designed to formally evaluate the child's ability to read, write, listen, think, or convey information.

The Selection and Presentation of Literature Influences the Success of a Literature Curriculum

The suitability of the selected literature and the presentation of the literature also influence the success of the literature curriculum. As teachers observe students' responses to literature and talk about literature with children, they also gain valuable insights about the effectiveness of the literature to help accomplish the instructional goals. When teachers review the literature for instructional purposes, they identify those selections that are successful for a pure literature approach rather than a literature-based approach, and selections that are suitable for independent reading rather than for a focus book.

Teaching is a reflective process. Teachers constantly review their strengths and weaknesses when presenting a literature selection. They also measure the success of the instructional strategies used in the presentation to accomplish the identified instructional goals. Throughout this book guidelines were suggested to help teachers in this assessment.

The reflection guides for each approach suggested in Chapter 11 help teachers judge the effectiveness of each approach. By using these guides and the informal assessments suggested previously, the teacher can determine the success of the total literature curriculum.

Summary

Figure 12.3 presents five principles and related components for teachers to use when designing and implementing a literature curriculum.

FIGURE 12.3   Principles for Designing a Literature Curriculum

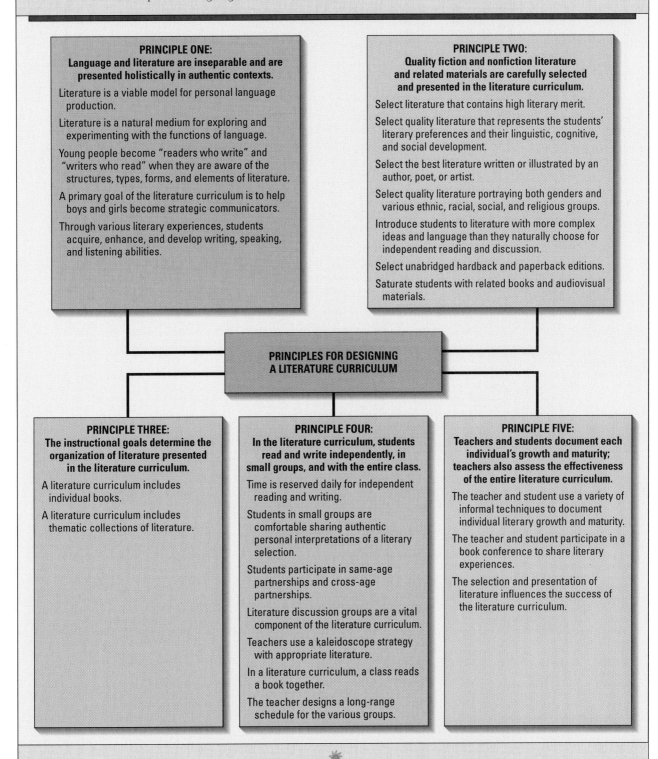

PRINCIPLE ONE:
Language and literature are inseparable and are presented holistically in authentic contexts.

Literature is a viable model for personal language production.

Literature is a natural medium for exploring and experimenting with the functions of language.

Young people become "readers who write" and "writers who read" when they are aware of the structures, types, forms, and elements of literature.

A primary goal of the literature curriculum is to help boys and girls become strategic communicators.

Through various literary experiences, students acquire, enhance, and develop writing, speaking, and listening abilities.

PRINCIPLE TWO:
Quality fiction and nonfiction literature and related materials are carefully selected and presented in the literature curriculum.

Select literature that contains high literary merit.

Select quality literature that represents the students' literary preferences and their linguistic, cognitive, and social development.

Select the best literature written or illustrated by an author, poet, or artist.

Select quality literature portraying both genders and various ethnic, racial, social, and religious groups.

Introduce students to literature with more complex ideas and language than they naturally choose for independent reading and discussion.

Select unabridged hardback and paperback editions.

Saturate students with related books and audiovisual materials.

PRINCIPLES FOR DESIGNING A LITERATURE CURRICULUM

PRINCIPLE THREE:
The instructional goals determine the organization of literature presented in the literature curriculum.

A literature curriculum includes individual books.

A literature curriculum includes thematic collections of literature.

PRINCIPLE FOUR:
In the literature curriculum, students read and write independently, in small groups, and with the entire class.

Time is reserved daily for independent reading and writing.

Students in small groups are comfortable sharing authentic personal interpretations of a literary selection.

Students participate in same-age partnerships and cross-age partnerships.

Literature discussion groups are a vital component of the literature curriculum.

Teachers use a kaleidoscope strategy with appropriate literature.

In a literature curriculum, a class reads a book together.

The teacher designs a long-range schedule for the various groups.

PRINCIPLE FIVE:
Teachers and students document each individual's growth and maturity; teachers also assess the effectiveness of the entire literature curriculum.

The teacher and student use a variety of informal techniques to document individual literary growth and maturity.

The teacher and student participate in a book conference to share literary experiences.

The selection and presentation of literature influences the success of the literature curriculum.

NOTES

The opening quotation is from Purves, A. C., Rogers, T., & Soter, A. O. 1990. *How Porcupines Make Love II: Teaching a Response-Centered Literature Curriculum.* New York: Longman. 175.

1. For additional information about a response-centered curriculum, see Purves, A. C., Rogers, T., & Soter, A. O. 1990. *How Porcupines Make Love II: Teaching a Response-Centered Literature Curriculum.* New York: Longman.

2. For additional information about the functions of language, see sources such as Allen, R. R., Brown, K. L. & Yatvin, J. 1986. *Learning Language through Communication.* Belmont, Calif.: Wadsworth; Tompkins, G. E., & Hoskisson, K. 1995. *Language Arts Content and Teaching Strategies.* (3d Ed.). Englewood Cliffs, N.J.: Merrill. 14–16, 243–44; Wells, G. 1973. *Coding Manual for the Description of Child Speech.* Bristol, England: School of Education, University of Bristol; Wepner, S. B., & Feeley, J. T. 1993. *Moving Forward with Literature.* New York: Merrill. 18; Wisconsin Department of Public Instruction. 1986. *A Guide to Curriculum Planning in English Language Arts.* Madison, Wis.: Bulletin No. 6360.

3. Paris, S. G., Lipson, M. Y., & Wixson, K. K. 1983. Issues concerning the acquisition of knowledge: Effects of vocabulary training on reading comprehension. *Review of Educational Research.* 53. 293–316.

4. Routman, R. 1994. *Invitations: Changing as Teachers and Learners K–12.* Portsmouth, N.H.: Heinemann. 134–59; Schmitt, M. C. 1990. A questionnaire to measure children's awareness of strategic reading processes. *The Reading Teacher.* 43(4). 454–58.

5. For additional information about Thinking Aloud, Reciprocal Teaching, and ReQuest techniques, see sources such as Baumann, J. F., Jones, L. A., & Seifert-Kessell, N. 1993. Using Think Alouds to enhance children's comprehension monitoring abilities. *The Reading Teacher.* 48(3). 184–93; Irwin, J. 1991. *Teaching Reading Comprehension Process.* New York: Prentice-Hall. 18–19, 190, 201–3; Tierney, R. J., Readence, J. E., & Dishner, E. K. 1990. *Reading Strategies and Practices: A Compendium.* (3d Ed.). Boston: Allyn & Bacon. 54–61, 81–85.

6. For additional information about the writing process and writing in the literature curriculum, see sources such as Atwell, N. 1987. *In the Middle: Writing, Reading, and Learning with Adolescents.* Portsmouth, N.H.: Boynton/Cook; Calkins, L. M. 1991. *Living between the Lines.* Portsmouth, N.H.: Heinemann; Graves, D. 1994. *A Fresh Look at Writing.* Portsmouth, N.H.: Heinemann; Shanahan, T. 1990. *Reading and Writing Together: New Perspectives for the Classroom.* Norwood, Mass.: Christopher-Gordon; Tompkins, G. E. 1994. *Teaching Writing: Balancing Process and Product.* (2d Ed.). New York: Merrill.

   For additional information about connecting literature and writing, see articles in *The Reading Teacher, Language Arts, Writing Teacher, The New Advocate,* and other professional journals. For example, Angeletti, S. R. 1993. Group writing and publishing: Building community in a second-grade classroom.

Language Arts. 70(6). October. 494–99; DeGroff, L. 1989. Developing writing processes with children's literature. *The New Advocate.* 2(2). Spring. 115–23; Farnan, N. 1989. Critical reading and writing through a reader response approach. *Writing Teacher.* 2(5). 36–38; Lapp, D., & Flood, J. 1993. Are there "real" writers living in your classroom? Implementing a writer-centered classroom. *The Reading Teacher.* 48(3). November. 254–58; Lunsford, S. H. 1997. "And they wrote happily ever after": Literature-based mini-lessons in writing. *Language Arts.* 74(1). January. 42–48; Person, D. G. 1991. Becoming a nation of writers: Writing as literature. Paper presented at the annual meeting of the International Reading Association. (*ERIC Document* Reproduction Services No. ED 334 598); Steen, P. 1991. Book diaries: Connecting free reading with instruction, home with school, and kids with books. *The Reading Teacher.* 45(4). April. 330–33.

7. For additional information about expository text structure, see Chapter 6 and the following sources: Armbruster, B. B., Anderson, T. H., & Ostertag, J. 1989. Teaching text structure to improve reading and writing. *The Reading Teacher.* 43(3). March. 130–37; Moore, S. R. 1995. Focus on research: Questions for research into reading-writing relationships and text structure knowledge. *Language Arts.* 72(8). December. 598–606; Salinger, T. 1993. *Models of Literacy Instruction.* New York: Merrill. 184–97.

8. For additional information about developing oral language, see sources such as Bragert, B. 1992. Act it out: Making poetry come alive. In Cullinan, B. E. (Ed.) *Invitation to Read: More Children's Literature in the Reading Program.* Newark, Del.: International Reading Association. 14–23; Brent, R., & Anderson, P. 1993. Developing children's classroom listening strategies. *The Reading Teacher.* 47(2). 122–26; Hiebert, E. H. 1990. Research directions: Starting with oral language. *Language Arts.* 67(1). 502–6; Klesius, J., & Goforth, F. S. 1987. Using poetry to improve listening comprehension. *New England Journal of Reading.* 22(1), Winter. 8–15.

9. De Lawer, J. 1992. Teaching literature: from clerk to explorer. In Langer, S. (Ed.). *Literature Instruction: Focus on Student Response.* Urbana, Ill.: National Council of Teachers of English. 101–30, at 113.

10. Backer, J., Colon, C., Davis, J., Harwayne, S., Pak, S., & Rhodes, R. P. 1997. Weaving literature into the school community. *The New Advocate.* 10(1). Winter. 79–93; Freeman, Y. S., Freeman, D., & Fennacy, J. 1997. California's reading revolution: What happened? *The New Advocate.* 10(1). Winter. 31–47; Veatch, J., & Cooter, R. B. 1986. The effect of teacher selection on reading achievement: The California Study. *Language Arts.* 63(4). 364–68.

11. For additional information about thematic collections of literature, see sources such as Allen, J., & Eisel, B. 1990. Yelling for books without losing your voice. *The New Advocate.* 3(2). 117–30; Hartman, D. K., & Hartman, J. 1993. Reading across text: Expanding the role of the reader. *The Reading Teacher.* 47(3). March. 202–11; Heine, P. 1991. The power of related books. *The Reading Teacher.* 45(1). 75–77;

Manning, M., & Manning, G. 1992. Strategy: Together we read. *Teaching Pre K–8.* 22(2). October. 37–139; Watson, D. J. (Ed.) 1987. *Ideas and Insights: Language Arts in the Elementary School.* Urbana, Ill.: National Council of Teachers of English. 23–59.

12. For additional information about the use of themes in the classroom, see sources such as Erwin, B., Hines, C., & Curtis, C. 1992. Thematic units: A Scottish approach to literature-based instruction. *Reading Horizons.* 33(2). 108–20; Goodman, K. S. 1991. In the mail. In Goodman, K. S., Bird, L. B., & Goodman, Y. M. (Eds.). *The Whole Language Catalog.* Santa Rosa, Calif.: American School. 432; Moss, J. F. 1994. *Using Literature in the Middle Grades: A Thematic Approach.* Norwood, Mass.: Christopher-Gordon; Pappas, C. C., Kiefer, B. Z., & Levstik, L. S. 1995. *An Integrated Language Perspective in the Elementary School.* (2d Ed.). White Plains, N.Y.: Longman; Spillman, C. V. 1995. *Integrating Language Arts through Literature in Elementary Classrooms.* Phoenix, Ariz.: Oryx.

13. For additional information about integrated units and interdisciplinary programs, see sources such as Jacobs, H. H. 1989. The interdisciplinary concept model: A step-by-step approach for developing integrated units of study. *Interdisciplinary Curriculum: Design and Implementation.* Arlington, Va.: Association for Supervision and Curriculum Development. 8, 53–65; Lipson, M. Y., Valencia, S. W., Wixon, K. K., & Peters, C. W. 1993. Integration and thematic teaching: Integration to improve teaching and learning. *Language Arts.* 70(4). April. 252–62; Theme cycles. 1994. *Primary Voices K–6.* 2(1). January.

14. For additional information about the thematic categories for the organization of literature, see sources such as Fogarty, R. 1991. *The Mindful School: How to Integrate the Curricula.* Palatine, Ill.: Skylight. 55; Sippola, A. E. 1991. When thematic units are not thematic units. *Reading Horizons.* 33(3). 217–23.

15. For additional ideas about designing thematic units, see sources such as Meinbach, A. M., Rothlein, L., & Fredericks, A. D. 1995. *The Complete Guide to Thematic Units: Creating the Integrated Curriculum.* Norwood, Mass.: Christopher-Gordon; Pappas, C. C., Kiefer, B. Z., & Levstik, L. S. 1995. 49–72; Routman, R. 1994. *Invitations.* Portsmouth, N.H.: Heinemann. 276–96.

16. For additional information about grouping students for literary study, see sources such as Anderson, R. C., Wilkson, I. A. G., & Mason, J. 1991. A microanalysis of the small-group, guided reading lesson: Effects of an emphasis on global story meaning. *Reading Research Quarterly.* 26(4). 417–41; Berghoff, B., & Egawa, K. 1991. No more "rocks": Grouping to give students control of their learning. *The Reading Teacher.* 44(8). April. 536–47; Colt, J. M. 1990. Support for new teachers in literature-based reading programs. *Journal of Reading.* 34(1). 64–66; Flood, J., Lapp, D., Flood, S., & Nagel, G. 1992. Am I allowed to group? Using flexible patterns for effective instruction. *The Reading Teacher.* 45(8). April. 608–16; Harp, B. 1989. When the principal asks: "What do we put in the place of ability

grouping?" *The Reading Teacher*. 42(7). 543–45; Hiebert, E. H., & Colt, J. 1989. Patterns of literature-based reading instruction. *The Reading Teacher*. 42(2). October. 14–20; Indrisano, R., & Paratore, J. R. 1991. Classroom contexts for literacy learning. In Flood, J., Jensen, J., Lapp, D., & Squire, J. 1991. *Handbooks of Research on Teaching the English Language Arts*. New York: Macmillan. 477–88; Reardon, J. S. 1989. The development of critical readers: A look into the classroom. *The New Advocate*. 1(1). Fall. 52–61.

17. For additional information about the value of motivation and self-selection of materials for reading and writing topics, see sources such as Gambrell, L. B. 1996. Creating classroom cultures that foster reading motivation. *The Reading Teacher*. 50(1). September. 14–25; Ohlhausen, M. M., & Jepsen, M. 1993. Lessons from Goldilocks: "Somebody's been choosing my books but I can make my own choices now!" *The New Advocate*. 5(2). Spring. 31–46; Pablo, E. R. 1986. Factors that promote the development of permanent interest in reading. In Cotton, E. G. (Ed.). *Proceedings of the Annual Symposium on Reading*. Guam: International Reading Association. 41–55; Skolnick, D. F. 1992. Reading relationships. *The New Advocate*. 5(2). Spring. 117–27.

18. For additional information about independent reading and writing, see sources such as Anderson, R. C., Hiebert, E. H., Scott, J. A., & Wilkinson, I. A. G. 1985. *Becoming a Nation of Readers*. Washington, D.C.: National Institute of Education. 76–82, 119; Anderson, R. C., Fielding, I. G., & Wilson, P. T. 1988. Growth in reading and how children spend their time outside of school. *Reading Research Quarterly*. 23. 285–304; Greaney, V., & Hegarty, M. 1987. Correlates of leisure-time reading. *Journal of Research in Reading*. 10(1). 3–20; Holt, S. B., & O'Tuel, F. S. 1990. The effect of sustained silent reading and writing on achievement and attitudes of seventh and eighth grade students reading two years below grade level. *Reading Improvement*. 27(4). 290–97; Morrow, L. M. 1991. Promoting voluntary reading. In Flood, J., Jensen, J., Lapp, D., & Squire, J. 1991. 681–90; McIntyre, E. 1990. Young children's reading strategies as they read self-selected books in school. *Early Childhood Research Quarterly*. 5(2). 265–77; Taylor, B. M., Frye, B. J., & Maruyama, G. M. 1990. Time spent reading and reading growth. *American Educational Research Journal*. 27(2). 351–62.

19. For additional information about implementing independent reading and writing, see sources such as Morrow, L. M., & Sharkey, E. A. 1993. Motivating independent reading and writing in the primary grades through social cooperative literacy experiences. *The Reading Teacher*. 47(2). October. 162–65; Routman, R. 1994. 41–69; *Suggestions for the Classroom: Teachers and Independent Reading*. (n.d.). Urbana-Champaign, Ill.: Center for the Study of Reading. 1–10.

20. The following sources present suggestions for scheduling independent reading and writing experiences: Cairney, T. H. 1991. *Other Worlds: The Endless Possibilities of Literature*. Portsmouth, N.H.: Heinemann; Schell, L. 1991. *How to Create an Independent Reading Program*. New York: Scholastic Professional Books. 32–36.

21. For additional information about single-age and cross-age partners, see sources such as Chapman, M. L. 1995. Designing literacy

learning experiences in a multiage classroom. *Language Arts*. 72(6). October. 416–28; Hart-Hewins, L., & Wells, J. 1990. *Real Books for Reading: Learning to Read with Children's Literature*. Portsmouth, N.H.: Heinemann. 71–72; Sharpley, A. M., & Sharpley, C. F. 1981. Peer-tutoring—A review of the literature. *Collected Original Resources in Education*. 5(3). 7–11; Topping, K. 1989. Peer tutoring and paired reading: Combining two powerful techniques. *The Reading Teacher*. 42(7). April. 488–72.

For additional information about peer interactions while writing, see sources such as Calkins, L. 1986. *The Art of Teaching Writing*. Portsmouth, N.H.: Heinemann; Tompkins, G. E. 1994. *Teaching Writing: Balancing Process and Product*. (2d Ed.). New York: Macmillan.

For additional information about cross-age tutoring, reading, and writing experiences, see Campbell, C. H., & Stewart, B. V. 1992. Project PEP. *The Reading Teacher*. 46(3). November. 264–66; Leland, C., & Fitzpatrick, R. 1993–1994. Cross-age interaction builds enthusiasm for reading and writing. *The Reading Teacher*. 47(4). December/January. 292–301; Morrice, C., & Simmons, M. 1991. Beyond reading buddies: A whole language cross-age program. *The Reading Teacher*. 44(8). May. 572–77; Robb, L. 1991. Building bridges: Eighth and third grades read together. *The New Advocate*. 4(3). Summer. 151–61.

22. For additional information about Literature discussion groups, see sources such as Close, E. E. 1992. Literature discussion: A classroom environment for thinking and sharing. *English Journal*. 81(5). 65–71; Eeds, M., & Wells, D. 989. Grand conversations: An exploration of meaning construction in literature study groups. *Research in the Teaching of English*. 23(1). 9–29; Evans, K. S. 1996. Creating spaces for equity? The role of positioning in peer-led literature discussions. *Language Arts*. 73(3). March. 194–202; Keegan, S., & Shrake, K. 1991. Literature study groups: An alternative to ability grouping. *The Reading Teacher*. 44(8). 542–47; Leal, D. J. 1993. The power of literary peer-group discussions: How children collaboratively negotiate meanings. *The Reading Teacher*. 47(2). October. 114–20; Lehman, B. A., & Scharer, P. L. 1996. Reading alone, talking together: The role of discussion in developing literary awareness. *The Reading Teacher*. 50(1). September. 26–35; McCutchen, D., Laird, A., & Graves, J. 1992. Literature study groups with at-risk readers: Extending the grand conversation. *Reading Horizons*. 33(4). 313–28; McMahon, S. I. 1994. Student-led book clubs: Transversing a river of interpretation. *The New Advocate*. 7(2). Spring. 109–25; Raphel, T. E., McMahon, S. I., Goatley, J. J., Boyd, F. B., Pardo, L. S., & Woodman, D. A. 1992. Research directions: Literature and discussion in the reading program. *Language Arts*. 69(1). September. 54–61; Short, K. G., & Pierce, K. M. (Eds.). 1990. *Talking about Books: Creating Literature Communities*. Portsmouth, N.H.: Heinemann; Villaume, S. K., Worden, T., Williams, S., Hopkins, L., & Rosenblatt, C. 1994. Five teachers in search of a discussion. *The Reading Teacher*. 47(6). 480–87; Watson, D., & Davis, S. 1988. Readers and texts in a fifth-grade classroom. *Literature in the Classroom: Readers, Texts, and Context*. Urbana, Ill.: National Council of Teachers of English. 59–68.

23. The term *teacher participant-facilitator* was suggested by Barbara Canterford in 1991. The "new" teacher: Participant and facilitator. *Language Arts*. 68(4). April. 286–91.

24. Indrisano, R., & Paratore, J. R. 1991. 485.

25. Numerous writings about cooperative groups are available. The researchers and writers cited the following theorists most often: David and Roger Johnson, S. Kagen, R. Slavin, and L. Vygotsky. The following books are recommended: Johnson, D. W., Johnson, R. R., Holubec, E. J., & Roy, P. 1984. *Circles of Learning: Cooperation in the Classroom*. Alexandria, Va.: Association for Supervision and Curriculum Development; Kagan, S. 1992. *Cooperative Learning*. Laguna Niguel, Calif.: Resources for Teachers; Slavin, R. E. 1986. *Ability Grouping and Student Achievement in Elementary School: A Best Evidence Synthesis*. Baltimore: Johns Hopkins University, Center for Research on Elementary and Middle Schools; Vygotsky, L. 1962. *Thought and Language*. Cambridge, Mass.: MIT Press. See also Vygotsky, L. 1978. *Mind in Society: The Development of Higher Psychological Processes*. Cambridge, Mass.: Harvard University Press.

26. For additional information about the evaluation of cooperative groups, see sources such as Bath, S. R. 1992. Trade-book minigroups: A cooperative approach to literature. *The Reading Teacher*. 46(3). November. 273–74; Johnson, D. W., Johnson, R. R., Holubec, E. J., & Roy, P. 1984; Pardeck, J. T., & Pardeck, J. A. 1990. Using development literature with collaborative groups. *Reading Improvement*. 27(4). 226–37.

27. For additional information about implementing cooperative literature discussion groups, see sources such as Baloche, L., & Platt, T. J. 1993. Sprouting magic beans: Exploring literature through creative questioning and cooperative learning. *Language Arts*. 70(4). April. 264–71; Bath, S. R. 1992. 272–75; Eeds, M., & Peterson, R. 1991. Teacher as curator: Learning to talk about literature. *The Reading Teacher*. 45(2). October. 118–26; Villaume, S. K., & Worden, T. 1993. Developing literature voices: The challenge of whole language. *Language Arts*. 70(6). October. 462–68; Wiseman, D. L., Many, J. E., & Altieri, J. 1992. Enabling complex aesthetic responses: An examination of three literary discussion approaches. In Kinzer, C. K., & Leu, D. J. (Eds.). *Literacy Research, Theory, and Practice: Views from Many Perspectives*. Chicago: National Reading Conference. 283–90; Urzua, C. 1992. Faith in learners through literature studies. *Language Arts*. 69(7). November. 49–51.

28. Salinger, T. 1993. *Models of Literacy Instruction*. New York: Merrill. 29–30.

29. For additional information about book conferences (conversations), see sources such as Cairney, T. H. 1991. 46–47; Goldenberg, C. 1992–1993. Instructional conversations: Promoting comprehension through discussion. *The Reading Teacher*. 46(4). December/January. 316–26; Hart-Hewins, L., & Wells, J. 1990. 45–47.

30. Squire, J. 1989. Research on reader response and the national literature initiative. Paper presented at the International Conference on English, East Anglia, England.

Literary Vocabulary

Allegory   Fiction in which the action and characters represent truths about human conduct or experiences.

Alliteration   The repetition of stressed, initial sounds of words. The repeated sound is generally made by a consonant and the words are usually consecutive words or words very close to one another within a sentence; e.g., "funny, furry, fox."

Allusion   A figurative or symbolic reference to a well-known event or character in life or in literature.

Annotation   A brief, descriptive summary of the major events in the plot. When applicable, information about the setting, theme, major characters' names, and an indication of the literary genre are included.

Antagonist   The major character(s) who creates the most conflict and actively opposes the protagonist.

Anthology   A book containing several selected stories, poems, plays, or songs. The selections may be written by one person or a number of people.

Assonance   The repetition of a vowel in stressed syllables without the repetition of consonants. An assonance is used as a substitute for a rhyme; e.g., "Slap" and "dash;" "fate" and "make;" "time" and "mind."

Bibliographic information   A listing of the author(s), date of publication, title of the work, name of the illustrator, place of publication, and publishing company.

Canon   Meritorious literature that has been sanctioned by literary authorities.

Cliffhanger   Unresolved suspense at the conclusion of a chapter.

Climax   The high point of the story where the reader does not know the outcome. At this point the conflict begins to be resolved.

Conflict   Tension or struggle between two opposing forces.

Connotation   Feelings and emotional associations surrounding a word or phrase.

Consonance   The recurrence or repetition of identical or similar consonants; e.g., " 'Twas a bit of 'a bun and a ben. . . ."

Conventions   Widely accepted or generally agreed upon stylistic devices used in literature; e.g., cliffhangers.

Creator   The author, artist, or poet who created a particular piece of literature.

Critic   A person who evaluates the quality of a literary selection.

Denotation   The explicit or dictionary meaning of a word.

Denouement   The outcome and resolution of the plot.

Didactic   Teaching a religious or moralistic lesson through literature. Pleasure or entertainment is a secondary purpose.

Excerpt   A passage or selection removed from a longer piece of literature.

Figurative language   The use of words and phrases in a nonliteral way to give new and/or unusual meanings to the language.

Flashback   Moving out of chronological order and looking at a previous event.

Foil   A character who is opposite or different from the protagonist. The foil emphasizes the protagonist's traits; events or settings may also be used as foils.

Hyperbole   A deliberate exaggeration that could not be meant literally; e.g., "She was hungry enough to eat a horse."

Idiom   An expression that is peculiar to a language, and whose meaning is not meant to be taken literally; e.g., "with a grain of salt."

Imagery   The use of vivid descriptions (words or phrases) that appeal to the senses and stimulate the imagination of the audience.

Internal rhyme   Rhyming words appearing inside a line of verse.

Irony   An event or outcome of an event that is different from what the reader expects or anticipates while reading.

Literary elements   The literary conventions of fiction, i.e., the theme, plot, characterization, setting, style, point-of-view, and format.

Literary genre A distinctive category of literary composition characterized by a particular style, form, or content. Evaluative criteria can be developed to objectively judge the literary merit and quality of the composition. The five literary genres are folk literature, fantasy, realistic fiction, nonfiction, and poetry.

Literary work, title, text, selection These terms are used to refer to a specific tale, story, book, play, poem, or verse.

Literature Any oral, written, or visual narrative containing imaginative language that realistically portrays thoughts, emotions, and experiences of the human condition. Literature provides insights and intellectual stimulation to the audience and relates to the interests and experiences of the reader and to his or her cognitive, literary, and emotional development.

Metaphor A figure of speech which implies a comparison of two unlike things to suggest a resemblance between them; e. g., "He is a proud lion."

Mood The atmosphere or emotional or subjective context felt within a text.

Motif A recurring thematic pattern or feature in a narrative.

Motive Something within a character that prompts her or him to action.

Nonfiction elements The criteria used to evaluate the quality of nonfiction literature, i.e., accuracy, currency, organizational structure, and format.

Onomatopoeia A word that represents or imitates the sound associated with the word or action named; e.g., "swoosh."

Parable A short narrative with one-dimensional characters that makes a point or explains an abstract idea.

Parody An amusing imitation of another piece of literature.

Personification Giving human traits to nonhuman beings or inanimate objects.

Problem An event that begins the action, conflict, or tension of a text.

Protagonist The principal or leading character of a story, poem, or drama.

Pun A play on words; putting words together to be humorous.

Satire An amusing look at human vices, foibles, or stupidity. The person is held up for contempt in an attempt to reform him or her.

Simile A vivid image developed by comparing two things that are alike or similar to one another. The comparison uses words such as "like," "as," "than," "similar to"; e.g., "She is like a beautiful flower."

Stereotype A character portrayed by showing only those traits expected of a particular group of people. This character does not possess individual traits.

Tone The attitude or mood brought forth in the narrative.

Trade books A book sold in a bookstore or found in libraries, not a textbook.

Description of Selected Literary Response Modes

Individuals use various visual and verbal modes to respond to literature. The responses are natural, spontaneous reactions to a story, poem or book. The responses may be private and totally unrecognized by another person or may be stimulated by adults or peers. Ideally, a Literary Response Mode (LRM) is selected by the individual to reflect his or her personal reaction to a literary selection. Occasionally, depending on the instructional goals, the teacher may suggest alternate modes that involve the students in writing, visual, or oral experiences.

Throughout this book various LRMs have been suggested for use with literature. This appendix provides additional information about the actual production of LRMs. The modes are categorized according to four dimensions:

Visual manipulative. A visual response that the person may manipulate.

Visual artistic. A visual response that highlights artistic modalities.

Verbal oral. A verbal response presented in an oral modality.

Verbal written. A verbal response produced in a written modality.

Naturally, because of the holistic nature of language a student may produce a modality in one mode and present it in another mode. For example, puppets are produced in the visual manipulative modality and presented in the verbal oral mode. Therefore, an LRM that we place in one category may overlap and also fit into other categories.

Before students produce selected LRMs, the teacher will discuss procedures for constructing LRMs and demonstrate how to present them.[1]

VISUAL MANIPULATIVE

The following are examples of visual manipulative LRMs:

Background setting display. Students will display commercial and original maps and other artifacts from the setting of a poem, story, or nonfiction material. Use the display with a book talk or in the literature center.

Bar graph. Use a bar graph to record data compiled from students' opinions about a literary selection or their expressed preferences about a variety of books or genres. Students compile the data and then record the information on graphs to be displayed in the room.

Board game. Using a poster board, young people create their own board games. Usually, squares are placed randomly over the face of the board. The first square is placed on the left side of the board to serve as a beginning point, and the last square is placed on the right side to end the game. Bits of advice and tasks for the players to perform are placed on the squares. Players must heed the advice or perform the tasks when their token lands on the square. Cards may be drawn when the player lands on certain squares. The cards may be the impetus for moving forward or back. How a child answers a question on the card may determine these moves. The questions may deal with content, story structure, creator information, or trivia information. (See LitBit under Verbal Written later in this appendix for additional ideas about preparing cards for games.)

Bound book. A bookbinding technique (sewing, brads, plastic bindings) is used to attach paper within covered boards to make a book. Students then write and illustrate a story or poem on the pages. (See Techniques for Making Books later in this appendix.)

Character clues. Clues about the personality or action of characters in books read by students are drawn or sketched on paper. For clarity, the student may write a caption under the drawing, but complete sentences or narratives should not be used. Each drawing is numbered. Students have a Character Clue Tally Card with the corresponding number and columns for Title, Author, and Name of Character. The drawings are passed around the room, and students complete their tally card if they know the information. After they view all drawings, the artist gives the number and related information about the book.

Classroom reading ship. Paint or cut a cardboard refrigerator box to form the sides of a ship. Place pillows inside the ship and encourage small groups of students to read in the ship. Students will earn the privilege of reading in the ship by adhering to specific guidelines. The construction of the ship can be a class project, or the teacher could structure the shell. The students research and paint the outside to resemble a ship of a given era. Other objects, such as a whale, can also be constructed. The ship is placed near the literature center.

Expository Text Structures Visuals. Five text structures are associated with expository narratives. The structures are simple listing, sequence, comparison/contrasts, cause and effect, and problem and solution. The structures and a visual representing each structure are discussed in Chapter 6. Students use the appropriate visual to record information presented in the literary selection.

File Folder Games. Students will prepare a file folder game for a particular literary selection or collection of books representing various literary genres. The game, which is similar to a board game, is placed on a file folder. The folders may be laminated for durability. A pocket attached to the outside cover will hold playing pieces needed for the game. (See Board Game above for additional ideas.)

Hero Bulletin Board. A permanent bulletin board related to literature remains in the class throughout the year. Groups of students change the display periodically to reflect a favorite literary hero selected from the books they read independently or in groups. At the beginning of the year, the class will develop the criteria for a hero and a process for evaluating credentials for selecting the character to receive hero status.

ID Bag. A student will collect artifacts representing an incident, the characters, setting, or a theme found in a story, poem, or book. The student will decorate a bag that gives clues about the literary selection but does not cite the author or title. While giving a book talk about the se-

lection, the speaker will display the bag and artifact. After the talk the class will ask questions to figure out the title and author of the selection. The speaker will answer the questions without giving this information. If the class does not identify the selection, the bag and perhaps the artifact are placed in the literature center until the class discovers the name and title of the selection.

Literary circle. Prepare a large circle on a chart or background, such as oil cloth or felt. The purpose is to give the children an opportunity to identify the incidents in a literary selection. The students will identify major incidents and draw a picture to represent each incident. Then, beginning at the top of the circle, the students will place the drawings in sequential order so that the selection concludes at the top.

Literary hanging. A literary hanging is similar to a banner or quilt. A hanging is a drawing or sketch prepared on fabric using quilting, embroidery, yarn, sequins, or other decorations to depict a particular incident in a book. The visual is placed on a piece of fabric and hung in the room, hallway, or media center. Students can produce the hanging on a computer.

Magazine ad. Students will prepare an advertisement, like those found in magazines, to persuade others to read a particular piece of literature. Students will study magazine advertisements, compare and contrast their formats, and select the most appropriate format for the particular piece of literature.

Mood path. Chart the characters' emotions by sketching the events. Color a strip at the top of the page to indicate the mood. For example, green might mean calm, brown could mean despair, blue might mean slightly unhappy, red could mean angry, and pink could indicate contentment and happiness.

Picture narrative circle. Identify the major events in a poem or book. Select the same number of groups of students as there are events. Each group will select an event. The group will sketch the event and draw a picture representing it. The drawings will be placed in the proper sequence on a large paper circle. The title and author of the selection will be placed in the center of the circle. Display the circle in the literature center or on the literature bulletin board.

Poster board replicas. Using poster board, cut out replicas of characters, paint or color them, and add magnetic tape to the back so they can be displayed on the chalkboard. The students may also manipulate these replicas to retell the story.

Prediction chart. Prepare a chart with two columns at the top: "What I Think Will Happen" and "What Actually

Happened." Before reading, place major events down the side of the chart, and allow the children to predict what will happen. After reading the selection, record what happened.

Prediction paper. Students will write predictions about a literary selection on special paper reserved for predictions. The paper can be various sizes, colors, and shapes. Students write the predictions before and during the reading of the selection.

Prediction pitcher. Girls and boys will make a prediction and place it in a plastic water pitcher or similar container. Students read, confirm, or modify the predictions while reading the narrative.

Pun fun. A picture album will be reserved for puns or other figurative language encountered while reading. The entire class develops the album. It is placed in the literature center. Students are encouraged to read the puns, add to the collection, and use puns when appropriate in original writing. A scrapbook containing other figurative language can be prepared in a similar manner.

Sentence strips. Tagboard strips are distributed to students who will write questions or probes about the theme, plot, or characters in the tale. The strips are used for sequencing the plot, to elicit responses from others, or for display on a thematic bulletin board.

Story map. Using an appropriate visual (i.e., a chart or transparency), students will identify and record the literary elements of a selection, including the setting, major characters, and plot development (beginning, major incidents, and conclusion). Students list the elements in sequence and draw pictures or sketches to accompany the identified elements.

Story scroll. Give a team a long sheet of paper, and have team members draw and color several incidents from a book or poem. Glue a dowel rod at the top and bottom of the paper. Roll the paper in scroll fashion and use it when giving a book talk. Attach a tassel to each dowel rod. Students can store the scrolls in a shoe box. A copy of the story or poem can be placed in the box and shared with other students.

Storyteller's apron. A specially designed apron with a bib is worn by the teller when sharing a story. Large pockets with storytelling motifs are attached to the apron. Visuals about the story are stored in the pockets and shown at the appropriate time.

Storytelling hat. The storyteller wears a special hat when telling a story. The hat can be made from velvet and decorated with feathers or pom-poms. Students can attach special objects about the story to the hat.

Tale-a-time line. Groups of students will identify the major incidents in a poem or book and draw sketches to represent the narrative on a continuous fold of computer paper. The author and title of the selection are written on a piece of construction paper and attached to the time line. A permanent time line without visuals can also be constructed. The students can prepare sketches for a particular selection and tape them in proper sequence to the time line. Different groups will prepare visuals for two books set in the same period. Appropriate visuals for one book will be placed at the top of the time line, while the other visuals are placed at the bottom. The students will compare the events.

VISUAL ARTISTIC

The following are examples of visual artistic LRMs:

All visual media. Students need many experiences with the various visual media used by artists in books with pictures, as described in Chapter 8.

Bumper sticker. A short motto or statement representing the theme or a major concept presented in a piece of literature is placed on a strip of paper. Place clear contact paper or other adhesive paper larger than the illustrated strip over the strip and then attach the strip to an object such as a car bumper.

Comic book sketches. Students will produce comic book sketches for a particular event or literary selection.

Compare folk art. Select a particular country or cultural group. Identify the folk art produced by that group, as found in books with pictures. Compare the media, styles, and techniques used by the artists. Later, have the students compare and contrast the folk art representative of several parallel cultures.

Construct a castle. Consult various sources to research castle architecture. (See D. Macaulay's *Castle* and other books.) Using available materials, construct a castle and display it in the room or school media center. Other buildings can also be constructed. See the architecture bibliography for suitable books.

Crayon batik. To create crayon batik, draw a scene with a heavy coating of crayons and cover the entire picture with black or blue tempera paint. The paint will adhere to the unwaxed portion of the picture and will make a background for the drawing.

Diorama. A diorama is a miniature three-dimensional replica of a scene from a literary selection. The diorama is constructed in a box. The front of the box is cut out. A background and objects related to the event are placed in the box. The box can be decorated with a suitable covering.

Enchanted creatures. After reading a book of fantasy, students will design and make enchanted creatures from paper, feathers, fabric, sequins, or any other materials that will give an enchanted appearance. The creatures may have the partial shape of real animals, birds, or humans, but with obvious changes to make them enchanted. *Alternate idea:* Students will use origami paper folding for the enchanted creatures.

Facial expression masks. Students will make masks from various media to express the perceived emotions of a character at different points in a story. Display the masks in the sequence of the narrative to depict the character's changes.

Golden love box. Wrap a small empty box in golden paper and suitable ribbon. Attach a poem about friendship or love to the box. Give it to a special friend.

Lapel pins or campaign buttons. Draw a design representing a piece of literature and use a commercial button-maker to make buttons. Use plastic-covered name tags. On the paper insert, write "Ask me about" and then draw a picture representing the book. A character's name or the book title can also be written on the paper. Children will wear the pins in the hallways. The pins encourage others to ask about the book. Campaign buttons can be made asking others to vote for a special book character. The class can compile voting results to select _____ for president (or principal).

Mind's eye image. Students will hear a story without seeing an artist's rendition of the events. They will create a picture or a series of drawings from their "mind's eye." They may sketch a picture or otherwise illustrate the story and share their creation with the class. Students' impressions will vary, and by sharing, the girls and boys will come to understand parts of the story that were not clear to them.

Montage. Students will collect pictures that reflect their interpretation of a book. The pictures are combined to form a collage. Paint and additional sketches and drawings can be added to the pictures. Photographs are effective to use with this LRM.

Mural. A mural is a large painting, usually created by many people working together. Tape a long sheet of butcher paper across a chalkboard or place it on the floor. Students plan where certain episodes or drawings will be placed, divide the work, and cooperatively paint, draw, or illustrate the poem or book using various suitable media.

Papier-mâché objects. The teacher will display and instruct students in the preparation of a papier-mâché object representing something portrayed in the selection. Consult the art teacher or an information book on making papier-mâché objects.

Potato printing. Cut a potato in half and carve a design in it with a blunt knife. Then dip the design on the potato into a shallow dish or tray containing tempera paint. The potato is then placed against a sheet of paper, and the design is "printed." Negative or positive designs are possible depending on whether the design is dug out of the potato or the background is carved out, leaving the design protruding. A Styrofoam tray such as those used to store food in the grocery store can be used instead of a potato.

Scratchboard technique. This artistic technique is similar to etching. The entire paper is colored with a heavy layer of crayons. Then, the paper is covered with smooth layers of paint. When the paint is dry, the top layer is scraped with a sharp instrument. The layer underneath is exposed to form a picture.

Shadow box. This three-dimensional visual represents a particular scene from a selection. The visual is placed inside a box (with a removable lid). Paint the inside of the box to represent the background of the selected scene. Objects are arranged in front of the background. Paper, sticks, or sand may be used to create the three-dimensional perspective. Most of the box lid is cut away and replaced with colored cellophane paper. The lid is placed on the box, and the viewer can look down into the box. A small peephole can also be placed at one end of the box, and a viewer can look into the hole. If additional light is needed, use a flashlight. Innovation is the key to this LRM.

Sketch an idea. After listening to a story, students will sketch an idea or character from the story and share with members of a small group. Discussion will occur as students compare their perceptions with those of the other students. Various media such as pencils, colored pencils, markers, and charcoal will be used.

Story board. Read a book about the story boards made by some artists when creating illustrations for books. Encourage a group of children to make a story board for an event in a novel without pictures.

Story quilt. Students are given nine-inch squares of muslin cloth. Have the students use fabric markers to draw favorite scenes from a literary selection. The title of the tale and the student's name should be included on the square. The squares should be sewn together, lined with another piece of cloth, and quilted as desired. A bright border would make the quilt attractive.

Thematic T-shirts. Using a variety of permanent markers or paint for fabrics, students will sketch a scene from their favorite folk literature selection on a T-shirt. The fabric and paint must be processed properly. Dyes can also be used to represent the mood of the poem or story.

Thumbprint drawings. Students will cover their thumbs (or fingertips) with ink from an ink pad. They will then place the inked thumbs (or fingertips) on a piece of paper. Using the thumbprints as faces, the students will use markers to draw original sketches of people or objects described in the selection.

Travelogue. This response includes pictures; a short description of the setting of a favorite book; geographical notes describing the characters' travels, persons met while traveling, and adventures experienced; and recommendations for inns, restaurants, and side trips.

Wanted poster. Students will use the proper format to advertise for a missing person. Characters found in a particular selection will be used for the poster.

VERBAL ORAL

The following are examples of verbal oral LRMs:

Brainstorming board. Use a newsprint tablet to record the ideas elicited from a brainstorming session. After the session, remove the paper and use it later for oral or written language productions. Encourage partners, triads, and small groups to use a brainstorming board when they are interpreting selections and planning personal language productions.

Buddy buzz. Give students time to talk about a book with a buddy. The "buddies" should be predetermined, so that when the signal is given for talking quietly (buzzing), they may begin. Sometimes the buddies are given a question to discuss, but often the time is unstructured for free responses.

Cast dinner party. After a group or class reads a favorite book, they will plan a dinner party for the book characters. First, they will write invitations to the characters. Next, they will decide the menu, selecting foods the characters enjoy. Finally, the group will plan entertainment the characters would enjoy. If possible, the group will present the dinner party and invite the administration and another class. Characters will be played by members of the class. They will talk about the food and entertainment they enjoy. They will serve a modified menu while the group presents the entertainment.

Chain-the-tale. Group students to prepare to role-play (or orally retell) a specified incident. While holding a long rope or thick strand of yarn, a student or teacher will begin the tale. When he or she stops, the students who are responsible for role-playing the next incident of the tale will take hold of the rope and present the event. Each group continues in the same manner. The audience will decide if the groups presented the incidents in the proper sequence. The strategy can be repeated with different participants.

Character-but-then-so frame. This technique for replicating stories allows students to see the character's initiative, followed by a problem (but), followed by a solution (then), followed by a resolution (so). For example, the man (character) wanted to marry the girl, (but) her family was so silly that he wanted to find people sillier than they were. (Then) he searched and found three sillies who were sillier than his girlfriend and her family, (so) he came back and they were married.

Character report card. Give book characters a report card. Have the students select criteria to be evaluated and a grading scale. Each team selects a book character and designs a report card for the character. For example, they might grade Red Riding Hood on critical thinking and bravery. Criteria for critical thinking might be as follows:

1. Asks questions to determine real identities.
2. Listens to the voice to determine if it is an impostor.
3. Asks questions but does not sense danger.
4. Accepts what she is told without question.

A 1 could correspond to A on a grading scale, 2 could correspond to B, 3 to C, and 4 to D—and if she gets a D, she may get eaten.

Character tag. Students are assigned a character from a poem or book read by the class. Place a six-inch square of poster board with the character's name on it around each student's neck and ask the student to assume the character's personality. The student asks questions the character might ask and plays games as the character might. The student is involved in various classroom activities, but must remain as the character for a designated period. After that time, the student reflects on his or her portrayal of the character.

Cleverest character contest. Students nominate and then vote on the cleverest character in a book. The students should develop criteria for "cleverness." Possible criteria might include the following:

Outsmarted others.

Answered riddles and questions.

Was considered smart and clever.

Had unusual answers.

Communication circles. In these circles, students may express their reactions to thoughts about a book if they follow rules, such as the following:

1. Everyone contributes to the discussion.
2. What they say is honest (thought to be true) and fair.
3. What they say is connected in some way to what was previously said.
4. Participants respect the rights of others, and only one person talks at a time.

Compare variants of a story, theme, or character. Students will find different variants of a theme or tale. They will compare the variants to the literature being read or share the variants with a group or class. The comparisons focus on similarities and differences in plot development, names of characters, events, behavior of characters, conclusion, language used, and settings. Variations of tales, stories, and poems from various cultural groups are interesting.

Conduct a trial. Discuss the procedures, roles, and responsibilities of persons involved in a trial. Let the students decide the character they want to portray. Give them time to plan their roles and actions. Then present the trial before persons knowledgeable about the incidents and characters on trial. A judge, lawyers, and jury will determine the fate of the character.

Credentialing process. When a student wishes to nominate a book hero, he or she must gather evidence that the character meets given criteria. Once gathered, the evidence may be presented to the class. The class will vote on whether the character is an appropriate hero for the bulletin board. Additional discussion, listing of criteria, and voting will be necessary to determine whether the candidate is a *likely* or *unlikely* hero.

Debates. Students take sides on an issue and prepare to orally present information to persuade others to accept their position. These debates will be prepared rather than spontaneous. Following the debate, students will vote to determine who has persuaded the most people.

Describe a character. Two students are paired and labeled A and B. After listening to a story or reading one without seeing pictures, student A will describe a character to B. Student B attempts to bring the image to mind as the character is described. Roles are then reversed, so both students have an opportunity to describe and to listen to a description.

Dramatizing action words. Children will act out the meaning of the words. For example, children may not understand the meaning of "tripping" and "tramping" in

"The Billy Goats Gruff" story, until they see someone demonstrating the actions for the words.

Imaginary campfire. Make a safe, but inviting campfire in the classroom using these simple props: a basket with a tall handle, a flashlight, and a yellow plastic garbage can liner. Place the flashlight inside the basket, turn the liner over the basket handle, and pull it down around the basket. Crunch the liner a bit. When the flashlight is on and the room lights are turned down, the basket appears to be a campfire.

Interview the character. After reading a book with several characters, different groups will write questions to interview a character about the events in the book and the reasons for the character's behavior. A member from another group will assume the role of the character and attempt to answer the questions, based on the information given in the text.

Jest for Fun. Students find a funny story about a book character or make up additional stories that could happen to the character.

Literature treasure hunt. Give the students clues representing information presented in fiction or nonfiction literature displayed in the room. The students will scan or read selections to determine the literature containing the clues. The students will share their selected literature and state why they chose the selection. Prizes such as time to read for pleasure will be awarded to students who identify the correct piece of literature.

Problem-searches. After reading a book a small group will write a short scenario describing a problem encountered by a character in the story. They will give the scenario to a group of students who have not read the book. The second group will have ten minutes to brainstorm and record various ways the character could solve the problem. The first group will tell the way the character solved the problem.

Questioning. After a class reads a poem or story, small groups will develop probes and prompts about the selection to ask other groups. The answers must be consistent to the events and characters in the book. The questions will stimulate creative or critical thinking and begin with stems such as the following:

How would. . . ?
What if. . . ?
Why do you suppose. . . ?
Imagine that. . . . .

Readers' Theatre Script: Two or more readers will prepare a dramatic script from a section of a book or a narrative poem. A narrator and other readers will assume the role of the characters in the selection and read the script.

Retelling a Narrative. After listening to a teacher read a story aloud, the students will retell the narrative. The teller may use visual aids or clues to help remember the sequence of the story.

Round Table Discussion. After reading a book or poem, students will sit around a table and discuss a topic of interest from the selection. After a topic is presented, the students will express personal views about it. Leadership of the group moves from one person to the next. A student may lead the discussion if he or she gives new, relevant information about the topic and encourages other group members to react to the topic.

Say What I Saw. A group will listen to a short story, poem, play, or excerpt from a book, students will draw an event from the selection. They give the picture to the person on their left side. This person, without showing the picture to the group, will describe it and "say what the other person saw" while listening to the selection.

Shadowtale. With two students playing each role, one will paraphrase the text, and immediately the other person playing the same role will *shadow* by saying what the character may *really* have been thinking.

Shareback. Groups of students form a consensus or draw conclusions about incidents, characters, and the like. They then share their conclusions orally with the rest of the class.

Storytelling (collective). Many people will tell a story by adding incidents to it. Sometimes props are used to keep the story going. Some props that have been useful in passing from one storyteller to another are bones, skeins of yarn, or objects that represent some aspect of a story.

Storytelling festival. Students learn the fundamentals of the art of storytelling and plan an afternoon or a Saturday event when they will tell stories to families, friends, or another class or grade level.

Storytelling skills. Storytellers use their voices to dramatically present a story. Using vocal expressions, such as intonation, pronunciation, articulation, rate, and emphasis, effectively is important, as is the use of nonverbal movements. Occasionally, visual props may be used, but the voice should be the most important element.

Survey. Under the guidance of a teacher, the children develop a list of questions to ask a group of people. They will decide what questions to ask, whom they should ask, and how the answers should be recorded. Students survey the selected people, record the responses, and share them with the class. The responses may be charted or graphed for visual information.

Theme cards. Themes from literature selections are written on cards. The cards are displayed for class discussion of the way the theme is portrayed in the selection. A group of students may receive individual cards for discussion and later group shareback.

Think aloud. Adults model for children they way they interpret literature. The teacher verbalizes what she or he thinks while reading the story and how she or he reflects on the reading and reaches an interpretation or reaction to the selection.

This is your life. A group will select a favorite creator and research the person's life to determine people who had an important influence on his or her professional development. One student will be selected to role-play the creator; another will be the narrator of the presentation. Other students will be the important people. Students will prepare for their roles and write out a script for the presentation. The group will review each script and organize the presentation. Simple costumes, photographs, or props are suitable. After planning with the teacher, the group will make the presentation to the class, media specialist, administrators, and other classes.

Triad recaps. Group three children for a discussion (recap) of a story they have read or heard. Each child is labeled A, B, or C. A and B recap the story. C is an observer and adds details or corrects misconceptions about the narrative.

VERBAL WRITTEN

The following are examples of verbal written LRMs:

Book links. A book link is similar to a book talk, except that it is written. The purpose of the book link is to introduce a book to another person and to entice the person to read it. The book link is short and highlights exciting, interesting events in the book. A collection of book links may represent a particular motif, subgenre, or theme.

Character continuum. Students will discuss and identify various personality traits of characters. They will select a character and place the subject on a continuum of various dichotomies. Include contrasts, such as smart versus dull and optimistic versus pessimistic.

X	X
SMART	DULL
X	X
OPTIMISTIC	PESSIMISTIC

Character webs. Place a character's name in a circle in the center of a large sheet of paper. Draw lines to the center, spiderweb fashion. Elicit information about the character from the students. Record similar information together. For example, words describing the personality of the character are clustered together, as are words describing the character's actions, emotions, integrity, and physical traits.

Copycat writing. Using a patterned narrative, compose another line, story, song, or poem. Students pattern the new creation after the old one with some changes in words or rhythm.

Describe a procedure. Students will write the procedure for conducting an activity, such as playing soccer or creating a product.

Descriptive name. Students will create a new name for an object or persons in a selection based on specific characteristics. This activity may originate with a study of Native Americans whose names were often descriptive, such as Sitting Bull or Running Bear. Students will write the name on their name tag and illustrate it. They might write a statement justifying their name choice. Girls and boys must be sensitive, select positive names, and avoid using stereotypical names.

Descriptive writing. The writer is encouraged to use a variety of vivid, descriptive words and phrases to describe particular objects, events, or characters from a selection. Students are encouraged to use language encountered in reading.

Diary entries. Students will write several entries in the first person, describing incidents involving a character from a tale.

Did you know? Students will select a favorite creator and write a "Did You Know?" similar to those included in this book. The writer focuses on interesting information about the person's life, such as why she or he writes for young people and the writing/artistic process or techniques she or he uses. Bibliographic sources for obtaining this information are listed in Appendix G.

Dramatic script. Students will write a script based on a favorite event in a book or a narrative poem. The script will be used for a dramatic presentation of the selection.

Epic book. Students will write a retelling of an old favorite epic (or tall tale). The story will be published in a bound Big Book. Large print and pictures will be included in the book. The creators will sit in the author's chair and read the book. Then they will display it in the classroom and media center.

Eyewitness report. Students will write a first-person, factual report of an incident portrayed in a selection.

Fax-the-facts. Faxes will be sent from one child to another, telling about an incident read in a book or poem.

The second child will send another fax, responding to the incident. This process can continue several times. The faxes are placed in a binder, where they can be read by others when selecting a book for personal reading.

Goal setting. Students determine their individual focus for the next grading period during a readers' or writers' workshop. Possible goals might be to read five more books than I read in the last period, to write five more drafts than I wrote in the last period, or to use more figurative language as I write.

Group write. This experience is also called "shared writing" or "paired writing." Children collaborate among themselves or with the teacher to produce a piece of work of which they are all considered authors.

Hero/heroine criteria. Students will list what makes a hero. These lists will be different based on the ages of the students and their ideas about what a hero is. Allow time for consensus building. If they do not agree on the criteria, a vote can be taken. Then students will write a character sketch of a book hero.

Interview the creator. After discussing techniques for interviewing people, two students will select a favorite creator and write out questions they would like him or her to answer. The students research the person's life and attempt to answer the questions. They write the questions and answers they discover in final edited form. The partners then read the interview to the class. Display artifacts and photographs of the person. The interview and photos are placed in a class scrapbook, "Our Favorite Creators." This idea could be modified, so students could interview book characters.

Letter to an advice column. Write a letter to an advice columnist asking specific questions about a character's life or dilemma. Another student will answer the letter.

LitBit. Students and teachers will write literal and critical questions, inferential probes, and involvement and extension prompts relating to the literary selection being read by a group or the class. The questions, probes, and prompts will be placed on cards and organized according to the literary selection. The cards are color-coded according to literary genre. A group uses the LitBit cards to stimulate discussion during or after reading or hearing a book. The cards can also be used with a board book.

Literary detectives. While reading literature, students will collect and record in their journal interesting, unique, nice-sounding words and phrases they want to use in their personal writing. The language is shared each week with the class. The class will decide the language they would like to have placed in the class literary thesaurus. The thesaurus is a shoe box with blank cards. The cards are color-coded to represent different types of language. Students record the language on the cards, and if appropriate, original definitions are placed on the back of the card. Throughout the next week, the cards are displayed on a bulletin board or word wall. Then the cards are placed in the shoe box. The box is placed in a prominent place in the writing center. Students are encouraged to review the words and use them in their personal communication. Each month the teacher will recognize students who have used the words appropriately in their writing or talking.

Literary letters. Students will write letters to or from a literary character and display them on a bulletin board designed especially for the letters.

Magazine story. Students will study, compare, and contrast the content, format, and organization of magazine articles. They will then write a magazine story about an event in the literary selection or write about an original event that they predict will happen at the conclusion of the selection.

Modern adaptation. Students will adapt an old story with modern language and actions. The story may be presented in written or dramatized form to other students.

Network of book links. The purpose of the network is to share book links with other students in a school or with students in different schools. A newspaper format could be used. Plan with other teachers the columns to be included, such as editorials, articles, pictures, maps, want ads, obituaries, and advertisements. The media specialist could be an active member of the editorial staff of the Literary Links. The link would serve two purposes: (1) it would recommend literature for independent reading, and (2) it would help teachers at various grade levels to identify literary selections students have read and enjoyed.

News report. Students will study, compare, and contrast news items to identify the format, content, and style of writing used by news reporters. Students will then write news reports related to a particular literary selection. The report will be included in a newspaper devoted to a particular selection, unit, or topic.

One question. Immediately after reading a story, students will write one question they would like to ask the author. The questions are shared during the discussion of the story. The best questions will be selected, and one person will write a letter to the author including one or two questions.

Partner journal. Two students will write in a journal. One student will write reflections, ideas, and questions to a partner. The partner will reply and add personal comments.

Play-it-again script. A pair of students will review each incident in a selection and the characters' actions and motives. The students will write a modification of part of the narrative, while retaining certain elements, such as the theme or major characters. Alternatively, the tale can be completely different. Then the students will write a script and present the incidents orally to other groups of students on the school television show.

Poetry collection. Students will write or collect (adding visuals) poems about friendship and love. Individuals or groups may complete the collection. They will publish it and give the poems to a loved one.

Pro and con chart. Students will select an issue. They will record on a class chart information obtained from nonfiction literature supporting the Pro or Con side of the issue. Pairs of students will prepare a written debate supporting one or the other side. The pairs will read the written debate. Then they will write additional information to support their side. Finally, the pairs will read the written debate again and conclude with extemporaneous speeches.

Research projects. Students will select areas of interest for further reading and thinking. After gathering data, students will prepare a report on their topic. They will write the reports and share them orally with other students.

Shared writing. Two or more students will compose an original piece of writing. The team will sit in the author's chair and read their writing.

Subgenre commercial. Students will write and present an enticing commercial to convince others that they should read a particular tale or verse from a given subgenre. Visuals or props are helpful. Encourage students to be extremely creative, "wild," or outlandish in choosing the content of their commercials, since the focus is on "selling" the selection.

Television report. Students will write an essay about a topic of interest to many others. They will include factual information in the essay and cite research sources. A group will hear and react to the essay. Selected essays will be read by the reporter on the school television network.

What if? incidents. Students will replace one important event in a plot and imagine another compatible event. In groups or pairs, they will discuss what might happen if the event were replaced with the second one. Individually or in groups, predictions will be written and shared with others. Students will compare the predictions and discuss whether they are consistent with other events and the characters' behavior.

Write an annotation. Using the summary statements given in this book and other annotations about books and selections, discuss the elements of an annotation. It should introduce the protagonists, antagonists, and other major characters and list the major conflicts and solutions reached by the characters. An annotation should be one to three paragraphs long and should be written in an interesting style in the present tense. The purpose of the annotation is to introduce a selection and entice the audience to read or hear it.

Write a conversation between characters. Students will write conversations that could transpire between characters in a selection. The ideas and dialogue must be authentic to the individual characters. Students should be grouped to represent the number of characters involved in the selected incident.

Write future events. Students will write what they predict will happen in the future to selected characters.

Write a variant. After comparing several variants of a tale, students will write an original story or poem by combining elements found in the variations.

Writers' workshop. A block of time is designated daily for students to write self-selected pieces of work. During the workshop, students will write, draft, edit, proofread, and share works from various styles and genres.

LRMS ELICITING VISUAL AND VERBAL RESPONSES

PUPPETS

Various types of puppets can be used including the following:

Hand puppets. From felt or soft fabric, cut a puppet with a head, a neck, and two arms. Include enough material to cover the arm of the puppeteer. Cut another piece of fabric the same shape and sew the shapes together leaving the bottom open. Decorate with suitable materials, such as fabric, buttons, sequins, beads, and other trimmings available at a craft store. To manipulate the puppet, place one hand inside the mitten. Insert the index finger inside the neck, the thumb in one arm, and the center or pointer finger in the other arm. Fold the fourth finger and little finger into the palm of the hand. (Encourage the puppeteer to use the fingers that feel comfortable.)

Fist puppets. The bare hand can be used for the face of a puppet. Fold the thumb under the fingers and use the bottom fingers for a mouth. Decorate the hand with washable markers. A scarf or large bandanna can be used to cover the arm. A hat can be placed on the top of the hand.

Glove puppets. The fingers of an inexpensive garden glove can be decorated to make five finger puppets.

Markers can be used, or interchangeable puppets can be made from pieces of felt, heavy material, or decorator balls. The material is cut in the appropriate size to fit on a finger of the glove and decorated with markers, sequins, small eyes, and other materials available in craft shops. Velcro is attached to the finger of the glove and the puppet piece.

Finger puppets. Cut a wide strip of paper to fit around a child's finger. The child draws a puppet face on the paper and decorates it with appropriate markers and craft materials. Tape the paper around the child's finger.

Sock puppets. Place a sock over the hand with the foot of the sock over the fingertips. Pull sock up over the arm. Fold the foot of the sock inside the finger and thumb to form a mouth. The mouth can be covered (sewn, glued, colored with a marker) with a contrasting material to highlight it. Decorate the sock over the top of the hand to give the puppet a personality. Use the hand to open and close the mouth when the puppet is speaking.

Box puppets. Cut a small milk carton or an individual serving cereal box on three sides to make two opened squares with a hinge to hold the two squares together. Fold the box so that one open square is on the top and one on the bottom. Place the fingers inside the top box square and the thumb inside the bottom half. Open and close the two box halves to suggest a puppet talking. Paint or decorate the box, making the inside of the mouth red. Exaggerated ears, eyes, and mouth give the puppet a personality.

Papier-mâché puppets. Cover a large tube to form the base of the puppet. Insert an inflated balloon at the top of the base. Carefully cover the balloon with layers of paper strips dipped in paste. Pop the balloon when the paper is dry. Add features to the puppet with paints, materials, and paper. Decorate. Hold the puppet face with the tube. Place a drawstring slipcover over the hand.

Paper bag puppets. Use the top of a folded paper bag as the face and body of a puppet. Place the mouth at the bottom of the flap. Place the hand inside the folded bag, and move the flap up and down to make the puppet talk. The inside of the flap is painted or decorated to highlight the mouth. To make an animal, human, or a creature puppet, use paper, materials, or paints on the ears, eyes, hair, nose, arms, feet, wings, tails, clothing, or feathers.

Flat puppets. Draw a silhouette of the puppet on lightweight cardboard (e.g., the inside of a cereal box). Draw facial and body features on one side of the paper. Attach a rod or tongue depressor to the back of the silhouette. Hold the puppet by the rod just below a table or stage. Move the puppet along the edge of the stage. To make a two-sided flat puppet, use two silhouettes. Place the rod between the two silhouettes and decorate both sides of the puppet.

Shadow puppets. Use a flat puppet for a shadow puppet. To present a shadow play, construct puppets, put up a sheet, place a light behind the sheet, and move the puppets behind the sheet and light. The puppet casts a shadow on the sheet.

Stick puppets. Cut a picture from a magazine or draw a picture of the desired puppet. Glue the picture to a piece of tagboard. Glue or tape the puppet to a wooden stick, plastic drinking straw, or wooden spoon.

Styrofoam ball puppets. Paint, pin, or glue objects on a Styrofoam ball. Make a hole in the bottom of the ball and insert a rod to hold the puppet. Complete the puppet head by draping material over the puppeteer's hand.

Rod puppets. Using a stick puppet as a base, attach the arms and legs separately with round head fasteners or hinges. To achieve movement, attach a rod to the body and jiggle the puppet. Older children can attach rods to the body and individual rods to the arms or legs and move the rods to achieve exaggerated movement.

Paper plate puppets. Fold a paper plate in half. Decorate the top of the plate and the mouth with paper, paints, or other materials. Attach arms, legs, and eyes. Attach a strip of paper near the fold on the top of the plate. Place the hand inside the paper to move the mouth. As a variation, decorate the front of a plate and attach a stick or straw at the back to form a handle. Cut out eyes on the plate to make a mask.

Object puppets. Use objects, such as fruit, vegetables, egg cartons, salt boxes, paper cups, and plastic or wooden spoons, to form the base of unique puppets. Use fabric, sequins, paper, and other objects to make a face and form the body. Insert rods or sticks in the puppet for the puppeteer to hold.

Mask puppets. Draw and cut a mask from heavy paper or lightweight cardboard. Decorate appropriately with a variety of materials or paints. Make sure the eyes are large enough for the puppeteer to see. The mask can be fastened around the head with yarn or ribbon. A mask can also be made by shaping a metal clothes hanger in a large oval. Fold the ends of the hanger together, and cover with fabric tape to make a holder for the mask. Pull one leg of a nylon stocking over the oval-shaped hanger. Attach extra stocking to the holder. Cut as needed. Make a face for the mask by attaching paper or materials to the stocking.

Board puppets. Cut a large piece of cardboard into the shape of a person, animal, creature, or object. Leave a place for the arms, face, and legs of the puppeteer. Decorate appropriately. The puppeteer wears the cardboard cutout, so it should be as large as the person.

String puppets or marionettes. Older students can make and manipulate marionettes. A marionette is a complex puppet with hinged body parts that are attached by strings to a control stick. This type of puppet requires both skill and practice to create and operate. It is usually considered too complicated for young children to operate, although they love to watch marionette performances staged by older students.

Egg carton puppets. Using thread or fishing line, string together segments of a Styrofoam egg carton to make a train, worm, or other objects. Decorate with faces and body parts. Place a heavy cord at the front of the object to pull it across the stage.

Puppets can be presented on a variety of stages:

Table stage. Use a classroom table turned on its side for a stage. The flat surface should face the audience. A simple background is attached to the flat surface. The puppeteer is behind the table and holds the puppet over the top of the table.

Doorway stage. Use a rope or expandable curtain rod at an opened doorway. Make a curtain from a piece of fabric and run it over the rod. Place the curtain at a comfortable level for the puppeteer. The puppets appear at the top of the curtain. Several individual pieces of fabric can be hung on a rod, allowing several puppets to be placed through the curtain.

Chair Stage. A cloth, sheet, or blanket may be draped over the handle of a broom placed across two chairs. The height of the stage can be easily adjusted by using chairs of different sizes.

Box Stage. A large cardboard box, such as an appliance box, is a suitable portable stage for a puppet show. The back of the box is cut away and a large hole is cut in the front of the box for the puppets to perform. The sides and bottom of the box are retained. The box is decorated. The puppeteers stand behind the box to manipulate the puppets.

Apron Stage. The apron stage is a three-part, folding-screen. Plywood, appliance boxes, or cutting boards, available at sewing shops are used. Usually, a hole is cut in the front of the screen for the puppet's performance. A curtain can be attached to cover the hole and be pulled back during the performance.

BOOK RECORDING DEVICES

Book recording devices are visual–verbal modes used by students to record the books read during a specified period. The device includes the title and author of the book read, the literary genre, and five or six words describing the learner's reaction to the book.

Book recording devices serve the following purposes:

1. They help students determine if they are reaching their reading goals.

2. They give the teacher or librarian valuable information about a child's reading habits and reactions to the literature.

3. They give students an opportunity to share their enthusiasm and personal recommendations about a particular piece of literature.

4. They serve as an informal indicator of the student's literary preferences.

5. They give adults information to use when introducing students to new titles or genres.

6. They often expand the literary interests of all members of the class.

Because this is a recording device and an advertisement of books, students may display the device on the literature bulletin board. Later, the completed device is placed in the student's literature portfolio. During a book conference the teacher and student will talk about the books recorded on the device. Learners usually record only the books they read, because it is not used as competition among class members. The device also provides a visual record of all of the books read by an entire class. For example, a paper bookworm slinking around the room or a train moving around the room represents the books read by all members of the class. The students enjoy showing visitors all of the books they have read.

An individual or group can use the following ideas for book recording devices to represent thematic topics, genres, or specific books. The ideas are easy to modify to meet the interest of the students and the teacher's purposes.[2]

Special Event Device: At Thanksgiving, students fill a cornucopia with food-shaped objects recording the books they have read during a specified time.

Alternate: Change background and visuals to represent different holidays or special events.

Focus Book Device. While the class or group read a focus book, they select an object representing the content highlighted in the book. They prepare visuals in the selected shape, record requested information about books read in-

dependently on the visual, and place it on a class bulletin board. For example, when students read John Gardiner's *Stone Fox*, they record information about their independent reading on a visual in the shape of a potato. They place the visuals on a bulletin board covered with burlap material to represent potato sacks.

Outer Space with Books. Design a bulletin board with a background representing outer space. Individuals record the title, author, and comments about science fiction and space-related information books they are reading or have read on a spaceship.

Feed the Squirrels. Display a large tree on the bulletin board and place several squirrels in the tree. One squirrel represents fiction, one represents poetry, and one represents nonfiction literature. The students prepare visuals in the shape of an acorn. Then when completing a selection, they write information about it on the acorn. Depending on the genre of the selection, the child places the visual around the fiction squirrel, the poetry squirrel, or the nonfiction squirrel. This visual gives the teacher information about the genre children chose to read. The teacher gives book talks to introduce students to various genres.

Travel around America with Tall Tales. Display a large map of the United States. Students record information about a tall tale they are reading on an object that represents the tall tale character. The students use visuals such as an apple for Johnny Appleseed, an axe for Paul Bunyan, or a sailing ship for Captain Stormalong. Students record requested information of the appropriate visual and place it on the map in the proper geographic setting of the tale. Encourage students to find events about a favorite character in different places in the United States. The bibliography lists various books with tall tale characters.

Reading Jigsaw. Cut up several large pictures to form a puzzle and prepare a backing piece to hold the puzzle. Put the pieces in an envelope. After reading a book the student selects a piece of the puzzle and writes requested information about the book on the puzzle piece. Then the student places the piece in the proper place to complete the puzzle.

Book Calendar. Give students a calendar for the month. Every time they spend a specified amount of time reading or responding to a book, they color the date on the calendar. This may be an independent activity or a group experience. The various colors could represent a genre.

Book Garden. Use a garden setting to form the background of a bulletin board. Whenever students read a book, they make a flower, leaves, birds, insects, or other objects found in a garden. They write requested responses on the object and place it in the suitable place on the bulletin board garden.

Genre Rainbow. Give each student a paper with a rainbow drawn on it. A legend at the bottom of the page identifies the color of a literary genre. After reading a book, a student colors a band of the rainbow in the color representing the literary genre of the book. In the spaces between the bands, they record requested reactions to the book. This device is placed on the literature bulletin board or in the student's literature portfolio.

Fill Your Personal Bookcase. A teacher gives the students a paper with a sketch of a bookcase and empty books in it. Students write the titles of the books they are reading on the spines of the books to fill up the bookcase. Individuals or groups can complete this device. For a group, the teacher sketches a large bookcase with empty books on the bulletin board. As members of the group read literature independently, they write the titles of the end of the books shown in the bookcase.

Literary Commentary. Place two attractive boxes in the classroom with blank index cards. After reading a book, a student writes the author, title, and a thought-proving question about an event or a character in the book. On the back of the card the student writes a personal comment about the book and signs his or her name and places the card in the box. The student then writes the answer to the question and the page number that verified the answer on a sheet of paper. Then the student writes the title, author, and his or her name on the bottom of

the page. This paper is placed in the companion box. After several students read the same book, they can use the answers and questions to play a game similar to *Jeopardy*. They can use the cards for a literature trivia game. After playing the game, they place the cards in a container in the literature center. The cards are arranged according to genre or topic and a student searching for a book to read independently can review the cards.

TECHNIQUES FOR MAKING BOOKS

When students place their writings in a bound book, the writings take on added importance, and the children feel that they are published writers. In some schools parent volunteers help type the manuscripts and bind the books in the school publishing center. Young people enjoy participating in the process of binding books. Since several techniques are available, children of all ages can make books such as the following:

Accordion Books. This type of book is made from a long strip of heavy paper. The paper is folded, accordion fashion, to make the pages for the book. Sometimes the beginning and ending folds are reinforced with cardboard. The children write and illustrate events in sequential order on the folded pages. When the book is completed, it can be folded, then gently pulled apart. Ribbon can be attached to the front and back pages to tie the book together for easy storing.

Pop-Up Books. After writing a story, decide the number of objects to show in the book. Use a file folder or large sheet of heavy paper. Make a pop-up tab for each object

A sample accordion book.

as follows: cut a tab one and one-half-inches wide and three inches deep from the fold. Open the paper, bring each tab inside the paper to the front of the paper. Close the paper again at the fold with the pop-up tab inside, fold the tab three inches deep from the fold of the paper. Open the paper and adjust the tab so that it stands out as a pop up tab. Paste an object on each pop-up tab. The author will read the story and show the pop-up book. Place the narrative in an envelope and store with the pop-up book. Display the pop-up book and story in the literature center.

Wordless Books. After reading and analyzing the format of a wordless book, a team of children can make an original wordless text. The visual sequence that depicts the storyline must be planned before drawing the story. The artists must be sure the pictures flow from one page to the next to tell a continuous story. The wordless book can be bound in a variety of ways.

Bound Books. Adults and students use a technique such as the following to make a bound book.[3] First, obtain a piece of oak tag (or a cereal box), adhesive paper (such as contact paper), scissors, typing paper, a long-arm stapler, and a roll of 2-inch-wide cloth tape. Use the following procedure to make the cover and pages of the book:

1. To make the hardboards of the cover, cut two pieces of oak tag slightly larger than the paper that will be used inside. The front and back of a cereal box is also good to use.
2. Cut two pieces of self-adhesive vinyl (contact paper) two inches wider and two inches longer than each hardboard.

3. Carefully peel the backing from one piece of vinyl, trying not to stretch the vinyl.
4. Place one hardboard on the vinyl. Fold the vinyl smoothly over the corners to cover the hardboard. Repeat the procedure for the second hardboard. The front and back covers are now completed.
5. Lay both covers on a piece of fabric tape, leaving extra tape at the top and bottom of the hardboard covers. Leave approximately one and one-half inches between the covers to make a spine for the book. Fold the extra tape over the top and bottom of the book covers.
6. Make the inside pages by folding four (or more, depending on the number of pages in the book) pieces of 8½-by-11-inch paper in half. Fold a piece of construction paper the same size on the outside of the pages. Use a long-arm stapler, or one mounted on a V-bracket, to staple across the pages and construction paper in three places. (The pages can be sewn on a machine or double hand-sewn with dental floss.) The construction paper becomes the endpages.

Use the following procedure to put the book together:

7. Place the pages on the spine of the book (the fabric tape), with the endpages next to the covers. Push the folder pages against the sticky part of the tape. Make sure they are firmly inside the tape. Close the covers over the pages.
8. Paste the endpages (construction paper) to the cover, leave approximately ½-inch of the sides of the covers showing. This allows extra room in the center for easy folding of the book.

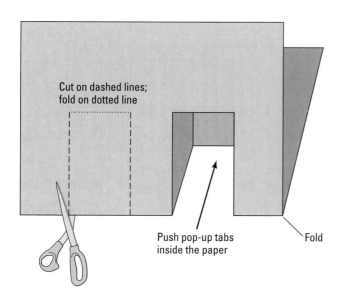

Cut on dashed lines; fold on dotted line

Push pop-up tabs inside the paper

Fold

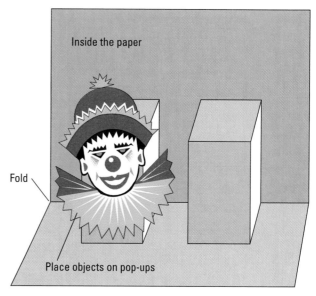

Inside the paper

Fold

Place objects on pop-ups

A sample pop-up book.

Step 5

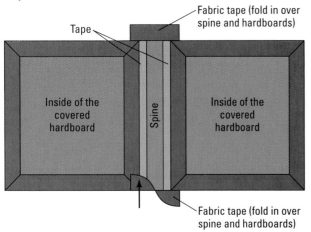

Tape

Fabric tape (fold in over spine and hardboards)

Inside of the covered hardboard

Spine

Inside of the covered hardboard

Fabric tape (fold in over spine and hardboards)

Steps 6–8

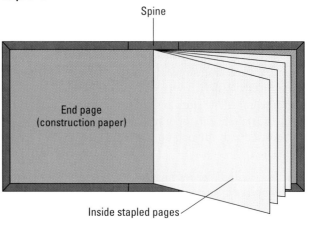

Spine

End page (construction paper)

Inside stapled pages

Making a cover and pages for a bound book.

Use the following procedure to finish the book:

9. Write the title and author's name on a self-adhesive label or a small piece of paper and glue it onto the cover. Add a picture if desired. Cover the front cover with a piece of clear contact paper.
10. Prepare a title page, a copyright page, and a dedication page. Place a brief biographical sketch of the author on the last page of the book.
11. After writing and editing the final version of the story, block the verbal narrative to determine where the illustrations should go. Use illustrations to help tell the story or complement the verbal narrative. Children could make a sketch or story board representing each page before placing the verbal and visual narratives in the book.
12. Copy one block of the verbal narrative onto the page and draw the picture (or glue the illustration on the page). Or leave room for the picture on the page. Continue writing blocks of verbal narrative and pasting or drawing illustrations to the pages of the book. Depending on the age of the children, they might write and illustrate the book on lined paper and glue the pages onto the pages of the book.
13. When the book is finished, share it with others.

Simple Folded Book. To make a simple folded book follow these instructions:

1. Fold a legal-size sheet of paper down the center of the length. Open.
2. Fold the paper across its width. Open. The paper should now have two folds (four sections).

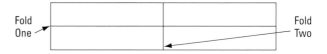

Fold One

Fold Two

3. Fold the paper along fold 1, which is the length of the paper.
4. With the crease of the paper upward, fold the left edge of the paper to the center crease.
5. Now fold the right edge of the paper to the center crease.
6. Open the entire sheet of paper. There should be four creases (eight sections) on the page.
7. Fold the paper again so that fold 2 is on top.
8. Tear (or cut) the paper in the center from the top fold to the center of the crease.

Tear along crease

9. Open the paper again and refold so that fold 1 is on top.
10. Hold each end of the paper and push the left and right ends toward the center.

Push right

Fold One Push left

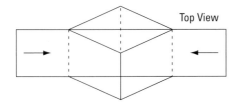

Top View

11. Fold into a square. The result is a four-section book.

Shape Book. To make a shape book, follow these instructions:

1. Using a pattern, cut the cover and pages according to the desired shape.
2. Staple across the top or sides.

Alternatively, the book can be made as follows:

1. Cut the front and back covers from a manila folder; be sure to leave the fold intact.
2. Fold several sheets of paper and cut according to a pattern, again leaving the fold intact.
3. Sew or staple the pages and cover together along the fold.

NOTES

1. This listing was adapted from Goforth, F. & Spillman, C. 1994. *Using Folk Literature in the Classroom: Encouraging Children to Read and Write.* Phoenix, Ariz.: Oryx. Pp. 171–186.
2. For additional ideas about book recording devices, see sources such as Schell, L. 1991. *How to Create an Independent Reading Program.* New York: Scholastic. 38–39.
3. This procedure for making a bound book was adapted from an article by Marzollo, J. 1991. Easy steps to bookmaking. *Instructor.* May. 40–42. Many books contain this basic procedure, such as Guthrie, C., Bentley, N. and Arnsteen, K. K. 1994. *The Young Author's Do-It-Yourself Book: How to Write, Illustrate, and Produce Your Own Book.* Illus. Katy Keck Arnsteen. Brookfield, Conn.: Millbrook.; Harste, J. C., Short, K. G. With Burke, C. *Creating Classrooms for Authors.* Portsmouth, NH: Heinemann. 238–242.; Stowell, C. 1994. *Step-By-Step Making Books.* New York: Kingfisher. (For 5–12 yrs.)

C

Major Awards Given for Children's Literature

INTERNATIONAL AWARD

The most prestigious international award is the *Hans Christian Andersen Award*, which was established in 1956 by the International Board on Books for Young People. The biennial award honors one living author and one living illustrator for her or his entire contribution to literature. Countries nominate an author and artist; then, a five-member committee representing different countries makes the final selection.

1956 Eleanor Farjeon (Great Britain).

1958 Astrid Lindgren (Sweden).

1960 Erich Kästner (Germany).

1962 Meindert Dejong (United States).

1964 René Guillot (France).

1966 *Author:* Tove Jansson (Finland).
Illustrator: Alois Carigiet (Switzerland).

1968 *Authors:* James Krüss (Germany); Jose Maria Sanchez-Silva (Spain).
Illustrator: Jiri Trnka (Czechoslovakia).

1970 *Author:* Gianni Rodari (Italy).
Illustrator: Maurice Sendak (United States).

1972 *Author:* Scott O'Dell (United States).
Illustrator: Ib Spang Olsen (Denmark).

1974 *Author:* Maria Gripe (Sweden).
Illustrator: Farshid Mesghali (Iran).

1976 *Author:* Cecil Bodker (Denmark).
Illustrator: Tatjana Mawrina (Union of Soviet Socialist Republics).

1978 *Author:* Paula Fox (United States).
Illustrator: Svend Otto S. (Denmark).

1980 *Author:* Bohumil Riha (Czechoslovakia).
Illustrator: Suekichi Akaba (Japan).

1982 *Author:* Lygia Bojunga Nunes (Brazil).
Illustrator: Zbigniew Rychlicki (Poland).

1984 *Author:* Christine Nostlinger (Austria).
Illustrator: Mitsumasa Anno (Japan).

1986 *Author:* Patricia Wrightson (Australia).
Illustrator: Robert Ingpen (Australia).

1988 *Author:* Annie M. G. Schmidt (Netherlands).
Illustrator: Dusan Kallay (Czechoslovakia).

1990 *Author:* Tormod Haugen (Norway).
Illustrator: Lisbeth Zwerger (Austria).

1992 *Author:* Virginia Hamilton (United States).
Illustrator: Kveta Pacovoska.

1994 *Author:* Michio Mado (Japan).
Illustrator: Jorg Muller (Switzerland).

1996 *Author:* Uri Orlev (Israel).
Illustrator: Klaus Ensikat (Germany).

NATIONAL AWARDS

CALDECOTT AWARDS

The Randolph Caldecott Medal was begun in 1938 by Frederic G. Melcher, editor of *Publisher's Weekly Magazine*. The award is named in honor of Randolph Caldecott, the English illustrator of note. A committee from the American Library Association awards the medal annually to the illustrator of the most distinguished picture book for children published in the United States during the preceding year. The artist must be a resident or citizen of the United States. Honor books are also recognized. In the following list, the award winner is presented in capital letters, the honor books are listed below the winner.

1938 ANIMALS OF THE BIBLE: A PICTURE BOOK. Text selected from the King James Bible by Helen Dean Fish. Illustrated by Dorothy O. Lathrop.   Stokes.
Seven Simeons by Boris Artzybasheff.   Viking.
Four and Twenty Blackbirds compiled by Helen Dean Fish. Illustrated by Robert Lawson.   Stokes.

1939   MEI LI by Thomas Handforth.   Doubleday.
The Forest Pool by Laura Adams Armer.   Longmans, Green.
Wee Gillis by Munro Leaf. Illustrated by Robert Lawson.   Viking.
Snow White and the Seven Dwarfs translated and illustrated by Wanda Gág.   Coward-McCann.
Barkis by Clare Turlay Newberry.   Harper.
Andy and the Lion by James Daugherty.   Viking.

1940   ABRAHAM LINCOLN by Ingri d'Aulaire and Edgar Parin d'Aulaire. Doubleday.
Cock-a-Doodle-Doo by Berta Hader and Elmer Hader.   Macmillan.
Madeline by Ludwig Bemelmans.   Simon and Schuster.
The Ageless Story by Lauren Ford.   Dodd, Mead.

1941   THEY WERE STRONG AND GOOD by Robert Lawson.   Viking.
April's Kittens by Clare Turlay Newberry.   Harper.

1942   MAKE WAY FOR DUCKLINGS by Robert McCloskey.   Viking.
An American ABC by Maud Petersham and Miska Petersham. Macmillan.
In My Mother's House by Ann Nolan Clark. Illustrated by Velino Herrera.   Viking.
Paddle-to-the-Sea by Holling Clancy Holling.   Houghton Mifflin.
Nothing at All by Wanda Gág.   Coward McCann.

1943   THE LITTLE HOUSE by Virginia Lee Burton.   Houghton Mifflin.
Dash and Dart by Mary Buff and Conrad Buff.   Viking.
Marshmallow by Clare Turlay Newberry.   Harper.

1944   MANY MOONS by James Thurber. Illustrated by Louis Slobodkin.   Harcourt.
Small Rain. Text arranged from the Bible by Jessie Orton Jones. Illustrated by Elizabeth Orton Jones.   Viking.
Pierre Pidgeon by Lee Kingman. Illustrated by Arnold Edwin Bare.   Houghton Mifflin.
Good-Luck Horse by Chih-Yi Chan. Illustrated by Plato Chan. Whittlesey.
Mighty Hunter by Berta Hader and Elmer Hader.   Macmillan.
A Child's Good Night Book by Margaret Wise Brown. Illustrated by Jean Charlot.   W. R. Scott.

1945   PRAYER FOR A CHILD by Rachel Field. Pictures by Elizabeth Orton Jones.   Macmillan.
Mother Goose. Compiled and illustrated by Tasha Tudor. Oxford.
In the Forest by Marie Hall Ets.   Viking.
Yonie Wondernose by Marguerite de Angeli.   Doubleday.
The Christmas Anna Angel by Ruth Sawyer. Illustrated by Kate Seredy.   Viking.

1946   THE ROOSTER CROWS by Maud Petersham and Miska Petersham.   Macmillan.
Little Lost Lamb by Margaret Wise Brown. Illustrated by Leonard Weisgard.   Doubleday.
Sing Mother Goose. Music by Opal Wheeler. Illustrated by Marjorie Torrey.   Dutton.
My Mother Is the Most Beautiful Woman in the World by Becky Reyher. Illustrated by Ruth C. Gannett.   Lothrop.
You Can Write Chinese by Kurt Wiese.   Viking.

1947   THE LITTLE ISLAND by Golden MacDonald. Illustrated by Leonard Weisgard.   Doubleday.
Rain Drop Splash by Alvin R. Tresselt. Illustrated by Leonard Weisgard.   Lothrop.
Boats on the River by Marjorie Flack. Illustrated by Jay Hyde Barnum.   Viking.
Timothy Turtle by Al Graham. Illustrated by Tony Palazzo. Robert Welch.
Pedro, Angel of Olvera Street by Leo Politi.   Scribner.
Sing in Praise by Opal Wheeler. Illustrated by Marjorie Torrey. Dutton.

1948   WHITE SNOW, BRIGHT SNOW by Alvin Tresselt. Illustrated by Roger Duvoisin.   Lothrop.
Stone Soup. Told and illustrated by Marcia Brown.   Scribner.

McElligot's Pool by Theodor S. Geisel (Dr. Seuss).   Random House.
Bambino the Clown by George Schreiber.   Viking.
Roger and the Fox by Lavinia R. Davis. Illustrated by Hildegard Woodward.   Doubleday.
Song of Robin Hood. Anne Malcolmson, ed. Illustrated by Virginia Lee Burton.   Houghton Mifflin.

1949   THE BIG SNOW by Berta Hader and Elmer Hader.   Macmillan.
Blueberries for Sal by Robert McCloskey.   Viking.
All Around the Town by Phyllis McGinley. Illustrated by Helen Stone.   Lippincott.
Juanita by Leo Politi.   Scribner.
Fish in the Air by Kurt Wiese.   Viking.

1950   SONG OF THE SWALLOWS by Leo Politi.   Scribner.
America's Ethan Allen by Stewart Holbrook. Illustrated by Lynd Ward.   Houghton Mifflin.
The Wild Birthday Cake by Lavinia R. Davis. Illustrated by Hildegard Woodward.   Doubleday.
Happy Day by Ruth Krauss. Illustrated by Marc Simont. Harper.
Henry-Fisherman by Marcia Brown.   Scribner.
Bartholomew and the Oobleck by Theodor S. Geisel (Dr. Seuss). Random House.

1951   THE EGG TREE by Katherine Milhous.   Scribner.
Dick Whittington and His Cat told and illustrated by Marcia Brown.   Scribner.
The Two Reds by Will (William Lipkind). Illustrated by Nicolas (Mordvinoff).   Harcourt.
If I Ran the Zoo by Theodor S. Geisel (Dr. Seuss).   Random House.
T-Bone the Baby-Sitter by Clare Turlay Newberry.   Harper.
The Most Wonderful Doll in the World by Phyllis McGinley. Illustrated by Helen Stone.   Lippincott.

1952   FINDERS KEEPERS by Will (William Lipkind). Illustrated by Nicolas (Mordvinoff).   Harcourt.
Mr. T. W. Anthony Woo by Marie Hall Ets.   Viking.
Skipper John's Cook by Marcia Brown.   Scribner.
All Falling Down by Gene Zion. Illustrated by Margaret Bloy Graham.   Harper.
Bear Party by William Pène du Bois.   Viking.
Feather Mountain by Elizabeth Olds.   Houghton Mifflin.

1953   THE BIGGEST BEAR by Lynd Ward.   Houghton Mifflin.
Puss in Boots. Told and illustrated by Marcia Brown.   Scribner.
One Morning in Maine by Robert McCloskey.   Viking.
Ape in a Cape by Fritz Eichenberg.   Harcourt.
The Storm Book by Charlotte Zolotow. Illustrated by Margaret Bloy Graham.   Harper.
Five Little Monkeys by Juliet Kepes.   Houghton Mifflin.

1954   MADELINE'S RESCUE by Ludwig Bemelmans.   Viking.
Journey Cake, Ho! by Ruth Sawyer. Illustrated by Robert McCloskey.   Viking.
When Will the World Be Mine? by Miriam Schlein. Illustrated by Jean Charlot.   W. R. Scott.
The Steadfast Tin Soldier translated by M. R. James. Adapted from Hans Christian Andersen. Illustrated by Marcia Brown. Scribner.
A Very Special House by Ruth Krauss. Illustrated by Maurice Sendak.   Harper.
Green Eyes by Abe Birnbaum.   Capitol.

1955   CINDERELLA by Charles Perrault. Illustrated by Marcia Brown. Harper.
Book of Nursery and Mother Goose Rhymes. Compiled and illustrated by Marguerite de Angeli.   Doubleday.
Wheel on the Chimney by Margaret Wise Brown. Illustrated by Tibor Gergely.   Lippincott.

1956   FROG WENT A-COURTIN' by John Langstaff. Illustrated by Feodor Rojankovsky.   Harcourt.

Play with Me by Marie Hall Ets. Viking.
Crow Boy by Taro Yashima. Viking.

1957 A TREE IS NICE by Janice May Udry. Illustrated by Marc Simont. Harper.
Mr. Penny's Race Horse by Marie Hall Ets. Viking.
1 Is One by Tasha Tudor. Oxford.
Anatole by Eve Titus. Illustrated by Paul Galdone. Whittlesey.
Gillespie and the Guards by Benjamin Elkin. Illustrated by James Daugherty. Viking.
Lion by William Pène du Bois. Viking.

1958 TIME OF WONDER by Robert McCloskey. Viking.
Fly High, Fly Low by Don Freeman. Viking.
Anatole and the Cat by Eve Titus. Illustrated by Paul Galdone. Whittlesey.

1959 CHANTICLEER AND THE FOX. Edited and illustrated by Barbara Cooney. Crowell.
The House That Jack Built by Antonio Frasconi. Crowell.
What Do You Say, Dear? by Sesyle Joslin. Illustrated by Maurice Sendak. W. R. Scott.
Umbrella by Taro Yashima. Viking.

1960 NINE DAYS TO CHRISTMAS by Marie Hall Ets and Aurora Labastida. Viking.
Houses from the Sea by Alice E. Goudey. Illustrated by Adrienne Adams. Scribner.
The Moon Jumpers by Janice May Udry. Illustrated by Maurice Sendak. Harper.

1961 BABOUSHKA AND THE THREE KINGS by Ruth Robbins. Illustrated by Nicolas Sidjakov. Parnassus.
Inch by Inch by Leo Lionni. Obolensky.

1962 ONCE A MOUSE by Marcia Brown. Scribner.
The Fox Went Out on a Chilly Night by Peter Spier. Doubleday.
Little Bear's Visit by Else Minarik. Illustrated by Maurice Sendak. Harper.
The Day We Saw the Sun Come Up by Alice Goudey. Illustrated by Adrienne Adams. Scribner.

1963 THE SNOWY DAY by Ezra Jack Keats. Viking.
The Sun Is a Golden Earring by Natalia Belting. Illustrated by Bernarda Bryson. Holt, Rinehart and Winston.
Mr. Rabbit and the Lovely Present by Charlotte Zolotow. Illustrated by Maurice Sendak. Harper & Row.

1964 WHERE THE WILD THINGS ARE by Maurice Sendak. Harper & Row.
Swimmy by Leo Lionni. Pantheon.
All in the Morning Early by Sorche Nic Leodhas. Illustrated by Evaline Ness. Holt, Rinehart and Winston.
Mother Goose and Nursery Rhymes by Philip Reed. Atheneum.

1965 MAY I BRING A FRIEND? by Beatrice Schenk de Regniers. Illustrated by Beni Montresor. Atheneum.
Rain Makes Applesauce by Julian Scheer. Illustrated by Marvin Bileck. Holiday.
The Wave by Margaret Hodges. Illustrated by Blair Lent. Houghton Mifflin.
A Pocketful of Cricket by Rebecca Caudill. Illustrated by Evaline Ness. Holt, Rinehart and Winston.

1966 ALWAYS ROOM FOR ONE MORE by Sorche Nic Leodhas. Illustrated by Nonny Hogrogian. Holt, Rinehart and Winston.
Hide and Seek Fog by Alvin Tresselt. Illustrated by Roger Duvoisin. Lothrop.
Just Me by Marie Hall Ets. Viking.
Tom Tit Tot. Joseph Jacobs, ed. Illustrated by Evaline Ness. Scribner.

1967 SAM, BANGS AND MOONSHINE by Evaline Ness. Holt, Rinehart and Winston.
One Wide River to Cross by Barbara Emberley. Illustrated by Ed Emberley. Prentice-Hall.

1968 DRUMMER HOFF by Barbara Emberley. Illustrated by Ed Emberley. Prentice-Hall.
Frederick by Leo Lionni. Pantheon.
Seashore Story by Taro Yashima. Viking.
The Emperor and the Kite by Jane Yolen. Illustrated by Ed Young. World Publishing.

1969 THE FOOL OF THE WORLD AND THE FLYING SHIP by Arthur Ransome. Illustrated by Uri Shulevitz. Farrar, Straus.
Why the Sun and the Moon Live in the Sky by Elphinstone Dayrell. Illustrated by Blair Lent. Houghton Mifflin.

1970 SYLVESTER AND THE MAGIC PEBBLE by William Steig. Windmill/Simon and Schuster.
Goggles by Ezra Jack Keats. Macmillan.
Alexander and the Wind-up Mouse by Leo Lionni. Pantheon.
Pop Corn and Ma Goodness by Edna Mitchell Preston. Illustrated by Robert Andrew Parker. Viking.
Thy Friend, Obadiah by Brinton Turkle. Viking.
The Judge by Harve Zemach. Illustrated by Margot Zemach. Farrar, Straus.

1971 A STORY, A STORY by Gail E. Haley. Atheneum.
The Angry Moon by William Sleator. Illustrated by Blair Lent. Atlantic-Little, Brown.
Frog and Toad Are Friends by Arnold Lobel. Harper & Row.
In the Night Kitchen by Maurice Sendak. Harper & Row.

1972 ONE FINE DAY by Nonny Hogrogian. Macmillan.
If All the Seas Were One Sea by Janina Domanska. Macmillan.
Moja Means One: Swahili Counting Book by Muriel Feelings. Illustrated by Tom Feelings. Dial.
Hildilid's Night by Cheli Duran Ryan. Illustrated by Arnold Lobel. Macmillan.

1973 THE FUNNY LITTLE WOMAN by Arlene Mosel. Illustrated by Blair Lent. Dutton.
Hosie's Alphabet by Hosea Baskin, Tobias Baskin, and Lisa Baskin. Illustrated by Leonard Baskin. Viking.
When Clay Sings by Byrd Baylor. Illustrated by Tom Bahti. Scribner.
Snow-White and the Seven Dwarfs by the Brothers Grimm, translated by Randall Jarrell. Illustrated by Nancy Ekholm Burkert. Farrar, Straus.
Anansi the Spider by Gerald McDermott. Holt, Rinehart and Winston.

1974 DUFFY AND THE DEVIL by Harve Zemach. Illustrated by Margot Zemach. Farrar, Straus.
The Three Jovial Huntsmen by Susan Jeffers. Bradbury.
Cathedral by David Macaulay. Houghton Mifflin.

1975 ARROW TO THE SUN. Adapted and illustrated by Gerald McDermott. Viking.
Jambo Means Hello: Swahili Alphabet Book by Muriel Feelings. Illustrated by Tom Feelings. Dial.

1976 WHY MOSQUITOES BUZZ IN PEOPLE'S EARS by Verna Aardema. Illustrated by Leo and Diane Dillon. Dial.
The Desert Is Theirs by Byrd Baylor. Illustrated by Peter Parnell. Scribner.
Strega Nona retold and illustrated by Tomie de Paola.

1977 ASHANTI TO ZULU: AFRICAN TRADITIONS by Margaret Musgrove. Illustrated by Leo and Diane Dillon. Dial.
The Amazing Bone by William Steig. Farrar, Straus.
The Contest by Nonny Hogrogian. Greenwillow.
Fish for Supper by M. B. Goffstein. Dial.
The Golem by Beverly Brodsky McDermott. Lippincott.
Hawk, I'm Your Brother by Byrd Baylor. Illustrated by Peter Parnall. Scribner.

1978 NOAH'S ARK by Peter Spier. Doubleday.
Castle by David Macaulay. Houghton Mifflin.
It Could Always Be Worse by Margot Zemach. Farrar, Straus.

1979 THE GIRL WHO LOVED WILD HORSES by Paul Goble. Bradbury.
Freight Train by Donald Crews.   Greenwillow.
The Way to Start a Day by Byrd Baylor. Illustrated by Peter Parnall.   Scribner's.

1980 OX-CART MAN by Donald Hall. Illustrated by Barbara Cooney. Viking.
Ben's Trumpet by Rachel Isadora.   Greenwillow.
The Treasure by Uri Shulevitz.   Farrar Straus.
The Garden of Abdul Gasazi by Chris Van Allsburg.   Houghton Mifflin.

1981 FABLES by Arnold Lobel.   Harper & Row.
The Bremen-Town Musicians by Ilse Plume.   Doubleday.
The Grey Lady and the Strawberry Snatcher by Molly Bang. Four Winds.
Mice Twice by Joseph Low.   Atheneum.
Truck by Donald Crews.   Greenwillow.

1982 JUMANJI by Chris Van Allsburg.   Houghton Mifflin.
A Visit to William Blake's Inn: Poems for Innocent and Experienced Travelers by Nancy Willard. Illustrated by Alice and Martin Provensen.   Harcourt Brace Jovanovich.
Where the Buffaloes Began by Olaf Baker. Illustrated by Stephen Gammell.   Warne.
On Market Street by Arnold Lobel. Illustrated by Anita Lobel. Greenwillow.
Outside Over There by Maurice Sendak.   Harper & Row.

1983 SHADOW by Blaise Cendrars. Illustrated by Marcia Brown. Scribner.
When I Was Young in the Mountains by Cynthia Rylant. Illustrated by Diane Goode.   Dutton.
A Chair for My Mother by Vera B. Williams.   Morrow.

1984 THE GLORIOUS FLIGHT: ACROSS THE CHANNEL WITH LOUIS BLERIOT, JULY 25, 1909 by Alice and Martin Provensen.   Viking.
Ten, Nine, Eight by Molly Bang.   Greenwillow.
Little Red Riding Hood by Trina Schart Hyman.   Holiday.

1985 SAINT GEORGE AND THE DRAGON adapted by Margaret Hodges. Illustrated by Trina Schart Hyman.   Little, Brown.
Hansel and Gretel by Rika Lesser. Illustrated by Paul O. Zelinsky.   Dodd.
The Story of Jumping Mouse by John Steptoe.   Lothrop.
Have You Seen My Duckling? by Nancy Tafuri.   Greenwillow.

1986 POLAR EXPRESS by Chris Van Allsburg.   Houghton Mifflin.
The Relatives Came by Cynthia Rylant. Illustrated by Stephen Gammell.   Bradbury.
King Bidgood's in the Bathtub by Audrey Wood. Illustrated by Don Wood.   Harcourt Brace Jovanovich.

1987 HEY AL by Arthur Yorinks. Illustrated by Richard Egielski. Farrar, Straus.
Alphabatics by Suse MacDonald.   Bradbury.
Rumpelstiltskin by Paul O. Zelinsky.   Dutton.
The Village of Round and Square Houses by Ann Grifalconi. Little, Brown.

1988 OWL MOON by Jane Yolen. Illustrated by John Schoenherr. Philomel.
Mufaro's Beautiful Daughters: An African Story. Adapted and illustrated by John Steptoe.   Lothrop.

1989 SONG AND DANCE MAN by Karen Ackerman. Illustrated by Stephen Gammell.   Knopf.
The Boy of the Three-Year Nap by Dianne Stanley. Illustrated by Allen Say.   Houghton Mifflin.
Free Fall by David Wiesner.   Lothrop.
Goldilocks and the Three Bears. Adapted and illustrated by James Marshall.   Dial.
Mirandy and Brother Wind by Patricia McKissack. Illustrated by Jerry Pinkney.   Knopf.

1990 LON PO PO: A RED RIDING HOOD STORY FROM CHINA. Adapted and illustrated by Ed Young.   Philomel.
Bill Peet: An Autobiography by Bill Peet.   Houghton Mifflin.
Color Zoo by Lois Ehlert.   Lippincott.
Herschel and the Hanukkah Goblins by Eric Kimmel. Illustrated by Trina Schart Hyman.   Holiday.
The Talking Eggs by Robert D. San Souci. Illustrated by Jerry Pinkney.   Dial.

1991 BLACK AND WHITE by David Macaulay.   Houghton Mifflin.
Puss in Boots by Charles Perrault. Translated by Malcolm Arthur. Illustrated by Fred Marcellino.   Farrar, Straus.
"More More More," Said the Baby by Vera B. Williams. Greenwillow.

1992 TUESDAY by David Wiesner.   Clarion.
Tar Beach by Faith Ringgold.   Crown.

1993 MIRETTE ON THE HIGH WIRE by Emily Arnold McCully. Putnam.
The Stinky Cheese Man and Other Fairly Stupid Tales by Jon Scieszka. Illustrated by Lane Smith.   Viking.
Working Cotton by Sherley Anne Williams. Illustrated by Carole Byard.   Harcourt Brace Jovanovich.
Seven Blind Mice by Ed Young.   Philomel.

1994 GRANDFATHER'S JOURNEY by Allen Say.   Houghton Mifflin.
Peppe the Lamplighter by Elisa Bartone. Illustrations by Ted Lewin.   Lothrop.
In the Small, Small Pond by Denise Fleming.   Holt.
Owen by Kevin Henkes.   Greenwillow.
Raven: A Trickster Tale from the Pacific Northwest by Gerald McDermott.   Harcourt Brace Jovanovich.
Yo! Yes? by Chris Raschka.   Orchard/Richard Jackson.

1995 SMOKY NIGHT by Eve Bunting. Illustrated by David Diaz. Harcourt Brace Jovanovich.
Swamp Angel by Anne Isaacs. Illustrated by Paul O. Zelinsky. Dutton.
John Henry by Julius Lester. Illustrated by Jerry Pinkney.   Dial.
Time Flies by Eric Rohmann.   Crown.

1996 OFFICER BUCKLE AND GLORIA by Peggy Rathmann.   Putnam.
Alphabet City by Stephen T. Johnson.   Viking.
Zin! Zin! Zin! by Lloyd Moss. Illustrated by Marjorie Priceman. Simon & Schuster.
The Faithful Friend by Robert D. San Souci. Illustrated by Brian Pinkney.   Simon & Schuster.
Tops and Bottoms by Janet Stevens.   Harcourt Brace Jovanovich.

1997 GOLEM by David Wisniewski.   Clarion
Hush!: A Thai Lullaby by Minfong Ho. Illustrated by Holly Meade.   Kroupa/Orchard.
The Graphic Alphabet. Illustrated by David Pelletier.   Orchard.
The Paperboy by Dav Pilkey.   Jackson/Orchard.
Starry Messenger by Peter Sis.   Foster/Farrar.

NEWBERY AWARDS

The *Newbery Medal* was begun in 1922 by Frederic G. Melcher, editor of the *Publisher's Weekly Magazine*. The award is named after John Newbery, the first English seller of books especially written for children. A committee of the Association for Library Service to Children (ALSC) of the American Library Association awards the medal annually to the most outstanding juvenile book published in the United States the previous year. The award is limited to authors who are residents or citizens of the United States. Honor books are also recognized. In the following list, the award winner is presented in capital letters, the honor books are listed below the winner.

1922 THE STORY OF MANKIND by Hendrik Van Loon. Boni & Liveright.
The Great Quest by Charles Boardman Hawes. Little, Brown.
Cedric the Forester by Bernard G. Marshall. Appleton.
The Old Tobacco Shop by William Bowen. Macmillan.
The Golden Fleece by Padraic Colum. Macmillan.
Windy Hill by Cornelia Meigs. Macmillan.

1923 THE VOYAGES OF DOCTOR DOLITTLE by Hugh Lofting. Stokes.
[No record of honor books.]

1924 THE DARK FRIGATE by Charles Boardman Hawes. Little, Brown.
[No record of honor books.]

1925 TALES FROM SILVER LANDS by Charles J. Finger. Illustrated by Paul Honoré. Doubleday.
Nicholas by Anne Carroll Moore. Putnam.
Dream Coach by Anne and Dillwyn Parrish. Macmillan.

1926 SHEN OF THE SEA by Arthur Bowie Chrisman. Illustrated by Else Hasselriis. Dutton.
The Voyagers by Padraic Colum. Macmillan.

1927 SMOKY, THE COWHORSE by Will James. Scribner.
[No record of honor books.]

1928 GAY NECK by Dhan Gopal Mukerji. Illustrated by Boris Artzybasheff. Dutton.
The Wonder-Smith and His Son by Ella Young. Longmans, Green.
Downright Dencey by Caroline Dale Snedeker. Doubleday.

1929 TRUMPETER OF KRAKOW by Eric P. Kelly. Illustrated by Angela Pruszynska. Macmillan.
The Pigtail of Ah Lee Ben Loo by John Bennett. Longmans, Green.
Millions of Cats by Wanda Gág. Coward-McCann.
The Boy Who Was by Grace T. Hallock. Dutton.
Clearing Weather by Cornelia Meigs. Little, Brown.
The Runaway Papoose by Grace P. Moon. Doubleday.
Tod of the Fens by Eleanor Whitney. Macmillan.

1930 HITTY, HER FIRST HUNDRED YEARS by Rachel Field. Illustrated by Dorothy P. Lathrop. Macmillan.
Pran of Albania by Elizabeth C. Miller. Doubleday.
The Jumping-Off Place by Marian Hurd McNeely. Longmans, Green.
A Daughter of the Seine by Jeanette Eaton. Harper.

1931 THE CAT WHO WENT TO HEAVEN by Elizabeth Coatsworth. Illustrated by Lynd Ward. Macmillan.
Floating Island by Anne Parrish. Harper.
The Dark Star of Itza by Alida Malkus. Harcourt.
Queer Person by Ralph Hubbard. Doubleday.
Mountains Are Free by Julia Davis Adams. Dutton.
Spice and the Devil's Cave by Agnes D. Hewes. Knopf.
Meggy McIntosh by Elizabeth Janet Gray. Doubleday.

1932 WATERLESS MOUNTAIN by Laura Adams Armer. Illustrated by Sidney Armer and the author. Longmans, Green.
The Fairy Circus by Dorothy Lathrop. Macmillan.
Calico Bush by Rachel Field. Macmillan.
Boy of the South Seas by Eunice Tietjens. Coward-McCann.
Out of the Flame by Eloise Lounsbery. Longmans, Green.
Jane's Island by Marjorie Hill Alee. Houghton Mifflin.
Truce of the Wolf by Mary Gould Davis. Harcourt.

1933 YOUNG FU OF THE UPPER YANGTZE by Elizabeth Foreman Lewis. Illustrated by Kurt Wiese. Winston.
Swift Rivers by Cornelia Meigs. Little.
The Railroad to Freedom by Hildegarde Swift. Harcourt.
Children of the Soil by Nora Burglon. Doubleday.

1934 INVINCIBLE LOUISA by Cornelia Meigs. Little, Brown.
Forgotten Daughter by Caroline Dale Snedeker. Doubleday.
Swords of Steel by Elsie Singmaster. Houghton Mifflin.
ABC Bunny by Wanda Gág. Coward-McCann.
Winged Girl of Knossos by Erick Berry. Appleton.
New Land by Sarah L. Schmidt. McBride.
Apprentices of Florence by Anne Kyle. Houghton Mifflin.

1935 DOBRY by Monica Shannon. Illustrated by Atanas Katchamakoff. Viking.
The Pageant of Chinese History by Elizabeth Seeger. Longmans, Green.
Davy Crockett by Constance Rourke. Harcourt.
A Day on Skates by Hilda Van Stockum. Harper.

1936 CADDIE WOODLAWN by Carol Ryrie Brink. Illustrated by Kate Seredy. Macmillan.
Honk the Moose by Phil Stong. Dodd, Mead.
The Good Master by Kate Seredy. Viking.
Young Walter Scott by Elizabeth Janet Gray. Viking.
All Sail Set by Armstrong Sperry. Winston.

1937 ROLLER SKATES by Ruth Sawyer. Illustrated by Valenti Angelo. Viking.
Phoebe Fairchild: Her Book by Lois Lenski. Stokes.
Whistler's Van by Idwal Jones. Viking.
The Golden Basket by Ludwig Bemelmans. Viking.
Winterbound by Margery Bianco. Viking.
Audubon by Constance Rourke. Harcourt.
The Codfish Musket by Agnes D. Hewes. Doubleday.

1938 THE WHITE STAG by Kate Seredy. Viking.
Bright Island by Mabel L. Robinson. Random House.
Pecos Bill by James Cloyd Bowman. Whitman.
On the Banks of Plum Creek by Laura Ingalls Wilder. Harper.

1939 THIMBLE SUMMER by Elizabeth Enright. Farrar & Rinehart.
Leader by Destiny by Jeanette Eaton. Harcourt.
Penn by Elizabeth Janet Gray. Viking.
Nino by Valenti Angelo. Viking.
"Hello, the Boat!" by Phyllis Crawford. Holt.
Mr. Popper's Penguins by Richard and Florence Atwater. Little, Brown.

1940 DANIEL BOONE by James H. Daugherty. Viking.
The Singing Tree by Kate Seredy. Viking.
Runner of the Mountain Tops by Mabel L. Robinson. Random House.
By the Shores of Silver Lake by Laura Ingalls Wilder. Harper.
Boy with a Pack by Stephen W. Meader. Harcourt.

1941 CALL IT COURAGE by Armstrong Sperry. Macmillan.
Blue Willow by Doris Gates. Viking.
Young Mac of Fort Vancouver by Mary Jane Carr. Crowell.
The Long Winter by Laura Ingalls Wilder. Harper.
Nansen by Anna Gertrude Hall. Viking.

1942 THE MATCHLOCK GUN by Walter D. Edmonds. Illustrated by Paul Lantz. Dodd, Mead.
Little Town on the Prairie by Laura Ingalls Wilder. Harper.
George Washington's World by Genevieve Foster. Scribner.
Indian Captive by Lois Lenski. Stokes.
Down Ryton Water by E. R. Gaggin. Viking.

1943 ADAM OF THE ROAD by Elizabeth Janet Gray. Illustrated by Robert Lawson. Viking.
The Middle Moffat by Eleanor Estes. Harcourt.
"Have You Seen Tom Thumb?" by Mabel Leigh Hunt. Stokes.

1944 JOHNNY TREMAIN by Esther Forbes. Illustrated by Lynd Ward. Houghton Mifflin.
These Happy Golden Years by Laura Ingalls Wilder. Harper.
Fog Magic by Julia L. Sauer. Viking.
Rufus M. by Eleanor Estes. Harcourt.
Mountain Born by Elizabeth Yates. Coward-McCann.

1945 RABBIT HILL by Robert Lawson. Viking.
The Hundred Dresses by Eleanor Estes. Harcourt.

The Silver Pencil by Alice Dalgliesh.   Scribner.
Abraham Lincoln's World by Genevieve Foster.   Scribner.
Lone Journey by Jeanette Eaton.   Harcourt.

1946   STRAWBERRY GIRL by Lois Lenski.   Lippincott.
Justin Morgan Had a Horse by Marguerite Henry.   Wilcox & Follett (Follett).
The Moved-Outers by Florence Crannell Means.   Houghton Mifflin.
Bhimsa, the Dancing Bear by Christine Weston.   Scribner.
New Found World by Katherine B. Shippen.   Viking.

1947   MISS HICKORY by Carolyn Sherwin Bailey. Illustrated by Ruth Gannett.   Viking.
The Wonderful Year by Nancy Barnes.   Messner.
Big Tree by Mary Buff and Conrad Buff.   Viking.
The Heavenly Tenants by William Maxwell.   Harper.
The Avion My Uncle Flew by Cyrus Fisher.   Appleton.
The Hidden Treasure of Glaston by Eleanore M. Jewett.   Viking.

1948   THE TWENTY-ONE BALLOONS by William Pène du Bois.   Viking.
Pancakes-Paris by Claire Huchet Bishop.   Viking.
Li Lun, Lad of Courage by Carolyn Treffinger.   Abingdon-Cokesbury.
The Quaint and Curious Quest of Johnny Longfoot by Catherine Besterman.   Bobbs-Merrill.
The Cow-Tail Switch by Harold Courlander and George Herzog.   Holt.
Misty of Chincoteague by Marguerite Henry.   Rand McNally.

1949   KING OF THE WIND by Marguerite Henry. Illustrated by Wesley Dennis.   Rand McNally.
Seabird by Holling Clancy Holling.   Houghton Mifflin.
Daughter of the Mountains by Louise Rankin.   Viking.
My Father's Dragon by Ruth S. Gannett.   Random House.
Story of the Negro by Arna Bontemps.   Knopf.

1950   THE DOOR IN THE WALL by Marguerite de Angeli.   Doubleday.
Tree of Freedom by Rebecca Caudill.   Viking.
Blue Cat of Castle Town by Catherine Coblentz.   Longmans, Green.
Kildee House by Rutherford Montgomery.   Doubleday.
George Washington by Genevieve Foster.   Scribner.
Song of the Pines by Walter Havighurst and Marion Havighurst.   Winston.

1951   AMOS FORTUNE, FREE MAN by Elizabeth Yates. Illustrated by Nora Unwin.   Aladdin.
Better Known as Johnny Appleseed by Mabel Leigh Hunt.   Lippincott.
Gandhi, Fighter without a Sword by Jeanette Eaton.   Morrow.
Abraham Lincoln, Friend of the People by Clara I. Judson.   Wilcox & Follett.
The Story of Appleby Capple by Anne Parrish.   Harper.

1952   GINGER PYE by Eleanor Estes.   Harcourt.
Americans before Columbus by Elizabeth Chesley Baity.   Viking.
Minn of the Mississippi by Holling Clancy Holling.   Houghton Mifflin.
The Defender by Nicholas Kalashnikoff.   Scribner.
The Light at Tern Rock by Julia L. Sauer.   Viking.
The Apple and the Arrow by Mary Buff.   Houghton Mifflin.

1953   SECRET OF THE ANDES by Ann Nolan Clark. Illustrated by Jean Charlot.   Viking.
Charlotte's Web by E. B. White.   Harper.
Moccasin Trail by Eloise J. McGraw.   Coward-McCann.
Red Sails for Capri by Ann Weil.   Viking.
The Bears on Hemlock Mountain by Alice Dalgliesh.   Scribner.
Birthdays of Freedom by Genevieve Foster.   Scribner.

1954   AND NOW MIGUEL by Joseph Krumgold. Illustrated by Jean Charlot.   Crowell.
All Alone by Clarie Huchet Bishop.   Viking.
Shadrach by Meindert DeJong.   Harper.

Hurry Home, Candy by Meindert DeJong.   Harper.
Theodore Roosevelt, Fighting Patriot by Clara I. Judson.   Follett.
Magic Maize by Mary Buff.   Houghton Mifflin.

1955   THE WHEEL ON THE SCHOOL by Meindert DeJong. Illustrated by Maurice Sendak.   Harper.
The Courage of Sarah Noble by Alice Dalgliesh.   Scribner.
Banner in the Sky by James Ramsey Ullman.   Lippincott.

1956   CARRY ON, MR. BOWDITCH by Jean Lee Latham.   Houghton Mifflin.
The Golden Name Day by Jennie D. Lindquist.   Harper.
The Secret River by Marjorie Kinnan Rawlings.   Scribner.
Men, Microscopes and Living Things by Katherine B. Shippen.   Viking.

1957   MIRACLES ON MAPLE HILL by Virginia Sorensen. Illustrated by Beth Krush and Joe Krush.   Harcourt.
Old Yeller by Fred Gipson.   Harper.
The House of Sixty Fathers by Meindert DeJong.   Harper.
Mr. Justice Holmes by Clara I. Judson.   Follett.
The Corn Grows Ripe by Dorothy Rhoads.   Viking.
The Black Fox of Lorne by Marguerite de Angeli.   Doubleday.

1958   RIFLES FOR WATIE by Harold Keith. Illustrated by Peter Burchard.   Crowell.
The Horsecatcher by Mari Sandoz.   Westminster.
Gone-away Lake by Elizabeth Enright.   Harcourt.
The Great Wheel by Robert Lawson.   Viking.
Tom Paine, Freedom's Apostle by Leo Gurko.   Crowell.

1959   THE WITCH OF BLACKBIRD POND by Elizabeth George Speare.   Houghton Mifflin.
The Family under the Bridge by Natalie S. Carlson.   Harper.
Along Came a Dog by Meindert DeJong.   Harper.
Chucaro by Francis Kalnay.   Harcourt.
The Perilous Road by William O. Steele.   Harcourt.

1960   ONION JOHN by Joseph Krumgold. Illustrated by Symeon Shimin.   Crowell.
My Side of the Mountain by Jean George.   Dutton.
America Is Born by Gerald Johnson.   Morrow.
The Gammage Cup by Carol Kendall.   Harcourt.

1961   ISLAND OF THE BLUE DOLPHINS by Scott O'Dell.   Houghton Mifflin.
America Moves Forward by Gerald Johnson.   Morrow.
Old Ramon by Jack Schaefer.   Houghton Mifflin.
The Cricket in Times Square by George Selden.   Farrar.

1962   THE BRONZE BOW by Elizabeth George Speare.   Houghton Mifflin.
Frontier Living by Edwin Tunis.   World Publishing.
The Golden Goblet by Eloise J. McGraw.   Coward-McCann.
Belling the Tiger by Mary Stolz.   Harper & Row.

1963   A WRINKLE IN TIME by Madeleine L'Engle.   Farrar.
Thistle and Thyme by Sorche Nic Leodhas.   Holt, Rinehart and Winston.
Men of Athens by Olivia Coolidge.   Houghton Mifflin.

1964   IT'S LIKE THIS, CAT by Emily Neville. Illustrated by Emil Weiss.   Harper & Row.
Rascal by Sterling North.   Dutton.
The Loner by Ester Wier.   McKay.

1965   SHADOW OF A BULL by Maia Wojciechowska. Illustrated by Alvin Smith.   Atheneum.
Across Five Aprils by Irene Hunt.   Follett.

1966   I, JUAN DE PAREJA by Elizabeth Borten de Treviño.   Farrar, Straus.
The Black Cauldron by Lloyd Alexander.   Holt, Rinehart and Winston.
The Animal Family by Randall Jarrell.   Pantheon.
The Noonday Friends by Mary Stolz.   Harper & Row.

1967   UP A ROAD SLOWLY by Irene Hunt.   Follett.
The King's Fifth by Scott O'Dell.   Houghton Mifflin.

Zlateh the Goat and Other Stories by Isaac Bashevis Singer. Harper & Row.
The Jazz Man by Mary Hays Weik.   Atheneum.

1968   FROM THE MIXED-UP FILES OF MRS. BASIL E. FRANKWEILER by E. L. Konigsburg.   Atheneum.
Jennifer, Hecate, Macbeth, William McKinley, and Me, Elizabeth by E. L. Konigsburg.   Atheneum.
The Black Pearl by Scott O'Dell.   Houghton Mifflin.
The Fearsome Inn by Isaac Bashevis Singer.   Scribner.
The Egypt Game by Zilpha Keatley Snyder.   Atheneum.

1969   THE HIGH KING by Lloyd Alexander.   Holt, Rinehart and Winston.
To Be a Slave by Julius Lester.   Dial.
When Shlemiel Went to Warsaw and Other Stories by Isaac Bashevis Singer.   Farrar, Straus.

1970   SOUNDER by William H. Armstrong.   Harper & Row.
Our Eddie by Sulamith Ish-Kishor.   Pantheon.
The Many Ways of Seeing: An Introduction to the Pleasures of Art by Janet Gaylord Moore.   World.
Journey Outside by Mary Q. Steele.   Viking.

1971   SUMMER OF THE SWANS by Betsy Byars.   Viking.
Kneeknock Rise by Natalie Babbitt.   Farrar, Straus.
Enchantress from the Stars by Sylvia Louise Engdahl.   Atheneum.
Sing Down the Moon by Scott O'Dell.   Houghton Mifflin.

1972   MRS. FRISBY AND THE RATS OF NIMH by Robert C. O'Brien.   Atheneum.
Incident at Hawk's Hill by Allan W. Eckert.   Little, Brown.
The Planet of Junior Brown by Virginia Hamilton.   Macmillan.
The Tombs of Atuan by Ursula K. LeGuin.   Atheneum.
Annie and the Old One by Miska Miles.   Atlantic-Little, Brown.
The Headless Cupid by Zilpha Keatley Snyder.   Atheneum.

1973   JULIE OF THE WOLVES by Jean Craighead George.   Harper & Row.
Frog and Toad Together by Arnold Lobel.   Harper & Row.
The Upstairs Room by Johanna Reiss.   Crowell.
The Witches of Worm by Zilpha Keatley Snyder.   Atheneum.

1974   THE SLAVE DANCER by Paula Fox.   Bradbury.
The Dark Is Rising by Susan Cooper.   Atheneum.

1975   M. C. HIGGINS THE GREAT by Virginia Hamilton.   Macmillan.
My Brother Sam Is Dead by James Collier and Christopher Collier.   Four Winds.
Philip Hall Likes Me. I Reckon Maybe by Bette Greene.   Dial.
The Perilous Gard by Elizabeth Pope.   Houghton Mifflin.
Figgs & Phantoms by Ellen Raskin.   Dutton.

1976   THE GREY KING by Susan Cooper.   Atheneum.
Dragonwings by Laurence Yep.   Harper & Row.
The Hundred Penny Box by Sharon Mathis.   Viking.

1977   ROLL OF THUNDER, HEAR MY CRY by Mildred D. Taylor.   Dial.
Abel's Island by William Steig.   Farrar, Straus.
A String in the Harp by Nancy Bond.   Atheneum.

1978   BRIDGE TO TERABITHIA by Katherine Paterson.   Crowell.
Anpao: An American Indian Odyssey by Jamake Highwater.   Lippincott.
Ramona and Her Father by Beverly Cleary.   Morrow.

1979   THE WESTING GAME by Ellen Raskin.   Dutton.
The Great Gilly Hopkins by Katherine Paterson.   Crowell.

1980   A GATHERING OF DAYS: A NEW ENGLAND GIRL'S JOURNAL, 1830–32 by Joan W. Blos.   Scribner.
The Road from Home: The Story of an Armenian Girl by David Kherdian.   Greenwillow.

1981   JACOB HAVE I LOVED by Katherine Paterson.   Crowell.
The Fledgling by Jane Langton.   Harper & Row.
Ring of Endless Light by Madeleine L'Engle.   Farrar, Straus.

1982   A VISIT TO WILLIAM BLAKE'S INN: POEMS FOR INNOCENT AND EXPERIENCED TRAVELERS by Nancy Willard. Illustrated by Alice and Martin Provensen.   Harcourt Brace Jovanovich.

1983   *Ramona Quimby, Age 8* by Beverly Cleary.   Morrow.
Upon the Head of the Goat: A Childhood in Hungary, 1939–1944 by Aranka Siegal.   Farrar, Straus.

1983   DICEY'S SONG by Cynthia Voigt.   Atheneum.
The Blue Sword by Robin McKinley.   Greenwillow.
Doctor De Soto by William Steig.   Farrar, Straus.
Graven Images by Paul Fleischman.   Harper & Row.
Homesick: My Own Story by Jean Fritz.   Putnam.
Sweet Whispers, Brother Rush by Virginia Hamilton.   Philomel.

1984   DEAR MR. HENSHAW by Beverly Cleary.   Morrow.
The Wish-Giver by Bill Brittain.   Harper & Row.
A Solitary Blue by Cynthia Voigt.   Atheneum.
The Sign of the Beaver by Elizabeth George Speare.   Houghton Mifflin.
Sugaring Time by Kathryn Lasky. Photographs by Christopher Knight.   Macmillan.

1985   THE HERO AND THE CROWN by Robin McKinley.   Greenwillow.
The Moves Make the Man by Bruce Brooks.   Harper & Row.
One-Eyed Cat by Paula Fox.   Bradbury.
Like Jake and Me by Mavis Jukes. Illustrated by Lloyd Bloom.   Knopf.

1986   SARAH, PLAIN AND TALL by Patricia MacLachlan.   Harper & Row.
Commodore Perry in the Land of the Shogun by Rhoda Blumberg.   Lothrop.
Dogsong by Gary Paulsen.   Bradbury.

1987   THE WHIPPING BOY by Sid Fleischman.   Greenwillow.
A Fine White Dust by Cynthia Rylant.   Bradbury.
On My Honor by Marion Dane Bauer.   Clarion.
Volcano by Patricia Lauber.   Bradbury.

1988   LINCOLN: A PHOTOBIOGRAPHY by Russell Freedman.   Clarion.
After the Rain by Norma Fox Mazer.   Morrow.
Hatchet by Gary Paulsen.   Bradbury.

1989   JOYFUL NOISE: POEMS FOR TWO VOICES by Paul Fleischman.   Harper & Row.
In the Beginning: Creation Stories from Around the World by Virginia Hamilton.   Harcourt.
Scorpions by Walter Dean Myers.   Harper & Row.

1990   NUMBER THE STARS by Lois Lowry.   Houghton Mifflin.
Afternoon of the Elves by Janet Taylor Lisle.   Orchard.
Shabanu: Daughter of the Wind by Suzanne Fisher Staples.   Knopf.
The Winter Room by Gary Paulsen.   Orchard.

1991   MANIAC MAGEE by Jerry Spinelli.   Little, Brown.
The True Confessions of Charlotte Doyle by Avi.   Orchard.

1992   SHILOH by Phyllis Reynolds Naylor.   Atheneum.
Nothing but the Truth by Avi.   Orchard.
The Wright Brothers by Russell Freedman.   Holiday.

1993   MISSING MAY by Cynthia Rylant.   Orchard/Richard Jackson.
What Hearts by Bruce Brooks.   HarperCollins.
The Dark-Thirty: Southern Tales of the Supernatural by Patricia McKissack. Illustrations by Brian Pinkney.   Knopf.
Somewhere in the Darkness by Walter Dean Myers.   Scholastic.

1994   THE GIVER by Lois Lowry.   Houghton Mifflin.
Crazy Lady! by Jane Leslie Conly.   HarperCollins.
Eleanor Roosevelt: A Life of Discovery by Russell Freedman.   Clarion.
Dragon's Gate by Laurence Yep.   HarperCollins.

1995   WALK TWO MOONS by Sharon Creech.   HarperCollins.
Catherine, Called Birdy by Karen Cushman.   Clarion.
The Ear, the Eye and the Arm by Nancy Farmer.   Orchard/Richard Jackson.

1996   THE MIDWIFE'S APPRENTICE by Karen Cushman.   Clarion.
What Jamie Saw by Carolyn Coman.   Front Street.
The Watsons Go to Birmingham—1963 by Christopher Paul Curtis.   Delacorte.

Yolonda's Genius by Carol Fenner.   McElderry.
The Great Fire by Jim Murphy.   Scholastic.

1997   THE VIEW FROM SATURDAY by E. L. Konigsburg.
Karl/Atheneum.
A Girl Named Disaster by Nancy Farmer.   Jackson/Orchard.
The Moonchild by Eloise McGraw.   McElderry.
The Thief by Megan Whalen Turner.   Greenwillow.
Belle Prater's Boy by Ruth White.   Farrar.

LAURA INGALLS WILDER AWARD

The *Laura Ingalls Wilder Award*, named in honor of the author of the *Little House* books and the first recipient of the award, is sponsored by the Association for Library Service to Children, a council of the American Library Association. Originally, the award was given every five years, but since 1980 it has been given every three years to a U.S. author or illustrator whose entire body of work has made a substantial and lasting contribution to children's literature. The award was established in 1954, and the books must be published in the United States.

1954   Laura Ingalls Wilder
1960   Clara Ingram Judson
1965   Ruth Sawyer
1970   E. B. White
1975   Beverly Cleary
1980   Theodore Geisel (Dr. Seuss)
1983   Maurice Sendak
1986   Jean Fritz
1989   Elizabeth George Speare
1992   Marcia Brown
1995   Virginia Hamilton

CORETTA SCOTT KING AWARD

The *Coretta Scott King Awards* are sponsored by the Social Responsibilities Round Table and the Association for Library Service, councils of the American Library Association. The annual awards were established in 1970 to recognize African-American authors and artists. The award is named for the widow of the civil right leader and Nobel Peace Prize winner, Dr. Martin Luther King, Jr. Since 1974 two awards are given, one to an African-American author and one to an African-American artist. The awards are given to books that are published the previous year and are recognized by the committee as educational and an inspiration to young readers.

1970   *Martin Luther King, Jr., Man of Peace* by Lillie Patterson.   Garrard.
1971   *Black Troubadour: Langston Hughes* by Charlemae Rollins.   Rand.
1972   *17 Black Artists* by Elton C. Fax.   Dodd.
1973   *I Never Had It Made* by Jackie Robinson (as told to Alfred Duckett).   Putnam.
1974   Text: *Ray Charles* by Sharon Bell Mathis.   Crowell.
Illustration: *Ray Charles* by Sharon Bell Mathis. Illustrated by George Ford.   Crowell.

1975   Text: *The Legend of Africana* by Dorothy Robinson.   Johnson.
Illustration: *The Legend of Africana* by Dorothy Robinson. Illustrated by Herbert Temple.   Johnson.

1976   Text: *Duey's Tale* by Pearl Bailey.   Harcourt.
Illustration: No award.

1977   Text: *The Story of Stevie Wonder* by James Haskins.   Lothrop.
Illustration: No award.

1978   Text: *Africa Dream* by Eloise Greenfield.   Day/Crowell.
Illustration: *Africa Dream* by Eloise Greenfield. Illustrated by Carole Bayard.   Day/Crowell.

1979   Text: *Escape to Freedom* by Ossie Davis.   Viking.
Illustration: *Something on My Mind* by Nikki Grimes. Illustrated by Tom Feelings.   Dial.

1980   Text: *The Young Landlords* by Walter Dean Myers.   Viking.
Illustration: *Cornrows* by Camille Yarbrough. Illustrated by Carole Bayard.   Coward.

1981   Text: *This Life* by Sidney Poitier.   Knopf.
Illustration: *Beat the Story-Drum, Pum-Pum* by Ashley Bryan. Atheneum.

1982   Text: *Let the Circle Be Unbroken* by Mildred D. Taylor.   Dial.
Illustration: *Mother Crocodile: An Uncle Amadou Tale from Senegal* adapted by Rosa Guy. Illustrated by John Steptoe.   Delacorte.

1983   Text: *Sweet Whispers, Brother Rush* by Virginia Hamilton. Philomel.
Illustration: *Black Child* by Peter Mugabane.   Knopf.

1984   Text: *Everett Anderson's Good-Bye* by Lucile Clifton.   Holt.
Illustration: *My Mama Needs Me* by Mildred Pitts Walter. Illustrated by Pat Cummings.   Lothrop.

1985   Text: *Motown and Didi* by Walter Dean Myers.   Viking.
Illustration: No award.

1986   Text: *The People Could Fly: American Black Folktales* by Virginia Hamilton.   Knopf.
Illustration: *Patchwork Quilt* by Valerie Flournoy. Illustrated by Jerry Pinkney.   Dial.

1987   Text: *Justin and the Best Biscuits in the World* by Mildred Pitts Walter.   Lothrop.
Illustration: *Half Moon and One Whole Star* by Crescent Dragonwagon. Illustrated by Jerry Pinkney.   Macmillan.

1988   Text: *The Friendship* by Mildred D. Taylor.   Dial.
Illustration: *Mufaro's Beautiful Daughters: An African Tale* retold and illustrated by John Steptoe.   Lothrop.

1989   Text: *Fallen Angels* by Walter Dean Myers.   Scholastic.
Illustration: *Mirandy and Brother Wind* by Patricia McKissack. Illustrated by Jerry Pinkney.   Knopf.

1990   Text: *A Long Hard Journey* by Patricia and Frederick McKissack. Walker.
Illustration: *Nathaniel Talking* by Eloise Greenfield. Illustrated by Jan Spivey Gilchrist.   Black Butterfly Press.

1991   Text: *Road to Memphis* by Mildred D. Taylor.   Dial.
Illustration: *Aida* retold by Leontyne Price. Illustrated by Leo and Diane Dillon.   Harcourt Brace Jovanovich.

1992   Text: *Now Is Your Time! The African-American Struggle for Freedom* by Walter Dean Myers.   HarperCollins.
Illustration: *Tar Beach* by Faith Ringgold.   Crown.

1993   Text: *The Dark-Thirty: Southern Tales of the Supernatural* by Patricia McKissack.   Knopf.
Illustration: *The Origin of Life on Earth: An African Creation Myth* by David A. Anderson. Illustrated by Kathleen Atkins Wilson.   Sight Productions.

1994   Text: *Toning the Sweep* by Angela Johnson.   Orchard.
Illustration: *Soul Looks Back in Wonder* by Tom Feelings.   Dial.

1995   Text: *Christmas in the Big House, Christmas in the Quarters* by Patricia and Frederick McKissack.   Scholastic.
Illustration: *The Creation* by James Weldon Johnson. Illustrated by James Ransome.   Holiday.

1996　Text: *Her Stories* by Virginia Hamilton. Illustrated by Leo and Diane Dillon.　Blue Sky Press.
　　　Illustration: *The Middle Passage: White Ships Black Cargo* written and illustrated by Ton Feelings.　Dial.
　　　The Faithful Friend written by Robert D. San Souci. Illustrated by Brian Pinkney.　Simon.

1997　Text: *Slam!* by Walter Dean Myers.　Scholastic.
　　　Illustration: *Minty: A Story of Young Harriet Tubman* by Alan Schroeder. Illustrated by Jerry Pinkney. Dial.

NCTE EXCELLENCE IN POETRY FOR CHILDREN

The *NCTE Excellence in Poetry for Children* is sponsored by the National Council of Teachers of English. The award is given every three years to a living American poet who has made a major contribution to juvenile poetry, ages 3–13 years.

1977　David McCord
1978　Aileen Fisher
1979　Karla Kuskin
1980　Myra Cohn Livingston
1981　Eve Merriam
1982　John Ciardi
1985　Lilian Moore
1988　Arnold Adoff
1991　Valerie Worth
1994　Barbara Esbensen

CHILDREN'S BOOK AWARD

The *Children's Book Award* is sponsored by the International Reading Association. The annual award is given to new authors of books for younger readers and books for older readers.

1975　*Transport 7-41-R* by T. Degens.　Viking.
1976　*Dragonwings* by Laurence Yep.　Harper & Row.
1977　*A String in the Harp* by Nancy Bond.　Atheneum.
1978　*A Summer to Die* by Lois Lowry.　Houghton Mifflin.
1979　*Reserved for Mark Anthony Crowder* by Alison Smith. Dutton.
1980　*Words by Heart* by Ouida Sebestyen.　Little, Brown.
1981　*My Own Private Sky* by Delores Beckman.　Dutton.
1982　*Good Night, Mr. Tom* by Michelle Magorian.　Harper & Row.
1983　*The Darkangel* by Meredith Ann Pierce.　Atlantic/Little, Brown.
1984　*Ratha's Creature* by Clare Bell.　Atheneum.
1985　*Badger on the Barge* by Janni Howker.　Greenwillow.
1986　*Prairie Songs* by Pam Conrad.　Harper & Row.
1987　*The Line Up Book* by Marisa Russo.　Greenwillow (picture book).
　　　After the Dancing Days by Marisa Russo.　Harper & Row (older readers).
1988　*The Third-Story Cat* by Leslie Baker.　Little (picture book).
　　　Ruby in the Smoke by Philip Pullman.　Knopf (older readers).

1989　*Rechenka's Eggs* by Patricia Polacco.　Philomel (picture book).
　　　Probably Still Nick Swanson by Virginia Euwer Wolff.　H. Holt (older readers).
1990　*No Star Nights* by Anna Egan Smucker. Illustrated by Steve Johnson.　Knopf (younger readers).
　　　Children of the River by Linda Crew.　Delacorte (older readers).
1991　*Is This a House for Hermit Crab?* by Megan McDonald. Illustrated by S. D. Schindler.　Orchard (younger readers).
　　　Under the Hawthorn Tree by Marita Conlon-McKenna. Holiday (older readers).
1992　*Ten Little Rabbits* by Virginia Grossman. Illustrated by Sylvia Long.　Chronicle (younger readers).
　　　Rescue Josh McGuire by Ben Mikaelsen.　Hyperion (older readers).
1993　*Old Turtle* by Douglas Wood. Illustrated by Cheng-Khee Chee. Pfeiffer-Hamilton (younger readers).
　　　Letters from Rifka by Karen Hesse.　Holt (older readers).
1994　*Sweet Clara and the Freedom Quilt* by Deborah Hopkinson. Illustrated by James Ransome.　Knopf (younger readers).
　　　Behind the Secret Window: A Memoir of a Hidden Childhood during World War Two by Nelly S. Toll.　Dial (older readers).
1995　*The Ledgerbook of Thomas Blue Eagle* by Juel Grutman and Gay Matthaei. Illustrated by Adam Czijanovic. (younger readers).
　　　Spite Fences by Trudy Krisher.　Delacorte (older readers).
1996　*More Than Anything Else* by Marie Bradby. Illustrated by Chris K. Soentplet.　Orchard/Jackson. (picture book).
　　　The King's Shadow by Elizabeth Adler.　Farrar. (older readers).
　　　The Case of the Mummified Pigs by Susan E. Quinlan. Illustrations by Jennifer Owings Dewey.　Boyds Mills (information book, older readers).

ORBIS PICTUS AWARD FOR OUTSTANDING NONFICTION FOR CHILDREN

The *Orbis Pictus Award for Outstanding Nonfiction for Children* is sponsored by the National Council of Teachers of English. The annual award, established in 1990, is given to outstanding nonfiction or informational children's books published in the United States the preceding year.

1990　*The Great Little Madison* by Jean Fritz.　Putnam.
　　　Honor Books:
　　　The Great American Gold Rush by Rhonda Blumberg.　Bradbury.
　　　The News About Dinosaurs by Patricia Lauber.　Bradbury.
1991　*Franklin Delano Roosevelt* by Russell Freedman.　Clarion.
　　　Honor Books:
　　　Arctic Memories by Normee Ekoomiak.　Holt.
　　　Seeing Earth from Space by Patricia Lauber.　Orchard.
1992　*Flight: The Journey of Charles Lindbergh* by Robert Burleigh. Illustrated by Mike Wimmer.　Philomel.
　　　Honor Books:
　　　Now Is Your Time! The African-American Struggle for Freedom by Walter Dean Myers.　HarperCollins.
　　　Prairie Vision: The Life and Times of Solomon Butcher by Pam Conrad.　HarperCollins.
1993　*Children of the Dust Bowl: The True Story of the School at Weedpatch Camp* by Jerry Stanley.　Crown.
　　　Honor Books:
　　　Talking with Artists by Pat Cummings.　Bradbury.
　　　Come Back, Salmon by Molly Cone.　Sierra.

1994 *Across America on an Emigrant Train* by Jim Murphy.   Clarion.
Honor Books:
To the Top of the World: Adventures with Arctic Wolves by Jim Brandenburg.   Walker.
Making Sense: Animal Perception and Communication by Bruce Brooks.   Farrar.

1995 *Safari beneath the Sea: The Wonder World of the North Pacific Coast* by Diane Swanson.   Sierra Club.
Honor Books:
Wildlife Rescue: The Work of Dr. Kathleen Ramsay by Jennifer Owings Dewey.   Boyds Mills.
Kids at Work: Lewis Hine and the Crusade against Child Labor by Russell Freedman.   Clarion.
Christmas in the Big House, Christmas in the Quarters by Patricia and Frederick McKissack.   Scholastic.

1996 *The Great Fire* by Jim Murphy.   Scholastic.
Honor Books:
Dolphin Man: Exploring the World of Dolphins by Laurence Pringle.   Atheneum.
Rosie the Riveter: Women Working on the Home Front in World War II by Penny Colman.   Crown.

1997 *Leonardo da Vinci* by Diane Stanley.   Morrow.
Honor Books:
Full Steam Ahead: The Race to Build a Transcontinental Railroad by Rhoda Blumberg.   National Geographic.
The Life and Death of Crazy Horse by Russell Freedman.   Holiday.
One World, Many Religions: The Ways We Worship by Mary Pope Osborne.   Knopf.

SCOTT O'DELL AWARD FOR HISTORICAL FICTION

The *Scott O'Dell Award for Historical Fiction* was established by noted children's novelist, Scott O'Dell, and is administered by the Advisory Committee of the Bulletin of the Center for Children's Books. This award is given to a distinguished work of historical fiction for children or adolescents that is set in the New World and written by a citizen of the United States.

1984 *The Sign of the Beaver* by Elizabeth George Speare.   Houghton Mifflin.
1985 *The Fighting Ground* by Avi.   Harper & Row.
1986 *Sarah, Plain and Tall* by Patricia MacLachlan.   Harper & Row.
1987 *Streams to the River, River to the Sea: A Novel of Sacagawea* by Scott O'Dell.   Houghton Mifflin.
1988 *Charlie Skedaddle* by Patricia Beatty.   Morrow.
1989 *The Honorable Prison* by Lyll Becerra de Jenkins.   Lodestar.
1990 *Shades of Gray* by Carolyn Reeder.   Macmillan.
1991 *A Time of Troubles* by Pieter van Raven.   Scribner.
1992 *Stepping on the Cracks* by Mary Downing Hahn.   Clarion.
1993 *Morning Girl* by Michael Dorris.   Hyperion.
1994 *Bull Run* by Paul Fleischman.   Harper & Row.
1995 *Under the Blood-Red Sun* by Graham Salisbury.   Delacorte.
1996 *The Bomb* by Theodore Taylor.   Harcourt Brace Jovanovich.
1997 *Jip: His Story* by Katherine Paterson.   Lodestar.

AWARDS SELECTED BY CHILDREN

Children in forty-one states read and select an outstanding book each year. Typically, children and adults nominate books, from which a master list is compiled by the responsible state committee. Throughout the year the children read or hear a designated number of books and vote for their favorite selection.

REPRESENTATIVE AWARDS GIVEN FOR JUVENILE BOOKS

Canada, England, Australia, and New Zealand give awards comparable to the Newbery and Caldecott Medals each year.

The *Jane Addams Children's Book Award* is an annual award established in 1953 by the Jane Addams Peace Association and the Women's International League for Peace and Freedom. The award honors the book that most effectively promotes peace, world community, and social justice.

The *Mildred L. Batchelder Award* is given to an American publisher for an outstanding book originally published in a country other than the United States, but later translated and published in the United States during the previous year. The award, which was established in 1968, is given by the Association for Library Service to Children (ALSC), a committee of the American Library Association.

The *Boston Globe* and *The Horn Book Magazine* have co-sponsored an award for outstanding writing and illustrations in children's books since 1967. Beginning in 1976, they have presented annual awards for outstanding fiction or poetry, outstanding nonfiction, and outstanding illustrations. *The Horn Book Magazine* publishes the recipients' acceptance speeches.

The *Christopher Award* is given by The Christophers, a humanitarian organization, to literature of artistic excellence that affirms the highest values of the human spirit.

The *Ezra Jack Keats Award* is given biennially to a promising new artist and a promising writer.

The *Phoenix Award* was established in 1985. The Children's Literature Association presents this award to a book, first published in English twenty years earlier, that has not received a major children's book award, but has proved, through time, to be a worthy, literary selection with enduring excellence.

The *Edgar Allan Poe Award* was established in 1967 for the best juvenile novel in the fields of mystery, suspense, crime, and intrigue. An award for the best young adult novel was established in 1989. The recipients receive a ceramic bust of Edgar Allan Poe. The Edgars are comparable to the Hollywood Oscars.

In addition to these awards, the following groups and publications establish lists of best books:

The American Library Association. Notable Children's Books and Best Books for Young Adults.

The Bulletin of the Center for Children's Books. The Bulletin Blue Ribbons appears in the January issue.

The Children's Book Council. "Children's Choices" are selected in cooperation with the International Reading Association and appear in the October issue of *The*

Reading Teacher. "Outstanding Science Trade Books for Children" are selected in cooperation with the National Science Teachers Association and appear in the March issue of *Science and Children.* "Notable Children's Trade Books in the Field of Social Studies" are selected in cooperation with the National Council of Social Studies and appear in the April/May issue of *Social Studies.*

The Horn Book Magazine. "Fanfare" appears in the March/April issue.

The School Library Journal. "Best Books" appear in the December issue.

See the Children's Book Council, *Children's Books Awards & Prizes* for a complete description and listing of all awards given for children's literature.

Censorship

The passion for freedom of the mind is strong and everlasting, which is fortunate because so is the passion to squelch it.

—A. M. Rosenthal, former editor,
New York Times

Censorship (from the Latin *censere* meaning to value or judge) is a phenomenon that has occurred across cultures and throughout history.[1] In ancient Greece, Plato suggested that all literature should be scrutinized—particularly the writings of Homer—so that only suitable works would be available to young readers. We can trace censorship in the United States to the English common law's concept of *in loco parentis*, which held, among other things, that educational institutions should act as parents and protect students from certain types of literature. The English settlers in America brought the idea of *in loco parentis* with them. It is interesting that the very colonists who came to the New World to find greater freedom immediately began limiting access to literature by controlling the printing presses through licensure.

Later, Thomas Bowdler sought to popularize his own notion of censorship—expurgation (cleansing of text). He found the works of Shakespeare to be particularly unfit. Bowdler was instrumental in the publication of *The Family Shakespeare*, in which anything morally offensive was eliminated from the plays. Unfortunately, in the process

the plays were also stripped of passion.[2] Bowdler and his fellow expurgators failed to realize that it is the moment of passion when writer and reader are joined through text that sets great writers apart from the rest. Expurgation in less flagrant form is still alive and well today. Anthony Comstock, who founded the New York Society for the Suppression of Vice, was another early American censor. He worked through the postal service to protect readers from objectionable literature. The current restrictions on sending obscene material through the mail are a reflection of Comstock's early efforts. More recently, the era of McCarthyism produced a plethora of censors with few opponents.[3] These censors sought to rid libraries of books with communist content—*Robin Hood* barely survived!

WHY CENSORSHIP?

Although one might think that censorship would be declining in our enlightened and democratic society of the 1990s, instances of censorship and attempted censorship are actually on the rise. Further, it is estimated that only 15 percent of censorship incidents are reported.[4] The reasons suggested for increasing censorship activity are as diverse as society itself:

This appendix was written by Melanie Fernandez, teacher, scholar, and activist for the reader's right to read.

Censorship has been most virulent where rapid population growth has occurred.[5]

Students are attaining higher levels of education than their parents, and education itself can be divisive and thus threatening.[6]

The communication environment is changing from being dominated by print to being dominated by images.[7]

Children frequently see stories through visual media rather than through books. Since electronic media are sometimes uninvited guests, parents feel they have less control and influence over the information that their children receive.

As children become aware of the world at a younger age, society's vision of childhood is changing. The new view has yet to be clearly defined, and adults feel uncertain about what will eventually emerge as the child's role.[8]

Finally, censorship increases when there is a feeling that the social fabric of society is in disrepair. This perception is prevalent across the United States today.[9]

The essence of education, the process of acquiring knowledge and searching for truth, is in direct opposition to censorship. In seeking to channel and shield readers from selected media by controlling printed thoughts and ideas, the censor takes a negative and reactionary stance that could lead to literary works being reduced to pictures and words and phrases being taken out of context and held up to an arbitrary standard of quality.[10] Unlike those who choose literature based upon personal preferences and trust others to do the same, censors seek to ban or label intellectual works that are in conflict with their own values and personal agenda.

WHO ARE TODAY'S CENSORS?

A variety of groups and individuals have attempted censorship at one time or another. For example, some feminist groups, racial and ethnic groups, advocates for the disabled, age-related groups, and religious groups have advocated censorship at some time, although it should be emphasized that by no means do all groups that fall into these categories favor censorship. In addition, this list is not all-inclusive—other groups of various types have also favored censorship.

In recent years, groups have become increasingly active in challenging schoolbooks. In 1983, only 17 percent of censorship incidents could be traced to a particular group. In 1987, 43 percent of the censorship incidents in public schools were traced to four groups affiliated with ultra-conservative organizations.[11] Even though efforts by groups to ban books have increased, their success rate has declined.[12] A major reason for their lack of success may be the resistance of professional groups, such as the American Library Association, the American Association of School Librarians, the International Reading Association, and the National Council of Teachers of English. In 1939, the American Library Association created The Library Bill of Rights, which has been amended several times to create a clear, concise statement on access to information and ideas.[13] In support of these principles, the National Council of Teachers of English published a statement, which also defines text selection procedures and criteria as important safeguards against censorship.[14]

In writing library policies, school districts often include statements and concepts from these organizations. The school districts that have accepted these principles thus form a large community fortified with common ideals. These established policies help protect books from censors, but even when policies are in place, they may be circumvented or ignored. Individuals or groups may gather community support and take their case to the school board without following the established procedures. Then some school board members may either remove or demand the removal of certain books from shelves. Administrators at all levels have taken it upon themselves to censor or control library materials without following established procedures.[15] Media specialists may engage in censorship activities by restricting access to materials or refusing to include certain books in the library collection.[16] In fact, as the number of successful attempts to censor or control books by groups has decreased, the percentage of successful censorship attempts by administrators, school board members, and staff has increased.[17] In some cases, school personnel or school boards may engage in censorship in an attempt to avert potential problems or law suits.[18]

CONSEQUENCES OF CENSORSHIP

Censorship, or even the threat of censorship, can have many consequences. Students learn that ideas are either good or bad, acceptable or unacceptable. They are given the idea that books and thoughts that are different or unpopular should be suppressed or eliminated. They see that with power and persistence knowledge may be controlled. The "pre-censorship" activities of publishers could be considered another consequence of censorship. Many publishers give authors guidelines before they write a text and edit completed works so as to please the largest possible audience. Authors are also often asked to create "school editions" of original writings.[19] Here expurgation becomes an economic issue.

WHAT IS THE TEACHER'S ROLE?

Educators have a responsibility to refuse to reject suitable books because of fear of censorship. Teachers and librarians must learn to distinguish among wise advice, advice that encourages self-censorship, and ambiguous advice that lies somewhere between self-censorship and recognition of community standards.[20] In contrast to the negative efforts of censorship, the task of book selection is a positive action that promotes quality literature for students. Censorship activities frequently focus upon individual words and phrases while the selection process involves the evaluation of the entire work. Adults who advocate selection instead of censorship respect children's intellectual freedom and believe that they have an obligation to be honest with them.[21] Giving children access to the best literature available is a manifestation of this respect for children's right to read. In selecting materials, individuals and committees operate from a set of standards agreed upon by the group or community. With selection criteria in place, school-based committees search for good literature to support the curriculum. In school systems with clear selection philosophies, policies, and procedures, fewer books are being removed from the shelves. Nevertheless, in 1990 a survey of 421 California school districts revealed that one-fourth of the districts did not have established selection policies.[22]

Communication with parents or guardians about children's reading material is also important. Teachers must communicate their purposes and prepare rationales for all works that are read in common. In one Texas school district, teachers conducted workshops for parents or guardians so they could read and discuss books that their children were reading. Everyone involved—teachers, parents, guardians, students—found the seminars to be helpful and satisfying. When parents or guardians work with teachers and learn about literature, they challenge few books.[23]

As literature becomes the vehicle for the curriculum, more classroom teachers, rather than media specialists, will be called upon to mediate challenges to literature. Fortified by good policies, good literature, and a passion for freedom of speech, teachers will meet the challenges with strength and dignity. As one author has put it, "The first book off the shelf is symbolic of every other item people want removed."[24]

WHAT SHOULD WE DO?

The following strategies can help teachers defend against censorship:

Before using a book with the entire class, decide why you want to use it, how it meets your goals, and what children will gain from exploring it.[25]

Remember to defend the right to read rather than the individual work being challenged.

Acknowledge that school personnel can make errors about selection.

Remember that most challenges come from sincere people who are interested in the well-being of children.

Keep current in the field.

Obtain selection criteria from your school media specialist and national professional organizations.

Communicate with parents.

Evaluate books with children.

Prepare a school policy statement.

Adopt a formal complaint procedure.

MOST FREQUENT OBJECTIONS

Books have been challenged on a variety of grounds. Here we will briefly summarize some of the objections raised most frequently.[26]

A frequent objection is that books contain anti-Christian themes. For example, Alvin Schwartz's *Scary Stories to Tell in the Dark* (1981) has been accused of advocating cannibalism, brutality, the practice of witchcraft, and violence. Katherine Paterson's *Bridge to Terabithia* (1977) has been accused of presenting a negative religious image. Some people object because some of the characters swear, using the words *Lord, damn,* and *hell.* Paterson's *The Great Gilly Hopkins* (1978) has also been criticized for its language and anti-Christian themes. It contains the words *Christ, hell, good god,* and *crap.* Characters also make comments about God that some people consider derogatory.

Some books are criticized for their sexual content. For example, Judy Blume's *Forever* (1975), *Are You There God, It's Me, Margaret* (1970), and *Dennie* (1973) are considered objectionable by people who wish to protect children from knowledge of certain topics. They argue that early exposure to sexual behavior in books leads to experimentation and permissive attitudes toward sex. Some parents or guardians object to Leslea Newman's *Heather Has Two Mommies* (1991) and Michael Willhoite's *Daddy's Roommate* (1991) because they feature gay and lesbian parents.

Another criticism is that some books treat women or various racial and ethnic groups in a derogatory manner. Mark Twain's *Adventures of Huckleberry Finn* (1884) has been criticized because Jim is gullible, simple-minded, and superstitious, and because the word *nigger* is used. Lynne Banks's *The Indian in the Cupboard* (1981) has been accused of portraying Native Americans in an offensive manner.

Books by Norma Klein, Betty Miles, and Judy Blume are frequently challenged as being anti-American and anti-family because they discuss divorce, extramarital living arrangements, maladjusted adults, and child abuse. The story of "Goldilocks and the Three Bears" has been criticized because Goldilocks gets off scot-free after committing petty larceny and vandalism.

Finally, some people object to books that discuss anything they find offensive. Roald Dahl's *The BFG* (1982) has been challenged for including violence by those who believe childhood should remain free of all reference to violence and war so as to avoid putting unnecessary stress on children. Dahl's *James and the Giant Peach* (1961) has been criticized by those who dislike tobacco because it mentions tobacco and snuff. It has also been attacked by those who object to the use of alcohol because it mentions wine. Similarly, Trina Hyman's illustrations for the Grimm Brothers' *Little Red Riding Hood* has been challenged for showing wine in a basket. Dr. Seuss's *The Lorax* (1971) was challenged in Oregon because it criminalized the forest industry.

In 1995–1996 the People for the American Way report the most frequently challenged books in the United States in rank order are as follows:[27]

Angelou, Maya, *I Know Why the Caged Bird Sings*.

Lowry, Lois, *The Giver*.

Twain, Mark, *The Adventures of Huckleberry Finn*.

Steinbeck, John, *Of Mice and Men*.

Walker, Alice, *The Color Purple*.

Cormier, Robert, *The Chocolate War*.

Anonymous, *Go Ask Alice*.

Salinger, J. D., *Catcher in the Rye*.

Peck, Robert, *A Day No Pigs Would Die*.

Wright, Richard, *Native Son*.

Paterson, Katherine, *Bridge to Terabithia*.

In 1994 the American Library Association's Office for Intellectual Freedom reported the most challenged books in the United States were as follows:[28]

Wilhoite, Michael, *Daddy's Roommate*.

Newman, Leslea, *Heather Has Two Mommies*.

Schwartz, Alvin, *Scary Stories to Tell in the Dark*.

Blume, Judy, *Forever*.

Schwartz, Alvin, *More Scary Stories to Tell in the Dark*.

Paterson, Katherine, *Bridge to Terabithia*.

Cormier, Robert, *The Chocolate War*.

Silverstein, Charles, *The New Joy of Gay Sex*.

Twain, Mark, *The Adventures of Huckleberry Finn*.

Salinger, J. D., *Catcher in the Rye*.

According to the People for the American Way the most frequently challenged books in the United States from 1982 to 1991 are as follows:

Steinbeck, John, *Of Mice and Men*.

Salinger, J. D., *The Catcher in the Rye*.

Cormier, Robert, *The Chocolate War*.

Twain, Mark, *The Adventures of Huckleberry Finn*.

Silverstein, Shel, *A Light in the Attic*.

Blume, Judy, *Forever*.

Blume, Judy, *Then Again, Maybe I Won't*.

Angelou, Maya, *I Know Why the Caged Bird Sings*.

Walker, Alice, *The Color Purple*.

In the school year 1991–1992 the People for the American Way reported 376 incidents of challenges to curricula, library and textbooks, student expression, and other components of public education. In 1995–1996 they reported 475 challenges to curricula and materials. This represents a twenty percent increase in the number of challenged materials from 1991 to 1996.[29]

NOTES

1. Cloonan, M. V. 1984. The censorship of the *Adventures of Huckleberry Finn:* An investigation. *Top of the News.* 40(2). 189–96; Moore, K. M. 1987. Abracadabra: Making the schoolbooks disappear! *Delta Kappa Gamma Bulletin.* Fall. 30–39; Pottorf, D. D., & Olthof, K. 1993. Censorship of children's books on the rise: Schools need to be prepared. *Reading Improvement.* 30(2). 66–75.

2. Pottorf, D. D., & Olthof, K. 1993.

3. Woods, L. B., & Robinson, C. 1982. Censorship: Changing reality. Paper presented at the annual convention of the American Library Association.

4. Moore, K. M. 1987.

5. Kister, K. 1989. Censorship in the sunshine state: Florida libraries respond. *Wilson Library Bulletin.* 64(3). 29–31.

6. Hansen, E. 1987. Censorship in schools: Studies and surveys. *School Library Journal.* 34(1). 123–25.

7. Jalongo, M., & Creany, A. D. 1991. Censorship in children's literature: What every educator should know. *Childhood Education.* 67(3). 143–48.

8. Jalongo, M., & Creany, A. D. 1991.

9. Jongsma, K. S. 1991. Concerns about censorship and intellectual freedom. *The Reading Teacher.* 45(2). 152–53.

10. Clark, E. 1986. A slow, subtle exercise in censorship. *School Library Journal.* 32(7). 93–6; Jalongo, M., & Creany, A. D. 1991.

11. Sims, B. F. 1987. Censorship and the quality of education. *Delta Kappa Gamma Bulletin.* Fall. 41–43.

12. Jalongo, M., & Creany, A. D. 1991. See 7, 16, 19, 21. *Childhood Education.*

13. American Library Association, 1996. Intellectual Freedom Manual. (5th Ed.) Chicago, Ill.

14. Prepared by SLATE and Standing Committee Against Censorship. 1996. Guidelines for selection of materials in English Language Arts Programs. Urbana, Ill.: National Council of Teachers of English. (An NCTE Standards Document.)

15. Jenkinson, E. B. 1985. The tale of tell city: An anti-censorship saga. Washington, D.C.: People for the American Way; Boardman, E. M. 1989. Staying in the kitchen: Notes on a censorship battle. *The Book Report.* 8(3). 28–32; Gottlieb, S. S. 1990. The right to read: Censorship in the school library. *ERIC Document* ED 319 067; Pico, S. 1990. An introduction to censorship. *School Library Media Quarterly.* 18(2). 84–87.

16. Jalongo, M., & Creany, A. D. 1991.

17. Hansen, E. 1987.

18. Kister, K. 1989.

19. Jalongo, M., & Creany, A. D. 1991.

20. Gottlieb, S. S. 1990.

21. Jalongo, M., & Creany, A. D. 1991.

22. Donelson, K. 1993. Steps toward the freedom to read. *The ALAN Review.* 20(2). 14–19.

23. Moore, K. M. 1987.

24. Loch-Wouters, M. 1991. Beginners' luck has just run out. *Journal of Youth Services in Libraries.* 4(3). 261–66.

25. Donelson, K. 1993.

26. McClure, A. 1995. Censorship of children's books. In Lehr, S. *Battling Dragons: Issues and Controversy in Children's Literature.* Portsmouth, N.H.: Heinemann. 3–30.

27. People for the American Way. 1995–1996. *Attacks on the Freedom to Learn.* Washington, D.C.

28. American Library Association. 1994. Survey from the Office for Intellectual Freedom. Chicago, Ill.

29. People for the American Way. 1990–1996. *Attacks on the Freedom to Learn.* Washington, D.C.

Also see two excellent books of readings:

Lehr, S. (Ed.). 1995. *Battling Dragons: Issues and Controversy in Children's Literature.* Portsmouth, N.H.: Heinemann.

Simmons, J. S. (Ed.). 1994. *Censorship: A Threat to Reading, Learning, Thinking.* International Reading Association.

Literary Link

McSWIGAN, M. 1942. *SNOW TREASURE*. ILLUS. ANDRÉ LABLANC. NEW YORK: SCHOLASTIC.

NOTE TO THE TEACHER: A variety of topics, questions, instructional strategies, and LRMs to use in the construction and create components naturally evolve from this book. When presenting the book the teachers use only those elements of the components that are compatible to the students' reactions to the text, their interests, and the teacher's instructional purposes and goals. The connect component suggests topics that the teacher can implement as desired. Therefore, the presentation of this book will vary from group to group. Teachers will not use all of the elements suggested for the various chapters with each group and they will modify specific strategies to meet the need of the students and the instructional goals.

SUMMARY

In the winter of 1940, Nazi troops parachuted into Peter Lundstrom's tiny Norwegian village and held it captive. The Norwegians had hidden nine million dollars in gold in snow caves by the village. To save the gold from the Nazis, Uncle Victor, a sea captain, ask Peter, Michael, Helga Thomsen, Lovisa (Peter's sister), and the other children to place the gold on their sleds, slide down the hill, and slip past the soldiers. At that point the villagers would place the gold on Uncle Victor's ship, who would take it to the United States for safekeeping until after World War II. The plan was dangerous. Would Peter and the others be able to keep the secret from the soldiers? Would the snow stay hard or would the rains come and melt the snow cave before they could remove all of the gold? What would they do when Jan Lasek, a Nazi soldier, discovered what they were doing? Would he expose the plan? Would Uncle Victor trust this Nazi soldier?

GENRE:	Historical realistic fiction (loosely based on fact).
THEME:	Dedicated teamwork is important for a worthwhile goal; the bravery and resourcefulness of children protecting their country; patriotism, responsibility.
SETTING:	Riswyk, a tiny village in northern Norway, near the Arctic Circle, winter, ice caves; 1940, during World War II.
ILLUSTRATIONS:	realistic, black and white line sketches.

IMPLEMENTATION:	(Check the grouping to be used:)
	LITERARY GROUPS: ____√____
	INDEPENDENT READING: ____√____
	PARTNER READING: ____√____
	WHOLE CLASS: ____√____
	OTHER GROUPS: Cooperative Groups During discussion and creating LRMs
APPROXIMATE TIME REQUIRED:	Five weeks, forty-five minutes each day
AGE OF STUDENTS:	10–13 years

486

| CURRICULAR AREAS: | Social Studies; Science (Weather); Sports. | LITERARY GOALS: | *Plot development:* critical issues; sequential; rising tension, action; several incidents moving to climax. |

CURRICULAR AREAS: Social Studies; Science (Weather); Sports.

CHARACTERS:
Peter Lundstrom: Twelve years old; leader; brave; (round, dynamic character).

Michael Berg: Twelve years old; Peter's friend; brave; (round, static character).

Helga Thomsen: Twelve years old; tomboy; quick-witted; strong; (round, static character).

Lovisa Lundstrom: Ten years old; Peter's sister; brave; (round, static character).

Uncle Victor: Leader; ship captain; intelligent; (round, static character).

Jan Lasek: Nazi Soldier; honest; brave; (round, static character).

LITERARY GOALS: *Plot development:* critical issues; sequential; rising tension, action; several incidents moving to climax.

Language: dialogue; easy: limited figurative language; some terminology typical of setting (place and time).

Other Literary element highlighted: foreshadowing.

INSTRUCTIONAL GOALS: Students will become knowledgeable about World War II; become familiar with Norway; vicariously experience the Norwegian winter, including sledding, ice caves, and the winter lifestyle near the Arctic Circle; differences in monetary systems; information about the weight and price of gold.

BEFORE READING : *CONNECT TO TEXT*

Focus on the following: Norway; World War II; skiing, sledding.

- Show Norway on a map; talk about the Arctic Circle and winter weather in Norway.
- Talk about fjords—label place names on a map.
- Discuss the setting: Norway, World War II, and the winter of 1940.
- Discuss winter sports, such as skiing, sledding, and snowball fights.

TEACHER READ ALOUD CHAPTERS 1 AND 2 *(pp. 1–13)*

Chapter 1: *Winter Fun (pp. 1–8)*   Peter, Michael, Helga, and Lovisa enjoyed sledding, skiing, throwing snowballs. Such was the life of Norwegian children near the Arctic Circle. Uncle Victor appeared earlier than expected. Why was he here and why did Mr. Lundstrom leave the house in such a hurry when Peter told him that his brother Victor was back?

Chapter 2: *The Plan (pp. 9–13)*   Peter was ready to try the plan. Would the other children be strong enough to help?

Construct: Focus on the plan and winter sports in Norway.

- Discuss winter sports.
- Use probes in summary statements.
- Where did the gold come from? Why was it so important for the plan to work?
- Discuss the plan and children's role.

Create: Focus on Characters; Setting; and Winter Sports.

- Talk about the four children; begin a character sketch of each.
- Create a story grammar web.
- Go to the media center to find books and information about Norway and winter sports.

- Provide index cards for Jeopardy game questions (Groups will challenge each other to win the game.)
- Display pictures of the region and winter sports.
- After reading each chapter in the book, each group will suggest a title for the chapter. Students suggested the titles in this Literary Link.

LitLog   Students will write daily in LitLog. They may use probes or prompts if necessary.

GROUP READING AND DISCUSSION: *CHAPTERS 3 AND 4 (pp. 14–23)*

Chapter 3: *The Defense Club (pp. 14–18)*   Peter was appointed the president of the Defense Club. Why do the club members need to practice air-raid drills?

Chapter 4: *Responsibilities of a President (pp. 19–23)*   Safeguarding all the gold in the Bank of Norway was a heavy responsibility. Peter was to lead the others to the cave without using flashlights since there were spies in the woods.

Construct: Focus on World War II; the Plot and the Characters.

- Can twenty-five children get nine million dollars of gold down the mountain on their sleds?
- Discuss an air-raid drill and an air-raid shelter.
- Why was Peter appointed President of the Defense Club?
- Who were the spies? The Russians? The Germans?
- What role did Norway play in World War II? Discuss background information about the war.
- How did the Nazis capture Norway? What role did Nazi soldiers play in occupied Norway?
- Identify Oslo on the map and label on the map.
- Discuss strengths and weakness of the plan.

Create: Focus on Norway's position in World War II.

- Begin a time line of the children's adventures. (Use a long piece of shelf paper, mark off each day in the story on the paper.)
- Continue preparing information cards for game about Norway, World War II.

PARTNER READING: CHAPTERS 5, 6, AND 7 (*pp. 24–37*)

Chapter 5: *The Cave (pp. 24–28)* For the first time Peter sees where the men have hidden the gold—thirteen hundred brick-size packages. Each brick contains eighteen and a half pounds of gold bullion—over twenty thousand kroner. In all there were 13 tons of gold bullion, nearly forty million kroner, around nine million dollars.

Chapter 6: *Germans Parachute Troops (pp. 29–32)* The people practiced air-raid drills and they hastily built air-raid shelters. Why?

Chapter 7: *The Teams (pp. 33–37)* Peter learns the importance of following orders, never talking to strangers, and working together in teams. Peter realized the danger of the job and the meaning of patriotism and love of country. Will the children be able to ride 'belly-grinder' on their sleds with seventy-five pounds of bullion worth 80,000 kroners or $20,000?

Construct: Focus on the plot, such as the gold bullion, the German soldiers, the ice cave, and sledding, the importance of teamwork, and patriotism.

- Discuss the weight, price of the gold bullion bricks.
- Describe the cave. How was it built? Why? What will happen if the weather turns warm as it is April?
- Why did the German troops parachute into the village? What happened when they came into the village?
- Why is teamwork important?
- What does patriotism mean to you?
- What does "belly-grinder" mean?
- What is a Kroner? How much was a Kroner worth in dollars in 1940? How much is a Kroner worth today?

Create: Focus on plot and continue the previous focus.

- Measure bullion, compare differences between Kroner and dollars. Make visuals representing size of each brick and monetary amount.
- Continue previous LRMs.
- Find poems or essays on teamwork and patriotism. Write statements, such as Patriotism is; Write a Bio-Poem or Acrostic Poem, such as, write the word TEAM down one side of a piece of paper; find words beginning with each letter to describe why students enjoy working in teams; for example, "Together we can tackle a big job."
- Give a book talk about the plot of the book for a group reading another book.

LITERARY GROUP READING AND DISCUSSION: CHAPTERS 8 AND 9 (*pp. 38–46*)

Chapter 8: *The Promise (pp. 38–42)* Peter, Michael, Helga, and Lovisa realize the importance of keeping the promise not to talk to the Germans. When they find Per Garson racing madly around and around on skis to cover Uncle Victor's tracks, they begin to understand the full impact of secrecy—after all they are working to save their country. Has Peter forgotten the location of the cave? Is he lost?

Chapter 9: *Billions & Sleds (pp. 43–46)* The details of the plan are so well organized that it will be difficult for the Germans to spot the cave. The children learn the need to pay attention to details, untying ropes, riding "belly-grinder," and building snowmen.

Construct: Focus on the plot.

- Discuss keeping your promises, What will happen if the children talk to the Germans? What would happen if your class was told not to talk to someone? What if you knew that by talking to someone you could get your favorite uncle, aunt, grandparent killed?
- Discuss patriotism: Do you love your country enough to risk your life for it?
- Discuss skiing and sledding: How difficult will it be for the children to guide their sleds with four bullions strapped to each sled?
- Discuss the details of each trip.

Create: Focus on patriotism, sledding, and careful planning.

- Math: Discuss weight and balance. Each group will discuss how much each brick bullion weighs. What problems will the children have balancing the bullion on their sleds? How will the younger children maneuver the sleds with that much weight? How will the older children help the younger children?

Task: How can you show others the weight of the bullion? What differences will the children experience maneuvering their sleds with that much gold on them?

- Begin a Buddy Journal. You and your buddy are on different teams. Write back and forth about your feelings of patriotism, working together to save the gold. (Remember, you must communicate in secret. The Nazis must never find your journal. You will take the gold down at different times of day. Figure out a way to pass your journals without anyone else seeing you, even your teacher.)

INDEPENDENT READING: CHAPTERS 10, 11, AND 12 (*pp. 47–61*)

Chapter 10: *Goose-Stepping Soldiers (pp. 47–51)* The worst had happened! The Nazis landed in the village. Soldiers were marching right up the sled tracks! Peter knew the children must face the Nazis, but did he have to run right into them?

Chapter 11: *Dumb Stupid Things (pp. 52–57)* Maybe Uncle Victor was wrong. The Germans seemed pleasant. After all the captain turned his men aside so that Peter could sled on the track.

The soldiers saw them all right—Peter, Helga, Michael, and Lovisa "playing" on their sleds. The captain did say, "I liked nothing better than to toboggan." The soldiers are so friendly!

Chapter 12: *Frau and Herr Holm* (pp. 58–62) The food and the conversation were wonderful! The children told about Peter almost sledding into the Nazi soldiers. The Holms were warm, friendly people, who thought the children were very brave. Why was Herr Holm worried about the "snow holding up?"

Construct: Focus on the plot and language.

- Vocabulary: *goose-stepping soldiers; toboggan; Viking boats; sentry; tarpaulin; knackebrod; Frau & Herr Holm; Ja.*
- Cooperative groups will find interesting, unusual language in the chapter. The selected vocabulary will be discussed, compared, and displayed.
- Discuss the children's reactions to the soldiers.

Create: Focus on the Nazis' reaction to Peter, his reaction to the soldiers, and the first ride.

- Each person will select a character and describe that character's reaction to the Nazis. Then the student will explain how he or she would feel in the same situation.
- In cooperative groups students will complete a Venn diagram with two circles. Each student will list in the left circle the reactions of the character that are different from their personal reactions. On the right circle students list their personal reactions that are different from the characters' reactions. In the center of the diagram students will list similar reactions. Students will mount individual diagrams on a group poster. Each group will discuss, compare, and contrast, the characters' reactions and students' reactions. Compare and contrast personal reactions among group members.
- Continue the time line; Make additional Jeopardy cards; Write in the Buddy Journals, describing reactions to the children's adventures in the last three chapters.
- Students will role play a conversation of the children telling the Holms about their adventure.
- Science: Research the average snow fall in northern Norway; find out how long the snow lasts; the length of a day and night at that time of year; and typical weather at that time of year. What will happen if the rain comes?
- Write predictions: Will the children be able to remove all of the gold? Why do you think so? Will the Nazis find the gold buried under the snowmen? Sign the predictions, fold the paper, place inside a covered box. Open the box when all have finished reading the book. Share and discuss reasons for predictions.
- Draw a line drawing similar to the artist's showing what would have happened if the soldiers had not moved.

PARTNER READING: CHAPTERS 13 AND 14 (pp. 62–74)

Chapter 13: *Rain* (pp. 62–68) The teams are chosen. In three weeks they have removed in each trip almost $20,000 in gold bullions, yet the cave is still full of gold. The soldiers are nice, yet not one child has spoken. Why haven't the Nazis become suspicious, or have they? What will the Germans do to the children if they find out about the plan?

Chapter 14: *Per Garson's Rheumatism* (pp. 69–74) The rains came and brought a blizzard. How could Per Garson know by the feeling in his bones that a blizzard was on the way?

Construct: Focus on the children's work and Per Garson's rheumatism.

- How do the children feel now? They have worked for three weeks, yet much gold is left in the cave. Have you ever had a hard job where it seemed that the faster you worked, the more work you had to do? Do you think they will finish the job in time?
- Why were the soldiers friendly with the children?
- Discuss Per Garson's rheumatism. How could he feel it in his bones?

Create: Focus on finishing a job and how the children feel in bad weather.

- Continue the time line, Jeopardy cards, add new characters to the character visual, and write in Buddy Journals.
- Make a mural of the community in winter and in the blizzard.
- Role-play the children's job.
- Debate pros and cons of talking to the friendly soldiers who were probably fathers with children at home in Germany riding their sleds.
- Survey adults about feeling the weather changing in their bones; report their responses to group members. Chart the responses and share them with other groups.

INDEPENDENT READING AND GROUP DISCUSSION: CHAPTERS 15 AND 16 (PP. 75–87)

Chapter 15: *The Children and the Commandant* (pp. 75–81) The children are worried about the blizzard. Could it prevent them from completing the plan? The children investigate the damage at the Germans' barracks and encounter the Commandant who teases Peter, attempts to get him to talk. Why? Will Peter break the vow of silence to defend himself?

Construct: Focus on the weather; Peter's courage.

- Describe blizzards.
- Discuss Per Garson.
- Why did the Commandant call Peter stupid?
- Who are Hitler's Youth?
- Explain the lifestyle of German children during the war.
- What did the Commandant think about the children?
- Who is stronger, Peter or the Commandant?
- Why did the Commandant threaten the children with school? What does this threat really mean to the children? Will they return to school? Can they return? Where is the schoolmaster?

Create: Focus on the weather and the actions of characters.

- One or two groups will research blizzards in Norway near the Arctic Circle.
- The groups will prepare a weather report for a radio station, explaining what will probably happen during the next week.
- Another group will research Hitler's Youth and chart the differences between the lives of Norwegian and German children during the war.
- Another group will review previous chapters and discuss Per Garson. They will add additional information about him to the character visual begun earlier.
- Compare and contrast Peter and the Commandant on a Character Attribute Chart (see Chapter 10).
- Role-play the Commandant's conversation with the children.
- Write a letter from one child to a relative living in another village describing the incident.

Chapter 16: *School is open! (pp. 82–87)* The villagers decide what to do about opening the school. Why does the blue-eyed Nazi want to be friendly with Peter and his mother?

Construct: Focus on the importance of not talking to the enemy; Wartime conspiracy.

- Why did the villagers keep the school closed?
- Why is it important not to talk when the enemy is present?
- Who is the blue-eyed Nazi? Why is he attempting to be friendly with the villagers?
- What kind of epidemic did the village experience?

Create: Focus on communicating with an enemy in wartime.

- Talk about wartime etiquette and not talking in the presence of the enemy.
- Talk about different visual slogans and the effectiveness of using them. Partners will design a slogan to remind children not to talk before enemies; place the slogan on a visual, with a symbol on it (for example, write the slogan "Words may hurt the plan" and place a large X over it).

PARTNER READING: CHAPTERS 17, 18, AND 19 (PP. 88–102)

Chapter 17: *The Riswyk Plague (pp. 88–93)* All of the children in the village contracted a mysterious, very contagious disease. The symptoms are spots and fever. They were so sick. The school could not open. Everyone was sick, but Peter, Michael, Helga, and Lovisa. When the children were leaving a load of gold under the snowmen, they heard something. Is someone watching them? Who could it be?

Construct: Focus on the epidemic; the person who is watching them; and the language in text.

- Vocabulary: *plague*; *quarantined*; *disinfecting*; *heathenish outlandish place*.

- Is it right for Dr. Aker to invent the plague?
- Isn't it amazing that none of the younger children in Peter, Michael, and Helga's families got sick?
- Why didn't Dr. Metzer check the children?
- How do you think the Germans feel about living in Riswyk? How do you know?
- Have you ever felt that someone was watching you when you were doing something that was a secret? Do you wonder why the children felt this way? Is it possible that they might be right?
- Discuss foreshadowing; help the children identify incidents during the chapter and elsewhere in the book.

Create: Focus on the plague; the author's use of foreshadowing.

- Write a definition for foreshadowing. Find and display examples of foreshadowing in books they are reading independently.
- Write in Buddy Journals as one sick child to another; question why the doctor invented the plague. Predict whether the Nazis will find out the reason for the mysterious disease.
- Role-play the conversation between Drs. Aker and Metzer.

Chapter 18: *The Mysterious German Soldier on Skis (pp. 94–97)* Everything was moving along so smoothly. Why didn't the Germans stop the children? Did the Nazis know how to ski? Peter saw a soldier skiing in the light of the sunset. Why was he there?

Construct: Focus on the setting; the mysterious German soldier on skis.

- Vocabulary: *curfew*; *Christiania turn*.
- Discuss the questions suggested in the chapter summary.
- Why did the German soldier learn to ski?
- What did northern Norway look like at this time of year? What month is it now?

Create: Focus on the setting.

- Draw a map of Riswyk showing the main action (plot) of the book.
- Have partners research "Christiania turn" and describe the procedure to the class.
- Write predictions about whom the Nazi soldier is watching and why he is watching the children. Place predictions in an envelope until the author explains, then check predictions.

Chapter 19: *Locating the Cleng Peerson (pp. 98–102)* The villagers realize Uncle Victor must be contacted about the Nazi soldier. How will Peter and his mother find him? Does he leave signs to help them find him?

Construction: Focus on the search for Uncle Victor and the *Cleng Peerson*.

- Why would Herr Holm violate the curfew? Can he outrun the soldiers? Why did he want a sheet? What did Frau Holm mean when she told Peter, "They'd have to be smart to catch that slippery Norseman?" What is the penalty for violating the curfew?

- How did Mother find Uncle Victor's boat?
- What do you think of Mother's plan with the other ladies? Will Peter go with his mother?

Create: Focus on the search for Uncle Victor.

- Children will create a conversation between Michael, Helga, and Lovisa estimating Peter's chances of finding Uncle Victor.

INDEPENDENT READING, FOLLOWED BY DISCUSSION GROUPS, CHAPTERS 20, 21, AND 22 (pp. 103–17)

Chapter 20: *Mother's Trip With the Children* (pp. 103–8) Frau Lundstrom and the other mothers took their children on a sled ride with the gold. They had to find out if the soldiers were suspicious. Peter met Mother at the snow soldiers, and to their surprise, Uncle Victor's boat was not there, or was it?

Construct: Focus on finding Uncle Victor.

- Discuss pp. 104–5. What is the Commandant doing with his hand?
- Do you think the Nazis were suspicious of the people? Why? Why not?
- Where is Uncle Victor's boat, the *Cleng Peerson?*
- Just as Peter and his mother spied Uncle Victor's boat, who spoke to them?
- Vocabulary: *Heil Hitler*; *boors*; *spar*; *boom*; *mast*; *hull*; *camouflage.*

Create: Focus on Mother's trip with the children.

- Dramatize a conversation between the Commandant and Lieutenant Sit-Down about Frau Lundstrum and the children. In the conversation indicate whether the Germans know about the plan. If so, what will they do to the people of Riswyk?
- Add the location of Uncle Victor's boat to the map.
- The children will prepare a Word Wall. Display the author and title of the book, draw a ship with camouflage, and add ship-related vocabulary on the wall.

Chapter 21: *The Norwegian Daniel Boone* (pp. 109–13) Peter and Frau Lundstrum have a conversation with Uncle Victor inside the ship. Even though Uncle Victor and Rolls watch the children deliver the gold, is it possible that there was someone there that they did not see? Will they deliver all of the gold in six weeks so that Uncle Victor can see New York again?

Construct: Focus on the plot.

- Describe Uncle Victor's pride in the *Cleng Peerson.*
- Explain how Uncle Victor can maneuver the *Cleng Peerson* to perform the tasks he needed to accomplish to get the gold.

- Locate and label Trondheim on a map.
- Dramatize the conversation with Uncle Victor including the possibility that someone is watching the children.
- Describe the mines and how Uncle Victor will depart.

Create: Focus on the plot.

- Draw a sketch of the inside of the *Cleng Peerson.*
- Prepare a banner of the Norwegian flag.
- Write to a buddy about the times Uncle Victor was not watching. Describe the children's feeling about their suspicion that someone is watching them. Predict who is watching and whether the Nazis know about their plan.

Chapter 22: *Frau Holm's Visitor* (pp. 114–17) After the visit with Uncle Victor, Peter was determined that Uncle Victor would sail on time. When Peter and his mother arrived at Frau Holm's home, she told them of a mysterious German soldier's visit to the barn. What did he want? Before long Peter will find out.

Construct: Focus on the visitor and the villager's determination to finish the plan in a hurry.

- Predict who the visitor is and why he was in the Holms' barn.
- Describe Peter's meeting with the stranger.

Create: Focus on the visitor.

- Each group will describe the visitor and record predictions.
- Role-play Peter's meeting with the visitor. What happened? Will he arrest Peter?

TEACHER READ ALOUD AND DISCUSSION: CHAPTERS 23, 24, AND 25 (pp. 118–34)

Chapter 23: *The Lonely Pole* (pp. 118–23) Peter thought the Nazis had finally decided to stop them, but Uncle Victor and Rolls captured the soldier who followed Peter. Peter, as president of the Defense Club, followed the men back to the ship to hear a strange story from a lonely Pole. Could they really believe why the Pole had followed the boys? Did he really want to go to the United States without a passport? Was this merely a sly German trick? What would Uncle Victor and Rolls do about the soldier?

Construct: Focus on the lonely German (Polish) soldiers' story.

- *Before reading:* discuss the illustration on page 119.
- As president of the Defense Club, Peter could order Helga to return without him. Discuss the importance of Helga following the rules at this time.
- Why was it important for Peter to follow Uncle Victor? Was this a wise move?
- The Pole's story is convincing, but do they believe him?
- What do you think Uncle Victor should do about the soldier?
- Why is the Pole's passport important?
- Vocabulary: *Pole*; *konditeri.*

Create: Focus on the plot.

- Complete the scene of the area.
- Update the time line and the character visual.
- Write several conversations to a buddy discussing the Pole's story. In the journal attempt to reach consensuses about his honesty.

Chapter 24: *Jan Lasek's Story (pp. 124–29)* Uncle Victor and Rolls listened to Lasek's story, but did they believe it? After all he could be a German spy. The German Gestapo were clever, trained liars!

Construct: Focus on Jan Lasek's story.

- Locate and label Cracow, Poland on a map. Discuss its location relative to Germany and Norway.
- Why did the Germans steal Lasek's passport?
- Who was the German Gestapo? Why did they have different outfits?
- What is the difference between a German Patriot and a Norwegian or Polish patriot? Which patriots did the United States support during World War II? Why?
- Discuss the German's treatment of Norway during World War II.
- Vocabulary: *patriot; fuhrer; Rumania; humiliation.*

Create: Focus on Jan Lasek's story and Poland's involvement in the war.

- Research Poland's involvement in World War II. Find out why a passport is so important.
- Continue the Buddy Journal. Discuss in the journal what you think about Jan's story.
- Individuals will write several sentences describing the Germans' treatment of Poland during the war. The class will orally discuss and compare the Germans' treatment of the Norwegians.

Chapter 25: *Is $250,000 Enough? (pp. 130–33)* As the Norwegians talk about what to do with Jan, German soldiers arrive near the ship, looking for Jan. Will they find the ship and the gold?

Construct: Focus on Uncle Victor's plan.

- Do you believe Jan's story?
- What is Uncle Victor's plan?
- How much gold is already on the ship?

Create: Focus on the future of the Norwegians and Jan.

- Write a radio program script between the Norwegians and Jan before and after the Germans arrive outside.
- Make a written prediction about what will happen to the Norwegians and Jan.
- Continue the time line.
- Begin a large Story Pyramid. Place it on the bulletin board. Use a large shaped colored paper as the base. Write on the

base the reason for the plan. On the next largest paper write the plan. Then prepare other building blocks from paper and write other important events from the book. The top block will be the conclusion of the story. As the children read the book they will use the time line and prepare blocks for the Pyramid.

PARTNER READING: CHAPTERS 26, 27, AND 28 (pp. 134–47)

Chapter 26: *We Fooled the Goose-Steppers! (pp. 134–38)* The Germans continue looking for Jan. Lovisa tells Peter about the hunt the night before while they make their snow soldiers that cover the last of the gold. We fooled the goose-steppers! They exclaim. The gold is out of the cave. Now all Uncle Victor has to do is to load it onto the ship and sail for America.

Construct: Focus on the children's celebration when they accomplished their goal.

- How was the goal accomplished?
- Predict whether the Germans will find Jan. Did Jan tell the truth? Will Uncle Victor get the gold onto the ship? Do the Germans suspect the children?

Create: Focus on the plot.

- Continue the time line and the Story Pyramid. Add to the character visual.
- Discuss and compare predictions.

Chapter 27: *The Snow Ball (pp. 139–142)* The Commandant demanded that the children tell him whether they had seen the German soldier. In a rage, because they would not answer him, the Commandant began knocking down Lovisa's snowman to show the children what the German Army could do to them. Afraid that the German would kick the gold, Peter threw a snowball that landed exactly on the Commandant's right ear. Peter started to run. Will the soldiers catch him? If so, what will happen to Peter?

Construct: Focus on Peter's actions.

- Would the children keep their solemn promise and not talk to the Nazis?
- What would you have done in Peter's place?
- Write a prediction about what will happen to Peter in the future.

Create: Focus on the plot.

- Continue LRMs from previous chapters.
- Discuss and compare predictions.

Chapter 28: *Peter's Fate (pp. 143–147)* A ring of German soldiers captured Peter. What will they do to him now? Will they kill him? Jan's story kept ringing in his ears. Yet, Peter knew he had helped save the gold. Uncle Victor can not save him now. He must sail to America now that all of the gold is loaded on his ship!

Construct: Focus on Peter's actions and the language in the text.

- Vocabulary: *foreigners*; *rabbit facing a pack of hounds*; *tussle*; *submit*; *barracks*; *conquerors* (p. 143); *sentries*; *court martial* (p. 145).
- Was it a good idea for Peter to throw the snowball?
- Write predictions about Peter's future.

Create: Focus on Peter.

- Cluster the language from World War II found in the book. Place the term *World War II* in the center of a large piece of paper. Write the language related to the soldiers and the war on the paper, by clustering similar or related language on the same spoke. Indicate the page number where the language was used; discuss the language and the reason for placing the language on the visual.
- Write on a sheet of paper what you think Peter's fate will be. Do not talk to peers. Fold the paper and give it to the teacher who will open the predictions when the book is finished.

TEACHER READ ALOUD AND DISCUSSION: CHAPTERS 29 AND 30 (*pp. 148–158*)

Chapter 29: *Follow him at all costs! (pp. 148–51)* The German soldier was Jan Lasek, the Pole! Uncle Victor had seen the soldiers capture Peter, but why was Jan here? Peter read Uncle Victor's note that told him to follow Jan wherever he went. Peter did. The next thing he knew he was in the water, freezing. Then they lifted him into another boat. Peter knew he was free!

Construct: Focus on Peter's escape.

- Does Uncle Victor believe Jan's story? How do you know?
- Did you believe they would escape?

Create: Focus on Peter's escape.

- Write a letter from Peter to Helga. Tell about his escape and his feelings about Jan.
- Write in the Buddy Journal discussing the events of this chapter. Discuss Peter, Jan, & Peter's future.

Chapter 30: *America (pp. 152–58)* Peter was surprised! He was going to America! The description of Jan's escape plan was breathtaking. He knew exactly how and when to arrive and how to return to the ship! He was a brave Pole who was determined to go to America!

Construct: Focus on Jan's escape plan and Peter's future.

- How was the *Cleng Peerson* camouflaged?
- Describe Jan's brave plan to escape from the Germans. Would it work?
- What are the benefits of growing up in a country where people are free?
- Why are Norwegians considered *liberty-loving people?*
- What does patriotism mean to you?
- What was the year of this adventure? How do you know?
- What happened in Riswyk when Peter did not return?
- Did the soldiers question Peter's family when he escaped from their prison? What did they do to his family?
- How long did the Nazis stay in the Norwegian village? Did the soldiers find out about the gold?
- What happened to Peter, Jan, and Uncle Victor after the war?
- What happened to the gold after the war?
- Is this a factual story? How do you know?

Magazines for Children

How many adults read magazines, but not books? Isn't it refreshing to pick up a magazine that is totally different from one's professional concerns and read short excerpts about a medical breakthrough, the new car models, the latest fashions, or recent political development? What a delight to pick up a magazine, look at the pictures, and read very little. Since adults acquire information, gain new insights, and stimulate their visual curiosities from reading magazines, we should give children the same pleasures. Recognizing that parents or guardians, grandparents, and other adults want to help their children develop a habit of reading for pleasure and information, publishers are producing a record number of magazines—between 150 and 250—aimed at young people three to fifteen years old.

Reluctant readers, to whom the thought of reading an entire book is overwhelming, will "thumb through" a magazine. Curious children wait eagerly for a new issue of their favorite magazine so they can find out more about a topic of interest. All children relish browsing through magazines, especially those with clear pictures, that contain articles about current happenings that are important to them at that particular time. Teachers realize magazines can entice children to read. Current information available in magazines can enhance social studies or science lessons. Also, teachers are interested in discovering which topics are currently captivating children. The wise teacher consults with the school media specialist and the public librarian and brings many of these reading materials into the classroom. This appendix provides a representative list, organized according to the major focus of the magazine. Because subscription rates change periodically, review current issues of magazines in bookstores and libraries.

MAGAZINES

ART AND WRITINGS BY CHILDREN

Boodle: By Kids for Kids, for 6–12 years. Each quarterly issue highlights poems, stories, and artwork submitted by the readers. Formerly called *Caboodle*. P.O. Box 1049, Portland, IN 47371.

Creative Kids, for 8–14 years. The six issues each year are filled with stories and poems by children. A variety of topics are included in each issue. Prufrock Press, P.O. Box 8813, Waco, TX 76714-8813. Phone: 800-998-2208.

ECONOMIC INTERESTS

Zillions, for 8–14 years. The six issues each year focus on consumer-related issues, such as the influence of advertisements and how to earn, manage, and save money. They also include the results of tests on various consumer items. Zillions Subscription Dept., P.O. Box 54861, Boulder, CO 80322-4861.

GENDER RELATED

American Girls, for 7–12 years. The six issues each year include fiction and nonfiction articles about history and lifestyles of the past and present. Additional adventures of characters in the American Girls series are included. American Girls Collection, P.O. Box 620190, Middleton, WI 53562-0190.

Boy's Life, for 7–17 years. The monthly issues highlight general topics of interest, such as hobbies, sports, history, science, and scouting projects and programs. Some fiction is included. Boy's Life, Boy Scouts of America, 1325 Walnut Hill Lane, P.O. Box 152350, Irving, TX 75015-2350.

Hopscotch, especially for girls 6–12 years. The six issues each year contain fiction, nonfiction, poems, games, crafts, and activities of interest to the young girl. P.O. Box 164, Bluffton, OH 45817-0164.

GENERAL: VARIETY OF TOPICS

Highlights for Children, for 4–12 years. This magazine has a larger circulation than any other magazine for children and is published twelve times a year. Regular features include scientific experiments, crafts, games, puzzles, hidden pictures, stories, and poems. P.O. Box 269, Columbus, OH 43216-0002.

Kids Discover, for 6–12 years. The ten issues each year focus on a theme such as buildings, oceans, or rain forests. Also included are photographs, puzzles, projects, and suggestions for further reading. 170 Fifth Ave., 6th Floor, New York, NY 10010.

3-2-1 Contact, for 8–14 years. The ten issues each year highlight various topics in the physical, natural, and social sciences. Photographs and art accompany fictional and informational articles, puzzles, and experiments. Children's Television Workshop, P.O. Box 53051, Boulder, CO 80306.

GLOBAL INTERESTS

Faces, for 8–14 years. The nine issues each year celebrate the diversity of our society. Lifestyles, values, customs, and celebrations from around the world are explored. The magazine explores and celebrates human diversity. Cobblestone Publishing, 7 School St., Peterborough, NH 03458. Phone: 603-924-7209.

Skipping Stones, for 7–14 years. The five issues each year highlight people from all areas of the world. The multicultural, multilingual approaches include original writings and illustrations from people of all ages. Crafts, ceremonies, songs, and games from around the world are included. Book reviews, a pen pal page, and a guide for adults are regular features. P.O. Box 3939, Eugene, OR 97403.

HISTORICAL INTERESTS

Calliope, for 8–15 years. The five issues each year focus on a topic in world history. Archaeology, crafts, and authentic information are covered through fiction and nonfiction articles, photographs, maps, and puzzles. Calliope, Cobblestone Publishing, 7 School St., Peterborough, NH 03458.

Cobblestone, for 8–15 years. The ten issues each year focus on a particular topic in American history. This magazine contains articles, photographs, activities, poems, puzzles, crafts, and contests all aimed at making history live. Cobblestone Publishing, 7 School St., Peterborough, NH 03458.

Ranger Rick, for 6–12 years. The monthly issues feature fiction and nonfiction articles about nature and natural history. This popular magazine also includes photographs, crafts, activities, poems, and plays. Subscribers become members of the Ranger Rick Nature Club. Also, see *Your Big Outdoors*, for 3–5 years. National Wildlife Federation, 8925 Leesburg Pike, Vienna, VA 22184-0001.

LITERARY INTERESTS

Cricket, for 7–14 years. This literary magazine, published twelve times a year, contains fiction and nonfiction stories, poems, arti-

cles, and illustrations by recognized creators of children's literature. The magazine accepts children's writings, and the cover is a special delight. Cricket, Carus Publishing, P.O. Box 593, Mt. Morris, IL 61054-0593. Phone: 800-827-0227.

Ladybug, for 2–7 years. The monthly issues contain read-aloud stories, illustrations, poetry, songs, and fun activities for younger children. The magazine also includes stories and art from creators of children's literature and a supplement for parents suggesting literature to share with youngsters. It is published by the publishers of *Cricket Magazine*, whose goal is to help children develop a habit of reading. Also, see *Spider* for 5–9 years. Carus Publishing, P.O. Box 593, Mt. Morris, IL 61054-0593.

Plays: The Drama Magazine for Young People, for 6–18 years. The seven issues each year provide eight to twelve original dramatic materials, such as skits, one-act plays, puppet shows, and other dramatic presentations and offer ideas for settings and costumes for elementary- to secondary-age students. 120 Boylston St., Boston, MA 02116-4615.

Stone Soup, for 6–13 years. The six issues each year feature art, poems, and stories written by children. Book reviews, photographs, and activities are also included in this literary magazine. Children's Art Foundation, P.O. Box 83, Santa Cruz, CA 95063.

Storyworks, for teachers. The six issues each year contain stories and art by well-known creators of children's literature. The magazine is designed for use in the classroom. Scholastic, P.O. Box 3710, Jefferson City, MO 65102-9957.

SCIENTIFIC INTERESTS

Chickadee, for 3–9 years. The ten issues each year highlight science and nature topics. Short, easy-to-read stories and poems, nonfiction articles, photographs, posters, puzzles, and science experiments are included in each issue. Also, see *Owl* for 8–14 years. Young Naturalist Foundation, 25 Boxwood Lane, Buffalo, NY 14227 or 179 John St., Suite 500, Toronto, Ont., Canada M5T 3G5.

Dolphin Log, for 7–15 years. The six issues each year feature articles about aquatic life, marine biology, ecology, science, and global issues concerning the water system. Regular features, puzzles, "Nature News," "Cousteau Adventure," and the cartoon series are enjoyed by the readers. The Cousteau Society, 870 Greenbrier Circle, Suite 402, Chesapeake, VA 23320.

National Geographic World, for 8–14 years. The monthly issues discuss geographic issues, natural history, and outdoor adventures of interest to young people. Colored photographs accompany the short articles, games, animal trading cards, posters, and crafts. Membership in the National Geographic Society is a part of the subscription. 11555 Darnestown Road, Gaithersburg, MD 20878.

Odyssey, for 8–14 years. The ten issues each year highlight a particular topic related to space exploration, weather, or astronomy. Colored photographs, illustrations, star charts, and activities accompany the articles. Readers are encouraged to interact with the editor. Cobblestone Publishing, 7 School St., Peterborough, NH 03458.

Scienceland, for 5–10 years. The eight issues each year feature science-related topics, such as animals, plants, or motion. Full-page colored illustrations supplement the fiction and nonfiction articles. Teachers can adapt each issue for various ages. Scienceland, 501 Fifth Avenue, Suite 2108, New York, NY 10017-6102.

ZooBooks, for 5–14 years. The monthly issues frequently highlight a particular animal. Photographs accompany the scientific articles about wildlife. Wildlife Education Limited, 9820 Willow Creek Road, Suite 300, San Diego, CA 92131-1112.

Sports Interests

Sports Illustrated for Kids, for 8–13 years. The monthly issues feature amateur and professional male and female athletes. Regular features include sports topics, advice for young athletes, various activities, comic strips, art by children, and posters. Time Magazine Co., P.O. Box 830609, Birmingham, AL 35283-0609.

ADDITIONAL REFERENCES

Brawner, L. C. 1994. Magazines for Children. *Book Links*. 3(6). July. 50–55. Offers ideas for using magazines in the classroom.

The Children's Writer's and Illustrator's Market. Cincinnati, OH: Writer's Digest. Annual.

Donavin, D. (Ed.). 1992. *Best of the Best for Children*. New York: American Library Association/Random House.

Fakih, K. O. 1991. *Of Cabbages and Kings: The Year's Best Magazine Writings for Kids*. New York: R. R. Bowker.

Jacobs, J. S., & Tunnell, M. O. 1999. *Children's Literature, Briefly*. Englewood Cliffs, NJ.: Merrill. 283–87.

Katz, B., & Katz, L. S. 1991. *Magazines for Young People: A Children's Magazine Guide Companion Volume*. New York: R. R. Bowker.

Richardson, S. 1991. *Magazines for Children*. Chicago, Ill.: American Library Association.

Stoll, D. R. (Ed.). 1997. *Magazines for Kids and Teens*. Newark, Del.: International Reading Association.

Book Selection Sources

REVIEW SOURCES

Appraisal, 605 Commonwealth Ave., Boston, MA 02215.
A quarterly publication of evaluative reviews of new children's and young adult science books.

Booklist, American Library Association, 50 E. Huron St., Chicago, IL 60611.
Published biweekly, except for July and August, this journal provides a guide to current print and nonprint materials recommended for purchase by small and medium-sized school media centers and public libraries. Also publishes annual book lists: "Editor's Choice," "ALA Notable Children's Books," "Best Books for Young Adults."

Bulletin of the Center for Children's Books, University of Illinois Press, 54 E. Gregory Dr., Champaign, IL 61820.
From September to July (July and August are combined), this bulletin reviews and rates current children's books. The books are classified according to grade/age level and subject areas. A booklist of outstanding books, "Bulletin Blue Ribbons," is published in the January issue. An annual index is included in the July/August issue.

Children's Book Review, 1204 New York Drive, Altadena, CA 91001-3146.
This quarterly magazine contains book and media reviews, colored pictures from the books, and articles of interest to teachers and media specialists. Several authors and illustrators are interviewed in each issue.

Horn Book Magazine, Horn Book, Inc., 14 Beacon St., Boston, MA 02108-3704.
This magazine, published six times per year, includes book reviews and articles about literature, interviews with creators, and news related to children's literature. The Newbery and Caldecott acceptance speeches are included in the July/August issue, with a biographical sketch of the recipient. The March/April issue contains the "Fanfare," a list of exemplary books selected by the reviewers.

School Library Journal, P.O. Box 1978, Marion, OH 43305-1978.
This monthly journal contains news, information, and reviews for children and young adult librarians. The "Best Books" list of outstanding books is included in the December issue.

BIBLIOGRAPHIES

A to Zoo: Subject Access to Children's Picture Books. 1993. By Carolyn W. and John A. Lima. 4th ed. New York: R. R. Bowker.
This bibliography lists 12,000 picture books. The historical development of picture books is presented in the introductory chapter. The books are organized according to author, illustrator, title, and subject.

Adventuring with Books: A Booklist for Pre-K–Grade 6. 1997. Edited by Wendy K. Sutton. 11th ed. Urbana, Ill.: National Council of Teachers of English.
This annotated bibliography lists recommended juvenile literature published since the last edition. The books are organized according to genre, subject, and author.

The Bookfinder: A Guide to Children's Literature about the Needs and Problems of Youth Aged 2–15. 1977, 1981, 1985, 1989. By Sharon Spredemann Dreyer. Circle Pines, Mn.: American Guidance Service.
Annotations of recommended books are indexed according to needs and problems of children and adults. A cumulative index of Volumes 1–3 is included in Volume 4.

Children's Books in Print. New York: R. R. Bowker.
All books in print are cited in this annual bibliography. The books are indexed according to title, author, and subject. Information about purchasing the books is also included.

The Children's Catalog. 1991. Edited by Juliette Yakov. 16th ed. New York: H. W. Wilson.
This bibliography is published every five years. A supplement is published each year. Recommended literature, magazines, and

professional resources are listed. The books are arranged according to author, title, and subject. Editions for older readers are also available.

The Elementary School Library Collection: A Guide to Books and Other Media. Edited by Lauren K. Lee. Williamsport, Pa.: Brodart.

Every two years a list of juvenile books, magazines, and non-print media are described. Selections are indexed according to subject, title, author, and illustrator.

Eyeopeners! and *Eyeopeners II.* 1988 and 1995. Edited by B. Kobrin. New York: Penguin Press.

Each book includes an annotated bibliography of over 500 non-fiction books organized according to topic. Also included are ideas for using the books in the classroom.

Horn Book Guide to Children's and Young Adult Books. Edited by Roger Sutton. Boston: Horn Book.

Since 1989, in March and September, this guide provides an annotated and rated listing of hardback books published the previous six months for young people aged two to eighteen years. Fiction is arranged according to age and nonfiction literature is classified according to the Dewey Decimal System. The titles are also arranged according to author, title, and subject.

Your Reading: A Booklist for Junior High and Middle School Students. 1993. Edited by C. Anne Webb. 9th ed. Urbana, Ill.: National Council of Teachers of English.

This annotated bibliography lists literature published in the early 1990s for young adult readers. It is frequently updated. Books are listed according to genre, title, author, and subject.

JOURNALS

The ALAN Review. National Council of Teachers of English, 111 W. Kenyon Rd., Urbana, IL 61801-1096.

Published three times a year, this periodical contains topics of interest related to young adult literature. Reviews of current young adult books are included.

Book Links: Connecting Books, Libraries, and Classrooms. Edited by Barbara Ellemann. American Library Association, 50 E. Huron St., Chicago, IL 60611.

This bimonthly magazine explores literature and topics related to literature that are of interest to teachers, librarians, library media specialists, booksellers, parents or guardians, and other adults. Thematic bibliographies and ways to use literature in the classroom are discussed in each issue.

CBC Features. Children's Book Council, 350 Scotland Rd., Orange, NJ 07050.

This semiannual newsletter contains news and information about literature, articles by experts in the field of children's literature, author profiles, and a list of free or inexpensive materials.

Children's Literature in Education: An International Quarterly. Human Sciences Press. 233 Spring St., New York, NY 10013-1578. A quarterly publication containing features about literature, author and artist interviews, critical reviews of books, current issues related to literature, conference information, and ideas for teaching children's literature.

Journal of Children's Literature. Children's Literature Assembly, National Council of Teachers of English, 1111 W. Kenyon Rd., Urbana, IL 61801-1096.

Articles related to literature and items of interest are published in this periodical.

Journal of Youth Services. American Library Association, 50 Huron St., Chicago, IL 60611.

This quarterly is published jointly by the ALSC and YALSA, JOTS of the American Library Association. Information for librarians about current trends and techniques, news, and reviews of professional resources are included in each issue.

Kirkus. Kikus Services, Inc., 200 Park Ave., S, New York, NY 10003. Published twice a month, this periodical reviews the most current children's literature.

Language Arts. National Council of Teachers of English, 1111 W. Kenyon Rd., Urbana, IL 61801-1096.

Annotations of children's books, reviews of professional resources, and ideas for teaching literature and language arts are included in each issue. Topics related to the teaching of language arts in the elementary and middle schools are the major focus of this professional journal, which is published monthly from September through April.

The New Advocate: For Those Involved with Young People and Their Literature. Edited by Kathy G. Short, Dana L. Fox, and Cyndi Giorgis. Christopher-Gordon Publishers, Inc., 480 Washington St., Norwood, MA 02062.

This quarterly journal contains issues related to the production and teaching of literature. Creator profiles and reviews of children's literature are also included.

The Reading Teacher. International Reading Association, 800 Barksdale Rd., P.O. Box 8139, Newark, DE 19714-8139.

Published from September to May, with a combination issue in December/January, this periodical highlights issues about teaching reading. Each issue contains a thematic review of children's books and teaching reading through literature. Professional book reviews and research reports are also included.

The United States Board on Books for Young People Newsletter. USBBY Secretariat, c/o International Reading Association, P.O. Box 8139, Newark, DE 19714-8139.

Published twice a year, this newsletter contains information and articles related to international children's literature. Reviews of international children's books are also included.

VOYA, Voices of Youth Advocates. Scarecrow Press, Dept. VOYA, 52 Liberty St., P.O. Box 4167, Metuchen, NY 08840. Literature for intermediate and young adults is reviewed in this bimonthly periodical. Each issue also contains a biography of a creator.

BIBLIOGRAPHIC SOURCES ABOUT AUTHORS AND ARTISTS

Authors and Artists for Young Adults. 12 volumes. Detroit, Mich.: Gale Research.

Blount, R. H. 1994. *The Address Book of Children's Authors and Illustrators.* Minneapolis, Minn.: Denison.

Copeland, J. S. & Copeland, V. L. 1993, 1994. *Speaking of Poets: Interviews with Poets who Write for Children and Young Adults 1 & 2.* Urbana, Ill.: National Council of Teachers of English.

Cummings, P. 1992, 1995. *Talking with Artists 1 & II.* New York: Bradbury.

Day, F. A. 1994. *Multicultural Voices in Contemporary Literature: A Resource for Teachers.* Portsmouth, N.H.: Heineman.

Gallo, D. R. (Ed.). 1990, 1993. *Speaking for Ourselves, Too: Autobiographical Sketches by Notable Authors of Books for Young Adults.* Urbana, Ill.: National Council of Teachers of English.

Kovacs, D. & Preller, J. 1991, 1993. *Meet the Authors and Illustrators.* Vols. 1 and 2. New York: Scholastic.

Marantz, S. & Marantz, K. 1992. *Artists of the Page.* Jefferson, N.C.: McFarland.

Martin, D. 1990. *The Telling Line.* New York: Delacorte.

McElmeel, S. 1990. *Bookpeople: A First Album, Grades 1–4.* Englewood, Col.: Libraries Unlimited.

———. 1990. *Bookpeople: A Second Album, Grades 3–9.* Englewood, Col.: Libraries Unlimited.

———. 1992. *Bookpeople: A Multicultural Album.* Englewood, Col.: Libraries Unlimited.

Norby, S., & Ryan, G. 1988, 1989. *Famous Children's Authors. Book One & Two.* Minneapolis, Minn.: Denison.

Roginski, J. 1985, 1989. *Behind the Covers: Interviews with Authors and Illustrators of Books for Children and Young Adults.* Vols. 1 and 2. Englewood, Col.: Libraries Unlimited.

Rollock, B. 1988. *Black Authors and Illustrators of Children's Books.* New York: Garland.

Silvey, A. (Ed.). 1995. *Children's Books and Their Creators: An Invitation to the Feast of Twentieth-Century Children's Literature.* Burlington, Mass.: Houghton Mifflin.

The Sixth Book of Junior Authors and Illustrators. 1989. New York: Wilson. (Also see vols. 1 through 5.)

Something about the Author. 77 vols. Detroit, Mich.: Gale Research.

Twentieth-Century Children's Writers. 1989. 3d ed. St. James.

Word, M. E. 1990. *Authors of Books for Young People.* 3d ed. Metuchen, N.J.: Scarecrow.

Williams, H. E. 1991. *African-American Authors and Illustrators for Children and Young Adults.* Chicago, Ill.: American Library Association.

Also see the bibliographies for Chapters 6 and 8 for autobiographies and biographies about various authors and illustrators.

TEACHER REFERENCES

Cullinan, B. E. & Galda, L. 1994. *Literature and the Child.* (3rd Ed.) Fort Worth: Harcourt Brace.

Hillman, J. 1995. *Discovering Children's Literature.* Englewood Cliffs, NJ: Merrill.

Huck, C. S., Hepler, S., Hickman, J., & Kiefer; B. Z. 1997. *Children's Literature in the Elementary School.* (6th Ed.) Madison, Wisc.: Brown & Benchmark.

Jacobs, J. S. & Tunnell, M. O. 1996. *Children's Literature, Briefly.* Englewood Cliffs, N.J.: Prentice-Hall.

Lukens, R. J. 1995. *A Critical Handbook of Children's Literature.* (5th Ed.) New York: HarperCollins.

Lynch-Brown, C. & Tomlinson, C. M. 1993. Boston, Mass.: Allyn and Bacon.

Nodelman, P. 1992. *The Pleasures of Children's Literature.* White Plains, N.Y.: Longman.

Norton, D. E. 1995. *Through the Eyes of a Child: An Introduction to Children's Literature.* (4th Ed.) Englewood Cliffs, N.J.: Merrill.

Rothlein, L. & Meinbach, A. M. 1996. *Legacies: Using Children's Literature in the Classroom.* New York: HarperCollins.

Routman, R. 1994. *Invitations: Changing as Teachers and Learners. K–12.* (Revision). Portsmouth, N.H.: Heinemann.

Russell, D. L. 1994. *Literature for Children: A Short Introduction.* (2nd Ed.) White Plains, N.J.: Longman.

Sutherland, Z. & Arbuthnot, M. H. 1991. *Children and Books.* (8th Ed.) New York: HarperCollins.

Publishers' Addresses

This list may not be correct. Due to mergers and acquisitions, many publishers' addresses and names have changed. Therefore, consult the most current edition of *Books in Print* or *Children's Books in Print* for an up-to-date listing.

Harry N. Abrams. Subsidiary of Times Mirror. 100 Fifth Ave., New York, NY. 10010. Orders to 120 Woodbine St., Bergenfield, NJ 07621. 800-345-1359.

Addison-Wesley Publishing Co. One Jacob Way, Reading, MA 01867.

Aladdin Books. 1230 Avenue of the Americas, New York, NY 10020.

Allyn and Bacon. A division of Simon and Schuster. 160 Gould St., Needham Heights, MA 02194.

Arte Publico Press. University of Houston, 4800 Calhoun, Houston, TX 77204-2090. 800-633-ARTE; fax 713-743-2847.

Atheneum. Imprint of Macmillan. 1230 Avenue of the Americas, New York, NY 10020. Orders to 100 Front St., Box 500, Riverside, NJ 08075. 800-257-5755.

Avon Books. 1350 Avenue of the Americas, New York, NY 10019.

Bantam Doubleday Dell. 666 Fifth Ave., New York, NY, 10103. Orders to 414 E. Gulf Road, Des Plaines, IL 60016. 800-223-6834.

Bantam Little Rooster Books. *See* Bantam Doubleday Dell.

Bantam Skylark Books. *See* Bantam Doubleday Dell.

Barron's Educational Series. P.O. Box 8040, 250 Wireless Boulevard, Hauppauge, NY 11788. 800-645-3476.

Peter Bedrick Books. 21112 Broadway, Suite 318, New York, NY 10023.

Beechtree Books. 1350 Avenue of the Americas, New York, NY 10019.

Berley Publishing Group. 200 Madison Ave., New York, NY 10010.

Black Butterfly Children's Books. Produced by Writers and Readers Publishing. Distributed by Publishers Group West, 4065 Hollis St., Emeryville, CA 94608. 800-788-3123.

R. R. Bowker. 121 Chanlon Road, New Providence, NJ 07974. 800-521-8110. Orders to P.O. Box 1001, Summit, NJ 07902-1001.

Boyds Mills Press. Division of Highlights Company. 815 Church St., Honesdale, PA 18431. Distributed by St. Martin's Press, 175 Fifth Ave., Room 1715, New York, NY 10010. 800-221-7945.

Boyds Mills Press/Caroline House. *See* Boyds Mills Press.

Boyds Mills Press/Wordsong. *See* Boyds Mills Press.

Bradbury Press. Imprint of Macmillan. 1230 Avenue of the Americas, New York, NY 10020. Orders to 100 Front St., Box 500, Riverside, NJ 08075. 800-257-5755.

Camelot. 1350 Avenue of the Americas. New York, NY 10019.

Candlewick Press. Distributed by Penguin USA. 2067 Massachusetts Ave., Cambridge, MA 02140. Orders to 120 Woodbine St., Bergenfield, NJ 07621. 800-526-0275.

Caroline House. Imprint of Green Hill. Distributed by National Book Network, 4720A Boston Way, Lanham, MD 20706-4310. 800-462-6420.

Carolrhoda Books. 241 First Ave. N., Minneapolis, MN 55401. 800-328-4929.

Checkerboard Press. 30 Vesey St., New York, NY 10007. 212-571-6300.

Chelsea House Publishers. 95 Madison Ave., New York, NY 10016.

Children's Book Press. 6400 Hollis St., Emeryville, CA 94608. 510-655-3395; fax 510-655-1978. Distributed by Bookpeople, 7900 Edgewater Drive, Oakland, CA 94621. 800-999-4650.

Children's Press. 5440 N. Cumberland Ave., Chicago, IL 60656.

Christopher-Gordon. 480 Washington St., Norwood, MA 02062. 617-762-5577.

Chronicle Books. Division of Chronicle Publishing, 275 Fifth St., San Francisco, CA 94103. 800-722-6657 (orders only).

Clarion Books. Imprint of Houghton Mifflin. 215 Park Ave. S., New York, NY 10003. Orders to Wayside Road, Burlington, MA 01803. 800-225-3362.

Cobblehill Books. Imprint of Dutton Children's Books, a division of Penguin USA. 375 Hudson St., New York, NY 10014. Orders to 120 Woodbine St., Bergenfield, NJ 07621. 800-526-0275.

Cobblestone Publishing. 7 School St., Peterborough, NH 03458. 603-924-7209.

Cooperative Children's Book Center. Orders to Publication Sales, Wisconsin Department of Public Instruction, P.O. Box 7841, Madison, WI 53707-7841. 800-243-8782.

Creative Education. Box 227, 123 S. Broad St., Mankato, MN 56001.

Crestwood House, 1230 Avenue of the Americas, New York, NY 10020.

Thomas Y. Crowell. Imprint of HarperCollins Children's Books. 10 East 53rd St., New York, NY 10022. Orders to 1000 Keystone Industrial Park, Scranton, PA 18512. 800-242-7737.

Crown Publishing Group. Affiliate of Random House. 201 E. 50th St., New York, NY 10022. Orders to 400 Hahn Road, Westminster, MD 21157. 800-733-3000 (orders); 800-726-0600 (inquiries).

Delacorte Press. Division of Bantam Doubleday Dell. Orders to 414 E. Gulf Road, Des Plaines, IL 60016. 800-223-6834.

Dell Publishing Co. 666 Fifth Ave., New York, NY 10103.

Dial Books. Division of Penguin USA. 375 Avenue of the Americas, New York, NY 10020. Orders to 120 Woodbine St., Bergenfield, NJ 07621. 800-526-0275.

Dial Books for Young Readers. *See* Dial Books.

Dillon Press. Imprint of Macmillan. 123 Avenue of the Americas, New York, NY 10020. Orders to 100 Front St., Riverside, NJ 08705. 800-257-5755.

Doubleday. Division of Bantam Doubleday Dell. 666 Fifth Ave., New York, NY 10103. Orders to Doubleday Consumer Services, P.O. Box 5071, Des Plaines, IL 60017-5071. 800-223-6834.

Doubleday Books for Young Readers. *See* Doubleday.

Dutton Children's Books. Division of Penguin USA. 375 Hudson St., New York, NY 10014. Orders to 120 Woodbine St., Bergenfield, NJ 07621. 800-526-0275.

ERIC Document Reproduction Service No. ED.

Farrar, Straus and Giroux. 19 Union Square W., New York, NY. 10003. 800-631-8571.

Four Winds Press. Imprint of Macmillan Children's Book Group. 1230 Avenue of the Americas, New York, NY 10020. Orders to 100 Front St., Riverside, NJ 08705. 800-257-5755.

Friends of the Cooperative Children's Book Center. P.O. Box 5288, Madison, WI 53705-0288. 608-222-1867.

David R. Godine, Publisher. Horticulture Hall, 200 Massachusetts Ave., Boston, MA 02115.

Good Books for Young Readers. P.O. Box 419, Main St., Intercourse, PA 17534. 800-762-7171; fax 717-768-3433.

Green Tiger Press. Imprint of Simon and Schuster. 1230 Avenue of the Americas, New York, NY 10020. 212-698-7000.

Greenwillow Books. Division of William Morrow. 1350 Avenue of the Americas, New York, NY 10019. Orders to 39 Plymouth St., P.O. Box 1219, Fairfield, NJ 07007. 800-843-9389.

Greenwood Press. Division of Greenwood Publishing Group. 88 Post Road W., P.O. Box 5007, Westport, CT 06881-5007. 800-225-5800 (orders only).

Grosset & Dunlap. 200 Madison Ave., New York, NY 10016.

Gryphon House. 3706 Otis St., Mt. Rainier, MD 20712.

Gulliver Books. 1250 Sixth Ave., San Diego, CA 92101.

Harcourt Brace Jovanovich. 1250 Sixth Ave., San Diego, CA 92101. Orders to 6277 Sea Harbor Drive, Orlando, FL 32887. 800-225-5425.

Harcourt Brace Jovanovich/Gulliver Books. *See* Harcourt Brace Jovanovich.

Harcourt Brace Jovanovich/Odyssey Books. *See* Harcourt Brace Jovanovich.

Harper and Row. Division of HarperCollins. Orders to 1000 Keystone Industrial Park, Scranton, PA 18512-4621. 800-242-7737 (800-982-4377 in Pennsylvania).

HarperCollins. 10 E. 53rd St., New York, NY 10022. Orders to 1000 Keystone Industrial Park, Scranton, PA 18512-4621. 800-242-7737 (800-982-4377 in Pennsylvania).

HarperCollins/Willa Perlman Books. *See* HarperCollins.

HarperCollins/Charlotte Zolotow Books. *See* HarperCollins.

Harper Trophy. *See* HarperCollins.

Heinemann. 361 Hanover St., Portsmouth, NH 03801-3912.

Henry Holt. 113 W. 19th St., New York, NY 10011. Orders to 4375 W. 1980 S., Salt Lake City, UT 84104. 800-488-5233.

Henry Holt/Red Feather Books. *See* Henry Holt.

Highsmith Press. W5527, P.O. Box 800, Fort Atkinson, WI 53538-0800. 800-558-2110 for information; fax 800-835-2329.

Hispanic Books. Distributors and publishers. 1665 West Grant Rd., Tucson, AZ 85745. 602-882-9484.

Holiday House. 425 Madison Ave., New York, NY 10017. 212-688-0085.

Houghton Mifflin. Orders to Wayside Road, Burlington, MA 01803. 800-225-3362.

Hyperion Books for Children. Division of Disney Book Publishing. 114 Fifth Ave., New York, Ny 10011. Distributed by Little, Brown. Orders to 200 West St., Waltham, MA 02254. 800-343-9204.

Ideals Publishing Corp. Egmont, Inc., U.S.A. 565 Marriot Drive, Nashville, TN 37210.

International Reading Association. 800 Barksdale Road, P.O. Box 8139, Newark, DE 19714-8139. Primary journal used: *The Reading Teacher.*

Jewish Publication Society. 1930 Chestnut St., Philadelphia, PA 19103.

Joy Street Books. 34 Beacon St., Boston, MA 02108.

Just Us Books. 301 Main St., Suite 22–24, Orange, NJ 07050. 201-676-4345.

Kane/Miller Book Publisher. Box 529, Brooklyn, NY 11231.

Alfred A. Knopf. Subsidiary of Random House. 201 E. 50th St., New York, NY 10022. Orders to 400 Hahn Road, Westminster, MD 21157. 800-733-3000.

Alfred A. Knopf/Borzoi Books. *See* Alfred A. Knopf.

Lee and Low Books. 228 E. 45th St., 14th Floor, New York, NY 10017. 212-867-6155; fax 212-338-9059. Distributed by Publishers Group West, 4065 Hollis St., Emeryville, CA 94608. 800-788-3123.

Lerner Publications. 241 First Ave. N., Minneapolis, MN 55401. 800-328-4929.

Lippincott Children's Books. Imprint of HarperCollins Children's Books. 10 East 53rd St., New York, NY 10022. Orders to 1000 Keystone Industrial Park, Scranton, PA 18512-4621. 800-638-3030.

Little, Brown. Division of Time Warner. 34 Beacon St., Boston, MA 02108. Orders to 200 West St., Waltham, MA 02254. 800-759-0190.

Little, Brown/Joy Street Books. *See* Little, Brown.

Lodestar Books. Imprint of Dutton Children's Books, a division of Penguin Books. 375 Hudson St., New York, NY 10014. Orders to Penguin USA, 120 Woodbine St., Bergenfield, NJ 07621. 800-526-0275.

Longman. Division of Addison-Wesley. Orders to 95 Church St., White Plains, NY 10601. 914-993-5000.

Longman Publishing. 10 Bank St., White Plains, NY 10606.

Lothrop, Lee and Shepard Books. Division of William Morrow. 1350 Avenue of the Americas, New York, NY 10014. Orders to 39 Plymouth St., P.O. Box 1219, Fairfield, NJ 07007. 800-237-0657.

Lothrop, Lee and Shepard Books/Mulberry Books. *See* Lothrop, Lee and Shepard Books.

Macmillan. 1230 Avenue of the Americas, New York, NY 10020. Orders to 100 Front St., Riverside, NJ 08075. 800-257-5755.

Margaret K. McElderry Books. Imprint of Macmillan Children's Books Group. 1230 Avenue of the Americas, New York, NY 10020. Orders to 100 Front St., Riverside, NJ 08075. 800-257-5755.

McGraw-Hill Book Co. 1221 Avenue of the Americas, New York, NY 10020.

Merrill. An imprint of Prentice Hall, a Simon and Schuster division. Englewood Cliffs, NJ 07632. (Note: In 1993 Merrill was an imprint of Macmillan Company.)

Julian Messner. Imprint of Simon and Schuster. 1230 Avenue of the Americas, New York, NY 10020. 212-698-7000.

William Morrow. 1350 Avenue of the Americas, New York, NY 10019. Orders to Wilmor Warehouse, P.O. Box 1219, 39 Plymouth St., Fairfield, NJ 07007. 800-237-0657.

Morrow Junior Books. *See* William Morrow.

John Muir Publications. P.O. Box 613, Santa Fe, NM 87504.

Mulberry Books. 1350 Avenue of the Americas, New York, NY 10019.

Network of Educators' Committees on Central America. P.O. Box 43509, Washington, DC 20010-9509. 202-429-0137.

New Society Publishers. 4527 Springfield Ave., Philadelphia, PA 19143. 215-382-6543.

North-South Books. 1133 Broadway, Suite 1016, New York, NY 10010. 800-282-8257.

Northland Publishing. P.O. Box 1389, Flagstaff, AZ 86002. 800-346-3257.

Orchard Books. Division of Franklin Watts. 387 Park Ave. S., New York, NY 10016. 800-672-6672.

Orchard Books/Richard Jackson Books. *See* Orchard Books.

Oryx Press. 4041 North Central Ave., Suite 700, Phoenix, AZ 85012-3397.

Oxford University Press. 200 Madison Ave., New York, NY 10016.

Oyate. 2702 Mathews St., Berkeley, CA 94702. 510-848-6700.

Pantheon Books. 201 E. 50th St., 27th Floor, New York, NY 10022.

Penguin USA. 375 Hudson St., New York, NY 10014.

Philomel Books. Imprint of the Putnam Publishing Group. 200 Madison Ave., New York, NY 10016. Orders to 390 Murray Hill Parkway, East Rutherford, NJ 07073. 800-631-8571.

Picture Book Studio. Box 919, 10 Central St., Saxonville, MA 01701. Orders to Simon and Schuster Children's Books, 15 Columbus Circle, New York, NY 10023. 800-223-2348; 800-223-2336 (orders only).

Price Stern Sloan. 11150 Olympic Boulevard, Suite 650, Los Angeles, CA 90064.

Puffin Books. 375 Hudson St., New York, NY 10014.

G. P. Putnam's Sons. Imprint of the Putnam Publishing Group. 200 Madison Ave., New York, NY 10016. Orders to 390 Murray Hill Parkway, East Rutherford, NJ 07073. 800-631-8571.

G. P. Putnam's Sons/Whitebird Books. *See* G. P. Putnam's Sons.

Random House. 201 E. 50th St., New York, NY 10022.

Rizzoli International Publications. 300 Park Ave. S., New York, NY 10010. 800-462-2387.

Rizzoli International Publications/National Museum of American Art, Smithsonian Scholastic. *See* Rizzoli International Publications.

Savanna Books. 858 Massachusetts Ave., Central Square, Cambridge, MA. 617-868-3423.

Scarecrow Press. Division of Grolier. Orders to 52 Liberty St., Box 4167, Metuchen, NJ 08840. 800-537-7107.

Scholastic. 555 Broadway, New York, NY 10012. Orders to P.O. Box 120, Bergenfield, NJ 07621. 800-325-6149 (orders only).

Scholastic/Apple Paperbacks. *See* Scholastic.

Scholastic/Cartwheel Books. *See* Scholastic.

Scholastic Hardcover Books. *See* Scholastic.

Scholastic Hardcover Books/Lucas Evans Books. *See* Scholastic.

Scholastic Hardcover Books/Byron Preiss–New China Pictures Books. *See* Scholastic.

Charles Scribner's Sons. Division of Macmillan. 1230 Avenue of the Americas, New York, NY 10020. Orders to 100 Front St., Riverside, NJ 08075. 800-257-5755.

Sierra Club Books/Little, Brown. Distributed by Little, Brown. Orders to 200 West St., Waltham, MA 02254. 800-759-0190.

Sights Productions. P.O. Box 101, Mt. Airy, MD 21771. 410-795-4582.

Silver Burdett Press. Division of Paramount Publishing. Orders to P.O. Box 2649, Columbus, OH 43216. 800-848-9500.

Simon and Schuster. 1230 Avenue of the Americas, New York, NY 10020. 212-698-7000.

Simon and Schuster Books for Young Readers. *See* Simon and Schuster.

Tambourine Books. Imprint of William Morrow. 1350 Avenue of the Americas, New York, NY 10019. Orders to Wilmor Warehouse, P.O. Box 1219, 39 Plymouth St., Fairfield, NJ 07007. 800-237-0657 (customer service).

Tilbury House. Distributed by Consortium Book Sales and Distribution. 1045 Westgate Drive, St. Paul, MN 55114-1065. 800-283-3572.

Troll Associates. Subsidiary of Educational Reading Services. 100 Corporate Drive, Mahwah, NJ 07430. 800-526-5289.

Tundra Books. Box 1030, Plattsburgh, NY 12901. In Canada: University of Toronto Press, 5201 Dufferin St., Downsview, Ontario M3H 5T8; 416-667-7791; fax 416-667-7832. In the United States: University of Toronto Press, 340 Nagel Drive, Buffalo, NY 14225; 716-683-4547.

Helaine Victoria Press. 911 N. College Ave., No. 3, Bloomington, IN 47404. 812-331-0444.

Viking Penguin. Division of Penguin USA. 375 Hudson St., New York, NY 10014. Orders to 120 Woodbine St., Bergenfield, NJ 07621. 800-526-0275.

Walker and Company. Division of Walker Publishing. 720 Fifth Ave., New York, NY 10019. 800-289-2553 (orders only).

Frederick Warne & Co. 375 Hudson St., New York, NY 10014.

Franklin Watts. Subsidiary of Grolier. 95 Madison Ave., New York, NY 10016. Orders to 5450 N. Cumberland Ave., Chicago, IL 60656. 800-672-6672.

Western Publishing Co. 1220 Mound Ave., Racine, WI 53404.

Whispering Coyote Press. 480 Newbury St., Suite 104, Danvers, MA 01923. 508-281-4995.

Whispering Coyote Press/Treld Bicknell Books. *See* Whispering Coyote Press.

Albert Whitman. 6340 Oakton St., Morton Grove, IL 60053. 800-155-7675.

Writers and Readers Publishing. 625 Broadway, 10th Floor, New York, NY 10012. 212-982-3158. Distributed by Publishers Group West, 4065 Hollis St., Emeryville, CA 94608. 800-788-3123.

Bibliography

CHAPTER 1

CHILDREN'S BOOKS MENTIONED IN THE CHAPTER

Adler, E. 1995. *The King's Shadow*. New York: Farrar, Straus, & Giroux. 12–16 yrs.

Avi. 1991. *Nothing but the Truth: A Documentary Novel*. New York: Orchard. 12–16 yrs.

———. 1995. *Poppy*. New York: Orchard/Jackson. 9–12 yrs.

Bradbury, M. 1995. *More Than Anything Else*. Illus. Chris K. Saentpict. New York: Orchard/Jackson. 7–11 yrs.

Bunting, E. 1995. *Once Upon a Time*. Photos John Pezaris. Katonah, N.Y.: Owen. 6–10 yrs.

Burnett, F. H. 1886 (New Ed., 1987). *The Secret Garden*. Illus. Tasha Tudor. New York: Harper & Row.

Cole, J. 1989. *Magic School Bus Inside the Human Body*. Illus. Bruce Degan. New York: Scholastic. 5–9 yrs.

Faulkner, K. 1996. *Wide Mouth Frog*. Illus. Jonathan Lambert. New York: Dial. 3–8 yrs.

Grimm, J. & W. Grimm. 1977. *Grimm's Tales for Young and Old*. Illus. George Cruickshank. New York: Doubleday. 7–12 yrs. *(Originally titled German Popular Tales, 1822.)*

Isaacs, A. 1994. *Swamp Angel*. Illus. Paul O. Zelinsky. New York: Dutton. 7–11 yrs.

Isaacson, P. M. 1993. *A Short Walk Around the Pyramids and Through the World of Art*. New York: Knopf. 8–14 yrs.

Konigsburg, E. L. 1996. *The View from Saturday*. New York: Karl/Atheneum. 10–14 yrs.

Lindberg, R. 1987. *The Midnight Farm*. Illus. Susan Jeffers. New York: Dial. 6–10 yrs.

Lovett, S. 1993. *Extremely Weird Snakes*. Photos. Santa Fe, N.M.: John Muir. 8–12 yrs.

Murphy, J. 1995. *The Great Fire*. Photos. New York: Scholastic. 8–12 yrs.

Myers, W. D. 1996. *Slam!* New York: Scholastic. 12–16 yrs.

Prelutsky, J. (Ed.) 1983. *Random House Book of Poetry*. Illus. Arnold Lobel. New York: Random House. 5–12 yrs.

Provensen, A. 1995. *My Fellow Americans: A Family Album*. San Diego, Calif.: Harcourt Brace. 9–14 yrs.

Quinland, S. E. 1995. *The Case of the Mummified Pigs*. Honesdale, Penn.: Boyds Mills. 8–12 yrs.

Schroeder, A. 1996. *Minty: A Story of Young Harriet Tubman*. Illus. Jerry Pinkney. 6–10 yrs.

Van Allsburg, C. 1981. *Jumanji*. Boston: Houghton Mifflin. 7–12 yrs.

Viorst, J. 1972. *Alexander and the Terrible, Horrible, No Good, Very Bad Day*. Illus. Ray Cruz. New York: Atheneum. 5–10 yrs.

White, E. B. 1952. *Charlotte's Web*. Illus. Garth Williams. New York: Harper & Row.

Wilder, L. I. 1935. (New Ed. 1953). *Little House on the Prairie*. Illus. Garth Williams. New York. Harper & Row. 6–12 yrs.

Williams, M. 1922. *The Velveteen Rabbit: Or How Toys Became Real*. Illus. William Nicholson. New York: Doubleday. 8–14 yrs.

Wisniewski, D. 1996. *Golem*. New York: Clarion. 7–11 yrs.

CHAPTER 2

CHILDREN'S BOOKS MENTIONED IN THE CHAPTER

Ahlberg, J. & A. Ahlberg. 1986. *The Jolly Postman or Other People's Letters*. Boston: Heinemann. 5–11 yrs.

Fleischman, P. 1988. *Rondo in C*. Illus. Janet Wentworth. New York: Harper & Row. 9–12 yrs.

Newberry, C. T. 1993. *April's Kittens*. New York: Harper & Row. 5–9 yrs.

Prelutsky, J. (Ed.) 1983. *The Random House Book of Poetry*. Illus. Arnold Lobel. New York: Random. 4–14 yrs.

Rathman, P. 1995. *Officer Buckle and Gloria*. New York: Putnam. 5–10 yrs.

Silverstein, S. 1974. *A Light in the Attic*. New York: HarperCollins. 6–14 yrs.

White, E. B. 1952. *Charlotte's Web*. Illus. Garth Williams. New York: HarperCollins. 8–12 yrs.

Yolen, J. 1987. *Owl Moon*. Illus. John Schoenherr. New York: Philomel. 6–10 yrs.

LIT SET

"Old Stormalong, the Deep-Water Sailman" in B. A. Botkin (Ed.). 1949. *The Treasury of American Folklore* (pp. 185–192). New York: Crown.

"Stormalong" in C. Carmer (Compiler). 1949. *America Sings* (pp. 30–34). New York: Knopf.

Felton, H. 1986. *True Tall Tales of Stormalong: Sail of the Seven Seas*. Englewood Cliffs, N.J.: Prentice-Hall.

Malcolmson, A. & D. J. McCormick. 1952. *Mr. Stormalong*. Boston: Houghton Mifflin.

"Stormalong" in M. P. Osborne. 1991. *American Tall Tales* (pp. 37–44). Engravings by M. McCurdy. New York: Knopf.

Shay, F. 1930. *Here's Audacity! American Legendary Heroes* (pp. 17–31). New York: Macaulay.

CHAPTER 3

CHILDREN'S BOOKS MENTIONED IN THE CHAPTER

Aardema, V. 1995. *How the Ostrich Got Its Long Neck: A Tale from the Akamba of Kenya*. Illus. Marcia Brown. New York: Scholastic. 5–9 yrs.

Ada, A. F. (Tran. Rosalma Zubizarreta). 1995. *Mediopollito I Half-Chicken*. Illus. Kim Howard. New York: Doubleday. 6–9 yrs.

Aesop's Fables. Illus. Lisbeth Zwerger. 1989. Saxonville, Mass.: Picture Book Studio. 7–10 yrs.

Alderson, B. 1995. *The Arabian Nights: Or Tales Told by Sheherezade during a Thousand Nights and One Night*. Illus. Michael Foreman. New York: Morrow. 9–12 yrs. *Books of Wonder series*.

Andersen, H. C. 1987 printing. *Andersen's Fairy Tales*. New York: Grosset & Dunlap. 6–12 yrs.

Asbjornsen, P. C. & Moe, J. E. 1922. *East o' the Sun and West o' the Moon*. Illus. Hedvig Collin. (New ed. 1953) New York, Macmillan. 9–12 yrs.

Baring-Gould, W. S. & C. 1962. *The Annotated Mother Goose*. New York: Bramhall.

Bawden, N. 1981. *William Tell*. Illus. P. Allamand. New York: Lothrop, Lee & Shepard. 9–12 yrs.

Berenzy, A. 1995. *Rapunzel*. New York: Henry Holt. 6–9 yrs.

Benjamin, F. 1995. *Skip across the Ocean: Nursery Rhymes from around the World*. Illus. Sheila Moxley. New York: Orchard. 3–9 yrs.

Briggs, R. 1966. *The Mother Goose Treasury*. London: Coward. 3–7 yrs.

Bruhac, J. 1995. *The Boy Who Lived with Bears: And Other Iroquois Stories*. Illus. Murv Jacob. New York: HarperCollins. 10–13 yrs.

Brusca, M. C. and Wilson, T. 1995. *Pedro Fools the Gringo: And Other Tales of a Latin American Trickster*. Illus. Maria Cristina Brusca. New York: Holt. 6–9 yrs.

Carrick, C. 1989. *Aladdin and the Wonderful Lamp*. Illus. D. Carrick. New York: Scholastic. 7–12 yrs.

Climo, S. 1995. *Atalanta's Race: A Greek Myth*. Illustrated by Alexander Koshkin. New York: Clarion. 5–9 yrs.

Cohn, A. L. (Comp.). *From Sea to Shining Sea: A Treasury of American Folklore and Folk Songs*. Illus. By 11 Caldecott winners. New York: Scholastic. 6–14 yrs.

Cole, J. 1982. *Best-Loved Folktales of the World*. Illus. J. K. Schwarz. Garden City, NY: Doubleday. 7–12 yrs.

Courlander, H. & Herzog, G. 1947. *The Cow-Tail Switch and Other West African Stories*. Illus. Madye Lee Chastain. New York: Holt. 9–12 yrs.

Cresswick, P. 1912. *Robin Hood*. Illus. N. C. Wyeth. New York: Scribner. 9–13 yrs.

D'Aulaire, I. & E. P. 1962. *D'Aulaire's Book of Greek Myths*. New York: Doubleday. 10–14 yrs.

———. 1967. *D'Aulaire's Norse Gods and Giants*. New York: Doubleday. 10–14 yrs.

de Angeli, M. 1954. *The Book of Nursery and Mother Goose Rhymes*. New York: Doubleday. 3–6 yrs.

de Paola, T. 1985. *Tomie de Paola's Mother Goose*. New York: Putnam. 4–7 yrs.

_____. 1983. *The Legend of the Bluebonnet: A Tale of Old Texas.* New York: Putnam. 7–10 yrs.

_____. 1988. *The Legend of the Indian Paintbrush.* New York: Putnam. 7–10 yrs.

_____. 1994. *The Legend of the Poinsettia.* New York: Putnam. 7–10 yrs.

Duncan, L. 1996. *The Magic of Spider Woman.* Illus. Shonto Begay. New York: Scholastic. 6–9 yrs.

Fisher, L. E. 1996. *William Tell.* New York: Farrar, Straus & Giroux. 9–13 yrs.

Fleishman, P. 1996. *Dateline: Troy.* Cambridge, Mass.: Candlewick. 12–16 yrs.

Forest, H. 1995. *Wonder Tales from Around the World.* Illus. David Boston. Little Rock, Ark.: August House. 12–16 yrs.

Galdone, 1984. *The Teeny Tiny Woman.* New York: Clarion. 4–8 yrs.

Gerson, M. (Ad.) 1992. *Why the Sky Is Far Away: A Nigerian Folktale.* Illus. C. Golembe. Boston, Mass.: Joy Street/Little. 8–12 yrs.

Greenaway, K. 1881. *Mother Goose, or the Old Nursery Rhymes.* Illus. K. Greenaway. London: Frederick Warne. 4–7 yrs.

_____. 1888. *The Pied Piper of Hamelin.* London: Fredrich-Warne. 7–10 yrs.

Grimm, J. & W. 1812. *Folk Tales for Children and the Home.* German Publication. 9–12 yrs.

_____. 1977. *Grimm's Tales for Young and Old.* New York: Doubleday. 8–12 yrs. (Original 1822, title *German Popular Tales.*)

_____. (Tran. Anthea Bell) 1996. *The Six Servants.* Illus. Sergei Goloshapov. New York: North-South. 7–11 yrs.

Hamilton, V. 1988. *In the Beginning: Creation Stories from Around the World.* Illus. David Shannon. Orlando, Fl.: Harcourt. 9–12 yrs.

_____. 1988. *The People Could Fly.* Illus. Leo and Diane Dillon. New York: Knopf. 8–12 yrs.

_____. 1992. *Many Thousand Gone: African Americans from Slavery to Freedom.* Illus. Leo and Diane Dillon. New York: Knopf. 8–12 yrs.

_____. 1995. *Her Stories: African American Folktales.* Illus. Leo and Diane Dillon. New York: Blue Sky.

_____. (ad.) 1996. *When Birds Could Talk and Bats Could Sing: The Adventures of Bruh Sparrow, Sis Wren, and Their Friends.* Illus. Barry Moser. New York: Blue Sky/Scholastic. 9–12 yrs.

Harris, J. C. 1986. *Jump! The Adventures of Brer Rabbit.* Illus. Barry Moser. Orlando, Fla.: Harcourt. 9–12 yrs.

Hayes, S. 1993. *The Candlewick Book of Fairy Tales.* Illus. P. J. Lynch. Cambridge, Mass.: Candlewick. 6–9 yrs.

Hill, E. 1982. *The Nursery Rhyme Peek-a-Book.* New York: Price-Stern. 2–5 yrs.

Hodges, M. (Reteller). 1993. *Saint Patrick and the Peddler.* Illus. Paul Brett Johnson. New York: Orchard. 6–9 yrs.

Impey, R. 1993. *Read Me a Fairy Tale: A Child's Book of Classic Fairy Tales.* Illus. Ian Beck, New York: Scholastic. 6–9 yrs.

Jeffers, S. 1979. *The Jovial Huntsmen.* New York: Macmillan. 4–7 yrs.

Jacobs, J. 1902. *English Fairy Tales,* 2 vols. Illus. John D. Batten. New York: Putnam. 8–12 yrs.

_____. 1892–1894. *Celtic Fairy Tales.* 2 volumes. London: David McNutt. 9–13 yrs.

_____. 1892. *Indian Fairy Tales.* London: David McNutt. 9–13 yrs.

Keats, E. J. 1987. *John Henry.* New York: Knopf. 7–10 yrs.

Kellogg, S. 1984. *Paul Bunyan.* New York: Morrow.

_____. 1986. *Pecos Bill.* New York: Morrow. 7–10 yrs.

_____. 1988. *Johnny Appleseed.* New York: Morrow. 7–10 yrs.

_____. 1992. *Mike Fink: A Tall Tale.* New York: Morrow. 7–10 yrs.

_____. 1995. *Sally Ann Thunder Ann Whirlwind Crockett: A Tall Tale.* New York: Morrow. 7–10 yrs.

Kherdian, D. (Reteller). 1992. *Feathers and Tails: Animal Fables From Around the World.* Illus. by Nonny Hogrogian. New York: Philomel. 6–11 yrs.

Kimmel, E. A. 1995. *The Adventures of Hershel of Ostropol.* Illus. Trina Schart Hyman. New York: Holiday. 8–12 yrs.

_____. 1992. *The Tale of Aladdin and the Wonderful Lamp: A Story of the Arabian Nights.* Illus. Ju-Hong Chen. New York: Holiday. 8–12 yrs.

Kurtz, J. (Ad.) 1996. *Miro in the Kingdom of the Sun.* Illus. by David Frampton. Burlington, Mass.: Houghton. 6–10 yrs.

Lang, A. (Tr.) 1898. (New Ed. 1991) *Tales from the Arabian Nights.* Illus. Edmund Dulac & others. Pleasantville, N.Y.: Reader's Digest.

_____. 1948. *The Blue Fairy Book.* Illus. Ben Kutcher. New York: McKay. 7–12 yrs.

_____. 1978. *Red Fairy Book.* Illus. Faith Jacques. New York: Dover. 7–12 yrs.

_____. 1978. *Green Fairy Book.* Illus. Antony Maitland. New York: Dover. 7–12 yrs.

_____. 1980. *Yellow Fairy Book.* Illus. Eric Blegvad. New York: Dover. 7–12 yrs.

_____. 1982. *Pink Fairy Book.* Illus. Colin McNaughton. New York: Dover. 7–12 yrs.

Lattimore, D. N. 1995. *Arabian Nights: Three Tales.* New York: HarperCollins/Cotler. 7–10 yrs.

Leeson, R. *The Story of Robin Hood.* Illus. by Barbara Lofthouse. New York: Kingfisher. 9–11 yrs.

Lester, J. 1987. *The Tales of Uncle Remus.* Illus. Jerry Pinkney. New York: Dial. 9–13 yrs.

_____. 1989. *How Many Spots Does a Leopard Have? And Other Tales.* New York: Scholastic. 9–13 yrs.

_____. 1994. *John Henry.* Illus. Jerry Pinkney. New York: Dial. 7–10 yrs.

Lobel, A. 1980. *Fables.* New York: Harper. 9–12 yrs.

_____. 1986. *The Random House Book of Mother Goose.* New York: Random House. 4–6 yrs.

Longfellow, H. W. 1983. *Hiawatha.* Illus. Susan Jeffers. New York: Dial. 8–12 yrs.

Maddern, E. 1993. *Rainbow Bird: An Aboriginal Folktale from Northern Australia.* Illus. Adrienne Kennaway. Boston, Mass.: Little. 6–9 yrs.

Marshall, J. 1979. *James Marshall's Mother Goose.* New York: Farrar. 3–6 yrs.

Martin, R. 1992. *The Rough-Face Girl.* Illus. David Shannon. New York: Putnam. 7–10 yrs.

McAllister, A. 1990. *When the Ark Was Full.* Illus. Michaela Bloomfield. New York: Dutton. 4–7 yrs.

McDermott, G. 1992. *Zomo: The Rabbit: A Trickster Tale from West Africa.* Orlando, Fla.: Harcourt, Brace, Jovanovich. 8–11 yrs.

_____. 1993. *Raven: A Trickster Tale from the Pacific Northwest.* Orlando, Fla.: Harcourt. 8–11 yrs.

McManus, P. F. 1996. *Never Cry "Arp!" and Other Great Adventures.* New York: Holt. 9–12 yrs.

Merrill, J. (Ad.). 1992. *The Girl Who Loved Caterpillars: A Twelfth-Century Tale from Japan.* Illus. Floyd Cooper. New York: Philomel. 7–11 yrs.

Moroney, L. 1995. *Moontellers: Myths of the Moon from Around the World.* Illus. Greg Shed. Flagstaff, Ariz.: Northland. 7–10 yrs.

Opie, I. 1988. *Tail Feathers from Mother Goose: The Opie Rhyme Book.* Illus. Maurice Sendak. Boston, Mass.: Little, Brown. 4–6 yrs.

Opie, I. & P. 1952. *Oxford Dictionary of Nursery Rhymes.* New York: Oxford University Press.

Osborne, M. P. 1991. *American Tall Tales.* Illus. Michael McCurdy. New York: Knopf. 7–12 yrs.

Peppe, R. 1985. *The House That Jack Built.* New York: Delacorte. 4–8 yrs.

Perrault, C. 1697. *Histories ou contes du temps passé; avec des moralites.* Illus. Gustave Dore. Paris (New ed. 1969) Mineola: N.Y.: Dover.

_____. 1729. *Contes de ma mere l'oye* (Tales of Mother Goose). Charing Cross: J. Pote.

Philip, N. (Ad.) 1994. *The Arabian Nights.* Illus. Sheila Moxley. New York: Orchard. 10–14 yrs.

_____. 1995. *The Illustrated Book of Myths: Tales and Legends of the World.* Illus. Nilesh Mistry. New York: Dorling. 10–13 yrs.

_____. 1996. *American Fairy Tales: From Rip Van Winkle to the Rootabaga Stories.* Illus. Michael McCurdy. New York: Hyperion. 11–16 yrs.

Picard, B. 1952. *The Odyssey of Homer Retold.* New York: Walack. 10–13 yrs.

_____. 1960. *The Iliad of Homer.* New York: Walck. 10–13 yrs.

Pilling, J. 1993. *Realms of Gold: Myths and Legends from Around the World.* Illus. Kady M. Denton. New York: Kingfisher. 9–12 yrs.

Pohrt, T. 1995. *Coyote Goes Walking.* New York: Farrar. 6–9 yrs.

Potter, B. 1995. *Beatrix Potter's Nursery Rhyme Book.* London: Warne. 5–9 yrs.

Provensen, A. & M. Provensen. 1976. *The Mother Goose Book.* New York: Random House. 3–6 yrs.

Purdy, C. 1985. *Iva Dunnit and the Big Wind.* Illus. Steven Kellogg. New York: Morrow. 7–10 yrs.

Rosen, M. (Ed.). 1992. *South and North and East and West.* Cambridge, Mass.: Candlewick. 7–12 yrs.

Rockwell, A. 1995. *The Acorn Tree and Other Folktales.* New York: Greenwillow. 5–9 yrs.

San Souci, R. D. 1993. *Young Guinevere.* Illus. Jamichael Henterly. New York: Doubleday. 9–13 yrs.

Sherman, J. 1996. *Trickster Tales: Forty Folk Stories from Around the World.* Illus. David Boston. Little Rock, Ark.: August House. 10–13 yrs.

Sierra, J. (Comp. and ad.) 1996. *Nursery Tales Around the World.* Illus. by Stefano Vitale. New York: Clarion. 3–7 yrs.

Songs from the Nursery, or Mother Goose's Melodies. 1719. Boston: Thomas Fleet.

Stanley, D. 1995. *Petrosinella: A Neapolitan Rapunzel.* New York: Dial. 5–10 yrs.

Steptoe, J. 1987. *Mufaro's Beautiful Daughters: An African Tale.* New York: Lothrop, Lee & Shepard. 7–12 yrs.

Stevens, J. 1985. *The House That Jack Built.* New York: Holiday. 5–9 yrs.

Stoutenberg, A. 1976. *American Tall Tales.* New York: Penguin. 9–13 yrs.

Sutcliff, R. 1995. *Black Ships Before Troy: The Story of the Iliad.* Illus. Alan Lee. New York: Delacorte. 11–16 yrs.

_____. 1996. *The Wanderings of Odysseus: The Story of the Odyssey.* Illus. Alan Lee. New York: Delacorte. 11–16 yrs.

Sutherland, Z. & Livingston, M. C. 1984. *The Scott, Foresman Anthology of Children's Literature.* Glenview, Ill.: Scott, Foresman. 5–16 yrs.

Talbott, H. 1995. *King Arthur and the Round Table.* New York: Morrow. 7–10 yrs.

Taylor, C. J. 1995. *The Monster from the Swamp: Native Legends of Monsters, Demons and Other Creatures.* Montreal: Tundra. 10–13 yrs.

Thurber, J. 1940. *Fables of Our Time and Famous Poems.* New York: Simon & Schuster. 8–11 yrs.

Tudor, T. 1944. *Mother Goose.* New York: Walck. 3–6 yrs.

Van Laan, N. 1995. *In a Circle Long Ago: A Treasury of Native Lore from North America.*

Illus. Lisa Desimini. New York: Apple Soup. 10–13 yrs.

Wiggin, K. D. & Smith, N. A. (Eds.). 1993. *The Arabian Nights: Their Best-Known Tales*. Illus. Maxfield Parrish. New York: Scribner. 10–16 yrs.

Wildsmith, B. 1963. *Brian Wildsmith's Mother Goose*. London: Watts. 3–6 yrs.

Wright, B. F. 1965. *The Real Mother Goose*. Illus. B. F. Wright. Stokie, Ill.: Rand McNally. 3–7 yrs.

Yolen, J. 1986. *Favorite Folktales from Around the World*. New York: Pantheon. 7–16 yrs.

_____. 1992. *Street Rhymes Around the World*. Honesdale, PA: Wordsong. 5–9 yrs.

Young, E. 1995. *Cat and Rat: The Legend of the Chinese Zodiac*. New York: Holt. 6–9 yrs.

Zeman, L. 1992. *Gilgamesh*. Platsburgh, NY: Tundra Books. 10–14 yrs.

_____. 1993. *The Revenge of Ishtar*. Platsburgh, NY: Tundra Books. 10–14 yrs.

_____. 1995. *The Last Quest of Gilgamesh*. Plattsburgh, NY: Tundra Books. 10–13 yrs.

FOLK LITERATURE COLLECTIONS

Asbojornsen, P. C., & J. Moe. 1988. *Popular Tales from the Norse*. Trans. Sir G. W. Dasent. Edinburgh: David Douglas. 7–11 yrs.

Botkin, B. A. (Ed.). 1949. *The Treasury of American Folklore*. New York: Crown. 6–13 yrs.

Brooke, William J. 1990. *A Telling of the Tales: Five Stories*. Illus. Richard Egielski. New York: Harper & Row. 8–13 yrs.

_____. 1992. *Untold Tales*. New York: HarperCollins. 10–13 yrs.

Brusca, Maria Cristina, and Tona Wilson. 1995. *When Jaguars Ate the Moon: And Other Stories about Animals and Plants of the Americas*. Illus. Maria Cristina Brusca. New York: Holt. 5–9 yrs.

Butler, F. 1987. *The Wide World All Around*. New York: Longman. 6–13 yrs.

Carle, Eric. 1976. *Eric Carle's Storybook: Seven Tales by the Brothers Grimm*. New York: Watts. 6–10 yrs.

Chase, R. 1943. *The Jack Tales*. Illus. B. Williams. Boston: Houghton Mifflin. 7–11 yrs.

_____. 1948. *Grandfather Tales*. Boston: Houghton Mifflin. 7–11 yrs.

Chorao, Kay. 1990. *The Child's Fairy Tale Book*. Illus. Kay Chorao. New York: Dutton. 4–8 yrs.

Clouston, W. A. 1968. *Popular Tales and Fictions: Their Migrations and Transformations*. Detroit: Singing Tree Press. 7–12 yrs.

Cohen, Daniel. 1995. *Real Vampires*. New York: Cobblehill. 10–16 yrs.

Cole, J. (Selector). 1982. *Best-Loved Folktales of the World*. Illus. J. K. Schwarz. New York: Doubleday. 6–13 yrs.

Darrell, M. (Ed.) 1972. *Once Upon a Time: The Fairy Tale World of Arthur Rackham*. New York: Viking. 7–11 yrs.

De la Mare, W. 1980. *Tales Told Again*. Illus. A. Howard. London: Faber Fanfares. 7–11 yrs.

De Regniers, B. S. 1966. *The Giant Book*. Illus. W. Cummings. New York: Atheneum. 7–11 yrs.

DeSpain, Pleasant. 1994. *Eleven Turtle Tales: Adventure Tales from around the World*. Illus. Joe Shlichta. Little Rock, Ark.: August. 10–15 yrs. American Storytelling Series. 7–11 yrs.

Dobbs, Rose. 1950. *Once Upon a Time: Twenty Cheerful Tales to Read and Tell*. Illus. F. Gag. New York: Random House. 7–12 yrs.

Eisen, Armand. (Ed.) 1992. *A Treasury of Children's Literature*. Boston: Houghton Mifflin/Ariel. 7–13 yrs.

Foster, J. R. 1955. *Great Folktales of Wit and Humor*. New York: Harper. 7–11 yrs.

Fox, P., & F. Vecchi. 1993. *Amzat and His Brothers: Three Italian Tales*. Illus. E. A. McCully. New York: Orchard/Jackson. 7–12 yrs.

Gag, W. 1979. *Tales from Grimm*. New York: Coward-McCann. 7–11 yrs.

Galloway, Priscilla. 1995. *Truly Grim Tales*. New York: Delacorte. 12–15 yrs. (eight revisionist fairy tales).

Giblin, James Cross. 1992. *The Truth about Unicorns*. Illus. Michael McDermott. New York: HarperCollins. 10–13 yrs.

Griffith, J. W., & C. H. Frey. 1981. *Classics of Children's Literature*. New York: Macmillan. 6–13 yrs.

Grimm, J. & W. (Tran. Lucy Crane) 1886. *Grimm's Household Stories*. Illus. Walter Crane. London: Routledge. (New York: Macmillan). 8–12 yrs.

_____. (Reteller V. Haviland). 1959. *Favorite Fairy Tales Told in Germany*. Illus. S. Suba. Boston: Little, Brown. 7–13 yrs.

_____. 1972. *The Complete Grimm Fairy Tales*. New York: Pantheon. 7–13 yrs.

_____. 1989. *The Frog King and Other Tales of the Grimm Brothers*. New York: Dutton. 6–12 yrs.

_____. 1992. *The Bremen Town Musicians* (ad. & ill. J. Stevens). Holiday. 7–10 yrs.

Gruenberg, S. M. 1942. *Favorite Stories Old and New*. Illus. K. Wiese. New York: Doubleday. 7–12 yrs.

Haviland, V. 1961. *Favorite Fairy Tales Told in Russia*. Illus. H. Danska. Boston: Little, Brown. 7–12 yrs.

_____. (Selector). 1972. *The Fairy Tale Treasury*. Illus. R. Briggs. New York: Dell. 7–12 yrs.

Hawthorne, H. 1892. *A Wonder Book for Girls and Boys*. New York: Ticknor, Reed, & Fields. 8–13 yrs.

Hayes, Sarah. 1993. *The Candlewick Book of Fairy Tales*. Illus. P. J. Lynch. Cambridge, Mass.: Candlewick. 5–8 yrs.

Impey, Rose. 1993. *Read Me a Fairy Tale: A Child's Book of Classic Fairy Tales*. Illus. Ian Beck. New York: Scholastic. 5–9 yrs.

Jacobs, J. (no date). *English Folk and Fairy Tales*. New York: Putnam. 8–13 yrs.

_____. 1894. *More English Fairy Tales*. London: David McNutt. 8–12 yrs.

Jafe, N., & S. Zeitlin (Adapter). 1993. *While Standing on One Foot: Puzzle Stories and Wisdom Tales from the Jewish Tradition*. Illus. J. Segal. New York: Holt. 7–12 yrs.

Kuskin, K. 1993. *A Great Miracle Happened There: A Chanukah Story*. Illus. R. A. Parker. New York: HarperCollins. 5–9 yrs.

Lang, Andrew. 1994. *A World of Fairy Tales*. Illus. Henry Justice Ford. New York: Dial. 5–8 yrs.

Leeds, B. 1990. *Fairy Tale Rap: "Jack and the Beanstalk" & Other Stories*. Illus. C. Hamilton. New York: Miramonte. 6–11 yrs.

Martignoni, M. E. (Ed.). 1955. *The Illustrated Treasury of Children's Literature*. New York: Grossett & Dunlap. 6–12 yrs.

Mayo, Margaret. 1995. *Tortoise's Flying Lesson*. Illus. Emily Bolam. San Diego: Harcourt Brace. 5–10 yrs.

Minard, R. 1975. *Womenfolk and Fairy Tales*. Illus. S. Klein. Boston: Houghton Mifflin. 7–12 yrs.

Morel, E. (Ed.) 1970. *Fairy Tales and Fables*. Illus. G. Frijikawa. New York: Grossett & Dunlap. 8–12 yrs.

Neil, P. 1991. *Fairy Tales of Eastern Europe*. Illus. L. Wilkes. New York: Clarion. 8–12 yrs.

Oodgeroo. 1994. *Dreamtime: Aboriginal Stories*. Illus. by Bronwyn Bancroft. New York: Lothrop, Lee, & Shepard. 9–11 yrs.

Perrault, C. 1967. *Perrault's Fairy Tales*. New York: Dover. 8–12 yrs.

_____. 1989. *Cinderella, and Other Tales from Perrault*. Illus. Michael Hague. New York: Henry Holt. 6–12 yrs.

Philip, Neil. 1994. *The Arabian Nights*. Illus. by Sheila Moxley. New York: Orchard. 9–11 yrs.

Rackham, A. (Ed.) 1930. *The Arthur Rackham Fairy Book*. New York: Lippincott. 7–12 yrs.

Richardson, F. 1972. *Great Children's Stories*. Northbrook, Ill.: Hubbard. 6–12 yrs.

Rockwell, A. 1988. *Puss in Boots and Other Stories*. New York: Macmillan. 7–11 yrs.

Ross, E. S. 1958. *The Buried Treasure and Other Picture Tales*. Illus. J. Cellini. New York: Lippincott. 7–12 yrs.

Ross, N. P. (Ed.). 1961. *The Life Treasury of American Folklore*. New York: Time. 7–12 yrs.

Rugoff, M. (Ed.) 1949. *A Harvest of World Folk Tales*. New York: Viking. 7–12 yrs.

Saltman, J. (Ed.) 1985. *The Riverside Anthology of Children's Literature*. Boston: Houghton Mifflin. 7–13 yrs.

San Souci, Robert D. 1994. *More Short and Shivery: Thirty Terrifying Tales*. Illus. by Katherine Coville and Jacqueline Rogers. New York: Delacorte. 9–11 yrs.

Shub, E. (trans.) 1971. *About Wise Men and Simpletons: Twelve Tales from Grimm*. New York: Macmillan. 7–12 yrs.

Shub, Elizabeth. 1994. *Seeing Is Believing*. Illus. by Rachel Isadora. New York: Greenwillow. 5–8 yrs.

Schwartz, Alvin. (Compiler and reteller). 1991. *Scary Stories 3: More Tales to Chill Your Bones*. Illus. Stephen Gammell. New York: HarperCollins. 9–13 yrs.

Schwartz, Howard, and Barbara Rush. (Compilers and retellers). 1991. *The Diamond Tree: Jewish Tales from around the World*. Illus. Uri Shulevitz. New York: HarperCollins. 8–12 yrs.

Schwartz, Howard. (Ad. and trans.) 1995. *Next Year in Jerusalem: 3000 Years of Jewish Stories*. Illus. by Neil Waldman. New York: Viking. 9–13 yrs.

Singer, I. B. 1966. *Zlateh the Goat and Other Stories*. Illus. M. Sendak. New York: Harper & Row. 8–12 yrs.

Spariosu, Mihai I., & Dezso Benedek. 1994. *Ghosts, Vampires, and Werewolves: Eerie Tales from Transylvania*. Illus. by Laszlo Kubinyi. New York: Orchard. 9–11 yrs.

Sutherland, Z., & M. C. Livingston. 1984. *The Scott, Foresman Anthology of Children's Literature*. Glenview, Ill.: Scott, Foresman. 6–14 yrs.

Tanaka, Beatrice. 1994. *Green Tales*. New York: Four Walls. 5–8 yrs.

Wiggin, Kate Douglas, & Nora A. Smith. (Eds.) 1993. *The Arabian Nights: Their Best-Known Tales*. Illus. Maxfield Parrish. New York: Scribner. 10–16 yrs.

Williams-Ellis, A. (Reteller). 1960. *Fairy Tales from the British Isles*. Illus. P. B. Baynes. New York: Warne. 7–12 yrs.

Wilson, B. K. 1966. *Greek Fairy Tales*. Illus. H. Toothill. River Grove, Ill.: Follett. 8–12 yrs.

Windham, Sophie. 1991. *Read Me a Story: A Child's Book of Favorite Tales*. Illus. Sophie Windham. New York: Scholastic. 3–8 yrs.

Yeats, W. B. (Compiler Neil Philip). 1990. *Fairy Tales of Ireland*. Illus. P. J. Lynch. New York: Delacorte. 10–12 yrs.

Yeoman, John. 1994. *The Singing Tortoise and Other Animal Folktales*. Illus. Quentin Blake. New York: Tambourine. 9–11 yrs.

SINGLE-STORY BOOKS

FOLKTALES AND FAIRY TALES

Afanasyev, Alexander Nikolayevich. (Reteller Lenny Hort). 1990. *The Fool and the Fish: A Tale from Russia*. Illus. Gennady Spirin. New York: Dial. 4–8 yrs.

Aksakov, Sergei. (Trans. Isadora Levin). 1989. *The Scarlet Flower: A Russian Folk Tale*. Illus. Boris Diodorov. San Diego: Harcourt Brace Jovanovich. 4–8 yrs.

Arnold, Caroline. 1989. *The Terrible Hodag*. Illus. Lambert Davis. San Diego: Harcourt Brace Jovanovich. 4–8 yrs.

Arnold, K. 1993. *Baba Yaga*. New York: North-South. 8–12 yrs.

Arnold, Tedd. 1991. *Ollie Forgot*. Illus. Tedd Arnold. New York: Dial/Pied Piper. 4–8 yrs. (noodlehead).

Arnold, Tim. 1993. *The Three Billy Goats Gruff*. New York: McElderry. 5–8 yrs.

Asbjornsen, P. C. & J. E. Moe. 1992. *The Man Who Kept House*. New York: McElderry. 5–8 yrs.

Barry, David. 1994. *The Rajah's Rice: A Mathematical Folktale from India*. Illus. by Donna Perrone. New York: Scientific American. 9–11 yrs.

Barton, Byron. 1991. *The Three Bears*. Illus. Byron Barton. New York: HarperCollins. 3–6 yrs.

———. 1993. *The Little Red Hen*. New York: HarperCollins. 4–6 yrs.

Bell, A. 1988. *The Golden Goose by Jacob and Wilhelm Grimm*. Illus. D. Duntz. New York: North-South. 7–11 yrs.

Bell, A. (Trans.) 1990. *The Merry Pranks of Till Eulenspiegel*. Illus. L. Zwerger. Saxonville, Mass.: Picture Book Studio.

———. 1992. *Jack in Luck*. Illus. Eve Tharlet. Saxonville, Mass.: Picture. 5–9 yrs.

Bernhard, Emery. 1994. *The Girl Who Wanted to Hunt: A Siberian Tale*. Illus. by Durga Bernhard. New York: Holiday. 5–9 yrs.

Black, F. (Reteller). 1991. *The Frog Prince*. Illus. W. Parmenter. Kansas City, Mo.: Andrews & McMeel. 6–9 yrs.

Birdseye, T. 1993. *Soap! Soap! Don't Forget the Soap! An Appalachian Folktale*. New York: Holiday. 5–8 yrs.

Brett, Jan. (Reteller). 1990. *Beauty and the Beast*. Illus. Jan Brett. New York: Clarion. 6–12 yrs.

Brett, Jan. (Adapter). 1989. *The Mitten: A Ukrainian Folktale*. Illus. Jan Brett. New York: Putnam. 4–8 yrs.

Brett, Jan. 1994. *Town Mouse, Country Mouse*. New York: Putnam. 5–8 yrs.

Brown, M. 1950. *Dick Whittington and His Cat*. New York: Scribners. 6–11 yrs.

———. 1988. *Cinderella*. New York: Macmillan. 6–11 yrs.

Bruchac, Joseph. *Gluskabe and the Four Wishes*. Illus. Christine Nyburg Shrader. New York: Cobblehill. 5–9 yrs.

Brusca, M. C., & T. Wilson. 1993. *The Cook and the King*. New York: Holt. 5–9 yrs.

Burkert, Nancy Ekholm. 1989. *Valentine and Orson*. Illus. Nancy Ekholm Burkert. New York: Farrar, Straus & Giroux/Floyd Yearout. 10–12.

Butler, Stephen. 1991. *Henny Penny*. Illus. Stephen Butler. New York: Tambourine. 3–6 yrs.

Carrick, C. 1989. *Aladin and the Wonderful Lamp*. Ill. D. Carrick. New York: Scholastic. 7–12 yrs.

Cech, John. 1992. *First Snow, Magic Snow*. Sharon McGinley-Nally. New York: Four Winds. 6–9 yrs.

Cecil, Laura. 1995. *The Frog Princess*. Illus. Emma Chichester Clark. New York: Greenwillow. 5–9 yrs.

Claverie, Jean. (Reteller). 1989. *The Three Little Pigs*. Illus. Jean Claverie. New York: North-South. 3–10 yrs.

Coady, C. (Reteller). 1992. *Little Red Riding Hood*. Illus. C. Coady. New York: Dutton. 7–11 yrs.

Compton, Joanne. 1994. *Ashpet: An Appalachian Tale*. Illus. by Kenn Compton. New York: Holiday. 5–8 yrs.

———. 1995. *Sody Sallyratus*. Illus. Kenn Compton. New York: Holt. 5–10 yrs.

Cook, Joel. 1993. *The Rats' Daughter*. Lanham, Md.: Caroline. 5–7 yrs.

Craig, J. 1986. *The Three Wishes*. Illus. Y. Salzman. New York: Scholastic. 7–10 yrs.

Croll, Carolyn. (Adapter). 1989. *The Little Snowgirl: An Old Russian Tale*. Illus. Carolyn Croll. New York: Putnam/Whitebird. 4–8 yrs.

———. 1991. *The Three Brothers: A German Folktale*. Illus. Carolyn Croll. New York: Putnam/Whitebird. 4–8 yrs.

Czernecki, Stefan, & Timothy Rhodes. 1993. *The Singing Snake*. Illus. Stefan Czernecki. New York: Hyperion. 5–7 yrs.

de Christopher, Marlowe. 1991. *Greencoat and the Swanboy*. Illus. Marlowe de Christopher. New York: Philomel. 4–10 yrs.

DeFelice, Cynthia, & Mary DeMarsh. 1995. *Three Perfect Peaches: A French Folktale*. Illus. Irene Trivas. New York: Orchard/Jackson. 5–9 yrs.

de Gerez, Tree. 1994. *When Bear Came Down from the Sky*. Illus. by Lisa Desimini. New York: Viking. 5–8 yrs.

Delamare, David. 1993. *Cinderella*. New York: Green Tiger. 5–8 yrs.

De la Mare, Walter. 1992. *The Turnip*. Illus. Kevin Hawkes. Boston: Godine. 5–9 yrs.

Demi. 1994. *The Firebird*. New York: Holt. 5–8 yrs.

Denise, Christopher. 1994. *The Fool of the World and the Flying Ship: A Russian Folktale from the Skazki of Polevoi*. New York: Philomel. 5–8 yrs.

de Paola, Tomie. 1989. *Tony's Bread: An Italian Folktale*. Illus. Tomie de Paola. New York: Putnam/Whitebird. 4–6 yrs.

———. 1994. *Christopher: The Holy Giant*. New York: Holiday. 5–8 yrs.

Deuchar, Ian. 1989. *The Prince and the Mermaid*. Illus. Ian Deuchar. New York: Dial. 4–8 yrs.

Dodson, B. 1979. *Lazy Jack*. Mahwah, N.J.: Troll. 6–9 yrs.

Donaldson, Julia. 1993. *A Squash and a Squeeze*. Illus. Axel Scheffler. New York: McElderry. 5–8 yrs.

Dugin, Andrej. (Adapter). 1993. *Dragon Feathers*. Illus. A. Dugin & Olga Dugin. Charlottesville, Va.: Thomasson-Grant. 9–12 yrs.

Dupre, Judith. 1993. *The Mouse Bride: A Mayan Folk Tale*. Illus. Fabricio Vanden Broeck. New York: Knopf. 5–8 yrs. *Umbrella series*.

Easton, S. 1991. *The Bremen Town Musicians*. Illus. M. Corcoran. Kansas City, Mo.: Andrews & McMeel. 5–9 yrs.

Emberley, Rebecca. 1995. *Three Cool Kids*. Boston: Little, Brown. 5–9 yrs.

Esterl, A. 1991. *The Fine, Round Cake*. Illus. A. Dugin & O. Dugin. New York: Four Winds. 5–8 yrs.

Evans, E. 1990. *Bremen Town Musicians*. Illus. J. Boddy. Morris Plains, N.J.: Unicorn. 5–9 yrs.

Falconer, E. Illus. 1990. *The House That Jack Built*. Nashville, Tenn.: Ideals. 5–9 yrs.

French, Vivian. 1993. *Why the Sea Is Salt*. Illus. Patrice Aggs. Cambridge, Mass.: Candlewick. 5–9 yrs.

———. 1995. *Red Hen and Sly Fox*. Illus. Sally Hobson. New York: Simon & Schuster. 5–9 yrs.

Gabler, Mirko. 1994. *Tall, Wide, and Sharp-Eye: A Czech Folktale*. New York: Holt. 5–8 yrs.

Gates, Frieda. 1994. *Owl Eyes*. Illus. by Yoshi Miyake. New York: Lothrop, Lee & Shepard. 5–8 yrs.

Gershator, Phillis. 1994. *Tukama Tootles the Flute: A Tale from the Antilles*. Illus. Synthia Saint James. New York: Orchard/Jackson. 5–8 yrs.

Ginsburg, Mirra. 1994. *The King Who Tried to Fry an Egg on His Head*. Illus. Will Hillenbrand. New York: Macmillan. 5–8 yrs.

Goldilocks and the Three Bears: A Peek-through-the-Window Book. Illus. Penny Ives. New York: Putnam. 1992. 3–6 yrs.

Goodall, J. 1990. *Puss in Boots*. New York: McElderry. 6–9 yrs.

Gordon, R. 1993. *Feather*. Illus. L. Dabocovich. New York: Macmillan. 5–9 yrs.

Greaves, Margaret. (Reteller). 1990. *Tattercoats*. Illus. Margaret Chamberlain. New York: Clarkson N. Potter. 5–10 yrs.

Greene, Carol. 1991. *The Old Ladies Who Liked Cats*. Illus. Loretta Krupinski. New York: HarperCollins. 6–10 yrs.

Greene, Jacqueline Dembar. 1992. *What His Father Did*. Illus. John O'Brien. Boston: Houghton Mifflin. 5–9 yrs.

Greenway, J. (Reteller). 1991. *The Three Billy Goats Gruff*. Illus. L. Lustig. Kansas City, Mo.: Andrews & McMeel. 5–9 yrs.

Gregory, Valiska. 1992. *Through the Mickle Woods*. Illus. Barry Moser. Boston: Little, Brown. 8–12 yrs.

Grimm, J. & W. (Reteller F. Pavel). 1961. *The Elves and the Shoemaker*. Illus. J. Hewitt. New York: Holt, Rinehart, & Winston. 5–9 yrs.

———. 1967. *The Elves and the Shoemaker*. Illus. K. Brandt. River Grove, Ill.: Follett. 5–9 yrs.

———. (Trans. E. Crawford). 1983. *Little Red Cap*. Illus. L. Zwergwer. New York: Morrow. 5–9 yrs.

———. (Reteller Alison Sage). 1990. *Rumpelstiltskin*. Illus. Gennady Spirin. New York: Dial. 6–11 yrs.

———. (Trans. Elizabeth D. Crawford). 1991. *Hansel and Gretel*. Illus. Lisbeth Zwerger. New York: Scholastic/Blue Ribbon. 6–10 yrs.

———. (Trans. and ad. Anthea Bell). 1992. *Jack in Luck*. Illus. by Eve Tharlet. Saxonville, Mass.: Picture Book Studio/Michael Neugebauer. 4–8 yrs.

———. 1992. *Snow White and Red Rose*. Illus. G. Spirin. New York: Philomel. 6–9 yrs.

———. (Trans. Anthea Bell). 1993. *Rumpelstiltskin: A Fairy Tale*. Illus. Bernadette Watts. New York: North-South. 5–9 yrs.

———. 1993. *Iron Hans*. Illus. M. Heyer. New York: Viking. 6–10 yrs.

———. (Reteller and illus. Mitsumasa Anno). 1993. *Anno's Twice Told Tales: The Fisherman and His Wife and The Four Clever Brothers*. New York: Philomel.

———. 1994. *Grimm's Fairy Tales*. Illus. Amanda Harvey. New York: Holt. 5–8 yrs. *Little Classics series*.

———. (Trans. Anthea Bell). 1995. *The Sleeping Beauty: A Fairy Tale*. Illus. Monika Laimgruber. New York: North-South. 5–9 yrs.

Grimm, Jakob Ludwig Karl. (Trans. Anthea Bell). 1995. *The Seven Ravens*. Illus. Henrietta Sauvant. New York: North-South. 5–7 yrs.

Haley, Gail E. (Reteller). 1991. *Puss in Boots*. Illus. Gail E. Haley. New York: Dutton. 4–10 yrs.

Haley, Gail E. 1990. *Sea Tale*. Illus. Gail E. Haley. New York: Dutton. 5–8 yrs.

———. 1992. *Mountain Jack Tales*. New York: Dutton. 10–12 yrs.

———. 1993. *Dream Peddler*. New York: Dutton. 6–9 yrs.

Hansard, Peter. 1995. *Jig, Fig, and Mrs. Pig*. Illus. Francesca Martin. Cambridge, Mass.: Candlewick. 5–9 yrs.

Hastings, S. 1993. *The Firebird*. Illus. R. Cartwright. Cambridge, Mass.: Candlewick. 7–10 yrs.

Haviland, Virginia. (Reteller). 1990. *The Talking Pot: A Danish Folktale*. Illus. Melissa Sweet. Boston: Little, Brown/Joy. 4–8 yrs.

Hilbert, M. 1978. *The Golden Goose*. Illus. M. Santa. River Grove, Ill.: Follett. 5–8 yrs.

Hobson, Sally. 1994. *Chicken Little*. New York: Simon & Schuster. 5–8 yrs.

Hodges, Margaret. (Compiler and reteller). 1991. *Hauntings: Ghosts and Ghouls from around the World*. Illus. David Wenzel. Boston: Little, Brown. 8–12 yrs.

———. 1993. *The Hero of Bremen*. Illus. Charles Mikolaycak. New York: Holiday. 5–8 yrs.

Huck, Charlotte. (Reteller). 1989. *Princess Furball*. Illus. Anita Lobel. New York: Greenwillow. 4–6 yrs.

Hunter, C. W. (Reteller). 1992. *The Green Gourd: A North Carolina Folktale*. Illus. Tony Griego. New York: Putnam/Whitebird. 4–8 yrs.

Hunter, Mollie. 1994. *Gilly Martin the Fox*. Illus. Dennis McDermott. New York: Hyperion. 5–8 yrs.

Isadora, Rachel. (Adapter). 1989. *The Princess and the Frog*. Illus. Rachel Isadora. New York: Greenwillow. 4–7 yrs.

Isadora, Rachel. 1994. *Firebird*. New York: Putnam. 5–8 yrs.

Jackson, Ellen. 1994. *Cinder Edna*. Illus. Kevin O'Malley. New York: Lothrop, Lee & Shepard. 6–10 yrs.

Jacobs, Joseph. (Compiler and editor). 1989. *Tattercoats*. Illus. Margot Tomes. New York: Putnam. 5–9 yrs.

Jarrell, R. (Trans.). 1980. *The Fisherman and His Wife*. New York: Farrar, Straus & Giroux. 6–10 yrs.

Johnston, Tony. 1992. *The Cowboy and the Black-Eyed Pea*. Illus. Warren Ludwig. New York: Putnam. 4–8 yrs.

Karlin, Barbara. (Reteller). 1989. *Cinderella*. Illus. James Marshall. Boston: Little, Brown. 5–8 yrs.

Kellogg, Steven. (Reteller). 1991. *Jack and the Beanstalk*. Illus. Steven Kellogg. New York: Morrow. 6+ yrs.

Kimmel, Eric A. (Reteller). 1990. *Nanny Goat and the Seven Little Kids*. Illus. Janet Stevens. New York: Holiday. 5–9 yrs.

———. 1991. *Bearhead: A Russian Folktale*. Illus. Charles Mikolaycak. New York: Holiday. 4–8 yrs.

———. 1992. *The Old Woman and Her Pig*. New York: Holiday. 5–9 yrs.

———. 1992. *The Tale of Aladdin and the Wonderful Lamp: A Story of the Arabian Nights*. New York: Holiday. 8–12 yrs.

———. (Reteller). 1992. *Boots and His Brothers: A Norwegian Tale*. Illus. by Kimberly Bulcken Root. New York: Holiday. 6–10 yrs.

———. 1993. *Asher and the Capmakers: A Hanukkah Story*. Illus. W. Hillenbrand. New York: Holiday. 7–12 yrs.

———. 1993. *The Gingerbread Man*. Illus. Megan Lloyd. New York: Holiday. 4–8 yrs.

———. 1993. *Three Sacks of Truth: A Story from France*. Illus. Robert Rayevsky. New York: Holiday. 6–9 yrs.

———. 1994. *Iron John: Adapted from the Brothers Grimm*. Illus. by Trina Schart Hyman. New York: Holiday. 9–11 yrs.

———. 1994. *I-Know-Not-What, I-Know-Not-Where: A Russian Tale*. Illus. by Robert Sauber. New York: Holiday. 9–11 yrs.

———. 1994. *The Three Princes: A Tale from the Middle East*. Illus. by Leonard Everett Fisher. New York: Holiday. 6–9 yrs.

Kirstein, Lincoln. (Reteller). 1992. *Puss in Boots*. Illus. Alain Vaes. Boston: Little, Brown. 5–10 yrs.

Krensky, Stephen. 1991. *The Missing Mother Goose*. Illus. Chris Demarest. New York: Doubleday. 5–8 yrs. (Mother Goose)

Kurtz, Jane. 1994. *Fire on the Mountain*. Illus. E. B. Lewis. New York: Simon & Schuster. 5–8 yrs.

———. (Ad.). 1996. *Miro in the Kingdom of the Sun*. Illus. David Frampton. Boston: Houghton Mifflin. 6–10 yrs.

Langley, Jonathan. (Reteller). 1992. *Rumpelstiltskin*. Illus. Jonathan Langley. New York: HarperCollins. 4–8 yrs.

———. 1993. *Goldilocks and the Three Bears*. New York: HarperCollins. 5–9 yrs.

Lewis, N. (Trans.) 1989. *The Frog Prince*. Illus. B. Schroeder. New York: North-South. 6–10 yrs.

Lewis, J. Patrick. 1994. *The Frog Princess: A Russian Folktale*. Illus. by Gennady Spirin. New York: Dial. 5–8 yrs.

Littledale, F. 1991. *The Elves and the Shoemaker*. New York: Scholastic. 5–9 yrs.

Litzinger, Rosanne. 1993. *The Old Woman and Her Pig: An Old English Tale*. Orlando, Fla.: Harcourt Brace Jovanovich. 5–9 yrs.

Lodge, Bernard. 1993. *Prince Ivan and the Firebird: A Russian Folk Tale*. Danvers, Mass.: Whispering. 32 pp. 5–9 yrs.

Lynch, P. J. 1992. *East O' the Sun and West O' the Moon*. Cambridge, Mass.: Candlewick. 8–12 yrs.

MacGill-Callahan, Sheila. 1995. *When Solomon Was King*. Illus. Stephen T. Johnson. New York: Dial. 5–10 yrs.

Maddern, Eric. 1993. *Rainbow Bird: An Aboriginal Folktale from Northern Australia*. Boston: Little, Brown. 5–9 yrs. (pourquoi)

Malkovych, Ivan. (Trans. Motria Onyschuk). 1995. *The Cat and the Rooster: A Ukrainian Folktale*. Illus. Kost' Lavro. New York: Knopf. 5–10 yrs.

Mantinband, G. 1993. *Three Clever Mice*. Illus. M. Gourbault. New York: Greenwillow. 5–9 yrs.

Marshall, James. (Reteller). 1990. *Hansel and Gretel*. Illus. James Marshall. New York: Dial. 5–9 yrs.

Martin, Claire. (Reteller). 1992. *Boots and the Glass Mountain*. Illus. Gennady Spirin. New York: Dial. 6–10 yrs.

Mathews, Judith, & Fay Robinson. 1994. *Nathaniel Willy, Scared Silly*. Illus. by Alexi Natchev. New York: Bradbury. 5–8 yrs.

Mayer, M. 1980. *East of the Sun & West of the Moon*. New York: Aladin. 8–12 yrs.

Mayer, Marianna. 1989. *The Prince and the Princess: A Bohemian Fairy Tale*. Illus. Jacqueline Rogers. New York: Bantam Skylark. 8–12 yrs.

———. (Reteller). 1989. *Twelve Dancing Princesses*. Illus. K. Y. Craft. New York: Morrow. 8–12 yrs. (est.). Notable 1989 Children's Trade Books in the Field of Social Studies.

———. 1994. *Baba Yaga and Vasilisa the Brave*. Illus. K. Y. Craft. New York: Morrow. 6–9 yrs.

Mayhew, James. 1993. *Koshka's Tales: Stories from Russia*. New York: Kingfisher. 9–12 yrs. (Collection).

McAllister, Angela. 1990. *When the Ark Was Full*. Illus. Michaela Bloomfield. New York: Dutton. 4–7. pourquoi.

———. 1991. *The Enchanted Flute*. Illus. Margaret Chamberlain. New York: Delacorte. 4–8 yrs.

McCaughrean, Geraldine. 1993. *Greek Myths*. Illus. Emma Chichester Clark. New York: McElderry. 10–13 yrs.

Meeker, Clare Hodgson. 1994. *A Tale of Two Rice Birds: A Folktale from Thailand*. Illus. Christine Lamb. Seattle: Sasquatch. 5–8 yrs.

Mills, Lauren. 1993. *Tatterhood and the Hobgoblins: A Norwegian Folktale*. Boston: Little, Brown. 9–12 yrs.

Minter, Frances. *Cinder-Elly*. Illus. G. Brian Karas. New York: Viking. 5–10 yrs.

Mollel, Tololwa M. 1993. *The King and the Tortoise*. Illus. Kathy Blankley. New York: Clarion. 5–9 yrs.

Montresor, Beni. 1989. *The Witches of Venice*. Illus. Beni Montresor. New York: Doubleday. 4–8 yrs.

Moodie, Fiona. 1993. *The Boy and the Giants*. Farrar, New York: Straus & Giroux. 5–9 yrs.

Morgan, Pierr. 1990. *The Turnip: An Old Russian Folktale*. Illus. Pierr Morgan. New York: Philomel. 5–9 yrs.

Morris, Ann. (Reteller). 1989. *The Cinderella Rebus Book*. Illus. LjilJana Rylands. New York: Orchard. 5–9 yrs.

Mosel, A. 1972. *The Funny Little Woman*. New York: Dutton. 6–9 yrs.

Moser, Barry. 1994. *Tucker Pfeffercorn: An Old Story Retold*. Boston: Little, Brown. 5–8 yrs.

Murphy, Claire Rudolf. 1993. *The Prince and the Salmon People*. Illus. Duane Pasco. New York: Rizzoli. 9–12 yrs.

Nesbit, E. 1989. *Melisande*. Illus. P. J. Lynch. San Diego: Harcourt Brace Jovanovich. 6–10 yrs.

Nimmo, Jenny. 1993. *The Witches and the Singing Mice*. Illus. Angela Barrett. New York: Dial. 5–9 yrs.

Olson, Arielle North. 1992. *Noah's Cats and the Devil's Fire*. Illus. Barry Moser. New York: Orchard. 5–9 yrs.

Oppenheim, Joanne. 1993. *The Christmas Witch: An Italian Legend*. Illus. Annie Mitra. New York: Bantam. 5–8 yrs. Bank Street Ready-to-Read series.

Orgel, Doris, & Ellen Schecter. 1994. *The Flower of Sheba*. Illus. Laura Kelly. New York: Bantam. 5–8 yrs. Bank Street Ready-to-Read series.

Ormerod, Jan, & David Lloyd. (Retellers). 1990. *The Frog Prince*. Illus. Jan Ormerod. New York: Lothrop, Lee & Shepard. 5–8 yrs.

Page, P. (Reteller). 1992. *The Traveling Musicians of Bremen*. Illus. K. Denton. Boston: Little, Brown. 5–9 yrs.

Page, P. K. (Reteller). 1992. *The Traveling Musicians of Bremen*. Illus. Kady MacDonald Denton. Boston: Little, Brown/Joy. 4–10 yrs.

Peppe, R. 1985. *The House That Jack Built*. Delacorte. 5–9 yrs.

Percy, Graham. (Illus.). 1992. *The Cock, the Mouse, and the Little Red Hen*. Cambridge, Mass.: Candlewick. 5–9 yrs.

Perrault, Charles. 1990. *Puss in Boots*. Illus. Fred Marcellino. New York: Farrar, Straus & Giroux. 7–10 yrs.

———. 1990. *Cinderella*. New York: Puffin. 5–9 yrs.

———. (Trans. Neil Philip and Nicoletta Simborowski). 1993. *The Complete Fairy Tales of Charles Perrault*. Illus. Sally Holmes. New York: Clarion. 9–12 yrs.

Plume. I. 1991. *Shoemaker and Elves*. Harbrace. 5–9 yrs.

Pollock, Penny. (Adapter). 1996. *The Turkey Girl: A Zuni Cinderella Story*. Illus. Ed Young. Boston: Little, Brown. 5–8 yrs.

Poole, J. 1991. *Snow White*. Illus. A. Barrett. New York: Knopf. 6–10 yrs.

Porter, Wesley. (Reteller). 1979. *The Hare, the Elephant, and the Hippo*. Illus. J. Behr. New York: Westport Group Book. 6–9 yrs.

Prose, Francine. 1996. *DybJuk: A Story Made in Heaven.* Illus. Mark Podwal. New York: Greenwillow. 5–8 yrs.

Rayevsky, Inna. (Reteller). 1990. *The Talking Tree: An Old Italian Tale.* Illus. Robert Rayevsky. New York: Putnam's. 5–10 yrs.

Richardson, I. M. (Ed.) 1988. *The Fisherman and His Wife.* Illus. G. Troll. New York: Lippincott. 6–9 yrs.

Riggio, Anita. 1994. *Beware the Brindlebeast.* Honesdale, Pa.: Boyds. 5–8 yrs.

Ross, T. 1990. *Mrs. Goat and Her Seven Little Kids.* New York: Atheneum. 5–9 yrs.

Ross, Tony. 1994. *Hansel and Gretel.* New York: Overlook. 5–8 yrs.

Rothenberg, Joan. 1995. *Yettele's Feathers.* New York: Hyperion. 5–10 yrs.

Rounds, Glen. 1992. *Three Little Pigs and the Big Bad Wolf.* Illus. Glen Rounds. New York: Holiday. 3–8 yrs.

———. (Reteller). 1993. *The Three Billy Goats Gruff.* Illus. Glen Rounds. New York: Holiday. 5–9 yrs.

Rowland, J. (Reteller). 1989. *The Elves and the Shoemaker.* Chicago: Calico. 5–9 yrs.

Sanfield, Steve. 1995. *Strudel, Strudel, Strudel.* Illus. Emily Lisker. New York: Orchard. 5–10 yrs.

San Souci, Robert D. (Reteller). 1988. *The Six Swans.* Illus. Daniel San Souci. New York: Simon & Schuster. 4–8 yrs.

———. 1990. *The White Cat: An Old French Fairy Tale.* Illus. Gennady Spirin. New York: Orchard. 4–8 yrs.

———. 1992. *The Tsar's Promise: A Russian Tale.* Illus. Lauren Mills. New York: Philomel. 5–10 yrs.

———. 1994. *The Hobyahs.* Illus. Alexi Natchev. New York: Doubleday. 7–10 yrs.

Sawyer, Ruth. 1994. *The Remarkable Christmas of the Cobbler's Sons.* Illus. Barbara Cooney. New York: Viking. 5–8 yrs.

Schaefer, Carole. 1994. *Lexa under the Midsummer Sky.* Illus. Pat Geddes. New York: Putnam/Whitebird. 5–8 yrs.

Schemer, Ursel. (Trans. Amy Gelman). 1990. *The Giant Apple.* Illus. Silke Brix-Henker. Minneapolis, Minn.: Carolrhoda. 6–10 yrs.

Schenk de Regniers, Beatrice. 1994. *Little Sister and the Month Brothers.* Illus. Margot Tomes. New York: Lothrop, Lee & Shepard. 5–8 yrs.

Schroeder, Alan. 1994. *The Stone Lion.* Illus. Todd L. W. Doney. Old Tappan, N.J.: Scribners. 5–8 yrs.

Shepard, Aaron. 1995. *The Gifts of Wali Dad: A Tale of India and Pakistan.* Illus. Daniel San Souci. New York: Atheneum. 5–10 yrs.

Shorto, R. 1990. *Cinderella, The Untold Story.* Illus. T. Lewis. Secaucus, N.J.: Birch Lane Press/Carol. 6–10 yrs.

Shulevitz, Uri. 1979. *The Treasure.* New York: Farrar, Straus & Giroux. 5–9 yrs.

———. 1993. *The Secret Room.* New York: Farrar, Straus & Giroux. 5–8 yrs.

———. (Adapter). 1995. *The Golden Goose.* Illus. by Uri Shulevitz. New York: Farrar, Straus & Giroux. 4–8 yrs.

Singer, Marilyn. 1995. *The Maiden on the Moor.* Illus. Troy Howell. New York: Morrow. 5–10 yrs.

Stanley, Diane. 1990. *Fortune.* Illus. Diane Stanley. New York: Morrow. 6–11 yrs.

———. 1995. *Petrosinella: A Neapolitan Rapunzel.* New York: Dial. 5–10 yrs. (Reissue, 1981, Warne).

Steele, Flora Annie. 1976. *Tattercoats.* New York: Bradbury. 5–9 yrs.

Stevens, Janet. (Reteller). 1992. *The Bremen Town Musicians.* Illus. Janet Stevens. New York: Holiday. 4–8 yrs.

Stevenson, S. 1992. *The Princess and the Pea.* New York: Doubleday. 5–9 yrs.

Stewig, John Warren. (Reteller). 1991. *Stone Soup.* Illus. Margot Tomes. New York: Holiday. 4–8 yrs.

Stow, J. 1992. *The House That Jack Built.* New York: Dial. 5–9 yrs.

Strangis, Joel. 1993. *Grandfather's Rock: An Italian Folktale.* Illus. Ruth Gamper. Burlington, Mass.: Houghton Mifflin. 5–8 yrs.

Thomson, Peggy. (Reteller). 1992. *The Brave Little Tailor.* Illus. James Warhola. New York: Simon & Schuster. 6–10 yrs.

Wegman, William. 1993. *Cinderella.* New York: Hyperion. 5–9 yrs.

Wells, Rosemary. 1990. *The Little Lame Prince.* Illus. Rosemary Wells. New York: Dial. 4–8 yrs.

Wilde, Oscar. 1989. *The Happy Prince.* Illus. Ed Young. New York: Simon & Schuster. 6–8 yrs.

Wilhelm, H. 1992. *The Bremen Town Musicians.* New York: Scholastic. 5–9 yrs.

Willard, Nancy. (Reteller). 1992. *Beauty and the Beast.* Illus. Barry Moser. San Diego: Harcourt Brace Jovanovich. 7–11 yrs.

Wilson, Barbara Ker. 1993. *Wishbones.* New York: Bradbury. 5–9 yrs.

Winthrop, Elizabeth. (Adapter). 1991. *Vasilissa the Beautiful: A Russian Folktale.* Illus. Alexander Koshkin. New York: HarperCollins. 6–11 yrs.

Wise, William. (Reteller). 1990. *The Black Falcon: A Tale from the Decameron.* Illus. Gillian Barlow. New York: Philomel. 6–10 yrs.

Wisniewski, David. 1990. *Elfwyn's Saga.* Illus. David Wisniewski. New York: Lothrop, Lee & Shepard. 6–10 yrs.

Wolkstein, Diane. (Reteller). 1991. *Oom Razoom; or, Go I Know Not Where, Bring Back I Know Not What: A Russian Tale.* Illus. Dennis McDermott. New York: Morrow. 4–8 yrs.

Yolen, Jane. 1991. *Wings.* Illus. D. Nolan. San Diego: Harcourt Brace Jovanovich. 5–9 yrs.

Zemach, H. 1963. *The Three Sillies.* Illus. M. Zemach. New York: Holt, Rinehart & Winston. 5–9 yrs.

Zimmerman, H. Werner. 1989. *Henny Penny.* Illus. H. Werner Zimmerman. New York: Scholastic. 4–8 yrs.

FABLES

Aesop. 1947. *Aesop's Fables.* Illus. F. Kredel. New York: Grosset & Dunlap. 6–11 yrs.

———. 1989. *Aesop's Fables.* Illus. L. Zwerger. Saxonville, Mass.: Picture Book Studio. 6–11 yrs.

Aesop's Fables. Illus. R. Rayevsky. New York: Morrow. 6–11 yrs.

Aliki. 1994. *The Gods and Goddesses of Olympus.* New York: HarperCollins. 5–8 yrs.

Anno, Mitsumasa. (Reteller). 1989. *Anno's Aesop: A Book of Fables by Aesop and Mr. Fox.* New York: Orchard. 5–11 yrs.

Babbitt, E. C. (Reteller). 1950. *Jataka Tales.* Illus. E. Young. New York: Appleton Century Crofts. 8–12 yrs.

Barnett, C. 1990. *Lion and the Mouse.* New York: NTC Publishers Group. 7–10 yrs.

Branston, Brian. 1994. *Gods and Heroes from Viking Mythology.* Illus. by Giovanni Caselli. New York: Bedrick. 10–13 yrs. *World Mythology series.*

Brown, M. 1961. *Once a Mouse.* New York: Scribners. 5–10 yrs.

Clark, Margaret. (Reteller). 1990. *The Best of Aesop's Fables.* Illus. Charlotte Voake. Boston: Little, Brown/Joy. 4–10 yrs.

Climo, Shirley. 1994. *Stolen Thunder: A Norse Myth.* Illus. Alexander Koshkin. New York: Clarion. 6–9 yrs.

Craig, Helen. (Reteller). 1992. *The Town Mouse and the Country Mouse.* Illus. Helen Craig. Cambridge, Mass.: Candlewick. 4–8 yrs.

Gaer, Joseph. 1955. *The Fables of India.* Illus. R. Monk. Boston: Little, Brown. 6–11 yrs.

Gatti, Anne. (Reteller). 1992. *Aesop's Fables.* Illus. Safaya Salter. San Diego: Harcourt Brace Jovanovich/Gulliver. 6–11 yrs.

Heins, Ethel. 1995. *The Cat and the Cook and Other Fables of Krylov.* Illus. Anita Lobel. New York: Greenwillow. 5–10 yrs.

Kherdian, David. (Reteller). 1992. *Feathers and Tails: Animal Fables from around the World.* Illus. Nonny Hogrogian. New York: Philomel. 6–11 yrs.

La Fontaine, J. 1982. *The Hare and the Tortoise.* Illus. B. Wildsmith. Oxford: Oxford University Press. 6–10 yrs.

———. 1986. *The Lion and the Rat.* Illus. B. Wildsmith. Oxford: Oxford University Press. 6–10 yrs.

McDonald, Suse, & Bill Oakes. (Retellers). 1990. *Once Upon Another: The Tortoise and the Hare.* Illus. Suse McDonald and Bill Oakes. New York: Dial. 5–8 yrs.

Paxton, Tom. (Reteller). 1991. *Androcles and the Lion, and Other Aesop's Fables.* Illus. Robert Rayevsky. New York: Morrow. 4–10 yrs. and up.

———. 1990. *Belling the Cat, and Other Aesop's Fables.* Illus. Robert Rayevsky. New York: Morrow. 4–11 yrs.

Rockwell, Anne. (Adapter). 1996. *The One-Eyed Giant and Other Monsters from the Greek Myth.* Illus. by Anne Rockwell. New York: Greenwillow. 7–9 yrs.

Ross, Anne. 1994. *Druids, Gods, and Heroes from Celtic Mythology.* Illus. Roger Garland and John Sibbick. New York: Bedrick, 10–13 yrs. *World Mythology series.*

Thuswaldner, Werner. 1994. *Aesop's Fables.* Illus. Gisela Durr. New York: North-South. 5–8 yrs.

Townsend, G. F. (Trans.). 1968. *Aesop's Fables.* New York: Doubleday. 7–10 yrs.

Wallis, Diz. (Reteller). 1991. *Something Nasty in the Cabbages.* Illus. Diz Wallis. Honesdale, Pa.: Boyds Mills Press/Caroline. 6–11 yrs.

Watts, Bernadette. (Reteller). 1992. *The Wind and the Sun: An Aesop Fable.* Illus. Bernadette Watts. New York: North-South. 5–8 yrs.

FOLK SONGS AND BALLADS

Carmer, C. (Collector). 1949. *America Sings.* New York: Knopf.

Chase, Richard. 1956. *American Folk Tales and Songs.* New York: New American.

Cohn, A. (Compiler). 1993. *From Sea to Shining Sea: A Treasury of American Folklore and Folk Songs.* Illus. eleven Caldecott Medal and four Caldecott Honor Book artists. New York: Scholastic. 7–14 yrs.

The Friendly Beasts: A Traditional Christmas Carol. 1991. Illus. Sarah Chamberlain. New York: Dutton. 3–8 yrs.

Goode, Diane. 1992. *Diane Goode's Book of Silly Stories and Songs.* New York: Dutton. 5–10 yrs. (sillies, noodleheads; songs).

Hart, Jane. 1989. *Singing Bee! A Collection of Favorite Children's Songs.* Illus. Anita Lobel. New York: Lothrop, Lee & Shepard. 4–12 yrs.

Headington, C. (Compiler). 1990. *Sweet Sleep: A Collection of Lullabies, Poems and Cradle Songs.* New York: Potter/Random House.

Krull, Kathleen. 1991. *I Know an Old Lady Who Swallowed a Fly.* Illus. Glen Rounds. New York: Holiday. 4–7 yrs.

_____. 1992. *Gonna Sing My Head Off*. Illus. A. Garns. New York: Knopf. 6–10 yrs.

Manson, Christopher. (Reteller). 1992. *A Farmyard Song: An Old Rhyme*. Illus. Christopher Manson. New York: North-South. 2–6 yrs.

McNally, Darcie. (Adapter). 1991. *In a Cabin in a Wood*. Illus. Robin Michal Koontz. New York: Cobblehill. 4–8 yrs.

Metropolitan Museum of Art, in association with the Buffalo Bill Historical Center. 1991. *Songs of the Wild West*. New York: Metropolitan Museum of Art and Simon & Schuster. 10–16 yrs.

Moser, Barry. (Reteller). 1992. *Polly Vaughn: A Traditional British Ballad*. Illus. Barry Moser. Boston: Little, Brown. 10–12 yrs.

Raffi. 1989. *Tingalayo*. Illus. K. Duke. New York: Crown. 5–10.

_____. 1990. *Baby Beluga*. Illus. A. Wolff. New York: Crown. 5–10 yrs.

Richardson, Jean. 1991. *Stephen's Feast*. Illus. Alice Englander. Boston: Little, Brown. 4–8 yrs.

Rosen, Michael. (Reteller). 1990. *Little Rabbit Foo Foo*. Illus. Arthur Robins. New York: Simon & Schuster. 4–8 yrs.

Schwartz, A. (Ed.) 1992. *And the Green Grass Grew All Around: Folk Poetry from Everyone*. Illus. S. Truesdell. New York: HarperCollins. 8–13 yrs.

Simon, Paul. 1991. *At the Zoo*. Illus. Valerie Michaut. New York: Doubleday/Bryon Preiss. 4–7 yrs.

Slavin, Bill. 1992. *The Cat Came Back: A Traditional Song*. Illus. Bill Slavin. Morton Grove, Ill.: Whitman. 6–11 yrs.

Sweet, Melissa. (Adapter). 1992. *Fiddle-I-Fee: A Farmyard Song for the Very Young*. Boston: Illus. Melissa Sweet. Boston: Little, Brown/Joy. 3–6 yrs.

Watson, Wendy. 1990. *Frog Went a-Courting*. Illus. Wendy Watson. New York: Lothrop, Lee & Shepard. 4–7 yrs.

Westcott, Nadine Bernard. (Adapter). 1989. *Skip to My Lou*. Illus. Nadine Bernard Westcott. Boston: Little, Brown/Joy. 3–7 yrs.

MYTHS

Alexander, R. L. 1947. *Famous Myths of the Golden Age*. New York: Random House. 9–12 yrs.

Al-Saleh, Khairat. 1995. *Fabled Cities, Princes, and Jinn from Arab Myths and Legends*. Illus. Rashad N. Salim. New York: Bedrick. 10–14 yrs. *World Mythology series*.

Climo, Shirley. 1995. *Atalanta's Race: A Greek Myth*. Illus. Alexander Koshkin. New York: Clarion. 5–9 yrs.

Fisher, Leonard Everett. 1990. *Jason and the Golden Fleece*. Illus. Leonard Everett Fisher. New York: Holiday. 7–10 yrs.

_____. 1991. *Cyclops*. Illus. Leonard Everett Fisher. New York: Holiday. 7–11 yrs.

Hutton, Warwick. 1993. *Perseus*. New York: McElderry. 7–10 yrs.

_____. 1994. *Persephone*. New York: McElderry. 5–8 yrs.

Mikolaycak, Charles. 1992. *Orpheus*. San Diego: Harcourt Brace.

Orgel, Doris. 1994. *Ariadne, Awake!* Illus. by Barry Moser. New York: Viking. 9–11 yrs.

Osborne, Mary Pope. (Reteller). 1989. *Favorite Greek Myths*. Illus. Troy Howell. New York: Scholastic. 8–12 yrs.

Pilling, A. 1993. *Realms of Gold: Myths and Legends from around the World*. Illus. K. M. Denton. New York: Kingfisher. 10–16 yrs.

Shepard, Aaron. 1993. *The Legend of Slappy Hooper: An American Tall Tale*. Illus. by Toni Goffe. New York: Scribner. 6–9 yrs.

Te Kanawa, Kiri. 1989. *Land of the Long White Cloud: Maori Myths, Tales and Legends*. Illus. Michael Foreman. Boston: Little, Brown/Arcade. 9–13 yrs.

Waldherr, Kris. 1993. *Persephone and the Pomegranate: A Myth from Greece*. New York: Dial. 7–10 yrs.

Williams, Marcia. 1992. *Greek Myths for Young Children*. Illus. Marcia Williams. Cambridge, Mass.: Candlewick. 9–12 yrs.

LEGENDS

de Paola, Tomie. 1993. *The Legend of the Persian Carpet*. Illus. Claire Ewart. New York: Putnam/Whitebird. 6–9 yrs.

_____. 1994. *The Legend of the Poinsettia*. New York: Putnam. 7–10 yrs.

Hawkes, Kevin. 1992. *His Royal Buckliness*. Illus. Kevin Hawkes. New York: Lothrop, Lee & Shepard. 6–10 yrs.

Hodges, Margaret. (Reteller). 1984. *Saint George and the Dragon*. Illus. Tina S. Hyman. Boston: Little, Brown. 9–12 yrs.

_____. 1990. *The Kitchen Knight: A Tale of King Arthur*. Illus. Trina Schart Hyman. New York: Holiday. 7–11 yrs.

_____. 1993. *Saint Patrick and the Peddler*. Illus. Paul Brett Johnson. New York: Orchard. 6–9 yrs.

Hodges, Margaret, & Margery Evernden. 1993. *Of Swords and Sorcerers: The Adventures of King Arthur and His Knights*. Illus. David Frampton. New York: Scribner. 10–13 yrs.

Husain, Shahrukh. 1995. *Demons, Gods, and Holy Men from Indian Myths and Legends*. Illus. Durga Prasad Das. New York: Bedrick. 10–14 yrs. *World Mythology series*. 10–13 yrs.

Lagerlof, S. 1990. *The Legend of the Christmas Rose*. New York: Holiday. 7–10 yrs.

Lanier, S. (Ed.) 1989. *The Boy's King Arthur*. New York: Scribner. 9–13 yrs.

Leeson, Robert. 1994. *The Story of Robin Hood*. Illus. by Barbara Lofthouse. New York: Kingfisher. 9–11 yrs.

Lemieux, Michele. 1993. *The Pied Piper of Hamelin*. New York: Morrow. 6–9 yrs.

Lister, R. 1990. *The Legend of King Arthur*. Illus. A. Baker. New York: Doubleday. 9–14 yrs.

Manson, Christopher. (Reteller). 1992. *The Tale of the Marvellous Blue Mouse*. Illus. Christopher Manson. New York: Henry Holt. 7–11 yrs.

Martin, Claire. 1991. *The Race of the Golden Apples*. Illus. Leo and Diane Dillon. New York: Dial. 6–10 yrs.

McCaughrean, Geraldine. 1989. *Saint George and the Dragon*. Illus. Nicki Palin. New York: Doubleday. 6–9 yrs.

Pyle, H. 1946. *The Merry Adventures of Robin Hood of Great Renown in Nottinghamshire*. New York: Scribner. 9–12 yrs.

_____. 1990. *King Arthur and the Magic Sword*. New York: Dial. 9–14 yrs.

Riordan, J. 1982. *Tales of King Authur*. Illus. by V. Ambrus. Skokie, Ill.: Rand McNally. 9–13 yrs.

San Souci, R. D. 1993. *Young Guinevere*. Illus. J. Henterly. New York: Doubleday. 8–12 yrs.

Scott, Bill. (Reteller). 1990. *Many Kinds of Magic: Tales of Mystery, Myth, and Enchantment*. Illus. Lisa Herriman. New York: Viking Penguin. 8–16 yrs.

Small, Terry. 1991. *The Legend of William Tell*. Illus. Terry Small. New York: Bantam/Little Rooster. 5–9 yrs.

Talbott, H. 1991. *King Arthur: The Sword in the Stone*. New York: Morrow. 9–12 yrs.

Wetterer, Margaret K. 1991. *The Boy Who Knew the Language of the Birds*. Illus. by Beth Wright. Minneapolis, Minn.: Carolrhoda. 7–10 yrs.

Williams, Marcia. 1995. *The Adventures of Robin Hood*. Cambridge, Mass.: Candlewick. 7–10 yrs.

Wilson, Barbara Ker. (Reteller). 1990. *The Turtle and the Island: A Folktale from Papua New Guinea*. Illus. Frane Lessac. New York: Lippincott. 6–10 yrs.

TALL TALES

Bowman, J. C. 1937. *Pecos Bill, the Greatest Cowboy of All Time*. Morton Grove, Ill.: Whitman. 9–13 yrs.

Emberley, Barbara. 1994. *The Story of Paul Bunyan*. Illus. by Ed Emberley. New York: Simon & Schuster. 5–8 yrs.

Felton, H. 1968. *True Tall Tales of Stormalong: Sail of the Seven Seas*. Englewood Cliffs, N.J.: Prentice-Hall. 9–12 yrs.

Kellogg, Steven. (Reteller). 1992. *Mike Fink: A Tall Tale*. Illus. Steven Kellogg. New York: Morrow. 5–10 yrs.

Kesey, Ken. 1990. *Little Tricker the Squirrel Meets Big Double the Bear*. Illus. Barry Moser. New York: Viking Penguin. 8–12 yrs.

Malcolmson, A., & D. J. McCormick. 1952. *Mr. Stormalong*. Boston: Houghton Mifflin. 8–12 yrs.

Manes, Stephen. 1990. *Some of the Adventures of Rhode Island Red*. Illus. William Joyce. New York: Lippincott. 8–12 yrs.

Roberts, L. 1964. *South from Hell-fer-Sartin*. Berea, Ky.: Council of Southern Mountains. 10–14 yrs.

San Souci, R. D. 1992. *Larger than Life: The Adventures of American Legendary Heroes*. Illus. A. Glass. New York: Doubleday. 10–13 yrs.

Shay, F. 1930. *Here's Audacity! American Legendary Heroes*. North Stratford, N.H.: Ayer. 12–16 yrs.

Small, T. 1992. *The Legend of Pecos Bill*. New York: Little Rooster. 3–6 yrs.

Stoutenburg, A. 1966. *American Tall Tales*. New York: Viking. 10–13 yrs.

Walker, P. R. 1993. *Big Men, Big Country*. Illus. J. Bernardin. San Diego: Harcourt Brace. 10–13 yrs.

NURSERY RHYMES

Baker, Keith. 1994. *Big Fat Hen*. San Diego: Harcourt.

Bolam, Emily. 1993. *The House That Jack Built*. New York: Dutton. 5–8 yrs.

Craig, Helen. 1993. *I See the Moon, and the Moon Sees Me: Helen Craig's Book of Nursery Rhymes*. New York: HarperCollins/Perlman. 4–7 yrs.

Crane, Walter. Illus. 1993. *Favorite Poems of Childhood*. New York: Green Tiger. 5–8 yrs.

_____. 1995. *Traditional Nursery Rhymes*. New York: Andrews. 5–9 yrs.

Folkard, Charles and various illustrators. 1993. *Rock-a-Bye Rhymes: Four Miniature Nursery Rhyme Books*. San Francisco: Chronicle. 5–8 yrs.

Goode, Diane. 1993. *The Little Books of Nursery Animals*. New York: Dutton. 3–6 yrs.

Hague, Michael. 1993. *Teddy Bear, Teddy Bear: A Classic Action Rhyme*. New York: Morrow. 3–6 yrs.

Hastings, S. 1990. *Miss Mary Mac All Dressed in Black: Tongue Twisters, Jump-Rope Rhymes, and Other Children's Lore from New England*. Little Rock, Ark.: August House. 5–12 yrs.

Lacome, Julie. 1993. *Walking through the Jungle*. Cambridge, Mass.: Candlewick. 3–6 yrs.

Lottridge, Celia Barker. 1994. *Ten Small Tales*. Illus. by Joanne Fitzgerald. New York: McElderry. 5–8 yrs.

Manson, Christopher. 1993. *The Tree in the Wood: An Old Nursery Song*. New York: North-South. 5–8 yrs.

Marks, A. 1992. *Ring-a-Ring o'Roses and a Ding, Dong, Bell: A Book of Nursery Rhymes.* Old Tappan, N.J.: Picture Book Studio. 5–8 yrs.

McKellar, Shona. 1993. *Counting Rhymes.* New York: Dorling. 5–8 yrs.

O'Malley, Kevin. 1993. *Who Killed Cock Robin?* New York: Lothrop, Lee & Shepard. 5–8 yrs.

Opie, Iona. (Ed.). 1992. *I Saw Esau: The Schoolchild's Pocket Book.* Illus. M. Sendak. Cambridge, Mass.: Candlewick. 5–8 yrs.

Ormerod, Jan. 1994. *Jan Ormerod's to Baby with Love.* New York: Lothrop, Lee & Shepard.

Oxenbury, Helen. 1992. (1985 reissue). *The Helen Oxenbury Nursery Story Book.* New York: Knopf. 5–9 yrs.

Rosenberg, Liz. 1994. *Mama Goose: A New Mother Goose.* Illus. by Janet Street. New York: Philomel. 5–8 yrs.

Sierra, Judy. (Comp. and ad.) 1996. *Nursery Tales Around the World.* Illus. by Stefano Vitale. New York: Clarion, 3–7 yrs.

Theobalds, Prue. 1994. (new ed. 1992). *For Teddy and Me.* New York: Bedrick. 3–6 yrs.

Voake, Charlotte. (Compiler). 1992. *The Three Little Pigs, and Other Favourite Nursery Stories.* Illus. Charlotte Voake. Cambridge, Mass.: Candlewick. 3–7 yrs.

Voce, Louise. 1994. *Over in the Meadow: A Traditional Counting Rhyme.* Cambridge, Mass.: Candlewick. 3–6 yrs.

TRICKSTER TALES

Edmonds, I. G. 1966. *Trickster Tales.* Illus. S. Morrison. Philadelphia: Lippincott. 5–10 yrs.

Hastings, R. (Reteller). 1991. *Reynard the Fox.* New York: Tambourine. 7–10 yrs.

Molted, T. M. 1993. *The King and the Tortoise.* Illus. K. Blankley. New York: Clarion. 5–9 yrs.

Stevens, Janet. 1995. *Tops and Bottoms.* San Diego: Harcourt. 5–10 yrs.

Vaes, Alain. 1994. *Reynard the Fox.* Orlando, Fla.: Turner. 5–8 yrs. (See also Uncle Remus, Coyote, Anansi, McDermott's Tales in Chapter 9.)

EPICS

Hutton, W. 1992. *The Trojan Horse.* New York: McElderry. 10–16 yrs.

McCaughrean, Geraldine. 1995. *The Odyssey.* Illus. Victor G. Ambrus. Oxford: Oxford University Press. 10–14 yrs.

Sutcliff, Rosemary. 1993. *Black Ships before Troy: The Story of The Iliad.* Illus. Alan Lee. New York: Delacorte. 12–16 yrs.

Zeman, Ludmila. 1993. *The Revenge of Ishtar.* Plattsburgh, N.Y.: Tundra. 10–14 yrs.

CHAPTER 4

CHILDREN'S BOOKS MENTIONED IN THE CHAPTER

Adams, R. 1974. *Watership Down.* New York: Macmillan. 12–18 yrs.

Alexander, L. 1964. *The Book of Three.* New York: Holt. 11–14 yrs.

Andersen, H. C. 1846. *Wonderful Stories for Children.* London: Chapman & Hall. 7–13 yrs.

Atwater, R. & F. 1938. *Mr. Popper's Penguins.* Illus. R. Lawson. Boston, Mass.: Little, Brown. 9–11 yrs.

Babbitt, N. 1975. *Tuck Everlasting.* New York: Farrar, Straus, & Giroux. 9–12 yrs.

Bang, M. 1980. *The Grey Lady and the Strawberry Snatcher.* New York: Four Winds. 7–12 yrs.

Banks, L. R. 1993. *The Magic Hare.* Illus. Barry Moser. 49 pp. New York: Morrow. 6–9 yrs.

Barrie, Sir J. M. 1950. *Peter Pan.* Illus. Nora S. Unwin. New York: Scribner's 10–13 yrs.

Baum, L. F. 1900. *The Wonderful Wizard of Oz.* Illus. W. W. Denslow. Chicago, Ill.: Hill. 10–13 yrs.

Boston, L. M. 1954. *The Children of Green Knowe.* Illus. P. Boston. Orlando, Fla.: Harcourt. 9–12 yrs.

Bunting, E. 1994. *Night of the Gargoyles.* Illus. David Wiesner. New York: Clarion. 8–12 yrs.

Clarke, P. 1964. *The Return of the Twelve.* Illus. Bernarda Bryson. New York: Coward. 9–12 yrs.

Collington, P. *Tooth Fairy.* New York: Knopf. 6–11 yrs.

Collodi, C. (Tran. E. Harden). 1988. *The Adventures of Pinocchio.* Illus. Poberto Innocenti. New York: Knopf. 9–13 yrs.

Cooper, S. 1973. *The Dark is Rising.* Illus. A. E. Cober. New York: Atheneum. 12–14 yrs.

Dahl, R. 1961. *James and The Giant Peach.* Illus. N. E. Burkert. New York: Bantam. 8–11 yrs.

———. 1972. *Charlie and the Chocolate Factory.* Illus. J. Schindelman. New York: Knopf. 8–11 yrs.

———. 1988. *Matilda.* Illus. Quentin Blake. New York: Viking Kestrel. 8–11 yrs.

de la Mare, W. 1925. *Broomsticks and Other Tales.* London: Constable. 8–12 yrs.

Gannett, R. 1986. *My Father's Dragon.* Illus. R. Gannett. New York: Random. 8–12 yrs.

Henkes, K. 1993. *Owen.* 32 pp. New York: Greenwillow. 5–8 yrs.

Heinlein, R. 1947. *Rocket Ship Galileo.* New York: Scribner. 10–16 yrs.

Hodges, M. (Ad. from *Faerie Queene*). 1984. *Saint George and the Dragon.* Illus. Trina Schart Hyman. Boston, Mass.: Little, Brown. 8–12 yrs.

Hunter, M. 1988. *The Mermaid Summer.* New York: HarperCollins. 9–12 yrs.

Jacques, B. 1987. *Redwall.* Illus. G. Chalk. New York: Philomel. 11–16 yrs.

Jones, D. W. 1995. *Cart and Cwidder.* New York: Greenwillow. 12–16 yrs.

Langston, J. 1962. *The Diamond in the Window.* Illus. Erik Blegvad. New York: Harper. 11–14 yrs.

———. 1980. *The Fledgling.* New York: Harper. 11–14 yrs.

L'Engle, M. 1962. *A Wrinkle in Time.* Farrar. 12–14 yrs.

Lewis, C. S. 1970. *The Lion, the Witch, the Wardrobe.* Illus. P. Baynes. New York: Macmillan. 10–12 yrs.

———. 1970. *The Magician's Nephew.* Illus. P. Baynes. New York: Macmillan. 10–12 yrs.

MacDonald, A. 1996. *The Spider Who Created the World.* Illus. by G. Brian Karas. New York: Orchard. 4–8 yrs.

Mahy, M. 1969. *A Lion in the Meadow.*

———. 1968. *There's a Nightmare in My Closet.* New York: Dial. 4–7 yrs.

Mayne, W. 1966. *Earthfasts.* New York: Dutton. 11–14 yrs.

McKillip, P. 1974. *The Forgotten Beasts of Eld.* New York: Atheneum. 11–14 yrs.

———. 1976. *The Riddle-Master of Hed.* New York: Atheneum. 12–16 yrs.

McKinley, R. 1985. *The Hero and the Crown.* New York: Greenwillow. 12–16 yrs.

Meddaugh, S. 1995. *Hog-Eye.* Burlington, Mass.: Houghton Mifflin. 6–9 yrs.

Nesbit, E. 1992. *Enchanted Castle.* Illus. P. Zelinsky. New York: Morrow. 10–13 yrs.

Nones, Eric Jon. 1995. *Angela's Wings.* New York: HarperCollins. 7–10 yrs.

Norton, M. 1965. *The Borrowers.* Illus. B. & J. Krush. Orlando, Fla.: Harcourt Brace Jovanovich. 8–13 yrs.

Philip, N. 1995. *Fairy Tales of Hans Christian Andersen.* Illus. Isabelle Brent. New York: Viking. 8–12 yrs.

Pochocki, E. 1993. *The Mushroom Man.* Illus. Barry Moser. 32 pp. New York: Green Tiger. 6–8 yrs.

Sendak, M. 1963. *Where the Wild Things Are.* New York: Harper. 5–10 yrs.

Slote, A. 1975. *My Robot Buddy.* New York: HarperCollins. 9–11 yrs.

Stine, R. L. 1992. *Welcome to Dead House.* New York: Scholastic. 8–11 yrs. *Goosebump Books.*

———. 1994. *The House of Evil: The First Horror.* New York: Scholastic. 12–16 yrs. *Fear Street Books.*

Tolkien, J. R. R. 1966. *The Hobbit.* Orlando, Fla.: Houghton Mifflin. 11–18 yrs.

Williams, M. B. 1970. *The Velveteen Rabbit.* Illus. Willian Nicholson. London: Heinemann. 7–16 yrs.

NOTABLE LITERARY FAIRY TALES

Alexander, Lloyd. 1992. *The Fortune-Tellers.* Illus. Trina S. Hyman. New York: Dutton. 6–10 yrs.

Andersen, H. C. (Trans. E. Haugaard). 1985. *Hans Andersen: His Classic Fairy Tales.* Illus. M. Foreman. New York: Doubleday. 9–12 yrs.

Browne, F. 1985. *Granny's Wonderful Chair.* Illus. K. Meadows. Harmondsworth, Middlesex: Penguin. 10–12 yrs.

Buehner, C. 1996. *Fanny's Dream.* Illus. Mark Buehner. New York: Dial. 5–9 yrs.

Coatsworth, Elizabeth. 1967. *The Cat Who Went to Heaven.* Illus. L. Ward. New York: Simon & Schuster. 10–12 yrs.

de la Mare, W. 1925. *Broomsticks and Other Tales.* London: Constable. 8–12 yrs.

———. 1927. *Told Again.* Illus. A. H. Watson. Oxford: Basil Blackwell. 6–12 yrs.

———. 1980. *Tales Told Again.* Merrimack. 7–11 yrs.

Farjeon, E. 1961. *Martin Pippin in the Apple Orchard.* Illus. R. Kennedy. New York: Lippincott. 12–14 yrs.

Fleischman, P. 1982. *Graven Images: Three Stories.* Illus. A. Glass. New York: Harper. 11–13 yrs.

Gannett, Ruth S. 1986. *My Father's Dragon.* Illus. by author. New York: Random House. 9–12 yrs.

Grahame, K. 1938. *The Reluctant Dragon.* Illus. E. Shepard. New York: Holiday. 10–12 yrs.

Helldorfer, M. C. *Jack, Skinny Bones, and the Golden Pancakes.* Illus. Elise Primavera. New York: Viking. 5–8 yrs.

Housman, L. 1905. *A Doorway in Fairyland.* Illus. C. & L. Housman. San Diego: Harcourt Brace. 10–12 yrs.

Kipling, R. 1991. *Just So Stories.* Woodcuts D. Frampton. New York: HarperCollins. 8–12 yrs.

Lang, Andrew (Ed.). 1981. *Prince Prigio and Prince Ricardo* (in: *The Chronicles of Pantouflia*). Illus. J. Titherington. Lincoln, Mass.: Godine. 10–12 yrs.

Munsch, Robert. 1980. *Paper Bag Princess.* Illus. Michael Martchenko. Buffalo, N.Y.: Firefly. 8–12 yrs.

Nesbit, Edith. 1973. *The Complete Book of Dragons.* Illus. E. Blegvad. New York: Dover. 10–12 yrs.

Paterson, Katherine. 1992. *The King's Equal*. Illus. Vladimir Vagin. New York: HarperCollins. 6–10 yrs.

Pyle, Howard. (verses by K. Pyle). 1943. *The Wonder Clock: or, Four & Twenty Marvelous Tales*. Illus. H. Pyle. 11–13 yrs.

Ruskin, J. 1978. *The King of the Golden River*. Illus. K. Turska. New York: Greenwillow. 7–11 yrs.

Saint-Exupery, A. de (Trans. K. Woods). 1968. *The Little Prince*. Illus. by author. San Diego: Harcourt Brace. 10–16 yrs.

Sandburg, Carl. 1930. *Potato Face*. San Diego: Harcourt Brace. 11–13 yrs.

———. 1974. *Rootabaga Pigeons*. Illus. M. & M. Petersham. San Diego: Harcourt Brace. 11–13 yrs.

———. 1990. *Rootabaga Stories*. Illus. M. & M. Petersham. San Diego: Harcourt Brace. 11–13 yrs.

Singer, Isaac Bashevis. 1966. *Zlateh the Goat & other Tales*. Illus. M. Sendak. New York: HarperCollins. 11–13 yrs.

Steig, W. 1996. *The Toy Brother*. HarperCollins/di Capua. 5–7 yrs.

Stockton, Frank. 1955. *Ting-A-Ling*. Illus. R. Floethe. New York: Scribners. 11–13 yrs.

Thackeray, William. 1947. *The Rose and the Ring*. Illus. J. Gilbert & P. Hogarth. New York: Pierpont Morgan Library. 10–13 yrs.

Thurber, James. 1990. *Many Moons*. Illus. M. Simont. San Diego: Harcourt Brace. 7–11 yrs.

Tolkien, J. R. R. 1965. *The Lord of the Rings* (trilogy). New York: Houghton Mifflin.

Van Allsburg, Chris. 1992. *The Widow's Broom*. Boston: Houghton Mifflin. 9–12 yrs.

Wilde, Oscar. 1978. *The Selfish Giant*. Illus. M. Foreman & F. Wright. New York: Routledge, Chapman & Hall. 6–9 yrs.

———. 1980. *The Happy Prince*. Illus. J. Claverie. New York: Oxford. 9–13 yrs.

———. 1991. *The Happy Prince and Other Stories*. Illus. C. Robinson. New York: Morrow. 10–12 yrs.

Yolen, Jane. 1967. *The Emperor and the Kite*. Illus. E. Young. World. 9–12 yrs.

———. 1974. *The Girl Who Cried Flowers and Other Tales*. Illus. D. Palladini. Crowell. 9–12 yrs.

———. 1989. *The Faery Flag: Stories and Poems of Fantasy and the Supernatural*. New York: Orchard. 10–12 yrs.

NOTABLE LOW FANTASY

Adams, Richard. 1974. *Watership Down*. New York: Macmillan. 12–18 yrs.

Atwater, Richard & Florence Atwater. 1938. *Mr. Popper's Penguins*. Illus. R. Lawson. Boston: Little, Brown. 9–11 yrs.

Babbitt, Natalie. 1975. *Tuck Everlasting*. New York: Farrar, Straus & Giroux. 9–12 yrs.

Banks, Lynne R. 1985. *The Indian in the Cupboard*. Illus. Brock Cole. New York: Doubleday. 10–12 yrs.

———. 1986. *The Return of the Indian*. Illus. W. Geldart. New York: Doubleday. 10–12 yrs.

———. 1989. *The Secret of the Indian*. Illus. T. Lewin. New York: Doubleday. 10–12 yrs.

———. 1993. *The Mystery of the Cupboard*. Illus. T. Newsom. New York: Morrow. 11–13 yrs.

Boston, L. M. 1954. *The Children of Green Knowe*. Illus. P. Boston. San Diego: Harcourt Brace. New York: Concord. 9–12 yrs.

Clarke, Pauline. 1964. *The Return of the Twelves*. Illus. B. Bryson. New York: Coward. 9–12 yrs.

Collodi, C. (Trans. C. D. Chiesa). 1989. *The Adventures of Pinocchio*. Illus. A. Mussino. New York: Simon & Schuster. 11–16 yrs.

Conly, Jane. 1986. *Rasco and the Rats of NIMH*. Illus. Leonard Lubin. New York: HarperCollins. 11–14 yrs.

———. 1990. *R-T, Margaret and the Rats of NIMH*. Illus. Leonard Lubin. New York: HarperCollins. 11–14 yrs.

Dahl, Roald. 1961. *James & The Giant Peach*. Illus. N. E. Burkert. New York: Knopf. 8–11 yrs.

———. 1964. *Charlie & the Chocolate Factory*. Illus. J. Schindelman. New York: Knopf. 8–11 yrs.

———. 1988. *Matilda*. Illus. Quentin Blake. New York: Viking Kestrel. 8–11 yrs.

Dr. Seuss. 1938. *The Five Hundred Hats of Bartholomew Cubbins*. New York: Random House. 7–9 yrs.

Godden, Rumer. 1947. *The Doll's House*. New York: Puffin. 8–11 yrs.

Grahame, Kenneth. 1982. *The Wind in the Willows*. Illus. M. Hague. 10–14 yrs.

Kingsley, C. 1976. *The Water-Babies*. Illus. L. Sambourne. New York: Garland. 10–12 yrs.

King-Smith, Dick. 1982. *Pigs Might Fly*. Illus. M. Payner. New York: Viking. 8–11 yrs.

———.1985. *Babe: The Gallant Pig*. Illus. M. Rayner. New York: Crown. 10–12 yrs.

———.1990. *Ace: The Very Important Pig*. Illus. L. Hemmant. New York: Crown. 10–12 yrs.

Kipling, R. 1981. *The Jungle Book*. Illus. V. G. Ambrus. 8–11 yrs.

Lawson, R. 1954. *A Tough Winter*. Illus. R. Lawson. New York: Viking. 8–12 yrs.

———. 1973. *Ben and Me*. Illus. author. New York: Dell. 10–12 yrs.

———. 1977. *Rabbit Hill*. Illus. author. New York: Puffin. 8–12 yrs.

———. 1989. *Robbut: A Tale of Tails*. North Haven, Conn.: Shoe String Press. 10–12 yrs.

Lindgren, Astrid. (Trans. F. Lamborn). 1977. *Pippi Longstocking*. Illus. L. Glanzman. New York: Puffin. 10–12 yrs.

Lofting, H. 1920. *The Story of Dr. Dolittle*. Illus. H. Lofting. New York: Lippincott. 8–12 yrs.

———. 1989. *Doctor Dolittle and the Green Canary*. New York: Delacorte. 10–12 yrs.

MacDonald, G. 1871. (New ed. 1952) *At the Back of the North Wind*. Illus. Arthur Hughes. New York: Macmillan.

Mahy, Margaret. 1982. *The Haunting*. New York: Simon & Schuster. 11–14 yrs.

Mayne, William. 1966. *Earthfasts*. New York: Dutton. 11–14 yrs.

Meddaugh, Susan. 1992. *Martha Speaks*. Illus. S. Meddaugh. Boston: Houghton Mifflin. 4–8 yrs.

Milne. A. A. 1970. *Winnie-the-Pooh*. Illus. E. Shepard. New York: Dell. 8–12 yrs.

Nesbit, Edith. 1959. *The Five Children and It*. Illus. J. S. Goodall. New York: Random House. 11–14 yrs.

———. 1991. *The Railway Children*. Illus. P. Kay. New York: Putnam. 10–12 yrs.

———. 1992. *Enchanted Castle*. Illus. P. Zelinsky. New York: Morrow. 10–12 yrs.

O'Brien, Robert. 1971. *Mrs. Frisby and the Rats of NIMH*. Illus. Z. Bernstein. New York: Scholastic. 11–14 yrs.

Pearce, P. 1979. *Tom's Midnight Garden*. Illus. S. Einzig. New York: Dell. 11–14 yrs.

Potter, Beatrix. 1902. *The Tale of Peter Rabbit*. London: Warne. 5–7 yrs.

Selden, George. 1960. *The Cricket in Times Square*. Illus. G. Williams. New York: Farrar, Straus & Giroux. 8–11 yrs.

———. 1981. *Chester Cricket's Pigeon Ride*. Illus. G. Williams. New York: Farrar, Straus & Giroux. 10–12 yrs.

Travers, Pamela L. 1981. *Mary Poppins*. Illus. M. Shepard. San Diego: Harcourt Brace. 9–12 yrs.

White, E. B. 1945. *Stuart Little*. Illus. G. Williams. New York: HarperCollins. 8–12 yrs.

———. 1952. *Charlotte's Web*. Illus. G. Williams. New York: HarperCollins. 7–12 yrs.

———. 1970. *Trumpet of the Swan*. New York: HarperCollins. 10–14 yrs.

Willard, Nancy. 1990. *The High Rise Glorious Skittle Skat Roarious Sky Pie Angel Food Cake*. Illus. Richard Jesse Watson. San Diego: Harcourt Brace. 6–12 yrs.

Williams, Margery. 1970. *The Velveteen Rabbit*. Illus. William Nicholson. London: Heinemann. 7–adult.

FANTASY LITERATURE BY CATEGORIES

ANIMAL FANTASIES

Adams, Richard. 1974. *Watership Down*. New York: Macmillan. 12–18 yrs.

Akkerman, Dinie. (Trans. Greta Kilburn). 1994. *King on the Beach*. Hauppauge, N.Y.: Barron. 6–8 yrs.

Allen, Jeffrey. 1987. *Nosey Mrs. Rat*. Illus. James Marshall. New York: Puffin.

Arkin, Alan. 1976. *Lemming Condition*. Illus. J. Sandin. New York: HarperCollins. 10–12 yrs.

Avi. 1995. *Poppy*. Illus. Brian Floca. New York: Jackson/Orchard. 10–13 yrs.

Axworthy, Anni. 1993. *Along Came Toto*. Cambridge, Mass.: Candlewick. 5–8 yrs.

Bancroft, Catherine and Hannah Coale Gruenberg. 1993. *Felix's Hat*. Illus. Hannah Coale Gruenberg. New York: Simon & Schuster. 5–8 yrs.

———. 1995. *That's Philomena*. Illus. Hannah Coale. New York: Simon & Schuster. 5–8 yrs.

Bassett, Jeni. 1995. *The Chicks' Trick*. New York: Dutton. 6–8 yrs.

Bemelmans, Ludwig. 1993. *Rosebud*. New York: Knopf. Umbrella series. 6–8 yrs.

Benchley, N. 1978. *Kilroy and the Gull*. Illus. J. Schoenherr. New York: HarperCollins. 11–13 yrs.

Black, Charles C. 1995. *The Royal Nap*. Illus. James Stevenson. New York: Viking. 5–9 yrs.

Boelts, Maribeth. 1994. *Dry Days, Wet Nights*. Illus. Kathy Parkinson. Morton Grove, Ill.: Whitman, Albert. 5–8 yrs.

Bomans, Godfried. (Trans. Regina Louise Kornblith). 1994. *Eric in the Land of the Insects*. Illus. Mark Richardson. Boston: Houghton Mifflin. 10–13 yrs.

Breathed, Berkeley. 1993. *Goodnight Opus*. Boston: Little, Brown. 5–7 yrs.

Brenner, Barbara. 1994. *Mr. Tall and Mr. Small*. Illus. Mike Shenon. New York: Holt. 5–7 yrs.

Brimner, Larry Dane. 1993. *Max and Felix*. Illus. Les Gray. Honesdale, Penn.: Boyd Mills. 5–8 yrs.

Brown, Ken. 1993. *Nellie's Knot*. New York: Simon & Schuster. 4–7 yrs.

Brown, Marc. 1993. *Arthur's Family Vacation*. Boston: Little, Brown. 4–7 yrs.

Brown, Paula. 1993. *Moon Jump*. New York: Viking. 4–6 yrs.

Brown, Ruth. 1993. *The Picnic*. New York: Dutton. 4–6 yrs.

Buchwald, Emilie. 1993. *Gildaen: The Heroic Adventures of a Most Unusual Rabbit*. Illus. Barbara Flynn. Minneapolis, Minn.: Milkweed. 10–13 yrs.

Burningham, John. 1994. *Courtney*. New York: Crown. 6–8 yrs.

Caple, Kathy. 1994. *The Wimp*. Boston: Houghton Mifflin. 5–7 yrs.

Carlstrom, Nancy White. 1994. *Happy Birthday, Jesse Bear!* Illus. Bruce Degen. New York: Simon & Schuster. 5–7 yrs.

Charles, Donald. 1994. *Ugly Bug*. New York: Dial. 5–7 yrs.

Chorao, Kay. 1988. *Cathedral Mouse*. New York: Dutton. 5–8 yrs.

Christelow, E. 1996. *Five Little Monkeys with Nothing to Do*. New York: Clarion. 3–6 yrs.

Cleary, B. 1965. *The Mouse and the Motorcycle*. Illus. L. Darling. Morrow. 8–10 yrs. (See also *Runaway Ralph*, 1970, and *Ralph S. Mouse*, 1982. 8–10 yrs.)

Cole, Sheila. 1993. *The Hen that Crowed*. Illus. Barbara Rogoff. New York: Lothrop, Lee & Shepard. 4–7 yrs.

Cooper, S. 1991. *Matthew's Dragon*. Illus. J. A. Smith. New York: Simon & Schuster. 5–8 yrs.

Corbalis, J. 1988. *Porcellus, The Flying Pig*. Illus. H. Craig. New York: Dial. 5–10 yrs.

Cunningham, J. 1962. *Macaroon*. Illus. E. Ness. New York: Pantheon. 8–12 yrs.

Cushman, Doug. 1992. *Aunt Eater's Mystery Vacation*. New York: HarperCollins. 6–9 yrs. I Can Read series.

Cuyler, Margery. 1993. *Buddy Bear and the Bad Guys*. Illus. Janet Stevens. Boston: Houghton Mifflin. 5–7 yrs.

Dahl, R. 1991. *The Enormous Crocodile*. Illus. Q. Blake. New York: Knopf. 6–9 yrs.

de Beer, Hans. (Trans. Marianne Martens). 1994. *Bernard Bear's Amazing Adventure*. New York: North-South. 5–7 yrs.

Dickinson, Peter. 1996. *Chuck and Danielle*. Illus. Kees de Kiefte. New York: Delacorte. 9–11 yrs.

Donovan. Mary Lee. 1993. *Papa's Bedtime Story*. Illus. Kimberly Bulcken Root. New York: Knopf. 4–6 yrs.

Dubanevich, Arlene. 1993. *Calico Cows*. New York: Viking. 4–7 yrs.

Edwards, Richard. 1994. *Moles Can Dance*. Illus. Caroline Anstey. Cambridge, Mass.: Candlewick. 5–7 yrs.

Egan, Tim. 1994. *Friday Night at Hodges' Cafe*. Boston: Houghton Mifflin. 5–8 yrs.

Evans, Katie. 1994. *Hunky Dory Found It*. Illus. Janet Morgan Stoeke. New York: Morrow. 5–7 yrs.

Ezra, Mark. 1994. *The Sleepy Dormouse*. Illus. Gavin Rowe. New York: Interlink. 4–6 yrs.

Fletcher, S. 1996. *Sign of the Dove*. New York: Atheneum/Karl. 9–12 yrs.

Fox, Mem. 1987. *Possum Magic*. Illus. J. Vivas. Nashville, Tenn.: Abingdon. 4–8 yrs.

Froehlich, Margaret. 1995. *That Kookoory!* Illus. Marla Frazee. San Diego: Harcourt Brace. 5–9 yrs.

Gerstein, M. 1991. *The New Creatures*. New York: HarperCollins. 5–8 yrs.

Gliori, Debi. 1995. *Mr. Bear's Picnic*. Racine, Wisc.: Western Publishing. 5–9 yrs.

Godden, Rumer. 1982. *The Mousewife*. Illus. H. Holder. New York: Viking. 7–9 yrs.

Goodman, J. E. 1996. *Bernard's Bath*. Illus. Dominic Catalano. Honesdale, Penn.: Boyds. 4–6 yrs.

Gravois, Jeanne M. 1994. *Quickly, Quigley*. Illus. Alison Hill. New York: Morrow. 4–6 yrs.

Gregory, Valiska. 1993. *Babysitting for Benjamin*. Illus. Lynn Munsinger. Boston: Little, Brown. 5–7 yrs.

Gross, L. 1996. *The Frog Who Wanted to Be a Singer*. Illus. Cynthia Jabar. New York: Kroupa/Orchard. 4–7 yrs.

Hadithi, Mwenye. 1993. *Baby Baboon*. Illus. Adrienne Kennaway. Boston: Little, Brown. 4–7 yrs.

Hall, Donald. 1994. *I Am the Dog, I Am the Cat*. Illus. Barry Moser. New York: Dial. 6–9 yrs.

Hawkes, Kevin. 1992. *Then the Troll Heard the Squeak*. New York: Puffin. 6–9 yrs.

Hayes, Ann. 1995. *Meet the Marching Smithereens*. Illus. Karmen Thompson. San Diego: Harcourt Brace. 5–9 yrs.

Heller, Nicholas. 1994. *Woody*. New York: Greenwillow. 5–7 yrs.

Henkes, Kevin. 1993. *Owen*. New York: Greenwillow. 5–8 yrs.

Hoban, Russell. 1993. *Bread and Jam for Frances*. Illus. Lillian Hoban. New York: HarperCollins. 4–7 yrs.

———. 1970. *A Bargain for Frances*. Illus. Lillian Hoban. New York: HarperCollins. I Can Read Books.

———. 1969. *Best Friends for Frances*. Illus. Lillian Hoban. New York: HarperCollins. 6–8 yrs.

———. 1964. *A Baby Sister for Frances*. Illus. Lillian Hoban. New York: HarperCollins. 4–6 yrs.

Hoff, Syd. 1993. *Captain Cat*. Illus. by Syd Hoff. New York: HarperCollins. 5–7 yrs. I Can Read Books.

Howe, James. 1992. *Return to Howliday Inn*. Illus. A. Daniel. New York: Simon & Schuster. 10–12 yrs.

———. 1993. *Rabbit Cadabra!* Illus. Alan Daniel. New York: Morrow. 7–10 yrs.

Hutchins, Pat. 1994. *Little Pink Pig*. New York: Greenwillow. 5–7 yrs.

Hurd, Thacher. 1996. *Art Dog*. Illus. Thacher Hurd. New York: HarperCollins, 5–8 yrs.

Inkpen, Mick. 1993. *Kipper's Birthday*. San Diego: Harcourt Brace. 5–7 yrs.

Jarrell, Randall. 1964. *The Bat-Poet*. Illus. M. Sendak. New York: Macmillan. 8–11 yrs.

———. 1965. *The Animal Family*. Illus. M. Sendak. New York: Pantheon. 9–14 yrs.

Jennings, Linda. 1995. *Tom's Tail*. Illus. Tim Warnes. Boston: Little, Brown. 5–9 yrs.

Johnson, Doug. 1993. *Never Babysit the Hippopotamuses!* Illus. Abby Carter. New York: Holt. 5–7 yrs.

Johnston, Tony. 1995. *The Iguana Brothers*. Illus. Mark Teague. New York: Scholastic. 6–9 yrs.

Jungman, Ann. 1993. *When the People Are Away*. Illus. Linda Birch. Honesdale, Penn.: Boyds Mills. 5–8 yrs.

Kasza, Keiko. 1995. *Grandpa Toad's Last Secret*. New York: Putnam. 6–9 yrs.

Kellogg, Steven. 1977. *The Mysterious Tadpole*. New York: Dial. 4–8 yrs.

———. 1987. *Prehistoric Pinkerton*. Dial. 5–8 yrs. (See also: *Tallyho, Pinkerton*, 1983, *Pinkerton, Behave!* 1979, and *A Rose for Pinkerton*, 1981.) 5–8 yrs.

King-Smith, D. 1987. *Harry's Mad*. Illus. J. Bennett. New York: Crown. 7–9 yrs.

———. 1993. *All Pigs Are Beautiful*. Illus. A. Jeram. Cambridge, Mass.: Candlewick. 5–8 yrs.

———. 1993. *The Cuckoo Child*. Illus. Leslie W. Bowman. New York: Hyperion. 9–12 yrs.

———. 1993 (reissue, 1985). *Babe: The Gallant Pig*. Illus. Mary Rayner. New York: Crown. 9–12 yrs.

———. 1994. *Three Terrible Trins*. Illus. by Mark Teague. New York: Crown. 10–13 yrs.

———. 1995. *The School Mouse*. Illus. by Cynthia Fisher. New York: Hyperion. 9–11 yrs.

———. 1996. *Mr. Potter's Pet*. Illus. by Mark Teague. New York: Hyperion. 7–9 yrs.

Koscielniak, Bruce. 1993. *Bear and Bunny Grow Tomatoes*. New York: Knopf. 4–6 yrs. Umbrella series.

Kulling, Monica. 1993. *Waiting for Amos*. Illus. Vicky Lowe. New York: Simon & Schuster. 5–7 yrs.

Levine, Arthur A. 1993. *Sheep Dreams*. Illus. Judy Lanfredi. New York: Dial. 5–7 yrs.

Lewison, Wendy Cheyette. 1993. *Shy Vi*. Illus. Stephen John Smith. New York: Simon & Schuster. 5–7 yrs.

Lionni, Leo. 1993. *A Color of His Own*. New York: Knopf. 4–7 yrs.

———. 1994. *An Extraordinary Egg*. New York: Knopf. 4–6 yrs.

Lisle, Janet Taylor. 1993. *Forest*. New York: Orchard/Jackson. 10–13 yrs.

London, Jonathan. 1993. *Hip Cat*. Illus. Woodleigh Hubbard. San Francisco: Chronicle. 7–9 yrs.

Mahy, Margaret. 1990. *The Great White Man-Eating Shark*. Illus. J. Allen. New York: Dial. 5–8 yrs.

———. 1993. *The Three-Legged Cat*. Illus. Jonathan Allen. New York: Viking. 6–8 yrs.

Marshall, James. 1986. *Wings: A Tale of Two Chickens*. New York: Viking. 6–9 yrs.

McBratney, Sam. 1995. *Guess How Much I Love You*. Illus. Anita Jeram. Cambridge, Mass.: Candlewick. 4–8 yrs.

McClure, Gillian. 1993. *The Christmas Donkey*. New York: Farrar, Straus & Giroux. 6–8 yrs.

McCully, Emily Arnold. 1994. *My Real Family*. San Diego: Harcourt Brace. 5–7 yrs.

McPhail, David. 1976. *Henry Bear's Park*. Boston: Little, Brown. 6–8 yrs.

Meddaugh, D. 1996. *Martha Blah Blah*. Burlington, Mass.: Lorraine/Houghton. 5–8 yrs.

Minarik, Else H. 1991. *The Little Girl & the Dragon*. New York: Greenwillow/Morrow. 3–6 yrs.

Miyamoto, Tadao. 1994. *Papa and Me*. Minneapolis, Minn.: Lerner Group. 4–6 yrs.

Moore, Inga. 1994. *A Big Day for Little Jack*. Cambridge, Mass.: Candlewick. 5–7 yrs.

Murphy, Jill. 1994. *A Quiet Night In*. Cambridge, Mass.: Candlewick. 4–7 yrs.

Naylor, Phyllis Reynolds. 1993. *The Grand Escape*. Illus. Alan Daniel. New York: Simon & Schuster. 9–12 yrs.

Novak, Matt. 1994. *Mouse TV*. New York: Orchard/Jackson. 5–7 yrs.

Oakley, Graham. 1972. *The Church Mouse*. New York: Simon & Schuster. 7–9 yrs.

Offen, Hilda. 1993. *Elephant Pie*. New York: Dutton. 5–7 yrs.

Oram, Hiawyn. 1995. *Badger's Bring Something Party*. Illus. Susan Varley. New York: Lothrop, Lee & Shepard. 5–9 yrs.

Paul, A. 1995. *The Tiger Who Lost His Stripes*. Illus. Michael Foreman. San Diego, Calif.: Harcourt Brace Jovanovich. 6–9 yrs.

Peet, Bill. 1970. *The Whingdingdilly*. Boston: Houghton Mifflin. 6–9 yrs.

Pilkey, Dav. 1993. *Dogzilla*. San Diego: Harcourt Brace. 6–9 yrs.

Porter, Sue. 1994. *Moose Music*. Racine, Wisc.: Western. 5–8 yrs.

Potter, B. 1951. *The Fairy Caravan*. New York: Warne. 9–12 yrs.

Potter, Katherine. 1993. *My Mother the Cat*. New York: Simon & Schuster. 5–7 yrs.

Raschka, C. 1996. *The Blushful Hippopotamus*. New York: Jackson/Orchard. 4–8 yrs.

Richardson, Judith Benet. 1993. *Come to My Party*. Illus. Salley Mavor. New York: Simon & Schuster. 4–8 yrs.

Rockwell, Anne. 1994. *The Way to Captain Yankee's*. New York: Simon & Schuster. 5–8 yrs.

Rockwell, Norman. 1994. *Willie Was Different*. Stockbridge, Mass.: Berkshire House. 5–7 yrs.

Rodell, Susanna. 1995. *Dear Fred*. Illus. Kim Gamble. New York: Ticknor & Fields. 5–9 yrs.

Root, Phyllis. 1994. *Sam Who Was Swallowed by a Shark*. Illus. Axel Scheffler. Cambridge, Mass.: Candlewick. 6–8 yrs.

Ross, T. 1978. *Hugo and Oddsock*. River Grove, Ill.: Follett. 5–9 yrs.

Samton, Sheila White. 1993. *Tilly and the Rhinoceros*. New York: Putnam. 4–7 yrs.

Saunders, Dave & Julie Saunders. 1994. *Storm's Coming*. New York: Simon & Schuster. 4–6 yrs.

Scamell, Ragnhild. 1996. *Buster's Echo*. Illus. Genevieve Webster. New York: HarperCollins/Perlman. 4–6 yrs.

Schlein, Miriam. 1993. *Just like Me*. Illus. Marilyn Janovitz. New York: Hyperion. 4–6 yrs.

_____. 1993. *The Way Mothers Are*. Illus. Joe Lasker. Morton Grove, Ill.: A. Whitman. 4–6 yrs.

Schmidt, Annie. (Trans. Lance Salway). 1994. *Minnie*. Illus. Kay Sather. Minneapolis, Minn.: Milkweed. 10–13 yrs.

Seidler, Tor. 1993. *The Wainscott Weasel*. Illus. Fred Marcellino. New York: HarperCollins/di Capua. 9–12 yrs.

Sharp, Margery. 1959. *The Rescuers*. Boston: Little, Brown. 8–12 yrs.

Silverman, Erica. 1994. *Don't Fidget a Feather!* Illus. S. D. Schindler. New York: Macmillan. 5–7 yrs.

Smith, Maggie. 1994. *Argo, You Lucky Dog*. New York: Lothrop, Lee & Shepard. 6–9 yrs.

Smucker, Anna Egan. 1994. *Outside the Window*. Illus. Stacey Schuett. New York: Knopf. 5–7 yrs.

Stanley, Diane. 1995. *Woe Is Moe*. Illus. Elise Primavera. New York: Putnam. 5–9 yrs.

Steig, William. 1976. *Abel's Island*. New York: Farrar, Straus & Giroux. 8–12 yrs.

_____. 1994. *Zeke Pippin*. New York: HarperCollins/di Capua. 6–8 yrs.

Stevenson, James. 1993. *The Pattaconk Brook*. New York: Greenwillow. 4–7 yrs.

Sykes, J. 1996. *This and That*. Illus. Tanya Linch. New York: Farrar. 2–5 yrs.

Teague, Mark. 1994. *Pigsty*. New York: Scholastic. 4–6 yrs.

Tompert, Ann. 1993. *Just a Little Bit*. Illus. Lynn Munsinger. Boston: Houghton Mifflin. 4–7 yrs.

Tryon, Leslie. 1994. *Albert's Thanksgiving*. New York: Simon & Schuster. 5–8 yrs.

Waber, Bernard. 1994. *Lyle at the Office*. Boston: Houghton Mifflin. 5–8 yrs.

Waddell, Martin. 1993. *Let's Go Home, Little Bear*. Illus. Barbara Firth. Cambridge, Mass.: Candlewick. 4–6 yrs.

Walsh, Ellen Stoll. 1993. *Hop Jump*. San Diego: Harcourt Brace. 4–6 yrs.

Wilson, Gina. 1995. *Prowlpuss*. Illus. David Parkins. Cambridge, Mass.: Candlewick. 5–9 yrs.

Wormell, Mary. 1995. *Hilda Hen's Happy Birthday*. Linocut. San Diego: Harcourt Brace. 4–8 yrs.

Zimmerman, Andrea and David Clemesha. 1995. *The Cow Buzzed*. Illus. Paul Meisel. New York: HarperCollins. 4–6 yrs.

NOTABLE HIGH FANTASY

Alexander, Lloyd. 1968. *The High King*. New York: Holt. 11–14 yrs.

_____. 1969. *Taran Wanderer*. New York: Dell. 11–14 yrs.

_____. 1980. *The Black Cauldron*. New York: Dell. 11–14 yrs.

_____. 1980. *The Book of Three*. New York: Dell. 11–14 yrs.

_____. 1980. *The Castle of Llyr*. New York: Dell. 11–14 yrs.

_____. 1982. *Westmark*. New York: Dell. 11–14 yrs.

Barrie, J. M. 1982. *Peter Pan*. Illus. T. S. Hyman. New York: Avon. 10–13 yrs.

Baum, L. Frank. 1982. *The Wizard of Oz*. Illus. M. Hague. New York: Holt. 10–13 yrs.

Carroll, L. 1993. *Alice's Adventures in Wonderland and Through the Looking Glass*. Illus. J. Tenniel. New York: Morrow/Books of Wonder. 10–16 yrs.

_____. 1981. *Through the Looking-Glass*. Cutchogue, N.Y.: Buccaneer. 10–16 yrs.

Cooper, Susan. 1966. *Over Sea, Under Stone*. Illus. M. Gill. San Diego: Harcourt Brace. 11–14 yrs.

_____. 1973. *The Dark Is Rising*. Illus. A. E. Cober. New York: Simon & Schuster. 12–14 yrs.

_____. 1973. *Greenwitch*. New York: McElderry. 11–14 yrs.

_____. 1975. *The Grey King*. Illus. M. Heslop. New York: Simon & Schuster. 11–14 yrs.

_____. 1977. *Silver on the Tree*. New York: Simon & Schuster. 12–14 yrs.

Dickinson, P. 1969. *The Weathermonger*. Boston: Little, Brown. 11–14 yrs.

_____. 1969. *Heartsease*. London: Gollancz. 11–14 yrs.

_____. 1970. *The Devil's Children*. London: Gollancz. 11–14 yrs.

Le Guin, Ursula K. 1968. *A Wizard of Earthsea*. Illus. R. Robbins. Boston: Houghton Mifflin. 12–16 yrs.

Lewis, C. S. 1953. *The Silver Chair*. Illus. P. Baynes. New York: Macmillan. 11–13 yrs.

_____. 1970. *The Horse and His Boy*. Illus. P. Baynes. New York: Macmillan. 11–16 yrs.

_____. 1970. *The Last Battle*. Illus. P. Baynes. New York: Simon & Schuster. 10–16 yrs.

_____. 1970. *The Lion, the Witch, and the Wardrobe*. Illus. P. Baynes. New York: Macmillan. 10–12 yrs.

_____. 1970. *The Magician's Nephew*. Illus. P. Baynes. New York: Macmillan. 10–12 yrs.

_____. 1970. *Prince Caspian: The Return to Narnia*. Illus. P. Baynes. New York: Macmillan. 11–13 yrs.

_____. 1970. *The Voyage of the Dawn Treader*. Illus. P. Baynes. New York: Macmillan. 11–14 yrs.

McKinley, Robin. 1982. *The Blue Sword*. New York: Greenwillow. 13–17 yrs.

_____. 1984. *The Hero and the Crown*. New York: Greenwillow. 12–16 yrs.

Norton, Mary. 1955. *The Borrowers Afield*. Illus. B. & J. Krush. San Diego: Harcourt Brace. 8–13 yrs.

_____. 1959. *The Borrowers Afloat*. Illus. B & J. Krush. San Diego: Harcourt Brace. 8–13 yrs.

_____. 1961. *The Borrowers Afloat*. Illus. B. & J. Krush. San Diego: Harcourt Brace. 8–13 yrs.

_____. 1965. *The Borrowers*. Illus. B. & J. Krush. San Diego: Harcourt Brace. 8–13 yrs.

_____. 1982. *The Borrowers Avenged*. Illus. B. & J. Krush. San Diego: Harcourt Brace. 8–13 yrs.

Pierce, Meredith. 1982. *The Darkangel*. Boston: Little, Brown. 12–16 yrs.

_____. 1984. *A Gathering of Gargoyles*. Boston: Little, Brown. 12–16 yrs.

_____. 1989. *The Pearl of the Soul of the World*. Boston: Little, Brown. 12–16 yrs.

Sendak, Maurice. 1963. *Where the Wild Things Are*. New York: HarperCollins. 5–10 yrs.

Tolkien, J. R. R. 1986. *The Hobbit*. Boston: Houghton Mifflin. 12–18 yrs.

_____. 1988. *The Lord of the Rings*. London: Unwin. 13–18 yrs. Separate titles are: 1986, *The Fellowship of the Ring*, Boston: Houghton Mifflin; 1986, *The Two Towers*, Boston: Houghton Mifflin; 1986, *The Return of the King*, Boston: Houghton Mifflin. 1986.

NOTABLE SCIENCE FICTION

Appleton, Victor. 1911. *Tom Swift and His Electric Rifle*. New York: Grosset & Dunlap. 9–12 yrs.

Baum, L. Frank. 1901. *Master Key: An Electrical Fairy Tale*. Bowen-Merrill. 10–18 yrs.

Christopher, John. 1967. *The White Mountains*. New York: Simon & Schuster. 12–14 yrs.

del Rey, L., C. Matschatt, & C. Carmer, (Eds.) 1954. *The Year after Tomorrow: An Anthology of Science Fiction Stories*. Winston. 11–13 yrs.

du Bois, W. P. 1947. *The Twenty-One Balloons*. New York: Viking. 10–14 yrs.

Heinlein, R. 1947. *Rocket Ship Galileo*. New York: Scribners. 10–16 yrs.

_____. 1955. *Tunnel in the Sky*. New York: Scribners. 12–14 yrs.

Hoover, H. M. 1990. *Away Is a Strange Place to Be*. New York: Dutton. 9–12 yrs.

Hunter, Norman. 1933. *The Incredible Adventure of Professor Branestawn*. Oxford: Bodley Head. 12–16 yrs.

L'Engle, Madeleine. 1962. *A Wrinkle in Time*. New York: Farrar, Straus & Giroux. 12–14 yrs.

Lowry, Lois. 1993. *The Giver*. Boston: Houghton Mifflin. 12–14 yrs.

Nesbit, Edith. 1959. *The Story of the Amulet*. New York: Penguin. 11–13 yrs.

Norton, A. 1952. *Star Man's Son*. San Diego: Harcourt Brace. 12–16 yrs.

Pratchett, Terry. 1991. *Wings*. New York: Delacorte. 10–12 yrs.

_____. 1991. *Diggers*. New York: Delacorte. 10–12 yrs. (See *Truckers*, 1990, also in Bromeliad Trilogy. 10–12 yrs.)

Rockwood, R. 1906. *Through the Air to the North Pole; or, The Wonderful Cruise of the Electric Monarch*. Cupples-Leon. 9–11 yrs.

Rubinstein, G. 1988. *Space Demons*. New York: Dial. 11–16 yrs.

_____. 1991. *Skymaze*. New York: Orchard. 11–16 yrs.

Sargent, P. 1983. *Earthseed*. New York: HarperCollins. 13–18 yrs.

Sleator, William. 1988. *The Duplicate*. New York: Dutton. 12–18 yrs.

_____. 1995. *Interstellar Pig*. New York: Dutton. 9–12 yrs.

_____. 1990. *Strange Attractors*. New York: Dutton. 13–18 yrs.

Verne, J. 1926. *Around the World in Eighty Days*. Dent. 13–18 yrs.

_____. 1956. *Twenty Thousand Leagues Under The Sea*. Heritage. 12–18 yrs.

Yep, Laurence. 1983. *Sweetwater*. New York: HarperCollins. 12–15 yrs.

FANCIFUL CREATURES

Benjamin, Saragil Katzman. 1994. *My Dog Ate It*. New York: Holiday. 9–12 yrs.

Berlan, Kathryn Hook. 1993. *Andrew's Amazing Monsters*. Illus. Maxie Chambliss. New York: Simon & Schuster. 4–7 yrs.

Bradshaw, Gillian. 1991. *The Dragon and the Thief*. New York: Greenwillow/Morrow. 11–13 yrs.

Brett, Jan. 1993. *Christmas Trolls*. New York: Putnam. 5–7 yrs.

Briggs, K. M. 1977. *Hobberdy Dick*. New York: Greenwillow. 11–14 yrs.

Brittain, B. 1990. *Professor Popkin's Prodigious Polish: A Tale of Coven Tree*. Illus. A. Glass. New York: HarperCollins. 10–12 yrs.

_____. 1981. *The Devil's Donkey*. New York: HarperCollins. 9–12 yrs.

Bulla, C. R. 1980. *My Friend the Monster*. Illus. M. Chesssare. New York: HarperCollins. 7–11 yrs.

Bunting, Eve. 1994. *Night of the Gargoyles*. Illus. David Wiesner. Boston: Houghton Mifflin. 7–9 yrs.

Butterworth, O. 1956. *Enormous Egg: You Won't Believe Your Eyes!* Illus. L. Darling. Boston: Little, Brown. 9–12 yrs.

Cameron, E. 1959. *The Terrible Churnadryne.* Boston: Little, Brown. 10–12 yrs.

———. 1975. *Marra's World.* Illus. K. Turska. New York: Greenwillow/Morrow. 7–9 yrs.

Cauley, L. R. 1988. *The Trouble with Tyrannosaurus Rex.* San Diego: Harcourt Brace. 6–10 yrs.

Cooper, Susan. 1993. *The Boggart.* New York: Simon & Schuster. 8–12 yrs.

Enright, Elizabeth. 1993. *Zeee.* Illus. Susan Gaber. San Diego: Harcourt Brace. 7–9 yrs.

Friesner, Esther M. 1993. *Wishing Season.* Illus. Frank Kelly Freas. New York: Simon & Schuster. Dragonflight Series. 12–14 yrs.

Gannett, Ruth S. 1948. *My Father's Dragon.* New York: Random House. 8–11 yrs. (See also other books in series.)

Glassman, Peter. 1994. *My Working Mom.* Illus. Tedd Arnold. New York: Morrow. 4–6 yrs.

Godden, Rumer. 1981. *The Dragon of Og.* Illus. P. Baynes. New York: Viking. 9–12 yrs.

Harris, Mark Jonathan. 1993. *Solay.* New York: Simon & Schuster. 9–12 yrs.

Hayward, Linda. 1995. *The Biggest Cookie in the World.* Illus. Joe Ewers. New York: Random/CTW. 5–9 yrs. Step into Reading series.

Heide, Florence Parry. 1993. *Timothy Twinge.* Illus. Barbara Lehman. New York: Lothrop, Lee & Shepard. 6–8 yrs.

Hoban, Russell. 1990. *Monsters.* Illus. Q. Blake. New York: Scholastic. 7–9 yrs.

Hooks, W. H. 1994. *Mean Jake and the Devils.* Illus. D. Zimmer. New York: Dial. 8–12 yrs.

Hunter, Mollie. 1977. *The Wicked One: A Story of Suspense.* New York: HarperCollins. 11–16 yrs.

———. 1977. *A Furl of Fairy Wind: Four Stories.* Illus. S. Gammell. New York: HarperCollins. 7–10 yrs. (See also *The Haunted Mountain: A Story of Suspense*, 11–14 yrs.; *The Kelpie's Pearls*, 10–12 yrs.; and *A Stranger Came Ashore*, 12–16 yrs.)

Jansson, Tove. (Trans. E. Portch). 1989. *Finn Family Moomintroll.* New York: Farrar, Straus & Giroux. (See other six books in series, 9–12 yrs.)

———. (Trans. E. Portch). 1991. *Comet in Moominland.* New York: Farrar, Straus & Giroux. 10–12 yrs.

———. (Trans. T. Warburton). 1991. *Moominsummer Madness.* New York: Farrar, Straus & Giroux. 10–12 yrs.

Kastner, E. (Trans. J. Kirkup). 1980. *The Little Man.* Illus. R. Schreiter. New York: Avon. 10–12 yrs. (See also sequel: *The Little Man and the Big Thief.*)

Kimmel, Eric. 1989. *Hershel and the Hanukkah Goblins.* Illus. T. C. Hyman. New York: Holiday. 6–9 yrs.

Kornblatt, Marc. 1994. *Eli and the Dimplemeyers.* Illus. Jack Ziegler. New York: Simon & Schuster. 5–7 yrs.

Krensky, Stephen. 1980. *The Earthquake Man.* New York: Scribners. 10–12 yrs.

Lisle, Janet Taylor. 1989. *Afternoon of the Elves.* New York: Orchard. 10–12 yrs.

———. 1994. *The Gold Dust Letters.* New York: Orchard/Jackson. 10–13 yrs.

Martin, Bill, Jr. 1993. *Old Devil Wind.* Illus. Barry Root. San Diego: Harcourt Brace. 6–8 yrs.

Mayne, William. 1994. *Hob & the Goblins.* Illus. by Norman Messenger. New York: Dorling Kindersley. 12–16 yrs.

Mazer, Anne. 1993. *The Oxboy.* New York: Knopf. 10–13 yrs.

McGraw, E. 1996. *The Moorchild.* New York: McElderry. 9–12 yrs.

McPhail, David. 1994. *The Glerp.* Morristown, N.J.: Silver Burdett. 6–8 yrs.

Montresor, B. 1989. *The Witches of Venice.* New York: Doubleday. 7–10 yrs.

Munsch, Robert. 1982. *Mud Puddle.* Buffalo, N.Y.: Firefly. 6–9 yrs.

Nesbit, E. 1980. *The Last of the Dragons.* Illus. P. Firmin. New York: McGraw-Hill. 10–12 yrs.

Novak, Matt. 1993. *The Last Christmas Present.* New York: Orchard/Jackson. 5–7 yrs.

Oppenheim, S. 1977. *The Selchie's Seed.* Illus. D. Goode. New York: Avon. 10–12 yrs.

Ormondroyd, E. 1957. *David and the Phoenix.* New York: Scholastic. 10–12 yrs.

Osborne, Mary Pope. 1994. *Molly and the Prince.* Illus. Elizabeth Sayles. New York: Knopf. 6–8 yrs.

Patron, Susan. 1993. *Bobbin Dustdobbin.* Illus. Mike Shenon. New York: Orchard/Jackson. 6–8 yrs.

Peck, Sylvia. 1989. *Seal Child.* Illus. R. A. Parker. New York: Morrow. 10–12 yrs.

Pierce, Tamora. 1994. *Wolf-Speaker.* New York: Simon & Schuster. 12–16 yrs. Immortals Series. (*Wild Magic*, 1992, is first in series).

Pilkey, Dav. 1993. *Dragon's Halloween.* New York: Orchard. 5–7 yrs.

Rosenberg, Liz. 1993. *Monster Mama.* Illus. Stephen Gammell. New York: Putnam. 4–7 yrs.

Ryder, Joanne. 1994. *A House by the Sea.* Illus. Melissa Sweet. New York: Morrow. 5–7 yrs.

Sabraw, J. 1989. *I Wouldn't Be Scared.* New York: Orchard/Jackson. 5–8 yrs.

Samton, Sheila White. 1993. *Oh, No!: A Naptime Adventure.* New York: Viking. 4–6 yrs.

Sargent, S. 1980. *Weird Henry Berg.* New York: Crown. 10–12 yrs.

Shannon, Margaret. 1993. *Elvira.* New York: Ticknor & Fields. 5–7 yrs.

Sis, Peter. 1993. *Komodo!* New York: Greenwillow. 6–9 yrs.

Slote, Elizabeth. 1993. *Nelly's Grannies.* New York: Morrow. 4–6 yrs.

Stanley, Diane. 1994. *The Gentleman & the Kitchen Maid.* Illus. Dennis Nolan. New York: Dial. 9–13 yrs.

Steig, William. 1990. *Shrek!* New York: Farrar, Straus & Giroux. 6–10 yrs.

Stridh, Kicki. 1994. *The Horrible Spookhouse.* Illus. Eva Eriksson. Minneapolis, Minn.: Lerner. 5–7 yrs.

Tanis, Joel E. & Jeff Grooters. 1993. *The Dragon Pack Snack Attack.* Illus. Joel E. Tanis. New York: Simon & Schuster. 5–8 yrs.

Ungerer, T. 1991. *Zeralda's Ogre.* New York: Delacorte. 6–9 yrs.

Van Allsburg, Chris. 1993. *The Sweetest Fig.* Boston: Houghton Mifflin. 6–10 yrs.

Van Pallandt, Nicolas. 1994. *Troll's Search for Summer.* New York: Farrar, Straus & Giroux. 7–9 yrs.

Velde, Vande V. 1992. *Dragon's Bait.* San Diego: Harcourt Brace. 12–14 yrs.

Whipple, L. (Compiler). 1991. *Dragons Dragons and Other Creatures that Never Were.* Illus. E. Carle. 10–12 yrs.

Wrede, Patricia C. 1991. *Searching for Dragons.* San Diego: Harcourt Brace. 10–12 yrs. (See also sequel: *Dealing with Dragons*, 1990, 10–12 yrs.)

Yep, Laurence. 1988. *Dragon of the Lost Sea.* New York: HarperCollins. 11–16 yrs.

Yolen, Jane H. 1982. *Dragon's Blood.* New York: Delacorte. 13–16 yrs.

———. 1990. *The Dragon's Boy.* New York: HarperCollins. 10–12 yrs.

———. 1991. *Greyling: A Picture Story from the Islands of Shetland.* New York: Putnam. 7–10 yrs.

Zambreno, Mary Frances. 1994. *Journeyman Wizard: A Magical Mystery.* San Diego: Harcourt Brace. 12–16 yrs.

FANCIFUL ADVENTURES

Aiken, Joan. 1996. *Cold Shoulder Road.* New York: Delacorte. 10–14 yrs.

Anderson, Joan. 1995. *Sally's Submarine.* Photographs by George Ancona. New York: Morrow. 5–8 yrs.

Avi. 1993. *City of Light, City of Dark: A Comic Book Novel.* Illus. Brian Floca. New York: Orchard/Jackson. 10–13 yrs.

Berger, Barbara. 1992. *Grandfather Twilight.* New York: Putnam. 4–7 yrs.

Berry, Liz. 1996. *The China Garden.* New York: Farrar, Straus & Giroux. 12–17 yrs.

Boland, Janice. 1995. *Annabel Again.* Illus. Megan Halsey. New York: Dial. 5–8 yrs.

Boston, L. M. 1976. *The Fossil Snake.* Illus. P. Boston. New York: Atheneum. 9–12 yrs.

———. 1959. *The River at Green Knowe.* Illus. P. Boston. San Diego: Harcourt Brace. 10–13 yrs. (See also *Sea Egg*, Harcourt Brace. 9–11 yrs.)

Brittain, B. 1983. *The Wish Giver: Three Tales of Coven Tree.* Illus. A. Glass. New York: HarperCollins. 9–12 yrs.

———. 1987. *Dr. Dredd's Wagon of Wonders.* New York: HarperCollins. 8–12 yrs.

Burgess, Barbara H. 1991. *Oren Bell.* New York: Delacorte. 8–10 yrs.

Cole, Babette. 1993. *Supermoo!* New York: Putnam. 4–7 yrs.

Corbett, Scott. 1960. *The Lemonade Trick.* Illus. P. Galdone. Boston: Little, Brown. 10–12 yrs. (See also other books in sequel.)

Cresswell, Helen. 1973. *The Bongleweed.* New York: Macmillan. 11–13 yrs.

Dahl, R. 1996. *James and the Giant Peach: A Children's Story.* Illus. Lane Smith. New York: Knopf. 9–12 yrs.

Demarest, Chris L. 1995. *My Blue Boat.* San Diego: Harcourt Brace. 5–9 yrs.

Dexter, Catherine. 1992. *The Gilded Cat.* New York: Morrow. 10–12 yrs.

Downer, Ann. 1989. *The Glass Salamander.* New York: Atheneum. 12–14 yrs. (See sequels: *The Spellkey Trilogy*, 1995, New York: Simon & Schuster; and *The Books of the Keepers*, 1993, New York: Simon & Schuster.)

Eager, Edward. 1954. *Half Magic.* Illus. N. M. Bodecker. San Diego: Harcourt Brace. 9–11 yrs.

———. 1970. *Magic or Not?* Illus. N. M. Bodecker. 10–12 yrs. (See *Knight's Castle*, 1989, San Diego: Harcourt Brace. 10–12 yrs.)

Embry, M. 1983. *The Blue-Nosed Witch.* New York: Bantam. 6–8 yrs.

Enright, Elizabeth. 1991. *Tatsinda.* Illus. K. T. Treherne. San Diego: Harcourt Brace. 7–9 yrs.

Estes, Eleanor. 1975. *The Witch Family.* Illus. E. Ardizzone. San Diego: Harcourt Brace. 8–11 yrs.

Farmer, Nancy. 1995. *The Warm Place.* New York: Orchard/Jackson. 11–14 yrs.

Farmer, P. 1974. *William and Mary: A Story.* New York: Atheneum. 11–13 yrs.

Fleischman, Sid. 1990. *The Midnight Horse.* Illus. P. Sis. New York: Greenwillow. 10–12 yrs.

Fletcher, Susan. 1989. *Dragon's Milk.* New York: Simon & Schuster. 11–13 yrs.

Fienberg, A. 1990. *Wiggy and Boa.* Illus. A. James. Boston: Houghton Mifflin. 10–12 yrs.

Friend, Catherine. 1994. *My Head Is Full of Colors.* Illus. Kiki. New York: Hyperion. 5–7 yrs.

Gage, W. 1963. *Miss Osborne-the-Mop.* Illus. P. Galdone. New York: Pocket. 10–12 yrs.

Garner, A. 1979. *The Owl Service.* New York: Philomel. 12–15 yrs.

———. 1979. *The Weirdstone of Brisingamen.* New York: Philomel. 12–14 yrs. (See also sequel: *The Moon of Gomrath*, 1981. 12–14 yrs.)

Gray, Libba Moore. 1994. *Small Green Snake.* Illus. Holly Meade. New York: Orchard. 5–7 yrs.

Goudge, Elizabeth. 1981. *Linnets and Valerians.* Illus. I. Ribbons. New York: Avon. 11–13 yrs. (See also: *The Little White Horse.* 1992. 12–15 yrs.)

Hamilton, Virginia. 1983. *The Magical Adventures of Pretty Pearl.* New York: HarperCollins. 12–16 yrs.

Hazen, Barbara S. 1989. *The Knight Who Was Afraid of the Dark.* Illus. T. Ross. New York: Dial. 5–8 yrs.

———. 1994. *The Knight Who Was Afraid to Fight.* Illus. Toni Goffe. New York: Dial. 5–8 yrs.

Heine, Helme. 1982. *King Bounce the First.* Barrigada, Guam: Alphabet Press. 4–6 yrs.

———. 1995. *Friends Go Adventuring.* Illus. by Helme Heine. New York: McElderry. 4–6 yrs.

Herge. 1994. *The Adventures of Tintin, Volume 1: Tintin in America, Cigars of the Pharaoh, The Blue Lotus; The Adventures of Tintin, Volume 2: The Broken Ear, The Black Island, King Ottokar's Sceptre; The Adventures of Tintin, Volume 3: The Crab with the Golden Claws, The Shooting Star, The Secret of the Unicorn.* Boston: Little, Brown. 10–13 yrs.

Hodges, Margaret. (Reteller). 1995. *Gulliver in Lilliput.* Illus. Kimberly Bulcken Root. New York: Holiday. 8–12 yrs.

Hunter, M. 1970. *The Walking Stones: A Story of Suspense.* Illus. T. S. Hyman. New York: HarperCollins. 10–12 yrs.

Jacques, Brian. 1987. *Redwall.* Illus. G. Chalk. New York: Putnam. 11–16 yrs. (See other books in sequel: *Mossflower*, 1988; *Mattimeo*, 1990; *Mariel of Redwall*, 1992; *Martin the Warrior*, 1994; *Salamandastron*, 1993. 11–16 yrs.)

———. 1994. *The Bellmaker.* Illus. Allan Curless. New York: Putnam. 11–16 yrs. Redwall series.

Jones, Diana W. 1988. *The Lives of Christopher Chant.* New York: Greenwillow. 11–13 yrs. (See also: *The Magicians of Caprona*, 1980; *Witch Week*, 1982. 11–13 yrs.)

———. 1990. *The Ogre Downstairs.* New York: Greenwillow. 12–14 yrs.

———. 1989. *Charmed Life.* New York: Greenwillow. 11–13 yrs.

Joyce, William. 1993. *Santa Calls.* New York: HarperCollins/Geringer. 6–9 yrs.

Kendall, Carol. 1990. *The Gammage Cup.* Illus. E. Blegvad. San Diego: Harcourt Brace. 11–14 yrs.

Kimmel, Margaret M. 1975. *Magic in the Mist.* Illus. T. C. Hyman. New York: Simon & Schuster. 6–8 yrs.

Kooiker, I. 1978. *The Magic Stone.* Illus. C. Hollander. New York: Morrow. 8–12 yrs. (See also *Legacy of Magic*, 1979. 10–12 yrs.)

Kumin, M. & A. Sexton. 1975. *The Wizard's Tears.* Illus. E. Ness. 6–9 yrs.

Langton, Jane. 1980. *Fledgling.* New York: HarperCollins. 11–14 yrs. (Three-book sequel.)

Lawrence, L. 1978. *Star Lord.* New York: HarperCollins. 12–16 yrs.

Lester, Alison. 1991. *The Journey Home.* Boston: Houghton Mifflin. 6–9 yrs.

Lillegard, Dee. 1993. *My Yellow Ball.* Illus. Sarah Chamberlain. New York: Dutton. 5–7 yrs.

Mahy, Margaret. 1989. *The Blood-and-Thunder Adventure on Hurricane Peak.* New York: Simon & Schuster. 10–12 yrs.

———. 1991. *Dangerous Spaces.* New York: Viking. 10–12 yrs.

———. 1993. *The Pirates' Mixed-up Voyage.* New York: Dial. 8–12 yrs.

Manushkin, Fran. 1993. *My Christmas Safari.* Illustrated by R. W. Alley. New York: Dial. 5–8 yrs.

McAllister, Angela. 1991. *The Enchanted Flute.* New York: Delacorte. 5–7 yrs.

McCarthy, Bobette. 1994. *Dreaming.* Cambridge, Mass.: Candlewick. 4–6 yrs.

McKean, T. 1991. *The Secret of the Seven Willows.* New York: Simon & Schuster. 10–12 yrs.

McPhail, David. 1993. *Santa's Book of Names.* Boston: Little, Brown. 5–7 yrs.

Morgan, Helen. 1994. *The Witch Doll.* New York: Puffin. 10–12 yrs.

Morpurgo, Michael. 1995. *Arthur, High King of Britain.* Illus. Michael Foreman. San Diego: Harcourt Brace. 10–14 yrs.

Napoli, Donna J. 1993. *The Magic Circle.* New York: Dutton. 12–14 yrs.

Norman, R. 1992. *Albion's Dream: A Novel of Terror.* New York: Delacorte. 10–12 yrs.

Norton, Mary. 1990. *Bed-Knob & Broomstick.* Illus. E. Blegvad. San Diego: Harcourt Brace. 10–12 yrs.

Pierce, M. A. 1990. *The Pearl of the Soul of the World.* New York: 12–14 yrs. (See also *Darkangel*, 1982. 12–14 yrs.)

Preussler, Ottfried. (Trans. A. Bell). 1973. *The Satanic Mill.* New York: Macmillan. 11–13 yrs.

Pittau, Francisco. 1993. *The Tightrope Walker.* Illus. Bernadette Gervais. New York: Lothrop, Lee & Shepard. 5–7 yrs.

Place, Francois. (Trans. William Rodarmor). 1993. *The Last Giants.* Lincoln, Mass.: Godine.

Samton, Sheila W. 1993. *Jenny's Journey.* New York: Puffin. 5–9 yrs.

Schneider, Antonie. (Trans. J. Alison James.) 1995. *You Shall Be King!* Illus. Christa Unzner. New York: North-South. 6–9 yrs.

Seibold, J. Otto and Vivian Walsh. 1993. *Mr. Lunch Takes a Plane Ride.* Illus. J. Otto Seibold. New York: Viking. 6–8 yrs.

Selden, George. 1985. *The Genie of Sutton Place.* New York: Farrar, Straus & Giroux. 11–13 yrs.

Smith, Maggie. 1991. *There's a Witch Under the Stairs.* New York: Lothrop, Lee & Shepard. 4–8 yrs.

Smith, Sherwood. 1990. *Wren to the Rescue.* San Diego: Harcourt Brace. 10–12 yrs.

———. 1993. *Wren's Quest.* San Diego: Harcourt Brace. 10–12 yrs. (Sequel.)

Stephens, Jane. 1993. *Katie's Too Big Coat.* Illus. Nancy Poydar. New York: Simon & Schuster. 6–8 yrs.

Sterman, Betsy & Samuel Sterman. 1993. *Backyard Dragon.* Illus. David Wenzel. New York: HarperCollins. 12–15 yrs.

Sun, Chyng Feng. 1994. *On a White Pebble Hill.* Illus. Chihsien Chen. Boston: Houghton Mifflin. 6–8 yrs.

Tarr, Judith. 1993. *His Majesty's Elephant.* San Diego: Harcourt Brace. 12–15 yrs.

Taylor, Lisa. 1993. *Beryl's Box.* Illus. Penny Dann. Hauppauge, N.Y.: Barron. 5–8 yrs.

Testa, Fulvio. 1993. *Time to Get Out.* New York: Morrow. 4–6 yrs.

Tomlinson, Theresa. 1995. *The Forestwife.* New York: Orchard. 11–15 yrs.

Turnbull, A. 1975. *The Frightened Forest.* Illus. G. Gaze. Seabury. 10–12 yrs.

Willis, Val. 1990. *The Surprise in the Wardrobe.* Illus. J. Shelley. New York: Farrar, Straus & Giroux. 7–9 yrs.

Wrightson, Patricia. 1979. *The Dark Bright Water.* New York: Atheneum. 11–14 yrs. (See also books in sequel: *The Ice Is Coming*, 1977, and *Journey Behind the Winds*, 1981. Related book: *The Nargun and the Stars*, 1974. 11–14 yrs.)

Wynne-Jones, Tim. 1993. *Zoom at Sea.* Illus. Eric Beddows. New York: HarperCollins/Geringer. 7–10 yrs.

Yolen, Jane. 1991. *Wizard's Hall.* San Diego: Harcourt Brace. 8–12 yrs.

GHOST FANTASIES

Aiken, Joan. 1980. *The Shadow Guests.* New York: Delacorte. 14–16 yrs.

Alcock, V. 1982. *The Haunting of Cassie Palmer.* New York: Delacorte. 12–16 yrs.

Brown, Ruth. 1993. *One Stormy Night.* New York: Dutton. 6–8 yrs.

Carlson, N. S. 1984. *Ghost in the Lagoon.* Illus. A. Glass. New York: Lothrop. 7–10 yrs.

Chesworth, Michael. 1993. *Party at the Ghost House.* Illus. Chris Demarest. New York: Reader's Digest. 6–8 yrs.

Conrad, Pam. 1990. *Stonewords: A Ghost Story.* New York: HarperCollins. 12–14 yrs.

Coombs, Patricia. 1980. *Dorrie and the Blue Witch.* New York: Dell. 7–10 yrs. (See also other books about Dorrie.)

Cresswell, Helen. 1977. *A Game of Catch.* New York: Macmillan. 9–12 yrs.

Curry, J. L. 1977. *Poor Tom's Ghost.* New York: Atheneum. 12–16 yrs.

Dickens, C. 1990. *A Christmas Carol.* Illus. R. Innocenti. Mankato, Minn.: Creative Education. 10–16 yrs.

Duquennoy, Jacques. 1994. *The Ghost's Dinner.* Racine, Wisc.: Western Publishing. 5–7 yrs.

Freeman, B. C. 1977. *A Haunting Air.* New York: Dutton. 10–13 yrs.

Garfield, Leon. 1987. *The Wedding Ghost.* Illus. C. Keeping. New York: Oxford University Press. 12–16 yrs.

———. 1988. *The Empty Sleeve.* New York: Delacorte. 10–14 yrs.

Hahn, Mary D. 1986. *Wait Till Helen Comes: A Ghost Story.* Boston: Houghton Mifflin. 10–12 yrs.

———. 1989. *The Doll in the Garden: A Ghost Story.* Boston: Houghton Mifflin. 10–12 yrs.

———. 1994. *Time for Andrew: A Ghost Story.* Boston: Houghton Mifflin. 10–13 yrs.

Hawkins, Colin & Jacqui Hawkins. 1993. *Come for a Ride on the Ghost Train.* Cambridge, Mass.: Candlewick. 6–9 yrs.

Hodges, M. 1991. *Hauntings: Ghosts and Ghouls from around the World.* Illus. D. Wenzel. Boston: Little, Brown. 10–12 yrs.

Hoffman, Mary. 1993. *The Four-Legged Ghosts.* Illus. Laura L. Seeley. New York: Dial. 8–11 yrs.

Irving, Washington. 1990. *The Legend of Sleepy Hollow.* Illus. A. Rackham. New York: Morrow. 12–16 yrs.

Jacques, Brian. 1991. *Seven Strange and Ghostly Tales.* New York: Putnam. 10–12 yrs.

Kushner, D. 1990. *The House of the Good Spirits.* Lester & Orpen Dennys. 12–15 yrs.

Leach, M. 1959. *The Thing at the Foot of the Bed and Other Scary Tales.* Illus. K. Werth. New York: Putnam. 10–14 yrs.

Lisle, Janet T. 1991. *The Lampfish of Twill.* Illus. W. A. Halperin. New York: Orchard/Jackson. 10–12 yrs.

Lively, Penelope. 1973. *The Ghost of Thomas Kempe.* New York: Dutton. 10–12 yrs. (See also: *The Revenge of Samuel Stokes,* 1981. 11–13 yrs.)

———. 1976. *A Stitch in Time.* New York: Dutton. 9–13 yrs. (See also: *The Wild Hunt of the Ghost Hounds,* 1971. 9–13 yrs.)

Mahy, Margaret. 1987. *The Tricksters.* New York: Simon & Schuster. 11–16 yrs.

———. 1991. *Dangerous Spaces.* New York: Viking. 8–12 yrs.

Mayne, W. 1978. *It.* New York: Greenwillow. 12–16 yrs.

Peck, Richard. 1975. *The Ghost Belonged to Me: A Novel.* New York: Viking. 11–16 yrs.

Price, Susan. 1992. *Ghost Song.* New York: Farrar, Straus & Giroux. 10–12 yrs.

Seabrooke, Brenda. 1995. *The Haunting of Holroyd Hill.* New York: Dutton. 9–13 yrs.

Shecter, B. 1974. *The Whistling Whirligig.* New York: HarperCollins. 11–14 yrs.

Tomalin, Ruth. 1979. *Gone Away.* Merrimack. 11–13 yrs.

Turner, Ann. 1991. *Rosemary's Witch.* New York: HarperCollins. 9–12 yrs.

Westall, Robert. 1991. *The Promise.* New York: Scholastic. 12–14 yrs.

Wright, Betty R. 1990. *The Ghost of Ernie P.* New York: Holiday. 10–12 yrs.

———. 1991. *The Scariest Night.* New York: Holiday. 10–12 yrs.

———. 1993. *The Ghost of Popcorn Hill.* Illus. K. Ritz. New York: Holiday. 8–12 yrs.

———. 1993. *The Ghost Witch.* Illus. Ellen Eagle. New York: Holiday. 10–13 yrs.

———. 1993. *The Ghosts of Mercy Manor.* New York: Scholastic. 10–13 yrs.

———. 1995. *Out of the Dark.* New York: Scholastic. 9–13 yrs.

———. 1996. *Haunted Summer.* New York: Scholastic. 9–12 yrs.

HUMOROUS FANTASY

Ahlberg, Janet & Allan Ahlberg. 1990. *Funnybones.* New York: Morrow. 5–7 yrs.

Allen, Jonathan. 1995. *Two-by-Two-by-Two.* New York: Dial. 6–10 yrs.

Aiken, Joan. 1987. *The Wolves of Willoughby Chase.* New York: Doubleday. 11–14 yrs.

Armour, Peter. 1993. *Stop That Pickle!* Illus. Andrew Shachat. Boston: Houghton Mifflin. 6–8 yrs.

Arnold, Tedd. 1993. *Green Wilma.* New York: Dial. 5–8 yrs.

Auch, Mary Jane. 1993. *Peeping Beauty.* New York: Holiday. 5–7 yrs.

Babbitt, N. 1971. *Goody Hall.* New York: Farrar, Straus & Giroux. 11–13 yrs.

Bender, Robert. 1994. *A Most Unusual Lunch.* New York: Dial. 5–7 yrs.

Bontemps, A. & Conroy, J. 1942. *The Fast Sooner Hound.* Boston: Houghton Mifflin. 6–10 yrs.

Borovsky, Paul. 1993. *The Strange Blue Creature.* New York: Hyperion. 4–6 yrs.

Brown, Jeff. 1964. *Flat Stanley.* New York: HarperCollins. 6–10 yrs.

Burningham, John. 1993. *Harvey Slumfenburger's Christmas Present.* Cambridge, Mass.: Candlewick. 5–7 yrs.

Butterworth, O. 1993. *Trouble with Jenny's Ear.* Boston: Little, Brown. 9–12 yrs.

Carter, Penny. 1993. *A New House for the Morrisons.* New York: Viking. 5–7 yrs.

Christelow, Eileen. 1994. *The Great Pig Escape.* Boston: Houghton Mifflin. 4–6 yrs.

Conlon-McKenna, Marita. 1993. *Little Star.* Illus. Christopher Coady. Boston: Little, Brown. 4–7 yrs.

Dahl, R. 1982. *The BFG.* Illus. Q. Blake. New York: Farrar, Straus & Giroux. 9–12 yrs.

Drescher, Henrik. 1994. *The Boy Who Ate Around.* New York: Hyperion. 6–8 yrs.

Egan, Tim. 1995. *Chestnut Cove.* Boston: Houghton Mifflin. 5–9 yrs.

Fleischman, Sid. 1978. *Jim Bridger's Alarm Clock, and Other Tall Tales.* Illus. E. Von Schmidt. New York: Dutton. 7–10 yrs.

———. 1980. *Humbug Mountain.* Illus. E. Von Schmidt. Boston: Little, Brown. 10–13 yrs.

———. 1981. *McBroom Tells the Truth.* Illus. W. Lorraine. Boston: Little, Brown. 8–10 yrs. (See other books in the McBroom series).

Fleming, I. 1964. *Chitty-Chitty Bang Bang: The Magical Car.* Illus. J. Burningham. New York: Random House. 10–12 yrs.

Hale, Lucretia. 1981. *The Complete Peterkin Papers.* Sharon. 10–13 yrs. 7–9 yrs.

Hearn, Diane Dawson. 1993. *Dad's Dinosaur Day.* New York: Simon & Schuster. 5–8 yrs.

Heide, Florence P. 1983. *The Shrinking of Treehorn.* Illus. E. Gorey. (Paper title: *The Adventures of Treehorn*). New York: Dell. 5–7 yrs.

Hoban, R. 1978. *How Tom Beat Captain Najork and His Hired Sportsmen.* Illus. Q. Blake. New York: Atheneum. 7–10 yrs.

Hoff, Syd. 1993. *Bernard on His Own.* Boston: Houghton Mifflin. 4–7 yrs.

Hoffman, Mary. 1993. *The Four-Legged Ghosts.* Illus. Laura L. Seeley. New York: Dial. 8–11 yrs.

Houck, Eric L., Jr. 1993. *Rabbit Surprise.* Illus. Dominic Catalano. New York: Crown. 4–7 yrs.

Hutchins, Pat. 1975. *The House That Sailed Away.* Illus. L. Hutchins. New York: Greenwillow/Morrow. 10–12 yrs.

———. 1977. *Follow That Bus!* Illus. L. Hutchins. New York: Greenwillow/Morrow. 7–10 yrs.

Johnson, Paul Brett. 1993. *The Cow Who Wouldn't Come Down.* New York: Orchard/Jackson. 5–7 yrs.

Kharms, Daniil. 1996. *First, Second.* Illus. Marc Rosenthal. New York: Farrar, Straus & Giroux. 6–9 yrs.

Kiser, Kevin. 1994. *Sherman the Sheep.* Illus. Rowan Barnes-Murphy. New York: Simon & Schuster. 5–7 yrs.

Lee, Tanith. 1991. *Black Unicorn.* Illus. H. Cooper. New York: Simon & Schuster. 12–15 yrs.

Lester, Helen. 1994. *Three Cheers for Tacky.* Illus. Lynn Munsinger. Boston: Houghton Mifflin. 5–7 yrs.

Lies, Brian. 1994. *Hamlet and the Enormous Chinese Dragon Kite.* Boston: Houghton Mifflin. 5–8 yrs.

Lillegard, Dee. 1995. *The Hee-Haw River.* Illus. Allan Eitzen. New York: Holt. 5–9 yrs.

London, Jonathan. 1995. *Froggy Learns to Swim.* Illus. Frank Remkiewicz. New York: Viking. 4–8 yrs.

Lustig, Michael & Esther Lustig. 1994. *Willy Whyner, Cloud Designer.* New York: Simon & Schuster. 6–8 yrs.

MacDonald, Betty. 1957. *Mrs. Piggle-Wiggle.* Illus. H. Knight. New York: HarperCollins. 7–11 yrs. (See three other books in sequel.)

Mahy, M. 1996. *Tingleberries, Tuckertubs, and Telephones: A Tale of Love and Ice-Cream.* Illus. Robert Staermose. New York: Viking. 9–12 yrs.

Mathews, Judith. 1993. *An Egg and Seven Socks.* Illus. Marylin Hafner. New York: HarperCollins. 5–8 yrs.

McKean, Thomas. 1994. *Hooray for Grandma Jo!* Illus. Chris L. Demarest. New York: Crown. 4–6 yrs.

McKee, David. 1993. *Zebra's Hiccups.* New York: Simon & Schuster. 4–6 yrs.

McNaughton, Colin. 1995. *Suddenly!* San Diego: Harcourt Brace. 5–9 yrs.

McPhail, David. 1993. *Pigs Aplenty, Pigs Galore!* New York: Dutton. 5–7 yrs.

Meddaugh, Susan. 1994. *Martha Calling.* Boston: Houghton Mifflin. 5–7 yrs.

Merrill, Jean. 1964. *The Pushcart War.* Illus. R. Solbert. Reading, Mass.: Addison-Wesley. 10–14 yrs.

———. 1974. *The Toothpaste Millionaire.* Boston: Houghton Mifflin. 10–12 yrs.

Nostlinger, Christine. (Trans. A. Bell). 1982. *Konrad.* Illus. C. Nicklaus. (British title: *Conrad: The Hilarious Adventures of a Factory-made Child,* 1976.) New York: Avon. 10–13 yrs.

Parish, Herman. 1995. *Good Driving, Amelia Bedelia.* Illus. Lynn Sweat. New York: Greenwillow. 5–9 yrs.

Pinkwater, Daniel M. 1976. *Lizard Music.* New York: Dodd. 10–12 yrs.

———. 1978. *The Hoboken Chicken Emergency.* Englewood Cliffs, N.J.: Prentice-Hall. 8–11 yrs.

Primavera, Elise. 1993. *The Three Dots.* New York: Putnam. 6–8 yrs.

Raskin, Ellen. 1974. *Figgs & Phantoms.* New York: Dutton. 11–14 yrs.

———. 1981. *The Tattooed Potato and Other Clues.* New York: Avon. 12–14 yrs.

Remkiewicz, Frank. 1994. *The Bone Stranger.* New York: Lothrop, Lee & Shepard. 7–9 yrs.

Richemont, Enid. 1993. *The Magic Skateboard.* Illus. Jan Ormerod. Cambridge, Mass.: Candlewick. 8–10 yrs.

Rodgers, Mary. 1972. *Freaky Friday.* New York: HarperCollins. 11–13 yrs. (See sequel: *A Billion for Boris* and *Summer Switch.*)

Ross, Christine. 1993. *The Whirlys and the West Wind.* Boston: Houghton Mifflin. 5–7 yrs.

Rounds, G. 1980. *Mr. Yowder, The Peripatetic Sigh Painter: Three Tall Tales.* New York: Holiday. 8–11 yrs. (See also five companion volumes about Mr. Yowder.)

Rubel, Nicole. 1993. *Conga Crocodile.* Boston: Houghton Mifflin. 6–8 yrs.

Scarry, Richard. 1993. *Huckle Cat's Busiest Day Ever.* New York: Random House. 4–6 yrs.

Schindel, John. 1993. *What's for Lunch?* Illus. Kevin O'Malley. New York: Lothrop, Lee & Shepard. 4–6 yrs.

Schotter, Roni. 1993. *When Crocodiles Clean Up.* Illus. Thor Wickstrom. New York: Simon & Schuster. 5–8 yrs.

Shannon, Margaret. 1993. *Elvira.* New York: Ticknor & Fields. 6–8 yrs.

Simon, F. 1996. *The Topsy-Turview.* Illus. Keren Ludlow. New York: Dial. 4–7 yrs.

Singer, Isaac B. (Trans. E. Shub). 1973. *The Fools of Chelm and Their History.* New York: Farrar, Straus & Giroux. 10–13 yrs.

Speed, Toby. 1995. *Two Cool Cows.* Illus. Barry Root. New York: Putnam. 5–9 yrs.

Steele, W. O. 1959. *Andy Jackson's Water Well.* Illus. M. Ramos. San Diego: Harcourt Brace. 9–12 yrs. (See also *Daniel Boone's Echo* and *Davy Crockett's Earthquake.*)

Wilker, L. 1996. *Alfonse, Where Are You?* New York: Crown. 4–6 yrs.

Wood, Audrey. 1994. *The Tickleoctopus.* Illus. Don Wood. San Diego: Harcourt Brace. 6–8 yrs.

IMAGINARY WORLDS

Alcock, Vivien. 1993. *Singer to the Sea God.* New York: Delacorte. 12–17 yrs.

Alexander, L. 1989. *The Jedera Adventure.* New York: Dutton. 10–12 yrs.

_____. 1991. *The Remarkable Journey of Prince Jen*. New York: Dutton. 10–12 yrs.

Alexander, Lloyd. 1995. *The Arkadians*. New York: Dutton. 10–13 yrs.

Babbitt, Lucy Cullyford. 1993. *Where the Truth Lies*. New York: Orchard/Jackson. 12–16 yrs.

Babbitt, N. 1969. *The Search for Delicious*. New York: Farrar, Straus & Giroux. 8–12 yrs.

Baum, L. Frank. 1993 (reissue, 1910). *The Emerald City of Oz*. Illus. Jon R. Neill. New York: Morrow. 10–14 yrs. Books of Wonder Series.

_____. 1994. *Little Wizard Stories of Oz*. Illus. John R. Neill. New York: Morrow. 7–10 yrs. Book of Wonder Series.

Blackwood, G. L. 1991. *Beyond the Door*. New York: Atheneum. 12+ yrs.

Bradshaw, Gillian. 1993. *Beyond the North Wind*. New York: Greenwillow. 12–16 yrs.

Carroll, Lewis. 1993. *Through the Looking Glass and What Alice Found There*. Illus. John Tenniel. New York: Morrow. 10–15 yrs.

Charnas, Suzy McKee. 1993. *The Kingdom of Kevin Malone*. San Diego: Harcourt Brace. 12–16 yrs.

Chetwin, Grace. 1993. *The Chimes of Alyafaleyn*. New York: Simon & Schuster. 12–16 yrs.

Coatsworth, E. J. 1963. *The Princess and the Lion*. Illus. E. Ness. 10–12 yrs.

Cresswell, Helen. 1994. *The Watchers: A Mystery at Alton Towers*. New York: Simon & Schuster. 10–13 yrs.

de Saint-Exupery, Antoine. (Trans. Katherine Woods). 1993. *The Little Prince*. San Diego: Harcourt Brace. 9–14 yrs.

Dickinson, Peter. 1994. *Shadow of a Hero*. New York: Delacorte. 12–17 yrs.

Fletcher, Susan. 1993. *Flight of the Dragon Kyn*. New York: Simon & Schuster. 12–16 yrs.

Gliori, Debi. 1994. *A Lion at Bedtime*. Hauppauge, N.Y.: Barron. 5–7 yrs.

Harris, R. 1983. *Prince of the Godborn*. New York: Greenwillow. 12+ yrs. (See also books in sequel: *Children of the Wind* and *The Dead Kingdom*.)

Heyer, Marilee. 1988. *The Forbidden Door*. New York: Viking/Kestrel. 5–9 yrs.

Hilgartner, Beth. 1991. *The Feast of the Trickster*. Boston: Houghton Mifflin. 12–16 yrs. (See also *Dreamweaver's Loom*, 1989. 12–16 yrs.)

Jansson, Tove. (Trans. Kingsley Hart). 1993. *Moominpappa at Sea*. New York: Farrar, Straus & Giroux.

Jones, Diana W. 1981. *The Homeward Bounders*. New York: Greenwillow. 12–16 yrs. (See also Dalemark Series: *Cart and Cwidder*, 1977; *Drowned Ammet*, 1978; and *The Spellcoats*, 1979; New York: Atheneum. 12–16 yrs.)

_____. 1991. *Castle in the Air*. New York: Greenwillow. 12–16 yrs. (See also: *Howl's Moving Castle*, 1986. 12–16 yrs.)

_____. 1995. *Cart and Cwidder*. New York: Greenwillow. 12–16 yrs. Dalemark Quartet Series.

_____. 1995. *Drowned Ammet*. New York: Greenwillow. 12–16 yrs. Dalemark Quartet Series.

_____. 1995. *The Spellcoats*. New York: Greenwillow. 12–16 yrs. Dalemark Quartet Series.

Juster, Norton. 1961. *The Phantom Tollbooth*. New York: Knopf. 11–13 yrs.

Kennedy, R. 1979. *The Lost Kingdom of Karnica*. Illus. U. Shulevitz. New York: Scribners. 7–10 yrs.

Le Guin, Ursula. 1988. *Catwings*. Illus. S. D. Schindler. New York: Orchard. 7–10 yrs.

_____. 1990. *The Farthest Shore*. New York: Simon & Schuster. 11–15 yrs.

_____. 1990. *Tehanu: The Last Book of Earthsea*. New York: Simon & Schuster. 12–16 yrs.

Lively, Penelope. 1994. *The Cat, the Crow, and the Banyan Tree*. Illus. Terry Milne. Cambridge, Mass.: Candlewick. 5–7 yrs.

MacDonald, George. 1984. *The Light Princess*. Illus. M. Sendak. New York: Farrar, Straus & Giroux. 8–13 yrs.

Mayne, W. 1990. *Antar and the Eagles*. New York: Delacorte. 10–12 yrs.

McAllister, Angela. 1994. *The Ice Palace*. Illus. Angela Barrett. New York: Putnam. 7–9 yrs.

_____. 1994. *The Wind Garden*. Illus. Claire Fletcher. New York: Lothrop, Lee & Shepard. 5–9 yrs.

McCaffrey, Anne. 1976. *Dragonsong*. New York: Simon & Schuster. 12–16 yrs. (See also books in sequel: *Dragonsinger*, 1977; *Dragondrums*, 1979. 12–16 yrs.)

McKillip, Patricia A. 1975. *The Forgotten Beasts of Eld*. New York: Atheneum. 12–16 yrs.

_____. 1978. *Heir of Sea and Firs*. New York: Atheneum. 12–16 yrs. (See also other books in Hed Sequel: *The Riddle-Master of Hed*, 1985; *The Harpist in the Wind*, 1979. 12–16 yrs.)

McKinley, Robin. 1978. *Beauty: A Retelling of the Story of Beauty and the Beast*. New York: HarperCollins. 9–13 yrs.

_____. 1982. *The Blue Sword*. New York: Greenwillow. 13–17 yrs.

McPhail, David. 1994. *Moony B. Finch, the Fastest Draw in the West*. Racine, Wisc.: Western. 5–7 yrs.

Molesworth, M. L. 1976. *The Cuckoo Clock*. New York: Garland. 10–12 yrs.

Murphy, Sheila R. 1992. *Silver Woven in My Hair*. New York: Simon & Schuster. 10–12 yrs.

Nichols, R. 1969. *A Walk out of the World*. San Diego: Harcourt Brace. 10–12 yrs.

Page, P. K. 1989. *A Flask of Sea Water*. Illus. L. Gal. New York: Oxford University Press. 10–12 yrs.

Pilkey, Dav. 1993. *Kat Kong*. San Diego: Harcourt Brace. 6–9 yrs.

Pope, Elizabeth. 1974. *The Perilous Gard*. Boston: Houghton Mifflin. 11–13 yrs.

Pullman, Philip. 1996. *The Golden Compass*. New York: Knopf. 11–15 yrs.

Reiser, Lynn. 1995. *Night Thunder and the Queen of the Wild Horses*. Illus. by Lynn Reiser. New York: Greenwillow. 5–8 yrs.

Riordan, J. 1980. *The Three Magic Gifts*. Illus. E. leCain. New York: Oxford. 5–9 yrs.

Rodda, Emily. 1991. *Finders Keepers*. Illus. Noela Young. New York: Greenwillow. 10–16 yrs.

Sanderson, Ruth. 1991. *The Enchanted Wood*. Boston: Little, Brown. 7–11 yrs.

Sleator, William. 1970. *Angry Moon*. Illus. B. Lent. Boston: Little, Brown. 8–12 yrs.

Snyder, Zilpha K. 1992. *Below the Root*. New York: Dell. 13–16 yrs.

Stickland, Henrietta. 1993. *The Christmas Bear*. Illus. Paul Stickland. New York: Dutton. 4–6 yrs.

Terlouw, J. 1977. *How to Become King*. Mamaroneck, N.Y.: Hastings. 12–14 yrs.

White, Theodore H. 1978. *The Sword in the Stone*. New York: Dell. 11–14 yrs.

Winterfeld, Harry. (Trans. K. Schabert). 1990. *Castaways in Lilliput*. Illus. W. Hutchinson. San Diego: Harcourt Brace. 10–12 yrs.

Winthrop, Elizabeth. 1993. *The Battle for the Castle*. New York: Holiday. 9–12 yrs. (Sequel to *A Castle in the Attic*, 1985, New York: Holiday.)

Woodruff, Elvira. 1994. *The Magnificent Mummy Maker*. New York: Scholastic. 10–13 yrs.

Wrede, Patricia C. 1993. *Calling on Dragons*. San Diego: Harcourt Brace. 9–12 yrs. Enchanted Forest Chronicles Series.

_____. 1993. *Talking to Dragons*. San Diego: Harcourt Brace. 10–13 yrs. (Fourth in Enchanted Forest Chronicles Series.)

Wynne-Jones, Tim. 1993. *Zoom Away*. Illus. Eric Beddows. New York: HarperCollins. 6–9 yrs.

Zettner, Pat. 1990. *The Shadow Warrior*. New York: Simon & Schuster. 12–14 yrs.

LITERARY FANTASY TALES

Ada, Alma Flor. 1994. *Dear Peter Rabbit*. Illus. Leslie Tryon. New York: Simon & Schuster. 5–8 yrs.

Aiken, J. 1974. *Not What You Expected: A Collection of Short Stories*. New York: Doubleday. 8–12 yrs.

_____. 1992. *A Foot in the Grave*. Illus. J. Pienkowski. New York: Viking. 10–12 yrs.

Allen, Jonathan. 1993. *Who's at the Door?* New York: Morrow. 5–8 yrs.

Andersen, Hans Christian. (Trans. E. Le Gallienne). 1965. *The Nightingale*. Illus. N. Burkert. New York: HarperCollins. 7–10 yrs.

_____. 1968. *The Little Match Girl*. Illus. B. Lent. Boston: Houghton Mifflin. 7–10 yrs.

_____. (Adaptor A. Ehrlich). 1982. *The Snow Queen*. Illus. S. Jeffers. New York: Dial. 8–10 yrs.

_____. (Trans. A. Stewart). 1985. *The Ugly Duckling*. Illus. M. Laimgruber. New York: Greenwillow. 5–10 yrs.

_____. 1989. *The Little Mermaid*. Illus. Katie Thamer Treherne. San Diego: Harcourt Brace Jovanovich. 7–10 yrs.

_____. 1989. *The Nightingale*. Illus. Alison Claire Darke. New York: Doubleday. 6–9 yrs.

_____. (Reteller Neil Philip). 1989. *The Snow Queen*. Illus. Sally Holmes. New York: Lothrop, Lee and Shepard. 6–10 yrs.

_____. (Reteller Deborah Hautzig). 1990. *Thumbelina*. Illus. Kaarina Kaila. New York: Knopf/Borzoi. 6–9 yrs.

_____. (Reteller Troy Howell). 1990. *The Ugly Duckling*. Illus. Troy Howell. New York: Putnam. 6–9 yrs.

_____. (Reteller James Riordan). 1991. *Thumbelina*. Illus. Wayne Anderson. New York: Putnam. 6–9 yrs.

_____. (Adaptor Deborah Hahn). 1991. *The Swineherd: Narrated by Himself and Acted by His Favorite Friends and Relatives*. Illus. Deborah Hahn. New York: Lothrop, Lee & Shepard. 5–10 yrs.

_____. (Reteller Riki Levinson). 1991. *The Emperor's New Clothes*. Illus. Robert Byrd. New York: Dutton Children's Books. 4–8 yrs.

_____. 1991. *Thumbelina*. Illus. Alison Claire Darke. New York: Doubleday. 6–9 yrs.

_____. (Trans. Naomi Lewis). 1992. *The Steadfast Tin Soldier*. Illus. P. J. Lynch. San Diego: Harcourt Brace Jovanovich/Gulliver Books. 5–10 yrs.

_____. (Reteller Tor Seidler). 1992. *The Steadfast Tin Soldier*. Illus. Fred Marcellino. New York: HarperCollins/Michael di Capua Books. 5–10 yrs.

_____. (Trans. Naomi Lewis). 1993. *The Snow Queen*. Illus. Angela Barrett. Cambridge, Mass.: Candlewick. 7–10 yrs.

_____. (Trans. Anthea Bell). 1995. *The Swineherd*. Illus. Lisbeth Zwerger. New York: North-South.

Armstrong, Jennifer. 1995. *King Crow*. Illus. Eric Rohmann. New York: Crown. 6–9 yrs.

Babbitt, Natalie. 1994. *Bub or the Very Best Thing*. New York: HarperCollins/di Capua. 5–7 yrs.

Banks, Lynne Reid. 1993. *The Magic Hare*. Illus. Barry Moser. New York: Morrow. 6–9 yrs.

Barracca, Debra & Sal Barracca. 1994. *A Taxi Dog Christmas*. Illus. Alan Ayers. New York: Dial. 5–7 yrs.

Bodkin, Odds. 1995. *The Banshee Train.* Illus. Ted Rose. Boston: Houghton Mifflin. 7–10 yrs.

Bordewich, Fergus M. 1994. *Peach Blossom Spring.* Illus. Yang Ming-Yi. New York: Simon & Schuster. 6–8 yrs.

Burningham, John. 1976. *Mr. Gumpy's Motor Car.* New York: HarperCollins. 4–6 yrs.

_____. 1994. *Avocado Baby.* New York: HarperCollins. 5–7 yrs.

Calhoun, Mary. 1994. *Henry the Sailor Cat.* Illus. Erick Ingraham. New York: Morrow. 4–6 yrs.

Calmenson, Stephanie. 1989. *The Principal's New Clothes.* Illus. Denise Brunkus. New York: Scholastic. 6–9 yrs.

Carle, Eric. 1995. *Walter the Baker.* New York: Simon & Schuster. 5–9 yrs.

Carlstrom, Nancy White. 1993. *Fish and Flamingo.* Illus. Lisa Desimini. Boston: Little, Brown. 4–7 yrs.

Clark, Elizabeth. 1994. *Father Christmas and the Donkey.* Illus. Jan Ormerod. New York: Viking. 6–9 yrs.

Coffelt, Nancy. 1995. *The Dog Who Cried Woof.* San Diego: Harcourt Brace. 5–9 yrs.

Curry, Jane L. 1989. *Little, Little Sister.* Illus. E. Blegvad. New York: Simon & Schuster. 5–7 yrs.

Dahl, R. 1991. *The Minpins.* Illus. P. Benson. New York: Viking. 5–8 yrs.

Day, David. 1993. *King of the Woods.* Illus. Ken Brown. New York: Simon & Schuster. 6–8 yrs.

Ehrlich, Amy. 1993. *Parents in the Pigpen, Pigs in the Tub.* New York: Dial. 6–8 yrs.

Gogol, Nikolai. (Reteller Catherine Cowan). 1995. *Nikolai Gogol's The Nose: As Retold for Children.* Illus. Kevin Hawkes. New York: Lothrop, Lee & Shepard. 6–9 yrs.

Harness, Cheryl. 1993. *The Queen with Bees in Her Hair.* New York: Holt. 6–8 yrs.

Joyce, William. 1995. *Dinosaur Bob and His Adventures with the Family Lazardo.* New York: HarperCollins/Geringer. 6–10 yrs.

Kajpust, Melissa. 1993. *A Dozen Silk Diapers.* Illus. Veselina Tomova. New York: Hyperion. 6–8 yrs.

Kleven, Elisa. 1994. *The Paper Princess.* New York: Dutton. 4–6 yrs.

Kroll, Steven. 1993. *Queen of the May.* Illus. Patience Brewster. New York: Holiday. 5–7 yrs.

Lamorisse, Albert. 1978. *The Red Balloon.* Illus. photos from movie. New York: Doubleday. 6–12 yrs.

Lawson, Julie. 1993. *The Dragon's Pearl.* Illus. P. Morin. Boston: Houghton Mifflin. 5–8 yrs.

Lehan, Daniel. 1993. *Wipe Your Feet!* New York: Dutton. 5–7 yrs.

Lewison, Wendy. 1995. *The Rooster Who Lost His Crow.* Illus. Thor Wickstrom. New York: Dial. 2–5 yrs.

London, Jonathan. 1993. *Into This Night We Are Rising.* Illus. G. Brian Karas. New York: Viking. 4–7 yrs.

McKenzie, Ellen K. 1993. *The King, the Princess, and the Tinker.* Illus. W. Low. New York: Holt. 10–12 yrs.

McNaughton, Colin. 1994. *Captain Abdul's Pirate School.* Cambridge, Mass.: Candlewick. 6–8 yrs.

Meeks, Arone Raymond. 1993. *Enora and the Black Crane.* New York: Scholastic. 6–8 yrs.

Melmed, Laura Krauss. 1994. *Prince Nautilus.* Illus. Henri Sorensen. New York: Lothrop, Lee & Shepard. 7–9 yrs.

Mostacchi, Massimo. (Trans. Andrew Clements.) 1995. *The Beast and the Boy.* Illus. Monica Miceli. New York: North-South. 6–9 yrs.

Nesbit, E. 1989. *Melisande.* Illus. P. J. Lynch. San Diego: Harcourt Brace. 5–7 yrs.

Obrist, J. 1984. *The Miser Who Wanted the Sun.* New York: Atheneum. 5–9 yrs.

Petach, Heidi. 1995. *Goldilocks and the Three Hares.* Illus. by Heidi Petach. New York: Putnam. 6–9 yrs.

Pochocki, Ethel. 1993. *The Mushroom Man.* Illus. Barry Moser. New York: Simon & Schuster. 6–8 yrs.

Polacco, Patricia. 1993. *Babushka Baba Yaga.* New York: Putnam. 5–8 yrs.

Ross, T. 1983. *The Three Pigs.* New York: Pantheon. 5–8 yrs.

Scamell, Ragnhild. 1993. *Three Bags Full.* Illus. Sally Hobson. New York: Orchard. 4–6 yrs.

_____. 1994. *Rooster Crows.* Illus. Judith Riches. New York: Morrow. 4–7 yrs.

Scheffler, Ursel. (Trans. J. Alison James). 1993. *The Return of Rinaldo the Sly Fox.* Illus. Iskender Gider. New York: North-South. 6–8 yrs.

Scieszka, Jon. 1989. *The True Story of the Three Little Pigs.* Illus. L. Smith. New York: Viking. 7–12 yrs.

_____. 1991. *The Frog Prince, Continued.* Illus. S. Johnson. New York: Viking. 7–12 yrs.

_____. 1992. *The Stinky Cheese Man: And Other Fairly Stupid Tales.* Illus. L. Smith. New York: Viking/Penguin. 7–11 yrs.

Seymour, Tres. 1993. *Hunting the White Cow.* Illus. Wendy Anderson Halperin. New York: Orchard/Jackson. 6–8 yrs.

Shecter, Ben. 1993. *When Will the Snow Trees Grow?* New York: HarperCollins/Zolotow. 6–8 yrs.

Smith, Lane. 1993. *The Happy Hocky Family.* New York: Viking. 6–11 yrs.

Sutcliff, Rosemary. 1993. *The Minstrel & the Dragon Pup.* Illus. Emma Chichester Clark. Cambridge, Mass.: Candlewick. 7–9 yrs.

Swift, Jonathan. (Reteller Ann Keay Beneduce). 1993. *Gulliver's Adventures in Lilliput.* Illus. Gennady Spirin. New York: Putnam. 8–10 yrs.

Turnbull, Ann. 1994. *Too Tired.* Illus. Emma Chicester Clark. San Diego: Harcourt Brace. 6–8 yrs.

Vaughan, Marcia. 1994. *Dorobo the Dangerous.* Illus. Kazuko Stone. Morristown, N.J.: Silver Burdett. 6–8 yrs.

Watson, Pete. 1994. *The Market Lady & the Mango Tree.* Illus. Mary Watson. New York: Morrow. 6–8 yrs.

Wisniewski, David. 1989. *The Warrior and the Wise Man.* New York: Lothrop, Lee & Shepard. 6–10 yrs.

Wood, Audrey. 1987. *Heckedy Peg.* Illus. D. Wood. San Diego: Harcourt Brace. 4–7 yrs.

Woolf, Virginia. 1991. *Nurse Lugton's Curtain.* Illus. J. Vivas. San Diego: Harcourt Brace. 6–9 yrs.

Yee, Wong Herbert. 1993. *Big Black Bear.* Boston: Houghton Mifflin. 5–7 yrs.

Zwerger, Lisbeth. (Compiler). (Trans. Anthea Bell). 1991. *Hans Christian Andersen Fairy Tales.* Illus. Lisbeth Zwerger. Saxonville, Mass.: Picture Book Studio/Michael Neugebauer. 4–9 yrs.

PERSONIFIED TOYS AND OTHER INANIMATE OBJECTS

Bailey, C. S. 1977. *Miss Hickory.* New York: Puffin. 8–10 yrs.

Banks, Lynne Reid. 1993. *The Mystery of the Cupboard.* Illus. Tom Newsom. New York: Morrow. 9–12 yrs.

Baum, L. Frank. 1995. *The Patchwork Girl of Oz.* Illus. John R. Neil. New York: Morrow. 9–12 yrs.

Burnett, Frances H. 1975. *Racketty-Packetty House.* Illus. H. Johnson. Lippincott. 8–11 yrs.

Cassedy, Sylvia. 1989. *Lucie Babbidge's House.* New York: HarperCollins. 10–12 yrs.

Conrad, Pam. 1989. *The Tub People.* Illus. R. Egielski. New York: HarperCollins. 6–9 yrs.

_____. 1993. *The Tub Grandfather.* Illus. Richard Egielski. New York: HarperCollins/Geringer. 6–8 yrs.

_____. 1994. *Doll Face Has a Party!* Illus. Brian Selznick. New York: HarperCollins/Geringer. 5–8 yrs.

Dedieu, Thierry. 1993. (Trans. George Wen). *The Little Christmas Soldier.* New York: Holt. 5–8 yrs.

Dickinson, Peter. 1994. *Time & the Clock Mice, Etcetera.* Illus. by Emma Chichester-Clark. New York: Delacorte. 10–13 yrs.

Field, Rachel L. 1937. *Hitty, Her First Hundred Years.* Illus. D. Lathrop. New York: Macmillan. 10–12 yrs.

Godden, Rumer. 1954. *Impunity Jane.* Illus. A. Adams. New York: Viking. 7–10 yrs.

Griffith, Helen V. 1993. *Doll Trouble.* Illus. Susan Condie Lamb. New York: Greenwillow. 9–12 yrs.

Heller, Nicholas. 1993. *Peas.* New York: Greenwillow. 5–7 yrs.

Hissey, Jane. 1994. *Ruff.* New York: Random House. 4–7 yrs.

Hoban, Russell. 1975. *Mouse and His Child.* Illus. L. Hoban. New York: Avon. 10–13 yrs.

Kennedy, Richard. 1985. *Amy's Eyes.* Illus. R. Egielski. New York: HarperCollins. 10–14 yrs.

King-Smith, Dick. 1993. *Lady Daisy.* Illus. Jan Naimo Jones. New York: Delacorte. 9–12 yrs.

Mark, Jan. 1993. *Fun with Mrs. Thumb.* Illus. Nicola Bayley. Cambridge, Mass.: Candlewick. 5–7 yrs.

Mariana. 1988. *Miss Flora McFlimsey and the Baby New Year.* Illus. C. W. Howe. New York: Lothrop, Lee & Shepard. 3–6 yrs.

McClintock, Barbara. 1994. *The Battle of Luke and Longnose.* Boston: Houghton Mifflin. 6–8 yrs.

McGinley, P. 1990. *The Most Wonderful Doll in the World.* Illus. H. Stone. New York: Scholastic. 5–8 yrs.

Mills, Elaine. 1994. *The Cottage at the End of the Lane.* New York: Crown. 5–7 yrs.

Milne, A. A. 1928. *The House at Pooh Corner.* Illus. E. H. Shepard. New York: Dutton. 9–13 yrs.

Nabb, Magdalen. 1993. *The Enchanted Horse.* Illus. Julek Heller. New York: Orchard. 9–12 yrs.

O'Connell, J. 1976. *The Dollhouse Caper.* Illus. E. Blegvad. Crowell. 10–13 yrs.

Polacco, Patricia. 1990. *Babushka's Doll.* New York: Simon & Schuster. 5–9 yrs.

Poltarnees, Welleran. 1993. *A Most Memorable Birthday.* Illus. Paul Cline & Judythe Sieck. New York: Simon & Schuster. 7–9 yrs.

Richardson, J. 1990. *Nicholas and the Rocking Horse.* Nashville, Tenn.: Hambleton-Hill. 5–7 yrs.

Sleator, William. 1975. *Among the Dolls.* Illus. T. S. Hyman. New York: Dutton. 10–12 yrs.

Tregarthen, E. 1972. *The Doll Who Came Alive.* Illus. N. Unwin. New York: Day. 8–10 yrs.

Waugh, Sylvia. 1994. *The Mennyms.* New York: Greenwillow. 10–13 yrs.

_____. 1995. *Mennyms in the Wilderness.* New York: Greenwillow. 10–14 yrs.

_____. 1996. *The Mennyms Under Siege.* New York: Greenwillow. 10–13 yrs.

Williams, Margery. 1991. *The Velveteen Rabbit: Or How Toys Become Real.* Illus. W. Nicholson. New York: Doubleday. 7–16 yrs.

Winthrop, Elizabeth. 1985. *The Castle in the Attic.* New York: Holiday. 10–12 yrs.

SCIENCE FANTASY/FICTION

Alcock, V. 1988. *The Monster Garden.* New York: Delacorte. 10–14 yrs.

Anderson, Joan. 1993. *Richie's Rocket.* Photographs George Ancona. New York: Morrow. 6–8 yrs.

Berry, J. R. 1973. *Dar Tellum Stranger from a Distant Planet*. Illus. E. Scull. New York: Walker. 6–8 yrs.

Bova, B. 1971. *Exiled from Earth*. New York: Dutton. 13–16 yrs.

Brennan, Herbie. 1995. *The Mystery Machine*. New York: Simon & Schuster. 9–12 yrs.

Brittain, Bill. 1994. *Shape-Changer*. New York: HarperCollins. 10–13 yrs.

Cameron, Eleanor. 1954. *The Wonderful Flight to the Mushroom Planet*. Boston: Little, Brown. 11–13 yrs.

Christopher, J. 1970. *The Guardians*. Hamish Hamilton. 12–14 yrs.

———. 1974. *The Prince in Waiting*. New York: Macmillan. 11–13 yrs.

———. 1976. *The Sword of the Spirits*. New York: Macmillan. 12–15 yrs.

———. *A Dusk of Demons*. New York: Simon & Schuster. 10–13 yrs.

Clarke, A. C. 1963. *Dolphin Island*. New York: Holt. 12–14 yrs.

Corbett, S. 1981. *The Deadly Hoax*. New York: Dutton. 11–13 yrs.

Coville, Bruce. 1993. *Aliens Ate My Homework*. Illus. Katherine Coville. New York: Pocket Books. 10–13 yrs.

———. 1994. *I Left My Sneakers in Dimension X*. Illus. Katherine Coville. New York: Pocket Books. 9–12 yrs. Rod Allbright Alien Adventure series.

Cross, Gillian. 1995. *New World*. New York: Holiday. 12–16 yrs.

Dereske, Jo. 1989. *The Lone Sentinel*. New York: Simon & Schuster. 12–14 yrs.

Dickinson, P. 1989. *Eva*. New York: Delacorte. 12–16 yrs.

———. 1993. *A Bone from a Dry Sea*. New York: Delacorte. 11–16 yrs.

Dexter, Catherine. 1995. *Alien Game*. New York: Morrow. 10–14 yrs.

Engdahl, Sylvia L. 1970. *Enchantress from the Stars*. New York: Atheneum. 12–16 yrs.

Farmer, Nancy. 1994. *The Ear, the Eye, and the Arm: A Novel*. New York: Orchard/Jackson. 12–14 yrs.

Faville, Barry. 1989. *The Return*. New York: Oxford University Press. 12–14 yrs.

Fine, Anne. 1993. *The Chicken Gave It to Me*. Illus. Cynthia Fisher. Boston: Little, Brown. 10–13 yrs.

Fisk, N. 1971. *Trillions*. New York: Viking Penguin. 12–14 yrs.

Gilden, Mel. 1989. *Outer Space & All That Junk*. New York: HarperCollins. 11–16 yrs.

Goldman, E. M. 1995. *The Night Room*. New York: Viking. 12–16 yrs.

Greer, Gery & Robert Ruddick. 1992. *Let Me Off This Spaceship!* New York: HarperCollins. 7–9 yrs.

Hamilton, Virginia. 1978. *Justice and Her Brothers*. New York: Greenwillow. 12–16 yrs.

Harding, L. 1979. *Misplaced Persons*. New York: HarperCollins. 13–15 yrs.

Harrison, H. 1975. *The California Iceberg*. New York: Walker. 8–12 yrs.

Hoover, H. M. 1981. *Another Heaven, Another Earth*. New York: Viking. 12–14 yrs.

———. 1995. *The Winds of Mars*. New York: Dutton. 11–14 yrs.

Howarth, Lesley. 1994. *MapHead*. Cambridge, Mass.: Candlewick. 10–13 yrs.

Huddy, Delia. 1976. *Time Piper*. New York: Viking Penguin. 13–16 yrs.

Hughes, M. 1985. *Devil on My Back*. New York: Atheneum. 10–14 yrs.

———. 1987. *The Dream Catcher*. New York: Atheneum. 10–15 yrs.

Hughes, Monica. 1994. *The Crystal Drop*. New York: Simon & Schuster. 10–13 yrs.

———. 1995. *The Golden Aquarians*. New York: Simon & Schuster. 12–16 yrs.

Jackson, J. & W. Perlmutter. 1973. *The Endless Pavement*. Illus. R. Cuffari. New York: Seabury. 7–9 yrs.

Jacobs, Paul S. 1994. *Sleepers, Wake*. New York: Scholastic. 12–14 yrs.

Johnson, A. & E. 1984. *Danger Quotient*. New York: HarperCollins. 12–16 yrs.

Jones, Diana Wynne. 1994. *Hexwood*. New York: Greenwillow. 12–15 yrs.

Jordan, Sherryl. 1995. *Winter of Fire*. New York: Scholastic. 12–18 yrs.

King-Smith, Dick. 1995. *Harriet's Hare*. New York: Crown. 10–13 yrs.

Klause, Annette Curtis. 1993. *Alien Secrets*. New York: Delacorte. 9–13 yrs.

Krudop, Walter Lyon. 1995. *Something Is Growing*. New York: Simon & Schuster. 5–9 yrs.

Lawrence, Louise. 1988. *Calling B for Butterfly*. New York: HarperCollins. 11–14 yrs.

———. 1993. *Keeper of the Universe*. Boston: Houghton Mifflin. 12–16 yrs.

L'Engle, Madeleine. 1973. *A Wind in the Door*. New York: Farrar, Straus & Giroux. 12–16 yrs.

———. 1978. *A Swiftly Tilting Planet*. New York: Farrar, Straus & Giroux. 12–16 yrs.

Leek, S. 1969. *The Tree That Conquered the World*. Englewood Cliffs, N.J.: Prentice-Hall. 8–10 yrs.

Levy, Elizabeth. 1993. *Something Queer in Outer Space*. Illus. Mordicai Gerstein. New York: Hyperion. 6–8 yrs. (Ninth book in series.)

Lewis, C. S. 1938. *Out of the Silent Planet*. Lane. 12–15 yrs.

———. 1943. *Perelandra*. Lane. 12–15 yrs.

———. 1945. *That Hideous Strength: A Modern Fairy-Tale for Grown-Ups*. Lane. (Abridged edition: *The Tortured Planet*, 1958, New York: Avon. 12–17 yrs.)

Lindbergh, Anne. 1994. *Nick of Time*. Boston: Little, Brown. 10–13 yrs.

Lord, B. 1967. *The Day the Spaceship Landed*. Illus. H. Berson. New York: Walck. 8–9 yrs. (See also *The Day the Spaceship Returns*, 1970.)

MacGregor, E. 1951. *Miss Pickerell Goes to Mars*. New York: McGraw-Hill. 8–10 yrs. (See also other books in sequel.)

Mahy, Margaret. 1994. *The Greatest Show off Earth*. Illus. by Wendy Smith. New York: Viking. 10–13 yrs.

McCaffrey, Anne. 1976. *Dragonsong*. New York: Simon & Schuster. 12–15 yrs.

McKillip, Patricia. 1984. *Moon-Flash*. New York: Atheneum. 12–16 yrs.

Morresy, J. 1974. *The Humans of Ziax II*. Walker. 7–9 yrs. (See also the sequel: *The Drought on Ziax II*, 1978. 7–9 yrs.)

———. 1975. *The Windows of Forever*. Walker. 8–10 yrs.

North, E. 1955. *The Ant Men*. New York: Winston. 12–14 yrs.

Norton, A. 1967. *Operation Time Search*. San Diego: Harcourt Brace. 12–14 yrs.

Norton, A. & D. Madlee. 1976. *Star Ka'at*. Walker. 8–10 yrs. (See also sequels: *Star Ka'at World*, 1978; *Star Ka'ats and the Plant People*, 1979; *Star Ka'ats and the Winged Warriors*, 1981. 8–10 yrs.)

Nourse, A. E. 1960. *Star Surgeon*. New York: McKay. 12–15 yrs.

O'Brien, Robert C. 1975. *Z for Zachariah*. New York: Simon & Schuster. 12–16 yrs.

Oppel, Kenneth. 1993. *Dead Water Zone*. Boston: Little, Brown. 12–15 yrs.

Pace, Sue. 1993. *The Last Oasis*. New York: Delacorte. 12–16 yrs.

Patchett, T. 1990. *Truckers*. New York: Delacorte. 10–12 yrs.

Pinkwater, Daniel. 1990. *Borgel*. New York: Simon & Schuster. 12–14 yrs.

Randall, F. E. 1976. *A Watcher in the Woods*. New York: Atheneum. 12–15 yrs.

Reynolds, A. 1985. *Kiteman of Karanga*. New York: Knopf. 12–14 yrs.

Rubinstein, B. 1990. *Beyond the Labyrinth*. New York: Orchard/Jackson. 12–16 yrs.

Ryan, Mary C. 1991. *Me, Two*. Boston: Little, Brown. 10–13 yrs.

Sadler, Marilyn. 1994. *Alistair and the Alien Invasion*. Illus. Roger Bollen. New York: Simon & Schuster. 7–10 yrs.

Schlee, Ann. 1981. *The Vandal*. New York: Crown. 12–14 yrs.

Service, Pamela. 1993. *Stinker's Return*. New York: Simon & Schuster. 10–13 yrs. (Sequel to *Stinker from Space*, 1988, New York: Simon & Schuster. 11–14 yrs.)

Skurzynski, Gloria. 1995. *Cyberstorm*. New York: Simon & Schuster. 10–15 yrs.

Sleator, William. 1986. *The Boy Who Reversed Himself*. New York: Dutton. 10–14 yrs.

———. 1993. *Others See Us*. New York: Dutton. 12–15 yrs.

———. 1995. *Interstellar Pig*. New York: Puffin. 11–14 yrs.

Slobodkin, L. 1993. *The Space Ship uinder the Apple Tree*. New York: Simon & Schuster. 8–10 yrs. (See also *The Space Ship Returns to the Apple Tree*, 1958; *The Three-Seated Space Ship*, 1962; *Round Trip Space Ship*, 1968; and *The Space Ship in the Park*, 1972.)

Slote, Alfred. 1981. *C.O.L.A.R.* A. Kramer. New York: HarperCollins. 10–12 yrs. (See also: *My Trip to Alpha I.*, 1992; *Omega Station*, 1986; and *The Trouble on Janus*, 1985; New York: HarperCollins.)

———. 1986. *My Robot Buddy*. New York: HarperCollins. 9–11 yrs.

Stevermer, C. 1992. *River Rats*. San Diego: Harcourt Brace. 10–12 yrs.

Walsh, J. P. 1981. *The Green Book*. New York: Macmillan. 8–10 yrs.

Williams, Travis. 1993. *Changes*. Kansas City, Mo.: Landmark. 8–11 yrs.

Yolen, Jane. 1980. *Commander Toad in Space*. Illus. B. Degen. New York: Putnam. 6–9 yrs.

SHORT STORY COLLECTIONS

Andersen, Hans Christian. 1992. *Seven Tales by H. C. Andersen*. Illus. M. Sendak. New York: HarperCollins. 7–12 yrs.

———. 1994. *Twelve Tales*. Illus. by Erik Blegvad. New York: Simon & Schuster. 9–12 yrs.

Berry, James. 1993. *The Future-Telling Lady and Other Stories*. New York: HarperCollins/Perlman. 9–12 yrs.

de Brunhoff, Jean and Laurent de Brunhoff. 1993. *Babar's Anniversary Album*. New York: Random House. 6–9 yrs.

Fox, Paula. 1981. *The Little Swineherd and Other Tales*. New York: Dell. 8–12 yrs.

Gardner, J. C. 1975. *Dragon, Dragon, and Other Timeless Tales*. New York: Knopf. 11–14 yrs.

Holmes, B. 1979. *Enchanted World: Pictures to Grow Up With*. New York: Oxford. 8–12 yrs.

Jones, Diana Wynne. 1993. *Stopping for a Spell: Three Fantasies*. Illus. Jos. A. Smith. New York: Greenwillow. 9–12 yrs. (three stories.)

Jones, Terry. 1993. *Fantastic Stories*. Illus. Michael Foreman. New York: Viking. 9–12 yrs.

Mahy, Margaret. 1993. *The Door in the Air*. Illus. D. Catchpole. New York: Dell. 10–12 yrs.

———. 1994. *Tick Tock Tales*. Illus. Wendy Smith. New York: Simon & Schuster. 7–11 yrs.

Marshall, James. 1991. *Rats on the Roof and Other Stories*. New York: Dial. 7–10 yrs.

McKinley, R. 1996. *The Door in the Hedge*. New York: Greenwillow. 12–16 yrs.

Potter, Beatrix. 1987. *The Tale of Jemima Puddle-Duck and Other Farmyard Tales*. New York: Warne. 6–9 yrs.

Westall, Robert. 1994. *Shades of Darkness: More of the Ghostly Best Stories of Robert Westall*. New York: Farrar, Straus & Giroux. 12–16 yrs.

Williams, J. 1978. *The Practical Princess and Other Liberating Fairy Tales*. New York: Parents' Magazine. 6–9 yrs.

Wrede, Patricia C. 1996. *Book of Enchantments*. San Diego: Harcourt Brace. 11–14 yrs.

Wynne-Jones, Tim. 1995. *Some of the Kinder Planets*. New York: Orchard/Kroupa. 10–14 yrs. (Nine stories)

Yolen, Jane. 1989. *Dream Weaver*. Illus. M. Hague. New York: Philomel. 10–14 yrs.

Yolen, Jane & Martin H. Greenberg (Eds.). 1989. *Things that Go Bump in the Night: A Collection of Original Stories*. New York: HarperCollins. 11–14 yrs.

TIME-SLIP FANTASY

Allan, M. E. 1975. *Romansgrove*. Illus. G. Owens. New York: Atheneum. 10–12 yrs.

Arthur, R. M. 1967. *Requiem for a Princess*. New York: Atheneum. 12–15 yrs.

Bond, Nancy. 1976. *A String in the Harp*. New York: Simon & Schuster. 12–16 yrs.

Collier, John. 1993. *In My Backyard*. New York: Viking. 6–8 yrs.

Cooney, Caroline B. 1996. *Out of Time*. New York: Delacorte. 12–16 yrs.

Curry, J. L. 1978. *The Bassumtyte Treasure*. New York: Atheneum. 11–13 yrs.

Davies, A. 1980. *Conrad's War*. New York: Crown. 11–13 yrs.

Dickinson, Peter. 1993. *A Bone from a Dry Sea*. New York: Delacorte. 12–16 yrs.

Dunlop, Eileen. 1989. *The Valley of Deer*. New York: Holiday. 12–14 yrs.

Farmer, P. 1996. *Penelope*. New York: McElderry. 12–15 yrs.

Fleischman, P. 1991. *Time Train*. Illus. C. Ewart. New York: HarperCollins. 4–8 yrs.

Griffin, Peni R. 1993. *Switching Well*. New York: Simon & Schuster. 12–14 yrs.

Hippely, Hilary Horder. 1994. *The Crimson Ribbon*. Illus. Jo Ellen McAllister Stammen. New York: Putnam. 7–9 yrs.

Hoppe, Joanne. 1992. *Dream Spinner*. New York: Morrow. 12–14 yrs.

Houghton, E. 1980. *Steps Out of Time*. New York: Lothrop, Lee & Shepard. 11–14 yrs.

Hurmence, Belinda. 1982. *A Girl Called Boy*. New York: Clarion/Houghton. 12–14 yrs.

Kindl, Patrice. 1993. *Owl in Love*. Boston: Houghton Mifflin. 12–17 yrs.

Levin, Betty. 1989. *The Keeping Room*. New York: Greenwillow. 13–16 yrs.

Lively, Penelope. 1974. *The House in Norham Gardens*. New York: Dutton. 12–14 yrs.

Lunn, Janet. 1983. *The Root Cellar*. New York: Simon & Schuster. 11–13 yrs.

Lyon, George-Ella. 1995. *Here & Then*. New York: Orchard/Jackson. 11–14 yrs.

McGraw, Eloise J. 1990. *A Really Weird Summer*. New York: Simon & Schuster. 12–14 yrs.

Pascal, F. 1977. *Hangin' Out with Cici*. New York: Viking. 12–15 yrs.

Peck, Richard. 1977. *Ghosts I Have Been*. New York: Viking. 12–16 yrs. (See also: *The Ghost Belonged to Me*, 1975; *The Dreadful Future of Blossom Culp*, 1983. 12–16 yrs.)

———. 1989. *Voices After Midnight*. New York: Delacorte. 12–14 yrs.

Pearson, Kit. 1991. *A Handful of Time*. New York: Puffin. 11–15 yrs.

Scieszka, Jon. 1993. *Your Mother Was a Neanderthal*. Illus. Lane Smith. New York: Viking. 9–12 yrs. Time Warp Trio Series.

———. 1995. *2095*. Illus. Lane Smith. New York: Viking. 9–11 yrs. Time Warp Trio Series.

Slepian, Jan. 1993. *Back to Before*. New York: Putnam. 10–13 yrs.

Smith, D. B. 1989. *Voyages*. New York: Viking. 12–14 yrs.

Stolz, M. 1975. *The Cat in the Mirror*. New York: HarperCollins. 11–13 yrs.

Sykes, P. 1976. *Mirror of Danger*. New York: Archway. 11–12 yrs.

Voigt, C. 1990. *On Fortune's Wheel*. New York: Simon & Schuster. 12–14 yrs. (See also: *Jackaroo*, 1985, New York: Simon & Schuster.)

Walsh, Jill. 1980. *A Chance Child*. New York: Avon. 12–16 yrs.

Westall, R. 1977. *The Wind Eye*. New York: Greenwillow/Morrow. 13–16 yrs.

———. 1978. *The Watch House*. New York: Greenwillow/Morrow. 12–16 yrs.

Wiseman, David. 1990. *Jeremy Visick*. Boston: Houghton Mifflin. 11–13 yrs.

CHAPTER 5

CHILDREN'S BOOKS MENTIONED IN THE CHAPTER

Ackerman, K. 1995. *Bingleman's Midway*. Illus. Barry Moser. Honesdale, Penn.: Boyds. 6–9 yrs.

Adler, C. S. 1995. *Courtyard Cat*. New York: Clarion. 8–11 yrs.

Alcock, V. 1992. *A Kind of Thief*. New York: Delacorte. 10–12 yrs.

Alcott, L. M. 1994. *Little Women: Or Meg, Jo, Beth, and Amy*. Boston: Little, Brown. 11–16 yrs.

———. 1971. *Jo's Boys*. New York: Grosset & Dunlap. 11–15 yrs.

Anaya, R. 1995. *The Farolitos of Christmas*. Illustrated by Edward Gonzales. New York: Hyperion. 6–9 yrs.

Anderson, L. 1989. *Stina*. Illus. Lena Anderson. New York: Greenwillow. 4–8 yrs.

———. 1991. *Stina's Visit*. Illus. Lena Anderson. New York: Greenwillow. 4–8 yrs.

Armstrong, J. 1995. *Black-Eyed Susan*. Illus. Emily Martindale. New York: Crown. 9–12 yrs.

Armstrong, W. H. 1969. *Sounder*. New York: HarperCollins. 10–12 yrs.

Arrington, F. 1994. *Stella's Bull*. Illus. Aileen Arrington. Boston: Houghton Mifflin. 5–8 yrs.

Avi, 1992. *"Who Was That Masked Man, Anyway?"* New York: Orchard/Jackson. 10–13 yrs.

Bartone, E. 1993. *Peppe the Lamplighter*. Illus. Ted Lewin. New York: Lothrop, Lee & Shepard. 7–10 yrs.

Base, G. 1988. *The Eleventh Hour: A Curious Mystery*. New York: Abrams. 8–12 yrs.

Bauer, M. D. 1986. *On My Honor*. New York: Clarion. 10–13 yrs.

Behn, H. 1963. *The Faraway Lurs*. New York: Putnam. 12–15 yrs.

Blume, J. 1970. *Are You There God? It's Me, Margaret*. New York: Bradbury. 10–12 yrs.

———. 1975. *Forever*. New York: Bradbury. 14–18 yrs.

———. 1990. *Fudge-a-mania*. New York: Dutton. 10–11 yrs.

Bunting, E. 1991. *Fly Away Home*. Illus. Ronald Himler. New York: Clarion. 9–12 yrs.

———. 1994. *Smoky Night*. Illus. David Diaz. San Diego: Harcourt Brace. 9–12 yrs.

Burnett, F. 1988. *The Secret Garden*. Illus. Tasha Tudor. New York: Viking. 10–13 yrs.

Burnford, S. 1961. *The Incredible Journey*. Illus. Carl Burger. Boston: Little, Brown. 10–13 yrs.

Burton, V. L. 1942. *The Little House*. Boston: Houghton Mifflin. 4–7 yrs.

Byars, B. 1970. *Summer of the Swan*. Illus. Ted CoConis. New York: Viking. 9–12 yrs.

———. 1977. *The Pinballs*. New York: HarperCollins. 11–13 yrs.

———. 1986. *Not-Just-Anybody Family*. New York: Delacorte. 9–12 yrs.

———. 1995. *Tarot Says Beware*. New York: Viking. 9–12 yrs. Herculeah Jones Mystery series.

Clapp, P. 1982. *Witches' Children: A Story of Salem*. New York: Lothrop, Penguin/Puffin. 11–14 yrs.

Cleary, B. 1981. *Ramona Quimby, Age 8*. New York: Morrow. 7–9 yrs.

———. 1983. *Dear Mr. Henshaw*. Illus. Paul O. Zelinsky. New York: Morrow. 9–12 yrs.

———. 1991. *Strider*. Illus. Paul O. Zelinsky. New York: Morrow. 8–12 yrs.

Cleaver, V. & B. Cleaver. 1969. *Where the Lillies Bloom*. Illus. James Spanfeller. New York: Lippincott. 10–13 yrs.

Coman, C. 1995. *What Jamie Saw*. Arden, N.C.: Front. 9–12 yrs.

Conford, E. 1988. *A Case for Jenny Archer*. Boston: Little, Brown. 9–12 yrs.

Conly, J. L. 1995. *Trout Summer*. New York: Holt. 12–15 yrs.

Cushman, K. 1994. *Catherine, Called Birdy*. New York: Clarion. 12–16 yrs.

Dalgliesh, A. 1954. *The Courage of Sarah Noble*. New York: Scribners. 7–10 yrs.

De Angeli, M. 1946. *Bright April*. Doubleday. 9–11 yrs.

———. 1949. *The Door in the Wall*. New York: Doubleday. 9–12 yrs.

DeJong, M. 1956. *The House of Sixty Fathers*. Illus. Maurice Sendak. New York: HarperCollins. 10–13 yrs.

de Paola, T. 1996. *The Baby Sister*. New York: Putnam. 6–9 yrs.

Dionetti, M. & Riggio, A. 1991. *Coal Mine Peaches*. New York: Orchard. 6–10 yrs.

Dixon, Franklin. 1927. *The Hardy Boys*. New York: Simon & Schuster. 7–12 yrs.

Dodge, M. M. 1865. *Hans Brinker, or The Silver Skates*. Illus. Hilda Van Stockum. New York: World. 10–12 yrs.

Estes, E. 1944. *The Hundred Dresses*. Illus. Louis Slobodkin. Orlando, Fla.: Harcourt Brace. 8–10 yrs.

Fine, A. 1994. *Flour Babies*. Boston: Little, Brown. 9–12 yrs.

Fitzhugh, L. 1964. *Harriet the Spy*. New York: HarperCollins. 10–13 yrs.

Forbes, E. 1942. *Paul Revere and the World He Lived In*. Boston: Houghton Mifflin.

———. 1969. *Johnny Tremain*. Boston: Houghton Mifflin. 10–13 yrs.

Gardiner, J. R. 1980. *Stone Fox*. Illus. Marcia Sewall. New York: Crowell. 9–11 yrs.

Gerrard, R. 1996. *Wagons West!* New York: Farrar, Straus & Giroux. 7–11 yrs.

Hamilton, V. 1974. *M. C. Higgins the Great*. New York: Macmillan. 11–14 yrs.

_____. 1984. *The House of Dies Drear*. New York: Macmillan. 11–13 yrs.

Hendershot, Judith. 1987. *In Coal Country*. Illus. Thomas B. Allen. New York: Knopf. 6–10 yrs.

Hermes, P. 1995. *On Winter's Wind: A Novel*. Boston: Little, Brown. 9–12 yrs.

Hickman, J. 1994. *Jericho*. New York: Greenwillow. 9–12 yrs.

Hinton, S. E. 1967. *The Outsiders*. New York: Viking. 13–18 yrs.

Hobbs, W. 1989. *Bearstone*. New York: Atheneum. 9–12 yrs.

_____. 1993. *Beardance*. New York: Atheneum. 10–13 yrs.

Houston, G. 1988. *The Year of the Perfect Christmas Tree*. Illus. Barbara Cooney. New York: Dial. 8–12 yrs.

_____. 1990. *Littlejim*. Illus. Thomas B. Allen. New York: Philomel. 8–12 yrs.

_____. 1992. *But No Candy*. Illus. Lloyd Bloom. New York: Philomel. 6–10 yrs.

_____. 1992. *My Great Aunt Arizona*. Illus. Susan Condie Lamb. New York: HarperCollins. 5–9 yrs.

_____. 1994. *Littlejim's Gift: An Appalachian Christmas Story*. Illus. Thomas B. Allen. New York: Philomel. 8–11 yrs.

_____. 1994. *Mountain Valor*. Illus. Thomas B. Allen. New York: Philomel. 11–13 yrs.

Howe, D. & J. Howe. 1979. *Bunnicula*. New York: Avon. 8–11 yrs.

_____. 1983. *The Celery Stalks at Midnight*. Illus. L. Morrill. New York: Atheneum. 8–11 yrs.

Howe, J. 1982. *Howliday Inn*. Illus. Lynn Musinger. New York: Atheneum. 9–11 yrs.

Hunt, I. 1978. *The Lottery Rose*. New York: Scribners. 10–14 yrs.

Isadora, R. 1991. *At the Crossroads*. New York: Greenwillow. 4–7 yrs.

_____. 1995. *Lili on Stage*. New York: Putnam. 7–10 yrs.

Keehn, S. M. 1991. *I Am Regina*. New York: Philomel. 10–14 yrs.

Keene, Carolyn. 1930. *The Bungalow Mystery*. New York: Grosset & Dunlap. 9–12 yrs. Nancy Drew Mystery Stories.

Kelly, E. 1928. *The Trumpeter of Krakow*. New York: Macmillan. 11–14 yrs.

Konigsburg, E. L. 1967. *From the Mixed-Up Files of Mrs. Basil E. Frankweiler*. New York: Atheneum. 10–13 yrs.

Lester, A. 1994. *My Farm*. Illus. Alison Lester. Boston: Houghton Mifflin. 5–8 yrs.

Lowery, L. 1987. *Rabble Starkey*. New York: Dell. 10–14 yrs.

_____. 1991. *Shilo*. New York: Atheneum. 10–13 yrs.

Macauley, D. 1990. *Black and White*. Boston: Houghton Mifflin. 6–12 yrs.

_____. 1995. *Shortcut*. Boston: Houghton/Lorraine. 7–10 yrs.

MacLachlan, P. 1985. *Sarah, Plain and Tall*. New York: HarperCollins. 7–10 yrs.

_____. 1993. *Baby*. New York: Delacorte. 10–12 yrs.

Mann, P. 1973. *My Dad Lives in a Downtown Hotel*. Illus. R. Cuffari. New York: Doubleday. 8–12 yrs.

McCloskey, R. 1941. *Make Way for Ducklings*. 1941. New York: Viking. 4–8 yrs.

_____. 1943. *Homer Price*. New York: Viking. 10–12 yrs.

_____. 1948. *Blueberries for Sal*. New York: Viking. 4–8 yrs.

McKay, H. 1995. *Dog Friday*. New York: McElderry. 9–12 yrs.

McSwigan, M. 1942. *Snow Treasure*. New York: Scholastic. 10–14 yrs.

Mills, L. 1991. *Rag Coat*. Boston: Little, Brown. 9–12 yrs.

Montgomery, L. M. 1908. *Anne of Green Gables*. New York: Grossett & Dunlap. 10–13 yrs.

Myers, W. D. 1988. *Scorpions*. New York: Harper & Row. 12–15 yrs.

Naylor, P. R. *Shilo*. New York: Atheneum. 10–13 yrs.

Nerlove, M. 1996. *Flowers on the Wall*. New York: McElderry. 6–10 yrs.

Newbery, J. 1744. *A Little Pretty Pocketbook*. London: Newbery Press.

_____. (publisher) 1765. *The History of Little Goody Two Shoes*. London: Newbery.

Nichol, B. 1994. *Beethoven Lives Upstairs*. Illus. Scott Cameron. New York: Orchard. 8–11 yrs.

O'Dell, S. 1960. *Island of the Blue Dolphins*. Boston: Houghton Mifflin. 10–14 yrs.

Paterson, K. 1973. *The Sign of the Chrysanthemum*. New York: Crowell. 11–14 yrs.

_____. 1974. *Of Nightingales That Weep*. New York: Crowell. 11–14 yrs.

_____. 1975. *The Master Puppeteer*. New York: Crowell.

_____. 1976. *The Bridge to Terabithia*. Illus. Donna Diamond. New York: HarperCollins. 10–12 yrs.

_____. 1978. *The Great Gilly Hopkins*. New York: HarperCollins. 10–13 yrs.

_____. 1979. *Angels and Other Strangers*. New York: Crowell. 9–13 yrs.

_____. 1980. *Jacob Have I Loved*. New York: HarperCollins. 10–14 yrs.

_____. 1983. *Rebels of the Heavenly Kingdom*. New York: Dutton. 9–12 yrs.

_____. 1985. *Come Sing, Jimmy Jo*. New York: Dutton. 10–13 yrs.

_____. 1990. *The Tale of the Mandarin Ducks*. Illus. Leo & Diane Dillon. New York: Lodestar. 7–11 yrs.

_____. 1991. *Lyddie*. New York: Lodestar. 10–14 yrs.

_____. 1994. *Flip-Flop Girl*. New York: Lodestar. 9–12 yrs.

Paulsen, G. 1983. *Dancing Carl*. New York: Bradbury. 9–13 yrs.

_____. 1987. *Hatchet*. New York: Bradbury. 9–13 yrs.

_____. 1989. *The Winter Room*. New York: Orchard. 11–13 yrs.

_____. 1991. *The Cookcamp*. New York: Orchard. 10–13 yrs.

_____. 1991. *The River*. New York: Delacorte. 11–14 yrs.

_____. 1985. *Dogsong*. New York: Bradbury. 10–14 yrs.

_____. 1993. *Nightjohn*. New York: Delacorte. 10–14 yrs.

_____. 1995. *The Tent*. Orlando, Fla.: Harcourt Brace. 11–16 yrs.

_____. 1996. *Brian's Winter*. New York: Delacorte. 10–14 yrs.

Peck, R. N. 1974. *Soup*. New York: Knopf. 9–12 yrs.

Rappaport, D. 1987. *Trouble at the Mines*. Illus. Joan Sandin. New York: Crowell. 10–13 yrs.

Reaver, C. 1994. *Bill*. New York: Delacorte. 11–13 yrs.

Reeder, C. 1993. *Moonshiner's Son*. New York: Macmillan. 11–15 yrs.

Rylant, C. 1991. *Appalachia: Voices of the Sleeping Birds*. Illus. Barry Moser. Orlando, Fla.: Harcourt Brace. 6–12 yrs.

Sachar, L. 1994. *Marvin Redpost: Alone in His Teacher's House*. Illus. Barbara Sullivan. New York: Random House. 7–9 yrs.

Sinclair, C. 1839. *Holiday House*. English writer.

Soto, G. 1991. *Baseball in April: and Other Stories*. San Diego, Calif.: Harcourt Brace Jovanovich. 12–14 yrs.

_____. 1992. *The Skirt*. Illus. Eric Velasquez. New York: Delacorte. 7–10 yrs.

Speare, E. G. 1953. *The Witch of Blackbird Pond*. Boston: Houghton Mifflin. 10–12 yrs.

_____. 1961. *The Bronze Bow*. Boston: Houghton Mifflin. 10–14 yrs.

_____. 1983. *Sign of the Beaver*. Boston: Houghton Mifflin. 10–12 yrs.

Spyri, J. 1962. *Heidi*. Illus. Greta Elgaard. New York: Macmillan. 9–11 yrs.

Steptoe, J. 1969. *Stevie*. New York: HarperCollins. 5–9 yrs.

Stevenson, R. L. 1981. *Treasure Island*. Illus. N. C. Wyeth. New York: Scribners. 10–14 yrs.

Sutcliff, R. 1978. *Sun Horse, Moon Horse*. New York: Dutton. 10–14 yrs.

Taylor, M. 1976. *Roll of Thunder, Hear My Cry*. New York: Dial. 10–14 yrs.

Twain, M. 1962. *The Adventures of Mark Twain*. Illus. John Falter. New York: Macmillan. 10–14 yrs.

Viorst, J. 1972. *Alexander and the Terrible, Horrible, No Good, Very Bad Day*. Illus. Ray Cruz. New York: Atheneum. 6–11 yrs.

_____. 1995. *Alexander, Who's Not (Do You Hear Me? I Mean It!) Going to Move*. Illus. Robin P. Glasser. New York: Atheneum. 6–10 yrs.

Voigt, C. 1981. *Homecoming*. New York: Atheneum. 12–15 yrs.

_____. 1982. *Dicey's Song*. New York: Atheneum. 12–15 yrs.

_____. 1983. *A Solitary Blue*. New York: Atheneum. 12–15 yrs.

Wells, R. 1993. *Waiting for the Evening Star*. Illus. Susan Jeffers. New York: Dial. 6–9 yrs.

White, R. 1988. *Sweet Creek Holler*. New York: Farrar, Straus & Giroux. 12–15 yrs.

Wilder, L. I. 1932. *Little House in the Big Woods*. Illus. Garth Williams. New York: HarperCollins. 7–12 yrs.

Williams, D. 1993. *Grandma Essie's Covered Wagon*. Illus. Wiktor Sadowski. New York: Knopf. 7–9 yrs.

Yolen, Jane. 1987. *Owl Moon*. Illus. John Schoenherr. New York: Putnam, Philomel. 6–12 yrs.

_____. 1988. *The Devil's Arithmetic*. New York: Viking. 11–15 yrs.

_____. 1992. *Encounter*. Illus. David Shannon. San Diego, Calif.: Harcourt Brace Jovanovich. 6–12 yrs.

_____. 1995. *Before the Storm*. Illus. Georgia Pugh. Honesdale, Penn.: Boyds Mills. 5–7 yrs.

REALISTIC LITERATURE ORGANIZED IN CATEGORIES

HISTORICAL PERIODS

Antiquity: 3,000 B.C.–500 A.D.

Behn, Harry. 1982. *The Faraway Lurs*. New York: Putnam. 12–15 yrs.

Bond, Nancy. 1976. *A String in the Harp*. New York: Macmillan/McElderry. 12–15 yrs.

Brett, Jan. 1988. *The First Dog*. San Diego: Harcourt Brace Jovanovich. 4–8 yrs.

Carter, Dorothy. 1978. *His Majesty, Queen Hatshepsut*. New York: HarperCollins. 10–12 yrs.

Denzel, Justin. 1988. *The Boy of the Painted Cave*. New York: Philomel. 10–14 yrs.

Dyer, T. A. 1990. *A Way of His Own*. Boston: Houghton Mifflin. 10–14 yrs.

Fleischman, Paul. 1996. *Dateline: Troy*. Illus. Gwen Frankfeldt and Glenn Morrow. Cambridge, Mass.: Candlewick. 12–17 yrs.

Furlong, Monica. 1987. *Wise Child*. New York: Knopf/Borzoi. 10–12 yrs.

Haugaard, Erik Christian. 1984. *The Samurai's Tale*. Boston: Houghton Mifflin. 12–15 yrs.

Hunter, Mollie. 1974. *The Stronghold*. New York: HarperCollins. 9–12 yrs.

Levitin, Sonia. 1994. *Escape from Egypt*. Boston: Little, Brown. 12–16 yrs.

Linevski, A. 1973. *An Old Tale Carved Out of Stone*. Trans. Maria Polushkin. New York: Crown. 10–14 yrs.

Manniche, Lise. 1982. *The Prince Who Knew His Fate*. New York: Philomel. 10–12 yrs.

McGraw, Eloise Jarvis. 1985. *Mara, Daughter of the Nile*. New York: Penguin. 12–15 yrs.

McKinley, Robin. 1994. *A Knot in the Grain and Other Stories*. New York: Greenwillow. 12–16 yrs.

Nolan, Dennis. 1989. *Wolf Child*. Illus. Dennis Nolan. New York: Macmillan. 7–10 yrs.

Osborne, Chester. 1984. *The Memory String*. New York: Atheneum. 8–12 yrs.

Pryor, Bonnie. 1988. *Seth of the Lion People*. New York: Morrow. 10–13 yrs.

Speare, Elizabeth George. 1961. *The Bronze Bow*. Boston: Houghton Mifflin. 10–14 yrs.

Steele, William O. 1979. *The Magic Amulet*. San Diego: Harcourt Brace. 10–14 yrs.

Sutcliff, Rosemary. 1954. *The Eagle of the Ninth*. Illus. C. Walter Hodges. New York: Walck. 12–15 yrs.

———. 1959. *The Lantern Bearers*. Illus. Charles Keeping. New York: Walck. 12–15 yrs.

———. 1978. *Song for a Dark Queen*. New York: Crowell. 10–14 yrs.

———. 1978. *Sun Horse, Moon Horse*. New York: Dutton. 10–14 yrs.

———. 1990. *The Shining Company*. New York: Farrar, Straus & Giroux. 12–15 yrs.

Treece, Henry. 1968. *The Dream-Time*. Bellevue, WA: Meredith. 11–14 yrs.

Turnbull, Ann. 1990. *Maroo of the Winter Caves*. New York: Clarion. 10–13 yrs.

Turner, Ann. 1987. *Time of the Bison*. Illus. Beth Peck. New York: Macmillan. 8–11 yrs.

Wibberley, Leonard. 1968. *Attar of the Ice Valley*. New York: Farrar, Straus & Giroux. 11–15 yrs.

Yarbra, Chelsea Quinn. 1984. *Locadio's Apprentice*. New York: HarperCollins. 11–14 yrs.

Middle Ages 500–1600 A.D.

Aliki. 1983. *A Medieval Feast*. New York: HarperCollins. 5–8 yrs.

Bulla, Clyde Robert. 1963. *Viking Adventure*. New York: Crowell. 7–10 yrs.

Carrick, Donald. 1988. *Harald and the Great Stag*. New York: Clarion. 6–9 yrs.

Cushman, Karen. 1994. *Catherine, Called Birdy*. New York: Clarion. 12–16 yrs.

———. 1995. *The Midwife's Apprentice*. New York: Clarion. 10–14 yrs.

Dana, Barbara. 1991. *Young Joan*. New York: HarperCollins/Charlotte Zolotow. 10–13 yrs.

De Angeli, Marguerite. 1949. *The Door in the Wall*. New York: Doubleday. 9–12 yrs.

Fleischman, Sid. 1987. *The Whipping Boy*. Illus. Peter Sis. Mahwah, N.J.: Troll. 8–12 yrs.

Goodall, J. S. 1987. *The Story of a Main Street*. New York: McElderry. 7–12 yrs.

Gray, Elizabeth Vining. 1942. *Adam of the Road*. Illus. Robert Lawson. New York: Viking. 12–15 yrs.

Haugaard, Erik Christian. 1963. *Hakon of Rogen's Saga*. Boston: Houghton Mifflin. 9–12 yrs.

Hilgartner, Beth. 1986. *A Murder for Her Majesty*. Boston: Houghton Mifflin. 12–14 yrs.

Hunt, Jonathan. 1989. *Illuminations*. New York: Bradbury. 8–12 yrs.

Hunter, Mollie. 1971. *The 13th Member*. New York: HarperCollins. 12–17 yrs.

Kelly, Eric. 1928. *The Trumpeter of Krakow*. New York: Macmillan. 11–14 yrs.

Lasker, Joe. 1986. *Tournament of Knights*. New York: Crowell. 9–12 yrs.

Llorente, Pilar Molina. (Trans. Robin Longshaw). 1993. *The Apprentice*. Illus. Juan Ramon Alonso. New York: Farrar, Straus & Giroux. 10–12 yrs.

Mccaffrey, Anne. 1996. *Black Horses for the King*. San Diego: Harcourt Brace. 12–16 yrs.

Morressy, John. 1996. *The Juggler*. New York: Holt. 12–17 yrs.

O'Dell, Scott. 1979. *The Captive*. Boston: Houghton Mifflin. 10–14 yrs.

———. 1980. *The Road to Damietta*. Boston: Houghton Mifflin. 12–16 yrs.

Skurzynski, Gloria. 1979. *What Happened in Hamelin*. New York: Four Winds. 10–14 yrs.

———. 1981. *Manwolf*. Boston: Houghton Mifflin. 10–14 yrs.

———. 1988. *The Minstrel in the Tower*. Illus. Julek Heller. New York: Random House/Stepping Stone Books. 6–8 yrs.

Smith, T. H. 1986. *Cry to the Night Wind*. New York: Viking. 10–12 yrs.

Stolz, Mary. 1988. *Pangur Ban*. New York: HarperCollins. 11–14 yrs.

———. 1990. *Bartholomew Fair*. New York: Greenwillow Books/Beech Tree. 11–14 yrs.

Temple, Frances. 1994. *The Ramsay Scallop*. New York: Jackson/Orchard. 12–15 yrs.

———. 1996. *The Bedouins' Gazelle*. New York: Jackson/Orchard. 12–15 yrs.

Vining, Elizabeth Gray. 1962. *I Will Adventure*. New York: Viking. 12–15 yrs.

Walsh, Jill Paton. 1983. *A Parcel of Patterns*. New York: Farrar, Straus & Giroux. 12–15 yrs.

Westall, Robert. 1993. *The Stones of Muncaster Cathedral*. New York: Farrar, Straus & Giroux. 12–15 yrs.

The World in 1492

Conrad, Pam. 1991. *Pedro's Journal: A Voyage with Christopher Columbus, August 3, 1492–February 14, 1493*. Illus. Peter Koeppen. Honesdale, Penn.: Boyds Mills/Caroline. 7–10 yrs.

Dorris, Michael. 1992. *Morning Girl*. New York: Hyperion. 8–12 yrs.

Foreman, Michael & Richard Seaver. 1992. *The Boy Who Sailed with Columbus*. Illus. Michael Foreman. Boston: Little, Brown/Arcade. 8–13 yrs.

Jacobs, Francine. 1992. *The Tainos: The People Who Welcomed Columbus*. New York: Putnam. 10–14 yrs.

Litowinsky, Olga. 1991. *The High Voyage: The Final Crossing of Christopher Columbus*. New York: Delacorte. 10–13 yrs.

Locker, Thomas. 1991. *The Land of Gray Wolf*. New York: Dial. 7–11 yrs.

Smith, Barry. 1992. *The First Voyage of Christopher Columbus, 1492*. Illus. Barry Smith. New York: Viking/Penguin. 4–8 yrs.

Yolen, Jane. 1992. *Encounter*. Illus. David Shannon. San Diego: Harcourt Brace Jovanovich. 6–12 yrs.

The World in the 17th Century (1600s)

Brighton, Catherine. 1987. *Five Secrets in a Box*. New York: Dutton. 4–7 yrs.

Burgess, Melvin. 1994. *Burning Issy*. New York: Simon & Schuster. 10–13 yrs.

Haugaard, Erik Christian. 1976. *A Messenger for Parliament*. Boston: Houghton Mifflin. 10–14 yrs.

Hort, Lenny. 1987. *The Boy Who Held Back the Sea*. Illus. Thomas Locker. New York: Dial. 4–8 yrs.

Sutcliff, Rosemary. 1984. *Bonnie Dundee*. New York: Dutton. 10–14 yrs.

Pilgrims and Colonial Period (1645–1700s)

Avi. 1994. *Encounter at Easton*. New York: Morrow. 9–12 yrs.

———. 1994. *Night Journeys*. New York: Morrow. 9–12 yrs.

Bowen, Gary. 1994. *Stranded at Plimoth Plantation 1626*. New York: HarperCollins. 9–12 yrs.

Bulla, Clyde Robert. 1956. *John Billington: Friend of Squanto*. New York: HarperCollins. 10–12 yrs.

———. 1981. *A Lion to Guard Us*. New York: HarperCollins. 10–12 yrs.

Campbell, Elizabeth. 1974. *Jamestown: The Beginning*. Boston: Little, Brown. 10–12 yrs.

Clapp, Patricia. 1982. *Witches' Children: A Story of Salem*. New York: Lothrop, Penguin/Puffin. 11–14 yrs.

Cooney, Barbara. 1988. *Island Boy*. New York: Viking/Kestrel. 4–8 yrs.

Dillon, Ellis. 1986. *The Seekers*. New York: Scribners. 13–16 yrs.

Fleischman, Paul. 1992. *Saturnalia*. New York: HarperKeypoint/Charlotte Zolotow Books. 10–14 yrs.

Harness, Cheryl. 1992. *Three Young Pilgrims*. Illus. Cheryl Harness. New York: Bradbury. 5–10 yrs.

Hudson, Jan. 1990. *Dawn Rider*. New York: Philomel. 10–15 yrs.

Lasky, Kathryn. 1994. *Beyond the Burning Time*. New York: Scholastic/Blue Sky. 12–16 yrs.

Luhrmann, Winifred Bruce. 1989. *Only Brave Tomorrows*. Boston: Houghton Mifflin. 10–14 yrs.

Monjo, F. N. 1991. *The House on Stink Alley*. New York: Dell. 10–12 yrs.

Mott, Michael. 1986. *Master Entrick*. New York: Dell. 13–16 yrs.

Petry, Ann. 1988. *Tituba of Salem Village*. New York: HarperCollins. 10–12 yrs.

Quackenbush, Robert. 1986. *Old Silver Legs Takes Over: A Story of Peter Stuyvesant*. Englewood Cliffs, N.J.: Prentice Hall. 6–9 yrs.

Rinaldi, Ann. 1992. *A Break with Charity: A Story about the Salem Witch Trials*. San Diego: Harcourt Brace Jovanovich/Gulliver. 10–16 yrs.

———. 1994. *A Stitch in Time*. New York: Scholastic. 12–16 yrs.

———. 1994. *Finishing Becca: A Story about Peggy Shippen and Benedict Arnold*. San Diego: Harcourt Brace/Gulliver. 12–16 yrs. American Colonies series.

Sewer, Marcia. 1986. *The Pilgrims of Plimoth*. New York: Atheneum. 7–11 yrs.

Speare, Elizabeth George. 1953. *The Witch of Blackbird Pond*. Boston: Houghton Mifflin. 10–12 yrs.

Spier, Peter. 1967. *The Legend of New Amsterdam*. New York: Doubleday. 7–11 yrs.

Wisler, G. Clifton. 1987. *This New Land*. Walker/American History Series. 9–12 yrs.

Thanksgiving

Anderson, Joan. 1984. *The First Thanksgiving Feast*. Photos George Ancona. New York: Clarion. 7–11 yrs.

Cohen, Barbara. 1983. *Molly's Pilgrim*. New York: Lothrop, Lee & Shepard. 7–11 yrs.

Dalgliesh, Alice. 1987. *The Thanksgiving Story*. New York: Macmillan. 7–11 yrs.

Sewall, Marcia. 1986. *People of the Breaking Day*. New York: Atheneum. 6–9 yrs.

Watson, Wendy. 1991. *Thanksgiving at Our House*. New York: Clarion. 7–10 yrs.

The World in the 18th Century (1700s)

Almedingen, E. M. 1983. *The Crimson Oak*. New York: Coward McCann. 11–14 yrs.

Calvert, Patricia. 1986. *Hadder MacColl*. New York: Viking Penguin/Puffin. 10–13 yrs.

Doherty, Berlie. 1994. *Street Child*. New York: Orchard. 9–12 yrs.

Garfield, Leon. 1965. *Jack Holborn*. Illus. Anthony Maitland. New York: Pantheon. 11–14 yrs.

_____. 1967. *Smith*. Illus. Anthony Maitland. New York: Pantheon. 11–14 yrs.

_____. 1989. *Young Nick and Jubilee*. Illus. Ted Lewin. New York: Delacorte. 10–15 yrs.

Sutcliff, Rosemary. 1989. *Flame Colored Taffeta*. New York: Farrar, Straus & Giroux. 12–15 yrs.

U.S. Pioneer and Revolutionary Period (1700–1800)

Avi. 1979. *Night Journeys*. New York: Pantheon. 8–11 yrs.

_____. 1984. *The Fighting Ground*. New York: Lippincott. 10–14 yrs.

Brady, Esther Wood. 1988. *Toliver's Secret*. New York: Crown. 10–12 yrs.

Brown, Drollene P. 1985. *Sybil Rides for Independence*. Morton Grove, Ill.: Whitman. 10–12 yrs.

Clapp, Patricia. 1977. *I'm Deborah Sampson: A Soldier in the War of the Revolution*. New York: Lothrop, Lee & Shepard. 9–12 yrs.

Collier, James Lincoln, & Christopher Collier. 1974. *My Brother Sam Is Dead*. New York: Four Winds. 10–14 yrs.

_____. 1981. *Jump Ship to Freedom*. New York: Delacorte. 9–12 yrs.

_____. 1983. *War Comes to Willy Freeman*. New York: Delacorte. 9–12 yrs.

Caudill, Rebecca. 1964. *The Far-off Land*. New York: Viking. 11–14 yrs.

_____. 1988. *Tree of Freedom*. New York: Viking\Puffin. 13–16 yrs.

Colver, Anne. 1970. *Bread-and-Butter Journey*. New York: Holt. 7–10 yrs.

Dalgliesh, Alice. 1954. *The Courage of Sarah Noble*. New York: Scribners. 7–10 yrs.

Forbes, Esther. 1969. *Johnny Tremain*. Boston: Houghton Mifflin. 10–13 yrs.

Fritz, Jean. 1967. *Early Thunder*. New York: Putnam. 12–16 yrs.

_____. 1958. *The Cabin Faced West*. New York: Coward. 7–10 yrs.

Gauch, Patricia Lee. 1992. *This Time, Tempe Wick?* Illus. Margot Tomes. New York: Putnam. 8–10 yrs.

Haugaard, Erik. 1990. *Cromwell's Boy*. Boston: Houghton Mifflin. 12–16 yrs.

Marko, Katherine McGlade. 1985. *Away to Fundy Bay*. Walker. 10–12 yrs.

McGovern, Ann. 1987. *Secret Soldier: The Story of Deborah Sampson*. New York: Macmillan/Four Winds. 10–13 yrs.

O'Dell, Scott. 1980. *Sarah Bishop*. Boston: Houghton Mifflin. 12–16 yrs.

_____. 1990. *My Name Is Not Angelica*. New York: Dell/Yearling. 8–12 yrs.

Rappaport, Doreen. 1988. *The Boston Coffee Party*. Illus. Emily Arnold McCully. New York: HarperCollins. 5–8 yrs.

Rinaldi, Ann. 1986. *Time Enough for Drums*. New York: Holiday House. 9–12 yrs.

_____. 1995. *The Secret of Sarah Revere*. San Diego: Harcourt Brace/Gulliver. 12–16 yrs. Great Episodes series.

Turner, Ann. 1992. *Katie's Trunk*. Illus. Ron Himler. New York: Macmillan. 6–10 yrs.

Siegel, Beatrice. 1985. *Sam Ellis's Island*. New York: Macmillan/Four Winds. 6–9 yrs.

Speare, Elizabeth George. 1983. *Sign of the Beaver*. Boston: Houghton Mifflin. 10–12 yrs.

Wibberley, Leonard. 1986. *John Treegate's Musket*. New York: Farrar, Straus & Giroux. 10–13 yrs.

Steele, William O. 1964. *Wayah of the Real People*. Illus. Isa Barnett. New York: Holt. 11–13 yrs.

The World in the 19th Century

Aiken, Joan. 1988. *The Teeth of the Gale*. New York: HarperCollins. 9–13 yrs. (Reprint of 1985; New York: Bradbury.)

Anderson, Rachel. 1995. *Black Water*. New York: Holt. 10–13 yrs.

Angell, Judie. 1985. *One Way to Ansonia*. New York: Bradbury. 10–14 yrs.

Avery, Gillian. 1994. *A Likely Lad*. Illus. Julie Downing. New York: Simon & Schuster. 9–12 yrs.

Avi. 1992. *The True Confessions of Charlotte Doyle*. New York: Avon/Flare. 10–15 yrs.

_____. 1996. *Beyond the Western Sea, Book One: The Escape from Home*. New York: Jackson/Orchard. 10–13 yrs.

Berry, James. 1992. *Ajeemah and His Son*. New York: HarperCollins/Perlman. 10–14 yrs.

Bilson, Geoffrey. 1982. *Death over Montreal*. Canada: Kids Can Press. 8–11 yrs.

Brandis, Marianne. 1982. *The Tinderbox*. Canada: Porcupine's Quill. 11–14 yrs.

Collier, Mary Jo. 1996. *The King's Giraffe*. Illus. Stephane Poulin. New York: Simon & Schuster. 6–10 yrs.

Crofford, Emily. 1991. *Born in the Year of Courage*. Minneapolis, Minn.: Carolrhoda. 10–14 yrs.

Garfield, Leon. 1987. *The December Rose*. New York: Viking Kestrel. 10–14 yrs.

German, Tony. 1985. *A Breed Apart*. Buffalo, New York: McClelland and Stewart. 11–14 yrs.

Greene, Jacqueline Dembar. 1994. *One Foot Ashore*. New York: Walker. 9–12 yrs.

Harris, Christie. 1957. *Cariboo Trail*. White Plains, N.Y.: Longman. 12–14 yrs.

Hautzig, Esther. 1992. *Riches*. Illus. Donna Diamond. New York: HarperCollins/Charlotte Zolotow. 8–12 yrs.

Hudson, Jan. 1989. *Sweetgrass*. New York: Philomel. 10–13 yrs.

Lunn, Janet. 1986. *Shadow in Hawthorn Bay*. New York: Scribners. 12–15 yrs.

Lutzeier, Elizabeth. 1991. *The Coldest Winter*. New York: Holiday. 10–15 yrs.

McCully, Emily Arnold. 1992. *Mirette on the High Wire*. New York: Putnam. 4–8 yrs.

Pullman, Philip. 1987. *Ruby in the Smoke*. New York: Knopf. 12–16 yrs.

_____. 1994. *The Tin Princess*. New York: Knopf. 12–16 yrs.

Schur, Maxine Rose. 1994. *The Circlemaker*. New York: Dial. 10–14 yrs.

Smucker, Barbara. *Underground to Canada*. Burr Ridge, Ill.: Clarke Irwin. 12–15 yrs.

Yep, Laurence. 1984. *The Serpent's Children*. New York: HarperCollins. 10–14 yrs.

Zei, Alki. 1979. *The Sound of Dragon's Feet*. New York: Dutton. 10–14 yrs.

The U.S. in the Early 19th Century

Avi. 1995. *The History of Helpless Harry: To Which Is Added a Variety of Amusing and Entertaining Adventures*. Illus. Paul O. Zelinsky. New York: Morrow. 10–13 yrs.

Blos, Joan. 1979. *A Gathering of Days: A New England Girl's Journal, 1830–32*. New York: Scribner. 7–11 yrs.

Conrad, Pam. 1989. *My Daniel*. New York: Harper & Row. 10–14 yrs.

Conlon-Mckenna, Marita. 1992. *Wildflower Girl*. Illus. Donald Teskey. New York: Holiday House. 10–14 yrs.

De Felice, Cynthia. 1990. *Weasel*. New York: Macmillan. 9–12 yrs.

Gaeddert, LouAnn. 1994. *Breaking Free*. New York: Atheneum/Karl. 9–12 yrs.

Goble, Paul. 1987. *Death of the Iron Horse*. New York: Bradbury. 5–9 yrs.

Highwater, Jamake. 1984. *Legend Days*. New York: HarperCollins. 10–14 yrs.

Hoobler, Dorothy, Thomas Hoobler, & Carey-Greenberg Associates. 1992. *A Promise at the Alamo: The Story of a Texas Girl*. Illus. Jennifer Hewitson. Morristown, N.J.: Silver Burdett. 9–12 yrs.

Hooks, William H. 1990. *The Ballad of Belle Dorcas*. Illus. Brian Pinkney. New York: Knopf/Borzoi. 6–10 yrs.

Johnston, Tony. 1988. *Yonder*. Illus. Lloyd Bloom. New York: Dial. 4–8 yrs.

Krensky, Stephen. 1995. *The Printer's Apprentice*. Illus. Madeline Sorel. New York: Delacorte. 11–13 yrs.

Levinson, Nancy Smiler. 1992. *Snowshoe Thompson*. New York: HarperCollins. 7–10 yrs.

Matas, Carol. 1993. *Sworn Enemies*. New York: Bantam. 12–15 yrs.

McPhail, David. 1992. *Farm Boy's Year*. New York: Atheneum. 5–7 yrs.

Minahan, John A. 1995. *Abigail's Drum*. Illus. Robert Quackenbush. New York: Pippin. 7–9 yrs.

Morrow, Barbara. 1991. *Edward's Portrait*. New York: Macmillan. 6–9 yrs.

O'Dell, Scott. *Island of the Blue Dolphins*. Boston: Houghton Mifflin. 10–14 yrs.

Sanders, Scott Russell. 1989. *Aurora Means Dawn*. Illus. Jill Kastner. New York: Bradbury. 6–9 yrs.

_____. 1992. *Warm as Wool*. Illus. Helen Cogancherry. New York: Bradbury. 6–10 yrs.

Wisler, G. Clifton. 1990. *Piper's Ferry: A Tale of the Texas Revolution*. New York: Lodestar. 10–14 yrs.

The U.S. in the Civil War Era

Alcott, Louisa M. 1994. *Jo's Boys: And How They Turned Out*. Boston: Little, Brown. 11–16 yrs.

_____. 1994. *Little Men: Life at Plumfield with Jo's Boys*. Boston: Little, Brown. 11–16 yrs.

_____. 1994. *Little Women: Or Meg, Jo, Beth, and Amy*. Boston: Little, Brown. 11–16 yrs.

Beatty, Patricia. 1984. *Turn Homeward, Hannalee*. New York: Morrow. 10–14 yrs.

_____. 1988. *Be Ever Hopeful, Hannalee*. New York: Morrow. 10–14 yrs.

_____. 1987. *Charley Skedaddle*. New York: Morrow. 11–14 yrs.

_____. 1991. *Jayhawker*. New York: Morrow. 10–14 yrs.

_____. 1992. *Who Comes with Cannons?* New York: Morrow. 10–14 yrs.

Beatty, Patricia & Phillip Robbins. 1990. *Eben Tyne, Powdermonkey*. New York: Morrow. 9–13 yrs.

Calvert, Patricia. 1994. *Bigger*. New York: Scribners. 10–13 yrs.

Donahue, John. 1994. *An Island Far from Home*. Minneapolis, Minn.: Carolrhoda. 11–14 yrs.

Fleischman, Paul. 1993. *Bull Run*. New York: HarperCollins/Geringer. 10–13 yrs.

Fox, Paula. 1973. *The Slave Dancer*. New York: Bradbury. 12–15 yrs.

Fritz, Jean. 1960. (New ed. 1987) *Brady*. Illus. Lynn Ward. New York: Coward. 9–12 yrs.

Gauch, Patricia L. 1990. *Thunder at Gettysburg*. Illus. Stephen Gammell. New York: Putnam. 10–12 yrs.

Hansen, Joyce. 1986. *Which Way Freedom?* New York: Walker. 11–14 yrs.

Hickman, Janet. 1978. *Zoar Blue*. New York: Macmillan. 9–12 yrs.

Hiser, Bernice T. 1986. *The Adventure of Charlie and His Wheat-Straw Hat: A Memorat*. Illus. Mary Szilagyi. Northbrook, Ill.: Dood, Mead. 5–7 yrs.

Houston, Gloria. 1994. *Mountain Valor*. Illus. Thomas B. Allen. New York: Philomel. 11–13 yrs.

Hunt, Irene. 1964. *Across Five Aprils*. River Grove, Ill.: Follett. 10–14 yrs.

Hurmence, Belinda. 1984. *Tancy*. Boston: Houghton/Clarion. 10–14 yrs.

Keith, Harold. 1954. *Rifles for Watie*. New York: Crowell. 12–15 yrs.

Lyon, George Ella. 1991. *Cecil's Story*. Illus. Peter Catalanotto. New York: Orchard. 4–8 yrs.

Lyons, Mary E. 1992. *Letters from a Slave Girl: The Story of Harriet Jacobs*. New York: Scribners. 10–13 yrs.

Monjo, F. N. 1970. *The Drinking Gourd*. New York: HarperCollins. 7–10 yrs.

Myers, Walter Dean. 1992. *The Righteous Revenge of Artemis Bonner*. New York: HarperCollins. 10–14 yrs.

Reeder, Carolyn. 1989. *Shades of Gray*. New York: Macmillan. 10–12 yrs.

Steele, William O. 1958. *The Perilous Road*. Illus. Paul Galdone. San Diego: Harcourt Brace. 11–16 yrs.

Turner, Ann. 1987. *Nettie's Trip South*. Illus. Ronald Himler. New York: Macmillan. 7–10 yrs.

Winter, Jeanette. 1988. *Follow the Drinking Gourd*. New York: Knopf. 8–11 yrs.

Wisler, G. Clifton. 1991. *Red Cap*. New York: Lodestar. 10–13 yrs.

The U.S. During the Western Expansion

Beatty, Patricia. 1989. *Sarah and Me and the Lady from the Sea*. New York: Morrow. 9–12 yrs.

_____. 1993. *The Nickel-Plated Beauty*. New York: Morrow. 9–12 yrs.

_____. 1994. *O the Red Rose Tree*. New York: Morrow. 9–12 yrs.

Brenner, Barbara. 1978. *Wagon Wheels*. New York: HarperCollins. 7–9 yrs.

Brink, Carol Ryrie. 1935. *Caddie Woodlawn*. New York: Macmillan. 8–11 yrs.

Coerr, Eleanor. 1986. *The Josefina Story Quilt*. New York: HarperCollins. 9–11 yrs.

_____. 1992. *The Big Balloon Race*. New York: HarperCollins. 10–12 yrs.

Conrad, Pam. 1985. *Prairie Songs*. New York: HarperCollins. 10–14 yrs.

Duffy, James. 1993. *Radical Red*. New York: Scribners. 9–12 yrs.

Fisher, Leonard Everelt. 1990. *The Oregon Trail*. New York: Holiday. 10–12 yrs.

Fleischman, Paul. 1985. *Coming-and-Going Men: Four Tales*. Illus. Randy Gaul. New York: HarperCollins. 11–14 yrs.

_____. 1991. *The Borning Room*. New York: HarperCollins. 10–13 yrs.

Fleischman, Sid. 1992. *Jim Ugly*. Illus. J. A. Smith. New York: Greenwillow. 10–12 yrs.

Fritz, Jean. 1958. *The Cabin Faced West*. Illus. Feodor Rojankovsky. New York: Putnam. 9–12 yrs.

Gerrard, Roy. 1989. *Rosie and the Rustlers*. New York: Farrar, Straus & Giroux. 5–9 yrs.

Hamilton, Virginia. 1989. *The Bells of Christmas*. Illus. Lambert Davis. San Diego: Harcourt Brace. 8–12 yrs.

Harvey, Brett. 1988. *Cassie's Journey: Going West in the 1860s*. Illus. Deborah Kogan Ray. New York: Holiday. 7–9 yrs.

Harvey, Brett. 1986. *My Prairie Year: Based on the Diary of Elenore Plaisted*. Illus. Deborah Kogan Ray. New York: Holiday. 7–9 yrs.

_____. 1990. *My Prairie Christmas*. Illus. Deborah Kogan Ray. New York: Holiday. 5–8 yrs.

Holland, Isabelle. 1990. *The Journey Home*. New York: Scholastic. 8–12 yrs.

_____. 1996. *The Promised Land*. New York: Scholastic. 9–11 yrs. (Sequel to *The Journey Home.*)

Hooks, William H. 1988. *Pioneer Cat*. Illus. Charles Robinson. New York: Random House/Stepping Stone. 6–8 yrs.

Howard, Ellen. 1987. *Edith Herself*. New York: Atheneum. 7–11 yrs.

_____. 1990. *Sister*. New York: Atheneum. 7–11 yrs.

_____. 1991. *The Chickenhouse House*. New York: Atheneum. 7–11 yrs.

Irwin, Foley. 1994. *Jim-Dandy*. New York: McElderry. 11–13 yrs.

Karr, Kathleen. 1990. *It Ain't Always Easy*. New York: Farrar, Straus & Giroux. 10–15 yrs.

_____. 1992. *Oh, Those Harper Girls!* New York: Farrar, Straus & Giroux. 12–15 yrs.

Kimmel, Eric A. 1990. *Four Dollars and Fifty Cents*. Illus. Glen Rounds. New York: Holiday. 6–10 yrs.

Lasky, Kathryn. 1983. *Beyond the Divide*. New York: Macmillan. 10–13 yrs.

Lawlor, Laurie. 1993. *George on His Own*. Illus. Toby Gowing. Morton Grove, Ill.: Whitman. 10–12 yrs.

Levin, Betty. 1990. *Brother Moose*. New York: Greenwillow. 10–14 yrs.

Love, D. Anne. 1995. *Bess's Log Cabin Quilt*. Illus. Ronald Himler. New York: Holiday. 9–11 yrs.

Lucas, Barbara M. 1993. *Snowed In*. Illus. Catherine Stock. New York: Bradbury. 5–8 yrs.

MacLachlan, Patricia. 1991. *Three Names*. Illus. Alexander Pertzoff. New York: HarperCollins. 7–11 yrs.

_____. 1994. *Skylark*. New York: HarperCollins. 11–13 yrs. (Sequel to *Sarah, Plain and Tall*.)

Martin, Bill, Jr., & John Archambault. 1987. *Knots on a Counting Rope*. New York: Holt. 7–11 yrs.

Meyer, Carolyn. 1992. *Where the Broken Heart Still Beats: The Story of Cynthia Ann Parker*. San Diego: Harcourt Brace Jovanovich/Gulliver. 8–12 yrs.

Moeri, Louise. 1981. *Save Queen of Sheba*. New York: Dutton. 9–12 yrs.

Morrow, Honore. 1954. *On to Oregon*. New York: Morrow. 9–12 yrs.

Myers, Anna. 1996. *Graveyard Girl*. New York: Walker. 9–12 yrs.

Nixon, Joan Lowery. 1987–1989. *The Orphan Train Quartet: A Family Apart; Caught in the Act; In the Face of Danger; A Place to Belong*. New York: Bantam. 12–15 yrs.

_____. 1989. *You Bet Your Britches Claude*. Illus. Tracey Campbell Pearson. New York: Viking. 6–9 yrs.

_____. 1994. *A Dangerous Promise*. New York: Delacorte. 12–16 yrs.

O'Dell, Scott. 1970. *Sing Down the Moon*. Boston: Houghton Mifflin. 10–14 yrs.

O'Dell, Scott & Elizabeth Hall. 1992. *Thunder Rolling in the Mountains*. Boston: Houghton Mifflin. 12–14 yrs.

Pellowski, Anne. 1982. *First Farm in the Valley: Anna's Story*. Illus. Wendy Watson. New York: Philomel. 7–10 yrs.

Polacco, Patricia. 1988. *The Keeping Quilt*. New York: Simon & Schuster. 5–9 yrs.

Rounds, Glen. 1991. *Cowboys*. Illus. Glen Rounds. New York: Holiday House. 3–7 yrs.

Turner, Ann. 1985. *Dakota Dugout*. Illus. Ronald Himler. New York: Macmillan. 8–10 yrs.

_____. 1989. *Grasshopper Summer*. New York: Macmillan. 10–13 yrs.

Van Leeuwen, Jean. 1992. *Going West*. Illus. Thomas B. Allen. New York: Dial. 5–9 yrs.

_____. 1994. *Bound for Oregon*. Illus. James Watling. New York: Dial. 9–12 yrs.

Wallace, Bill. 1987. *Red Dog*. New York: Holiday. 9–12 yrs.

Whelan, Gloria. 1993. *Night of the Full Moon*. Illus. Leslie Bowman. New York: Knopf. 9–11 yrs.

Woodruff, Elvira. 1994. *Dear Levi: Letters from the Overland Trail*. Illus. Beth Peck. New York: Knopf. 9–12 yrs.

The World in the Early 1900s

Anderson, Margaret. 1980. *The Journey of the Shadow Bairns*. New York: Knopf. 11–13 yrs.

Bosse, Malcolm. 1993. *Deep Dream of the Rain Forest*. New York: Farrar, Straus & Giroux. 12–15 yrs.

Holman, Felice. 1983. *The Wild Children*. New York: Scribners. 9–12 yrs.

Lasky, Kathryn. 1981. *The Night Journey*. New York: Warne. 10–14 yrs.

Leighton, Maxinne Rhea. 1992. *An Ellis Island Christmas*. Illus. Dennis Nolan. New York: Viking Penguin. 3–8 yrs.

Mayerson, Evelyn. 1990. *The Cat Who Escaped from Steerage*. New York: Scribners. 10–13 yrs.

Oberman, Sheldon. 1994. *The Always Prayer Shawl*. Illus. Ted Lewin. Honesdale, Penn.: Boyds Mill. 5–7 yrs.

Shefelman, Janice. 1992. *A Peddler's Dream*. Illus. Tom Shefelman. Boston: Houghton Mifflin. 6–10 yrs.

Westall, Robert. 1994. *Christmas Spirit: Two Stories*. Illus. John Lawrence. New York: Farrar, Straus & Giroux. 9–12 yrs.

Zei, Alki. (Trans. Edward Fenron). 1968. *Wildcat Under Glass*. New York: Holt. 11–15 yrs.

The U.S. in the Early 1900s

Adler, Susan. 1986. *Meet Samantha*. Middleton, Wisc.: Pleasant. 9–12 yrs.

Allen, Thomas B. 1989. *On Granddaddy's Farm*. New York: Knopf/Borzoi. 4–7 yrs.

Blos, Joan W. 1994. *Brooklyn Doesn't Rhyme*. Illus. Paul Birling. New York: Scribners. 9–12 yrs.

Cameron, Eleanor. 1971. *A Room Made of Windows*. Boston: Little, Brown. 10–12 yrs.

_____. 1977. *Julia and the Hand of God*. Illus. Gail Owens. New York: Dutton. 9–12 yrs.

_____. 1982. *That Julia Redfern*. Illus. Gail Owens. New York: Dutton. 9–12 yrs.

_____. 1984. *Julia's Magic*. Illus. Gail Owens. New York: Dutton. 9–12 yrs.

_____. 1988. *The Private Worlds of Julia Redfern*. New York: Dutton. 9–12 yrs.

Coats, Laura Jane. 1991. *The Almond Orchard*. New York: Macmillan. 7–11 yrs.

Cohen, Barbara. 1983. *Molly's Pilgrim*. Illus. Michael J. Deraney. New York: Lothrop, Lee & Shepard. 5–8 yrs.

Collier, James L. 1991. *My Crooked Family*. New York: Simon & Schuster. 12–16 yrs.

Cooney, Barbara. 1990. *Hattie and the Wild Waves: A Story from Brooklyn*. New York: Viking Penguin. 3–8 yrs.

Cross, Verda. 1992. *Great-Grandma Tells of Threshing Day*. Illus. Gail Owens. Morton Grove, Ill.: Whitman. 6–11 yrs.

Fleischman, Paul. 1990. *Shadow Play*. Illus. Eric Beddows. New York: Harper & Row/Charlotte Zolotow. 4–8 yrs.

Green, Connie Jordan. 1992. *Emmy.* New York: McElderry. 10–13 yrs.

Gregory, Kristiana. 1992. *Earthquake at Dawn.* San Diego: Harcourt Brace Jovanovich/ Gulliver. 10–15 yrs.

Harvey, Brett. 1987. *Immigrant Girl: Becky of Eldridge Street.* Illus. Deborah Kogan Ray. New York: Holiday. 7–10 yrs.

Hooks, William H. 1982. *Circle of Fire.* New York: Macmillan/McElderry. 11–13 yrs.

Howard, Elizabeth Fitzgerald. 1989. *Chita's Christmas Tree.* Illus. Floyd Cooper. New York: Bradbury. 5–8 yrs.

Kroll, Stephen. 1989. *The Hokey-Pokey Man.* Illus. Deborah K. Ray. New York: Holiday. 5–7 yrs.

Leighton, Maxine R. 1992. *An Ellis Island Christmas.* Illus. Dennis Nolan. New York: Viking. 5–11 yrs.

Leonard, Laura. 1989. *Saving Damaris.* New York: Atheneum/Karl. 8–12 yrs.

Levinson, Riki. 1986. *I Go with My Family to Grandma's.* Illus. Diane Goode. New York: Dutton. 4–10 yrs.

———. 1993. *Soon, Annala.* Illus. Julie Downing. New York: Orchard/Jackson. 5–8 yrs.

Lovelace, Maud Hart. 1940. (New ed.1994) *Betsy-Tacy.* Illus. Lois Lenski. New York: HarperCollins. 9–12 yrs.

Mayne, William. 1993. *Low Tide.* New York: Delacorte. 12–15 yrs.

McDonald, Megan. 1991. *The Potato Man.* Illus. Ted Lewin. New York: Orchard/Jackson. 5–8 yrs.

———. 1992. *The Great Pumpkin Switch.* Illus. Ted Lewin. New York: Orchard/Jackson. 4–7 yrs.

Morris, Linda Lowe. 1991. *Morning Milking.* Illus. David DeRan. New York: Picture Book Studio. 6–8 yrs.

Nixon, Joan Lowry. 1992. *Land of Hope.* New York: Bantam. 11–14 yrs. (See also other books in Ellis Island Series)

O'Kelly, Mattie Lou. 1991. *Moving to Town.* Boston: Little, Brown. 7–9 yrs.

Precek, Katharine Wilson. 1989. *Penny in the Road.* Illus. Patricia Cullen-Clark. New York: Macmillan. 4–8 yrs.

Sandin, Joan. 1981. *The Long Way to a New Land.* New York: HarperCollins. 8–10 yrs.

———. 1989. *The Long Way Westward.* New York: HarperCollins. 8–10 yrs.

Sauerwein, Leigh. 1994. *The Way Home.* Illus. Miles Hyman. New York: Farrar, Straus & Giroux. 12–15 yrs.

Sawyer, Ruth. 1995. *Roller Skates.* Illus. Valenti Angelo. New York: Viking. 9–11 yrs.

Shefelman, Janice. 1992. *A Peddler's Dream.* Illus. Tom Shefelman. Boston: Houghton Mifflin. 6–9 yrs.

Sherman, Eileen Bluestone. 1990. *Independence Avenue.* Philadelphia, Penn.: Jewish Publication Society. 10–14 yrs.

Stevens, Carla. 1992. *Lily and Miss Liberty.* Illus. Deborah Kogan Ray. New York: Scholastic. 10–12 yrs.

Thesman, Jean. 1996. *The Ornament Tree.* Boston: Houghton Mifflin. 10–13 yrs.

Wallace, Bill. 1992. *Buffalo Gal.* New York: Holiday House. 11–15 yrs.

Weitzman, David. 1991. *Thrashin' Time: Harvest Days in the Dakotas.* Boston: Godine. 10–13 yrs.

Wiegand, Roberta. 1984. *The Year of the Comet.* New York: Bradbury. 11–14 yrs.

Wiggin, Kate Douglas. 1994. *Rebecca of Sunnybrook Farm.* Illus. Helen Mason Grose. New York: Morrow. 9–12 yrs.

Wyman, Andrea. 1991. *Red Sky at Morning.* New York: Holiday House. 10–14 yrs.

Yee, Paul. 1991. *Roses Sing on New Snow: A Delicious Tale.* Illus. Harvey Chan. New York: Macmillan. 9–11 yrs.

Yektai, Niki. 1992. *The Secret Room.* New York: Orchard. 9–12 yrs.

Yep, Laurence. 1979. *Dragonwings.* New York: HarperCollins 9–12 yrs.

World War I

Corcoran, Barbara. 1989. *The Private War of Lillian Adams.* New York: Atheneum/Karl. 9–12 yrs.

Dank, Milton. 1980. *Khaki Wings.* New York: Delacorte. 12–14 yrs.

Foreman, Michael. 1994. *War Game.* New York: Arcade. 9–12 yrs.

Frank, Rudolf. (Trans. Patricia Crampton). 1986. *No Hero for the Kaiser.* Illus. Klaus Steffens. New York: Lothrop, Lee & Shepard. 10–15 yrs.

Houston, Gloria. 1988. *The Year of the Perfect Christmas Tree.* Illus. Barbara Cooney. New York: Dial.

Kinsey-Warnock, Natalie. 1991. *The Night the Bells Rang.* New York: Dutton. 10–13 yrs.

Mukerji, Djam Gopal. 1927. *Gay-Neck: The Story of a Pigeon.* Illus. Boris Artzybasheff. New York: Dutton. 10–14 yrs.

Rostkowski, Margaret. 1986. *After the Dancing Days.* New York: HarperCollins. 12–16 yrs.

Skurzynski, Gloria. 1992. *Good-bye, Billy Radish.* New York: Bradbury. 10–14 yrs.

Smith, Barry. 1991. *Minnie and Ginger.* New York: Crown. 6–9 yrs.

Voigt, Cynthia. 1988. *Tree by Leaf.* New York: Atheneum. 10–14 yrs.

Between the Wars

Ackerman, Karen. 1990. *Just Like Max.* Illus. George Schmidt. New York: Knopf. 5–9 yrs.

Ames, Mildred. 1980. *The Dancing Madness.* New York: Delacorte. 12–14 yrs.

Antel, Nancy. 1993. *Hard Times: A Story of the Depression.* Illus. J. Watling. New York: Viking. 10–12 yrs.

Avi. 1994. *Smugglers' Island.* (Original title: *Shadrach's Crossing.* 1983. New York: Morrow.) 9–12 yrs.

Belton, Sandra. 1993. *From Miss Ida's Porch.* Illus. Floyd Cooper. New York: Four Winds. 6–9 yrs.

Cannon, Bettie. 1987. *A Bellsong for Sarah Raines.* New York: Scribners. 12–15 yrs.

Clifford, Eth. 1987. *The Man Who Sang in the Dark.* Illus. Mary Beth Owens. Boston: Houghton Mifflin. 9–11 yrs.

Corcoran, Barbara. 1988. *The Sky Is Falling.* New York: Atheneum/Karl. 11–13 yrs.

Crew, Linda. 1995. *Fire on the Wind.* New York: Delacorte. 12–16 yrs.

Crofford, Emily. 1981. *A Matter of Pride.* Illus. Jim LaMarche. Minneapolis, Minn.: Carolrhoda. 7–9 yrs.

Cuneo, Mary Louise. 1993. *Anne Is Elegant.* New York: HarperCollins. 10–12 yrs.

Delton, Judy. 1987. *Kitty from the Start.* Boston: Houghton Mifflin. 8–10 yrs.

Disher, Garry. 1993. *The Bamboo Flute.* New York: Ticknor & Fields. 10–13 yrs.

Edwards, Pat. 1987. *Nelda.* Boston: Houghton Mifflin. 10–13 yrs.

Gates, Doris. 1940. *Blue Willow.* Illus. Paul Lantz. New York: Viking. 10–14 yrs.

Greene, Constance C. 1980. *Dotty's Suitcase.* New York: Viking. 8–11 yrs.

Hendershot, Judith. 1987. *In Coal Country.* Illus. Thomas B. Allen. New York: Knopf. 8–11 yrs.

Hooks, William H. 1982. *Circle of Fire.* New York: Atheneum. 9–12 yrs.

Houston, Gloria. 1990. *Littlejim.* Illus. Thomas B. Allen. New York: Philomel. 8–12 yrs.

Hunter, Bernice Thurman. 1981. *That Scatterbrain Booky.* New York: Scholastic-TAB. 12–15 yrs.

Huntington, Lee P. 1984. *Maybe a Miracle.* Illus. Neil Wildman. New York: Putnam. 7–9 yrs.

Kherdisn, David. 1989. *A Song for Uncle Harry.* New York: Philomel. 9–12 yrs.

Koller, Jackie French. 1991. *Nothing to Fear.* San Diego: Harcourt Brace/Gulliver. 11–14 yrs.

Levinson, Riki. 1990. *Watch the Stars Come Out.* Illus. Diane Goode. New York: Dutton. 6–10 yrs.

———. 1992. *Boys Here-Girls There.* Illus. Karen Ritz. New York: Lodestar. 8–10 yrs.

Lyon, George Ella. 1988. *Borrowed Children.* New York: Watts. 10–14 yrs.

Mazer, Harry. 1986. *Cave Under the City.* New York: HarperCollins. 9–12 yrs.

Mills, Claudia. 1985. *What about Annie?* New York: Walker. 12–14 yrs.

Mitchell, Margaree King. 1993. *Uncle Jed's Barbershop.* Illus. James Ransome. New York: Simon & Schuster. 6–8 yrs.

Myers, Anna. 1992. *Red-Dirt Jessie.* New York: Walker. 8–10 yrs.

Naylor, Phyllis Reynolds & Lura Schiedl Reynolds. 1988. *Maudie in the Middle.* Illus. Judith Gwyn Brown. New York: Atheneum/Karl. 10–13 yrs.

Olsen, Violet. 1987. *View from the Pighouse Roof.* New York: Atheneum. 10–13 yrs.

Pinkney, Gloria. 1994. *Jean Back Home.* Illus. Jerry Pinkney. New York: Dial. 5–8 yrs.

Reeder, Carolyn. 1991. *Grandpa's Mountain.* New York: Macmillan. 11–15 yrs.

Rosenblum, Richard. *My Block.* New York: Atheneum. 5–7 yrs.

Rylant, Cynthia. 1982. *When I Was Young in the Mountains.* Illus. Diane Goode. New York: Dutton. 5–9 yrs.

Snyder, Zilpha Keatley. 1965. *The Velvet Room.* Illus. Alton Raible. Magnolia, Mass.: Peter Smith.

———. 1994. *Cat Running.* New York: Delacorte. 9–12 yrs.

Taylor, Mildred. 1976. *Roll of Thunder, Hear My Cry.* New York: Dial. 10–14 yrs.

———. 1981. *Let the Circle Be Unbroken.* New York: Dial. 10–14 yrs.

———. 1985. *Song of the Trees.* New York: Dial. 11–14 yrs.

———. 1987. *The Friendship.* New York: Dial. 11–14 yrs.

———. 1990. *Mississippi Bridge.* Illus. Max Ginsburg. New York: Dial. 12–15 yrs.

Weaver, Lydia. 1992. *Child Star: When Talkies Came to Hollywood.* Illus. Michele Laporte. New York: Viking. 11–15 yrs.

Whitmore, Arvella. 1990. *The Bread Winner.* Boston: Houghton Mifflin. 9–13 yrs.

Williams, Sherley Anne. 1992. *Working Cotton.* Illus. Carol Byard. San Diego: Harcourt Brace. 7–10 yrs.

The World During World War II

Anderson, Rachel. 1993. *Paper Faces.* New York: Holt. 10–13 yrs.

Bawden, Nina. 1988. *Henry.* Illus. Joyce Powzyk. New York: Lothrop, Lee & Shepard. 9–12 yrs.

———. 1993. *The Real Plato Jones.* New York: Clarion. 10–13 yrs.

Benchley, Nathaniel. 1974. *Bright Candles: A Novel of the Danish Resistance.* New York: Harper & Row. 10–15 yrs.

Bergman,Tamar. (Trans. Michael Swirsky). 1991. *Along the Tracks.* Boston: Houghton Mifflin. 12–15 yrs.

Chang, Margaret, & Raymond Chang. 1990. *In the Eye of the War.* New York: Macmillan. 10–12 yrs.

De Jong, Meindert. 1956. *House of Sixty Fathers.* New York: HarperCollins. 8–12 yrs.

Gallaz, Christophe & Roberto Innocenti. 1985. *Rose Blance*. Illus. Roberto Innocenti. Burlington, WI: Creative Education. 9–15 yrs.

Hill, Susan. 1991. *The Glass Angels*. Illus. Valerie Littlewood. Cambridge, Mass.: Candlewick. 9–13 yrs.

Hughes, Monica. 1986. *Blaine's Way*. Burr Ridge, Ill.: Irwin. 15 yrs.

Little, Jean. 1972. *From Anna*. New York: HarperCollins. 10–12 yrs.

Lowry, Lois. 1989. *Number the Stars*. Boston: Houghton Mifflin. 10–13 yrs.

Magorian, Michelle. 1982. *Good Night, Mr. Tom*. New York: HarperCollins. 11–14 yrs.

Maruki, Toshi. 1980. *Hiroshima No Pika*. New York: Lothrop, Lee & Shepard. 8–12 yrs.

Matas, Carol. 1989. *Lisa's War*. New York: Scribners. 10–13 yrs.

McSwaig, Marie. 1942. *Snow Treasure*. Illus. Mary Reardon. New York: Dutton. 9–12 yrs.

Mori, Hana. (Trans. Tamiko Kurosaki and Elizabeth Crowe) 1993. *Jirohattan*. Illus. Elizabeth Crowe. Honolulu: Bess Press. 10–13 yrs.

Morimoto, Junko. 1987. *My Hiroshima*. New York: Viking. 10–13 yrs.

Morpurgo, Michael. 1991. *Waiting for Anya*. New York: Viking Penguin. 10–14 yrs.

Oppenheim, Shulamith Levey. 1992. *The Lily Cupboard*. Illus. Ronald Himler. New York: HarperCollins/Zolotow. 6–8 yrs.

Pearson, Kit. 1989. *The Sky Is Falling*. New York: Viking. 10–13 yrs.

———. 1992. *Looking at the Moon*. New York: Viking. 10–13 yrs.

———. 1994. *The Lights Go On Again*. New York: Viking. 10–13 yrs.

Pelgrom, Els. (Trans. Maryka and Rafael Rudnik) 1980. *The Winter When Time Was Frozen*. New York: Morrow. 9–12 yrs.

Pople, Maureen. 1986. *The Other Side of the Family*. New York: Holt, Rinehart & Winston. 10–14 yrs.

Reuter, Bjarne. (Trans. Anthea Bell) 1994. *The Boys from St. Petri*. New York: Dutton. 12–15 yrs.

Sachs, Marilyn. 1973. *A Pocket Full of Seeds*. Illus. Ben Stahl. New York: Doubleday. 12–15 yrs.

Siegal, Aranka. 1981. *Upon the Head of the Goat: A Childhood in Hungary 1939–44*. New York: Farrar, Straus & Giroux. 12–16 yrs.

Vos, Ida. (Trans. Terese Edelstein and Inez Smidt). 1996. *Dancing on the Bridge of Avignon*. Boston: Houghton Mifflin. 9–12 yrs.

Westall, Robert. 1991. *The Kindgom by the Sea*. New York: Farrar, Straus & Giroux. 10–13 yrs.

Wild, Margaret. 1991. *Let the Celebrations Begin!* Illus. Julie Vivas. New York: Orchard. 7–10 yrs.

Zei, Alki. (Trans. Edward Fenton). 1972. *Petro's War*. New York: Dutton. 12–15 yrs.

The U.S. in World War II

Ackerman, Karen. 1992. *When Mama Retires*. Illus. Alexa Grace. New York: Knopf. 6–7 yrs.

Cormier, Robert. 1990. *Other Bells for Us to Ring*. Illus. Deborah Kogan Ray. New York: Delacorte. 9–12 yrs.

Greene, Bette. 1973. *The Summer of My German Soldier*. New York: Dial. 11–15 yrs.

Hahn, Mary Downing. 1991. *Stepping on the Cracks*. New York: Clarion. 10–13 yrs.

Houston, Gloria. 1992. *But No Candy*. Illus. Lloyd Bloom. New York: Philomel. 6–10 yrs.

McKinley, Robin. 1992. *My Father Is in the Navy*. Illus. Martine Gourbault. New York: Greenwillow. 4–7 yrs.

Ray, Deborah Kogan. 1990. *My Daddy Was a Soldier: A World War II Story*. New York: Holiday. 8–12 yrs.

Rylant, Cynthia. 1993. *I Had Seen Castles*. San Diego: Harcourt Brace. 12–15 yrs.

Stevenson, James. 1992. *Don't You Know There's a War On?* New York: Greenwillow. 6–10 yrs.

Yolen, Jane. 1991. *All Those Secrets of the World*. Illus. Leslie Baker. Boston: Little, Brown. 7–10 yrs.

Jewish Experiences During World War II and Holocaust

Aaron, Chester. 1982. *Gideon*. New York: HarperCollins/Lippincott. 12–15 yrs.

Baillie, Allan. 1994. *Rebel*. Illus. Di Wu. New York: Ticknor & Fields. 6–9 yrs.

Dillon, Eilis. 1992. *Children of Bach*. New York: Scribners. 10–13 yrs.

Drucker, Malka & Michael Halperin. 1993. *Jacob's Rescue: A Holocaust Story*. New York: Bantam Skylark. 12–14 yrs.

Hautzig, Ester. 1968. *The Endless Steppe*. New York: HarperCollins. 10–14 yrs.

Heuck, Sigrid. (Trans. Rika Lesser). 1988. *The Hideout*. New York: Dutton. 9–12 yrs.

Kerr, Judith. 1972. *When Hilter Stole Pink Rabbit*. New York: Coward McCann. 10–13 yrs.

Laird, Christa. 1990. *Shadow of the Wall*. New York: Greenwillow. 12+ yrs.

Leitner, Isabella (with Irving A. Leitner). 1992. *The Big Lie: A True Story*. Illus. Judy Pedersen. New York: Scholastic. 8–12 yrs.

Levitin, Sonia. 1989. *Silver Days*. New York: Atheneum. 10–15 yrs.

———. 1993. *Journey to America*. Illus. Charles Robinson. New York: Atheneum. 10–13 yrs.

Levoy, Myron. 1987. *Alan and Naomi*. New York: HarperCollins/Trophy. 12–14 yrs.

Nerlove, Miriam. 1996. *Flowers on the Wall*. Illus. Miriam Nerlove. New York: McElderry. 5–8 yrs.

Orlev, Uri. (Trans. Hillel Halkin) 1983. *The Island on Bird Street*. Boston: Houghton Mifflin. 9–13 yrs.

———. 1991. (Trans. Hillel Halkin) *The Man from the Other Side*. Boston: Houghton Mifflin. 12–15 yrs.

———. 1993. (Trans. Hillel Halkin) *Lydia, Queen of Palestine*. Boston: Houghton Mifflin. 10–15 yrs.

Ray, Karen. 1994. *To Cross a Line*. New York: Jackson/Orchard. 13–15 yrs.

Reiss, Johanna. 1972. *The Upstairs Room*. New York: Crowell. 10–14 yrs.

Richter, Hans Peter. (Trans. Edith Kroll) 1970. *Friedrich*. New York: Holt. 10–14 yrs.

Vos, Ida. (Trans. Terese Edelstein & Inez Smidt) 1991. *Hide and Seek*. Boston: Houghton Mifflin. 10–13 yrs.

———. (Trans. Terese Edelstein & Inez Smidt) 1993. *Anna Is Still Here*. Boston: Houghton Mifflin. 10–13 yrs.

———. (Trans. Terese Edelstein & Inez Smidt) 1995. *Dancing on the Bridge of Avignon*. Boston: Houghton Mifflin. 10–15 yrs.

———. (Trans. Terese Edelstein & Inez Smidt). 1996. *Dancing on the Bridge of Avignon*. Boston: Houghton Mifflin. 9–12 yrs.

Yolen, Jane. 1990. *The Devil's Arithmetic*. New York: Penguin. 12–15 yrs.

Late 1940s to Late 1980s

Baillie, Allan. 1992. *Little Brother*. New York: Viking. 11–13 yrs.

Bauer, Marion Dane. 1983. *Rain of Fire*. New York: Clarion. 10–13 yrs.

Bunting, Eve. 1990. *The Wall*. Illus. Ronald Himler. Boston: Houghton Mifflin/Clarion. 8–12 yrs.

Clark, Ann Nolan. 1978. *To Stand Against the Wind*. New York: Viking. 11–13 yrs.

Cleary, Beverly. 1950–1957. *Henry Huggins Series*. New York: Morrow. 9–11 yrs.

———. 1968–1984. *Romana Quimby Series*. New York: Morrow. 9–11 yrs.

de Jenkins, Lyll Becerra. 1988. *The Honorable Prison*. New York: Lodestar. 12–15 yrs.

Doyle, Brian. 1984. *Angel Square*. New York: Groundwood. 9–12 yrs.

Freeman, Suzanne. 1996. *The Cuckoo's Child*. New York: Greenwillow. 11–14 yrs.

Gantos, Jack. 1994. *Heads or Tails: Stories from the Sixth Grade*. New York: Farrar, Straus & Giroux. 9–12 yrs.

Giff, Patricia Reilly. 1991. *The War Began at Supper; Letters to Miss Loria*. Illus. Betsy Lewin. New York: Dell. 8–12 yrs.

Gilson, Jamie. 1985. *Hello, My Name Is Scrambled Eggs*. Illus. John Wallner. New York: Lothrop, Lee & Shepard. 10–12 yrs.

Hahn, Mary Downing. 1988. *December Stillness*. New York: Clarion. 12–14 yrs.

Hartling, Peter. (Trans. Elizabeth D. Crawford) 1988. *Crutches*. New York: Lothrop, Lee & Shepard. 9–14 yrs.

Heide, Florence Parry & Judith Heide Gilliland. 1992. *Sami and the Time of the Troubles*. Illus. Ted Lewin. New York: Clarion. 8–12 yrs.

Herlihy, Dirlie. 1988. *Ludie's Song*. New York: Dial. 11–15 yrs.

Hest, Amy. 1990. *Fancy Aunt Jess*. Illus. Amy Schwartz. New York: Morrow. 5–7 yrs.

Hewitt, Marsha, & Claire MacKay. 1981. *One Proud Summer*. London: The Women's Press. 10–15 yrs.

Johnsto4n, Julie. 1993. *Hero of Lesser Causes*. Boston: Joy Street. 10–12 yrs.

Kordon, Klaus. (Trans. Elizabeth D. Crawford) 1992. *Brothers Like Friends*. New York: Philomel. 10–15 yrs.

Levitin, Sonia. 1993. *Annie's Promise*. New York: Atheneum. 12–16 yrs.

Lingard, Joan. 1991. *Between Two Worlds*. New York: Lodestar. 12–15 yrs.

Lutzeier, Elizabeth. 1992. *The Wall*. New York: Holiday. 10–15 yrs.

Nelson, Theresa. 1989. *And One for All*. New York: Orchard/Jackson. 11–15 yrs.

Paik, Min. 1988. *Aekyung's Dream*. Children's Book Press. 6–9 yrs.

Paterson, Katherine. 1989. *Park's Quest*. New York: Puffin. 11–15 yrs.

Paulsen, Gary. 1993. *Harris and Me: A Summer Remembered*. San Diego: Harcourt Brace. 12–16 yrs.

Qualey, Marsha. 1994. *Come In from the Cold*. Boston: Houghton Mifflin. 12–16 yrs.

Rinaldi, Ann. 1996. *Keep Smiling Through*. San Diego: Harcourt Brace. 9–12 yrs.

Sacks, Margaret. 1989. *Beyond Safe Boundaries*. New York: Lodestar. 12–15 yrs.

Slepian, Jan. 1990. *Risk n' Roses*. New York: Putnam. 11–14 yrs.

Smucker, Anna Egan. 1989. *No Star Nights*. Illus. Steve Johnson. New York: Knopf/Borzoi. 7–10 yrs.

Talbert, Marc. 1992. *The Purple Heart*. New York: HarperCollins. 10–13 yrs.

LITERARY CATEGORIES

ADVENTURE STORIES

Avi, 1992. *"Who Was That Masked Man, Anyway?"* New York: Orchard/Jackson. 10–13 yrs.

Byars, Betsy. 1993. *McMummy*. New York: Viking.

Coles, William E., Jr. 1996. *Another Kind of Monday*. New York: Atheneum. 13–17 yrs.

George, Jean Craighead. 1987. *Water Sky*. New York: Harper & Row. 10–14 yrs.

———. 1989. *Shark beneath the Reef*. New York: HarperCollins. 9–12 yrs.

Greer, Gery & Bob Ruddick. 1987. *This Island Isn't Big Enough for the Four of Us!* New York: Crowell. 10–13 yrs.

Haarhoff, Dorian. 1992. *Desert December.* Illus. Leon Vermeulen. New York: Clarion. 7–9 yrs.

Helldorfer, Mary Claire. 1991. *Sailing to the Sea.* Illus. Loretta Krupinski. New York: Viking Penguin. 5–8 yrs.

Hobbs, Will. 1992. *The Big Wander.* New York: Atheneum. 11–15 yrs.

———. 1993. *Beardance.* New York: Atheneum. 10–13 yrs.

Hurwitz, Johanna. 1993. *The Up and Down Spring.* Illus. Gail Owens. New York: Morrow. 9–12 yrs.

Karr, Kathleen. 1993. *Gideon and the Mummy Professor.* New York: Farrar, Straus & Giroux. 10–12 yrs.

Kingman, Lee. 1986. *The Luck of the Miss L.* Boston: Houghton Mifflin. 8–11 yrs.

Lindbergh, Anne. 1985. *The Worry Week.* Illus. Kathryn Hewitt. San Diego: Harcourt Brace Jovanovich. 10–12 yrs.

Lyon, George Ella. 1990. *Come a Tide.* Illus. Stephen Gammell. New York: Orchard/Jackson. 4–7 yrs.

Marino, Jan. 1993. *For the Love of Pete: A Novel.* Boston: Little, Brown. 10–14 yrs.

Myers, Walter Dean. 1986. *Ambush in the Amazon.* New York: Viking Penguin/Puffin. 9–12 yrs.

Polacco, Patricia. 1993. *The Bee Tree.* New York: Philomel. 5–8 yrs.

Radin, Ruth Yaffe. 1989. *High in the Mountains.* Illus. Ed Young. New York: Macmillan. 5–10 yrs.

Rand, Gloria. 1989. *Salty Dog.* Illus. Ted Rand. New York: Holt. 9–11 yrs.

Sachs, Elizabeth-Ann. 1992. *Kiss Me, Janie Tannenbaum.* New York: Atheneum/Karl. 11–13 yrs.

Sebestyen, Ouida. 1994. *Out of Nowhere.* New York: Orchard/Kroupa. 12–16 yrs.

Stevenson, Robert Louis. 1994. *David Balfour.* Illus. N. C. Wyeth. New York: Scribners. 12–16 yrs. (Sequel to *Kidnapped.*)

Taylor, Theodore. 1989. *Sniper.* San Diego: Harcourt Brace Jovanovich. 10–13 yrs.

Twain, Mark. 1994. *The Adventures of Huckleberry Finn.* Illus. Steven Kellogg. New York: Morrow. 10–16 yrs. Books of Wonder series.

SURVIVAL STORIES

Avi. 1992. *Man from the Sky.* New York: Morrow. 10–12 yrs.

———. 1994. *The Barn.* New York: Orchard/Jackson. 9–12 yrs.

Baillie, Allan. 1992. *Adrift.* New York: Viking. 10–12 yrs.

Burnford, Sheila. 1961. *The Incredible Journey.* Illus. Carl Burger. Boston: Little, Brown. 10–13 yrs.

Cleaver, Vera & Bill Cleaver. 1969. *Where the Lillies Bloom.* Illus. James Spanfeller. New York: Lippincott. 10–13 yrs.

Cole, Brock. 1987. *The Goats.* New York: HarperCollins. 11–13 yrs.

Cooney, Caroline B. 1995. *Flush Fire.* New York: Scholastic. 12–15 yrs.

*Cottonwood, Joe. 1992. *Danny Ain't.* New York: Scholastic. 11–13 yrs.

†Cross, Gillian. 1985. *On the Edge.* New York: Holiday. 12–15 yrs.

DeFelice, Cynthia. 1994. *Lostman's River.* New York: Macmillan. 9–12 yrs.

†Duncan, Lois. 1989. *Don't Look Behind You.* New York: Delacorte. 12–15 yrs.

†Fox, Paula. 1991. *Monkey Island.* New York: Orchard. 12–15 yrs.

George, Jean Craighead. 1959. *My Side of the Mountain.* New York: Dutton. 11–14 yrs.

———. 1972. *Julie of the Wolves.* Illus. John Schoenherr. New York: Harper & Row. 11–14 yrs.

———. 1983. *The Talking Earth.* New York: HarperCollins. 10–13 yrs.

———. 1990. *On the Far Side of the Mountain.* New York: Dutton. 8–12 yrs.

———. 1994. *Julie.* Illus. Wendell Minor. New York: HarperCollins. 10–14 yrs.

*Hamilton, Virginia. 1971. *The Planet of Junior Brown.* New York: Macmillan. 11–13 yrs.

†Harris, Rosemary. 1982. *Zad.* Farber & Farber. 12–15 yrs.

Hill, Kirkpatrick. 1993. *Winter Camp.* New York: McElderry. 9–12 yrs.

†Holman, Felice. 1974. *Slake's Limbo.* New York: Scribners. 12–15 yrs.

Houston, James. 1977. *Frozen Fire.* New York: Atheneum. 12–15 yrs.

———. 1982. *Black Diamond.* New York: Atheneum. 12–15 yrs.

Hunt, Irene. 1987. *No Promises in the Wind.* New York: Berkeley. 11–14 yrs.

Levin, Betty. 1995. *Fire in the Wind.* New York: Greenwillow. 9–14 yrs.

London, Jack. 1994. *The Call of the Wild.* Illus. Barry Moser. New York: Macmillan. 9–12 yrs.

Manley, Joan B. 1995. *She Flew No Flags.* Boston: Houghton Mifflin. 11–14 yrs.

†Moeri, Louise. 1981. *Save Queen of Sheba.* New York: Dutton. 10–13 yrs.

———. 1984. *Downwind.* New York: Dutton. 12–15 yrs.

*Myers, Walter Dean. 1978. *It Ain't All for Nothin'.* New York: Viking. 12–15 yrs.

* ———. 1988. *Scorpions.* New York: Harper & Row. 12–15 yrs.

Naylor, Phyllis Reynolds. 1994. *The Fear Place.* New York: Atheneum. 9–12 yrs.

Paulsen, Gary. 1989. *The Voyage of the Frog.* New York: Orchard/Jackson. 10–15 yrs.

———. 1993. *Dogteam.* Illus. Ruth Wright Paulsen. New York: Delacorte. 7–10 yrs.

Pendergrafts, Patricia. 1991. *As Far as Mill Springs.* New York: Philomel. 10–12 yrs.

†Rardin, Susan Lowry. 1984. *Captive in a Foreign Land.* Boston: Houghton Mifflin. 11–14 yrs.

Ruckman, Ivy. 1984. *Night of the Twister.* New York: Crowell. 10–13 yrs.

Sperry, Armstrong. 1940. *Call It Courage.* New York: Macmillan. 11–14 yrs.

Spinelli, Jerry. 1990. *Maniac Magee.* Boston: Little, Brown. 11–14 yrs.

Staples, Suzanne Fisher. 1993. *Haveli.* New York: Knopf. 13–16 yrs.

Sweeney, Joyce. 1996. *Free Fall.* New York: Delacorte. 12–15 yrs.

Taylor, Theodore. 1969. *The Cay.* New York: Doubleday. 10–13 yrs.

———. 1993. *Timothy of the Cay.* San Diego: Harcourt Brace. 10–13 yrs. (Sequel to *The Cay*)

Thesman, Jean. 1992. *When the Road Ends.* Boston: Houghton Mifflin. 11–13 yrs.

Voigt, Cynthia. 1981. *Homecoming.* New York: Atheneum. 12–15 yrs.

———. 1982. *Dicey's Song.* New York: Atheneum. 12–15 yrs.

Waddell, Martin. 1996. *The Kidnapping of Suzie Q.* Cambridge, Mass.: Candlewick. 12–15 yrs.

†Watson, James. 1983. *Talking in a Whisper.* London: Victor Gollancz. 12–15 yrs.

Wild, Margaret. 1991. *Let the Celebrations Begin!* Illus. Julie Vivas. New York: Orchard. 3–6 yrs.

Wisler, G. Clifton. 1993. *Jericho's Journey.* New York: Lodestar. 9–12 yrs.

REALISTIC ANIMALS

Domesticated (Pets)

Abercrombie, Barbara. 1993. *Michael and the Cats.* Illus. Mark Grahm. New York: McElderry. 4–7 yrs.

Auch, Mary Jane. 1994. *The Latchkey Dog.* Illus. by Cat Bowman Smith. Boston: Little, Brown. 10–12 yrs.

Aylesworth, Jim. 1989. *Mother Halverson's New Cat.* Illus. Toni Goffe. New York: Atheneum. 5–8 yrs.

Baker, Leslie. 1992. *The Antique Store Cat.* Boston: Little, Brown. 5–8 yrs.

Bonsall, Crosby. 1986. *The Amazing, the Incredible Super Dog.* New York: Harper & Row. 5–9 yrs.

Borton, Lady. 1993. *Fat Chance!* Illus. Deborah Kogan Ray. New York: Philomel. 5–7 yrs.

Broome, Errol. 1994. *Tangles.* Illus. Ann James. New York: Knopf. 8–12 yrs.

Brown, Marc. 1993. *Arthur's New Puppy.* Boston: Little, Brown. 4–7 yrs.

Brown, Ruth. 1986. *Our Cat Flossie.* New York: Dutton. 3–7 yrs.

———. 1987. *Our Puppy's Vacation.* New York: Dutton. 3–5 yrs.

Burns, Theresa. 1989. *You're Not My Cat.* New York: Lippincott. 6–9 yrs.

Carle, Eric. 1990. *The Very Quiet Cricket.* New York: Philomel. 3–6 yrs.

Doherty, Berlie. 1993. *Snowy.* New York: Dial. 5–7 yrs.

Ernst, Lisa. 1994. *Campbell Walter's Tail.* New York: Bradbury. 5–7 yrs.

Gardiner, John Reynolds. 1980. *Stone Fox.* Illus. Marcia Sewell. New York: Crowell. 9–12 yrs.

Godden, Rumer. 1992. *Listen to the Nightingale.* New York: Viking. 10–13 yrs.

Gordon, Gaelyn. 1992. *Duckat.* Illus. Chris Gaskin. New York: Scholastic. 2–6 yrs.

Gottlieb, Dale. 1989. *Big Dog.* Illus. Dale Gottlieb. New York: Morrow. 3–7 yrs.

Haas, Jessie. 1993. *A Horse like Barney.* New York: Greenwillow. 9–12 yrs.

———. 1994. *Uncle Daney's Way.* New York: Greenwillow. 11–14 yrs.

———. 1996. *Be Well, Beware.* Illus. Jos. A. Smith. New York: Greenwillow. 8–10 yrs. (See also: *Beware the Mare*, 1993; and *A Blue for Beware*, 1995.)

Hall, Lynn. 1986. *Danger Dog.* New York: Scribners. 10–12 yrs.

———. 1992. *Windsong.* New York: Scribners. 10–12 yrs.

Haywood, Carolyn. 1990. *Eddie's Friend Boodles.* Illus. Catherine Stock. New York: Morrow. 7–10 yrs.

Henkes, Kevin. 1995. *Protecting Marie.* New York: Greenwillow. 11–14 yrs.

Hesse, Karen. 1993. *Lester's Dog.* Illus. Nancy Carpenter. New York: Crown. 5–8 yrs.

High, Linda. 1995. *Oatman Maizie.* New York: Holiday. 10–14 yrs.

NOTE: Most books about the Jewish experience and most fiction about war eras are survival stories.

* Survival on the streets

† International intrigue and kidnapping

Hindley, Judy. 1990. *Mrs. Mary Malarky's Seven Cats.* Illus. Denise Teasdale. New York: Orchard. 4–7 yrs.

Joosse, Barbara M. 1992. *Nobody's Cat.* New York: HarperCollins. 5–7 yrs.

Keller, Holly. 1992. *Furry.* New York: Greenwillow. 5–7 yrs.

Kharms, Daniil. (Trans. Jamey Gambrell) 1993. *The Story of a Boy Named Will, Who Went Sledding Down the Hill.* Illus. Vladimir Radunsky. New York: North-South. 4–6 yrs.

King-Smith, Dick. 1992. *Pretty Polly.* Illus. Marshall Peck. New York: Crown. 9–11 yrs.

Kjelgaar, Jim. 1956. *Big Red.* Illus. Bob Kuhn. New York: Holiday. 10–13 yrs.

Knight, E. (Wells, R., reteller). 1995. *Lassie Come Home.* Illus. Susan Jeffers. New York: Holt. 7–10 yrs.

Lindenbaum, Pija. (Reteller Gabrielle Charbonnet) 1992. *Boodil My Dog.* New York: Holt. 5–9 yrs.

Little, Jean. 1985. *Lost and Found.* Illus. Leoung O'Young. New York: Viking Kestrel. 7–9 yrs.

Martin, Ann M. 1985. *Me and Katie (the Pest).* Illus. Blanche Sims. New York: Holiday. 7–10 yrs.

Martin, Jacqueline Briggs. 1992. *The Finest Horse in Town.* Illus. Susan Gaber. New York: HarperCollins. 7–10 yrs.

McNulty, Faith. 1994. *A Snake in the House.* Illus. Ted Rand. New York: Scholastic. 5–9 yrs.

Moore, Inga. 1991. *Six-Dinner Sid.* New York: Simon & Schuster. 6–10 yrs.

Monson, A. M. 1992. *The Deer Stand.* New York: Lothrop, Lee & Shepard. 11–13 yrs.

Naylor, Phyllis Reynolds. 1991. *Shiloh.* New York: Atheneum. 10–13 yrs.

Newberry, Clare Turlay. 1993. *April's Kittens.* New York: HarperCollins. 4–7 yrs.

Nodset, Joan L. 1993. *Come Here Cat.* Illus. Steven Kellogg. New York: HarperCollins. 5–7 yrs.

Ormerod, Jan. 1989. *Kitten Day.* New York: Lothrop, Lee & Shepard. 3–6 yrs.

Parnall, Peter. 1993. *Water Pup.* New York: Macmillan. 10–12 yrs.

Pomerantz, Charlotte. 1993. *The Outside Dog.* Illus. Jennifer Plecas. New York: HarperCollins. 5–8 yrs.

Rawls, Wilson. 1961. *Where the Red Fern Grows.* New York: Doubleday. 9–12 yrs.

Rylant, Cynthia. 1989. *Henry and Mudge Get the Cold Shivers: The Seventh Book of Their Adventures.* Illus. Sucie Stevenson. New York: Bradbury. 5–7 yrs.

Samuels, Barbara. 1986. *Duncan and Dolores.* New York: Bradbury. 4–7 yrs.

Schwartz, Amy. 1987. *Oma and Bobo.* New York: Bradbury. 5–9 yrs.

Scott, Ann Herbert. 1993. *A Brand Is Forever.* Illus. Ronald Himler. New York: Clarion. 6–9 yrs.

Spooner, J. B. 1994. *The Story of the Little Black Dog.* Illus. Terre Lamb Seeley. New York: Arcade. 5–8 yrs.

Strommen, Judith Bernie. 1993. *Champ Hobarth.* New York: Holt. 10–12 yrs.

Sharmat, Marjorie Weinman. 1991. *I'm the Best!* Illus. Will Hillenbrand. New York: Holiday. 6–9 yrs.

Taylor, Theodore. 1981. *The Trouble with Tuck.* New York: Doubleday. 9–13 yrs.

———. 1991. *Tuck Triumphant.* New York: Doubleday. 9–13 yrs.

Thiele, Colin. 1978. *Storm Boy.* Illus. John Schoenherr. New York: HarperCollins. 12–15 yrs.

Thomas, Jane Resh. 1981. *The Comeback Dog.* Illus. Troy Howell. Boston: Houghton Mifflin. 10–13 yrs.

Updike, David. 1993. *The Sounds of Summer.* Illus. Robert Andrew Parker. New York: Pippin. 5–8 yrs.

Whitmore, Arvella. 1985. *You're a Real Hero, Amanda.* Boston: Houghton Mifflin. 9–13 yrs.

Wilhelm, Hans. 1985. *I'll Always Love You.* New York: Crown. 3–7 yrs.

Wild, Margaret. 1994. *Toby.* Illus. Noela Young. New York: Ticknor & Fields. 5–8 yrs.

Animals in Their Natural Environment

Allen, Judy. 1992. *Tiger.* Illus. Tudor Humphries. Cambridge, Mass.: Candlewick. 6–9 yrs.

Baker, Alan. 1991. *Two Tiny Mice.* Illus. Alan Baker. New York: Dial. 3–8 yrs.

Blyler, Allison. 1991. *Finding Foxes.* Illus. Robert J. Blake. New York: Philomel. 6–8 yrs.

Brett, Jan. 1985. *Annie and the Wild Animals.* New York: Harper & Row. 5–9 yrs.

Carlstrom, Nancy White. 1990. *Moose in the Garden.* Illus. Lisa Desimini. New York: Harper & Row. 3–8 yrs.

———. 1991. *Goodbye Geese.* Illus. Ed Young. New York: Philomel. 4–6 yrs.

Carter, Anne. 1986. *Ruff Leaves Home.* Illus. John Butler. Centerview, Mo.: Carter. 4–7 yrs.

———. 1987. *Bella's Secret Garden.* Illus. John Butler. Centerview, Mo.: Carter. 3–7 yrs.

Corcoran, Barbara. 1993. *Wolf at the Door.* New York: Atheneum/Karl. 10–13 yrs.

Cross, Gillian. 1993. *The Great American Elephant Chase.* New York: Holiday. 12–15 yrs.

Dugan, Barbara. 1993. *Leaving Home with a Pickle Jar.* Illus. Karen Lee Baker. New York: Greenwillow. 5–7 yrs.

Ehlert, Lois. 1990. *Feathers for Lunches.* San Diego: Harcourt Brace Jovanovich. 3–8 yrs.

Evans, Sanford. 1993. *Naomi's Geese.* New York: Simon & Schuster. 8–12 yrs.

Geisert, Arthur. 1993. *Oink Oink.* Boston: Houghton Mifflin. 6–10 yrs.

George, William T. 1989. *Box Turtle at Long Pond.* Illus. Lindsay Barrett George. New York: Greenwillow. 5–8 yrs.

Haas, Jessie. 1993. *Beware the Mare.* New York: Greenwillow. 7–9 yrs.

Henry, Marguerite. 1954. *Justin Morgan Had a Horse.* Illus. Wesley Dennis. Skokie, Ill.: Rand McNally. 9–12 yrs.

———. 1963. *Misty of Chincoteague.* Illus. Wesley Dennis. Skokie, Ill.: Rand McNally. 8–11 yrs.

———. 1976. *King of the Wind.* Illus. Wesley Dennis. Skokie, Ill.: Rand McNally. 9–12 yrs.

Ichikawa, Satomi. 1991. *Nora's Duck.* New York: Philomel. 6–8 yrs.

Kuskin, Karla. 1992. *Which Horse Is William?* New York: Greenwillow. 5–7 yrs.

Locker, Thomas. 1985. *The Mare on the Hill.* New York: Dial. 5–10 yrs.

London, Jack. 1968. *Call of the Wild.* Illus. Charles Pickard. New York: Dutton. 12–15 yrs.

McDonald, Megan. 1990. *Is This a House for Hermit Crab?* Illus. S. D. Schindler. New York: Orchard/Jackson. 3–7 yrs.

McNulty, Faith. 1986. *The Lady and the Spider.* New York: Dial. 5–8 yrs.

Morrison, Dorothy Naful. 1987. *Whisper Again.* New York: Atheneum. 10–13 yrs.

Murphy, Jim. 1989. *The Call of the Wolves.* Illus. Mark Alan Weatherby. New York: Scholastic. 4–8 yrs.

Pedersen, Judy. 1989. *The Tiny Patient.* Illus. Judy Pedersen. New York: Knopf/Borzoi. 4–8 yrs.

Peyton, K. M. 1992. *Poor Badger.* New York: Delacorte. 8–12 yrs.

Pryor, Bonnie. 1991. *Greenbrook Farm.* Illus. Mark Graham. New York: Simon & Schuster. 6–10 yrs.

Rawlings, Marjorie Kinnan. 1938. *The Yearling.* Illus. Edward Shenton. New York: Scribners. 12–14 yrs.

Rogers, Jean. 1985. *The Secret Moose.* Illus. Jim Fowler. New York: Greenwillow. 7–9 yrs.

Ryder, Joanne. 1989–91. *Catching the Wind; Lizard in the Sun; Winter Whale.* Michael Rothman. New York: Morrow. 4–7 yrs.

Rylant, Cynthia. 1985. *Every Living Thing.* Illus. S. D. Schindler. New York: Bradbury. 10–12 yrs.

Schoenherr, John. 1991. *Bear.* New York: Philomel. 4–8 yrs.

Springer, Nancy. 1987. *A Horse to Love.* Harper & Row. 9–11 yrs.

Vyner, Sue. 1992. *The Stolen Egg.* Illus. Tim Vyner. New York: Viking Penguin. 4–6 yrs.

Wellington, Monica. 1990. *Seasons of Swans.* New York: Dutton. 3–7 yrs.

Williams, Barbara. 1985. *Mitzi and the Elephants.* Illus. Emily Arnold McCully. New York: Dutton. 8–10 yrs.

Yolen, Jane. 1993. *Honkers.* Illus. Leslie Baker. Boston: Little, Brown. 5–8 yrs.

Mysteries

Ackerman, Karen. 1995. *Bingleman's Midway.* Illus. Barry Moser. Honesdale, Penn.: Boyds Mills. 6–9 yrs.

Adler, David. 1981. *Cam Jansen & the Mystery of the Dinosaur Bones.* New York: Viking. 6–9 yrs.

———. 1985. *Cam Jansen and the Mystery at the Monkey House.* Illus. Susanna Natti. New York: Viking Kestrel. 7–9 yrs.

———. 1985. *The Fourth Floor Twins and the Fish Snitch Mystery.* Illus. Irene Trivas. New York: Viking Kestrel. 7–9 yrs.

———. 1985. *The Fourth Floor Twins and the Fortune Cookie Chase.* Illus. Irene Trivas. New York: Viking Kestrel. 7–9 yrs.

———. 1986. *My Dog and the Green Sock Mystery.* Illus. Dick Gackenbach. New York: Holiday. 6–8 yrs.

———. 1987. *My Dog and the Birthday Mystery.* Illus. Dick Gackenbach. Holiday. 4–8 yrs.

Alexander, Sue. 1990. *World Famous Muriel and the Magic Mystery.* Illus. Marla Frazee. New York: Crowell. 5–8 yrs.

Arden, William. 1974. *Mystery of the Dead Man's Riddle.* New York: Random House. 9–12 yrs.

Avi. 1989. *The Man Who Was Poe.* New York: Orchard. 11–15 yrs.

———. 1991. *Windcatcher.* New York: Macmillan. 10–12 yrs.

Base, Grahame. 1988. *The Eleventh Hour.* New York: Harry Abrams. 9–13 yrs.

Bawden, Nina. 1978. *Rebel on a Rock.* New York: HarperCollins. 10–12 yrs.

———. 1979. *The Robbers.* New York: Lothrop, Lee & Shepard. 10–12 yrs.

———. 1991. *A Handful of Thieves.* New York: Clarion. 10–12 yrs.

———. 1991. *The Witch's Daughter.* New York: Clarion. 10–13 yrs.

———. 1992. *The House of Secrets.* New York: Clarion. 10–12 yrs.

Bonsai, Crosby. 1963. *The Case of the Hungry Stranger.* New York: HarperCollins. 6–8 yrs.

———. 1965. *The Case of the Cat's Meow.* New York: HarperCollins. 6–8 yrs.

Brittain, Bill. 1989. *My Buddy, the King.* New York: HarperCollins. 10–12 yrs.

Bunting, Eve. 1988. *Is Anybody There?* New York: Lippincott. 9–12 yrs.

———. 1992. *Coffin On a Case.* New York: HarperCollins. 10–13 yrs.

Byars, Betsy. 1994. *The Dark Stairs: A Herculeah Jones Mystery.* New York: Viking. 9–12 yrs.

Carmody, Isobelle. 1994. *The Gathering*. New York: Dial.

Christian, Mary Blount. 1986. *Merger on the Orient Expressway*. Illus. Kathleen Collins Howell. New York: Dutton. 8–10 yrs. Determined Detectives Series.

Clifford, Eth. 1987. *Harvey's Marvelous Monkey Mystery*. Boston: Houghton Mifflin. 8–11 yrs.

———. 1989. *I Hate Your Guts, Ben Brooster*. Boston: Houghton Mifflin. 9–12 yrs.

Conford, Ellen. 1988. *A Case for Jenny Archer*. Boston: Little, Brown. 9–12 yrs.

Cross, Gilbert B. 1986. *Mystery at Loon Lake*. New York: Atheneum. 10–12 yrs.

Cross, Gillian. 1991. *Wolf*. New York: Holiday. 12–15 yrs.

Curry, Jane Louise. 1991. *What the Dickens!* New York: McElderry/Macmillan. 10–12 yrs.

DeClements, Barthe. 1991. *Wake Me at Midnight*. New York: Viking Penguin. 8–12 yrs.

DeFelice, Cynthia. 1993. *The Light on Hogback Hill*. New York: Macmillan. 7–10 yrs.

Deleon, Eric. 1988. *Pitch and Hasty Check It Out*. New York: Orchard/Jackson. 8–11 yrs.

Dicks, Terrance. 1980. *The Case of the Cinema Swindle*. New York: Elsevier/Nelson. 10–12 yrs.

Dillon, Eilis. 1989. *The Island of Ghosts*. New York: Scribners. 10–13 yrs.

Duncan, Lois. 1974. *Down a Dark Hall*. Boston: Little, Brown. 12–15 yrs.

———. 1981. *Stranger with My Face*. Boston: Little, Brown. 12–15 yrs.

———. 1984. *Third Eye*. Boston: Little, Brown. 12–15 yrs.

Eisenberg, Lisa. 1987. *Mystery at Snowshoe Mountain Lodge*. New York: Dial. 10–14 yrs.

Galbraith, Kathryn Osebold. 1985. *Something Suspicious*. New York: McElderry. 8–12 yrs.

George, Jean Craighead. 1991. *Who Really Killed Cock Robin?* New York: HarperCollins. 10–13 yrs.

———. 1992. *The Missing 'Gator of Gumbo Limbo: An Ecological Mystery*. New York: HarperCollins. 11–13 yrs.

———. 1993. *The Fire Bug Collection*. New York: HarperCollins. 10–13 yrs.

Giff, Patricia Reilly. 1989. *Garbage Juice for Breakfast*. Illus. Blanche Sims. New York: Dell/Yearling. 6–9 yrs.

Greenberg, Daniel A. 1992. *The Great Baseball Card Hunt: A Southside Sluggers Baseball Mystery*. New York: Simon & Schuster. 9–12 yrs.

———. 1992. *The Missing Championship Ring: A Southside Sluggers Baseball Mystery*. New York: Simon & Schuster. 9–12 yrs.

Griffin, Peni R. 1992. *The Treasure Bird*. New York: McElderry. 10–12 yrs.

Haas, Dorothy. 1988. *To Catch a Crook*. New York: Clarion. 8–11 yrs.

Hahn, Mary Downing. 1988. *Following the Mystery Man*. New York: Avon. 11–13 yrs.

Hamilton, Virginia. 1984. *The House of Dies Drear*. New York: Macmillan. 11–13 yrs.

———. 1987. *Mystery of Drear House*. New York: Greenwillow. 11–13 yrs.

Hass, E. A. 1986. *Incognito Mosquito Takes to the Air*. New York: Random House. 9–12 yrs.

Heisel, Sharon E. 1993. *Wrapped in a Riddle*. Boston: Houghton Mifflin. 9–12 yrs.

Hildick, E. W. 1986. *The Case of the Muttering Mummy*. Illus. Blanche Sims. New York: Macmillan. 9–11 yrs. McGurk Mystery Series.

———. 1988. *The Case of the Wandering Weathervanes*. Illus. Denise Brunkus. Macmillan. 9–11 yrs. McGurk Mystery Series.

———. 1994. *The Case of the Fantastic Footprints: A McGurk Mystery*. New York: Macmillan. 9–12 yrs. (See also other books in series.)

Howe, James. 1985. *What Eric Knew*. New York: Atheneum. 10–12 yrs. Sebastian Barth Mystery Series.

Howe, Deborah & James Howe. 1979. *Bunnicula*. New York: Avon. 8–11 yrs.

———. 1982. *Howliday Inn*. Illus. L. Munsinger. New York: Atheneum. 8–11 yrs.

———. 1983. *The Celery Stalks at Midnight*. Illus. L. Morrill. New York: Atheneum. 8–11 yrs.

———. 1990. *Dew Drop Dead: A Sebastian Barth Mystery*. New York: Atheneum. 10–13 yrs.

Hughes, Dean. 1985. *Nutty and the Case of the Mastermind Thief*. New York: Atheneum. 9–11 yrs.

Kehret, Peg. 1987. *Deadly Stranger*. Northbrook, Ill.: Dodd, Mead. 9–11 yrs.

Klein, Robin. 1987. *People Might Hear You*. New York: Viking Kestrel. 11–14 yrs.

Konigsburg, E. L. 1967. *From the Mixed-Up Files of Mrs. Basil E. Frankweiler*. New York: Atheneum. 10–13 yrs.

Kwitz, Mary DeBall. 1991. *The Bell Tolls at Mousehaven Manor*. New York: Scholastic. 10–13 yrs.

Lasky, Kathryn. 1993. *A Voice in the Wind*. San Diego: Harcourt Brace. 8–12 yrs. (See also: *Double Trouble Squared*; *Shadows in the Water*.)

Levy, Elizabeth. 1982. *Something Queer Is Going On*. New York: Dell. 6–9 yrs.

———. 1994. *School Spirit Sabotage: A Brian and Pea Brain Mystery*. Illus. George Ulrich. New York: HarperCollins. 9–12 yrs.

Littke, Lael. 1992. *The Mystery of Ruby's Ghost*. Salt Lake City: Cinnamon/Tree/Deseret. 10–13 yrs.

Maccarone, Grace. 1987. *The Haunting of Grade Three*. Illus. Kelly Oechsli. New York: Scholastic/Lucky Star. 7–9 yrs.

Macken, Walter. 1966. *Island of the Great Yellow Ox*. New York: Simon & Shuster. 10–13 yrs.

Mahy, Margaret. 1995. *The Other Side of Silence*. New York: Viking. 12–14 yrs.

Morpurgo, Michael. 1996. *The Wreck of the Zanzibar*. Illus. François Place. New York: Viking. 9–12 yrs.

Naylor, Phyllis Reynolds. 1986. *The Bodies in the Bessledorf Hotel*. New York: Atheneum. 9–11 yrs. Bernie Magruder Mystery Series.

———. 1990. *Bernie and the Bessledorf Ghost*. New York: Atheneum. 9–11 yrs.

Newman, Robert. 1985. *The Case of the Murdered Players*. New York: Atheneum. 11–13 yrs.

———. 1986. *The Case of the Indian Curse*. New York: Atheneum. 10–14 yrs.

Nixon, Joan Lowery. 1994. *Shadowmaker*. New York: Delacorte. 11–15 yrs.

Otfinoski, Steven. 1992. *The Stolen Signs: A Southside Sluggers Baseball Mystery*. New York: Simon & Schuster. 9–12 yrs.

———. 1992. *Who Stole Home Plate?: A Southside Sluggers Baseball Mystery*. New York: Simon & Schuster. 9–12 yrs.

Pearce, Philippa. 1985. *The Way to Sattin Shore*. New York: Viking Puffin. 12–15 yrs.

Petersen, P. J. 1987. *The Freshman Detective Blues*. New York: Delacorte. 11–13 yrs.

Powell, Pamela. 1992. *The Turtle Watchers*. New York: Viking. 10–12 yrs.

Prather, Ray. 1992. *Fish and Bones*. New York: HarperCollins. 10–13 yrs.

Pryor, Bonnie. 1994. *Marvelous Marvin and the Wolfman Mystery*. Illus. Melissa Sweet. New York: Morrow. 9–12 yrs.

Pullman, Philip. 1992. *The Broken Bridge*. New York: Knopf. 12–15 yrs.

Raskin, Ellen. 1978. *The Westing Game*. New York: Dutton. 11–13 yrs.

Roberts, Willo Davis. 1975. *The View from the Cherry Tree*. New York: Atheneum. 10–12 yrs.

———. 1989. *What Could Go Wrong?* New York: Atheneum. 10–12 yrs.

Roennfeldt, Mary. 1992. *What's That Noise?* Illus. Robert Roennfeldt. New York: Orchard. 3–6 yrs.

Roos, Kelley, & Stephen Roos. 1986. *The Incredible Cat Caper*. Illus. Katherine Coville. New York: Dell/Yearling. 8–11 yrs.

Ross, Ramon R. 1993. *Harper & Moon*. New York: Karl/Atheneum. 13–16 yrs.

Service, Pamela. 1994. *Phantom Victory*. New York: Scribners. 10–12 yrs.

Sharmat, Marjorie W. 1981. *Nate the Great & the Missing Key*. New York: Putnam. 7–9 yrs.

———. 1982–92. *Nate the Great and the Halloween Hunt; Nate the Great and the Musical Note; Nate the Great and the Stolen Base; Nate the Great Goes Down in the Dumps*. Illus. Marc Simont. New York: Putnam. 7–9 yrs.

———. 1985. *Nate the Great and the Fishy Prize*. Illus. Marc Simont. New York: Coward-McCann. 7–9 yrs.

———. 1986. *Nate the Great Stalks Stupidweed*. Illus. Marc Simont. New York: Coward-McCann. 6–9 yrs.

Sharmat, Marjorie Weinman, & Rosalind Weinman. 1993. *Nate the Great and the Pillowcase*. New York: Delacorte. 7–9 yrs.

Simon, Seymour. 1980. *Einstein Anderson: Science Sleuth*. New York: Puffin Penguin. 10–12 yrs.

———. 1980. *Einstein Anderson Shocks His Friends*. New York: Puffin Penguin. 10–12 yrs.

———. 1981. *Einstein Anderson Makes up for Lost Time*. New York: Puffin Penguin. 10–12 yrs.

———. 1982. *Einstein Anderson Lights up the Sky*. New York: Puffin Penguin. 10–12 yrs.

———. 1983. *Einstein Anderson Sees Through the Invisible Man*. New York: Puffin Penguin. 10–12 yrs.

Singer, Marilyn. 1985. *A Clue in Code*. Illus. Judy Glasser. New York: Harper & Row. 8–10 yrs. Sam & Dave Mystery Series.

———. 1986. *Where There's a Will, There's a Wag*. Illus. Andrew Glass. New York: Holt. 9–12 yrs.

———. 1989. *The Hoax on You*. Illus. Richard Williams. New York: Harper & Row. 8–12 yrs.

Sobol, Donald J. 1971. *Encyclopedia Brown Tracks Them Down*. Illus. Leonard Shortall. New York: Crowell. 7–11 yrs.

———. 1973. *Encyclopedia Brown Takes the Case*. Illus. Leonard Shortall. New York: Nelson. 7–11 yrs.

———. 1982. *Encyclopedia Brown Sets the Pace*. Illus. Ib Ohisson. New York: Scholastic/Four Winds. 7–11 yrs.

———. 1986. *Encyclopedia Brown and the Case of the Mysterious Handprints*. Illus. Gail Owens. New York: Bantam Books/Skylark. 7–11 yrs.

———. 1988. *Encyclopedia Brown and the Case of the Treasure Hunt*. New York: Bantam. 7–11 yrs.

———. 1990. *Encyclopedia Brown and the Case of the Disgusting Sneakers*. Illus. Gail Owens. New York: Morrow. 7–11 yrs.

———. 1994. *Encyclopedia Brown and the Case of the Two Spies*. Illus. Eric Velasquez. New York: Delacorte. 9–12 yrs. (See also other books in series.)

Stevenson, James. 1995. *The Bones in the Cliff*. New York: Greenwillow.

Taylor, Theodore. 1991. *The Weirdo*. San Diego: Harcourt Brace. 12–15 yrs.

Townsend, John Rowe. 1986. *Tom Tiddler's Ground*. New York: HarperCollins. 12–15 yrs.

Trease, Geoffrey. 1989. *A Flight of Angels*. Minneapolis, Minn.: Lerner. 9–13 yrs.

Turner, Ann. 1995. *One Brave Summer*. New York: HarperCollins. 10–13 yrs.

Vivelo, Jackie. 1985. *Super Sleuth: Twelve Solve-It-Yourself Mysteries*. New York: Putnam. 8–12 yrs.

_____. 1986. *Beagle in Trouble: Super Sleuth II; Twelve Solve-It-Yourself Mysteries*. New York: Putnam. 8–12 yrs.

Voigt, Cynthia. 1992. *The Vandemark Mummy*. New York: Fawcett Juniper. 10–13 yrs.

Wells, Rosemary. 1980. *When No One Was Looking*. New York: Dial. 12–15 yrs.

Wright, Betty Ren. 1989. *Rosie and the Dance of the Dino*. New York: Holiday. 10–12 yrs.

_____. 1991. *The Scariest Night*. New York: Holiday. 10–12 yrs.

_____. 1995. *Nothing but Trouble*. Illus. Jacqueline Rogers. New York: Holiday. 9–12 yrs.

HUMOROUS BOOKS

Ahlberg, Allan. 1995. *The Giant Baby*. Illus. Fritz Wegner. New York: Viking. 9–12 yrs.

Arnold, Tedd. 1994. *The Signmaker's Assistant*. New York: Dial. 7–10 yrs.

Blume, Judy. 1990. *Fudge-a-Mania*. New York: Dutton. 7–11 yrs. (See also other books with Fudge.)

Brittain, Bill. 1989. *My Buddy, the King*. New York: Harper & Row. 9–12 yrs.

Burch, Robert. 1980. *Ida Early Comes Over the Mountain*. New York: Viking. 10–12 yrs.

_____. 1983. *Christmas with Ida Early*. New York: Viking. 10–12 yrs.

Byars, Betsy. 1991. *The Seven Treasure Hunts*. Illus. Jennifer Barrett. New York: HarperCollins. 7–11 yrs.

_____. 1991. *Wanted . . . Mud Blossom*. Illus. Jacqueline Rogers. New York: Delacorte. 9–11 yrs. (See also other books in Popular Realistic Series.)

Carris, Joan. 1990. *The Greatest Idea Ever*. Illus. Carol Newsom. New York: Lippincott. 8–12 yrs.

Cleary, Beverly. 1981. *Ramona Quimby, Age Eight*. New York: Morrow. 8–11 yrs. (See also Popular Realistic Series.)

Conford, Ellen. 1992. *Dear Mom, Get Me Out of Here!* Boston: Little, Brown. 10–12 yrs.

Danziger, Paula. 1989. *Everyone Else's Parents Said Yes*. New York: Delacorte. 9–12 yrs.

_____. 1990. *Make Like a Tree and Leave*. New York: Delacorte. 9–12 yrs.

_____. 1992. *Earth to Matthew*. New York: Delacorte. 9–12 yrs.

Gilson, Jamie. 1987. *Hobie Hanson, You're Weird*. Illus. Elise Primavera. New York: Lothrop, Lee & Shepard. 9–11 yrs.

_____. 1989. *Hobie Hanson: Greatest Hero of the Mall*. Illus. Anita Riggio. New York: Lothrop, Lee & Shepard. 8–12 yrs.

Gleeson, Libby. 1993. *Uncle David*. Illus. Armin Greder. New York: Tambourine. 5–8 yrs.

Goode, Diane. 1991. *Where's Our Mama?* New York: Dutton. 3–7 yrs.

Grossman, Bill. 1990. *The Guy Who Was Five Minutes Late*. Illus. Judy Glasser. New York: Harper & Row. 3–6 yrs.

Hall, Lynn. 1991. *Dagmar Schultz and the Green-Eyed Monster*. New York: Macmillan. 10–12 yrs.

Hurwitz, Johanna. 1981. *Adventures of Ali Baba Bernstein*. Illus. Gail Owens. New York: Scholastic. 9–11 yrs.

Hutchins, Pat. 1989. *Rats!* Illus. Laurence Hutchins. New York: Greenwillow. 6–10 yrs.

James, Mary. 1994. *Frankenlouse*. New York: Scholastic. 12–16 yrs.

Kline, Suzy. 1991. *Horrible Harry and the Green Slime*. Illus. Remkiewicz. New York: Viking/Puffin. 9–11 yrs.

Koertge, Ron. 1992. *The Harmony Arms*. Boston: Joy Street. 12–16 yrs.

Levine, Evan. 1991. *Not the Piano, Mrs. Medley!* Illus. S. D. Schindler. New York: Orchard/Jackson. 4–7 yrs.

Lillie, Patricia. 1991. *When the Rooster Crowed*. Illus. Nancy Winslow Parker. New York: Greenwillow. 3–6 yrs.

Lowry, Lois. 1991. *Anastasia at This Address*. Boston: Houghton Mifflin. 8–12 yrs. (See also Popular Realistic Series.)

_____. 1992. *Attaboy, Sam!* Illus. Diane de Groat. Boston: Houghton Mifflin. 8–11 yrs.

Mahy, Margaret. 1990. *The Great White Man-Eating Shark: A Cautionary Tale*. Illus. Jonathan Allen. New York: Dial. 5–8 yrs.

Manes, Stephen. 1990. *Chocolate-Covered Ants*. New York: Scholastic. 8–12 yrs.

_____. 1991. *Make Four Million Dollar$ by Next Thursday!* Illus. George Ulrich. New York: Bantam/Skylark. 8–12 yrs.

McClosky, Robert. 1943. *Homer Price*. New York: Viking. 10–12 yrs.

Milstein, Linda. 1993. *Amanda's Perfect Hair*. Illus. Susan Meddaugh. New York: Tambourine. 5–7 yrs.

Paulsen, Gary. 1990. *The Boy Who Owned the School: A Comedy of Love*. New York: Orchard/Jackson. 11–14 yrs.

Peck, Robert Newton. 1990. *Higbee's Halloween*. New York: Walker. 10–12 yrs.

_____. 1992. *Soup in Love*. Illus. Charles Robinson. New York: Delacorte. 9–12 yrs. (See also Popular Realistic Series.)

Pinkwater, Daniel. 1989. *Uncle Melvin*. New York: Macmillan. 5–8 yrs.

Porte, Barbara. 1991. *Fat Fanny, Beanpole Bertha, and the Boys*. New York: Orchard. 9–11 yrs.

Quattlebaum, Mary. 1994. *Jackson Jones and the Puddle of Thorns*. Illus. Melodye Rosales. New York: Delacorte. 10–13 yrs.

Rattigan, Jama Kim. 1994. *Truman's Aunt Farm*. Illus. G. Brian Kara. Boston: Houghton Mifflin. 5–8 yrs.

Remkiewicz, Frank. 1992. *Greedyanna*. New York: Lothrop, Lee & Shepard. 4–8 yrs.

Robertson, Keith. 1966. *Henry Reed's Think Tank*. New York: Viking. 9–11 yrs. (See also Popular Realistic Series.)

Robinson, Barbara. 1994. *The Best School Year Ever*. New York: HarperCollins. 9–12 yrs. (See also *The Best Christmas Pageant Ever*, 1988, New York: HarperCollins.)

Rockwell, Norman. 1973. *How to Eat Fried Worms*. Chicago: Watts. 10–13 yrs.

Sachar, Louis. 1989. *Wayside School Is Falling Down*. Illus. Joel Schick. New York: Lothrop, Lee & Shepard. 8–10 yrs.

_____. 1992. *Marvin Redpost: Kidnapped at Birth?* Illus. Neal Hughes. New York: Random House. 7–9 yrs. A First Stepping Stone Book.

Sachs, Marilyn. 1993. *Thirteen Going On Seven*. New York: Dutton. 10–12 yrs.

Samuels, Barbara. 1992. *What's So Great about Cindy Snappleby?* New York: Orchard. 3–6 yrs.

Spinelli, Jerry. 1990. *The Bathwater Gang*. Illus. Meredith Johnson. Boston: Little, Brown/Springboard. 7–11 yrs.

Stevenson, Sucie. 1989. *Jessica the Blue Streak*. New York: Orchard/Jackson. 5–8 yrs.

Taylor, William. 1992. *Knitwits*. New York: Scholastic. 10–13 yrs.

Tusa, Tricia. 1989. *Sherman and Pearl*. New York: Macmillan. 4–8 yrs.

Wilson, Sarah. 1990. *The Day That Henry Cleaned His Room*. New York: Simon & Schuster. 4–8 yrs.

Woodruff, Elvira. 1991. *Show and Tell*. Illus. Denise Brunkus. New York: Holiday. 4–8 yrs.

THEMATIC CATEGORIES

(MANY RECOMMENDED BOOKS PUBLISHED SINCE 1989)

FAMILY LIVING

Traditional Families

Bunting, Eve. 1991. *Sharing Susan*. New York: HarperCollins. 10–12 yrs.

Cleary, Beverly. 1977. *Ramona and Her Father*. Illus. Alan Tiegreen. New York: Morrow. 8–11 yrs.

_____. 1979. *Ramona and Her Mother*. Illus. Alan Tiegreen. New York: Morrow. 8–11 yrs. (See also Popular Realistic Series.)

Cole, Barbara Hancock. 1990. *Texas Star*. Illus. Barbara Minton. New York: Orchard/Jackson. 4–7 yrs.

Collier, James Lincoln. 1989. *The Winchesters*. New York: Avon/Flare. 10–13 yrs.

Cresswell, Helen. 1994. *Posy Bates, Again!* Illus. Kate Aldous. New York: Macmillan. 9–12 yrs.

Cutler, Jane. 1992. *Family Dinner*. Illus. Philip Caswell. New York: Farrar, Straus & Giroux. 10–12 yrs.

Dorflinger, Carolyn. 1994. *Tomorrow Is Mom's Birthday*. Illus. Iza Trapani. Dallas, TX: Whispering Coyote. 4–6 yrs.

Gardella, Tricia. 1993. *Just Like My Dad*. Illus. Margo Apple. New York: HarperCollins. 5–8 yrs.

Greenwald, Sheila. 1992. *Rosy Cole Discovers America*. Illus. Sheila Greenwald. Boston: Joy Street. 8–11 yrs.

Haas, Jessie. 1996. *Clean House*. Illus. Yossi Abolafia. New York: Greenwillow. 7–9 yrs.

Hughes, Shirley. 1982. *Alfie Gets in First*. New York: Lothrop, Lee & Shepard. 5–7 yrs.

_____. 1983. *Alfie's Feet*. New York: Lothrop, Lee & Shepard. 5–7 yrs.

_____. 1984. *Alfie Gives a Hand*. New York: Lothrop, Lee & Shepard. 5–7 yrs.

_____. 1985. *An Evening at Alfie's*. New York: Lothrop, Lee & Shepard. 5–7 yrs.

_____. 1993. *The Alfie Collection*. New York: Morrow/Tupelo. 5–7 yrs.

Hurwitz, Johanna. 1995. *Elisa in the Middle*. Illus. Lillian Hoban. New York: Morrow. 6–9 yrs.

Ish-Kishor, Sulamith. 1992. *Our Eddie*. New York: Knopf. 11–13 yrs.

Jensen, Kathryn. 1989. *Pocket Change*. New York: Scholastic. 11–14 yrs.

Johnson, Dolores. 1994. *Papa's Stories*. Illus. D. Johnson. New York: Macmillan. 5–8 yrs.

Kaplow, Robert. 1992. *Alessandra in Between*. New York: HarperCollins. 12–15 yrs.

Kimmelman, Leslie. 1989. *Fannie's Fruits*. Illus. Petra Mathers. New York: Harper & Row. 5–7 yrs.

Lowry, Lois. 1979. *Anastasia Krupnik*. Boston: Houghton Mifflin. 9–11 yrs. (See also Popular Realistic Series.)

_____. 1992. *Attaboy, Sam!* Illus. Diane de Groat. Boston: Houghton Mifflin. 8–11 yrs.

_____. 1995. *Anastasia, Absolutely*. Burlington, Mass.: Houghton Mifflin. 9–12 yrs. (See also series.)

MacLachlan, Patricia. 1988. *The Facts and Fictions of Minna Pratt*. New York: Harper & Row. 9–12 yrs.

Martin, Ann M. 1991. *Eleven Kids, One Summer*. New York: Holiday. 8–11 yrs.

Miklowitz, Gloria D. 1989. *Suddenly Super Rich.* New York: Bantam. 10–12 yrs.

Mills, Claudia. 1990. *Dynamite Dinah.* New York: Macmillan. 9–12 yrs.

Pevsner, Stella. 1996. *Would My Fortune Cookie Lie?* New York: Clarion. 10–13 yrs.

Rylant, Cynthia. 1989. *Henry and Mudge and the Forever Sea: The Sixth Book of Their Adventures.* Illus. Sucie Stevenson. New York: Bradbury. 6–8 yrs.

———. 1992. *Henry and Mudge and the Long Weekend.* New York: Bradbury.

Small-Hector, Irene. 1992. *Jonathan and His Mommy.* Illus. Michael Hays. Boston: Little, Brown. 4–6 yrs.

Schotter, Roni. 1993. *A Fruit and Vegetable Man.* Illus. Jeanette Winter. Boston: Little, Brown. 6–8 yrs.

Soto, Gary. 1993. *Too Many Tamales.* Illus. Ed Martinez. New York: Putnam. 4–7 yrs.

Spohn, David. 1993. *Home Field.* New York: Lothrop, Lee & Shepard. 6–9 yrs.

Viorst, Judith. 1972. *Alexander and the Terrible, Horrible, No Good, Very Bad Day.* Illus. Ray Cruz. New York: Atheneum. 6–12 yrs.

Wardlaw, Lee. *Seventh-Grade Weirdo.* New York: Scholastic. 11–13 yrs.

Ware, Cheryl. 1996. *Sea Monkey Summer.* New York: Jackson/Orchard. 9–11 yrs.

Wood, Audrey. 1990. *Weird Parents.* New York: Dial. 4–8 yrs.

Yolen, Jane. 1987. *Owl Moon.* Illus. John Schoenherr. New York: Putnam/Philomel. 6–12 yrs.

Interactions in a One-Parent Family

Anderson, Janet. 1994. *The Key into Winter.* Illus. David Soman. Morton Grove, Ill.: Whitman. 5–8 yrs.

Angell, Judie. 1993. *Yours Truly: A Novel.* New York: Orchard/Jackson. 12–15 yrs.

Auch, Mary Jane. 1991. *Mom Is Dating Weird Wayne.* New York: Bantam/Skylark. 8–12 yrs.

*———. 1992. *Out of Step.* New York: Holiday. 7–10 yrs.

Bechard, Margaret. 1994. *Really No Big Deal.* New York: Viking. 9–12 yrs.

Bond, Nancy. 1994. *Truth to Tell.* New York: McElderry. 12–16 yrs.

Brooks, Bruce. 1992. *What Hearts.* New York: HarperCollins/Geringer. 10–14 yrs.

Broome, Errol. 1993. *Dear Mr. Sprouts.* New York: Knopf. 10–14 yrs.

Cooper, Susan. 1993. *Danny and the Kings.* Illus. Jos. A. Smith. New York: McElderry. 5–8 yrs.

Ferris, Jean. 1993. *Relative Strangers.* New York: Farrar, Straus & Giroux. 12–15 yrs.

Fine, Anne. 1989. *My War with Goggle-Eyes.* Boston: Little, Brown. 11–14 yrs.

*———. 1996. *Step by Wicked Step.* Boston: Little, Brown. 10–14 yrs.

French, Simon. 1993. *Change the Locks.* New York: Scholastic. 10–13 yrs.

Gauthier, Bertrand. 1993. *Zachary in Camping Out; Zachary in the Championship; Zachary in I'm Zachary; Zachary in the Wawabongbong; Zachary in the Winner.* Illus. Daniel Sylvestre. Milwaukee, Wisc.: Gareth Sevens. 3–6 yrs. Just Me and My Dad series.

Hughes, Dean. 1994. *The Trophy.* New York: Knopf. 9–12 yrs.

*Jukes, Mavis. 1984. *Like Jake & Me.* Illus. Lloyd Bloom. New York: Knopf. 7–10 yrs.

Mazer, Norma Fox. 1990. *C, My Name Is Cal.* New York: Scholastic. 9–12 yrs.

Molinar, Dorothy E. & Stephan H. Fenton. 1991. *Who Will Pick Me Up When I Fall?* Illus. Irene Trivas. Morton Grove, Ill.: Whitman. 6–8 yrs.

Murphy, Jill. 1988. *Worlds Apart.* New York: Putnam. 10–13 yrs.

Naylor, Phyllis Reynolds. 1995. *Being Danny's Dog.* New York: Atheneum. 10–13 yrs.

*Petersen, P. J. 1993. *I Want Answers and a Parachute.* New York: Simon & Schuster. 9–12 yrs.

Pfeffer, Susan Beth. 1989. *Dear Dad, Love Laurie.* New York: Scholastic. 8–12 yrs.

Reiss, Kathryn. 1993. *Dreadful Sorry.* San Diego: Harcourt Brace. 12–15 yrs.

Rodowsky, Colby. 1994. *Hannah in Between.* New York: Farrar, Straus & Giroux. 12–16 yrs.

*———. 1995. *Sydney, Invincible.* New York: Farrar, Straus & Giroux. 10–15 yrs.

Sachs, Marilyn. 1990. *At the Sound of the Beep.* New York: Dutton. 11–14 yrs.

Shreve, Susan. 1995. *The Formerly Great Alexander Family.* Illus. Chris Cart. New York: Tambourine.

Slepian, Jan. 1993. *Back to Before.* New York: Philomel. 9–11 yrs.

*Tamar, Erika. 1994. *The Things I Did Last Summer.* San Diego: Harcourt Brace. 12–16 yrs.

Thesman, Jean. 1994. *Cattail Moon.* Boston: Houghton Mifflin. 12–16 yrs.

Van Leeuwen, Jean. 1996. *Blue Sky, Butterfly.* New York: Dial. 10–12 yrs.

Williams, Vera B. 1993. *Scooter.* New York: Greenwillow. 9–11 yrs.

Wolff, Virginia. 1993. *Make Lemonade.* New York: Holt. 12–15 yrs.

Interactions with Siblings

Adler, C. S. 1989. *One Sister Too Many.* New York: Macmillan. 10–12 yrs.

Caseley, Judith. 1993. *Sophie and Sammy's Library Sleepover.* New York: Greenwillow. 5–7 yrs.

Blume, Judy. 1993. *Here's to You, Rachel Robinson.* New York: Orchard/Jackson. 12–15 yrs.

Byars, Betsy. 1994. *The Golly Sisters Ride Again.* Illus. Sue Truesdell. New York: HarperCollins. 6–8 yrs.

Fitzgerald, John D. 1995. *The Great Brain Is Back.* Illus. Diane de Groat. New York: Dial. 10–13 yrs.

Herzig, Alison Cragin & Jane Lawrence. 1994. *Mali the Wimp of the World.* New York: Viking. 9–12 yrs.

Hurwitz, Johanna. 1996. *Even Stephen.* Illus. Michael Dooling. New York: Morrow. 10–13 yrs.

Kerr, M. E. 1994. *Deliver Us from Evie.* New York: HarperCollins. 12–16 yrs.

Krensky, Stephen. 1992. *Lionel and Louise.* New York: Dial. 7–9 yrs.

Maguire, Gregory. 1994. *Missing Sisters.* New York: McElderry. 11–14 yrs.

Metzger, Lois. 1992. *Barry's Sister.* New York: Atheneum. 12–15 yrs.

Paterson, Katherine. 1980. *Jacob Have I Loved.* New York: HarperCollins. 10–14 yrs.

Pevsner, Stella. 1993. *I'm Emma: I'm a Quint.* New York: Clarion. 10–14 yrs.

Pfeffer, Susan Beth. 1992. *Twin Troubles.* Illus. Libby Carter. New York: Holt. 6–9 yrs. Redfeather Series.

Schertle, A. 1991. *Witch Hazel.* Illus. Margot Tomes. New York: HarperCollins. 7–9 yrs.

Shreve, Susan. 1995. *Zoe and Columbo.* Illus. Gregg Thorkelson. New York: Tambourine. 7–9 yrs.

Willey, Margaret. 1996. *Facing the Music.* New York: Delacorte. 12–15 yrs.

Williams, Carol Lynch. 1993. *Kelly and Me.* New York: Delacorte. 11–13 yrs.

Grandparents

Ackerman, Karen. 1992. *Song and Dance Man.* Illus. Stephen Gammell. New York: Knopf/Dragonfly. 6–11 yrs.

Addy, Sharon Hart. 1989. *A Visit with Great-Grandma.* Illus. Lydia Halverson. Morton Grove, Ill.: Whitman. 4–8 yrs.

Anderson, Lena. 1989. *Stina.* Illus. Lena Anderson. New York: Greenwillow. 4–8 yrs.

———. 1991. *Stina's Visit.* Illus. Lena Anderson. New York: Greenwillow. 4–8 yrs.

Arkin, A. 1995. *Some Fine Grandpa!* Illus. Dirk Zimmer. New York: HarperCollins. 6–12 yrs.

Bahr, Mary. 1992. *The Memory Box.* Illus. David Cunninghom. Morton Grove, Ill.: Whitman. 8–9 yrs.

Bawden, Nina. 1996. *Granny the Pad.* New York: Clarion. 10–12 yrs.

Blos, Joan W. 1989. *The Grandpa Days.* Illus. Emily Arnold McCully. New York: Simon & Schuster. 3–7 yrs.

Bunting, Eve. 1989. *The Wednesday Surprise.* Illus. Donald Carrick. New York: Clarion. 6–9 yrs.

———. 1994. *Sunshine Home.* Illus. Diane de Groat. New York: Clarion. 5–8 yrs.

Caseley, Judith. 1991. *Dear Annie.* New York: Greenwillow. 4–7 yrs.

Christiansen, C. B. 1994. *I See the Moon.* New York: Atheneum. 9–12 yrs.

Creech, A. 1994. *Walk Two Moons.* New York: HarperCollins. 11–16 yrs.

Cutler, Jane. 1993. *Darcy and Gran Don't Like Babies.* Illus. Susannah Ryan. New York: Scholastic. 4–7 yrs.

Delton, Judy & Dorothy Tucker. 1985. *My Grandma's in a Nursing Home.* Morton Grove, Ill.: Whitman. 7–10 yrs.

dePaola, Tomie. 1981. *Now One Foot, Now the Other.* New York: Putnam. 5–9 yrs.

Derby, Pat. 1994. *Grams, Her Boyfriend, My Family, and Me.* New York: Farrar, Straus & Giroux. 12–15 yrs.

Dionetti, Michelle. 1991. *Coal Mine Peaches.* Illus. Anita Riggio. New York: Orchard. 4–7 yrs.

Duffey, Betsy. 1995. *Utterly Yours, Booker Jones.* New York: Viking. 9–12 yrs.

Dugan, Barbara. 1992. *Loop the Loop.* New York: Greenwillow. 5–8 yrs.

Flournoy, Valerie. 1985. *The Patchwork Quilt.* Illus. Jerry Pinkney. New York: Dial. 6–9 yrs.

———. 1995. *Tanya's Reunion.* Illus. Jerry Pinkney. New York: Dial. 6–10 yrs.

Fox, Mim. 1985. *Wilfred Gordon McDonald Partridge.* Illus. Julie Vivas. Brooklyn, N.Y.: Kane/Miller. 6–9 yrs.

Fox, Paula. 1993. *Western Wind: A Novel.* New York: Orchard/Jackson. 10–13 yrs.

Greenfield, Eloise. 1991. *Grandpa's Face.* Illus. Floyd Cooper. New York: Putnam. 6–10 yrs.

Guback, Georgia. 1994. *Luka's Quilt.* Illus. Georgia Guback. New York: Greenwillow. 4–7 yrs.

---

*Step-parent/family

Guthrie, Donna. 1985. *Grandpa Doesn't Know It's Me.* New York: Human Sciences Press. 7–10 yrs.

Henkes, K. *Good-bye, Curtis.* Illus. Marisabina Russo. New York: Greenwillow. 4–8 yrs.

Hest, Amy. 1993. *Weekend Girl.* Illus. Harvey Stevenson. New York: Morrow. 5–8 yrs.

Hines, Anna G. 1988. *Grandma Gets Grumpy.* New York: Clarion. 7–10 yrs.

Hirschi, Ron. 1991. *Harvest Song.* Illus. Deborah Haeffele. New York: Cobblehill/Dutton. 7–9 yrs.

Howard, Elizabeth. 1991. *Aunt Flossie's Hats (and Crab Cakes Later).* New York: Clarion. 6–10 yrs.

Hurwitz, H. A. & H. Wasburn. (Ed. Mara H. Wasburn.) 1993. *Dear Hope . . . Love, Grandma.* Los Angeles: Alef Design. 9–12 yrs.

Johnston, Tony. 1991. *Grandpa's Song.* Illus. Brad Sneed. New York: Dial. 5–9 yrs.

Jukes, Mavis. 1993. *Blackberries in the Dark.* Illus. Thomas B. Allen. New York: Knopf. 8–10 yrs.

Ketner, Mary Grace. 1991. *Granzy Remembers.* Illus. Barbara Sparks. New York: Atheneum. 9–12 yrs.

Kinsey-Warnock, Natalie. 1989. *The Canada Geese Quilt.* Illus. Leslie W. Bowman. New York: Cobblehill. 9–13 yrs.

Koertge, Ron. 1994. *Tiger, Tiger, Burning Bright.* New York: Kroupa/Orchard. 11–14 yrs.

Leighton, A. O. 1995. *A Window of Time.* Lake Forest, Calif.: Nadja. 5–10 yrs.

Mahy, Margaret. 1996. *Tingleberries, Tuckertubs and Telephones.* Illus. Robert Staermose. New York: Viking. 8–10 yrs.

Masters, Susan Rowan. 1995. *Summer Song.* New York: Clarion. 9–12 yrs.

Mazer, Norma Fox. 1987. *After the Rain.* New York: Morrow. 11–15 yrs.

Miller, Jim W. 1989. *Newfound.* New York: Orchard/Jackson. 12–15 yrs.

Moore, Elaine. 1988. *Grandma's Promise.* New York: Lothrop, Lee & Shepard.

Nelson, Vauda. 1988. *Always Gramma.* New York: Putnam. 6–9 yrs.

Pearson, Susan. 1987. *Happy Birthday Grampie.* New York: Dial. 5–9 yrs.

Polacco, Patricia. 1992. *Mrs. Katz and Tush.* New York: Bantam. 6–10 yrs.

Roe, Eileen. 1989. *Staying with Grandma.* Illus. Jacquline Rogers. New York: Bradbury. 1–6 yrs.

Ross, K. & A. Ross. 1995. *Cemetery Quilt.* Illus. Rosanne Kaloustian. Boston: Houghton Mifflin. 6–12 yrs.

Russo, Marisabina. 1991. *A Visit to Oma.* Illus. Marisabina Russo. New York: Greenwillow. 4–7 yrs.

Rylant, Cynthia. 1985. *The Relatives Came.* New York: Bradbury. 6–9 yrs.

Shecter, B. 1996. *Great-Uncle Alfred Forgets.* New York: HarperCollins. 4–8 yrs.

Sheldon, Dyan. 1990. *The Whales' Song.* Illus. Gary Blythe. New York: Dial. 4–8 yrs.

Spinelli, Jerry. 1996. *Crash.* New York: Knopf. 10–14 yrs.

Thomas, Elizabeth. 1992. *Green Beans.* Illus. Vicki Jo Redenbaugh. Minneapolis, Minn.: Carolrhoda. 5–8 yrs.

Trevor, William. 1994. *Juliet's Story.* New York: Simon & Schuster. 9–12 yrs.

Whitelaw, Nancy. 1991. *A Beautiful Pearl.* Morton Grove, Ill.: Whitman. 7–9 yrs.

Willner-Pardo, G. 1994. *Hunting Grandma's Treasures.* Illus. Walter Lyon Krudop. New York: Clarion. 7–12 yrs.

Winslow, B. 1995. *Dance on a Sealskin.* Illus. Teri Sloat. Seattle, Wash.: Alaska. 6–12 yrs.

Wright, Betty Ren. 1991. *The Cat Next Door.* New York: Holiday. 6–8 yrs.

Woodruff, Elvira. 1992. *Dear Napoleon, I Know You're Dead, But . . . .* Illus. Noral & Jess Woodruff. New York: Holiday. 10–15 yrs.

Other Extended

Ackerman, Karen. 1990. *Just Like Max.* Illus. George Schmidt. New York: Knopf/Borzoi. 4–8 yrs.

Baldwin, Nina. 1990. *The Outside Child.* New York: Lothrop, Lee & Shepard. 9–12 yrs.

Coman, Carolyn. 1993. *Tell Me Everything.* New York: Farrar, Straus & Giroux. 11–14 yrs.

Ellis, Sarah. 1995. *Out of the Blue.* New York: McElderry. 11–15 yrs.

Honeycutt, N. 1993. *Whistle Home.* Illus. Annie Cannon. New York: Orchard/Jackson. 5–8 yrs.

Johnson, Emily Rhoads. 1992. *A House Full of Strangers.* New York: Cobblehill. 9–11 yrs.

Mahy, Margaret. 1993. *A Fortunate Name.* New York: Delacorte. 9–12 yrs.

Pinkney, Gloria Jean. 1994. *The Sunday Outing.* Illus. Jerry Pinkney. New York: Dial. 5–8 yrs.

Rodowsky, Colby. 1992. *Jenny and Grand Old Great-Aunts.* Illus. Barbara J. Roman. New York: Bradbury. 8–10 yrs.

Stolz, Mary. 1992. *Stealing Home.* New York: HarperCollins. 10–12 yrs.

Stowe, Cynthia. 1992. *Dear Mom, in Ohio for a Year.* New York: Scholastic. 10–13 yrs.

PERSONAL RELATIONSHIPS

Adjusting

Brancato, Robin. 1989. *Winning.* New York: Knopf/Borzoi Sprinters. 10–13 yrs.

Byars, Betsy. 1992. *Bingo Brown's Guide to Romance.* New York: Viking Penguin. 10–13 yrs.

Doherty, Berlie. 1992. *Dear Nobody.* New York: Orchard. 12–15 yrs.

Ferguson, Alane. 1993. *Stardust.* New York: Bradbury. 7–10 yrs.

Gibbons, Faye. 1989. *King Shoes and Clown Pockets.* New York: Morrow. 9–12 yrs.

Greene, Constance C. 1988. *Monday, I Love You.* New York: HarperCollins. 12–15 yrs.

Hahn, Mary Downing. 1993. *The Wind Blows Backward.* New York: Clarion. 12–15 yrs.

Hamilton, Morse. 1994. *Yellow Blue Bus Means I Love You.* New York: Greenwillow. 12–15 yrs.

Kerr, M. E. 1993. *Linger.* New York: HarperCollins. 12–15 yrs.

Lehrman, Robert. 1990. *Separations.* New York: Viking Penguin. 10–14 yrs.

Mazer, Norma Fox. 1990. *Babyface.* New York: Morrow. 12–16 yrs.

Mills, Claudia. 1993. *Dinah in Love.* New York: Macmillan. 9–13 yrs.

Murphy, Catherine Frey. 1993. *Alice Dodd and the Spirit of Truth.* New York: Macmillan. 11–13 yrs.

Murrow, Liza Ketchum. 1993. *Twelve Days in August.* New York: Holiday. 12–15 yrs.

Park, Barbara. 1981. *The Kid in the Red Jacket.* New York: Knopf. 9–11 yrs.

Patron, Susan. 1993. *Maybe Yes, Maybe No, Maybe Maybe.* Illus. Dorothy Donahue. New York: Orchard. 10–12 yrs.

Paulsen, Gary. 1993. *Sisters/Hermanas.* San Diego: Harcourt Brace. 12–15 yrs.

Roybal, Laura. 1994. *Billy.* Boston: Houghton Mifflin. 12–16 yrs.

Skinner, David. 1995. *The Wrecker.* New York: Simon & Schuster. 9–12 yrs.

Slepian, Jan. 1988. *The Broccoli Tapes.* New York: Philomel. 8–12 yrs.

Smith, Janice Lee. 1992. *Nelson in Love: An Adam Joshua Valentine's Day Story.* Illus. Dick Gackenbach. New York: HarperCollins. 7–9 yrs.

Turnbull, Ann. 1996. *Room for a Stranger.* Cambridge, Mass.: Candlewick. 10–12 yrs.

Wynne-Jones, Tim. 1995. *The Book of Changes.* New York: Orchard/Kroupa. 9–12 yrs. (Seven short stories)

Maturing

Avery, Gillian. 1992. *Maria Escapes.* Illus. Scott Snow. New York: Simon & Schuster. 10–12 yrs.

Bennett, James. 1994. *Dakota Dream.* New York: Scholastic. 12–15 yrs.

Berger, Fredericka. 1993. *The Green Bottle and the Silver Kite.* New York: Greenwillow. 10–12 yrs.

Brooks, Martha. 1994. *Traveling On into the Light and Other Stories.* New York: Orchard/Kroupa. 12–16 yrs.

Brown, Marc. 1993. *D. W. Rides Again!* Boston: Little, Brown. 4–7 yrs.

Caseley, Judith. 1992. *My Father, the Nutcase.* New York: Knopf. 12–15 yrs.

Coman, Carolyn. 1993. *Tell Me Everything.* New York: Farrar, Straus & Giroux. 12–14 yrs.

Conly, Jane Leslie. 1993. *Crazy Lady.* New York: HarperCollins. 11–14 yrs.

Cullen, Lynn. 1996. *The Three Lives of Harris Harper.* New York: Clarion. 10–13 yrs.

DeVito, Cara. 1993. *Where I Want to Be.* Boston: Houghton Mifflin. 12–16 yrs.

Duffey, Betsy. 1994. *Coaster.* New York: Viking. 9–12 yrs.

Farmer, Nancy. 1993. *Do You Know Me.* Illus. Shelley Jackson. New York: Orchard. 10–14 yrs.

Fox, Paula. 1984. *One-Eyed Cat.* New York: Bradbury. 10–13 yrs.

Greene, Patricia Baird. 1993. *The Sabbath Garden.* New York: Lodestar. 12–15 yrs.

Greene, Carol. 1992. *The Golden Locket.* Illus. Marcia Sewall. San Diego: Harcourt Brace. 4–7 yrs.

Graham, Bob. 1992. *Rose Meets Mr. Wintergarten.* Cambridge, Mass.: Candlewick. 5–7 yrs.

Gifaidi, David. 1993. *Toby Scudder, Ultimate Warrior.* New York: Clarion. 9–12 yrs.

Guy, Rosa. 1992. *Billy the Great.* Illus. Caroline Binch. New York: Delacorte. 5–8 yrs.

Hamilton, Virginia. 1993. *Plain City.* New York: Blue Sky. 12–15 yrs.

Hermes, Patricia. 1993. *Someone to Count On.* Boston: Little, Brown. 10–12 yrs.

Hurwitz, Johanna. 1993. *Make Room for Elisa.* Illus. Lillian Hoban. New York: Morrow. 5–7 yrs.

Klass, Sheila Solomon. 1993. *Rhino.* Illus. Keith Birdsong. New York: Scholastic. 12–15 yrs.

Kiser, Susan. 1993. *The Catspring Somersault Flying One-Handed Flip-Flop.* Illus. Peter Catalanotto. New York: Orchard/Jackson. 4–7 yrs.

Lipsyte, Robert. 1993. *The Chief.* New York: HarperCollins. 12–15 yrs.

Lynch, Chris. 1993. *Shadow Boxer.* New York: HarperCollins. 12–15 yrs.

McClain, Ellen Jaffe. 1994. *No Big Deal.* New York: Lodestar. 12–16 yrs.

McKenna, Colleen O'Shaughnessy. 1992. *The Brightest Light.* New York: Scholastic. 12–16 yrs.

Mead, Alice. 1994. *Crossing the Starlight Bridge.* New York: Bradbury. 8–11 yrs.

Mori, Kyoko. 1993. *Shizuko's Daughter.* New York: Holt. 12–15 yrs.

Naylor, Phyllis Reynolds. 1993. *Alice in April.* New York: Atheneum/Karl. 12–14 yrs.

———. 1994. *Alice in-Between.* New York: Karl/Atheneum. 12–14 yrs.

Orgel, Doris. 1996. *The Princess and the God.* New York: Jackson/Orchard. 11–14 yrs.

Reeder, Carolyn. 1993. *Moonshiner's Son.* New York: Macmillan. 10–15 yrs.

Seymour, Tres. 1994. *Life in the Desert.* New York: Orchard/Jackson. 12–16 yrs.

Slepian, Jan. 1995. *Pinocchio's Sister.* New York: Philomel. 10–13 yrs.

Vail, Rachel. 1992. *Do-Over.* New York: Orchard/Jackson. 12–15 yrs.

Werlin, Nancy. 1994. *Are You Alone on Purpose?* Boston: Houghton Mifflin. 12–16 yrs.

Wittlinger, Ellen. 1993. *Lombardo's Law.* Boston: Houghton Mifflin. 12–15 yrs.

Coping

Death/Grief

Adler, C. S. 1993. *Daddy's Climbing Tree.* New York: Clarion. 10–12 yrs.

Bauer, Marion Dane. 1994. *A Question of Trust.* New York: Scholastic.

Brooks, Bruce. 1990. *Everywhere.* New York: Harper & Row. 9–13 yrs.

Buchanan, Dawna Lisa. 1992. *The Falcon's Wing.* New York: Orchard/Jackson. 11–13 yrs.

de Jenkins, Lyll Becerra. 1993. *Celebrating the Hero.* New York: Lodestar. 12–15 yrs.

Hamilton, Virginia. 1990. *Cousins.* New York: Philomel. 10–13 yrs.

Hesse, Karen. 1994. *Phoenix Rising.* New York: Holt. 11–15 yrs.

Hest, Amy. 1995. *The Private Notebook of Katie Roberts, Age 11.* Illus. Sonja Lamut. Cambridge, Mass.: Candlewick. 10–12 yrs.

High, Linda Oatman. 1995. *Hound Heaven.* New York: Holiday. 9–12 yrs.

Howard, Ellen. 1993. *The Tower Room.* New York: Atheneum/Karl. 9–13 yrs.

Johnston, Julie. 1994. *Adam and Eve and Pinch-Me.* Boston: Little, Brown. 12–15 yrs.

Klein, Robin. 1994. *Seeing Things.* New York: Viking. 11–14 yrs.

Laird, Elizabeth. 1989. *Loving Ben.* New York: Delacorte. 10–15 yrs.

Lanton, Sandy. 1991. *Daddy's Chair.* Rockville, Md.: Kar-Ben. 6–9 yrs.

Madenski, Melissa. 1991. *Some of the Pieces.* Illus. Deborah Kogan Ray. Boston: Little, Brown. 4–8 yrs.

Marino, Jan. 1995. *The Mona Lisa of Salem Street: A Novel.* Boston: Little, Brown. 10–14 yrs.

Miska, Miles. 1985. *Annie and the Old One.* Illus. Peter Parnall. Boston: Little, Brown. 8–12 yrs.

Nelson, Vaunda Micheaux. 1995. *Possibles.* New York: Putnam. 9–12 yrs. (Papa.)

Rodowsky, Colby. 1996. *Remembering Mog.* New York: Farrar, Straus & Giroux. 12–15 yrs.

Rylant, Cynthia. 1992. *Missing May.* New York: Orchard/Jackson. 11–15 yrs.

Smith, Barbara A. 1993. *Somewhere Just Beyond.* New York: Atheneum. 9–11 yrs.

Smith, Jane Denitz. 1994. *Mary by Myself.* New York: HarperCollins. 9–12 yrs.

Thomas, Jane Resh. 1988. *Saying Good-bye to Grandma.* Illus. Marcia Sewall. New York: Clarion. 6–9 yrs.

Thurman, Chuck. 1989. *A Time for Remembering.* Illus. Elizabeth Sayles. New York: Simon & Schuster. 4–8 yrs.

Vigna, Judith. 1991. *Saying Goodbye to Daddy.* Morton Grove, Ill.: Whitman. 5–7 yrs.

Wilson, Johnniece Marshall. 1990. *Robin on His Own.* New York: Scholastic. 8–12 yrs.

Illness and Disability

•Ackerman, Karen. 1991. *The Broken Boy.* New York: Philomel. 10–14 yrs. (Emotionally disturbed friend)

†Amadeo, Diana M. 1989. *There's a Little Bit of Me in Jamey.* Illus. Judith Friedman. Morton Grove, Ill.: Whitman. 6–9 yrs. (Leukemia)

•Anderson, Rachel. 1992. *The Bus People.* New York: Holt. 12–15 yrs. (Special education children)

•Auch, Mary Jane. 1990. *Kidnapping Kevin Kowalski.* New York: Holiday. 8–10 yrs. (Accident; mental problems)

Bohlmeijer, Arno. 1996. *Something Very Sorry.* Boston: Houghton Mifflin. 9–11 yrs. (Automobile accident)

•Busselle, Rebecca. 1988. *Bathing Ugly.* New York: Orchard. 10–13 yrs. (Overweight)

•Booth, Barbara D. 1991. *Mandy.* Illus. Jim LaMarche. New York: Lothrop, Lee & Shepard. 6–12 yrs. (Deafness)

•Byars, Betsy. 1970. *Summer of the Swan.* Illus. Ted CoConis. New York: Viking. 9–12 yrs. (Mentally disabled boy)

†Butler, Beverly. 1993. *Witch's Fire.* New York: Cobblehill. 8–12 yrs. (Blindness)

•Calvert, Patricia. 1993. *Picking Up the Pieces.* New York: Scribners. 11–14 yrs. (Wheelchair)

•Carrick, Carol. 1985. *Stay Away from Simon.* New York: Clarion. 7–10 yrs. (Mentally disabled boy)

•Carlson, Nancy. 1990. *Arnie and the New Kid.* New York: Viking. 5–7 yrs. (Wheelchair; physical disabilities)

•Casley, Judith. 1991. *Harry and Willy and Carrothead.* New York: Greenwillow. 5–8 yrs. (Physical disabilities)

†Cohen, Barbara. 1990. *The Long Way Home.* Illus. Diane de Groat. New York: Lothrop, Lee & Shepard. 10–14 yrs. (Mother's chemotherapy)

•Covington, Dennis. 1991. *Lizard.* New York: Delacorte. 11–14 yrs. (Physical discrimination)

•Cowen-Fletcher, Jane. 1993. *Mama Zooms.* New York: Scholastic. 4–7 yrs. (Wheelchair)

†Crofford, Emily. 1994. *A Place to Belong.* Minneapolis, Minn.: Carolrhoda. 11–14 yrs. (Clubfoot, poverty)

†Davis, Deborah. 1994. *My Brother Has AIDS.* New York: Atheneum/Karl. 12–16 yrs.

•Damrell, Liz. 1991. *With the Wind.* Illus. Stephen Marchesi. New York: Orchard/Jackson. 5–8 yrs. (Physical disability, horseback riding)

†Fraustino, Lisa Rowe. 1995. *Ash: A Novel.* New York: Orchard. 11–16 yrs. (Schizophrenia)

•Fleming, Virginia. 1993. *Be Good to Eddie Lee.* Illus. Floyd Cooyer. New York: Philomel. 6–9 yrs. (Down syndrome)

•Feuer, Elizabeth. 1990. *Paper Doll.* Farrar, Straus & Giroux. 11–14 yrs. (Physically disabled, cerebral palsy)

†Girard, Linda. 1991. *Alex, the Kid with AIDS.* 1990. Morton Grove, Ill.: Whitman. 7–10 yrs.

•Hall, Lynn. 1990. *Halsey's Pride.* New York: Scribners. 12–14 yrs. (Epilepsy)

†Hesse, Karen. 1995. *A Time of Angels.* New York: Hyperion. 12–15 yrs.

•Hines, Anna G. 1993. *Gramma's Walk.* New York: Greenwillow. 5–7 yrs.

†Jordan, MaryKate. 1989. *Losing Uncle Tim.* Illus. Judith Friedman. Morton Grove, Ill.: Whitman. 7–11 yrs. (AIDS)

†Keller, Holly. 1989. *The Best Present.* Illus. Holly Keller. New York: Greenwillow. 4–7 yrs. (Grandmother sick in hospital)

Levin, Betty. 1995. *Fire in the Wind.* New York: Greenwillow. 9–12 yrs. (Disability; family relationships)

•Little, Jean. 1972. *From Anna.* Illus. Joan Sandin. New York: Harper & Row. 9–12 yrs. (Girl with poor eyesight placed in special education class)

•———. 1995. *Mine for Keeps.* New York: Viking. 11–14 yrs. (Cerebral palsy)

•Mayne, William. 1989. *Gideon Ahoy!* New York: Delacorte. 10–14 yrs. (Brain-damaged and deaf brother)

†Mathers, Petra. 1995. *Kisses from Rosa.* Illus. Petra Mathers. New York: Apple Soup/Knopf. 5–8 yrs.

†Nelson, Theresa. 1994. *Earthshine.* New York: Orchard/Jackson. (Father dying of AIDS)

•Osofsky, Audrey. 1992. *By Buddy.* Illus. Ted Rand. 5–8 yrs. (Wheelchair-muscular dystrophy)

•Powers, Mary Ellen. 1986. *Our Teacher's in a Wheelchair.* Morton Grove, Ill.: Whitman. 5–6 yrs.

†Roth, Susan L. 1989. *We'll Ride Elephants through Brooklyn.* Illus. Susan L. Roth. New York: Farrar, Straus & Giroux. 3–6 yrs. (Grandfather ill)

•Rubin, Susan Goldman. 1993. *Emily Good as Gold.* San Diego: Browndeer. 11–14 yrs. (Adjusting to developmental disability)

•Russo, Marisabina. 1992. *Alex Is My Friend.* New York: Greenwillow. 5–8 yrs. (Physical disabilities stop young boy from playing ball)

•Shreve, Susan. 1991. *The Gift of the Girl Who Couldn't Hear.* New York: Tambourine. 9–12 yrs.

•Sirof, Harriet. 1993. *Because She's My Friend.* New York: Atheneum. 11–15 yrs. (Physical)

•Slepian, Jan. 1980. *The Alfred Summer.* New York: Macmillan. 9–13 yrs. (Cerebral palsy)

•Snyder, Carol. 1989. *Dear Mom and Dad, Don't Worry.* New York: Bantam. 11–14 yrs. (Spinal injury)

•Springer, Nancy. 1991. *Colt.* New York: Dial. 10–13 yrs. (Physically disabled rides a horse)

†Thiele, Colin. 1990. *Jodie's Journey.* New York: HarperCollins. 9–13 yrs. (Arthritis)

•Thompson, Mary. 1992. *My Brother Matthew.* Bethesda, Md.: Woodbine House. 5–8 yrs. (Disability)

•Voigt, Cynthia. 1986. *Izzy, Willy-Nilly.* New York: Atheneum. 12–15 yrs. (Physical)

•Werlin, Nancy. 1994. *Are You Alone on Purpose?* Boston: Houghton Mifflin. 12–16 yrs. (Autistic twin)

Williams, Karen Lynn. 1995. *A Real Christmas This Year.* New York: Clarion. 9–12 yrs. (Multiple-disabled brother)

•Wison, Nancy Hope. 1994. *The Reason for Janey.* New York: Macmillan. 11–14 yrs. (Mentally disabled)

†Ziefert, Harriet. 1991. *When Daddy Had the Chicken Pox.* Illus. Lionel Kalish. New York: HarperCollins. 4–8 yrs.

Achieving

Career, Special Interests, Sports

‡Barnes, Joyce A. 1994. *The Baby Grand, the Moon in July, and Me.* New York: Dial. 12–15 yrs.

‡Byars, Betsy. 1984. *The Computer Nut.* New York: Viking. 9–12 yrs.

*Calhoun, B. B. (Creator Lucy Ellis) 1990. *The Pink Parrots: All That Jazz.* Boston: Little, Brown/Sports Illustrated for Kids. 8–11 yrs. (See also rest of series about the Pink Parrot Baseball Team.)

*Christopher, Matt. 1987. *Red-Hot Hightops.* Boston: Little, Brown. 9–13 yrs.

---

† ILLNESS
• DISABILITY

* SPORTS
‡ CAREER, SPECIAL INTERESTS

_____. 1991. *Skateboard Tough*. Boston: Little, Brown. 10–12 yrs.

_____. 1992. *Return of the Home Run Kid*. Illus. Paul Casale. Boston: Little, Brown. 9–12 yrs. (Sequel to *The Kid Who Only Hit Homers*.)

‡Collier, James Lincoln. 1994. *The Jazz Kid*. New York: Holt. 11–14 yrs.

‡Conford, Ellen. 1993. *Nibble, Nibble, Jenny Archer*. Illus. Diane Palmisciano. Boston: Little, Brown. 7–10 yrs. Springboard Series.

*Crutcher, Chris. 1987. *The Crazy Horse Electric Game*. 1987. New York: Greenwillow. 12–16 yrs.

*Deuker, Carl. 1993. *Heart of a Champion*. Boston: Joy Street. 12–16 yrs.

‡Duder, Tessa. 1986. *Jellybean*. New York: Viking, Kestrel. 10–12 yrs.

* _____. 1992. *Alex in Rome*. Boston: Houghton Mifflin. 13–15 yrs.

‡Fleischman, Paul. 1988. *Rondo in C*. Illus. Janet Wentworth. New York: Harper & Row. 7–12 yrs.

‡Godden, Rumer. 1992. *Listen to the Nightingale*. New York: Viking Penguin. 7–11 yrs.

*Hallowell, T. 1990. *Shot from Midfield*. New York: Puffin. 8–12 yrs.

*Hite, Sid. 1995. *An Even Break*. New York: Holt. 10–13 yrs.

*Hughes, Dean. 1990. *Angel Park All Stars: Big Base Hit*. New York: Knopf. 8–12 yrs.

‡Isadora, Rachel. 1993. *Lili at Ballet*. New York: Putnam. 6–9 yrs.

*Jackson, Alison. 1991. *Crane's Rebound*. Illus. Diane Dawson Hearn. New York: Dutton. 8–11 yrs.

*Kelly, Jeffrey. 1987. *The Basement Baseball Club*. Boston: Houghton Mifflin 9–12 yrs.

*Kline, Suzy. 1988. *Herbie Jones and the Monster Ball*. New York: Putnam. 7–11 yrs.

‡MacLachlan, Patricia. 1988. *The Facts and Fictions of Minna Pratt*. New York: Harper & Row. 9–12 yrs.

‡McDonnell, Christine. 1987. *Just for the Summer*. New York: Viking. 8–10 yrs.

*Myers, Walter Dean. 1988. *Me, Mop, and the Moondance Kid*. New York: Delacorte.

_____. 1992. *Mop, Moondance, and the Nagasaki Knights*. New York: Delacorte. 10–12 yrs.

‡Nichol, Barbara. 1994. *Beethoven Lives Upstairs*. Illus. Scott Cameron. New York: Orchard. 8–11 yrs.

*Rabe, Berniece. 1986. *Margaret's Moves*. Illus. Julie Downing. New York: Dutton.

‡Schick, Eleanor. 1987. *Art Lessons*. New York: Greenwillow. 7–9 yrs.

_____. 1992. *I Have Another Language: The Language Is Dance*. New York: Macmillan. 5–7 yrs.

*Schulman, L. M. (Selector). 1990. *Random House Book of Sports Stories*. New York: Random House. 7–16 yrs.

*Slote, Alfred. 1990. *The Trading Game*. New York: Lippincott. 10–12 yrs.

‡Smith, Doris Buchanan. 1987. *Karate Dancer*. New York: Putnam. 10–13 yrs.

*Weaver, Will. 1993. *Striking Out*. New York: HarperCollins. 12–15 yrs.

*Wolfe, L. E. 1990. *The Case of the "Missing" Playbook and Other Mysteries*. Boston: Little, Brown/Sports Illustrated for Kids. 9–12 yrs. (The first of four books with Jack B. Quick, the sports detective.)

‡Zelver, Patricia. 1994. *The Wonderful Towers of Watts*. Illus. Frane Lessac. New York: Tambourine. 5–8 yrs.

*Zirpoli, Jane. 1988. *Roots in the Outfield*. Boston: Houghton Mifflin. 9–12 yrs.

FRIENDSHIPS

Aamundsen, Nina Ring. 1990. *Two Short and One Long*. Boston: Houghton Mifflin. 9–12 yrs.

Aylesworth, Jim. 1989. *Mr. McGill Goes to Town*. Illus. Thomas Graham. New York: Holt. 4–8 yrs.

Bawden, Nina. 1989. *The Outside Child*. New York: Lothrop, Lee & Shepard. 10–12 yrs.

Barbour, Karen. 1989. *Nancy*. San Diego: Harcourt Brace Jovanovich. 4–7 yrs.

Bedard, Michael. 1992. *Emily*. Illus. Barbara Cooney. New York: Doubleday. 6–9 yrs.

Bledsoe, Lucy Jane. 1995. *The Big Bike Race*. Illus. Sterling Brown. New York: Holiday. 9–12 yrs.

Bridgers, Sue Ellen. 1993. *Keeping Christina*. New York: HarperCollins. 12–15 yrs.

Brisson, Pat. 1989. *Your Best Friend, Kate*. Illus. Rick Brown. New York: Bradbury. 7–10 yrs.

Bunting, Eve. 1992. *Summer Wheels*. Illus. Thomas B. Allen. San Diego: Harcourt Brace Jovanovich. 6–10 yrs.

Byars, Betsy. 1981. *The Cybil War*. New York: Viking. 10–13 yrs.

Calnum, Michael. 1992. *Breaking the Fall*. New York: Viking. 12–15 yrs.

Cameron, Ann. 1987. *Julian's Glorious Summer*. New York: Pantheon. 9–11 yrs.

Cave, Hugh B. 1989. *Conquering Kilmarnie*. New York: Macmillan. 10–15 yrs.

Champion, Joyce. 1993. *Emily and Alice*. Illus. Sucie Stevenson. San Diego: Harcourt Brace/Gulliver. 5–7 yrs.

Clifton, Lucille. 1992. *Three Wishes*. Illus. Michael Hays. New York: Doubleday. 5–8 yrs.

Conford, Ellen. 1979. *Anything for a Friend*. Boston: Little, Brown. 10–14 yrs.

Corcoran, Barbara. 1989. *The Potato Kid*. New York: Atheneum/Karl. 9–12 yrs.

Cramer, Alexander. 1994. *A Night in Moonbeam County*. New York: Scribners. 12–16 yrs.

Crowley, Michael. 1993. *Shack and Back*. Illus. Abby Carter. Boston: Little, Brown. 5–9 yrs.

Crutcher, Chris. 1993. *Staying Fat for Sarah Byrnes*. New York: Greenwillow. 13–16 yrs.

Danziger, Paula. 1994. *Amber Brown Is Not a Crayon*. Illus. Tony Ross. New York: Putnam. 7–8 yrs.

Fosburgh, Lisa. 1989. *Afternoon Magic*. New York: Macmillan. 10–13 yrs.

Greene, Constance. 1969. *A Girl Called Al*. Illus. Byron Barton. New York: Viking. 10–13 yrs.

Haas, Jessie. 1995. *A Blue for Beware*. Illus. Jos. A. Smith. New York: Greenwillow. 10–13 yrs.

Haseley, Dennis. 1994. *Getting Him*. New York: Farrar, Straus & Giroux. 9–12 yrs.

Havill, Juanita. 1993. *Jamaica and Brianna*. Illus. Anne Sibley O'Brien. Boston: Houghton Mifflin. 5–7 yrs.

Henkes, Kevin. 1992. *Words of Stone*. New York: Greenwillow. 10–14 yrs.

Hest, Amy. 1992. *Pajama Party*. Illus. Irene Trivas. New York: Morrow. 8–10 yrs.

Howker, Janni. 1995. *The Topiary Garden*. Illus. Anthony Browne. New York: Orchard. 11–13 yrs.

Hurwitz, Johanna. 1979. *Aldo Applesauce*. Illus. John Wallner. New York: Morrow. 9–11 yrs.

_____. 1995. *Ozzie on His Own*. Illus. Eileen McKeating. New York: Morrow. 9–12 yrs.

Johnson, Scott. 1994. *Overnight Sensation*. New York: Atheneum. 13–15 yrs.

Kehret, Peg. 1994. *The Richest Kids in Town*. New York: Cobblehill. 9–12 yrs.

Kherdian, David. 1991. *The Great Fishing Contest*. Illus. Nonny Hogrogian. New York: Philomel. 7–10 yrs.

Lawlor, Laurie. 1995. *Gold in the Hills*. New York: Walker. 10–13 yrs.

Leverich, Kathleen. 1995. *Best Enemies Forever*. Illus. Walter Lorraine. New York: Greenwillow. 7–10 yrs.

Lillie, Patricia. 1989. *Jake and Rosie*. New York: Greenwillow. 6–8 yrs.

Lisle, Janet Taylor. 1989. *Afternoon of the Elves*. New York: Orchard. 9–11 yrs.

Little, Jean. 1970. *Look Through My Window*. Illus. Joan Sandin. New York: HarperCollins. 11–13 yrs.

_____. 1971. *Kate*. New York: HarperCollins. 11–13 yrs.

_____. 1989. *Hey World, Here I Am!* Illus. Sue Truesdell. New York: HarperCollins. 11–13 yrs.

Lowery, Lois. 1987. *Rabble Starkey*. Boston: Houghton Mifflin. 12–13 yrs.

McKenna, Colleen O'Shaughnessy. 1989. *Fifth Grade: Here Comes Trouble*. New York: Scholastic. 8–12 yrs.

Miller, Mary Jane. 1993. *Fast Forward*. New York: Viking. 10–13 yrs.

Naylor, Phyllis Reynolds. 1989. *Alice in Rapture, Sort of*. New York: Atheneum/Karl. 10–12 yrs. (Sequel to *The Agony of Alice*.)

_____. 1992. *Josie's Troubles*. Illus. Shelley Matheis. New York: Atheneum. 9–11 yrs.

_____. 1993. *The Boys Start the War*. New York: Delacorte. 10–12 yrs.

_____. 1993. *The Girls Get Even*. New York: Delacorte. 10–12 yrs. (Sequel to above.)

_____. 1994. *All but Alice*. New York: Atheneum/Karl. 11–13 yrs.

_____. 1994. *Boys against Girls*. New York: Delacorte. 9–12 yrs.

_____. 1996. *Alice in Lace*. Karl/Atheneum. 10–13 yrs.

Orgel, Doris. 1990. *Nobodies and Somebodies*. New York: Puffin. 8–12 yrs.

Paterson, Kathryn. 1976. *Bridge to Terabithia*. Illus. Donna Diamond. New York: HarperCollins. 10–13 yrs.

Pearson, Gayle. 1993. *The Fog Doggies and Me*. New York: Atheneum. 10–12 yrs.

Pendergraft, Patricia. 1989. *Brushy Mountain*. New York: Philomel. 10–14 yrs.

Philbrick, Rodman. 1993. *Freak the Mighty*. New York: Blue Sky. 13–16 yrs.

Polacco, Patricia. 1992. *Picnic at Mudsock Meadow*. New York: Putnam. 4–8 yrs.

Rodowsky, Colby. 1990. *Dog Days*. Illus. Kathleen Collins Howell. New York: Farrar, Straus & Giroux. 7–11 yrs.

Ross, Tony. 1991. *A Fairy Tale*. Boston: Little, Brown. 4–8 yrs.

Rylant, Cynthia. 1992. *An Angel for Solomon Singer*. Illus. Peter Catalanotto. New York: Orchard/Jackson. 6–11 yrs.

Schenker, Dona. 1994. *Fearsome's Hero*. New York: Knopf. 10–12 yrs.

Seabrooke, Brenda. 1992. *The Bridges of Summer*. New York: Cobblehill. 12–15 yrs.

Sharmat, Marjorie Weinman & Mitchell Sharmat. 1989. *The Pizza Monster*. Illus. Denise Brunkus. New York: Delacorte. 5–8 yrs.

Sinykin, Sheri Cooper. 1993. *Slate Blues*. New York: Lothrop, Lee & Shepard. 13–15 yrs.

* SPORTS
‡ CAREER, SPECIAL INTERESTS

Smith, Susan Mathias. 1994. *The Booford Summer.* Illus. Andrew Glass. New York: Clarion. 9–12 yrs.

Snyder, Zilpha Keatley. 1993. *Fool's Gold.* New York: Delacorte. 10–15 yrs.

Spinelli, Eileen. 1992. *Somebody Loves You, Mr. Hatch.* Illus. Paul Yalowitz. New York: Bradbury. 5–7 yrs.

Spinelli, Jerry. 1991. *Fourth Grade Rats.* Illus. Paul Casale. New York: Scholastic. 7–9 yrs.

Vail, Rachel. 1994. *Ever After.* New York: Jackson/Orchard. 11–14 yrs.

———. 1996. *Daring to Be Abigail.* New York: Jackson/Orchard. 10–12 yrs.

Willis, Meredith Sue. 1994. *The Secret Super Powers of Marco.* New York: HarperCollins. 9–12 yrs.

Winthrop, Elizabeth. 1989. *The Best Friends Club: A Lizzie and Harold Story.* Illus. Martha Weston. New York: Lothrop, Lee, & Shepard. 4–7 yrs.

Woodson, Jacqueline. 1993. *Between Madison and Palmetto.* New York: Delacorte. 9–13 yrs.

INTERACTIONS IN SCHOOL

Allard, Harry. 1977. *Miss Nelson Is Missing.* Illus. James Marshall. Boston: Houghton Mifflin. 6–9 yrs.

———. 1982. *Miss Nelson Is Back.* Illus. James Marshall. Boston: Houghton Mifflin. 6–9 yrs.

———. 1985. *Miss Nelson Has a Field Day.* Illus. James Marshall. Boston: Houghton Mifflin. 6–9 yrs.

Avi. 1987. *Romeo and Juliet Together (and ALIVE!) AT LAST.* New York: Orchard. 11–13 yrs.

Baehr, Patricia. 1989. *School Isn't Fair!* Illus. R. W. Alley. New York: Four Winds. 4–6 yrs.

Betancourt, Jeanne. 1993. *My Name is Brain Brian.* New York: Scholastic. 10–12 yrs.

Birdseye, Tom. 1993. *Just Call Me Stupid.* New York: Holiday. 10–13 yrs.

Blacker, Terence. 1993. *Homebird.* New York: Bradbury. 13–14 yrs.

Bunting, Eve. 1990. *Our Sixth-Grade Sugar Babies.* New York: Lippincott. 9–12 yrs.

———. 1992. *Our Teacher's Having a Baby.* Illus. Diane de Groat. New York: Clarion. 6–8 yrs.

Cantos, Jack. 1994. *Heads or Tails: Stories from the Sixth Grade.* New York: Farrar, Straus & Giroux. 9–13 yrs.

Carrick, Carol. 1988. *Left Behind.* Illus. Donald Carrick. New York: Clarion. 5–8 yrs.

Chang, Heidi. 1988. *Elaine, Mary Lewis, and the Frogs.* New York: Crown. 8–10 yrs.

Cleary, Beverly. 1990. *Muggie Maggie.* Illus. Kay Life. New York: Morrow. 8–10 yrs.

Cooney, Caroline B. 1987. *Among Friends.* New York: Bantam. 12–15 yrs.

Danziger, Paula. 1995. *Amber Brown Goes Fourth.* Illus. Tony Ross. New York: Putnam. 7–10 yrs.

de Groat, Diane. 1996. *Roses Are Pink, Your Feet Really Stink.* Illus. Diane de Groat. New York: Morrow. 5–8 yrs.

Delton, Judy. 1991. *My Mom Made Me Go to School.* Illus. Lisa McCue. New York: Delacorte. 5–8 yrs.

Denslow, Sharon Phillips. 1993. *Bus Riders.* New York: Four Winds. 5–7 yrs.

Denton, Terry. 1990. *The School for Laughter.* Boston: Houghton Mifflin. 5–8 yrs.

Duffey, Betsy. 1993. *How to Be Cool in the Third Grade.* New York: Viking. 8–10 yrs.

Dugan, Barbara. 1994. *Good-bye, Hello.* New York: Greenwillow. 9–12 yrs.

Duncan, Lois. 1988. *Wonder Kid Meets the Evil Lunch Snatcher.* Boston: Little, Brown. 10–12 yrs.

Giff, Patricia Reilly. 1984. *The Beast in Ms. Rooney's Room.* New York: Delacorte. 7–10 yrs.

Gilson, Jamie. 1991. *Sticks and Stones and Skeleton Bones.* Illus. Dee deRosa. New York: Lothrop, Lee & Shepard. 8–11 yrs.

———. 1994. *It Goes EEEEEEEEEEEEE!* Illus. Diane de Groat. Boston: Houghton Mifflin. 6–8 yrs.

Gleitzman, Morris. 1995. *Blabber Mouth.* San Diego: Harcourt Brace. 11–14 yrs.

Hayes, Daniel. 1993. *No Effect.* Boston: Godine. 12–15 yrs.

Hennessy, B. G. 1990. *School Days.* Illus. Tracey Campbell Pearson. New York: Viking Penguin. 3–8 yrs.

Hermes, Patricia. 1990. *I Hate Being Gifted.* New York: Putnam. 10–13 yrs.

Hoffman, Phyllis. 1991. *Meatball.* Illus. Emily Arnold McCully. New York: HarperCollins/Zolotow. 2–7 yrs.

Holmes, Barbara Ware. 1989. *Charlotte Shakespeare and Annie the Great.* Illus. John Himmelman. New York: Harper & Row. 9–12 yrs.

Honeycutt, Natalie. 1986. *The All-New Jonah Twist.* New York: Bradbury. 7–9 yrs.

———. 1988. *The Best-Laid Plans of Jonah Twist.* New York: Bradbury. 7–9 yrs.

———. 1992. *Juliet Fisher and the Foolproof Plan.* New York: Bradbury. 7–9 yrs.

———. 1993. *Lydia Jane and the Baby-Sitter Exchange.* New York: Bradbury. 9–12 yrs.

Hopper, Nancy J. 1993. *I Was a Fifth-Grade Zebra.* New York: Dial. 9–12 yrs.

Hurwitz, Johanna. 1987. *Class Clown.* Illus. Sheila Hamanaka. New York: Morrow. 8–11 yrs.

———. 1988. *Teacher's Pet.* Illus. Sheila Hamanaka. New York: Morrow. 8–11 yrs.

———. 1990. *Class President.* Illus. Sheila Hamanaka. New York: Morrow. 8–11 yrs.

———. 1991. *School's Out.* Illus. Sheila Hamanaka. New York: Morrow. 8–11 yrs.

———. 1992. *Roz and Ozzie.* Illus. Eileen McKeating. New York: Morrow. 7–10 yrs.

———. 1994. *School Spirit.* Illus. Karen Dugan. New York: Morrow. 9–12 yrs.

Jabar, Cynthia. 1989. *Alice Ann Gets Ready for School.* Boston: Little, Brown. 4–6 yrs.

Klein, Norma. 1987. *Herbie Jones and the Class Gift.* Illus. Richard Williams. New York: Putnam. 7–9 yrs.

Levy, Elizabeth. 1992. *Keep Ms. Sugarman in the Fourth Grade.* New York: HarperCollins. 8–10 yrs.

Littke, Lael. 1992. *Getting Rid of Rhoda.* 1992. Salt Lake City: CinnamonTree/Deseret. 10–13 yrs.

Lowry, Lois. 1991. *Your Move, J. P.!* New York: Dell/Yearling. 9–12 yrs.

Martin, Ann. 1992. *Rachel Parker, Kindergarten Show-Off.* Illus. Nancy Poydar. New York: Holiday. 4–7 yrs.

———. 1984. *Stage Fright.* New York: Holiday. 9–11 yrs.

McCants, William D. 1993. *Anything Can Happen in High School: (And It Usually Does).* San Diego: Browndeer. 12–15 yrs.

McKenna, Colleen O'Shaughnessy. 1989. *Fourth Grade Is a Jinx.* New York: Scholastic. 8–12 yrs.

———. 1993. *Good Grief . . . Third Grade.* Illus. Richard Williams. New York: Scholastic. 7–9 yrs.

Mills, Claudia. 1989. *After Fifth Grade, the World!* New York: Macmillan. 8–10 yrs.

———. 1992. *Dinah for President.* New York: Macmillan. 10–12 yrs.

———. 1994. *The Secret Life of Bethany Barrett.* New York: Macmillan. 10–13 yrs.

———. 1996. *Dinah Forever.* New York: Farrar, Straus & Giroux. 9–12 yrs.

Morris, Judy K. 1989. *The Kid Who Ran for Principal.* New York: Lippincott. 8–12 yrs.

Myers, Laurie. 1993. *Earthquake in the Third Grade.* Illus. Karen Ritz. New York: Clarion. 7–9 yrs.

Park, Barbara. 1992. *Junie B. Jones the Stupid Smelly Bus.* Illus. Denise Brunkus. New York: Random House. 6–10 yrs.

———. 1993. *Junie B. Jones and a Little Monkey Business.* New York: Random House. 6–10 yrs.

Pinkwater, Daniel. 1983. *I Was a Second Grade Werewolf.* New York: Dutton. 6–9 yrs.

Pilling, Ann. 1988. *The Big Pink.* New York: Viking. 8–10 yrs.

Potter, Katherine. 1994. *Spike.* Illus. Katherine Potter. New York: Simon & Schuster. 7–9 yrs.

Roberts, Brenda C. 1993. *Sticks and Stones, Bobbie Bones.* New York: Scholastic. 10–12 yrs.

Roberts, Willo Davis. 1986. *The Magic Book.* New York: Atheneum. 10–12 yrs.

Robinson, Barbara. 1972. *The Best Christmas Pagent Ever.* Illus. Judith Gwyn Brown. New York: HarperCollins. 8–10 yrs.

Roe, Eliane Corbeil. 1989. *Circle of Light.* New York: Harper & Row. 10–15 yrs.

Rogers, Jean. 1988. *Dinosaurs Are 568.* New York: Greenwillow. 5–7 yrs.

Sachar, Louis. 1987. *Sixth Grade Secrets.* New York: Scholastic. 8–11 yrs.

———. 1987. *There's a Boy in the Girls' Bathroom.* New York: Knopf/Borzoi. 9–12 yrs.

———. 1995. *Wayside School Gets a Little Stranger.* Illus. Joel Schnick. New York: Morrow. 10–13 yrs.

Shreve, Susan. 1984. *The Flunking of Joshua T. Bates.* Illus. Diane de Groat. New York: Knopf. 9–12 yrs.

———. 1993. *Joshua T. Bates Takes Charge.* Illus. Dan Andreasen. New York: Knopf. 10–12 yrs.

———. 1993. *Amy Dunn Quits School.* New York: Tambourine. 9–12 yrs.

Snyder, Zilpha Keatly. 1991. *Libby on Wednesday.* New York: Dell/Yearling. 10–13 yrs.

Strauch, Eileen Walsh. 1993. *Hey You, Sister Rose.* New York: Tambourine. 10–12 yrs.

Schwartz, Am. 1982. *Bea and Mr. Jones.* New York: Macmillan. 4–7 yrs.

Tolan, Stephanie S. 1993. *Save Halloween!* New York: Morrow. 10–12 yrs.

Voigt, Cynthia. 1996. *Bad Girls.* New York: Scholastic. 10–13 yrs.

Waggoner, Karen. 1992. *The Lemonade Babysitter.* Illus. Dorothy Donohue. Boston: Little, Brown/Joy Street. 4–7 yrs.

Wallace, Bill. 1992. *The Biggest Klutz in Fifth Grade.* New York: Holiday. 9–12 yrs.

Weinman, Marjorie & Mitchell Sharmat. 1989. *The Princess of the Fillmore Street School.* Illus. Denise Brunkus. New York: Delacorte. 5–8 yrs.

Wyman, Andrea. 1994. *Faith, Hope, and Chicken Feathers.* New York: Holiday. 11–13 yrs.

Zach, Cheryl. 1992. *Benny and the No-Good Teacher.* Illus. Janet Wilson. New York: Bradbury. 8–10 yrs.

SOCIETAL CONCERNS

Ackerman, Karen. 1991. *The Leaves in October.* New York: Atheneum. 10–13 yrs.

Avi. 1993. *Punch with Judy.* Illus. Emily Lisker. New York: Bradbury. 13–16 yrs.

Barre, Shelley A. 1993. *Chive*. New York: Simon & Schuster. 9–12 yrs.

Barbour, Karen. 1991. *Mr. Bow Tie*. San Diego: Harcourt Brace. 5–9 yrs.

Bawden, Nina. 1991. *The Witch's Daughter*. New York: Clarion. 10–12 yrs.

Bunting, Eve. 1991. *Fly Away Home*. Illus. Ronald Himler. New York: Clarion. 9–12 yrs.

_____. 1994. *Smoky Night*. Illus. David Diaz. San Diego: Harcourt Brace. K–3.

Byars, Betsy. 1977. *The Pinballs*. New York: HarperCollins. 11–13 yrs.

_____. 1985. *Cracker Jackson*. Illus. Diane de Groat. New York: Viking. 12–15 yrs.

Charbonneau, Eileen. 1996. *Honor to the Hills*. New York: Tor. 12–15 yrs.

Cohn, Janice. 1994. *Why Did It Happen? Helping Children Cope in a Violent World*. New York: Morrow. 5–9 yrs.

Coman, Carolyn. 1995. *What Jamie Saw*. Arden, N.C.: Front Street. 10–13 yrs.

Collier, James Lincoln & Christopher Collier. 1992. *The Clock*. Illus. Kelly Maddox. New York: Delacorte. 11–13 yrs.

Corcoran, Barbara. 1991. *Stay Tuned*. New York: Atheneum. 12–15 yrs.

Deem, James M. 1994. *Three NBs of Julian Drew*. Boston: Houghton Mifflin. 12–16 yrs.

DeClements, Barthe. 1993. *The Pickle Song*. New York: Viking. 8–12 yrs.

DeFelice, Cynthia. 1990. *Weasel*. New York: Macmillan. 10–13 yrs.

DiSalvo-Ryan, DyAnne. 1991. *Uncle Willie and the Soup Kitchen*. New York: Morrow. 5–9 yrs.

Fox, Paula. 1991. *Monkey Island*. New York: Orchard, Watts. 12–15 yrs.

Grant, Cynthia D. 1993. *Uncle Vampire*. New York: Atheneum. 12–15 yrs.

Grove, Vicke. 1990. *The Fastest Friend in the West*. New York: Putnam. 12–15 yrs.

Guthrie, Donna. 1988. *A Rose for Abby*. Illus. Donna Hockerman. Nashville, Tenn.: Abingdon. 5–8 yrs.

Harris, Mary. 1989. *Come the Morning*. New York: Bradbury. 12–15 yrs.

Hodge, Merle. 1993. *For the Life of Laetitia*. New York: Farrar, Straus & Giroux. 10–12 yrs.

Holman, Felice. 1990. *Secret City, USA*. New York: Scribners. 12–15 yrs.

Hughes, Dean. 1989. *Family Pose*. New York: Atheneum. 9–13 yrs.

Johnson, Angela. 1993. *Toning the Sweep*. New York: Orchard/Jackson. 13–15 yrs.

Jones, Adrienne. 1987. *Street Family*. New York: HarperCollins. 12–16 yrs.

Jones, Rebecca C. 1991. *Matthew and Tilly*. Illus. Beth Peck. New York: Dutton. 3–6 yrs.

Lee, Marie G. 1994. *Saying Goodbye*. Boston: Houghton Mifflin. 13–18 yrs.

Llorente, Pilar Molina. (Trans. Robin Longshaw). 1993. *The Apprentice*. Illus. Jan Ramon Alonso. New York: Farrar, Straus & Giroux. 12–16 yrs.

Lowery, Linda. 1994. *Laurie Tells*. Illus. John Eric Karpinski. Minneapolis, Minn.: Carolrhoda. 10–12 yrs.

Luger, Harriett. 1996. *Bye, Bye, Bali Kai*. San Diego: Browndeer/Harcourt Brace. 10–16 yrs.

Mahon, K. L. 1994. *Just One Tear*. New York: Lothrop, Lee & Shepard. 10–14 yrs.

Marsden, John. 1994. *Letters from the Inside*. Boston: Houghton Mifflin. 12–16 yrs.

Mazer, Norma Fox. 1989. *Silver*. New York: Avon/Flare. 10–15 yrs.

_____. 1993. *Out of Control*. New York: Morrow. 12–15 yrs.

Mazzio, Joann. 1993. *Leaving Eldorado*. Boston: Houghton Mifflin. 12–15 yrs.

Mccully, Emily Arnold. 1996. *The Bobbin Girl*. Illus. Emily Arnold McCully. New York: Dial. 8–10 yrs.

McDaniel, Lurlene. 1993. *Baby Alicia Is Dying*. New York: Bantam. 12–15 yrs.

Mead, Alice. 1995. *Junebug*. New York: Farrar, Straus & Giroux. 9–12 yrs. (Urban gang; maturing)

Nelson, Theresa. 1992. *The Beggars' Ride*. New York: Orchard/Jackson. 13–15 yrs.

Nelson, Vaunda Micheaux. 1993. *Mayfield Crossing*. Illus. Leonard Jenkins. New York: Putnam. 10–12 yrs.

Paterson, Katherine. 1978. *The Great Gilly Hopkins*. New York: HarperCollins. 10–13 yrs.

_____. 1991. *Lyddie*. New York: Lodestar. 10–14 yrs.

Pennebaker, Ruth. 1996. *Don't Think Twice*. New York: Holt. 12–17 yrs.

Pinkwater, Jill. 1991. *Tails of the Bronx*. New York: Macmillan. 9–13 yrs.

Porte, Barbara Ann. 1994. *Something Terrible Happened: A Novel*. New York: Orchard/Jackson. 12–16 yrs.

Qualey, Marsha. 1993. *Revolutions of the Heart*. Boston: Houghton Mifflin. 13–16 yrs.

Ruby, Lois. 1993. *Miriam's Well*. New York: Scholastic. 12–15 yrs.

Taylor, Clark. 1992. *The House That Crack Built*. Illus. Jan Thompson Dicks. San Francisco: Chronicle. 8–12 yrs.

Taylor, Mildred D. 1990. *Mississippi Bridge*. Illus. Max Ginsburg. New York: Dial. 12–15 yrs.

Temple, Frances. 1993. *Grab Hands and Run*. New York: Orchard/Jackson. 12–15 yrs.

Testa, Maria. 1995. *Dancing Pink Flamingos and Other Stories*. Minneapolis, Minn.: Lerner. 12–15 yrs. (Ten short stories)

Tolan, Stephanie S. 1992. *Sophie and the Sidewalk Man*. Illus. Susan Avishai. New York: Four Winds. 7–9 yrs.

Voigt, Cynthia. 1994. *When She Hollers*. New York: Scholastic. 12–16 yrs.

Wallace, Bill. 1994. *Blackwater Swamp*. New York: Holiday House. 11–14 yrs.

Wilson, Jacqueline. 1996. *Elsa, Star of the Shelter*. Illus. Nick Sharratt. Morton Grove, Ill.: Whitman. 9–11 yrs.

Wine, Jeanine. 1989. *Silly Tillie*. Khei, HI: Good Books. 5–9 yrs.

Wojciechowski, Susan. 1989. *Patty Dillman of Hot Dog Fame*. New York: Orchard. 10–14 yrs.

Woodson, Jacqueline. 1992. *Maizon at Blue Hill*. New York: Delacorte. 11–13 yrs.

Yep, Laurence. 1991. *The Star Fisher*. New York: Morrow. 9–10 yrs.

_____. 1993. *Dragon's Gate*. Illus. Charles Lilly. New York: HarperCollins. 13–16 yrs.

Young, Ronder Thomas. 1993. *Learning by Heart*. Boston: Houghton Mifflin. 10–12 yrs.

CULTURAL LIFESTYLES AND TRADITIONS

(See also Comprehensive bibliographies in Chapter 9)

Beatty, Patricia. 1981. *Lupita Mañana*. New York: Beech Tree. 12–15 yrs.

Brooks, Bruce. 1990. *Everywhere*. New York: HarperCollins. 11–14 yrs.

Bruchac, Joseph. 1993. *Fox Song*. Illus. Paul Morin. New York: Philomel. 5–8 yrs.

Crew, Linda. 1989. *Children of the River*. New York: Delacorte. 12–16 yrs.

Dooley, Norah. 1991. *Everybody Cooks Rice*. Illus. Peter J. Thornton. Minneapolis, Minn.: Carolrhoda. 4–9 yrs.

Finley, Mary Peace. 1993. *Soaring Eagle*. New York: Simon & Schuster. 10–13 yrs.

Garland, Sherry. 1993. *Shadow of the Dragon*. San Diego: Harcourt Brace. 12–15 yrs.

Guy, Rosa. 1989. *The Ups and Downs of Carl Davis III*. New York: Delacorte. 10–14 yrs.

Levin, Ellen. 1989. *I Hate English!* Illus. Steve Bjorkman. New York: Scholastic. 6–9 yrs.

Meyer, Carolyn. 1993. *White Lilacs*. San Diego: Gulliver. 12–15 yrs.

Miles, Calvin. 1993. *Calvin's Christmas Wish*. Illus. Dolores Johnson. New York: Viking. 4–7 yrs.

Myers, Walter Dean. 1988. *Scorpions*. New York: HarperCollins. 12–16 yrs.

_____. 1990. *The Mouse Rap*. New York: Harper & Row. 8–12 yrs.

Namioka, L. 1992. *Yang the Youngest and His Terrible Ear*. Illus. Kees de Kiefte. Boston: Joy/Little, Brown. 9–11 yrs.

Paulsen, Gary. 1987. *The Crossing*. New York: Orchard. 12–15 yrs.

_____. 1993. *Sisters/Hermanas*. San Diego: Harcourt Brace. 12–16 yrs.

Polacco, Patricia. 1989. *Uncle Vova's Tree*. New York: Philomel. 4–8 yrs.

_____. 1990. *Just Plain Fancy*. New York: Bantam/Little Rooster. 4–8 yrs.

_____. 1992. *Chicken Sunday*. New York: Philomel. 4–8 yrs.

Soto, Gary. 1992. *The Skirt*. Illus. Eric Velasquez. New York: Delacorte. 7–10 yrs.

_____. 1993. *Local News*. San Diego: Harcourt Brace. 10–14 yrs.

Tan, Amy. 1992. *The Moon Lady*. Illus. Gretchen Schields. New York: Macmillan. 7–10 yrs.

Wright, Richard. 1994. *Rite of Passage*. HarperCollins. 12–16 yrs.

INTERNATIONAL LITERATURE

(See also Bibliographies for World: All Historical Periods in Chapters 5 & 6)

Appiah, Sonia. 1989. *Amoko and Efua Bear*. Illus. Carol Easmon. New York: Macmillan. 4–8 yrs.

Baker, Jeannie. 1991. *Window*. New York: Greenwillow. 7–12 yrs.

Brooks, M. 1992. *Two Moons in August*. Boston: Little, Brown. 11–14 yrs.

Carlstrom, Nancy White. 1990. *Light: Stories of a Small Kindness*. Illus. Lisa Desimini. Boston: Little, Brown. 8–12 yrs.

Casey, Maude. 1994. *Over the Water*. New York: Holt. 12–14 yrs.

Castaneda, Omar S. 1994. *Imagining Isabel*. New York: Lodestar. 12–16 yrs.

Clarke, J. 1993. *Al Capsella Takes a Vacation*. New York: Holt. 12–15 yrs.

Crew, Gary. 1994. *No Such Country*. New York: Simon & Schuster. 12–16 yrs.

Dolkay, Vedat. (Trans. Guner Ener). 1994. *Sister Shako and Kolo the Goat: Memories of My Childhood in Turkey*. New York: Lothrop, Lee & Shepard. 11–13 yrs.

Dodd, L. 1992. *Hairy Maclary's Showbusiness*. Milwaukee, Wisc.: Gareth Stevens. 6–10 yrs.

Dorros, Arthur. 1991. *Tonight Is Carnaval.* Illus. Club de Madres Virgen del Carmen of Lima, Peru. New York: Dutton. 5–8 yrs. (Andes Mountains of South America)

Ellis, Sarah. 1991. *Pick-up Sticks.* New York: McElderry. 11–14 yrs.

French, F. 1991. *Anancy and Mr. Dry-Bone.* Boston: Little, Brown. 6–9 yrs.

Grover, Wayne. 1993. *Ali and the Golden Eagle.* New York: Greenwillow. 12–15 yrs.

Heide, Florence Parry & Judith Heide Gilliland. 1990. *The Day of Ahmed's Secret.* Illus. Ted Lewin. New York: Lothrop, Lee & Shepard. 6–9 yrs.

Hill, A. 1995. *The Burnt Stick.* Illus. Mark Sofilas. Burlington, Mass.: Houghton Mifflin. 9–12 yrs. (Australia)

Hoestlandt, J. (Trans. Mark Polizzoti). 1995. *Star of Fear, Star of Hope.* Illus. Johanna Kang. New York: Walker. 8–11 yrs. (France)

Ibbitson, J. 1991. *1812: Jeremy and the General.* New York: Macmillan. 11–14 yrs.

Isadora, Rachel. 1991. *At the Crossroads.* Illus. Rachel Isadora. New York: Greenwillow. 4–7 yrs.

———. 1992. *Over the Green Hills.* Illus. Rachel Isadora. New York: Greenwillow. 4–8 yrs.

Jacobs, Shannon K. 1991. *Song of the Giraffe.* Illus. Pamela Johnson. Boston: Little, Brown/Springboard. 7–9 yrs.

Klein, Robin. 1987. *Hating Alison Ashley.* New York: Viking Kestrel.

———. 1992. *All in the Blue Unclouded Weather.* New York: Viking. 11–14 yrs.

Major, Kevin. 1989. *Blood Red Ochre.* New York: Delacorte. 12–15 yrs.

Matas, C. 1991. *The Race.* New York: HarperCollins. 11–14 yrs.

Meeks, Arone Raymond. 1993. *Enora and the Black Crane.* New York: Scholastic. 5–8 yrs.

Mennen, Ingrid, and Niki Daly. 1992. *Somewhere in Africa.* Illus. Nicolaas Maritz. New York: Dutton. 3–8 yrs.

Neville, Emily Cheney. 1991. *The China Year.* New York: HarperCollins. 10–14 yrs.

Nohotima, P. 1991. *Parera Parera.* Illus. E. Williamson. Palmerston North: New Zealand Natural Heritage Foundation. 7–10 yrs.

Orlev, U. (Trans. Hillel Halkin) 1995. *The Lady with the Hat.* Burlington, Mass.: Houghton Mifflin. 11–16 yrs. (Palestine; Poland; Italy; Cyprus)

Pearson, Kit. 1992. *Looking at the Moon.* New York: Viking. 12–15 yrs.

Pettepiece, Thomas & Anatoly Aleksin, (Eds.). 1990. *Face to Face: A Collection of Stories by Celebrated Soviet and American Writers.* New York: Philomel. 12–16 yrs.

Pomerantz, Charlotte. 1989. *The Chalk Doll.* Illus. Frane Lessac. New York: Lippincott. 3–7 yrs.

Sacks, Margaret. 1992. *Themba.* Illus. Wil Clay. New York: Lodestar. 9–12 yrs.

Schami, Rafik. (Trans. Rika Lesser) 1990. *A Hand Full of Stars.* New York: Dutton. 12–15 yrs.

Schermbrucker, Reviva. 1991. *Charlie's House.* Illus. Niki Daly. New York: Viking Penguin. 3–8 yrs.

Semel, Nava. (Trans. Hillel Halkin). 1995. *Flying Lessons.* New York: Simon. 9–12 yrs. (Israel; coping with death of mother)

Soto, Gary. 1992. *Pacific Crossing.* San Diego: Harcourt Brace. 11–14 yrs.

Staples, Suzanne Fisher. 1989. *Shabanu: Daughter of the Wind.* New York: Knopf. 12–16 yrs.

Temple, Frances. 1992. *Taste of Salt: A Story of Modern Haiti.* New York: Orchard/Jackson. 12–16 yrs.

Walker, Kate. 1993. *Peter.* Houghton Mifflin. 14–16 yrs.

Whelan, Gloria. 1992. *Goodbye, Vietnam.* New York: Knopf. 11–14 yrs.

Williams, Karen Lynn. 1991. *Galimoto.* Illus. Catherine Stock. New York: Mulberry. 4–8 yrs.

Williams, Michael. 1992. *Crocodile Burning.* New York: Lodestar. 13–16 yrs.

Yep, Laurence. 1994. *The Boy Who Swallowed Snakes.* Illus. Jean & Mou-Sien Tseng. New York: Scholastic. 4–6 yrs.

Zheleznikov, Vladimir (Trans. Antonina W. Bouis). *Scarecrow.* New York: Lippincott. 10–15 yrs.

NATURE

Aldag, Kurt. 1992. *Some Things Never Change.* Illus. Ken Rush. New York: Macmillan. 8–11 yrs.

Bjork, Christina (Trans. Joan Sandin). 1989. *Linnea's Almanac.* Illus. Lena Anderson. R & S Books. 6–10 yrs.

Chall, Martha Wilson. 1992. *Up North at the Cabin.* Illus. Steve Johnson. New York: Lothrop, Lee & Shepard. 5–8 yrs.

Clark, Emma Chichester. 1993. *Across the Blue Mountains.* San Diego: Harcourt Brace/Gulliver. 5–8 yrs.

Cotler, Joanna. 1990. *Sky Above, Earth Below.* Illus. Joanna Cotler. New York: Harper & Row/Charlotte Zolotow. 3–6 yrs.

Cowcher, Helen. 1990. *Antarctica.* New York: Farrar, Straus & Giroux. 4–8 yrs.

Cross, Verda. 1992. *Great-Grandma Tells of Threshing Day.* Illus. Gail Owens. Morton Grove, Ill.: Whitman. 7–10 yrs.

Emberley, Michael. 1993. *Welcome Back, Sun.* Boston: Little, Brown. 4–7 yrs.

Florian, Douglas. 1989 *Nature Walk.* New York: Greenwillow. 3–7 yrs.

Franklin, Kristine L. 1994. *The Shepherd Boy.* Illus. Jill Kastner. New York: Atheneum. 5–7 yrs. (Spanish ed.: *El niño pastor.*)

Hamilton, Virginia. 1992. *Drylongso.* Illus. Jerry Pinkney. San Diego: Harcourt Brace Jovanovich. 10–12 yrs.

Heiligman, Deborah. 1990. *Into the Night.* Illus. Melissa Sweet. New York: Harper & Row. 4–8 yrs.

Hol, Coby. 1989. *A Visit to the Farm.* New York: North-South. 4–8 yrs.

Johnson, Herschel. 1989. *A Visit to the Country.* Illus. Romare Bearden. New York: Harper & Row. 2–8 yrs.

Klass, David. 1994. *California Blue.* New York: Scholastic. 11–13 yrs.

Levin, Betty. 1994. *Starshine and Sunglow.* Illus. Jos. A. Smith. New York: Greenwillow. 9–12 yrs.

Lyon, George Ella. 1992. *Who Came Down That Road?* Illus. Peter Catalanotto. New York: Orchard/Jackson. 4–7 yrs.

Mitchell, Barbara. 1993. *Down Buttermilk Lane.* Illus. John Sandford. New York: Lothrop, Lee & Shepard. 5–8 yrs.

Parnall, Peter. 1989. *Quiet.* New York: Morrow. 5–9 yrs.

Reeder, Carolyn. 1991. *Grandpa's Mountain.* New York: Macmillan. 10–13 yrs.

Rockwell, Anne. 1989. *Apples and Pumpkins.* Illus. Lizzy Rockwell. New York: Macmillan. 4–8 yrs.

———. 1989. *My Spring Robin.* Illus. Harlow Rockwell & Lizzy Rockwell. New York: Macmillan. 2–4 yrs.

Schlein, Miriam. 1990. *The Year of the Panda.* Illus. Kam Mak. New York: Crowell. 8–12 yrs.

Shannon, George. 1993. *Climbing Kansas Mountains.* Illus. Thomas B. Allen. New York: Bradbury. 5–8 yrs.

Tresselt, Alvin. 1992. *The Gift of the Tree.* Illus. Henri Sorensen. New York: Lothrop, Lee & Shepard. 4–8 yrs.

Turner, Ann. 1989. *Heron Street.* Illus. Lisa Desimini. New York: Harper & Row/Zolotow. 6–9 yrs.

Vaughan, Marcia. 1992. *The Sea-Breeze Hotel.* New York: HarperCollins/Perlman. 7–9 yrs.

Weller, Francis Ward. 1991. *I Wonder If I'll See a Whale.* Illus. Ted Lewin. New York: Philomel. 4–8 yrs.

Weiner, David. 1990. *Hurricane.* New York: Clarion. 5–10 yrs.

Williams, David. 1990. *Walking to the Creek.* Illus. Thomas B. Allen. New York: Knopf/Borzoi. 5–8 yrs.

Wittmann, Patricia. 1993. *Scrabble Creek.* Illus. Nancy Poydar. New York: Macmillan. 5–7 yrs.

Yolen, Jane. 1992. *Letting Swift River Go.* Illus. Barbara Cooney. Boston: Little, Brown. 6–10 yrs.

STORIES OF MUSIC

Fonteyn, Margot (Reteller). 1989. *Swan Lake.* Illus. Trina Schart Hyman. San Diego: Harcourt Brace Jovanovich/Gulliver. 8–16 yrs.

Greaves, Margaret (Reteller). 1989. *The Magic Flute: The Story of Mozart's Opera.* Illus. Francesca Crespi. New York: Holt. 6–8 yrs.

Hollyer, Belinda. 1995. *Stories from Classical Ballet.* Illus. Sophy Williams. New York: Viking. 10–13 yrs.

Isadora, Rachel (Adapter). 1991. *Swan Lake.* Illus. Rachel Isadora. New York: Putnam. 8–12 yrs.

Kroll, Steven. 1994. *By the Dawn's Early Light: The Story of the Star-Spangled Banner.* Illus. Dan Andreasen. New York: Scholastic. 8–11 yrs.

McCaughrean, G. (Reteller). 1995. *The Random House Book of Stories from the Ballet.* Illus. Angela Barrett. New York: Random. 9–12 yrs.

Price, Leontyne (Reteller). 1990. *Aida.* Illus. Leo & Diane Dillon. San Diego: Harcourt Brace Jovanovich/Gulliver. 8–15 yrs.

Reisfeld, R. 1996. *This Is the Sound: The Best of Alternate Rock.* Photos. New York: Aladdin. 11–16 yrs.

San Souci, Robert (Reteller). 1992. *The Firebird.* Illus. Kris Waldherr. New York: Dial. 6–9 yrs.

Verdy, Violette. 1991. *Of Swans, Sugarplums and Satin Slippers: Ballet Stories for Children.* Illus. Marcia Brown. New York: Scholastic. 7–11 yrs.

Werner, Vivian (Reteller). 1992. *Petrouchka: The Story of the Ballet.* Illus. John Collier. New York: Viking Penguin/Bryon Press. 8–14 yrs.

POPULAR REALISTIC SERIES
(See also Series Listed in Previous Bibliographies)

PRIMARY

Allard, Harry.

Miss Nelson Is Missing. 1977. Illus. James Stevenson. Boston: Houghton Mifflin.

Miss Nelson Has a Field Day. 1985. Illus. James Stevenson. Boston: Houghton Mifflin.

Miss Nelson Is Back. 1982. Illus. James Stevenson. Boston: Houghton Mifflin.

Hughes, Shirley.
The Alfie Collection. 1993. New York: Tupelo.
Alfie Gets in First. 1982. New York: Lothrop, Lee & Shepard.
Alfie's Feet. 1983. New York: Lothrop, Lee & Shepard.
Alfie Gives a Hand. 1984. New York: Lothrop, Lee & Shepard.
An Evening at Alfie's. 1985. New York: Lothrop, Lee & Shepard.

Rylant, Cynthia.
Henry and Mudge: The First Book. 1987. New York: Bradbury.
Henry and Mudge in the Green Time. 1987. New York: Bradbury.
Henry and Mudge Under the Yellow Moon. 1987. New York: Bradbury.
Henry and Mudge in Puddle Trouble. 1987. New York: Bradbury.
Henry and Mudge in the Sparkle Days. 1988. New York: Bradbury.
Henry and Mudge and the Forever Sea. 1989. New York: Bradbury.
Henry and Mudge Get the Cold Shivers. 1989. Bradbury.
Henry and Mudge and the Happy Cat. 1990. New York: Bradbury.
Henry and Mudge Take the Big Test. 1991. New York: Bradbury.
Henry and Mudge and the Long Weekend. 1992. New York: Bradbury.

Smith, Janice Lee.
The Monster in the Third Dresser Drawer. 1981. New York: HarperCollins.
The Kid Next Door and Other Headaches. 1984. New York: HarperCollins.
The Show-and-Tell War: and Other Stories About Adam Joshua. 1988. New York: HarperCollins.
It's Not Easy Being George. 1989. New York: HarperCollins.

INTERMEDIATE

Byars, Betsy.
Blossom Promise. 1982. New York: Delacorte.
Not-Just-Anybody Family. 1986. New York: Delacorte.
Blossoms and the Green Phantom. 1987. New York: Delacorte.
Blossoms Meet the Vulture Lady. 1986. New York: Delacorte.

Cameron, Ann.
Stories Julian Tells. 1981. New York: Pantheon.
More Stories Julian Tells. 1986. New York: Pantheon.
Julian's Glorious Summer. 1987. New York: Pantheon.
Julian, Dream Doctor. 1990. New York: Pantheon.

Cleary, Beverly.
Dear Mr. Henshaw. 1983. New York: Morrow.
Strider. 1991. New York: Morrow.
Ramona, the Brave. 1975. New York: Morrow.
Ramona and Her Father. 1977. New York: Morrow.
Ramona and Her Mother. 1979. New York: Morrow.
Ramona Quimby, Age 8. 1981. New York: Morrow.
Henry Huggins. 1950. New York: Morrow & Avon/Camelot.
Henry and Beezus. 1952. New York: Morrow.
Henry and the Paper Route. 1954. New York: Morrow.
Henry and Ribsy. 1957. New York: Morrow.
Henry and the Clubhouse. 1962. New York: Morrow.

Conford, Ellen.
A Case for Jenny Archer. 1988. Boston: Little, Brown.
A Job for Jenny Archer. 1988. Boston: Little, Brown.
Jenny Archer, Author. 1989. Boston: Little, Brown.
What's Cooking, Jenny Archer? 1989. Boston: Little, Brown.
Jenny Archer to the Rescue. 1990. Illus. Diane Palmisciano. Boston: Little, Brown.
Can Do, Jenny Archer. 1991. Boston: Little, Brown.
Nibble, Nibble, Jenny Archer. 1993. Boston: Little, Brown.

Cooper, Ilene.
Frances Takes a Chance. 1991. New York: Knopf & Knopf/Bullseye.
Frances Dances. 1991. New York: Knopf & Knopf/Bullseye.
Frances Foureyes. 1991. New York: Knopf & Knopf/Bullseye.
Frances and Friends. 1991. New York: Knopf & Knopf/Bullseye.

Hurwitz, Johanna.
Much Ado about Aldo. 1978. New York: Morrow & Penguin/Puffin.
Aldo Applesauce. 1979. New York: Morrow & Penguin/Puffin.
Aldo Ice Cream. 1981. New York: Morrow & Penguin/Puffin.
Aldo Peanut Butter. 1990. New York: Morrow & Penguin/Puffin.
Rip-Roaring Russell. 1983. New York: Morrow.
Russell Rides Again. 1985. New York: Morrow.
Russell and Elisa. 1989. New York: Morrow.
Russell Sprouts. 1987. New York: Morrow.
School's Out. 1992. New York: Morrow.

Kline, Suzy.
Herbie Jones and the Class Gift. 1987. New York: Putnam.
Herbie Jones and the Monster Ball. 1988. New York: Putnam.

Lowry, Lois.
Anastasia Krupnik. 1979. Boston: Houghton Mifflin.
Anastasia Again! 1981. Boston: Houghton Mifflin.
Anastasia at Your Service. 1982. Boston: Houghton Mifflin.
Anastasia, Ask Your Analyst. 1984. Boston: Houghton Mifflin.
Anastasia on Her Own. 1985. Boston: Houghton Mifflin.
Anastasia Has the Answers. 1986. Boston: Houghton Mifflin.
Anastasia and Her Chosen Career. 1987. Boston: Houghton Mifflin.
Anastasia at This Address. 1991. Boston: Houghton Mifflin.
All About Sam. 1988. Boston: Houghton Mifflin.

Martin, Ann.
Baby Sitter's Club. 1986–. New York: Scholastic.

Naylor, Phyllis.
The Agony of Alice. 1985. New York: Atheneum.
Alice in Rapture, Sort of. 1989. New York: Atheneum.
Reluctantly Alice. 1991. New York: Atheneum.
All but Alice. 1992. New York: Atheneum.
Alice in April. 1993. New York: Atheneum.
Alice In-Between. 1994. New York: Atheneum.
Alice in Lace. 1996. New York: Atheneum. 10–13 yrs.

Pascal, Francine.
Sweet Valley High series. 1985–. New York: Bantam.
Sweet Valley Twins series. 1985–. New York: Bantam.

Peck, Robert Newton.
Soup. 1974. New York: Knopf.
Soup and Me. 1975. New York: Knopf.
Soup for President. 1978. New York: Knopf.
Soup's Drum. 1980. New York: Knopf.
Soup on Wheels. 1981. New York: Knopf.
Soup in the Saddle. 1983. New York: Knopf.
Soup's Goat. 1984. New York: Knopf.
Soup on Ice. 1985. New York: Knopf.
Soup on Fire. 1987. New York: Knopf.
Soup's Uncle. 1988. New York: Knopf.
Soup's Hoop. 1990. New York: Knopf.
Soup in Love. 1992. New York: Knopf.

Wilder, Laura Ingalls.
Little House in the Big Woods. 1932. New York: HarperCollins.
Farmer Boy. 1933. New York: HarperCollins.
Little House on the Prairie. 1935. New York: HarperCollins.
On the Banks of Plum Creek. 1939. New York: HarperCollins.
By the Shores of Silver Lake. 1939. New York: HarperCollins.
The Long Winter. 1940. New York: HarperCollins.
Little Town on the Prairie. 1941. New York: HarperCollins.
These Happy Golden Years. 1943. New York: HarperCollins.

ADVANCED

Alcott, Louisa May.
Little Women. 1868. Boston: Little, Brown. (Other editions available.)
Little Men. 1871. (New ed. 1987) New York: Scholastic.
Jo's Boys. 1873. (New ed. 1971) New York: Grosset & Dunlap.

DeClements, Barthe.
Five Finger Discount. 1989. New York: Delacorte.
Monkey See. Monkey Do. 1990. New York: Delacorte.
Breaking Out. 1991. New York: Delacorte.

Fitzgerald, John D.
The Great Brain. 1967. New York: Dial.
More Adventures of the Great Brain. 1969. New York: Dial.
Me and My Little Brain. 1971. New York: Dial.
The Great Brain at the Academy. 1972. New York: Dial.
The Great Brain Reforms. 1973. New York: Dial.
The Return of the Great Brain. 1974. New York: Dial.
The Great Brain Does it Again. 1975. New York: Dial.
The Great Brain Is Back. 1995. Illus. Diane de Groat. New York: Dial. 10–13 yrs.

Greene, Constance C.
A Girl Called Al. 1969. New York: Viking.
I Know You, Al. 1975. New York: Viking.
Your Old Pal, Al. 1979. New York: Viking.
Just Plain Al. 1986. New York: Viking.
Al's Blind Date. 1989. New York: Viking.
Al(exandra) the Great. 1992. New York: Viking.

Knudson, R. R.
Zanballer. 1972. New York: Penguin/Puffin.
Zanbanger. 1977. New York: HarperCollins.
Zanboomer. 1978. New York: HarperCollins.
Zan Hagen's Marathon. 1984. New York: Farrar, Straus & Giroux.

Nixon, Joan Lowery.
The Orphan Train Quartet, 1987–1989. New York: Bantam:
   A Family Apart.
   Caught in the Act.
   In the Face of Danger.
   A Place to Belong.
   A Dangerous Promise. 1994. New York: Delacorte. 12–16 yrs.

CHAPTER 6

CHILDREN'S BOOKS MENTIONED IN THE CHAPTER

Abrams First Impressions Series, such as Rubin, Susan Goldman. 1995. *Frank Lloyd Wright.* New York: Abrams. 12–16 yrs.

Adler, D. 1992. *A Picture Book of Jesse Owens.* New York: Holiday. 6–9 yrs. Picture Book Series.

_____. 1995. *A Picture Book of Patrick Henry.* New York: Holiday. 6–9 yrs. Picture Book Series.

Aliki. 1988. *A Weed Is a Flower: The Life of George Washington Carver.* New York: Simon & Schuster. 7–9 yrs.

_____. 1989. *My Five Senses.* New York: HarperCollins. 4–6 yrs.

Anderson, J. 1993. *Earth Keepers.* Photos George Ancona. San Diego: Gulliver Green. 10–13 yrs.

Anno, M. 1986. *Anno's Counting Book.* New York: Harper & Row. 6–9 yrs.

Ardley, N. 1992. *The Science Book of Energy.* Photos. Dave King. San Diego, Calif.: Gulliver/Harcourt Brace. 10–12 yrs.

Arnold, T. 1995. *Five Ugly Monsters.* New York: Cartwheel. 4–7 yrs. Story Corner series.

Atelsek, J. 1993. *All About Computers.* Illus. Debra Murow. Emeryville, Calif.: Ziff Davis Press. 10–14 yrs.

Bannatyne-Cugnet, Jo. 1992. *Prairie Alphabet.* Illus. Yvette Moore. Plattsburg, N.Y.: Tundra. 8–11 yrs.

Base, G. 1986. *Animalia.* New York: Abrams. 8–11 yrs.

Bauer, M. & E. R. Peyser. 1939. *How Music Grew from Prehistoric Times to the Present Day.* New York: London. 8–12 yrs.

Brandenburg, J. 1993. *To the Top of the World: Adventures with Arctic Wolves.* New York: Walker. 9–12 yrs.

Branley, F. 1989. *What Happened to the Dinosaurs?* Illus. Marc Simont. New York: Crowell. 8–10 yrs. Let's-Read-and-Find-Out Science Books series.

Brooks, B. 1991. *Predator.* Color photos. New York: Farrar, Straus & Giroux. 9–14 yrs.

_____. 1993. *Making Sense: Animal Perception and Communication.* Photos. New York: Farrar, Straus & Giroux. 11–15 yrs. Knowing Nature Series.

Brown, C. 1992. *City Sounds.* New York: Greenwillow. 6–8 yrs.

Brust, B. W. 1992. *The Amazing Paper Cuttings of Hans Christian Andersen.* Photos. New York: Ticknor & Fields. 9–12 yrs.

Bynes, John. 1987. *How Maps Are Made.* Facts on File. 10–14 yrs.

Cherry, L. 1994. *The Armadillo from Amarillo.* Illus. L. Cherry. San Diego, Calif.: Gulliver Green/Harcourt Brace. 9–12 yrs.

Chinery, M. 1994. *Questions and Answers About Seashore Animals.* Illus. Wayne Ford, Mick Loates, & Myke Taylor. New York: Kingfisher. 8–12 yrs.

Christian, M. B. 1993. *Who'd Believe John Colter?* Illus. Laszlo Kubinyi. New York: Macmillan. 10–13 yrs.

Cleary, B. 1988. *A Girl from Yamhill: A Memoir.* New York: Morrow. 11–16 yrs.

_____. 1995. *My Own Two Feet: A Memoir.* New York: Morrow. 12–16 yrs.

Cole, J. 1986. *The Magic School Bus at the Waterworks.* Illus. Bruce Degan. New York: Scholastic. 8–11 yrs.

_____. 1995. *My New Kitten.* Photos Margaret Miller. New York: Morrow. 4–8 yrs.

Cushman, D. 1993. *The ABC Mystery.* New York: HarperCollins. 6–9 yrs.

Daugherty, J. 1939. *Daniel Boone.* New York: Viking. 10–13 yrs.

d'Aulaire, I. & E. d'Aulaire. 1939. *Abraham Lincoln.* New York: Doubleday. 9–12 yrs.

David, R. 1993. *Growing Up in Ancient Egypt.* Mahwah, N.J.: Troll. 8–12 yrs.

Feelings, M. 1975. *Mojo Means One: A Swahili Counting Book.* Illus. Tom Feelings. New York: Dial. 6–9 yrs.

Fenton, C. L. 1935. *Along the Hill.* Cited in Meigs, Eaton, Nesbitt, & Viguers, 1953. *A Critical History of Children's Literature* (p. 527). New York: Macmillan.

Few, R. 1993. *Macmillan Children's Guide to Endangered Animals.* New York: Macmillan. 10–15 yrs.

Filipovic, Z. (Trans. Christina Pribichevich-Zoric). 1994. *Zlata's Diary: A Child's Life in Sarajevo.* Photos. New York: Viking. 10–13 yrs.

Fireside, B. J. 1994. *Is There a Woman in the House . . . or Senate?* Photos. Morton Grove, Ill.: Whitman. 10–13 yrs.

Fish, H. D. 1937. *Animals of the Bible.* Illus. Dorothy Lathrop. New York: Lippincott. 6–10 yrs.

Fisher, L. E. 1995. *Gandhi.* New York: Atheneum. 10–14 yrs.

Fitch, F. 1944. *One God: The Ways We Worship Him.* New York: Lothrop, Lee & Shepard. 11–14 yrs.

Fleischman, P. 1988. *Joyful Noise: Poems for Two Voices.* Illus. Eric Beddows. New York: HarperCollins. 8–12 yrs.

Fleischman, S. 1996. *The Abracadabra Kid.* Photos. New York: Greenwillow. 12–15 yrs.

Fleming, D. 1992. *Count!* New York: Holt. 3–6 yrs.

_____. 1996. *Where Once There Was a Wood.* New York: Utah: Holt. 5–8 yrs.

Foster, G. 1944. *Abraham Lincoln's World.* New York: Scribner's. 10–13 yrs.

Frank, A. 1967. *Anne Frank: Diary of a Young Girl.* New York: Doubleday. 10–16 yrs.

Freedman, R. 1961. *Teenagers Who Made History.* New York: Holiday. 12–16 yrs.

_____. 1969. *How Animals Learn.* New York: Holiday. 8–12 yrs.

_____. 1980. *Immigrant Kids.* New York: Dutton. 8–13 yrs.

_____. 1983. *Children of the Wild West.* New York: Clarion. 10–13 yrs.

_____. 1987. *Lincoln: A Photo Biography.* Burlington, Mass.: Houghton Mifflin. 10–14 yrs.

_____. 1988. *Buffalo Hunt.* New York: Holiday. 9–14 yrs.

_____. 1993. *Eleanor Roosevelt: A Life of Discovery.* Photos & documents. New York: Clarion. 10–13 yrs. 1994 Newbery Honor Book.

Fritz, Jean. 1973. *And Then What Happened, Paul Revere?* Illus. Margot Tomes. New York: Putnam. 9–12 yrs.

_____. 1982. *Homesick: My Own Story.* New York: Putnam. 11–16 yrs.

_____. 1989. *The Great Little Madison.* New York: Putnam. 10–15 yrs.

Garne, S. T. 1994. *One White Sail: A Caribbean Counting Book.* Illus. Lisa Etre. New York: Simon & Schuster. 3–6 yrs.

Gates, P. 1995. *Nature Got There First.* New York: Kingfisher. 9–12 yrs.

Geisert, A. 1992. *Pigs from 1 to 10.* Burlington, Mass.: Houghton Mifflin. 5–8 yrs.

George, J. C. 1971. *All Upon a Stone.* New York: Crowell. 10–13 yrs.

Ghermon, B. 1992. *E. B. White: Some Writer!* New York: Atheneum. 11–15 yrs.

Gibbons, G. 1985. *Check It Out! A Book about Libraries.* San Diego: Harcourt Brace Jovanovich. 6–10 yrs.

_____. 1987. *Deadline! From News to Newspaper.* New York: HarperCollins. 8–12 yrs.

_____. 1987. *Weather Forecasting.* Illus. G. Gibbons. New York: Four Winds. 7–12 yrs.

_____. 1990. *Weather Words and What They Mean.* New York: Holiday. 8–12 yrs.

_____. 1992. *Recycle! A Handbook for Kids.* Boston: Little, Brown. 9–12 yrs.

_____. 1992. *Say Woof!: The Day of a Country Veterinarian.* New York: Macmillan. 6–10 yrs.

Giblin, J. C. 1993. *Cross Be Seated: A Book about Chairs.* Photos. New York: HarperCollins. 10–12 yrs.

Grimes, N. 1995. *C Is for City.* Illus. Pat Cummings. New York: Lothrop, Lee & Shepard. 4–8 yrs.

Grover, M. 1995. *Amazing and Incredible Counting Stories!: A Number of Tall Tales.* San Diego: Harcourt Brace/Browndeer. 7–10 yrs.

Hamilton, V. 1988. *Anthony Burns: The Defeat and Triumph of a Fugitive Slave.* New York: Knopf. 11–15 yrs.

Harris, G. 1990. *Ancient Egypt.* Photos & Illus. New York: Facts on File. 10–16 yrs.

Hatay, N. 1993. *Charlie's ABC.* New York: Hyperion. 3–6 yrs.

Helman, A. 1995. *O Is for Orca: A Pacific Northwest Alphabet Book.* Color Photos. Art Wolfe. Seattle, Wash.: Sasquatch. 5–9 yrs.

Hesse, K. 1992. *Letters from Rifka.* New York: Holt. 11–14 yrs.

Hillyer, V. M. & E. G. Huey. 1933. *A Child's History of Art.* Cited in Meigs, Eaton, Nesbitt, & Viguers, 1953 . *A Critical History of Children's Literature* (p. 575). New York: Macmillan.

Hirschi, R. 1992. *Desert.* Photos. New York: Dell. 7–11 yrs. Discover My World Series.

Hoban, Tana. 1990. *Exactly the Opposite.* Photos. New York: Greenwillow. 2–5 yrs.

Honda, T. 1992. *Wild Horse Winter.* San Francisco, Calif.: Chronicle. 10–12 yrs.

Hubbard, W. 1992. *The Friendship Book.* San Francisco, Calif.: Chronicle. 6–9 yrs.

Jenkins, S. 1995. *Flip-Flap.* New York: Dorling Kindersley. 2–5 yrs.

Johnson, N. 1989. *The Battle of Gettysburg.* New York: Simon & Schuster. 10–14 yrs.

Johnson, S. 1995. *Alphabet City.* Color photos. New York: Viking. 7–10 yrs.

Judson, C. I. 1950. *Abraham Lincoln, Friend of the People.* River Grove, Ill.: Follett. 11–13 yrs.

Kendall, R. 1994. *Russian Girl: Life in an Old Russian Town.* Photos. New York: Scholastic. 8–11 yrs.

Kenna, Kathleen. 1995. *A People Apart.* Photos Andrew Stawicki. Burlington, Mass.: Houghton Mifflin. 9–12 yrs.

Kindersly, B. & A. Kindersly. 1995. *Children Just Like Me.* London: Dorling Kindersley. In association with U.N. Children's Fund. 8–12 yrs.

Kitchen, B. 1992. *Somewhere Today.* Cambridge, Mass.: Candlewick. 8–11 yrs.

Knight, A. S. (Adapter Lillian Schlissel). 1993. *The Way West: Journal of a Pioneer Woman.* Illus. Michael McCurdy. New York: Simon & Schuster. 5–9 yrs.

Langley, G. 1990. *The Age of Dinosaurs.* Illus. Mike Atkinson. Nashville, Tenn.: Ideals Children's Books. 9–12 yrs.

La Prade, E. 1927. *Alice in Orchestralia.* Garden City, N.Y.: Doubleday, Page & Co. 8–12 yrs.

Lasky, K. 1983. *Sugaring Time.* Photos Christopher Knight. New York: Macmillan. 10–14 yrs.

Latham, J. L. 1955. *Carry on Mr. Bowditch.* Illus. J. Cosgrave. Burlington, Mass.: Houghton Mifflin. 10–16 yrs.

Lauber, Patricia. 1986. *Volcano: The Eruption and Healing of Mount St. Helens.* New York: Bradbury. 10–14 yrs.

_____. 1995. *Who Eats What?: Food Chains and Food Webs.* Illus. Holly Keller. New York: HarperCollins. 5–9 yrs.

_____. 1996. *Hurricanes: Earth's Mightiest Storms.* Photos. New York: Scholastic. 9–12 yrs.

Lawrence, R. D. 1990. *Wolves.* Photos Dorothy Siemens. Boston: Sierra/Little, Brown. 8–12 yrs.

Lawson, R. 1939. *Ben and Me.* Boston: Little, Brown. 8–11 yrs.

_____. 1953. *Mr. Revere & I.* Boston: Little, Brown. 8–11 yrs.

_____. 1956. *Captain Kidd's Cat.* Boston: Little, Brown. 8–11 yrs.

Leedy, L. 1992. *The Monster Money Book.* New York: Holiday. 5–8 yrs.

_____. 1995. *2 × 2 = Boo!: A Set of Spooky Multiplication Stories.* New York: Holiday. 6–9 yrs.

Leighton, M. R. 1992. *An Ellis Island Christmas.* Illus. Dennis Nolan. New York: Viking. 9–12 yrs.

Lenski, L. 1934. *The Little Auto.* New York: McKay. 3–6 yrs.

Lester, J. 1973. *To Be a Slave.* Illus. Tom Feelings. New York: Dial. 11–14 yrs.

Levine, E. 1993. *If Your Name Was Changed at Ellis Island.* Illus. Wayne Parmenter. New York: Scholastic. 9–12 yrs.

The Lifesize Animal Counting Book. 1994. Color photos. New York: Dorling Kindersley. 2–5 yrs.

Linton, R. & Adelin. 1947. *Man's Way from Cave to Skyscraper.* Cited in Meigs, Eaton, Nesbitt, & Viguers, 1953. *A Critical History of Children's Literature* (p. 573). New York: Macmillan.

Little, J. 1995. *His Banner Over Me.* New York: Viking. 10–14 yrs.

Macdonald, F. 1991. *A Medieval Cathedral.* Illus. John James. New York: Peter Bedrick. 10–14 yrs.

Martinet, J. 1993. *The Year You Were Born series: 1983; 1984; 1986; 1987.* Illus. Judy Lafredic. New York: Tambourine. 9–12 yrs.

MacKinnon, D. 1993. *How Many?* Photos Anthea Sieveking. New York: Dial. 3–6 yrs.

_____. 1995. *My World of Words.* Photos Geoff Dann. Hauppauge, N.Y.: Barron's. 3–5 yrs.

Mahon, K. L. 1994. *Just One Tear.* New York: Lothrop, Lee & Shepard. 10–14 yrs.

Mason, A. 1994. *The Children's Atlas of Civilizations.* Brookfield, Conn.: Millbrook. 9–16 yrs.

Mayer, W. D. 1993. *Brown Angels: An Album of Pictures and Verse.* Photos. New York: HarperCollins. 8–13 yrs.

Mccauley, D. 1988. *The Way Things Work.* Burlington, Mass.: Houghton Mifflin. 9–16 yrs.

McCloskey, Robert. 1957. *Time of Wonder.* New York: Viking. 8–12 yrs.

Meigs, C. 1968. *Invincible Louisa.* Boston: Little, Brown. 12–16 yrs.

Meltzer, M. 1964–67. *In Their Own Words: A History of the American Negro.* New York: Crowell. (See also 1984, *The Black Americans: A History in Their Own Words,* New York: Crowell. A revision of the three volumes published in 1964–1967.) 11–16 yrs.

Meltzer, M. 1995. *Hold Your Horses! A Feedbag Full of Facts and Fables.* New York: HarperCollins. 8–12 yrs.

Merbrew, W. C. & L. C. Riley. 1996. *Television: What's Behind What You See.* New York: Farrar, Straus, & Giroux. 9–12 yrs.

Merriam, E. 1992. *Goodnight to Annie: An Alphabet Lullaby.* Illus. Carol Schwartz. New York: Hyperion. 3–7 yrs.

_____. 1993. *Twelve Ways to Get to Eleven.* Illus. Bernie Karlin. New York: Simon & Schuster. 5–9 yrs.

Micklethwait, L. 1992. *I Spy: An Alphabet in Art.* Reproductions. New York: Greenwillow. 6–12 yrs.

Millard, A. 1996. *Pyramids.* New York: Kingfisher. 10–16 yrs.

Modesitt, J. 1992. *Sometimes I Feel Like a Mouse: A Book About Feelings.* Illus. Robin Spowart. New York: Scholastic. 6–9 yrs.

Monjo, F. N. 1970. *The One Bad Thing about Father.* Illus. Rocco Negri. New York: Harper & Row. 9–12 yrs.

_____. 1971. *The Vicksburg Veteran.* Illus. Douglas Gorsline. New York: Simon and Schuster. 9–12 yrs.

_____. 1973. *Me and Willie and Pa: The Story of Abraham Lincoln and His Son Tad.* Illus. Douglas Gorsline. New York: Simon & Schuster. 9–12 yrs.

_____. 1973. *Poor Richard in France.* Illus. Brinton Turkle. New York: Dell. 9–12 yrs.

_____. 1974. *Grand Papa and Ellen Aroon.* Illus. Richard Cuffari. New York: Holt, Rinehart & Winston. 9–12 yrs.

_____. 1974. *King George's Head Was Made of Lead.* Illus. Margaret Tomes. New York: Coward, McCann and Geoghegan. 9–12 yrs.

_____. 1975. *Letters to Horseface: Being the Story of Wolfgang Amadeus Mozart's Journey to Italy, 1769–1770, When He Was a Boy of Fourteen.* Illus. Don Bolognese & Elaine Raphael. New York: Viking. 9–12 yrs.

Moss, L. 1995. *Zin! Zin! Zin! A Violin.* Illus. Marjorie Priceman. New York: Simon & Schuster. 6–9 yrs.

Mullins, P. 1994. *V for Vanishing: An Alphabet of Endangered Animals.* New York: HarperCollins. 6–13 yrs.

Murphy, J. 1993. *Across America on an Emigrant Train.* Photographs. New York: Clarion. 12–15 yrs.

_____. 1995. *The Great Fire.* Photos. New York: Scholastic. 10–13 yrs.

_____. 1996. *A Young Patriot: The American Revolution as Experienced by One Boy.* New York: Clarion. 10–14 yrs.

Musgrove, M. 1976. *Ashanti to Zulu: African Traditions.* Illus. Leo & Diane Dillon. New York: Dial. 11–14 yrs.

Myers, Jack (ed.) 1991. *Can Birds Get Lost? And Other Questions About Animals.* Illus. John Rice, Tome & Mimi Powers. Honesdale, Penn.: Boyd Mills. 8–13 yrs.

Myers, W. D. 1993. *Brown Angels: An Album of Pictures and Verses.* Photos. New York: HarperCollins. 6–14 yrs.

Neimark, A. 1992. *Diego Rivera: Artist of the People.* New York: HarperCollins. 10–13 yrs.

Nightingale, S. 1992. *Pink Pigs Aplenty.* Orlando, Fla.: Harcourt Brace. 4–6 yrs.

_____. *Number Pops.* 1995. Snapshot. 2–5 yrs.

Owen's *Meet the Author Collection,* including Rylant, Cynthia. 1992. *Best Wishes.* Photos Carol Ontal. Katonah, N.Y.: Owen. 7–12 yrs. Meet the Author Collection.

Owens, M. B. 1993. *Counting Cranes.* New York: Little, Brown. 6–8 yrs.

Paparone, P. (Illustrator). 1995. *Five Little Ducks: An Old Rhyme.* New York: North-South. 2–5 yrs.

Paschkis, J. 1995. *So Happy/So Sad.* New York: Holt. 6–9 yrs.

Peet, Bill. 1989. *Bill Peet: An Autobiography.* Burlington, Mass.: Houghton Mifflin. 6–13 yrs.

Perl, L. 1989. *The Great Ancestor Hunt.* Photos & drawings Erika Weihs. New York: Clarion. 11–15 yrs.

Petersham, M. & M. Petersham. 1933. *The Story Book of Things We Use.* New York: Doubleday. 7–10 yrs.

Platt, R. 1992. *Stephen Biestys Incredible Cross-Sections.* Illus. Steven Biesty. New York: Knopf. 10–14 yrs.

_____. 1994. *Castle.* Illus. Stephen Biesty. New York: Dorling Kindersley. 10–14 yrs.

Pollock, S. 1995. *The Atlas of Endangered Resources.* New York: Facts on File. 8–12 yrs.

Powell, C. 1995. *A Bold Carnivore: An Alphabet of Predators.* London: Roberts. 5–9 yrs.

Provensen, A. 1995. *My Fellow Americans: A Family Album.* Orlando, Fla.: Harcourt Brace. 9–12 yrs.

Ray, M. L. 1994. *Shaker Boy.* Illus. Jeanette Winter. San Diego: Browndeer/Harcourt Brace. 6–9 yrs.

Reed, W. M. 1930. *The Earth for Sam.* Orlando, Fla.: Harcourt Brace. 6–9 yrs.

Ridington, R. & J. Ridington 1992. *People of the Trail: How Northern Forest Indians Lived.* Illus. Ian Babson. Vancover, B. C.: Douglas & McIntyre Ltd. 10–12 yrs.

Rikys, B. 1992. *Red Bear.* New York: Dial. 2–5 yrs.

Rogasky, B. 1988. *Smoke and Ashes: The Story of the Holocaust.* Photos. New York: Holiday. 12–16 yrs.

Rosher, J. 1992. *Ancient Egypt.* New York: Viking. 10–14 yrs.

Roth, S. L. 1991. *Marco Polo: His Notebook.* New York: Doubleday. 8–12 yrs.

Rotner, S. 1996. *Action Alphabet.* Photos. New York: Atheneum. 3–6 yrs.

Ryan, P. M. 1994. *One Hundred Is a Family.* Illus. Benrei Huang. New York: Hyperion. 4–6 yrs.

Sanders, E. 1995. *"What's Your Name?" From Ariel to Zoe.* Illus. Marilyn Sanders. New York: Holiday. 5–9 yrs.

Say, A. 1993. *Grandfather's Journey.* Burlington, Mass.: Houghton Mifflin. 7–11 yrs.

Schami, R. (Trans. R. Lesser). 1989. *A Hand Full of Stars.* New York: Dutton. 11–14 yrs.

Scieszka, J. 1995. *Math Curse.* Illus. Lane Smith. New York: Viking. 7–10 yrs.

Selsam, M. E. 1966. *Benny's Animals, and How He Put Them in Order.* Illus. Arnold Lobel. New York: Harper. 6–9 yrs.

Sharmat, M. W. 1992. *The 329th Friend.* Illus. Cyndy Szekeres. New York: Four Winds. 5–9 yrs.

Sharratt, N. 1995. *Rocket Countdown.* Cambridge, Mass.: Candlewick. 2–5 yrs.

Siebert, D. 1988. *Mojave.* Illus. Wendell Minor. New York: Crowell. 9–13 yrs.

_____. 1989. *Heartland.* Illus. Wendell Minor. New York: Crowell. 8–13 yrs.

Simon, S. 1988. *Galaxies.* Color photos. New York: Mulberry. 7–12 yrs.

_____. 1992. *Snakes.* Color photos. New York: HarperCollins. 7–11 yrs.

_____. 1996. *The Heart: Our Circulatory System.* Photos. New York: Morrow. 9–12 yrs.

_____. 1996. *Wildfires.* New York: Morrow. 9–14 yrs.

Sobol, R. and J. Sobol. 1993. *Seal Journey.* Photos Richard Sobol. New York: Cobblehill. 5–9 yrs.

Stanley, D. 1996. *Leonardo da Vinci.* New York: Morrow. 9–12 yrs.

Stanley, D. & P. Vennema. 1994. *Cleopatra.* Illus. Diane Stanley. New York: Morrow. 9–11 yrs.

Stanley, J. 1992. *Children of the Dust Bowl.* Photos. New York: Crown. 10–13 yrs.

Sturges, P. 1995. *Ten Flashing Fireflies.* Illus. Anna Vojtech. New York: North-South. 5–9 yrs.

Sullivan, C. 1992. *Numbers at Play: A Counting Book.* Paintings & photos. New York: Rizzoli. 7–12 yrs.

Tresselt, A. 1948. *White Snow, Bright Snow.* Illus. Roger Duvoisin. New York: Lothrop, Lee & Shepard. 5–8 yrs.

Turner, G. T. 1989. *Take a Walk in Their Shoes.* Illus. Elton C. Fax. New York: Puffin. 11–14 yrs.

Udry, J. M. 1957. *A Tree Is Nice.* Illus. Marc Simont. New York: HarperCollins. 4–7 yrs.

UNICEF. 1994. *I Dream of Peace: Images of War Children of Former Yugoslavia.* Illus. & photographs. New York: UNICEF/HarperCollins. 11–16 yrs.

United Nations Editors. 1994. *Rescue Mission Planet Earth: A Children's Edition of Agenda 21.* New York: Kingfisher. 9–16 yrs.

Updike, J. 1995. *A Helpful Alphabet of Friendly Objects.* Photos David Updike. New York: Knopf. 5–9 yrs.

Wallwork, A. 1993. *No Dodos: A Counting Book of Endangered Animals.* New York: Scholastic. 5–7 yrs.

Ward, G. C. & K. Burns, with P. R. Walker. 1994. *Baseball the American Epic: Who Invented the Game?* Photos. New York: Knopf. 10–16 yrs.

Weems, Mason. 1880. *The Life and Memorable Acts of George Washington.* Cited in Sutherland, Zena & Arbuthnot, May H. 1991. *Children and Books.* (8th Ed.). New York: HarperCollins. p. 455.

Weston, M. 1992. *Bea's Four Bears.* New York: Clarion. 3–6 yrs.

Whatley, B. & R. Smith. 1995. *Whatley's Quest.* Illus. Bruce Whatley. New York: HarperCollins. 5–9 yrs.

Whiteley, O. (Selector Jane Boulton). 1994. *Only Opal: The Diary of a Young Girl.* Illus. Barbara Cooney. New York: Philomel. 5–9 yrs.

Willard, N. 1981. *A Visit to William Blake's Inn: Poems for Innocent and Experienced Travelers.* Illus. Alice & Martin Provensen. Orlando, Fla.: Harcourt Brace. 10–14 yrs.

Van Loon, H. W. 1921. *The Story of Mankind.* New York: Liveright. 12–17 yrs.

Viorst, J. 1994. *The Alphabet from Z to A: (With Much Confusion on the Way).* Illus. Richard Hull. New York: Atheneum. 8–13 yrs.

Yates, E. 1951. *Amos Fortune, Free Man.* New York: Aladdin. 12–14 yrs.

Zim, H. S. & S. Bleeker. 1970. *Life and Death.* Illus. Rene Martin. New York: Morrow. 9–12 yrs.

NONFICTION LITURATURE ORGANIZED ACCORDING TO HISTORICAL PERIODS

ANTIQUITY: 3,000 B.C.–500 A.D.

Biographies

Lattimore, Deborah Nourse. 1991. *The Sailor Who Captured the Sea: A Story of the Book of Kells.* Illus. Deborah Nourse Lattimore. New York: HarperCollins. 7–10. Fictionalized. Notable 1991 Children's Trade Books in the Field of Social Studies.

Stanley, Diane & Peter Vennema. 1994. *Cleopatra.* Illus. Diane Stanley. New York: Morrow. 9–11 yrs.

Information Books

Baquedano, Elizabeth. 1993. *Aztec, Inca, and Maya.* Photos Michael Zabe & David Rudkin. New York: Knopf. 10 yrs.–adult.

Beattie, Owen & John Geiger, with Shelley Tanaka. 1992. *Buried in Ice.* New York: Scholastic/Madison. 8–12 yrs.

Courtalon, Corinne. 1988. *On the Banks of the Pharaoh's Nile.* Ossining, N.Y.: Young Discovery. 7–11 yrs.

David, Rosalie. 1993. *The Giant Book of the Mummy.* New York: Lodestar/Dutton. 8–12 yrs.

——. 1993. *Growing Up in Ancient Egypt.* Mahwah, N.J.: Troll. 8–12 yrs.

Dawson, Imogen. 1994. *Food and Feasts in the Middle Ages.* Photos. Morristown, N.J.: Silver Burdett/New Discovery. 10–14 yrs. Food and Feasts Series.

Der Manuelian, Peter. 1993. *Hieroglyphs from A to Z.* New York: Rizzoli. 8–13 yrs.

Giblin, James Cross. 1990. *The Riddle of the Rosetta Stone.* New York: Crowell. 10–14 yrs.

Harris, Geraldine. 1990. *Ancient Egypt.* Photos & illus. New York: Facts on File. 10–16 yrs.

Hicks, Peter. 1995. *Sports and Entertainment.* New York: Thomson. 10–13 yrs. Legacies series.

Isaacson, Philip M. 1993. *A Short Walk Around the Pyramids and Through the World of Art.* Photos. New York: Knopf. 10 yrs.–adult. Notable Children's Trade Books in the Field of Social Studies 1994.

James, Simon. 1992. *Ancient Rome.* New York: Viking/Penguin. 8–12 yrs.

Koenig, Vivian. 1992. *The Ancient Egyptians.* Illus. Veronique Ageorges. Brookfield, Conn.: Millbrook. 10–15 yrs.

Lasky, Kathryn. 1989. *Traces of Life: The Origins of Humankind.* Illus. Whitney Powell. New York: Morrow. 10–16 yrs.–adult.

Lazo, Caroline. 1993. *Terra Cotta Army of Emperor Qin.* Morristown, N.J.: Silver Burdett/New Discovery. 10–14 yrs.

Leroi-Gourhan, Andre. (Trans. Claire Jacobson). 1989. *The Hunters of Prehistory.* New York: Atheneum. 10–15 yrs. Notable 1989 Children's Trade Books in the Field of Social Studies.

Loverance, Rowena. 1993. *Ancient Greece.* Illus. Bill LeFever & others. New York: Viking. 10 yrs.–adult. Notable Children's Trade Books in the Field of Social Studies 1993.

Macdonald, Fiona. 1995. *A Samurai Castle.* Illus. David Antram & John James. New York: Bedrick. 9–12 yrs. Inside Story series.

——. 1995. *A Viking Town.* Illus. Mark Bergin. New York: Bedrick. 9–12 yrs. Inside Story series.

Martell, H. M. 1995. *The Kingfisher Book of the Ancient World: From the Ice Age to the Fall of Rome.* New York: Kingfisher. 9–12 yrs.

Meyer, Carolyn, and Charles Gallenkamp. 1995. *The Mystery of the Ancient Maya.* New York: McElderry. 12–16 yrs.

Place, R. 1995. *Bodies from the Past.* New York: Thomson Learning: Digging Up the Past series.

Putnam, Jim. 1993. *Mummy.* Illus. Peter Hayman. New York: Knopf. 10–17 yrs. Notable Children's Trade Books in the Field of Social Studies 1994.

Reeves, Nicholas. 1992. *Into the Mummy's Tomb.* New York: Scholastic. 9–12 yrs.

Roehrig, Catherine. 1990. *Fun with Hieroglyphs.* New York: Viking. 9–16 yrs.

Sattler, Helen Roney. 1993. *The Earliest Americans.* Illus. Jean Day Zallinger. New York: Clarion. 10–16 yrs. Notable Children's Trade Books in the Field of Social Studies 1994.

Steele, Philip. 1994. *Food and Feasts in Ancient Rome.* Photos. Morristown, N.J.: Silver Burdett/New Discovery. 10–14 yrs. Food and Feasts Series.

Trumble, K. 1996. *Cat Mummies.* Illus. Laszlo Kubinyi. New York: Clarion. 9–12 yrs.

Wilcox, Charlotte. 1993. *Mummies & Their Mysteries.* Photos. Minneapolis, Minn.: Carolrhoda. 10–13 yrs. Outstanding Science Trade Books for Children for 1994; Notable Children's Trade Books in the Field of Social Studies 1994.

PREHISTORIC LIFE

Aliki. 1990. *Fossils Tell of Long Ago.* Illus. Aliki. New York: Crowell. 6–10. Let's-Read-and-Find-Out Science Book; Outstanding Science Trade Books for Children in 1990.

Arnold, Caroline. 1993. *Dinosaurs All Around: An Artist's View of the Prehistoric World.* Photos Richard Hewett. New York: Clarion. 10–12 yrs.

Branley, Franklyn. 1989. *What Happened to the Dinosaurs?* Illus. Marc Simont. New York: Crowell. 8–10 yrs. Let's-Read-and-Find-Out Science Books series; Notable Children's Trade Books in Science, 1989.

Dixon, Dougal. 1993. *Dougal Dixon's Dinosaurs.* Photos and prints. Honesdale, Penn.: Boyds Mill. 10–16 yrs. Outstanding Science Trade Books for Children for 1994.

Funston, Sylvia. 1992. *Dinosaur Question and Answer Book.* Boston: Little, Brown. 9–12 yrs.

Lasky, Kathryn. 1990. *Dinosaur Dig.* Photos Christopher G. Knight. New York: Morrow. 8–11 yrs. Outstanding Science Trade Books for Children in 1990.

Lauber, Patricia. 1989. *The News about Dinosaurs.* New York: Simon & Schuster/Bradbury. 8–12 yrs.

Lindsay, William. 1991. *Great Dinosaur Atlas.* Illus. Giulano Fornari. Morristown, N.J.: Silver Burdett/Julian Messner. 9–12 yrs.

McGowan, Chris. 1993. *Discover Dinosaurs.* Reading, Mass.: Addison Wesley. 8–12 yrs.

Most, Bernard. 1989. *The Littlest Dinosaurs.* Illus. B. Most. San Diego: Harcourt Brace Jovanovich. 4–7 yrs.

Mullins, Patricia. 1993. *Dinosaur Encore.* New York: HarperCollins/Perlman. 5–8 yrs.

Peters, David. 1989. *A Gallery of Dinosaurs and Other Early Reptiles.* Illus. D. Peters. New York: Knopf/Borzoi. 8–12 yrs. Notable Children's Trade Books in Science, 1989.

Sattler, Helen Roney. 1990. *The New Illustrated Dinosaur Dictionary.* Illus. Joyce Powzyk. New York: Lothrop, Lee & Shepard. 7 yrs.–adult.

——. 1992. *Stegosaurs.* Illus. Turi MacCombie. New York: Lothrop, Lee & Shepard. 9–13 yrs.

Simon, Seymour. 1990. *New Questions and Answers about Dinosaurs.* Illus. Jennifer Dewey. New York: Morrow. 6–12 yrs.

Whitfield, Philip. 1992. *Macmillan Children's Guide to Dinosaurs and Other Prehistoric Animals.* New York: Macmillan. 9–12 yrs.

The Visual Dictionary of Dinosaurs. 1993. Photos Andy Crawford. New York: Dorling Kindersley. 10 yrs.–adult.

MIDDLE AGES: 500 AD–16TH CENTURY

Biographies

Aliki. 1989. *The King's Day: Louis XIV of France.* New York: Crowell. 7–11 yrs.

Brooks, Polly Schoyer. 1983. *Queen Eleanor, Independent Spirit of the Medieval World: A Biography of Eleanor of Aquitaine.* New York: Lippincott. 12–16 yrs.

——. 1990. *Beyond the Myth: The Story of Joan of Arc.* New York: Lippincott. 12–16 yrs.

Dramer, Kim. 1990. *Kublai Khan.* New York: Chelsea House. 10–14 yrs.

Fisher, Leonard Everett. 1993. *Gutenberg.* New York: Macmillan. 10–12 yrs.

Fritz, Jean. 1994. *Around the World in a Hundred Years: From Henry the Navigator to Magellan.* Illus. Anthony Bacon Venti. New York: Putnam. 10–14 yrs.

Hull, Mary. 1995. *The Travels of Marco Polo.* San Diego: Lucent. 12–16 yrs.

Roth, Susan L. 1991. *Marco Polo: His Notebook.* New York: Doubleday. 8–12 yrs. Fictionalized version

Simon, Charnan. 1991. *Leif Eriksson and the Vikings: The Norse Discovery of America.* Danbury, Conn.: Children's Press. 10–14 yrs.

Information Books

Adams, Brian. 1989. *Medieval Castles.* New York: Watts. 9–12 yrs.

Andronik, Catherine M. 1989. *Quest for a King: Searching for the Real King Arthur.* New York: Atheneum. 10–15 yrs.

Biesty, Stephen. 1994. *Stephen Biesty's Cross-Sections Castle.* New York: Dorling Kindersley. 7–14 yrs.

Caselli, Giovanni. 1987. *A Cathedral Builder.* New York: Peter Bedrick. 10–13 yrs.

_____. 1988. *The Middle Ages.* New York: Peter Bedrick. 10–13 yrs.

Clare, John D. (Ed.) 1992. *The Vikings.* Photos. San Diego: Gulliver. 10–16 yrs.

_____. 1993. *Fourteenth Century Town.* San Diego: Harcourt Brace. 10–16 yrs.

Clements, Gillian. 1990. *The Truth about Castles.* Illus. Gillian Clements. Minneapolis, Minn.: Carolrhoda. 7–11 yrs.

Corbishley, Mike. 1990. *Cultural Atlas for Young People: The Middle Ages.* New York: Facts On File. 10–14 yrs.

Gravett, Christopher. 1993. *Knight.* Photos Geoff Dann. New York: Knopf. 10 yrs.–adult.

Howarth, Sarah. 1992. *Medieval People.* Brookfield, Conn.: Millbrook. 10–13 yrs.

_____. 1993. *The Middle Ages.* New York: Viking. 10–13 yrs.

Howe, J. (Illustrator). 1995. *Knights.* New York: Orchard. 9–12 yrs. Paper engineering.

Lasker, Joe. 1986. *A Tournament of Knights.* New York: HarperCollins. 8–13 yrs.

Macaulay, David. 1973. *Cathedral: The Story of Its Construction.* Boston: Houghton Mifflin. 9–13 yrs.

_____. 1977. *Castle.* Boston: Houghton Mifflin. 9–13 yrs.

Macdonald, Fiona. 1991. *A Medieval Cathedral.* Illus. John James. New York: Peter Bedrick. 10–14 yrs. (See other books in the Inside Story series: *A Greek Temple; An Egyptian Pyramid; A Roman Fort.*)

_____. 1993. *The Middle Ages.* New York: Facts on File. 10–15 yrs.

Maestro, Betsy & Giulio. 1991. *The Discovery of the Americas.* New York: Mulberry. 9–13 yrs.

McKissack, Patricia & Fredrick McKissack. 1994. *The Royal Kingdoms of Ghana, Mali and Songhay: Life in Medieval Africa.* Photos. New York: Holt. 12–16 yrs.

Osband, Gillian. 1991. *Castles.* Illus. Robert Andrew. New York: Orchard. 9–12 yrs.

Pearson, Anne. 1994. *The Vikings.* Color photos. New York: Viking. 10–13 yrs. See also Through History series.

Perdrizet, Marie-Pierre. 1992. *The Cathedral Builders.* Illus. Eddy Krahenbuhl. Brookfield, Conn.: Millbrook. 10–14 yrs.

Ruby, Jennifer. 1990. *Costume in Context: Medieval Times.* North Pomfret, Vt.: Trafalgar/Batsford, U.K. 11–14 yrs.

Steele, Philip. 1995. *Castles.* Color illus. New York: Kingfisher. 10–13 yrs.

Wilson, Elizabeth B. 1994. *Bibles and Bestiaries: A Guide to Illuminated Manuscripts.* New York: Farrar, Straus & Giroux. 11–15 yrs.

Yue, Charlotte & David Yue. 1994. *Armour.* Boston: Houghton Mifflin. 11–14 yrs.

THE WORLD IN THE 1490S

Biographies

Adler, David A. 1991. *A Picture Book of Christopher Columbus.* Illus. John & Alexandra Wallner. New York: Holiday. 8–12 yrs.

Alper, Ann Fritzpatrick. 1991. *Forgotten Voyager: The Story of Amerigo Vespucci.* Minneapolis, Minn.: Carolrhoda. 9–13 yrs.

Anderson, Joan. 1991. *Christopher Columbus: From Vision to Voyage.* Photos George Ancona. New York: Dial. 7–10 yrs.

Fisher, Leonard Everett. 1990. *Prince Henry the Navigator.* Illus. L. E. Fisher. New York: Macmillan. 10–14 yrs.

Levinson, Nancy Smiler. 1990. *Christopher Columbus: Voyager to the Unknown.* New York: Lodestar/Dutton. 9–12 yrs.

Meltzer, Milton. 1990. *Columbus and the World Around Him.* Danbury, Conn.: Watts. 10–14 yrs.

Sis, Peter. 1991. *Follow the Dream.* Illus. Peter Sis. New York: Knopf. 7–12 yrs.

West, Delno C. & Jean M. West. 1991. *Christopher Columbus.* New York: Atheneum. 11–15 yrs.

Information Books

Brenner, Barbara. 1991. *If You Were There in 1492.* Illus. Julie Downing. New York: Simon & Schuster.

Columbus, Christopher (Selector Steve Lowe). 1992. *The Log of Christopher Columbus: The First Voyage: Spring, Summer and Fall, 1492.* Illus. Robert Sabuda. New York: Philomel. 6–12 yrs.

Finkelstein, Norman H. 1989. *The Other 1492.* New York: Beech Tree. 10–16 yrs.

Howarth, Sarah. 1993. *The Middle Ages.* Illus. Bill LeFever and others. New York: Viking. 10–16 yrs.

Jacobs, Francine. 1992. *The Tinos.* New York: Putnam. 10–17 yrs.

Lauber, Patricia. 1992. *Who Discovered America? Mysteries and Puzzles of the New World.* Illus. Mike Eagle. New York: HarperCollins. 8–11 yrs.

Maestro, Betsy. 1991–92. *The Discovery of the Americas. The Discovery of the Americas Activities Book.* Illus. Giulio Maestro. New York: Lothrop, Lee & Shepard. 7–10 yrs.

Marzollo, Jean. 1991. *In 1492.* Illus. Steve Bjorkman. New York: Scholastic. 7–9 yrs.

Roop, Peter & Connie Roop (Ed.). 1990. *I, Columbus: My Journal 1492–3.* Illus. Peter E. Hanson. Walker. 9–12 yrs.

Ventura, Piero. 1992. *1492, The Year of the New World.* New York: Putnam. 10–16 yrs.

17TH CENTURY: U.S. PILGRIMS AND COLONIAL PERIOD (1645–1700S)

Biography

Kessel, Joyce K. 1983. *Squanto and the First Thanksgiving.* Illus. Lisa Donze. Minneapolis, Minn.: Carolrhoda. 7–11 yrs.

Information Books

Barrett, T. 1995. *Growing Up in Colonial America.* Black-and-white reproductions. Brookfield, Conn.: Millbrook. 9–12 yrs. American Children series.

George, Jean Craighead. 1993. *The First Thanksgiving.* Illus. Thomas Locker. New York: Philomel. 5–9 yrs.

Penner, Recht. 1991. *Eating the Plates.* New York: Macmillan. 8–11 yrs.

San Souci, Robert. 1991. *N. C. Wyeth's Pilgrims.* Illus. from Wyeth's murals. San Francisco: Chronicle. 10–14 yrs.

Sewell, Marcia. 1990. *People of the Breaking Day.* Illus. M. Sewell. New York: Atheneum. 9–12 yrs.

Waters, Kate. 1989. *Sarah Morton's Day: A Day in the Life of a Pilgrim Girl.* Photos Russ Kendall. New York: Scholastic. 5–9 yrs.

_____. 1993. *Samuel Eaton's Day: A Day in the Life of a Pilgrim Boy.* Photos Russ Kendall. New York: Scholastic. 6–9 yrs.

18TH CENTURY: U.S. PIONEER AND REVOLUTIONARY PERIOD

Biographies

Adler, David A. 1990. *A Picture Book of Benjamin Franklin.* Illus. John & Alexandra Wallner. New York: Holiday. 7–10 yrs.

_____. 1990. *A Picture Book of Thomas Jefferson.* Illus. John & Alexandra Wallner. New York: Holiday. 7–10 yrs.

_____. 1995. *A Picture Book of Paul Revere.* Illus. John & Alexandra Wallner. New York: Holiday. Picture Book Biography series.

Fritz, Jean. 1992. *George Washington's Mother.* Illus. DyAnne DiSalvo-Ryan. New York: Grosset & Dunlap. 7–9 yrs.

Giblin, James Cross. 1992. *George Washington: A Picture Book Biography.* Illus. Michael Dooling. New York: Scholastic. 5–8 yrs.

_____. 1994. *Thomas Jefferson: A Picture Book Biography.* Illus. Michael Dooling. New York: Scholastic. 7–10 yrs.

Martin, Joseph Plumb. (Ed. George F. Scheer.) 1995. *Yankee Doodle Boy: A Young Soldier's Adventures in the American Revolution Told Himself.* Illus. Victor Mays. New York: Holiday. 10–13 yrs.

Meltzer, Milton. 1986. *George Washington and the Birth of Our Nation.* Danbury, Conn.: Watts. 10–14 yrs.

_____ 1988. *Benjamin Franklin: The New American.* Danbury, Conn.: Watts. 12–14 yrs.

_____. 1992. *Thomas Jefferson: The Revolutionary Aristocrat.* Danbury, Conn.: Watts. 12–14 yrs.

Osborne, Mary Pope. 1990. *The Many Lives of Benjamin Franklin.* New York: Dial. 9–12 yrs.

_____. 1991. *George Washington.* New York: Dial. 10–14 yrs.

Wallner, Alexandra. 1994. *Betsy Ross.* Illus. A. Wallner. New York: Holiday. 7–9 yrs.

Information Books

Brenner, Barbara. 1994. *If You Were There in 1776.* Photos. New York: Simon & Schuster/Bradbury. 9–12 yrs.

Dolan, E. F. 1995. *The American Revolution: How We Fought the War of Independence.* Archival black-and-white illus. Brookfield, Conn.: Millbrook. 9–12 yrs.

Grant, R. G. 1995. *1848: Year of Revolution.* Color reproductions & maps. New York: Thomson Learning. 9–12 yrs. Revolution! series.

19TH CENTURY

World: Biographies

Marrin, Albert. 1991. *Napoleon and the Napoleonic Wars.* New York: Viking/Penguin. 10–15 yrs.

Milton, Nancy. 1992. *The Giraffe That Walked to Paris.* Illus. Roger Roth. New York: Crown. 9–11 yrs.

Wormser, Richard. 1990. *Pinkerton: America's First Private Eye.* Walker. 10–13 yrs.

U.S.: Biographies

Blumberg, Rhoda. 1992. *Jumbo.* Illus. Jonathan Hunt. New York: Simon & Schuster/Bradbury. 9–12 yrs.

_____. 1993. *Bloomers!* Illus. Mary Morgan. New York: Bradbury. 5–8 yrs.

Christian, Mary Blount. 1993. *Who'd Believe John Colter?* Illus. Laszlo Kubinyi. New York: Macmillan. 10–13 yrs. (fictionalized).

Fradin, Dennis Brindell. 1992. *Hiawatha: Messenger of Peace.* New York: McElderry. 12–15 yrs.

McPherson, Stephanie Sammartino. 1994. *Peace and Bread: The Story of Jane Addams.* Minneapolis, Minn.: Carolrhoda. 10–15 yrs.

Ray, Mary Lyn. 1994. *Shaker Boy.* Illus. Jeanette Winter. San Diego: Browndeer/Harcourt Brace. 6–9 yrs. (fictionalized)

Roop, Peter & Connie Roop. (Eds.). 1993. *Off the Map: The Journals of Lewis and Clark.* Illus. Tim Tanner. New York: Walker. 10–13 yrs.

Rowland, Della. 1989. *The Story of Sacajawea, Guide to Lewis and Clark*. Illus. Richard Leonard. New York: Dell/Yearling. 11–13 yrs.

Salmon, Marylynn. 1994. *The Limits of Independence: American Women, 1760–1800*. New York: Oxford. 12–17 yrs.

Sigerman, Harriet. 1994. *Laborers for Liberty: America's Women, 1865–1890*. New York: Oxford. 12–17 yrs.

Information Books

Blake, Arthur, & Pamela Dailey. 1995. *The Gold Rush of 1849: Staking a Claim in California*. Art & photos. Danbury, Conn.: Millbrook. 10–13 yrs. Spotlight on American History series.

Christiansen, Candace. 1993. *The Ice Horse*. Illus. Thomas Locker. New York: Dial. 6–12 yrs.

Duncan, Lois. 1993. *The Circus Comes Home: When the Greatest Show on Earth Rode the Rails*. Photos Joseph Janney Steinmetz. New York: Doubleday. 10–13 yrs.

Harness, Cheryl. 1995. *The Amazing Impossible Erie Canal*. New York: Macmillan. 6–9 yrs.

Langley, Andrew. 1994. *The Industrial Revolution*. New York: Viking. 10–13 yrs. See Through History series

U.S. CIVIL WAR ERA

(SEE ALSO "SLAVERY" BIBLIOGRAPHY IN CHAPTER 9)

Biographies

Archer, Jules. 1995. *A House Divided: The Lives of Ulysses S. Grant and Robert E. Lee*. New York: Scholastic. 10+ yrs.

Freedman, Russell. 1987. *Lincoln: A Photobiography*. Photos. Boston: Houghton Mifflin. 10–14 yrs.

Marrin, Albert. 1994. *Unconditional Surrender: U. S. Grant and the Civil War*. New York: Atheneum. Photos. 12–15 yrs.

Meltzer, Milton (Ed.). 1993. *Lincoln in His Own Words*. Illus. Stephen Alcorn. San Diego: Harcourt Brace. 10–16 yrs.

Read, Thomas Buchanan. 1993. *Sheridan's Ride*. Illus. Nancy Winslow Parker. New York: Greenwillow. 10–16 yrs.

Stevens, Bryna. 1992. *Frank Thompson: Her Civil War Story*. B & W photographs and reproductions. New York: Macmillan. 10–12 yrs.

Sullivan, George. 1994. *Mathew Brady: His Life and Photographs*. Photos. New York: Cobblehill. 12–15 yrs.

Turner, Ann. 1987. *Nettie's Trip South*. Illus. Ronald Himler. New York: Macmillan. 9–12 yrs.

Wisler, G. Clifton. 1991. *Red Cap*. New York: Lodestar/Dutton. 12–15 yrs.

Information Books

Ashabranner, Brent. 1992. *A Memorial for Mr. Lincoln*. Photos Jennifer Ashabranner. New York: Putnam. 10–15 yrs.

Bolotin, N. & A. Herb. 1995. *For Home and Country: A Civil War Scrapbook*. New York: Lodestar/Dutton. 9–12 yrs. Young Reader's History of the Civil War series.

Chang, Ina. 1991. *A Separate Battle: Women and the Civil War*. New York: Lodestar/Dutton. 12–15 yrs.

Cox, Clinton. 1991. *Undying Glory: The Story of the Massachusetts 54th Regiment*. New York: Scholastic. 12–15 yrs.

Fleischman, Paul. 1993. *Bull Run*. Woodcuts David Frampton. New York: HarperCollins. 10–16 yrs.

Hansen, Joyce. 1993. *Between Two Fires: Black Soldiers in the Civil War*. Prints & photos. Danbury, Conn.: Watts. Adult.

Lincoln, A. 1995. *The Gettysburg Address*. Illus. Michael McCurdy. Burlington, Mass.: Houghton Mifflin. 7–11 yrs.

Ray, Delia. 1991. *Behind the Blue and Gray: The Soldier's Life in the Civil War*. New York: Lodestar/Dutton. 10–15 yrs.

St. George, Judith. 1991. *Mason and Dixon's Line of Fire*. New York: Putnam. 10–15 yrs.

Smith, Carter (Ed.). 1993. *One Nation Again: A Sourcebook on the Civil War*. Danbury, Conn.: Millbrook. 10–16 yrs.

_____. 1993. *1863: The Crucial Year*. Danbury, Conn.: Millbrook. 10 yrs–adult.

_____. 1993. *The First Battles*. Danbury, Conn.: Millbrook. 10 yrs–adult.

_____. 1993. *Prelude to War*. Danbury, Conn.: Millbrook. 10 yrs–adult.

U.S. WESTERN EXPANSION

Biographies

Conrad, Pam. 1991. *Prairie Visions: The Life and Times of Solomon Butcher*. Photos Solomon Butcher. New York: HarperCollins. 11–14 yrs.

Cox, Clinton. 1993. *The Forgotten Heroes: The Story of the Buffalo Soldiers*. Prints & photos. New York: Scholastic. 10–16 yrs.

Harvey, Brett. 1986. *My Prairie Year*. New York: Holiday. 10–14 yrs.

Herda, D. J. 1995. *Outlaws of the American West*. Photos. Danbury, Conn.: Millbrook. 10–13 yrs.

Klausner, Janet. 1993. *Sequoyah's Gift: A Portrait of the Cherokee Leader*. New York: HarperCollins. 10–12 yrs.

Knight, Amelia Stewart (Adaptor Lillian Schlissel). 1993. *The Way West: Journal of a Pioneer Woman*. Illus. Michael McCurdy. New York: Simon & Schuster. 5–9 yrs.

Kroll, Steven. 1996. *Pony Express!* Illus. Dan Andreasen. New York: Scholastic. 8–10 yrs.

Lavender, D. 1996. *Snowbound: The Tragic Story of the Donner Party*. Photos. New York: Holiday. 10–15 yrs.

Madsen, Susan Arrington. 1994. *I Walked to Zion: True Stories of Young Pioneers on the Morman Trail*. Salt Lake City: Cinnamon Tree/Deseret. 11–14 yrs.

Miller, Brandon Marie. 1995. *Buffalo Gals: Women of the Old West*. Minneapolis, Minn.: Lerner. 10–13 yrs.

Murphy, Jim. 1995. *The Great Fire*. Photos. New York: Scholastic. 10–13 yrs.

Murphy, V. R. (Ed. Karen Zeinert). 1996. *Across the Plains in the Donner Party*. With letters by James Reed. Photos. Linnet. 11–16 yrs.

Russell, Marion (Adaptor Ginger Wadsworth). 1993. *Along the Santa Fe Trail: Marion Russell's Own Story*. Illus. James Watling. Morton Grove, Ill.: Whitman. 10–16 yrs.

San Souci, R. D. 1995. *Kate Shelley: Bound for Legend*. Illus. Max Ginsburg. New York: Dial. 5–8 yrs.

Young, Carrie. 1991. *Nothing to Do But Stay: My Pioneer Mother*. University of Iowa Press. 12–15 yrs.

Information Books

Alter, Judith. 1989. *Growing up in the Old West*. Danbury, Conn.: Franklin Watts/First Books. 8–12 yrs.

Anderson, Joan. 1989. *Spanish Pioneers of the Southwest*. Photos George Ancona. New York: Lodestar/Dutton. 10–12 yrs.

Bial, Raymond. 1993. *Frontier Home*. Color photos R. Bial. Boston: Houghton Mifflin. 9–13 yrs.

Brown, Lois. 1993. *Tales of the Wild West*. New York: Rizzoli. 12–16 yrs.

Cobb, Mary. 1995. *The Quilt-Block History of Pioneer Days: With Projects Kids Can Make*. Illus. Jan Davey Ellis. Brookfield, Conn.: Millbrook. 10–13 yrs.

Erickson, Paul. 1994. *Daily Life in a Covered Wagon*. Color photos. Washington, D.C.: Preservation. 10–13 yrs.

Fraser, Mary Ann. 1995. *In Search of the Grand Canyon*. B&W drawings. New York: Holt. 10–13 yrs. Redfeather series.

Granfield, Linda. 1994. *Cowboy: An Album*. Photos. New York: Ticknor & Fields. 9–13 yrs.

Greenlaw, M. Jean. 1993. *Ranch Dressing: The Story of Western Wear*. Photos. New York: Lodestar/Dutton. 9–16 yrs.

Greenwood, Barbara. 1995. *A Pioneer Sampler: The Daily Life of a Pioneer Family in 1840*. Illus. Heather Collins. New York: Ticknor & Fields. 10–12 yrs.

Marrin, Albert. 1993. *Cowboys, Indians, and Gunfighters: The Story of the Cattle Kingdom*. New York: Atheneum. 12–15 yrs.

Morris, Juddi. 1994. *The Harvey Girls: The Women Who Civilized the West*. Photos. New York: Walker. 12–14 yrs.

Patent, D. H. 1995. *West by Covered Wagon: Retracing the Pioneer Trails*. Color photos & illus. William Munzo. New York: Walker. 9–12 yrs.

Rounds, Glen. 1995. *Sod Houses on the Great Plain*. New York: Holiday. 6–9 yrs.

Scott, Ann Herbert. 1993. *Cowboy Country*. Illus. Ted Lewin. New York: Clarion. 5–9 yrs.

Steedman, Scott. 1994. *A Frontier Fort on the Oregon Trail*. New York: Bedrick. 10–13 yrs.

Sullivan, Charles. 1993. *Cowboys*. Archival & contemporary photos. New York: Rizzoli. 8–12 yrs.

Woodruff, Elvira. 1994. *Dear Levi: Letters from the Overland Trail*. Illus. Beth Peck. New York: Knopf. 8–12 yrs.

Van Der Linde, Laurel. 1993. *The Pony Express*. Photos. New York: Simon & Schuster. 11–14 yrs.

20TH CENTURY: EARLY 1900s

Biographies: World

Hesse, Karen. 1992. *Letters from Rifka*. New York: Holt. 11–14 yrs.

Kherdian, David. 1979. *The Road from Home: The Story of an Armenian Girl*. New York: Greenwillow. 12–16 yrs.

Rappaport, Doreen. (Ed.). 1990. *American Women: Their Lives in Their Words*. New York: HarperCollins. 11–16 yrs.

Biographies: U.S.

Adler, David A. 1991. *A Picture Book of Eleanor Roosevelt*. Illus. Robert Casilla. New York: Holiday. 8–12 yrs.

Blos, Joan. 1991. *The Heroine of the Titanic: A Tale both True and Otherwise of the Life of Molly Brown*. Illus. Tennessee Dixon. New York: Morrow. 10–13 yrs.

Brown, F. G. 1995. *Daisy and the Girl Scouts: The Story of Juliette Gordon Low*. Photos & drawings. Morton Grove, Ill.: Whitman. 8–12 yrs.

Coleman, Penny. 1994. *Mother Jones and the March of the Mill Children*. Brookfield, Conn.: Millbrook. 10–13 yrs.

Collins, David. 1991. *Charles Lindbergh: Hero Pilot*. New York: Chelsea House. 9–12 yrs.

Cowen, Ida & Irene Gunther. 1985. *Spy for Freedom: The Story of Sarah Aaronsohn*. New York: Lodestar/Dutton. 11–13 yrs.

Freedman, Russell. 1993. *Eleanor Roosevelt: A Life of Discovery*. Photos & documents. New York: Clarion. 10–13 yrs.

Fritz, J. 1995. *You Want Women to Vote, Lizzie Stanton?* Illus. DyAnne DiSalvo-Ryan. New York: Putnam. 9–12 yrs.

Haskins, James. 1986. *Shirley Temple Black: Actress to Ambassador.* Illus. Donna Ruff. New York: Viking. 7–11 yrs.

Houston, Gloria. 1992. *My Great-Aunt Arizona.* Illus. Susan Condie Lamb. New York: HarperCollins. 5–9 yrs.

Hyatt, P. R. 1995. *Coast to Coast with Alice.* Photos. Minneapolis, Minn.: Carolrhoda. 9–12 yrs.

Meltzer, Milton. 1985. *Dorothea Lange: Life Through the Camera.* Illus. Donna Diamond. New York: Viking. 10–14 yrs.

Osinski, Alice. 1989. *Franklin D. Roosevelt.* Danbury, Conn.: Childrens. 9–12 yrs.

Quackenbush, Robert. 1990. *Clear the Cow Pasture, I'm Coming in for a Landing: A Story of Amelia Earhart.* New York: Simon & Schuster. 7–9 yrs. (See also Pearce, Carol, *Amelia Earhart,* New York: Facts on File and Lauber, Patricia, *Lost Star: The Story of Amelia Earhart,* New York: Scholastic)

Stanley, Jerry. 1992. *Children of the Dust Bowl: The True Story of the School at Weedpatch Camp.* Photos. New York: Crown. 10–13 yrs.

Stevenson, James. 1994. *Fun/No Fun.* New York: Greenwillow. 5–9 yrs.

Warren, A. 1996. *Orphan Train Rider: One Boy's True Story.* Photos. Burlington, Mass.: Houghton Mifflin. 9–14 yrs.

Whiteley, Opal (Selector Jane Boulton). 1994. *Only Opal: The Diary of a Young Girl.* Illus. Barbara Cooney. New York: Philomel. 5–9 yrs.

Information: World

Parker, N. W. 1996. *Locks, Crocs, & Skeeters: The Story of the Panama Canal.* New York: Greenwillow. 9–12 yrs.

Tanaka, S. 1996. *On Board the Titanic.* Illus. Ken Marschall. New York: Hyperion/Madison. 9–12 yrs. I Was There Books.

Information Books: U.S.

Bosco, Peter. 1991. *World War I.* New York: Facts on File. 12–14 yrs.

Goldston, Robert. 1978. *The Road Between the Wars: 1918–1941.* New York: Dial. 12–14 yrs.

Jantzen, Steven L. 1990. *Hooray for Peace, Hurrah for War: The United States During World War I.* New York: Facts on File. 12–14 yrs.

Levinson, Nancy Smiler. 1994. *Turn of the Century: Our Nation One Hundred Years Ago.* Reproductions, b & w photos. New York: Lodestar/Dutton. 10–13 yrs.

Meltzer, Milton. 1991. *Brother, Can You Spare a Dime? The Great Depression, 1929–1933.* New York: Facts On File. 12–15 yrs.

Our Century: 1900–1910. 1993. Milwaukee, Wisc.: Gareth Stevens. B&W photos. 9–11 yrs. (See also *Our Century: 1910–1920*)

Schraff, Anne E. 1990. *The Great Depression and the New Deal: America's Economic Collapse and Recovery.* Danbury, Conn.: Watts. 12–14 yrs.

Wallner, Alexandra. 1992. *Since 1920.* Illus. A. Wallner. New York: Doubleday. 8–12 yrs.

WORLD WAR II ERA

Biographies & Information Books: World

Besson, J. (Trans. Carol Volk). 1995. *October 45: Childhood Memories of the War.* Orlando, Fla.: Creative/Harcourt Brace. 9–12 yrs. (France)

Colman, Penny. 1995. *Rosie the Riveter: Women Working on the Home Front in World War II.* B & W photos. New York: Crown. 10–13 yrs.

Ippisch, Hanneke. 1996. *Sky: A True Story of Resistance During World War II.* New York: Simon & Schuster. 12–16 yrs.

Katz, William Loren, & Marc Crawford. 1989. *The Lincoln Brigade: A Picture History.* New York: Atheneum. 12–16 yrs. (Spanish Civil War, 1936–39).

Lawson, Don. 1980. *An Album of World War II Home Fronts.* Danbury, Conn.: Watts. 12–16 yrs.

Marx, Trish. 1994. *Echoes of World War II.* Photos. Minneapolis, Minn.: Lerner. 11–15 yrs.

Sherrow, Victoria. 1992. *Amsterdam.* New York: Simon & Schuster. 10–12 yrs. Cities at War series

———. 1992. *London.* New York: Simon & Schuster. 10–12 yrs. Cities at War series

Biographies U.S.

Deschamps-Adams, Helene (Ed. Karyn Monget). 1995. *Spyglass: An Autobiography.* New York: Holt. 12–18 yrs. Edge Series.

Nicholson, Dorinda Makanaonalani Stagner. 1993. *Pearl Harbor Child: A Child's View of Pearl Harbor—from Attack to Peace.* Photos. Honolulu: Arizona Memorial Museum Association. 11–14 yrs.

Stevenson, James. 1986. *When I Was Nine.* New York: Greenwillow. 7–11 yrs.

———. 1987. *Higher on the Door.* New York: Greenwillow. 7–11 yrs.

———. 1992. *Don't You Know There's A War On?* Illus. J. Stevenson. New York: Greenwillow. 9–12 yrs.

Information Books U.S.

Baker, Patricia. 1992. *Fashions of a Decade: The 1940s.* Illus. Robert Price. New York: Facts On File. 10–14 yrs.

Devaney, John. 1991. *America Goes to War: 1941; America Fights the Tide: 1942; America on the Attack: 1943.* New York: Walker. 12–16 yrs.

———. 1995. *America Triumphs: 1945.* B & W Photos. New York: Walker. 12–16 yrs. World War II series.

Duden, Jane. 1989. *1940s.* Morristown, N.J.: Silver Burdett. 12–15 yrs.

Finkelstein, Norman H. 1993. *Sounds in the Air: The Golden Age of Radio.* New York: Scribners. 12–16 yrs.

Krull, Kathleen. 1995. *V Is for Victory: America Remembers World War II.* New York: Knopf/Apple Soup. 10–12 yrs.

Leonard, Thomas M. 1977. *Day by Day: The Forties.* New York: Facts on File. Adult.

Our Century: 1940–1950. 1993. Milwaukee, Wisc.: Gareth Stevens. 12–16 yrs.

Whitman, Sylvia. 1992. *"V" Is for Victory: The American Home Front during World War II.* Prints & photos. Minneapolis, Minn.: Lerner. 10–16 yrs.

JEWISH EXPERIENCES DURING WORLD WAR II

Biographies

Adler, David A. 1993. *A Picture Book of Anne Frank.* Illus. Karen Ritz. New York: Holiday. 8–12 yrs.

———. 1994. *Hilde and Eli: Children of the Holocaust.* Illus. Karen Ritz. New York: Holiday. 8–12 yrs.

Atkinson, Linda. 1985. *In Kindling Flame: The Story of Hannah Senesh, 1921–1944.* New York: Lothrop, Lee & Shepard. 12–15 yrs.

Bernheim, Mark. 1980. *Father of the Orphans: The Story of Janusz Korczak.* New York: Lodestar/Dutton. 11–16 yrs. Jewish Biography series.

Bresnick-Perry, Roslyn. 1993. *Leaving for America.* Illus. Mira Reisberg. Danbury, Conn.: Children's Press. 6–9 yrs.

Drucker, Malka & Michael Halperin. 1993. *Jacob's Rescue: A Holocaust Story.* New York: Bantam Doubleday Dell. 10–16 yrs.

Frank, Anne. 1967. *Anne Frank: Diary of a Young Girl.* New York: Doubleday. 10–16 yrs.

Greenfeld, Howard. 1993. *The Hidden Children.* Photos. New York: Ticknor & Fields. 10–14 yrs.

Haas, G. 1995. *Tracking the Holocaust.* Archival photos & maps. Minneapolis, Minn.: Lerner/Runestone. 9–12 yrs.

Handler, Andrew & Susan V. Meschel. (Compilers). 1993. *Young People Speak: Surviving the Holocaust in Hungary.* Prints & photos. Danbury, Conn.: Watts. Adult.

Ippisch, H. 1996. *Sky: A True Story of Resistance During World War II.* Photos & documents. New York: Simon & Schuster. 11–16 yrs.

Kosterina, Nina (Trans. Mira Ginsburg). 1970. *The Diary of Nina Kosterina.* Camelot. 12–16 yrs.

Leitner, Isabella & Irving A. Leitner. 1992. *The Big Lie: A True Story.* Illus. Judy Pedersen. New York: Scholastic. 10–12 yrs.

Linnea, Sharon. 1993. *Raoul Wallenberg: The Man Who Stopped Death.* Philadelphia, Penn.: Jewish Publication Society. 12–15 yrs.

Perl, L. & M. B. Lazan. 1996. *Four Perfect Pebbles: A Holocaust Story.* Photos. New York: Greenwillow. 11–15 yrs.

Toll, Nelly S. 1993. *Behind the Secret Window.* New York: Dial. 12 yrs.–adult.

Van der Rol, Ruud, & Rian Verhoeven. 1993. *Anne Frank: Beyond the Diary, a Photographic Remembrance.* New York: Viking. 12–16 yrs.

Information Books

Adler, David A. 1989. *We Remember the Holocaust.* New York: Holt. 11–15 yrs.

Backrach, Susan D. 1994. *Tell Them We Remember: The Story of the Holocaust.* Photos from U.S. Holocaust Memorial Museum. Boston: Little, Brown. 10–15 yrs.

Oppenheim, Shulamith Levey. 1992. *The Lily Cupboard.* Illus. Ronald Himler. New York: HarperCollins. 8–11 yrs.

Rosenberg, Maxine B. 1994. *Hiding to Survive: Stories of Jewish Children Rescued from the Holocaust.* Photos. New York: Clarion. 11–15 yrs.

1950s TO LATE 1980s

(SEE ALSO CIVIL RIGHTS BIBLIOGRAPHY IN CHAPTER 9)

Biographies

Atkin, S. Beth. 1993. *Voices from the Fields: Children of Migrant Farmworkers Tell Their Stories.* Photos S. B. Atkin. Boston: Joy Street/Little, Brown. 10–17 yrs.

Fleming, Tom. 1993. *Harry S. Truman, President.* Photos. New York: Walker. 10–13 yrs.

Medina, Juan. 1992. *A Migrant Family.* Photos Larry Dane Brimner. Minneapolis, Minn.: Lerner. 9–12 yrs.

Rappaport, Dorreen. 1993. *Tinker vs. Des Moines: Student Rights on Trial.* New York: HarperCollins. 12–15 yrs.

Information Books

Backrach, Susan D. 1994. *Tell Them We Remember: The Story of the Holocaust.* Photos from United States Holocaust Memorial Museum. Boston: Little, Brown. 10–15 yrs.

Becker, Elizabeth. 1992. *America's Vietnam War: A Narrative History.* New York: Clarion. 12–16 yrs.

Denenberg, Barry. 1995. *Voices from Vietnam.* New York: Scholastic. 12–16 yrs.

Hoobler, Dorothy & Thomas Hoobler. 1990. *Vietnam: Why We Fought: An Illustrated History.* New York: Knopf/Borzoi. 10–15 yrs.

Marrin, Albert. 1992. *America and Vietnam: The Elephant and the Tiger.* New York: Viking. 12–16 yrs.

Myers, Walter Dean. 1993. *A Place Called Heartbreak: A Story of Vietnam.* Illus. Frederick Porter. Chatham, N.J.: Raintree/Steck-Vaughn. 10–14 yrs. (Stories of America)

Warren, James. 1990. *A Portrait of a Tragedy: America and the Vietnam War.* Photos J. Warren. New York: Lothrop, Lee & Shepard. 11–16 yrs.

Wormser, Richard L. 1993. *Three Faces of Vietnam.* Photos. Danbury, Conn.: Watts. 12–16 yrs.

CONTEMPORARY PERIOD

Biographies

Ashabranner, Brent. 1994. *A New Frontier: The Peace Corps in Eastern Europe.* Photos Paul Conklin. New York: Cobblehill. 10–16 yrs.

Filipovic, Zlata (Trans. Christina Pribichevich-Zoric). 1994. *Zlata's Diary: A Child's Life in Sarajevo.* Photos. New York: Viking. 10–13 yrs.

Schami, Rafik. (Trans. Rika Lesser). 1989. *A Hand Full of Stars.* New York: Dutton. 11–14 yrs.

Senna, Carl. 1992. *Colin Powell: A Man of War and Peace.* New York: Walker. 8–12 yrs.

Information Books

Cozic, Charles P. (Compiler). 1994. *Israel: Opposing Viewpoints.* San Diego: Greenhaven. 12–16 yrs. (Opposing Viewpoints).

Greenberg, K. 1994. *Terrorism: The New Menace.* Brookfield, Conn.: Millbrook. 12–16 yrs.

King, John. 1991. *The Gulf War.* Morristown, N.J.: Dillon/Silver Burdett. 10–15 yrs.

Morris, Ann. 1990. *When Will the Fighting Stop? A Child's View of Jerusalem.* Photos Lilly Rivlin. New York: Atheneum. 8–12 yrs.

Salak, John, III. 1993. *The Los Angeles Riots: America's Cities in Crisis.* Brookfield, Conn.: Millbrook. 12–17 yrs.

UNICEF. 1994. *I Dream of Peace: Images of War Children of Former Yugoslavia.* Photos & illus. New York: UNICEF/HarperCollins. 11 yrs. and up.

BIOGRAPHIES AND INFORMATION BOOKS ORGANIZED ACCORDING TO TOPIC

ADVENTURERS

Ash, Ruth, & Deborah Gore Ohrn. (Eds.) (Introduction Gloria Steinem.) 1995. *Herstory: Women Who Changed the World.* Photos & drawings. New York: Viking. 12–18 yrs.

Blos, Joan W. 1996. *Nellie Bly's Monkey: His Remarkable Story in His Own Words.* Illus. Catherine Stock. New York: Morrow. 7–11 yrs.

Chrisp, P. 1995. *The Whalers.* Color photos & re-productions. New York: Thomson Learning. 9–12 yrs. Remarkable World series.

Jacobs, Francine. 1994. *A Passion for Danger: Nansen's Artic Adventures.* Illus. & photos. New York: Putnam. 11–15 yrs.

Marrin, Albert. 1995. *The Sea King: Sir Francis Drake and His Times.* New York: Atheneum. 10–12 yrs.

McCully, E. A. 1995. *The Pirate Queen.* New York: Putnam. 9–12 yrs.

Rappaport, Doreen. 1991. *Living Dangerously: American Women Who Risked Their Lives for Adventure.* New York: HarperCollins. 9–13 yrs.

Stanley, Diane. 1995. *The True Adventure of Daniel Hall.* New York: Dial. 9–12 yrs.

Stefoff, Rebecca. 1992. *Women of the World.* New York: Oxford. 10–16 yrs.

Van Meter, V. & D. Gutman. 1995. *Taking Flight: My Story.* New York: Viking. 9–12 yrs.

Wood, Ted. 1996. *Iditarod Dream: Dusty and His Sled Dogs Compete in Alaska's Jr. Iditarod.* Photos Ted Wood. New York: Walker. 9–12 yrs.

Information Books

Crisman, Ruth. 1993. *Racing the Iditarod Trail.* Morristown, N.J.: Dillon/Silver Burdett. 10–13 yrs.

Brandenburg, Jim. (Ed. Joann Bren Guernsey). 1995. *An American Safari: Adventures on the North American Prairie.* Color photos. New York: Walker. 9–12 yrs.

Lincoln, M. 1995. *The Pirate's Handbook.* Petersborough, NH: Cobblehill. 9–12 yrs.

Pirotta, S. 1995. *Pirates and Treasure.* Color photos & reproductions. New York: Thomson Learning. 9–12 yrs. Remarkable World series.

Platt, Richard. 1995. *Pirate.* Photos Tina Chambers. New York: Knopf. 10–14 yrs. Eyewitness series.

Wulffson, Don L. 1989. *More Incredible True Adventures.* New York: Cobblehill. 9–12 yrs.

———. 1991. *Amazing True Stories.* Illus. John R. Jones. New York: Cobblehill. 9–12 yrs.

ARCHITECTURE

Biographies

Boulton, Alexander O. 1993. *Frank Lloyd Wright, Architect: A Picture Biography.* New York: Rizzoli. 11–16 yrs.

Hudson, Karen. 1993. *Paul R. Williams, Architect.* New York: Rizzoli. 10–15 yrs.

Rubin, Susan Goldman. 1994. *Frank Lloyd Wright.* New York: Abrams. 12–17 yrs. First Impressions Series.

Information Books

Arnold, Caroline. 1992. *The Ancient Cliff Dwellers of Mesa Verde.* Photos Richard Hewett. New York: Clarion. 8–13 yrs.

Ancona, George. 1995. *Cutters, Carvers, and the Cathedral.* Color photos. New York: Lothrop, Lee & Shepard. 9–12 yrs.

Ashabranner, Brent. 1992. *A Memorial for Mr. Lincoln.* Photos Jennifer Ashabranner. New York: Putnam. 12–16 yrs.

Bial, Raymond. 1993. *Amish Home.* Color photos. Boston: Houghton Mifflin. 9–13 yrs.

———. 1994. *Shaker Home.* Color photos. Boston: Houghton Mifflin. 10–12 yrs.

Boring, Mel. 1985. *Incredible Constructions and the People Who Built Them.* New York: Walker. 11–14 yrs.

Brown, David J. 1992. *The Random House Book of How Things Were Built.* New York: Random House. 11–14 yrs.

Churchill, E. Richard. 1990. *Building with Paper.* New York: Sterling. 11–16 yrs.

Clinton, Susan. 1986. *I Can Be an Architect!* Danbury, Conn.: Children's Press. 9–12 yrs.

Conrad, P. 1995. *Our House: The Stories of Levittown.* Illus. Brian Selznick. New York: Scholastic. 9–12 yrs.

Crosbie, Michael J. & Steve Rosenthal. 1993. *Architecture Shapes.* Washington, D.C.: Preservation Press. 6–10 yrs. (See also *Architecture Colors, Architecture Counts.*)

D'Alelio, Jane. 1989. *I Know That Building! Discovering Architecture with Activities and Games.* Washington, D.C.: Preservation Press. 8–11 yrs.

Dorros, Arthur. 1992. *This Is My House.* New York: Scholastic. 5–10 yrs.

Eisen, David. 1992. *Fun With Architecture.* New York: Viking. 10–16 yrs.

Gaughenbaugh, Michael & Herbert Camburn. 1993. *Old House, New House: A Child's Exploration of American Architectural Styles.* Illus. Herbert Camburn. Washington, D.C.: Preservation Press. 10–14 yrs.

Gibbons, Gail. 1986. *Up Goes the Skyscraper!* New York: Four Winds/Aladdin. 6–8 yrs.

———. 1990. *How a House Is Built.* Illus. Gail Gibbons. New York: Holiday. 6–8 yrs.

Giblin, James Cross. 1988. *Let There Be Light: A Book about Windows.* Photos and prints. New York: HarperCollins. 11–16 yrs. (See also *The Skyscraper Book,* New York: HarperCollins.)

———. 1993. *Be Seated: A Book about Chairs.* Photos. New York: HarperCollins. 10–12 yrs.

Glenn, Patricia. 1993. *Under Every Roof: A Kids' Style and Field Guide to the Architecture of American Houses.* Illus. Joe Stites. Washington, D.C.: Preservation Press. 10–15 yrs.

Hernandez, Xavier. 1992. *San Rafael: A Central American City Through the Ages.* Illus. Jordi Ballonga & Josep Escofet. Boston: Houghton Mifflin. 11–16 yrs. (See also *Barmi: A Mediterranean City through the Ages* and *Lebek: A City of Northern Europe through the Ages,* Boston: Houghton Mifflin.)

Hogner, Franz. 1986. *From Blueprint to House.* Minneapolis, Minn.: Carolrhoda. 5–9 yrs.

Isaacson, Philip M. 1988. *Round Buildings, Square Buildings, and Buildings That Wiggle like a Fish.* Photos P. M. Isaacson. New York: Knopf. 10–16 yrs.

Macaulay, David. 1980. *Unbuilding.* Boston: Houghton Mifflin. 9–16 yrs. (See also *Cathedral, Castle, and City,* Boston: Houghton Mifflin.)

Manning, M. 1994. *A Ruined House.* Cambridge, Mass.: Candlewick. 6–8 yrs. Read and Wonder series.

Morris, Ann. 1992. *Houses and Homes.* Photos Ken Heyman. New York: Lothrop, Lee & Shepard. 7–9 yrs.

Platt, Richard. 1992. *Incredible Cross-Sections.* Illus. Stephen Biesty. New York: Knopf. 10–15 yrs.

Radford, Derek. 1992. *Building Machines and What They Do.* Cambridge, Mass.: Candlewick. 5–7 yrs.

Rickard, Graham. 1989. *Mobile Homes.* Minneapolis, Minn.: Lerner. 7–10 yrs.

Robbins, Ken. 1991. *Bridges.* Color photos K. Robbins. New York: Dial. 5–9 yrs.

Seltzer, Isadore. 1992. *The House I Live In: At Home in America.* New York: Macmillan. 6–10 yrs.

Ventura, Piero. 1993. *Houses: Structures, Method, and Ways of Living.* Boston: Houghton Mifflin. 8–11 yrs.

The Visual Dictionary of Buildings. 1993. Photos and illus. New York: Dorling Kindersley. 9–14 yrs. Eyewitness Visual Dictionary Series.

Weiss, Harvey. 1988. *Shelters: From Tepee to Igloo.* New York: HarperCollins. 8–13 yrs.

Wilkinson, Philip. 1993. *Amazing Buildings.* Illus. Paola Donati & Studio Illibill. New York: Dorling Kindersley. 9–14 yrs.

———. 1995. *Building.* Photos Dave King & Geoff Dann. New York: Knopf. 10–13 yrs. Eyewitness Series.

Williamson, Ray A. & Jean Guard Monroe. 1993. *First Houses: Native American Homes and Sacred Structures.* Boston: Houghton Mifflin. 9–13 yrs.

Wood, Richard. 1995. *Architecture.* New York: Thomson Learning. 10–13 yrs. Legacies Series.

Zelver, Patricia. 1994. *The Wonderful Towers of Watts.* Illus. Frank Lessac. New York: Tambourine. 5–8 yrs.

CONSERVATION, ECOLOGY, AND RAIN FORESTS

Biographies: Naturalists, Biologists

Dewey, Jennifer Owings. 1994. *Wildlife Rescue: The Work of Dr. Kathleen Ramsay.* Honesdale, Penn.: Boyds Mills. 9–11 yrs.

Forsyth, Adrian. 1988. *Through A Tropical Jungle.* New York: Simon & Schuster. 10–14 yrs.

Heinrich, Bernd. 1990. *An Owl in the House: A Naturalist's Diary.* Boston: Little, Brown. 10–14 yrs.

Krensky, Stephen. 1992. *Four Against the Odds: The Struggle to Save Our Environment.* New York: Scholastic. 10–14 yrs.

Ransom, Candice F. 1993. *Listening to Crickets: A Story About Rachel Carson.* Illus. Shelly O. Haas. Minneapolis, Minn.: Carolrhoda. 10–13 yrs.

Ring, Elizabeth. 1993. *Henry David Thoreau: In Step with Nature.* Sketches, pictures, journal excerpt. Brookfield, Conn.: Millbrook. 10–14 yrs. Gateway Greens Biography.

Shulman, Jeffrey & Teresa Rogers. 1992. *Gaylord Nelson: A Day for the Earth.* New York: 21st Century. 9–12 yrs.

Wadsworth, Ginger. 1992. *Rachel Carson: Voice for the Earth.* Photos. Minneapolis, Minn.: Lerner. 10–12 yrs.

Information Books

Aldis, Rodney. 1992. *Town and Cities.* Photos, illus., maps. Morristown, N.J.: Dillon/Silver Burdett. 10–13 yrs. Ecology Watch Series.

Amsel, Sherri. 1992. *A Wetland Walk.* Illus. S. Amsel. Brookfield, Conn.: Millbrook. Unpaged. 7–9 yrs.

Anderson, Joan. 1993. *Earth Keepers.* Photos George Ancona. San Diego, Calif.: Harcourt Brace/Gulliver Green. 10–13 yrs.

Arnosky, Jim. 1989. *In the Forest: A Portfolio of Paintings.* Illus. J. Arnosky. New York: Lothrop, Lee & Shepard. 6–10 yrs.

Baker, Lucy. 1990. *Life in the Rain Forests.* New York: Scholastic. 10–12 yrs.

Benson, Laura Lee. 1994. *This Is Our Earth.* Illus. John Carrozza. Watertown, Mass.: Charlesbridge. 7–9 yrs.

Brown, Laurie Krasny & Marc Brown. 1992. *Dinosaurs to the Rescue!: A Guide to Protecting Our Planet.* Illus. Marc Brown. Boston: Joy Street. 5–8 yrs.

Cherry, Lynne. 1990. *The Great Kapok Tree.* San Diego: Harcourt Brace. 4–8 yrs.

———. 1992. *A River Ran Wild: An Environmental History.* San Diego: Harcourt Brace/Gulliver. 10–12 yrs.

Chief Seattle. 1991. *Brother Eagle, Sister Sky: A Message from Chief Seattle.* Illus. Susan Jeffers. New York: Dial. 9–16 yrs.

Clements, Andew. 1992. *Mother Earth's Counting Book.* Illus. Lonni Sue Jonson. New York: Simon & Schuster/Picture Book Studio. 7–10 yrs.

Cone, Molly. 1992. *Come Back, Salmon: How a Group of Dedicated Kids Adopted Pigeon Creek and Brought It Back to Life.* Photos Sidnee Wheelwright. San Francisco, Calif.: Sierra Club. 9–12 yrs.

Cowcher, Helen. 1988. *Rain Forests.* New York: Farrar, Straus & Giroux. 6–12 yrs.

Cowcher, Helen & Jeannie Baker. 1987. *Where the Forest Meets the Sea.* New York: Greenwillow. 6–12 yrs.

Dolan, Edward F. 1991. *Our Poisoned Sky.* New York: Cobblehill. 10–16 yrs.

Dorros, Arthur. 1990. *Rain Forest Secrets.* Illus. A. Dorros. New York: Scholastic. 6–9 yrs.

Dunphy, Madeline. 1993. *Here Is the Arctic Winter.* Illus. Alan James Robinson. New York: Hyperion. 8–11 yrs.

Durell, Ann, Jean Craighead George, & Katherine Paterson. (Eds.). 1993. *The Big Book for Our Planet.* New York: Dutton. 8–12 yrs. (Ecology)

Edwards, Richard. 1993. *The Tall Oaktrees.* Illus. Caroline Crossland. New York: Tambourine. 5–9 yrs.

Elkington, John, Julia Hailes, Douglas Hill, & Joel Makower. 1990. *Going Green: A Kid's Handbook to Saving the Planet.* Illus. Tony Ross. New York: Viking/Penguin/Tilden. 8–12 yrs.

George, Jean Craighead. 1990. *One Day in the Tropical Rain Forest.* New York: Crowell. 8–12 yrs.

Geraghty, Paul. 1992. *Stop that Noise!* Illus. P. Geraghty. New York: Crown. 9–12 yrs.

Gibbons, G. 1993. *Nature's Tree Umbrella: Tropical Rain Forests.* New York: Holt. 6–8 yrs.

Godkin, Celia. 1993. *Wolf Island.* Illus. C. Godkin. New York: Freeman/Scientific American. 7–11 yrs.

Holmes, Anita. 1993. *I Can Save the Earth: A Kid's Handbook for Keeping Earth Healthy and Green.* Illus. David Neuhaus. Morristown, N.J.: Silver Burdett/Julian Messner. 9–12 yrs.

Iverson, Diane. 1993. *I Celebrate Nature.* Illus. D. Iverson. Nevada City, Calif.: Dawn Publishing. 6–9 yrs.

Jam, Teddy. 1993. *The Year of Fire.* Illus. Ian Wallace. New York: McElderry. 10–13 yrs.

Johnson, Rebecca L. 1990. *The Greenhouse Effect.* Charts, diagrams & photos. Minneapolis, Minn.: Lerner. 12–16 yrs.

Kalman, Bobbie. 1991. *Kid Heroes of the Environment.* Berkeley, Calif.: Earth Works. 9–12 yrs.

———. 1991. *Reducing, Reusing, and Recycling.* New York: Crabtree. 8–12 yrs.

Koch, Michelle. 1993. *World Water Watch.* Illus. M. Koch. New York: Greenwillow. 5–9 yrs.

Lasky, Kathryn. 1992. *Surtsey: The Newest Place on Earth.* Photos Christopher G. Knight. New York: Hyperion. 8–12 yrs.

Lauber, Patricia. 1991. *Summer of Fire: Yellowstone 1988.* New York: Orchard. 9 yrs.–adult.

Lewington, Anna (Adapter). 1993. *Antonio's Rain Forest.* Photos Edward Parker. Minneapolis, Minn.: Carolrhoda. 10–16 yrs.

Lewis, Barbara. 1991. *Kid's Guide to Social Action.* Minneapolis, Minn.: Free Spirit. 9–13 yrs.

Lord, Suzanne. 1993. *Garbage: The Trashiest Book You'll Ever Read.* New York: Scholastic. 9–12 yrs.

Love, Ann & Jane Drake. 1992. *Take Action: An Environmental Book for Kids.* Illus. Pat Cupples. New York: Tambourine. 9–12 yrs. World Wildlife Fund.

Lowery, Linda, & Marybeth Lorbiecki. 1993. *Earthwise at School.* Illus. David Mataya. Minneapolis, Minn.: Carolrhoda. 9–12 yrs. (See also other books in series.)

Mallory, Kenneth. 1992. *Water Hole: Life in a Rescued Tropical Forest.* Danbury, Conn.: Watts. 9–12 yrs.

Matthews, Downs. 1993. *Arctic Summer.* Photos Dan Guravich. New York: Simon & Schuster. 8–11 yrs.

McVey, Vicki. 1993. *The Sierra Club Kid's Guide to Planet Care and Repair.* Illus. Martha Weston. San Francisco: Sierra Club. 10–16 yrs.

Mullins, Patricia. 1994. *V for Vanishing: An Alphabet of Endangered Animals.* Illus. P. Mullins. New York: HarperCollins. 7–16 yrs.

Patent, D. H. 1996. *Children Save the Rain Forest.* Photos Dan L. Perlman. New York: Cobblehill. 11–14 yrs.

Perez, Ed. 1993. *A Look Around Rain Forests.* Photos Mel Crawford. St. Petersburg, Fla.: Willowisp. 9–12 yrs.

Petrash, Carol. 1992. *Earthways: Simple Environmental Activities for Young Children.* Beltsville, Md.: Gryphon House. 9–12 yrs.

Pringle, Laurence. 1990. *Global Warming.* Color photos. New York: Arcade. 10–14 yrs.

———. 1991. *Living Treasure: Saving Earth's Threatened Biodiversity.* Illus. Irene Brady. New York: Morrow. 8–13 yrs.

———. 1993. *Oil Spills: Damage, Recovery, and Prevention.* Photos. New York: Morrow. 9–13 yrs.

———. 1995. *Vanishing Ozone: Protecting Earth from Ultraviolet Radiation.* B & W photos. New York: Morrow. 10–14 yrs. Save-the-Earth series.

Rand, Gloria. 1992. *Prince William.* Illus. Ted Rand. New York: Holt. 8–12 yrs.

Ranger Rick Editors. 1986. *Wonders of the Jungle.* Vienna, Va.: Ranger Rick Magazine. 10–14 yrs.

Rowland-Entwistle, Theodore. 1987. *Jungles and Rainforests.* Morristown, N.J.: Silver. 9–12 yrs.

Shel, Anne. 1993. *What to Do About Pollution.* Illus. Irene Trivas. New York: Orchard. 8–11 yrs.

Siy, Alexandra. 1991. *Ancient Forests; Arctic National Wildlife Refuge; Hawaiian Islands; Native Grasslands.* Color photos. Morristown, N.J.: Dillon/Silver Burdett. 9–13 yrs.

———. 1993. *The Brazilian Rain Forest.* Morristown, N.J.: Dillon/Silver Burdett. 9–13 yrs. Circle of Life Series.

Smucker, Anna Egan. 1994. *No Star Nights.* New York: Knopf. 10–14 yrs.

Stwertka, Eve & Albert Stwertka. 1993. *Cleaning Up: How Trash Becomes Treasure.* Illus. Mena Dolobowsky. Morristown, N.J.: Silver Burdett/Julian Messner. 10–12 yrs. At Home with Science Series.

Sullivan, George. 1992. *Disaster! The Destruction of Our Planet.* B & W photos. New York: Scholastic. 10–16 yrs.

Taylor, Barbara. 1992. *Rain Forest: A Close-up Look at the Natural World of a Rain Forest.* Photos Frank Greenaway. New York: Dorling Kindersley. 9–13 yrs. Look Closer Series.

Temple, Lannis. (Ed). 1993. *Dear World: How Children Around the World Feel About Our Environment.* New York: Random House. 9–12 yrs.

United Nations Editors. 1994. *Rescue Mission Planet Earth: A Children's Edition of Agenda 21.* New York: Kingfisher. 9–16 yrs.

Winner, Cherie. 1993. *Salamanders.* Photos C. Winner. Minneapolis, Minn.: Carolrhoda. 10–13 yrs.

Wood, A. J. 1992. *Look Again! The Second Ultimate Spot-the-Difference Book.* Illus. April Wilson. New York: Dial. All ages.

Yolen, Jane. 1993. *Welcome to the Green House.* Illus. Laura Regan. New York: Putnam. 8–12 yrs.

Zak, Monica (Trans. Nancy Schimmel). 1992. *Save My Rainforest.* Illus. Bengt-Arne Runnerstrom. Volcano, Calif.: Volcano. 10–14 yrs. (Narrative.) Notable 1992 Children's Trade Books in the Field of Social Studies.

ECONOMICS

Biographies

Aaseng, Nathan. 1990. *From Rags to Riches: People Who Started Businesses from Scratch.* Minneapolis, Minn.: Lerner. 10–14 yrs.

McKissack, Patricia & Fredrick McKissack. 1992. *Madam C. J. Walker: Self-Made Millionaire.* Springfield, N.J.: Enslow. 7–10 yrs.

Information Books

Barkin, Carp & Elizabeth James. 1990. *Jobs for Kids*. Illus. Roy Doty. New York: Lothrop, Lee & Shepard. 10–14 yrs.

Berstein, Daryl. 1992. *Better than a Lemonade Stand! Small Business Ideas for Kids*. Hillsboro, Or.: Beyond Words. 9–13 yrs.

Burns, Peggy. 1995. *Stores and Markets*. Color photos. New York: Thomson Learning. 10–13 yrs. Stepping through History series.

Dolan, Edward F. 1995. *Your Privacy: Protecting It in a Nosy World*. New York: Cobblehill. 12–16 yrs.

Gay, Kathlyn. 1992. *Caution! This May be an Advertisement: A Teen Guide to Advertising*. Danbury, Conn.: Watts. 12–14 yrs.

Kent, Zachary. 1990. *The Story of the New York Stock Exchange*. Danbury, Conn.: Children's Press. 9–12 yrs.

Lewin, T. 1996. *Market!* New York: Lothrop, Lee & Shepard. 7–10 yrs.

Maestro, Betsy. 1993. *The Story of Money*. Illus. Giulio Maestro. New York: Clarion. 10–16 yrs.

Maybury, Richard J. 1993. *Whatever Happened to Penny Candy?* Placerville, Calif.: Bluestocking Press. 12–15 yrs.

Parker, Nancy Winslow. 1995. *Money, Money, Money: The Meaning of the Art and Symbols on United States Paper Currency*. New York: HarperCollins. 10–13 yrs.

Rendon, Marion B. & Rachel Kranz. 1992. *Straight Talk About Money*. New York: Facts on File. 12–15 yrs.

Wilkinson, Elizabeth. 1989. *Making Cents: Every Kid's Guide to Money*. Illus. Martha Weston. Boston: Little, Brown. 9–12 yrs.

Watt, Elaine & Stan Hinden. 1991. *The Money Book and Bank*. Illus. Arnie Levin. New York: Tambourine. 10–13 yrs.

Young, Robin. 1991. *Stock Market*. Minneapolis, Minn.: Lerner. 11–14 yrs.

GOVERNMENT

Biographies

Adler, David A. 1991. *A Picture Book of John F. Kennedy*. Illus. Robert Casilla. New York: Holiday. 7–10 yrs.

Ayer, Eleanor H. 1995. *Ruth Bader Ginsburg: Fire and Steel on the Supreme Court*. Morristown, N.J.: Dillon/Silver Burdett. 10–13 yrs. People in Focus series.

Blue, Rose, & Corinne J. Naden. 1995. *The White House Kids*. Brookfield, Conn.: Millbrook. 10–13 yrs.

Bober, Natalie S. 1995. *Abigail Adams: Witness to a Revolution*. Black & white reproductions. New York: Atheneum. 12–17 yrs.

Colman, Penny. 1993. *A Woman Unafraid: The Achievements of Frances Perkins*. New York: Atheneum. 12–15 yrs.

Fireside, Bryna J. 1994. *Is There a Woman in the House . . . or Senate?* Photos. Morton Grove, Ill.: Whitman. 10–13 yrs.

Fritz, Jean. 1989. *The Great Little Madison*. New York: Putnam. 10–14 yrs.

———. 1991. *Bully for You, Teddy Roosevelt!* Illus. Mike Wimmer. New York: Putnam. 10–14 yrs.

Kovalchik, Sally. (Compiler). 1993. *Dear Mr. President*. Illus. G. Brian Karas. New York: Workman. 5–8 yrs.

Harrison, Barbara & Daniel Terris. 1992. *A Twilight Struggle: The Life of John Fitzgerald Kennedy*. Photos. New York: Lothrop, Lee & Shepard. 10–12 yrs.

Jaspersohn, William. 1992. *Senator: A Profile of Bill Bradley in the U.S. Senate*. Harcourt Brace Jovanovich. 12–15 yrs.

Jones, R. C. 1996. *The President Has Been Shot: True Stories of the Attacks on Ten U.S. Presidents*. Photos. New York: Dutton. 9–13 yrs.

Siegel, Beatrice. 1989. *George and Martha Washington at Home in New York*. Illus. Frank Aloise. New York: Simon & Schuster/Four Winds. 9–12 yrs.

Sobol, Richard. 1994. *Governor: In the Company of Ann W. Richards, Governor of Texas*. Photos R. Sobol. New York: Cobblehill. 10–13 yrs.

Whitelaw, Nancy. 1992. *Thedore Roosevelt Takes Charge*. Prints & photos. Morton Grove, Ill.: Whitman. 12–17 yrs.

Wisniewski, David. 1992. *Sundiata: Lion King of Mali*. New York: Clarion. 5–8 yrs.

Information Books

Ashabranner, Melissa J. & Brent Ashabranner. 1989. *Counting America: The Story of the United States Census*. New York: Putnam. 10–15 yrs.

Brenner, Barbara. 1995. *The United Nations Fiftieth Anniversary Book*. Color photos. New York: Atheneum. 12–14 yrs.

Carter, Jimmy. 1993. *Talking Peace: A Vision for the Next Generation*. New York: Dutton. 12–16 yrs.

Fireside, Harvey & Sarah Betsy Fuller. 1994. *Brown v. Board of Education: Equal Schooling for All*. Springfield, N.J.: Enslow. 12–16 yrs.

Gay, Kathlyn. 1994. *The New Power of Women in Politics*. Springfield, N.J.: Enslow. 12–16 yrs.

Goldish, Meish. 1994. *Our Supreme Court*. Brookfield, Conn.: Millbrook. 11–15 yrs.

Haas, Carol. 1994. *Engel v. Vitale: Separation of Church and State*. Springfield, N.J.: Enslow. 12–16 yrs.

Herda, D. J. 1994. *The Dred Scott Case: Slavery and Citizenship*. Springfield, N.J.: Enslow. 12–16 yrs.

———. 1994. *New York Times v. United States: National Security and Censorship*. Springfield, N.J.: Enslow. 12–16 yrs.

———. 1994. *Roe v. Wade: The Abortion Question*. Springfield, N.J.: Enslow. 12–16 yrs.

Hilton, Suzanne. 1992. *A Capital Capital City, 1790–1814*. New York: Atheneum. 10–12 yrs.

Hoig, Stan. 1990. *A Capital for the Nation*. New York: Cobblehill. 8–12 yrs.

Meltzer, Milton. 1989. *American Politics: How It Really Works*. Illus. David Small. New York: Morrow. 11–15 yrs.

Pascoe, Elaine. 1993. *Freedom of Expression: The Right to Speak Out in America*. Brookfield, Conn.: Millbrook. 12–16 yrs. Issue and Debate series.

Provensen, Alice. 1990. *The Buck Stops Here: The Presidents of the United States*. Illus. Alice Provensen. New York: Harper & Row. 9–12 yrs. Notable 1990 Children's Trade Books in the Field of Social Studies.

Riley, Gail Blasser. 1994. *Miranda v. Arizona: Rights of the Accused*. Springfield, N.J.: Enslow. 9–11 yrs.

St. George, Judith. 1990. *The White House: Cornerstone of a Nation*. New York: Putnam. 10–16 yrs.

Sherrow, Victoria. 1995. *Gideon v. Wainright: Free Legal Counsel*. B & W photos. Springfield, N.J.: Enslow. 10–14 yrs. Landmark Supreme Court Cases series.

Smith, Carter. (Ed.). 1993. *The Founding Presidents: A Sourcebook on the U.S. Presidency*. Prints & photos. Brookfield, Conn.: Millbrook. 10–16 yrs.

Spies, Karen. 1994. *Our Presidency*. Brookfield, Conn.: Millbrook. 11–15 yrs.

Steins, Richard. 1994. *Our Elections*. Brookfield, Conn.: Millbrook. 11–15 yrs.

Waters, Kate. 1991. *The Story of the White House*. New York: Scholastic. 5–8 yrs.

Weber, Michael. 1994. *Our Congress*. Brookfield, Conn.: Millbrook. 9–11 yrs.

Zeinert, Karen. 1995. *Free Speech: From Newspapers to Music Lyrics*. Photos. Springfield, N.J.: Enslow. 12–16 yrs. Issues in Focus series.

HUMAN BODY, HEALTH, AND DEVELOPMENT

Biographies

Adler, David A. 1990. *A Picture Book of Helen Keller*. Illus. John & Alexandra Wallner. New York: Holiday. 7–10 yrs.

Ashabranner, Brent. 1994. *A New Frontier: The Peace Corps in Eastern Europe*. New York: Cobblehill. 9–11 yrs.

Drimmer, Frederick. 1985. *The Elephant Man*. New York: Putnam. 12–18 yrs.

Emmert, Michelle. 1989. *I'm the Big Sister Now*. Illus. Gail Owens. Morton Grove, Ill.: Whitman. 7–11 yrs.

Greenberg, Keith Elliot. 1992. *Magic Johnson: Champion with a Cause*. Minneapolis, Minn.: Lerner. 10–12 yrs.

Heron, Ann. (Ed.). 1994. *Two Teenagers in Twenty: Writings Gay and Lesbian Youth*. Boston: Alyson. 15–18 yrs.

Keller, Helen. 1954. *The Story of My Life*. New York: Doubleday/Scholastic. 12–16 yrs.

Kudlinsi, Kathleen V. 1991. *Helen Keller*. New York: Puffin. 9–12 yrs.

Little, Jean. 1988. *Little Little: A Writer's Education*. New York: Viking. 10–13 yrs.

———. 1992. *The Stars Come Out Within*. New York: Viking. 7–12 yrs.

White, Ryan, & Ann Marie Cunningham. 1991. *Ryan White: My Own Story*. New York: Dial. 10–16 yrs.

Information Books

Aliki. 1990. *My Feet. My Hands*. Illus. Aliki. New York: Crowell. 3–6 yrs. Let's-Read-and-Find-Out Science Book.

Allison, Linda. 1976. *Blood and Guts*. Boston: Little, Brown. 9–12 yrs.

Allison, Linda & Tom Ferguson. 1991. *Stethoscope Book & Kit*. Illus. L. Allison. Reading, Mass.: Addison Wesley. 7–11 yrs.

Aronson, Billy. 1993. *They Came from DNA*. Illus. Danny O'Leary. New York: Freeman/Scientific American. 13–16 yrs.

Berger, M. 1995. *Germs Make Me Sick!* Illus. Marylin Hafner. New York: HarperCollins. 5–8 yrs. Let's-Read-and-Find-Out Science series.

Bergman, Thomas. 1989. *Finding A Common Language: Children Living with Deafness*. Photos T. Bergman. Milwaukee, Wisc.: Gareth Stevens. 9–12 yrs.

———. 1989. *On Our Own Terms: Children Living with Physical Handicaps*. Photos T. Bergman. Milwaukee, Wisc.: Gareth Stevens. 9–11 yrs.

———. 1989. *Seeing in Special Ways: Children Living with Blindness*. Photos T. Bergman. Milwaukee, Wisc.: Gareth Stevens. 9–12 yrs.

Brown, Laurie Krasny & Marc Brown. 1990. *Dinosaurs Alive and Well! A Guide to Good Health*. Illus. Laurie Krasny Brown & Marc Brown. Boston: Little, Brown/Joy. 4–8 yrs.

Bruun, Ruth Dowling & Bertel Bruun. 1989. *The Brain: What It Is, What It Does*. Illus. Peter Bruun. New York: Greenwillow. 9–12 yrs.

Bunnett, Rochelle. 1993. *Friends in the Park*. Illus. Carl Sahlhoff. New York: Checkerboard. 5–6 yrs.

Cole, B. 1993. *Mommy Laid an Egg!: Or Where Do Babies Come From?* San Francisco, Calif.: Chronicle. 4–7 yrs.

Cole, J. 1993. *How You Were Born*. Photos Margaret Miller. New York: Morrow. 5–8 yrs.

Cumbaa, Stephen. 1991. *Bones Book*. New York: Workman. 9–12 yrs.

Dahl, Tessa. 1990. *Babies, Babies, Babies*. Illus. Siobhan Dodds. New York: Viking/Penguin. 2–6 yrs.

De Saint Phalle, Niki. 1986. *AIDS: You Can't Catch It Holding Hands*. Venice, Calif.: Lapis Press. 6–10 yrs.

Dolmetsch, P. & G. Mauricette. 1987. *Teens Talk About Alcohol and Alcoholism*. Dolphin. 10–16 yrs.

———. 1992. *I'm Growing!* Illus. author. New York: HarperCollins. 3–7 yrs. Let's-Read-and-Find-Out Science Book.

Donnelly, Judy & S. A. Kramer. 1993. *Survive! Could You?* Illus. Gonzalez Vincente. New York: Random House. 10–13 yrs. Read It to Believe It! series.

Drimmer, Frederick. 1991. *Born Different: Amazing Stories of Very Special People*. New York: Bantam Skylark. 10–12 yrs.

Dwight, Laura. 1992. *We Can Do It!* Photos. New York: Checkerboard. 5–7 yrs.

Eyewitness Book. 1988. *Skeleton*. New York: Knopf. 7–14 yrs.

Fassler, David & Kelly McQueen. 1990. *What's a Virus, Anyway?: The Kid's Book about AIDS*. Burlington, Ver.: Waterfront Books. 5–10 yrs.

Fiedler, Jean & Hal Fiedler. 1990. *Be Smart about Sex: Facts for Young People*. Springfield, N.J.: Enslow. 12–16 yrs.

Ford, Michael Thomas. 1992. *100 Questions and Answers about AIDS: A Guide for Young People*. New York: Macmillan/New Discovery. 11–16 yrs.

Giblin, J. C. 1995. *When Plague Strikes: The Black Death, Smallpox, AIDS*. Illus. David Frampton. New York: HarperCollins. 11–18 yrs.

Gravelle, K. & J. Gravelle. 1996. *The Period Book: Everything You Don't Want to Ask (but Need to Know)*. Illus. Debbie Palen. New York: Walker. 10–14 yrs.

Greenberg, Lorna. 1992. *AIDS: How It Works in the Body*. Danbury, Conn.: Watts. 10–14 yrs.

Haldane, Suzanne. 1991. *Helping Hands: How Monkeys Assist People Who Are Disabled*. Photos S. Haldane. New York: Dutton. 8–12 yrs.

Hall, David E. 1993. *Living with Learning Disabilities: A Guide for Students*. Minneapolis, Minn.: Lerner. 9–11 yrs.

Harris, Robie H. 1994. *It's Perfectly Normal: A Book about Changing Bodies Growing Up, Sex, and Sexual Health*. Illus. Michael Emberley. Cambridge, Mass.: Candlewick. 10–15 yrs.

Hausherr, Rosmarie. 1989. *Children and the AIDS Virus: A Book for Children, Parents, and Teachers*. Photos R. Hausherr. New York: Clarion. 10–15 yrs.

Howe, James. 1994. *The Hospital Book*. Photos Mal Warshaw. New York: Morrow. 10–13 yrs.

Hyde, Margaret O. and Elizabeth H. Forsyth. 1990. *Medical Dilemmas*. New York: Putnam. 12–16 yrs.

———. 1995. *Know about Smoking*. Photos. New York: Walker. 10–14 yrs.

Knight, M. B. 1994. *Welcoming Babies*. Illus. Anne Sibley O'Brien. St. Paul, Minn.: Tilbury. 5–8 yrs.

Krementz, Jill. 1992. *How It Feels to Live with a Physical Disability*. New York: Simon & Schuster. 12–14 yrs.

Kriegsman, Kay Harris et al. 1992. *Taking Charge: Teenagers Talk About Life and Physical Disabilities*. Bethesda, Md.: Woodbine House. 12–15 yrs.

Kuklin, Susan. 1986. *Thinking Big: The Story of a Young Dwarf*. New York: Lothrop, Lee & Shepard. 9–12 yrs.

Landau, Elaine. 1993. *Rabies*. New York: Lodestar/Dutton. 10–12 yrs.

LeVert Suzanne. 1993. *Teens Face to Face with Chronic Illness*. Morristown, N.J.: Silver Burdett/Julian Messner. 12–15 yrs.

London, Jonathan. 1993. *Voices of the Wild*. Illus. Wayne McLoughlin. New York: Crown. 6–12 yrs.

Markle, Sandra. 1991. *Outside and Inside You*. Illus. & photos S. Markle. 9–12 yrs.

Parker, Steve. 1993. *The Body Atlas*. Illus. Giuliano Fornari. New York: Dorling Kindersley. 10–16 yrs.

Peters, David. 1991. *From the Beginning: The Story of Human Evolution*. Illus. D. Peters. New York: Morrow. 8–12 yrs.

Pirner, Connie. 1994. *Even Little Kids Get Diabetes*. Morton Grove, Ill.: Whitman. 6–8 yrs.

Ro, Cynthia. 1993. *When Learning Is Tough: Kids Talk about Their Learning Disabilities*. Photos Elena Dorfman. Morton Grove, Ill.: Whitman. 9–11 yrs.

Sutton, Roger. 1994. *Hearing Us Out: Voices from the Gay and Lesbian Community*. Photos Lisa Ebright. Boston: Little, Brown. 12–16 yrs.

Suzuki, David & Barbara Hehner. 1991. *Looking at the Body*. New York: Wiley. 7–12 yrs.

The Visual Dictionary of the Human Body. 1991. New York: Dorling Kindersley. 12–16 yrs.

Walker, Lou Ann. 1994. *Hand, Heart, and Mind: The Story of the Education of America's Deaf People*. Photos. New York: Dial. 12–16 yrs.

Western, Joan & Ronald Wilson. 1991. *The Human Body*. Mahwah, N.J.: Troll. 9–13 yrs.

Westheimer, Dr. Ruth. 1993. *Dr. Ruth Talks to Kids: Where You Came From, How Your Body Changes, and What Sex Is All About*. Illus. Diane de Groat. New York: Macmillan. 10–14 yrs.

"What's Inside My Body?" 1991. New York: Dorling Kindersley. 6–8 yrs.

Wiener, Lori S., Aprille Best, & Philip A. Pizzo (Ed.). 1994. *Be a Friend: Children Who Live with HIV Speak*. Morton Grove, Ill.: Whitman. 9–11 yrs.

INVENTIONS

Biographies

Haskins, Jim. 1991. *Outward Dreams: Black Inventors and Their Inventions*. New York: Walker. 12–15 yrs.

Kendall, Martha E. 1995. *Steve Wozniak: The Man Who Grew the Apple*. Photos. New York: Walker. 10–12 yrs.

St. George, Judith. 1992. *Dear Dr. Bell . . . Your friend, Helen Keller*. New York: Putnam. 10–12 yrs.

Streissguth, Tom. 1995. *Rocket Man: The Story of Robert Goddard*. B & W photos. Minneapolis, Minn.: Carolrhoda. 10–12 yrs.

Towle, Wendy. 1993. *The Real McCoy: The Life of an African-American Inventor*. Illus. Wil Clay. New York: Scholastic. 10–14 yrs.

Information Books

Asimov, Isaac. 1989. *How Did We Find Out about Microwaves?* Illus. Erika Kors. New York: Walker. 10–12 yrs. How Did We Find Out series.

———. 1990. *How Did We Find Out about Lasers?* Illus. Erika Kors. New York: Walker. 10–12 yrs.

Bendick, Jeanne. 1992. *Eureka! It's an Automobile!* Illus. Sal Murdocca. Brookfield, Conn.: Millbrook. 9–11 yrs.

Berger, Melvin. 1989. *Switch On, Switch Off*. Illus. Carol Croll. New York: Crowell. 6–9 yrs. Let's-Read-and-Find-Out Science Book.

Bolick, Nancy O'Keefe & Sallie G. Randolph. 1990. *Shaker Inventions*. Illus. Melissa Francisco. New York: Walker. 12–15 yrs.

Coombs, Karen Mueller. 1995. *Flush: Treating Wastewater*. Photos Jerry Boucher. Minneapolis, Minn.: Carolrhoda. 8–11 yrs.

Finkelstein, Norman H. 1993. *Sounds in the Air: The Golden Age of Radio*. Photos. New York: Scribners. 12–15 yrs.

Hindley, Judy A. 1993. *A Piece of String Is a Wonderful Thing*. Illus. Margaret Chamberlain. Cambridge, Mass.: Candlewick. 5–8 yrs. Read and Wonder series.

Jones, C. F. 1996. *Accidents May Happen: Fifty Inventions Discovered by Mistake*. Illus. John O'Brien. New York: Delacorte. 9–12 yrs.

Kuklin, Susan. 1994. *From Head to Toe: How a Doll Is Made*. Photos S. Kuklin. New York: Hyperion. 7–10 yrs.

Simon, Seymour. 1985. *Bits and Bytes*. Illus. E. & B. Emberley. New York: Crowell. 9–12 yrs.

———. 1986. *Turtle Talk: A Beginner's Book of LOGO*. Illus. B.& E. Emberley. New York: Crowell. 7–9 yrs.

Skurzynski, Gloria. 1993. *Get the Message: Telecommunications in Your High-Tech World*. Color photos. New York: Simon & Schuster/Bradbury. 10–12 yrs.

———. 1994. *Know the Score: Video Games in Your High-Tech World*. Photos. New York: Simon & Schuster/Bradbury. 9–14 yrs. Your High-Tech World.

Wakin, E. 1996. *How TV Changed America's Mind*. Photos. New York: Lothrop, Lee & Shepard. 12–16 yrs.

LITERATURE

Autobiographies & Biographies of Authors & Poets

Autobiographies

Aardema, Verna. 1993. *A Bookworm Who Hatched*. Photos Dede Smith. Katonah, N.Y.: Owen. 7–12 yrs. Meet the Author Collection.

Ashabranner, Brent. 1990. *The Times of My Life: A Memoir*. New York: Dutton. 10–15 yrs.

Bernier-Grand, Carmen T. 1995. *Poet and Politician of Puerto Rico: Don Luis Muñoz Marin*. New York: Orchard. 10–13 yrs. Latino.

Brown, Margaret Wise (Adaptor Joan W. Blos). 1994. *The Days Before Now*. Illus. Thomas B. Allen. New York: Simon & Schuster. 5–9 yrs.

Bulla, Clyde Robert. 1985. *A Grain of Wheat: A Writer Begins*. Boston: Godine. 7–12 yrs.

Bunting, Eve. 1995. *Once Upon a Time*. Photos John Pezaris. Katonah, N.Y.: Owen. 6–10 yrs. Meet the Author Series.

Byars, Betsy. 1992. *The Moon and I*. Morristown, N.J.: Silver Burdett/Julian Messner. 10–14 yrs.

Cleary, Beverly. 1988. *A Girl from Yamhill: A Memoir*. New York: Morrow. 11–16 yrs.

———. 1995. *My Own Two Feet*. New York: Morrow. 11–16 yrs.

Cole, J. 1996. *On the Bus with Joanna Cole: A Creative Autobiography*. Portsmouth, N.H. 9–16 yrs.

Cooper, S. 1996. *Dreams and Wishes: Essays on Writing for Children*. New York: McElderry. 10–16 yrs.

Dahl, Roald. 1984. *Boy: Tales of Childhood*. New York: Farrar, Straus & Giroux. 11–16 yrs.

Duncan, Lois. 1982. *Chapters: My Growth as a Writer*. Boston: Little, Brown. 11–16 yrs.

Faber, Doris, & Harold Faber. 1995. *Great Lives: American Literature*. Photos. New York: Atheneum. 10–12 yrs. Great Lives series.

Fox, Mem. 1992. *Dear Mem Fox: I Read All Your Books, Even the Pathetic Ones*. San Diego: Harcourt Brace. 12–16 yrs.

Fritz, Jean. 1982. *Homesick: My Own Story*. New York: Putnam. 11–16 yrs.

———. 1993. *Surprising Myself*. Katonah, N.Y.: Owen. 7–12 yrs. Meet the Author Collection.

Goble, Paul. 1994. *Hau Kola/Hello Friend*. Photos Gerry Perrin. Katonah, N.Y.: Owen. 6–11 yrs. Meet the Author series.

Greenfield, Eloise & Lessie Jones Little. 1979. *Childtimes: A Three Generation Memoir*. New York: HarperCollins. 11–16 yrs.

Henry, Marguerite. 1980. *Illustrated Marguerite Henry*. Illus. Wesley Dennis. Skokie, Ill.: Rand McNally. 9–13 yrs.

Hentoff, Nat. 1986. *Boston Boy*. New York: Knopf. 12–16 yrs.

Hopkins, Lee Bennett. 1993. *The Writing Bug*. Katonah, N.Y.: Owen. 7–12 yrs. Meet the Author Collection.

Howe, James. 1994. *Playing with Words*. Katonah, N.Y.: Owen. 7–12 yrs. Meet the Author Collection.

Kuskin, Karla. 1995. *Thoughts, Pictures, and Words*. Photos Nicholas Kuskin. Katonah, N.Y.: Owen. 6–10 yrs. Meet the Author Series.

Lyons, Mary E. 1995. *Keeping Secrets: The Girlhood Diaries of Seven Women Writers*. Photos. New York: Holt. 12–16 yrs.

Mahy, Margaret. 1995. *My Mysterious World*. Photos David Alexander. Katonah, N.Y.: Owen. 6–10 yrs. Meet the Author series.

Martin, Rafe. 1992. *A Storyteller's Story*. Photos Jill Krementz. Katonah, N.Y.: Owens. 7–12 yrs.

Meaker, Marijane. 1983. *Me, Me, Me, Me, Me, Not a Novel M. E. Kerr*. New York: HarperCollins. 11–15 yrs.

Meltzer, Milton. 1988. *Starting from Home: A Writer's Beginnings*. New York: Viking. 11–16 yrs.

Naylor, Phyllis Reynolds. 1986. *How I Came to Be a Writer*. New York: Aladdin. 11–16 yrs.

Nesbit, E. 1988. *Long Ago When I Was Young*. New York: Dial. 11–16 yrs.

Paulsen, Gary. 1990. *Woodsong*. New York: Simon & Schuster/Bradbury. 11–16 yrs.

———. 1994. *Father Water, Mother Woods*. New York: Delacorte. 11–16 yrs.

Peck, Richard. 1991. *Anonymously Yours: A Memoir*. Morristown, N.J.: Silver Burdett/Julian Messner. 13–16 yrs. My Own Words series.

Polacco, Patricia. 1994. *Firetalking*. Photos Lawrence Migdale. Katonah, N.Y.: Owen. 6–11 yrs. Meet the Author series.

Potter, Beatrix. 1982. *Beatrix Potter's Americans: Selected Letters*. Boston: Horn Book. 12–16 yrs.

———. 1989. *The Journal of Beatrix Potter. 1881–1987*. New York: Warne. 12–16 yrs.

Reef, Catherine. 1995. *Walt Whitman*. Photos. New York: Clarion. 10–12 yrs.

———. 1996. *John Steinbeck*. Photos. New York: Clarion. 12–15 yrs.

Rylant, Cynthia. 1984. *Waiting to Waltz: A Childhood*. Illus. Stephen Gammell. New York: Simon & Schuster/Bradbury. 9–12 yrs.

———. 1989. *But I'll Be Back Again: An Album*. New York: Orchard. 9–12 yrs.

———. 1992. *Best Wishes*. Photos Carol Ontal. Katonah, N.Y.: Owens. 7–12 yrs. Meet the Author Collection.

Stevenson, J. 1995. *I Had a Lot of Wishes*. New York: Greenwillow. 8–11 yrs.

Sutcliff, Rosemary. 1992. *Blue Remembered Hills*. New York: Farrar, Straus, & Giroux. 9–16 yrs.

Thwaite, Ann. 1994. *The Brilliant Career of Winnie-the-Pooh: The Definitive History of the Best Bear in All the World*. Photos. New York: Dutton. 12–16 yrs.

Turk, Ruth. 1995. *Lillian Hellman: Rebel Playwright*. B & W photos. Minneapolis, Minn.: Lerner. 10–12 yrs.

Uchida, Yoshiko. 1991. *The Invisible Thread: A Memoir by the Author of* The Best Bad Thing. Morristown, N.J.: Silver Burdett/Julian Messner. 10–16 yrs.

Wilder, Laura Ingalls (Setting Rose Wilder Lane). 1994. *On the Way Home: A Diary of a Trip from South Dakota to Mansfield, Missouri in 1894*. New York: HarperCollins. 12+ yrs.

———. (Ed. Roger Lea MacBride); historical setting Margot Patterson Doss). 1994. *West from Home: Letters of Laura Ingalls Wilder, San Francisco, 1915*. New York: HarperCollins. 12+ yrs.

Yates, E. 1996. *Spanning Time: A Diary Keeper Becomes a Writer*. Petersborough, N.H.: Cobblestone. 9–14 yrs.

Yep, Laurence. 1991. *The Lost Garden: A Memoir the Author of Dragonwings*. Morristown, N.J.: Silver Burdett/Julian Messner. 11–14 yrs.

Yolen, Jane. 1992. *A Letter from Phoenix Farm*. Photos Jason Stemple. Katonah, N.Y.: Owen. 7–12 yrs. Meet the Author series.

Zindel, Paul. 1992. *The Pigman & Me*. New York: HarperCollins/Zolotow. 10–12 yrs.

Biographies

Anderson, Madelyn Klein. 1993. *Edgar Allan Poe: A Mystery*. Photos. Danbury, Conn.: Watts. Gr. 7–10. Impact Biographies.

Andronik, Catherine M. 1993. *Kindred Spirit: A Biography of L. M. Montgomery, Creator of Anne of Green Gables*. New York: Atheneum. 10–13 yrs.

Asher, Sandy. 1987. *Where Do You Get Your Ideas? Helping Young Writers Begin*. Illus. Susan Hellard. New York: Walker. 11–16 yrs.

Bassett, L. 1987. *Very Truly Yours, Charles L. Dodgson, Alias Lewis Carroll*. New York: Lothrop, Lee & Shepard. 12–16 yrs.

Bjork, Christina. (Trans. Scan Sandin). 1993. *The Other Alice: The Story of Alice Liddell and Alice in Wonderland*. Illus. Inga-Karin Eriksson. New York: Farrar, Straus & Giroux. 10–13 yrs.

Blair, Gwenda. 1981. *Laura Ingalls Wilder*. New York: Putnam. 10–13 yrs.

Bober, Natalie. 1991. *A Restless Spirit: The Story of Robert Frost*. New York: Holt. 11–16 yrs.

Brighton, Catherine. 1994. *The Brontes: Scenes from the Childhood of Charlotte, Branwell, Emily and Anne*. Illus. C. Brighton. San Francisco: Chronicle. 6–9 yrs.

Bruce, Harry. 1992. *Maud: The Life of L. M. Montgomery*. New York: Bantam. 11–16 yrs.

Brust, Beth Wagner. 1992. *The Amazing Paper Cuttings of Hans Christian Andersen*. Photos. New York: Ticknor & Fields. 9–12 yrs.

Campbell, Patricia J. 1989. *Presenting Robert Cormier*. New York: Macmillan. 13–16 yrs.

Carpenter, A. S. 1990. *Frances Hodgson Burnett: Beyond the Secret Garden*. Minneapolis, Minn.: Lerner. 11–16 yrs.

Carpenter, Angelica Shirley, & Jean Shirley. 1992. *L. Frank Baum: Royal Historian of Oz*. Minneapolis, Minn.: Lerner. 10–15 yrs.

Collins, D. R. 1989. *Country Artist: A Story about Beatrix Potter*. Minneapolis, Minn.: Carolrhoda. 11–15 yrs.

———. 1989. *To the Point: A Story about E. B. White*. Minneapolis, Minn.: Carolrhoda. 11–15 yrs.

Cox, C. 1995. *Mark Twain: America's Humorist, Dreamer, Prophet*. New York: Scholastic. 9–12 yrs.

Daly, Jay. 1989. *Presenting S. E. Hinton*. New York: Dell. 12–15 yrs.

Drake, William. 1991. *The First Wave: Women Poets in America, 1915–1945*. New York: Macmillan. 12–16 yrs.

Duggleby, J. 1996. *Artist in Overalls: The Life of Grant Wood*. Paintings, lithographs, photographs & illustrations. San Francisco, Calif.: Chronicle. 9–11 yrs.

Fritz, Jean. 1994. *Harriet Beecher Stowe and the Beecher Preachers*. Photos. New York: Putnam. 11–14 yrs.

Ghermon, Beverly. 1992. *E. B. White: Some Writer!* New York: Atheneum. 11–15 yrs.

Giff, Patricia Reilly. 1989. *Laura Ingalls Wilder: Growing Up in the Little House*. New York: Viking. 10–12 yrs.

Gonzales, Doreen. 1991. *Madeleine L'Engle: Author of A Wrinkle in Time*. New York: Dillon. 10–13 yrs.

Greene, Carol. 1991. *Hans Christian Andersen: Prince of Storytellers*. Danbury, Conn.: Children's Book Press. 11–16 yrs.

Harlan, Judith. 1989. *Sounding the Alarm: A Biography of Rachel Carson*. New York: Macmillan. 12–16 yrs.

Hurwitz, Johanna. 1989. *Astrid Lindgren: Storyteller to the World*. New York: Viking/Puffin. 11–16 yrs. Woman of Our Times Series.

Johnston, Norma. 1991. *Louisa May: The World and Works of Louisa Alcott*. New York: Simon & Schuster/Four Winds. 12–15 yrs.

———. 1994. *Harriet: The Life and World of Harriet Beecher Stowe*. New York: Simon & Schuster/Four Winds. 12–15 yrs.

Kamen, Gloria. 1985. *Kipling: Storyteller of East and West*. New York: Atheneum. 11–15 yrs.

Knudson, R. R. 1992. *The Wonderful Pen of May Swenson*. New York: Macmillan. 10–13 yrs.

Krull, Kathleen. 1994. *Lives of the Writers: Comedies, Tragedies (and What the Neighbors Thought)*. Illus. Kathryn Hewitt. San Diego: Harcourt Brace. 10–14 yrs.

Kudlinski, Kathleen V. 1988. *Rachel Carson: Pioneer of Ecology*. New York: Viking. 13–16 yrs.

Lasky, Kathryn & Meribah Knight. 1993. *Searching for Laura Ingalls: A Reader's Journey*. Photos Christopher G. Knight. New York: Macmillan. 9–12 yrs.

Lyons, Mary E. 1990. *Sorrow's Kitchen: The Life and Folklore of Zora Neale Hurston*. New York: Scribners. 10–15 yrs.

Meigs, Cornelia. 1968. *Invincible Louisa*. Boston: Little, Brown. 12–16 yrs.

Murphy, Jim. 1993. *Across America on an Emigrant Train*. Photos. New York: Clarion. 12–15 yrs.

Nilsen, Aileen Pace. 1990. *Presenting M. E. Kerr*. New York: Dell. 12–16 yrs.

Norris, Jerrie. 1990. *Presenting Rosa Guy*. New York: Dell. 12–16 yrs.

Perl, Lila. 1995. *Isaac Bashevis Singer: The Life of a Storyteller*. Illus. Donna Ruff. Philadelphia, Penn.: Jewish Publication Society. 10–12 yrs.

Porter, A. P. 1992. *Jump at de Sun: The Story of Zora Neale Hurston.* Minneapolis, Minn.: Carolrhoda Books. 10–12 yrs.

Quackenbush, Robert. 1984. *Mark Twain? What Kind of Name Is That? A Story of Samuel Langhorne Clemens.* New York: Simon & Schuster. 9–14 yrs.

———. 1986. *Who Said There's No Man on the Moon? Jules Verne.* New York: Simon & Schuster. 11–16 yrs.

Smith, Lucinda. 1989. *Women Who Write.* Morristown, N.J.: Silver Burdett/Julian Messner. 12–16 yrs.

Stanley, Diane, & Peter Vennema. 1992. *Bard of Avon: The Story of William Shakespeare.* Illus. Diane Stanley. New York: Morrow.

Stefoff, Rebecca. 1994. *Herman Melville.* New York: Simon & Schuster. 12–16 yrs.

Taylor, Judy. 1987. *Beatrix Potter: Artist, Storyteller and Countrywoman.* New York: Warne. 12–16 yrs.

———. 1988. *Beatrix Potter 1866–1943: The Artist and Her Work.* New York: Warne. 12–16 yrs.

———. 1990. *Beatrix Potter's Letters.* New York: Warne. 12–16 yrs.

———. 1992. *Letters to Children from Beatrix Potter.* New York: Warne. 9–12 yrs.

Teeters, Peggy. 1992. *Jules Verne: The Man Who Invented Tomorrow.* New York: Walker. 10–16 yrs.

Thaxter, Celia. 1992. *Celia's Island Journal.* Adapter & illus. Loretta Krupinski. Boston: Little, Brown. 5–8 yrs.

Tingum, J. 1995. *E. B. White: The Elements of a Writer.* B & W illus. Minneapolis, Minn.: Lerner. 9–12 yrs.

Walker, Alice. 1974. *Langston Hughes, American Poet.* New York: HarperCollins. 12–16 yrs.

Wallner, A. 1995. *Beatrix Potter.* New York: Holiday. 5–8 yrs.

Weidt, Maryann N. 1989. *Presenting Judy Blume.* New York: Macmillan/Twayne. 11–16 yrs.

Anthologies

Bauer, Caroline Feller. 1994. *Thanksgiving: Stories and Poems.* Illus. Nadine Bernard Westcott. New York: HarperCollins. 9–11 yrs.

Bauer, Marion Dane (Ed.). 1994. *Am I Blue?: Coming Out from the Silence.* New York: HarperCollins. 13–18 yrs.

Brown, Marc. 1994. *Scared Silly!: A Book for the Brave.* Boston: Little, Brown. 5–8 yrs.

Cohen, Daniel. 1994. *The Ghost of Elvis: And Other Celebrity Spirits.* New York: Putnam. 9–11 yrs.

Cole, J. & S. Calmenson. 1995. *Ready . . . Set . . . Read—and Laugh!: A Funny Treasury for Beginning Readers.* New York: Doubleday. 5–8 yrs.

Dann, Penny. 1993. *A Little Book of Courage.* Illus. P. Dann. Plymouth, Minn.: Child's World. 5–8 yrs.

———. 1993. *A Little Book of Friendship.* Illus. P. Dann. Plymouth, Minn.: Child's World. 5–8 yrs.

Ehrlich, Amy (Ed.). 1996. *When I Was Your Age: Original Stories about Growing Up.* Photos. Cambridge, Mass.: Candlewick. 10–13 yrs.

Goode, Diane. 1994. *Diane Goode's Book of Scary Stories and Songs.* New York: Dutton. 5–8 yrs.

Franklin, Kristine L. (Ed.). 1996. *Out of the Dump: Writings and Photos by Children of Guatemala.* Photos. New York: Lothrop, Lee & Shepard. 9–12 yrs.

Hamanaka, S. 1995. *On the Wings of Peace.* Various artists. New York: Clarion. 9–13 yrs.

Pellowski, A. 1995. *The Storytelling Handbook: A Young People's Collection of Unusual Tales and Helpful Hints on How to Tell Them.* Illus. Martha Stoberock. New York: Simon & Schuster. 9–12 yrs.

Porte, B. A. 1996. *Black Elephant with a Brown Ear (in Alabama).* Illus. Bill Traylor. New York: Greenwillow. 12–16 yrs.

Thomas, Roy. 1994. *Come Go with Me: Old-Timer Stories from the Southern Mountains.* Illus. Laszlo Kubinyi. New York: Farrar, Straus & Giroux. 10–13 yrs.

MATHEMATICS

Biographies

Cwiklik, R. 1987. *Albert Einstein and the Theory of Relativity.* Hauppauge, N.Y.: Barron's Educational Series. 10–14 yrs.

Latham, J. L. 1955. *Carry On, Mr. Bowditch.* Illus. J. Cosgrave. Boston: Houghton Mifflin. 10–16 yrs.

Lasky, Katherine. 1994. *The Librarian Who Measured the Earth.* Illus. Kevin Hawkes. Boston: Little, Brown. 8–10 yrs.

Terry, L. 1964. *The Mathmen.* Illus. P. A. Hutchison; mathematical drawings J. Techet. New York: McGraw-Hill. 10–16 yrs.

Information Books

Adler, David A. 1977. *Roman Numerals.* Illus. Ron Barton. New York: HarperCollins. 9–11 yrs.

Adler, I. 1990. *Mathematics.* Illus. R. Miller. New York: Doubleday. 8–12 yrs.

Anno, Masaichiro & Mitsumasa Anno. 1983. *Anno's Mysterious Multiplying Jar.* New York: Philomel. 8–12 yrs.

Anno, Mitsumasa. 1982. *Anno's Math Games.* New York: Philomel. 5–9 yrs.

———. 1989. *Anno's Math Games II.* Illus. Mitsumasa Anno. New York: Philomel. 6–10 yrs. Notable Children's Trade Books in Science, 1989.

———. 1991. *Anno's Math Games III.* Illus. M. Anno. New York: Philomel. 6–9 yrs.

———. 1995. *Anno's Magic Seeds.* Illus. M. Anno. New York: Philomel. 5–9 yrs.

Birch, David. 1993. *The Kings' Chessboard.* New York: Puffin. 8–16 yrs.

Burns, M. 1975. *The I Hate Mathematics! Book.* Boston: Little, Brown. 8–14 yrs.

———. 1982. *Math for Smarty Pants.* Illus. Martha Weston. Boston: Little, Brown. 9–14 yrs.

Chwast, Seymour. 1993. *12 Circus Rings.* San Diego: Harcourt Brace. 4–8 yrs.

Crews, Donald. 1986. *Ten Black Dots.* New York: Greenwillow. 6–9 yrs.

Dennis, J. Richard. 1971. *Fractions Are Parts of Things.* Illus. Donald Crews. New York: HarperCollins. 7–10 yrs.

Falwell, Cathryn. 1993. *Feast for Ten.* Illus. C. Falwell. New York: Clarion. 4–8 yrs.

Froman, Robert. 1978. *Angles Are Easy as Pie.* Illus. Ron Barton. New York: HarperCollins. 7–11 yrs.

———. 1978. *The Greatest Guessing Game.* Illus. Giola Flammenghi. New York: HarperCollins. 7–11 yrs.

Geisert, Arthur. 1996. *Roman Numerals I to MM/Numerabilia Romana Uno ad Duo Mila.* Illus. Arthur Geisert. Boston: Lorraine/Houghton Mifflin. 7–10 yrs.

Gillen, Patricia Bellan. 1988. *My Signing Book of Numbers.* Illus. P. Gillen. Washington, DC (dist.): Kendall Green. 4–8 yrs.

Hague, K. 1986. *Numbears.* Illus. Michael Hague. New York: Holt. 2–6 yrs.

Hamm, Diane Johnston. 1991. *How Many Feet in the Bed?* New York: Simon & Schuster. 5–9 yrs.

Hulme, Joy N. 1991. *Sea Squares.* Illus. Carol Schwartz. New York: Disney Press/Hyperion. 5–9 yrs.

Hutchins, Pat. 1986. *The Doorbell Rang.* Pippin. Illus. Gregory Filling. New York: Greenwillow. 7–11 yrs.

Keller, Charles. 1991. *Take Me to Your Liter: Science and Math Jokes.* Illus. Gregory Filling. Ann Arbor, Mich.: Pippin. 7–11 yrs.

Leedy, Loreen. 1994. *Fraction Action.* Illus. author. New York: Holiday. 6–9 yrs.

Lionni, Leo. 1960. *Inch by Inch.* New York: Astor-Honor. 6–9 yrs.

Markle, S. 1995. *Measuring Up!: Experiments, Puzzles, and Games Exploring Measurement.* Color photos & graphics. New York: Atheneum. 4–6 yrs.

McCarthy, Patricia. 1990. *Ocean Parade.* New York: Dial. 6–9 yrs.

McMillan, Bruce. 1986. *Counting Wildflowers.* New York: Lothrop, Lee & Shepard. 5–7 yrs.

———. 1991. *Eating Fractions.* New York: Scholastic. 5–7 yrs.

Mogensen, J. 1990. *The 46 Little Men.* New York: Greenwillow. 8–12 yrs.

Mori, T. 1986. *Socrates and the Three Little Pigs.* Illus. M. Anno. New York: Philomel. 7–12 yrs.

Morozumi, Atsuko. 1990. *One Gorilla.* New York: Farrar, Straus & Giroux. 6–9 yrs.

Muller, Robert. 1990. *The Great Book of Math Teasers.* Illus. Norbert Schrader. New York: Sterling. 10–14 yrs.

Owen, Annie. 1988. *Annie's One to Ten.* New York: Knopf. 5–8 yrs.

Phillips, Louis. 1985. *263 Brain Busters: Just How Smart Are You Anyway?* Illus. James Stevenson. New York: Viking. 9–12 yrs.

Pinczes, Elinor J. 1993. *One Hundred Hungry Ants.* Boston: Houghton Mifflin. 5–9 yrs.

Pragoff, Fiona. 1987. *How Many?* New York: Doubleday. 4–8 yrs.

Ross, Catherine Sheldrick. 1992. *Circles.* Illus. Bill Slavin. Reading, Mass.: Addison Wesley. 8–14 yrs.

Schwartz, D. 1985. *How Much Is a Million?* Illus. S. Kellogg. New York: Lothrop, Lee & Shepard. 5–12 yrs.

———. 1989. *If You Made a Million.* Illus. Steven Kellogg. New York: Lothrop, Lee & Shepard. 7–10 yrs.

Shepard, S. 1991. *International Business Bird.* New York: Holt. 6–12 yrs.

Tallarico, T. 1991. *What's Wrong Here? At School.* Chicago: Kidsbooks. 8–12 yrs.

Wells, Robert E. 1993. *Is a Blue Whale the Biggest Thing There Is?* Illus. R. E. Wells. Morton Grove, Ill.: Whitman. 5–9 yrs.

Wyler, Rose & Mary Elting. 1992. Math Fun Series: *Test Your Luck; Money Puzzlers; Tricky Lines and Shapes; Pocket Calculator.* Morristown, N.J.: Silver Burdett/Julian Messner. 9–14 yrs.

MUSIC

(SEE ALSO STORIES OF MUSIC IN CHAPTER 5)

Biographies: Composers

Arkin, David. 1968. *The Twenty Children of Johann Sebastian Bach.* Seattle, Wash.: Ritchie Press. 7–10 yrs.

Downing, Julie, & R. J. Monjo. 1991. *Mozart Tonight.* New York: Simon & Schuster/Bradbury. 8–10 yrs. (Fictionalized)

Kamen, Gloria. 1996. *Hidden Music: The Life of Fanny Mendelssohn.* Illus. Gloria Kamen. New York: Simon & Schuster. 11–16 yrs.

Mitchell, Barbara. 1987. *America, I Hear You: A Story about George Gershwin*. Minneapolis, Minn.: Carolrhoda. 9–12 yrs.

Monjo, F. N. 1975. *Letters to Horseface: Being the Story of Wolfgang Amadeus Mozart's Journey to Italy, 1769–1770, When He Was a Boy of Fourteen*. New York: Viking. 9–12 yrs. (Fictionalized)

Nichols, Janet. 1990. *American Music Makers: An Introduction to American Composers*. New York: Walker. 12–15 yrs.

Silverman, Jerry. 1994. *Songs and Stories from the American Revolution*. Brookfield, Conn.: Millbrook. 9–11 yrs.

Stevens, Bryna. 1990. *Handel and the Famous Sword Swallower of Halle*. Illus. Ruth Tietjen Councell. New York: Philomel. 7–10 yrs.

Switzer, E. 1995. *The Magic of Mozart: Mozart, The Magic Flute, and the Salzburg Marionettes*. Photos Costas. New York: Atheneum/Karl. 9–12 yrs.

Thompson, Wendy. 1991. *Wolfgang Amadeus Mozart*. New York: Viking. 11–16 yrs.

———. 1991. *Ludwig van Beethoven*. New York: Viking. 11–16 yrs.

Ventura, Piero. 1989. *Great Composers*. Illus. Piero Ventura. New York: Putnam. 7–16 yrs.

Weil, Lisl. 1991. *Wolferl: The First Six Years in the Life of Wolfgang Amadeus Mozart, 1756–1762*. Illus. Lisl Weil. New York: Holiday. 8–10 yrs.

Biographies: Performers

Beirne, Barbara. 1990. *A Pianist's Debut*. Minneapolis, Minn.: Carolrhoda. 9–12 yrs.

Brighton, Catherine. 1989. *Nijinsky: Scenes from the Childhood of the Great Dancer*. Illus. Catherine Brighton. New York: Doubleday. 6–9 yrs.

Collier, J. L. 1991. *Duke Ellington*. New York: Macmillan. 12–15 yrs.

Dolan, Sean. 1994. *Johnny Cash*. B & W photos. New York: Chelsea. 12+ yrs. Pop Culture Legends Series.

Faber, Doris. 1992. *Calamity Jane: Her Life and Her Legend*. Boston: Houghton Mifflin. 10–12 yrs.

Garfunkel, Trudy. 1995. *Letter to the World: The Life and Dances of Martha Graham*. B & W photos. Boston: Little, Brown. 10–13 yrs.

Haskins, James. 1985. *Diana Ross Star Supreme*. New York: Puffin. 8–12 yrs.

———. 1990. *Black Dance in America: A History through Its People*. New York: Crowell. 12–16 yrs. Nonfiction. Coretta Scott King Honor Book (Writing)

Levine, Ellen. 1995. *Anna Pavlova: Genius of the Dance*. B & W photos. New York: Scholastic. 10–12 yrs.

Lewis-Ferguson, Julinda. 1994. *Alvin Ailey, Jr.: A Life in Dance*. New York: Walker. Photos. 10–13 yrs.

Nardo, Don. 1994. *John Wayne*. B & W photos. New York: Chelsea. 12+ yrs. Pop Culture Legends series.

O'Connor, Barbara. 1994. *Barefoot Dancer: The Story of Isadora Duncan*. Photos. Minneapolis, Minn.: Carolrhoda. 11–14 yrs.

Scordato, Mark, & Ellen Scordato. 1995. *The Three Stooges*. New York: Chelsea. 12+ yrs. Filmography. Pop Culture Legends series.

Information Books

Anderson, Joan. 1993. *Twins on Toes: A Ballet Debut*. Photos George Ancona. New York: Lodestar/Dutton. 10–13 yrs.

Bellvile, Cheryl Walsh. 1986. *Theater Magic: Behind the Scenes at a Children's Theater*. Minneapolis, Minn.: Carolrhoda. 10–16 yrs.

Fleisher, Paul. 1993. *The Master Violinmaker*. Photos David Saunders. Boston: Houghton Mifflin. 5–9 yrs.

Greenberg, Keith Eliot. 1988. *Rap*. Minneapolis, Minn.: Lerner. 10–12 yrs.

Hammerstein, Oscar II. 1992. *A Real Nice Clambake*. Illus. Nadine Bernard Westcott. Boston: Joy Street. 5–8 yrs.

Hausherr, Rosmarie. 1992. *What Instrument Is This?* New York: Scholastic. 6–9 yrs.

Hayes, Ann & Karen Thompson. 1991. *Meet the Orchestra*. Illus. A. Hayes & K. Thompson. San Diego: Harcourt Brace/Gulliver. 8–12 yrs.

Jones, K. Maurice. 1994. *Say It Loud: The Story of Rap Music*. Photos. Brookfield, Conn.: Millbrook. 12–14 yrs.

Kindersley, D. 1989. *Music*. New York: Random House. 9–16 yrs. Eyewitness Books Series.

Krementz, Jill. 1986. *A Very Young Dancer*. New York: Dell. 9–12 yrs.

Krull, Kathleen. 1992. *Lives of the Musicians: Good Times, Bad Times (and What the Neighbors Thought)*. Illus. Kathryn Hewitt. San Diego: Harcourt Brace. 10–16 yrs.

Morris, Ann. 1994. *Dancing to America*. Illus. Paul Kolnik. New York: Dutton. 9–11 yrs.

Paxton, Arthur K. 1987. *Making Music*. New York: Atheneum. 7–10 yrs.

Pillar, Marjorie. 1991. *Join the School Band*. New York: HarperCollins. 8–12 yrs.

RELIGION

Biographies

dePaola, Tomie. 1992. *Patrick: Patron Saint of Ireland*. New York: Holiday. 5–9 yrs.

Dunlop, Eileen. 1996. *Tales of St. Patrick*. New York: Holiday. 11–14 yrs.

Fisher, Leonard Everett. 1995. *Moses: Retold from the Bible*. New York: Holiday. 10–13 yrs.

Gauch, Patricia Lee. 1994. *Noah*. New York: Philomel. 5–9 yrs.

Haskin, Jim. 1992. *Amazing Grace*. Brookfield, Conn.: Millbrook. 10–14 yrs.

Wolkstein, Diane. 1996. *Esther's Story*. Illus. Juan Wijngaard. New York: Morrow. 9–11 yrs.

Information Books

Adams, Georgie (Reteller). 1995. *The Bible Storybook: Ten Tales from the Old and New Testaments*. Illus. Peter Utton. New York: Dial. 5–9 yrs.

Alrunon, Richard. 1989. *Growing Up Amish*. New York: Atheneum. 9–13 yrs.

Brent, I. (Trans.). 1992. *Noah's Ark*. Illus. I. Brent. Boston: Little, Brown. 4–8 yrs.

Cousins, Lucy (Trans.). 1993. *Noah's Ark*. Illus. L. Cousins. Cambridge, Mass.: Candlewick. 9–12 yrs.

dePaola, Tomie. 1995. *Tomie dePaola's Book of the Old Testament: New International Version*. Illus. T. dePaola. New York: Putnam. 5–9 yrs.

Drucker, Malka. 1992. *A Jewish Holiday ABC*. Illus. Rita Pocock. San Diego: Harcourt Brace/Gulliver. 5–9 yrs.

Eisler, Colin (Compiler and ed.). 1992. *David's Songs: His Psalms and Their Story*. Illus. Jerry Pinkney. New York: Dial. 8–12 yrs.

Faber, Doris. 1991. *The Amish*. Illus. Michael E. Erkel. New York: Doubleday. 7–11 yrs. Notable 1991 Children's Trade Books in the Field of Social Studies.

Ganeri, Anita (Adapter). 1996. *Out of the Ark: Stories from the World's Religions*. Illus. Jackie Morris. San Diego: Harcourt Brace. 7–12 yrs.

Gellman, Marc. 1989. *Does God Have a Big Toe? Stories about Stories in the Bible*. Illus. Oscar de Mejo. New York: Harper & Row. 7–13 yrs.

Gellman, Marc & Thomas Hartman. 1995. *How Do You Spell God?: Answers to the Big Questions from Around the World*. Illus. Jos. A. Smith. New York: Morrow. 10–13 yrs.

Goldin, Barbara Diamond. 1994. *The Passover Journey: A Seder Companion*. Illus. Neil Waldman. New York: Viking. 8–12 yrs.

Hennessy, B. G. 1993. *The First Night*. Illus. Steele Johnson & Lou Fancher. New York: Viking. 5–8 yrs.

Keats, Ezra Jack. 1994. *God Is in the Mountain*. New York: Holt. 7–10 yrs.

Kuskin, Karla. 1993. *A Great Miracle Happened There: A Chanukah Story*. Illus. Robert Andrew Parker. New York: HarperCollins/Perlman. 5–8 yrs.

Mitchell, Barbara. 1993. *Down Buttermilk Lane*. Illus. John Sandford. New York: Lothrop, Lee & Shepard. 6–9 yrs.

Ray, Jane (Trans.). 1990. *Noah's Ark*. Illus. J. Ray. New York: Dutton. All ages.

Reid, Barbara. 1993. *Two by Two*. Illus. B. Reid. New York: Scholastic. 7–12 yrs.

Sabuda, R. (Illus.) *The Twelve Days of Christmas: A Pop-Up Celebration*. New York: Simon & Schuster. 5–12 yrs.

Stoddard, Sandol. 1992. *The Doubleday Illustrated Children's Bible*. Illus. Tony Chen. New York: Doubleday. 10–13 yrs.

———. (Comp.). 1992. *Prayers, Praises, and Thanksgivings*. Illus. Rachel Isadora. New York: Dial. 8–15 yrs.

Strom, Yale. 1990. *A Tree Still Stands: Jewish Youth in Eastern Europe Today*. Photos. Y. Strom. New York: Philomel. 8–13 yrs.

SCIENCE

Biographies

Bernstein, Joanne E., & Rose Blue, with Alan Jay Gerber. 1990. *Judith Resnik: Challenger Astronaut*. New York: Lodestar/Dutton. 10–14 yrs.

Dash, Joan. 1991. *The Triumph of Discovery: Women Scientists Who Won the Nobel Prize*. Morristown, N.J.: Silver Burdett/Julian Messner. 10–16 yrs.

Evans, J. Edward. 1993. *Charles Darwin: Revolutionary Biologist*. Photos & drawings. Minneapolis, Minn.: Lerner. 10–16 yrs.

Fisher, Leonard Everett. 1992. *Galileo*. New York: Macmillan. 10–12 yrs.

Fleischman, Paul. 1992. *Townsend's Warbler*. New York: HarperCollins/Charlotte Zolotow. 9–12 yrs.

Ireland, Karin. 1989. *Albert Einstein*. Morristown, N.J.: Silver Burdett. 10–14 yrs. Pioneers in Change series.

Mowat, Farley. 1987. *Woman in the Mists: The Story of Dian Fossey and the Mountain Gorillas of Africa*. New York: Warner. 12–15 yrs.

Pflaum, Rosalynd. 1993. *Marie Curie and Her Daughter Irene*. Photos. Minneapolis, Minn.: Lerner. 10–16 yrs.

Pringle, Laurence. 1989. *Bearman: Exploring the World of Black Bears*. Photos Lynn Rogers. New York: Scribners. 7–10 yrs.

———. 1991. *Batman*. New York: Scribners. 7–10 yrs.

———. 1993. *Jackal Woman: Exploring the World of Jackals*. Photos Patricia D. Moehlman. New York: Scribners. 10–12 yrs.

Simon, Sheridan. 1991. *Stephen Hawking: Unlocking the Universe*. Morristown, N.J.: Dillon/Silver Burdett. 10–12 yrs. People in Focus book.

Wilson, J. 1996. *The Ingenious Mr. Peale: Painter, Patriot and Man of Science.* Photos. New York: Atheneum. 11–14 yrs.

Information Books: General Concepts

Bulla, Clyde Robert. 1994. *What Makes a Shadow?* Illus. June Otani. New York: HarperCollins. Let's-Read-and-Find-Out Science Series.

Cobb, Vicki. 1989–91. *For Your Own Protection: Stories Science Photos Tell; Fun and Games: Stories Science Photos Tell; Natural Wonders: Stories Science Photos Tell.* New York: Lothrop, Lee & Shepard. 8–12 yrs.

Eldin, Peter. 1992. *Troll's Student Handbook.* Mahwah, N.J.: Troll Associates. 10–15 yrs.

Gallant, Roy A. 1989. *Before the Sun Dies: The Story of Evolution.* New York: Macmillan. 11–14 yrs.

Gamlin, Linda. 1993. *Eyewitness Science: Evolution.* Prints & photos. New York: Dorling Kindersley. 10–16 yrs.

Lavies, Bianca. 1993. *Compost Critters.* Photos B. Lavies. New York: Dutton. 10–13 yrs. Outstanding Science Trade Books for Children for 1994.

Lauber, Patricia. 1995. *Who Eats What?: Food Chains and Food Webs.* Illus. Holly Keller. New York: HarperCollins. 5–9 yrs.

Newmark, Ann. 1993. *Eyewitness Science: Chemistry.* Photos Dorling Kindersley. 12–16 yrs.

Skurzynski, Gloria. 1994. *Zero Gravity.* New York: Simon & Schuster/Bradbury. 9–11 yrs.

Thomson, David. 1991. *Visual Magic.* Illus. D. Thomson. New York: Dial. 6–10 yrs.

Wadsworth, Ginger. 1992. *Rachel Carson: Voice of the People.* Photos. Minneapolis, Minn.: Learner. 10–12 yrs.

Information Books: General & Experiments

Ardley, Neil. 1992. *The Science Book of Energy; The Science Book of Machines.* Photos Dave King. San Diego: Harcourt Brace/Gulliver. 10–12 yrs.

———. 1992. *The Science Book of Hot and Cold; The Science Book of the Senses.* Photos Clive Streeter. San Diego: Harcourt Brace/Gulliver. 10–12 yrs.

Bulla, Clyde Robert. 1994. *What Makes a Shadow?* Illus. June Otani. New York: HarperCollins. 5–8 yrs.

Richards, Roy. 1991. *101 Science Tricks: Fun Experiments with Everyday Materials.* Illus. Alex Pang. New York: Sterling. 7–12 yrs.

White, Laurence B., Jr. & Ray Broekel. 1991. *Shazam! Simple Science Magic.* Illus. Meyer Seltzer. Morton Grove, Ill.: Whitman. 8–12 yrs.

Zubrowski, B. 1994. *Making Waves: Finding Out about Rhythmic Motion.* Illus. Roy Doty. New York: Morrow. 9–11 yrs.

SPORTS

Biographies

Adler, David. 1989. *Jackie Robinson: He Was the First.* New York: Holiday. 7–12 yrs.

———. 1992. *A Picture Book of Jesse Owens.* New York: Holiday. 10–12 yrs.

Appel, Marty. 1992. *Joe DiMaggio.* New York: Chelsea. 10–12 yrs.

Aaseng, Nathan. 1983. *Baseball's Brilliant Managers.* Minneapolis, Minn.: Lerner. 9–12 yrs.

———. 1984. *Hockey's Fearless Goalies.* Minneapolis, Minn.: Lerner. 8–11 yrs.

———. 1985. *Carl Lewis: Legend Chaser.* Minneapolis, Minn.: Lerner. 8–12 yrs.

Bauleke, Ann. 1993. *Kirby Puckett: Fan Favorite.* Photos. Minneapolis, Minn.: Lerner. 9–12 yrs.

Donohue, Shibhan. 1993. *Kristi Yamaguchi: Artist on Ice.* Minneapolis, Minn.: Lerner. 9–12 yrs.

Frommer, Harvey. 1985. *Baseball's Hall of Fame.* Danbury, Conn.: Watts. 9–12 yrs.

Gilbert, Thomas W. 1992. *Lee Trevino.* New York: Chelsea. 10–15 yrs.

Goedecke, Christopher J. 1992. *The Wind Warrior: The Training of a Karate Champion.* Photos Rosmarie Hausher. New York: Simon & Schuster/Four Winds. 9–12 yrs.

Goldstein, Margaret J. 1992. *Brett Hull: Hockey's Top Gun.* Minneapolis, Minn.: Lerner. 9–12 yrs.

Goldenbock, Peter. 1990. *Teammates.* Illus. Paul Bacon. San Diego: Harcourt Brace. 9–12 yrs.

Grabowski, John. 1992. *Sandy Koufax.* New York: Chelsea. 9–12 yrs.

Greenberg, Keith Elliot. 1992. *Magic Johnson: Champion with a Cause.* Minneapolis, Minn.: Lerner. 9–12 yrs.

Humphrey, Kathryn Long. 1988. *Satchel Paige.* Danbury, Conn.: Watts. 8–12 yrs.

Jacobs, William Jay. 1994. *They Shaped the Game: Ty Cobb, Babe Ruth, Jackie Robinson.* Photos. New York: Scribners.

Johnson, Rick L. 1991. *Bo Jackson: Baseball/Football Superstar.* Morristown, N.J.: Dillon/Silver Burdett. 7–10 yrs. Taking Part Biography.

Kavanagh, Jack. 1992. *Walter Johnson.* New York: Chelsea. 9–12 yrs.

———. 1994. *Honus Wagner.* B & W photos. New York: Chelsea 10–13 yrs. Baseball Legends series.

Knudson, R. R. 1985. *Babe Didrikson.* New York: Viking. 8–10 yrs.

Krull, K. 1996. *Wilma Unlimited: How Wilma Rudolph Became the World's Fastest Woman.* Illus. David Diaz. Orlando, Fla.: Harcourt Brace. 7–12 yrs.

Littlefield, Bill. 1993. *Champions: Stories of Ten Remarkable Athletes.* Illus. Bernie Fuchs. Boston: Little, Brown. 10–12 yrs.

Macht, Norman L. 1991. *Christy Mathewson.* New York: Chelsea. 9–12 yrs.

———. 1992. *Cy Young.* New York: Chelsea. 9–12 yrs.

———. 1991. *Satchel Paige.* New York: Chelsea. 9–12 yrs.

———. 1994. *Tom Seaver.* B & W photos. New York: Chelsea. 10–13 yrs. Baseball Legends series.

Macy, Sue. 1993. *A Whole New Ball Game: The Story of the All-American Girls Professional Baseball League.* Prints & photos. New York: Holt. 12–16 yrs.

Macy, S. 1996. *Winning Ways: A Photohistory of American Women in Sports.* Photos. New York: Holt. 12–16 yrs.

Morris, A. 1996. *Karate Boy.* Photos David Katzenstein. New York: Dutton. 6–9 yrs.

Ryan, Nolan & Harvey Frommer. 1990. *Throwing Heat: The Autobiography of Nolan Ryan.* New York: Avon. 12–15 yrs.

Scott, Richard. 1987. *Jackie Robinson.* New York: Chelsea. 9–12 yrs.

Sullivan, George. 1993. *In-Line Skating: A Complete Guide for Beginners.* Photos. New York: Cobblehill. 9–12 yrs.

Walker, Paul Robert. 1988. *Pride of Puerto Rico: The Life of Roberto Clemente.* San Diego: Harcourt Brace. 9–12 yrs.

Weber, Bruce. 1986. *Magic Johnson/Larry Bird.* New York: Avon. 12–16 yrs.

Weidhorn, Manfred. 1993. *Jackie Robinson.* Photos. New York: Atheneum. 10–16 yrs.

Weissberg, Ted. 1991. *Arthur Ashe.* New York: Chelsea. 12–16 yrs.

Information Books

Anderson. Joan. 1996. *Batboy: An Inside Look at Spring Training.* Photos Matthew Cavanaugh. New York: Lodestar/Dutton. 8–10 yrs.

Appel, Marty. 1988. *The First Book Of Baseball.* New York: Crown. 9–11 yrs.

Barrett, Norman. 1988. *Hang Gliding.* Danbury, Conn.: Watts. 9–13 yrs.

———. 1988. *Skydiving.* Danbury, Conn.: Watts. 9–13 yrs.

Boyd, Brendan, and Robert Garrett. 1989. *Hoops: Behind the Scenes with the Boston Celtics.* Photos Henry Horenstein. Boston: Little, Brown/Pond. 9–12 yrs.

Diamond, Arthur. 1994. *Muhammad Ali.* B & W photos. San Diego: Lucent. 10–13 yrs. Importance of . . . Series.

Egan, Terry, Stan Friedmann & Mike Levine. 1992. *The Macmillan Book of Baseball Stories.* New York: Macmillan. 9–12 yrs.

Gait, Margot Fortunato. 1995. *Up to the Plate: The All American Girls Professional Baseball League.* Sepia-tone photos. Minneapolis, Minn.: Lerner. 10–12 yrs.

Goedecke, Christopher J. 1992. *The Wind Warrior: The Training of a Karate Champion.* Photos Rosemarie Hausher. New York: Simon & Schuster/Four Winds. 10–12 yrs.

Graham, Ian. 1995. *Sports.* Color photos. Chatham, N.J.: Raintree. 10–12 yrs. Science Spotlight series.

Gryski, Camilla. 1991. *Hands On, Thumbs Up.* Reading, Mass.: Addison Wesley. 8–12 yrs.

Hammond, Tim. 1988. *Sports.* New York: Knopf. 7–14 yrs. An Eyewitness Book.

Hanmer, Trudy J. 1994. *The All-American Girls Professional Baseball League.* New York: New Discovery. 10–13 yrs. American Events series.

Hautzig, David. 1995. *One Thousand Miles in Twelve Days: Pro Cyclists on Tour.* Photos. New York: Orchard. 10–12 yrs.

Hollander, Phyllis & Zander Hollander. 1990. *More Amazing But True Sports Stories.* New York: Scholastic/Associated Features. 9–12 yrs.

Horenstein, Henry. 1988. *Spring Training.* New York: Macmillan. 7–12 yrs.

Isberg, Emily. 1989. *Peak Performance: Sports, Science, and the Body in Action.* Simon & Schuster/NOVABOOKS. 9–12 yrs.

Jackman, Joan. 1995. *The Young Gymnast.* Color photos; foreword Shannon Miller. New York: Dorling Kindersley. 10–12 yrs.

Jensen, Julie. 1995. *Beginning Golf.* Color photos Andy King. Minneapolis, Minn.: Lerner. 10–12 yrs. Beginning Sports series.

———. 1995. *Beginning Soccer.* Color photos Andy King. Minneapolis, Minn.: Lerner. 10–12 yrs. Beginning Sports series.

———. 1995. *Beginning Tennis.* Color photos Andy King. Minneapolis, Minn.: Lerner. 10–12 yrs. Beginning Sports series.

———. 1995. *Beginning Volleyball.* Color photos Andy King. Minneapolis, Minn.: Lerner. 10–12 yrs. Beginning Sports series.

Knudson, R. R. & May Swenson. (Compilers) 1988. *American Sports Poems.* New York: Orchard. 11–16 yrs.

Krementz, Jill. 1986. *A Very Young Skater.* New York: Dell. 9–12 yrs.

Lankford, Mary D. 1992. *Hopscotch around the World.* Illus. Karen Milone. New York: Morrow. 8–12 yrs.

Madden, John. 1988. *The First Book Of Football.* New York: Crown. 10–13 yrs.

Margolies, Jacob. 1993. *The Negro Leagues: The Story of Black Baseball.* Prints & photos. Danbury, Conn.: Watts. 12–16 yrs.

Metil, Luana, & Jace Townsend. 1995. *The Story of Karate: From Buddhism to Bruce Lee.* B & W photos. Minneapolis, Minn.: Lerner. 10–12 yrs. Sports Legacy series.

Ritter, Lawrence S. 1990. *The Story of Baseball.* New York: Morrow. 10–12 yrs.

———. 1995. *Leagues Apart: The Men and Times of the Negro Baseball Leagues.* Illus. Richard Merkin. New York: Morrow. 10–12 yrs.

Rolfe, J. 1990. *Sureballs: Wacky Facts to Bat Around.* Boston: Little, Brown/Sports Illus. for Kids. 9–14 yrs.

Schmidt, Diane. 1990. *I Am a Jesse White Tumbler.* Photos Diane Schmidt. Morton Grove, Ill.: Whitman. 8–11 yrs.

Schulman, L. M. (Compiler). 1990. *The Random House Book of Sports Stories.* Illus. Thomas B. Allen. New York: Random House. 9–13 yrs.

Solomon, Chuck. 1988. *Our Soccer League.* New York: Crown. 5–9 yrs.

Sullivan, George. 1986. *Baseball Backstage: A Behind-the-Scenes Look at the New York Yankees.* New York: Holt. 9–13 yrs.

———. 1987. *All About Football.* Northbrook, Ill.: Dodd. 9–13 yrs.

Tallow, Peter. 1988. *The Olympics.* Charlottesville, Va.: Bookwrights. 8–12 yrs.

Thayer, Ernest Lawrence. 1988. *Casey At The Bat.* New York: Putnam. 10–16 yrs.

Ward, Geoffrey C., Ken Burns, & S. A. Kramer. 1994. *Twenty-Five Great Moments.* New York: Knopf. 11–16 yrs. Baseball, the American Epic series.

Ward, Geoffrey C., Ken Burns, & Jim O'Connor. 1994. *Shadow Ball: The History of the Negro Leagues.* New York: Knopf. Baseball, the American Epic series.

Ward, Geoffrey C., Ken Burns, & Paul Robert Walker. 1994. *Who Invented the Game?* New York: Knopf. 9–11 yrs. Baseball, the American Epic series.

Young, Robert. 1993. *Sports Cards.* Morristown, N.J.: Dillon/Silver Burdett. 9–12 yrs.

Transportation

Biographies

Berliner, Don. 1990. *Before the Wright Brothers.* B & W archival photos. Minneapolis, Minn.: Lerner. 10–16 yrs.

———. 1990. *The World Aerobatics Championships.* Minneapolis, Minn.: Lerner. 10–16 yrs.

Brown, Don. 1993. *Ruth Law Thrills a Nation.* New York: Ticknor & Fields. 6–9 yrs.

Burleigh, Robert. 1991. *Flight: The Journey of Charles Lindbergh.* Illus. Mike Wimmer. New York: Philomel. 7–10 yrs.

Denenberg, Barry. 1996. *An American Hero: The True Story of Charles A. Lindbergh.* Photos. New York: Scholastic. 12–17 yrs.

Freedman, Russell. 1991. *The Wright Brothers: How They Invented the Airplane.* Photos Wilbur & Orville Wright. New York: Holiday. 10–16 yrs.

Hart, Philip S. 1992. *Flying Free: America's First Black Aviators.* Photos. Minneapolis, Minn.: Lerner. 9–13 yrs. (collection).

Hook, Jason. 1989. *The Wright Brothers.* Illus. Peter Lowe. Charlottesville, Va.: Bookwrights. 9–12 yrs.

Marquardt, Mac. 1989. *Wilbur, Orville and the Flying Machine.* Illus. Mike Eagle. Chatham, N.J.: Raintree. 6–9 yrs.

Provensen, Alice & Martin Provensen. 1983. *The Glorious Flight: Across the Channel with Louis Bleriot.* New York: Viking. 6–9 yrs.

Swanson, J. 1991. *David Bushnell and His Turtle: The Story of America's First Submarine.* Illus. Mike Eagle. New York: Atheneum. 10–13 yrs.

Wallner, A. 1996. *The First Air Voyage in the United States: The Story of Jean Pierre Blanchard.* New York: Holiday. 5–8 yrs.

Information Books

Ayres, Carter M. 1990. *Pilots and Aviation.* Minneapolis, Minn.: Lerner. 10–16 yrs.

Baer, Edith. 1990. *This Is the Way We Go to School: A Book about Children around the World.* Illus. Steven Bjorkman. New York: Scholastic. 3–7 yrs.

Bellville, Cheryl Walsh. 1993. *Flying in a Hot Air Balloon.* Photos C. Bellville. Minneapolis, Minn.: Carolrhoda. 8–12 yrs.

Blanchard, Anne. 1992. *Navigation: A 3-Dimensional Exploration.* Illus. Irvine Peacock. New York: Orchard. 8–12 yrs.

Brown, Laurie Krasny & Marc Brown. 1988. *Dinosaurs Travel: A Guide for Families on the Go.* Illus. Marc Brown. Boston: Little, Brown/Joy Street. 4–8 yrs.

Churchill, E. Richard. 1990. *Instant Paper Airplanes.* New York: Sterling. 8–12 yrs.

Eyewitness Series Editors. 1990. *Flying Machine.* New York: Knopf. 8–12 yrs.

Fisher, Leonard Everett. 1992. *Tracks across America: The Story of the American Railroad, 1825–1900.* New York: Holiday. 10–12 yrs.

Francis, Neil. 1988. *Super Flyers.* Reading, Mass.: Addison Wesley. 8–12 yrs.

Fraser, Maryann. 1993. *Ten Mile Day and the Building of the Transcontinental Railroad.* Illus. M. Fraser. New York: Holt. 9–12 yrs.

Gibbons, Gail. 1992. *The Great St. Lawrence Seaway.* Illus. Gail Gibbons. New York: Morrow. 9–12 yrs.

———. 1995. *Bicycle Book.* New York: Holiday. 5–8 yrs.

Johnson, Neil. 1991. *Fire and Silk: Flying in a Hot Air Balloon.* Photos N. Johnson. Boston: Little, Brown/Joy Street. 4–8 yrs.

Johnstone, Michael. 1994. *Look Inside Cross-Sections Planes.* Illus. Hans Jenssen. New York: Dorling Kindersley. 10–14 yrs.

Kaufmann, John. 1989. *Voyager.* Illus. J. Kaufmann; introduction Burt Rutans & Jeanna Yeager. Springfield, N.J.: Enslow. 11–16 yrs.

Lindblom, Steven. 1991. *Fly the Hot Ones.* Boston: Houghton Mifflin. 9–12 yrs.

Macaulay, David. 1993. *Ship.* Boston: Houghton Mifflin. 10–12 yrs.

Maurer, Richard. 1990. *Airborne.* Illus. Brian Lies. New York: Simon & Schuster. 10–16 yrs.

McVey, Vicki. 1989. *The Sierra Club Wayfinding Book.* Illus. Martha Weston. Boston: Little, Brown. 9–12 yrs.

Moseley, Keith. 1989. *Steam Locomotives: A Three-Dimensional Book.* Illus. Brian Bartle & Brian Watson. New York: Orchard. 6–10 yrs.

Moser, Barry. 1993. *Fly! A Brief History of Flight Illustrated.* Illus. B. Moser. New York: HarperCollins. 10–16 yrs.

Platt, Richard. 1993. *Stephen Biesty's Incredible Cross-Sections Man-of-War.* Illus. Stephen Biesty. New York: Dorling Kindersley. 11–15 yrs.

Powledge, Fred. 1995. *Working River.* B & W photos. New York: Farrar, Straus & Giroux. 10–13 yrs.

Robbins, Ken. 1989. *Boats.* Photos K. Robbins. New York: Scholastic. 3–8 yrs.

———. 1991. *Bridges.* Photos K. Robbins. New York: Dial. 4–8 yrs.

Rotner, S. 1995. *Wheels Around.* Color photos. Boston: Houghton Mifflin. 5–8 yrs.

Siebert, Diane. 1993. *Plane Song.* Illus. Vincent Nasta. New York: HarperCollins. 10–16 yrs.

Tanaka, Shelley. 1993. *The Disaster of the Hindenburg: The Last Flight of the Greatest Airship Ever Built.* Prints & photos. New York: Scholastic Hardcover. 10–16 yrs.

Tessendorf, K. C. 1988. *Barnstormers and Daredevils.* New York: Atheneum. 11–14 yrs.

Wormser, Richard. 1994. *Hoboes: Wandering in America, 1870–1940.* Photos. New York: Walker. 11–14 yrs.

Yepsen, Roger. 1993. *City Trains: Moving Through America's Cities Rail.* Photos. New York: Macmillan. 10–12 yrs.

INFORMATION BOOKS ORGANIZED ACCORDING TO TOPICS

Alphabet Books

Agard, J. 1993. *The Calypso Alphabet.* Illus. Jennifer Bent. New York: Henry Holt. 5–8 yrs.

Alda, A. 1993. *Arlene Alda's ABC.* Photos. Berkeley, Calif.: Tricycle Press. 4–8 yrs.

Andersen, K. 1993. *Born an Alphabet in Five Acts.* Illus. Flint Born. New York: Dial. 4–8 yrs.

Argent, K. 1989. *Animal Capers.* Illus. Kerry Argent. New York: Dial. 3–7 yrs.

Aylesworth, J. 1992. *The Folks in the Valley: A Pennsylvania/Dutch ABC.* Illus. Stefano Vitale. New York: HarperCollins. 3–10 yrs.

Baker, A. 1994. *Black and White Rabbit's ABC.* New York: Kingfisher. 2–4 yrs. Little Rabbit series.

Bayer, J. 1984. *A My Name Is Alice.* Illus. Steven Kellogg. New York: Dial. 5–9 yrs.

Bernhard, D. *Alphabeasts: A Hide and Seek Alphabet Book.* New York: Holiday. 4–7 yrs.

Blake, Q. 1989. *Quentin Blake's ABC.* New York: Knopf/Borzoi. 4–6 yrs.

Bourke, L. 1991. *Eye Spy: A Mysterious Alphabet.* San Francisco, Calif.: Chronicle. 7–12 yrs.

Boynton, S. 1987. *A Is for Angry: An Animals and Adjective Alphabet.* New York: Workman. 6–10 yrs.

Brown, M. W. 1994. *Sleepy ABC.* Illus. Esphyr Slobodkina. New York: HarperCollins. 4–6 yrs.

Brown, R. 1991. *Alphabet Times Four: An International ABC.* New York: Dutton. 6–11 yrs.

Browne, B. 1991. *Antler, Bear, Canoe: A Northwoods Alphabet Year.* Boston: Little, Brown/Joy Street. 4–8 yrs.

Browne, P. 1995. *African Animals ABC.* Boston: Sierra. 5–9 yrs.

Burningham, J. 1993. *John Burningham's ABC.* New York: Crown. 5–7 yrs.

Cohen, N. 1993. *From Apple to Zipper.* Illus. Donna Kern. New York: Macmillan. 5–8 yrs.

Cousins, L. 1995. *Maisy's ABC.* Cambridge, Mass.: Candlewick. 2–5 yrs.

Cox, L. 1990. *Crazy Alphabet.* Illus. Rodney McRae. New York: Orchard. 3–6 yrs.

Crowther, R. 1995. *Robert Crowther's Incredible Animal Alphabet.* Cambridge, Mass.: Candlewick. 2–5 yrs.

Demi. 1985. *Demi's Find the Animal ABC.* New York: Putnam/Sandcastle. 4–9 yrs.

Dodd, L. 1994. *The Minister's Cat ABC.* Gareth Stevens. 7–11 yrs.

Downie, J. 1988. *Alphabet Puzzle.* New York: Lothrop, Lee & Shepard. 5–10 yrs.

Duke, K. 1983. *The Guinea Pig ABC.* New York: Dutton. 5–9 yrs.

Edwards, M. 1992. *Alef-Bet: A Hebrew Alphabet Book.* New York: Lothrop, Lee & Shepard. 5–8 yrs.

Ehlert, Lois. 1989. *Eating the Alphabet: Fruits and Vegetables from A to Z*. Illus. L. Ehlert. Orlando, Fla.: Harcourt Brace Jovanovich. 3–8 yrs.

Elliot, D. 1991. *A Alphabet of Rotten Kids*. Illus. Oscar de Mejo. New York: Philomel. 6–11 yrs.

Etling, M. & M. Folsom. 1980. *Q is for Duck*. Illus. Jack Kent. New York: Clarion. 6–8 yrs.

Folsom, M. & M. Folsom. 1985. *Easy as Pie: A Guessing Game of Sayings*. Illus. Jack Kent. New York: Clarion. 9–12 yrs.

Garten, J. 1994. *The Alphabet Tale*. Illus. Muriel Batherman. New York: Greenwillow. 3–6 yrs.

Goennel, H. 1993. *Heidi's Zoo: An Un-Alphabet Book*. New York: Tambourine. 4–6 yrs.

Gordon, R. K. 1990. *A Canadian ABC: An Alphabet Book for Kids*. Illus. Thoreau MacDonald. University of Toronto Press/Penumbra. 8–12 yrs.

Grover, M. 1993. *The Accidental Zucchini: An Unexpected Alphabet*. New York: Browndeer. 4–6 yrs.

Hepworth, C. 1992. *Antics! An Alphabetical Anthology*. New York: Putnam. 6–12 yrs.

Howland, N. 1994. *ABC Drive!: A Car Trip Alphabet*. New York: Clarion. 2–5 yrs.

Hyman, T. S. 1993. *A Little Alphabet*. New York: Morrow. 4–6 yrs. Books of Wonder series.

Jacobs, L. 1994. *Alphabet of Girls*. Illus. B. Ohlsson. New York: Holt. 6–12 yrs.

Janovitx, M. 1994. *Look Out, Bird!* New York: North-South. 3–6 yrs.

Jonas, A. 1990. *Aardvarks, Disembark!* New York: Greenwillow. 4–7 yrs.

Kellogg, S. 1987. *Aster Aardvark's Alphabet Adventures*. New York: Morrow. 7–11 yrs.

King-Smith, D. 1992. *Alphabeasts*. Illus. Quentin Blake. New York: Macmillan. 8–12 yrs.

Kitamura, S. 1992. *From Acorn to Zoo: And Everything in Between in Alphabetical Order*. New York: Farrar, Straus & Giroux. 4–7 yrs.

Lear, E. 1992. *A Was Once an Apple Pie*. Illus. Julie Lacome. New York: Candlewick. 4–7 yrs.

Lecourt, N. 1991. *Abracadabra to Zigzag*. Illus. Barbara Lehman. New York: Lothrop, Lee & Shepard. 7–10 yrs.

Lessac, F. 1994. *Caribbean Alphabet*. New York: Tambourine. 4–6 yrs.

Lobel, A. 1990. *Alison's Zinnia*. New York: Greenwillow. 3–11 yrs.

———. 1994. *Away from Home*. New York: Greenwillow. 6–8 yrs.

Lyon, G. E. 1989. *A B Cedar: An Alphabet of Trees*. Illus. Tom Parker. New York: Orchard. 4–8 yrs.

MacKinnon, D. 1992. *My First ABC*. Photos Anthea Sieveking. Hauppauge, N.Y.: Barron's. 3–6 yrs.

MacDonald, S. 1986. *Alphabatics*. New York: Bradbury. 5–10 yrs.

Mahurin, T. 1995. *Jeremy Kooloo*. New York: Dutton. 3–6 yrs.

Marshall, J. 1995. *Look Once, Look Twice*. New York: Ticknor & Fields. 4–7 yrs.

Maurer, D. 1993. *Annie, Bea, and Chi Chi Dolores: A School Day Alphabet*. New York: Orchard. 3–6 yrs.

Mayers, F. C. 1988. *ABC Musical Instruments from the Metropolitan Museum of Art*. New York: Abrams. 6–13 yrs. (See also other books in series: *ABC Egyptian Art from the Brooklyn Museum*; *ABC The Museum of Modern Art, New York*; *ABC Museum of Fine Arts, Boston*.)

Merriam, E. 1989. *Where Is Everybody? An Animal Alphabet*. Illus. Diane de Groat. New York: Simon and Schuster. 3–6 yrs.

Neumeier, M. & B. Glaser. 1985. *Action Alphabet*. New York: Greenwillow. 5–9 yrs.

Owens, M. B. 1990. *A Caribou Alphabet*. New York: Farrar, Straus & Giroux/Sunburst. 3–6 yrs.

Patterson, B. Illustrated 1992. *Baby's ABC*. New York: Grosset. 2–4 yrs.

Phillips, T. 1989. *Day Care ABC*. Illus. Dora Leder. Morton, Grove, Ill.: Whitman. 2–7 yrs.

Rankin, L. 1991. *The Handmade Alphabet*. New York: Dial. 5–10 yrs.

Rubin, C. E. (Selector). 1989. *ABC Americana from the National Gallery of Art*. Paintings. Orlando, Fla.: Harcourt Brace Jovanovich/Gulliver. 6–14 yrs.

Sardegna, J. 1994. *K Is for Kiss Good Night: A Bedtime Alphabet*. Illus. Michael Hays. New York: Doubleday. 4–6 yrs.

Sarasas, C. 1964. *The ABCs of Origami: Paper Folding for Children*. Rootstown, Oh.: Tuttle. 6–12 yrs.

Sharon, L. & B. Sharon. 1992. *Sing A to Z*. Illus. Kim LaFave. New York: Crown. 6–13 yrs.

Shelby, A. 1991. *Potluck*. Illus. Irene Trivas. New York: Orchard. 3–6 yrs.

Simpson, Gretchen Dow. 1991. *Gretchen's abc*. New York: HarperCollins/Laura Geringer. 3–6 yrs.

Sloat, T. 1989. *From Letter to Letter*. New York: Puffin Unicorn. 5–9 yrs.

Snow, A. 1991. *The Monster Book of A B C Sounds*. New York: Dial. 2–10 yrs.

Steig, Jeanne. 1992. *Alpha Beta Chowder*. Illus. William Steig. New York: HarperCollins. 8–11 yrs.

Stock, C. 1988. *Alexander's Midnight Snack: A Little Elephant's ABC*. New York: Clarion. 3–6 yrs.

Sullivan, C. 1991. *Alphabet Animals*. New York: Rizzoli. 6–12 yrs.

Tryon, L. 1991. *Albert's Alphabet*. New York: Atheneum. 5–9 yrs.

Tucker, S. 1995. *A Is for Astronaut: My First Lift-the-Flap ABC*. New York: Simon & Schuster. 2–5 yrs.

Van Allsburg, C. 1987. *The Z Was Zapped*. New York: Clarion. 7–13 yrs.

Wilks, M. 1986. *The Ultimate Alphabet*. New York: Holt. 8–16 yrs.

Wilner, I. 1991. *A Garden Alphabet*. Illus. Ashley Wolff. New York: Dutton. 4–6 yrs.

Wood, J. 1993. *Animal Parade*. New York: Bradbury. 4–7 yrs.

AERONAUTICS AND SPACE

Asimov, Isaac. 1991. *The Asteroids. Space Garbage*. New York: Dell/Yearling. 7–12 yrs.

Branley, Franklyn M. 1988. *Uranus: The Seventh Planet*. Illus. Yvonne Buchanan. New York: Crowell. 9–11 yrs.

———. 1994. *Venus: Magellan Explores Our Twin Planet*. New York: HarperCollins. 9–11 yrs.

Bensusen. New York: Lodestar/Dutton. 10–15 yrs. (Sixth book in *Mysteries of the Universe Series*)

———. 1989. *Shooting Stars*. Illus. Holly Keller. New York: Crowell. 5–9 yrs. Let's-Read-and-Find-Out Science Books.

———. 1990. *Superstar: The Supernova of 1987*. Illus. True Kelley. New York: Crowell. 8–12 yrs.

Castaldo, N. F. 1996. *Sunny Days and Starry Night*. Williamson, MA: Williamson. 2–6 yrs.

Couper, Heather & Nigel Henbest. 1986. *Galaxies and Quasars*. Danbury, Conn.: Watts. 9–12 yrs.

Curlee, L. 1996. *Ships of the Air*. Illus. Lynn Curlee. Boston: Houghton Mifflin. 9–12 yrs.

Dickinson, T. 1996. *Exploring the Night Sky: The Equinox Astronomy Guide for Beginners*. Buffalo, N.Y.: Camden House/Firefly. 6–10 yrs.

———. 1996. *Exploring the Sky by Day: The Equinox Guide to Weather and the Atmosphere*. Buffalo, N.Y.: Camden House/Firefly. 6–10 yrs.

Embury, Barbara, with Thomas D. Couch. 1990. *The Dream Is Alive: A Flight of Discovery Aboard the Space Shuttle*. New York: Harper Row/Somerville. 6–14 yrs.

Harris, Alan & Paul Weissman. 1990. *The Great Voyager Adventure: A Guided Tour through the Solar System*. Morristown, N.J.: Silver Burdett/Julian Messner. 10–15 yrs.

Hirst, Robin & Sally Hirst. 1990. *My Place in Space*. Illus. Roland Harvey & Joe Levine. New York: Orchard. 6–14 yrs.

Jenkins, S. 1996. *Looking Down*. Burlington, Mass.: Houghton Mifflin. 6–13 yrs.

Johnstone, M. 1994. *Look Inside Cross-Sections Planes*. Illus. Hans Jensen. New York: Dorling Kindersley. 9–12 yrs.

Jones, Brian. 1991. *Space: A Three-Dimensional Journey*. Illus. Richard Clifton-Dey. New York: Dial. 7–10 yrs.

Kelch, Joseph W. 1990. *Small Worlds: Exploring the 60 Moons of Our Solar System*. Morristown, N.J.: Silver Burdett/Julian Messner. 11–15 yrs.

Lauber, Patricia. 1990. *Seeing Earth from Space*. New York: Orchard. 10–15 yrs.

Maurer, Richard. 1989. *Junk In Space*. New York: Simon & Schuster. 10–14 yrs.

Moore, P. 1996. *The Starry Sky*. Illus. Paul Doherty. Brookfield, Conn.: Cooper Beach/Millbrook. 4–8 yrs.

National Geographic Editors. 1989. *Exploring Your Solar System*. Washington, D.C.: National Geographic. 9–13 yrs.

Night Sky Action Pack: An Interactive Journey Through the Night Sky. 1996. New York: Dorling Kindersley. 6–12 yrs.

Ride, Sally & Tam O'Shaughnessy. 1994. *The Third Planet: Exploring the Earth from Space*. New York: Crown. 10–14 yrs.

Rosen, S. 1996. *Can You Catch a Falling Star?* Illus. Dean Lindberg. Minneapolis, Minn.: Carolrhoda. 5–8 yrs.

Skurzynski, Gloria. 1994. *Zero Gravity*. New York: Simon & Schuster/Bradbury. 8–11 yrs.

Simon, Seymour. 1991. *Galaxies*. Color photos. New York: Mulberry. 7–11 yrs.

———. 1991. *Space Worlds: A Dictionary*. Illus. Randy Chewning. New York: HarperCollins. 7–11 yrs.

———. 1992. *Our Solar System*. Color photos. New York: Morrow. 5–10 yrs.

———. 1992. *Mercury. Venus*. Color photos. New York: Morrow. 5–10 yrs.

———. 1994. *Comets, Meteors, and Asteroids*. New York: Morrow. 9–11 yrs.

Stott, C. 1996. *I Wonder Why Stars Twinkle: and Other Questions About Space*. New York: Kingfisher. 4–9 yrs.

Verba, Joan Marie. 1991. *Voyager: Exploring the Outer Planets*. Minneapolis, Minn.: Lerner. 11–15 yrs.

Verdet, J. P. 1996. *Earth, Sky and Beyond: A Journey through Space*. Illus. Pierre Bon. New York: Lodestar/Dutton. 6–12 yrs.

Visual Dictionary of the Earth. 1993. New York: Dorling Kindersley. 10–16 yrs. Eyewitness Visual Dictionaries.

Vogt, Gregory L. 1994. *Venus*. Minneapolis, Minn.: Carolrhoda. 1–14 yrs.

ANIMALS

Characteristics and Behavior of Animals

Arnosky, Jim. 1995. *I See Animals Hiding*. New York: Scholastic. 5–9 yrs.

Barkan, Joanne. 1991. *Creatures That Glow*. New York: Doubleday. 7–11 yrs.

Batten, Mary. 1992. *Nature's Tricksters: Animals and Plants That Aren't What They Seem*. Illus. Lois Lovejoy. Boston: Sierra Club/Little, Brown. 8–17 yrs.

Brooks, Bruce. 1993. *Making Sense: Animal Perception and Communication*. Photos. New York: Farrar, Straus & Giroux. 11–15 yrs. Knowing Nature Series.

Clarke, Barry. 1990. *Amazing Frogs and Toads*. Photos Jerry Young. New York: Knopf/Borzoi. 4–12 yrs.

Dewey, Jennifer Owings. 1989. *Can You Find Me? A Book about Animal Camouflage*. Illus. J. O. Dewey. New York: Scholastic. 4–7 yrs.

———. 1991. *Animal Architecture*. Illus. J. O. Dewey. New York: Orchard. 5–10 yrs.

Dorros, Arthur. 1991. *Animal Tracks*. Illus. A. Dorros. New York: Scholastic. 3–7 yrs.

Feldman, Eve B. 1992. *Animals Don't Wear Pajamas: A Book about Sleeping*. Illus. Mary Beth Owens. New York: Holt. 3–6 yrs.

Facklam, Margery. 1994. *What Does the Crow Know?: The Mysteries of Animal Intelligence*. Illus. Pamela Johnson. San Francisco: Sierra. 10–14 yrs.

Fleming, Denise. 1994. *Barnyard Banter*. Illus. Denise Fleming. New York: Holt. 16 mos.–3 yrs.

George, Jean Craighead. 1992. *The Moon of the Chickarees; The Moon of the Fox Pups; The Moon of the Salamanders*. Illus. Norman Adams; Don Rodell; Marlene Hill Wernor. New York: HarperCollins. 8–12 yrs.

Hirschi, Ron. 1993. *A Time for Babies*. Photos R. Hirschi. New York: Cobblehill. 6–9 yrs.

Jenkins, Steve. 1995. *Biggest, Strongest, Fastest*. New York: Ticknor & Fields. 5–9 yrs.

Johnson, Rebecca L. 1989. *The Secret Language: Pheromones in the Animal World*. Minneapolis, Minn.: Lerner. 10–13 yrs.

Kitchen, Bert. 1992. *Somewhere Today*. Illus. B. Kitchen. Cambridge, Mass.: Candlewick. 8–11 yrs.

Landau, Elaine. 1993. *Rabies*. Photos E. Landau. New York: Lodestar/Dutton. 6–12 yrs.

Machotka, Hana. 1992. *Breathtaking Noses*. Photos. New York: Morrow. 5–8 yrs.

———. 1994. *Terrific Tails*. New York: Morrow. 5–9 yrs.

Mirocha. 1992. *Awesome Animal Actions; Baffling Bird Behavior; Freaky Fish Facts; Incredible Insect Instincts*. Illus. Paul Mirocha. New York: HarperCollins/HarperFestival. 5–9 yrs. Amazing Nature Pop-up Books.

Morris, Desmond. 1993. *The World of Animals*. Illus. Peter Barrett. New York: Viking. 10–12 yrs.

Myers, Jack (Ed.). 1991. *Can Birds Get Lost? And Other Questions About Animals*. Illus. John Rice, Tome & Mimi Powers. Honesdale, Penn.: Boyd Mills. 8–13 yrs.

Parsons, Alexandra. 1990. *Amazing Birds; Amazing Cats; Amazing Mammals; Amazing Poisonous Animals; Amazing Snakes; Amazing Spiders*. Photos. New York: Knopf. 9–13 yrs.

Patent, Dorothy Hinshaw. 1995. *Why Mammals Have Fur*. Photos William Muhoz. New York: Cobblehill. 5–9 yrs.

Presnall, Judith Janda. 1993. *Animals that Glow*. Photos. Danbury, Conn.: Watts. 7–10 yrs.

Rauzon, Mark J. 1993. *Horns, Antlers, Fangs, and Tusks*. Color photos. New York: Lothrop, Lee & Shepard. 5–8 yrs.

———. 1993. *Skin, Scales, Feathers, and Fur*. New York: Lothrop, Lee & Shepard. 5–8 yrs.

Riha, Susanne. 1989. *Animals in Winter*. Illus. Susanne Riha. Minneapolis, Minn.: Carolrhoda. 8–10 yrs.

Royston, Angela. 1991–92. *Chick; Duck; Frog; Kitten; Puppy; Rabbit*. Photos Jane Burton; Kim Taylor; Barrie Danbury. New York: Lodestar/Dutton. 3–7 yrs.

Silverstein, Alvin, Virginia Silverstein & Robert Silverstein. 1992. *Smell, the Subtle Sense*. Illus. Ann Neumann. New York: Morrow. 10–12 yrs.

Smith, Trevor. 1990. *Amazing Lizards*. Photos Jerry Young. New York: Knopf/Borzoi. 4–12 yrs.

DOMESTICATED ANIMALS

Cats

Clutton-Brock, Juliet. *Cats*. New York: Knopf. 9–12 yrs. Eyewitness Books.

Cole, Joanna. 1995. *My New Kitten*. Photos Margaret Miller. New York: Morrow. 5–9 yrs.

Fogle, Bruce. 1991. *Know Your Cat*. New York: Dorling Kindersley. 10–14 yrs.

Hirschi, Ron. 1991. *What Is a Cat? Where Do Cats Live?* Photos Linda Quartman. New York: Walker. 5–9 yrs.

Jessel, Camilla. 1992. *The Kitten Book*. Photos. Cambridge, Mass.: Candlewick. 2–5 yrs.

Dogs

Arnold, Caroline. 1991. *Guide Dog: Puppy Grows Up*. Photos Richard Hewett. San Diego: Harcourt Brace. 9–12 yrs.

Ashabranner, Brent. 1990. *Crazy about German Shepherds*. Photos Jennifer Ashabranner. New York: Cobblehill. 10–13 yrs.

Calmenson, Stephanie. 1994. *Rosie: A Visiting Dog's Story*. Photos Justin Sutcliffe. New York: Clarion. 7–9 yrs.

Cohen, Susan & Daniel Cohen. 1989. *What Kind of a Dog Is That?* Photos. New York: Dutton. 9–12 yrs.

Cooper, Michael. 1988. *Racing Sled Dogs*. Photos. New York: Clarion. 8–12 yrs.

Crisman, Ruth. 1993. *Racing the Iditarod Trail*. Photos. Morristown, N.J.: Dillon/Silver Burdett. 10–13 yrs.

Curtis, Patricia. 1989. *Dogs on the Case: Search Dogs Who Help Save Lives and Enforce the Law*. Photos David Cupp. New York: Lodestar/Dutton. 10–16 yrs.

Jessel, Camilia. 1992. *The Puppy Book*. Photos. Cambridge, Mass.: Candlewick. 5–8 yrs.

Kramer, S. A. 1993. *Adventure in Alaska: An Amazing True Story of the World's Longest, Toughest, Dog Sled Race*. Illus. Karen Meyer; photos. New York: Random House. 8–12 yrs. Read It To Believe It!

Patent, Dorothy Hinshaw. 1993. *Dogs: The Wolf Within*. Photos William Munoz. Minneapolis, Minn.: Carolrhoda. Understanding Animals Series. 9–12 yrs.

Squire, Ann. 1991. *Understanding Man's Best Friend*. New York: Macmillan. 9–12 yrs.

Horses

Ancona, George. 1992. *Man and Mustang*. New York: Macmillan. 10–12 yrs. Photo essay.

Cole, Joanna. 1996. *Riding Silver Star*. New York: Morrow. 7–9 yrs.

Frydenborg, Kay. 1992. *Who Harnessed the Horse? The Story of Animal Domestication*. Illus. Steven Parton. Boston: Little, Brown. 9–14 yrs.

———. 1994. *They Dreamed of Horses: Careers for Horse Lovers*. Illus. & photos. Tanya Wood. New York: Walker. 10–15 yrs.

Hansard, Peter A. 1994. *A Field Full of Horses*. Illus. Kenneth Lilly. Cambridge, Mass.: Candlewick. 5–8 yrs. Read and Wonder Series.

Hirschi, Ron. 1989. *What Is a Horse? Where Do Horses Live?* Photos Linda Quartman Younker & Ron Hirschi. New York: Walker. 6–9 yrs.

Jauck, Andrea & Larry Points. 1993. *Assateague*. New York: Macmillan. 9–12 yrs.

Jurmain, Suzanne. 1989. *Once Upon a Horse: A History of Horses and How They Shaped Our History*. New York: Lothrop, Lee & Shepard. 10–16 yrs. Notable 1989 Children's Trade Books in the Field of Social Studies.

McFarland, Cynthia. 1993. *Hoofbeats: The Story of a Thoroughbred*. Photos C. McFarland. New York: Atheneum. 7–12 yrs.

Paten, Dorothy Hinshaw. 1994. *Horses*. Photos William J. Munoz. Minneapolis, Minn.: Carolrhoda. 10–13 yrs. Understanding Animals Series.

Rodenas, Paula. 1991. *Horses and Horsemanship*. Book designer Jane Byers Bierhorst. New York: Random House. 11–17 yrs.

Saville, Lynne. 1989. *Horses in the Circus Ring*. Photos L. Saville. New York: Dutton. 5–9 yrs.

———. 1991. *The Ultimate Horse Book*. New York: Dorling Kindersley. 8–15 yrs.

Others

Clayton, Gordon. 1993. *Calf*. Photos G. Clayton. New York: Dorling Kindersley. 2–5 yrs. See How They Grow series.

King-Smith, Dick. 1993. *All Pigs Are Beautiful*. Illus. Anita Jeram. Cambridge, Mass.: Candlewick. 5–8 yrs. Read and Wonder Series.

———. 1995. *I Love Guinea Pigs*. Illus. Anita Jeram. Cambridge, Mass.: Candlewick. 5–9 yrs.

Ling, Bill. 1993. *Pig*. Photos B. Ling. New York: Dorling Kindersley. 4–6 yrs. See How They Grow series.

Ziefert, Harriet. 1993. *Let's Get a Pet*. Illus. Mavis Smith. New York: Viking. 5–9 yrs.

WILD ANIMALS

Elephants

Arnold, Caroline. 1993. *Elephant*. Photos Richard Hewett. New York: Morrow. 10–12 yrs.

Grace, Eric S. 1993. *Elephants: The Sierra Club Wildlife Library*. Illus. & photos Dorothy Slems. San Francisco, Calif.: Sierra Club. 9–11 yrs.

Le Tord, Bijou. 1993. *Elephant Moon*. Illus. B. Le Tord. New York: Bantam Doubleday Dell. 8–11 yrs.

Patent, Dorothy Hinshaw. 1991. *African Elephants*. Photos. New York: Holiday. 9–12 yrs.

———. 1994. *Deer and Elk*. Photos William Nunoz. New York: Clarion. 10–13 yrs.

Payne, Katharine. 1992. *Elephants Calling*. Photos. New York: Crown. 10–12 yrs. Face to Face with Science series.

Riley, L. C. 1995. *Elephants Swim*. Illus. Steve Jenkins. Boston: Houghton Mifflin. 5–8 yrs.

Schlein, Meriam. 1990. *Elephants*. Photos. New York: Atheneum/Aladdin. 9–12 yrs.

Schmidt, Jeremy. 1994. *In the Village of the Elephants*. Photos Ted Wood. New York: Walker. 10–12 yrs.

Sobol, Richard. 1995. *One More Elephant: The Fight to Save Wildlife in Uganda*. Color photos. New York: Cobblehill. 10–13 yrs.

Yoshida, Toshi. 1989. *Elephant Crossing*. Illus. T. Yoshida. New York: Philomel. 8–10 yrs.

Others

Ackerman, Diane. 1991. *The Moon Whale Light*. New York: Random House. 12–16 yrs.

Arnold, Caroline. 1989–91. *Cheetah; Flamingo; Hippo; Orangutan; Snake; Wild Goat.* Photos Richard Hewett. New York: Morrow. 7–14 yrs. Notable Children's Trade Books in Science, 1989.

———. 1993. *Monkey.* Photos Richard Hewett. New York: Morrow. 10–12 yrs.

———. 1996. *Bat.* Photos Richard Hewett. New York: Morrow. 10–13 yrs.

———. 1996. *Fox.* Photos Richard Hewett. New York: Morrow. 9–13 yrs.

Arnosky, Jim. 1989. *Crinkleroot's Book of Animal Tracking.* Illus. J. Arnosky. New York: Simon & Schuster/Bradbury. 7–11 yrs.

Bare, Colleen Stanley. 1993. *Never Grab a Deer the Ear.* New York: Cobblehill. 5–8 yrs.

Bash, Barbara. 1993. *Shadows of Night: The Hidden World of the Little Brown Bat.* San Francisco: Sierra Club. 5–8 yrs.

Berman, Ruth. 1992. *American Bison.* Photos Cheryl Walsh Bellville. Minneapolis, Minn.: Carolrhoda. 7–10 yrs. Nature Watch series.

Bird, E. J. 1990. *How Do Bears Sleep?* Illus. E. J. Bird. Minneapolis, Minn.: Carolrhoda. 4–8 yrs.

Brandenburg, Jim. 1993. *To the Top of the World: Adventures with Arctic Wolves.* Photos. New York: Walker. 10–17 yrs.

Bowen, Betsy. 1991. *Antler Bear Canoe.* Boston: Little, Brown. 9–12 yrs.

———. 1993. *Tracks in the Wild.* Illus. B. Bowen. Boston: Little, Brown. 9–12 yrs.

Brooks, Bruce. 1991. *Nature Design.* Color photos. New York: Farrar, Straus & Giroux. 9–14 yrs.

———. 1991. *Predator.* Color photos. New York: Farrar, Straus & Giroux. 9–14 yrs.

Clark, Margaret Goff. 1993. *The Endangered Florida Panther.* Photos. New York: Cobblehill. 10–14 yrs.

Darling, Kathy. 1993. *Kangaroos: On Location.* Photos K. Darling. New York: Lothrop, Lee & Shepard. 10–12 yrs.

Davolls, Linda. 1994. *Tano & Binti: Two Chimpanzees Return to the Wild.* Illus. Andy DaVolls. New York: Clarion. 5–8 yrs.

Halton, Cheryl M. 1991. *Those Amazing Bats.* Morristown, N.J.: Dillon/Silver Burdett. 9–12 yrs.

Hewett, Joan. 1993. *Tiger, Tiger, Growing Up.* Photos Richard Hewett. New York: Clarion. 7–9 yrs.

Hilker, Cathryn Hosea. 1992. *A Cheetah Named Angel.* Photos C. H. Hilker. Danbury, Conn.: Watts. 8–11 yrs.

Hofer, Angelika, Gunter Ziesler & Jonathon Scott. 1988–91. *The Lion Family; The Leopard Family in Books.* Photos authors. New York: Simon & Schuster/Picture Book. 8–12 yrs.

Johnston, Ginny & Judy Cutchins. 1990. *Windows on Wildlife.* New York: Morrow. 7–12 yrs.

Jones, Frances. 1992. *Nature's Deadly Creatures: A Pop-up Exploration.* Illus. Andrew Robinson & Tony Smith. New York: Dial. 8–12 yrs.

Kitchen, Bert. 1990. *Gorilla/Chinchilla, and Other Animal Rhymes.* Illus. B. Kitchen. New York: Dial. 7–12 yrs.

Lawrence, R. D. 1990. *Wolves.* Photos Dorothy Siemens. Boston: Little, Brown.

Lemmon, Tess. 1993. *Apes.* Illus. John Butler. New York: Ticknor & Fields. 7–11 yrs.

Lewis, Sharon. 1990. *Tiger!* Illus. Linda Roberts. New York: HarperCollins. 6–10 yrs.

Lindblad, Lisa. 1994. *The Serengeti Migration: Africa's Animals on the Move.* Photos Sven-Olof Lindblad. New York: Hyperion. 8–12 yrs.

London, Jonathan. 1993. *The Eyes of Gray Wolf.* Illus. Jon Van Zyle. San Francisco: Chronicle. 9–12 yrs.

Martin, James. 1993. *Hiding Out: Camouflage in the Wild.* Photos Art Wolfe. New York: Crown. 10–13 yrs.

Matthews, D. 1995. *Arctic Foxes.* Color photos Dan Guravich & Nikita Ovsyanikov. New York: Simon & Schuster. 5–9 yrs.

Murphy, Jim. 1993. *Backyard Bear.* Illus. J. Greene. New York: Scholastic. 5–9 yrs.

Perenyi, Constance. 1993. *Wild Wild West: Wildlife Habitats of Western North America.* Illus. C. Perenyi. Seattle, Wash.: Sasquatch. 6–12 yrs.

Robinson, Sandra Chisholm. 1991. *Mountain Lion.* Rinehart, Roberts: Ninot, Colo.: 8–12 yrs.

Rinard, Judith. 1992. *Lion Cubs and Their World.* Washington, D.C.: National Geographic. 4–7 yrs. Action Book: pop-up.

Ryden, Hope. 1991. *Your Cat's Wild Cousins.* Photos Hope Ryden. New York: Lodestar/Dutton. 8–12 yrs.

———. 1994. *Joey: The Story of a Baby Kangaroo.* Color photos. New York: Tambourine. 5–8 yrs.

Sattler, Helen Roney. 1989. *Giraffes, the Sentinels of the Savannas.* Illus. Christopher Santoro. New York: Lothrop, Lee & Shepard. 8–12 yrs.

Selsam, Millicent E. & Joyce Hunt. 1989. *Keep Looking!* Illus. Normand Chartier. New York: Macmillan. 6–9 yrs.

Simon, Seymour. 1991. *A First Look at Bats.* Illus. Harriett Springer. New York: Walker. 6–9 yrs.

———. 1991. *Big Cats.* New York: HarperCollins. 5–12 yrs.

———. 1993. *Wolves.* Photos. New York: HarperCollins. 6–12 yrs.

Stirling, Ian. 1992. *Bears.* Photos Aubrey Lang. San Francisco, Calif.: Sierra Club. 10–13 yrs.

Stuart, Dee. 1993. *The Astonishing Armadillo.* Photos. Minneapolis, Minn.: Carolrhoda. 8–12 yrs.

Yoshida, Toshi. 1989. *Young Lions.* Illus. T. Yoshida. New York: Philomel. 8–10 yrs.

BIRDS

Arnold, Caroline. 1993. *On the Brink of Extinction: The California Condor.* Photos Michael Wallace. San Diego, Calif.: Harcourt Brace/Gulliver Green. 10–12 yrs.

Arnosky, Jim. 1992. *Crinklerott's Guide to Knowing Birds.* New York: Simon & Schuster/Bradbury. 8–13 yrs.

———. 1995. *All about Owls.* New York: Scholastic. 5–8 yrs.

Bash, Barbara. 1990. *Urban Roosts: Where Birds Nest in the Cities.* Illus. B. Bash. Boston: Little, Brown. 6–9 yrs.

Bernhard, Emery. 1994. *Eagles: Lions of the Sky.* Illus. Durga Bernhard. New York: Holiday. 5–9 yrs.

Biel, Timothy. 1990. *Owls.* Creative Education. 7–9 yrs.

Boice, Tara. 1992. *If You Find a Baby Bird: How to Protect and Care for Wild Baby Birds.* Illus. Marjorie Sagar & Ernest C. Simmons. Redington Shores, Fla.: Seawind. 8–10 yrs.

Brown, Mary Barrett. 1992. *Wings along the Waterway.* New York: Orchard. 10–12 yrs.

Casey, Denise. 1993. *Bid Birds.* Photos Jackie Gilmore. New York: Cobblehill. 7–9 yrs.

Epple, Wolfgana. 1992. *Barn Owls.* Photos Manfred Rogl. Minneapolis, Minn.: Carolrhoda. 8–11 yrs.

Esbensen, Barbara Juster. 1991. *Tiger with Wings: The Great Horned Owl.* Illus. Mary Barrett Brown. New York: Orchard. 8–11 yrs.

Fitchter, George S. 1994. *Cardinals, Robins, and Other Birds.* Illus. Patricia Topper. Racine, Wisc.: Golden Books. 9–12 yrs.

Gibbons, Gail. 1991. *The Puffins Are Back!* Illus. G. Gibbons. New York: HarperCollins. 8–11 yrs.

Gove, Doris. 1985. *Miracle at Rock: A Puffin's Story.* Illus. Bonnie Bishop. Camden, Maine: Down East Books. 10–12 yrs.

Heinrich, Bernd. 1990. *An Owl in the House: A Naturalist's Diary.* Boston: Joy Street/Little, Brown. 11–14 yrs.

Hiller, Ilo. 1989. *Introducing Birds to Young Naturalists: From Texas Parks & Wildlife Magazine.* College Station, Tex.: Texas A & M University Press. 9–12 yrs.

Hirschi, Ron. 1989. *The Mountain Bluebird.* Photos Galen Burred. New York: Cobblehill. 7–11 yrs.

Horton, Tom. 1991. *Swanfall: Journey of the Tundra Swans.* Photos David Harp. New York: Walker. 7–10 yrs.

Hume, Rob. 1993. *Birdwatching.* New York: Random House. 10–16 yrs.

Johnson, S. A. 1995. *Raptor Rescue!: An Eagle Flies Free.* Color photos Ron Winch. New York: Dutton. 5–8 yrs.

Kappeler, Markus. 1991. *Owls.* Milwaukee, Wisc.: Gareth Stevens. 8–12 yrs.

Lerner, Carol. 1994. *Backyard Birds of Winter.* New York: Morrow. 9–11 yrs.

Ling, Mary. 1992. *See How They Grow: Owl.* Photos Kim Taylor. New York: Dorling Kindersley. 5–8 yrs.

Markle, Sandra. 1994. *Outside and Inside Birds.* Photos. New York: Simon & Schuster/Bradbury. 7–9 yrs.

Maynard, Thane. 1993. *Saving Endangered Birds: Ensuring a Future in the Wild.* Photos. Danbury, Conn.: Watts. 8–12 yrs.

McMillan, Bruce. 1993. *Penguins at home: Gentoos of Antarctica.* Boston: Houghton Mifflin. 10–14 yrs.

———. 1995. *Nights of the Pufflings.* Color photos. Boston: Houghton Mifflin. 5–9 yrs.

———. 1995. *Puffins Climb, Penguins Rhyme.* Color photos. San Diego: Harcourt Brace/Gulliver. 3–6 yrs.

Patent, Dorothy Hinshaw. 1992. *Feathers.* Photos William Munoz. New York: Cobblehill. 10–12 yrs.

———. 1993. *Ospreys.* Photos William Munoz. New York: Clarion. 9–12 yrs.

Ryder, Joanne. 1992. *Dancers in the Garden.* Illus. Judith Lopez. San Francisco, Calif.: Sierra Club. 6–9 yrs.

Sattler, Helen Roney. 1989. *The Book of Eagles.* Illus. Jean Day Zallinger. New York: Lothrop, Lee & Shepard. 8–12 yrs.

———. 1995. *The Book of North American Owls.* Illus. Jean Day Zallinger. New York: Clarion. 9–12 yrs.

Snedden, Robert. 1993. *What Is a Bird?* Boston: Little, Brown. 6–9 yrs.

Stone, Lynn M. 1993. *Vultures.* Photos L. M. Brown. Minneapolis, Minn.: Carolrhoda. 10–13 yrs.

Vernon, Adele. 1991. *The Hoiho: New Zealand's Yellow-Eyed Penguin.* Photos Dean Schneider. New York: Putnam. 9–12 yrs.

BOTANY

Applebaum, Diana. 1993. *Giants in the Land.* Illus. Michael McCurdy. Boston: Houghton Mifflin. 9–12 yrs.

Arnosky, Jim. 1992. *Crinkleroot's Guide to Knowing Trees.* New York: Simon & Schuster/Bradbury. 5–9 yrs.

Barone, Kathy. 1994. *The Tree of Time*. Yosemite National Park: Yosemite Association. 8–11 yrs.

Bash, Barbara. 1994. *Ancient Ones: The World of the Old-Growth Douglas Fir*. Boston: Little, Brown. 7–11 yrs.

Brenner, Barbara & May Garelick. 1992. *The Tremendous Tree Book*. Illus. Fred Brenner. Honesdale, Penn.: Boyds Mills. 5–8 yrs.

Burns, Diane L. 1990. *Sugaring Season: Making Maple Syrup*. Photos Cheryl Walsh Bellville. Minneapolis, Minn.: Carolrhoda. 6–11 yrs.

Coldrey, Jennifer. 1989. *Strawberry*. Photos George Bernard. Morristown, N.J.: Silver Burdett/Stopwatch. 3–6 yrs.

Collier, John. 1993. *The Backyard*. Illus. J. Collier. New York: Viking. 6–9 yrs.

Cowcher, Helen. 1993. *Whistling Thorn*. New York: Scholastic. 8–12 yrs.

Dowden, Anne Ophells. 1994. *The Blossom on the Bough: A Book of Trees*. New York: Ticknor & Fields. 10–12 yrs.

_____. 1994. *From Flower to Fruit*. New York: Ticknor & Fields. 10–12 yrs.

_____. 1994. *Poisons in Our Path: Plants That Harm and Heal*. Illus. A. O. Dowden. New York: HarperCollins. 10–12 yrs.

Gackenbach, Dick. 1992. *Mighty Tree*. San Diego: Gulliver/Harcourt, Brace, Jovanovich. 7–9 yrs.

Gibbons, Gail. 1991. *From Seed to Plant*. Illus. Gail Gibbons. New York: Holiday. 4–8 yrs.

Hindley, Judy. 1990. *The Tree*. Illus. Alison Wisenfeld. New York: Potter. 6–10 yrs.

Hines, Gary. 1993. *Flying Firefighters*. Illus. Anna Grossnickle Hines. New York: Clarion. 7–10 yrs.

Hiscock, Bruce. 1991. *The Big Tree*. New York: Atheneum. 6–9 yrs.

Holmes, Anita. 1993. *Flowers for You: Blooms for Every Month*. Illus. Virginia Wright-Frierson. New York: Simon & Schuster/Bradbury. 9–12 yrs.

Jaspersohn, William. 1991. *Cranberries*. Photos. Boston: Houghton Mifflin. 7–10 yrs.

Jordan, Sandra. 1993. *Christmas Tree Farm*. Photos. New York: Orchard. 5–8 yrs.

King, Elizabeth. 1990. *The Pumpkin Patch*. Photos Elizabeth King. New York: Dutton. 4–8 yrs.

_____. 1993. *Backyard Sunflower*. Photos E. King. New York: Dutton. 5–9 yrs.

Lampton, Christopher. 1991. *Forest Fire*. Photos C. Lampton. Brookfield, Conn.: Millbrook. 9–12 yrs.

Lauber, Patricia. 1994. *Be a Friend to Trees*. Illus. Holly Keller. New York: HarperCollins. 6–9 yrs. Let's-Read-and-Find-Out Science Series.

Lerner, Carol. 1988. *Moonseed and Mistletoe: A Book of Poisonous Wild Plants*. New York: Morrow. 9–12 yrs.

_____. 1990. *Dumb Cane and Daffodils: Poisonous Plants in the House and Garden*. New York: Morrow. 9–12 yrs.

_____. 1993. *Plants That Make You Sniffle and Sneeze*. New York: Morrow. 9–12 yrs.

Lyons, George Ella. 1989. *ABCedar: An Alphabet of Trees*. Illus. Tom Parker. New York: Orchard. 8–11 yrs.

Maestro, Betsy. 1992. *How Do Apples Grow?* Illus. Giulio Maestro. New York: HarperCollins. 5–8 yrs. Let's-Read-and-Find-Out Science series.

Markle, Sandra. 1993. *Outside and Inside Trees*. New York: Simon & Schuster/Bradbury. 5–8 yrs.

Meltzer, Milton. 1992. *The Amazing Potato: A Story in Which the Incas, Conquistadors, Marie Antoinette, Thomas Jefferson, Wars, Famines, Immigrants, and French Fries All Play a Part*. New York: HarperCollins. 8–12 yrs.

Patent, Dorothy Hinshaw. 1990. *Yellowstore Fires: Flames and Rebirth*. Photos William Munoz & others. New York: Holiday. 8–12 yrs.

Robbins, Ken. 1990. *A Flower Grows*. Illus. Ken Robbins. New York: Dial. 6–9 yrs.

Straub, Frank. 1993. *Yellowstone's Cycle of Fire*. Minneapolis, Minn.: Carolrhoda. 9–11 yrs.

Tresselt, Alvin. 1992. *The Gift of the Tree*. Illus. Henri Sorensen. New York: Lothrop, Lee & Shepard 5–8 yrs.

Vogel, Carole G. & Kathryn A. Goldner. 1990. *The Great Yellowstone Fire*. Photos. Boston: Little, Brown. 7–10 yrs.

Wexler, Jerome. 1992. *Wonderful Pussy Willows*. Color photos. New York: Dutton. 5–8 yrs.

_____. 1993. *Jack-in-the-Pulpit*. Color photos. New York: Dutton. 5–8 yrs.

_____. 1994. *Queen Anne's Lace*. Color photos. Morton Grove, Ill.: Whitman. 7–9 yrs.

_____. 1995. *Sundew Stranglers: Plants That Eat Insects*. Color photos. New York: Dutton. 9–12 yrs.

CANADA

Bourgeois, Paulette. 1991–92. *Canadian Fire Fighters; Canadian Postal Workers; Canadian Police Officers, and Canadian Garbage Collectors*. Illus. Kim LaFave. 4–8 yrs.

Granfield, Linda. 1992. *Canada Votes*. Illus. Craig Terlson. Kids Can. 10–13 yrs.

Harrison, Ted. 1993. *O Canada*. Illus. T. Harrison. New York: Ticknor & Fields. 8–11 yrs.

Lunn, Janet & Christopher Moore. 1992. *The Story of Canada*. Illus. Alan Daniel. Lanham, Md.: National Book Network/Key Porter. 11–16 yrs.

Parry, Caroline. 1987. *Let's Celebrate*. Kids Can. 10–14 yrs.

Reynolds, Marilynn. 1993. *Belle's Journey*. Illus. Stephen McCallum. Custer, Wash.: Orca. 7–10 yrs.

Temple, Frances Nolting. 1993. *Grab Hands and Run*. New York: Orchard. 10–16 yrs.

Thompson, Sheila. 1991. *Cheryl's Potlatch*. Color photos & illus. S. Thompson. Yinka Deene. 8–12 yrs.

CAREERS

Anderson, Joan. 1989. *The American Family Farm: A Photo Essay by George Ancona*. Photos George Ancona. San Diego: Harcourt Brace Jovanovich. 9–12 yrs.

Ancona, George. 1990. *Riverkeeper*. Photos G. Ancona. New York: Macmillan. 9–13 yrs.

Ashabranner, Brent. 1989. *People Who Make a Difference*. Photos Paul Conklin. New York: Cobblehill. 10–15 yrs.

Black, Judy. 1994. *Fashion*. Color photos. Morristown, N.J.: Silver Burdett/Crestwood. 12–16 yrs. Now Hiring series.

Bryant, Jennifer. 1991. *Ubel Velez*. Photos. New York: Holt/21st Century. 10–14 yrs.

Burns, Peggy. 1995. *The Mail*. Color photos. New York: Thomson Learning. 10–12 yrs. Stepping through History series.

Cody, Tod. 1996. *The Cowboy's Handbook: How to Become a Hero of the Wild West*. Photos. New York: Cobblehill. 8–11 yrs.

Crisfield, Debbie. 1994. *Radio*. Color photos. Morristown, N.J.: Silver Burdett/Crestwood. 12–16 yrs. Now Hiring series.

Cummins, J. 1996. *The Inside-Outside Book of Libraries*. Illus. Roxie Munro. New York: Dutton. 5–9 yrs.

Day, Nancy. 1996. *Sensational TV: Trash or Journalism?* Photos. Springfield, N.J.: Enslow. 11–14 yrs. Issues in Focus Series.

Easton, Patricia Harrison. 1991. *Stable Girl*. Color photos Herb Ferguson. San Diego: Harcourt Brace. 9–12 yrs.

Grossman, Patricia. 1991. *The Night Ones*. Illus. Lydia Dabcovich. San Diego: Harcourt Brace. 4–8 yrs.

Hewett, Joan. 1991. *Public Defender*. New York: Lodestar/Dutton. 10–14 yrs.

Horenstein, Henry. 1994. *My Mom's a Vet*. Photos H. Horenstein. Cambridge, Mass.: Candlewick. 9–12 yrs.

Jackson, Donna M. 1996. *The Bone Detectives: How Forensic Anthropologists Solve Crimes and Uncover Mysteries of the Dead*. Photos Charlie Fellenbaum. Boston: Little, Brown. 9–13 yrs.

Jaspersohn, William. 1994. *My Hometown Library*. Photos W. Jaspersohn. Boston: Houghton Mifflin. 8–12 yrs.

Johnson, Jean. 1988. *Librarians A to Z*. Photos J. Johnson. New York: Walker. 5–8 yrs.

Klinting, L. 1996. *Bruno the Carpenter*. Illus. Lars Klinting. New York: Holt. 5–8 yrs.

Miller, Margaret. 1990. *Who Uses This?* Photos. New York: Greenwillow. 4–9 yrs.

Scott, Elaine. 1991. *Safe in the Spotlight*. Photos E. Scott. New York: Morrow. 10–14 yrs.

Serrian, Michael. 1994. *Film*. Color photos. Morristown, N.J.: Silver Burdett Crestwood. 12–16 yrs. Now Hiring series.

Weil, Lisl. 1990. *Let's Go to the Library*. Illus. Lisl Weil. New York: Holiday. 10–12 yrs.

Wolf, Sylvia. 1994. *Focus: Five Women Photographers*. Morton Grove, Ill.: Whitman. 10–13 yrs.

COMMUNICATION

Aliki. 1993. *Communication*. New York: Greenwillow. 5–8 yrs.

Ancona, George & Mary Beth Ancona. 1989. *Handtalk Zoo*. Photos G. Ancona. New York: Simon & Schuster/Four Winds. 8–10 yrs.

Bauer, Marion Dane. 1992. *What's Your Story?: A Young Person's Guide to Writing Fiction*. New York: Clarion. 10–12 yrs.

Burns, Peggy. 1995. *News*. Color photos. New York: Thomson Learning. 10–13 yrs. Stepping through History series.

Gibbons, Gail. 1993. *Puff . . . flash . . . bang! A Book about Signals*. Illus. G. Gibbons. New York: Morrow. 6–8 yrs.

Granfield, Linda. 1994. *Extra! Extra!: The Who, What, Where, When, and Why of Newspapers*. Illus. Bill Slavin. New York: Orchard. 9–11 yrs.

Guthrie, Donna, Nancy Bentley & Katy Keck Arnsteen. 1994. *The Young Author's Do-It-Yourself Book: How to Write, Illustrate, and Produce Your Own Book*. Illus. Katy Keck Arnsteen. Brookfield, Conn.: Millbrook. 5–8 yrs.

Leedy, Loreen. 1991. *Messages in the Mailbox: How to Write a Letter*. Illus. L. Leedy. New York: Holiday. 7–10 yrs.

_____. 1992. *My First 100 Words in Spanish and English*. New York: Simon & Schuster. 6–10 yrs.

Schwartz, Perry. 1991. *How to Make Your Own Video*. Minneapolis, Minn.: Lerner. 10–15 yrs.

Stowell, Charlotte. 1994. *Step-by-Step Making Books*. Illus. Jim Robins. New York: Kingfisher. 9–12 yrs.

COUNTING BOOKS

Alda, A. 1992. *Sheep, Sheep, Sheep, Help Me Fall Asleep*. New York: Doubleday. 6–8 yrs.

Anholt, C. and L. Anholt. 1994. *One, Two, Three, Count with Me*. New York: Viking. 3–6 yrs.

Baker, A. 1994. *Gray Rabbit's 1, 2, 3.* New York: Kingfisher. 2–4 yrs. Little Rabbit series.

Bowen, B. 1995. *Gathering: A Northwoods Counting Book.* Boston: Little, Brown. 7–10 yrs.

Brisson, P. 1993. *Benny's Pennies.* Illus. Bob Barner. New York: Doubleday. 3–6 yrs.

Cherrill, P. 1995. *Ten Tiny Turtles: A Crazy Counting Book.* New York: Ticknor & Fields. 5–8 yrs.

Chwast, S. 1993. *The Twelve Circus Rings.* San Diego, Calif.: Gulliver. 5–8 yrs.

Coats, L. 1994. *One Hungry Baby: A Bedtime Counting Rhyme.* Illus. Sue Hellard. New York: Crown. 2–5 yrs.

Hunt, J. & L. Hunt. 1995. *One Is a Mouse.* New York: Macmillan. 3–6 yrs.

Loomis, Christine. 1994. *One Cow Coughs: A Counting Book for the Sick and Miserable.* Illus. Pat Dypold. New York: Ticknor & Fields. 4–6 yrs.

Marzollo, J. 1994. *Ten Cats Have Hats: A Counting Book.* Illus. David McPhail. New York: Cartwheel. 2–5 yrs.

Milstein, L. 1995. *Coconut Mon.* Illus. Cheryl Munro Taylor. New York: Tambourine. 5–9 yrs.

Murphy, C. 1995. *Chuck Murphy's One to Ten Pop-Up Surprises!* New York: Simon & Schuster. 3–6 yrs.

Nadler, E. 1994. *Tiny Tippy Truck.* Concept & design David Bennett Books Ltd. New York: Little. 2–5 yrs.

Pace, D. 1995. *Shouting Sharon: A Riotous Counting Rhyme.* New York: Artists. 3–6 yrs.

Pallotta, Jerry. 1992. *The Icky Bug Counting Book.* Illus. Ralph Masiello. Watertown, Mass.: Charlesbridge. 6–9 yrs.

Paterson, B. 1992. *Baby's 1 2 3: A Counting Song.* Illus. B. Paterson. New York: Grosset. So Tall Board Book series.

Rocklin, J. 1993. *Musical Chairs and Dancing Bears.* Illus. Laure de Matharel. New York: Holt. 4–6 yrs.

Smith, M. 1995. *Counting Our Way to Maine.* New York: Orchard/Kroupa. 6–9 yrs.

van der Meer, R. & A. van der Meer. 1992. *Funny Hats: A Lift-the-Flap Counting Book with a Surprise Gift.* New York: Random House. 2–4 yrs.

Wise, W. 1993. *Ten Sly Piranhas: A Counting Story in Reverse (A Tale of Wickedness – and Worse!).* Illus. Victoria Chess. New York: Dial. 6–8 yrs.

CONCEPT BOOKS

Me, Myself, and I

Anholt, C. & L. Anholt. 1991. *What I Like.* New York: Putnam. 3–6 yrs.

———. 1992. *All about You.* New York: Viking. 3–6 yrs.

———. 1992. *Kids.* Cambridge, Mass.: Candlewick. 4–6 yrs.

Blake, Q. 1994. *Simpkin.* New York: Viking. 5–8 yrs.

Browne, A. 1989. *Things I Like.* New York: Knopf/Dragonfly. 3–6 yrs.

Burningham, J. 1993. *Would You Rather.* New York: HarperCollins. 4–6 yrs.

Henderson, K. 1994. *Bounce Bounce Bounce.* Illus. Carol Thompson. Cambridge, Mass.: Candlewick. 1–3 yrs.

———. 1994. *Bumpety Bump.* Illus. Carol Thompson. Cambridge, Mass.: Candlewick. 1–3 yrs.

Hughes, S. 1993. *Bouncing.* Cambridge, Mass.: Candlewick. 3–6 yrs.

———. 1993. *Giving.* Cambridge, Mass.: Candlewick. 3–6 yrs.

———. 1994. *Chatting.* Cambridge, Mass.: Candlewick. 3–6 yrs.

———. 1994. *Hiding.* Cambridge, Mass.: Candlewick. 3–6 yrs.

Kunhardt, E. 1992. *Red Day, Green Day.* Illus. Marylin Hafner. New York: Greenwillow. 3–5 yrs.

Macdonald, M. 1995. *Rosie and the Poor Rabbits.* Illus. Melissa Sweet. New York: Atheneum. 5–7 yrs.

Miller, M. 1994. *My Five Senses.* Photos Margaret Miller. New York: Simon & Schuster. 2–5 yrs.

Ogburn, J. K. 1995. *The Noise Lullaby.* Illus. John Sandford. New York: Lothrop, Lee & Shepard.

Silbaugh, E. 1996. *Let's Play Cards!* Illus. Jef Kaminsky. New York: Simon & Schuster. 7–9 yrs. Ready-to-Read series.

Tews, S. 1993. *Nettie's Gift.* Illus. Elizabeth Sayles. New York: Clarion. 4–6 yrs.

Yoon, Jung-Huyn. 1996. *Popposites: A Lift, Pull, and Pop Book of Opposites.* Photos. New York: Dorling Kindersley. 2–4 yrs. Paper engineering.

Science

Bishop, R. 1994. *In the Forest.* Illus. R. Bishop; paper engineer Ruth Mawdsley. New York: Simon & Schuster. 1–4 Yrs. Little Nature Pop series.

———. 1994. *Look at Insects.* Paper engineer Ruth Mawdsley. New York: Simon & Schuster. 1–4 yrs. Little Nature Pop Series.

Borden, L. 1989. *Caps, Hats, Socks, and Mittens: A Book about the Four Seasons.* Illus. Lillian Hoban. New York: Scholastic. 2–6 yrs.

Couture, C. 1993. *A Walk in the Woods.* New York: Farrar, Straus & Giroux. 5–7 yrs.

Dunphy, M. 1993. *Here Is the Arctic Winter.* Illus. Alan James Robinson. New York: Hyperion. 5–8 yrs.

Ehlert, L. 1993. *Nuts to You!* Orlando, Fla.: Harcourt Brace. 4–7 yrs.

Fleming, D. 1993. *In the Small, Small Pond.* New York: Holt. 5–8 yrs. 1994 Caldecott Honor book.

Gerstein, M. & S. Y. Harris. 1995. *Daisy's Garden.* New York: Hyperion. 5–9 yrs.

Greeley, V. 1994. *The Acorn's Story.* New York: Macmillan. 5–8 yrs.

Hansard, P. 1994. *Wag Wag Wag.* Illus. Barbara Firth. Cambridge, Mass.: Candlewick. 3–6 yrs.

Hazelaar, C. 1995. *Dogs Everywhere.* New York: Knopf. 5–9 yrs.

Le Tord, B. 1993. *Elephant Moon.* New York: Doubleday. 6–8 yrs.

London, J. 1994. *Condor's Egg.* Illus. James Chaffee. San Francisco, Calif.: Chronicle. 6–8 yrs.

Paschkis, J. 1994. *So Sleepy/Wide Awake.* New York: Holt. 4–6 yrs.

Robert Taylor Elementary School Students. 1994. *A Day in the Desert.* St. Petersburg, Fla.: Willowisp. 4–7 yrs.

Wells, R. 1994. *Night Sounds, Morning Colors.* Illus. David McPhail. New York: Dial. 5–7 yrs.

Wexler, J. 1995. *Everyday Mysteries.* Color photos. New York: Dutton. 5–8 yrs.

Social Science, Cultures, and History

Allen, J. 1993. *What Is a Wall, After All?* Illus. Alan Baron. Cambridge Mass.: Candlewick. 6–8 yrs.

Brown, M. W. 1993. *The Little Fireman.* Illus. Esphyr Slobodkina. New York: HarperCollins. 4–6 yrs.

Desimini, L. 1994. *My House.* New York: Holt. 5–7 yrs.

Hartman, G. 1994. *As the Roadrunner Runs: A First Book of Maps.* Illus. Cathy Bobak. New York: Bradbury. 6–9 yrs.

Lyon, G. E. 1994. *Mama Is a Miner.* Illus. Peter Catalanotto. New York: Orchard. 6–8 yrs.

Mandel, P. 1994. *Red Cat, White Cat.* Illus. Clare Mackie. New York: Holt. 4–6 yrs.

McGuire, R. 1994. *Night Becomes Day.* New York: Viking. 5–7 yrs.

Provensen, A. and M. Provensen. 1994. *Town and Country.* Orlando, Fla.: Browndeer. 5–7 yrs.

Tucker, K. 1994. *Do Pirates Take Baths?* Illus. Nadine Bernard Westcott. Morton Grove, Ill.: Whitman. 5–7 yrs.

Zolotow, C. 1995. *When the Wind Stops.* Illus. Stefano Vitale. New York: HarperCollins. 5–9 yrs.

Shapes, Colors, Time

Baker, A. 1994. *Brown Rabbit's Shape Book.* New York: Kingfisher. 2–4 yrs. Little Rabbit series.

Burningham, J. 1994. *First Steps: Letters, Numbers, Colors, Opposites.* Cambridge, Mass.: Candlewick. 2–5 yrs.

Dodds, D. A. 1994. *The Shape of Things.* Illus. Julie Lacome. Cambridge, Mass.: Candlewick. 4–6 yrs.

Edmonds, W. 1994. *Big Book of Time.* Illus. Helen Marsden. New York: Writers and Reader's. 9–11 yrs.

MacKinnon, D. 1992. *What Shape?* Photos Anthea Sieveking. New York: Dial. 2–5 yrs.

Shapiro, A. 1992. *Circles. Squares. Triangles.* Illus. Bari Weissman. New York: Dial. 1–5 yrs.

INFORMATIONAL STORYBOOKS

Agell. C. 1994. *I Slide into the White of Winter.* St. Paul, Minn.: Tilbury. 5–7 yrs.

———. 1994. *Wind Spins Me Around in the Fall.* St. Paul, Minn.: Tilbury. 5–7 yrs.

Brandenburg, J. (Joann Bren Guerney, Ed.) 1995. *An American Safari: Adventures on the North American Prairie.* New York: Walker. 9–12 yrs.

Carle, E. 1969. *The Very Hungry Caterpillar.* New York: Philomel. 4–8 yrs.

———. 1995. *The Very Lonely Firefly.* New York: Philomel. 4–8 yrs. (Fourth in series.)

Christelow, E. 1992. *Don't Wake Up Mama!: Another Five Little Monkeys Story.* New York: Clarion. 5–8 yrs.

Cole, Joanna. 1989. *The Magic School Bus Inside the Human Body.* Illus. Bruce Degen. New York: Scholastic. 8–11 yrs.

———. 1992. *The Magic School Bus on the Ocean Floor.* Illus. Bruce Degen. New York: Scholastic. 8–11 yrs.

———. 1994. *The Magic School Bus in the Time of the Dinosaurs.* Illus. Bruce Degen. New York: Scholastic. 8–11 yrs.

———. 1995. *The Magic School Bus Inside a Hurricane.* Illus. Bruce Degen. New York: Scholastic. 7–10 yrs.

———. 1996. *The Magic School Bus in a Beehive.* Illus. Bruce Degen. New York: Scholastic. 8–12 yrs.

Cooney, N. E. 1993. *Chatterbox Jamie.* Illus. Marylin Hafner. New York: Putnam. 2–4 yrs.

French, V. 1995. *Spider Watching.* Illus. Alison Wisenfeld. Cambridge, Mass.: Candlewick. 6–9 yrs. Read and Wonder Series.

Kasperson, J. 1995. *Little Brother Moose.* Illus. Karlyn Holman. Nevada City, Calif.: Dawn. 6–9 yrs.

Lewin, B. 1995. *Booby Hatch.* New York: Clarion. 6–10 yrs.

Lewin, T. 1993. *Amazon Boy.* New York: Macmillan. 6–8 yrs.

London, J. 1995. *Honey Paw and Lightfoot.* Illus. Jon Van Zyle. San Francisco, Calif.: Chronicle. 8–10 yrs.

———. 1996. *Red Wolf Country.* Illus. Daniel San Souci. New York: Dutton. 8–11 yrs.

Lucas, B. M. 1993. *Snowed In.* Illus. Catherine Stock. New York: Bradbury. 7–9 yrs.

McCarthy, B. 1992. *Ten Little Hippos.* New York: Bradbury. 4–7 yrs.

Merriam, E. 1992. *Train Leaves the Station.* Illus. Dale Gottlieb. New York: Holt/Martin. 4–7 yrs.

Penner, L. R. 1996. *Monster Bugs.* Illus. Pamela Johnson. New York: Random House. 6–9 yrs. Step into Reading.

Ryder, J. 1995. *Bears Out There.* Illus. Jo Ellen McAllister-Stammen. New York: Atheneum. 5–9 yrs.

Schwartz, H. B. 1993. *Backstage with Clawdio.* Illus. David Catrow. New York: Knopf. 6–8 yrs.

Skofield, J. 1993. *Ground and Around.* Illus. James Graham Hale. New York: HarperCollins. 4–6 yrs.

Slawson, M. B. 1994. *Apple Picking Time.* Illus. Deborah Kogan Ray. New York: Crown. 5–7 yrs.

Stock, C. 1993. *Where Are You Going Manyoni?* New York: Morrow. 6–8 yrs.

Walters, M. P. 1995. *Darkness.* Illus. Marcia Jameson. New York: Simon & Schuster. 5–9 yrs.

Walton, R. 1993. *How Many, How Many, How Many.* Illus. Cynthia Jabar. Cambridge, Mass.: Candlewick. 3–6 yrs.

Willis, J. 1993. *Earth Weather as Explained by Professor Xargle.* Illus.Tony Ross. New York: Dutton. 6–9 yrs.

DIVERSE LIFESTYLES & COMMUNITIES IN THE U.S. AND WORLD

Ashabranner, Brent. 1989. *Born to the Land: An American Portrait.* Photos Paul Conklin. New York: Putnam. 10–16 yrs.

———. 1991. *An Ancient Heritage: The Arab-American Minority.* Photos. Paul S. Conklin. New York: HarperCollins. 9–15 yrs.

Ayer, Eleanor H. 1992. *Berlin.* New York: Simon & Schuster/New Discovery. 10–12 yrs. Cities at War series.

Bial, Raymond. 1992. *County Fair.* Boston: Houghton Mifflin. 10–12 yrs.

Buettner, Dan. 1994. *Sovietrek: A Journey by Bicycle Across Russia.* Illus. D. Buettner. Minneapolis, Minn.: Lerner. 10–15 yrs.

Burke, Patrick. 1995. *Germany.* Color photos. New York: Thomson Learning. 12–14 yrs. Modern Industrial World series.

Charbonneau, Claudette & Patricia Slade Lander. 1993. *The Land and People of Norway.* Photos & maps. New York: HarperCollins. 12–17 yrs.

Chester, Jonathan. 1995. *A for Antarctica.* Color photos. Berkeley, Calif.: Tricycle. 5–9 yrs.

Chicoine, Stephen, & Brent Ashabranner. 1995. *Lithuania: The Nation That Would Be Free.* Photos. Stephen Chicoine. New York: Cobblehill. 10–14 yrs.

di Franco, J. Philip. 1995. *The Italian Americans.* Photos. New York: Chelsea. 10–14 yrs. Immigrant Experience series.

Ganeri, Anita. 1994. *I Remember Bosnia.* Color photos. Chatham, N.J.: Raintree. 6–10 yrs. Why We Left series.

Geography Department, Lerner Publications. 1992. *Estonia. Latvia. Lithuania. Russia.* Minneapolis, Minn.: Lerner. 8–12 yrs. The Then and Now series.

Goodwin, Bob, & Candi Perez. 1995. *A Taste of Spain.* Color photos. New York: Thomson Learning. 10–13 yrs. Food around the World series.

Gordon, Ginger. 1993. *My Two Worlds.* Photos Martha Cooper. New York: Clarion. 6–12 yrs.

Graff, Nancy Price. 1992. *The Call of the Running Tide: A Portrait of an Island Family.* Photos Richard Howard. Boston: Little, Brown. 8–12 yrs.

Hoig, Stan. 1995. *It's the Fourth of July!* B & W photos & reproductions. New York: Cobblehill. 10–14 yrs.

Hoobler, Dorothy & Thomas Hoobler. 1995. *Irish American Family Album.* Photos, engravings. New York: Oxford. 10–14 yrs. American Family Albums series.

Huff, Barbara A. 1990. *Greening the City Streets: The Story of Community Gardens.* Photos Peter Ziebel. New York: Clarion. 8–12 yrs.

Jacobsen, Kathy. 1993. *My New York.* Boston: Little, Brown. 5–9 yrs.

Johnson, Rebecca L. 1995. *Science on the Ice: An Antarctic Journal.* Color photos. Minneapolis, Minn.: Lerner. 10–13 yrs.

Kendall, Russ. 1992. *Eskimo Boy: Life in an Inupiaq Eskimo Village.* Photos R. Kendall. New York: Scholastic. 5–8 yrs.

———. 1994. *Russian Girl: Life in an Old Russian Town.* Photos R. Kendall. New York: Scholastic. 8–11 yrs.

Krull, Kathleen. 1995. *Bridges to Change: How Kids Live on a South Carolina Sea Island.* Color photos David Hautzig. New York: Lodestar/Dutton. World of My Own series.

Kuklin, Susan. 1992. *"How My Family Lives In America."* Photos S. Kuklin. New York: Simon & Schuster/Bradbury. 7–10 yrs.

Lester, Alison. 1994. *My Farm.* Illus. A. Lester. Boston: Houghton Mifflin. 5–8 yrs.

Liptak, Karen. 1993. *Endangered Peoples.* Photos. Danbury, Conn.: Watts. 12–15 yrs. Impact Books.

Margolies, Barbara M. 1994. *Warriors, Wigmen, and the Crocodile People: Journeys in Papua New Guinea.* Photos B. Margolies. New York: Simon & Schuster/Four Winds. 8–12 yrs.

Munro, Roxie. 1989–92. *The Inside-Outside Book of London; The Inside-Outside Book of Paris.* Illus. Roxie Munro. New York: Dutton. All ages. Inside-Out series.

Nye, Naomi Shihab. 1994. *Sitti's Secrets.* Illus. Nancy Carpenter. New York: Simon & Schuster/Four Winds. 5–7 yrs.

Pitkanen, Matti A., with Reijo Harkonen. 1991. *The Children of Egypt.* Photos. M. A. Pitkanen. Minneapolis, Minn.: Carolrhoda. 8–11 yrs. World's Children series.

Pitkanen, Matti A., with Ritva Lehtinen & Kari E. Nurmi. 1991. *Grandchildren of the Incas.* Photographs. Minneapolis, Minn.: Carolrhoda. 8–11 yrs. World's Children series.

Raimondo, Lois. 1994. *The Little Lama of Tibet.* Photos Lois Raimondo. New York: Scholastic. 8–11 yrs.

Sage, James. 1993. *Where the Great Bear Watches.* Illus. Lisa Flather. New York: Viking. 5–8 yrs.

Stewart, Gail B. 1994. *Life during the French Revolution.* San Diego, Calif.: Lucent. 12–16 yrs. The Way People Live series.

Strom, Yale. 1993. *Uncertain Roads: Searching for the Gypsies.* Photos Y. Strom. New York: Simon & Schuster/Four Winds. 10–14 yrs.

Tresselt, Alvin. 1990–91. *Wake Up, City! Wake Up, Farm!* Illus. Carolyn Ewing. New York: Lothrop, Lee & Shepard. 3–6 yrs.

Van Rynbach, Iris. 1991. *Everything from a Nail to a Coffin.* Illus. Iris Van Rynbach. New York: Orchard. 7–9 yrs.

Vitebsky, Piers. 1994. *The Saami of Lapland.* Photos. New York: Thomson Learning. 9–12 yrs. Threatened Cultures Series.

Wilds, Kazumi Inose. 1994. *Hajime in the North Woods.* Illus. K. Wilds. New York: Arcade. 6–10 yrs.

EARTH SCIENCE

Ballard, Robert D., with Rick Archbold. 1990. *The Lost Wreck of the Isis.* Illus. Wesley Lowe & Ken Marshall. New York: Scholastic/Madison. 9–12 yrs.

Barasch, Lynne. 1993. *A Winter Walk.* Illus. L. Barasch. New York: Ticknor & Fields. 5–8 yrs.

Branley, Franklyn M. 1990. *Earthquakes.* Illus. Richard Rosenblum. New York: Crowell. 7–10 yrs. Let's-Read-and-Find-Out Science Books.

Cobb, Vicki. 1989. *This Place Is Dry.* Illus. Barbara Lavallee. New York: Walker. 7–9 yrs.

Cole, Joanna. 1987. *The Magic Bus Inside the Earth.* Illus. Bruce Degan. New York: Scholastic. 8–11 yrs.

DeWitt, Lynda. 1991. *What Will the Weather Be?* Illus. Carolyn Croll. New York: HarperCollins. 8–10 yrs. Let's-Read-and-Find-Out Science Books series.

Dorros, Arthur. 1989. *Feel the Wind.* Illus. A. Dorros. New York: Crowell. 4–8 yrs. Let's-Read-and-Find-Out Science Book.

Dunphy, Madeline. 1993. *Here Is the Arctic Winter.* Illus. Alan James Robinson. New York: Hyperion. 5–9 yrs.

Goodman, Billy. 1991. *Natural Wonders and Disasters.* Boston: Little, Brown. 8–12 yrs. Planet Earth series.

Jackson, Ellen. 1994. *The Winter Solstice.* Illus. J. D. Ellis. Brookfield, Conn.: Millbrook. 10–13 yrs.

Lauber, Patricia. 1990. *How We Learned the Earth Is Round.* Illus. Megan Lloyd. New York: Crowell. 6–10 yrs. Let's-Read-and-Find-Out Science Book.

Meltzer, Milton. 1993. *Gold: The True Story of Why People Search for It, Mine It, Trade It, Steal It, Mint It, Hoard It, Shape It, Wear It, Fight and Kill for It.* Photos. New York: HarperCollins. 10–12 yrs.

Nirgiotis, N. 1996. *Volcanoes: Mountains That Blow Their Tops.* Illus. Michael Radencich. New York: Grosset & Dunlap. 6–9 yrs. All Aboard Reading series.

Ranger Rick. 1989. *Wild About Weather.* Vienna, Vir.: National Wildlife. 11–14 yrs.

Robbins, K. 1995. *Air: The Elements.* Color photos. New York: Holt. 10–13 yrs.

Simon, Seymour. 1990. *Deserts.* New York: Morrow. Color photos. 7–10 yrs.

———. 1991. *Earthquakes.* New York: Morrow. 6–10 yrs.

———. 1993. *Weather.* Photos. New York: Morrow. 5–9 yrs.

———. 1994. *Mountains.* Photos. New York: Morrow. 9–12 yrs.

———. 1994. *Winter across America.* New York: Hyperion. 5–8 yrs.

Tripp, Nathaniel. 1994. *Thunderstorms!* Illus. Juan Wijngaard. New York: Dial. 9–12 yrs.

Usborne Editors. 1987. *The Usborne Book of Weather Facts.* Tulsa, Okla.: Usborne. 9–11 yrs.

Walker, Sally M. 1994. *Volcanoes: Earth's Inner Fire.* Minneapolis, Minn.: Carolrhoda. 9–11 yrs.

Wyatt, Valerie. 1990. *Weatherwatch.* Illus. Pat Cupples. Reading, Mass.: Addison Wesley. 8–12 yrs.

ENCYCLOPEDIAS, ATLASES, AND MAPS

Adams, S., J. Briquebec & A. Kramer. 1991. *Illustrated Atlas of World History.* New York: Random House. 10–17 yrs.

Anthony, Susan C. 1991. *An Almanac of Essential Information.* Anchorage, Ala.: IRC. 8–14 yrs.

Biesty, Steven. 1992. *Incredible Cross-Sections.* Illus. Richard Platt. New York: Knopf. 10–14 yrs.

Bunting, Jane. 1995. *The Children's Visual Dictionary*. Illus. David Hopkins. New York: Dorling Kindersley. 4–9 yrs.

Bynes, John. 1987. *How Maps Are Made*. New York: Facts on File. 10–14 yrs.

Cassidy, John. 1991. *Explorabook*. Palo Alto, Calif.: Klutz. 7–12 yrs.

Children's Atlas of the Environment. 1991. Skokie, Ill.: Rand McNally. 7–12 yrs.

Children's Atlas of World Wildlife. 1990. Skokie, Ill.: Rand McNally. 7–13 yrs.

Clouse, Nancy L. 1990. *Puzzle Maps U.S.A.* New York: Holt. 7–11 yrs.

Cultural Atlas for Young People Series: Africa; Ancient America; Ancient Egypt; Ancient Greece; Ancient Rome; The Middle Ages. 6 vols. New York: Facts On File. 7–16 yrs.

The Doubleday Atlas of the United States of America. 1990. New York: Doubleday. 10–14 yrs.

Ferrel, Robert H. 1991. *Atlas of American History*. New York: Facts on File. 7–16 yrs.

Hammond Basic Map Skills. 1991. Maplewood, N.J.: Hammond. 8–13 yrs.

Hartman, Gail. 1991. *As the Crow Flies: A First Book of Maps*. Illus. Harvey Stevenson. New York: Simon & Schuster/Bradbury. 6–9 yrs.

Kelley, Kevin W. 1991. *The Home Planet*. Reading, Mass.: Addison Wesley. 7–14 yrs.

Kerrod, Robin. 1992. *The Children's Space Atlas*. Brookfield, Conn.: Millbrook. 9–14 yrs.

King, Celia. 1991. *The Seven Natural Wonders of the World*. San Francisco: Chronicle. 9–14 yrs.

Knowlton, Jack. 1985. *Maps and Globes*. Illus. Harriet Barton. New York: HarperCollins. 7–11 yrs.

Lambert, David. 1992. *The Children's Animal Atlas*. Brookfield, Conn.: Millbrook. 7–11 yrs.

Mason, Antony. 1994. *The Children's Atlas of Civilizations*. Brookfield, Conn.: Millbrook. 9–16 yrs. (See also other books in series.)

National Geographic Picture Atlas of Our World. 1991. Washington, D.C.: National Geographic. 8–16 yrs.

Parker, Steve. 1990. *How Things Work*. New York: Random House. 8–12 yrs.

Rand McNally Children's World Atlas. 1991. Skokie, Ill.: Rand McNally. 7–14 yrs.

Rand McNally Classroom Atlas. 1991. Skokie, Ill.: Rand McNally. 7–14 yrs.

Random House Editors. 1991. *Random House Children's Encyclopedia*. New York: Random House. 7–16 yrs.

Reader's Digest Editors. 1991. *How Science Works; How Nature Works*. New York: Reader's Digest. 11–16 yrs.

Van Rose, Susanna. 1994. *The Earth Atlas*. Illus. Richard Bonson. New York: Dorling Kindersley. 9–11 yrs.

The Visual Dictionary of Everyday Things. 1991. New York: Dorling Kindersley. 10–14 yrs.

Weiss, Harvey. 1991. *Maps: "Getting fom Here to There."* Illus. H. Weiss. Boston: Houghton Mifflin. 9–12 yrs.

FAMILY RELATIONSHIPS

A Family that Fights. 1991. Morton Grove, Ill.: Whitman. 6–11 yrs.

Banish, Roslyn & Jennifer Jordan-Wong. 1992. *A Forever Family*. Photos. New York: HarperCollins. 10–12 yrs. (Interracial adoption.)

Bernstein, Joanne E. & Bryna Fireside. 1991. *Special Parents, Special Children*. Photos Michael Bernstein. Morton Grove, Ill.: Albert Whitman. 10–13 yrs.

Bendall, Pamela & Sam Bendall. 1990. *Kids For Sail*. Custer, Wash.: Orca. 10–14 yrs.

Bial, R. 1995. *Portrait of a Farm Family*. Color photos. Burlington, Mass.: Houghton Mifflin. 9–12 yrs.

Bode, Janet. 1992. *Kids Still Having Kids: People Talk About Teen Pregnancy*. Illus. Stan Mack. Danbury, Conn.: Watts. 12–18 yrs.

Brown, M. & L. Brown. 1986. *Dinosaurs Divorce*. Boston: Little, Brown. 6–12 yrs.

Dinner, Sherry H. 1989. *Nothing to Be Ashamed of: Growing Up with Mental Illness in Your Family*. New York: Lothrop, Lee & Shepard. 10–15 yrs.

Greenspun, Adele Aron. 1991. *Daddies*. Photos Adele Aron Greenspun. New York: Philomel. 5–10 yrs.

Goldentyer, Debra. 1995. *Parental Divorce*. B & W photos. Chatham, N.J.: Raintree. 12–17 yrs. Teen Hot Line series.

Krementz, Jill. 1982. *How It Feels to Be Adopted*. New York: Knopf. 10–16 yrs.

———. 1984. *How It Feels When Parents Divorce*. New York: Knopf. 7–12 yrs.

Kroll, Virginia. 1994. *Beginnings: How Families Came to Be*. Illus. Stacey Schuett. Morton Grove, Ill.: Whitman. 6–11 yrs.

LeShan, Eda. 1978. *What's Going to Happen to Me? When Parents Separate or Divorce*. New York: Simon & Schuster/Four Winds. 11–15 yrs.

Lewis, Deborah Shaw & Gregg Lewis. 1995. *When You Were a Baby*. Design & hand-tinting Gary Gnidovic. Atlanta, Ga.: Peachtree. 5–9 yrs.

Liptak, Karen. 1993. *Adoption Controversies*. Danbury, Conn.: Watts. 12–16 yrs. The Changing Family Series.

Mahon, K. L. 1994. *Just One Tear*. New York: Lothrop, Lee & Shepard. 10–14 yrs.

Martinet, Jeanne. 1992. *The Year You Were Born*. Illus. Judy Lanfredi. New York: Tambourine. 10–14 yrs. (Information also available for 1983, 1984, 1985.)

Morris, Ann. 1990. *Loving*. Photos Ken Heyman. New York: Lothrop, Lee & Shepard. 3–7 yrs.

Patent, Dorothy Hinshaw. 1991. *A Family Goes Hunting*. Illus. William Munoz. New York: Clarion. 9–12 yrs.

Porterfield, K. 1985. *Coping with an Alcoholic Parent*. New York: Facts on File. 11–16 yrs.

Rogers, Fred. 1995. *Let's Talk about It: Adoption*. Photos Jim Judkis. New York: Putnam. 4–6 yrs. First Experiences series.

Rosenberg, Maxine B. 1984. *Being Adopted*. New York: Lothrop, Lee & Shepard. 8–16 yrs.

———. 1989. *Growing Up Adopted*. New York: Simon & Schuster/Bradbury. 10–15 yrs.

Ryerson, E. 1985. *When Your Parent Drinks Too Much*. New York: Facts on File. 11–16 yrs.

Seixas, Judith S. 1989. *Living with a Parent Who Takes Drugs*. New York: Greenwillow. 9–15 yrs.

Senisi, Ellen B. 1993. *Brothers & Sisters*. Photos. New York: Scholastic. 5–8 yrs.

Sobol, H. 1984. *We Don't Look Like Our Mom and Dad*. New York: Putnam/Coward. 10–14 yrs.

Worth, Richard. 1992. *Single-Parent Families*. Prints & photos. Danbury, Conn.: Watts. 12–18 yrs.

GEOGRAPHY

Bell, Neill. 1982. *The Book of Where; or, How to Be Naturally Geographic*. Illus. Richard Wilson. Boston: Little, Brown. 9–14 yrs.

Blandford, Percy W. 1992. *The New Explorer's Guide to Using Maps and Compasses*. Blue Ridge Summit, Penn.: TAB Books. 11–16 yrs.

Brownstone, David M. & Irene M. Franck. 1989. *Natural Wonders of America*. New York: Atheneum. 8–12 yrs.

Cherry, Lynne. 1994. *The Armadillo from Amarillo*. Illus. L. Cherry. San Diego: Gulliver Green/Harcourt Brace. 9–12 yrs.

Cooper, Rod & Emilie Cooper. 1993. *Journey through Australia*. Color photos/drawings. Mahwah, N.J.: Troll. 10–12 yrs. Journey Through series.

Donnelly, Judy. 1991. *All Around the World*. Illus. True Kelley. New York: Putnam. 7–9 yrs.

Gerberg, Mort. 1991. *Geographunny: A Book of Global Riddles*. New York: Clarion. 9–12 yrs.

Gottfried, Ted. 1994. *Lia: Desert Land in Conflict*. Brookfield, Conn.: Millbrook. 12–15 yrs.

Husain, Shahrukh. 1993. *Mecca*. Photos (Holy Cities). Morristown, N.J.: Dillon/Silver Burdett. 10–15 yrs.

Kandoian, Ellen. 1989. *Is Anybody Up?* Illus. E. Kandoian. 4–8 yrs.

King, John. 1993. *Bedouin*. Photos. Chatham, N.J.: Raintree/Steck-Vaughn. 10–13 yrs. Threatened Cultures.

Kreikemeier, Gregory Scott. 1993. *Come with Me to Africa: A Photographic Journey*. Photos. G. Kreikemeier. Racine, Wisc.: Golden. 10–14 yrs.

Leedy, Loreen. 1992. *Blast Off to Earth! A Look at Geography*. Illus. L. Leedy. New York: Holiday. 7–10 yrs.

Margolies, Barbara A. 1990. *Rehema's Journey: A Visit in Tanzania*. Photos. B. Margolies. New York: Scholastic. 7–10 yrs.

———. 1993. *Warriors, Wigmen, and Crocodile People: Journeys in Papua New Guinea*. New York: Simon & Schuster/Four Winds. 10–12 yrs.

———. 1994. *Olbalbal: A Day in Maasailand*. Photos B. Margolies. New York: Simon & Schuster/Four Winds. 8–11 yrs.

McVey, Vicki. 1989. *The Sierra Club Wayfinding Book*. Illus. Martha Weston. San Francisco: Sierra Club, dist. Little, Brown. 11–14 yrs.

Sheldon, Dyan. 1994. *Love, Your Bear Pete*. Cambridge, Mass.: Candlewick. 5–8 yrs.

HANDICRAFTS & PROJECTS

Anderson, Yvonne. 1991. *Make Your Own Movies and Videotapes*. Photos, diagrams, drawings. Boston: Little, Brown. 10–16 yrs.

Ayture-Scheele, Zulal (Trans. Elisabeth E. Reinersmann). 1990. *Beautiful Origami*. Photos Gerhard Burrock. New York: Sterling. 5–9 yrs.

Bial, Raymond. 1996. *With Needle and Thread: A Book About Quilts*. Illus. Raymond Bial. Boston: Houghton Mifflin. 9–11 yrs.

Churchill, E. Richard. 1991. *Terrific Paper Toys*. Illus. James Michaels. New York: Sterling. 8–12 yrs.

Corwin, Judith Hoffman. 1989. *The Home. The School*. Illus. Judith Hoffman Corwin. Franklin Danbury, Conn.: Watts. 5–9 yrs. The Colonial American Crafts.

Emberley, Ed. 1992. *Ed Emberley's Thumbprint Drawing Box*. Illus. E. Emberley. Boston: Little, Brown. 4–8 yrs.

Hawcock, David. 1989. *Making Paper Warplanes*. Illus. David Hawcock. New York: Sterling. David and Charles. 7–13 yrs.

Irvine, J. 1996. *How to Make Holiday Pop-Ups*. Illus. Linda Hendry. New York: Morrow. 9–12 yrs.

Jenkins, Patrick. 1991. *Animations*. Illus. P. Jenkins. Reading, Mass.: Addison Wesley. 7–12 yrs.

Jensen, V. 1996. *Carving a Totem Pole*. Photos. New York: Holt. 7–10 yrs.

Keeler, Patricia A., & Francis X. McCall, Jr. 1995. *Unraveling Fibers*. New York: Atheneum. 9–12 yrs.

Lewis, Brenda Ralph. 1991. *Stamps! A Young Collector's Guide.* New York: Lodestar/Dutton. 5–9 yrs.

Morgan, Terri & Shmuel Thaler. 1991. *Photography: Take Your Best Shot.* Photos authors. Minneapolis, Minn.: Lerner. 10–16 yrs.

Paul, Ann Whitford. 1991. *Eight Hands Round: A Patchwork Alphabet.* Illus. Jeanette Emter. New York: HarperCollins. 5–8 yrs.

Sherrow, Victoria. 1992. *Huskings, Quiltings, and Barn Raisings: Work-Play Parties in Early America.* Illus. Laura LoTurco. New York: Walker. 10–14 yrs.

Solga, Kim. 1991. *Make Prints!; Make Gifts!; Draw!; or Paint!* Cincinnati, Oh.: North Light. 7–12 yrs.

Tofts, Hannah (Writer & ed. Diane James). 1990. *The Paint Book; The Paper Book; The Print Book; The 3-D Paper Book.* Photos Jon Barnes. New York: Simon & Schuster. 6–12 yrs.

Walter, F. Virginia. 1992. *Fun with Paper Bags and Cardboard Tubes.* Photos Walter Kaiser. New York: Sterling/Tamos. 6–12 yrs.

Westray, Kathleen. 1993. *A Color Sampler.* New York: Ticknor & Fields. 6–9 yrs.

Zubrowski, B. 1995. *Shadow Play: Making Pictures with Light and Lenses.* Illus. Roy Doty. New York: Morrow. 9–12 yrs.

HISTORY: UNITED STATES

Ashabranner, Brent. 1990. *A Grateful Nation: The Story of Arlington National Cemetery.* Photos Jennifer Ashabranner. New York: Putnam. 10–15 yrs.

——. 1993. *Still a Nation of Immigrants.* Photos Jennifer Ashabranner. New York: Cobblehill. 12–15 yrs.

Bresnick-Perry, Roslyn. 1992. *Leaving for America.* Illus. Mita Reisbery. Emeryville, Calif.: Children's Book Press. 8–11 yrs.

Dash, Joan. 1996. *We Shall Not Be Moved; The Women's Factory Strike of 1909.* Photos. New York: Scholastic. 10–14 yrs.

Fleming, Thomas. 1989. *Behind the Headlines: The Story of American Newspapers.* New York: Walker. 9–12 yrs.

Fry, Annette R. 1994. *The Orphan Trains.* Photos. New York: New Discovery. 11–15 yrs. American Events series.

Gibbons, Gail. 1990. *Beacons of Light: Lighthouses.* Illus. Gail Gibbons. New York: Morrow. 8–12 yrs.

Graff, Nancy Price. 1993. *Where the River Runs: A Portrait of a Refugee Family.* Photos Richard Howard. Boston: Little, Brown. 10–16 yrs.

Maestro, Betsy. 1996. *Coming to America: The Story of Immigration.* Illus. Susannah Ryan. New York: Scholastic. 6–9 yrs.

McKissack, Patricia & Frederick McKissack. 1989. *A Long Hard Journey: The Story of the Pullman Porter.* New York: Walker. 12–16 yrs. American History Series for Young People.

Provensen, Alice. 1995. *My Fellow Americans: A Family Album.* Illus. Alice Provensen. San Diego, Calif.: Browndeer/Harcourt. 10–16 yrs.

Rowan, N. R. 1994. *Women in the Marines: The Boot Camp Challenge.* Photos. Minneapolis, Minn.: Lerner. 11–15 yrs.

Smith, Howard E., Jr. 1989. *All about Arrowheads and Spear Points.* Illus. Jennifer Owings Dewey. New York: Holt. 9–12 yrs.

Watkin, Edward with Daniel Watkin. 1993. *Photos That Made U.S. History: Volume 1: From the Civil War Era to the Atomic Age.* New York:

Walker. adult. *Volume II: From the Cold War to the Space Age.* New York: Walker. 12–16 yrs.

HISTORY: WORLD

Ganeri, Anita. 1994. *I Remember India.* Photos Tim Page. Chatham, N.J.: Raintree. 6–10 yrs. Why We Left series.

——. 1994. *I Remember Palestine.* Photos Tim Page. 6–10 yrs. Chatham, N.J.: Raintree. Why We Left series.

Littlewood, Valerie. 1992. *Scarecrow!* Illus. Valerie Littlewood. New York: Dutton. 7–10 yrs.

McIntosh, Jane. 1994. *Archeology.* Photos Geoff Brightling. New York: Knopf. 10–13 yrs. Eyewitness series.

Putnam, James. 1994. *Pyramid.* Photos Geoff Brightling. New York: Knopf. 10–13 yrs. Eyewitness series.

Rathe, Gustave. 1992. *The Wreck of the Barque Stefano off the North West Cape of Australia in 1875.* New York: Farrar, Straus & Giroux. 12–15 yrs.

Sisulu, Elinor Batezat. 1996. *The Day Gogo Went to Vote.* Illus. Sharon Wilson. Boston: Little, Brown. 5–8 yrs.

Wheatley, Nadia. 1992. *My Place.* Illus. Donna Rawlins. Brooklyn, N.Y.: Kane/Miller. 10–12 yrs.

HUMAN RELATIONSHIPS

Aliki. 1990. *Manners.* Illus. Aliki. New York: Greenwillow. 5–9 yrs.

Blume. Judy. 1986. *Letters to Judy.* New York: Putnam. 10–16 yrs.

Bode, Janet. 1993. *Death Is Hard to Live With: Teenagers and How They Cope with Loss.* Illus. Stan Mack. New York: Delacorte. 12–16 yrs.

——. 1995. *Trust and Betrayal: Real Life Stories of Friends and Enemies.* New York: Delacorte. 12–16 yrs.

Brooks, Bruce. 1993. *Boys Will Be.* New York: Holt. 12–15 yrs.

Brown, Laurie Krasny. 1996. *When Dinosaurs Die: A Guide to Understanding Death.* Illus. Laurie Krasny Brown & Marc Brown. Boston: Little, Brown. 5–9 yrs.

Buehner, Caralyn. 1995. *It's a Spoon, Not a Shovel.* Illus. Mark Buehner. New York: Dial. 5–9 yrs.

Deem, James M. 1994. *How to Read Your Mother's Mind.* Illus. True Kelley. Boston: Houghton Mifflin. 9–13 yrs.

Donnelly, Judy & S. A. Kramer. 1993. *Survive! Could You?* Illus. Gonzales Vicente. New York: Random House. 8–10 yrs. Read It To Believe It! Series.

Fry, Virginia Lynn. 1995. *Part of Me Died, Too: Stories of Creative Survival among Bereaved Children and Teenagers.* New York: Dutton. 12–18 yrs.

Hyde, Margaret O. 1992. *Peace and Friendship/Mir i druzhba: Russian and American Teens Meet.* New York: Cobblehill. 10–15 yrs.

LeShan, Eda. 1992. *What Makes You So Special?* New York: Dial. 10–13 yrs.

INSECTS AND SPIDERS

Bernhard, Emery. 1993. *Dragonfly.* Illus. Durga Bernhard. New York: Holiday. 6–9 yrs.

Brenner, Barbara. 1993. *Where's That Insect?* Illus. Carol Schwartz. New York: Scholastic. 5–9 yrs.

Dewey, Jennifer Owings. 1992. *Spiders Near and Far.* New York: Dutton. 7–10 yrs.

Epstein, Sam & Beryl Epstein. 1989. *Bugs for Dinner? The Eating Habits of Neighborhood Creatures.* Illus. Walter Gaffney-Kessell. New York: Macmillan. 7–12 yrs.

Esbensen, Barbara Juster. 1993. *Playful Slider: The North American River Otter.* Illus. Mary Barrett Brown. Boston: Little, Brown. 5–9 yrs.

Facklam, Margery. 1994. *The Big Bug Book.* Illus. Paul Facklam. Boston: Little, Brown. 8–12 yrs.

——. 1996. *Creepy, Crawly, Caterpillars.* Illus. Paul Facklam. Boston: Little, Brown. 7–10 yrs.

French, Vivian. 1993. *Caterpillars Caterpillar.* Illus. Charlotte Voake. Cambridge, Mass.: Candlewick. 5–9 yrs. Read and Wonder series.

Goor, Ron & Nancy Goor. 1990. *Insect Metamorphosis: From Egg to Adult.* Photos Ron Goor. New York: Atheneum. 7–11 yrs.

Harwood, Lynne. 1994. *Honeybees at Home.* Gardiner, Maine.: Tilbury . 7–9 yrs.

Hickman, Pamela M. 1991. *Bugwise.* Illus. Judie Shore. Reading, Mass.: Addison Wesley. 9–11 yrs.

Hopf, Alice L. 1990. *Spiders.* Photos Ann Moreton. New York: Cobblehill. 5–10 yrs.

Johnson, Sylva A. 1994. *A Beekeeper's Year.* Photos Nick Von Ohlen. Boston: Little, Brown. 9–12 yrs.

Lasky, Kathryn. 1993. *Monarchs.* Photos Christopher G. Knight. San Diego, Calif.: Harcourt Brace/Gulliver Green. 10–13 yrs.

Kneidel, Sally. 1994. *Pet Bugs: A Kid's Guide to Catching and Keeping Touchable Insects.* Illus. Mauro Megellan. New York: Wiley. 8–13 yrs.

Markle, Sandra. 1994. *Outside and Inside Spiders.* New York: Simon & Schuster/Bradbury. 10–12 yrs.

McLaughlin, Molly. 1989. *Dragonflies.* New York: Walker. 6–10 yrs.

Myers, Susan. 1991. *Insect Zoo.* Photos Richard Hewett. New York: Lodestar/Dutton. 9–12 yrs.

Pringle, Laurence. 1990. *Killer Bees.* New York: Morrow. 8–12 yrs.

Royston, Angela. 1992. *What's Inside? Insects.* Photos & illus. Richard Manning. New York: Dorling Kindersley. 6–9 yrs.

Silver, Donald M. 1993. *One Small Square: Backyard.* Illus. Patricia J. Wynne. New York: Freeman. 9–11 yrs.

Souza, D. M. 1991. *Insects around the House; Insects in the Garden; What Bit Me?* Minneapolis, Minn.: Carolrhoda. 6–9 yrs. Creatures All Around Us series.

Tesar, Jenny. 1993. *Insects.* Illus. J. Tesar. Woodbridge, Conn.: Blackbirch. 9–12 yrs.

MACHINES

Appelbaum, Diana. 1993. *Giants in the Land.* Illus. Michael McCurdy. Boston: Houghton Mifflin. 5–9 yrs.

Brown, C. 1995. *Tractor.* New York: Greenwillow. 4–6 yrs.

Burnie, David. 1991. *Machines and How They Work.* New York: Dorling Kindersley. 8–12 yrs.

Geisert, B. 1995. *Haystack.* Illus. Arthur Geisert. Burlington, Mass.: Houghton Mifflin. 5–8 yrs.

Horvatic, Anne. 1989. *Simple Machines.* Photos Stephen Bruner. New York: Dutton. 7–10 yrs.

Llewellyn, Claire. 1992. *My First Book of Time.* Color photos. New York: Dorling Kindersley. 5–8 yrs.

Macaulay, David. 1988. *The Way Things Work.* Boston: Houghton Mifflin. 9–16 yrs.

Marston, Hope Irvin. 1993. *Big Rigs.* Photos. New York: Cobblehill. 5–8 yrs.

NATURAL SCIENCE

Collier, John. 1993. *The Backyard.* Illus. John Collier. New York: Viking. 6–9 yrs.

Cutchins, J. & G. Johnson. 1995. *Are Those Animals REAL?: How Museums Prepare Wildlife Exhibits.* Color photos. New York: Morrow. 10–13 yrs.

George, Jean Craighead. 1993. *Dear Rebecca, Winter Is Here.* Illus. Loretta Krupinski. New York: HarperCollins. 5–9 yrs.

Hirschi, Ron. 1990–91. *Fall; Spring; Summer; Winter.* Photos Thomas D. Mangelsen. New York: Cobblehill. 3–8 yrs.

Hisock, Bruce. 1993. *The Big Storm.* Illus. B. Hisock. New York: Atheneum. 5–9 yrs.

Johnson, Rebecca L. 1993. *Investigating the Ozone Hole.* Photos. Minneapolis, Minn.: Lerner. 12–17+ yrs.

Lauber, Patricia. 1986. *Volcano: The Eruption and Healing of Mount St. Helens.* New York: Bradbury. 10–14 yrs.

Matthews, Downs. 1993. *Arctic Summer.* Photos Dan Guravich. New York: Simon & Schuster. 10–12 yrs.

Pandell, Karen. 1993. *Land of Dark, Land of Light: The Arctic National Wildlife Refuge.* Photos Fred Bruemmer. New York: Dutton. 6–12 yrs.

Quinlan, Susan E. 1995. *The Case of the Mummified Pigs: And Other Mysteries in Nature.* Illus. Jennifer Owings Dewey. Honesdale, Penn.: Boyds Mills. 9–12 yrs.

Taylor, Barbara. 1992. *Coral Reef.* Photos Jane Burton. New York: Dorling Kindersley. 4–6 yrs. Look Closer series.

––––––. 1992. *Desert Life.* Photos Frank Greenaway. New York: Dorling Kindersley. 4–6 yrs. Look Closer series.

––––––. 1992. *Pond Life.* Photos Frank Greenaway. New York: Dorling Kindersley. 4–6 yrs. Look Closer series.

––––––. 1992. *Rain Forest.* Photos Frank Greenaway. New York: Dorling Kindersley. 4–6 yrs. Look Closer series.

Eyewitness Visual Dictionaries. 1993. *The Visual Dictionary of the Earth.* Photos. New York: Dorling Kindersley. 10–16 yrs.

––––––. 1993. *The Visual Dictionary of the Universe.* Photos. New York: Dorling Kindersley. 10–16 yrs.

NUTRITION & COOKING

Blain, D. 1991. *Boxcar Children Cookbook.* Illus. L. K. Deal & E. M. Neill. Morton Grove, Ill.: Whitman. 7–12 yrs.

Bravo, O. 1995. *Olga's Cup and Saucer: A Picture Book with Recipes.* New York: Holt. 6–10 yrs.

Cole, H. 1995. *Jack's Garden.* New York: Greenwillow. 6–9 yrs.

George, Jean Craighead. 1995. *Acorn Pancakes, Dandelion Salad, and Thirty-Eight Other Wild Recipes.* Illus. Paul Mirocha. New York: HarperCollins. 9–12 yrs.

Hausherr, Rosmarie. 1994. *What Food Is This?* Photos R. Hausherr. New York: Scholastic. 4–8 yrs.

Katzen, Mollie & Ann Henderson. 1994. *Pretend Soup and Other Real Recipes: A Cookbook for Preschoolers and Up.* Illus. Mollie Katzen. Berkeley, Calif.: Tricycle. 4–6 yrs.

King, Elizabeth. 1995. *Chile Fever: A Celebration of Peppers.* Color photos. New York: Dutton. 9–12 yrs.

Krizmanic, Judy. 1994. *A Teen's Guide to Going Vegetarian.* Illus. Matthew Wawiorka. New York: Viking. 12–15 yrs.

Micucci, Charles. 1992. *The Life and Times of the Apple.* New York: Orchard. 5–8 yrs.

Monroe, Luck. 1993. *Creepy Cuisine: Revolting Recipes That Look Disgusting but Taste Divine.* Illus. Dianne O'Quinn Burke. New York: Random House. 10–13 yrs.

Priceman, Marjorie. 1994. *How to Make an Apple Pie and See the World.* Illus. M. Priceman. New York: Knopf. 5–9 yrs.

Rockwell, Anne. 1993. *Pots and Pans.* Illus. Lizzy Rockwell. New York: Macmillan. 3–6 yrs.

Scobey, Joan. 1993. *The Fannie Farmer Junior Cookbook.* Illus. Patience Brewster. Boston: Little, Brown. 10–13 yrs.

Snedden, R. 1996. *Yuck!: A Big Book of Little Horrors.* Photos. New York: Simon & Schuster. 7–10 yrs.

Walker, B. M. 1995. *The Little House Cookbook: Frontier Foods from Laura Ingalls Wilder's Classic Stories.* Illus. Garth Williams. New York: HarperCollins. 9–12 yrs.

STATES IN THE UNITED STATES

Buckley, Virginia. 1986. *State Birds.* Illus. Arthur & Alan Singer. New York: Lodestar/Dutton. 8–11 yrs.

Costabel, Eva Deutsch. 1993. *The Early People of Florida.* New York: Atheneum. 10–12 yrs.

Haban, Rita D. 1989. *How Proudly They Wave.* Minneapolis, Minn.: Lerner. 9–12 yrs.

Plummer, James. 1983. *A Gift from Maine.* Portland, Maine: Gannett. 10–14 yrs.

Swanson, June. 1990. *I Pledge Allegiance.* Minneapolis, Minn.: Carolrhoda. 7–11 yrs.

"Hello U.S.A." 1991–93. Lerner. 9–11 yrs. (Information about each state available in the series.)

SOCIETAL CONCERNS

Archer, Jules. 1994. *Rage in the Streets: Mob Violence in America.* San Diego: Harcourt Brace. 12–16 yrs.

Ashabranner, Brent. 1994. *Dark Harvest: Migrant Farmworkers in America.* Photos Paul Conklin. Linnet. 12–16 yrs.

Bernards, Neal. 1991. *Gun Control.* San Diego: Lucent. 11–14 yrs.

Berck, Judith. 1992. *No Place to Be: Voices of Homeless Children.* Photos. Boston: Houghton Mifflin. 12–15 yrs.

Freedman, Russell. 1994. *Kids at Work: Lewis Hine and the Crusade against Child Labor.* New York: Clarion. 9–11 yrs.

Greenberg, Keith E. 1992. *Erik Is Homeless.* Photos Carol Halebian. Minneapolis, Minn.: Lerner. 10–14 yrs.

Guernsey, JoAnn Bren. 1995. *Sexual Harassment: A Question of Power.* B&W photos. Minneapolis, Minn.: Lerner. 12–16 yrs. Frontline series.

Harris, Jack. 1990. *Gun Control.* Morristown, N.J.: Silver Burdett/Crestwood. 11–15 yrs.

Hinojosa, Maria. 1995. *Crews: Gang Members Talk to Maria Hinojosa.* Photos German Perez. San Diego: Harcourt Brace. 12–16 yrs.

Hoose, Phillip. 1993. *It's Our World, Too!: Stories of People Who Are Making a Difference.* Illus. B&W photos. Boston: Joy Street. 10–12 yrs.

Hubbard, Jim. 1991. *Shooting Back: A Photographic View of Life Homeless Children.* Selected photos by children. San Francisco: Chronicle. 11–17 yrs.

Hyde, Margaret O. 1989. *The Homeless: Profiling the Problem.* Springfield, N.J.: Enslow. 11–15 yrs.

Kaufman, Curt & Gita Kaufman. 1987. *Hotel Boy.* Photos C. Kaufman. New York: Atheneum. 7–10 yrs.

Knight, Margy Burns. 1992. *Talking Walls.* Illus. Anne Sibley O'Brien. St. Paul, Minn.: Tilbury. 10–17 yrs.

Kosof, Anna. 1988. *Homeless in America.* Photos. Danbury, Conn.: Watts. 11–15 yrs.

Kraft, Betsy Harvey. 1995. *Mother Jones: One Woman's Fight for Labor.* B & W photos. New York: Clarion. 10–13 yrs.

Kronenwetter, Michael. 1993. *Under Eighteen: Knowing Your Rights.* Springfield, N.J.: Enslow. 12–18 yrs. Issues in Focus series.

––––––. 1994. *The Peace Commandos: Nonviolent Heroes in the Struggle Against War and Injustice.* New York: New Discovery. 12–16 yrs. Timestop Books.

Kuklin, Susan. 1993. *Speaking Out: Teenagers Take on Race, Sex, and Identity.* Photos S. Kuklin. New York: Putnam. 13–16 yrs.

––––––. 1989. *Fighting Back.* Photos S. Kuklin. New York: Putnam. 13–16 yrs.

––––––. 1991. *What Do I Do Now?* Photos S. Kuklin. New York: Putnam. 13–16 yrs.

––––––. 1996. *Irrepressible Spirit: Conversations with Human Rights Activists.* Photos. New York: Putnam. 12–18 yrs.

Meltzer, Milton. 1990. *Crime in America.* New York: Morrow. 12–15 yrs.

––––––. 1994. *Cheap Raw Material.* New York: Viking. (Child labor.)

––––––. 1994. *Who Cares? Millions Do: A Book about Altruism.* New York: Walker. 12–16 yrs.

Newton, David E. 1992. *Gun Control: An Issue for the Nineties.* Springfield, N.J.: Enslow. 12–16 yrs.

Nichelason, Margery G. 1994. *Homeless or Helpless?* New York: Lerner. 11–16 yrs.

O'Neill, Terry. 1990. *The Homeless: Distinguishing between Fact and Opinion.* San Diego, Calif.: Greenhaven. 11–15 yrs.

Osborn, Kevin. 1994. *Everything You Need to Know about Bias Incidents.* New York: Rosen. 12–13 yrs.

Patent, Dorothy Hinshaw. 1992. *Places of Refuge: Our National Wildlife Refuge System.* Photos William Munoz. New York: Clarion. 10–12 yrs.

Pringle, Laurence. 1989. *The Animal Rights Controversy.* San Diego, Calif.: Harcourt Brace Jovanovich. 9–13 yrs.

Rappaport, Doreen. 1993. *Tinker vs. Des Moines: Student Rights on Trial.* Prints, photos, diagrams. New York: HarperCollins. 10–16 yrs.

––––––. *The Alger Hiss Trial.* 1993. Prints, photos, diagrams. New York: HarperCollins. 10–17 yrs.

Rosen, Michael. 1992. *Home: A Collaboration of Thirty Distinguished Authors and Illustrators of Children's Books to Aid the Homeless.* Illus. various artists. New York: HarperCollins. 10–14 yrs.

St. Pierre, Stephanie. *Everything You Need to Know When a Parent Is in Jail.* New York: Rosen. 9–11 yrs.

Taylor, Clark. 1992. *The House that Crack Built.* Illus. Jan Thompson Dicks. San Francisco, Calif.: Chronicle. 10–17 yrs.

Wolf, Bernard. 1995. *Homeless.* Color photos. New York: Orchard. 5–9 yrs.

Wood, A. J. 1992. *Errata: A Book of Historical Errors.* Illus. Hemesh Alles. New York: Green Tiger Press. 10–16 yrs.

WATERLIFE, REPTILES, & AMPHIBIANS

Adams, Georgie. 1993. *Fish Fish Fish.* Illus. Brigitte Wilgoss. New York: Dial. 5–9 yrs.

Aliki. 1993. *My Visit to the Aquarium.* Illus. Aliki. New York: HarperCollins. 7–12 yrs.

Arnold, Caroline. 1991. *Snakes.* Photos Richard Hewett. New York: Morrow. 9–12 yrs.

––––––. 1994. *Killer Whale.* New York: Morrow. New York: Morrow.

––––––. 1994. *Sea Lion.* New York: Morrow. 9–11 yrs.

Arnosky, Jim. 1991. *Come Out, Muskrats.* Illus. Jim Arnosky. New York: Mulberry. 4–8 yrs.

––––––. 1992. *Otters under Water.* Illus. Jim Arnosky. New York: Putnam. 3–6 yrs.

Baker, Lucy. 1990. *Snakes.* Color photos. New York: Puffin. 8–11 yrs.

Bare, Colleen Stanley. 1989. *Never Kiss an Alligator!* Photos C. Bare. New York: Cobblehill. 6–8 yrs.

Bendick, Jeanne. 1992. *Exploring an Ocean Tide Pool*. Illus. Todd Telander. New York: Henry Holt/Redfeather. 7–10 yrs.

Berger, Melvin. 1992. *Look Out for Turtles!* Illus. Megan Lloyd. New York: HarperCollins. 7–10 yrs.

Bernhard, Emery. 1995. *Salamanders*. Illus. Durga Bernhard. New York: Holiday. 5–9 yrs.

Carrick, Carol. *Whaling Days*. Illus. David Frampton. New York: Clarion. 5–8 yrs.

Cerullo, Mary M. 1993. *Sharks: Challengers of the Deep*. Photos Jeffrey L. Rotman. New York: Cobblehill. 10–16 yrs.

_____. 1994. *Lobsters: Gangsters of the Sea*. Photos Jeffrey L. Rotman. New York: Cobblehill. 10–12 yrs.

Challand, Helen J. 1992. *Disappearing Wetlands*. Danbury, Conn.: Children's Press. 11–15 yrs.

Conant, Roger. 1992. *Peterson First Guide to Reptiles and Amphibians*. Boston: Houghton Mifflin. 7–11 yrs.

Cossl, Olga. 1991. *Harp Seals*. Photos. Minneapolis, Minn.: Carolrhoda. 5–13 yrs. Nature Watch Book.

Cousteau Society. 1991–92. *Dolphins; Penguins; Seals; Turtles*. Photos Cousteau Society. New York: Simon & Schuster/Simon & Schuster. 3–7 yrs.

Dorros, Arthur. 1991. *Follow the Water from Brook to Ocean*. New York: HarperCollins. 7–10 yrs. Let's-Read-and-Find-Out Science Book.

Downer, Ann. 1992. *Spring Pool: A Guide to the Ecology of Temporary Ponds*. Danbury, Conn.: Watts/New England Aquarium. 9–14 yrs.

Gibbons, Gail. 1991. *Sharks*. Illus. G. Gibbons. New York: Holiday. 6–9 yrs.

_____. 1991. *Whales*. Illus. G. Gibbons. New York: Holiday. 6–10 yrs.

_____. 1993. *Frogs*. Illus. G. Gibbons. New York: Holiday. 5–8 yrs.

_____. 1995. *Sea Turtles*. New York: Holiday. 5–8 yrs.

Gilliand, Judith Heide. 1993. *River*. Illus. Joyce Powzyk. New York: Clarion. 9–12 yrs.

Gourley, Catherine. 1995. *Hunting Neptune's Giants: True Stories of American Whaling*. Photos Mystic Seaport Museum. Brookfield, Conn.: Millbrook. 9–11 yrs.

Gowell, Elizabeth Tayntor. 1993. *Sea Jellies: Rainbows in the Sea*. Prints & photos. Danbury, Conn.: Watts. 7–12 yrs.

Greenway, Thereas. 1993. *Swamp Life: A Close-up Look at the Natural World of a Swamp*. Photos Kim Taylor & Jane Burton. New York: Dorling Kindersley. 6–10 yrs.

Grover, Wayne. 1990. *Dolphin Adventure: A True Story*. Illus. Jim Fowler. New York: Greenwillow. 8–12 yrs.

Guiberson, Brenda Z. 1993. *Lobster Boat*. Illus. Megan Lloyd. New York: Holt. 5–9 yrs.

_____. 1996. *Into the Sea*. Illus. Alix Berenzy. New York: Holt. 6–10 yrs.

Johnston, Ginny & Judy Cutchins. 1991. *Slippery Babies: Young Frogs, Toads, and Salamanders*. New York: Morrow. 8–12 yrs.

Johnson, Rebecca L. 1992. *The Great Barrier Reef: A Living Laboratory*. Minneapolis, Minn.: Lerner. 6–11 yrs.

Julivert, Maria Angels. 1993. *The Fascinating World of Snakes*. Hauppauge, N.Y.: Barron's. 9–12 yrs.

Kraus, Scott & Kenneth Mallory. 1993. *The Search for the Right Whale*. Photos. New York: Crown. 10–13 yrs.

Lauber, Patricia. 1990. *An Octopus Is Amazing*. Illus. Holly Keller. New York: Crowell/Let's-Read-and-Find-Out Science Books. 6–9 yrs.

Lavies, Bianca. 1990. *The Secretive Timber Rattlesnakes*. Color photos B. Lavies. New York: Dutton. 9–11 yrs.

_____. 1992. *The Atlantic Salmon*. Photos. New York: Dutton. 10–12 yrs.

_____. 1993. *A Gathering of Garter Snakes*. Photos. New York: Dutton. 10–12 yrs.

_____. 1994. *Mangrove Wilderness: Nature's Nursery*. New York: Dutton. 8–12 yrs.

Leedy, Loreen. 1993. *Tracks in the Sand*. Illus. L. Leedy. New York: Bantam Doubleday Dell. 5–8 yrs.

Liptak, Karen. 1991. *Saving Our Wetlands and Our Wildlife*. Danbury, Conn.: Watts. 9–12 yrs.

Machotka, Hana. 1993. *Outstanding Outsides*. New York: Morrow. 5–7 yrs.

Maestro, Betsy. 1990. *A Sea Full of Sharks*. Illus. Giulio Maestro. New York: Scholastic. 6–9 yrs.

_____. 1992. *Take a Look at Snakes*. Illus. Giulio Maestro. New York: Scholastic. 7–10 yrs.

Mallory, Kenneth & Andrea Conley. 1989. *Rescue of the Stranded Whales*. New York: Simon & Schuster/New England Aquarium. 6–10 yrs.

Markle, Sandra. 1995. *Outside and Inside Snakes*. Color photos. New York: Macmillan. 5–9 yrs.

Martin, James. 1993. *Tentacles: The Amazing World of Octopus, Squid, and Their Relatives*. Photos & drawings. New York: Crown. 10–13 yrs.

Matthews, Downs. 1994. *Wetlands*. Photos Dan Guravich. New York: Simon & Schuster. 7–11 yrs.

McCloskey, Robert. 1957. *Time of Wonder*. Illus. R. McCloskey. New York: Viking. 9–12 yrs.

McDonald, Megan. 1990. *Is This a House for a Hermit Crab?* Illus. S. D. Schindler. New York: Orchard/Jackson. 4–7 yrs.

McFarlane, Sheryl. 1993. *Waiting for the Whales*. Illus. Ron Lightburn. New York: Philomel. 5–9 yrs.

McMillan, Bruce. 1992. *Going on a Whale Watch*. Photos B. McMillan. New York: Scholastic. 9–12 yrs.

_____. 1993. *A Beach for the Birds*. Photos B. McMillan. Boston: Houghton Mifflin. 9–12 yrs.

_____. 1993. *Penguins at Home: Gentoos of Antarctica*. Photos B. McMillan. Boston: Houghton Mifflin. 7–12 yrs.

Orr, Katherine. 1993. *Story of a Dolphin*. Illus. K. Orr. Minneapolis, Minn.: Carolrhoda. 7–12 yrs.

Parker, Nancy Winslow & Joan Richards Wright. *Frogs, Toads, Lizards, and Salamanders*. Illus. author. New York: Greenwillow. 6–9 yrs.

Paten, Dorothy Hinshaw. 1993. *Killer Whales*. Photos John K. B. Ford. New York: Holiday. 5–8 yrs.

_____. 1994. *The American Alligator*. New York: Clarion. 9–11 yrs.

Peters, Lisa Westberg. 1991. *Water's Way*. Illus. Ted Rand. Boston: Little, Brown/Arcade. 6–8 yrs.

Pfeffer, Wendy. 1994. *From Tadpole to Frog*. Illus. Holly Keller. New York: HarperCollins. 5–8 yrs.

Pratt, Kristin Joy. 1994. *A Swim through the Sea*. Illus. K. Pratt. Nevada City, Calif.: Dawn. 9–13 yrs.

Pringle, Laurence. 1995. *The Dolphin Man: Exploring the World of Dolphins*. New York: Atheneum. 10–13 yrs.

_____. 1995. *Coral Reefs: Earth's Undersea Treasures*. Color photos. New York: Simon & Schuster. 9–12 yrs.

Reyonds, Jan. 1993. *Amazon Basin: Vanishing Cultures*. San Diego: Harcourt Brace. 7–12 yrs.

Robbins, Ken. 1994. *Water: The Elements*. New York: Holt. 9–11 yrs.

Rood, Ronald. 1994. *Wetlands*. Illus. Marlene Hill Donnelly. New York: HarperCollins. 9–11 yrs.

Simon, Seymour. 1989. *Whales*. Color photos. New York: Crowell. 5–9 yrs.

_____. 1990. *Oceans*. Color photos. New York: Morrow. 5–9 yrs.

_____. 1992. *Snakes*. Color photos. New York: HarperCollins. 5–9 yrs.

_____. 1995. *Sharks*. Color photos. New York: HarperCollins. 5–8 yrs.

Sobol, Richard & Jonah Sobol. 1993. *Seal Journey*. Photos Richard Sobol. New York: Cobblehill. 5–9 yrs.

Swanson, Diane. 1995. *Safari Beneath the Sea: The Wonder World of the North Pacific Coast*. Photos Royal British Columbia Museum. San Francisco: Sierra Club Books. 10–13 yrs.

Wallace, Karen. 1993. *Think of a Beaver*. Illus. Mick Manning. Cambridge, Mass.: Candlewick. 5–8 yrs. Read and Wonder Series

_____. 1993. *Think of an Eel*. Illus. Mike Bostock. Cambridge, Mass.: Candlewick. 5–8 yrs. Read and Wonder Series.

Waters, John F. 1991. *Watching Whales*. Photos. New York: Cobblehill. 8–10 yrs.

_____. 1994. *Deep-Sea Vents: Living Worlds without Sun*. Photos. New York: Cobblehill. 8–12 yrs.

Wells, Robert E. 1993. *Is a Blue Whale the Biggest Thing?* Morton Grove, Ill.: Whitman. 5–8 yrs.

White, Sandra Verrill & Michael Filisky. 1989. *Sterling: The Rescue of a Baby Harbor Seal*. New York: Crown/New England Aquarium Books. 7–10 yrs.

Wu, Norbert. 1991. *Life in the Oceans*. Boston: Little, Brown. 8–12 yrs. Planet Earth series.

Yolen, Jane. 1992. *Letting Swift River Go*. Illus. Barbara Cooney. Boston: Little, Brown. 10–13 yrs.

Ziter, Cary B. 1989. *When Turtles Come to Town*. Photos Chuck Bigger. Franklin Danbury, Conn.: Watts/First Books. 8–10 yrs.

Zoehfeld, Kathleen Weidner. 1994. *What Lives in a Shell?* Illus. Helen K. Davie. New York: HarperCollins. 5–8 yrs. Let's-Read-and Find-Out Science series.

ZOOLIFE

Curtis, Patricia. 1991. *Animals and the New Zoos*. Photos. New York: Lodestar/Dutton. 11–15 yrs.

Florian, Douglas. 1992. *At the Zoo*. Illus. D. Florian. New York: Greenwillow. 4–7 yrs.

Henley, Claire. 1992. *At the Zoo*. Illus. C. Henley. New York: Hyperion. 4–7 yrs.

Irvine, Georgine. 1991. *The Work of the Zoo Doctors at the San Diego Zoo*. New York: Simon & Schuster. 9–11 yrs.

Johnston, Ginny & Judy Cutchins. 1990. *Windows on Wildlife*. Color photos. New York: Morrow. 9–12 yrs.

Machotka, Hana. 1990. *What Do You Do at a Petting Zoo?* Photos. New York: Morrow. 4–8 yrs.

McMillan, Bruce. 1992. *The Baby Zoo*. Photos. New York: Scholastic. 10–12 yrs.

Most, Bernard. 1992. *Zoodles*. San Diego: Harcourt Brace. 7–10 yrs.

Ormerod, Jan. 1990. *"When We Went to the Zoo."* Illus. J. Ormerod. New York: Lothrop, Lee & Shepard. 4–7 yrs.

Rinard, Judith. 1992. *At the Zoo*. Washington, D.C.: National Geographic. 4–7 yrs.

Smith, Roland. 1993. *Inside the Zoo Nursery*. Photos William Munoz. New York: Cobblehill. 10–14 yrs.

Thomson, Peggy. 1988. *Keepers and Creatures at the National Zoo*. Photos Paul Conklin. New York: Crowell. 10–14 yrs.

LITSET: UNITED STATES CIVIL WAR

(SEE CHAPTER 9 FOR ADDITIONAL BOOKS)

UNDERGROUND RAILROAD

Brill, M. T. 1993. *Allen Jay and the Underground Railroad*. Illus. Janice Lee Porter. Minneapolis, Minn.: Carrolrhoda. 7–10 yrs.

Cosner, S. 1991. *The Underground Railroad*. New York: Watts. 12–14 yrs.

Gorrell, G. K. 1997. *North Star to Freedom: The Story of the Underground Railroad*. Photos. New York: Delacorte. 11–16 yrs.

Hamilton, V. 1968. *The House of Dies Drear*. New York: Macmillan. 11–15 yrs.

Haskins, J. 1993. *Get On Board: The Story of the Underground Railroad*. New York: Scholastic. 10–14 yrs.

Monjo, F. N. 1993. *The Drinking Gourd: A Story of the Underground Railroad*. Illus. Fred Brenner. New York: HarperCollins. 7–9 yrs.

Ringgold, F. 1992. *Aunt Harriet's Underground Railroad in the Sky*. New York: Crown. 7–11 yrs.

Ruby, L. 1994. *Steal Away Home*. New York: Macmillan. 9–13 yrs.

Wright, C. C. 1994. *Journey to Freedom: A Story of the Underground Railroad*. Illus. Gershom Griffith. New York: Holiday. 7–10 yrs.

CIVIL WAR

Information Books

The American Heritage Illustrated History of the United States. Volume 8: The Civil War. 1988. New York: American Heritage. 10–14 yrs.

Ashabranner, B. 1992. *A Memorial for Mr. Lincoln*. Photos. New York: Putnam's. 10–15 yrs.

Beller, S. P. 1995. *To Hold This Ground: A Desperate Battle at Gettysburg*. New York: McElderry. 11–14 yrs.

Bolotin, N. & Herb, A. 1995. *For Home and Country: A Civil War Scrapbook*. New York: Lodestar. 10–14 yrs.

Chang, I. 1991. *A Separate Battle: Women and the Civil War*. New York: Lodestar. 12–15 yrs.

Cox, C. 1991. *Undying Glory: The Story of the Massachusetts 54th Regiment*. New York: Scholastic. 12–15 yrs.

Dorf, P. 1994. *Highlights and Sidelights of the Civil War*. Middletown, Conn.: Southfarm. 11–14 yrs.

Fleischman, P. 1993. *Bull Run*. Woodcuts by David Frampton. New York: HarperCollins. 10–16 yrs.

Hansen, J. 1993. *Between Two Fires: Black Soldiers in the Civil War*. Prints & Photos. New York: Watts.

Johnson, N. 1989. *The Battle of Gettysburg*. New York: Four Winds. 9–14 yrs.

Kent, Z. 1994. *The Civil War: "A House Divided."* Hillside, N.J.: Enclow. 11–15 yrs.

Lincoln, A. 1995. *The Gettysburg Address*. Illus. Michael McCurdy. Boston: Houghton. 9–13 yrs.

Meltzer M. 1980. *All Times, All Peoples: A World History of Slavery*. New York: HarperCollins. 10–15 yrs.

Meltzer, M. 1989. *Voices from the Civil War: A Documentary History of the Great American Conflict*. New York: HarperTrophy. 11–14 yrs.

Mettger, Z. 1994. *Reconstruction: America after the Civil War*. New York: Lodestar. 11–14 yrs.

Murphy, J. 1992. *The Long Road to Gettysburg*. New York: Clarion. 10–14 yrs.

Ray, D. 1990. *A Nation Torn: The Story of How the Civil War Began*. New York: Lodestar. 10–14 yrs.

Robertson, J. I., Jr. 1992. *Civil War! America Becomes One Nation*. New York: Knopf. 11–14 yrs.

Rogers, J. 1994. *The Antislavery Movement*. New York: Facts on File. 12–16 yrs.

Smith, C. 1993. *Prelude to War*. Brookfield, Conn.: Milbrook. 12–14 yrs.

———. (Ed.) 1993. *One Nation Again: A Sourcebook on the Civil War*. Brookfield, Conn.; Milbrook. 10–16 yrs.

———. (Ed.) 1993. *1863: The Crucial Year*. Brookfield, Conn.: Milbrook. 10–16 yrs.

———. (Ed.) 1993. *The First Battles*. Brookfield, Conn.: Milbrook. 10–16 yrs.

St. George, J. 1991. *Mason and Dixon's Line of Fire*. New York: Putnam. 10–15 yrs.

Poetry Collections

Hopkins, L. B. (Ed.) 1994. *Hand in Hand: An American History Through Poetry*. Illus. Peter M. Fiore. New York: Simon & Schuster. 9–13 yrs.

Philip, N. (Ed.) 1995. *Singing America: Poems That Define a Nation*. Illus. Michael McCurdy. New York: Viking. 12–16 yrs.

Biographies

Archer, J. 1995. *A House Divided: The Lives of Ulysses S. Grant and Robert E. Lee*. New York: Scholastic. 10–16 yrs.

Burchard, P. 1995. *Charlotte Forten: A Black Teacher in the Civil War*. New York: Crown. 10–14 yrs.

Chang, I. 1991. *A Separate Battle: Women and the Civil War*. New York: Lodestar. 11–14 yrs.

Collins, D. R. 1994. *Shattered Dreams: The Story of Mary Todd Lincoln*. Greensboro, N.C.: Morgan Reynolds. 11–15 yrs.

Colman, P. 1992. *Spies! Women in the Civil War*. Cincinnati, Ohio: Shoe Tree. 11–14 yrs.

Cooper, M. L. 1994. *From Slave to Civil War Hero: The Life and Times of Robert Smalls*. New York: Lodestar. 10–14 yrs.

Everett, G. 1993. *John Brown: One Man Against Slavery*. Illus. Jacob Lawrence. New York: Rizzoli. 9–14 yrs.

Fleming, T. 1988. *Band of Brothers: West Point in the Civil War*. New York: Walker. 10–14 yrs.

Freedman, R. 1987. *Lincoln: A Photobiography*. Photos. Boston: Houghton Mifflin. 10–14 yrs.

Fritz, J. 1979. *Stonewall*. Illus. Stephen Gammell. New York: Putnam. 10–14 yrs.

———. 1993. *Just a Few Words, Mr. Lincoln: The Story of the Gettysburg Address*. Illus. Charles Robinson. New York: Putnam. 7–10 yrs.

Goldman, M. 1992. *Nat Turner and the Southampton Revolt of 1831*. New York: Watts. 12–14 yrs.

Hamilton, L. 1988. *Clara Barton*. New York: Chelsea. 12–16 yrs.

Hansen, J. 1986. *Which Way Freedom?* New York: Walker. 10–14 yrs.

Haskins, J. 1992. *Amazing Grace: The Story Behind the Song*. Brookfield, Conn.: Milbrook. 10–13 yrs.

Kent, Z. 1987. *The Story of Sherman's March to the Sea*. Illus. Ralph Canaday. Chicago, Ill.: Children's Press. 7–11 yrs.

Lyons, M. E. 1993. *Stitching Stars: The Story Quilts of Harriet Powers*. New York: Scribner. 11–14 yrs.

Marrin, A. 1994. *Virginia's General: Robert E. Lee and the Civil War*. New York: Atheneum. 12–16 yrs.

———. 1994. *Unconditional Surrender: U.S. Grant and the Civil War*. Photos. New York: Atheneum. 12–15 yrs.

Meltzer, M. 1965. *Tongue of Flame: The Life of Lydia Maria Child*. New York: HarperCollins. 10–14 yrs.

———. (Ed.) 1993. *Lincoln in His Own Words*. Illus. Stephen Alcorn. San Diego, Calif.: Harcourt Brace. 10–16 yrs.

Mettger, Z. 1994. *Till Victory Is Won: Black Soldiers in the Civil War*. New York: Lodestar. 11–14 yrs.

Murphy, J. 1990. *The Boys' War: Confederate and Union Soldiers Talk About the Civil War*. New York: Clarion. 9–13 yrs.

Nixon, J. L. 1994. *A Dangerous Promise*. New York: Delacorte. 11–14 yrs.

O'Dell, S. 1976. *The Two Hundred Ninety*. Boston: Houghton. 11–14 yrs.

Perez, N. A. 1984. *The Slopes of War*. Boston: Houghton. 11–14 yrs.

Ray, D. 1991. *Behind the Blue and Gray: The Soldier's Life in the Civil War*. New York: Lodestar. 11–14 yrs.

Read, T. B. 1993. *Sheridan's Ride*. Illus. Nancy Winslow Parker. New York: Greenwillow. 10–16 yrs.

Reit, S. 1988. *Behind Rebel Lines: The Incredible Story of Emma Edmonds, Civil War Spy*. San Diego, Calif.: Harcourt. 11–14 yrs.

Rosen, M. J. 1995. *A School for Pompey Walker*. Illus. Aminah Brenda Lynn Robinson. San Diego, Calif.: Harcourt. 7–10 yrs.

Shura, M. F. 1991. *Gentle Annie: The True Story of a Civil War Nurse*. New York: Scholastic. 11–14 yrs.

Stepto, M. 1994. *Our Song, Our Toil: The Story of American Slavery as Told by Slaves*. Brookfield, Conn.: Milbrook. 10–14 yrs.

Stevens, B. 1992. *Frank Thompson: Her Civil War Story*. Photos & reproductions. New York: Macmillan. 10–12 yrs.

Sullivan, G. 1994. *Mathew Brady: His Life and Photographs*. Photos. New York: Cobblehill. 12–15 yrs.

Turner, A. 1987. *Nettie's Trip South*. Illus. Ronald Himler. New York: Macmillan. 9–12 yrs.

Whitter, J. G. 1992. *Barbara Frietchie*. Illus. Nancy Winslow Parker. New York: Greenwillow. 6–9 yrs.

Wisler, G. C. 1991. *Red Cap*. New York: Lodestar/Cutton. 12–15 yrs.

———. 1994. *Mr. Lincoln's Drummer*. New York: Lodestar. 11–15 yrs.

Yates, E. 1967. *Amos Fortune, Free Man*. Illus. Nora S. Unwin. New York: Dutton. 10–14 yrs.

Books with Pictures: Fiction

Ackerman, K. 1990. *The Tin Heart*. Illus. Michael Hays. New York: Atheneum. 6–10 yrs.

Gauch, P. L. 1990. *Thunder at Gettysburg*. Illus. Stephen Gammell. New York: Putnam. 9–12 yrs.

Polacco, P. 1994. *Pink and Say.* New York: Philomel. 11–14 yrs.

Wright, C. C. 1995. *Wagon Train: A Family Goes West in 1865.* Illus. Gershom Griffith. New York: Holiday. 7–9 yrs.

Fiction

Armstrong, J. 1996. *The Dreams of Mairhe Mehan.* New York: Knopf. 12–16 yrs.

Banim, L. 1995. *A Thief on Morgan's Plantation.* New York: Silver Moon. 9–12 yrs.

Blos, J. 1979. *A Gathering of Days: A New England Girl's Journal. 1830–1832.* New York: Scribner. 11–14 yrs.

Brink, C. R. 1935 (reissue 1973). *Caddie Woodlawn.* Illus. Trina Schart Hyman. New York: Macmillan. 11–15 yrs.

Clapp, P. 1986. *The Tamarack Tree.* New York: Lathrop. 12–16 yrs.

Climo, S. 1987. *A Month of Seven Days.* New York: HarperCollins. 10–14 yrs.

DeAngeli, M. 1940. *Thee, Hannah!* New York: Doubleday. 9–12 yrs.

Forrester, S. 1995. *Sound the Jubilee.* New York: Lodestar. 11–15 yrs.

Hansen, J. 1994. *The Captive.* New York: Scholastic. 10–13 yrs.

Hurmence, B. 1982. *A Girl Called Boy.* Boston: Houghton. 11–14 yrs.

Kassem, L. 1986. *Listen for Rachel.* New York: Avon. 11–14 yrs.

Stolz, M. 1994. *Cezanne Pinto: A Memoir.* New York: Knopf. 11–14 yrs.

CHAPTER 7

CHILDREN'S BOOKS MENTIONED IN THE CHAPTER

Adler, D. B. 1983. *The Carsick Zebra and Other Animal Riddles.* Illus. Tomie de Paolo. New York: Bantam. 7–11 yrs.

Adoff, A. 1973. *Black Is Brown Is Tan.* Illus. Emily Arnold McCully. New York: Harper & Row. 6–10 yrs.

———. 1986. *Sports Pages.* Illus. Steve Kuzma. New York: Lippincott. 9–12 yrs.

Adshead, G. & A. Duff. 1948. *Gladys Adshead's An Inheritance of Poetry.* Decorations Nora S. Unwin. Boston: Houghton Mifflin. 9–13 yrs.

Aldis, D. 1952. *All Together: A Child's Treasury of Verse.* Illus. Helen D. Jameson, Marjorie Flack, & Margaret Freeman. New York: Putnam. 5–9 yrs.

Allingham, W. 1887. *Rhymes for Young Folks.* Cited in Huber, M. B. 1965. *Story and Verse for Children.* New York: Macmillan. 6–14 yrs.

Arbuthnot, M. H. & S. Root. 1968. *Time for Poetry.* Illus. Arthur Paul. Chicago, Ill.: Scott, Foresman. 4–14 yrs.

Association for Childhood Education, Literature Committee. 1962. *Sung Under the Silver Umbrella.* Illus. Dorothy Lathrop. New York: Macmillan. 4–9 yrs.

Aylesworth, J. 1994. *My Son John.* Illus. David Frampton. New York: Holt. 3–6 yrs.

Begay, S. 1995. *Navajo: Visions and Voices across the Mesa.* New York: Scholastic. 9–14 yrs.

Behn, H. 1949. *The Little Hill.* San Diego, Calif.: Harcourt Brace. 9–12 yrs.

———. 1964. *Cricket Song.* Pictures from Japanese masters. New York: Harcourt Brace & World. 8–12 yrs.

Belloc, H. 1992. *Matilda Who Told Lies.* Illus. Steven Kellogg. New York: Dial. 5–8 yrs.

———. 1992. *Matilda Who Told Lies.* Illus. Posy Simmonds. New York: Knopf. 5–9 yrs.

Benet, R. & S. V. Benet. 1933. *A Book of Americans.* Illus. Charles Child. New York: Holt. 8–14 yrs.

Bennet, J. (Selector). 1987. *Noisy Poems.* Illus. Nick Sharratt. New York: Oxford University Press. 5–8 yrs.

Blake, W. 1966. *Songs of Innocence.* Illus. Ellen Raskin. New York: Doubleday.

———. 1927. *Songs of Experience.* London: E. Beun.

Bodecker, N. M. 1974. *Let's Marry Said the Cherry.* New York: McElderry/Macmillan. 7–10 yrs.

Bouchard, D. 1995. *If You're Not from the Prairie.* Images by Henry Ripplinger. New York: Atheneum. 9–13 yrs.

Brewton, J. E. 1937. *Under the Tent of the Sky.* New York: Macmillan. 5–9 yrs.

Brooks, G. 1956. *Bronzeville Boys and Girls.* New York: HarperCollins. 7–11 yrs.

Browning, R. 1970. *The Pied Piper of Hamelin.* Illus. Lieselotte Schwarz. London: Scroll Press. 7–14 yrs.

Bruchac, J. 1995. *The Earth Under Sky Bear: Native American Poems of the Land.* Illus. Thomas Locker. New York: Philomel. 9–13 yrs.

Bruchac, J. & J. London. 1992. *Thirteen Moons on Turtle's Back: A Native American Year of Moons.* Illus. Thomas Locker. New York: Philomel. 8–12 yrs.

Bryan, A. 1992. *Sing to the Sun.* New York: HarperCollins. 6–12 yrs.

Bunyan, J. 1686. *A Book for Boys & Girls or Country Rhymes for Children.* Cited in Z. Sutherland & M. H. Arbuthnot, 1991. *Children and Books* (8th ed., p. 57). New York: HarperCollins.

Carlstrom, N. W. 1992. *Northern Lullaby.* Illus. Leo & Diane Dillon. New York: Philomel. 5–8 yrs.

Carroll, L. 1977. *Jabberwocky.* Illus. Jane Breskin Zalben. London: Warne. 9–14 yrs.

Chandra, D. 1990. *Balloons and Other Poems.* New York: Farrar, Straus & Giroux. 9–12 yrs.

Ciardi, J. 1959. *The Reason for the Pelican.* Illus. Madeleine Gekiere. New York: Lippincott. 5–9 yrs.

———. 1989. *The Hopeful Trout and Other Limericks.* Illus. Susan Meddaugh. Boston: Houghton Mifflin. 8–12 yrs.

Clifton, L. 1970. *Some of the Days of Everett Anderson.* Illus. Evaline Ness. New York: Holt. 5–7 yrs.

Cole, J. 1989. *Anna Banana: 101 Jump-Rope Rhymes.* Illus. Alan Tiegreen. New York: Morrow. 6–11 yrs.

Cole, J. & S. Calmenson. (Compiler). 1990. *Miss Mary Mack, and Other Children's Street Rhymes.* Illus. Alan Tiegreen. New York: Morrow. 7–12 yrs.

Cole, W. 1955. *Humorous Poetry for Children.* Illus. Ervine Metzl. Cleveland, Ohio: World. 8–13 yrs.

———. 1964. *Beastly Boys and Ghastly Girls.* Illus. Tomi Ungerer. Cleveland, Ohio: World. 8–13 yrs.

———. 1981. *Poem Stew.* Illus. Karen Ann Weinhaus. New York: Lippincott. 8–12 yrs.

Conklin, H. 1920. *Poems by a Little Girl.* New York: Lippincott. 6–10 yrs.

cummings, e. e. 1989. *Hist Wist.* Illus. Deborah Kogan Ray. New York: Crown. 5–12 yrs.

de Angeli, M. 1954. *Book of Nursery and Mother Goose Rhymes.* New York: Doubleday. 4–7 yrs.

de la Mare, W. 1947. *Songs of Childhood.* Illus. Elinore Blaisdell. New York: Holt. (Original title *Rhymes and Verses, Collected Poems for Children.*) 6–12 yrs.

de Regniers, B. S. 1958. *Something Special.* Illus. Irene Haas. San Diego, Calif.: Harcourt Brace. 3–6 yrs.

de Regniers, B. S., E. Moore, M. M. White, & J. Carrel (Compilers). 1988. *Sing a Song of Popcorn: Every Child's Book of Poems.* Illus.

nine Caldecott winners. New York: Scholastic. 5–15 yrs.

Dyer, J. (Compiler). 1996. *Animal Crackers: A Delectable Collection of Pictures, Poems, and Lullabies for the Very Young.* Illus. Jane Dyer. Boston, Mass.: Little, Brown. 4–9 yrs.

Eliot, T. S. 1939. *Old Possum's Book of Practical Cats.* San Diego, Calif.: Harcourt Brace Jovanovich. 10–16 yrs.

Esbensen, B. J. 1965. *Swing Around the Sun.* Minneapolis, Minn.: Lerner. 6–9 yrs.

———. 1986. *Words with Wrinkled Knees: Animal Poems.* Illus. John Stadler. New York: Crowell. 6–12 yrs.

Evans, D. 1992. *Monster Soup and Other Spooky Poems.* Illus. Jacqueline Rogers. New York: Scholastic. 5–9 yrs.

Ferris, H. 1957. *Favorite Poems, Old and New.* Illus. Leonard Weisgard. New York: Doubleday. 6–14 yrs.

Field, E. 1904. *Poems of Childhood.* Illus. Maxfield Parrish. New York: Scribners. 6–12 yrs.

———. 1990. *The Gingham Dog and the Calico Cat.* Illus. Janet Stevens. New York: Philomel. 4–10 yrs.

Field, R. 1926. *Taxis and Toadstools.* New York: Macmillan. 7–12 yrs.

Fisher, A. 1960. *Going Barefoot.* New York: Crowell. 7–12 yrs.

———. 1963. *Cricket in a Thicket.* Illus. Feodor Rojankovsky. New York: Scribners. 5–8 yrs.

———. 1980. *Out in the Dark and Daylight.* Illus. Gail Owens. New York: Harper. 6–10 yrs.

Florian, D. 1994. *Beast Feast.* San Diego, Calif.: Harcourt Brace. 5–9 yrs.

———. 1994. *Bing Bang Boing.* Illus. D. Florian. San Diego, Calif.: Harcourt Brace. 9–12 yrs.

Fleischman, P. 1988. *Joyful Noise: Poems for Two Voices.* Illus. Eric Beddows. New York: Harper and Row/Zolotow. 6–14 yrs.

Frost, R. 1959. *You Come Too; Favorite Poems of Robert Frost for Young Readers.* Illus. Thomas W. Nason. New York: Holt. 9–16 yrs.

———. 1978. *Stopping by Woods on a Snowy Evening.* Illus. Susan Jeffers. New York: Dutton. 7–14 yrs.

———. 1988. *Birches.* Illus. Ed Young. New York: Holt. 8–12 yrs.

Fyleman, R. 1944. *Fairies and Chimneys.* New York: Doubleday. 8–10 yrs.

Geismer, B. P. & A. B. Suter. 1945. *Very Young Verse.* Cited in Dora Smith. *Fifty Years of Children's Books.* Champaign, Ill.: National Council of Teachers of English.

Giovanni, N. 1987. *Spin a Soft Black Song.* New York: Farrar, Straus & Giroux. 10–13 yrs.

Graham, J. B. 1994. *Splish Splash.* Illus. Steve Scott. Boston: Houghton Mifflin/Ticknor & Fields. 6–9 yrs.

Greenfield, E. 1978. *Honey, I Love and Other Love Poems.* Illus. Leo & Diane Dillon. New York: HarperCollins. 9–12 yrs.

_____. 1991. *Night on Neighborhood Street.* Illus. Jan Spivey Gilchrist. New York: Dial. 9–12 yrs.

Hirshfelder, A. C. & B. Singer (Compilers). 1992. *Rising Voices: Writings of Young Native Americans.* New York: Scribners. 10–16 yrs.

Hoberman, M. A. 1959. *Hello and Good-by.* Illus. Norman Hoberman. Boston: Little, Brown. 4–9 yrs.

_____. 1991. *Fathers, Mothers, Sisters, Brothers.* Boston, Mass.: Little, Brown. 4–9 yrs.

Holman, F. 1970. *At the Top of My Voice and Other Poems.* Illus. Edward Gorey. New York: Norton. 8–11 yrs.

Houston, J. (Ed.). 1972. *Songs of the Dream People.* New York: Atheneum. 10–16 yrs.

Huang, Tze-si (Trans.). 1992. *In the Eyes of the Cat: Japanese Poetry for All Seasons.* Illus. Demi. New York: Holt. 7–12 yrs.

Hughes, L. 1952. *The Dream Keeper and Other Poems.* Illus. Helen Sewell. New York: Knopf. 12–16 yrs.

Janeczko, P. B. 1994. *Poetry from A to Z: A Guide for Young Writers.* Illus. Cathy Bobak. New York: Bradbury. 10–15 yrs.

Joseph, L. 1990. *Coconut Kind of Day: Island Poems.* Illus. Sandra Speidel. New York: Lothrop, Lee & Shepard. 6–12 yrs.

Kennedy, X. J. 1975. *One Winter Night in August & Other Nonsense Jingles.* New York: McElderry/Macmillan. 5–10 yrs.

Kennedy, X. J. & D. Kennedy. 1992. *Talking like the Rain: A First Book of Poems.* Illus. Jane Dyer. Boston, Mass.: Little, Brown. 7–14 yrs.

Kuskin, K. 1980. *Dogs & Dragons, Trees & Dreams.* New York: Harper. 10–13 yrs.

_____. 1991. *Roar and More.* New York: HarperCollins. 6–9 yrs.

Lansky, B. 1991. *Kids Pick the Funniest Poems.* Illus. Steve Carpenter. Deephaven, Minn.: Meadowbrook Press. 6–12 yrs.

Lear, E. 1976. *The Complete Book of Nonsense.* New York: Garland. 8–14 yrs.

_____. 1987. *The Owl and the Pussy-Cat.* Illus. Paul Galdone. Boston: Houghton Mifflin. 5–10 yrs.

_____. 1986. *The Owl and the Pussycat.* Illus. Lorinda Bryan Cauley. New York: Putnam. 5–8 yrs.

_____. 1987. *The Owl and the Pussycat.* Illus. Paul Galdone. New York: Clarion. 5–8 yrs.

_____. 1987. *The Owl and the Pussycat.* Illus. Claire Littlejohn. New York: Harper & Row/Pop-up. 5–8 yrs.

_____. 1991. *The Owl and the Pussycat.* Illus. Jan Brett. New York: Putnam. 4–8 yrs.

_____. 1991. *The Owl and the Pussycat.* Illus. Helen Cooper. New York: Dial. 4–8 yrs.

_____. 1991. *The Owl and the Pussy-Cat.* Illus. Louise Voce. New York: Lothrop, Lee & Shepard. 4–8 yrs.

Lee, D. 1978. *Garbage Delight.* Illus. Frank Newfeld. Burlington, Maine: Houghton Mifflin. 7–13 yrs.

_____. 1983. *Jelly Belly.* Illus. J. Wijngaard. New York: Bedrick. 7–12 yrs.

Levy, C. A. 1994. *A Tree Place and Other Poems.* Illus. Robert Sabuda. New York: Macmillan. 8–12 yrs.

Lewis, J. P. 1990. *A Hippopotamusn't, and Other Animal Verses.* Illus. Victoria Chess. New York: Dial. 3–8 yrs.

_____. 1991. *Two-legged, Four-legged, No legged Rhymes.* Illus. Pamela Paparone. New York: Knopf. 8–12 yrs.

_____. 1991. *Earth Verse and Water Rhymes.* New York: Atheneum. 8–12 yrs.

_____. 1995. *Ridicholas Nicholas: More Animal Poems.* Illus. Victoria Chess. New York: Dial. 5–9 yrs.

Lines, K. 1954. *Lavender's Blue, A Book of Nursery Rhymes.* Illus. Harold Jones. New York: Watts. 4–8 yrs.

Livingston, M. C. 1958. *Whispers and Other Poems.* Illus. Jacqueline Chwast. San Diego, Calif.: Harcourt Brace. 9–12 yrs.

_____. 1989. *Birthday Poems.* New York: Holiday. 8–12 yrs.

Longfellow, H. W. 1985. *Paul Revere's Ride.* Illus. Nancy Winslow Parker. New York: Greenwillow. 10–16 yrs.

_____. 1990. *Paul Revere's Ride.* Illus. Ted Rand. New York: Dutton. 10–16 yrs.

Lucas, E. V. 1897. *A Book of Verses for Children.* London: Richards. 3–8 yrs.

McCord, D. 1952. *Far and Few: Rhymes of the Never Was and Always Is.* Illus. Henry B. Lane. Boston: Little, Brown. 5–9 yrs.

_____. 1993. *A Hippo's A Heap: And Other Animal Poems.* Illus. Laura Rader. Honesdale, Penn.: Wordsong. 5–9 yrs.

Merriam, E. 1962. *There Is No Rhyme for Silver.* Illus. Joseph Schindelman. New York: Atheneum. 9–13 yrs.

Milne, A. A. 1924. *When We Were Very Young.* Illus. Ernest Shepard. New York: Dutton. 4–9 yrs.

_____. 1927. *Now We Are Six.* Illus. Ernest Shepard. New York: Dutton. 9–12 yrs. (Both collections named as *The World of Christopher Robin,* 1958, illus. Ernest Shepard, New York: Dutton.)

Moore, C. 1971. *A Visit from St. Nicholas.* Illus. T. J. Boyd. New York: Simon & Schuster. 6–14 yrs. (See also contemporary versions.)

Moore, L. 1976. *I Feel the Same Way.* Illus. Robert Quackenbush. New York: Macmillan. 6–12 yrs.

Moss, J. 1991. *The Other Side of the Door.* Illus. Chris Demarest. New York: Bantam. 7–12 yrs.

Myers, W. D. 1993. *Brown Angels: An Album of Pictures and Verses.* Photos. New York: HarperCollins. 6–14 yrs.

Nash, O. 1942. *Good Intentions.* Boston: Little, Brown. 10–14 yrs.

Nurse Lovechild. 1788. *Tommy Thumb's Pretty Song Book.* Worcester, Mass.: Isaiah Thomas. 6–12 yrs.

O'Neill, M. 1961. *Hailstones and Halibut Bones.* Illus. Leonard Weisgard. New York: Doubleday. 5–12 yrs.

_____. 1966. *Words, Words, Words.* New York: Doubleday. 6–12 yrs.

_____. 1966. *What Is That Sound?* New York: Atheneum. 6–12 yrs.

_____. 1968. *Take A Number.* New York: Doubleday. 6–12 yrs.

Petersham, M. & M. Petersham. 1945. *The Rooster Crows.* New York: Macmillan. 4–8 yrs.

Philip, N. 1995. *Songs Are Thoughts: Poems of the Inuit.* Illus. Maryclare Foa. New York: Orchard. 10–13 yrs.

Plotz, H. 1955. *Imagination's Other Place: Poems of Science and Math.* Illus. Clare Leighton. New York: Crowell. 12–16 yrs.

_____. 1957. *Untune the Sky: Poems for Music and the Dance.* Boston: Little, Brown. 10–16 yrs.

Prelutsky, J. 1967. *A Gopher in the Garden and Other Animal Poems.* Illus. Robert Leydenfrost. New York: Macmillan. 9–12 yrs.

_____. 1984. *The New Kid on the Block.* Illus. James Stevenson. New York: Greenwillow. 8–14 yrs.

_____. 1990. *Something BIG Has Been Here.* Illus. James Stevenson. New York: Greenwillow. 5–14 yrs.

_____. 1996. *A Pizza the Size of the Sun.* Illus. James Stevenson. New York: Greenwillow. 5–14 yrs.

Prelutsky, J. (Ed.). 1983. *The Random House Book of Poetry for Children.* Illus. Arnold Lobel. New York: Random House. 4–16 yrs.

Rands, W. B. 1899. *Lilliput Lyrics.* 8–12 yrs. Cited in Margaret Gillespie, 1970. *History and Trends.* Boston, Mass.: Little, Brown.

Read, H. 1956. *This Way, Delight, a Book of Poetry for the Young.* Illus. Juliet Kepes. New York: Pantheon. 8–13 yrs.

Richards, L. E. 1955. *In My Nursery.* 6–10 yrs. (Combined with other poems and published as *Tirra Lirra, Rhymes Old and New.* 1955. Illus. Marguerite Davis. Boston: Little, Brown.)

Riley, J. W. 1891. *Rhymes of Childhood.* Indianapolis: Bowen-Merrill. 6–14 yrs.

Roberts, E. M. 1922. *Under the Tree.* Illus. F. D. Bedford. New York: Viking. 6–10 yrs.

Roethke, T. 1961. *I Am! Says the Lamb.* Illus. Robert Leydenfrost. New York: Doubleday. 10–16 yrs.

Roscoe, W. 1807. *Butterfly's Ball.* London: Harris. 6–9 yrs.

Rosen, M. 1989. *We're Going on a Bear Hunt.* Illus. Helen Oxenbury. New York: McElderry. 4–8 yrs.

_____. 1993. *The Kingfisher Book of Children's Poetry.* Illus. Alice Englander. New York: Kingfisher. 9–13 yrs.

Rossetti, C. 1924. *Sing Song, a Nursery Rhyme Book for Children.* New York: Macmillan. 5–9 yrs.

Sandburg, C. 1930. *Early Moon.* Illus. James Dougherty. San Diego, Calif.: Harcourt Brace. 10–14 yrs.

Singer, M. 1989. *Turtle in July.* Illus. Jerry Pinkney. New York: Macmillan. 7–15 yrs.

Sky-Peck, K. (Ed.). 1991. *Who Has Seen the Wind? An Illustrated Collection of Poetry for Young People.* Museum of Fine Arts, Boston. New York: Rizzoli. 7–14 yrs.

Soto, G. 1990. *Fire in My Hands: A Book of Poems.* New York: Scholastic. 10–16 yrs.

Silverstein, S. 1974. *Where the Sidewalk Ends: Poems and Drawings.* New York: Harper & Row. 5–14 yrs.

_____. 1981. *A Light in the Attic.* New York: Harper. 5–14 yrs.

_____. 1996. *Falling Up.* New York: HarperCollins. 5–14 yrs.

Smith, W. J. 1990. *Laughing Time: Collected Nonsense.* Illus. Fernando Krahn. New York: Farrar, Straus & Giroux. 7–12 yrs.

Sneve, V. D. H. 1989. *Dancing Teepees: Poems of American Indian Youth.* Illus. Stephen Gammel. New York: Holiday. 10–14 yrs.

Starbird, K. 1960. *Speaking of Cows.* Illus. Rita Fava. New York: Lippincott. 5–10 yrs.

Stevenson, R. L. 1965. *A Child's Garden of Verses.* Illus. Jessie Wilcox Smith. New York: Scribners. 5–10 yrs. (See also contemporary versions.)

Taylor, A. & J. Taylor. 1977. *Original Poems for Infant Minds.* New York: Garland. 5–11 yrs.

Teasdale, S. 1930. *Stars To-night: Verses Old and New for Boys and Girls.* Illus. Dorothy Lathrop. New York: Macmillan. 8–12 yrs.

Thayer, Ernest. 1989. *Casey at the Bat.* Illus. Wallace Tripp. New York: Putnam. 8–13 yrs. (See also contemporary versions.)

Thompson, B. (Ed.). 1967. *Silver Pennies.* Decorations by Ursula Arndt. New York:

Macmillan. (Now titled *All the Silver Pennies*.)
6–12 yrs.

Tippett, J. S. 1927. *I Live in a City*. New York: Harper. 5–7 yrs.

Untermeyer, L. 1935. *Rainbow in the Sky*. Illus. Reginald Birch. San Diego, Calif.: Harcourt Brace. 7–12 yrs.

Viorst, J. 1981. *If I Were in Charge of the World, and Other Worries: Poems for Children and Their Parents*. Illus. Lynne Cherry. New York: Atheneum. 8–14 yrs.

———. 1995. *Sad Underwear and Other Complications: More Poems for Children and Their Parents*. Illus. Richard Hull. New York: Atheneum. 10–12 yrs.

Watson, C. 1971. *Father Fox's Pennyrhymes*. Illus. Wendy Watson. New York: Crowell. 8–10 yrs.

Watts, I. 1866. *Divine and Moral Songs*. London: Nisbet. 6–14 yrs.

Westcott, N. B. 1994. *Never Take a Pig to Lunch: And Other Poems about the Fun of Eating*. New York: Orchard. 7–14 yrs.

Whipple, L. (Ed.). 1991. *Eric Carle's Dragons and Creatures That Never Were*. Illus. Eric Carle. New York: Philomel. 5–9 yrs.

———. (Compiler). 1989. *Animals Animals*. Illus. Eric Carle. New York: Philomel. 7–12 yrs.

Willard, N. 1981. *A Visit to William Blake's Inn: Poems for Innocent and Experienced Travelers*. Illus. Alice & Martin Provensen. San Diego, Calif.: Harcourt Brace. 10–14 yrs.

———. 1991. *Pish, posh, Said Hieronymus Bosch*. Illus. Leo, Diane, & Lee Dillon. San Diego, Calif.: Harcourt Brace. 10–14 yrs.

Wiggin, K. D. & N. A. Smith. 1903. *Golden Numbers*. McClure. 7–12 yrs.

———. 1903. *The Posy Ring*. McClure. 7–12 yrs.

Worth, V. 1972. *Small Poems*. Illus. N. Babbitt. New York: Farrar, Straus & Giroux. 7–12 yrs.

———. 1987. *All the Small Poems*. Illus. Natalie Babbitt. New York: Farrar, Straus & Giroux. 7–12 yrs.

Yolen, J. 1980. *How Beastly! A Menagerie of Nonsense Poems*. Illus. James Marshall. New York: Collins. 6–12 yrs.

———. 1991. *Bird Watch: A Book of Poetry*. Illus. Ted Lewin. New York: Philomel. 8–13 yrs.

———. (Compiler). 1992. *Street Rhymes around the World*. Illus. seventeen international artists. Honesdale, Penn.: Wordsong. 5–10 yrs.

PROSE MENTIONED IN THE CHAPTER

Aardema, V. 1975. *Why Mosquitoes Buzz in People's Ears*. Illus. Leo & Diane Dillon. New York: Dial. 8–12 yrs.

Ardley, N. 1989. *Eyewitness Book of Music*. New York: Dorling Kindersley. 8–12 yrs.

Bang, M. 1980. *The Grey Lady and the Strawberry Snatcher*. New York: Four Winds. 7–12 yrs.

Chimery, M. 1994. *Question and Answers about Seashore Animals*. New York: Kingfisher. 8–10 yrs.

Cooper, F. 1994. *Coming Home: From the Life of Langston Hughes*. New York: Philomel. 9–12 yrs.

de Paolo, T. 1978. *The Popcorn Book*. New York: Holiday. 6–10 yrs.

Demi. 1992. *Demi's Dragons and Fantastic Creatures*. New York: Holt. 5–8 yrs.

Hobbs, W. 1989. *Bearstone*. New York: Avon. 9–13 yrs.

Lowery, L. 1993. *The Giver*. Boston: Houghton Mifflin. 11–16 yrs.

Yep, L. 1991. *The Star Fisher*. New York: Morrow. 10–14 yrs.

Young, E. 1989. *Lon Po Po: A Red-Riding Hood Story from China*. New York: Philomel. 7–11 yrs.

POETRY ANTHOLOGIES

Abdul, Raoul (Adapter). 1972. *The Magic of Black Poetry*. Illus. Dane Burr. New York: Dodd. 8–12 yrs.

Adoff, Arnold (Ed.). 1973. *The Poetry of Black America: An Anthology of the 20th Century*. New York: HarperCollins. 11–16 yrs.

———. 1977. *Celebrations: A New Anthology of Black American Poetry*. River Grove, Ill.: Follett. 11–16 yrs.

Agard John, & Grace Nichols (Compilers). 1994. *A Caribbean Dozen: Poems from Caribbean Poets*. Illus. Cathie Felstead. Cambridge, Mass.: Candlewick. 9–12 yrs.

Benchely Paddy (Ed.). 1981. *Drumming in the Sky: Poems from "Stories and Rhymes."* Illus. Priscilla Lamont. London: British Broadcasting Corporation. 8–12 yrs.

Berry, James. 1995. *Classic Poems to Read Aloud*. Illus. James Mayhew. New York: Kingfisher. 10–13 yrs.

Bierhorst, John (Ed.). 1983. *The Sacred Path: Spells, Prayers, and Power Songs of the American Indians*. New York: Morrow. 12–16 yrs.

———. 1994. *On the Road of Stars: Native American Night Poems and Sleep Charms*. Illus. Judy Pedersen. New York: Macmillan. 5–9 yrs.

Big Bear's Treasury: A Children's Anthology. 1992. Illus. various artists. Cambridge, Mass.: Candlewick. 4–8 yrs.

Blishen, Edward. 1964. *The Oxford Book of Poetry for Children*. Illus. Brian Wildsmith. New York: Oxford University. 9–13 yrs.

Bober, N. S. (Ed.). 1989. *Let's Pretend: Poems of Flight and Fancy*. New York: Viking Kestrel. 9–14 yrs.

Booth, David. (Compiler). 1989. *'Til All the Stars Have Fallen*. New York: Penguin. 8–12 yrs.

———. 1990. *Voices on the Wind: Poems for All Seasons*. Illus. Michele Lemieux. New York: Morrow. 8–16 yrs.

Brenner, Barbara. 1994. *The Earth Is Painted Green: A Garden of Poems about Our Planet*. Illus. S. D. Schindler. New York: Scholastic. 9–14 yrs.

Brent, Isabelle (Selector). *Cameo Cats*. 1992. Illus. Isabelle Brent. Boston: Little, Brown. 6–12 yrs.

———. 1994. *All Creatures Great and Small*. Illus. I. Brent. Boston: Little, Brown. 5–9 yrs.

Brewton, John E. 1940. *Gaily We Parade*. New York: Macmillan. 5–12 yrs.

———. 1949. *Bridled with Rainbows*. New York: Macmillan. 4–8 yrs.

Brewton, Sara & John Brewton. 1969. *Shrieks at Midnight: Macabre Poems, Eerie and Humorous*. Illus. Ellen Raskin. New York: Crowell. 9–13 yrs.

Brown, Marc (Compiler). 1994. *Scared Silly: A Book for the Brave*. Illus. M. Brown. Boston: Little, Brown. 6–9 yrs.

Bruchac, Joseph & Jonathan London. 1992. *Thirteen Moons on Turtle's Back: A Native American Year of Moons*. Illus. Thomas Locker. New York: Philomel. 7–12 yrs.

Bryan, Ashley (Selector). 1991. *All Night, All Day: A Child's First Book of African-American Spirituals*. Illus. A. Bryan. New York: Atheneum. 7–11 yrs.

Carlson, Lori M. (Ed.). 1994. *Cool Salsa: Bilingual Poems on Growing Up Latino in the United States*. New York: Holt. 12–15 yrs.

Carson, Jo (Ed.). 1989. *Stories I Ain't Told Nobody Yet*. New York: Watts. 9–13 yrs.

Clark, E. C. 1991. *I Never Saw a Purple Cow*. Boston: Little, Brown. 4–7 yrs.

Clise, Michele Durkson (Compiler). 1994. *Ophelia's Bedtime Book: A Collection of Poems to Read and Share*. New York: Viking. 5–9 yrs.

Cole, William (Compiler). 1960. *Poems of Magic and Spells*. Illus. Peggy Bacon. Cleveland: World. 9–12 yrs.

———. 1984. *A New Treasury of Children's Poetry*. New York: Doubleday. 7–13 yrs.

Cullinan, Bernice E. (Ed.). 1995. *A Jar of Tiny Stars. Poems by NCTE Award-Winning Poets*. Illus. Andi MacLeod & Marc Nadel. Honesdale, Penn.: Wordsong/Boyds Mills. 8–10 yrs.

Dakos, Kalli. 1993. *Don't Read This Book, Whatever You Do: More Poems about School*. Illus. G. Brian Karas. New York: Four Winds.

De la Mare, Walter. 1961. *Tom Tiddler's Ground, a Book of Poetry for Children*. Drawings Margery Gill. New York: Knopf. 6–12 yrs.

———. 1957. *Come Hither*. 3rd ed. Illus. Warren Chappell. New York: Knopf. 6–12 yrs.

———. 1986. *The Voice*. Illus. & comp. Catherine Brighton. New York: Delacorte. All ages.

Demi. 1993. *Demi's Secret Garden*. New York: Holt. 9–12 yrs.

De Gerez, Toni. 1981. *My Song Is a Piece of Jade: Poems of Ancient Mexico in English and Spanish*. Illus. William Stark. Boston: Little, Brown. 9–12 yrs.

de Paola, Tomie (Compiler). 1988. *Tomie de Paola's Book of Poems*. Illus. T. de Paola. New York: Putnam. 7–12 yrs.

Downie, Mary Alice & Barbara Robertson. 1984. *The New Wind Has Wings: Poems from Canada*. Illus. Elizabeth Cleaver. New York: Oxford. 9–14 yrs.

Duffy, Carol Ann (Compiler). 1994. *I Wouldn't Thank You for a Valentine: Poems for Young Feminists*. Illus. Trisha Rafferty. New York: Holt. 12–15 yrs.

Dunning, Stephen, Edward Lueders, & Hugh Smith (Compilers). 1967. *Reflections on a Gift of Watermelon Pickle, and Other Modern Verse*. New York: Lothrop, Lee & Shepard. 10–16 yrs.

———. 1969. *Some Haystacks Don't Even Have Any Needle*. Glenview, Ill.: Scott, Foresman. 10–16 yrs.

Dyer, Jane. (Compiler). 1996. *Animal Crackers: A Delectable Collection of Pictures, Poems, and Lullabies for the Very Young*. Illus. Jane Dyer. Boston: Little, Brown. 6–8 yrs.

Elledge, Scott (Ed.). 1990. *Wider than the Sky: Poems to Grow Up With*. New York: HarperCollins. 7–12 yrs.

Farber, Norma & M. C. Livingston. 1987. *These Small Stones*. New York: HarperCollins. 8–12 yrs.

Feelings, Tom (Compiler). 1993. *Soul Looks Back in Wonder*. New York: Dial. 5–8 yrs.

Freedman, R. 1987. *Lincoln: A Photobiography*. Photos. New York: Clarion. 10–16 yrs.

Glaser, I. J. 1995. *Dreams of Glory: Poems Starring Girls*. Illus. Pat Lowery Collins. New York: Atheneum. 10–13 yrs.

Gordon, Ruth. 1993. *Peeling the Onion: An Anthology of Poems*. New York: HarperCollins/Zolotow. 9–12 yrs.

———. 1995. *Pierced by a Ray of Sun: Poems about the Times We Feel Alone*. New York: HarperCollins. 12–18 yrs.

Hall, Donald (Ed.). 1985. *The Oxford Book of Children's Verse in America*. New York: Oxford University Press. 9–12 yrs.

Hopkins, Lee Bennett (Compiler). 1970. *Me!* New York: Seabury. 7–12 yrs.

_____. 1982. *Circus! Circus!* Illus. J. O'Brien. New York: Knopf.

_____. 1983. *The Sky Is Full of Song*. New York: Harper & Row. 7–12 yrs.

_____. 1983. *A Song in Stone: City Poems*. Photos Anna H. Audette. New York: Crowell. 7–12 yrs.

_____. 1984. *Surprises*. New York: Harper & Row. 7–12 yrs.

_____. 1985. *Creatures*. Illus. Stella Ormai. San Diego: Harcourt Brace Jovanovich. 6–12 yrs.

_____. 1986. *Best Friends*. New York: Harper & Row. 7–12 yrs.

_____. 1987. *Click, Rumble, Roar: Poems about Machines*. Photos Anna Held Audette. New York: Crowell. 8–12 yrs.

_____. 1987. *Dinosaurs*. Illus. Murray Tinkelman. San Diego: Harcourt Brace Jovanovich. 9–12 yrs.

_____. 1988. *Voyages: Poems by Walt Whitman*. San Diego: Harcourt Brace Jovanovich. 12–16 yrs.

_____. 1989. *More Surprises*. New York: Harper & Row. 7–12 yrs.

_____. 1989. *Still As a Star*. Boston: Little, Brown. 7–12 yrs.

_____. 1990. *Good Books, Good Times!* Illus. Harvey Stevenson. New York: Harper & Row/Charlotte Zolotow. 5–12 yrs.

_____. 1991. *Happy Birthday*. Illus. Hilary Knight. New York: Simon & Schuster. 5–9 yrs.

_____. 1991. *On the Farm*. Illus. Laurel Molk. Boston: Little, Brown. 4–10 yrs.

_____. 1991. *Side by Side: Poems to Read Together*. Illus. Hilary Knight. New York: Simon & Schuster. 4–12 yrs.

_____. 1992. *Flit, Flutter, Fly!: Poems about Bugs and Other Crawly Creatures*. Illus. Peter Palagonia. New York: Doubleday. 5–8 yrs.

_____. 1992. *Questions: Poems*. Illus. Carolyn Croll. New York: HarperCollins/Zolotow. I Can Read Series. 5–9 yrs.

_____. 1992. *Ring Out, Wild Bells: Poems about Holidays and Seasons*. Illus. Karen Baumann. San Diego: Harcourt Brace. 5–9 yrs.

_____. 1992. *Through Our Eyes: Poems and Pictures about Growing Up*. Photos Jeffrey Dunn. Boston: Little, Brown. 10–13 yrs.

_____. 1992. *To the Zoo: Animal Poems*. Illus. John Wallner. Boston: Little, Brown. 5–9 yrs.

_____. 1993. *Beat the Drum: Independence Day Has Come: Poems for the Fourth of July*. Illus. Tomie de Paola. Honesdale, Penn.: Wordsong. 5–9 yrs.

_____. 1993. *Easter Buds Are Springing: Poems for Easter*. Illus. Tomie de Paola. Honesdale, Penn.: Wordsong. 5–8 yrs.

_____. 1993. *Extra Innings: Baseball Poems*. Illus. Scott Medlock. San Diego: Harcourt Brace. 9–12 yrs.

_____. 1993. *Good Morning to You, Valentine: Poems for Valentine's Day*. Illus. Tomie de Paola. Honesdale, Penn.: Wordsong. 5–8 yrs.

_____. 1993. *It's about Time!* Illus. Matt Novak. New York: Simon & Schuster. 5–8 yrs.

_____. 1993. *Ragged Shadows: Poems of Halloween Night*. Illus. Giles Laroche. Boston: Little, Brown. 5–8 yrs.

_____. 1994. *April Bubbles Chocolate: An ABC of Poetry*. Illus. Barry Root. New York: Simon & Schuster. 5–9 yrs.

_____. 1994. *Weather*. Illus. Melanie Hall. New York: HarperCollins. 5–9 yrs. I Can Read series.

_____. 1995. *Blast Off!: Poems about Space*. Illus. Melissa Sweet. New York: HarperCollins. 5–8 yrs. I Can Read Book.

_____. 1995. *Hand in Hand: An American History through Poetry*. New York: Simon & Schuster. 9–12 yrs.

_____. 1995. *Small Talk: A Book of Short Poems*. Illus. Susan Bager. San Diego: Harcourt Brace. 5–9 yrs.

Huck, Charlotte. 1993. *Secret Places*. Illus. Lindsay Barrett George. New York: Greenwillow. 5–8 yrs.

Hudson, Wade. 1993. *Pass It On: African-American Poetry for Children*. Illus. Floyd Cooper. New York: Scholastic. 5–8 yrs.

Hyun, Peter (Ed.). 1986. *Korea's Favorite Tales and Lyrics*. Illus. Dong-il Park. Tuttle/Seoul International. 5–10 yrs.

Jacobs, Leland. 1971. *All about Me*. Champaign, Ill.: Garrard. 9–12 yrs.

_____. 1993. *Is Somewhere Always Far Away?: Poems about Places*. Illus. Jeff Kaufman. New York: Holt/Martin. 5–8 yrs.

_____. 1994. *Alphabet of Girls*. Illus. Ib Ohlsson. New York: Holt/Martin. 5–9 yrs.

Janeczko, Paul (Ed.). 1981. *Don't Forget to Fly: A Cycle of Modern Poems*. New York: Bradbury. 12–16 yrs.

_____. 1987. *Going Over to Your Place: Poems for Each Other*. New York: Bradbury. 12–16 yrs.

_____. 1987. *This Delicious Day*. New York: Orchard Books. 9–12 yrs.

_____. 1990. *The Place My Words Are Looking For: What Poets Say About and Through Their Work*. New York: Bradbury. 9–15 yrs.

_____. 1991. *Preposterous: Poems of Youth*. New York: Watts.

_____. 1993. *Looking for Your Name: A Collection of Contemporary Poems*. New York: Orchard/Jackson. 12–16 yrs.

Janeczko, P. B. 1995. *Wherever Home Begins: 100 Contemporary Poems*. New York: Orchard/Jackson. 12–16 yrs.

Jones, Hettie. 1993. *The Trees Stand Shining: Poetry of the North American Indians*. Illus. Robert Andrew Parker. New York: Dial. 7–12 yrs.

Kemp, Gene (Ed.). 1983. *Ducks and Dragons: Poems for Children*. Illus. Carolyn Dinan. New York: Puffin. 8–12 yrs.

Kennedy, X. J. & Dorothy M. Kennedy (Eds.). 1982. *Knock at a Star: A Child's Introduction to Poetry*. Illus. Karen A. Weinhaus. Boston: Little, Brown. 8–12 yrs.

Kennedy, Dorothy M. (Compiler). 1993. *I Thought I'd Take My Rat to School: Poems for September to June*. Illus. Abby Carter. Boston: Little, Brown. 8–10 yrs.

Lalicki, Barbara (Ed.). 1944. *If There Were Dreams to Sell*. Illus. Margot Tomes. New York: Lothrop, Lee & Shepard. 7–11 yrs.

Larrick, Nancy (Ed.). 1965. *Piper, Pipe that Song Again*. New York: Random House. 7–13 yrs.

_____. 1968. *Piping Down the Valleys Wild*. New York: Dell. 7–13 yrs.

_____. 1983. *When the Dark Comes Dancing: A Bedtime Poetry Book*. Illus. John Wallner. New York: Putnam. 3–8 yrs.

_____. 1991. *To the Moon and Back: A Collection of Poems*. Illus. Catharine O'Neill. New York: Delacorte. 6–9 yrs.

Larrick, Nancy & Wendy Lamb (Eds.). 1991. *To Ride a Butterfly: Original Pictures, Stories, Poems, and Songs for Children by Fifty-two Distinguished Authors and Illustrators*. New York: Bantam Doubleday Dell. 8–16 yrs.

Larrick, Nancy. 1992. *The Night of the Whippoorwill*. Illus. David Ray. New York: Philomel. 8–14 yrs.

Lessac, Frane (Collector). 1994. *Caribbean Canvas*. Illus. F. Lessac. Honesdale, Penn.: Boyds/Wordsong. 5–8 yrs.

Lewis, Richard. 1966. *Miracles: Poems by Children of the English-Speaking World*. New York: Simon & Schuster. 9–14 yrs.

_____. 1968. *Of This World: A Poet's Life in Poetry*. Photos Helen Buttfield. New York: Dial. 10–14 yrs.

Livingston, M. C. (Ed.). 1994. *Riddle-Me Rhymes*. Illus. Rebecca Perry. New York: McElderry. 9–14 yrs.

Loveday, John (Ed.). 1981. *Over the Bridge: An Anthology of New Poems*. Illus. Michael Foreman. New York: Kestrel, Penguin. 9–15 yrs.

Mado, Michio (Trans. the Empress Michiko of Japan). 1992. *The Animals: Selected Poems*. Illus. Mitsumasa Anno. New York: McElderry. 10–12 yrs.

Marshall, James. 1993. *Pocketful of Nonsense*. Racine, Wisc.: Western/Artists.

Mathias, Beverly. 1992. *Reader's Digest Children's Book of Poetry*. Illus. Alan Snow. New York: Reader's Digest Kids. 3–5 yrs.

Mayer, Mercer (Ed.). 1977. *A Poison Tree and Other Poems*. Illus. M. Mayer. New York: Scribners. 10–14 yrs.

Moore, Lilian (Compiler). 1992. *Sunflakes: Poems for Children*. Illus. Jan Ormerod. New York: Clarion. 7–14 yrs.

Moore, Lilian & Judith Thurman (Compilers). 1974. *To See the World Afresh*. New York: Atheneum. 7–12 yrs.

_____. 1979. *Go with the Poem*. New York: McGraw-Hill. 7–12 yrs.

Morton, Miriam (Ed.). 1972. *The Moon Is Like a Silver Sickle: A Celebration of Poetry by Russian Children*. Illus. Eros Keith. New York: Simon & Schuster. 9–14 yrs.

Nister, Ernest. 1992. *Hide-and-Seek: An Antique Book of Turning Pictures*. New York: Philomel. 6–12 yrs.

Nye, Naomi Shihab. 1992. *This Same Sky: A Collection of Poems from Around the World*. New York: Four Winds. 10–12 yrs.

_____. (Compiler). 1995. *The Tree Is Older Than You Are: A Bilingual Gathering of Poems & Stories from Mexico with Paintings by Mexican Artists*. Photos. New York: Simon & Schuster. 10–14 yrs.

Opie, Iona, & Peter Opie (Eds.). 1973. *The Oxford Book of Children's Verse*. New York: Oxford University Press.

Philip, Neil. 1992. *Poems for the Young*. Illus. John Lawrence. Boca Raton, Flor.: Stewart. 5–8 yrs.

_____. 1995. *Songs Are Thoughts: Poems of the Inuit*. Illus. Maryclare Foa. New York: Orchard. 10–13 yrs.

Pooley, Sarah (Ed.). 1988. *A Day of Rhymes*. New York: Knopf. 3–6 yrs.

Radley, Gail (Ed.). 1992. *Rainy Day Rhymes*. Illus. Ellen Kandoian. Boston: Houghton Mifflin. 5–9 yrs.

Rosen, Michael (Ed.). 1992. *Home*. New York: HarperCollins/Zolotow. 6–12 yrs. (Thirteen authors & illustrations; poems & essays about home; various cultures & art styles.)

_____. 1993. *Poems for the Very Young*. Illus. Bob Graham. New York: Kingfisher. 5–9 yrs.

Schwartz, Alvin (Compiler). 1992. *And the Green Grass Green All Around: Folk Poetry from Everyone*. Illus. Sue Truesdell. New York: HarperCollins. 5–8 yrs.

_____. 1989. *I Saw You in the Bathtub, and Other Folk Rhymes*. Illus. Syd Hoff. New York: Harper & Row. 5–8 yrs.

Slater, Teddy (Ed.). 1993. *Eloise Wilkin's Babies: A Book of Poems*. Illus. Eloise Wilkin. Racine, Wisc.: Golden. 2–5 yrs.

Slier, D. (Ed.). 1991. *Make a Joyful Sound: Poems for Children by African-American Poets*. New York: Checkerboard Press. 9–12 yrs.

Steele, S. & M. Styles (Eds.). 1991. *Mother Gave a Shout: Poems by Women and Girls*. Volcano, Calif.: Volcano Press. 12–16 yrs.

Strickland, Dorothy S. & Michael R. Strickland. 1994. *Families: Poems Celebrating the African-American Experience*. Illus. John Ward. Honesdale, Penn.: Wordsong/Boyds Mills. 5–9 yrs.

Sullivan, Charles (Ed.). 1994. *Here Is My Kingdom: Hispanic-American Literature and Art for Young People*. New York: Abrams. 7–14 yrs.

Townsend, John Rowe (Ed.). 1974. *Modern Poetry*. New York: Lippincott. 9–13 yrs.

Volavkova, Hana (Ed.). 1993. *I Never Saw Another Butterfly*. New York: Pantheon. 10–16 yrs. (Poetry and drawings by children in the Terezin Concentration Camp during World War II.)

Walsh, Caroline. 1993. *The Little Book of Poems*. Illus. Gilly Marklew. New York: Kingfisher. 5–8 yrs.

Wolman, Bernice. 1992. *Taking Turns: Poetry to Share*. Illus. Catherine Stock. New York: Atheneum. 5–8 yrs.

Wood, Nancy. 1993. *Spirit Walker*. Illus. Frank Howell. New York: Doubleday. 12–16 yrs.

POETRY COLLECTIONS

Adoff, Arnold. 1975. *Make a Circle, Keep Us In: Poems for a Good Day*. Illus. Ronald Himler. New York: Delacorte. 6–10 yrs.

———. 1978. *City Sandwich*. New York: Greenwillow. 6–9 yrs.

———. 1981. *Outside-inside Poems*. Illus. John Steptoe. New York: Lothrop, Lee & Shepard. 9–13 yrs.

———. 1982. *All the Colors of the Race*. Illus. John Steptoe. New York: Lothrop, Lee & Shepard. 9–15 yrs.

———. 1994. *My Black Me: A Beginning Book of Black Poetry*. New York: Dutton. 9–12 yrs.

———. 1995. *Slow Dance Heart Break Blues*. Photos William Cotton. New York: Lothrop, Lee & Shepard. 12–16 yrs.

———. 1995. *Street Music: City Poems*. Illus. Karen Barbour. New York: HarperCollins. 8–12 yrs.

Asch, F. 1978. *City Sandwich*. New York: Greenwillow. 6–9 yrs.

———. 1979. *Country Pie*. New York: Greenwillow. 6–9 yrs.

Bagert, Brod. 1993. *Chicken Socks and Other Contagious Poems*. Illus. Tim Ellis. Honesdale, Penn.: Boyds/Wordsong. 9–12 yrs.

———. 1992. *Let Me Be . . . the Boss: Poems for Kids to Perform*. Illus. G. L. Smith. Honesdale, Penn.: Wordsong. 5–8 yrs.

Base, Graeme. 1986. *Animalia*. New York: Abrams. 8–12 yrs.

Begay, Shonto. 1995. *Navajo: Visions and Voices across the Mesa*. New York: Scholastic. 12–16 yrs.

Benjamin, A. 1993. *Nickel Buys a Rhyme*. Illus. Karen Lee Schmidt. New York: Morrow. 5–9 yrs.

Bennett, Jill. 1980. *Roger Was a Razor Fish*. New York: Lothrop, Lee & Shepard. 6–11 yrs.

———. 1981. *Days Are Where We Live and Other Poems*. New York: Lothrop, Lee & Shepard. 5–9 yrs.

———. 1982. *Tiny Tim: Verses for Children*. Illus. Helen Oxenbury. New York: Delacorte. 5–9 yrs.

———. 1989. *Spooky Poems*. Boston: Little, Brown. 6–11 yrs.

Blos, Joan. 1992. *A Seed, a Flower, a Minute, an Hour*. Illus. Hans Poppel. New York: Simon & Schuster. 5–8 yrs.

Bodecker, N. M. 1976. *Hurry, Hurry Mary Dear! And Other Nonsense Poems*. New York: Atheneum/McElderry. 7–10 yrs.

———. 1983. *Snowman Sniffles, and Other Verse*. New York: Atheneum. 8–10 yrs.

Brooks, Gwendolyn. 1949. *Annie Allen*. New York: HarperCollins. 9–12 yrs.

Byars, Betsy. 1988. *Beans on the Roof*. Illus. Melodye Rosaes. New York: Delacorte. 9–12 yrs.

Carroll, L. (M. C. Livingston, selector). 1973. *Poems of Lewis Carroll*. New York: Crowell. 10–16 yrs.

Causley, Charles. 1973. *Figgie Hobbin*. Illus. Trina Schart Hyman. New York: Walker. 8–12 yrs.

Chute, M. 1957. *Around and About*. New York: Dutton. 8–12 yrs.

Chandra, Deborah. 1990. *Balloons and Other Poems*. New York: Farrar, Straus & Giroux. 7–13 yrs.

———. 1993. *Rich Lizard and Other Poems*. Illus. Leslie Bowman. New York: Farrar, Straus & Giroux. 9–12 yrs.

Ciardi, John. 1959. *The Reason for the Pelican*. Illus. Madeleine Gekiere. New York: Lippincott. 5–9 yrs.

———. 1961. *The Man Who Sang the Sillies*. Illus. Edward Gorey. New York: Lippincott. 5–9 yrs.

———. 1985. *Doodle Soup*. Illus. Merle Nacht. Boston: Houghton Mifflin. 7–11 yrs.

———. 1990. *Mummy Took Cooking Lessons and Other Poems*. Illus. Merle Nacht. Boston: Houghton Mifflin. 9–12 yrs.

———. 1993. *Someone Could Win a Polar Bear*. Illus. Edward Gorey. Honesdale, Penn.: Wordsong. 5–9 yrs.

———. 1994. *The Reason for the Pelican*. Honesdale, Penn.: Boyds/Wordsong. 5–8 yrs.

Clifton, Lucille. 1970. *Some of the Days of Everett Anderson*. New York: Holt. 7–10 yrs.

———. 1974. *Everett Anderson's Year*. New York: Holt, Rinehart & Winston. 7–10 yrs.

Duncan, Lois. 1982. *From Spring to Spring: Poems and Photographs*. Louisville, KY: Westminster. 10–14 yrs.

Eccleshare, Julia (Collector). 1994. *First Poems*. Illus. Selina Young. New York: Bedrick. 5–9 yrs.

Esbensen, Barbara Jester. 1984. *Cold Stars and Fireflies*. Illus. S. Bonners. New York: Crowell. 9–12 yrs.

———. 1992. *Who Shrank My Grandmother's House?: Poems of Discovery*. Illus. Eric Beddows. New York: HarperCollins. 9–12 yrs.

Farjeon, Eleanor. 1965. *Then There Were Three*. Illus. Isobel & John Morton-Sale. New York: Lippincott. 7–11 yrs.

Field, Eugene. 1897. *Songs of Childhood*. New York: Scribners. 4–8 yrs.

Field, Rachel. 1957. *Poems*. New York: Macmillan. 4–8 yrs.

Frank, Josette (Ed.). 1982. (New ed. 1988) *Poems to Read to the Very Young*. Illus. Eloise Wilkin. New York: Random. 6–9 yrs.

Froman, Robert. 1974. *Seeing Things: A Book of Poems*. New York: Crowell. 7–11 yrs.

Giovanni, Nikki. 1973. *Ego-tripping*. New York: Lawrence Hill. 9–12 yrs.

———. 1980. *Vacation time: Poems for children*. New York: Morrow. 9–14 yrs.

———. 1985. *Spin a Soft Black Song*. Illus. George Martins. New York: Hill & Wang. 9–16 yrs.

———. 1994. *Knoxville, Tennessee*. Illus. Larry Johnson. New York: Scholastic. 5–9 yrs.

Goldstein, Bobbye S. 1989. *Bear in Mind*. New York: Penguin. 5–10 yrs.

Greenfield, Eloise. 1988. *Under the Sunday Tree*. Illus. Amos Ferguson. New York: Harper & Row. 5–10 yrs.

———. 1988. *Nathaniel Talking*. New York: Writers & Readers/Black Butterfly. 9–12 yrs.

———. 1991. *Night on Neighborhood Street*. Illus. Jan Spivey Gilchrist. New York: Dial. 6–16 yrs.

Grimes, Nikki. 1978. *Something on My Mind*. Illus. T. Feelings. New York: Dial. 7–10 yrs.

———. 1994. *Meet Danitra Brown*. Illus. Floyd Cooper. New York: Lothrop, Lee & Shepard. 5–9 yrs.

Gunning, Monica. 1993. *Not a Copper Penny in Me House: Poems from the Caribbean*. Illus. Frane Lessac. Honesdale, Penn.: Boyds/Wordsong. 5–8 yrs.

Heide, Florence Parry. 1996. *Oh, Grow Up!: Poems to Help You Survive Parents, Chores, School, and Other Afflictions*. Illus. Nadine Bernard Westcott. New York: Kroupa/Orchard. 7–10 yrs.

Hennessy, B. G. 1992. *Sleep Tight*. Illus. Anthony Carnabuci. New York: Viking. 3–6 yrs.

Hill, Helen. 1977. *Straight on Till Morning: Poems of the Imaginary World*. Illus. Ted Lewin. New York: Crowell. 10–16 yrs.

Hopkins, L. B. 1995. *Been to Yesterdays: Poems of a Life*. Illus. Charlene Rendeiro. Honesdale, Penn.: Wordsong. 10–13 yrs.

Hopkins, Lee Bennett. 1995. *Good Rhymes, Good Times: Original Poems*. Illus. Frane Lessac. New York: HarperCollins. 5–9 yrs.

Hughes, Langston. 1959. *Selected Poems of Langston Hughes*. New York: Knopf. 10–16 yrs.

———. 1994. *The Dream Keeper and Other Poems*. Illus. Brian Pinkney. New York: Knopf. 10–16 yrs.

———. 1994. *The Sweet and Sour Animal Book*. Illus. students from the Harlem School of the Arts. New York: Oxford. 5–8 yrs. Lana and Peter Opie Library of Children's Literature Series.

Hughes, Shirley. 1995. *Rhymes for Annie Rose*. Illus. Shirley Hughes. New York: Lothrop, Lee & Shepard. 2–5 yrs.

Jabar, Cynthia. 1992. *Shimmy Shake Earthquake: Don't Forget to Dance Poems*. Boston: Joy Street. 5–7 yrs.

Janeczko, Paul B. 1993. *Stardust Hotel: Poems*. Illus. Dorothy Leech. New York: Orchard/Jackson. 12–16 yrs.

Katz, Bobbi. 1992. *Upside Down and Inside Out: Poems for All Your Pockets*. Illus. Wendy Watson. Honesdale, Penn.: Wordsong. 5–9 yrs.

Kennedy, X. J. 1982. *Did Adam Name the Vinegarroon?* Boston: Godine. 6–9 yrs.

———. 1986. *Brats*. New York: McElderry. 6–9 yrs.

———. 1985. *The Forgetful Wishing Well: Poems for Young People*. Illus. Monica Incisa. New York: McElderry. 8–12 yrs.

———. 1989. *Ghastlies, Goops and Pincushions*. Illus. Ron Barrett. New York: McElderry. 8–12 yrs.

———. 1990. *Fresh Brats*. New York: McElderry. 8–12 yrs.

———. 1993. *Drat These Brats!* Illus. James Watts. New York: Simon & Schuster. 5–11 yrs.

Kuskin, Karla. 1958. *In the Middle of the Trees*. New York: Harper & Row. 6–9 yrs.

———. 1972. *Any Me I Want to Be*. New York: Harper & Row. 6–9 yrs.

———. 1975. *Near the Window Tree*. New York: Harper & Row. 6–9 yrs.

———. 1980. *Dogs and Dragons, Trees and Dreams*. New York: Harper & Row. 9–13 yrs.

———. 1992. *Soap Soup, and Other Verses*. Illus. K. Kuskin. New York: HarperCollins/Zolotow. 5–12 yrs. I Can Read Book.

Lawrence, D. H. 1982. *Birds, Beasts and the Third Thing*. Illus. & sel. Alice & Martin Provensen. New York: Viking. 9–14 yrs.

Lear, E. 1995. *The Owl and the Pussy-Cat: And Other Nonsense Poems*. Illus. Michael Hague. New York: North-South. 5–9 yrs.

_____. 1995. *The Pelican Chorus and Other Nonsense*. Illus. Fred Marcelino. New York: HarperCollins/de Capua. 5–9 yrs.

Lewis, J. Patrick. 1991. *Earth Verse and Water Rhymes*. New York: Atheneum. 8–12 yrs.

_____. 1991. *Two-Legged, Four-Legged, No-Legged Rhymes*. Illus. Pamela Paparone. New York: Knopf. 8–12 yrs.

_____. 1994. *The Fat-Cats at Sea*. Illus. Victoria Chess. New York: Apple Soup. 5–8 yrs.

_____. 1994. *July Is a Mad Mosquito*. Illus. Melanie W. Hall. New York: Atheneum. 5–9 yrs.

Lillegard, Dee. 1993. *Do Not Feed the Table*. Illus. Keikl Narahashi. New York: Doubleday. 5–9 yrs.

Little, Jean. 1989. *Hey World, Here I Am!* Illus. Sue Truesdell. New York: Harper & Row. 8–12 yrs.

Livingston, Myra Cohn. 1965. *The Moon and a Star and Other Poems*. San Diego: Harcourt Brace.

_____. 1972. *Listen, Children, Listen: An Anthology of Poems for the Very Young*. Illus. Trina Schart Hyman. San Diego: Harcourt Brace Jovanovich. 6–10 yrs.

_____. 1972. *The Malibu and Other Poems*. Illus. J. Spanfeller. New York: Atheneum. 6–11 yrs.

_____. 1974. *The Way Things Are and Other Poems*. Illus. Jenni Oliver. New York: Atheneum. 6–11 yrs.

_____. 1976. *4-Way Stop*. Illus. J. Spanfeller. New York: Atheneum. 6–11 yrs.

_____. 1979. *O Sliver of Liver*. Illus. Iris Van Rynbach. New York: Atheneum. 7–12 yrs.

_____. 1982. *A Circle of Seasons*. Illus. L. E. Fisher. New York: Holiday. 7–12 yrs.

_____. 1984. *Sky Songs*. Illus. L. E. Fisher. New York: Holiday. 9–12 yrs.

_____. 1985. *Worlds I Know*. Illus. T. Arnold. New York: McElderry. 7–12 yrs.

_____. 1989. *Up in the Air*. Illus. L. E. Fisher. New York: Holiday. 7–12 yrs.

_____. 1989. *Dilly Dilly Piccalilli: Poems for the Very Young*. New York: McElderry. 9–12 yrs.

_____. 1989. *Remembering, and Other Poems*. New York: McElderry. 5–12 yrs.

_____. 1992. *I Never Told and Other Poems*. New York: McElderry. 9–12 yrs.

_____. 1992. *Light and Shadow*. Photos Barbara Rogasky. New York: Holiday. 6–10 yrs.

_____. 1993. *Roll Along: Poems on Wheels*. New York: McElderry. 9–12 yrs.

_____. 1994. *Animal, Vegetable, Mineral: Poems about Small Things*. New York: HarperCollins. 9–13 yrs.

_____. 1994. *Flights of Fancy and Other Poems*. New York: McElderry. 9–12 yrs.

Lobel, Arnold. 1985. *Whiskers and Rhymes*. New York: Greenwillow. 6–10 yrs.

Mahy, Margaret. 1989. *Nonstop Nonsense*. Illus. Quentin Blake. New York: McElderry. 7–10 yrs.

Margolis, R. 1984. *Secrets of a Small Brother*. New York: Macmillan. 6–9 yrs.

McCord, David. 1969. *Every Time I Climb a Tree*. Illus. Marc Simont. Boston: Little, Brown. 5–9 yrs.

_____. 1975. *The Star in the Pail*. Illus. M. Simont. Boston: Little, Brown. 6–10 yrs.

_____. 1986. *All Small*. Boston: Little, Brown. 6–10 yrs.

_____. 1986. *One at a Time: His Collected Poems for the Young*. Illus. Henry Kane. Boston: Little, Brown. 6–10 yrs.

_____. 1992. *All Day Long: Fifty Rhymes of the Never Was and Always Is*. Boston: Little, Brown. 8–12 yrs.

McNaughton, Colin. 1994. *Making Friends with Frankenstein: A Book of Monstrous Poems and Pictures*. Cambridge, Mass.: Candlewick. 5–9 yrs.

Merriam, Eve. 1964. *It Doesn't Always Have to Rhyme*. Illus. Malcolm Spooner. New York: Atheneum. 9–12 yrs.

_____. 1976. *Rainbow Writing*. New York: Atheneum. 9–13 yrs.

_____. 1984. *Jamboree: Rhymes for All Times*. Illus. Walter Gaffney-Kessell. New York: Dell. 9–13 yrs.

_____. 1985. *Blackberry Ink*. Illus. Hans Wilhelm. New York: Morrow. 6–10 yrs.

_____. 1986. *Fresh Paint*. Illus. D. Frampton. New York: Macmillan. 7–11 yrs.

_____. 1987. *Halloween ABC*. Illus. Lane Smith. New York: Macmillan. 8–12 yrs.

_____. 1988. *You Be Good and I'll Be Night: Jump-on-the-Bed Poems*. Illus. Karen Lee Schmidt. New York: Morrow. 3–9 yrs.

_____. 1989. *Chortles: New and Selected Wordplay Poems*. New York: Morrow. 9–13 yrs.

_____. 1989. *A Poem for a Pickle: Funnybone Verse*. Illus. Sheila Hamanaka. New York: Morrow. 4–8 yrs.

_____. 1994. *Higgle Wiggle: Happy Rhymes*. Illus. Hans Wilhelm. New York: Morrow. 5–9 yrs.

Miller, Cameron & Dominique Falla. 1995. *Woodlore*. Illus. Cameron Miller & Dominique Falla. New York: Ticknor & Fields. 9–12 yrs.

Moore, Lilian. 1973. *Sam's Place*. Illus. Talivaldis Stubis. New York: Atheneum. 6–12 yrs.

_____. 1975. *See My Lovely Poison Ivy*. Illus. Diane Dawson. New York: Atheneum. 9–12 yrs.

_____. 1982. *Something New Begins*. Illus. M. J. Dunton. New York: Atheneum.

Moore, L. 1995. *I Never Did That Before*. Illus. Lillian Hoban. New York: Atheneum/Karl. 2–5 yrs.

Moos, Elaine. 1977. *From Morn to Midnight*. Illus. Satomi Ichikawa. New York: Crowell. 6–9 yrs.

Morgenstern, Christian (Trans. Anthea Bell). 1995. *Christian Morgenstern: Lullabies, Lyrics, and Gallows Songs*. Illus. Lisbeth Zwerger. New York: North–South. 5–9 yrs.

Morrison, Lillian. 1992. *Whistling the Morning In*. Illus. Joel Cook. Honesdale, Penn.: Wordsong. 5–9 yrs.

Moss, Jeff. 1989. *The Butterfly Jar*. Illus. Chris Demarest. New York: Bantam 7–12 yrs.

Myers, Walter Dean. 1993. *Brown Angels: An Album of Pictures and Verse*. New York: HarperCollins. 6–12 yrs.

Navasky, Bruno (Selector & trans.). 1993. *Festival in My Heart: Poems by Japanese Children*. New York: Abrams. 9–12 yrs.

Nerlove, Miriam. 1985. *I Made a Mistake*. Illus. M. Nerlove. New York: McElderry. 5–9 yrs.

Nikola-Lisa, W. 1994. *Bein' with You This Way*. Illus. Michael Bryant. New York: Lee & Low. 5–9 yrs.

Olaleye, Isaac. 1995. *The Distant Talking Drum: Poems from Nigeria*. Illus. Frane Lessac. Honesdale, Penn.: Wordsong. 5–9 yrs.

Paraskevas, Betty. 1993. *Junior Kroll*. Illus. Michael Paraskevas. San Diego: Harcourt Brace. 5–8 yrs.

_____. 1994. *Junior Kroll and Company*. Illus. Michael Paraskevas. San Diego: Harcourt Brace. 5–9 yrs.

_____. 1994. *A Very Kroll Christmas*. Illus. Michael Paraskevas. San Diego: Harcourt Brace. 5–9 yrs.

Pomerantz, Charlotte. 1993. *The Tamarindo Puppy and Other Poems*. Illus. Byron Barton. New York: Greenwillow. 5–8 yrs.

_____. 1993. *Halfway to Your House*. Illus. Gabrielle Vincent. New York: Greenwillow. 5–8 yrs.

_____. 1993. *If I Had a Paka: Poems in Eleven Languages*. Illus. Nancy Tafuri. New York: Greenwillow. 5–8 yrs.

Prelutsky, Jack. 1978. *The Queen of Eene*. Illus. Victoria Chess. New York: Greenwillow. 9–12 yrs.

_____. 1980. *The Headless Horseman Rides Tonight*. Illus. Arnold Lobel. New York: Greenwillow. 9–14 yrs.

_____. 1980. *Rolling Harvey Down the Hill*. Illus. Victoria Chess. New York: Greenwillow. 9–12 yrs.

_____. 1982. *The Baby Uggs Are Hatching*. Illus. James Stevenson. New York: Greenwillow. 9–12 yrs.

_____. 1982. *The Sheriff of Rottenshot*. Illus. Victoria Chess. New York: Greenwillow. 9–12 yrs.

_____. 1983. *It's Valentine's Day*. Illus. Vossi Abola Ela. New York: Greenwillow. 4–8 yrs.

_____. 1986. *Read-Aloud Rhymes*. Illus. Marc Brown. New York: Knopf. 4–7 yrs.

_____. 1986. *Ride a Purple Pelican*. Illus. G. Williams. New York: Greenwillow. 5–9 yrs.

_____. 1988. *Tyrannosaurus Was a Beast: Dinosaur Poems*. Illus. Arnold Lobel. New York: Greenwillow. 4–10 yrs.

_____. 1990. *Beneath a Blue Umbrella*. Illus. Garth Williams. New York: Greenwillow. 7–16 yrs. Companion to *Ride a Purple Pelican*.

_____. 1990. *Something BIG Has Been Here*. Illus. James Stevenson. New York: Greenwillow. 5–14 yrs.

_____. 1991. *For Laughing Out Loud: Poems to Tickle Your Funnybone*. New York: Knopf. 6–14 yrs.

_____. 1993. *A Nonny Mouse Writes Again!* Illus. Marjorie Priceman. New York: Knopf. 5–8 yrs.

_____. 1993. *The Dragons Are Singing Tonight*. Illus. Peter Sis. New York: Greenwillow. 5–9 yrs.

_____. 1996. *Monday's Troll*. Illus. Peter Sis. New York: Greenwillow. 8–11 yrs.

Roethke, Theodore. (Beatrice Roethke & Stephen Lushing, selectors). 1973. *Dirty Dinky and Other Creatures*. New York: Doubleday. 5–8 yrs.

Rossetti, Christina. 1992. *The Skylark*. New York: Dial. 8–12 yrs.

Roth, S. L. 1991. *Gypsy Bird Song*. New York: Farrar, Straus & Giroux. 7–10 yrs.

Ryder, Joanne. 1995. *Without Words*. Photos Barbara Sonneborn. San Francisco: Sierra Club. 5–9 yrs.

Rylant, Cynthia. 1984. *Waiting to Waltz: A Childhood*. Illus. Stephen Gammell. New York: Bradbury. 11–14 yrs.

_____. 1990. *Soda Jerk*. Illus. Peter Catalanotto. New York: Orchard/Jackson. 12–16 yrs.

_____. 1994. *Something Permanent*. Photos. Walker Evans. San Diego: Harcourt Brace. 12–16 yrs.

Schertle, Alice. 1994. *How Now, Brown Cow?* Illus. Amanda Schaffer. San Diego: Browndeer/Harcourt Brace. 6–10 yrs.

Simmie, Lois. 1988. *Auntie's Knitting a Baby*. Illus. Anne Simmie. New York: Orchard. 8–12 yrs.

Singer, Marilyn. 1994. *Family Reunion*. Illus. R. W. Alley. New York: Macmillan. 5–8 yrs.

Smith, William J. 1957. *Boy Blue's Book of Beasts*. Boston: Little, Brown. 9–13 yrs.

_____. 1992. *Big and Little*. Illus. Don Bolognese. Honesdale, Penn.: Wordsong. 5–9 yrs.

Snyder, Z. K. 1969. *Today Is Saturday*. Illus. J. Arms. New York: Atheneum. 9–14 yrs.

Soto, Gary. 1992. *Neighborhood Odes*. Illus. David Diaz. San Diego: Harcourt Brace. 9–14 yrs.

Spooner, Michael A. 1993. *Moon in Your Lunch Box*. Illus. Ib Ohlsson. New York: Holt. 6–12 yrs. Redfeather series.

Starbird, Kaye. 1979. *The Covered Bridge House*. Illus. Jim Arnosky. New York: Four Winds. 7–11 yrs.

Steele, M. 1988. *Anna's Summer Songs*. New York: Scholastic. 9–12 yrs.

Stevenson, James. 1995. *Sweet Corn: Poems*. New York: Greenwillow. 5–9 yrs.

Stevenson, Robert Louis. (Michael Hague compiler). 1988. *The Land of Nod and Other Poems for Children*. Illus. M. Hague. New York: Holt. 9–12 yrs.

———. 1992. *A Child's Garden of Verses*. Illus. Jannat Messenger. New York: Dutton. 5–8 yrs.

Swenson, May. 1993. *The Complete Poems to Solve*. Illus. Christy Hale. New York: Macmillan. 9–12 yrs.

Thomas, Joyce Carol. 1993. *Brown Honey in Broomwheat Tea*. Illus. Floyd Cooper. New York: HarperCollins. 5–9 yrs.

Thurman, J. 1976. *Flashlight*. Illus. R. Rubel. New York: Atheneum. 9–12 yrs.

Tippett, J. S. 1973. *Cricket Cricket! The Best Loved Poems of James S. Tippett*. New York: HarperCollins. 7–12 yrs.

Tucker, Kathy. 1994. *Do Pirates Take Baths?* Illus. Nadine Bernard Westcott. Morton Grove, Ill.: Whitman. 3–7 yrs.

Turner, Ann. 1986. *Street Talk*. Illus. Catherine Stock. Boston: Houghton Mifflin. 8–12 yrs.

———. 1992. *Rainflowers*. Illus. Robert J. Blake. New York: HarperCollins/Zolotow. 3–8 yrs.

Ulrich, George. 1992. *The Spook Matinee and Other Scary Poems for Kids*. New York: Delacorte. 5–9 yrs.

Updike, John. 1965. *A Child's Calendar*. Illus. Nancy E. Burkert. New York: Knopf. 6–9 yrs.

Viorst, Judith. 1995. *Sad Underwear and Other Complications: More Poems for Children and Their Parents*. Illus. Richard Hull. New York: Atheneum. 10–13 yrs.

Weil, Zaro. 1992. *Mud, Moon and Me*. Illus. Jo Burroughes. Boston: Houghton Mifflin. 5–8 yrs.

Westcott, Nadine Bernard. 1987. *Peanut Butter and Jelly: A Play Rhyme*. New York: Dutton. 5–9 yrs.

Wilbur, Richard. 1995. *Runaway Opposites*. San Diego: Harcourt Brace. 5–9 yrs.

Willard, Nancy. 1989. *East of the Sun & West of the Moon: A Play*. Illus. Barry Moser. San Diego: Harcourt Brace Jovanovich. 8–12 yrs.

Wilner, Isabel. 1977. *The Poetry Troupe: Poems to Read Aloud*. New York: Scribners. 6–10 yrs.

Wilson, Sarah. 1992. *June Is a Tune That Jumps on a Stair*. New York: Simon & Schuster. 5–8 yrs.

Wong, Janet S. 1994. *Good Luck Gold: And Other Poems*. New York: McElderry. 10–13 yrs.

Worth, Valerie. 1976. *More Small Poems*. Illus. Natalie Babbitt. New York: Farrar, Straus & Giroux. 9–12 yrs.

———. 1978. *Still More Small Poems*. Illus. Natalie Babbitt. New York: Farrar, Straus & Giroux. 9–12 yrs.

———. 1986. *Small Poems Again*. Illus. Natalie Babbitt. New York: Farrar, Straus & Giroux. 9–14 yrs.

———. 1987. *All the Small Poems*. Illus. Natalie Babbitt. New York: Farrar, Straus & Giroux. 9–12 yrs.

———. 1992. *At Christmastime*. Illus. Antonia Frasconi. New York: HarperCollins/di Capua. 5–9 yrs.

———. 1994. *All the Small Poems and Fourteen More*. Illus. Natalie Babbitt. New York: Farrar, Straus & Giroux. 10–14 yrs.

Yolen, Jane 1993. *What Rhymes with Moon?* Illus. Ruth Tietjen Councell. New York: Philomel. 5–8 yrs.

———. 1995. *Water Music: Poems for Children*. Photos Jason Stemple. Honesdale, Penn.: Wordsong. 10–13 yrs.

———. 1996. *Sacred Places*. Illus. David Shannon. Orlando, Fla.: Harcourt Brace. 10–15 yrs.

Zolotow, Charlotte. 1967. *All that Sunlight*. New York: Harper & Row. 5–9 yrs.

———. 1970. *River Winding*. Illus. Regina Shekerjian. Manchester, N.H.: Abelard-Schuman. 5–9 yrs.

———. 1978. *River Winding*. Illus. Kazue Mizumura. New York: Crowell. 5–9 yrs.

———. 1993. *Snippets: A Gathering of Poems, Pictures, and Possibilities*. Illus. Melissa Sweet. New York: HarperCollins. 5–9 yrs.

INDIVIDUAL POEMS

Allingham, William. 1989. *The Fairies*. Illus. Michael Hague. New York: Holt. 4–8 yrs.

Angelou, Maya. 1993. *Life Doesn't Frighten Me*. Illus. Jean-Michel Basquiat. New York: Stewart Tobari & Chang. 9–12 yrs.

Base, Graeme. 1992. *The Sign of the Seahorse: A Tale of Greed and High Adventure in Two Acts*. New York: Abrams. 8–14 yrs.

Baylor, Byrd. 1992. *One Small Blue Bead*. Illus. Ronald Himler. New York: Scribners. 7–11 yrs.

Benjamin, Alan. 1994. *Buck*. Illus. Carol Morley. New York: Simon & Schuster. 5–7 yrs.

Blake, William. 1993. *The Tyger*. San Diego: Harcourt Brace Jovanovich. 10–16 yrs.

Bouchard, David. 1995. *If You're Not from the Prairie*. Illus. Henry Ripplinger. New York: Atheneum. 6–11 yrs.

Brown, Beatrice Curtis. 1978. *Jonathan Bing*. New York: Lothrop, Lee & Shepard. 7–10 yrs.

Brown, Margaret Wise. 1995. *The Diggers*. Illus. Daniel Kirk. New York: Hyperion. 5–8 yrs.

Brown, Ruth. 1988. *Ladybug, Ladybug*. New York: Dutton. 2–8 yrs.

Browning, Robert. 1988. *The Pied Piper of Hamelin*. Illus. & revised by Terry Small. Harcourt Brace Jovanovich/Gulliver. 8–12 yrs.

———. 1993. *The Pied Piper of Hamelin*. Illus. Kate Greenaway. New York: Random House/Derrydale. 6–10 yrs.

Burket, Nancy E. 1989. *Valentine & Orson*. New York: Farrar, Straus & Giroux. 10–14 yrs.

Carroll, Lewis. 1986. *The Walrus and the Carpenter*. Illus. Jane Breskin Zalben. New York: Holt. 6–12 yrs.

———. 1992. *Lewis Carroll's Jabberwocky*. Illus. Jane Breskin Zalben. Honesdale, Penn.: Boyds Mills. 9–12 yrs.

Carryl, Charles E. 1994. *The Walloping Window-Blind*. Illus. Ted Rand. New York: Arcade. 5–8 yrs.

Cauley, Lorinda Bryan. 1992. *Clap Your Hands*. New York: Putnam. 4–7 yrs.

Cawthorne, William A. 1989. *Who Killed Cockatoo?* Illus. Rodney McRead. New York: Farrar Straus & Giroux. 8–12 yrs.

Cherry, Lynne. 1994. *The Armadillo from Amarillo*. San Diego: Harcourt Brace/Gulliver Green. 7–9+ yrs.

Chorao, Kay. 1986. *The Baby's Good Morning Book*. New York: Dutton. 2–4 yrs.

Christelow, Eileen. 1989. *Five Little Monkeys Jumping on the Bed*. New York: Clarion. 2–6 yrs.

Ciardi, John. 1995. *The Reason for the Pelican*. Illus. Dominic Catalan. Honesdale, Penn.: Boyds/Wordsong. 5–9 yrs.

Clifton, Lucille. 1992. *Everett Anderson's Friend*. Illus. Ann Grifalconi. New York: Holt. 7–12 yrs.

———. 1992. *Everett Anderson's 1 2 3*. Illus. Ann Grifalconi. New York: Holt. 7–12 yrs.

———. 1992. *Everett Anderson's Year*. Illus. Ann Grifalconi. New York: Holt. 7–12 yrs.

Cole, William. 1993. *Have I Got Dogs!* Illus. Margot Apple. New York: Viking. 7–11 yrs.

Coleridge, Samuel Taylor. 1992. *The Rime of the Ancient Mariner*. Illus. Ed Young. New York: Atheneum. 12–16 yrs.

Coltman, Paul. 1985. *Tog the Ribber; or, Granny's Tale*. Illus. Gillian McClure. New York: Farrar, Straus & Giroux. 10–12 yrs.

———. 1989. *Witch Watch*. Illus. Gillian McClure. New York: Farrar, Straus & Giroux. 6–10 yrs.

Cooper, Melrose. 1993. *I Got a Family*. Illus. Dale Gottlieb. New York: Holt. 7–11 yrs.

Cory, Fanny Y. 1992. *The Fairy Alphabet of F. Y. Cory*. Helena, Mon.: American World Geographic. 5–8 yrs.

Crebbin, June. 1995. *The Train Ride*. Illus. Stephen Lambert. Cambridge, Mass.: Candlewick. 5–8 yrs.

cummings, e. e. 1989. *Hist Wist*. Illus. Deborah Kogan Ray. New York: Crown. 5–12 yrs.

Dabcovich, Lydia. 1992. *The Keys to My Kingdom: A Poem in Three Languages*. New York: Lothrop, Lee & Shepard. 9–12 yrs.

Dr. Seuss. 1993. *Oh, the Places You'll Go!* New York: Random House. 10–16 yrs.

Dragonwagon, Crescent. 1986. *Half a Moon and One Whole Star*. Illus. Jerry Pinkney. New York: Macmillan. 5–8 yrs.

Edwards, Roland. 1992. *Tigers*. Illus. Judith Riches. New York: Tambourine. 3–8 yrs.

Emberley, Barbara. 1967. *Drummer Hoff*. Illus. Ed Emberley. Englewood Cliffs, N. J.: Prentice-Hall. 5–9 yrs.

Evans, Lezlie. 1995. *Rain Song*. Illus. Cynthia Jabar. Boston: Houghton Mifflin. 3–6 yrs.

Farjeon, Eleanor. 1990. *Cats Sleep Anywhere*. Illus. Mary Price Jenkins. New York: Lippincott. 4–7 yrs.

Field, E. 1995. *Wynken, Blynken, and Nod*. Illus. Johanna Westerman. New York: North-South. 5–9 yrs.

Field, Rachel. 1990. *A Road Might Lead to Anywhere*. Illus. Giles Laroche. Boston: Little, Brown. 5–10 yrs.

Fields, J. 1988. *The Green Lion of Zion Street*. New York: McElderry. 5–10 yrs.

Florian, Douglas. 1990. *A Beach Day*. New York: Greenwillow. 3–10 yrs.

Fox, Mem. 1993. *Time for Bed*. Illus. Jane Dyer. San Diego: Harcourt Brace/Gulliver. 4–7 yrs.

Gerrard, Roy. 1994. *Croco'nile*. Illus. R. Gerrard. New York: Farrar, Straus & Giroux. 5–8 yrs.

Greenspun, Adele Aron. 1992. *Daddies*. Photos. New York: Philomel. 5–8 yrs.

Grossman, Bill. 1993. *Cowboy Ed*. Illus. Florence Wint. New York: HarperCollins/Geringer. 5–8 yrs.

———. 1995. *The Banging Book*. Illus. Robert Zimmerman. New York: HarperCollins/Geringer. 5–9 yrs.

Halak, Glenn. 1992. *A Grandmother's Story*. New York: Green Tiger. 5–8 yrs.

Hale, Sarah Josepha. 1995. *Mary Had a Little Lamb*. Illus. Salley Mavor. New York: Orchard/Kroupa. 3–6 yrs.

Herford, Oliver. 1992. *The Most Timid in the Land: A Bunny Romance*. Illus. Sylvia Long. San Francisco: Chronicle. 5–8 yrs.

_____. 1993. *The Rubaiyat of a Persian Kitten.* New York: Rizzoli. 9–12 yrs.

Hood, Thomas. *Before I Go to Sleep.* Illus. Mary Jane Begin-Callanan. New York: Putnam. 5–7 yrs.

Highwater, Jamake. 1981. *Moonsong Lullaby.* New York: Lothrop, Lee & Shepard. 5–9 yrs.

_____. 1995. *Songs for the Seasons.* Illus. Sandra Speidel. New York: Lothrop, Lee & Shepard. 5–9 yrs.

Hoberman, M. A. 1995. *The Cozy Book.* Illus. Betty Fraser. San Diego, Calif.: Browndeer. 5–9 yrs.

Hughes, Shirley. 1988. *Out and About.* New York: Lothrop, Lee & Shepard. 5–9 yrs.

_____. 1995. *Rhymes for Annie Rose.* New York: Lothrop, & Lee & Shepard. 5–9 yrs.

Jacobs, Howard. (Ed.). 1992. *"Trosclair" Cajun Night before Christmas.* Illus. James Rice. Pelican. 5–9 yrs.

James, Betsy. 1991. *He Wakes Me.* Illus. Helen K. Davie. New York: Orchard. 5–9 yrs.

Jenkin-Pearce, Susie. 1993. *The Seashell Song.* Illus. Claire Fletcher. New York: Lothrop, Lee & Shepard. 5–8 yrs.

Johnson, James Weldon. 1993. *The Creation.* Illus. C. Golembe. Boston: Little, Brown. 9–16 yrs.

_____. 1994. *The Creation.* Illus. James Ransome. New York: Holiday. 6–16 yrs.

Kipling, Rudyard. 1987. *Gunga Din.* San Diego: Harcourt Brace Jovanovich. 12–16 yrs.

Krauss, Ruth. 1987. *Big and Little.* Illus. Mary Szilagyi. New York: Scholastic. 5–7 yrs.

Kuskin, Karla. 1994. *City Dog.* New York: Clarion. 3–5 yrs.

_____. 1994. *City Noise.* Illus. Renee Flower. New York: HarperCollins. 5–8 yrs.

_____. 1994. *Patchwork Island.* Illus. Petra Mathers. New York: HarperCollins. 5–9 yrs.

Lauture, Denize. 1993. *Father and Son.* Illus. Jonathan Green. New York: Philomel. 5–8 yrs.

Lawrence, Jacob. 1993. *Harriet and the Promised Land.* New York: Simon & Schuster. 5–8 yrs.

Lear, Edward. 1986. *The Owl and the Pussycat.* Illus. Lorinda Bryan Cauley. New York: Putnam. 5–8 yrs.

_____. 1987. *The Owl and the Pussycat.* Illus. Paul Galdone. New York: Clarion. 5–8 yrs.

_____. 1987. *The Owl and the Pussycat.* Illus. Claire Littlejohn. New York: Harper & Row/Pop-up. 5–8 yrs.

_____. 1989. *The Jumblies.* Illus. Ted Rand. New York: Putnam. 3–9 yrs.

_____. 1991. *The Owl and the Pussycat.* Illus. Jan Brett. New York: Putnam. 4–8 yrs.

_____. 1991. *The Owl and the Pussycat.* Illus. Helen Cooper. New York: Dial. 4–8 yrs.

_____. 1991. *The Owl and the Pussy-Cat.* Illus. Louise Voce. New York: Lothrop, Lee & Shepard. 4–8 yrs.

_____. 1993. *The Table and the Chair.* Illus. Tom Powers. New York: HarperCollins. 4–8 yrs.

_____. 1995. *The New Vestments.* Illus. DeLoss McGraw. New York: Simon & Schuster. 5–9 yrs.

Leuck, Laura. 1994. *Sun Is Falling Night Is Calling.* Illus. Ora Eitan. New York: Simon & Schuster. 4–6 yrs.

Lindbergh, Reeve. 1990. *Johnny Appleseed.* Illus. Kathy Jakobsen. Boston: Little, Brown. 9–12 yrs.

_____. 1992. *View from the Air: Charles Lindbergh's Earth and Sky.* Photos Richard Brown. New York: Viking. 9–12 yrs.

_____. 1993. *Grandfather's Lovesong.* Illus. Rachel Isadora. New York: Viking. 6–8 yrs.

_____. 1993. *There's a Cow in the Road!* Illus. Tracey Campbell Pearson. New York: Dial. 6–9 yrs.

Livingston, Myra Cohn. 1986. *Higgledy-Piggledy: Verses and Pictures.* Illus. Peter Sis. New York: McElderry. 4–9 yrs.

Lobel, Arnold. 1984. *The Rose in My Garden.* Illus. Anita Lobel. New York: Greenwillow. 9–12 yrs.

_____. 1985. *Whiskers and Rhymes.* Illus. A. Lobel. New York: Greenwillow. 5–9 yrs. Children's Choice, 1985.

Longfellow, Henry Wadsworth. 1963. *Paul Revere's Ride.* Illus. Paul Galdone. New York: Crowell. 8–12 yrs.

_____. 1984. *Hiawatha's Childhood.* Illus. Errol LeCain. New York: Farrar, Straus & Giroux. 10–16 yrs.

_____. 1983. *Hiawatha.* Illus. Susan Jeffers. New York: Dial. 9–14 yrs.

_____. 1988. *Hiawatha.* Illus. Keith Mosely. New York: Putnam. 9–11 yrs.

_____. 1993. *The Children's Hour.* Illus. Glenna Lang. Lincoln, Mass.: Godine. 5–8 yrs.

Lyon, George Ella. 1989. *Together.* Illus. Vera Rosenberry. New York: Orchard. 4–6 yrs.

Marshall, Samuel. (Trans. Richard Pevear). 1989. *The Pup Grew Up!* Illus. Vladimir Radunsky. New York: Holt. 4–8 yrs.

Merriam, Eve. 1993. *Quiet, Please.* Illus. Sheila Hamanaka. New York: Simon & Schuster. 6–10 yrs.

_____. 1995. *Bam, Bam, Bam.* Illus. Dan Yaccarino. New York: Holt/Martin. 5–9 yrs.

Millay, Edna St. Vincent. 1994. *The Ballad of the Harp-Weaver.* Illus. Beth Peck. New York: Philomel. 6–12 yrs.

Moore, Clement Clarke. 1975. *The Night Before Christmas.* Illus. Tasha Tudor. Skokie, Ill.: Rand McNally. 5–12 yrs.

_____. 1980. *The Night Before Christmas.* Illus. Tomie de Paola. New York: Holiday. 5–12 yrs.

_____. 1992. *The Night Before Christmas.* Illus. Anita Lobel. New York: Knopf. 5–12 yrs.

_____. 1992. *The Night Before Christmas.* Illus. Joyce Patti. New York: Stewart Tabori & Chang. 5–12 yrs.

_____. 1994. *The Night Before Christmas.* Illus. Julie Downing. New York: Bradbury. 5–12 yrs.

_____. 1995. *The Night before Christmas.* Illus. Ted Rand. New York: North-South. 5–12 yrs.

Moore, Lilian. 1992. *Adam Mouse's Book of Poems.* Illus. Kathleen Garry McCord. New York: Atheneum/Karl. 5–9 yrs.

Nash, Ogden. 1980. *Custard and Company: Poems.* Sel. & illus. Quentin Blake. Boston: Little, Brown. 8–12 yrs.

_____. 1991. *The Adventures of Isabel.* Illus. James Marshall. Boston: Little, Brown/Joy. 5–10 yrs.

_____. 1995. *The Tale of Custard the Dragon.* Illus. Lynn Munsinger. Boston: Little, Brown. 5–9 yrs.

_____. 1996. *Custard the Dragon and the Wicked Knight.* Illus. Lynn Munsinger. Boston: Little, Brown. 5–8 yrs.

Noyles, Alfred. 1981. *The Highwayman.* Illus. Charles Keeping. New York: Oxford. 12–16 yrs.

O'Donnell, Elizabeth Lee. 1993. *Sing Me a Window.* Illus. Melissa Sweet. New York: Morrow. 5–8 yrs.

O'Hurgin, S. 1991. *The Ghost Horse of the Mommies.* Lincoln, Mass.: Godine. 12–16 yrs.

Paraskevas, Betty. 1993. *The Strawberry Dog.* Illus. Michael Paraskevas. New York: Dial. 5–8 yrs.

Prater, John. 1992. *"No!" Said Joe.* Cambridge, Mass.: Candlewick. 5–7 yrs.

Read, Thomas Buchanan. 1993. *Sheridan's Ride.* Illus. Nancy Winslow Parker. New York: Greenwillow. 5–8 yrs.

Salter, M. J. 1989. *The Moon Comes Home.* New York: Knopf.

Sandburg, Carl. 1993. *Arithmetic.* Illus. Ted Rand. San Diego: Harcourt Brace. 7–12 yrs.

Schmidt, Annie M. G. (Trans. Henrietta Ten Harmsel). 1992. *Pink Lemonade.* Illus. Timothy Foley. Grand Rapids, Mich.: Eerdmans. 12–16 yrs.

Schwartz, Delmore. 1979. *"I Am Cherry Alive," the Little Girl Said.* New York: Harper & Row. 7–11 yrs.

Seabrooke, Brenda. 1990. *Judy Scuppernong.* Illus. Ted Lewin. New York: Cobblehill. 10–16 yrs.

Sendak, Maurice. 1993. *We Are All in the Dumps with Jack and Guy.* New York: HarperCollins. 9–16 yrs.

Serfozo, Mary. 1992. *Dirty Kurt.* Illus. Nancy Poydar. New York: McElderry. 4–6 yrs.

Service, Robert W. 1988. *The Shooting of Dan McGrew.* Illus. Ted Harrison. Lincoln, Mass.: Godine. 11–16 yrs.

Shaw, Nancy. 1991. *Sheep in a Shop.* Illus. Margot Apple. Boston: Houghton Mifflin. 2–5 yrs. Companion title: *Sheep in a Jeep.*

_____. 1989. *Sheep on a Ship.* Illus. Margot Apple. Boston: Houghton Mifflin. 2–6 yrs.

_____. 1992. *Sheep Out to Eat.* Illus. Margot Apple. Boston: Houghton Mifflin. 4–8 yrs.

_____. 1994. *Sheep Take a Hike.* Illus. Margot Apple. Boston: Houghton Mifflin. 4–6 yrs.

Siebert, Diane. 1988. *Mojave.* Illus. W. Minor. New York: Crowell. 9–16 yrs.

_____. 1989. *Heartland.* Illus. Wendell Minor. New York: Crowell. 9–16 yrs.

_____. 1990. *Train Song.* Illus. Mike Wimmer. New York: Crowell. 9–16 yrs.

_____. 1991. *Sierra.* Illus. Wendell Minor. New York: HarperCollins. 9–16 yrs.

_____. 1993. *Plane Song.* Illus. Vincent Nasta. New York: HarperCollins. 9–16 yrs.

Singer, Marilyn. 1992. *In My Tent.* Illus. Emily Arnold McCully. New York: Macmillan. 5–8 yrs.

Southey, Robert. 1992. *The Cataract of Lodore.* Illus. David Catrow. New York: Holt. 5–8 yrs.

Stafford, William. 1992. *The Animal that Drank Up Sound.* Illus. Debra Frasier. San Diego: Harcourt Brace Jovanovich. 3–8 yrs.

Stevenson, Robert Louis. 1988. *Block City.* Illus. Ashley Wolff. New York: Dutton. 3–8 yrs.

_____. 1990. *My Shadow.* Illus. Ted Rand. New York: Putnam. 4–8 yrs.

_____. 1993. *From a Railway Carriage.* Illus. Llewellyn Thomas. New York: Viking. 5–9 yrs.

Stewart, Sarah 1995. *The Library.* Illus. David Small. New York: Farrar, Straus & Giroux. 6–10 yrs.

Stolz, Mary Bartholomew. 1990. *Fair.* New York: Greenwillow. 10–16 yrs.

Stutson, Caroline. 1993. *By the Light of the Halloween Moon.* Illus. Kevin Hawkes. New York: Lothrop, Lee & Shepard. 5–8 yrs.

Sweeney, Jacqueline. 1993. *Katie and the Night Noises.* Illus. Arden Johnson. Mahwah, N.J.: BridgeWater. 5–8 yrs.

Tagore, Rabindranath. 1992. *Paper Boats.* Illus. Grayce Bochak. Honesdale, Penn.: Boyds Mills Caroline. 6–9 yrs.

Taylor, Jane. 1992. *Twinkle, Twinkle, Little Star.* Illus. Michael Hague. New York: Morrow. 3–6 yrs. Books of Wonder series.

Teichman, Mary. 1993. *Merry Christmas: A Victorian Verse.* Illus. M. Teichman. New York: HarperCollins. 5–9 yrs.

Temple, Charles. 1992. *On the Riverbank.* Illus. Melanie Hall. Boston: Houghton Mifflin. 7–11 yrs.

Thayer, Ernest Lawrence. 1995. *Casey at the Bat.* Illus. Gerald Fitzgerald. New York: Atheneum. 5–9 yrs.

Titherington, Jeanne. 1989. *A Child's Prayer*. Illus. J. Titherington. New York: Greenwillow. 2–6 yrs.

Treece, Henry. 1992. *The Magic Wood*. Illus. Barry Moser. New York: HarperCollins/Perlman. 4–8 yrs.

Tryon, Leslie. 1992. *Albert's Play*. New York: Atheneum. 6–8 yrs.

Turner, Ethel. 1989. *Walking to School*. Illus. Peter Gouldthorpe. New York: Orchard. 4–7 yrs.

Van Vorst, M. L. 1988. *A Norse Lullaby*. Illus. Margot Tomes. New York: Lothrop, Lee & Shepard. 3–8 yrs.

Whittier, John Greenleaf. 1992. *Barbara Frietchie*. Illus. Nancy Winslow Parker. New York: Greenwillow. 10–16 yrs.

Willard, Nancy. 1993. *The Sorcerer's Apprentice*. Illus. Leo & Diane Dillon. New York: Blue Sky/Scholastic. 5–8 yrs.

———. 1993. *A Starlit Somersault Downhill*. Illus. Jerry Pinkney. Boston: Little, Brown. 5–7 yrs.

Wood, Audrey. 1992. *Silly Sally*. San Diego: Harcourt Brace Jovanovich.

Yolen, Jane. 1995. *The Ballad of the Pirate Queens*. Illus. David Shannon. San Diego: Harcourt Brace. 8–12 yrs.

Young, Ruth. 1992. *Golden Bear*. Illus. Rachel Isadora. New York: Viking. 4–7 yrs.

Zelinsky, Paul O. 1993. *The Maid and the Mouse and the Odd-Shaped House: A Story in Rhyme*. New York: Dutton. 7–12 yrs.

Ziefert, Harriet. 1990. *Parade*. Illus. Saul Mandel. New York: Bantam/Little Rooster Books. 2–6 yrs.

THEMATIC POETRY BOOKS

All of Lee Bennet Hopkins' anthologies are themed.

ALPHABET BOOKS

Aylesworth, Jim. 1992. *Old Black Fly*. Illus. Stephen Gammel. New York: Holt. 5–7 yrs.

Cassedy, Sylvia. 1987. *Roomrimes*. Illus. Michele Chessare. New York: Crowell. 9–12 yrs.

———. 1993. *Zoomrimes: Poems about Things That Go*. Illus. Michele Chessare. New York: HarperCollins. 5–9 yrs.

Lalicki, Barbara. 1994. *If There Were Dreams to Sell*. Illus. Margot Tomes. New York: Four Winds. 5–8 yrs.

Martin, Bill, Jr. & John Archambault. 1989. *Chicka Chicka Boom Boom*. New York: Simon & Schuster. 4–8 yrs.

Steig, Jeanne. 1992. *Alpha Beta Chowder*. Illus. William Steig. New York: HarperCollins/di Capua. 5–8 yrs.

Viorst, Judith. 1994. *The Alphabet from Z to A: With Much Confusion on the Way*. Illus. Richard Hull. New York: Atheneum. 10–13 yrs.

Yolen, Jane. 1995. *Alphabestiary: Animal Poems from A to Z*. Illus. Allan Eitzen. Honesdale, Penn.: Boyds Mills. 10–13 yrs.

ANIMAL BOOKS

Armour, Richard. 1970. *A Dozen Dinosaurs*. Illus. Paul Galdone. New York: McGraw-Hill. 8–12 yrs.

Carter, Anne (Ed.). 1991. *Birds, Beasts, and Fishes: A Selection of Animal Poems*. New York: Macmillan. 8–12 yrs.

Chapman, Jean (Ed.). 1986. *Cat Will Rhyme with Hat: A Book of Poems*. Illus. Peter Parnall. New York: Scribners. 5–14 yrs.

Cole, William (Ed.). 1992. *A Zooful of Animals*. Illus. Lynn Munsinger. Boston: Houghton Mifflin. 9–12 yrs.

Daniel, M. 1989. *A Child's Treasury of Animal Verse*. New York: Dial. 7–10 yrs.

de Regniers, Beatrice Schenk. 1985. *This Big Cat and Other Cats I've Known*. Illus. Alan Daniel. New York: Crown. 5–10 yrs.

Edwards, Richard. 1988. *A Mouse in My Roof*. New York: Delacorte. 7–11 yrs.

———. 1992. *The Word Party*. Illus. John Lawrence. New York: Delacorte. 10–12 yrs.

———. 1993. *Moon Frog: Animal Poems for Young Children*. Illus. Sarah Fox-Davies. Cambridge, Mass.: Candlewick. 5–9 yrs.

Eliot, T. S. 1939. *Mr. Mistoffelees with Mungojerrie and Rumpelteazer*. Illus. Errol LeCain. San Diego: Harcourt Brace. 9–12 yrs. (Poems about mischievous cats.)

Hague, Kathleen. 1989. *Bear Hugs*. Illus. Michael Hague. New York: Holt. 2–7 yrs.

Harrison, Michael & Christopher Stuart-Clark. 1992. *The Oxford Book of Animal Poems*. Illus. various artists. New York: Oxford. 9–12 yrs.

Heard, Georgia. 1992. *Creatures of Earth, Sea, and Sky*. Illus. Jennifer Owings Dewey. Honesdale, Penn.: Wordsong. 5–8 yrs.

Hoberman, Mary Ann. 1991. *A Fine Fat Pig, and Other Animal Poems*. Illus. Malcah Zeldis. New York: HarperCollins. 6–11 yrs.

Hooper, Patricia. 1987. *A Bundle of Beasts*. Illus. Mark Steele. Boston: Houghton Mifflin. 7–10 yrs.

Hubbell, Patricia. 1988. *The Tigers Brought Pink Lemonade*. Illus. Ju-Hong Chen. New York: Atheneum. 6–9 yrs.

Hughes, Ted. 1981. *Under the North Star*. Illus. Leonard Baskin. New York: Viking. 8–11 yrs.

Hulme, Joy N. 1993. *What If?: Just Wondering If Poems*. Illus. Valeri Gorbachev. Honesdale, Penn.: Wordsong. 5–9 yrs.

King-Smith, Dick. 1992. *Alphabeasts*. Illus. Quentin Blake. New York: Macmillan. 5–8 yrs.

Larrick, N. (Ed.). 1988. *Cats Are Cats*. Illus. Ed Young. New York: Philomel. 8–14 yrs.

———. 1990. *Mice Are Nice*. Illus. Ed Young. New York: Philomel. 8–14 yrs.

Livingston, Myra Cohn (Ed.). 1987. *Cat Poems*. Illus. Trina Schart Hyman. New York: Holiday. 5–12 yrs.

———. 1990. *Dog Poems*. Illus. Leslie Morrill. New York: Holiday. 9–12 yrs.

Lobel, A. 1985. *Whiskers and Rhymes*. Fairfield, N.J.: Greenwillow. 5–9 yrs.

Marzollo, Jean (Adapter). 1989. *The Teddy Bear Book*. Illus. Ann Schweninger. New York: Dial. 2–7 yrs.

McLoughland, Beverly. 1993. *A Hippo's A Heap: And Other Animal Poems*. Illus. Laura Rader. Honesdale, Penn.: Wordsong. 5–9 yrs.

Osborne, Mary Pope (Ed.). 1990. *Bears, Bears, Bears: A Treasury of Stories, Songs, and Poems about Bears*. Illus. Karen Lee Schmidt. Morristown, N.J.: Silver Burdett. 3–7 yrs.

Prelutsky, Jack. 1967. *A Gopher in the Garden & Other Animal Poems*. Illus. Robert Leydenfrost. New York: Macmillan. 8–12 yrs.

Richardson, Polly. 1992. *Animal Poems*. Illus. Meg Rutherford. Hauppauge, N.Y.: Barron's. 5–9 yrs.

Robb, L. 1995. *Snuffles and Snouts*. Illus. Steven Kellogg. New York: Dial. 5–9 yrs.

Schertle, A. 1995. *Advice for a Frog*. Illus. Norman Green. New York: Lothrop, Lee & Shepard. 5–9 yrs.

Singer, Marilyn. 1993. *It's Hard to Read a Map with a Beagle on Your Lap*. Illus. Clement Oubrerie. New York: Holt. 5–9 yrs.

Spilka, Arnold. 1994. *Monkeys Write Terrible Letters and Other Poems*. Honesdale, Penn.: Boyds/Wordsong. 5–9 yrs.

Springer, N. 1994. *Music of Their Hooves*. Honesdale, Penn.: Boyds Mills. 8–12 yrs.

ILLUSTRATED POETRY BOOKS

Axelrod, Alan. (Comment.) 1991. *Songs of the Wild West*. Art reproductions from Metropolitan Museum of Art. New York: Simon & Schuster. 5–15 yrs.

Bouchard, D. 1996. *Voices from the Wild: An Animal Sensagoria*. Paintings Don Parker. San Francisco, Calif.: Chronicle. 6–12 yrs.

Bunting, E. 1994. *Night of the Gargoyles*. Illus. David Wiesner. New York: Clarion. 10–14 yrs.

Goldstein, B. S. (Selector). 1992. *Inner Chimes: Poems on Poetry*. Illus. Jane B. Zalben. Honesdale, Penn.: Wordsong. 5–15 yrs.

Greenfield, E. 1978. *Honey, I Love*. Illus. Diane & Leo Dillon. New York: Crowell. 6–9 yrs.

Highwater, J. 1995. *Songs for the Seasons*. Illus. Sandra Speidel. New York: Lothrop, Lee & Shepard. 9–12 yrs.

Hopkins, L. B. 1995. *Small Talk: A Book of Short Poems*. Illus. Susan Gaber. San Diego, Calif.: Harcourt Brace. 7–11 yrs.

Kennedy, K. J. & D. M. (Compilers). 1992. *Talking Like the Rain*. Illus. Jane Dyer. Boston, Mass.: Little, Brown. 7–12 yrs.

Larrick, N. 1988. *Cats Are Cats*. Illus. Ed Young. New York: Philomel. 7–12 yrs.

Lear, E. 1995. *The Pelican Chorus and Other Nonsense*. Illus. Fred Marcellino. New York: HarperCollins/di Capua. 7–12 yrs.

Lindbergh, R. 1990. *Johnny Appleseed*. Illus. K. Jakobsen. Boston, Mass.: Joy Street. 8–12 yrs.

Livingston, M. C. 1989. *Up in the Air*. Illus. L. E. Fisher. New York: Holiday. 8–12 yrs.

Mahy, M. 1994. *The Christmas Tree Tangle*. Illus. Anthony Kerins. New York: McElderry. 7–12 yrs.

Merriam, E. 1995. *Bam, Bam, Bam*. Illus. Dan Yaccarino. New York: Holt/Martin. 7–11 yrs.

Rogasky, B. 1994. *Winter Poems*. Illus. Trina S. Hyman. New York: Scholastic. 6–12 yrs.

Ryder, J. 1985. *Inside the Turtle's Shell*. Illus. S. Bonners. New York: Macmillan. 7–12 yrs.

Siebert, D. 1993. *Plane Song*. Illus. Vincent Nasta. New York: HarperCollins. 7–12 yrs.

Sky-Peck, K. (Ed.). 1991. *Who Has Seen the Wind? An Illustrated Collection of Poetry for Young People*. Art reproductions from Boston Museum of Fine Arts. New York: Rizzoli. 7–12 yrs.

Spires, E. 1995. *With One White Wing: Puzzles in Poems and Pictures*. Illus. Erik Blegvad. New York: McElderry. 5–9 yrs.

Stevenson, J. 1995. *Sweet Corn: Poems*. Westport, Conn.: Greenwillow. 5–9 yrs.

Sullivan, C. (Ed.) 1989. *Imaginary Gardens: American Poetry and Art for Young People*. Paintings. New York: Abrams. 7–14 yrs.

Whipple, L. (Compiler). 1994. *Celebrating America: A Collection of Poems and Images of the American Spirit*. Paintings from Art Institute in Chicago. New York: Philomel. 9–13 yrs.

Wilbur, R. 1995. *Runaway Opposites*. Illus. Henrik Drescher. San Diego, Calif.: Harcourt Brace. 5–9 yrs.

Willard, N. 1993. *The Sorcerer's Apprentice*. Illus. Leo & Diane Dillon. New York: Blue Sky/Scholastic. 7–12 yrs.

Yolen, J. 1995. *The Ballad of the Pirate Queens.* Illus. David Shannon. San Diego, Calif.: Harcourt Brace. 7–9 yrs.

THE ARTS & LITERATURE BOOKS

Adoff, Arnold. 1988. *Greens.* Illus. B. Lewin. New York: Lothrop, Lee & Shepard.

Atwood, Ann. 1979. *Haiku: The Mood of the Earth.* Photos A. Atwood. New York: Scribners. 9–14 yrs.

Behn, Harry. 1964. *Cricket Songs: Japanese Haiku.* Pictures selected from Sesshu & other Japanese masters. San Diego: Harcourt, Brace & World. 9–16 yrs.

Carryl, Charles E. 1992. *The Walloping Window-Blind.* Illus. Ted Rand. New York: Arcade. 5–8 yrs.

Cassedy, Sylvia & Kunihiro Suetake (Trans.). 1967. *Birds, Frogs, and Moonlight.* New York: Doubleday. 7–12 yrs.

———. 1992. *Red Dragonfly on My Shoulder.* Illus. Molly Bang. New York: HarperCollins. 7–12 yrs.

Ciardi, John. 1989. *The Hopeful Trout, and Other Limericks.* Illus. Susan Meddaugh. Boston: Houghton Mifflin. 6–14 yrs.

de Gasztold, Carmen Bernos (Trans. Rumer Godden). 1992. *Prayers from the Ark.* Illus. Barry Moser. New York: Viking. 10–13 yrs.

Goldstein, Bobbe S. (Compiler). 1992. *Inner Chimes: Poems on Poetry.* Illus. Jane Breskin Zalben. Honesdale, Penn.: Wordsong. 5–8 yrs.

Graham, Joan Bransfield. 1994. *Splish Splash.* Illus. Steve Scott. New York: Ticknor & Fields. 6–9 yrs.

Higginson, William J. 1991. *Wind in the Long Grass: A Collection of Haiku.* Illus. Sandra Speidel. New York: Simon & Schuster. 10–14 yrs.

Hopkins, Lee Bennett (Compiler). 1992. *Rainbows Are Made: Poems by Carl Sandburg.* San Diego: Harcourt Brace Jovanovich. 12–16 yrs.

Issa et al., (Trans. Jean Merrill & Ronni Solbert; sel. by R. H. Blyth and Nobuyaki Yuasa). 1969. *A Few Flies and I: Haiku by Issa.* Illus. Ronni Solbert. New York: Pantheon. 10–15 yrs.

Lear, Edward (Lady Stachey, ed.). 1942. *The Complete Nonsense Book.* New York: Dodd.

———. 1943. *Nonsense Omnibus.* London: Warne. 8–14 yrs.

———. 1964. *The Nonsense Books of Edward Lear.* New York: New American Library. 8–14 yrs.

———. 1969. *The Quangle-Wangle's Hat.* Illus. Helen Oxenbury. New York: Watts. 8–14 yrs.

———. (Brian Alderson, sel.) 1982. *A Book of Bosh.* New York: Penguin. 8–12 yrs.

———. 1982. (Myra C. Livingston, ed.) *How Pleasant to Know Mr. Lear: Edward Lear's Selected Works.* New York: Holiday. 10–16 yrs.

———. 1983. *An Edward Lear Alphabet.* Illus. Carol Newsom. New York: Lothrop, Lee & Shepard. 4–8 yrs.

———. 1990. *Of Pelicans and Pussycats: Poems and Limericks.* Illus. Jill Newton. New York: Dial. 6–12 yrs.

———. 1992. *A Was Once an Apple Pie.* Illus. Julie Lacome. Cambridge, Mass.: Candlewick. 5–9 yrs.

———. 1992. *Daffy Down Dillies: Silly Limericks.* Illus. John O'Brien. Honesdale, Penn.: Boyds Mills/Caroline. 8–12 yrs.

Lear, Edward & Lewis Carroll. 1993. *Owls and Pussy-Cats: Nonsense Verse.* Illus. Nicki Palin. New York: Bedrick. 8–12 yrs.

Livingston, Myra Cohn (Ed.). 1991. *Lots of Limericks.* Illus. Rebecca Perry. New York: McElderry/Macmillan. 9–13 yrs.

Lobel, Arnold. 1983. *The Book of Pigericks: Pig Limericks.* New York: Harper & Row. 7–10 yrs.

Manley, Molly. 1994. *Talkaty Talker: Limericks.* Illus. Janet Marshall. Honesdale, Penn.: Boyds Mills. 5–9 yrs.

Rossetti, Christina. 1992. *Color.* Illus. Mary Teichman. New York: HarperCollins. 3–6 yrs.

Solt, Mary Ellen (Ed.). 1980. *Concrete Poetry: A World View.* Bloomington: Indiana University Press. 8–12 yrs.

Sullivan, Charles. 1992. *Circus.* Photos. New York: Rizzoli. 5–8 yrs. Adventures in Art series.

———. 1993. *Cowboys.* Illus. various artists. New York: Rizzoli. 5–8 yrs. Adventures in Art series.

Yolen, Jane. 1987. *The Three Bears Rhyme Book.* Illus. Jane Dyer. San Diego: Harcourt Brace Jovanovich. 8–12 yrs.

———. 1995. *A Sip of Aesop.* Illus. Karen Barbour. New York: Blue Sky/Scholastic. 7–10 yrs.

BIRD BOOKS

Adoff, Arnold. 1982. *Birds: Poems.* Illus. Troy Howell. New York: Lippincott. 8–12 yrs.

Day, David. 1993. *Aska's Birds.* Illus. Warabe Aska. New York: Doubleday. 5–8 yrs.

Fleischman, Paul. 1985. *I Am Phoenix: Poems for Two Voices.* Illus. by Ken Nutt. New York: Harper & Row/Zolotow. 10–15 yrs.

Florian, Douglas. 1996. *On the Wing: Bird Poems and Paintings.* Illus. Douglas Florian. San Diego: Harcourt Brace. 5–8 yrs.

Remkiewicz, Frank. 1995. *Fiona Raps It Up.* New York: Lothrop, Lee & Shepard. 6–10 yrs.

Yolen, Jane. 1990. *Bird Watch: A Book of Poetry.* Illus. Ted Lewin. New York: Philomel. 8–13 yrs.

CELEBRATION BOOKS

Carlstrom, N. W. 1995. *Who Said Boo?: Halloween Poems for the Very Young.* Illus. R. W. Alley. New York: Simon & Schuster. 3–6 yrs.

Chorao, K. 1995. *The Book of Giving: Poems of Thanks, Praise, and Celebration.* New York: Dutton. 5–9 yrs.

Farber, Norma & M. C. Livingston. 1993. *When It Snowed That Night.* Illus. Petra Mathers. New York: HarperCollins/Geringer. 5–8 yrs.

Goldstein, Bobbye S. 1993. *Birthday Rhymes, Special Times.* Illus. Jose Aruego & Ariane Dewey. New York: Doubleday. 5–8 yrs.

Kennedy, X. J. 1992. *The Beasts of Bethlehem.* Illus. Michael McCurdy. New York: McElderry. 6–12 yrs.

Livingston, Myra Cohn. 1978. *Callooh! Callay! Holiday Poems for Young Readers.* Illus. Janet Stevens. New York: Atheneum. 9–12 yrs.

———. 1984. *Christmas Poems.* Illus. Trina Schart Hyman. New York: Holiday. 8–12 yrs.

———. 1985. *Celebrations.* Illus. Leonard Everett Fisher. New York: Holiday. 5–10 yrs.

———. 1985. *Thanksgiving Poems.* Illus. Stephen Gammell. New York: Holiday. 9–12 yrs.

———. 1986. *Poems for Jewish Holidays.* Illus. Lloyd Bloom. New York: Holiday. 10–12 yrs.

———. 1987. *New Year's Poems.* Illus. Margot Tomes. New York: Holiday. 4–8 yrs.

———. 1989. *Halloween ABC.* New York: Macmillan. 8–12 yrs.

Metaxas, Eric. 1995. *The Birthday ABC.* Illus. Tim Raglin. New York: Simon & Schuster. 5–9 yrs.

Philip, Neil. 1995. *Singing America: Poems That Define a Nation.* Illus. Michael McCurdy. New York: Viking. 10–13 yrs.

Whitman, Walt. 1991. *I Hear America Singing.* Illus. Robert Sabuda. New York: Philomel. 10–16 yrs.

Yolen, Jane. 1993. *Mouse's Birthday.* Illus. Bruce Degan. New York: Putnam. 4–7 yrs.

———. 1995. *The Three Bears Holiday Rhyme Book.* Illus. Jane Dyer. San Diego: Harcourt Brace. 5–9 yrs.

EXPERIENCES WITH FOOD BOOKS

Adoff, Arnold. 1979. *Eats: Poems.* Illus. Susan Russo. New York: Lothrop, Lee & Shepard. 8–12 yrs.

———. 1989. *Chocolate Dreams.* Illus. Turi MacCombie. New York: Lothrop, Lee & Shepard. 8–12 yrs.

Goldstein, Bobbie S. 1992. *What's on the Menu?* Illus. Chris L. Demarest. New York: Viking. 5–9 yrs.

Lee, Dennis. 1991. *The Ice Cream Store.* Illus. David McPhail. New York: HarperCollins. 7–12 yrs.

Rosen, Michael. 1994. *The Greatest Table: A Banquet to Fight against Hunger.* Illus. sixteen artists. San Diego: Harcourt Brace. 5–9 yrs.

Rosen, M. 1996. *Food Fight.* San Diego, Calif.: Harcourt Brace. 7–12 yrs.

Yolen, Jane. 1992. *Tasty Poems.* Illus. Nick Sharratt. New York: Oxford. 5–9 yrs.

GAME BOOKS

Boardman, B. (Compiler). 1993. *Red Hot Peppers.* Illus. Diane Boardman. Seattle, Wash.: Sasquatch. 6–12 yrs.

Booth, D. (Ed.). 1993. *Doctor Knickerbocker and Other Rhymes.* Illus. Maryann Kovalski. New York: Ticknor & Fields. 9–12 yrs.

Cole, J. & S. Calmenson (Compiler). 1991. *The Eentsy, Weentsy Spider: Fingerplays and Action Rhymes.* Illus. Alan Tiegreen. New York: Morrow. 3–8 yrs.

———. 1995. *Yours till Banana Splits: 201 Autograph Rhymes.* New York: Morrow. 5–8 yrs.

Crews, D. 1986. *Ten Black Dots.* New York: Greenwillow. 4–7 yrs.

Esbensen, B. 1995. *Dance with Me Poems.* Illus. Megan Lloyd. New York: HarperCollins. 4–8 yrs.

Lankford, M. D. 1992. *Hopscotch Around the World.* Illus. Karen Milone. New York: Morrow. 8–12 yrs.

Spires, E. 1995. *With One White Wing: Puzzles in Poems and Pictures.* Illus. Erik Blegvad. New York: McElderry. 5–9 yrs.

Walsh, E. S. 1993. *Hop Jump.* Orlando, Fla.: Harcourt Brace. 5–7 yrs.

Westcott, N. B. 1987. *Peanut Butter and Jelly: A Play Rhyme.* New York: Dutton. 5–8 yrs.

———. 1988. *The Lady with the Alligator Purse.* Boston, Mass.: Little, Brown/Joy. 5–9 yrs.

Wood, Don. 1982. *Quick as a Cricket.* West Orange, N.J.: Child's Play International. 5–8 yrs.

HISTORY BOOKS

Lewis, Claudia. 1987. *Long Ago in Oregon.* Illus. Joel Fontaine. New York: Harper & Row/Zolotow. 8–12 yrs.

———. 1991. *Up in the Mountains and Other Poems of Long Ago.* Illus. Joel Fontaine. New York: HarperCollins. 9–12 yrs.

Little, Lessie Jones. 1988. *Children of Long Ago.* Illus. Jan Spivey Gilchrist. New York: Philomel. 5–9 yrs.

Livingston, Myra Cohn (Ed.). 1992. *Let Freedom Ring: A Ballad of Martin Luther King, Jr.* Illus. Samuel Byrd. New York: Holiday. 5–8 yrs.

———. 1993. *Abraham Lincoln: A Man for All the People.* Illus. Samuel Byrd. New York: Holiday. 6–9 yrs.

Panzer, Nora (Ed.). 1994. *Celebrate America in Poetry and Art.* Art, photos from Smithsonian Institution. New York: Hyperion. 10–16 yrs.

Philip, Neil. 1995. *Singing America: Poems That Define a Nation.* Illus. Michael McCurdby. New York: Viking. 10–13 yrs.

Turner, Ann. 1993. *Grass Songs.* Illus. Barry Moser. San Diego: Harcourt Brace. 12–16 yrs.

MAGICAL CREATURE BOOKS

Barker, Cicely Mary A. 1992. *A Treasury of Flower Faires.* New York: Warne. 9–12 yrs.

———. 1993. *The Flower Fairies Changing Seasons: A Sliding Picture Book.* New York: Warne. 5–12 yrs.

———. 1993. *World of Flower Fairies.* New York: Warne. 9–12 yrs.

de la Mare, Walter. 1989. *Peacock Pie: A Book of Rhymes.* Illus. Louise Brierley. New York: Holt. 5–12 yrs.

Florian, Douglas. 1993. *Monster Motel.* San Diego: Harcourt Brace. 5–9 yrs.

Fosters, John. 1992. *Dragon Poems.* Illus. Korky Paul. New York: Oxford. 10–13 yrs.

Heide, Florence Parry. 1992. *Grim and Ghastly Goings-On.* Illus. Victoria Chess. New York: Lothrop, Lee & Shepard. 5–9 yrs.

Livingston, Myra Cohs (Ed.). 1982. *Why Am I So Cold?* New York: Atheneum. 9–14 yrs.

Wallace, Daisy. 1976. *Monster Poems.* New York: Holiday House. 6–12 yrs.

———. 1979. *Ghost Poems.* Illus. Tomie de Paola. New York: Holiday. 6–12 yrs.

———. 1980. *Fairy Poems.* Illus. Trina Schart Hyman. New York: Holiday. 6–9 yrs.

Yolen, Jane 1989. *The Faery Flag: Stories and Poems of Fantasy and the Supernatural.* New York: Watts. 7–10 yrs.

———. 1994. *How Beastly!: A Menagerie of Nonsense Poems.* Illus. James Marshall. Honesdale, Penn.: Boyds/Wordsong. 5–9 yrs.

———. 1994. *Beneath the Ghost Moon.* Illus. Laurel Molk. Boston: Little, Brown. 7–10 yrs.

MATHEMATICS BOOKS

O'Neill, Mary. 1968. *Take a Number.* New York: Doubleday. 6–12 yrs.

Linden, Ann Marie. 1992. *One Smiling Grandma: A Caribbean Counting Book.* Illus. Lynne Russell. New York: Dial. 6–9 yrs.

Merriam, Eve. 1992. *Train Leaves the Station.* Illus. Dale Gottlieb. New York: Holt. 4–7 yrs.

Pinczes, Elinor. 1995. *A Remainder of One.* Illus. Bonnie MacKain. Boston: Houghton Mifflin. 6–9 yrs.

Wise, William. 1993. *Ten Sly Piranhas: A Counting Story in Reverse (A Tale of Wickedness—and Worse!).* Illus. Victoria Chess. New York: Dial. 4–8 yrs.

NATURE BOOKS

Adoff, Arnold. 1991. *In for Winter, Out for Spring.* San Diego: Harcourt Brace Jovanovich.

Behn, Harry. 1949. *Trees.* Illus. James Endicott. New York: Holt/Martin.

———. 1953. *Windy Morning.* Illus. Harry Behn. San Diego: Harcourt Brace. 9–12 yrs.

———. 1956. *Wizard in the Well.* Illus. Harry Behn. San Diego: Harcourt Brace. 9–12 yrs.

Brown, Margaret Wise. 1993. *Under the Sun and the Moon and Other Poems.* Illus. Tom Leonard. New York: Hyperion. 5–9 yrs.

Buchanan, Ken & Debby Buchanan. 1992. *Lizards on the Wall.* Illus. Betty Schweitzer-Johnson. Tuscon, Ariz.: Harbinger. 5–9 yrs. (Whiptail lizards.)

Causley, Charles (Ed.). 1981. *Salt-Sea Verse.* Illus. Anthony Maitland. New York: Kestrel/Puffin. 9–12 yrs.

Coleman, Mary Ann. 1993. *The Dreams of Hummingbirds: Poems from Nature.* Illus. Robert Masheris. Morton Grove, Ill.: Whitman. 9–12 yrs.

Coleridge, Sara. 1986. *January Brings the Snow: A Book of Months.* Illus. Jenni Oliver. New York: Dial. 3–6 yrs.

Cuneo, Mary Louise. 1993. *How to Grow a Picket Fence.* Illus. Nadine Bernard Westcott. New York: HarperCollins. 6–8 yrs.

Daniel, Mark (Ed.). 1991. *A Child's Treasury of Seaside Verse.* New York: Dial. 6–16 yrs.

Fisher, Arleen. 1963. *Listen Rabbit.* Illus. Symeon Shimin. New York: Crowell. 8–10 yrs.

———. 1969. *In One Door and Out the Other: A Book of Poems.* Illus. Lillian Hoban. New York: Crowell. 6–10 yrs.

———. 1971. *Feathered Ones and Furry.* Illus. Eric Carle. New York: Crowell. 7–12 yrs.

———. 1983. *Rabbits, Rabbits.* Illus. Gail Nieman. New York: Harper & Row. 8–12 yrs.

———. 1986. *When It Comes to Bugs.* Illus. Chris & Bruce Degen. New York: Harper & Row. 5–10 yrs.

———. 1988. *The House of a Mouse.* Illus. Joan Sandin. New York: Harper & Row/Zolotow. 3–7 yrs.

———. 1991. *Always Wondering: Some Favorite Poems of Aileen Fisher.* Illus. Joan Sandin. New York: HarperCollins/Zolotow. 7–12 yrs.

Frank, Josette (Ed.). 1990. *Snow toward Evening: A Year in a River Valley.* Illus. Thomas Locker. New York: Dial. 5–12 yrs.

Harvey, Anne (Ed.). 1922. *Shades of Green.* Illus. John Lawrence. New York: Greenwillow. 10–13 yrs.

Hughes, Ted. 1975. *Season Songs.* Illus. Leonard Baskin. New York: Viking. 12–16 yrs.

———. 1976. *Moon-Whales and Other Moon Poems.* Illus. Leonard Baskin. New York: Viking. 12–16 yrs.

Jacobs, Leland. 1964. *Poetry for Young Scientists.* New York: Holt, Rinehart & Winston. 9–12 yrs.

———. 1971. *Poetry for Summer.* Champaign, Ill.: Garrard. 9–12 yrs.

———. 1993. *Just Around the Corner: Poems about the Seasons.* Illus. Jeff Kaufman. New York: Holt/Martin. 5–8 yrs.

Johnston, Tony. 1994. *Three Little Bikers.* Illus. G. Brian Karas. New York: Knopf. 5–7 yrs. Umbrella series.

Keillor, Garrison. 1995. *Cat, You Better Come Home.* Illus. Steve Johnson & Lou Fancher. New York: Viking. 6–10 yrs.

Levy, Constance. A. 1991. *I'm Going to Pet a Worm Today and Other Poems.* Illus. Ronald Himler. New York: McElderry. 9–12 yrs.

———. 1994. *Tree Place and Other Poems.* Illus. Robert Sabuda. New York: McElderry. 9–12 yrs.

Livingston, Myra Cohn. 1986. *Earth Songs.* Illus. Leonard Everett Fisher. New York: Holiday. 10–14 yrs.

———. 1986. *Sea Songs.* Illus. Leonard Everett Fisher. New York: Holiday. 10–14 yrs.

———. 1990. *If the Owl Calls Again: A Collection of Owl Poems.* Woodcuts Atonio Frasconi. New York: McElderry/Macmillan. 9–12 yrs.

———. 1992. *If You Ever Meet a Whale.* Illus. Leonard Everett Fisher. New York: Holiday. 5–9 yrs.

Marsh, James. 1991. *Bizarre Birds and Beasts.* Illus. James Marsh. New York: Dial. 7–11 yrs.

McLean, Janet 1995. *Dog Tales.* Illus. Andrew McLean. New York: Ticknor & Fields. 6–9 yrs.

Merriam, Eve. 1992. *The Singing Green: New and Selected Poems for All Seasons.* Illus. Kathleen Collins Howell. New York: Morrow. 10–13 yrs.

Moon, Pat. 1993. *Earth Lines: Poems for the Green Age.* New York: Greenwillow. 9–12 yrs.

Paladino, Catherine (Ed.). 1993. *Land, Sea, and Sky: Poems to Celebrate the Earth.* Boston: Joy Street. 9–12 yrs.

Robinson, Fay. 1993. *A Frog inside My Hat: A First Book of Poems.* Illus. Cyd Moore. Mahwah, N.J.: BridgeWater. 5–8 yrs.

Rosen, Michael (Ed.). 1992. *Itsy-Bitsy Beasties: Poems from Around the World.* Illus. Alan Baker. Minneapolis, Minn.: Carolrhoda. 5–8 yrs.

Ryder, Joanne. 1985. *Inside Turtle's Shell, and Other Poems of the Field.* Illus. Susan Bonners. New York: Macmillan. 7–11 yrs.

———. 1988. *Step into the Night.* Illus. D. Nolan. New York: Four Winds. 6–11 yrs.

———. 1989. *Mockingbird Morning.* Illus. Dennis Nolan. New York: Four Winds. 6–9 yrs.

———. 1990. *Under Your Feet.* Illus. Dennis Nolan. New York: Four Winds. 6–9 yrs.

———. 1991. *Hello, Tree!* Illus. M. Hays. New York: Dutton. 6–11 yrs.

Shaw, Alison. 1995. *Until I Saw the Sea: A Collection of Seashore Poems.* New York: Holt. 5–9 yrs.

Singer, Marilyn. 1994. *Sky Words.* Illus. Deborah Kogan Ray. New York: Macmillan. 5–9 yrs.

Stafford, William (Selectors Jerry Watson & Laura Apol Obbink). 1994. *Learning to Live in the World: Earth Poems.* San Diego: Harcourt Brace. 12–16 yrs.

Steele, Mary Q. 1989. *Anna's Garden Songs.* Illus. Lena Anderson. New York: Greenwillow. 4–7 yrs.

Turner, Ann. 1994. *Moon for Seasons.* Illus. Robert Noreika. New York: Macmillan. 7–10 yrs.

Yolen, Jane. 1993. *Weather Report: Poems.* Illus. Annie Gusman. Honesdale, Penn.: Wordsong. 9–12 yrs.

PERSONAL RELATIONSHIP BOOKS

Anglund, Joan Walsh. 1992. *Love Is a Baby.* San Diego: Harcourt Brace/Gulliver. 5–8 yrs.

———. 1993. *Peace Is a Circle of Love.* San Diego: Harcourt Brace/Gulliver. 5–8 yrs. (Stylized woodcuts.)

de Regniers, Beatrice Schenk. 1988. *A Week in the Life of Best Friends, and Other Poems of Friendship.* Illus. Nancy Doyle. New York: Scholastic. 10–13 yrs.

———. 1988. *The Way I Feel. Sometimes.* Illus. Susan Meddaugh. New York: Clarion. 6–10 yrs.

Dickinson, Emily. (Ed. Rumer Godden) 1969. *Letter to the World.* Illus. Prudence Seward. New York: Macmillan. 10–14 yrs.

———. (Selector Karen Ackerman). 1990. *A Brighter Garden.* Illus. Tasha Tudor. New York: Philomel. 8–12 yrs.

Duffy, C. A. 1996. *Stopping for Death: Poems of Death and Loss.* Illus. Trisha Rafferty. New York: Holt. 12–18 yrs.

Fletcher, R. 1996. *Buried Alive: The Elements of Love.* Photos Andrew Moore. New York: Atheneum. 12–16 yrs.

Gutmann, Bessie Pease. 1994. *I Love You: Verses and Sweet Sayings.* Illus. B. Gutmann. New York: Grosset & Dunlap. 5–9 yrs.

Hoberman, Mary Ann. 1991. *Fathers, Mothers, Sisters, Brothers.* Boston: Little, Brown. 9–12 yrs.

Livingston, Myra Cohn (Ed.). 1988. *Poems for Mothers.* Illus. Deborah Kogan Ray. New York: Holiday. 7–12 yrs.

———. 1990. *Poems for Grandmothers.* Illus. Patricia Cullen-Clark. New York: Holiday. 5–8 yrs.

———. 1992. *A Time to Talk: Poems of Friendship.* New York: McElderry. 12–16 yrs.

Marsh, James. 1993. *From the Heart: Light-Hearted Verse.* New York: Dial. 12–16 yrs.

Nye, N. S. & Janeczke, P. B. 1996. *I Feel a Little Jumpy Around You: A Book of Her Poems & His Poems Collected in Pairs.* New York: Simon & Schuster. 12–16 yrs.

Singer, M. 1996. *All We Needed to Say: Poems about School from Tanya and Sophie.* Photos Lorna Clark. New York: Atheneum. 9–12 yrs.

Thomas, J. C. 1995. *Gingerbread Days.* Illus. Floyd Cooper. New York: HarperCollins. 6–10 yrs.

Walsh, C. 1995. *A Little Book of Love.* Illus. Susan Field. New York: Kingfisher. 10–13 yrs.

———. 1995. *A Little Book of Friendship.* Illus. Rosamund Fowler. New York: Kingfisher. 10–13 yrs.

RIDDLES, PUNS, LANGUAGE PLAY

Beisner, M. *Catch That Cat! A Picture Book of Rhymes and Puzzles.* Illus. Monika Beisner. New York: Farrar, Straus and Giroux.4–8 yrs.

Bierhorst, J. (Ed.). 1992. *Lightning inside You, and Other Native American Riddles.* Illus. Louise Brierley. New York: Morrow. 7–11 yrs.

Buck, N. 1995. *Creepy Crawly Critters: And Other Halloween Tongue Twisters.* Illus. Sue Truesdell. New York: HarperCollins. 5–9 yrs.

Calmenson, S. 1989. *What Am I? Very First Riddles.* Illus. Karen Gundersheimer. New York: Harper and Row. 4–7 yrs.

Gomi, T. 1991. *Who Ate It? Who Hid It?* Illus. Taro Gomi. Brookfield, Conn.: Millbrook. 2–6 yrs.

Gordon, J. R. 1991. *Hide and Shriek: Riddles about Ghosts and Goblins.* Illus. Susan Slattery. Minneapolis, Minn.: Lerner. 5–10 yrs.

Hall, K. & L. E. Hall. 1992. *Spacey Riddles.* Illus. Simms Taback. New York: Dial. 4–8 yrs.

Koontz, R. M. 1992. *I See Something You Don't See: A Riddle-Me Picture Book.* New York: Cobblehill. 4–8 yrs.

Lewis, J. P. 1996. *Riddle-icious.* Illus. Debbie Tilley. New York: Knopf. 7–10 yrs.

Livingston, M. C. 1990. *My Head Is Red, and Other Riddle Rhymes.* Illus. Tere LoPrete. New York: Holiday. 6–9 yrs.

Marzollo, Jean. 1992. *I Spy: A Book of Picture Riddles.* Photos Walter Wick. New York: Scholastic/Cartwheel. 2–7 yrs.

Maestro, G. 1989. *Riddle Roundup: A Wild Bunch to Beef Up Your Word Power.* New York: Clarion. 7–10 yrs.

McMillan, B. 1990. *One Sun: A Book of Terse Verse.* New York: Holiday. 4–7 yrs.

———. 1991. *Play Day: A Book of Terse Verse.* Photos. New York: Holiday. 4–7 yrs.

Milnes, G. (Compiler). 1990. *Granny Will Your Dog Bite, and Other Mountain Rhymes.* Illus. Kimberly Bulcken Root. New York: Knopf/Borzoi. 4–10 yrs.

Most, B. 1992. *Zoodles.* Illus. Bernard Most. San Diego, Calif.: Harcourt Brace Jovanovich. 3–8 yrs.

Nims, B. L. 1989. *Where Is the Bear at School?* Illus. Madelaine Gill. Morton Grove, Ill.: Whitman. 2–6 yrs.

Spires, E. 1995. *With One White Wing: Puzzles in Poems and Pictures.* Illus. Erik Blegvad. New York: McElderry. 7–9 yrs.

Walton, R. & A. Walton. 1991. *Ho Ho Ho! Riddles about Santa Claus.* Illus. Susan Slattery Burke. Minneapolis, Minn.: Lerner. 5–10 yrs.

SPORTS BOOKS

Knudson, R. R. & May Senson. 1988. *American Sports Poems.* New York: Watts. 9–16 yrs.

Morrison, Lillian (Ed.). 1977. *The Sidewalk Racer and Other Poems of Sports and Motion.* New York: Lothrop, Lee & Shepard. 8–14 yrs.

———. 1988. *Rhythm Road: Poems to Move To.* New York: Lothrop, Lee & Shepard. 7–10 yrs.

———. 1992. *At the Crack of the Bat: Baseball Poems.* Illus. Steve Cieslawski. New York: Hyperion. 9–12 yrs.

———. 1995. *Slam Dunk: Basketball Poems.* Illus. Bill James. New York: Hyperion. 10–13 yrs.

Thayer, Ernest Lawrence. 1988. *Casey at the Bat: A Ballad of the Republic, Sung in the Year 1888.* Additional text by illus. Patricia Polacco. New York: Putnam. 9–16 yrs.

SONGS AND MUSIC BOOKS

Traditional

Brett, Jan (Illus.). 1986. *Twelve Days of Christmas.* New York: Dodd. 4–12 yrs.

Cauley, L. B. (Reteller.) 1989. *Old MacDonald Had a Farm.* New York: Putnam. 4–8 yrs.

Chamberlain, Sarah (Illus.). 1991. *The Friendly Beasts: A Traditional Christmas Carol.* New York: Dutton. 5–12 yrs.

Delacre, L. (Ed.). 1989. *Arroz con Leche: Popular Songs and Rhymes from Latin America.* New York: Scholastic. 9–16 yrs.

Engvick, W. (Ed.). 1965. *Lullabies and Night Songs.* New York: Harper & Row. 4–7 yrs.

Geis, J. 1992. *Where the Buffalo Roam.* Nashville, Tenn.: Ideals. 5–9 yrs.

Gutman, Bessie Pease (Illus.). 1990–1991. *I Love You: Verses and Sweet Sayings; Nursery Poems and Prayers; Nursery Songs and Lullabies.* New York: Grosset & Dunlap. 5–12 yrs.

Jones, C. (Compiler). 1989. *Old MacDonald Had a Farm.* Illus. Carol Jones. Boston: Houghton Mifflin. 4–8 yrs.

Koontz, Robin M. (Illus.). 1988. *This Old Man: The Counting Song.* New York: Putnam. 5–12 yrs.

Kovalski, Maryann (Illus.). 1986. *Sharon, Lois and Bram's Mother Goose: Songs, Finger Rhymes, Tickling Verses, Games & More.* Boston, Mass.: Little, Brown/Joy Street. 2–6 yrs.

Langstaff, J. 1991. *Climbing Jacob's Ladder.* Illus. Ashley Bryan. New York: McElderry. 6–13 yrs.

Larrick, N. (Compiler). 1989. *Songs from Mother Goose: With the Traditional Melody for Each.* Illus. Robin Spowart. New York: Harper & Row. 2–6 yrs.

Manson, C. 1992. *A Farmyard Song: An Old Rhyme with New Pictures.* New York: North-South. 2–5 yrs.

Medearis, A. S. 1992. *The Zebra-Riding Cowboy: A Folk Song from the Old West.* Illus. Maria Christina Brusca. New York: Holt. 4–8 yrs.

Rounds, G. 1989. *Old MacDonald Had a Farm.* New York: Holiday. 3–7 yrs.

Trapani, I. 1993. *The Itsy Bitsy Spider.* Danvers, Mass.: Whispering Coyote Press. 4–7 yrs.

———. 1993. *I'm a Little Tea Pot.* Danvers, Mass.: Whispering Coyote Press. 4–7 yrs.

Yolen, J. (Ed.). 1986. *The Lullaby Song Book.* Illus. Charles Mikolaycak. San Diego, Calif.: Harcourt, Brace, Jovanovich. 4–7 yrs.

———. 1994. *Sleep Rhymes around the World.* Illus. various artists. Honesdale, Penn.: Boyds/Wordsong. 5–10 yrs.

OTHER SONGS AND COLLECTIONS

Axelrod, Alan (Comment). 1991. *Songs of the Wild West.* Art reproductions from Metropolitan Museum of Art. New York: Simon & Schuster. 5–15 yrs.

Carle, E. 1993. *Today Is Monday.* New York: Philomel. 4–8 yrs.

Carlstrom, N. W. 1993. *Swim the Silver Sea, Joshie Otter.* Illus. Ken Kuroi. New York: Philomel. 4–9 yrs.

Carroll, L. (Music Don Harper). 1979. *Songs from Alice.* Illus. Charles Folkard. New York: Holiday. 10–16 yrs.

Flander, M. & D. Swann. 1991. *The Hippopotamus Song: A Muddy Love Story.* Illus. Nadine Bernard Westcott. Boston, Mass.: Little Brown/Joy Street. 5–9 yrs.

Gasron, E. (Ed.). 1986. *The Laura Ingalls Wilder Songbook.* Illus. Garth Williams. New York: Harper. 9–11 yrs.

Glazer, T. 1988. *Tom Glazer's Treasury of Songs for Children.* New York: Doubleday. 4–7 yrs.

Go In and Out the Window: An Illustrated Songbook for Young People. 1987. New York: Metropolitan Museum of Art/Holt. 4–16 yrs.

Guthrie, W. with M. M. Guthrie. 1992. *Woody's 20 Grow Big Songs.* New York: HarperCollins. 5–16 yrs.

Hammerstein, O., II. 1992. *A Real Nice Clambake.* Illus. Nadine Bernard Westcott. Boston, Mass.: Little, Brown/Joy Street. 4–8 yrs.

Hart, J. (Ed.). 1989. *Singing Bee! A Collection of Favorite Children's Songs.* Illus. Anita Lobel. New York: Lothrop, Lee & Shepard. 4–7 yrs.

Higginsen, V. 1995. *This Is My Song!: A Collection of Gospel Music for the Family.* Illus. Brenda Joysmith. New York: Crown. 9–12 yrs.

Hughes, L. 1995. *The Book of Rhythms.* Illus. Matt Wawiorka. New York: Oxford. 9–12 yrs. Iona and Peter Opie Library of Children's Literature series.

Key, F. S. 1973. *The Star Spangled Banner.* Illus. Peter Spier. New York: Doubleday. 4–16 yrs.

Keats, E. J. (Illus.). 1987. *The Little Drummer Boy.* Illus. Ezra Jack Keats. (Illus.) 1987. New York: Macmillan. 5–12 yrs.

Livingston, M. C. 1995. *Call Down the Moon: Poems of Music.* New York: McElderry. 10–13 yrs.

Nelson, E. L. 1985. *The Great Rounds Songbook.* Illus. Joyce Behr. New York: Sterling. 3–12 yrs.

Norworth, J. 1993. *Take Me Out to the Ballgame.* Illus. Alec Gillman. New York: Four Winds. 8–12 yrs.

Oram, H. (Music Carl Davis). 1993. *A Creepy Crawly Song Book.* Illus. Satoshi Kitamura. New York: Farrar, Straus & Giroux. 5–9 yrs.

Osofsky, A. 1992. *Dreamcatcher.* Illus. Ed Young. New York: Orchard. 4–6 yrs.

Paparone, P. 1994. *Who Built the Ark?* New York: Simon & Schuster. 6–9 yrs.

———. 1993. *The Sesame Street Songbook.* Illus. David Prebenna. New York: Macmillan. 4–9 yrs.

Raffi. 1987. *The Raffi Singable Songbook.* Illus. Joyce Yamamoto. New York: Crown. 4–8 yrs.

———. 1989. *Five Little Ducks.* Illus. Jose Aruego & Ariane Dewey. New York: Crown. 3–7 yrs.

———. 1990. *Baby Beluga.* Illus. Ashley Wolff. New York: Crown. 3–7 yrs.

Strickland, M. R. 1993. *Poems That Sing to You.* Illus. Alan Leiner. Honesdale, Penn.: Boyds/Wordsong. 9–12 yrs.

Taylor, J. 1992. *Twinkle, Twinkle, Little Star.* Illus. Michael Hague. New York: Morrow. 2–6 yrs.

Titherington, J. 1992. *Baby's Boat.* New York: Greenwillow. 3–5 yrs.

Tolkien, J. R. R. 1992. *Bilbo's Last Song.* Illus. Pauline Baynes. New York: Knopf. 10–16 yrs.

Weiss, N. (Ed.). 1987. *If You're Happpy and You Know It: Eighteen Story Songs.* New York: Greenwillow. 4–7 yrs.

Winn, M. (Ed.). 1974. *The Fireside Book of Children's Songs.* New York: Simon & Schuster 4–7 yrs.

Young, R. 1992. *Golden Bear.* Illus. Rachel Isadora. New York: Viking Penguin. 2–6 yrs.

Yolen, J. 1990. *Dinosaur Dances.* Illus. Bruce Degen. New York: Putnam. 7–11 yrs.

Zelinsky, P. O. 1990. *The Wheels on the Bus.* New York: Dutton. 3–8 yrs.

NONFICTION BOOKS ABOUT POETRY FOR CHILDREN AND ADULTS

Armour, Maureen W. 1994. *Poetry, the Magic Language: Children Learn to Read and Write It*. Englewood, Colo.: Teacher Ideas Press. (A bibliography of children's poetry books arranged thematically.)

Bauer, Caroline Feller (Ed.). 1986. *Snowy Day: Stories and Poems*. Illus. Margot Tomes. New York: HarperCollins. 4–8 yrs. Children's Choice. (Includes stories and poems by popular authors, crafts, recipes, and snow trivia; a bibliography of snow-related books are cited.)

Chatton, Barbara. 1993. *Using Poetry Across the Curriculum: A Whole Language Approach*. Phoenix, Ariz.:Oryx. (Practical teaching ideas and examples of student's writings are cited.)

Esbensen, Barbara Juster. 1975. A *Celebration of Bees*. Minneapolis, Minn.: Winston Press. (The poet shares ideas about writing poetry.)

Livingston, Myra Cohn. 1991. *Poem-Making: Ways to Begin Poetry*. New York: HarperCollins/Zolotow.

9–16 yrs. (The poet shares ideas about writing poetry; the voices of poetry; its sounds, rhymes, rhythms, language, and forms; and poetic examples.)

Steinberg, Judith W. 1994. *Reading and Writing Poetry: A Guide for Teachers*. New York: Scholastic (The book gives instructional ideas and examples of students' writings.)

CHAPTER 8

CHILDREN'S BOOKS MENTIONED IN THE CHAPTER

Aardema, V. 1975. *Why Mosquitos Buzz in People's Ears*. Illus. Leo & Diane Dillon. New York: Dial. 7–11 yrs.

Adler, D. 1996. *Young Cam Jansen and the Missing Cookie*. Illus. Susanna Natti. New York: Viking. 6–9 yrs.

Adler, D. A. 1995. *One Yellow Daffodil: A Hanukkah Story*. Illus. L. Bloom. San Diego: Gulliver. 7–10 yrs.

Akass, S. 1993. *Number Nine Duckling*. Illus. Alex Ayliffe. Honesdale, Penn.: Boyds Mills. 3–6 yrs.

Anderson, L. 1991. *Bunny Fun*. New York: Farrar, Straus & Giroux. 3–6 yrs.

Anholt, C. & L. Anholt. 1995. *What Makes Me Happy?* Cambridge, Mass.: Candlewick. 3–6 yrs.

Anno, M. 1975. *Anno's Alphabet*. New York: Crowell. 6–10 yrs.

———. 1981. *Anno's Journey*. New York: Philomel. 7–11 yrs.

———. 1982. *Anno's Counting House*. New York: Philomel. 6–9 yrs.

Argent, K. 1991. *Happy Birthday, Wombat!* Boston: Little, Brown/Joy. 1–5 yrs.

Arkhurst, J. C. 1964. *The Adventures of Spider*. Illus. J. Pinkney. Boston, Mass.: Little. 8–14 yrs.

Arnold, T. 1993. *Green Wilma*. New York: Dial. 5–9 yrs.

Artzybasheff, B. 1937. *Seven Simeons*. In Bland, D., *A History of Book Illustrating*, p. 398. New York: World.

Babbitt, N. 1975. *Tuck Everlasting*. New York: Farrar, Straus & Giroux. 10–13 yrs.

Baker, J. 1991. *Windows*. New York: Greenwillow. 7–11 yrs.

———. 1995. *The Story of Rosy Dock*. New York: Greenwillow. 7–11 yrs.

Bang, M. 1980. *The Grey Lady and the Strawberry Snatcher*. New York: Four Winds. 7–12 yrs.

———. 1985. *The Paper Crane*. New York: Greenwillow. 6–10 yrs.

Barrie, J. M. 1906. (New eds. 1930 & 1950). *Peter Pan in Kensington Gardens*. Illus. Arthur Rackham. New York: Scribners. 10–13 yrs.

Bemelmans, L. 1937. *Madeline*. New York: Dutton. 5–8 yrs.

Bewick, J. 1792. *The Looking Glass for the Mind*. Cited in M. C. Gillespie, 1970. *History and Trends* (p. 108). Dubuque, Iowa: Brown.

Bewick, T. 1779. A *Pretty Book of Pictures for Masters and Misses or Tommy Trip's History of Beast and Birds*. In Gillespie, M. C. 1970. *History and Trends*, p. 108. Dubuque, Iowa: Brown.

Bewick, T. & J. Bewick. 1784. *The Select Fables of Aesop and Others*. In M. C. Gillespie, 1970. *History and Trends* (p. 108). Dubuque, Iowa: Brown.

Blake, W. 1789. *Songs of Innocence*. Cited in M. C. Gillespie, 1970. *History and Trends* (p. 108). Dubuque, Iowa: Brown.

Brandenburg, J. (Joann Bren Guerney, Ed.) 1995. *An American Safari: Adventures on the North American Prairie*. New York: Walker. 9–12 yrs.

Brett, J. 1995. *Armadillo Rodeo*. New York: Putnam. 6–9 yrs.

Brooke, L. 1903. *Johnny Crow's Garden*. London: Warne. 5–9 yrs.

Brown, M. 1954. *Cinderella*. New York: Scribners. 5–9 yrs.

———. 1961. *Once a Mouse*. New York: Scribners. 6–9 yrs.

———. 1982. *Shadows*. New York: Scribners. 10–13 yrs.

Brown, M. 1996. *Arthur Goes to School*. New York: Random. 3–5 yrs.

Browne, A. 1983. *Gorilla*. New York: Knopf. 5–9 yrs.

Bunting, E. 1994. *The Smoky Night*. Illus. David Diaz. San Diego, Calif.: Harcourt Brace. 7–10 yrs.

———. 1996. *Going Home*. Illus. David Diaz. New York: Cotler/HarperCollins. 6–9 yrs.

Burton, V. L. 1942. *The Little House*. Boston: Houghton Mifflin. 5–9 yrs.

———. 1939. *Mike Mulligan and His Steamshovel*. Boston: Houghton Mifflin. 5–9 yrs.

Caldecott, R. 1978. *The Diverting History of John Gilpin*. London: New York: Warne. 5–9 yrs.

Carle, Eric. 1969. *The Very Hungry Caterpillar*. New York: Philomel. 4–8 yrs.

———. 1995. *The Very Lonely Firefly*. New York: Philomel. 5–8 yrs.

———. 1995. *The Honeybee and the Robber: A Moving/Picture Book*. New York: Philomel. 6–9 yrs.

Carroll, L. 1977. *Alice's Adventures in Wonderland*. Illus. John Tenniel. New York: Philomel. 11–14 yrs.

Coatsworth, E. 1930. *The Cat Who Went to Heaven*. Illus. Lynd Ward. New York: Macmillan. 9–12 yrs.

Coles, R. 1995. *The Story of Ruby Bridges*. Illus. George Ford. New York: Scholastic. 6–10 yrs.

Collington, P. 1995. *The Tooth Fairy*. New York: Barzoi/Knopf. 7–11 yrs.

Cooney, B. (Adapter). 1958. *Canticleer and the Fox*. Illus. B. Cooney. New York: HarperCollins. 7–10 yrs.

Cousins, L. 1991. *Farm Animals*. New York: Tambourine. 12 mo.–26 mo.

Crane, W. 1985. *The House That Jack Built*. London: Warne. 7–10 yrs.

Crews, D. 1980. *Truck*. New York: Greenwillow. 4–7 yrs.

Cruikshank, G. 1853–1854. *George Cruikshank's Fairy Library*. 4 vols. London: David Bogue.

Curtiss, A. B. 1996. *Hallelujah, A Cat Comes Back*. Escondido, Calif.: Old Castle Publ. Co. 8–11 yrs.

Dahl, R. 1982. *B.F.G.* Illus. Quentin Blake. New York: Farrar, Straus & Giroux. 10–13 yrs.

D'Aulaire, I. & E. P. D'Aulaire. 1936. *George Washington*. New York: Doubleday. 8–10 yrs.

de Brunhoff, J. 1937. *The Story of Babar*. New York: Random. 5–8 yrs.

de Paola, T. 1973. *Nana Upstairs, Nana Downstairs*. New York: Putnam. 7–10 yrs.

———. 1975. *Strega Nona*. Englewood Cliffs, N.J.: Prentice Hall. 5–9 yrs.

de Regniers, B. S. et al. (Compilers). 1988. *Sing a Song of Popcorn: Every Child's Book of Poems*. Illus. nine Caldecott Medal artists. New York: Scholastic. 6–13 yrs.

Demi. 1990. *The Empty Pot*. New York: Holt. 9–11 yrs.

———. 1996. *Buddha*. New York: Holt. 9–11 yrs.

Dr. Seuss [Geisel, T.]. 1937. *And to Think that I Saw It on Mulberry Street*. New York: Vanguard. 6–9 yrs.

———. 1957. *The Cat in the Hat*. New York: Random House. 4–8 yrs.

Duvoisin, R. 1943. *The Three Sneezes*. In Bland, D. 1958, *A History of Book Illustrating*, p. 398. New York: World.

———. 1950. *Petunia*. New York: Knopf. 5–8 yrs.

Ehlert, L. 1988. *Planting a Rainbow*. San Diego, Cal.: Harcourt Brace Jovanovich. 4–7 yrs.

———. 1989. *Color Zoo*. New York: Lippincott. 3–5 yrs. Caldecott Honor Book, 1990.

Faulkner, K. 1996. *Wide Mouth Frog*. Illus. Jonathan Lambert. New York: Dial. 4–7 yrs.

Feelings, M. 1975. *Mojo Means One: A Swahili Counting Book*. Illus. Tom Feelings. New York: Dial. 6–9 yrs.

Fish, H. 1938. *Animals of the Bible*. Illus. D. P. Lathrop. Philadelphia: Lippincott. 6–10 yrs.

Fisher, L. E. 1986. *The Great Wall of China*. New York: Macmillan. 9–12 yrs.

Flack, M. 1933. *The Story About Ping*. Illus. Kurt Wiese. New York: Viking. 6–9 yrs.

Fleming, D. 1996. *Where Once There Was a Wood*. New York: Henry Holt. 3–6 yrs.

Flieschman, P. 1988. *Rondo in C*. Illus. Janet Wentworth. New York: Harper & Row. 8–12 yrs.

Gag, Wanda. 1928. *Millions of Cats*. New York: Coward-McCann. 5–9 yrs.

Geisert, B. & A. Geisert. 1995. *Haystack*. Boston: Houghton Mifflin. 7–10 yrs.

Goodall, J. 1980. *Paddy's New Hat*. New York: Atheneum. 4–9 yrs.

———. 1990. *Puss in Boots*. New York: Macmillan. 9–12 yrs.

Grahame, K. 1908. *The Wind in the Willows*. Illus. E. H. Shepard. New York: Scribners. 11–13 yrs.

Gray, L. M. 1995. *My Mama Had a Dancing Heart*. Illus. Raul Colon. New York: Orchard/Kroupa. 7–10 yrs.

Greenaway, K. 1878. *Under the Window*. London: Warne. 5–9 yrs.

———. 1881. *Mother Goose*. London: Warne. 5–9 yrs.

———. 1880. A *Apple Pie*. London: Warne. 5–9 yrs.

Grimm, J. & W. Grimm. 1986. *Rumpelstiltskin*. Illus. Paul Zelinsky. New York: Dutton. 8–12 yrs.

Hall, D. 1979. *Ox-Cart Man*. Illus. Barbara Cooney. New York: Viking. 5–9 yrs.

Harris, J. C. 1892. *Uncle Remus Tales*. Illus. A. B. Frost. Boston: Houghton Mifflin. 8–12 yrs.

Hoban, R. 1964. *A Baby Sister for Frances*. New York: Harper & Row. 6–9 yrs.

Hoban, T. 1972. *Push Pull, Empty Full: A Book of Opposites*. New York: Macmillan. 4–6 yrs.

———. 1995. *Colors Everywhere*. New York: Greenwillow. 5–9 yrs.

Hodges, M. 1984. *Saint George and the Dragon*. Illus. Trina Schart Hyman. Boston: Little Brown. 8–11 yrs.

———. (Reteller). 1995. *Gulliver in Lilliput*. Illus. Kimberly Bulcken Root. New York: Holiday. 8–12 yrs.

Hyman, T. S. 1983. *Little Red Riding Hood*. New York: Holiday. 8–12 yrs.

Irving, W. 1961. *Sketch Book*. Illus. Arthur Rackham. New York: New American Library Dutton. 10–16 yrs. (Included "Rip Van Winkle" and "The Legend of Sleepy Hollow").

Jeffer, S. 1989. *The Three Jovial Huntsmen*. New York: Macmillan. 5–9 yrs.

Johnson, A. 1994. *Joshua by the Sea*. New York: Orchard. 12 mo.–26 mo.

Johnson, S. 1995. *Alphabet City*. New York: Viking. 4–8 yrs.

Jonas, A. 1983. *Round Trip*. New York: Greenwillow. 9–11 yrs.

Joose, B. 1996. *I Love You the Purplest*. Illus. Mary Whyte. San Francisco, Calif.: Chronicle. 5–9 yrs.

Keats, E. J. 1962. *The Snowy Day*. New York: Viking. 4–8 yrs.

Kimmel, E. 1989. *Hershel and the Hanukkah Goblins*. Illus. Trina Schart Hyman. New York: Holiday. 7–10 yrs.

Kirk, D. 1995. *Miss Spider's Wedding*. New York: Scholastic. 7–10 yrs.

Kroll, V. 1993. *Naomi Knows It's Springtime*. Illus. J. Kastner. Lanham, Mary.: Caroline House. 6–9 yrs.

Lamb, C. & M. Lamb. 1806. *Tales from Shakespeare*. Illus. Arthur Rackham. (Reissue, 1988. Illus. Elizabeth S. Elliott. New York: Crown.)

Lattimore, D. N. 1989. *Why There Is No Arguing in Heaven: A Mayan Myth*. New York: HarperCollins. 9–11 yrs.

Lear, E. 1946. *A Book of Nonsense*. New York: Dodd Mead. 7–10 yrs.

Lenski, L. 1932. *The Little Family*. New York: Doubleday. 4–6 yrs.

Leslie, A. 1992. *Play Kitten Play: Ten Animal Fingerwiggles*. Cambridge, Mass.: Candlewick. 6 mo.–2 yrs.

Lionni, L. 1962. *Inch by Inch*. New York: Astor. 4–7 yrs.

———. 1963. *Swimmy*. New York: Knopf. 4–7 yrs.

Lobel, A. 1970. *Frog and Toad Are Friends*. New York: HarperCollins. 5–9 yrs.

London, J. 1994. *Call of the Wild*. Illus. Barry Moser. New York: Macmillan. 10–14 yrs.

London, Jonathan. 1995. *Honey Paw and Lightfoot*. Illus. Jon Van Zyle. San Francisco, Cal.: Chronicle. 8–12 yrs.

Louie, A. 1982. *Yeh-Shen: A Cinderella Story from China*. Illus. Ed Young. New York: Philomel. 8–12 yrs.

Macaulay, D. 1973. *Cathedral: The Story of Its Construction*. Boston: Houghton Mifflin. 10–13 yrs.

———. 1990. *Black and White*. Illus. David Macaulay. Boston: Houghton Mifflin. 10–15 yrs.

Mayer, M. 1967. *A Boy, a Dog, and a Frog*. New York: Dial. 5–8 yrs.

———. 1968. *There's A Nightmare in My Closet*. New York: Dial. 5–9 yrs.

McCloskey, R. 1948. *Blueberries for Sal*. New York: Viking. 5–8 yrs.

———. 1952. *One Morning in Maine*. New York: Viking. 5–8 yrs.

———. 1969. *Make Way for Ducklings*. New York: Viking. 5–9 yrs.

McCully, E. A. 1995. *The Pirate Queen*. New York: Putnam. 5–9 yrs.

McDermott, G. 1974. *Arrow to the Sun: A Pueblo Indian Tale*. New York: Viking. 7–10 yrs.

———. 1992. *Zomo the Rabbit*. New York: Harcourt Brace Jovanovich. 9–11 yrs.

McKissack, P. 1988. *Mirandy and Brother Wind*. Illus. J. Pinkney. New York: Knopf. 8–12 yrs.

McMillan, B. 1995. *Night of the Pufflings*. Boston: Houghton Mifflin. 5–9 yrs.

Merrill, J. (Adapter). 1992. *The Girl Who Loved Caterpillars: A Twelfth-Century Tale from Japan*. Illus. Floyd Cooper. New York: Philomel. 7–12 yrs.

Milne, A. A. 1924. *When We Were Very Young*. Illus. E. H. Shepard. New York: Dutton. 6–12 yrs.

———. 1974. *Winnie the Pooh*. Illus. E. H. Shepard; colored by Hilda Scott. New York: Dell. 9–12 yrs.

Minarik, E. 1957. *Little Bear*. Illus. Maurice Sendak. New York: HarperCollins. 5–9 yrs.

Moore, C. 1823. (New ed. 1971). *The Night Before Christmas*. Illus. T. Tudor. Skokie, Ill.: Rand McNally. 5–12 yrs.

Moore, F. 1995. *I Gave Thomas Edison My Sandwich*. Illus. Donna Kae Nelson. Morton Grove, Ill.: Whitman. 7–10 yrs.

Murphy, C. *Chuck Murphy's One to Ten Pop-Up Surprises!* New York: Little Simon. 3–6 yrs.

Murphy, J. 1993. *Across America on an Emigrant Train*. Photos. New York: Clarion. 12–15 yrs.

Myers, W. D. 1993. *Brown Angels: An Album of Pictures and Verse*. New York: HarperCollins. 7–11 yrs.

Ness, E. 1966. *Sam Bangs & Moonshine*. New York: Farrar, Straus & Giroux. 8–11 yrs.

Nicholson, W. 1926. *Clever Bill*. New York: Doubleday. 8–12 yrs.

Noll, S. 1994. *Lucky Morning*. New York: Greenwillow. 5–7 yrs.

Oppenheim, S. 1995. *The White Stone in the Castle Wall*. Illus. L. Tait. Montreal Quebec, Canada.: Tundra. 8–12 yrs.

Parish, H. 1995. *Good Driving, Amelia Bedelia*. Illus. Lynn Sweat. New York: Greenwillow. 5–9 yrs.

Parish, P. 1992. *Amelia Bedelia*. Illus. Fritz Siebel. New York: HarperCollins. 6–9 yrs.

Paterson, B. 1992. *In My House*. New York: Holt. 1–2 yrs.

Peet, B. 1965. *Chester the Worldly Pig*. Boston: Houghton Mifflin. 5–9 yrs.

———. 1974. *The Wump World*. Boston: Houghton. 5–9 yrs.

———. 1974. *Merle, the High-Flying Squirrel*. Boston: Houghton. 5–9 yrs.

Perrault, C. (Trans. Malcolm Arthur). 1990. *Puss in Boots*. Illus. Fred Marcellino. New York: Di Capua. 9–12 yrs.

Piatti, C. 1964. *The Happy Owl*. New York: Atheneum. 5–8 yrs.

———. 1966. *Celestino Piatti's Animal ABC*. New York: Atheneum. 5–8 yrs.

Platt, K. 1992. *Big Max Series*. Illus. Robert Lopshire. New York: HarperCollins. 6–9 yrs.

Politi, L. 1949. *Song of the Swallows*. New York: Scribners. 5–9 yrs.

Porte, B. 1995. *Chickens! Chickens!* New York: Orchard. 5–8 yrs.

Potter, B. 1902. *The Tales of Peter Rabbit*. London: Warne. 4–8 yrs.

Prelutsky, J. 1984. *The New Kid on the Block*. Illus. J. Stevenson. New York: Greenwillow. 6–14 yrs.

Provensen, A. 1995. *My Fellow Americans*. San Diego: Harcourt. 9–14 yrs.

Pyle, H. 1968. *The Merry Adventures of Robin Hood of Great Renown in Nottinghamshire*. Illus. H. Pyle. New York: Scribners. 11–15 yrs.

Rathmann, P. 1995. *Officer Buckle and Gloria*. New York: Putnam. 7–10 yrs.

Rey, H. A. 1941. *Curious George*. Boston: Houghton Mifflin. 4–9 yrs.

Ringold, F. 1992. *Aunt Harriet's Underground Railroad in the Sky*. New York: Crown. 5–9 yrs.

Rohman, E. 1994. *Time Flies*. New York: Crown. 6–9 yrs.

Roscoe, W. 1807. *Roscoe's Butterfly's Ball*. Illus. William Mulready. London: J. Harris.

Rylant, C. 1991. *Henry and Mudge and the Long Weekend*. Illus. Sucie Stevenson. New York: Bradbury. 6–9 yrs.

San Souci, R. D. 1992. *Sukey and the Mermaid*. Illus. Brian Pinkney. New York: Four Winds. 10–13 yrs.

Say, A. 1993. *Grandfather's Journey*. Boston: Houghton Mifflin. 9–12 yrs.

Schories, P. 1991. *Mouse Around*. New York: Farrar, Straus & Giroux. 5–9 yrs.

Schroeder, A. 1996. *Minty: A Story of Young Harriet Tubman*. Illus. Jerry Pinkney. New York: Dial. 8–11 yrs.

Schutt, S. 1995. *Somewhere in the World Right Now*. New York: Knopf. 8–12 yrs.

Scieszka, J. 1992. *The Stinky Cheese Man and Other Fairly Stupid Tales*. Illus. Lane Smith. New York: Viking. 9–11 yrs.

Sendak, M. 1963. *Where the Wild Things Are*. New York: Harper & Row. 6–10 yrs.

Sharmat, M. W. 1981. *Nate the Great and the Missing Key*. New York: Putnam. 7–10 yrs.

Steig, W. 1969. *Sylvester and the Magic Pebble*. New York: Simon & Schuster. 8–12 yrs.

———. 1982. *Dr. Desoto*. New York: Farrar, Straus & Giroux. 9–12 yrs.

Steptoe, J. 1969. *Stevie*. New York: Harper & Row. 5–10 yrs.

———. 1987. *Mufaro's Beautiful Daughters: An African Tale*. New York: Lothrop, Lee & Shepard. 9–12 yrs.

The Tall Book of Mother Goose. Illus. Feodor Rojankovsky. 1942. New York: Harper & Bros. 3–7 yrs.

Twain, M. [Samuel Clemens]. 1986. *The Adventures of Huckleberry Finn*. Illus. E. W. Kemble. New York: Penguin. 10–16 yrs.

Van Allsburg, C. 1979. *The Garden of Abdul Gasazi*. Boston: Houghton Mifflin. 9–12 yrs.

———. 1981. *Jumanji*. Boston: Houghton Mifflin. 9–12 yrs.

———. 1985. *The Polar Express*. Boston: Houghton Mifflin. 6–16 yrs.

———. 1991. *The Wretched Stone*. Boston: Houghton Mifflin. 6–12 yrs.

———. 1992. *The Widow's Broom*. Boston: Houghton Mifflin. 9–12 yrs.

Ward, Lynd. 1952. *The Biggest Bear*. Boston: Houghton Mifflin. 5–8 yrs.

———. 1930. *Madman's Drum*. In Richey, V. H. & Puckett, K. E. 1992, *Wordless/Almost Wordless Picture Books: A Guide*, Foreward Englewood, Colo.: Libraries Unlimited.

Weisner, D. 1988. *Free Fall*. New York: Lothrop, Lee & Shepard. 9–12 yrs.

———. 1990. *Hurricane*. New York: Clarion. 8–12 yrs.

———. 1991. *Tuesday*. New York: Clarion. 9–12 yrs.

_____. 1992. *June 29, 1999.* New York: Clarion. 8–12 yrs.

White, E. B. 1952. *Charlotte's Web.* Illus. Garth Williams. New York: Harper & Row. 8–12 yrs.

Wilder, L. I. 1995. *The Little House Series.* Illus. Garth Williams. New York: HarperCollins. 8–13 yrs.

Wildsmith, B. 1963. *Brian Wildsmith's Mother Goose.* New York: Watts. 4–9 yrs.

Wisniewski, D. 1996. *Golem.* New York: Clarion. 9–12 yrs.

Yaccarino, D. 1996. *If I Had a Robot.* New York: Viking. 5–8 yrs.

Yashima, T. 1955. *Crow Boy.* New York: Viking. 6–9 yrs.

Yolen, J. 1979. *The Dream Weaver.* Illus. Michael Hague. New York: Philomel. 9–12 yrs.

Young, E. 1989. *Lon Po Po: A Red Riding Hood Story from China.* New York: Philomel. 6–11 yrs.

Zelinsky, P. O. 1990. *The Wheels on the Bus.* New York: Dutton. 3–6 yrs.

AUTOBIOGRAPHIES & BIOGRAPHIES OF ARTISTS

AUTOBIOGRAPHIES

Blegvad, Erik. 1979. *Self-Portrait: Erik Blegvad.* Reading, Mass.: Addison-Wesley. 7–12 yrs.

Crews, Donald. 1991. *Bigmamma's.* New York: Greenwillow. 7–10 yrs.

de Paola, Tomie. 1989. *The Art Lesson.* New York: Putnam. 6–10 yrs.

Foreman, Michael. 1990. *War Boy: A Country Childhood.* New York: Arcade. 10–13 yrs.

Goble, Paul. 1994. *Hau Kola Hello Friend.* New York: Owens. 7–12 yrs. Meet the Author Collection.

Hyman, Trina Schart. 1989. *Self-Portrait: Trina Schart Hyman.* New York: HarperCollins. 7–11 yrs.

O'Kelley, Mattie Lou. 1983. *From the Hills of Georgia: An Autobiography in Paintings,* Boston: Little, Brown. 9–12 yrs.

Peet, Bill. 1989. *Bill Peet: An Autobiography.* Boston: Houghton Mifflin. 8–16 yrs.

Polacco, Patricia. 1994. *Firetalking.* New York: Owens. 7–12 yrs. Meet the Author Collection.

Zemach, Margot. 1981. *A Self-Portrait: Margot Zemach.* Reading, Mass.: Addison-Wesley. 8–12 yrs.

BIOGRAPHIES: ARTISTS

Agee, J. 1988. *The Incredible Paint of Felix Clousseau.* New York: Farrar, Straus & Giroux. 8–12 yrs.

Berman, Avis. 1993. *James McNeill Whistler.* New York: Abrams. 12–15 yrs. First Impressions series.

Bonafoux, Pascal. 1992. *A Weekend with Rembrandt.* New York: Rizzoli. 10–12 yrs. Weekend With series.

Bryant, Jennifer Fisher. 1995. *Henri de Toulouse-Lautrec: Artist.* New York: Chelsea House. 12–18 yrs. Great Achievers: Lives of the Physically Challenged Series.

Clement, Claude. 1986. *The Painter and the Wild Swan.* Illus. Frederic Clement. New York: Dial. 10–14 yrs. (Japanese painter Teiji.)

Cech, John. 1994. *Jacques-Henri Lartigue: Boy with a Camera.* New York: Four Winds. 9–11 yrs.

Cummings, Pat (Editor). 1992. *Talking with Artists.* Photos. New York: Bradbury. 10–12 yrs.

_____. 1995. *Talking with Artists, Volume Two.* Photos. New York: Simon & Schuster. 10–14 yrs.

Engel, D. & F. B. Freedman. 1995. *Ezra Jack Keats: A Biography with Illustrations.* New York: Silver Moon. 9–12 yrs.

Fischetto, Laura. 1993. *Michael the Angel.* Illus. Letizia Galli. New York: Doubleday. 5–9 yrs.

Garland, Michael. 1995. *Dinner at Magritte's.* New York: Dutton. 7–11 yrs.

Greenberg, J. & S. Jordan. 1995. *The American Eye: Eleven Artists of the Twentieth Century.* New York: Delacorte. 12–16 yrs.

Greenfeld, Howard. 1990. *Marc Chagall.* New York: Abrams. 12–16 yrs.

_____. 1993. *Paul Gauguin.* New York: Abrams. 12–16 yrs. First Impressions series.

Gherman, Beverly. 1986. *Georgia O'Keeffe: The Wideness and Wonder of Her World.* New York: Atheneum. 12–16 yrs.

Hughes, Andrew. 1995. *Van Gogh.* Hauppauge, N.Y.: Barron's. 10–13 yrs. Famous Artists Series.

Kastner, Joseph. 1992. *John James Audubon.* Color reproductions. New York: Abrams. 10–12 yrs. Impressions series.

Krull, K. 1995. *Lives of the Artists: Masterpieces, Messes (And What the Neighbors Thought).* Illus. Kathryn Hewitt. San Diego, Calif.: Harcourt Brace. 9–14 yrs.

Johnson, Jane. 1994. *The Princess and the Painter.* New York: Farrar, Straus & Giroux. 7–9 yrs.

Lyons, Mary E. 1993. *Starting Home: The Story of Horace Pippin, Painter.* New York: Scribners. 10–13 yrs. African-American Artists and Artisans series.

Mason, Antony. 1995. *Monet.* Hauppauge, N.Y.: Barron's. 10–13 yrs. Famous Artists Series.

_____. 1995. *Picasso.* Hauppauge, N.Y.: Barron's. Famous Artists Series.

McLanathan, Richard. 1990. *Leonardo da Vinci.* New York: Abrams. 12–16 yrs.

_____. 1995. *Peter Paul Rubens.* B & W & color reproductions. New York: Abrams. 12–17 yrs. First Impressions.

Meryman, Richard. 1991. *Andrew Wyeth.* New York: Abrams. 12–16 yrs.

Meyers, Susan E. 1991. *Mary Cassatt.* New York: Abrams. 12–16 yrs. First Impressions series.

_____. 1994. *Edgar Degas.* New York: Abrams. 12–17 yrs. First Impressions series.

Muhlberger, Richard. 1993. *What Makes a Monet?; What Makes a Bruegel a Bruegel?* Photos. Metropolitan Museum of Art/New York: Viking. *What Makes A . . . A . . .* Series. 12–15 yrs.

National Gallery of Canada & Anne Newlands. 1989. *Meet Edgar Degas.* New York: Lippincott. 6–16 yrs.

Neimark, Anne E. 1992. *Diego Rivera: Artist of the People.* New York: HarperCollins. 8–12 yrs. (Fictionalized biography.)

Plain, Nancy. 1994. *Mary Cassatt: An Artist's Life.* Morristown, N.J.: Dillon. 9–11 yrs. People in Focus series.

Plazy, Gilles. 1993. *A Weekend with Rousseau.* New York: Rizzoli. 10–12 yrs. Weekend With series.

Raboff, Ernest. 1987. *Leonardo Da Vinci: Art For Children; Pablo Picasso; Pierre-Auguste Renoir; Rembrandt.* New York: Lippincott. 10–13 yrs.

_____. 1988. *Marc Chagall; Michelangelo; Raphael; Van Gogh.* New York: HarperCollins. 10–13 yrs.

Richmond, Robin. 1991. *Introducing Michelangelo.* Boston: Little, Brown. 10–13 yrs.

Rodari, Florian. 1993. *A Weekend with Velazquez.* Color reproductions. New York: Rizzoli. 10–12 yrs. Weekend With series.

_____. (Trans. Joan Knioght). 1994. *A Weekend with Matisse.* New York: Rizzoli. 10–12 yrs. Weekend With series.

Romei, Francesca. 1995. *Leonardo da Vinci: Artist, Inventor, and Scientist of the Renaissance.* Illus. L. R. Galante & Andrea Ricciardi. Reproductions and other visuals. New York: Peter Bedrick. 10–14 yrs. Masters of Art Series.

Roop, Peter & Connie Roop (Eds). 1993. *Capturing Nature: The Writings and Art of John James Audubon.* Illus. Rick Farley. New York: Walker. 10–12 yrs.

Salvi, Francesco. 1995. *The Impressionists: The Origins of Modern Painting.* Illus. L. R. Galante & Andrea Ricciardi. Reproductions and other visuals. New York: Peter Bedrick. 10–14 yrs. Masters of Art Series.

Sills, Leslie. 1989. *Inspirations: Stories About Women Artists.* Illus. Ann Fay. Morton Grove, Ill.: Whitman. 10–14 yrs.

_____. 1993. *Visions: Stories about Women Artists.* Morton Grove, Ill.: Whitman. 10–14 yrs.

Skira-Venturi, Rosabianca. 1992. *A Weekend with Degas.* New York: Rizzoli. 10–12 yrs. A Weekend With series.

_____. (Trans. Ann Keay Beneduce). 1994. *A Weekend with Van Gogh.* New York: Rizzoli. 9–11 yrs. Weekend With series.

Sturgis, Alexander. 1994. *Introducing Rembrandt.* Color reproductions. Boston: Little, Brown. 9–11 yrs. Introducing the Artist series.

Turner, Robyn Montana. 1991. *Georgia O'Keeffe.* Boston: Little, Brown. 10–12 yrs. Portraits of Women Artists for Children series.

_____. 1992. *Mary Cassatt.* Boston: Little, Brown. 10–12 yrs. Portraits of Women Artists for Children series.

_____. 1993. *Faith Ringgold.* Boston: Little, Brown. 10–12 yrs. Portraits of Women Artists for Children series.

_____. 1993. *Frida Kahlo.* Boston: Little, Brown. 9–12 yrs. Portraits of Women Artists for Children series.

_____. 1994. *Dorothea Lange.* Boston: Little, Brown. 9–11 yrs. Portraits of Women Artists for Children series.

Ventura, Piero. 1989. *Michelangelo's World.* Illus. P. Ventura. New York: Putnam. 8–15 yrs.

Waldron, Ann. 1992. *Francisco Goya.* Color reproductions. New York: Abrams. 10–12 yrs.

Walker, Lou Ann. 1994. *Roy Lichtenstein: The Artist at Work.* Photos Michael Abramson. New York: Lodestar. 9–13 yrs.

Winter, Jonah. 1991. *Diego.* Illus. Jeanette Winter. New York: Knopf. 12–16 yrs.

_____. 1995. *Cowboy Charlie: The Story of Charles M. Russell.* Paintings. San Diego, Calif.: Harcourt Brace. 6–10 yrs.

Von Habsburg, Geza. 1994. *Carl Faberge.* New York: Abrams. 12–16 yrs. First Impressions series.

Zheng Zhensun & Alice Low. 1990. *A Young Chinese Painter: The Life and Paintings of Wang Yani China's Extraordinary Young Artist.* Photos Zheng Zhensun. New York: Scholastic/Byron Preiss-New China Pictures Books. 10–16 yrs.

BIOGRAPHIES: VISUAL ARTS

Ayer, Eleanor H. 1992. *Photographing the World: Margaret Bourke-White.* Photos. Morristown, N.J.: Dillon. 10–13 yrs.

Ford, Barbara. 1989. *Walt Disney.* New York: Walker. 9–12 yrs.

Gardner, Jane Mylum. 1993. *Henry Moore: From Bones and Stones to Sketches and Sculptures.* New York: Four Winds. 5–9 yrs.

Goldberg, Vicki. 1986. *Margaret Bourke-White.* New York: HarperCollins.

Lasky, Kathryn. 1992. *Think like an Eagle: At Work with a Wildlife Photographer.* Photos Christopher G. Knight & Jack Swedberg. Boston: Joy/Little, Brown. 10–13 yrs.

Mitchell, Barbara. 1986. *Click! A Story About George Eastman.* Minneapolis, Minn.: Carolrhoda. 8–11 yrs.

Sufrin, Mark. 1987. *Focus on America: Profiles of Nine Photographers.* New York: Scribners. 10–13 yrs.

Sullivan, George. 1994. *Mathew Brady: His Life and Photographs*. New York: Cobblehill. 9–11 yrs.

Wolf, Sylvia. 1994. *Focus: Five Women Photographers*. Photos. Morton Grove, Ill.: Whitman. 11–14 yrs.

INFORMATION BOOKS: ART AND CRAFTS

Baylor, Bird. 1987. *When Clay Sings*. New York: Scribners. 7–14 yrs.

Blizzard, Gladys S. 1992. *Come Look with Me: Exploring Landscape Art with Children*. Reproductions. Charlottesville, Vir.: Thomasson-Grant. 5–8 yrs.

Bolton, Linda. 1993. *Hidden Pictures*. New York: Dial. 5–9 yrs.

Botemans, Jack. 1986. *Paper Capers: An Amazing Array of Games, Puzzles, and Tricks*. New York: Holt. 12–16 yrs.

Bunchman, Janis & Stephanie Bissell Briggs. 1994. *Pictures and Poetry*. Worcester, Mass.: Davis. 9–11 yrs.

Chapman, G. & P. Robson. 1995. *Making Shaped Books*. Brookfield, Conn.: Millbrook. 5–10 yrs.

Chermayeff, Jane. 1990. *First Words*. New York: Abrams. 5–9 yrs.

———. 1991. *First Shapes*. Reproductions from Paris museums. New York: Abrams. 5–9 yrs.

Christelow, E. 1995. *What Do Authors Do?* New York: Clarion. 5–9 yrs.

Coleman, A. D. 1995. *Looking at Photographs: Animals*. Photos. San Francisco: Chronicle. 9–13 yrs.

Collins, Pat Lowery. 1992. *I Am an Artist*. Illus. Robin Brickman. Brookfield, Conn.: Millbrook. 9–13 yrs.

Costabel, Eva Deutsch. 1987. *The Pennsylvania Dutch Craftsmen and Farmers*. New York: Atheneum. 10–12 yrs.

Davidson, Rosemary. 1994. *Take a Look: An Introduction to the Experience of Art*. Photos. New York: Viking. 11–15 yrs.

Desimini, Lisa. 1994. *My House*. Illus. L. Desimini. New York: Holt. 4–7 yrs.

Falwell, Cathryn. 1994. *The Letter Jesters*. New York: Ticknor & Fields. 5–8 yrs. (Art of printing.)

Fisher, Leonard. 1986. *Symbol Art: Thirteen From Around The World*. New York: Four Winds. 11–15 yrs.

Frame, Paul. 1986. *Drawing Reptiles*. Danbury, Conn.: Watts. 12–14 yrs.

Glubok, Shirley. 1994. *Painting*. New York: Scribners. 9–11 yrs.

Greenberg, Jan & Sandra Jordan. 1991. *The Painter's Eye: Learning to Look at Contemporary American Art*. New York: Delacorte. 10–16 yrs.

———. 1993. *The Sculptor's Eye: Looking at Contemporary American Art*. New York: Delacorte. 12–15 yrs.

Hautzig, Ester. 1986. *Make It Special: Cards, Decorations, and Party Favors For Holidays and Other Special Occasions*. New York: Macmillan. 8–12 yrs.

Martin, Judy. 1994. *Painting and Drawing*. Brookfield, Conn.: Millbrook. 9–11 yrs. First Guide series.

———. 1995. *Impressionism*. Reproductions. New York: Thomson Learning. 12–17 yrs. Art and Artists Series.

Micklethwait, Lucy. 1991. *Color. Lines. Shapes. Stories*. Museum of Modern Art and New York: Delacorte. 5–10 yrs.

———. 1992. *I Spy: An Alphabet in Art*. New York: Greenwillow. 6–14 yrs.

———. 1993. *I Spy Two Eyes: Numbers in Art*. New York: Greenwillow. 6–9 yrs.

———. 1994. *I Spy a Lion: Animals in Art*. New York: Greenwillow. 5–8 yrs.

Miller, Cameron & Dominique Falla. 1995. *Woodlore*. New York: Ticknor & Fields. 5–9 yrs.

———. *Paint and Painting*. 1994. New York: Scholastic. 10–13 yrs. Voyages of Discovery series.

Peppin, Anthea. 1991–92. *Nature in Art; People in Art; Places in Art*. Illus. Helen Williams. Brookfield, Conn.: Millbrook. 7–12 yrs. Stories in Art.

Pluckrose, Henry. 1988. *Crayons Paints*. Danbury, Conn.: Watts. 8–12 yrs.

Ridley, Pauline. 1995. *Modern Art*. Reproductions. New York: Thomson Learning. 12–17 yrs. Art and Artists Series.

Roalf, Peggy. 1992. *Looking at Paintings* series: *Families; Horses; Landscapes; Seascapes*. Color reproductions. New York: Hyperion. 8–12 yrs.

———. 1993. *Looking at Paintings* series: *Children; Circus; Flowers; Self-Portraits; Dogs; Musicians*. Color reproductions. New York: Hyperion. 8–12 yrs.

Rylant, Cynthia. 1986. *All I See*. Illus. Peter Catalanotto. New York: Orchard. 7–12 yrs.

Seymour, Rowan. 1994. *The National Gallery ABC*. New York: Rizzoli/Universe. 7–17 yrs.

Sirett, Dawn. 1994. *My First Paint Book*. New York: Dorling Kindersley. 5–8 yrs.

Swain, G. 1995. *Bookworks: Making Books by Hand*. Illus. Jennifer Hagerman. Photos Andy King. Minneapolis, Minn.: Carolrhoda. 9–13 yrs.

Tucker, Jean S. 1994. *Come Look with Me: Discovering Photographs with Children*. Charlottesville, Vir.: Thomasson-Grant. 9–11 yrs. Come Look with Me series.

Welton, Jude. 1994. *Drawing: A Young Artist's Guide*. New York: Dorling Kindersley. 9–11 yrs.

Westray, Kathleen. 1993. *A Color Sampler*. Illus. K. Westray. New York: Ticknor & Fields. 7–10 yrs.

———. 1994. *Picture Puzzler*. Illus. K. Westray. New York: Ticknor & Fields. 7–10 yrs. (Optical illusion.)

Wilson, Elizabeth B. 1994. *Bibles and Bestiaries: A Guide to Illuminated Manuscripts*. New York: Farrar, Straus & Giroux. 12–18 yrs.

Wilson, Keith. 1994. *Photography*. New York: Random House. 9–11 yrs.

Willard, Nancy. 1991. *Pish, Posh, Said Hieronymus Bosch*. Illus. Diane & Leo Dillon. San Diego, Calif.: Harcourt Brace Jovanovich. All ages. Fictionalized.

Woolf, Felicity. 1989. *Picture This*. New York: Doubleday. 10–16 yrs.

Yenawine, Philip. 1991. *Color. Lines. Shapes. Stories*. New York: Museum of Modern Art and Delacorte. 5–9 yrs. Art Books for Children series.

———. 1993. *People; Places*. New York: Delacorte. 5–9 yrs. Art Books for Children series.

OUTSTANDING LITERATURE REPRESENTING VARIOUS ARTISTIC MEDIA, STYLES, BOOK DESIGN, TYPES OF BOOKS WITH PICTURES

(Exemplary books with pictures are cited throughout the genre bibliographies)

MEDIA AND GRAPHIC TECHNIQUES USED BY ARTISTS

Watercolor

Ackerman, Karen. 1994. *By the Dawn's Early Light*. Illus. Catherine Stock. New York: Atheneum. 5–8 yrs.

Arnold, M. D. 1995. *Heart of a Tiger*. Illus. Jamichael Henterly. New York: Dial. 6–9 yrs.

Base, Grahame. 1992. *The Sign of the Seahorse*. Illus. G. Base. New York: Abrams. 10–13 yrs.

Beard, D. B. 1995. *The Pumpkin Man from Piney Creek*. Illus. Laura Kelly. New York: Simon & Schuster. 6–9 yrs.

Borovsky, Paul. 1994. *The Fish That Wasn't*. New York: Hyperion. 5–8 yrs.

Browne, Eileen. 1994. *Tick-Tock*. Illus. David Parkins. Cambridge, Mass.: Candlewick. 4–6 yrs.

Brutschy, Jennifer. 1994. *Celeste and Crabapple Sam*. Illus. Eileen Christelow. New York: Lodestar. 6–8 yrs.

Carlstrom, Nancy White. 1993. *Wishing at Dawn in Summer*. Illus. Diane Worfolk Allison. Boston: Little, Brown. 4–7 yrs. Family life.

Donovan, M. L. 1995. *Snuffles Makes a Friend*. Illus. Caroline Anstey. Cambridge, Mass.: Candlewick. 5–9 yrs. Gund Children's Library series. With pencil.

Dyer, Jan. 1996. *Animal Cracker*. Boston: Little, Brown. 5–9 yrs.

Ellsworth, Barry. 1995. *The Little Stream*. Salt Lake City: Bonneville Classic Books.

French, Vivian. 1993. *Once upon a Time*. Illus. John Prater. Cambridge, Mass.: Candlewick.

Fuchs, D. M. 1995. *A Bear for All Seasons*. Illus. Kathryn Brown. New York: Holt. 4–8 yrs. With colored pencil.

Gerrard, Roy. 1996. *Wagons West!* New York: Farrar, Straus & Giroux. 10–12 yrs.

Giannini, Enzo. 1993. *Zorina Ballerina*. New York: Simon & Schuster. 5–7 yrs.

Hayes, Ann. 1995. *Meet the Marching Smithereens*. Illus. Karmen Thompson. San Diego, Calif.: Harcourt Brace. 5–9 yrs.

Ichikawa, S. 1995. *Isabela's Ribbons*. New York: Philomel. 5–8 yrs.

James, J. A. 1995. *Eucalyptus Wings*. Illus. Demi. New York: Atheneum. 6–9 yrs. With ink, gold highlights.

Kasza, Keiko. 1993. *The Rat and the Tiger*. New York: Putnam. 5–7 yrs.

Ketteman, H. 1995. *The Christmas Blizzard*. Illus. James Warhola. New York: Scholastic. 5–9 yrs.

Levine, Ellen. 1995. *The Tree That Would Not Die*. Illus. Ted Rand. New York: Scholastic.

London, Jonathan. 1995. *Froggy Learns to Swim*. Illus. Frank Remkiewicz. New York: Viking. 4–8 yrs.

Loomis, Christine. 1995. *The Hippo Hop*. Illus. Nadine Bernard Westcott. Boston: Houghton Mifflin. 6–9 yrs.

McBratney, Sam. 1995. *Guess How Much I Love You*. Illus. Anita Jeram. Cambridge, Mass.: Candlewick. 4–8 yrs.

McGeorge, Constance W. 1994. *Boomer's Big Day*. Illus. Mary Whyte. San Francisco: Chronicle. 4–6 yrs.

Mills, Claudia. 1994. *Phoebe's Parade*. Illus. Carolyn Ewing. New York: Macmillan. 4–7 yrs.

Nethery, M. 1996. *Hannah and Jack*. Illus. Mary Morgan. New York: Atheneum. 5–9 yrs. With gouache.

Nones, Eric. 1995. *Angela's Wings*. New York: HarperCollins. 8–11 yrs.

Oram, Hiawyn. 1995. *Badger's Bring Something Party*. Illus. Susan Varley. New York: Lothrop, Lee & Shepard. 5–9 yrs.

Rossi, Joyce. 1995. *The Gullywasher*. Flagstaff, Ariz.: Northland. 7–9 yrs. Watercolor.

Rylant, Cynthia. 1996. *The Old Woman Who Named Things*. Illus. Kathryn Brown. San Diego, Calif.: Harcourt Brace. 8–11 yrs.

Schertle, A. 1995. *Down the Road*. Illus. E. B. Lewis. San Diego, Calif.: Browndeer. 5–9 yrs.

Schoenherr, John. 1995. *Rebel*. Illus. J. Schoenherr. New York: Philomel. 3–6 yrs.

Seabrooke, B. 1995. *The Swan's Gift*. Illus. Wenhai Ma. Cambridge, Mass.: Candlewick. 7–10 yrs.

Waddell, M. 1995. *Once There Were Giants*. Illus. Penny Dale. Cambridge, Mass.: Candlewick.

Wiesner, David. 1991. *Tuesday*. Illus. D. Wiesner. New York: Clarion. 9–12 yrs.

Wiesner, J. 1992. *June 29,1999*. Illus. J. Wiesner. New York: Clarion. 9–12 yrs.

Gouache

Aruego, Jose (Reteller). 1988. *Rockabye Crocodile*. Illus. by Ariane Dewey. New York: Greenwillow. 4–6 yrs.

Ball, Duncan. 1994. *Grandfather's Wheelything*. Illus. by Cat Bowman Smith. New York: Simon & Schuster. 6–9 yrs.

Base, Graeme. 1987. *Animalia*. New York: Abrams. 8–12 yrs.

———. 1988. *The Eleventh Hour: A Curious Mystery*. New York: Abrams. 10–12 yrs.

Berenzy, Alix. 1995. *Rapunzel*. New York: Henry Holt. 9–11 yrs.

Cohen, Barbara. 1988. *The Donkey's Story*. Illus. by Susan Jeanne Cohen. New York: Lothrop, Lee & Shepard, 6–10 yrs.

Cooney, Barbara. 1988. *Island Boy*. Illus. by Barbara Cooney. New York: Viking/Kestrel. 4–8 yrs.

Cunningham, D. 1996. *A Crow's Journey*. Morton Grove, Ill.: Whitman. 4–6 yrs.

Ford, Miela. 1995. *Sunflower*. Illus. Sally Noll. New York: Greenwillow. 5–9 yrs.

Gaffney, T. R. 1996. *Grandpa Takes Me to the Moon*. Illus. Barry Root. New York: Tambourine. 5–8 yrs. With watercolor.

Gerstein, Mordecai. 1987. *The Mountain of Tibet*. Illus. by Mordecai Gerstein. New York: Harper. 7–13 yrs.

Hofmeyr, Dianne. 1995. *Do the Whales Still Sing?* Illus. Jude Daly. New York: Dial. 6–9 yrs.

Hutchins, Pat. 1994. *Three-Star Billy*. New York: Greenwillow. 4–6 yrs.

Hollinshead, Marilyn. 1994. *The Nine Days Wonder*. Illus. by Pierr Morgan. New York: Philomel. 6–8 yrs.

Hutchins, P. 1996. *Titch and Daisy*. New York: Greenwillow. 4–8 yrs. Stylized art.

Johnston, T. 1988. *Yonder*. Illus. Lloyd Bloom. New York: Dial. 9–11 yrs.

Joose, Barbara M. 1995. *The Morning Chair*. Illus. Marcia Sewall. New York: Clarion. 6–9 yrs.

Levine, Arthur A. 1995. *Bono and Nonno*. Illus. Judy Lanfredi. New York: Tambourine. 5–8 yrs.

Lindberg, Reve. 1987. *The Midnight Farm*. Illus. Susan Jeffers. New York: Dial. 4–7 yrs.

Lobel, Anita. 1994. *Away from Home*. New York: Greenwillow. 6–8 yrs.

McDermott, Gerald. 1992. *Zomo: The Rabbit: A Trickster Tale from West Africa*. San Diego, Calif.: Harcourt, Brace, Jovanovich. 9–12 yrs.

MacDonald, Amy. 1996. *The Spider Who Created the World*. Illus. G. Brian Karas. Kroupa/New York: Orchard. 4–7 yrs. With acrylic.

Plotz, Helen (Compiler). 1988. *A Week of Lullabies*. Illus. by Marisabina Russo. New York: Greenwillow. 3–6 yrs.

Russo, Marisabina. 1986. *The Line Up Book*. New York: Greenwillow. 3–6 yrs.

———. 1994. *I Don't Want to Go Back to School*. New York: Greenwillow. 6–8 yrs.

Stanley, Diane & Vennema, Peter. 1994. *Cleopatra*. Illus. Diane Stanley. New York: Morrow. 10–12 yrs.

Steptoe, J. 1987. *Mufaro's Beautiful Daughters: An African Tale*. New York: Lothrop, Lee & Shepard. 8–12 yrs.

Tregebov, Rhea. 1993. *The Big Storm*. Illus. by Maryann Kovalski. New York: Hyperion. 5–7 yrs.

Yaccarmo, Dan. 1993. *Big Brother Mike*. New York: Hyperion. 5–7 yrs.

Tempera

Carson, J. 1992. *You Hold Me and I'll Hold You*. Illus. Annie Cannon. New York: Orchard/Jackson. 6–9 yrs. With watercolor, colored pencil, collage; abstract mood.

Feelings, M. 1974. *Majo Means One*. Dial. 7–11 yrs. With ink.

———. 1975. *Jambo Means Hello*. New York: Dial. 7–11 yrs. With ink.

Langstaff, John (Compiler). 1987. *What a Morning! The Christmas Story in Black Spirituals*. New York: Simon & Schuster. 7–12 yrs.

Mayer, Marianna (Reteller). 1988. *Iduna and the Magic Apples*. Illus. Laszlo Gal. New York: Macmillan. 6–10 yrs.

Mayer, M. 1968. *There's A Nightmare in My Closet*. Illus. M. Mayer. New York: Dial. 7–11 yrs.

Sendak, M. 1963. *Where the Wild Things Are*. New York: Harper & Row. 6–10 yrs. With ink.

Oil/Acrylic Paint

Ballard, Robin. 1995. *Carnival*. New York: Greenwillow. 5–9 yrs.

Bruchac, J. & J. London. 1992. *Thirteen Moons on Turtle's Back*. Illus. Thomas Locker. New York: Philomel. 5–9 yrs.

Bunting, Eve. 1994. *Flower Garden*. Illus. Kathryn Hewitt. San Diego, Calif.: Harcourt Brace. 4–6 yrs.

Carlstrom, Nancy White. 1993. *What Does the Rain Play?* Illus. Henri Sorensen. New York: Macmillan. 4–6 yrs.

Carr, J. 1996. *Dark Day, Light Night*. Illus. James Ransome. New York: Hyperion. 4–6 yrs.

Cooper, Floyd. 1994. *Coming Home: From the Life of Langston Hughes*. New York: Philomel. 10–16 yrs.

Dedieu, Thierry (Trans. by George Wen). 1993. *The Little Christmas Soldier*. New York: Holt. 5–8 yrs.

Dillon, Leo & Diane Dillon (Illus.). 1995. *Her Stories: African American Folk Tales, Fairy Tales, and True Tales*. New York: Scholastic/Blue Sky. 11–16 yrs.

Erdrich. 1996. *Grandmother's Pigeon*. Illus. Jim La Marche. New York: Hyperion. 9–12 yrs.

Ferguson, A. 1996. *Tumbleweed Christmas*. Illus. Tom Sully. New York: Simon & Schuster. 5–8 yrs.

Fisher, Leonard Everett. 1995. *Gandhi*. New York: Atheneum. 10–16 yrs.

Frank, John. 1994. *Erin's Voyage*. Illus. Dena Schutzer. New York: Simon & Schuster. 5–7 yrs.

George, Jean Craighead. 1995. *To Climb a Waterfall*. Illus. Thomas Locker. New York: Philomel. 7–11 yrs.

Gershator, P. 1995. *Sambalena Show-Off*. Illus. Leonard Jenkins. New York: Simon & Schuster. 6–9 yrs. Acrylic.

Honeycutt, Natalie. 1993. *Whistle Home*. Illus. Annie Cannon. New York: Orchard/Jackson. 5–7 yrs.

Houston, Gloria. 1988. *The Year of the Perfect Christmas Tree*. Illus. Barbara Cooney. New York: Dial. 7–12 yrs.

Howard, Elizabeth Fitzgerald. 1991. *Aunt Flossie's Hats (and Crab Cakes Later)*. Illus. James Ransome. New York: Clarion. 9–12 yrs.

Isaacs, Anne. 1994. *Swamp Angel*. New York: Dutton. 9–12 yrs.

Jewell, Nancy. 1994. *Christmas Lullaby*. Illus. Stefano Vitale. New York: Clarion. 5–8 yrs.

Kalman, Esther. 1994. *Tchaikovsky Discovers America*. Illus. Laura Fernandez & Rick Jacobson. New York: Orchard. 9–12 yrs.

Kinsey-Warnock, Natalie. 1993. *When Spring Comes*. Illus. Stacey Schuett. New York: Dutton. 5–8 yrs.

Kiser, SuAnn. 1994. *The Hog Call to End All!* Illus. John Steven Gurney. New York: Orchard/Jackson. 5–8 yrs.

Lesser, Rika (Reteller). 1984. *Hansel and Gretel*. Illus. Paul Zelinsky. New York: Dodd, Mead. 8–12 yrs.

Marzollo, Jean. 1995. *Sun Song*. Illus. Laura Regan. New York: HarperCollins. 5–9 yrs.

McCutcheon, M. 1995. *Grandfather's Christmas Camp*. New York: Clarion. 6–9 yrs.

Ringgold, Faith. 1991. *Tar Beach*. New York: Crown. 9–11 yrs.

Rush, Ken. 1993. *The Seltzer Man*. New York: Macmillan. 5–8 yrs.

Ryder, Joanne. 1994. *My Father's Hands*. Illus. Mark Graham. New York: Morrow. 5–7 yrs.

Rylant, Cynthia. 1995. *Dog Heaven*. Illus. C. Rylant. New York: Blue Sky/Scholastic. 5–8 yrs.

Sorensen, Henri. 1995. *New Hope*. New York: Lothrop, Lee & Shepard. 6–9 yrs.

Wells, Rosemary. 1994. *Lucy Comes to Stay*. Illus. Mark Graham. New York: Dial. 6–8 yrs.

Yolen, Jane. 1992. *Encounter*. Illus. David Shannon. San Diego, Calif.: Harcourt Brace Jovanovich. 10–13 yrs.

Zolotow, C. 1995. *The Old Dog*. Illus. James Ransome. New York: HarperCollins. 5–10 yrs.

Pencils, Pastels, Crayons, Oil Pastels

Anderson, L. H. 1996. *Turkey Pox*. Illus. Dorothy Donohue. Morton Grove, Ill.: Whitman. 5–8 yrs. Color pencil and watercolor.

Baillie, Allan. 1994. *Rebel*. Illus. Di Wu. New York: Ticknor & Fields. 7–9 yrs. Pencil & watercolor.

Borden, Louise. 1993. *Albie the Lifeguard*. Illus. Elizabeth Sayles. New York: Scholastic. 4–6 yrs. Pastels.

Burton, Virginia. 1939. *Mike Mulligan and His Steam Shovel*. Boston: Houghton Mifflin. 5–9 yrs. Crayon.

Coffelt, Nancy. 1994. *Tom's Fish*. San Diego: Harcourt Brace/Gulliver. 4–7 yrs. Oil-pastel drawings.

Crebbin, June. 1995. *The Train Ride*. Illus. Stephen Lambert. Cambridge, Mass.: Candlewick. 5–8 yrs. Chalk pastels.

Dewey, Ariane. 1993. *The Sky*. New York: Green Tiger. 4–6 yrs. Chalk pastels.

Enderle, Judith Ross & Stephanie Gordon Tessler. 1993. *A Pile of Pigs*. Illus. Charles Jordan. Honesdale, Penn.: Boyds Mills. 4–6 yrs. Color pencil.

Erlbruch, W. 1995. *Leonard*. New York: Orchard. 6–9 yrs. Pastel chalk.

Fisher, Leonard Everett. 1996. *William Tell*. New York: Farrar, Straus & Giroux. 6–10 yrs. Pastel chalk.

Fleischman, P. 1988. *Rondo in C*. Illus. Janet Wentworth. New York: Harper & Row. 8–12 yrs. Pastel.

Fowler, Susi Gregg. 1993. *When Joel Comes Home*. Illus. by Jim Fowler. New York: Greenwillow. 6–8 yrs. Color pencil.

Fromental, Jean-Luc. 1995. *Broadway Chicken*. New York: Hyperion. 9–12 yrs. Dry pastelles.

Ginsburg, Mirra. 1994. *The Old Man and His Birds*. Illus. Donna Ruff. New York: Greenwillow. 7–9 yrs. Pastels.

Gray, Libba Moore. 1995. *My Mamma Had a Dancing Heart*. Illus. Raul Colon. New York: Orchard. 5–9 yrs. Watercolor, color & litho pencil.

Griffith, Helen V. 1994. *Dream Meadow*. Illus. Nancy Barnet. New York: Greenwillow. 6–8 yrs. Color pencil.

Heckman, Philip. 1996. *Waking Upside Down.* Illus. Dwight Been. New York: Atheneum. 5–8 yrs. Color pencil.

Lewis, Kim. 1993. *First Snow.* Cambridge, Mass.: Candlewick. 4–6 yrs. Pencil.

McLean, Janet. 1995. *Dog Tales.* Illus. Andrew McLean. New York: Ticknor & Fields. 6–9 yrs. Color pencil.

Newberry, Clare T. 1993. *April's Kittens.* New York: HarperCollins. 6–9 yrs. Charcoal.

Nielsen, L. F. 1995. *Jeremy's Muffler.* Illus. Christine M. Schneider. New York: Atheneum. Crayon.

Peet, Bill. 1989. *Bill Peet: An Autobiography.* Boston: Houghton Mifflin. 10–14 yrs. Pencil.

Perrault, Charles (Trans. Malcolm Arthur). 1990. *Puss in Boots.* Illus. Fred Marcellino. New York: Di Capua. 9–12 yrs. Pastel.

Pfeffer, W. 1995. *Marta's Magnets.* Illus. Gail Piazza. New York: Silver Burdett. 6–9 yrs. Color pencils.

Polacco, Patricia. 1995. *My Ol' Man.* New York: Philomel. 6–9 yrs. Watercolor & pencil.

Rydell, Katy. 1994. *Wind Says Good Night.* Illus. David Jorgensen. Boston: Houghton Mifflin. 4–6 yrs. Color pencil.

Sherrow, Victoria. 1994. *Chipmunk at Hollow Tree Lane.* Illus. Allen Davis. Norwalk, Conn.: Soundprints. 5–7 yrs. Color pencil.

Stevens, Janet. 1995. *Tops & Bottoms.* Illus. J. Stevens. San Diego, Calif.: Harcourt Brace. 7–10 yrs. Watercolor, colored pencil, grosso.

Strub, Susanne. 1993. *My Cat and I.* New York: Tambourine. 4–6 yrs. Crayon & marker.

———. 1993. *My Dog, My Sister, and I.* New York: Tambourine. 4–6 yrs. Crayon & marker.

Tryon, Leslie. 1993. *Albert's Field Trip.* New York: Atheneum. 5–7 yrs. Color pencil & watercolor.

Van Allsburg, Chris. 1984. *The Mysteries of Harris Burdick.* Boston: Houghton Mifflin. 9–14 yrs. Litho pencil.

———. 1985. *The Polar Express.* Boston: Houghton Mifflin. 7–16 yrs. Color Conte crayon.

———. 1992. *The Widow's Broom.* Boston: Houghton Mifflin. 10–13 yrs. Litho pencil.

———. 1995. *Bad Day at Riverbend.* Boston: Houghton Mifflin. 7–10 yrs. B & W line drawings & crayons.

Weiss, Nicki. 1993. *Stone Men.* New York: Greenwillow. 6–8 yrs. Pastels & pencil.

Young, Ed (Adapter). 1995. *Donkey Trouble.* Illus. E. Young. New York: Atheneum. 5–8 yrs. Pastels on brown paper.

Black and White

Christian, Peggy. 1995. *The Bookstore Mouse.* Illus. Gary Lippincott. San Diego, Calif.: Harcourt Brace. 10–14 yrs.

Curtiss, A. B. 1996. *Hallelujah, A Cat Comes Back.* Escondido, Calif.: Old Castle Publ. Co. 7–14 yrs.

Dahl, Roald. 1961. *James and the Giant Peach.* Illus. Nancy Ekholm Burkert. New York: Puffin. 8–12 yrs.

———. 1970. *Fantastic Mr. Fox.* Illus. Tony Ross. New York: Puffin. 6–9 yrs.

Fisher, Leonard Everett. 1986. *The Great Wall of China.* New York: Macmillan. 9–12 yrs. Pen.

Macaulay, David. 1973. *Cathedral: The Story of Its Construction.* Illus. D. Macaulay. Boston: Houghton Mifflin. 10–13 yrs.

Philip, N. (Ed.). 1995. *Singing America.* Illus. Michael McCurdy. New York: Viking. 10–16 yrs.

Prelutsky, Jack. 1984. *The New Kid on the Block.* Illus. James Stevenson. New York: Greenwillow. 6–14 yrs.

Silverstein, S. 1964. *The Giving Tree.* Illus. S. Silverstein. New York: Harper & Row. 6–14 yrs.

Steig, William. 1984. *CDC?* Illus. W. Steig. New York: Farrar, Straus & Giroux. 8–14 yrs.

Van Allsburg, Chris. 1979. *The Garden of Abdul Gasazi.* Boston: Houghton Mifflin. 9–12 yrs.

———. 1981. *Jumanji.* Boston: Houghton Mifflin. 9–12 yrs.

———. 1982. *Ben's Dream.* Boston: Houghton Mifflin. 9–12 yrs.

———. 1995. *Bad Day at Riverbend.* Boston: Houghton Mifflin. 5–9 yrs.

Viorst, J. 1978. *Alexander and the Terrible, Horrible, Very Bad Day.* Illus. Ray Cruz. New York: Simon & Schuster. 6–13 yrs.

———. 1995. *Alexander, Who's Not (Do You Hear Me?) Going (I Mean It) to Move.* Illus. Robin Preiss Glasser. New York: Atheneum. 7–12 yrs.

Weilerstein, Sadie Rose. 1995. *K'tonton's Yom Kippur Kitten.* Illus. Joe Boddy. Philadelphia: Jewish Publication Society. 7–10 yrs.

Collage

Akass, Susan. 1993. *Number Nine Duckling.* Illus. Alex Ayliffe. Honesdale, Penn.: Boyds Mills. 3–6 yrs.

Baker, Jeannie. 1991. *Windows.* New York: Greenwillow. 7–11 yrs.

———. 1995. *The Story of Rosy Dock.* New York: Greenwillow. 8–12 yrs.

Bang, Molly. 1985. *The Paper Crane.* New York: Greenwillow. 6–10 yrs.

———. 1991. *Yellow Ball.* Illus. M. Bang. New York: Morrow. 2–6 yrs.

Brown, Marcia. 1982. *Shadow.* New York: Scribners. 10–13 yrs.

Bunting, Eve. 1994. *The Smoky Night.* Illus. David Diaz. San Diego, Calif.: Harcourt Brace. 7–10 yrs.

Carle, Eric. 1995. *Walter the Baker.* New York: Simon & Schuster. 4–8 yrs.

———. 1996. *Little Cloud.* New York: Philomel. 4–8 yrs.

Crimi, Carolyn. 1995. *Outside, Inside.* Illus. Linnea Asplind Riley. New York: Simon & Schuster. 6–9 yrs.

Dorros, Arthur. 1991. *Abuela.* Illus. Elisa Kleven. New York: Dutton. 6–9 yrs.

———. 1995. *Isla.* Illus. Elisa Kleven. New York: Dutton. 6–9 yrs.

Ehlert, Lois. 1989. *Color Zoo.* New York: Lippincott. 3–5 yrs. Caldecott Honor Book, 1990.

———. 1992. *Circus.* New York: HarperCollins. 3–6 yrs.

———. 1995. *Mole Hill: A Woodland Tale.* San Diego, Calif.: Harcourt Brace. 6–9 yrs.

Feeling, Tom (Ed.). 1993. *Soul Looks Back in Wonder.* New York: Dial. 10–16 yrs.

Fleming, Denise. 1992. *Lunch.* New York: Holt. 3–6 yrs.

———. 1995. *Barnyard Banter.* New York: Holt. 6–9 yrs.

———. 1996. *Where Once There Was a Wood.* New York: Henry Holt. 4–7 yrs.

Frank, John. 1993. *Odds 'n' Ends Alvy.* Illus. G. Brian Karas. New York: Four Winds. 5–7 yrs.

Hall, Zoe. 1994. *It's Pumpkin Time!* Illus. Shari Halpern. New York: Scholastic/Blue Sky. 5–7 yrs.

Halsey, Megan. 1994. *Jump for Joy: A Book of Months.* New York: Bradbury. 5–8 yrs.

Johnson, Stephen. 1995. *Alphabet City.* Illus. Stephen Johnson. New York: Viking. 5–12 yrs.

Keats, Ezra Jack. 1964. *The Snowy Day.* Illus. E. J. Keats. New York: Viking. 4–8 yrs.

———. 1964. *Whistle for Willie.* Illus. E. J. Keats. New York: Viking. 4–8 yrs.

Lionni, Leo. 1962. *Inch by Inch.* New York: Astor-Honor. 4–7 yrs.

———. 1963. *Swimmy.* Illus. L. Lionni. New York: Knopf. 4–7 yrs.

———. 1967. *Frederick.* New York: Pantheon. 4–7 yrs.

———. 1995. *A Flea Story: I Want to Stay Here! I Want to Go There!* New York: Knopf. 6–10 yrs.

Martin, B. 1967. *Brown Bear, Brown Bear, What Do You See?* (Illus. E. Carle). New York: Holt.

Mullins, Patricia. 1994. *V for Vanishing: An Alphabet of Endangered Animals.* New York: HarperCollins. 5–10 yrs.

Riordan, J. 1995. *My G-r-r-reat Uncle Tiger.* Illus. Alex Ayliffe. Atlanta, Ga.: Peachtree. 5–8 yrs.

Roth, Susan L. 1993. *Princess.* New York: Hyperion. 5–7 yrs.

Schneider, Elisa. 1988. *The Merry-Go-Round Dog.* Illus. E. Schneider. New York: Knopf. 4–7 yrs.

Stow, J. 1995. *Growing Pains.* Mahwah, N.J.: BridgeWater. 5–8 yrs. Textured, childlike.

Sykes, J. 1996. *This and That.* Illus. Tanya Linch. New York: Farrar, Straus & Giroux. 2–5 yrs. Torn and painted paper.

Walsh, Ellen. 1994. *Stoll Pip's Magic.* San Diego, Calif.: Harcourt Brace. 5–7 yrs.

———. 1996. *Samantha.* San Diego, Calif.: Harcourt Brace. 4–6 yrs. Cut-paper mice.

Woodcut/Engraving and Linocut

Andersen, Hans Christian. (Trans. Carl Malmerg). 1964. *The Steadfast Tin Soldier.* Illus. Robert M. Quackenbush. New York: Holt, Rinehart & Winston. 7–10 yrs.

Brown, M. 1961. *Once a Mouse.* Illus. M. Brown. New York: Scribners. 6–9 yrs.

Emberley, Barbara. 1967. *Drummer Hoff.* Illus. Ed Emberley. Englewood Cliffs, N.J.: Prentice-Hall. 5–9 yrs.

Geisert, Arthur. 1986. *Pigs from A to Z.* Boston: Houghton Mifflin. 8–12 yrs.

Grimm, J. & W. Grimm. (Trans. Werner Linz). 1964. *Little Red-Cap.* Illus. Susan Blair. New York: Holt, Rinehart & Winston. 7–11 yrs.

MacLachlan, Patricia. 1995. *What You Know First.* Illus. Barry Moser. New York: HarperCollins/Cotler. 7–10 yrs. Wood engravings, some color.

Oliver, N. 1995. *The Best Beak in Boonaroo Bay.* Golden, Colo.: Fulcrum. 7–10 yrs. Hand-colored linocuts; informational story book.

Osborne, Mary Pope. 1991. *American Tall Tales.* Illus. Michael McCurdy. New York: Knopf. 10–13 yrs.

Reich, Janet. 1993. *Gus and the Green Thing.* New York: Walker. 4–6 yrs.

Tejima, Keizaburo. 1987. *Fox's Dream.* New York: Philomel. 6–9 yrs.

———. 1987. *Owl Lake.* New York: Philomel. 6–9 yrs.

———. 1988. *Swan Sky.* New York: Philomel. 6–9 yrs.

Wolff, Ashley. 1984. *A Year of Birds.* New York: Dutton. 6–9 yrs.

———. 1989. *A Year of Beasts.* New York: Dutton. 6–9 yrs.

———. 1993. *Stella and Roy.* New York: Dutton. 4–6 yrs.

Wormell, Mary. 1994. *Hilda Hen's Search.* San Diego, Calif.: Harcourt Brace. 5–7 yrs.

———. 1995. *Hilda Hen's Happy Birthday.* San Diego, Calif.: Harcourt Brace. 4–8 yrs.

Scratchboard

Cooney, B. 1958. *Chanticleer and the Fox.* Illus. B. Cooney. New York: Crowell. 7–10 yrs.

Jabar, Cythina (Illus.). 1996. *The Frog Who Wanted to Be a Singer.* New York: Kroupa/Orchard. 4–7 yrs.

Hall, Donald. 1994. *Lucy's Christmas.* Illus. Michael McCurdy. Browndeer. 5–8 yrs.

_____. 1995. *Lucy's Summer*. Illus. Michael McCurdy. San Diego: Harcourt Brace/Browndeer. 8–11 yrs.

San Souci, Robert D. 1992. *Sukey and the Mermaid*. Illus. Brian Pinkney. 10–13 yrs.

_____. 1995. *The Faithful Friend*. New York: Simon & Schuster. 10–14 yrs.

Schur, Maxine. 1994. *Rose Day of Delight: A Jewish Sabbath in Ethiopia*. Illus. Brian Pinkney. New York: Dial. 7–9 yrs.

Sierra, J. 1992. *The Elephant's Wrestling Match*. Illus. Brian Pinkney. New York: Lodestar. 5–8 yrs.

Soto, G. 1995. *Chato's Kitchen*. Illus. Susan Guevara. New York: Putnam. 6–10 yrs.

Thomas, S. M. 1995. *Putting the World to Sleep*. Illus. Bonnie Christensen. Boston: Houghton Mifflin. 4–8 yrs. With watercolors.

Walton, Rick. 1993. How Many, How Many, How Many. Illus. Cynthia Jabar. Cambridge, Mass.: Candlewick. 3–6 yrs.

Photography and Photo Essays

Anderson, J. 1996. *Cowboys: Roundup on an American Ranch*. Photos. George Ancona. New York: Scholastic. 9–12 yrs.

Asch, Frank. 1996. *Sawgrass Poems: A View of the Everglades*. Color photos Ted Levin. San Diego, Calif.: Harcourt Brace. 9–12 yrs.

Bunnett, R. 1993. *Friends in the Park*. Photos Carl Sahlhoff. New York: Checkerboard. 3–6 yrs.

Crews, Nina. 1996. *I'll Catch the Moon*. Illus. N. Crews. New York: Greenwillow. 4–7 yrs. Photocollage.

Davis, L. 1994. *P. B. Bear's Birthday Party*. Photos. New York: Dorling Kindersley. 4–6 yrs.

Freedman, Russell. 1980. *Immigrant Kids*. New York: Dutton. 10–13 yrs.

_____. 1988. *Buffalo Hunt*. Photos & paintings. New York: Holiday. 10–17 yrs.

Hautzig, David. 1996. *Pedal Power: How a Mountain Bike is Made*. Photos. New York: Lodestar. 9–12 yrs.

Hoban, Tana. 1995. *Animal, Vegetable, or Mineral?* New York: Greenwillow. 4–7 yrs.

_____. 1996. *Just Look*. Photos. New York: Greenwillow. 3–6 yrs.

Isaacson, P. M. 1995. *Round Buildings, Square Buildings, and Buildings That Wiggle Like a Fish*. Color photos. New York: Knopf. 9–12 yrs.

Korab, Balthazar. 1985. *Archabet: An Architectural Alphabet*. Photos. Washington, D.C.: Preservation Press. 6–12 yrs.

Krementz, Jill. 1978. *The Very Young Gymnast*. Photos. J. Krementz. New York: Knopf. 10–13 yrs. (See also other books in series.)

Levi, Steven C. 1996. *Cowboys of the Sky: The Story of Alaska's Bush Pilots*. Photos. New York: Walker. 12–16 yrs.

Lillie, Patricia. 1993. *When This Box Is Full*. Illus. Donald Crews. New York: Greenwillow. 5–7 yrs.

Maass, R. 1993. *When Summer Comes*. New York: Holt. 6–8 yrs.

_____. 1993. *When Winter Comes*. New York: Holt. 6–8 yrs.

Magee, Doug & Robert Newman. 1992. *Let's Fly from A to Z*. Photos D. Magee & R. Newman. New York: Cobblehill. 8–12 yrs.

Mayer, Walter Dean. 1993. *Brown Angels: An Album of Pictures and Verse*. Photos. New York: HarperCollins. 9–12 yrs.

McMillan, B. 1993. *Mouse Views: What the Class Pet Saw*. New York: Holiday. 5–7 yrs.

Miller, M. 1993. *Can You Guess?* Color photos. New York: Greenwillow. 4–6 yrs.

_____. 1996. *Now I'm Big*. Photos. New York: Greenwillow. 4–6 yrs.

Morris, A. 1995. *Weddings*. Photos. New York: Lothrop, Lee & Shepard. 3–6 yrs.

Rotner, S. & K. Kreisler. 1993. *Ocean Day*. Color photos Shelley Rotner. New York: Macmillan. 4–8 yrs.

_____. 1994. *Citybook*. Photos. New York: Orchard. 7–10 yrs.

Simon, S. 1994. *Comets, Meteors, and Asteroids*. Colored photos. New York: Harper. 9–12 yrs.

Waters, K. *The Mysterious Horseman: An Adventure in Prairietown, 1836*. Photos Marjory Dressler. New York: Scholastic. 6–9 yrs.

Wegman, William. 1994. *ABC*. Photos. New York: Hyperion. 7–10 yrs. (See also: *Cinderella; Little Red Riding Hood*.)

Wexler, Jerome. 1995. *Everyday Mysteries*. Photos. New York: Dutton. 7–10 yrs.

Zolotow, C. 1993. *The Moon Was the Best*. Photos Tana Hoban. New York: Greenwillow. 6–9 yrs.

ARTISTIC STYLES

Realistic Art

Bang, Molly. 1983. *Dawn*. Illus. M. Bang. New York: Morrow. 5–8 yrs.

Bates, Artie Ann. 1995. *Ragsale*. Illus. Jeff Chapman-Crane. Boston: Houghton Mifflin. 7–10 yrs.

Brown, Margaret Wise. 1996. *A Child's Good Morning Book*. Illus. Jean Charlot. New York: HarperCollins. 4–7 yrs.

Bunting, Eve. 1989. *The Wednesday Surprise*. Illus. Donald Carrick. New York: Clarion/Houghton. 6–9 yrs.

_____. 1994. *Sunshine Home*. Illus. Diane de Groat. New York: Clarion. 4–7 yrs.

Clark, Ann Nolan (Reteller). 1979. *In the Land of the Small Dragon*. Illus. Tony Chen. New York: Viking. 4–9 yrs.

Cooney, Barbara. 1982. *Miss Rumphius*. New York: Viking. 7–10 yrs.

Cauley, Lorinda Bryan. 1988. *The Trouble with Tyrannosaurus Rex*. Illus. L. B. Cauley. San Diego, Calif.: Harcourt, Brace, Jovanovich. 6–10 yrs.

Dyer, J. 1996. *Animal Cracker*. Boston, Mass.: Little Brown. 5–9 yrs.

Friedrich, Elizabeth. 1996. *Leah's Pony*. Illus. Michael Garland. Honesdale, Penn.: Boyds Mills. 10–12 yrs.

George, Lindsay Barrett. 1987. *William and Boomer*. Illus. L. B. George. New York: Greenwillow. 4–7 yrs.

Hakkinen, Anita. 1995. *Summer Legs*. Illus. Abby Carter. New York: Holt. 5–9 yrs.

Hoban, Russell. 1960. *Bedtime for Frances*. Illus. Garth Williams. New York: HarperCollins. 4–6 yrs.

Isadora, Rachel. 1988. *The Pirates of Bedford Street*. Illus. R. Isadora. New York: Greenwillow. 5–8 yrs.

Kimmel, Eric. 1989. *Hershel and the Hanukkah Goblins*. Illus. Trina Schart Hyman. New York: Holiday. 6–9 yrs.

Krudop, Walter Lyon. 1993. *Blue Claws*. New York: Atheneum. 5–8 yrs.

Loh, Morag. 1987. *Tucking Mommy In*. Illus. Donna Rawlins. New York: Orchard. 5–8 yrs.

MacLachlan, Patricia. 1994. *All the Places to Love*. Illus. Mike Wimmer. New York: HarperCollins. 5–8 yrs.

Pearson, Susan. 1987. *Happy Birthday, Grampa*. Illus. Ronald Himler. New York: Dial. 5–9 yrs.

Perkins, L. R. 1995. *Home Lovely*. New York: Greenwillow. 7–10 yrs.

Say, Allen. 1993. *Grandfather's Journey*. Boston: Houghton Mifflin. 9–12 yrs.

Schoenherr, J. 1995. *Rebel*. New York: Philomel. 6–9 yrs. Watercolor; informational story book.

Vainio, P. (Trans. Anthea Bell). 1995. *The Christmas Angel*. New York: North-South. 6–9 yrs.

Vyner, Sue. 1995. *Swim for Cover!: Adventure on the Coral Reef*. Illus. Tim Vyner. New York: Crown. 6–10 yrs.

Weidt, M. 1995. *Daddy Played Music for the Cows*. Illus. Henri Sorensen. New York: Lothrop, Lee & Shepard. 7–10 yrs.

Yolen, Jane. 1987. *Owl Moon*. Illus. John Schoenherr. New York: Putnam. 7–11 yrs.

Expressionistic

Ackerman, Karen. 1988. *Song and Dance Man*. Illus. Stephen Gammell. New York: Knopf. 5–9 yrs.

Armstrong, Jennifer. 1994. *The Whittler's Tale*. Illus. Valery Vasiliev. New York: Tambourine. 6–8 yrs.

Bartone, Elisa. 1993. *Peppe the Lamplighter*. Illus. Ted Lewin. New York: Lothrop, Lee & Shepard. 7–10 yrs.

Bemelmans, Ludwig. 1939. *Madeline*. Illus. L. Bemelmans. New York: Viking. 5–8 yrs.

Bouchard, David. 1995. *If You're Not from the Prairie*. Images Henry Ripplinger. New York: Atheneum. 8–12 yrs.

Burningham, John. 1994. *Cannonball Simp*. Cambridge, Mass.: Candlewick. 5–7 yrs.

Bunting, Eve. 1993. *Someday a Tree*. Illus. Ronald Himler. New York: Clarion. 5–8 yrs.

de Paolo, T. 1975. *Strega Nona*. New York: Simon & Schuster. 5–9 yrs. Stylized.

_____. 1996. *The Baby Sister*. New York: Putnam. 5–9 yrs.

DeFelice, Cynthia. 1994. *Mule Eggs*. Illus. Mike Shenon. New York: Orchard/Jackson. 6–8 yrs.

Demarest, Chris L. 1995. *My Blue Boat*. San Diego, Calif.: Harcourt Brace. 5–9 yrs.

Doro, A. 1996. *Twin Pickle*. Illus. Clare Mackie. New York: Holt/Martin. 5–8 yrs.

Erdrich, L. 1996. *Grandmother's Pigeon*. Illus. Jim La Marche. New York: Hyperion. 7–9 yrs.

Foreman, Michael. 1974. *War and Peas*. Illus. M. Foreman. New York: Crowell. 8–14 yrs.

Giovanni, Nikki. 1996. *The Genie in the Jar*. Illus. by Chris Raschka. New York: Henry Holt. 8–11 yrs.

Hastings, Selina (Reteller). 1988. *The Man Who Wanted to Live Forever*. Illus. Reg Cartwright. New York: Holt. 7–10 yrs.

MacDonald, Amy. 1996. *The Spider Who Created the World*. Illus. G. Brian Karas. New York: Orchard Books. 7–9 yrs.

Matthews, Andrew. 1993. *Crackling Brat*. Illus. Tomek Bogacki. New York: Holt. 6–8 yrs.

Nodset, Joan L. 1993. *Go Away, Dog*. Illus. Crosby Bonsall. New York: HarperCollins. 4–6 yrs.

Nolen, Jerdine. 1994. *Harvey Potter's Balloon Farm*. Illus. Mark Buehner. New York: Lothrop, Lee & Shepard. 5–8 yrs.

Rayner, Mary. 1993. *Garth Pig Steals the Show*. New York: Dutton. 5–7 yrs.

Scieszka, Jon. 1994. *The Book That Jack Wrote*. Illus. Daniel Adel. New York: Viking. 7–11 yrs.

Shange, Ntozake. 1994. *I Live in Music*. Illus. Romare Bearden. New York: Stewart, Tabori & Chang. 12–16 yrs.

Spohn, Kate. 1994. *Broken Umbrellas*. New York: Viking. 7–9 yrs.

Wittmann, Patricia. 1993. *Scrabble Creek*. Illus. Nancy Poydar. New York: Macmillan. 5–7 yrs.

Waddell, Martin. 1992. *Owl Babies*. Illus. Patrick Benson. Cambridge, Mass.: Candlewick. 6–9 yrs.

Walter, Mildred Pitt. 1995. *Darkness*. Illus. Marcia Jameston. New York: Simon & Schuster. 9–12 yrs.

Wildsmith, Brian. 1964. *The North Wind and the Sun*. Danbury, Conn.: Watts. 9–12 yrs.

Yashima, Taro. 1967. *Seashore Story*. Illus. T. Yashima. New York: Viking. 7–10.

Impressionistic

Alexander, S. 1992. *Hobart Maggie's Whopper*. Illus. Deborah Kogan Ray. New York: Macmillan. 6–9 yrs.

Bunting, Eve. 1994. *Night of the Gargoyles*. Illus. David Wiesner. New York: Clarion. 10–14 yrs.

Carlstrom, Nancy White. 1993. *How Does the Wind Walk?* Illus. Deborah Kogan Ray. New York: Macmillan. 5–9 yrs.

Howard, E. F. 1993. *Mac and Marie and the Train Toss Surprise*. Illus. Gail Gordon Carter. New York: Four Winds. 6–9 yrs.

Howe, James. 1987. *I Wish I Were a Butterfly*. Illus. Ed Young. San Diego: Harcourt Brace. 8–11 yrs.

Kiser, SuAnn. 1993. *The Catspring Somersault Flying One-Handed Flip-Flop*. Illus. Peter Catalanotto. New York: Orchard/Jackson. 5–7 yrs.

Krudop, Walter Lyon. 1995. *Something Is Growing*. New York: Atheneum. 5–9 yrs.

Lyon, G. E. 1992. *Who Came Down That Road?* Illus. Peter Catalanotto. New York: Orchard/Jackson. 6–9 yrs.

McCully, Emily Arnold. 1992. *Mirette on the Highwire*. Illus. E. A. McCully. New York: Putnam. 7–11 yrs.

———. 1993. *The Amazing Felix*. New York: Putnam. 6–8 yrs.

———. 1995. *The Pirate Queen*. New York: Putnam. 9–12 yrs.

McKissack, P. C. 1992. *A Million Fish . . . More or Less*. Illus. Dena Schutzer. New York: Knopf. 7–10 yrs.

Paulsen, Gary. 1995. *The Tortilla Factory*. Illus. Ruth Wright Paulsen. San Diego, Calif.: Harcourt Brace. 5–8 yrs.

Seymour, Tres. 1993. *Pole Dog*. Illus. David Soman. New York: Orchard/Jackson. 6–9 yrs.

Widerberg, Siv. (Trans. Tiina Nunnally). 1993. *Suddenly One Day*. Illus. Anna Walfridson. New York: Farrar, Straus & Giroux. 5–7 yrs.

Folk Art (Naive)

(See also Chapter 9 for additional examples representing parallel cultures)

Atkins, Jeannine. 1995. *Aani and the Tree Huggers*. Illus. Venantius J. Pinto. New York: Lee & Low. 7–10 yrs.

Begay, Shanto (Ed.). 1995. *Navajo: Visions and Voices across the Mesa*. Illus. Shanto Begay. New York: Scholastic. 10–16 yrs.

Bruchac, J. 1995. *The Earth Under Sky Bear's Feet: Native American Poems of the Land*. Illus. Thomas Locker. New York: Philomel. 10–16 yrs.

Carlstrom, Nancy White. 1993. *How Does the Wind Walk?* Illus. Deborah Kogan Ray. New York: Macmillan. 5–9 yrs.

Chocolate, Debbie. 1996. *Kente Cloth*. Illus. John Ward. New York: Walker & Co. 6–9 yrs.

Clements, Andrew. 1995. *Who Owns the Cow?* Illus. Joan Landis. New York: Clarion. 5–8 yrs.

French, V. 1995. *Oliver's Vegetables*. Illus. Alison Bartlett. New York: Orchard. 5–8 yrs.

Gag, Wanda. 1928. *Millions of Cats.*. New York. Coward-McCann. 4–8 yrs.

Goble, Paul. 1978. *The Girl Who Loved Wild Horses*. New York: Bradbury. 6–9 yrs.

Hall, Donald. 1979. *Ox-Cart Man*. Illus. Barbara Cooney. New York: Viking. 5–9 yrs.

Howard, Kim. 1994. *In Wintertime*. New York: Lothrop, Lee & Shepard. 5–7 yrs.

Imai, Miko. 1994. *Little Lumpty*. Cambridge, Mass.: Candlewick. 4–7 yrs.

Lewis, Paul Own. 1995. *Storm Boy*. Hillsboro, Ore.: Beyond Words Pub. Co. 7–9 yrs.

Mathers, P. 1995. *Kisses from Rosa*. New York: Apple Soup. 6–9 yrs.

Mayer, M. 1995. *Turandot*. Illus. Winslow Pels. New York: Morrow. 7–10 yrs.

Merrill, Jean (Adapter). 1992. *The Girl Who Loved Caterpillars: A Twelfth-Century Tale from Japan*. Illus. Floyd Cooper. New York: Philomel. 7–11 yrs.

Philip, Neil (Ed.). 1995. *Songs Are Thoughts: Poems of the Inuit*. Illus. Maryclare Foa. New York: Orchard. 10–12 yrs.

Polacco, Patricia. 1992. *Chicken Sunday*. New York: Philomel. 7–10 yrs.

Rahaman, V. 1996. *O Christmas Tree*. Illus. Frane Lessac. Honesdale, Penn.: Boyds Mills. 6–9 yrs. Naive.

Ray, Mary Lyn. 1994. *Shaker Boy*. Illus. Jeanette Winter. San Diego: Harcourt Brace/Browndeer. 7–9 yrs.

Young, Ed. 1989. *Lon Po Po: A Red-Riding Hood Story from China*. New York: Philomel. 6–11 yrs.

Humorous

Ahlberg, Jan & Allan Ahlberg. 1986. *The Jolly Postman*. Illus. Authors. Boston: Little, Brown. 5–9 yrs.

Burningham, J. 1996. *The Shopping Basket*. Cambridge, Mass.: Candlewick. 5–8 yrs.

Denton, Kady MacDonald. 1995. *Would They Love a Lion?* Illus. K. M. Denton. Kingfisher. 5–9 yrs.

de Paola, Tomie. 1993. *Strega Nona Meets Her Match*. Illus. T. de Paola. New York: Putnam. 5–8 yrs.

Dr. Suess [Geisel, Ted]. 1937. *And to Think that I Saw It on Mulberry Street*. Illus. T. Geisel. Hale. 6–9 yrs.

Glaser, Linda. 1993. *Stop That Garbage Truck!* Illus. Karen Lee Schmidt. Morton Grove, Ill.: Whitman. 4–7 yrs.

Ericsson, Jennifer A. 1993. *No Milk!* Illus. Ora Eitan. New York: Tambourine. 3–6 yrs.

Grossman, Bill. 1995. *The Banging Book*. Illus. Robert Zimmerman. New York: HarperCollins/Geringer. 5–9 yrs.

Hafner, M. 1995. *Mommies Don't Get Sick!* Cambridge, Mass.: Candlewick. 5–9 yrs.

Hardy, T. 1996. *Lost Cat*. Illus. David Goldin. Boston: Houghton Mifflin. 6–9 yrs.

Hassett, John & Ann Hassett. 1993. *Junior: A Little Loon Tale*. Illus. John Hassett. Camden, Maine: Down East. 6–8 yrs.

Holleyman, Sonia. 1993. *Mona the Brilliant*. New York: Doubleday. 5–7 yrs.

Johnson, Crockett. 1963. *Harold's A.B.C.* Illus. C. Johnson. New York: HarperCollins. 3–7 yrs.

Karms, D. (Trans. Richard Pevear). 1996. *First, Second*. Illus. Marc Rosenthal. New York: Farrar, Straus & Giroux. 5–8 yrs.

Kitamura, S. 1996. *Sheep in Wolves' Clothing*. New York: Farrar, Straus & Giroux. 6–9 yrs.

Koscielniak, B. 1995. *Geoffrey Groundhog Predicts the Weather*. Boston: Houghton Mifflin. 6–9 yrs.

Loomis, Christine. 1994. *We're Going on a Trip*. Illus. Maxie Chambliss. New York: Morrow. 5–7 yrs.

Luttrell, Ida. 1993. *Mattie's Little Possum Pet*. Illus. Betsy Lewin. New York: Atheneum. 5–7 yrs.

Martin, Jane Read & Patricia Marx. 1993. *Now Everybody Really Hates Me*. Illus. Roz Chast. New York: HarperCollins. 5–7 yrs.

Meddaugh, S. 1996. *Martha Blah Blah*. Boston: Houghton Mifflin. 6–9 yrs.

Moss, Lloyd. 1995. *Zin Zin a Violin*. Illus. Marjorie Priceman. New York: Simon & Schuster. 7–10 yrs.

Nolen, J. 1994. *Harvey Potter's Balloon Farm*. Illus. Mark Buehner. New York: Lothrop, Lee & Shepard. 5–8 yrs.

Petach, H. 1995. *Goldilocks and the Three Hares*. New York: Putnam. 7–10 yrs.

Palatini, M. 1995. *Piggie Pie!* Illus. Howard Fine. New York: Clarion. 5–9 yrs.

Raschka, C. 1995. *Can't Sleep*. New York: Orchard/Jackson. 4–7 yrs.

Rathmann, Peggy. 1995. *Officer Buckle & Gloria*. New York: Putnam. 7–10 yrs.

Schubert, Ingrid & Dieter Schubert. 1994. *Wild Will*. Minneapolis, Minn.: Carolrhoda. 5–7 yrs.

Shields, Carol Diggory. 1993. *I Am Really a Princess*. Illus. Paul Meisel. New York: Dutton. 4–6 yrs.

Shipton, J. 1995. *No Biting, Horrible Crocodile!* Racine, Wis.: Artists. 3–6 yrs.

Silver, N. 1995. *Cloud Nine*. Illus. Jan Ormerod. New York: Clarion. 4–7 yrs.

Simon, Francesca. *The Topsy-Turvies*. Illus. Keren Ludlow. New York: Dial. 4–7 yrs.

Steig, W. 1996. *The Toy Brother*. New York: di Capua. 5–7 yrs.

Stevenson, J. 1995. *The Worst Goes South*. New York: Greenwillow. 5–9 yrs.

Wild, Margaret. 1994. *Our Granny*. Illus. Julie Vivas. New York: Ticknor & Fields. 6–8 yrs.

Wolff, Ferida. 1993. *Seven Loaves of Bread*. Illus. Katie Keller. New York: Tambourine. 6–8 yrs.

Artistic Elements

Aesop's Fables. Illus. Lisbeth Zwerger. 1989. Saxonville, Mass.: Picture Book Studio. 8–12 yrs. Space; arrangement; perspective.

Biggs, R. 1995. *The Man*. New York: Random House. 8–11 yrs. Arrangement; cartoons.

Bottner, B. 1995. *Hurricane Music*. Illus. Paul Yalowitz. New York: Putnam. 6–9 yrs. Soft colors, rounded shapes.

Brown, M. W. 1995. *Little Donkey Close Your Eyes*. Illus. Ashley Wolff. New York: HarperCollins. 5–9 yrs. Strong outlines, rich color, texture.

Caseley, J. 1995. *Mr. Green Peas*. New York: Greenwillow. 5–9 yrs. Folk art; vivid color; patterns.

Cooper, H. 1996. *Little Monster Did It!* Illus. Helen Cooper. New York: Dial. 4–6 yrs.

Ehlert, L. 1995. *Snowballs*. San Diego, Calif.: Harcourt Brace. 6–9 yrs. Space, paper cutouts, well-designed.

Grover, M. 1996. *Circles & Squares Everywhere*. San Diego, Calif.: Harcourt, Brace/Browndeer Press. 4–8 yrs. Geometric shapes; bold color; native art.

Ingman, B. 1995. *When Martha's Away*. Boston: Houghton Mifflin. 6–9 yrs. Large, spacious illustrations; line drawings, simple shapes, and bright textured colors.

McGuire, R. 1995. *What Goes Around Comes Around*. New York: Viking. 6–9 yrs. Line & shape.

McLerran, A. 1996. *The Year of the Ranch*. Illus. Kimberly Bulcken Root. New York: Viking. 6–9 yrs. Varied shapes; placement across pages; watercolor & pencil.

Namioka, L. (Reteller). 1995. *The Loyal Cat*. Illus. Aki Sogabe. San Diego, Calif.: Browndeer. 7–10 yrs. Watercolor; airbrush; lines; texture.

Noll, S. 1994. *Lucky Morning*. New York: Greenwillow. 5–7 yrs. Shapes, large typeface.

Owen, R. *The Ibis and the Egret*. Illus. Robert Sabuda. New York: Philomel. 6–8 yrs. Lines and varied perspectives.

Pilkey, D. 1996. *The Paperboy*. New York: Orchard/Jackson. 7–10 yrs. Balance; geometric shapes.

Platt, R. 1992. *Stephen Biesty's Incredible Cross-Sections.* Illus. Stephen Biesty. New York: Borzoi/Knopf. 9–16 yrs. Detailed.

Purdy, Carol. 1985. *Iva Dunnit and the Big Wind.* Illus. Steven Kellogg. New York: Dial. 9–12 yrs. Lines & details.

Walsh, J. P. 1996. *Connie Came to Play.* Illus. Stephen Lambert. New York: Viking. 3–6 yrs. Simple figures against white background.

Yaccarino, D. 1996. *If I Had a Robot.* New York: Viking. 5–8 yrs. Geometric shapes; robot morphs from shape to shape, color to color.

PHYSICAL ELEMENTS OF BOOKS

Appelt, K. 1995. *Bayou Lullaby.* Illus. Neil Waldman. New York: Morrow. 4–8 yrs. White type on black page.

Glass, A. 1995. *Folks Call Me Appleseed John.* New York: Doubleday. 6–9 yrs. Map on endpapers.

Heller, Catherine. 1995. *Snow White.* Illus. Karen Stolper. New York: Carol/Birch Lane. 3–6 yrs. Upside Down tale: one side Snow White's story; other side Stepmother's story.

Howard, A. 1996. *When I Was Five.* San Diego, Calif.: Harcourt Brace. 4–6 yrs. Handwritten text; mixed-media.

Isaacs, A. *Swamp Angel.* New York: Dutton. 9–12 yrs. Oils on veneer; wood borders.

Jackson, E. 1995. *The Impossible Riddle.* Illus. Alison Winfield. Danvers, Mass.: Whispering Coyote. 6–9 yrs. Borders.

Johnston, T. 1994. *The Old Lady and the Birds.* Illus. Stephanie Garcia. San Diego, Calif.: Harcourt Brace. 5–8 yrs. Framed; texture; large type; white space.

Kirk, D. 1994. *Miss Spider's Tea Party.* New York: Scholastic. 5–9 yrs. Hand print; endpapers.

Kroll, V. 1993. *Naomi Knows It's Springtime.* Illus. Jill Kastner. Honesdale, Penn.: Boyds Mills/Caroline. 6–9 yrs. Unconventional typeface.

Oberman, S. 1995. *The White Stone in the Castle Wall.* Illus. Les Tait. Plattsburgh, N.Y.: Tundra. Map on endpapers; informational story book.

Titherington, J. 1995. *Sophy and Auntie Pearl.* New York: Greenwillow. 6–9 yrs. Large bold black type; hidden image of an angel on each page.

Truus. 1993. *What Kouka Knows.* New York: Lothrop, Lee & Shepard. 4–6 yrs. Bold shapes and patterns.

Vagin, V. & F. Asch. 1995. *Insects from Outer Space.* New York: Scholastic. 7–10 yrs. Border.

Van Laan, N. 1995. *Sleep, Sleep, Sleep: A Lullaby for Little Ones around the World.* Illus. Holly Meade. Boston, Mass.: Boston: Little, Brown. 3–7 yrs. Collage; endpaper stylized map of continents.

Book Design

Appelt, Kathi. 1995. *Bayou Lullaby.* Illus. Neil Waldman. New York: Morrow. 4–8 yrs. White type on black page.

Bottner, Barbara. 1995. *Hurricane Music.* Illus. Paul Yalowitz. New York: Putnam. 6–9 yrs. Rounded shapes.

Brett, Jan. 1995. *Armadillo Rodeo.* New York: Putnam & Grossett. 9–12 yrs. Border.

Briggs, Raymond. 1995. *The Man.* Illus. R. Briggs. New York: Random House. 8–11 yrs. Panels; cartoon balloons.

Brown, Marc. 1995. *D. W. the Picky Eater.* Boston: Little, Brown. 5–9 yrs. Unity text & visuals.

Caseley, Judith. 1995. *Mr. Green Peas.* New York: Greenwillow. 5–9 yrs. Preschool & folk art; patterns.

Demi. 1996. *Buddha.* Illus. Demi. New York: Henry Holt. 10–12 yrs. Small & large pictures blend; balance visual & verbal text.

Geisert, Bonnie & Arthur Geisert. 1995. *Haystack.* Boston: Houghton Mifflin. 9–12 yrs. Etchings; lines.

Grover, Max. 1996. *Circles & Squares Everywhere.* San Diego: Harcourt Brace/Browndeer. 4–8 yrs. Naive geometric shapes.

Heller, Catherine. 1995. *Snow White.* Illus. Karen Stolper. New York: Carol/Birch Lane. 3–6 yrs. Upside Down Book.

Hodges, Margaret (Adapter). 1984. *Saint George and the Dragon.* Illus. Trina Schart Hyman. Boston: Little, Brown. 10–13 yrs. Border. (Adapted from *Faerie Queene*.)

Isaacs, Anne. 1994. *Swamp Angel.* New York: Dutton. 9–12 yrs. Oil on wood; borders.

Johnston, Tony. 1994. *The Old Lady and the Birds.* Illus. Stephanie Garcia. San Diego: Harcourt Brace. 5–8 yrs. Texture, large type space; borders.

Kirk, David. 1994. *Miss Spider's Tea Party.* New York: Scholastic. 5–9 yrs. Hand print; endpapers.

———. 1995. *Miss Spider's Wedding.* New York: Scholastic. 6–9 yrs.

Owen, Roy. 1993. *The Ibis and the Egret.* Illus. Robert Sabuda. New York: Philomel. 6–8 yrs. Perspectives.

Provensen, Alice. 1995. *My Fellow Americans: A Family Album.* San Diego, Calif.: Harcourt Brace. 8–14 yrs. Large book; endpapers; visual arrangement.

Platt, Richard. 1992. *Stephen Biesty's Incredible Cross-Sections.* Illus. Stephen Biesty. New York: Borzoi/Knopf. 8–14 yrs. Detailed drawings; paper engineering.

Poltarnees, Welleran (Adapter). 1994. *Martin and Tommy.* Illus. M. Krestjanoff. New York: Green Tiger. 5–7 yrs. Overall design.

Porte, Barbara. 1995. *Chickens! Chickens!* New York: Orchard. 6–10 yrs. Arrangement; shapes.

Purdy, Carol. 1985. *Iva Dunnit and the Big Wind.* Illus. Steven Kellogg. New York: Dial. 9–12 yrs. Detailed lines & wind.

Root, Phyllis. 1996. *Aunt Nancy and Old Man Trouble.* Illus. David Parkins. Cambridge, Mass.: Candlewick. 5–7 yrs. Monochrome silhouettes; watercolor.

Scieszka, Jon. 1992. *The Stinky Cheese Man and Other Fairly Stupid Tales.* Illus. Lane Smith. New York: Viking. 7–12 yrs. Unique design.

Truus. 1993. *What Kouka Knows.* New York: Lothrop, Lee & Shepard. 4–6 yrs. Bold shapes; limited color; arrangement.

Vagin, V. & Frank Asch. 1995. *Insects from Outer Space.* New York: Scholastic. 6–9 yrs. Border; pictures & text inside frames; busy.

Willard, Nancy. 1991. *Pish Posh, Said Hieronymus Bosch.* Illus. Lee, Leo, & Diane Dillon. San Diego, Calif.: Harcourt Brace. 8–12 yrs. Pictures inside sculptured picture frame; hand lettering.

VARIOUS TYPES OF BOOKS WITH PICTURES

Informational Storybooks

(See also Chapter 6 bibliography for specific topics)

Adler, D. A. 1995. *One Yellow Daffodil: A Hanukkah Story.* Illus. Lloyd Bloom. San Diego, Calif.: Gulliver.

Agell, Charlotte. 1994. *I Slide into the White of Winter.* St. Paul, Minn.: Tilbury. 5–7 yrs.

———. 1994. *Wind Spins Me Around in the Fall.* St. Paul, Minn.: Tilbury. 5–7 yrs.

Brandenburg, Jim. (Joann Bren Guerney, Ed.) 1995. *An American Safari: Adventures on the North American Prairie.* New York: Walker. 9–12 yrs.

Carle, Eric. 1969. *The Very Hungry Caterpillar.* New York: Philomel. 4–8 yrs.

———. 1995. *The Very Lonely Firefly.* New York: Philomel. 4–8 yrs. (Fourth in series.)

Cole, Joanna. 1995. *My New Kitten.* Photos Margaret Miller. New York: Morrow. 5–9 yrs.

———. 1995. *The Magic School Bus Inside a Hurricane.* Illus. Bruce Degen. New York: Scholastic. 7–10 yrs.

Cooney, Nancy Evans. 1993. *Chatterbox Jamie.* Illus. Marylin Hafner. New York: Putnam. 2–4 yrs.

Fleming, D. 1993. *In the Small, Small Pond.* New York: Holt. 3–6 yrs.

———. 1996. *Where Once There Was a Wood.* New York: Henry Holt.

French, Vivian. 1995. *Spider Watching.* Illus. Alison Wisenfeld. Cambridge, Mass.: Candlewick. 6–9 yrs. Read and Wonder Series.

George, L. B. 1995. *In the Snow: Who's Been Here?* New York: Greenwillow. 6–9 yrs.

Lewin, Ted. 1993. *Amazon Boy.* Illus. T. Lewin. New York: Macmillan. 6–8 yrs.

Lewin, Betsy. 1995. *Booby Hatch.* Illus. B. Lewin. New York: Clarion. 6–10 yrs.

London, Jonathan. 1995. *Honey Paw and Lightfoot.* Illus. Jon Van Zyle. San Francisco: Chronicle. 6–9 yrs.

———. 1995. *Master Elk and the Mountain Lion.* Illus. Wayne McLoughlin. New York: Crown. 7–10 yrs. Information story book.

Lucas, Barbara M. 1993. *Snowed In.* Illus. Catherine Stock. New York: Bradbury. 7–9 yrs.

Martin, J. B. 1995. *Washing the Willow Tree Loon.* Illus. Nancy Carpenter. New York: Simon & Schuster. 7–10 yrs.

McMillan, B. 1995. *Grandfather's Trolley.* Hand-tinted photos. Cambridge, Mass.: Candlewick. 6–9 yrs. Photo essay.

Miller, M. 1996. *Now I'm Big.* Photos. New York: Greenwillow. 4–6 yrs.

Moss, L. 1995. *Zin! Zin! Zin! A Violin.* Illus. Marjorie Priceman. New York: Simon & Schuster. 6–9 yrs.

Penner, Lucille Recht. 1996. *Monster Bugs.* Illus. Pamela Johnson. New York: Random House. 1996. 6–9 yrs. Step into Reading.

Peters, L. 1995. *Westberg Meg and Dad Discover Treasure in the Air.* Illus. Deborah Durland DeSaix. New York: Holt. 7–10 yrs.

Ryder, Joanne. 1995. *Bears Out There.* Illus. Jo Ellen McAllister-Stammen. New York: Atheneum. 5–9 yrs.

Skofield, James. 1993. *Ground and Around.* Illus. James Graham Hale. New York: HarperCollins. 4–6 yrs.

Slawson, Michele Benoit. 1994. *Apple Picking Time.* Illus. Deborah Kogan Ray. New York: Crown. 5–7 yrs.

Stock, Catherine. 1993. *Where Are You Going Manyoni?* New York: Morrow. 6–8 yrs.

Wallner, Alexandra. 1996. *The First Air Voyage in the United States: The Story of Jean Pierre Blanchard.* Illus. Alexandra Wallner. New York: Holiday. 5–8 yrs.

Willis, Jeanne. 1993. *Earth Weather as Explained by Professor Xargle.* Illus. Tony Ross. New York: Dutton. 6–8 yrs.

VARIOUS CATEGORIES OF BOOKS WITH PICTURES

Board Books

Alexander, Martha. 1993. *Willy's Boot.* Cambridge, Mass.: Candlewick. 12 mo.–26 mo. (See also: *Lily and Willy; Where's Willy?;* and *Good Night, Lily.*)

Allen, Jonathan. 1992. *Big Owl, Little Towel.* New York: Tambourine. 18 mo.–3 yrs.

———. 1992. *One with a Bun.* New York: Tambourine. 18 mo.–3 yrs. (See also: *Purple*

Sock, Pink Sock; Up the Steps, Down the Slide.) Playful Board Books series.

Bond, Michael. 1992. *Paddington at the Seashore.* New York: HarperCollins. 1–4 yrs. (See also: *Paddington Goes Shopping; Paddington in the Kitchen; Paddington Takes a Bath.*)

Brown, M. 1996. *Arthur Goes to School.* New York: Random House. 3–5 yrs.

Cousins, Lucy. 1991. *Farm Animals.* New York: Tambourine. 12 mo.–26 mo. (See also: *Country Animals; Garden Animals; Pet Animals.*)

de Paola, Tomie. 1988. *Baby's First Christmas.* New York: Putnam. 1–2 yrs. (See also: *My First Chanukah; My First Passover; My First Easter; My First Halloween; My First Thanksgiving.*)

Dickens, Lucy. 1991. *Playtime.* New York: Viking. 12 mo.–26 mo.

Gellman, Ellie. 1985. *It's Rosh Hashanah!* Illus. Katherine Janus Kahn. Rockville, Md.: Kar-Ben. 1–2 yrs. (See also: *It's Chanukah!*)

Gomi, Taro. 1991. *Guess Who? A Peek-a-Boo Book.* San Francisco: Chronicle. 12 mo.–26 mo. (See also: *Guess What?* and *There's a Mouse in the House.*)

Greenaway, Elizabeth. 1994. *Cat Nap.* New York: Random House. 6 mo.–2 yrs.

Greenway, Shirley. 1992. *Color Me Bright.* Halesite, N.Y.: Whispering Coyote Press. 12 mo.–26 mo. (See also: *Here's Ears, A Tale of Tails,* and *Legs and All.*)

Groner, Judye & Madeline Wikler. 1991. *Let's Make Latkes.* Illus. Sally Springer. Rockville, Md.: Kar Ben. 18 mo.–26 mo.

Hathon, Elizabeth. 1993. *My Fuzzy Friends.* Photos E. Hathon. New York: Grosset. 3–6 yrs. Pudgy Board Book series. (See also: *Sleepy Time.*)

Hawkins, Colin & Jacqui Hawkins. 1992. *Hey Diddle Diddle.* Cambridge, Mass.: Candlewick. 12 mo.–26 mo. (See also: *Humpty Dumpty.*)

Hoban, Tana. 1985. *Panda, Panda.* New York: Greenwillow. 6 mo.–2 yrs.

_____. 1985. *What Is It?* New York: Greenwillow. 6 mo.–2 yrs.

Holabird, Katharine. 1992. *Christmas with Angelina.* Illus. Helen Craig. New York: Random House. 1–2 yrs.

Hudson, Cheryl Willis. 1992. *Good Morning Baby.* Illus. George Ford. New York: Scholastic. 6 mo.–2 yrs. (See also: *Good Night Baby.*)

Hughes, Fiona. 1993. *On the Farm: A Photographic Fares Book.* New York: Peter Bedrick. 1–3 yrs.

Inkpen, M. 1995. *Wibbly Pig Can Dance!* Racine, Wis.: Artists. 1–3 yrs.

_____. 1995. *Wibbly Pig Can Make a Tent.* Racine, Wis.: Artists. 1–3 yrs.

_____. 1995. *Wibbly Pig Is Upset.* Racine, Wis.: Artists. 1–3 yrs.

_____. 1995. *Wibbly Pig Likes Bananas.* Racine, Wis.: Artists. 1–3 yrs.

_____. 1995. *Wibbly Pig Makes Pictures.* Racine, Wis.: Artists. 1–3 yrs.

_____. 1995. *Wibbly Pig Opens His Presents.* Racine, Wis.: Artists. 1–3 yrs.

Johnson, Angela. 1994. *Joshua by the Sea.* New York: Orchard. 12 mo.–26 mo. (See also: *Mama Bird, Baby Birds, Joshua's Night Whispers,* and *Rain Feet.*)

Keats, E. J. 1996. *The Snowy Day.* New York: Viking. 3–6 yrs.

Lester, Alison. 1989. *Bibs and Boots.* New York: Viking. 12 mo.–26 mo. (See also: *Crashing and Splashing, Happy and Sad,* and *Bumping and Bouncing.*)

Leslie, Amanda. 1992. *Play Kitten Play: Ten Animal Fingerwiggles.* Cambridge, Mass.: Candlewick. 6 mo.–2 yrs.

Lewison, Wendy. 1993. *Happy Thanksgiving!* Illus. Mary Morgan. New York: Grosset. 1–2 yrs.

_____. 1993. *Christmas Cookies.* Illus. Mary Morgan. New York: Grosset. 1–2 yrs.

MacDonald, Amy. 1992. *Let's Play.* Illus. Maureen Roffey. Cambridge, Mass.: Candlewick. 6 mo.–2 yrs.

MacKinnon, Debbie. 1994. *Things to Cuddle.* Photos Geoff Dann. New York: Bantam. 12 mo.–26 mo.

Maris, Ron. 1992. *Ducks Quack.* Cambridge, Mass.: Candlewick. 6 mo.–2 yrs.

Morgan, Mary. 1989. *The Pudgy Merry Christmas Book.* New York: Grosset. 1–2 yrs.

_____. 1990. *Wee Seasons.* New York: Grosset. 12 mo.–26 mo.

_____. *On the Beach: What Can You Find?* 1993. New York: Dorling Kindersley. 12 mo.–26 mo. (See also: *Around the House, On the Farm,* and *In the Yard.*)

Oxenburg, Helen. 1995. *I Hear.* Cambridge, Mass.: Candlewick. 6 mo.–2 yrs. (See also: *I Can, I See,* and *I Touch.*)

Paterson, Bettina. 1992. *In My House.* New York: Holt. 1–2 yrs. (See also: *In My Yard, My Clothes, My Toys.*)

_____. 1993. *Busy Witch.* New York: Grosset. 1–2 yrs. (See also: *Scaredy-Ghost, Merry ABC.*)

Pragoff, Fiona. 1994. *Baby Days.* New York: Simon & Schuster. 6 mo.–2 yrs. (See also: *Baby Plays, Baby Says,* and *Baby Ways.*)

Richards, Kelly Frick. 1991. *Merry Christmas!* Illus. Lisa Kopper. New York: Grosset. 1–2 yrs.

Ross, T. 1996. *Bedtime.* San Diego, Calif.: Red Wagon. 2–5 yrs. (See also other books in the series: *Pets; Shapes; Weather.*)

Sheehan, Nancy. 1993. *Families.* Photos N. Sheehan. New York: Grosset. 3–6 yrs. Pudgy Board Book series.

Slier, Debby. 1985. *What Do Babies Do?* Photos D. Slier. New York: Random House. 6 mo.–2 yrs.

_____. 1992. *All My Things.* Photos. Laura Dwight. New York: Checkerboard. 1–2 yrs. (See also: *Me and My Grandma, Me and My Grandpa.*)

Spinelli, E. 1995. *Naptime, Laptime.* Illus. Melissa Sweet. New York: Cartwheel/Scholastic. 18 mo.–3 yrs. Thick pages.

Sweet, Melissa. 1993. *Little Chick.* New York: Grosset. 1–2 yrs.

Tucker, Sian. 1993. *The Little Boat.* New York: Simon & Schuster. 12 mo.–26 mo. (See also: *The Little Plane, The Little Train,* and *The Little Car.*)

Walsh, E. S. 1995. *Mouse Count.* San Diego, Calif.: Red Wagon. 2–5 yrs.

_____. 1996. *Mouse Paint.* San Diego, Calif.: Red Wagon. 2–5 yrs.

Wells, Rosemary. 1985. *Max's Breakfast.* New York: Dial. 12 mo.–26 mo. (See also: *Max's New Suit* and *Max's First Word.*)

Wijngaard, Juan. 1991. *Cat.* New York: Crown. 12 mo.–26 mo. (See also: *Dog, Bear,* and *Duck.*)

Witt, Dick. 1993. *Let's Look at My World.* New York: Scholastic. 6 mo.–2 yrs.

Yee, P. 1995. *Let's Eat.* New York: Viking. 2–4 yrs.

_____. 1995. *Let's Go.* New York: Viking. 2–4 yrs.

_____. 1995. *Let's Make Friends.* New York: Viking. 2–4 yrs.

_____. 1995. *Let's Play.* New York: Viking. 2–4 yrs.

Ziefert, Harriet. 1992. *Big to Little, Little to Big.* Illus. Susan Baum. New York: HarperCollins. 18 mo.–3 yrs. (See also: *Clothes On, Clothes Off; Count Up, Count Down; Empty to Full, Full to Empty.*)

Ziefert, Harriet & Simms Taback. 1985. *On Our Way to the Water.* New York: HarperCollins. 12 mo.–26 mo. (See also: *On Our Way to the Barn, On Our Way to the Forest,* and *On Our Way to the Zoo.*)

Toy Books (Paper-Engineering)

Action Pops. 1995. Color photos. New York: Snapshot. 2–5 yrs.

Agee, Jon. 1993. *Flapstick: Ten Ridiculous Rhymes with Flaps.* New York: Dutton. 6–8 yrs.

Anderson, Wayne. 1995. *The Perfect Match.* New York: Dorling Kindersley. 7–11 yrs.

Angel, Marie. 1992. *Marie Angel's Exotic Alphabet: A Lift-the-Flap Alphabetic Safari.* Illus. by Marie Angel. New York: Dial. 2–6 yrs.

Argent, Kerry. 1991. *Happy Birthday, Wombat!* Illus. Kerry Argent. Boston: Little, Brown/Joy Street. 1–5 yrs.

Bradman, Tony & Margaret Chamberlain. 1989. *Who's Afraid of the Big Bad Wolf?* Illus. Margaret Chamberlain. New York: Macmillan/Aladdin. 3–6 yrs.

Brown, Rick. 1994. *What Rhymes with Snake?: A Word and Picture Flap Book.* New York: Tambourine. 2–5 yrs.

Bishop, Roma. 1994. *On a Safari.* Illus. R. Bishop; paper engineering Ruth Mawdsley. New York: Simon & Schuster. 1–2 yrs. Little Nature Pop series. (See also: *See the Dinosaurs.*)

Carle, E. 1995. *The Very Busy Spider.* New York: Philomel. 2–5 yrs. Collage.

_____. 1995. *The Honeybee and the Robber: A Moving/Picture Book.* New York: Philomel. 6–9 yrs.

Carter, David A. 1993. *I'm Shy.* New York: Simon & Schuster. 3–6 yrs.

_____. 1993. *Says Who?: A Pop-Up Book of Animal Sounds.* New York: Simon & Schuster.

Coleridge, Sara. 1989. *January Brings the Snow: A Seasonal Hide-and-Seek.* Illus. Elizabeth Falconer. New York: Orchard. 3–6 yrs.

Crowther, Robert. 1993. *Animal Rap!* Cambridge, Mass.: Candlewick. 3–6 yrs. Noisy Pop-Up Book series.

_____. 1993. *Animal Snap!* Cambridge, Mass.: Candlewick. 3–6 yrs. Noisy Pop-Up Book series.

_____. 1996. *Pop-Up Olympics.* Cambridge, Mass.: Candlewick. 10–16 yrs.

Damon, E. 1995. *A Kaleidoscope of Kids.* New York: Dial. 6–9 yrs. Lift-the-flap.

de Beer, Hans. 1993. *Little Polar Bear: A Pop-Up Book.* New York: North-South. 5–7 yrs.

Dijs, Carla. 1992. *Who Sees You?: At the Pond.* New York: Putnam. 3–6 yrs.

_____. 1992. *Who Sees You?: In the Jungle.* New York: Grosset. 3–6 yrs.

_____. 1993. *Who Sees You?: At Night.* New York: Grosset. 3–6 yrs.

_____. 1993. *Who Sees You?: Underground.* New York: Grosset. 3–6 yrs. Little Pop-and-Peek series.

_____. 1995. *Hurry Home, Hungry Frog: A Pop Up Book.* New York: Simon & Schuster. 3–6 yrs.

_____. 1995. *Say No, Little Fish: A Pop-Up Book.* New York: Simon & Schuster. 3–6 yrs.

Farm Pops. 1995. Color photos. New York: Snapshot. 2–5 yrs.

Faulkner, Keith. 1996. *Wide Mouth Frog.* Illus. Jonathan Lambert. New York: Dial.

Fritz, Jean. 1992. *The Great Adventure of Christopher Columbus: A Pop-up Book.* Illus. Tomie de Paola. New York: Putnam and Grosset. 5–9 yrs.

Grindley, Sally. 1992. *Shhh!* Illus. Peter Utton. Boston: Little, Brown/Joy Street. 4–8 yrs.

Hill, Eric. 1992. *Spot Goes to a Party.* New York: Putnam. 2–5 yrs. Spot series.

Irvine, J. 1996. *How to Make Holiday Pop-Ups.* Illus. Linda Hendry. New York: Morrow. 9–12 yrs. Origami.

Moerbeek, Kees. 1993. *New at the Zoo Two: A Mix-and-Match Pop-Up Book.* New York: Random House. 4–7 yrs.

Moseley, Keith. 1991. *It Was a Dark and Stormy Night: A Pop-Up Mystery Whodunit.* Illus. by Linda Birkinshaw. New York: Dial. 8–10 yrs.

Murphy, Chuck. 1995. *Chuck Murphy's One to Ten Pop-Up Surprises!* New York: Simon & Schuster. 3–6 yrs.

Noisy Pops. 1995. Color photos. New York: Snapshot. 2–5 yrs.

Potter, Beatrix. 1991. *Beatrix Potter's Peter Rabbit: A Lift-the-Flap Rebus Book.* Illus. Colin Twinn. New York: Warne. 4–8 yrs.

Price, Mathew. 1993. *Peekaboo!* Illus. Jean Claverie. New York: Knopf. 3–6 yrs.

Sabuda, Robert. 1994. *The Knight's Castle: A Pop-Up Book.* Racine, Wis. Western/Artists. 5–12 yrs.

———. *The Twelve Days of Christmas: A Pop-Up Celebration.* Illus. R. Sabuda. Boston, Mass.: Simon & Schuster. 6–12 yrs. Sculptured pop-ups, largely white silhouettes.

Smyth, Iain. 1994. *The Mystery of the Russian Ruby: A Pop-Up Whodunit.* New York: Dutton. 6–10 yrs.

Souhami, J. 1995. *Old MacDonald.* Designer Paul McAlinden. New York: Orchard. 2–5 yrs.

Tilden, Ruth. 1994. *Cat Tricks: Ruth Tilden's Pop-Up Kitty Cats.* New York: Simon & Schuster. 3–5 yrs.

van der Meer, Ron & Atie van der Meer. 1992. *Funny Hats: A Lift-the-Flap Counting Book with a Surprise Gift.* New York: Random House. 3–6 yrs.

Wijngaard, J. 1995. *Buzz! Buzz!* Illus. J. Wijngaard. New York: Lodestar. 2–5 yrs. Pull-tabs.

Wyllie, S. 1995. *Bear Buys a Car.* Illus. Jonathan Allen. New York: Dial. 2–5 yrs. Wheels turn, hoods pop open, animals shift.

Yoon, Jung-Huyn. 1996. *Popposites: A Lift, Pull, and Pop Book of Opposites.* Designer J. Yoon. New York: Dorling Kindersley. 2–5 yrs.

Zelinsky, Paul O. 1990. *The Wheels on the Bus.* Illus. Paul O. Zelinsky. New York: Dutton. 3–6 yrs. ALA Notable Children's Books, 1991.

Photo Essay

(Additional books are cited in Chapter 6 and 7 bibliographies)

Alda, Arlene Arlene. 1993. *Alda's ABC.* Berkeley, Calif.: Tricycle. 3–7 yrs.

Bunnett, Rochelle. 1993. *Friends in the Park.* Photos Carl Sahlhoff. New York: Checkerboard. 3–6 yrs.

Davis, Lee. 1994. *P. B. Bear's Birthday Party.* Photos. New York: Dorling Kindersley. 4–6 yrs.

Maass, Robert. 1993. *When Summer Comes.* New York: Holt. 6–8 yrs.

———. 1993. *When Winter Comes.* New York: Holt. 6–8 yrs.

MacKinnon, Debbie. 1992. *What Shape?* Photos Anthea Sieveking. New York: Dial. 3–6 yrs.

McMillan, Bruce. 1993. *Mouse Views: What the Class Pet Saw.* New York: Holiday. 5–7 yrs.

———. 1995. *Nights of the Puffings.* Boston: Houghton Mifflin.

Miller, Margaret. 1993. *Can You Guess?* Color photos. New York: Greenwillow. 4–6 yrs.

———. 1996. *Now I'm Big.* Photos Margaret Miller. New York: Greenwillow. 4–6 yrs.

Morris, Ann. 1995. *Weddings.* Photos. New York: Lothrop, Lee & Shepard. 3–6 yrs.

Rotner, Shelley & Ken Kreisler. 1993. *Ocean Day.* Color photos. Shelley Rotner New York: Macmillan. 4–8 yrs.

———. 1994. *Citybook.* Photos Shelley Rotner. New York: Orchard. 7–10 yrs.

Simon, Seymour. 1994. *Comets, Meteors, and Asteroids.* Color photos. New York: HarperCollins. 9–12 yrs.

Waters, Kate. 1993. *Samuel Eaton's Day: A Day in the Life of a Pilgrim Boy.* Photos Russ Kendall. New York: Scholastic. 6–9 yrs.

———. 1994. *The Mysterious Horseman: An Adventure in Prairietown, 1836.* Photos Marjory Dressler. New York: Scholastic. 6–9 yrs.

Zolotow, Charlotte. 1993. *The Moon Was the Best.* Photos Tana Hoban. New York: Greenwillow. 6–9 yrs.

Picture Story Books

Ackerman, Karen. 1995. *The Sleeping Porch.* Illus. Elizabeth Sayles. New York: Morrow. 6–9 yrs.

Ahlberg, J. & A. Ahlberg. 1995. *The Jolly Pocket Postman.* Boston, Mass.: Little, Brown. 6–12 yrs.

Alexander, Martha. 1995. *You're a Genius, Blackboard Bear.* Cambridge, Mass.: Candlewick. 5–9 yrs.

Aliki. 1995. *Best Friends Together Again.* New York: Greenwillow. 5–9 yrs.

Allen, Pamela. 1993. *Belinda.* New York: Viking. 3–6 yrs.

Anholt, Laurence. 1995. *The New Puppy.* Illus. Catherine Anholt. Racine, Wis.: Western. 4–8 yrs.

Ballard, Robin. 1994. *Good-bye, House.* New York: Greenwillow. 5–8 yrs.

Barber, Antonia. 1993. *Gemma and the Baby Chick.* Illus. Karin Littlewood. New York: Scholastic. 5–8 yrs.

Bauer, Marion Dane. 1995. *When I Go Camping with Grandma.* Illus. Allen Garns. Mahwah, N.J.: BridgeWater. 6–10 yrs.

Birney, Betty G. 1994. *Tyrannosaurus Tex.* Illus. John O'Brien. Boston: Houghton Mifflin. 6–9 yrs.

Boelts, Maribeth. 1995. *Summer's End.* Illus. Ellen Kandoian. Boston: Houghton Mifflin. 6–9 yrs.

Borton, Lady. 1993. *Fat Chance!* Illus. Deborah Kogan Ray. New York: Philomel. 5–7 yrs.

Brown, M. 1995. *D. W. the Picky Eater.* Boston, Mass.: Little, Brown. 5–9 yrs.

———. 1993. *D. W. Thinks Big.* Boston: Joy Street. 4–7 yrs.

———. 1993. *Arthur's New Puppy.* Boston: Little, Brown. 5–7 yrs.

Boelts, Maribeth. 1995. *Summer's End.* Illus. Ellen Kandoian. Boston: Houghton Mifflin. 6–9 yrs.

Borton, Lady. 1993. *Fat Chance!* Illus. Deborah Kogan Ray. New York: Philomel. 5– 7 yrs.

Bunting, Eve. 1996. *Train to Somewhere.* Illus. Ronald Himler. New York: Clarion. 6–9 yrs.

Calmenson, Stephanie. 1994. *Hotter Than a Hot Dog!* Illus. Elivia. Boston: Little, Brown. 4–6 yrs.

Carr, Jan. 1996. *The Nature of the Beast.* Illus. G. Brian Karas. New York: Tambourine. 5–8 yrs.

Caseley, Judith. 1994. *Mama, Coming and Going.* New York: Greenwillow. 5–7 yrs.

———. 1996. *Slumber Party!* Illus. J. Caseley. New York: Greenwillow. 5–8 yrs.

Chmielarz, Sharon. 1994. *Down at Angel's.* Illus. Jill Kastner. New York: Ticknor & Fields. 6–9 yrs.

Clark, Emma Chichester. 1993. *Across the Blue Mountains.* San Diego: Harcourt Brace/Gulliver. 7–9 yrs.

Cooper, Helen. 1993. *The Bear under the Stairs.* New York: Dial. 4–7 yrs.

Crews, Donald. 1995. *Sail Away.* New York: Greenwillow. 6–10 yrs.

Cutler, J. 1996. *Mr. Carey's Garden.* Illus. G. Brian Karas. Boston: Houghton Mifflin. 6–9 yrs.

de Paola, Tomie. 1993. *Strega Nona Meets Her Match.* New York: Putnam. 5–8 yrs.

———. 1993. *Tom.* New York: Putnam. 5–8 yrs.

Dugan, Barbara. 1992. *Loop the Loop.* Illus. James Stevenson. New York: Greenwillow. 6–9 yrs.

Ernst, Lisa Campbell. 1994. *The Luckiest Kid on the Planet.* New York: Bradbury. 6–8 yrs.

Falk, Barbara Bustetter. 1993. *Grusha.* New York: HarperCollins/Geringer. 5–7 yrs.

Geisert, Arthur. 1994. *After the Flood.* Boston: Houghton Mifflin. 6–9 yrs.

Gleeson, Libby. 1994. *The Great Big Scary Dog.* Illus. Armin Greder. New York: Tambourine. 4–6 yrs.

Gibbons, F. 1995. *Night in the Barn.* Illus. Erick Ingraham. New York: Morrow. 6–9 yrs.

Ginsburg, Mirra. 1993. *Good Morning, Chick.* Illus. Byron Barton. New York: Tupelo. 3–6 yrs.

Greenstein, E. 1996. *Mrs. Rose's Garden.* New York: Simon & Schuster. 4–7 yrs.

Griffith, Helen V. 1993. *Grandaddy and Janetta.* Illus. James Stevenson. New York: Greenwillow. 7–9 yrs.

Haas, Jessie. 1994. *Mowing.* Illus. Jos. A. Smith. New York: Greenwillow. 5–7 yrs.

———. 1995. *No Foal Yet.* Illus. Jos. A. Smith. New York: Greenwillow. 6–9 yrs.

Hartmann, Wendy. 1993. *All the Magic in the World.* Illus. Niki Daly. New York: Dutton. 9–12 yrs.

Hershey, Kathleen. 1993. *Cotton Mill Town.* Illus. Jeannette Winter. New York: Dutton. 5–7 yrs.

Hest, A. 1995. *In the Rain with Baby Duck.* Illus. Jill Barton. Cambridge, Mass.: Candlewick. 3–6 yrs.

Hoestlandt, Jo. (Trans. Mark Polizzoti). 1995. *Star of Fear, Star of Hope.* Illus. Johanna Kang. New York: Walker. 9–14 yrs.

Isaacs, Anne. 1994. *Swamp Angel.* Illus. Paul O. Zelinsky. New York: Dutton. 7–9 yrs.

Jones, Rebecca C. 1995. *Great-Aunt Martha.* Illus. Shelley Jackson. New York: Dutton. 7–10 yrs.

Joseph, Daniel M. & Lydia J. Joseph. 1993. *Mendel All Dressed Up and Nowhere to Go.* Illus. Normand Chartier. Boston: Houghton Mifflin. 4–6 yrs.

Keller, H. 1995. *Rosata.* New York: Greenwillow. 6–9 yrs.

Mahy, Margaret. 1994. *The Rattlebang Picnic.* Illus. Steven Kellogg. New York: Dial. 6–8 yrs.

Manushkin, Fran. 1994. *Peeping and Sleeping.* Illus. Jennifer Plecas. New York: Clarion. 4–6 yrs.

Marshall, James. 1995. *Wings: A Tale of Two Chickens.* New York: Viking. 6–9 yrs.

Marshall, James. 1992. *Fox Outfoxed.* New York: Dial. 6–9 yrs.

Martin, C. L. G. 1995. *The Blueberry Train.* Illus. Angela Trotta Thomas. New York: Atheneum. 6–9 yrs.

Martin, Antoinette Truglio. 1993. *Famous Seaweed Soup.* Illus. Nadine Bernard Westcott. Morton Grove, Ill.: Whitman. 4–7 yrs.

Mayne, W. 1996. *Pandora.* Illus. Dietlind Blech. New York: Knopf. 5–9 yrs.

McCully, Emily Arnold. 1994. *My Real Family.* San Diego: Harcourt Brace/Browndeer. 5–7 yrs.

McDonald, Megan. 1995. *Insects Are My Life.* Illus. Paul Brett Johnson. New York: Orchard/Jackson. 6–9 yrs.

McNeal, T. & L. McNeal. 1996. *The Dog Who Lost His Bob.* Illus. John Sandford. Morton Grove, Ill.: Whitman. 5–8 yrs.

Neitzel, Shirley. 1995. *The Bag I'm Taking to Grandma's*. Illus. Nancy Winslow Parker. New York: Greenwillow. 4–8 yrs.

Oppenheim, S. L. 1995. *The Hundredth Name*. Illus. Michael Hays. Honesdale, Penn.: Boyds Mills. 7–10 yrs.

Oxenbury, Helen. 1993. *Tom and Pippo on the Beach*. Cambridge, Mass.: Candlewick. 2–4 yrs.

Patron, Susan. 1994. *Dark Cloud Strong Breeze*. Illus. Peter Catalanotto. New York: Orchard/Jackson. 5–7 yrs.

Pinkney, B. 1995. *JoJo's Flying Side Kick*. New York: Simon & Schuster. 5–9 yrs.

Potter, Katherine. 1994. *Spike*. Illus. K. Potter. New York: Simon & Schuster. 6–8 yrs.

Provensen, Alice & Martin Provensen. 1994. *An Owl and Three Pussycats*. San Diego: Harcourt Brace/Browndeer. 5–7 yrs.

Purdy, Carol. 1994. *Mrs. Merriwether's Musical Cat*. Illus. Petra Mathers. New York: Putnam. 5–7 yrs.

Ransom, C. F. 1995. *When the Whippoorwill Calls*. Illus. Kimberly Bulcken Root. New York: Tambourine. 7–10 yrs.

Raschka, Chris. 1995. *Can't Sleep*. Illus. C. Raschka. New York: Jackson/Orchard. 3–5 yrs.

Rathmann, Peggy. 1994. *Good Night, Gorilla*. Illus. P. Rathmann. New York: Putnam. 6–8 yrs.

Ray, Mary Lyn. 1994. *Alvah and Arvilla*. Illus. Barry Root. San Diego, Calif.: Harcourt Brace. 5–7 yrs.

Reiser, Lynn. 1993. *Tomorrow on Rocky Pond*. New York: Greenwillow. 4–6 yrs.

Rice, Eve. 1993. *Benny Bakes a Cake*. New York: Greenwillow. 3–6 yrs.

Root, P. 1996. *Aunt Nancy and Old Man Trouble*. Illus. David Parkins. Cambridge, Mass.: Candlewick. 5–7 yrs.

Rosen, Michael J. 1992. *Elijah's Angel: A Story for Chanukah and Christmas*. Illus. Aminah Brenda & Lynn Robinson. San Diego, Calif.: Harcourt Brace. 7–9 yrs.

Rush, Ken. 1994. *Friday's Journey*. New York: Orchard. 6–9 yrs.

Saul, C. P. 1995. *Someplace Else*. Illus. Barry Root. New York: Simon & Schuster. 6–9 yrs.

Schwartz, Amy. 1994. *A Teeny Tiny Baby*. New York: Orchard/Jackson. 4–7 yrs.

Stevens, Kathleen. 1994. *Aunt Skilly and the Stranger*. Illus. Robert Andrew Parker. New York: Ticknor & Fields. 7–9 yrs.

Stewart, Sarah. 1995. *The Library*. Illus. David Small. New York: Farrar, Straus & Giroux. 6–10 yrs.

Sundvall, V. L. (Trans. Kjersti Board). 1995. *Santa's Winter Vacation*. Illus. Olof Landstrom. New York: R&S. 5–9 yrs.

Thomassie, Tynia. 1995. *Feliciana Feydra LeRoux: A Cajun Tall Tale*. Illus. Cat Bowman Smith. Boston: Little, Brown. 7–11 yrs.

Tunnell, Michael O. 1993. *Chinook!* Illus. Barry Root. New York: Tambourine. 6–8 yrs.

Vaughan, Marcia. 1995. *Whistling Dixie*. Illus. Barry Moser. New York: HarperCollins. 6–9 yrs.

Waber, Bernard. 1995. *Do You See a Mouse?* Boston: Houghton Mifflin. 5–9 yrs.

Welch, Willy. 1995. *Playing Right Field*. Illus. Marc Simont. New York: Scholastic. 6–10 yrs.

Wells, Rosemary. 1993. *Waiting for the Evening Star*. Illus. Susan Jeffers. New York: Dial. 6–10 yrs.

———. 1995. *Max and Ruby's Midas: Another Greek Myth*. New York: Dial. 6–9 yrs.

Willis, Jeanne. 1994. *In Search of the Giant*. Illus. Ruth Brown. New York: Dutton. 5–7 yrs.

Wooldridge, Connie Nordhielm (Adapter). 1995. *Wicked Jack*. Illus. Will Hillenbrand. New York: Holiday. 5–8 yrs.

Wordless Books

Alexander, Martha. 1970. *Bobo's Dream*. New York: Dial. 3–6 yrs.

Aliki. 1995. *Tabby: A Story in Pictures*. New York: HarperCollins. 3–6 yrs.

Anderson, Lena. 1991. *Bunny Fun; Bunny Box; Bunny Story; Bunny Party; Bunny Bath; Bunny Surprise*. New York: Farrar, Straus & Giroux. 3–6 yrs.

Anno, Mitsumasa. 1981. *Anno's Journey*. New York: Philomel. 7–11 yrs.

———. 1986. *Anno's Counting Book*. New York: Harper & Row. 6–9 yrs.

Aruego, J. 1971. *Look What I Can Do*. New York: Scribners. 3–6 yrs.

Banyai, Istvan. 1995. *Zoom*. New York: Viking. 6–10 yrs.

———. 1995. *Re-zoom*. Illus. I. Banyai. New York: Viking. 7–10 yrs.

Blake, Q. 1996. *Clown*. Illus. Quentin Blake. New York: Holt. 5–8 yrs.

Biggs, R. 1995. *The Man*. New York: Random House. 8–11 yrs.

Billout, Guy. 1993. *The Journey*. Mankato, Minn.: Creative. 6–9 yrs.

Briggs, Raymond. 1986. *The Snowman*. New York: Random House. 8–12 yrs.

———. 1994. *The Bear*. New York: Random House. 4–6 yrs.

———. 1995. *The Man*. New York: Random House. 8–11 yrs.

Brown, Craig. 1989. *The Patchwork Farmer*. Illus. L. Brown. New York: Greenwillow. 4–6 yrs.

Bruna, D. 1984. *Miffy's Dream*. Los Angeles: Price, Stern, Sloan. 3–6 yrs.

Butterworth, Nick. 1991. *Amanda's Butterfly*. Illus. N. Butterworth. New York: Delacorte. 3–6 yrs.

Carle, Eric. 1987. *Do You Want to Be My Friend?* New York: Harper & Row. 3–6 yrs.

Charlip, Remy & Jerry Joyner. 1994. *Thirteen*. New York: Four Winds. 6–10 yrs.

Coffin, Josse. 1993. *Yes*. New York: Lothrop, Lee & Shepard. 3–6 yrs.

Collington, Peter. 1988. *My Darling Kitten*. New York: Knopf. 7–11 yrs.

———. 1990. *On Christmas Eve*. New York: Knopf. 7–11 yrs.

———. 1993. *The Midnight Circus*. New York: Knopf. 7–11 yrs.

———. 1995. *Tooth Fairy*. New York: Borzoi/Knopf. 7–11 yrs.

Crews, Donald. 1985. *Truck*. New York: Penguin. 6–9 yrs.

Cristini, E. & L. Puricello 1983. *In the Wood*. Austria: Verlag Neugebauu. 7–11 yrs.

Curro, E. 1963. *The Great Circus Parade*. New York: Holt, Rinehart & Winston. 3–6 yrs.

Day, Alexandra. 1992. *Carl Goes Shopping*. New York: Farrar, Straus & Giroux. 3–7 yrs.

———. 1992. *Carl's Afternoon in the Park*. New York: Farrar, Straus & Giroux. 3–7 yrs.

———. 1992. *Carl's Christmas*. New York: Farrar, Straus & Giroux. 3–7 yrs.

———. 1993. *Carl's Masquerade*. New York: Farrar, Straus & Giroux. 5–8 yrs.

———. 1994. *Carl Makes a Scrapbook*. New York: Farrar, Straus & Giroux. 7–9 yrs.

———. 1995. *Carl's Birthday*. New York: Farrar, Straus & Giroux. 3–6 yrs.

———. 1995. *Carl Goes to Daycare*. New York: Farrar, Straus & Giroux. 2–5 yrs. Board book edition.

Day, David. 1991. *Aska's Animals*. Illus. Warabe Aska. New York: Doubleday. 7–13 yrs.

de Groat, Diane. 1977. *Alligator's Toothache*. New York: Crown. 6–9 yrs.

de Paola, Tomie. 1978. *Pancakes for Breakfast*. New York: Holiday House. 3–6 yrs.

———. 1979. *Flicks*. San Diego, Calif.: Harcourt Brace Jovanovich. 9–12 yrs.

———. 1983. *Sing Pierrot, Sing*. San Diego, Calif.: Harcourt Brace. 3–6 yrs.

Dupasquier, P. 1990. *I Can't Sleep*. New York: Orchard. 7–9 yrs.

Felix, Monique. 1991. *The Wind*. New York: Stewart, Tabori & Chang. 7–11 yrs. (See also other books by author.)

Geisert, Arthur. 1991. *Oink*. Boston: Houghton Mifflin. 7–12 yrs.

———. 1993. *Oink Oink*. Boston: Houghton Mifflin. 6–10 yrs.

Gelman, R. & J. Kent. 1984. *More Spaghetti, I Say!* New York: Scholastic. 3–6 yrs.

Gill, Madelaine. 1993. *The Spring Hat*. New York: Simon & Schuster. 4–6 yrs.

Goodall, John. 1968. *The Adventures of Paddy Pork*. San Diego, Calif.: Harcourt Brace Jovanovich. 6–10 yrs. (See also other books in series.)

———. 1983. *Shrewbettina's Birthday*. San Diego, Calif.: Harcourt Brace Jovanovich. 6–10 yrs.

———. 1990. *Puss in Boots*. New York: Macmillan. 9–12 yrs.

Graham, Alastair. 1991. *Full Moon Soup; or, The Fall of the Hotel Splendide*. Illus. Alastair Graham. New York: Dial. 4–7 yrs.

Hoban, Tana. 1975. *Dig, Drill, Dump, Fill*. New York: Greenwillow. 3–6 yrs.

———. 1976. *Big Ones, Little Ones*. Photos T. Hoban. New York: Greenwillow. 3–6 yrs.

———. 1990. *Shadows and Reflections*. New York: Greenwillow. 2–9 yrs.

———. 1992. *Look Up, Look Down*. New York: Greenwillow. 3–6 yrs.

———. 1993. *Black on White*. New York: Greenwillow. 6 mo.–2 yrs.

Hughes, S. 1986. *Up and Up*. New York: Lothrop, Lee & Shepard. 5–9 yrs.

Jenkin-Pearce, S. 1988. *The Enchanted Garden*. Oxford: Oxford Press. 8–12 yrs.

Jenkins, S. 1995. *Looking Down*. Boston: Houghton Mifflin. 7–10 yrs.

Keats, Ezra. 1973. *Sh! Doggie*. Danbury, Conn.: Watts. 3–6 yrs.

Krahn, Fredrick. 1976. *Sebastian and the Mushroom*. New York: Delacorte. 7–11 yrs. (See also other books in series.)

Karlin, Bernie. 1992. *Shapes: Three Little Board Books*. New York: Simon & Schuster. 3–6 yrs.

Lapointe, C. 1995. *Out of Sight! Out of Mind!* San Diego, Calif.: Creative/Harcourt. 6–9 yrs.

Maizlish, Lisa. 1996. *The Ring*. Photos Lisa Maizlish. New York: Greenwillow. 4–6 yrs.

McCully, Emily. 1984. *Picnic*. New York: Harper & Row. 6–9 yrs.

———. 1987. *School*. New York: Harper Trophy. 6–9 yrs.

Mariotti, M. 1982. *Humands*. R. Marchiori. La Jolla, Calif.; Green Tiger Press. 7–11 yrs.

———. 1983. *Hanimals*. Illus. R. Marchiori. New York: Green Tiger Press. 7–11 yrs.

Mayer, Mercer. 1967. *A Boy, a Dog, and a Frog*. New York: Dial. 5–9 yrs.

———. 1977. *Frog Goes to Dinner*. New York: Dial. 5–9 yrs.

———. 1978. *Hiccup*. New York: Dial. 5–9 yrs.

———. 1980. *Frog, Where Are You?* New York: Dial. 5–9 yrs.

Mayo, Virginia. 1993. *Don't Forget Me, Santa Claus*. Hauppauge, N.Y.: Barron's. 5–8 yrs.

Mogensen, J. 1990. *The 46 Little Men*. New York: Greenwillow. 8–12 yrs.

Oakley, Graham. 1980. *Graham Oakley's Magical Changes*. New York: Atheneum/Macmillan. 10–16 yrs.

Ormerod, Jan. 1984. *Moonlight*. New York: Penguin. 3–6 yrs.

Rikys, Bodel. 1992. *Red Bear*. New York: Dial. 3–6 yrs.

Rohmann, Eric. 1994. *Time Flies*. New York: Crown. 6–9 yrs.

Rubinstein, Gillian. 1993. *Dog In, Cat Out*. Illus. Ann James. New York: Ticknor & Fields. 4–6 yrs.

Schories, Patricia. 1991. *Mouse Around*. New York: Farrar, Straus & Giroux. 7–11 yrs.

Schubert, D. 1987. *Where's My Monkey?* New York: Dial. 5–9 yrs.

Sara. 1991. *Across Town*. Illus. Sara. New York: Orchard. 3–7 yrs.

Sis, Peter. 1992. *An Ocean World*. Illus. P. Sis. New York: Greenwillow. 3–9 yrs.

Spier, Peter. 1981. *Noah's Ark*. Illus. P. Spier. New York: Doubleday. 7–11 yrs.

———. 1982. *Peter Spier's Rain*. New York: Doubleday. 7–11 yrs.

———. 1983. *Christmas*. New York: Doubleday. 7–11 yrs.

———. 1984. *Dreams*. New York: Doubleday. 7–11 yrs.

Tafuri, Nancy. 1988. *Junglewalk*. New York: Morrow. 6–10 yrs.

———. 1990. *Follow Me!* Illus. N. Tafuri. New York: Greenwillow. 4–9 yrs.

Turkle, B. 1976. *Deep in the Forest*. New York: Dutton. 7–10 yrs.

Ward, Lynn. 1930. *Madman's Drum*. Cited in Virginia H. Richey & Katharyn E. Puckett, 1992. *Wordless/Almost Wordless Picture Books: A Guide*. Englewood, Colo.: (Foreword) Libraries Unlimited.

———. 1973. *The Silver Pony: A Story in Pictures*. Boston: Houghton Mifflin. 8–13 yrs.

Wouters, Anne. 1991. *This Book Is for Us*. Illus. A. Wouters. New York: Dutton. 2–5 yrs.

———. 1991. *This Book Is Too Small*. Illus. A. Wouters. New York: Dutton. 2–5 yrs.

Wiesner, David. 1988. *Free Fall*. New York: Lothrop, Lee & Shepard. 8–12 yrs.

———. 1991. *Tuesday*. New York: Lothrop, Lee & Shepard. 7–11 yrs.

Wildsmith, Brian. 1982. *Trunk*. Oxford: Oxford Press. 6–9 yrs.

———. 1984. *Whose Shoes?* Oxford: Oxford Press. 5–9 yrs.

Language Play and Participation Books

Akass, Susan. 1995. *Swim, Number Nine Duckling*. Illus. Alex Ayliffe. Honesdale, Penn.: Boyds Mills. 3–6 yrs. Predictable Text.

Arnold, Tedd. 1995. *No More Water in the Tub?* Illus. T. Arnold. New York: Dial. 4–8 yrs. Participation.

Baer, Gene. 1989. *Thump, Thump, Rat-a-Tat-Tat*. Illus. Lois Ehlert. New York: Harper & Row/ZolotowBooks. 2–7 yrs. Fiction; onomatopoeic text.

Capucilli, Alyssa Satin. 1995. *Inside a Barn in the Country: A Rebus Read-Along Story*. Illus. Tedd Arnold. New York: Cartwheel. 2–5 yrs. Cumulative rhymes; participation book.

Carlstrom, Nancy White. 1992. *Baby-O*. Illus. Sucie Stevenson. Boston: Little, Brown. 3–6 yrs. Onomatopoeic refrains.

Catalanotto, Peter. 1990. *Mr. Mumble*. Illus. Peter Catalanotto. New York: Orchard/Jackson. 4–7 yrs. Participation book.

Cauley, Lorinda Bryan. 1992. *Clap Your Hands*. Illus. Lorinda Bryan Cauley. New York: Putnam. 3–6 yrs. Participation book.

Cazet, Denys. 1994. *Nothing at All*. New York: Orchard/Jackson. 4–6 yrs. R.F.; Repetitive phrase; silly words.

Enderle, Judith Ross & Stephanie Gordon Tessler. 1996. *Nell Nugget and the Cow Caper*. Illus. Paul Yalowitz. New York: Simon & Schuster. 5–8 yrs. Predictable text, sounds.

Falwell, Cathryn. 1991. *Clowning Around*. Illus. C. Falwell. New York: Orchard. 3–6 yrs. Participation book.

Fox, Mem. 1992. *Shoes from Grandpa*. Illus. Patricia Mullins. New York: Orchard. 3–6 yrs. Cumulative text.

Gordon, Jeffie Ross. 1991. *Six Sleepy Sheep*. Illus. John O'Brien. Honesdale, Penn.: Boyds Mills/Caroline. 2–6 yrs. Alliterative prose; counting.

Heller, Ruth. 1990. *Merry-Go-Round: A Book about Nouns*. Illus. R. Heller. New York: Grosset & Dunlap. 6–12 yrs. Vocabulary.

Hilton, Nette. 1990. *Prince Lachlan*. Illus. Ann James. New York: Orchard. 3–6 yrs. Repetitive phrases and onomatopoeia.

Hubbard, Patricia. 1996. *My Crayons Talk*. Illus. G. Brian Karas. New York: Martin/Holt. 3–6 yrs. Repetitive phrases; scribbly drawings.

Kitchen, Bert. 1992. *Somewhere Today*. Illus. B. Kitchen. Cambridge, Mass.: Candlewick: 5–9 yrs. Repetitive phrases; information.

Knutson, Kimberley. 1993. *Ska-tat!* New York: Macmillan. 5–7 yrs. Onomatopoeia.

Linscott, Jody. 1991. *Once Upon A to Z: An Alphabet Odyssey*. Illus. Claudia Porges Holland. New York: Doubleday. 4–8 yrs. Alliterative stories.

Macaulay, David. 1990. *Black and White*. Illus. David Macaulay. Boston: Houghton Mifflin. 10–15 yrs. Caldecott Winner, 1991. Interpret four stories in one book.

MacCarthy, Patricia. 1991. *Herds of Words*. Illus. Patricia MacCarthy. New York: Dial. 3–6 yrs. Collective nouns.

Martin, Bill, Jr., & John Archambault. 1989. *Chicka Chicka Boom Boom*. Illus. Lois Ehlert. New York: Simon & Schuster. 2–6 yrs.

———. 1994. *The Maestro Plays*. Illus. Vladimir Radunsky. New York: Holt. 4–6 yrs. Rhyming adverbs; instruments in an orchestra.

———. 1996. *"Fire! Fire!" Said Mrs. McGuire*. Illus. Richard Egielski. San Diego: Harcourt Brace. 3–6 yrs. Rhyming; wordplay.

Merriam, Eve. 1992. *Fighting Words*. Illus. David Small. New York: Morrow. 5–10 yrs. Words.

Newcome, Zita. 1996. *Toddlerobics*. Illus. Zita Newcome. Cambridge, Mass.: Candlewick. 2–4 yrs. Bouncy rhymes, participation book.

Parish, Herman. 1995. *Good Driving, Amelia Bedelia*. Illus. Lynn Sweat. New York: Greenwillow. 5–9 yrs. Literal interpretation of words.

Parish, Peggy. 1992. *Amelia Bedelia*. Illus. Fritz Siebel. New York: HarperCollins. 6–9 yrs. I Can Read series. Literal interpretation of words.

Rockwell, Anne. 1995. *NO! NO! NO!* New York: Macmillan. 3–6 yrs. Predictable text.

Stevenson, James. 1990. *Quick! Turn the Page!* Illus. J. Stevenson. New York: Greenwillow. 4–7 yrs. Participation book.

Walter, Virginia. 1995. *"Hi, Pizza Man!"* Illus. Ponder Goembel. New York: Orchard/Jackson. 5–9 yrs. Repetitive language play.

Williams, Sue. 1990. *I Went Walking*. Illus. Julie Vivas. San Diego, Calif.: Harcourt Brace Jovanovich/Gulliver. 3–7 yrs. Predictable, rhyming couplets.

Yektai, Niki. 1989. *What's Silly?* Illus. Susannah Ryan. New York: Clarion. 2–8 yrs. Predictable text; word play.

Early Readers

Allen, Laura Jean. 1992. *Rollo and Tweedy and the Ghost at Dougal Castle*. New York: HarperCollins. 5–8 yrs. I Can Read series.

Bonsall, Crosby. 1992. *The Case of the Hungry Stranger*. New York: HarperCollins. 6–8 yrs. I Can Read series.

Byars, Betsy. 1996. *My Brother, Ant*. Illus. Marc Simont. New York: Viking. 6–8 yrs.

Calmenson, Stephanie. 1994. *Marigold and Grandma on the Town*. Illus. Mary Chalmers. New York: HarperCollins. 6–9 yrs. I Can Read series.

Champion, Joyce. 1995. *Emily and Alice Again*. Illus. Sucie Stevenson. San Diego: Harcourt Brace/Gulliver. 6–9 yrs.

Coerr, Eleanor. 1992. *The Big Balloon Race*. Illus. Carolyn Croll. New York: HarperCollins. 6–9 yrs. I Can Read series. Biographical sketch.

———. 1995. *Buffalo Bill and the Pony Express*. Illus. Don Bolognese. New York: HarperCollins. 7–10 yrs. I Can Read series. Fictionalized biography.

Fox, Mem. 1994. *Tough Boris*. Illus. Kathryn Brown. San Diego, Calif.: Harcourt Brace. 6–9 yrs.

Hall, Donald. 1994. *The Farm Summer 1942*. Illus. Barry Moser. New York: Dial. 8–10 yrs.

Hest, Amy. 1994. *Nannies for Hire*. Illus. Irene Trivas. New York: Morrow. 7–10 yrs.

Krensky, Stephen. 1992. *Lionel and Louise*. Illus. Susanna Natti. New York: Dial. 6–8 yrs. Easy-to-Read series.

———. 1994. *Lionel in the Winter*. Illus. Susanna Natti. New York: Dial. 6–8 yrs. Easy-to-Read series.

Levinson, Nancy Smiler. 1992. *Snowshoe Thompson*. Illus. Joan Sandin. New York: HarperCollins. 6–9 yrs. I Can Read series. Biographical sketch.

McCully, Emily Arnold. 1993. *Grandmas at Bat*. New York: HarperCollins. 6–8 yrs. I Can Read series.

Mclerran, Alice. 1996. *The Year of the Ranch*. Illus. Kimberly Bulcken Root. New York: Viking. 6–9 yrs.

Platt, Kim. 1992. *Big Max*. Illus. Robert Lopshire. New York: HarperCollins. 6–9 yrs. I Can Read series.

Rylant, Cynthia. 1994. *Mr. Putter and Tabby Pour the Tea*. Illus. Arthur Howard. San Diego, Calif.: Harcourt Brace. 6–8 yrs.

———. 1994. *Mr. Puffer and Tabby Bake the Cake*. Illus. Arthur Howard. San Diego, Calif.: Harcourt Brace. 6–8 yrs.

———. 1994. *Mr. Putter and Tabby Walk the Dog*. Illus. Arthur Howard. San Diego, Calif.: Harcourt Brace. 6–8 yrs.

Thurber, James. 1994. *The Great Quillow*. Illus. Steven Kellogg. San Diego, Calif.: Harcourt Brace. 9–12 yrs. Contemporary classic sketch.

Van Leeuwen, Jean. 1992. *Oliver and Amanda's Halloween*. Illus. Ann Schweninger. New York: Dial. 6–8 yrs. Easy-to-Read series.

Chapter Books & Short Stories

Byars, Betsy. 1994. *The Golly Sisters Ride Again*. Illus. Sue Truesdell. New York: HarperCollins. 7–9 yrs. I Can Read series. Five historical stories.

Caseley, Judith. 1994. *Harry and Arney*. New York: Greenwillow. 7–9 yrs.

Doherty, Berlie. 1994. *Willa and Old Miss Annie*. Illus. Kim Lewis. Cambridge, Mass.: Candlewick. 7–9 yrs. Three short stories of friendship.

Griffith, Helen V. 1995. *Grandaddy's Stars*. Illus. James Stevenson. New York: Greenwillow. 6–9 yrs. Chapter book.

Hesse, Karen. 1994. *Sable*. Illus. Marcia Sewall. New York: Holt. 7–9 yrs. Redfeather series. Chapter book.

Macaulay, David. 1995. *Shortcut.* Illus. D. Macaulay. Boston: Houghton Mifflin. 7–10 yrs. Chapter book.

Marshall, James. 1993. *Rats on the Range and Other Stories.* New York: Dial. 6–8 yrs. Eight short stories.

———. 1993. *Fox on Stage.* New York: Dial. 6–8 yrs. Easy-to-Read series. Three stories.

Novak, Matt. 1996. *Newt.* Illus. M. Novak. New York: HarperCollins. 6–8 yrs. Chapter book.

Stevenson, James. 1994. *The Mud Flat Olympics.* New York: Greenwillow. 7–9 yrs. Chapter book.

———. 1995. *A Village Full of Valentines.* New York: Greenwillow. 7–9 yrs. Chapter book.

Van Leeuwen, Jean. 1994. *Two Girls in Sister Dresses.* Illus. Linda Benson. New York: Dial. 6–8 yrs. Chapter book.

Waggoner, Karen. 1995. *Partners.* Illus. Cat Bowman Smith. New York: Simon & Schuster. 7–10 yrs. Chapter book.

York, Carol Beach. 1994. *The Key to the Playhouse.* Illus. John Speirs. New York: Scholastic. 7–10 yrs. Chapter book.

Illustrated Books

Burnford, Sheila. 1961. *The Incredible Journey.* Illus. Carl Burger. New York: Bantam. 11–13 yrs.

Carroll, Lewis. 1977. *Through the Looking Glass.* Illus. John Tenniel. New York: St. Martin's. 11–16 yrs.

———. 1977. *Alice's Adventures in Wonderland.* Illus. John Tenniel. New York: Philomel. 11–14 yrs.

Christian, Peggy. 1995. *The Bookstore Mouse.* Illus. Gary A. Lippincott. San Diego, Calif.: Yolen/Harcourt Brace. 10–13 yrs.

Collodi, Carlo (Trans. E. Harden). 1988. *The Adventures of Pinocchio.* Illus. Roberto Innocenti. New York: Knopf. 11–14 yrs.

Hodges, Margaret (Reteller). 1995. *Gulliver in Lilliput.* Illus. Kimberly Bulcken Root. New York: Holiday. 8–12 yrs.

Lawson, Robert. 1944. *Rabbit Hill.* Illus. R. Lawson. New York: Puffin. 10–13 yrs.

London, J. 1994. *Call of the Wild.* Illus. Barry Moser. New York: Macmillan. 10–14 yrs.

Pyle, Howard. 1968. *The Merry Adventures of Robin Hood of Great Renown in Nottinghamshire.* Illus. H. Pyle. New York: Scribners. 11–15 yrs.

Milne, A. A. 1974. *Winnie-the-Pooh.* Illus. E. H. Shepard; Colored by Hilda Scott. New York: Dell. 9–12 yrs.

Stevenson, Robert Louis. 1994. *David Balfour.* Illus. N. C. Wyeth. New York: Scribners. 12–16 yrs.

Twain, Mark [Samuel Clemens]. 1994. *The Adventures of Huckleberry Finn.* Illus. Steven Kellogg. 10–15 yrs.

White, E. B. 1945. *Stuart Little.* Illus. Garth Williams. New York: Harper & Row. 8–12 yrs.

———. 1952. *Charlotte's Web.* Illus. Garth Williams. New York: Harper & Row. 8–12 yrs.

———. 1970. *The Trumpet of the Swan.* Illus. Edward Frascino. New York: Harper & Row. 9–13 yrs.

Wilder, Laura Ingalls. 1995. *The Little House Series.* Illus. Garth Williams. New York: HarperCollins. 8–13 yrs.

CHAPTER 9

CHILDREN'S BOOKS MENTIONED IN THE CHAPTER

Aardema, V. 1975. *Why Mosquitoes Buzz in People's Ears.* New York: Dial. 6–9 yrs.

Banks, L. R. 1981. *The Indian in the Cupboard.* New York: Doubleday. 9–12 yrs.

Bannerman, H. 1996. *The Story of Little Babaj.* Illus. Fred Marcellino. New York: de Capua/Harper. 5–8 yrs.

Beatty, P. 1981. *Lupita Mañana.* New York: Morrow. 9–14 yrs.

Belpre, P. 1961. *Perez and Martina.* Illus. C. Sanchez. New York: Viking Penguin. 7–10 yrs.

———. 1972. *The Dance of the Animals.* Illus. P. Galdone. New York: Warne. 7–10 yrs.

Bierhorst, J. 1971. *In the Trail of the Wind: American Indian Poems and Ritual Orations.* New York: Farrar, Straus & Giroux. 11–14 yrs.

———. 1986. *The Mythology of North America.* New York: Morrow.

Bruchac, J. 1995. *Gluskabe and the Four Wishes.* Illus. C. N. Shrader. Bergenfield, N.J.: Cobblehill. 6–9 yrs.

Bryan, A. (Selector). 1974. *Walk Together Children: Black American Spirituals.* Illus. A. Bryan. New York: Antheneum. 6–12 yrs.

———. 1977. *The Dancing Granny.* New York: Atheneum. 6–10 yrs.

Bunting, E. 1994. *Smoky Night.* Illus. D. Diaz. San Diego: Harcourt Brace. 9–12 yrs.

Crew, L. 1989. *Children of the River.* New York: Delacorte. 12–16 yrs.

Demi. 1980. *Liang and His Magic Brush.* New York: Holt. 6–10 yrs.

———. 1991. *The Artist and the Architect.* New York: Holt. 7–10 yrs.

———. 1991. *Chingis Khan.* New York: Holt. 8–11 yrs.

———. 1993. *Demi's Dragons and Fantastic Creatures.* New York: Holt. 5–9 yrs.

———. 1995. *The Stonecutter.* New York: Crown. 5–9 yrs.

———. 1996. *Buddha.* New York: Holt. 8–12 yrs.

Dorris, M. 1992. *Morning Girl.* New York: Hyperion. 10–15 yrs.

———. 1994. *Guest.* New York: Hyperion. 10–15 yrs.

Dorros, A. 1995. *Isla.* Illus. Elisa Kleven. New York: Dutton. 7–10 yrs.

Ellsworth, B. 1995. *The Little Stream.* Salt Lake City, Utah: Bonneville Classic Books. 8–12 yrs.

Feelings, M. 1974. *Jambo Means Hello: A Swahili Alphabet Book.* Illus. T. Feelings. New York: Dial. 7–10 yrs.

———. 1976. *Moja Means One: A Swahili Book.* Illus. T. Feelings. New York: Dial.

Feelings, T. (Ed.). 1993. *Soul Looks Back in Wonder.* New York: Dial. 7–12 yrs.

Garaway, M. J. 1993. *Askii and His Grandfather.* Tucson, Ariz.: Treasure Chest. 8–11 yrs.

———. 1993. *The Old Hogan.* Tucson, Ariz.: Old Hogan Publishing. 8–11 yrs.

Garza, C. L. (As told to Harriet Rohmer). 1990. *Family Pictures/Cuadros de Familia.* San Francisco, Calif.: Children's Book. 7–10 yrs.

Giovanni, N. 1987. *Spin a Soft Black Song.* New York: Farrar, Straus & Giroux. 8–12 yrs.

Greenfield, E., 1975. *Me and Neesie.* New York: HarperCollins. 7–10 yrs.

———. 1978. (New ed. 1986). *Honey, I Love and Other Love Poems.* New York: HarperCollins. 5–9 yrs.

Hamanaka, S. 1990. *The Journey: Japanese Americans, Racism, and Renewal.* New York: Orchard. 10–16 yrs.

Hamilton, V. 1967. *Zeely.* Illus. S. Shimin. New York: Macmillan. 9–12 yrs.

———. 1974. *M. C. Higgins the Great.* New York: Macmillan. 10–14 yrs.

———. 1992. *Drylongso.* Illus. J. Pinkney. San Diego.: Harcourt. 9–13 yrs.

Harris, J. C. 1892. *Uncle Remus and His Friends.* Boston: Houghton Mifflin. 8–13 yrs.

Highwater, J. 1977. *ANPAO: An American Indian Odyssey.* Illus. Fritz Scholder. New York: Harper. 10–16 yrs.

———. 1978. *Many Smokes, Many Moons: A Chronology of American Indian History Through Indian Art.* New York: HarperCollins. 11–16 yrs.

———. 1984. *Legend Days.* New York: HarperCollins. 11–16 yrs. Ghost Horse trilogy.

———. 1985. *Ceremony of Innocence.* New York: HarperCollins. 11–16 yrs. Ghost Horse trilogy.

———. 1986. *I Wear the Morning Star.* New York: HarperCollins. 11–16 yrs. Ghost Horse trilogy.

Howard, E. F. 1991. *Aunt Flossie's Hats (and Crab Cakes Later).* Paintings James Ransome. New York: Clarion. 6–10 yrs.

Hoyt-Goldsmith, D. 1995. *Apache Rodeo.* New York: Holiday. 9–12 yrs.

Hughes, L. 1962. *Dream Keeper.* New York: Knopf. 9–16 yrs.

Jackson, J. 1945. *Call Me Charley.* Illus. D. Speigel. New York: Harper & Row. 8–11 yrs.

Jeffers, S. 1991. *Brother Eagle, Sister Sky: A Message from Chief Seattle.* New York: Dial. 9–16 yrs.

Johnson, J. W. 1927. (New ed. 1994). *The Creation.* Illus. J. E. Rasome. New York: Holiday. 7–11 yrs.

Joosse, B. 1991. *Mama, Do You Love Me?* Illus. Barbara Lavallee. San Francisco, Calif.: Chronicle. 5–9 yrs.

Kline, S. 1993. *Son Lee in Room 2B.* Illus. F. Remkiewicz. New York: 5–7 yrs.

Lee, M. G. 1993. *If It Hadn't Been for Yoon Jun.* Boston: Houghton. 10–13 yrs.

———. 1994. *Saying Goodbye.* Boston: Houghton. 12–16 yrs.

Lester, J. (Reteller). 1987. *The Tales of Uncle Remus: The Adventures of Brer Rabbit.* Illus. Jerry Pinkney. New York: Dutton/Dial. 10–14 yrs.

———. 1994. *The Last Tales of Uncle Remus.* Illus. Jerry Pinkney. New York: Dial. 10–13 yrs.

———. 1996. *Sam and the Tigers: A New Telling of Little Black Sambo.* Illus. Jerry Pinkney. New York: Dial. 5–8 yrs.

Lord, B. B. 1984. *In the Year of the Boar and Jackie Robinson.* New York: HarperCollins. 9–12 yrs.

McKissack, P. 1988. *Mirandy and Brother Wind.* New York: Knopf. 7–10 yrs.

McMillan B. 1991. *Eating Fractions.* New York: Scholastic. 8–11 yrs.

Meltzer, M. 1984. *The Black Americans: A History in Their Own Words.* New York: Crowell. 10–16 yrs.

Mohr, N. 1979. *Felita.* Illus. Ray Cruz. New York: Dial. 9–12 yrs.

———. 1986. *Going Home.* New York: Dial. 10–13 yrs.

———. 1986. *Nilda.* New York: Dial. 10–13 yrs.

———. 1986. *El Bronx Remembered.* Houston: Arte Publico. 12–16 yrs.

———. 1988. *In Nueva York.* Houston: Arte Publico. 12–16 yrs.

Musgrove, M. 1976. *Ashanti to Zulu: African Traditions.* Illus. Leo & Diane Dillon. New York: Dial. 8–11 yrs.

Myers, W. D. 1975. *Sam, Cool Clyde, and Stuff.* New York: Viking. 10–14 yrs.

———. 1991. *Now Is Your Time!: The African-American Struggle for Freedom.* New York: Harper. 10–16 yrs.

Namioka, L. 1992. *Yang the Youngest and His Terrible Ear.* Illus. K. de Kiefte. Boston: Little, Brown/Joy Street. 9–11 yrs.

———. 1995. *Yang the Third and Her Impossible Family.* Illus. K. de Kiefte. Boston: Little, Brown. 8–10 yrs.

Nikola-Lisa, W. 1994. *Bein' With You This Way.* Illus. M. Bryant. New York: Lee & Low. 5–9 yrs.

Nones, E. J. 1995. *Angela's Wings.* New York: HarperCollins. 7–11 yrs.

Parks, R. & J. Haskins. 1992. *Rosa Parks: My Story.* Photos. New York: Dial. 12–16 yrs.

Paterson, K. 1973. *The Sign of the Chrysanthemum.* New York: HarperCollins. 11–15 yrs.

———. 1974. *Of Nightingales that Weep.* New York: HarperCollins. 11–15 yrs.

———. 1975. *The Master Puppeteer.* New York: HarperCollins. Illus. Haru Wells. 11–15 yrs.

Paulsen, G. 1995. *The Tortilla Factory.* Illus. Ruth Wright Paulsen. San Diego, Calif.: Harcourt Brace. 7–11 yrs.

Pinkwater, J. 1991. *Tails of the Bronx: A Tale of the Bronx.* New York: Macmillan. 9–12 yrs.

Ringgold, F. 1991. *Tar Beach.* New York: Crown. 6–10 yrs.

San Souci, R. D. 1995. *The Faithful Friend.* Illus. Brian Pinkney. New York: Simon & Schuster. 10–16 yrs.

Say, A. 1982. *The Bicycle Man.* Boston: Houghton. 5–9 yrs.

———. 1990. *El Chino.* Boston: Houghton. 12–16 yrs.

———. 1993. *Grandfather's Journey.* Boston: Houghton. 6–10 yrs.

Soto, G. 1990. *A Fire in My Hands.* New York: Scholastic. 11–16 yrs.

———. 1990. *Baseball in April and Other Stories.* San Diego: Harcourt. 11–16 yrs.

———. 1991. *Taking Sides.* San Diego: Harcourt. 11–16 yrs.

———. 1992. *Neighborhood Odes.* Illus. David Diaz. San Diego: Harcourt. 11–16 yrs.

———. 1992. *The Skirt.* Illus. Eric Velasquex. New York: Delacorte. 7–10 yrs.

———. 1993. *Too Many Tamales.* Illus. Ed Martinez. New York: Putnam. 4–7 yrs.

———. 1993. *Local News.* San Diego: Harcourt. 10–14 yrs.

Steptoe, J. 1969. *Stevie.* New York: HarperCollins. 5–8 yrs.

———. 1987. *Mufaro's Beautiful Daughters.* New York: Lothrop. 8–12 yrs.

Taylor, M. 1976. *Roll of Thunder, Hear My Cry.* New York: Dial. 10–14 yrs.

Thomas, J. C. 1992. *A Gathering of Flowers: Stories about Being Young in America.* New York: HarperCollins. 11–16 yrs.

Tompert, A. 1993. *Bamboo Hats and a Rice Cake.* Illus. Demi. New York: Crown. 6–10 yrs.

Uchida, Y. 1971. *Journey to Topaz.* Illus. D. Carrick. New York: Scribner's. 11–16 yrs.

———. 1991. *The Invisible Thread.* Englewood Cliffs, N.J.: Messner. 11–16 yrs.

Watkins, Y. K. 1994. *My Brother, My Sister, and I.* New York: Bradbury. 12–15 yrs.

Yashima, M. & T. Yashima. 1977. *Momo's Kitten.* New York: Puffin. 4–7 yrs.

Yashima, T. 1953. *The Village Tree.* New York: Viking. 8–11 yrs.

———. 1954. *Plenty to Watch.* New York: Viking. 6–9 yrs.

———. 1955. *Crow Boy.* New York: Viking. 7–11 yrs.

———. 1958. *Umbrella.* New York: Viking. 7–11 yrs.

———. 1961. *Momo's Kitten.* New York: Viking. 4–7 yrs.

———. 1962. *Youngest One.* New York: Viking. 4–7 yrs.

———. 1967. *Seashore Story.* New York: Viking. 7–10 yrs.

Yep, L. 1975. *Dragonwings.* New York: HarperCollins. 10–14 yrs.

———. 1977. *Child of the Owl.* New York: Harper & Row. 11–15 yrs.

———. 1979. *Sea Glass.* New York: HarperCollins. 10–14 yrs.

———. 1989. *The Rainbow People.* Illus. D. Wiesner. New York: HarperCollins. 10–16 yrs.

———. 1991. *The Star Fisher.* New York: Morrow. 10–14 yrs.

Yolen, J. 1992. *Encounter.* Illus. D. Shannon. San Diego: Harcourt. 8–12 yrs.

Young, E. 1989. *Lon Po Po: A Red-Riding Hood Story from China.* New York: Philomel. 7–11 yrs.

Zhensun, Zheng & A. Low. 1991. *A Young Painter: The Life and Paintings of Wang Yani—China's Extraordinary Young Artist.* Photos. Zheng Zhensun. New York: Scholastic/ Byron Press-New China Pictures Books. 10–14 yrs.

MULTI-ETHNIC LITERATURE
BOOKS WITH PICTURES
Family

Adoff, Arnold. 1991. *Hard to Be Six.* Illus. Cheryl Hanna. New York: Lothrop, Lee & Shepard. 5–8 yrs.

Davol, Marguerite W. 1993. *Black, White, Just Right!* Morton Grove, Ill.: Whitman. 6–8 yrs.

Mills, Claudia. 1992. *A Visit to Amy-Claire.* Illus. Sheila Hamanaka. New York: Macmillan. 5–8 yrs.

Rosenberg, Maxine B. 1991. *Brothers and Sisters.* Photos George Ancona. New York: Clarion. 8–10 yrs.

Swope, S. 1989. *The Araboolies of Liberty Street.* Illus. Berry Root. New York: Clarkson N. Potter. 9–14 yrs.

Wilson, Beth P. 1990. *Jenny.* Illus. Dolores Johnson. New York: Macmillan. 6–8 yrs.

Friendship

Guy, Rosa. 1992. *Billy the Great.* Illus. Caroline Binch. New York: Delacorte.

Havill, Juanita. 1993. *Jamaica and Brianna.* Illus. Anne Sibley O'Brien. Boston: Houghton Mifflin. 5–7 yrs. (See also *Jamaica's Find,* 1986; *Jamaica Tag-Along,* 1989.)

———. 1995. *Jamaica's Blue Marker.* Illus. Anne Sibley O'Brien. Boston: Houghton Mifflin. 4–6 yrs.

Gikow, Louise & Ellen Weiss, 1993. *For Every Child, a Better World.* Illus. Bruce McNally. Muppet/Golden. 5–8 yrs.

Martin, Ann. 1992. *Rachel Parker, Kindergarten Show-off.* Illus. Nancy Poydar. New York: Holiday. 5–8 yrs.

Polacco, Patricia. 1992. *Chicken Sunday.* New York: Philomel. 5–9 yrs.

———. 1992. *Mrs. Katz and Tush.* Illus. Patricia Polacco. New York: Bantam Little Rooster Books. 5–8 yrs.

Raschka, Chris. 1993. *Yo! Yes?* New York: Orchard/ Jackson. 4–7 yrs.

Samton, Sheila White. 1991. *Jenny's Journey.* Illus. J. Samton. New York: Viking Penguin. 4–8 yrs.

Williams, Vera B. 1990. *"More More More," Said the Baby: Three Love Stories.* Illus. V. B. Williams. New York: Greenwillow. 4–6 yrs.

Neighborhood

Bunting, Eve. 1992. *Summer Wheels.* Illus. Thomas B. Allen. San Diego: Harcourt Brace Jovanovich. 6–10 yrs.

———. 1994. *Smoky Night.* Illus. David Diaz. San Diego: Harcourt Brace. 8–11 yrs.

Hughes, Shirley. 1991. *Wheels: A Tale of Trotter Street.* Illus. Shirley Hughes. New York: Lothrop, Lee & Shepard. 5–8 yrs.

Levine, Arthur A. 1993. *Pearl Moscowitz's Last Stand.* Illus. Robert Roth. New York: Tambourine. 6–8 yrs.

Medearis, A. S. 1995. *Treemonisha.* Illus. Michael Bryant. New York: Holt. 10–15 yrs.

Patrick, Denise Lewis. 1993. *The Car Washing Street.* Illus. John Ward. New York: Tambourine. 6–8 yrs.

Sage, James. 1991. *The Little Band.* Illus. Keiko Narahashi. New York: McElderry. 4–8 yrs.

Smalls-Hector, Irene. 1992. *Jonathan and His Mommy.* Illus. Michael Hays. Boston: Little, Brown. 4–7 yrs.

Tamar, E. 1996. *The Garden of Happiness.* Illus. Barbara Lambase. San Diego, Calif.: Harcourt Brace. 6–9 yrs.

Torres, Leyla. 1993. *Subway Sparrow.* New York: Farrar, Straus & Giroux. 6–8 yrs.

Walker, Alice. 1991. *Finding the Green Stone.* Illus. Catherine Deeter. San Diego: Harcourt Brace Jovanovich. 7–10 yrs.

Celebration

George, Jean Craighead. 1993. *The First Thanksgiving.* Illus. Thomas Locker. New York: Philomel. 6–9 yrs.

Nikola-Lisa, W. 1994. *Bein' with You This Way.* Illus. Michael Bryant. New York: Lee & Low. 6–10 yrs.

Concept

Agell, Charlotte. 1994. *Dancing Feet.* San Diego: Harcourt Brace/Gulliver. 5–8 yrs.

Emberley, Rebecca. 1990. *Taking a Walk: A Book in Two Languages/Caminando: Un Libro en Dos Lenguas.* Illus. R. Emberley. Boston: Little, Brown. 4–6 yrs.

Garne, S. T. 1992. *One White Sail.* Illus. Lisa Etre. New York: Green Tiger. 3–6 yrs.

MacKinnon, Debbie. 1992. *My First ABC.* Photos Anthea Sieveking. Hauppauge, N.Y.: Barron's. 2–6 yrs.

McMillan, Bruce. 1991. *Eating Fractions.* Photos B. McMillan. New York: Scholastic. 6–9 yrs.

Miller, Mary Beth & George Ancona. 1991. *Handtalk School.* Photos George Ancona. New York: Four Winds. 5–11 yrs.

Morris, Ann. 1994. *Loving.* Photos Ken Heyman. New York: Mulberry. 6–10 yrs. (See also: *On the Go: Hats, Hats, Hats;* and *Bread, Bread, Bread.*)

———. 1992. *Tools.* Photos. Ken Heyman. New York: Lothrop, Lee and Shepard. 6–9 yrs.

Tales from Around the World

Baumgartner, Barbara. 1994. *Crocodile! Crocodile!: Stories Told around the World.* Illus. Judith Moffatt. New York: Dorling Kindersley. 6–11 yrs.

Gale, David (Ed.). 1993. *Don't Give Up the Ghost: The Delacorte Book of Original Ghost Stories.* New York: Delacorte. 10–13 yrs.

Hamilton, Virginia. 1990. *The Dark Way: Stories from the Spirit World.* Illus. Lambert Davis. San Diego: Harcourt Brace Jovanovich. 9–16 yrs.

Meyer, Carolyn. 1994. *Rio Grande Stories.* San Diego: Harcourt Brace/Gulliver. 10–13 yrs.

Osborne, Mary Pope. 1993. *Mermaid Tales from around the World.* Illus. Troy Howell. New York: Scholastic. 10–13 yrs.

Ray, Jane. Illus. 1993. *Magical Tales from Many Lands.* New York: Dutton. 10–13 yrs.

San Souci, Robert D. 1993. *Cut from the Same Cloth: American Women of Myth, Legend, and Tall Tale.* Illus. Brian Pinkney. New York: Philomel. 10–13 yrs.

Shannon, George. 1994. *Still More Stories to Solve: Fourteen Folktales from Around the World.* Illus. Peter Sis. New York: Greenwillow. 7–10 yrs. (See also: *Stories to Solve.*)

Yep, Laurence. 1995. *Tree of Dreams: Ten Tales from the Garden of Night.* Illus. Isadore Seltzer. Mahwah, N.J.: BridgeWater. 10–14 yrs.

REALISTIC NOVELS

Families

Hughes, Dean. 1989. *Family Pose.* New York: Atheneum. 12–14 yrs.

Pinkwater, Jill. 1991. *Tails of the Bronx: A Tale of the Bronx.* New York: Macmillan. 9–12 yrs.

Porte, Barbara Ann. 1987. *I Only Made Up the Roses.* New York: Greenwillow. 12–14 yrs.

Quattlebaum, Mary. 1994. *Jackson Jones and the Puddle of Thorns.* Illus. Melodye Rosales. New York: Delacorte. 10–13 yrs.

Spinelli, Jerry. 1990. *Maniac Magee.* Boston: Little, Brown. 9–16 yrs.

Friends/School

Nelson, Vaunda Micheaux. 1993. *Mayfield Crossing.* Illus. Leonard Jenkins. New York: Putnam. 10–12 yrs.

Regan, Dian Curtis. 1992. *The Curse of the Trouble Dolls.* Illus. Michael Chesworth. New York: Holt/Red Feather. 7–10 yrs.

Soto, Gary. 1992. *Pacific Crossing.* San Diego: Harcourt Brace. 11–14 yrs.

History

Polacco, Patricia. 1994. *Pink and Say.* New York: Philomel. 8–12 yrs.

Biography

Barboza, Steven. 1992. *I Feel like Dancing: A Year with Jacques d'Amboise and the National Dance Institute.* Photos Carolyn George d'Amboise. New York: Crown. 8–14 yrs.

INFORMATION BOOKS

Families

Greenspun, Adele Aron. 1991. *Daddies.* Illus. Adele Aron Greenspun. New York: Philomel. 4–6 yrs.

Jenness, Aylette. 1990. *Families: A Celebration of Diversity, Commitment, and Love.* Photos. Aylette Jenness. Boston: Houghton Mifflin. 8–13 yrs. (See also: Rebecca Clay's *Ties That Bind. Families and Community.*)

Lakin, Patricia. 1995. *Family Around the World.* Woodbridge Conn.: Blackbirch. 8–14 yrs.

Menzel, Peter. 1994. *Material World: A Global Family Portrait.* San Francisco: Sierra Club. 8–14 yrs.

Rosenberg, Maine B. *Talking about Stepfamilies.* 1990. New York: Simon & Schuster. 10–14 yrs. (See also: *Growing Up Adopted* and *Not My Family*)

Sketch, Robert. 1995. *Who's in a Family?* Illus. Laura Nienhaus. Berkeley, Calif.: Tricycle. 5–9 yrs.

Friendship

Dolphin, Laurle. 1993. *Neve Shalom/Wahat al-Salam: Oasis of Peace.* Photos Ben Dolphin. New York: Scholastic. 10–13 yrs.

Neighborhood

Jenness, Aylette. 1993. *Come Home with Me: A Multicultural Treasure Hunt.* Video frames D'Arcy Marsh; illus. Laura DeSantis; photos Max Belcher. New York: New Press. 10–13 yrs.

Immigration

Anastos, Phillip, & Chris French. 1991. *Illegal: Seeking the American Dream.* Photos P. Anastos & Chris French. New York: Rizzoli. 12–16 yrs.

Kuklin, Susan. 1992. *How My Family Lives in America.* Illus. Susan Kuklin. New York: Bradbury. 5–7 yrs.

Lawlor, Veronica. 1995. *I Was Dreaming to Come to America: Memories from the Ellis Island Oral History Project.* Collage illustrations. New York: Viking. 10–13 yrs.

Levine, Ellen. 1993. *If Your Name Was Changed at Ellis Island.* Illus. Wayne Parmenter. New York: Scholastic. 10–13 yrs.

Social Issues

Banfield, Susan. 1995. *Ethnic Conflicts in Schools.* B & W photos. Springfield, N.J.: Enslow. 12–16 yrs. Multicultural Issues series.

Lang, Paul. 1995. *The English Language Debate: One Nation, One Language?* B & W photos. Springfield, N.J.: Enslow. 12–16 yrs. Multicultural Issues series.

Information

Hausherr, Rosmarie. 1992. *What Instrument Is This?* New York: Scholastic. 5–10 yrs.

Jaffe, Nina. 1994. *Patakin: World Tales of Drums and Drummers.* Illus. Ellen Eagle. New York: Holt. 10–13 yrs.

Knight, Margy Burns. 1994. *Welcoming Babies.* Illus. Anne Sibley O'Brien. St. Paul, Minn.: Tilbury. 7–11 yrs.

History

Mettger, Zak. 1994. *Reconstruction: America after the Civil War.* New York: Lodestar. 12–16 yrs. Young Readers' History of the Civil War series.

Piggins, Carol Ann. 1993. *A Multicultural Portrait of the Civil War.* Tarrytown, N.Y.: Cavendish. 12–16 yrs. Perspectives series.

Press, David P. 1993. *A Multicultural Portrait of Professional Sports.* Color, B & W photos. Tarrytown, N.Y.: Cavendish. 12–16 yrs. Perspectives series.

Press, Petra. 1993. *A Multicultural Portrait of the Move West.* Tarrytown, N.Y.: Cavendish. 12–16 yrs. Perspectives series.

Washburne, Carolyn Kott. 1993. *A Multicultural Portrait of Colonial Life.* Tarrytown, N.Y.: Cavendish. 12–16 yrs. Perspectives series.

Wright, David K. 1993. *A Multicultural Portrait of Life in the Cities.* Tarrytown, N.Y.: Cavendish. 12–16 yrs. Perspectives series.

POEMS, SONGS, STORIES, GAMES

Anthologies: Poems & Stories

Berck, Judith. 1992. *No Place to Be: Voices of Homeless Children.* Boston: Houghton Mifflin. 10–16 yrs.

Durell, Ann, & Marilyn Sachs (Eds.). 1990. *The Big Book for Peace.* New York: Dutton. 7–12 yrs.

Larrick, Nancy, & Wendy Lamb (Eds.). 1991. *To Ride a Butterfly: Original Stories, Poems, and Songs for Children by Fifty-two Distinguished Authors and Illustrators.* New York: Bantam Doubleday Dell. 5–10 yrs.

Rosen, Michael J. (Ed.). 1992. *Home: A Collection of Thirty Distinguished Authors and Illustrators of Children's Books to Aid the Homeless.* New York: HarperCollins/Zolotow. 8–12 yrs.

Stories

Carlstrom, Nancy White. 1990. *Light: Stories of a Small Kindness.* Illus. Lisa Desimini. Boston: Little, Brown. 9–12 yrs.

Gallo, Donald R. 1993. *Join In: Multiethnic Short Stories by Outstanding Writers for Young Adults.* New York: Delacorte. 12–16 yrs.

Mazer, Anne (Intro.). 1993. *America Street: A Multicultural Anthology of Stories.* New York: Persea. 12–16 yrs.

Sauerwein, Leigh. 1994. *The Way Home.* Illus. Miles Hyman. New York: Farrar, Straus & Giroux. 12–16 yrs.

Thomas, Joyce Carol (Ed.). 1990. *A Gathering of Flowers: Stories about Being Young in America.* New York: Harper & Row. 11–14 yrs.

Poetry

Dabovich, Lydia. 1992. *The Keys to My Kingdom: A Poem in Three Languages.* Illus. Lydia Dabovich. New York: Lothrop, Lee & Shepard. 5–8 yrs.

Giovanni, Nikki (Ed.). 1994. *Grandmothers.* New York: Holt. 12–17 yrs.

Glenn, Mel. 1991. *My Friend's Got This Problem, Mr. Candler: High School Poems.* Photos. Michael J. Bernstein. New York: Clarion. 10–16 yrs.

Nye, Naomi Shihab (Compiler). 1992. *This Same Sky: A Collection of Poems from around the World.* New York: Four Winds. 8–13 yrs.

Pomerantz, Chalotte. 1993. *If I Had a Paka: Poems in Eleven Languages.* Illus. Nancy Tafuri. New York: Greenwillow. 5–9 yrs.

Shields, C. D. 1995. *Lunch Money: And Other Poems about School.* Illus. Paul Meisel. New York: Dutton. 5–9 yrs.

Games

Lankford, Mary D. (Ed.). 1992. *Hopscotch around the World.* Illus. Karen Milone. New York: Morrow. 5–10 yrs.

Yolen, Jane (Ed.). 1992. *Street Rhymes around the World.* Illus. Seventeen international artists. Honesdale, Penn.: Boyds Mills/Wordsong. 4–10 yrs.

AFRICAN AMERICAN LITERATURE

BOOKS WITH PICTURES

Family

Barber, Barbara E. 1994. *Saturday at the New You.* Illus. Anna Rich. New York: Lee & Low. 6–8 yrs.

Barrett, J. 1989. *Willie's Not the Hugging Kind.* Illus. Pat Cummings. New York: Harper & Row. 6–9 yrs.

Best, Cari. 1995. *Red Light, Green Light, Mama and Me.* Illus. Niki Daly. New York: Kroupa: Oyrchard. 3–6 yrs.

Bogart, Jo Ellen. 1990. *Daniel's Dog.* Illus. Janet Wilson. New York: Scholastic. 5–8 yrs.

Clifton, Lucille. 1983. *Everett Anderson's Goodbye.* New York: Holt, 5–9 yrs.

Cummings, Pat. 1985. *Jimmy Lee Did It.* New York: Lothrop, Lee & Shepard. 4–8 yrs.

———. 1991. *Clean Your Room, Harvey Moon.* Illus. P. Cummings. New York: Bradbury. 4–7 yrs.

Eisenberg, Phyllis Rose. 1992. *You're My Nikki.* Illus. Jill Kastner. New York: Dial. 4–8 yrs.

Falwell, Cathryn. 1993. *Feast for 10.* Illus. C. Falwell. New York: Clarion. 2–5 yrs.

Greenfield, Eloise. 1991. *Daddy and I.* Illus. Jan Spivey Gilchrist. New York: Writers & Readers/Black Butterfly. 1–5 yrs.

———. 1991. *First Pink Light.* Illus. Jan Spivey Gilchrist. New York: Writers & Readers/Black Butterfly. 5–8 yrs.

Hill, Elizabeth Starr. 1990. *Evan's Corner.* Illus. Sandra Speidel. New York: Viking Penguin. 3–8 yrs.

Howard, Elizabeth Fitzgerald. 1995. *Papa Tells Chita a Story.* Illus. Floyd Cooper. New York: Simon & Schuster. 7–10 yrs.

Hudson, Wade et al. 1991. *Jamal's Busy Day.* Illus. George Ford. East Orange, N.J.: Just Us Books. 5–7 yrs.

Jackson, I. 1996. *Somebody's New Pajamas*. Illus. David Soman. New York: Dial. 6–9 yrs.

Johnson, Angela. 1989. *Tell Me a Story, Mama*. Illus. David Soman. New York: Orchard. 5–8 yrs.

_____. 1990. *Do Like Kyla*. Illus. James E. Ransome. New York: Orchard/Jackson. 3–7 yrs.

_____. 1991. *One of Three*. Illus. David Soman. New York: Orchard. 4–7 yrs.

_____. 1995. *Shoes Like Miss Alice's*. Illus. Ken Page. New York: Orchard/Jackson. 5–9 yrs.

Johnson, Dolores. 1990. *What Will Mommy Do When I'm at School?* Illus. Dolores Johnson. New York: Macmillan. 4–6 yrs.

_____. 1994. *Papa's Stories*. Illus. D. Johnson. New York: Macmillan. 5–8 yrs.

Medearis, Angela Shelf. 1995. *Poppa's New Pants*. Illus. John Ward. New York: Holiday. 5–9 yrs.

Moss, Marissa. 1994. *Mel's Diner*. Mahwah, N.J.: BridgeWater. 6–8 yrs.

Porte, Barbara Ann. 1995. *Chickens! Chickens!* Illus. Greg Henry. New York: Orchard/Jackson. 6–10 yrs.

Ringgold, Faith. 1991. *Tar Beach*. Illus. Faith Ringgold. New York: Crown. 7–11 yrs.

Scott, Ann Herbert. 1992. *Sam*. Illus. Symeon Shimin. New York: Philomel 5–8 yrs.

Shelby, Anne. 1990. *We Keep a Store*. Illus. John Ward. New York: Orchard. 5–8 yrs.

Smalls-Hector, Irene. 1992. *Jonathan and His Mommy*. Illus. Michael Hays. Boston: Little, Brown. 4–7 yrs.

Temple, C. 1996. *Train*. Illus. Larry Johnson. Boston: Houghton Mifflin. 6–9 yrs.

Thomassie, T. 1996. *Mimi's Tutu*. Illus. Jan Spivey Gilchrist. New York: Scholastic. 6–9 yrs.

Walter, Mildred Pitts. 1990. *Two and Too Much*. Illus. Pat Cummings. New York: Bradbury. 4–7 yrs.

Williams, Sherley Anne. 1992. *Working Cotton*. Illus. Carole Byard. San Diego: Harcourt Brace Jovanovich. 6–10 yrs.

Wyeth, Sharon Dennis. 1995. *Always My Dad*. Illus. Raul Colin. New York: Knopf/Apple Soup. 6–9 yrs.

Yarbrough, C. 1996. *The Little Tree Growin' in the Shade*. Illus. Tyrone Geter. New York: Putnam. 6–9 yrs.

Grandparents

Belton, Sandra. 1994. *May'naise Sandwiches and Sunshine Tea*. Illus. Gail Gordon Carter. New York: Four Winds. 5–7 yrs.

Crews, Donald. 1991. *Bigmama's*. Illus. D. Crews. New York: Greenwillow. 5–8 yrs.

Curtis, Gavin. 1990. *Grandma's Baseball*. Illus. Gavin Curtis. New York: Crown. 6–9 yrs.

Flournoy, Valerie. 1985. *The Patchwork Quilt*. New York: Dial. 7–10 yrs.

Fox, Mem. 1994. *Sophie*. Illus. Aminah Brenda Lynn Robinson. San Diego: Harcourt Brace. 5–8 yrs.

Greenfield, Eloise. 1993. *William and the Good Old Days*. Illus. Jan Spivey Gilchrist. New York: HarperCollins. 6–9 yrs.

Haskins, Francine. 1992. *Things I Like about Grandma*. Illus. F. Haskins. Emeryville, Calif.: Children's Book Press. 4–8 yrs.

Igus, Toyomi. 1992. *When I Was Little*. Illus. Higgins Bond. East Orange, N.J.: Just Us Books. 6–9 yrs.

Johnson, Angela. 1990. *When I Am Old with You*. Illus. David Soman. New York: Orchard/Jackson. 4–7 yrs.

_____. 1993. *Julius*. Illus. Dav Pilkey. New York: Orchard/Jackson. 5–8 yrs.

Johnson, P. B. & C. Lewis. 1996. *Lost*. Illus. Paul Brett Johnson. New York: Orchard. 6–9 yrs.

Johnston, T. 1996. *Fishing Sunday*. Illus. Barry Root. New York: Tambourine. 6–9 yrs.

Stolz, Mary. 1988. *Storm in the Night*. Illus. Pat Cummings. New York: HarperCollins. 6–9 yrs.

Extended Family

Caines, Jeannette. 1982. *Just Us Women*. Illus. Pat Cumins. New York: HarperCollins. 5–8 yrs.

Howard, Elizabeth Fitzgerald. 1993. *Mac and Marie and the Train Toss Surprise*. Illus. Gail Gordon Carter. New York: Four Winds. 6–9 yrs.

_____. 1996. *What's in Aunt Mary's Room?* Illus. Cedric Lucas. New York: Clarion. 6–9 yrs.

Mitchell, Margaree King. 1993. *Uncle Jed's Barbershop*. Illus. James Ransome. New York: Simon & Schuster. 6–8 yrs.

Patrick, Denise Lewis. 1993. *Red Dancing Shoes*. Illus. James E. Ransome. New York: Tambourine. 4–7 yrs.

Pinkney, Gloria Jean. 1992. *Back Home*. Illus. Jerry Pinkney. New York: Dial. 5–9 yrs.

_____. 1992. *Jean Back Home*. Illus. Jerry Pinkney. New York: Dial. 5–8 yrs.

_____. 1994. *The Sunday Outing*. Illus. Jerry Pinkney. New York: Dial. 5–8 yrs.

Rodriguez, Anita. 1993. *Aunt Martha and the Golden Coin: An Aunt Martha Story*. New York: Potter. 6–8 yrs.

Friendship

Children

Clifton, Lucille. 1992. *Three Wishes*. Illus. Michael Hays. New York: Doubleday. 5–8 yrs.

Greenfield, Eloise. 1991. *Big Friend, Little Friend*. Illus. Jan Spivey Gilchrist. New York: Writers & Readers/Black Butterfly. 1–5 yrs.

Hutchins, Pat. 1993. *My Best Friend*. New York: Greenwillow. 5–8 yrs.

Johnson, Angela. 1992. *The Leaving Morning*. Illus. David Soman. New York: Orchard/Jackson. 4–7 yrs.

Johnson, Dolores. 1992. *The Best Bug to Be*. Illus. D. Johnson. New York: Macmillan. 4–8 yrs.

Older Friends

Barrett, Mary Brigid. 1994. *Sing to the Stars*. Illus. Sandra Speidel. Boston: Little, Brown. 6–8 yrs.

Battle-Lavert, Gwendolyn. 1994. *The Barber's Cutting Edge*. Illus. Raymond Holbert. Emeryville, Calif.: Children's Press. 5–7 yrs.

Belton, Sandra. 1993. *From Miss Ida's Porch*. Illus. Floyd Cooper. New York: Four Winds. 6–9 yrs.

Gray, Libba Moore. 1993. *Dear Willie Rudd*. Illus. Peter M. Fiore. New York: Simon & Schuster. 7–10 yrs.

_____. 1993. *Miss Tizzy*. Illus. Jada Rowland. New York: Simon & Schuster. 5–8 yrs.

_____. 1995. *My Mama Had a Dancing Heart*. Illus. Raul Colon. New York: Orchard. Ages 4–8 yrs.

Johnson, Dolores. 1991. *What Kind of Baby-sitter Is This?* Illus. D. Johnson. New York: Macmillan. 5–8 yrs.

Kroll, Virginia. 1994. *Pink Paper Swans*. Illus. Nancy L. Clouse. Grand Rapids, Mich.: Eerdmans. 6–9 yrs.

Milich, Melissa. 1995. *Can't Scare Me!* Illus. Tyrone Geter. New York: Doubleday. 6–9 yrs.

Rupert, Rona. 1993. *Straw Sense*. Illus. Mike Dooling. New York: Simon & Schuster. 6–8 yrs.

Maturing

Cameron, A. 1995. *The Stories Huey Tells*. Illus. Roberta Smith. New York: Knopf. 7–10 yrs.

Everyday Experiences

Albert, Burton. 1991. *Where Does the Trail Lead?* Illus. Brian Pinkney. New York: Simon and Schuster. 3–7 yrs.

Bang, Molly. 1994. *One Fall Day*. New York: Greenwillow. 5–7 yrs.

Crews, Donald. 1992. *Shortcut*. Illus. Donald Crews. New York: Greenwillow. 5–8 yrs.

Cummings, Pat. 1992. *Petey Moroni's Camp Runamok Diary*. Illus. P. Cummings. New York: Bradbury. 6–9 yrs.

De Veaux, Alexis. 1987. *An Enchanted Hair Tale*. New York: HarperCollins. 4–8 yrs.

Dragonwagon, Crescent. 1990. *Home Place*. Illus. Jerry Pinkney. New York: Macmillan. 6–9 yrs.

Duncan, Alice Faye. 1995. *Willie Jerome*. Illus. Tyrone Geter. New York: Macmillan. 6–9 yrs.

Greenfield, Eloise. 1991. *I Make Music*. Illus. Jan Spivey Gilchrist. New York: Writers & Readers/Black Butterfly. 1–5 yrs. Board book.

_____. 1991. *My Doll, Keshia*. Illus. Jan Spivey Gilchrist. New York: Writers & Readers/Black Butterfly. 1–5 yrs. Board book.

Hort, Lenny. 1991. *How Many Stars in the Sky?* Illus. James E. Ransome. New York: Tambourine. 5–9 yrs.

Hru, Dakari. 1996. *The Magic Moonberry Jump Ropes*. Illus. E. B. Lewis. New York: Dial. 6–9 yrs.

Johnson, Angela. 1993. *The Girl Who Wore Snakes*. Illus. James E. Ransome. New York: Orchard/Jackson. 5–7 yrs.

Lotz, Karen E. 1993. *Can't Sit Still*. Illus. Colleen Browning. New York: Dutton. 5–7 yrs.

Pinkney, Brian. 1994. *Max Found Two Sticks*. New York: Simon & Schuster. 5–8 yrs.

Rochelle, Belinda. 1994. *When Jo Louis Won the Title*. Illus. Larry Johnson. Boston: Houghton Mifflin. 6–8 yrs.

Schertle, Alic. 1995. *Down the Road*. Illus. E. B. Lewis. San Diego: Browndeer/Harcourt Brace. 4–7 yrs.

Schroeder, A. 1995. *Carolina Shout!* Illus. Bernie Fuchs. New York: Dial. 6–12 yrs.

Serfozo, Mary. 1990. *Rain Talk*. Illus. Keiko Narahashi. New York: McElderry. 4–8 yrs.

Weiss, G. D. & B. Thiele. 1995. *What A Wonderful World*. Illus. Ashley Bryan. New York: Atheneum. 4–8 yrs.

Williams, Vera B. 1986. *Cherries and Cherry Pits*. New York: Greenwillow. 5–8 yrs.

Wood, A. 1996. *The Red Racer*. New York: Simon & Schuster. 6–9 yrs.

Young, Ruth. 1992. *Golden Bear*. Illus. Rachel Isadora. New York: Viking Penguin. 2–6 yrs.

Imagination

Baker, A. 1996. *I Thought I Heard*. Brookfield, Conn.: Copper Beech. 4–6 yrs.

Blackman, Malorie. 1993. *Girl Wonder and the Terrific Twins*. Illus. Lis Toft. New York: Dutton. 6–8 yrs.

Collis, Annabel. 1993. *You Can't Catch Me!* Boston: Joy Street. 3–7 yrs.

Cummings, Pat. 1994. *Carousel*. New York: Bradbury. 4–6 yrs.

Greenfield, Eloise. 1989. *Africa Dream*. New York: Crowell. 6–9 yrs. (See also *Grandpa's Face*, 1988.)

Manushkin, Fran. 1993. *My Christmas Safari*. Illus. R. W. Alley. New York: Dial. 5–8 yrs.

Mendez, Phil. 1989. *The Black Snowman*. Illus. Carole Byard. New York: Scholastic. 6–10 yrs.

Miller, W. 1996. *The Conjure Woman*. Illus. Terea D. Shaffer. New York: Atheneum. 6–9 yrs.

Nolen, Jerdine. 1994. *Harvey Potter's Balloon Farm*. Illus. Mark Buehner. New York: Lothrop, Lee & Shepard. 5–8 yrs.

Steig, William. 1992. *Doctor De Soto Goes to Africa*. New York: HarperCollins/di Capua. 6–9 yrs.

Cultural Pride

Grifalconi, Ann. 1990. *Osa's Pride*. Illus. Ann Grifalconi. Boston: Little, Brown. 5–9 yrs.

Hooks, W. H. 1995. *Freedom's Fruit.* Illus. James Ransome. New York: Knopf. 6–9 yrs.

Kroll, Virginia. 1992. *Masai and I.* Illus. Nancy Carpenter. New York: Four Winds. 6–8 yrs.

———. 1993. *Africa Brothers and Sisters.* Illus. Vanessa French. New York: Four Winds. 6–9 yrs.

———. 1993. *Wood-Hoopoe Willie.* Illus. Katherine Roundtree. Watertown, Mass.: Charlesbridge. 6–9 yrs.

Mederis, Angela Shelf. 1994. *Our People.* Illus. Michael Bryant. New York: Atheneum. 5–7 yrs.

Ringgold, Faith. 1993. *Dinner at Aunt Connie's House.* New York: Hyperion. 6–9 yrs.

Smith, Eddie. 1994. *A Lullaby for Daddy.* Illus. Susan Anderson. Lawrenceville, N.J.: Africa World. 5–8 yrs.

Yarbrough, Camille. 1981. *Cornrows.* New York: Coward, 6–9 yrs.

Celebrations:

Fiction

Clifton, Lucille. 1991. *Everett Anderson's Christmas Coming.* Illus. Jan Spivey Gilchrist. New York: Holt. 4–8 yrs.

Flournoy, V. & V. Flournoy. 1995. *Celie and the Harvest Fiddler.* Illus. James E. Ransome. New York: Tambourine. 6–9 yrs.

Miles, Calvin. 1993. *Calvin's Christmas Wish.* Illus. Dolores Johnson. New York: Viking. 4–7 yrs.

Rosen, Michael J. 1992. *Elizah's Angel.* Illus. Aminah Brenda Lynn Robinson. San Diego: Harcourt Brace. 8–10 yrs.

Information Books

Brady, April A. 1995. *Kwanzaa Karamu: Cooking and Crafts for a Kwanzaa Feast.* Illus. Barbara Knutson. Photos Robert L. Wolfe & Diane Wolfe. Minneapolis, Minn.: Carolrhoda. 10–13 yrs.

Chocolate, Deborah Newton. 1990. *Kwanzaa.* Danbury, Conn.: Children's Press. 5–9 yrs.

———. 1992. *My First Kwanzaa Book.* Illus. Cal Massey, New York: Scholastic/Cartwheel. 5–8 yrs.

Hoyt-Goldsmith, Diane. 1993. *Celebrating Kwanzaa.* Photos Lawrence Migdale. New York: Holiday. 5–9 yrs.

McClester, Cedric. 1990. *Kwanzaa: Everything You Always Wanted to Know.* New York: Gumbs & Thomas, 11–16 yrs.

Pinkney, Andrea Davis. 1993. *Seven Candles for Kwanzaa,* Illus. Brian Pinkney. New York: Dial. 5–9 yrs.

Porter, A. P. 1991. *Kwanzaa.* Illus. Janice Lee Porter. Minneapolis, Minn.: Carolrhoda. 5–7 yrs. On My Own series.

History

Brenner, Barbara. 1993. *Wagon Wheels.* Illus. Don Bolognese. New York: HarperCollins. 7–9 yrs. I Can Read series.

Coleman, Evelyn. 1994. *The Foot Warmer and the Crow.* Illus. Daniel Minter. New York: Macmillan. 7–9 yrs.

Hopkinson, Deborah. 1993. *Sweet Clara and the Freedom Quilt.* Illus. James Ransome. New York: Knopf. 8–10 yrs.

Medearis, Angela Shelf. 1991. *Dancing with the Indians.* Illus. Samuel Byrd. New York: Holiday. 6–10 yrs.

Ringgold, Faith. 1992. *Aunt Harriet's Underground Railroad in the Sky.* Illus. Faith Ringgold. New York: Crown. 7–11 yrs.

Smalls-Hector, Irene. 1991. *Irene and the Big, Fine Nickel.* Illus. Tyrone Geter. Boston: Little, Brown. 5–8 yrs.

———. 1996. *Ebony Sea.* Illus. Jon Onye Lockard. Stamford, Conn.: Longmeadow. 6–9 yrs.

Wright, Courtni C. 1994. *Jumping the Broom.* Illus. Gershom Griffith. New York: Holiday. 7–10 yrs.

African Setting

Grimsdell, Jeremy. 1993. *Kalinzu: A Story from Africa.* New York: Kingfisher. 6–8 yrs.

Isadora, Rachel. 1991. *At the Crossroads.* Illus. R. Isadora. New York: Greenwillow. 6–8 yrs.

———. 1992. *Over the Green Hills.* Illus. R. Isadora. New York: Greenwillow. 5–8 yrs.

Kennaway, Adrienne. 1992. *Little Elephant's Walk.* New York: HarperCollins/Perlman. 5–8 yrs.

Lewin, Hugh. 1983. *Jafta and the Wedding.* Minneapolis, Minn.: Carolrhoda. 4–8 yrs.

———. 1994. *Jafta: The Homecoming.* Illus. Lisa Kopper. New York: Knopf. 5–7 yrs. Umbrella series.

MacDonald, Suse. 1995. *Nanta's Lion: A Search-and Find Adventure.* New York: Morrow. 6–10 yrs.

Matthews, Mary. 1996. *Magid Fasts for Ramadan.* Illus. E. B. Lewis. New York: Clarion. 8–9 yrs.

Olaleye, Isaac. 1994. *Bitter Bananas.* Illus. Ed Young. Honesdale, Penn.: Boyds Mills. 7–9 yrs.

Onyefulu, Ifeoma. 1993. *A Is for Africa.* Photos. New York: Cobblehill. 5–8 yrs.

———. 1996. *Ogbo: Sharing Life in an African Village.* Photos. Ifeoma Onyefulu. San Diego: Gulliver/Harcourt Brace. 6–9 yrs.

Sisulu, E. B. 1996. *The Day Gogo Went to Vote: South Africa, April 1994.* Illus. Sharon Wilson. Boston: Little, Brown. 7–9 yrs.

Stanley, Sanna. *The Rains Are Coming.* New York: Greenwillow. 5–7 yrs.

Stock, Catherine. 1993. *Where Are You Going Manyoni?* New York: Morrow. 6–8 yrs.

Vyner, Sue. 1992. *The Stolen Egg.* Illus. Tim Vyner. New York: Viking. 5–8 yrs.

Watson, Pete. 1994. *The Market Lady and the Mango Tree.* Illus. Mary Watson. New York: Tambourine. 6–8 yrs.

Williams, Karen Lynn. 1990. *Galimoto.* Illus. Catherine Stock. New York: Lothrop, Lee & Shepard/Mulberry. 5–8 yrs.

———. 1991. *When Africa Was Home.* Illus. Floyd Cooper. New York: Orchard/Jackson. 4–8 yrs.

FOLK LITERATURE

African-American Tales

Bowman, J. C. 1942. *John Henry.* Illus. R. LaGrove. Morton Grove, Ill.: Whitman. 9–12 yrs.

Hamilton, Virginia. 1985. *The People Could Fly: American Black Folktales.* Illus. Leo & Diane Dillon. New York: Knopf. 10–14 yrs.

———. 1993. *Many Thousand Gone: African Americans from Slavery to Freedom.* Illus. Leo & Diane Dillon. New York: Knopf. 10–14 yrs.

———. 1996. *When Birds Could Talk and Bats Could Sing: The Adventures of Bruh Sparros, Sis Wren, and Their Friends.* Illus. Barry Moser. New York: Blue Sky. 5–10 yrs.

Haskins, James. 1994. *The Headless Haunt: And Other African-American Ghost Stories.* Illus. Ben Otero. New York: HarperCollins. 10–13 yrs.

Hooks, William H. 1990. *The Ballad of Belle Dorcas.* Illus. Brian Pinkney. New York: Knopf/Borzoi. 9–13 yrs.

———. 1996. *Freedom's Fruit.* Illus. James Ransome. New York: Knopf. 9–12 yrs.

Keats, E. J. 1965. *John Henry: An American Legend.* New York: Pantheon. 9–12 yrs.

Lester, Julius. 1989. *How Many Spots Does a Leopard Have? and Other Tales.* Illus. David Shannon. New York: Scholastic. 5–10 yrs.

———. 1994. *John Henry.* Illus. Jerry Pinkney. New York: Dial. 9–12 yrs.

Lyons, Mary E. (Compiler). 1991. *Raw Head, Bloody Bones: African American Tales of the Supernatural.* New York: Scribners. 10–14 yrs.

McKissack, Patricia C. 1992. *The Dark Thirty: Southern Tales of the Supernatural.* Illus. Brian Pinkney. New York: Knopf/Borzoi. 8–14 yrs.

Medearis, A. S. 1995. *The Freedom Riddle.* Illus. John Ward. New York: Lodestar. 7–10 yrs.

Myers, W. D. 1996. *How Mr. Monkey Saw the Whole World.* Illus. Synthia Saint James. New York: Doubleday. 3–6 yrs.

San Souci, Robert D. 1989. *The Boy and the Ghost.* Illus. J. Brian Pinkney. New York: Simon & Schuster. 7–11 yrs.

———. 1992. *Sukey and the Mermaid.* Illus. Brian Pinkney. New York: Four Winds. 8–12 yrs.

———. 1995. *The Faithful Friend.* Illus. Brian Pinkney. New York: Simon & Schuster. 5–10 yrs.

Sierra, Judy (Adapter). 1996. *Wiley and the Hairy Man.* Illus. Brian Pinkney. New York: Lodestar. 5–8 yrs.

Small, Terry. 1994. *The Legend of John Henry.* New York: Doubleday. 7–10 yrs.

Wahl, Jan (Reteller). 1991. *Tailypo!* Illus. Wil Clay. New York: Holt. 5–10 yrs.

———. 1992. *Little Eight John.* Illus. Wil Clay. New York: Lodestar. 6–9 yrs.

African Tales

Aardema. 1977. *Who's in Rabbit's House?* New York: Dial. 6–9 yrs.

———. 1981. *Bringing the Rain to Kapiti Plain.* New York: Dial. 5–9 yrs.

———. 1989. *Rabbit Makes a Monkey of Lion.* New York: Dial. 6–9 yrs.

———. 1991. *Traveling to Tondo: A Tale of the Nkundo of Zaire.* Illus. Will Hillenbrand. New York: Knopf/Borzoi. 6–9 yrs.

———. 1992. *Anansi Finds a Fool: An Ashanti Tale.* Illus. Bryna Waldman. New York: Dial. 5–9 yrs.

———. 1993. *Sebgugugu the Glutton: A Bantu Tale from Rwanda.* Illus. Nancy L. Clouse. Grand Rapids, Mich.: Eerdmans. 6–9 yrs.

———. 1994. *Misoso: Once upon a Time Tales from Africa.* Illus. Reynold Ruffins. New York: Apple Soup. 7–11 yrs.

———. 1995. *Jackal's Flying Lesson: A Khoikhoi Tale.* Illus. Dale Gottlieb. New York: Apple Soup. 5–9 yrs.

Anderson-Sankofa, David A. 1991. *The Origin of Life on Earth: An African Creation Myth.* Illus. Kathleen Atkins Wilson. Mt. Airy, Md.: Sights Productions. 9–12 yrs. Coretta Scott King Illustration Award, 1993.

Arnott, K. 1962. *African Myths and Legends.* Illus. J. Kiddill-Monroe. New York: Walck. 9–13 yrs.

Barbosa, Rogerio Andrade (Trans. Feliz Guthrie). 1993. *African Animal Tales.* Illus. Cisa Fittipaldi. Volcano, Calif.: Volcano. 6–10 yrs.

Berry, James (Adapter). 1996. *Don't Leave an Elephant to Go and Chase a Bird.* Illus. Ann Grifalconi. New York: Simon & Schuster. 5–8 yrs.

Bryan, Ashley. 1993. *The Story of Lightning and Thunder.* New York: Atheneum/Karl. 6–9 yrs.

———. 1993. *The Ox of the Wonderful Horns and Other African Folktales.* New York: Atheneum. 10–12 yrs.

Cashford, Jules. 1993. *The Myth of Isis and Osiris.* Boston: Barefoot. 10–13 yrs.

Chocolate, Deborah (Adapter). 1993. *Talk, Talk: An Ashanti Legend.* Illus. D. Albers. Mahwah, N.J.: Troll. 7–10 yrs.

Climo, S. 1989. *The Egyptian Cinderella.* Illus. R. Heller. New York: Harper Trophy. 7–10 yrs.

Daly, Niki (Reteller). 1995. *Why the Sun and Moon Live in the Sky.* Illus. N. Day. New York: Lothrop, Lee & Shepard. 5–9 yrs.

Day, Nancy Raines. 1995. *The Lion's Whiskers: An Ethiopian Folktale.* Illus. Ann Grifalconi. New York: Scholastic. 5–9 yrs.

Dee, Ruby. 1988. *Two Ways to Count to Ten*. New York: Holt. 6–9 yrs.

———. 1991. *Tower to Heaven*. Illus. Jennifer Bent. New York: Holt. 6–10 yrs.

Deetlefs, Rene. 1995. *Tabu and the Dancing Elephants*. Illus. Lyn Gilbert. New York: Dutton. 5–9 yrs.

Fairman, Tony (Reteller). 1992. *Bury My Bones but Keep My Words: African Tales for Retelling*. Illus. Meshack Asare. New York: Holt. 10–14 yrs.

Faulkner, William J. 1995. *Brer Tiger and the Big Wind*. Illus. Roberta Wilson. New York: Morrow. 5–9 yrs.

Ford, Bernette. 1994. *The Hunter Who Was King: And Other African Tales*. Illus. George Ford. New York: Hyperion. 5–9 yrs.

Gatti, Anne. 1995. *Tales from the African Plains*. Illus. Gregory Alexander. New York: Dutton. 10–14 yrs.

Gershator, Phillis. 1994. *The Iroko-Man: A Yoruba Folktale*. Illus. Holly C. Kim. New York: Orchard/Jackson. 5–9 yrs.

Gerson, Mary-Joan (Reteller). 1992. *Why the Sky Is Far Away: A Nigerian Folktale*. Illus. Carla Golembe. Boston: Little, Brown/Joy Street. 7–10 yrs.

———. 1994. *How Night Came from the Sea: A Story from Brazil*. Illus. Carla Golembe. Boston: Little, Brown. 7–10 yrs.

Haley, Gail. 1970. *A Story, a Story*. New York: Atheneum. 6–9 yrs.

Harris, Joel Chandler (Adapter Van Dyke Parks). 1989. *Jump On Over! The Adventures of Brer Rabbit and His Family*. Illus. Barry Moser. San Diego: Harcourt Brace Jovanovich. 7–12 yrs.

Heady, E. B. 1965. *Jambo Sungura: Tales from East Africa*. Illus. R. Frankenberg. New York: Norton. 9–12 yrs.

Jaquith, Priscilla. 1995. *Bo Rabbit Smart for True: Tall Tales from the Gullah*. Illus. Ed Young. New York: Philomel. 5–10 yrs.

Kimmel, Eric A. (Reteller). 1992. *Anansi Goes Fishing*. Illus. Janet Stevens. New York: Holiday. 6–9 yrs.

———. 1995. *Rimonah of the Flashing Sword: A North African Tale*. Illus. Omar Rayyan. New York: Holiday. 5–10 yrs.

Knappert, Jan. 1994. *Kings, Gods, and Spirits from African Mythology*. Illus. Francesca Pelizzoli. New York: Bedrick. 10–13 yrs. World Mythology series.

Knutson, Barbara (Reteller). 1990. *How the Guinea Fowl Got Her Spots: A Swahili Tale of Friendship*. Illus. B. Knutson. Minneapolis, Minn.: Carolrhoda. 5–8 yrs.

———. 1993. *Sungura and Leopard: A Swahili Trickster Tale*. Boston: Little, Brown. 7–10 yrs.

Laird, Elizabeth. 1987. *The Road to Bethlehem: An Ethiopian Nativity*. New York: Holt. 6–10 yrs.

Lester, Julius (Reteller). 1990. *Further Tales of Uncle Remus: The Misadventures of Brer Rabbit, Brer Fox, Brer Wolf, the Doodang, and Other Creatures*. Illus. Jerry Pinkney. New York: Dial. 7–12 yrs. (See also sequel: *More Tales of Uncle Remus: Further Adventures of Brer Rabbit, His Friends, Enemies, and others*.)

Lyons, Mary E. 1995. *The Butter Tree: Tales of Bruh Rabbit*. Illus. Mireille Vautier. New York: Holt. 5–10 yrs.

Maddern, Eric. 1993. *The Fire Children: A West African Creation Tale*. Illus. Frane Lessac. New York: Dial. 7–11 yrs.

Martin, Francesca. 1992. *The Honey Hunters: A Traditional African Tale*. Illus. F. Martin. Cambridge, Mass.: Candlewick. 5–9 yrs.

McDermott, Gerald. 1992. *Zomo the Rabbit: A Trickster Tale from West Africa*. Illus. G. McDermott. San Diego: Harcourt Brace Jovanovich. 5–10 yrs.

———. 1994. *The Magic Tree: A Tale from the Congo*. Illus. G. McDermott. New York: Holt. 7–10 yrs.

Medearis, Angela Shelf. 1994. *The Singing Man: Adapted from a West African Folktale*. Illus. Terea Shaffer. New York: Holiday. 10–13 yrs.

———. 1995. *Too Much Talk*. Illus. Stefano Vitale. Cambridge, Mass.: Candlewick. 4–7 yrs.

Medicott, M. 1995. *The River that Went to the Sky: Twelve Tales by African Storytellers*. Illus. Ademola Akintola. New York: Kingfisher. 6–9 yrs.

Mollel, Tololwa M. 1990. *The Orphan Boy: A Maasai Story*. Illus. Paul Morin. New York: Clarion. 7–12 yrs.

———. 1991. *Rhinos for Lunch and Elephants for Supper! A Maasai Tale*. Illus. Barbara Spurll. New York: Clarion. 5–8 yrs.

———. 1992. *A Promise to the Sun: An African Story*. Illus. Beatriz Vidal. Boston: Little, Brown/Joy Street. 7–11 yrs.

———. 1994. *The Flying Tortoise: An Igbo Tale*. Illus. Barbara Spurll. New York: Clarion.

Onyefulu, Obi. 1994. *Chinye: A West African Folk Tale*. Illus. Evie Safarewicz. New York: Viking. 7–10 yrs.

Oyono, E. 1995. *Gollo and the Lion*. Illus. Laurent Corvaisier. New York: Hyperion. 5–9 yrs.

Pollock, P. (Adapter). 1996. *The Turkey Girl: A Zuni Cinderella Story*. Illus. Ed Young. Boston: Little, Brown. 5–8 yrs.

Rappaport, Doreen. 1995. *The New King*. Illus. E. B. Lewis. New York: Dial. 5–10 yrs.

Roddy, Patricia. 1994. *Api and the Boy Stranger: A Village Creation Tale*. Illus. Lynne Russell. New York: Dial. 5–9 yrs.

Rosen, Michael. 1993. *How Giraffe Got Such a Long Neck . . . And Why Rhino Is So Grumpy*. Illus. John Clementson. New York: Dial. 6–10 yrs.

Sanfield, Steve. 1989. *The Adventures of High John the Conqueror*. Illus. John Ward. New York: Orchard/Jackson. 8–12 yrs.

San Souci, Robert D. 1989. *Talking Eggs*. New York: Dial. 9–12 yrs.

Shute, Linda. 1995. *Rabbit Wishes*. New York: Lothrop, Lee & Shepard. 5–10 yrs.

Sierra, Judy. 1992. *The Elephant's Wrestling Match*. Illus. Brian Pinkney. New York: Lodestar. 5–8 yrs.

Souhami, J. 1996. *The Leopard's Drum: An Asante Tale from West Africa*. Boston: Little, Brown. 6–9 yrs.

Steptoe, John. 1987. *Mufaro's Beautiful Daughters: An African Tale*. New York: Lothrop, Lee & Shepard. 7–10 yrs.

Stewart, D. 1996. *Gift of the Sun: A Tale from South Africa*. Illus. Jude Daly. New York: Farrar, Straus & Giroux. 4–6 yrs.

Williams, Sheron. 1992. *And in the Beginning*. Illus. Robert Roth. New York: Atheneum. 8–11 yrs.

Wisniewski, David. 1992. *Sundiata: Lion King of Mali*. Illus. D. Wisniewski. New York: Clarion. 6–10 yrs.

Tadjo, Veronique (Reteller). 1989. *Lord of the Dance: An African Retelling*. Illus. Veronique Tadjo. New York: Lippincott. 6–10 yrs.

FANTASY/LITERARY FOLK TALES

Alexander, Lloyd. 1992. *The Fortune-Tellers*. Illus. Trina Schart Hyman. New York: Dutton. 5–9 yrs.

Hamilton, Virginia. 1978. *Justice and Her Brothers*. New York: Greenwillow. 12–16 yrs.

———. 1982. *Sweet Whispers, Brother Rush*. New York: Putnam/Philomel. 12–16 yrs.

———. 1991. *The All Jahdu Storybook*. Illus. Barry Moser. San Diego: Harcourt Brace Jovanovich. 8–11 yrs.

———. 1992. *Drylongso*. Illus. Jerry Pinkney. San Diego: Harcourt Brace Jovanovich. 9–13 yrs.

———. 1995. *Jaguarundi*. Illus. Floyd Cooper. New York: Scholastic/Blue Sky. 7–10 yrs.

McKissack, Patricia C. 1992. *A Million Fish . . . More or Less*. Illus. Dena Schutzer. New York: Knopf/Borzoi. 6–10 yrs.

Myers, Walter Dean. 1995. *The Story of the Three Kingdoms*. Illus. Ashley Bryan. New York: HarperCollins. 7–10 yrs.

REALISTIC NOVELS: HISTORICAL FICTION

Collier, James Lincoln & Christopher Collier. 1994. *With Every Drop of Blood*. New York: Delacorte. 10–13 yrs.

Guccione, Leslie Davis. 1995. *Come Morning*. Minneapolis, Minn.: Carolrhoda. 9–11 yrs.

Myers, Walter Dean. 1994. *The Glory Field*. New York: Scholastic. 12–16 yrs.

Slavery

Armstrong, Jennifer. 1992. *Steal Away*. New York: Orchard Books/Richard. 10–14 yrs.

Forrester, Sandra. 1995. *Sound the Jubilee*. New York: Lodestar. 10–12 yrs.

Hamilton, Virginia. 1968. *The House of Dies Drear*. New York: Macmillan. 11–15 yrs. See also sequel: *The Mystery of Drear House*.

Hopkinson, Deborah. 1993. *Sweet Clara and the Freedom Quilt*. Illus. James Ransome. New York: Knopf. 8–12 yrs.

Lester, Julius. 1982. *This Strange New Feeling*. New York: Dial. 12–15 yrs.

Lyons, Mary E. 1992. *Letters from a Slave Girl: The Story of Harriet Jacobs*. New York: Scribners. 12–16 yrs.

McKissack, Patricia C. & Fredrick L. McKissack. 1994. *Christmas in the Big House, Christmas in the Quarters*. Illus. John Thompson. New York: Scholastic. 10–13 yrs.

———. 1996. *Rebels Against Slavery: American Slave Revolts*. Photos. New York: Scholastic. 11–15 yrs.

Monjo, F. N. 1993. *The Drinking Gourd: A Story of the Underground Railroad*. Illus. Fred Brenner. New York: HarperCollins. 7–9 yrs. I Can Read series.

Paulsen, Gary. 1993. *Nightjohn*. New York: Delacorte. 10–13 yrs.

Rosen, M. J. 1995. *A School for Pompey Walker*. Illus. Aminah Brenda Lynn Robinson. San Diego, Calif.: Harcourt Brace. 9–12 yrs.

Ruby, Lois. 1994. *Steal Away Home*. New York: Macmillan. 10–13 yrs.

Stolz, Mary. 1994. *Cezanne Pinto: A Memoir*. New York: Knopf. 12–16 yrs.

Turner, Glennette Tilley. 1994. *Running for Our Lives*. Illus. Samuel Byrd. New York: Holiday. 12–14 yrs.

Wright, Courtni C. 1994. *Journey to Freedom: A Story of the Underground Railroad*. Illus. Gershom Griffith. New York: Holiday. 7–9+ yrs.

After the Civil War

Hamilton, Virginia. 1989. *Bells of Christmas*. San Diego: Harcourt Brace Jovanovich. 9–12 yrs.

Myers, Walter Dean. 1992. *The Righteous Revenge of Artemis Bonner*. New York: HarperCollins. 10–16 yrs.

Porter, Connie. 1993. *Addy Learns a Lesson: A School Story*. Illus. Melodye Rosales. Pleasant. 10–13 yrs. American Girls Collection.

———. 1993. *Meet Addy: An American Girl*. Illus. Melodye Rosales. Middleton, Wisc.: Pleasant. 10–13 yrs. American Girls Collection.

_____. 1994. *Addy Saves the Day: A Summer Story.* Illus. Bradford Brown, Renee Graef, & Geri Strigenz Bourget. Middleton, Wisc.: Pleasant. 7–9 yrs. American Girls series.

_____. 1994. *Happy Birthday, Addy!: A Springtime Story.* Illus. Bradford Brown, Renee Graef, & Geri Strigenz Bourget. Middletown, Wisc.: Pleasant. 7–9 yrs. American Girls series.

Wright, Courtni C. 1995. *Wagon Train: A Family Goes West in 1865.* Illus. Gershom Griffith. New York: Holiday. 7–10 yrs.

Early 20th Century

Collier, James Lincoln. 1994. *The Jazz Kid.* New York: Holt. 11–14 yrs.

Meyer, Carolyn. 1993. *White Lilacs.* San Diego: Harcourt Brace/Gulliver. 12–16 yrs.

Taylor, Mildred D. 1976. *Roll of Thunder, Hear My Cry.* New York: Dial. 10–15 yrs. (See also sequels: *Song of the Trees,* 1975; *The Friendship,* 1987; *The Gold Cadillac,* 1987; *The Road to Memphis,* 1990.)

_____. 1990. *Mississippi Bridge.* Illus. Max Ginsburg. New York: Dial. 10–13 yrs.

_____. 1995. *The Well: David's Story.* New York: Dial. 10–13 yrs.

Higginsen, Vy (with Tonya Bolden). 1992. *Mama, I Want to Sing.* New York: Scholastic. 11–16 yrs.

Civil Rights Period

Curtis, Christopher Paul. 1995. *The Watsons Go to Birmingham—1963.* New York: Delacorte. 11–14 yrs.

Davis, Ossie. 1992. *Just like Martin.* New York: Simon and Schuster. 10–16 yrs.

Krisher, Trudy. 1994. *Spite Fences.* New York: Delacorte. 12–16 yrs.

Moore, Yvette. 1991. *Freedom Songs.* New York: Orchard. 12–16 yrs.

Prather, Ray. 1992. *Fish and Bones.* New York: HarperCollins. 12–15 yrs.

Young, Ronder Thomas. 1993. *Learning by Heart.* Boston: Houghton Mifflin. 10–13 yrs.

Contemporary Period

Family

Banks, Jacqueline. 1994. *Turner the New One.* Boston: Houghton Mifflin. 10–13 yrs.

_____. 1995. *Egg-Drop Blues.* Boston: Houghton Mifflin. 10–13 yrs.

Barnes, Joyce A. 1994. *The Baby Grand, the Moon in July, and Me.* New York: Dial. 12–16 yrs.

Boyd, Candy Dawson. 1993. *Chevrolet Saturdays.* New York: Macmillan. 10–13 yrs.

Cameron, Ann. 1981. *The Stories Julian Tells.* New York: Pantheon Books. 6–9 yrs. (See also *More Stories Julian Tells,* 1986; *Julian, Secret Agent* 1988; *Julian, Dream Doctor; Julian's Glorious Summer* 1987.)

Fenner, Carol. 1995. *Yolonda's Genius.* New York: McElderry. 10–13 yrs.

Greenfield, Eloise. 1992. *Koya DeLaney and the Good Girl Blues.* New York: Scholastic. 10–13 yrs.

Grifalconi, Ann. 1995. *Not Home.* Boston: Little, Brown. 10–13 yrs.

Guy, Rosa. 1989. *The Ups and Downs of Carl Davis III.* New York: Delacorte. 10–14 yrs.

Hamilton, Virginia. 1967. *Zeely.* New York: Macmillan. 9–12 yrs.

_____. 1990. *Cousins.* Illus. Jerry Pinkney. New York: Philomel. 9–12 yrs.

_____. 1993. *Plain City.* New York: Scholastic/Blue Sky. 12–16 yrs.

Johnson, Angela. 1993. *Toning the Sweep.* New York: Orchard/Jackson. 12–17 yrs.

_____. 1995. *Humming Whispers.* New York: Orchard. 11–16 yrs.

Mathis, Sharon Bell. 1972. *Teacup Full of Roses.* New York: Puffin. 12–16 yrs.

_____. 1974. *Listen for the Fig Tree.* New York: Puffin. 12–16 yrs.

_____. 1975. *The Hundred Penny Box.* Illus. Diane & Leo Dillon. New York: Viking. 8–12 yrs.

Myers, Walter Dean. 1992. *Somewhere in the Darkness.* New York: Scholastic. 12–16 yrs.

Pinkney, Andrea Davis. 1995. *Hold Fast to Dreams.* New York: Morrow. 10–14 yrs.

Quattlebaum, Mary. 1994. *Jackson Jones and the Puddle of Thorns.* Illus. Melodye Rosales. New York: Delacorte. 10–13 yrs.

Stolz, Mary. 1991. *Go Fish.* Illus. Pat Cummings. New York: HarperCollins. 7–11 yrs.

_____. 1992. *Stealing Home.* New York: HarperCollins. 10–12 yrs.

_____. 1994. *Coco Grimes.* New York: HarperCollins. 10–13 yrs.

Tate, Eleanora. 1980. *Just an Overnight Guest.* New York: Dial. 10–13 yrs.

Thomas, Joyce Carol. 1992. *When the Nightingale Sings.* New York: HarperCollins. 12–16 yrs.

Walter, Mildred P. 1986. *Justin and the Best Biscuits in the World.* New York: Lothrop, Lee & Shepard. 7–10 yrs.

Williams-Garcia, Rita. 1995. *Like Sisters on the Homefront.* New York: Lodestar. 11–15 yrs.

Woodson, Jacqueline. 1991. *The Dear One.* New York: Delacorte. 12–16 yrs.

_____. 1995. *From the Notebooks of Melanin Sun.* New York: Scholastic/Blue Sky. 12–16 yrs.

Wyeth, Sharon Dennis. 1994. *The World of Daughter McGuire.* New York: Delacorte. 10–13 yrs.

Yarbrough, Camille. 1994. *Tamika and the Wisdom Rings.* Illus. Anna Rich. New York: Random. 8–12 yrs. First Stepping Stone series.

Maturing

Cameron, A. 1995. *The Stories Huey Tells.* Illus. Roberta Smith. New York: Knopf. 7–10 yrs.

Friendship

Boyd, Candy Dawson. 1985. *Breadsticks and Blessing Places.* New York: Macmillan. 10–15 yrs.

Booth, Coleen E. 1992. *Going Live.* New York: Scribners. 10–14 yrs.

Burgess, Barbara Hood. 1994. *The Fred Field.* New York: Delacorte. 12–16 yrs. (See also *Oren Bell.*)

Cottonwood, J. 1996. *Babcock.* New York: Scholastic. 10–14 yrs.

Draper, Sharon M. 1994. *Tears of a Tiger.* New York: Atheneum. 12–16 yrs.

Eskridge, Ann E. 1994. *The Sanctuary.* New York: Cobblehill. 10–13 yrs.

Greene, Patricia Baird. *The Sabbath Garden.* New York: Lodestar. 12–16 yrs.

Hewett, L. 1996. *Soulfire.* New York: Dutton. 12–15 yrs.

Moore, Emily. 1988. *Whose Side Are You On?* New York: Farrar, Straus & Giroux. 10–14 yrs.

Myers, Walter Dean. 1990. *The Mouse Rap.* New York: Harper and Row. 11–16 yrs.

_____. 1988. *Me, Mop, and the Moondance Kid.* New York: Delacorte. 9–13 yrs.

_____. 1988. *Scorpions.* New York: HarperCollins. 12–16 yrs.

_____. 1992. *Mop, Moondance, and the Nagasaki Knights.* New York: Delacorte. 9–12 yrs.

_____. 1994. *Darnell Rock Reporting.* New York: Delacorte. 10–16 yrs.

Roberts, Brenda C. 1993. *Sticks and Stones, Bobbie Bones.* New York: Scholastic. 10–12 yrs.

Woodson, Jacqueline. 1990. *Last Summer with Maizon.* New York: Delacorte. 10–16 yrs.

_____. 1992. *Maizon at Blue Hill.* New York: Delacorte. 10–16 yrs.

_____. 1993. *Between Madison and Palmetto.* New York: Delacorte. 9–13 yrs.

_____. 1994. *I Hadn't Meant to Tell You This.* New York: Delacorte. 12–16 yrs.

Wyman, Andrea. 1994. *Faith, Hope, and Chicken Feathers.* New York: Holiday. 11–13 yrs.

Cultural Pride

Tate, Eleanora. 1987. *The Secret of Gumbo Grove.* Danbury, Conn.: Watts. 10–16 yrs.

_____. 1990. *Thank You, Dr. Martin Luther King, Jr.!* Danbury, Conn.: Watts. 9–12 yrs.

Walter, Mildred Pitts. 1989. *Have a Happy . . . : A Novel.* Illus. Carole Byard. New York: Lothrop, Lee & Shepard. 9–12 yrs.

Yarbrough, Camille. 1989. *The Shimmershine Queens.* New York: Putnam. 11–14 yrs.

African Setting

Case, Dianne. 1991. *Love, David.* Illus. Dan Andreasen. New York: Lodestar. 10–12 yrs.

Naidoo, Beverley. 1986. *Journey to Jo'burg: A South African Story.* New York: Lippincott. 10–14 yrs.

_____. 1990. *Chain of Fire.* Illus. Eric Velasquez. New York: HarperCollins. 12–16 yrs.

Rupert, Janet E. 1994. *The African Mask.* New York: Clarion.

Sacks, Margaret. 1992. *Themba.* Illus. Wil Clay. New York: Lodestar. 11–14 yrs.

Williams, Michael. 1992. *Crocodile Burning.* New York: Lodestar. 12–16 yrs.

NONFICTION LITERATURE

Slavery

Biographies

Adler, David A. 1992. *A Picture Book of Harriet Tubman.* Illus. Samuel Byrd. New York: Holiday. 7–10 yrs.

Banta, Melissa. 1993. *Frederick Douglass.* B & W photos. New York: Chelsea House. 10–13 yrs. Junior World Biographies series.

Barrett, Tracy. 1993. *Nat Turner and the Slave Revolt.* Brookfield, Conn.: Millbrook. 10–13 yrs. Gateway Civil Rights series.

Bennett, Evelyn. 1993. *Frederick Douglass and the War against Slavery.* Brookfield, Conn.: Millbrook. 10–13 yrs. Gateway Civil Rights series.

Bland, Celia. 1993. *Harriet Beecher Stowe.* B & W photos. New York: Chelsea House. 10–13 yrs. Junior World Biographies series.

Coil, Suzanne M. 1993. *Harriet Beecher Stowe.* Prints & photos. Danbury, Conn.: Watts. 12–16 yrs.

Cooper, Michael L. 1994. *From Slave to Civil War Hero: The Life and Times of Robert Smalls.* B & W photos, reproductions. New York: Lodestar. 10–13 yrs. Rainbow Biography series.

Elish, Dan. 1993. *Harriet Tubman and the Underground Railroad.* Brookfield, Conn.: Millbrook. 10–13 yrs. Gateway Civil Rights series.

Equiano, Olaudah (Adapter Ann Cameron; introduction Henry Louis Gates, Jr.). 1995. *The Kidnapped Prince: The Life of Olaudah Equiano.* New York: Knopf. 10–12 yrs. (Originally published 1789.)

Everett, Gwen. 1993. *John Brown: One Man against Slavery.* Illus. Jacob Lawrence. New York: Rizzoli. 9–12 yrs.

Fritz, Jean. 1994. *Harriet Beecher Stowe and the Beecher Preachers.* Photos. New York: Putnam. 11–14 yrs.

Hamilton, Virginia. 1988. *Anthony Burns: The Defeat and Triumph of a Fugitive Slave.* New York: Knopf. 12–16 yrs.

Johnson, Dolores. 1993. *Now Let Me Fly: The Story of a Slave Family.* New York: Macmillan. 8–10 yrs.

_____. 1994. *Seminole Diary: Remembrances of a Slave.* New York: Macmillan. 8–10 yrs.

Johnston, Norma. 1994. *Harriet: The Life and World of Harriet Beecher Stowe.* New York: Four Winds. 12–15 yrs.

Lyons, Mary E. 1992. *Letters from a Slave Girl.* New York: Scribners. 12 yrs.–adult. (**fictionalized**; based on Harriet Jacobs's 1861 autobiography *Incidents in the Life of a Slave Girl.*)

_____. 1994. *Master of Mahogany: Tom Day, Free Black Cabinetmaker.* New York: Scribners. 10–13 yrs.

McClard, Megan. 1990. *Harriet Tubman: Slavery and the Underground Railroad.* Morristown, N.J.: Silver Burdett. 10–14 yrs.

McCurdy, Michael (Ed. & Illus.). 1994. *Escape from Slavery: The Boyhood of Frederick Douglass in His Own Words.* New York: Knopf. 10–13 yrs.

McKissack, Patricia C. & Fredrick McKissack. 1992. *Sojourner Truth: Ain't I a Woman?* New York: Scholastic. 9–13 yrs.

_____. 1996. *Rebels Against Slavery: American Slave Revolts.* Photos. New York: Scholastic. 11–15 yrs.

Pinkney, Andrea Davis. 1994. *Dear Benjamin Banneker.* Illus. Brian Pinkney. San Diego: Harcourt Brace/Gulliver. 7–10 yrs.

Warner, Lucille Schulberg (Adapter). 1993. *From Slave to Abolitionist: The Life of William Wells Brown.* New York: Dial. 12–16 yrs.

Information Books

Bial, Raymond. 1995. *The Underground Railroad.* Color photos. Boston: Houghton Mifflin. 10–13 yrs.

Cox, Clinton. 1991. *Undying Glory: The Story of the Massachusetts 54th Regiment.* Photos. New York: Scholastic. 10–14 yrs.

Feelings, Tom. 1995. *The Middle Passage: White Ships, Black Cargo.* New York: Dial. 12–16 yrs.

Haskins, Jim. 1993. *Get on Board: The Story of the Underground Railroad.* B & W photos & drawings. New York: Scholastic. 10–14 yrs.

Katz, William Loren. 1990. *Breaking the Chains: African-American Slave Resistance.* New York: Atheneum. 12–16 yrs.

Lester, Julius. 1993. *Long Journey Home: Stories from Black History.* New York: Dial. 12–16 yrs.

Mettger, Zak. 1994. *Till Victory Is Won: Black Soldiers in the Civil War.* New York: Lodestar. 12–16 yrs. Young Readers' History of the Civil War series.

Paulson, Timothy J. 1994. *Days of Sorrow, Years of Glory, 1831–1850: From the Nat Turner Revolt to the Fugitive Slave Law.* New York: Chelsea House. 10–13 yrs. Milestones in Black American History series.

Rappaport, Doreen. 1991. *Escape from Slavery: Five Journeys to Freedom.* Illus. Charles Lilly. New York: HarperCollins. 9–12 yrs.

Stepto, Michele (Ed.). 1994. *Our Song, Our Toil: The Story of American Slavery as Told by Slaves.* Paintings & B & W photos. Brookfield, Conn.: Millbrook. 10–13 yrs.

Sullivan, George. 1994. *Slave Ship: The Story of the Henrietta Marie.* Photos. New York: Cobblehill. 10–13 yrs.

Late 19th through Early 20th Centuries

Biographies

Bundles, A'Lelia Perry. 1993. *Madam C. J. Walker.* New York: Chelsea House. 12–16 yrs. Black Americans of Achievement series.

Calvert, Roz. 1993. *Zora Neal Hurston.* B & W photos. New York: Chelsea House. 11–14 yrs. Junior World Biographies series.

Cooper, Floyd. 1994. *Coming Home: From the Life of Langston Hughes.* New York: Philomel. 10–13 yrs.

Colman, Penny. 1992. *Spies! Women in the Civil War.* Cincinnati, Ohio: Shoe Tree Press. 10–15 yrs.

Cox, Clinton. 1993. *The Forgotten Heroes: The Story of the Buffalo Soldiers.* New York: Scholastic. 12–16 yrs.

Davis, Ossie. 1982. *Langston: A Play.* New York: Delacorte. 11–15 yrs.

Everett, Gwen. 1991. *Lil Sis and Uncle Willie: A Story Based on the Life and Paintings of William H. Johnson.* Illus. William H. Johnson. New York: Rizzoli International Publications/National Museum of American Art, Smithsonian Institution. 7–10 yrs.

Ferris, Jeri. 1994. *What I Had Was Singing: The Story of Marian Anderson.* B & W photos. Minneapolis, Minn.: Carolrhoda. 10–13 yrs. Trailblazers series.

Hudson, Karen E. 1994. *The Will and the Way: Paul R. Williams, Architect.* B & W photos. New York: Rizzoli. 10–13 yrs.

Lyons, Mary E. 1990. *Sorrow's Kitchen: The Life and Folklore of Zora Neale Hurston.* New York: Scribners. 12–16 yrs.

_____. 1993. *Starting Home: The Story of Horace Pippin, Painter.* New York: Scribners. 10–13 yrs. African-American Artists and Artisans series.

_____. 1993. *Stitching Stars: The Story Quilts of Harriet Powers.* New York: Scribners. 10–13 yrs. African-American Artists and Artisans series.

_____. 1994. *Deep Blues: Bill Traylor, Self-Taught Artist.* New York: Scribners. 10–13 yrs. African-American Artists and Artisans series.

Miller, William. 1994. *Zora Hurston and the Chinaberry Tree.* Illus. Cornelius Van Wright & Ying-Hwa Hu. New York: Lee & Low. 7–11 yrs.

Nickens, Bessie. 1994. *Walking the Log: Memories of a Southern Childhood.* New York: Rizzoli. 10–13 yrs.

Porter, A. P. 1992. *Jump at de Sun: The Story of Zora Neale Hurston.* Minneapolis, Minn.: Carolrhoda. 8–11 yrs.

Swanson, Gloria M. & Margaret V. Ott. 1994. *I've Got an Idea!: The Story of Frederick McKinley Jones.* B & W photos. Minneapolis, Minn.: Runestone. 10–13 yrs.

Information Books

Chu, Daniel & Bill Shaw. 1995. *Going Home to Nicodemus: The Story of an African American Frontier Town and the Pioneers Who Settled It.* Photos. Morristown, N.J.: Silver Burdett/Messner. 11–15 yrs.

Cooper, Michael L. 1995. *Bound for the Promised Land: The Great Black Migration.* Photos. New York: Lodestar. 10–14 yrs.

Lawrence, Jacob (With a poem by Walter Dean Myers). 1993. *The Great Migration: An American Story.* New York: HarperCollins. 6–9 yrs.

Civil Rights Period

Biographies

Adler, David A. 1993. *A Picture Book of Rosa Parks.* Illus. Robert Casilla. New York: Holiday. 6–9 yrs. Picture Book Biography series.

Adoff, Arnold. 1970. *Malcolm X.* Illus. John Wilson. New York: HarperCollins. 10–14 yrs.

Archer, Jules. 1993. *They Had a Dream: The Civil Rights Struggle from Frederick Douglass to Marcus Garvey to Martin Luther King and Malcolm X.* B & W photos. New York: Viking. 12–16 yrs. Epoch Biographies series.

Bray, Rosemary L. 1995. *Martin Luther King.* Illus. Malcah Zeldis. New York: Greenwillow. 10–12 yrs.

Cavan, Seamus. 1993. *W. E. B. Du Bois and Racial Relations.* Brookfield, Conn.: Millbrook. 10–13 yrs. Gateway Civil Rights series.

_____. 1993. *Thurgood Marshall and Equal Rights.* Brookfield, Conn.: Millbrook. 10–13 yrs. Gateway Civil Rights series.

Collins, David R. 1992. *Malcolm X: Black Rage.* Morristown, N.J.: Dillon. 12–17 yrs.

Colman, Penny. 1993. *Fannie Lou Hamer and the Fight for the Vote.* Brookfield, Conn.: Millbrook. 10–13 yrs. Gateway Civil Rights Series.

Cwiklik, Robert A. 1993. *Philip Randolph and the Labor Movement.* Brookfield, Conn.: Millbrook. 10–13 yrs. Gateway Civil Rights series.

_____. 1993. *Stokely Carmichael and Black Power.* Brookfield, Conn.: Millbrook. 10–13 yrs. Gateway Civil Rights series.

Darby, Jean. 1990. *Martin Luther King, Jr.* Minneapolis, Minn.: Lerner. 10–14 yrs.

Elish, Dan. 1994. *James Meredith and School Desegregation.* B & W photos. Brookfield, Conn.: Millbrook. 10–13 yrs. Gateway Civil Rights series.

Freedman, Suzanne. 1994. *Ida B. Wells-Barnett and the Antilynching Crusade.* B & W photos. Brookfield, Conn.: Millbrook. 10–13 yrs. Gateway Civil Rights series.

Haskins, Jim. 1993. *I Have a Dream: The Life and Words of Martin Luther King, Jr.* B & W photos. Brookfield, Conn.: Millbrook. 12–16 yrs.

Hull, Mary. 1994. *Rosa Parks.* B & W photos. New York: Chelsea House. 10–13 yrs. Black Americans of Achievement series.

Jakoubek, Robert E. 1994. *James Farmer and the Freedom Rides.* B & W photos. Brookfield, Conn.: Millbrook. 10–13 yrs. Gateway Civil Rights series.

_____. 1994. *Walter White and the Power of Organized Protest.* B & W photos. Brookfield, Conn.: Millbrook. 10–13 yrs. Gateway Civil Rights series.

King, Coretta Scott. 1993. *My Life with Martin Luther King, Jr.* B & W photos. New York: Holt. 12–16 yrs.

Lazo, Caroline. 1994. *Martin Luther King, Jr.* B & W photos. Morristown, N.J.: Dillon. 10–13 yrs. Peacemakers series.

Livingston, Myra Cohn. 1992. *Let Freedom Ring: A Ballad of Martin Luther King, Jr.* Illus. Samuel Byrd. New York: Holiday. 7–10 yrs.

Lowery, Linda. 1987 *Martin Luther King Day.* Minneapolis, Minn.: Carolrhoda. 6–9 yrs.

Marzollo, Jean. 1993. *Happy Birthday, Martin Luther King.* Illus. J. Brian Pinkney. New York: Scholastic. 4–6 yrs.

Medearis, Angela Shelf. 1994. *Dare to Dream: Coretta Scott King and the Civil Rights Movement.* Illus. Anna Rich. New York: Lodestar. 10–13 yrs. Rainbow Biography series.

Myers, Walter. 1993. *Malcolm X: By Any Means Necessary.* New York: Scholastic. 12–16 yrs.

Rochelle, Belinda. 1993. *Witnesses to Freedom: Young People Who Fought for Civil Rights.* B & W photos. New York: Lodestar. 10–13 yrs.

Shirley, David. 1994. *Malcolm X.* B & W photos. New York: Chelsea House. 10–13 yrs. Junior World Biographies series

Information Books

Bullard, Sara. 1993. *Free at Last: A History of the Civil Rights Movement and Those Who Died in the Struggle.* B & W photos. New York: Oxford. 12–16 yrs.

Coies, Robert. 1995. *The Story of Ruby Bridges*. Illus. George Ford. New York: Scholastic. 6–10 yrs.

Duncan, Alice Faye. 1995. *The National Civil Rights Museum Celebrates Everyday People*. Color, B & W photos; illus. J. Gerard Smith. Mahwah, N.J.: BridgeWater. 10–14 yrs.

Haskins, Jim. 1992. *The Day Martin Luther King, Jr., Was Shot: A Photo History of the Civil Rights Movement*. Photos & drawings. New York: Scholastic. 10–14 yrs.

———. 1993. *The March on Washington*. Photos. New York: HarperCollins. 10–16 yrs.

———. 1994. *The Scottsboro Boys*. New York: Holt. 12–16 yrs.

———. 1995. *Freedom Rides: Journey for Justice*. Photos. New York: Hyperion. 10–14 yrs.

Levine, Ellen. 1993. *Freedom's Children: Young Civil Rights Activists Tell Their Own Stories*. New York: Putnam. 12–16 yrs.

McKissack, Patricia C. 1986. *Our Martin Luther King Book*. Danbury, Conn.: Children's Press. 5–9 yrs.

McKissack, Patricia & Frederick McKissack. 1987. *The Civil Rights Movement in America*. Danbury, Conn.: Children's Press. 12–16 yrs.

O'Neill, Laurie A. 1994. *Little Rock: The Desegregation of Central High*. B & W photos. Brookfield, Conn.: Millbrook. 10–13 yrs. Spotlight on American History series.

Powledge, Fred. 1993. *We Shall Overcome: Heroes of the Civil Rights Movement*. New York: Scribners. 12–16 yrs.

Siegel, Beatrice. 1992. *The Year They Walked: Rosa Parks and the Montgomery Bus Boycott*. New York: Four Winds. 9–12 yrs.

———. 1994. *Murder on the Highway: The Viola Liuzo Story*. Photos. New York: Four Winds. 10–14 yrs.

Walter, Mildred Pitts. 1992. *Mississippi Challenge*. New York: Bradbury. 11–16 yrs.

Weisbrot, Robert. 1994. *Marching toward Freedom, 1957–1965: From the Founding of the Southern Christian Leadership Conference to the Assassination of Malcolm X*. B & W photos. New York: Chelsea House. 10–13 yrs. Milestones in Black American History series.

Contemporary Period

The Arts: Biographies

Awmiller, C. 1996. *This House on Fire: The Story of the Blues*. Photos. New York: Watts. 9–12 yrs. African-American Experience Series.

Bernotas, Bob. 1993. *Spike Lee: Filmmaker*. Springfield, N.J.: Enslow. 12–16 yrs. People to Know series.

Blue, Rose, & Corinne J. Naden. 1995. *Whoopi Goldberg*. New York: Chelsea House. Black Americans of Achievement series.

Century, Douglas. 1994. *Toni Morrison*. B & W photos. New York: Chelsea House. 10–13 yrs. Black Americans of Achievement series.

Collier, James Lincoln. 1991. *Duke Ellington*. New York: Macmillan. 10–16 yrs.

Course, Leslie. 1994. *Dizzy Gillespie and the Birth of Bebop*. B & W photos. New York: Atheneum. 12–16 yrs.

Haskins, Jim. 1988. *Bill Cosby: America's Most Famous Father*. New York: Walker. 11–16 yrs.

Igus, T. 1996. *Going Back Home: An Artist Returns to the South*. Illus. Michel Wood. San Francisco, Calif.: Children's Book Press. 9–12 yrs.

Jones, Hettie. 1995. *Big Star Fallin' Mama: Five Women in Black Music*. B & W photos. New York: Viking. 12–16 yrs.

Lewis-Ferguson, Julinda. 1994. *Alvin Ailey, Jr.: A Life in Dance*. B & W photos. New York: Walker. 10–13 yrs.

Lyons, M. E. 1996. *Painting Dreams: Minnie Evans, Visionary Artist*. Photos. Boston: Houghton Mifflin. 9–12 yrs.

Medearis, Angela Shelf. 1994. *Little Louis and the Jazz Band: The Story of Louis "Satchmo" Armstrong*. Illus. Anna Rich. New York: Lodestar. 10–13 yrs. Rainbow Biography series.

Nicholson, Lois P. 1994. *Oprah Winfrey*. B & W photos. New York: Chelsea House. 10–13 yrs. Black Americans of Achievement series.

Osofsky, A. 1996. *Free to Dream: The Making of a Poet: Langston Hughes*. New York: Lothrop, Lee & Shepard. 11–14 yrs.

Pinkney, Andrea Davis. 1993. *Alvin Ailey*. Illus. Brian Pinkney. New York: Hyperion. 5–9 yrs.

Porte, B. A. 1996. *Black Elephant with a Brown Ear (in Alabama)*. Illus. Bill Traylor. New York: Greenwillow. 12–16 yrs.

Shapiro, Miles. 1994. *Maya Angelou*. B & W photos. New York: Chelsea House. 10–13 yrs. Black Americans of Achievement series.

Turner, Robyn Montana. 1993. *Faith Ringgold*. Boston: Little, Brown. 10–13 yrs. Portraits of Women Artists for Children series.

The Arts: Information Books

Haskins, James. 1990. *Black Dancers in America: A History through Its People*. Photos J. Haskins. New York: Crowell. 10–16 yrs.

Jones, K. Maurice. 1994. *Say It Loud: The Story of Rap Music*. Photos. Brookfield, Conn.: Millbrook. 12–16 yrs.

Kuklin, Susan. 1987. *Reaching for Dreams: A Ballet from Rehearsal to Opening Night*. New York: Lothrop, Lee & Shepard. 11–16 yrs.

Sullivan, Charles (ed.). 1991. *Children of Promise: African-American Literature and Art for Young People*. New York: Abrams. 12–17 yrs.

Government: Biographies

Banta, Melissa. 1994. *Colin Powell*. B & W photos. New York: Chelsea House. 11–14 yrs. Junior World Biographies series

Haskins, James. 1992. *I Am Somebody!: A Biography of Jesse Jackson*. Springfield, N.J.: Enslow. 12–16 yrs.

———. 1992. *Thurgood Marshall: A Life for Justice*. New York: Holt. 11–14 yrs.

McKissack, Patricia C. 1989. *Jesse Jackson: A Biography*. New York: Scholastic. 10–12 yrs.

Senna, Carl. 1992. *Colin Powell: A Man of War and Peace*. New York: Walker. 10–16 yrs.

Siegel, Beatrice. 1995. *Marian Wright Edelman: The Making of a Crusader*. Photos. New York: Simon & Schuster. 10–12 yrs.

Government: Information Books

Fleming, Robert. 1995. *Rescuing a Neighborhood: The Bedford-Stuyvesant Volunteer Ambulance Corps*. Photos Porter Gifford. New York: Walker. 10–12 yrs.

Haskins, Francine. 1991. *I Remember "121."* Illus. Francine Haskins. Emeryville, Calif.: Children's Book Press. 5–9 yrs.

Schmidt, Diane. 1990. *I Am a Jesse White Tumbler*. Photos. Diane Schmidt. Morton Grove, Ill.: Whitman. 8–12 yrs.

Sports: Biographies

Aaseng, Nathan. 1994. *Barry Sanders: Star Running Back*. B & W photos. Springfield, N.J.: Enslow. 10–13 yrs. Sports Reports series.

Adler, David A. 1992. *A Picture Book of Jesse Owens*. Illus. Robert Casilla. New York: Holiday. 6–9 yrs.

Bjarkman, Peter C. 1994. *Ernie Banks*. B & W photos. New York: Chelsea House 10–13 yrs. Baseball Legends series.

Brashler, William. 1994. *The Story of Negro League Baseball*. B & W photos. New York: Ticknor & Fields. 10–13 yrs.

Collins, David R. 1994. *Arthur Ashe: Against the Wind*. B & W photos. Morristown, N.J.: Dillon. 12–16 yrs. People in Focus series.

Dolan, Sean. 1993. *Magic Johnson*. B & W photos. New York: Chelsea House. 12–16 yrs. Black Americans of Achievement series.

———. 1993. *Michael Jordan*. B & W photos. New York: Chelsea House. 12–16 yrs. Black Americans of Achievement series.

Evans, J. Edward. 1993. *Jerry Rice: Touchdown Talent*. B & W photos. Minneapolis, Minn.: Lerner. 10–13 yrs. Sports Achievers series.

Frankl, Ron. 1994. *Wilt Chamberlain*. B & W photos. New York: Chelsea House. 10–13 yrs. Basketball Legends series.

Goldstein, Margaret J. & Jennifer Larson. 1994. *Jackie Joyner-Kersee: Superwoman*. B & W photos. Minneapolis, Minn.: Lerner. 10–13 yrs. Achievers series.

Golenbock, Peter. 1990. *Teammates*. Illus. Paul Bacon. San Diego: Harcourt Brace Jovanovich/Gulliver. 7–10 yrs. (Jackie Robinson & Pee Wee Reese)

Klots, Steve. 1994. *Carl Lewis*. B & W photos. New York: Chelsea House. 10–13 yrs. Black Americans of Achievement series.

Kruli, Kathleen. 1996. *Wilma Unlimited: How Wilma Rudolph Became the World's Fastest Woman*. Illus. David Diaz. San Diego: Harcourt Brace. 6–9 yrs.

Lipsyte, Robert. 1994. *Joe Louis: A Champ for All America*. B & W photos. New York: HarperCollins. 10–13 yrs. Superstar Lineup series.

———. 1994. *Michael Jordan: A Life above the Rim*. B & W photos. New York: HarperCollins. 10–13 yrs. Superstar Lineup series.

Littlefield, Bill. 1993. *Champions: Stories of Ten Remarkable Athletes*. Illus. Bernie Fuchs. Boston: Little, Brown. 10–13 yrs.

Macy, S. 1996. *Winning Ways: A Photohistory of American Women in Sports*. Photos. New York: Holt. 12–16 yrs.

McKissack, Patricia C. & Fredrick McKissack, Jr. 1994. *Black Diamond: The Story of the Negro Baseball Leagues*. New York: Scholastic. 10–13 yrs.

Moss, N. 1996. *W.E.B. DuBois: Civil Rights Leader*. Photos. New York: Chelsea. 9–12 yrs. Junior World Biographies series.

Moutoussamy-Ashe, Jeanne. 1993. *Daddy and Me: A Photo Story of Arthur Ashe and His Daughter, Camera*. B & W photos. New York: Knopf. 5–9 yrs.

Nicholson, Lois P. 1994. *Michael Jackson*. B & W photos. New York: Chelsea House. 10–13 yrs. Black Americans of Achievement series.

Pettit, J. 1996. *Maya Angelou: Journey of the Heart*. Photos. New York: Lodestar. 9–12 yrs. A Rainbow Biography series.

Pinkney, A. D. 1996. *Bill Pickett: Rodeo-Ridin' Cowboy*. Illus. Brian Pinkney. San Diego, Calif.: Gulliver/Harcourt Brace. 7–10 yrs.

Puckett, Kirby. 1993. *Be the Best You Can Be*. Color, B & W photos. Minneapolis, Minn.: Waldman. 5–9 yrs.

Quackenbush, Robert. 1994. *Arthur Ashe and His Match with History*. New York: Simon & Schuster. 7–10 yrs.

Rennert, Richard Scott. 1993. *Henry Aaron*. B & W photos. New York: Chelsea House. 12–16 yrs. Black Americans of Achievement series.

Ringgold, F. 1995. *My Dream of Martin Luther King*. New York: Crown. 6–10 yrs.

Rivers, Glenn & Bruce Brooks. 1994. *Those Who Love the Game: Glenn "Doc" Rivers on Life in the NBA and Elsewhere.* B & W photos. New York: Holt. 12–16 yrs.

Santella, A. 1996. *Jackie Robinson Breaks the Color Line.* Archival photos. Chicago, Ill.: Children's Press. 9–12 yrs. Cornerstones of Freedom series.

Savage, Jeff. 1994. *Thurman Thomas: Star Running Back.* B & W photos. Springfield, N.J.: Enslow. 10–13 yrs. Sports Reports series.

Schulman, A. 1996. *Muhammad Ali: Champion.* Photos. Minneapolis, Minn.: Lerner. 9–12 yrs.

Schroeder, A. 1996. *Minty: A Story of Young Harriet Tubman.* Illus. Jerry Pinkney. New York: Dial. 6–9 yrs.

Shirley, David. 1993. *Satchel Paige.* New York: Chelsea House. 12–16 yrs. Black Americans of Achievement series.

Townsend, Brad. 1994. *Shaquille O'Neal: Center of Attention.* Color, B & W photos. Minneapolis, Minn.: Lerner. 10–13 yrs. Achievers series.

Turk, R. 1996. *Ray Charles: Soul Man.* Photos. Minneapolis, Minn.: Lerner. 9–12 yrs.

Weidhorn, Manfred. 1993. *Jackie Robinson.* B & W photos. New York: Atheneum. 12–16 yrs.

Wyeth, J., Jr. 1996. *Diana Ross.* New York: Chelsea. 12–16 yrs. Black Americans of Achievement Series.

Sports: Information Books

Cooper, Michael L. 1993. *Playing America's Game: The Story of Negro League Baseball.* B & W photos. New York: Lodestar. 10–13 yrs.

Falwell, Cathryn. 1992. *Shape Space.* Illus. C. Falwell. New York: Clarion. 4–8 yrs.

Biographical Collections

Hamilton, Virginia. 1995. *Her Stories: African American Folktales, Fairy Tales, and True Tales.* Illus. Leo & Diane Dillon. New York: BlueSky/Scholastic. 11–16 yrs.

Hart, Philip S. 1992. *Flying Free: America's First Black Aviators.* Minneapolis, Minn.: Lerner. 10–14 yrs.

Haskins, Jim. 1991. *Outward Dreams: Black Inventors and Their Inventions.* New York: Walker. 10–15 yrs.

_____. 1992. *Against All Opposition: Black Explorers in America.* New York: Walker. 10–16 yrs.

_____. 1992. *One More River to Cross: The Stories of Twelve Black Americans.* New York: Scholastic. 10–14 yrs.

_____. 1995. *Black Eagles: African Americans in Aviation.* B & W photos. New York: Scholastic. 10–12 yrs.

McKissack, Patricia & Fredrick McKissack. 1994. *African-American Inventors.* Brookfield, Conn.: Millbrook. 10–13 yrs. Proud Heritage Series.

_____. 1994. *African American Scientists.* B & W photos. Brookfield, Conn.: Millbrook. 10–13 yrs. Proud Heritage series.

_____. 1995. *Red-Tail Angels: The Story of the Tuskegee Airmen of World War II.* Photos. New York: Walker. 10–14 yrs.

Miller, Robert H. 1992. *Reflections of a Black Cowboy: Book Four, Mountain Men.* Illus. Richard Leonard. Morristown, N.J.: Silver Burdett. 9–12 yrs.

Sterling, Dorothy. 1984. *We Are Your Sisters: Black Women in the 19th Century.* New York: Norton. 12–18 yrs.

Turner, Glennette Tilley. 1989. *Take a Walk in Their Shoes.* New York: Dutton. 11–16 yrs.

African American History

Meltzer, Milton. 1984. *Black Americans: A History in Their Own Words.* New York: Crowell. 12–16 yrs.

Myers, Walter Dean. 1991. *Now Is Your Time! The African-American Struggle for Freedom.* New York: HarperCollins. 12–16 yrs.

Nardo, Don. 1994. *Braving the New World, 1619–1784: From the Arrival of the Enslaved Africans to the End of the American Revolution.* New York: Chelsea House. 10–13 yrs. Milestones in Black American History series.

Perseverance. 1993. B & W photos. New York: Time-Life. 12–16 yrs. African Americans: Voices of Triumph series.

Biographies

Denenberg, Barry. 1991. *Nelson Mandela: "No Easy Walk to Freedom."* New York: Scholastic. 10–14 yrs.

Hoobler, Dorothy & Thomas Hoobler. 1992. *Mandela: The Man, the Struggle, the Triumph.* Danbury, Conn.: Watts. 12–15 yrs.

Hughes, Libby. 1992. *Nelson Mandela: Voice of Freedom.* Morristown, N.J.: Dillon. 10–16 yrs.

Moore, Reavis. 1994. *Native Artists of Africa.* Photos, drawings, sketches. Santa Fe, N.M.: Muir. 10–13 yrs. Rainbow Warrior Artists series.

Onyefulu, I. 1996. *Ogbo: Sharing Life in an African Village.* Color photos. San Diego: Harcourt Brace/Gulliver. 6–10 yrs.

Roberts, Jack L. 1995. *Nelson Mandela: Determined to Be Free.* Color, B & W photos. Brookfield, Conn.: Millbrook. 10–12 yrs. Gateway Biography series.

Stanley, Diane & Peter Vennema. 1988. *Shaka: King of the Zulus.* New York: Morrow. 11–16 yrs.

_____. 1994. *Cleopatra.* Illus. Diane Stanley. New York: Morrow. 9–11 yrs.

Wisniewski, David. 1992. *Sundiata: Lion King of Mali.* Illus. David Wisniewski. New York: Clarion. 9–12 yrs.

Information Books

Angelou, Maya. 1994. *My Painted House, My Friendly Chicken, and Me.* Photos Margaret Courtney-Clarke. New York: Crown. 6–9 yrs.

Barboza, Steven. 1994. *Door of No Return: The Legend of Goree Island.* New York: Cobblehill. 10–13 yrs.

Brandenburg, Jim (JoAnn Bren Guernsey Ed.). 1994. *Sand and Fog: Adventures in Southern Africa.* New York: Walker. 10–13 yrs.

Ellis, Veronica F. 1990. *Afrobets First Book about Africa.* East Orange, N.J.: Just Us Books. 6–9 yrs.

Feelings, Muriel. 1974. *Jambo Means Hello: Swahili Alphabet Book.* New York: Dial. 6–9 yrs.

Goodsmith, Lauren. 1994. *The Children of Mauritania: Days in the Desert and by the River Shore.* Color photos. Minneapolis, Minn.: Carolrhoda. 10–13 yrs. World's Children series.

Gordon, Sheila. 1990. *The Middle of Somewhere: A Story of South Africa.* New York: Orchard/Jackson. 9–12 yrs.

Haskins, Jim, & Joann Biondi. 1995. *From Afar to Zulu: A Dictionary of African Cultures.* B & W photos. New York: Walker. 10–13 yrs.

Hermes, Jules. 1995. *The Children of Morocco.* Color photos. Minneapolis, Minn.: Carolrhoda. 10–13 yrs. World's Children series.

Illustrated History of South Africa: The Real Story. 1989. New York: Random. 12–18+ yrs.

Koslow, Philip. 1994. *Centuries of Greatness: The West African Kingdoms, 750–1900.* B & W photos. New York: Chelsea House. 10–13 yrs. Milestones in Black American History series.

_____. 1995. *Ancient Ghana: The Land of Gold.* New York: Chelsea House. 10–13 yrs. Kingdoms of Africa series.

_____. 1995. *Hausaland: The Fortress Kingdoms.* New York: Chelsea House. 10–13 yrs. Kingdoms of Africa series.

_____. 1995. *Kanem-Borno: One Thousand Years of Splendor.* New York: Chelsea House. 10–13 yrs. Kingdoms of Africa series.

_____. 1995. *Mali: Crossroads of Africa.* New York: Chelsea House. 10–13 yrs. Kingdoms of Africa series.

_____. 1995. *Songhay: The Empire Builders.* New York: Chelsea House. 10–13 yrs. Kingdoms of Africa series.

Kreikemeier, Gregory Scott. 1993. *Come with Me to Africa: A Photographic Journey.* Color photos. Racine, Wisc.: Golden. 10–13 yrs.

Magubane, Peter. 1982. *Black Child.* New York: Knopf. 11–16 yrs.

Matthews, Jo. 1994. *I Remember Somalia.* Color photos. Chatham, N.J.: Raintree. 6–9 yrs. Why We Left series.

Meisel, Jacqueline Drobis. 1994. *South Africa at the Crossroads.* Color, B & W photos. Brookfield, Conn.: Millbrook. 10–13 yrs. Headliners series.

Mennen, Ingrid & Niki Daly. 1992. *Somewhere in Africa.* Illus. Nicolaas Maritz. New York: Dutton. 6–8 yrs.

Obadiah. 1987. *I Am a Rastafarian.* Danbury, Conn.: Watts. 7–11 yrs.

Ofosu-Appiah, L. H. 1993. *People in Bondage: African Slavery Since the 15th Century.* Photos. Minneapolis, Minn.: Runestone. 12–15 yrs.

Onyefulu, Ifeoma. 1995. *Emeka's Gift: An African Counting Story.* New York: Cobblehill. 6–9 yrs.

Onyefulu, I. 1996. *Ogbo: Sharing Life in an African Village.* Color photos. San Diego: Harcourt Brace/Gulliver. 6–10 yrs.

Paton, Jonathan. 1990. *The Land and People of South Africa.* New York: HarperCollins. 12–16 yrs.

Reynolds, Jan. 1991. *Sahara: Vanishing Cultures.* Photos Jan Reynolds. San Diego: Harcourt Brace Jovanovich. 8–11 yrs.

Smith, Chris. 1993. *Conflict in Southern Africa.* New York: Macmillan. 11–16 yrs.

Zaslavsky, Claudia. 1980. *Count on Your Fingers African Style.* New York: Crowell. 5–9 yrs.

Poetry, Stories, Songs, Games

Adedjouma, D. (Compiler & ed.). 1996. *The Palm of My Heart: Poetry by African American Children.* Illus. Gregory Christie. New York: Lee & Low. 9–14 yrs.

Adoff, Arnold. 1991. *In for Winter, Out for Spring.* Illus. Jerry Pinkney. San Diego: Harcourt Brace Jovanovich. 5–9 yrs.

_____. 1994. *My Black Me: A Beginning Book of Black Poetry.* New York: Dutton. 10–13 yrs.

Allison, Diane Worfolk. 1992. *This Is the Key to the Kingdom.* Illus. Diane Worfolk Allison. Boston: Little, Brown. 5–8 yrs.

Bolden, Tonya (Ed.). 1994. *Rites of Passage: Stories about Growing Up by Black Writers from around the World.* New York: Hyperion. 12–16 yrs.

Bryan, Ashley (compiler). 1991. *All Night, All Day: A Child's First Book of African-American Spirituals.* Illus. Ashley Bryan. New York: Atheneum. 6–12 yrs.

Creative Fire. 1994. B & W & color photos. New York: Time-Life. 12–16 yrs.

Giovanni, Nikki. 1994. *Knoxville, Tennessee.* Illus. Larry Johnson. New York: Scholastic. 6–10 yrs.

_____. (Ed.). 1994. *Grand Mothers: Poems, Reminiscences, and Short Stories about the Keepers of Our Traditions.* New York: Holt. 12–16 yrs.

_____. (Compiler & ed.). 1996. *The Genie in the Jar.* Illus. Chris Raschka. New York: Holt. 5–9 yrs.

_____. 1996. *Shimmy Shimmy Shimmy Like My Sister Kate: Looking at the Harlem Renaissance through Poems.* New York: Holt. 13–18 yrs.

Greenfield, Eloise. 1986. *Honey, I Love and Other Love Poems.* New York: HarperCollins. 5–9 yrs.

_____. 1989. *Nathaniel Talking.* New York: Writers & Readers/Black Butterfly. 6–10 yrs.

_____. 1991. *Night on Neighborhood Street.* Illus. Jan Spivey Gilchrist. New York: Dial. 5–12 yrs.

Grimes, Nikki. 1994. *Meet Danitra Brown.* Illus. Floyd Cooper. New York: Lothrop, Lee & Shepard. 6–10 yrs.

Grimes, N. 1996. *Come Sunday.* Illus. Michael Bryant. Grand Rapids, Mich.: Eerdmans. 5–9 yrs.

Hale, Sarah Josepha. 1990. *Mary Had a Little Lamb.* Photos Bruce McMillan. New York: Scholastic. 3–7 yrs.

Haskins, Jim. 1987. *Black Music in America; A History through Its People.* New York: Crowell. 12–16 yrs.

Hauser, Pierre. 1995. *Great Ambitions: From the "Separate but Equal" Doctrine to the Birth of the NAACP (1896–1909).* B & W photos. New York: Chelsea House. 10–13 yrs. Milestones in Black American History series.

Hudson, Wade. 1993. *Pass It On: African-American Poetry for Children.* Illus. Floyd Cooper. New York: Scholastic. 5–9 yrs.

Hughes, Langston. 1962. *Dream Keeper.* New York: Knopf. 9–12 yrs.

_____. 1994. *The Dream Keeper and Other Poems.* Illus. Brian Pinkney. New York: Knopf. 10–16 yrs.

_____. 1994. *The Sweet and Sour Animal Book.* New York: Oxford. 6–10 yrs. Iona and Peter Opie Library of Children's Literature series.

_____. 1994. *Black Misery.* Illus. Arouni. New York: Oxford. 10–13 yrs. Iona and Peter Opie Library of Children's Literature series.

Johnson, James Weldon. 1993. *Lift Every Voice and Sing.* Illus. Elizabeth Catlett. New York: Walker. 10–13 yrs.

_____. 1994. *The Creation.* Illus. James E. Ransome. New York: Holiday. 7–11 yrs.

Jones, K. Maurice. 1994. *Say It Loud!: The Story of Rap Music.* B & W, color photos. Brookfield, Conn.: Millbrook. 12–16 yrs.

Langstaff, John. 1987. *What a Morning! The Christmas Story in Black Spirituals.* New York: Macmillan. 4–8 yrs.

_____. (Compiler & ed.). 1991. *Climbing Jacob's Ladder: Heroes of the Bible in African-American Spirituals.* Illus. Ashley Bryan. New York: McElderry. 4–10 yrs.

Lauture, Denize. 1992. *Father and Son.* Illus. Jonathan Green. New York: Philomel. 6–9 yrs.

Lawrence, Jacob. 1993. *Harriet and the Promised Land.* New York: Simon & Schuster. 5–9 yrs.

Little, Lessie Jones. 1988. *Children of Long Ago.* New York: Philomel. 6–9 yrs.

Livingston, Myra Cohn. 1994. *Keep On Singing: A Ballad of Marian Anderson.* Illus. Samuel Byrd. New York: Holiday. 6–9 yrs.

Mathis, Sharon Bell. 1991. *Red Dog, Blue Fly: Football Poems.* Illus. Jan Spivey Gilchrist. New York: Viking Penguin. 6–10 yrs.

Medearis, Angela Shelf (Compiler). 1992. *The Zebra-Riding Cowboy: A Folk Song from the Old West.* Illus. Maria Cristina Brusca. New York: Holt. 6–12 yrs.

_____. 1995. *Treemonisha.* Illus. Michael Bryant. New York: Holt. 8–10 yrs.

Monceaux, Morgan. 1994. *Jazz: My Music, My People.* New York: Knopf. 10–13 yrs.

Myers, Walter Dean. 1993. *Brown Angels: An Album of Pictures and Verse.* Photos. New York: HarperCollins. 5–10 yrs.

Price, Leontyne (Reteller). 1990. *Aida.* Illus. Leo & Diane Dillon. San Diego: Harcourt Brace Jovanovich/Gulliver. 10–16 yrs.

Rollins, Charlemae Hill. 1993. *Christmas Gif': An Anthology of Christmas Poems, Songs, and Stories Written by and about African-Americans.* Illus. Ashley Bryan. New York: Morrow. 10–13 yrs.

Slier, Deborah (Ed.). 1991. *Make a Joyful Sound: Poems for Children by African-American Poets.*

Illus. Cornelius Van Wright & Ying-Hwa Hu. New York: Checkerboard. 8–12 yrs.

Silverman, Jerry. 1993. *African Roots.* B & W photos. New York: Chelsea House. 10–13 yrs. Traditional Black Music series.

_____. 1993. *Children's Songs.* New York: Chelsea House. 10–13 yrs. Traditional Black Music series.

_____. 1993. *Slave Songs.* B & W photos. New York: Chelsea House. 10–13 yrs. Traditional Black Music series.

_____. 1994. *Gospel Songs.* New York: Chelsea House. 10–13 yrs. Traditional Black Music series.

_____. 1994. *Work Songs.* B & W photos. New York: Chelsea House. 6–10 yrs. Traditional Black Music series.

_____. 1996. *Just Listen to This Song I'm Singing: African-American History through Song.* Photos & reproductions. Brookfield, Conn.: Millbrook. 9–12 yrs.

Strickland, Dorothy S. & Michael R. Strickland. 1994. *Families: Poems Celebrating the African American Experience.* Illus. John Ward. Honesdale, Penn.: Boyds/Wordsong. 5–9 yrs.

Sullivan, Charles (Ed.). 1991. *Children of Promise: African-American Literature and Art for Young People.* New York: Abrams. 10–16 yrs.

Tate, Eleanora E. 1992. *Front Porch Stories at the One-Room School.* Illus. Eric Velasquez. New York: Bantam Skylark. 8–13 yrs.

Thomas, J. C. 1995. *Gingerbread Days.* Illus. Floyd Cooper. New York: HarperCollins/Cotler. 5–9 yrs.

Walker, David A., & James Haskins. 1986. *Double Dutch.* Springfield, N.J.: Enslow. 9–14 yrs.

CARIBBEAN LITERATURE

(Literature from Cuba, Hispaniola, Dominican Republic, Haiti, Jamaica, Lesser Antilles, Virgin Islands, and Trinidad. Puerto Rican Literature is in **Hispanic Literature.**)

BOOKS WITH PICTURES

Agard, John. 1989. *The Calypso Alphabet.* Illus. Jennifer Brent. New York: Holt. 5–8 yrs.

Binch, Caroline. 1994. *Gregory Cool.* New York: Dial. 5–8 yrs.

Buffett, Jimmy & Savannah Jane Buffett. 1988. *The Jolly Man.* Illus. Lambert Davis. San Diego: Harcourt Brace. 5–8 yrs. Book with audiocassette.

Bunting, Eve. 1988. *How Many Days to America? A Thanksgiving Story.* Illus. Beth Peck. New York: Clarion. 5–9 yrs.

Carlstrom, Nancy White. 1992. *Baby-O.* Illus. Sucie Stevenson. Boston: Little, Brown. 3–8 yrs.

Charles, Faustin (Compiler). 1996. *A Caribbean Counting Book.* Illus. Roberta Arenson. Boston: Houghton Mifflin. 5–8 yrs.

Garcia, Richard. 1987. *My Aunt Otilia's Spirits/Los Espiritus de Mi Tia Otilia.* Illus. Robin Cherin & Roger Reyes. Translated into Spanish, Jesus Guerrero Rea. Emeryville, Calif.: Children's Book Press. 6–9 yrs.

Garne, S. T. 1992. *One White Sail: A Caribbean Counting Book.* Illus. Lisa Etre. New York: Green Tiger. 4–7 yrs.

Gershator, Phillis. 1994. *Rata-pata-scata-fata: A Caribbean Story.* Illus. Holly Meade. Boston: Little, Brown. 5–8 yrs.

Greenberg, Melanie Hope. 1994. *Aunt Lilly's Laundromat.* New York: Dutton. 7–9 yrs.

Hayes, Sarah. 1986. *Happy Christmas Gemma.* New York: Lothrop, Lee & Shepard. 4–8 yrs.

Hoffman, Mary. 1991. *Amazing Grace.* Illus. Caroline Binch. New York: Dial. 5–9 yrs.

_____. 1995. *Boundless Grace.* Illus. Caroline Binch. New York: Dial. 7–10 yrs.

Joseph, Lynn. 1992. *An Island Christmas.* Illus. Catherine Stock. New York: Clarion. 4–8 yrs.

_____. 1994. *Jasmine's Parlour Day.* Illus. Ann Grifalconi. New York: Lothrop, Lee & Shepard. 5–7 yrs.

Keller, Holly. 1992. *Island Baby.* Illus. Holly Keller. New York: Greenwillow. 6–9 yrs.

Lauture, Denize. 1996. *Running the Road to ABC.* Illus. Reynold Ruffins. New York: Simon & Schuster. 4–7 yrs.

Lessac, Frane. 1984. *My Little Island.* New York: HarperCollins. 5–8 yrs.

_____. 1994. *Caribbean Alphabet.* New York: Tambourine. 4–6 yrs.

_____. 1994. *Caribbean Canvas.* Honesdale, Penn.: Boyds/Wordsong. 6–10 yrs.

Orr, Katherine. 1990. *My Grandpa and the Sea.* Illus. Katherine Orr. Minneapolis, Minn.: Carolrhoda. 5–9 yrs.

Pomerantz, Charlotte. 1989. *The Chalk Doll.* Illus. Frane Lessac. New York: Lippincott. 3–7 yrs.

Powell, Pamela. 1992. *The Turtle Watchers.* New York: Viking. 7–11 yrs.

Van Laan, Nancy. 1995. *Mama Rocks, Papa Sings.* Illus. Roberta Smith. New York: Knopf. 5–8 yrs.

FOLK LITERATURE

Agard, John, & Grace Nichols. 1995. *No Hickory, No Dickory, No Dock: Caribbean Nursery Rhymes.* Illus. Cynthia Jabar. Cambridge, Mass.: Candlewick. 5–10 yrs.

Berry, J. (Adapter). 1996. *Don't Leave an Elephant to Go and Chase a Bird.* Illus. Ann Grifalconi. New York: Simon & Schuster. 5–8 yrs. (African tale—Jamaican tradition.)

Bryan, Ashley. 1985. *The Cat's Purr.* New York: Atheneum. 5–8 yrs.

_____. (Reteller). 1989. *Turtle Knows Your Name.* Illus. Ashley Bryan. New York: Atheneum/Karl. 3–7 yrs.

Gleeson, Brian. 1992. *Anansi.* Illus. Steven Guarnaccia. New York: Simon & Schuster. 5–8 yrs. We All Have Tales series.

Gonzalez, Lucia M. 1994. *The Bossy Gallito/El Gallo de Bodas: A Traditional Cuban Folktale.* Illus. Lulu Delacre. New York: Scholastic. 5–9 yrs.

Joseph, Lynn. 1991. *A Wave in Her Pocket: Stories from Trinidad.* Illus. Brian Pinkney. New York: Clarion. 9–13 yrs.

_____. 1994. *The Mermaid's Twin Sister: More Stories from Trinidad.* Illus. Donna Perrone. New York: Clarion. 10–13 yrs.

Sherlock, Philip M. 1988. *West Indian Folktales.* Illus. Joan Kiddell Monroe. New York: Oxford. 11–16 yrs.

Shute, Linda. 1995. *Rabbit Wishes.* New York: Lothrop, Lee & Shepard. 5–10 yrs.

Stow, Jenny (Illus.). 1992. *The House That Jack Built.* New York: Dial. 5–8 yrs.

Temple, Frances. 1994. *Tiger Soup: An Anansi Story from Jamaica.* New York: Orchard/Jackson. 7–10 yrs.

Turenne des Pres, François. 1994. *Children of Yayoute: Folk Tales of Haiti.* New York: Universe. 10–13 yrs.

Wolkstein, Diane. 1978. *The Magic Orange Tree, and Other Haitian Folktales.* Illus. Elsa Henriquez. New York: Knopf. 10–16 yrs.

_____. 1981. *The Banza.* Illus. Marc Brown. New York: Dial. 5–8 yrs.

LITERARY FOLK TALES

French, Fiona. 1991. *Anancy and Mr. Dry-Bone.* Illus. F. French. Boston: Little, Brown. 9–11 yrs.

REALISTIC NOVELS

Berry, James. 1988. *A Thief in the Village and Other Stories.* New York: Orchard. 12–16 yrs.

_____. 1992. *Ajeemah and His Son.* New York: HarperCollins/Ella Perlman. 11–16 yrs.

Gantos, J. 1995. *Jack's New Power: Stories from a Caribbean Year.* New York: Farrar, Straus & Giroux. 11–15 yrs.

Hamilton, Virginia. 1985. *Junius Over Far.* New York: HarperCollins. 12–16 yrs.

Hyppolite, Joanne. 1995. *Seth and Samona.* Illus. Colin Bootman. New York: Delacorte. 11–15 yrs.

O'Dell, Scott. 1990. *My Name Is Not Angelica.* New York: Dell/Yearling Books. 8–12 yrs.

Perera, Hilda. 1992. *Kiki: A Cuban Boy's Adventure In America.* Miami, Fla.: Pickering Press. 10–14 yrs.

Taylor, Theodore. 1993. *Timothy of the Cay.* San Diego: Harcourt Brace. 12–16 yrs. (Sequel to *The Cay.*)

Temple, Frances. 1992. *Taste of Salt: A Story of Modern Haiti.* New York: Orchard/Jackson. 11–16 yrs.

BIOGRAPHIES

Ada, Alma Flor. 1994. *Where the Flame Trees Bloom.* Illus. Antonio Martorell. New York: Atheneum. 10–13 yrs.

Gleiter, Ian & Kathleen Thompson. 1990. *Jose Marti.* Illus. Les Didier. Translated Alma Flor Ada. Chatham, N.J.: Raintree. 9–12 yrs. Raintree biography series.

Hoobler, Thomas & Dorothy Hoobler. 1990. *Toussaint L'Ouverture.* New York: Chelsea House. 12–16 yrs.

INFORMATION BOOKS

Broberg, Merle. 1989. *Barbados.* New York: Chelsea House. 9–12 yrs.

Charles, F. (Compiler.). 1996. *A Caribbean Counting Book.* Illus. Roberta Arenson. Boston: Lorraine/Houghton Mifflin. 5–8 yrs.

Coldish, Meish. 1995. *Crisis in Haiti.* Brookfield, Conn.: Millbrook. 10–13 yrs. Headliners series.

_____. 1987. *Haiti in Pictures.* Minneapolis, Minn.: Lerner. 9–12 yrs.

Grenquist, Barbara. 1991. *Cubans.* Danbury, Conn.: Watts. 10–17 yrs.

Haskins, James. 1982. *The New Americans: Cuban Boat People.* Hillside, N.J.: Enslow, 10–16 yrs.

Hubley, John & Penny Hubley. 1985. *A Family in Jamaica.* Minneapolis, Minn.: Lerner. 9–12 yrs.

Kaufman, Cheryl. 1988. *Cooking the Caribbean Way.* Minneapolis, Minn.: Lerner. 10–13 yrs.

Linden, Ann Marie. 1992. *One Smiling Grandma: A Caribbean Counting Book.* Illus. Lynne Russell. New York: Dial. 4–8 yrs.

Lye, Keith. 1988. *Take a Trip to Jamaica.* Danbury, Conn.: Watts. 7–10 yrs.

McKenley, Yvonne. 1995. *A Taste of the Caribbean.* New York: Thomson. 10–13 yrs. Food around the World series.

Morris, Emily. 1991. *Cuba.* New York: Steck-Vaughn. 10–14 yrs.

Orr, Katherine. 1993. *Story of a Dolphin.* Minneapolis, Minn.: Carolrhoda. 6–9 yrs.

Rice, Earle, Jr. 1994. *The Cuban Revolution.* B & W photos. San Diego: Lucent. 12–16 yrs. World History series.

POETRY, SONGS, STORIES

Adoff, Arnold. 1988. *Flamboyan.* Illus. Karen Barbour. San Diego: Harcourt Brace. 5–8 yrs.

Agard, John & Grace Nichols. 1994. *A Caribbean Dozen: Poems from Caribbean Poets.* Illus. Cathie Felstead. Cambridge, Mass.: Candlewick. 5–9 yrs.

Berry, James. 1991. *When I Dance.* Illus. Karen Barbour. San Diego: Harcourt Brace Jovanovich. 12–16 yrs.

_____. 1994. *Celebration Song.* Illus. Louise Brierly. New York: Simon & Schuster. 4–6 yrs.

Bryan, Ashley. 1974. *Walk Together Children: Black American Spirituals.* New York: Aladdin. 5–12 yrs.

_____. 1992. *Sing to the Sun.* Illus. Ashley Bryan. New York: HarperCollins. 5–11 yrs.

Burgie, Irving. 1992. *Caribbean Carnival: Songs of the West Indies.* Illus. Frane Lessac. New York: Tambourine. 6–11 yrs.

Greenfield, Eloise. 1988. *Under the Sunday Tree.* Illus. Amos Ferguson. New York: HarperCollins. 9–12 yrs.

Joseph, Lynn. 1990. *Coconut Kind of Day: Island Poems.* Illus. Sandra Speidel. New York: Lothrop, Lee & Shepard. 6–12 yrs.

Lear, Edward. 1990. *The Owl and the Pussycat.* Illus. Jan Brett. New York: Putnam. 4–8 yrs.

Mattox, Cheryl Warren. 1989. *Shake It to the One that You Love the Best.* Oakley, Calif.: Warren-Mattox. 5–12 yrs.

Raffi. 1989. *Tinfisalayo.* Illus. Kate Duke. New York: Crown. 5–8 yrs.

Stow, Jenny (Illus.). 1992. *The House That Jack Built.* 1992. New York: Dial. 5–8 yrs.

ASIAN LITERATURE

BOOKS WITH PICTURES

Family

Calhoun, Mary. 1990. *While I Sleep.* Illus. Ed Young. New York: Morrow. 4–7 yrs.

Friedman, Ina R. 1984. *How My Parents Learned to Eat.* Illus. Allen Say. Boston: Houghton Mifflin. 4–7 yrs.

Heo, Yumi. 1994. *One Afternoon.* New York: Orchard. 5–7 yrs.

Ho, Minfong. 1996. *Hush!: A Thai Lullaby.* Illus. Holly Meade. New York: Kroupa/Orchard. 2–5 yrs.

Horton, Barbara Savadge. 1992. *What Comes in Spring?* Illus. Ed Young. New York: Knopf/Borzoi. 3–6 yrs.

Mochizuki, Ken. 1995. *Heroes.* Illus. Dom Lee. New York: Lee & Low. 7–12 yrs.

Schotter, Roni. 1993. *A Fruit and Vegetable Man.* Illus. Jeanette Winter. Boston: Little, Brown. 6–8 yrs.

Sun, Chyng Feng. 1994. *Mama Bear.* Illus. Lolly Robinson. Boston: Houghton Mifflin. 5–7 yrs.

Surat, Michelle Maria. 1983. *Angel Child, Dragon Child.* Illus. Vo-Dinh Mai. Chatham, N.J.: Raintree. 5–9 yrs.

Tsutsui, Yoriko. 1987. *Before the Picnic.* Illus. Akiko Hayashi. New York: Philomel. 3–5 yrs.

Friendship

Armstrong, Jennifer. 1993. *Chin Yu Min and the Ginger Cat.* Illus. Mary Grandpre. New York: Crown. 7–9 yrs.

Ashley, Bernard. 1991. *Cleversticks.* Illus. Derek Brazell. New York: Crown. 3–6 yrs.

Kline, Suzy. 1994. *Song Lee and the Hamster Hunt.* Illus. Frank Remkiewicz. New York: Viking. 7–9 yrs.

Grandparents

Bond, Ruskin. 1991. *Cherry Tree.* Illus. Allan Eitzen. Honesdale, Penn.: Boyds Mills Press/Caroline. 6–8 yrs.

Breckler, Rosemary K. 1992. *Hoang Breaks the Lucky Teapot.* Illus. Adrian Frankel. Boston: Houghton Mifflin. 5–8 yrs.

Choi, Sook Nyul. 1993. *Halmoni and the Picnic.* Illus. Karen M. Dugan. Boston: Houghton Mifflin. 6–9 yrs.

Garland, Sherry. 1993. *The Lotus Seed.* Illus. Tatsuro Kiuchi. San Diego: Harcourt Brace. 7–9 yrs.

Guback, Georgia. 1994. *Luka's Quilt.* New York: Greenwillow. 5–7 yrs.

Keller, Holly. 1994. *Grandfather's Dream.* New York: Greenwillow. 6–9 yrs.

Reddix, Valerie. 1991. *Dragon Kite of the Autumn Moon.* Illus. Jean & Mou-sien Tseng. New York: Lothrop, Lee & Shepard. 9–11 yrs.

Sakai, Kimiko. 1990. *Sachiko Means Happiness.* Illus. Tomie Arai. Emeryville, Calif.: Children's Book Press. 7–11 yrs.

Overcoming a Problem

Lee, Jeanne M. 1991. *Silent Lotus.* Illus. Jeanne M. Lee. New York: Farrar, Straus & Giroux. 7–10 yrs.

Say, Allen. 1995. *Stranger in the Mirror.* Illus. Allen Say. Boston: Houghton Mifflin. 5–8 yrs.

Celebration

Rattigan, Jama Kim. 1993. *Dumpling Soup.* Illus. Lillian Hsu-Flanders. Boston: Little, Brown. 7–10 yrs.

Say, Allen. 1991. *Tree of Cranes.* Illus. Allen Say. Boston: Houghton Mifflin. 4–8 yrs.

Cultural Pride

Godden, Rumer. 1990. *Fu-Dog.* Pictures Valerie Littlewood. New York: Viking. 9–12 yrs.

Lee, Huy Voun. 1994. *At the Beach.* New York: Holt. 6–9 yrs.

Nones, Susan Miho. 1995. *The Last Dragon.* Illus. Chris K. Soentpiet. New York: Clarion. 6–9 yrs.

History

Coerr, Eleanor. 1993. *Sadako.* Illus. Ed Young. New York: Putnam. 7–10 yrs.

Kodama, Tatsuharu (Trans. Kazuko Hokumen-Jones). 1995. *Shin's Tricycle.* Illus. Noriyuki Ando. New York: Walker. 8–11 yrs.

Krensky, Stephen. 1994. *The Iron Dragon Never Sleeps.* Illus. John Fulweiler. New York: Delacorte. 8–11 yrs.

Maruki, Toshi. 1980. *Hiroshima No Pika.* New York: Lothrop, Lee & Shepard. 9–12 yrs.

Nature

Porte, Barbara Ann. 1993. *"Leave That Cricket Be, Alan Lee."* Illus. Donna Ruff. New York: Greenwillow. 6–9 yrs.

Ryder, Joanne. 1992. *Dancers in the Garden.* Illus. Judith Lopez. San Francisco: Sierra. 6–8 yrs.

INFORMATIONAL STORYBOOKS

Axworthy, Anni. 1992. *Anni's India Diary.* Illus. Anni Axworthy. Danvers, Mass.: Whispering Coyote Press/Treld Bicknell. 7–10 yrs.

Ichikawa, Satomi. 1991. *Nora's Duck.* Illus. Satomi Ichikawa. New York: Philomel. 5–8 yrs.

Svend, Otto S. 1985. *Children of the Yangtze River.* New York: Viking/Pelham. 6–9 yrs.

Chinese Setting

Allen, Judy. 1992. *Tiger.* Illus. Tudor Humphries. Cambridge, Mass.: Candlewick. 7–10 yrs.

Hearn, Lafcadio. (Reteller Margaret Hodges). 1989. *The Voice of the Great Bell.* Illus. Ed Young. Boston: Little, Brown. 6–9 yrs.

Levinson, Riki. 1988. *Our Home Is the Sea.* Paintings Dennis Luzak. New York: Dutton. 5–9 yrs.

Tan, Amy. 1992. *The Moon Lady.* Illus. Gretchen Schields. New York: Macmillan. 9–12 yrs.

Japanese Setting

Baker, Keith. 1989. *The Magic Fan.* Illus. K. Baker. San Diego: Harcourt Brace Jovanovich. 5–9 yrs.

Brenner, Barbara. 1996. *Chibi: A True Story from Japan.* Illus. June Otani. New York: Clarion. 4–8 yrs.

Hayashi, Akiko. 1991. *Aki and the Fox.* Illus. Akiko Hayashi. New York: Doubleday. 5–8 yrs.

Ikeda, Daisaku (Trans. Gearaldine McCaughrean). 1991. *The Cherry Tree*. Illus. Brian Goldsmith. New York: Knopf/Borzoi. 7–9 yrs.

Johnson, Ryerson. 1992. *Kenji and the Magic Geese*. Illus. Jean & Mou-sien Tseng. New York: Simon & Schuster. 7–11 yrs.

Nakawatari Harutaka. (Trans. Susan Matsui). 1992. *The Sea and I*. New York: Farrar, Straus & Giroux. 6–8 yrs.

Say, Allen. 1982. *The Bicycle Man*. Illus. Allen Say. Boston: Houghton Mifflin. 5–9 yrs.

Takeshita, Fumlko (Trans. Ruth Kanagy). 1988. *The Park Bench*. Illus. Mamoru Suzuki. Brooklyn, N.Y.: Kane-Miller. 6–9 yrs.

Tsutsui, Yoriko. 1987. *Anna's Secret Friend*. Illus. Akiko Hayashi. New York: Viking Kestrel. 4–6 yrs.

FOLK LITERATURE

Chinese Tales

Birdseye, Tom. 1990. *A Song of Stars: An Asian Legend*. Illus. Ju-Hong Chen. New York: Holiday. 6–10 yrs.

Brooke, William J. 1993. *A Brush with Magic*. Illus. Michael Koelsch. New York: HarperCollins. 7–11 yrs.

Chang, Margaret & Raymond Chang. 1994. *The Cricket Warrior: A Chinese Tale*. Illus. Warwick Hutton. New York: McElderry. 7–10 yrs.

Demi. 1980. *Liang and the Magic Paintbrush*. New York: Holt. 6–10 yrs.

_____. 1990. *The Empty Pot*. Illus. Demi. New York: Holt. 6–10 yrs.

_____. 1990. *The Magic Boat*. Illus. Demi. New York: Holt. 6–10 yrs.

_____. 1995. *The Stonecutter*. New York: Crown. 5–9 yrs.

Drummond, Allan. 1992. *The Willow Pattern Story*. Illus. Allan Drummond. New York: North-South. 9–12 yrs.

Fang, Linda. 1995. *The Ch'i-lin Purse: A Collection of Ancient Chinese Stories*. Illus. Jeanne M. Lee. New York: Farrar, Straus & Giroux. 10–15 yrs.

Greene, E. 1996. *Ling-Li and the Phoenix Fairy: A Chinese Folktale*. Illus. Zong-Zhou Wang. New York: Clarion. 6–10 yrs.

Hooks, W. 1992. *Peach Boy*. New York: Little Rooster. 5–8 yrs. Bank Street Ready to Read.

Hong, Lily Toy. 1993. *Two of Everything*. Morton Grove, Ill.: Whitman. 6–10 yrs.

Han, Jay (Trans.). 1993. *Why Snails Have Shells: Minority and Han Folktales from China*. Illus. Li Ji. Honolulu: Univ. of Hawaii Press. 10–13 yrs.

Hillman, Elizabeth. 1992. *Min-Yo and the Moon Dragon*. Illus. John Wallner. San Diego: Harcourt Brace Jovanovich. 6–10 yrs.

Hong, Lily Toy (Reteller). 1991. *How the Ox Star Fell from Heaven*. Illus. Lily Toy Hong. Morton Grove, Ill.: Whitman. 6–10 yrs.

Kendall, Carol. 1988. *Wedding of the Rat Family*. Illus. James Watts. New York: Macmillan/McElderry. 9–12 yrs.

Leaf, Margaret. 1987. *Eyes of the Dragon*. Illus. Ed Young. New York: Lothrop, Lee & Shepard. 7–11 yrs.

Lee, Jeanne M. 1982. *Legend of the Milky Way*. New York: Holt. 9–12 yrs. (See also *Legend of the Li River*.)

_____. 1995. *The Song of Mu Lan*. Arden, N.C.: Front Street Books. 9–12 yrs.

Li, Zeru. 1987. *The Cowherd and the Girl Weaver*. Illus. Liu Yi. Beijing. 7–10 yrs.

Louie, Ai-Ling. 1982. *Yeh-Shen: A Cinderella Story from China*. Illus. Ed Young. New York: Philomel. 8–11 yrs.

Ma, Leong (Trans. James Anderson). 1991. *A Letter to the King*. Illus. Leong Va. New York: HarperCollins. 6–9 yrs.

Mahy, Margaret. 1990. *The Seven Chinese Brothers*. Illus. Jean & Mou-sien Tseng. New York: Scholastic. 7–11 yrs.

Meyer, Marianna. 1995. *Turandot*. Illus. Winslow Pels. New York: Morrow. 11–15 yrs.

Miller, Moira. 1989. *The Moon Dragon*. Illus. Ian Deuchar. New York: Dial. 5–9 yrs.

Mui, Y. T. (Ruth Tabrah, Ed.; adapters Robert B. Goodman & Robert A. Spicer). 1974. *The Magic Brush*. Honolulu: Island Heritage. 6–10 yrs.

Pattison, Darcy. 1991. *The River Dragon*. Illus. Jean & Mou-sien Tseng. New York: Lothrop, Lee & Shepard. 10–13 yrs.

Rappaport, Doreen (Reteller). 1991. *The Journey of Meng: A Chinese Legend*. Illus. Yang Ming-Yi. New York: Dial. 7–11 yrs.

_____. 1995. *The Long-Haired Girl: A Chinese Legend*. Illus. Yang Ming-Yi. New York: Dial. 5–10 yrs.

Sian-Tek, L. 1948. *More Folk Tales from China*. New York: John Day.

So, Meilo (Reteller). 1992. *The Emperor and the Nightingale*. Illus. Meilo So. New York: Bradbury. 7–11 yrs.

Tan, Amy. 1994. *The Chinese Siamese Cat*. Illus. Gretchen Schields. New York: Simon & Schuster. 11–15 yrs.

Torre, Betty L. (Reteller). 1990. *The Luminous Pearl: A Chinese Folktale*. Illus. Carol Inouye. New York: Orchard. 7–10 yrs.

Va, Leong (Trans. James Anderson). 1991. *A Letter to the King*. Illus. Leong Va. New York: HarperCollins. 7–11 yrs.

Wang, Rosalind C. 1995. *The Treasure Chest: A Chinese Tale*. Illus. Will Hillenbrand. New York: Holiday. 5–10 yrs.

Wang, Rosalind C. (Reteller). 1991. *The Fourth Question: A Chinese Tale*. Illus. Ju-Hong Chen. New York: Holiday. 7–10 yrs.

Wilson, Barbara Ker. 1993. *Wishbones: A Folk Tale from China*. Illus. Meilo So. New York: Bradbury. 6–10 yrs.

Yacowitz, Caryn (Adapter). 1992. *The Jade Stone: A Chinese Folktale*. Illus. Ju-Hong Chen. New York: Holiday. 8–12 yrs.

Yee, Paul. 1991. *Roses Sing on New Snow: A Delicious Tale*. Illus. Harvey Chan. New York: Macmillan. 6–11 yrs.

Yeh Chun-Chan & Alan Baillie. 1991. *Bawshou Rescues the Sun*. Illus. Michelle Powell. New York: Scholastic. 9–12 yrs.

Yen, Clora. 1991. *Why the Rat Comes First: A Story of the Chinese Zodiac*. Illus. Hideo C. Yoshido. Danbury, Conn.: Children's Press. 9–12 yrs.

Yep, Laurence. 1989. *The Rainbow People*. Illus. David Wiesner. New York: Harper & Row. 10–16 yrs.

_____. 1991. *Tongues of Jade*. Illus. David Wiesner. New York: HarperCollins. 10–16 yrs.

_____. 1993. *The Man Who Tricked a Ghost*. Illus. Isadore Seltzer. Mahwah, N.J.: BridgeWater. 6–10 yrs.

_____. 1993. *The Shell Woman and the King: A Chinese Folktale*. Illus. Yang Ming-Yi. New York: Dial. 7–10 yrs.

_____. 1994. *The Ghost Fox*. Illus. Jean Tseng & Mou-sien Tseng. New York: Scholastic. 10–13 yrs.

_____. 1994. *The Junior Thunder Lord*. Illus. Robert Van Nutt. Mahwah, N.J.: BridgeWater. 7–10 yrs.

_____. 1995. *Tiger Woman*. Illus. Robert Roth. Mahwah, N.J.: BridgeWater. 6–9 yrs.

Young, Ed (Trans.). 1989. *Lon Po Po: A Red-Riding Hood Story from China*. New York: Philomel. 7–11 yrs.

_____. 1992. *Seven Blind Mice*. New York: Philomel. 4–8 yrs.

_____. 1993. *Red Thread*. New York: Philomel. 8–11 yrs.

_____. 1994. *Little Plum*. New York: Philomel. 7–10 yrs.

_____. (Adapter) 1995. *Night Visitors*. New York: Philomel. 6–9 yrs.

Zhang, Song Nan. 1994. *Five Heavenly Emperors: Chinese Myths of Creation*. Plattsburgh, N.Y.: Tundra. 10–13 yrs.

Japanese Tales

Bryan, Ashley. 1988. *Sh-ko and His Eight Wicked Brothers*. Illus. Fumio Yoshimura. New York: Atheneum. 5–9 yrs.

Compton, Patricia A. (Reteller). 1991. *The Terrible EEK: A Japanese Tale*. Illus. Sheila Hamanaka. New York: Simon & Schuster. 6–10 yrs.

Edmonds, I. G. 1994. *Ooka the Wise: Tales of Old Japan*. Illus. Sanae Yamazaki. 10–13 yrs.

Hamanaka, Sheila. 1993. *Screen of Frogs: An Old Tale*. New York: Orchard/Jackson. 7–10 yrs.

Ikeda, Daisaku (Trans. Geraldine McCaughrean). 1990. *The Snow Country Prince*. Illus. Brian Wildsmith. New York: Knopf/Borzoi. 7–11 yrs.

Ishii, Momoko (Trans. Katherine Paterson). 1987. *The Tongue-Cut Sparrow*. Illus. Suekichi Akoba. New York: Lodestar. 7–9 yrs.

Johnston, Tony (Adapter). 1990. *The Badger and the Magic Fan: A Japanese Folktale*. Illus. Tomie de Paola. New York: Putnam/Whitebird. 6–9 yrs.

Laurin, Anne. 1981. *Perfect Crane*. Illus. Charles Mikolaycak. New York: Harper & Row. 9–12 yrs.

Levine, Arthur A. 1994. *The Boy Who Drew Cats: A Japanese Folktale*. Illus. Frederic Clement. New York: Dial. 7–10 yrs.

Long, J. F. 1996. *The Bee and the Dream: A Japanese Tale*. Illus. Kaoru Ono. New York: Dutton. 6–10 yrs.

Martin, R. 1996. *Mysterious Tales of Japan*. Illus. Tatsuro Kiuchi. New York: Putnam. 10–13 yrs.

Matsutani, Miyoko (Trans. Alvin Tresselt). 1968. *The Crane Maiden*. Illus. Chihiro Iwasaki. New York: Parents Magazine. 7–10 yrs.

Mayer, M. 1995. *Turandot*. Illus. Winslow Pels. New York: Morrow. 8–11 yrs.

McCoy, Karen Kawamoto. 1993. *A Tale of Two Tengu: A Japanese Folktale*. Illus. Koen Fossey. Morton Grove, Ill.: Whitman. 6–9 yrs.

McDermott, Gerold. 1975. *The Stonecutter*. New York: Puffin. 6–9 yrs.

Merrill, Jean (Adapter). 1992. *The Girl Who Loved Caterpillars: A Twelfth-Century Tale from Japan*. Illus. Floyd Cooper. New York: Philomel. 6–10 yrs.

Morimoto, Junko. 1986. *The Inch Boy*. New York: Viking. 6–9 yrs.

Namioka, Lensey (Reteller). 1995. *The Loyal Cat*. Illus. Aki Sogabe. San Diego: Harcourt Brace. Browndeer. 4–8 yrs.

Okawa, Essei. 1985. *Urashima Taro: The Fisherman and the Grateful Turtle*. Illus. Koichi Murakami. Union City, Calif.: Heian International. 5–9 yrs.

Quayle, Eric (Compiler). 1989. *The Shining Princess, and Other Japanese Legends*. Illus. Michael Foreman. New York: Arcade. 8–12 yrs.

Richard, Franchise. 1994. *On Cat Mountain*. Illus. Anne Buguet. New York: Putnam. 5–9 yrs.

Sakade, Florence (Ed.). 1958. *Japanese Children's Favorite Stories*. Illus. Yosbisuke Kurosaki. Boston: Tuttle. 7–10 yrs.

_____. (Ed.) 1958. *Kintaro's Adventures and Other Japanese Children's Stories*. Illus. Yoshio Hayashi. Boston: Tuttle. 7–10 yrs.

San Souci, Robert D. (Reteller). 1992. *The Samurai's Daughter: A Japanese Legend*. Illus. Stephen T. Johnson. New York: Dial. 7–11 yrs.

Schroeder, Alan. 1994. *Lily and the Wooden Bowl*. Illus. Yoriko Ito. New York: Doubleday. 7–10 yrs.

Shute, Linda. 1986. *Momotaro, the Peach Boy*. New York: Lothrop, Lee & Shepard. 5–9 yrs.

Snyder, Diane. 1988. *The Boy of the Three Year Nap*. Illus. Allen Say. Boston: Houghton Mifflin. 5–9 yrs.

Stamm, Claus. 1990. *Three Strong Women: A Tall Tale from Japan*. Pictures Jean & Mou-sien Tseng. New York: Viking. 6–10 yrs.

Tejima. 1990. *Ho-Limlim: A Rabbit Tale from Japan*. Illus. Tejima. New York: Philomel. 7–11 yrs.

Tompert, Ann. 1993. *Bamboo Hats and a Rice Cake*. Illus. Demi. New York: Crown. 6–10 yrs.

Uchida, Yoshiko. 1977. *The Dancing Kettle and Other Japanese Folk Tales*. San Diego: Harcourt Brace Jovanovich. 8–13 yrs.

———. 1993. *The Magic Purse*. Illus. Keiko Narahashi. New York: McElderry. 7–11 yrs.

———. 1994. *The Wise Old Woman*. Illus. Martin Springett. New York: McElderry. 7–10 yrs.

Wells, R. 1996. *The Farmer and the Poor God: A Folktale from Japan*. Illus. Yoshi. New York: Simon & Schuster. 6–9 yrs.

Williams, Carol Ann. 1995. *Tsubu the Little Snail*. Illus. Tatsuro Kiuchi. New York: Simon & Schuster. 5–10 yrs.

Yagawa, Sumiko (Trans. Katherine Paterson). 1981. *The Crane Wife*. Illus. Suekichi Akaba. New York: Morrow. 7–11 yrs.

Korean Tales

Climo, Shirley. 1993. *The Korean Cinderella*. Illus. Ruth Heller. New York: HarperCollins. 6–9 yrs.

Ginsburg, Mirra. 1988. *The Chinese Mirror*. Illus. Margot Zemach. San Diego: Harcourt Brace. 6–9 yrs.

Han, Suzanne Chowder. 1994. *The Rabbit's Judgment*. Illus. Yumi Heo. New York: Holt. 6–9 yrs.

Heo, Y. (Adapter & illus.) 1996. *The Green Frogs: A Korean Folktale*. Boston: Houghton Mifflin. 4–6 yrs.

Hubbard, Woodleigh (Illus.). 1993. *The Moles and the Mireuk: A Korean Folktale*. Illus. Woodleigh Hubbard. Boston: Houghton Mifflin. 6–9 yrs.

Jaffe, Nina (Adapter). 1995. *Older Brother, Younger Brother: A Korean Folktale*. Illus. Wenhai Ma. New York: Viking. 6–9 yrs.

O'Brien, Anne Sibley. 1993. *The Princess and the Beggar: A Korean Folktale*. New York: Scholastic. 7–10 yrs.

Plunkett, Stephanie Haboush. (Ed.). 1993. *Sir Whong and the Golden Pig*. Illus. Oki S. Han. New York: Dial. 7–10 yrs.

Rhee, Nami. 1993. *Magic Spring: A Korean Folktale*. New York: Putnam. 5–9 yrs.

Schecter, Ellen. 1993. *Sim Chung and the River Dragon: A Folktale from Korea*. New York: Bantam. 5–9 yrs.

Watkins, Yoko Kawashima. 1992. *Tales from the Bamboo Grove*. Illus. Jean & Mou-sien Tseng. New York: Bradbury. 9–12.

Vietnamese Tales

Garland, Sherry. 1993. *Why Ducks Sleep on One Leg*. Illus. Jean & Mou-sien Tseng. New York: Scholastic. 7–11 yrs.

Vuong, Lynette Dyer. 1993. *The Golden Carp: And Other Tales from Vietnam*. Illus. Manabu Saito. New York: Lothrop, Lee & Shepard. 10–13 yrs.

Vuong, Lynette Dyer. 1993. *Sky Legends of Vietnam*. Illus. Vo-Dinh Mai. New York: HarperCollins. 10–13 yrs.

Tales from Other Asian Countries

Blia, Xiong (Adapter Cathy Spagnoli). 1989. *Nine-in-One Grr! Grr! A Folktale from the Hmong People of Laos*. Illus. Nancy Hom. Emeryville, Calif.: Children's Book Press. 5–9 yrs.

Gretchen, Sylvia (Adapter). 1990. *Hero of the Land of Snow*. Illus. Julia Witwer. Berkeley, Calif.: Dharma Publishing. 7–10 yrs. (Adapted from the Tibetan epic tale of Gesar.)

Ho, Minfong & Saphan Ros. 1995. *The Two Brothers*. Illus. Jean & Mou-sien Tseng. New York: Lothrop, Lee & Shepard. 5–10 yrs.

Mayer, Marianna. 1990. *Golden Swan: An East Indian Tale of Love from The Mahabharata*. Illus. Robert Sauber. New York: Bantam Skylark Books/Timeless Tales. 10–13 yrs.

San Souci, R. D. (Adapter). 1996. *Pedro and the Monkey*. Illus. Michael Hays. New York: Morrow. 4–7 yrs.

Waite, M. P. 1996. *Jojofu*. Illus. Yoriko Ito. New York: Lothrop, Lee & Shepard. 5–8 yr.

Yep, Laurence. 1995. *Tree of Dreams: Ten Tales from the Garden of Night*. Illus. Isadore Seltzer. Mahwah, N.J.: BridgeWater. 10–14 yrs.

Literary Folk Tale

Demi. 1991. *The Artist and the Architect*. Illus. Demi. New York: Holt. 7–10 yrs.

Paterson, Katherine. 1990. *The Tale of the Mandarin Ducks*. Illus. Leo & Diane Dillon. New York: Lodestar. 7–12 yrs.

Yee, Paul. 1991. *Roses Sing on New Snow: A Delicious Tale*. Illus. Harvey Chan. New York: Macmillan. 6–11 yrs.

Yep, Laurence. 1994. *The Boy Who Swallowed Snakes*. Illus. Jean & Mou-sien Tseng. New York: Scholastic. 7–9 yrs.

Zimelman, Nathan. 1992. *The Great Adventure of Wo El*. Illus. Julie Downing. New York: Macmillan. 6–9 yrs.

Fantasy: Picture Story Books

Armstrong, Jennifer. 1995. *Wan Hu Is in the Stars*. Illus. Barry Root. New York: Tambourine. 6–9 yrs.

Hillman, Elizabeth. 1992. *Min-Yo and the Moon Dragon*. Illus. John Wallner. San Diego: Harcourt Brace. 6–9 yrs.

Gajadin, Chitra (Reteller; adapter Rabindranath Tagore). 1992. *Amal and the Letter from the King*. Illus. Helen Ong. Honesdale, Penn.: Boyds Mills Press/Caroline. 10–13 yrs.

Melmed, Laura Krauss. 1993. *The First Song Ever Sung*. Illus. Ed Young. New York: Lothrop, Lee & Shepard. 6–8 yrs.

Singer, Marilyn. 1994. *The Painted Fan*. Illus. Wenhai Ma. New York: Morrow. 8–10 yrs.

Sun, Chyng Feng. 1993. *Square Beak*. Illus. Chihsien Chen. Boston: Houghton Mifflin. 7–10 yrs.

———. 1994. *On a White Pebble Hill*. Illus. Chihsien Chen. Boston: Houghton Mifflin. 6–8 yrs.

Vaughan, Marcia. 1994. *Dorobo the Dangerous*. Illus. Kazuko Stone. Morristown, N.J.: Silver Burdett. 6–8 yrs.

Yee, Wong Herbert. 1993. *Big Black Bear*. Boston: Houghton Mifflin. 5–7 yrs.

Yep, Laurence. 1993. *The Butterfly Boy*. Illus. Jeanne M. Lee. New York: Farrar, Straus & Giroux. 6–8 yrs.

Novels: Fantasy

Alexander, Lloyd. 1991. *The Remarkable Journey of Prince Jen*. New York: Dutton. 11–16 yrs.

Namioka, Lensey. 1989. *Island of Ogres*. New York: HarperCollins. 12–15 yrs.

Contemporary Realistic Fiction

Kline, S. 1995. *Song Lee and the Leech Man*. Illus. Frank Remkiewicz. New York: Viking. 8–12 yrs.

Mori, K. 1995. *One Bird*. New York: Holt. 12–16 yrs.

Historical Fiction:

Russell, C. Y. 1995. *Water Ghost*. Illus. C. Zhong-Yuan Zhang. Honesdale, Penn.: Boyds Mills. 11–14 yrs.

Japan: Feudal Period-1600s

Haugaard, Erik Christian. 1984. *The Samurai's Tale*. Boston: Houghton Mifflin. 12–16 yrs.

———. 1991. *The Boy and the Samurai*. Boston: Houghton Mifflin. 10–16 yrs.

Namioka, Lensey. 1992. *The Coming of the Bear*. New York: HarperCollins. 11–15 yrs.

Paterson, Katherine. 1973. *The Sign of the Chrysanthemum*. New York: HarperCollins. 11–15 yrs.

———. 1974. *Of Nightingales that Weep*. New York: HarperCollins. 11–15 yrs.

———. 1975. *The Master Puppeteer*. Illus. Haru Wells. New York: HarperCollins. 11–15 yrs.

Asian Immigration to U.S.: History

Chetin, Helen. 1982. *Angel Island Prisoner*. Illus. Jan Lee. Berkeley, Calif.: New Seed Press. 11–16 yrs. English, Chinese.

Goldin, Barbara Diamond. 1994. *Red Means Good Fortune: A Story of San Francisco's Chinatown*. Illus. Wenhai Ma. New York: Viking. 11–15 yrs.

Krensky, Stephen. 1994. *The Iron Dragon Never Sleeps*. Illus. John Fulweiler. New York: Delacorte. 11–15 yrs.

Lim, Genny. 1982. *Wings for Lai Ho*. Illus. Andrea Ja. San Francisco: East/West. 8–10 yrs.

Yep, Lawrence. 1985. *Mountain Light*. New York: Harper & Row. 12–16 yrs.

———. 1993. *Dragon's Gate*. Illus. Charles Lilly. New York: HarperCollins. 12–17 yrs.

World War II

Choi, Sook Nyul. 1991. *Year of Impossible Goodbyes*. Boston: Houghton Mifflin. 10–16 yrs.

Salisbury, Graham. 1994. *Under the Blood-Red Sun*. New York: Delacorte. 10–13 yrs.

Yep, Laurence. 1995. *Hiroshima: A Novella*. New York: Scholastic. 10–16 yrs.

Vietnam War

Paterson, Katherine. 1988. *Park's Quest*. New York: Dutton. 12–16 yrs.

Whelan, Gloria. 1992. *Goodbye, Vietnam*. New York: Knopf/Borzoi. 12–16 yrs.

Living in Two Worlds

Crew, Linda. 1989. *Children of the River*. New York: Delacorte. 12–16 yrs.

Garland, Sherry. 1993. *Shadow of the Dragon*. San Diego: Harcourt Brace. 12–16 yrs.

Gogol, Sara. 1992 *Vatsana's Lucky New Year*. Minneapolis, Minn.: Lerner. 9–12 yrs.

Kanazawa, Tooru. 1989. *Sushi and Sourdough*. Seattle: Univ. of Washington Press. 12–16 yrs.

Kidd, Diana. 1991. *Onion Tears*. Illus. Lucy Montgomery. New York: Orchard. 8–10 yrs.

Kraus, Joanna Halpert. 1992. *Tall Boy's Journey*. Illus. Karen Ritz. Minneapolis, Minn.: Carolrhoda. 9–12 yrs.

Levitt, Solute. 1993. *The Golem and the Dragon Girl*. New York: Dial. 11–15 yrs.

Namioka, Lensey. 1994. *April and the Dragon Lady*. San Diego: Harcourt/Browndeer. 11–14 yrs.

Neville, Emily Cheney. 1991. *The China Year*. New York: HarperCollins. 10–14 yrs.

Ruby, Lois. 1984. *This Old Man*. Boston: Houghton Mifflin. 11–15 yrs.

Yep, Laurence. 1977. *Child of the Owl*. New York: HarperCollins. 11–15 yrs.

———. 1991. *The Star Fisher*. New York: Morrow. 10–14 yrs.

Family Support

Adler, C. S. 1995. *Youn Hee and Me*. San Diego: Harcourt Brace. 9–12 yrs.

Chinn, Karen. 1995. *Sam and the Lucky Money*. Illus. Cornelius Van Wright & Ying-Hwa Hu. New York: Lee & Low. 11–15 yrs.

Namioka, Lensey. 1992. *Yang the Youngest and His Terrible Ear*. Illus. Kees de Kiefte. Boston: Little, Brown/Joy Street. 9–11 yrs.

_____. 1995. *Yang the Third and Her Impossible Family*. Illus. Kees de Kiefte. Boston: Little, Brown. 8–10 yrs.

Salisbury, Graham. 1992. *Blue Skin of the Sea: A Novel in Stories*. New York: Delacorte. 10–14 yrs.

Yep, Laurence. 1995. *Later, Gator*. New York: Hyperion. 9–13 yrs.

Friendship

Howard, Ellen. 1988. *Her Own Song*. New York: Atheneum. 11–15 yrs.

Kline, Suzy. 1993. *Song Lee in Room 2B*. Illus. Frank Remkiewicz. New York: Viking 5–7 yrs.

Cultural Pride

Lee, Marie G. 1993. *If It Hadn't Been for Yoon Jun*. Boston: Houghton Mifflin. 10–13 yrs.

_____. 1994. *Saying Goodbye*. Boston: Houghton Mifflin. 12–16 yrs.

Okimoto, Jean Davies. 1995. *Talent Night*. New York: Scholastic. 12–16 yrs.

Mori, Kyoko. 1993. *Shizuko's Daughter*. New York: Holt. 12–16 yrs. Edge series.

Yep, Laurence. 1995. *Thief of Hearts*. New York: HarperCollins. 10–13 yrs.

Animals

Schlein, Miriam. 1990. *The Year of the Panda*. Illus. Kam Mak. New York: Crowell. 8–12 yrs.

NONFICTION LITERATURE

Japanese Internment in U.S. During World War II

Davis, Donlel S. 1982. *Behind Barbed Wire: The Imprisonment of Japanese Americans during World War II*. New York: Dutton. 10–15 yrs.

Garrigue, Sheila. 1985. *The Eternal Spring of Mr. Ito*. New York: Bradbury. 12–16 yrs.

Hamanaka, Sheila. 1990. *The Journey: Japanese Americans, Racism, and Renewal*. Illus. S. Hamanaka. New York: Orchard. 10–16 yrs.

Ho, Mingfong. 1990. *Rice Without Rain*. New York: Lothrop, Lee & Shepard. 12–15 yrs.

_____. 1991. *The Clay Marble*. New York: Farrar, Straus & Giroux. 12–15 yrs.

Houston, Jeanne Wakatsuki & James D. Houston. 1983. *Farewell to Manzanar*. New York: Bantam. 10–16 yrs.

Irwin, Hodley. 1987. *Kim/Kimi*. New York: Macmillan/McElderry. 12–16 yrs.

Kogawa, Joy. 1988. *Naomi's Road*. New York: Oxford. 10–14 yrs.

Means, Florence Cannell. 1993. *The Moved-Outers*. New York: Walker. 10–14 yrs.

Mochizuki, Ken. 1993. *Baseball Saved Us*. Illus. Dom Lee. New York: Lee & Low. 9–12 yrs.

Japanese American Journey: The Story of a People. 1985. Edited by the Japanese American Curriculum Project Staff. San Mateo, Calif.: JACP, Inc. 10–14 yrs.

Savin, Marcia. 1992. *The Moon Bridge*. New York: Scholastic. 10–14 yrs.

Stanley, Jerry. 1994. *I Am an American: A True Story of Japanese Internment*. B & W photos. New York: Crown. 10–13 yrs.

Takashima, Shizuye. 1991. *A Child in Prison Camp*. Plattsburgh, N.Y.: Tundra. 12–16 yrs.

Thesman, Jean. 1993. *Molly Donnelly*. Boston: Houghton Mifflin. 12–15 yrs.

Uchida, Yoshiko. 1971. *Journey to Topaz*. Illus. Donald Carrick. New York: Scribners. 10–14 yrs.

_____. 1978. *Journey Home*. New York: Macmillan/McElderry. 11–15 yrs.

_____. 1981. *A Jar of Dreams*. New York: Macmillan/McElderry. 11–15 yrs.

_____. 1991. *The Invisible Thread*. Morristown, N.J.: SilverBurdett/Messner. 10–14 yrs.

_____. 1993. *The Bracelet*. Illus. Joanna Yardley. New York: Philomel. 6–8 yrs.

Autobiographies

Fritz, Jean. 1982. *Homesick: My Own Story*. Illus. Margot Tomes, photos. New York: Putnam. 12–16 yrs.

Morimoto, Junko (Trans. Isao Morimoto). 1990. *My Hiroshima*. New York: Viking. 6–10 yrs.

Say, Allen. 1994. *The Ink-Keeper's Apprentice*. Boston: Houghton Mifflin. 12–16 yrs.

Watkins, Yoko Kawashima. 1986. *So Far from the Bamboo Grove*. New York: Lothrop, Lee & Shepard. 12–16 yrs.

_____. 1994. *My Brother, My Sister, and I*. New York: Bradbury. 12–15 yrs.

Yep, Laurence. 1991. *The Lost Garden*. Morristown, N.J.: Silver Burdett/Messner. 10–14 yrs.

Biographies

Beirne, Barbara. 1990. *A Pianist's Debut: Preparing for the Concert Stage*. Photos B. Beirne. Minneapolis, Minn.: Carolrhoda. 9–12 yrs.

Coerr, Eleanor. 1977. *Sadako and the Thousand Paper Cranes*. Illus. Ronald Himler. New York: Putnam. 9–12 yrs.

Demi. 1991. *Chingis Khan*. New York: Holt. 8–11 yrs.

Havill, Juanita. 1993. *Sato and the Elephants*. Illus. Jean & Mou-Sien Tseng. New York: Lothrop, Lee & Shepard. 7–12 yrs.

Hoyt-Goldsmith, Diane. 1992. *Hoang Anh*. Photos Lawrence Migdale. New York: Holiday. 9–11 yrs.

Humphrey, Judy. 1987. *Genghis Khan*. New York: Chelsea House. 12–16 yrs. World Leaders Past and Present Series.

Say, Allen. 1990. *El Chino*. Illus. Allen Say. Boston: Houghton Mifflin. 7–11 yrs.

_____. 1993. *Grandfather's Journey*. Boston: Houghton Mifflin. 7–9 yrs.

Stanley, Fay. 1991. *The Last Princess: The Story of Princess Ka'iulani of Hawaii*. Illus. Diane Stanley. New York: Four Winds. 10–15 yrs.

Biographical Collection

Morey, Janet Nomura & Wendy Dunn. 1992. *Famous Asian Americans*. New York: Cobblehill. 10–16 yrs.

Information Books

General Info

Bode, Janet. 1989. *New Kids on the Block: Oral Histories of Immigrant Teens*. Danbury, Conn.: Watts. 12–16 yrs.

Knight, Margy Burns. 1992. *Talking Walls*. Illus. Anne Sibley O'Brien. St. Paul, Minn.: Tilbury. 9–12 yrs.

Takaki, Ronald (Adapter Rebecca Stefoff). 1994. *Democracy and Race: Asian Americans and World War II*. B & W photos. New York: Chelsea House. 12–16 yrs. Asian-American Experience series.

_____. 1994. *Spacious Dreams: The First Wave of Asian Immigration*. B & W photos & reproductions. New York: Chelsea House. 12–16 yrs. Asian American Experience series.

_____. (With Carol Takaki) 1995. *Strangers at the Gates Again: Asian American Immigration after 1965*. B & W photos. New York: Chelsea House. 12–16 yrs. Asian American Experience Series.

China

Bandon, Alexandra. 1994. *Chinese Americans*. New York: New Discovery. 11–15 yrs.

Behrens, June. 1982. *Gung Hay Fat Choy (Happy New Year)*. Photos. compiled by Terry Behrens. Danbury, Conn.: Children's Press. 5–8 yrs. Festivals and Holidays Series.

Brown, Tricia. 1987. *Chinese New Year*. Photos Fran Ortiz. New York: Holt. 6–10 yrs.

Daley, William. 1995. *The Chinese Americans*. Color, B & W photos. New York: Chelsea House. 10–14 yrs. Immigrant Experience series.

Fisher, Leonard Everett. 1986. *The Great Wall of China*. New York: Macmillan. 9–12 yrs.

Fritz, Jean. 1988. *China's Long March: 6,000 Miles of Danger*. New York: Putnam. 12–16 yrs.

Ganeri, Anita. 1994. *I Remember China*. Photos Tim Page. Chatham, N.J.: Raintree. 6–10 yrs. Why We Left series.

Goldstein, Peggy. 1991. *Long Is a Dragon: Chinese Writing for Children*. Berkeley, Calif.: Pacific View Press. 11–15 yrs.

Hoobler, Dorothy & Thomas Hoobler. 1993. *The Chinese American Family Album*. New York: Oxford. 11–15 yrs.

Kort, Michael G. 1995. *China under Communism*. Brookfield, Conn.: Millbrook. 12–16 yrs.

Krull, Kathleen. 1994. *City within a City: How Kids Live in New York's Chinatown*. Color photos David Hautzig. New York: Lodestar. 10–13 yrs. World of My Own series.

Mayberry, Jodine. 1990. *Chinese*. Danbury, Conn.: Watts. 11–15 yrs.

Takaki, Ronald (Adapter Rebecca Stefoff). 1994. *Ethnic Islands: The Emergence of Urban Chinese America*. B & W photos. New York: Chelsea House. 12–16+ yrs. Asian-American Experience series.

_____. 1994. *Journey to Gold Mountain: The Chinese in Nineteenth-Century America*. B & W photos & reproductions. New York: Chelsea House. 12–16 yrs. Asian American Experience series.

Tan, Jennifer. 1989. *Food in China*. Vero Beach, Fla.: Rourke. 11–15 yrs.

Tang, Yungmei. 1981 *China, Here We Come!: Visiting the People's Republic of China*. New York: Putnam. 11–14 yrs.

Thompson, Peggy. 1991. *City Kids in China*. Photos Paul S. Conklin. New York: HarperCollins. 10–13 yrs.

Vander Els, Betty. 1984. *We Live in China*. A Living Here Book. Charlottesville, Vir.: Bookwright. 12–16 yrs.

_____. 1987. *Leaving Point*. New York: Farrar, Straus & Giroux. 12–16 yrs.

Wolf, Bernard. 1988. *In the Year of the Tiger*. Photos. New York: Macmillan. 12–16 yrs.

Yee, Paul. *Tales from Gold Mountain: Stories of the Chinese in the New World*. Illus. Simon Ng. 1990. New York: Simon & Schuster. 11–15 yrs.

Yu Ling. 1982. *Cooking the Chinese Way*. Minneapolis, Minn.: Lerner. 11–15 yrs.

Japan

Araki, Nancy & I Sue M. Horil. *Matsuri! Festival! Japanese American Celebrations and Activities*. 1985. Union City, Calif.: Heilan International. 10–15 yrs.

Blumberg, Rhoda. 1985. *Commodore Perry in the Land of the Shogun*. New York: Lothrop, Lee & Shepard. 12–16 yrs.

Brown, Tricia. 1995. *Konnichiwa!: I Am a Japanese American Girl*. Photos Kazuyoshi Arai. New York: Holt. 6–9 yrs.

Downer, Lesley. 1995. *Japan*. Color photos. New York: Thomson Learning. 10–14 yrs. Modern Industrial World series.

Elkin, Judith. 1987. *A Family in Japan*. Photos. Stuart Atkin. Minneapolis, Minn.: Lerner. 7–11 yrs. Families the World Over Series.

Greene, Carol. 1983. *Japan*. Danbury, Conn.: Children's Press. 9–12 yrs. Enchantment of the World Series.

Hamanaka, Sheila. 1990. *The Journey: Japanese Americans, Racism, and Renewal*. Paintings S. Hamanaka. New York: Orchard. 11–16 yrs.

Honda, Tetsuya. 1992. *Wild Horse Winter*. Illus. T. Honda. San Francisco: Chronicle. 8–10 yrs.

Kitano, Harry. 1987. *Japanese Americans*. New York: Chelsea House. 10–16 yrs.

Kudilnski, Kathleen V. 1991. *Pearl Harbor Is Burning: A Story of World War II*. New York: Viking. 7–12 yrs.

Kuklin, Susan. 1995. *Kodomo: Children of Japan*. Color photos. New York: Putnam. 6–9 yrs.

Sherrow, Victoria. 1994. *Hiroshima*. New York: New Discovery. 12–16 yrs. Timestop series.

Takaki, Ronald. (Adapter Rebecca Stefoff). 1994. *Issei and Nisei: The Settling of Japanese America*. B & W photos. New York: Chelsea House. 11–15 yrs. Asian American Experience series.

Tames, Richard. 1981. *Japan in the Twentieth Century*. London: Batsford Academic & Educational. 12–16 yrs. Twentieth Century World History Series.

————. 1982. *The Japanese*. London: Batsford Academic & Educational. 12–16 yrs. Today's World Series.

————. 1986. *Japan: The Land and Its People*. Morristown, N.J.: Silver Burdett. 12–16 yrs. Silver Burdett Countries Series.

Wells, Ruth. 1992. *A to Zen: A Book of Japanese Culture*. Illus. Yoshi. Saxonville, Mass.: Picture Book Studio. 7–12 yrs.

Korea

Ashby, Gwynneth. 1987. *A Family in South Korea*. Minneapolis, Minn.: Lerner. 7–11 yrs.

Bandon, Alexandra. 1994. *Korean Americans*. B & W photos. New York: New Discovery. 12–16 yrs. Footsteps to America series.

Bachrach, Deborah. 1991. *The Korean War*. San Diego: Lucent. 11–16 yrs.

Chung, Okwha & Judy Monroe. 1988. *Cooking the Korean Way*. Minneapolis, Minn.: Lerner. 11–15 yrs.

Farley, Carol. 1991. *Korea: Land of the Morning Calm*. Morristown, N.J.: Dillon. 11–15 yrs.

Haskins, Jim. 1989. *Count Your Way through Korea*. Illus. Dennis Hockerman. Minneapolis, Minn.: Carolrhoda. 6–10 yrs.

Jacobsen, Karen. 1989. *Korea*. Danbury, Conn.: Children's Press. 6–10 yrs.

Koh, Frances M. 1990. *Korean Holidays and Festivals*. Illus. Liz B. Dodson. Minneapolis, Minn.: East West Press. 7–11 yrs.

Lehrer, Brian. 1995. *The Korean Americans*. Color, B & W photos. New York: Chelsea House. 10–14 yrs. Immigrant Experience series.

McGowen, Tom. 1993. *The Korean War*. Danbury, Conn.: Watts. 11–16 yrs.

McMahon, Patricia. 1993. *Chi-hoon: A Korean Girl*. Photos Michael F. O'Brien. Honesdale, Penn.: Boyds Mills Press/Caroline. 8–10 yrs.

McNair, Sylvia. 1986. *Korea*. Danbury, Conn.: Children's Press. 11–13 yrs.

Nahm, Andrew. 1983. *A Panorama of 5000 Years: Korean History*. Elizabeth, N.J.: Hollym International. 11–15 yrs.

Nash, Amy. 1991. *North Korea*. New York: Chelsea House. 11–15 yrs.

Solberg, S. E. 1991. *Land and People of Korea*. New York: HarperCollins. 12–16 yrs.

————. 1989. *South Korea in Pictures*. 1989. Minneapolis, Minn.: Lerner. 11–14 yrs.

Takaki, Ronald (Adapter Rebecca Stefoff). 1994. *From the Land of Morning Calm: The Koreans in America*. B & W photos. New York: Chelsea House. 12–16 yrs.

Yoo, Yushin. 1987. *Korea the Beautiful: Treasures of the Hermit Kingdom*. Murray, Ky.: Golden Pond Press. 11–15 yrs.

————. 1990. *The Making of Modern Korea*. Murray, Ky.: Golden Pond Press. With video-cassette. 11–15 yrs.

Vietnam

Bandon, Alexandra. 1994. *Vietnamese Americans*. B & W photos. New York: New Discovery. 12–16 yrs. Footsteps to America series.

Brown, Tricia. 1991. *Lee Ann: The Story of a Vietnamese-American Girl*. Photos Ted Thai. New York: Putnam. 7–10 yrs.

Hoyt-Goldsmith, Diana. 1992. *A Vietnamese-American Boy*. Photos Lawrence Migdale. New York: Holiday. 9–12 yrs.

Huynh, Quang Nhuong. 1982. *The Land I Lost*. Illus. Vo-Dinh Mai. New York: Harper & Row. 10–14 yrs.

Matthews, Jo. 1994. *I Remember Vietnam*. Photos Tim Page. 6–10 yrs. Chatham, N.J.: Raintree. Why We Left series.

O'Connor, Karen. 1992. *Dan Thuy's New Life in America*. Minneapolis, Minn.: Lerner. 9–12 yrs.

Other Asian Countries

Feeney, Stephanie. 1985. *Hawaii Is a Rainbow*. Photos Jeff Reese. Honolulu: University of Hawaii Press. 5–8 yrs.

Reynolds, Jan. 1991. *Himalaya: Vanishing Cultures*. Photos Jan Reynolds. San Diego: Harcourt Brace Jovanovich. 8–11 yrs.

Takaki, Ronald (Adapter Rebecca Stefoff). 1994. *In the Heart of Filipino America: Immigrants from the Pacific Isles*. B & W photos. New York: Chelsea House. 12–16 yrs. Asian-American Experience series.

————. 1994. *India in the West: South Asians in America*. B & W photos. New York: Chelsea House. 12–16 yrs. Asian-American Experience series.

————. 1994. *Raising Cane: The World of Plantation Hawaii*. B & W photos. New York: Chelsea House. 12–16 yrs. Asian American Experience series.

Yu, Ling. 1990. *A Family in Taiwan*. Photos Chen Mingjeng. Minneapolis, Minn.: Lerner. 10–14 yrs.

Poetry & Stories

Carlson, Lori (Ed.). 1994. *American Eyes: New Asian American Short Stories for Young Adults*. New York: Holt. 12–16 yrs.

Cassedy, Sylvia, & Kunihiro Suetake (Trans). 1992. *Red Dragonfly on My Shoulder*. Illus. Molly Bang. New York: HarperCollins. 7–10 yrs.

Demi (Compiler; Trans. Tze-si Huang). 1992. *In the Eyes of the Cat: Japanese Poetry for All Seasons*. Illus. Demi. New York: Holt. 9–14 yrs.

————. 1993. *Demi's Dragons and Fantastic Creatures*. New York: Holt. 5–9 yrs.

Ho, M. 1996. *Hush!: A Thai Lullaby*. Illus. Holly Meade. New York: Orchard. 4–7 yrs.

————. (Compiler & trans). 1996. *Maples in the Mist: Children's Poems from the Tang Dynasty*. Illus. Jean & Mou-sien Tseng. New York: Lothrop, Lee & Shepard. 4–8 yrs.

Lee, Jeanne M. 1995. *The Song of Mulan*. Illus. J. Lee. Front Street Books. 7–10 yrs.

Mado, Michio (Trans. Empress Michiko of Japan). 1992. *The Animals: Selected Poems*. Illus. Mitsumasa Anno. New York: McElderry. 8–12 yrs.

Navasky, Bruno (Selector & Trans.) 1993. *Festival in My Heart: Poems by Japanese Children*. New York: Abrams. 10–13 yrs.

101 Favorite Songs Taught in Japanese Schools. 1983. Illus. Sachiko Higuchi. Essays and translations by Ichiro Nakano. The Japan Times. 8–14 yrs.

Shannon, G. 1996. *Spring: A Haiku Story*. Illus. Malcah Zeldis. New York: Greenwillow. 6–9 yrs.

Tagore, Rabindranath. 1992. *Paper Boats*. Illus. Grayce Bochak. Honesdale, Penn.: Boyds Mills/Caroline. 6–10 yrs.

Wong, Janet S. 1994. *Good Luck Gold: And Other Poems*. New York: McElderry. 10–13 yrs.

Wong, J. S. 1996. *A Suitcase of Seaweed and Other Poems*. New York: McElderry. 9–12 yrs.

Yep, Laurence (Ed.). 1993. *American Dragons: Twenty-Five Asian American Voices*. New York: HarperCollins. 12–16 yrs.

Chinese Americans: Videos

The Bamboo Brush. 1982; released 1983. 25 min. Produced by Seaton McLean, Michael MacMillan, and Janice Platt for Atlantis Films and Canadian Broadcasting Corp. Directed Sturla Gunnarsson. Altschul Group Corp., 1560 Sherman Ave., Evanston, IL 60201. 11–15 yrs.

The Emperor and the Nightingales. 1987. 40 min. Produced by Sony Video. Baker & Taylor, 501 S. Gladiolus, Momence, IL 60954. 11–15 yrs.

Holidays for Children Video: Chinese New Year. 1994. 30 min. Produced by Schlessinger Video Productions. Library Video Co., P.O. Box 1110, Dept. B. Bala Cynwyd, PA 19004. 10–15 yrs.

Multicultural Peoples of North America: Chinese Americans. 1993. 30 min. Produced by Schlessinger Video Productions. Library Video Co., P.O. Box 1110, Dept. B. Bala Cynwyd, PA 19004. 10–15 yrs.

Adult Resources

Coleman, Craig S. 1994. *Social Studies Guide on Korea for High School Teachers*. Korea Society of Los Angeles, 5505 Wilshire Blvd., Los Angeles, CA 90036.

Discover Japan: Words, Customs, and Concepts. Vol. 1 and 2. 1988. Kodansha International, 114 Fifth Ave., New York, NY 10011.

Li, Marjorie N. & Peter Li. 1990. *Understanding Asian Americans: A Curriculum Resource Guide*. Neal-Schuman.

Makino, Yasuko. 1985. *Japan through Children's Literature: An Annotated Bibliography*. 2d edition. Greenwood.

Richie, Donald. 1978. *Introducing Japan*. Kodansha International, 114 Fifth Ave., New York, NY 10011.

U.S. Sources for Obtaining Books from and about Japan

Charles E. Tuttle Company, 28 S. Main St., P.O. Box 410, Rutland, VT 05702.

Kinokuniya Book and Gallery, Fashion Island, 401 Newport Center Dr., Suite 315, Atrium Court, Newport Beach, CA 92660.

Taino Stories

Belpre, Pura. 1978. *The Rainbow-Colored Horse*. Illus. Antonio Martorell. New York: Warne. 7–11 yrs.

Crespo, George. 1993. *How the Sea Began: A Taino Myth*. New York: Clarion. 7–11 yrs.

Dorris, Michael. 1992. *Morning Girl*. New York: Hyperion. 10–15 yrs. Scott O'Dell Award for Historical Fiction, 1993.

Jacobs, Francine. 1992. *The Tainos: The People Who Welcomed Columbus*. Illus. Patrick Collins. New York: Putnam. 11–16 yrs.

Jaffe, N. (Adapter). 1996. *The Golden Flower: A Taino Myth from Puerto Rico*. Illus. Enrique O. Sanchez. New York: Simon & Schuster. 4–7 yrs.

Yolen, Jane. 1992. *Encounter*. Illus. David Shannon. San Diego: Harcourt Brace Jovanovich. 8–12 yrs.

HISPANIC LITERATURE

BOOKS WITH PICTURES

Family

Ackerman, Karen. 1994. *By the Dawn's Early Light*. Illus. Catherine Stock. New York: Atheneum. 5–9 yrs.

Alphin, Elaine Marie. 1996. *A Bear for Miguel*. Illus. Joan Sandin. New York: HarperCollins. 6–8 yrs. I Can Read Books.

Best, Cari. 1994. *Taxi! Taxi!* Illus. Dale Gottlieb. Boston: Little, Brown. 5–8 yrs.

Bunting, Eve. 1990. *The Wall*. Illus. Ronald Himler. New York: Clarion. 4–8 yrs.

———. 1996. *Going Home*. Illus. David Diaz. New York: Cotler/HarperCollins. 6–8 yrs. (Migrant.)

Carlstrom, Nancy White. 1994. *Barney Is Best*. Illus. James Graham Hale. New York: HarperCollins. 5–7 yrs.

Cowley, J. 1996. *Gracias: The Thanksgiving Turkey*. Illus. Joe Cepeda. New York: Scholastic. 5–8 yrs.

Czernecki, Stefan & Timothy Rhodes. 1994. *The Hummingbirds' Gift*. Illus. Stefan Czernecki. New York: Hyperion. 6–8 yrs.

Dorros, Arthur. 1993. *Radio Man/Don Radio: A Story in English and Spanish*. New York: HarperCollins. 5–7 yrs.

Flora, James. *The Fabulous Firework Family*. 1955. San Diego: Harcourt Brace. 5–9 yrs.

McLerran, Alice. 1992. *I Want to Go Home*. Illus. Jill Kastner. New York: Tambourine. 5–8 yrs.

Mora, Pat. 1992. *A Birthday Basket for Tia*. Illus. Cecily Lang. New York: Macmillan. 4–8 yrs.

———. 1996. *Uno, Dos, Tres: One, Two, Three*. Illus. Barbara Lavallee. New York: Clarion. 6–9 yrs.

Roe, Eileen. 1991. *Con Mi Hermano/With My Brother*. Illus. Robert Casilla. New York: Bradbury. 4–7 yrs.

Schoberle, Cecile. 1990. *Esmeralda and the Pet Parade*. Illus. Cecile Schoberle. New York: Simon and Schuster. 5–8 yrs.

Soto, Gary. 1993. *Too Many Tamales*. Illus. Ed Martinez. New York: Putnam. 4–7 yrs.

Stanek, Muriel. 1989. *I Speak English for My Mom*. Illus. Judith Friedman. Morton Grove, Ill.: Whitman. 7–10 yrs.

Thomas, Jane Resh. 1994. *Lights on the River*. Illus. Michael Dooling. New York: Hyperion. 5–9 yrs.

Torres, Leyla. 1995. *Saturday Sancocho*. New York: Farrar, Straus & Giroux. 5–9 yrs. Spanish language edition, *El Sancocho del sabado*.

Weiss, Nicki. 1992. *On a Hot, Hot Day*. Illus. Nicki Weiss. New York: Putnam. 3–7 yrs.

Winter, J. 1996. *Josefina*. San Diego, Calif.: Harcourt Brace. 4–8 yrs.

Grandparents

Argueta, Manlio. 1990. *Magic Dogs of the Volcanos/Los Perros Magicos de los Volcanes*. Illus. Elly Simmons. Emeryville, Calif.: Children's Book Press. 6–12 yrs.

Bunting, Eve. 1994. *A Day's Work*. Illus. Ronald Himler. New York: Clarion. 5–9 yrs.

Castaneda, Omar S. 1993. *Abuelo's Weave*. Illus. Enrique O. Sanchez. New York: Lee & Low. 5–9 yrs.

Dorros, Arthur. 1991. *Abuela*. Illus. Elisa Kleven. New York: Dutton. 8–10 yrs.

———. 1995. *Isla*. Illus. Elisa Kleven. New York: Dutton. 8–10 yrs.

Havill, Juanita. 1992. *Treasure Nap*. Illus. Elivia Savadier. Boston: Houghton Mifflin. 4–8 yrs.

Johnston, Tony. 1992. *Lorenzo, the Naughty Parrot*. Illus. Leo Politi. San Diego: Harcourt Brace Jovanovich. 5–8 yrs.

Meyer, L. 1993. *Grandma's Helper*. Illus. M. Passicot. Glenview, Ill.: Scott, Foresman. 5–9 yrs. Big book.

Nodar, Carmen Santiago. 1992. *Abuelita's Paradise/El Paraiso de Abuelita*. Illus. Diane Paterson. Morton Grove, Ill.: Whitman. 5–8 yrs.

Pomerantz, Charlotte. 1993. *The Outside Dog*. Illus. Jennifer Plecas. New York: HarperCollins. 6–8 yrs. I Can Read series.

Friendship

Anzaldua, Gloria. 1993. *Friends from the Other Side/Amigos del otro lado*. Illus. Consuelo Mendez. Emeryville, Calif.: Children's Book Press. 7–9 yrs.

Atkinson, Mary. 1979. *Maria Teresa*. Illus. Christina Engla Eber. Chapel Hill, N.C.: Lollipop Power. 6–9 yrs.

Fern, Eugene. 1991. *Pepito's Story*. New York: Yarrow Press. 5–8 yrs.

Hayes, Joe. 1996. *A Spoon for Every Bite*. Illus. Rebecca Leer. New York: Orchard. 5–8 yrs.

Reiser, Lynn. 1993. *Margaret and Margarita/Margarita y Margaret*. Illus. L. Reiser. New York: Greenwillow. 4–7 yrs.

Scott, Ann Herbert. 1994. *Hi*. Illus. Glo Coalson. New York: Philomel. 5–7 yrs.

Taha, Karen T. 1986. *A Gift for Tia Rosa*. Illus. Dee de Rosa. Minneapolis: Dillon. 6–9 yrs.

Celebration

Anaya, Rudolfo A. 1987. *The Farolitos of Christmas: A New Mexican Christmas Story*. Illus. Richard C. Sandoval. Sante Fe: New Mexico Magazine. 5–12 yrs.

Bruni, Mary Ann Smothers. 1981. *Rosita's Christmas Wish*. Illus. Thom Ricks. San Antonio: TexArt Services. 7–10 yrs.

Cruz, Manuel & Ruth Cruz. 1981. *A Chicano Christmas Story/Un Cuento Navideño Chicano*. Illus. Manuel Cruz. South Pasadena, Calif.: Bilingual Educational Services. 5–9 yrs.

Dorros, Arthur. 1991. *Tonight Is Carnaval*. Illus. the Club de Madras. Virgen del Carmen of Lima, Peru. New York: Dutton. 6–10 yrs.

Ets, Marie Hall & Aurora Labastida. 1959. *Nine Days to Christmas*. Illus. Marie Hall Ets. New York: Viking. 5–9 yrs.

Grifalconi, Ann. 1994. *The Bravest Flute: A Story of Courage in the Mayan Tradition*. Boston: Little, Brown. 7–9 yrs.

Krull, Kathleen. 1994. *Maria Molina and the Days of the Dead*. Illus. Enrique O. Sonchez. New York: Simon & Schuster. 6–9 yrs.

Martel, Cruz. 1987. *Yagua Days*. Illus. Jerry Pinkney. New York: Dial. 5–9 yrs.

Mora, Pat. 1994. *Pablo's Tree*. Illus. Cecily Lang. New York: Macmillan. 5–9 yrs.

Riehecky, Xonet. 1993. *Cinco de Mayo*. Illus. Krystyna Stasiak. Danbury, Conn.: Children's Press. 5–9 yrs.

Van Laan, N. 1996. *La Boda: A Mexican Wedding Celebration*. Illus. Andrea Arroyo. Boston: Little, Brown. 6–9 yrs.

Cultural Pride

Komaiko, Leah. 1992. *Aunt Elaine Does the Dance from Spain*. Illus. Petra Mathers. New York: Doubleday. 6–9 yrs.

Lachtman, Ofelia Dumos. 1995. *Pepita Talks Twice/Pepita habla dos veces*. Illus. Alex Pardo DeLange. Houston, Tex.: Piñata. 5–9 yrs.

Markel, Michelle. 1995. *Gracias, Rosa*. Illus. Diane Paterson. Morton Grove, Ill.: Whitman. 5–9 yrs.

Wing, N. 1996. *Jalapeno Bagels*. Illus. Robert Casilla. New York: Atheneum. 7–10 yrs.

Informational Story Books

Hewett, Joan. 1990. *Laura Loves Horses*. Photos Richard Hewett. New York: Clarion. 7–10 yrs.

Folk Literature

Hispanic-American Tales

Hayes, Joe. 1992. *Everyone Knows Gato Pinto: More Tales from Spanish New Mexico*. Illus. Lucy Jelinek. Santa Fe, N.M.: Mariposa. 9–12 yrs. (See also: *The Day It Snowed Tortillas*.)

Van Etten, Teresa Pijoan de. 1990. *Spanish-American Folktales*. Little Rock, Ark.: August House. 6–12 yrs.

Mexican Tales

Aardema, Verna (Reteller). 1991. *Borreguita and the Coyote: A Tale from Ayutla, Mexico*. Illus. Petra Mathers. New York: Knopf/Borzoi. 6–9 yrs.

Albert, B. 1996. *Journey of the Nightly Jaguar: Inspired by an Ancient Mayan Myth*. Illus. Robert Roth. New York: Atheneum. 6–9 yrs.

Atencio, Paulette. 1991. *Cuentos from My Childhood: Legends and Folktales of Northern New Mexico*. Santa Fe: Museum of New Mexico Press. 9–14 yrs.

Bidet, Ran. 1969. *The Fence: A Mexican Tale*. New York: Delacorte. 6–9 yrs.

Bierhorst, John (Trans.). 1990. *Spirit Child: A Story of the Nativity*. Illus. Barbara Cooney. New York: Greenwillow. 4–8 yrs.

Brenner, Anita (Reteller). 1992. *The Boy Who Could Do Anything and Other Mexican Folk Tales*. Illus. Jean Charlot. North Haven, Conn.: Linnet. 6–11 yrs.

de Paola, Tomie (Reteller). 1980. *The Lady of Guadalupe*. New York: Holiday. 9–12 yrs.

———. 1994. *The Legend of the Poinsettia*. New York: Putnam. 5–8 yrs.

Gerson, M. J. 1995. *People of Corn: A Mayan Story*. Illus. Carla Golembe. Boston: Little, Brown. 5–9 yrs.

Griego, Margot C. et al. 1981. *Tortillitas Para Mama and Other Nursery Rhymes*. Illus. Barbara Cooney. New York: Holt. 5–8 yrs.

Johnston, Tony. 1994. *The Tale of Rabbit and Coyote*. Illus. Tomie de Paola. New York: Putnam. 6–9 yrs.

Kimmel, Eric A. *The Witch's Face: A Mexican Tale*. Illus. Fabricio Vanden Broeck. New York: Holiday. 8–11 yrs.

Kouzel, Daisy, (Adapter & trans.). 1977. *The Cuckoo's Reward: A Folktale from Mexico in Spanish and English/El Premio del Cuco: Cuento Popular de México en Español y Inglés*. Illus. Earl Thollander. New York: Doubleday. 5–9 yrs.

Kurtycz, Marcos, & Ana Garcia Kobeth (Adapters; Felicia M. Hall trans.). 1984. *Tigers and Opossums: Animal Legends*. Illus. M. Kurtycz & A. Kobeth. Boston: Little, Brown. 9–12 yrs.

Lattimore, Deborah Nourse. 1987. *The Name of Peace: A Tale of the Aztecs*. New York: HarperCollins. 8–12 yrs.

Lewis, Richard. 1991. *All of You Was Singing*. Illus. Ed Young. New York: Atheneum. 8–11 yrs.

Lopez de Mariscal, Blanca. 1995. *The Harvest Birds/Los pajaros de la cosecha*. Illus. Enrique Flores. Emeryville, Calif.: Children's Book Press. 6–9 yrs.

Lyons, Grant. 1972. *Tales the People Tell in Mexico*. Morristown, N.J.: Silver Burdett/Messner. 6–10 yrs.

Martinez, Alejandro Cruz (text Rosalma Zubizarreta, Harriet Rohmer, & David Schecter). 1991. *The Woman Who Outshone*

the Sun: The Legend of Lucia Zenteño/La
Mujer que Brillaba Aun Mas que el Sol: La
Leyenda d e Lucia Zenteño. Illus. Fernando
Olivera. Emeryville, Calif.: Children's Book.
9–12 yrs.

Ober, Hal. 1994. *How Music Came to the World:
An Ancient Mexican Myth.* Illus. Carol Ober.
Boston: Houghton Mifflin. 7–10 yrs.

Rohmer, Harriet & Mary Anchondo (Adapters).
1988. *How We Came to the Fifth World/Como
Vinimos al Quinto Mundo.* Illus. Graciela
Carrillo. Emeryville, Calif.: Children's Book.
7–12 yrs.

Soto, G. 1996. *The Old Man and His Door.* Illus.
Joe Cepeda. New York: Putnam. 4–6 yrs.

South American Tales

Alexander, Ellen. 1989. *Llama and the Great
Flood: A Folktale from Peru.* Illus. E. Alexander.
New York: Crowell. 9–14 yrs.

Belting, Natalia M. 1992. *Moon Was Tired of
Walking on Air.* Illus. Will Hillenbrand.
Boston: Houghton Miflin. 5–9 yrs.

Blackmore, Vivien (Reteller). 1984. *Why Corn Is
Golden: Stories about Plants.* Illus. Susana
Martinez-Ostos. Boston: Little, Brown. 5–9 yrs.

Brusca, Maria Cristina & Tona Wilson (Retellers).
1992. *The Blacksmith and the Devil/El Herrero
y el Diablo.* Illus. Maria Cristina Brusca. New
York: Holt. 8–11 yrs.

Ehlert, Lois (Trans. Amy Prince). 1992. *Moon
Rope: A Peruvian Folktale/Un lazo a la tuna:
Una leyenda Peruana.* Illus. Lois Ehlert. San
Diego: Harcourt Brace Jovanovich. 5–8 yrs.

Gifford, Douglas. 1983. *Warriors, Gods, and Spirits
from Central and South American Mythology.*
Illus. John Sibbick. New York: Schocken.
11–16 yrs. World Mythologies Series.

————. 1994. *Warriors, Gods, and Spirits from
Central and South American Mythology.* Illus.
John Sibbick. New York: Bedrick. 10–13 yrs.
World Mythology series.

Lattimore, Deborah Nourse. 1989. *Why There Is
No Arguing in Heaven: A Mayan Myth.* Illus.
D. Lattimore. New York: Harper & Row.
9–14 yrs.

Martinez, Cruz Alejandro (Ad. Rosalma
Zubizarreta, Harriet Rohmer, & Davis
Schecter). 1991. *The Woman Who Outshone
the Sun/La Mujer Que Brillaba Aun Mas Que
el Sol.* Emeryville, Calif.: Children's Book
Press. 5–8 yrs.

Rohmer, Harriet (Adapter). 1989. *Uncle Nacho's
Hat/El Sombrero del Tio Nacho.* Illus. Veg
Reisberg. Emeryville, Calif.: Children's Book
Press. 5–8 yrs.

Rohmer, Harriet (Adapter; trans. Alma Flor Ada &
Rosalma Zubizarreta). 1982. *The Legend of
Food Mountain/La Leyenda de la Montana de
Alimento.* Illus. Graciela Carrillo. Emeryville,
Calif.: Children's Book. 8–12 yrs.

Rohmer, Harriet, Octavio Chow, & Morris Vidaure
(Trans. Rosalma Zubizarreta & Alma Flor Ada).
1987. *The Invisible Hunters: A Legend from the
Miskito Indians of Nicaragua/Los Cazadores
Invisibles: Una Leyenda de los Indios Miskitos
de Nicaragua.* Illus. Joe Sam. San Francisco:
Children's Book Press. 7–12 yrs.

Rohmer, Harriet & Dorminster Wilson (Trans.
Rosalma Zubizarreta & Alma Flor Ada). 1988.
*Mother Scorpion Country: A Legend from the
Miskito Indians of Nicaragua/La Tierra de la
Madre Escorpion: Una Leyenda de los Indios
Miskitos de Nicaragua.* Illus. Virginia Stearns.
Emeryville, Calif.: Children's Book. 7–12 yrs.

Stiles, Martha Bennett (Reteller). 1992. *James the
Vine Puller: A Brazilian Folktale.* Illus. Larry
Thomas. Minneapolis, Minn.: Carolrhoda.
6–10 yrs.

Van Laan, Nancy (Adapter). 1991. *The Legend of El
Dorado: A Latin American Tale.* Illus. Beatriz
Vidal. New York: Knopf/Borzoi. 7–12 yrs.

Volkmer, Jane Anne (Reteller; trans. Lori Ann
Schatschneider). 1990. *Song of the Chirimia:
A Guatemalan Folktale/La Musica de la Chirimia:
Folklore Guatemalteco.* Illus. Jane Anne Volkmer.
Minneapolis, Minn.: Carolrhoda. 8–11 yrs.

Puerto Rican Tales

Belpre, Pura. 1973. *Once in Puerto Rico.* Illus.
Christine Price. New York: Warne. 5–9 yrs.

————. 1991. *Perez and Martina: A Puerto Rican
Folktale/Perez y Martina.* Illus. Carlos
Sanchez. New York: Viking Penguin. 7–10 yrs.

Mohr, Nicholasa & Antonio Martorell. 1995. *The
Song of el Coqui: And Other Tales of Puerto
Rico.* New York: Viking. 5–10 yrs.

Pitre, Felix. 1993. *Juan Bobo and the Pig: A Puerto
Rican Folktale.* Illus. Christy Hale. New York:
Lodestar. 6–9 yrs.

Simms, Laura. 1991. *The Squeaky Door.* Illus.
Sylvie Wickstrom. New York: Crown. 3–6 yrs.

Spanish Tales

Janda, J. 1986. *The Legend of the Holy Child of
Atocha.* Illus. William Hart McNichols. New
York and Mahwah, N.J.: Paulist Press. 5–9 yrs.

Prieto, Mariana. 1962. *The Wise Rooster/El Gallo
Sabio.* Illus. Lee Smith. Day. 5–8 yrs.

Schon, Isabel (Collector & translator) with R. R.
Chalquest. 1983. *Doña Blanca and Other
Hispanic Nursery Rhymes and Games.*
Denison. 5–9 yrs.

Literary Folk Tales

Ada, Alma Flor (Trans. Bernice Randall). 1991.
The Gold Coin. Illus. Neil Waldman. New
York: Atheneum. 7–11 yrs.

Alexander, Lloyd. 1992. *The Fortune-Tellers.* Illus.
Trina Schart Hyman. New York: Dutton.
5–9 yrs.

Argueta, Manlio (Trans. Stacey Ross). 1990. *Magic
Dogs of the Volcanoes/Los Perros Magicos de los
Volcanes.* Illus. Elly Simmons. Emeryville,
Calif.: Children's Book. 7–11 yrs.

Blanco, Alberto (Trans. Barbara Paschke). 1992.
The Desert Mermaid/La Sirena del Desierto.
Illus. Patricia Revah. Emeryville, Calif.:
Children's Book. 7–10 yrs.

Gollub, Matthew. 1994. *The Moon Was at a Fiesta.*
Illus. Leovigildo Martinez. New York:
Tambourine. 6–8 yrs.

Johnston, Tony. 1995. *Alice Nizzy Nazzy: The
Witch of Santa Fe.* Illus. Tomie de Paola. New
York: Putnam. 6–9 yrs.

Wisniewski, David. 1991. *Rain Player.* Illus. David
Wisniewski. New York: Clarion. 8–10 yrs.

Fantasy: Picture Story Books

Garcia, Maria. 1986. *The Adventures of Connie and
Diego/Las Aventuras de Connie y Diego.* Illus.
Malaquias Montoya. Emeryville, Calif.:
Children's Book Press/Imprenta de Libros
Infantiles. 9–12 yrs.

Johnston, Tony. 1995. *The Iguana Brothers: A Tale
of Two Lizards.* Illus. Mark Teague. New York:
Scholastic/Blue Sky. 6–9 yrs.

Parkison, Jami. 1994. *Pequena the Burro.* Illus.
Itoko Maeno. Kansas City, Mo.: Marsh film.
6–9 yrs.

Soto, Gary. 1995. *Chato's Kitchen.* Illus. Susan
Guevara. New York: Putnam. 5–9 yrs.

REALISTIC NOVELS

Family

Alphin, E. M. 1996. *A Bear for Miguel.* Illus. Joan
Sandin. New York: HarperCollins. 6–8 yrs. I
Can Read Books.

Garcia, Richard. 1987. *My Aunt Otilia's Spirits/Los
Espiritos de Mi Tia Otilia.* Illus. Robin Cherin
& Roger I. Reyes. San Francisco: Children's
Book Press. 9–12 yrs.

Rosen, Michael J. 1995. *Bonesy and Isabel.* Illus.
James Ransome. San Diego: Harcourt Brace.
7–9 yrs.

Spurr, E. 1995. *Lupe and Me.* Illus. Enrique O.
Sanchez. San Diego, Calif.: San Diego:
Harcourt Brace/Gulliver. 7–10 yrs.

Friends

Hurwitz, Johanna. 1991. *Class President.* Illus.
Sheila Hamanaka. New York:
Scholastic/Apple. 10–12 yrs.

Mazzio, Joan. 1992. *The One Who Came Back.*
Boston: Houghton Mifflin. 11–16 yrs.

Soto, Gary. 1994. *Crazy Weekend.* New York:
Scholastic. 10–13 yrs.

————. 1995. *Boys at Work.* Illus. Robert Casilla.
New York: Delacorte. (Sequel to *The Pool
Party.*)

————. 1995. *Summer on Wheels.* New York:
Scholastic. 12–14 yrs.

Community Support

Kurusa (Trans. Karen Englander). 1985. *The
Streets Are Free.* Illus. Monika Doppert.
Annick. 9–12 yrs.

Velasquez, Gloria. 1994. *Juanita Fights the School
Board.* Houston, Tex.: Pinata Books. 12–14 yrs.
(See also sequel, *Maya's Divided World.*)

Cultural Pride

Ada, Alma Flor (Trans. Ana M. Cerro). 1993. *My
Name Is Maria Isabel.* Illus. K. Dyble
Thompson. New York: Atheneum. 9–11 yrs.
Spanish-language edition, *Me llamo Maria
Isabel.*

Soto, Gary. 1991. *Taking Sides.* San Diego:
Harcourt Brace Jovanovich. 10–16 yrs.

————. 1992. *The Skirt.* Illus. Eric Velasquez. New
York: Delacorte. 7–10 yrs.

Taylor, Theodore. 1992. *Maria: A Christmas Story.*
San Diego: Harcourt Brace Jovanovich. 8–12 yrs.

Living in Two Worlds

Betancourt, T. Ernesto. 1985. *The Me Inside of
Me.* Minneapolis, Minn.: Lerner, 11–16 yrs.

Castaneda, Omor S. 1991. *Among the Volcanoes.*
New York: Lodestar. 12–16 yrs.

Gordon, Ginger. 1993. *My Two Worlds.* Photos
Martha Cooper. New York: Clarion. 6–9 yrs.

Mohr, Nicholasa. 1979. *Felita.* Illus. Ray Cruz.
New York: Dial. 9–12 yrs.

————. 1986. *Going Home.* New York: Dial.
10–13 yrs. (See also: *Nilda.*)

Paulsen, Gary. 1993. *Sisters/Hermanas.* San Diego:
Harcourt Brace. 12–17 yrs.

Soto, Gary. 1994. *Jesse.* San Diego: Harcourt
Brace. 12–16 yrs.

Thomas, Piri. 1978. *Stories from El Barrio.* New
York: Knopf. 12–16 yrs.

Illegal Immigrants

Beatty, Patricia. 1981. *Lupita Mañana.* New York:
Morrow/Beech Tree. 11–14 yrs.

Buss, Fran Leeper (with Daisy Cubias). 1991.
Journey of the Sparrows. New York: Lodestar.
12–16 yrs.

History

de Trevino, Elizabeth Borton. 1991. *El Guero: A
True Adventure Story.* New York: Farrar, Straus
& Giroux. 10–14 yrs.

Gross, Virginia T. 1993. *The President Is Dead: A
Story of the Kennedy Assassination.* Illus. Dan
Andreasen. New York: Viking. 10–13 yrs. Once
upon America series.

Merino, Jose Mario (Trans. Helen Lane). 1991. *The Gold of Dreams.* New York: Farrar, Straus & Giroux. 10–14 yrs.

Neugeboren, Soy. 1989. *Poli: A Mexican Boy In Early Texas.* Illus. Tom Leomon. San Antonio, Tex.: Corona. 12–16 yrs.

O'Dell, Scott. 1977. *Carlota.* Boston: Houghton Mifflin. 10–14 yrs.

Adventure

Bogin, Magda. 1991. *Cervantes's Don Quixote: Being a Faithful Translation and Adaptation by Magda Bogin of the First Part of Cervantes's Original Classic.* Illus. M. Duel Boix. New York: Stewart, Tabori & Chang. 12–16 yrs. (See also Margaret Hodges' adaptation, *Don Quixote and Sancho Panza,* Illus. Stephen Marchesi.)

Bragg, Bea. 1989. *The Very First Thanksgiving: Pioneers on the Rio Grande.* Illus. Antonio Costro. Tucson, Ariz.: Harbinger. 9–12 yrs.

Quest

George, Jean Craighead. 1989. *Shark Beneath the Reef.* New York: HarperCollins. 12–15 yrs.

Animal

Kidney, Francis. 1958. *Chucaro: Wild Pony of the Pampas.* Illus. Julian de Miskey. New York: Walker. 11–14 yrs.

BIOGRAPHIES

The Arts

Amdur, Melissa. 1993. *Anthony Quinn.* B & W photos & drawings. New York: Chelsea House. 12–16 yrs. Hispanics of Achievement series.

———. 1993. *Linda Ronstadt.* New York: Chelsea House. 12–16 yrs. Hispanics of Achievement series.

Beardley, John. 1991. *Pablo Picasso.* New York: Abrams. 12–15 yrs.

Braun, Barbara. 1994. *A Weekend with Diego Rivera.* New York: Rizzoli. 10–13 yrs. Weekend With series.

Cockcroft, James. 1991. *Diego Rivera.* New York: Chelsea House. 12–16 yrs.

Dolan, Sean. 1993. *Gabriel Garcia Marquez.* B & W photos. New York: Chelsea House. 12–16 yrs. Hispanics of Achievement series.

Ducker, Malka. 1991. *Frida Kahlo: Torment and Triumph In Her Life and Art.* New York: Bantam. 12–18 yrs.

Garza, Hedda. 1991. *Joan Baez.* New York: Chelsea House. 12–16 yrs.

———. 1993. *Pablo Casals.* B & W photos & drawings. New York: Chelsea House. 12–16 yrs. Hispanics of Achievement series.

Gonzalez, Fernando. 1993. *Gloria Estefan: Cuban-American Singing Star.* Brookfield, Conn.: Millbrook. 10–13 yrs. Hispanic Heritage series.

Horgrove, Jim. 1990. *Diego Rivera: Mexican Muralist.* Danbury, Conn.: Children's Press. 10–14 yrs.

Martinez, Elizabeth Coonrod. 1994. *Edward James Olmos: Mexican-American Actor.* Brookfield, Conn.: Millbrook. 10–14 yrs. Hispanic Heritage series.

Roman, Joseph. 1993. *Octavio Paz.* B & W photos. New York: Chelsea House. 12–16 yrs. Hispanics of Achievement series.

West, Alan. 1994. *Jose Marti: Man of Poetry, Soldier of Freedom.* Brookfield, Conn.: Millbrook. 10–14 yrs. Hispanic Heritage series.

Winter, Jeanette (text Jonah Winter; trans. Amy Price). 1991. *Diego.* New York: Knopf/Borzoi. 5–8 yrs.

Autobiographies

Hunter, Latoya. 1992. *The Diary of Latoya Hunter: My First Year in Junior High.* New York: Crown. 10–14 yrs.

Lomas Garza, Carmen (as told to Harriet Rohmer). 1990. *Family Pictures/Cuadros de Familia.* Illus. Carmen Lomas Garza. Emeryville, Calif.: Children's Book. 7–10 yrs.

Mohr, Nicholasa. 1994. *Nicholasa Mohr: Growing Up inside the Sanctuary of My Imagination.* B & W photos. Morristown, N.J.: Silver Burdett/Messner. 12–16 yrs.

Villacana, Eugenio. 1972. *Viva Morella.* New York: M. Evans. 9–12 yrs.

Government

Codye, Corinn. 1989. *Vilma Martinez.* Illus. Susi Kilgore. 1989. Chatham, N.J.: Raintree/Steck-Vaughn. 9–12 yrs.

de Trevino, Elizabeth Barton. 1974. *Juarez: Man of Law.* New York: Farrar, Straus & Giroux. 9–12 yrs.

Henry, Christopher E. 1994. *Henry Cisneros.* New York: Chelsea House. 12–16 yrs.

Martinez, Elizabeth Coonrod. 1993. *Henry Cisneros: Mexican-American Leader.* Brookfield, Conn.: Millbrook. 10–13 yrs. Hispanic Heritage series.

Roberts, Maurice. 1986. *Henry Cisneros: Mexican American Mayor.* Danbury, Conn.: Children's Press. 9–12 yrs. Picture Book Biographies.

Wepman, Dennis. 1986. *Benito Juarez.* 1986. New York: Chelsea House. 10–14 yrs.

Military Leaders

Adler, David A. 1992. *A Picture Book of Simon Bolivar.* Illus. Robert Casilla. New York: Holiday. 8–10 yrs.

de Varona, Frank. 1993. *Miguel Hidalgo y Costilla: Father of Mexican Independence.* Brookfield, Conn.: Millbrook. 10–13 yrs. Hispanic Heritage series.

O'Brien, Steven. 1994. *Pancho Villa.* B & W photos. New York: Chelsea House. 10–13 yrs. Hispanics of Achievement series.

Ragan, John David. 1989. *Emiliano Zapata.* New York: Chelsea House. 12–18 yrs.

Rouverol, Jean. 1972. *Pancho Villa.* New York: Doubleday. 12–18 yrs.

Activists

Cedeño, Maria E. 1993. *Cesar Chavez: Labor Leader.* Brookfield, Conn.: Millbrook. 10–15 yrs.

Roberts, Maurice. 1986. *Cesar Chavez and La Causa.* Danbury, Conn.: Children's Press. 9–12 yrs. Picture Book Biographies.

Sports

Gilbert, Thomas W. 1991. *Roberto Clemente.* New York: Chelsea House. 12–16 yrs.

Sabin, Louis. 1992. *Roberto Clemente: Young Baseball Hero.* Illus. Marie DeJohn. Mahwah, N.J.: Troll. 6–9 yrs.

Walker, Paul Robert. 1991. *Pride of Puerto Rico: The Life of Roberto Clemente.* Harcourt Brace Jovanovich/Odyssey. 9–12 yrs.

West, Alan. 1993. *Roberto Clemente: Baseball Legend.* Brookfield, Conn.: Millbrook. 10–13 yrs. Hispanic Heritage series.

Other Hispanic Heroes

Clinton, Susan Maloney. 1990. *Everett Alvarez, Jr.: A Hero for Our Times.* Danbury, Conn.: Children's Press. 12–16 yrs.

Duran, Gloria. 1993. *Malinche: Slave Princess of Cortez.* North Haven, Conn.: Shoe String/Linnet. 12–16 yrs.

Fernandez, Jose B. 1994. *Jose de San Martin: Latin America's Quiet Hero.* Paintings, B & W photos. Brookfield, Conn.: Millbrook. 10–13 yrs. Hispanic Heritage series.

Goldberg, Jake. 1993. *Miguel de Cervantes.* B & W photos & drawings. New York: Chelsea House. 12–16 yrs. Hispanics of Achievement series.

Hoobler, Dorothy, Thomas Hoobler, & Carey-Greenberg Associates. 1992. *A Promise at the Alamo: The Story of a Texas Girl.* Illus. Jennifer Hewitson. Morristown, N.J.: Silver Burdett. 9–12 yrs.

Koslow, Philip. 1993. *El Cid.* B & W photos & drawings. New York: Chelsea House. 12–16 yrs. Hispanics of Achievement series.

Martinez, Elizabeth Coonrod. 1994. *Sor Juana: A Trailblazing Thinker.* Paintings, B & W photos. Brookfield, Conn.: Millbrook. 10–13 yrs. Hispanic Heritage series.

Biographical Collections

Meltzer, Milton. 1982. *The Hispanic Americans.* Photos. Morrie Campi & Catherine Neren. New York: Crowell. 10–15 yrs.

Morey, Janet, & Wendy Dunn. 1989. *Famous Mexican Americans.* Photos. New York: Cobblehill. 10–16 yrs.

INFORMATION BOOKS

Celebrations

Ancona, George. 1993. *Pablo Remembers: The Fiesta, the Day of the Dead.* New York: Lothrop, Lee & Shepard. 5–9 yrs.

———. 1995. *Fiesta U.S.A.* Color photos. New York: Lodestar. 5–10 yrs.

Hoyt-Goldsmith, Diane. 1994. *Day of the Dead. A Mexican-American Celebration.* Photos Lawrence Migdale. New York: Holiday. 4–7 yrs.

Lankford, Mary D. 1994. *Quinceañera: A Latina's Journey to Womanhood.* Photos Jesse Herrera. Brookfield, Conn.: Millbrook. 10–14 yrs.

Lasky, Kathryn. 1994. *Days of the Dead.* Photos Christopher G. Knight. New York: Hyperion. 10–13 yrs.

Perl, Lila. 1983. *Piñatas and Paper Flowers: Holidays of the Americas in English and Spanish/Piñatas y Flores de Papel: Fiestas de las Americas en Ingles y Espanol.* Illus. Victoria de Larrea. New York: Clarion. 9–12 yrs. (Spanish version by Alma Flor Ada.)

Presilla, Maricel E. 1994. *Feliz Nochebuena, Feliz Navidad: Christmas Feasts of the Hispanic Caribbean.* Illus. Ismael Espinosa Ferrer. New York: Holt. 4–6 yrs.

Ray, Jane (Compiler). 1991. *The Story of Christmas/La Historia de Navidad.* Illus. Jane Ray. New York: Dutton. 12–16 yrs.

Silverthorne, Elizabeth. 1992. *Fiesta! Mexico's Great Celebrations.* Illus. Jan Davey Ellis. Brookfield, Conn.: Millbrook. 8–12 yrs.

Explorers

Marrin, Albert. 1989. *Inca and Spaniard: Pizarro and the Conquest of Peru.* New York: Atheneum. 12–16 yrs.

Hispanic American Pioneers

Anderson, Joan. 1989. *Spanish Pioneers of the Southwest.* Photos George Ancona. New York: Lodestar. 7–12 yrs.

Morey, J. N. & W. Dunn. 1996. *Famous Hispanic Americans.* Photos. New York: Cobblehill. 9–12 yrs.

Contemporary Hispanic Americans

Brown, Tricia. 1986. *Hello Amigos.* Photos Fran Ortiz. New York: Holt. 6–9 yrs.

Catalano, Julie (Introduction Patrick Moynihan). 1988. *The Mexican Americans.* New York: Chelsea House. 11–16 yrs. The Peoples of North America Series.

Cockeroft, James D. 1995. *Latinos in the Making of the United States.* Danbury, Conn.: Watts. 12–16 yrs. *Hispanic Experience in the Americas* series.

Harlan, Judith. 1988. *Hispanic Voters: A Voice in American Politics.* Photos. Danbury, Conn.: Watts. 10–16 yrs.

Hewett, Joan. 1990. *Hector Lives in the United States Now: The Story of a Mexican-American Child.* Photos Richard R. Hewett. New York: HarperCollins. 10–13 yrs.

Hoobler, Dorothy & Thomas Hoobler. 1994. *The Mexican American Family Album.* B & W photos. New York: Oxford. 12–16 yrs. American Family Albums series.

Krull, Kathleen. 1994. *The Other Side: How Kids Live in a California Latino Neighborhood.* Color photos David Hautzig. New York: Lodestar. 10–14 yrs. World of My Own series.

Lakin, Patricia. 1994. *Everything You Need to Know When a Parent Doesn't Speak English.* Photos. New York: Rosen. 12–16 yrs. Need to Know Library series.

Pinchot, Jane. 1989. *The Mexicans in America.* Minneapolis: Lerner. 10–15 yrs. The In America Series.

Sinnott, Susan. 1991. *Extraordinary Hispanic Americans.* Danbury, Conn.: Children's Press. 11–16 yrs. (See also: *Hispanic American Biography, Hispanic/American Chronology,* and *Hispanic American Voices.*)

Migrant Workers in the U.S.

Altman, Linda Jacobs. 1994. *Migrant Farm Workers: The Temporary People.* Danbury, Conn.: Watts. 10–15 yrs.

Ashabranner, Brent. 1993. *Dark Harvest: Migrant Farmworkers in America.* Photos Paul Conklin. North Haven,Conn.: Shoe String/Linnet. 10–15 yrs.

Atkin, S. Beth. 1993. *Voices from the Fields: Children of Migrant Farmworkers Tell Their Stories.* Boston: Little, Brown. 10–15 yrs.

Brimner, Larry Dane. 1992. *A Migrant Family.* Minneapolis, Minn.: Lerner. 9–12 yrs.

De Ruiz, Dana Catherine & Richard Larios. 1993. *La Causa: The Migrant Farm Workers' Story.* Illus. Rudy Gutierrez. Chatham, N.J.: Raintree/Steck-Vaughn. 10–14 yrs.

Mexico

Arnold, Caroline. 1994. *City of the Gods: Mexico's Ancient City of Teotihuacan.* Photos Richard Hewett. New York: Clarion. 10–13 yrs.

Ashabranner, Brent. 1986. *Children of the Maya.* New York: Putnam. 10–16 yrs.

Baquedano, Elizabeth. 1993. *Aztec, Inca, and Maya.* Photos Michel Zabe. New York: Dorling Kindersley. 10–13 yrs. Eyewitness series.

Batemon, Penny 1988. *Aztecs and Incas: AD 1300–1532.* Illus. Rob Shone. Danbury, Conn.: Watts. 10–14 yrs.

Beck, Barbara L. 1983. *The Ancient Maya.* Danbury, Conn.: Watts. 10–16 yrs.

———. 1983. *The Aztecs.* Danbury, Conn.: Watts. 10–16 yrs.

Brenner, Barbara. 1991. *If You Were There in 1492.* New York: Bradbury. 11–15 yrs.

Calderwood, Michael & Gabriel Brena. 1990. *Mexico, A Higher Vision: An Aerial Journey from Past to Present.* Photos Michael Calderwood. La Jolla, Calif.: ALTI Publishing. 12–16 yrs.

Defrates, Joanna. 1993. *What Do We Know about the Aztecs?* Color photos & illustrations. New York: Bedrick. 10–13 yrs. What Do We Know About series.

Diaz Del Castillo, Bernal. 1988. *Cortez and the Conquest of Mexico by the Spaniards in 1521.* North Haven, Conn.: Shoe String/Linnet. 12–16 yrs.

Glubek, Shirley. 1968. *The Art of Ancient Mexico.* New York: HarperCollins. 9–12 yrs.

Grossman, Patricia. 1994. *Saturday Market.* Illus. Enrique O. Sanchez. New York: Lothrop, Lee & Shepard. 6–9 yrs.

Haskins, Jim. 1989. *Count Your Way through Mexico.* Illus. Helen Myers. Minneapolis, Minn.: Carolrhoda. 10–14 yrs.

Irizarry, Carmen. 1987. *Passport to Mexico.* Danbury, Conn.: Watts. 10–14 yrs.

James, Ian. 1989. *Inside Mexico.* Danbury, Conn.: Watts. 10–15 yrs.

Lewis, Thomas P. 1987. *Hill of Fire.* Illus. Joan Sandin. New York: Harper & Row. 5–9 yrs. I Can Read Book and Cassette Library Series.

Lye, Keith. 1982. *Take a Trip to Mexico.* 1982. Danbury, Conn.: Watts. 7–10 yrs.

McKissack, Patricia. 1985. *Aztec Indians.* Danbury, Conn.: Children's Press. 7–10 yrs.

———. 1985. *The Maya.* Danbury, Conn.: Children's Press. 9–12 yrs. New True Books.

Meltzer, Milton. 1974. *Bound for the Rio Grande: The Mexican Struggle, 1845–1850.* New York: Knopf. 12–18 yrs.

Mills, Bronwyn. 1992. *The Mexican War.* New York: Facts On File. 12–18 yrs.

Moran, Tom. 1987. *A Family In Mexico.* Color photos. Minneapolis, Minn.: Lerner. 9–12 yrs.

Neurath, Marie. 1966. *They Lived Like This: The Ancient Maya.* Illus. John Ellis. Danbury, Conn.: Watts. 9–12 yrs.

Stein, R. Conrad. 1984. *Mexico.* Danbury, Conn.: Children's Press. 10–14 yrs.

Villacana, Eugenio. 1972. *Viva Morella.* Illus. Elsa Manriquez. New York: Evans. 10–13 yrs.

Wood, Tim. 1992. *The Aztecs.* Color photos, overlays. New York: Viking. 10–13 yrs. See Through History series.

South America

Brusca, Maria Cristina. 1991. *On the Pampas.* Illus. Maria Cristina Brusca. New York: Holt. 5–8 yrs.

Gofen, Ethel Coro. 1991. *Argentina.* Tarrytown, N.Y.: Marshall Cavendish. 12–16 yrs.

Puerto Rico

Hauptly, Denis J. 1991. *Puerto Rico: An Unfinished Story.* New York: Atheneum. 12–16 yrs.

Central America

Hernandez, Xavier (Trans. Kathleen Leverich). 1992. *San Rafael: A Central American City through the Ages.* Illus. Jordi Ballonga & Josep Escofet. Boston: Houghton Mifflin. 12–16 yrs.

Ecology

Cherry, Lynne. 1990. *The Great Kapok Tree: A Tale of the Amazon Rain Forest.* Illus. L. Cherry. San Diego: Harcourt Brace Jovanovich/Gulliver. 8–12 yrs.

Gelman, Rita G. 1991. *Dawn to Dusk in the Galapagos: Flightless Birds, Swimming Lizards and Other Fascinating Creatures.* Photos Tui de Roy. Boston: Little, Brown. 11–15 yrs.

George, Jean Craighead. 1990. *One Day in the Tropical Rain Forest.* Illus. Gory Allen. New York: HarperCollins. 11–15 yrs.

Lewington, Anna (Adapter). 1993. *Antonio's Rain Forest.* Photos Edward Parker. Minneapolis, Minn.: Carolrhoda. 8–11 yrs.

Zak, Monica (Trans. Nancy Schimmel). 1991. *Save My Rainforest.* Illus. Bengt-Arne Runnerstrom. Volcano, Calif.: Volcano. 9–12 yrs.

General Information

Martin, Albert. 1991. *The Spanish-American War.* New York: Atheneum. 12–16 yrs.

Poynter, Margaret. 1992. *The Uncertain Journey: Stories of Illegal Aliens in El Norte.* New York: Atheneum. 12–16 yrs.

Santos, Richard G. 1981. *Origin of Spanish Names/Como te Llamas y Porque te Llamas Asi.* Illus. Humberto N. Cavazos. Photos Cynthia Ann Santos & Deborah A. Zamora. San Antonio: Richard G. Santos. 9–12 yrs.

Shubert, Adrian. 1992. *The Land and People of Spain.* New York: HarperCollins. 11–16 yrs.

POETRY, SONGS, SHORT STORIES

Aparicio, Frances R. (Ed.). 1994. *Latino Voices.* Brookfield, Conn.: Millbrook. 12–16 yrs. Writers of America series.

Carlson, L. M. (Ed.) 1996. *Barrio Streets Carnival Dreams: Three Generations of Latino Artistry.* Photos. New York: Holt. 12–16 yrs.

Carlson, Lori M., & Cynthia L. Ventura (Ed.). 1990. *Where Angels Glide at Dawn: New Stories from Latin America.* Illus. Jose Ortega. New York: Lippincott. 10–16 yrs.

Carlson, Lori M. 1994. *Cool Salsa: Bilingual Poems on Growing Up Latino in the United States.* New York: Holt. 12–16 yrs. Edge series.

Cofer, Judith Ortiz. 1995. *An Island Like You: Stories of the Barrio.* New York: Orchard/Kroupa. 12–16 yrs.

Cumpian, Carlos. 1994. *Latino Rainbow: Poems about Latino Americans.* Illus. Richard Leonard. Danbury, Conn.: Children's Press. 10–14 yrs.

De Gerez, Toni (Adapter). 1984. *My Song Is a Piece of Jade: Poems of Ancient Mexico in English and Spanish/Mi Canción es un Pedazo de Jade: Poemas del Mexico Antiguo en Ingles y Espanol.* Illus. William Stark. Boston: Little, Brown. 9–12 yrs.

Delacre, Lulu (Selector). 1989. *Arroz con Leche: Popular Songs and Rhymes from Latin America.* Illus. L. Delacre. New York: Scholastic. 5–9 yrs.

———. 1990. *Las Navidades: Popular Christmas Songs from Latin America.* Illus. Lulu Delacre. New York: Scholastic/Lucas Evans. 5–11 yrs.

Gershator, David & Phillis Gershator. 1995. *Bread Is for Eating.* Illus. Emma Shaw-Smith. New York: Holt. 6–9 yrs.

Gonzalez, Ralfka & Anna Ruiz (Compilers & illus.) (Introduction Sandra Cisneros). *My First Book of Proverbs/Mi Primer Libro De Dichos.* Emeryville, Calif.: Children's Book Press. 5–8 yrs.

Johnston, T. 1996. *My Mexico/Mexico Mio.* Illus. F. John Sierra. New York: Putnam. 7–11 yrs.

Medearis, Angela Shelf (Compiler). 1992. *The Zebra-Riding Cowboy: A Folk Song from the Old West.* Illus. Maria Cristina Brusca. New York: Holt. 5–12 yrs.

Nye, N. S. 1995. *The Tree Is Older than You Are: A Bilingual Gathering of Poems and Stories from Mexico with Paintings by Mexican Artists.* Paintings. New York: Simon & Schuster. 10–13 yrs.

Nye, Naomi Shihab. 1995. *The Tree Is Older Than You Are: A Bilingual Gathering of Poems and Stories from Mexico.* Illus. Mexican artists. New York: Simon & Schuster. 12–16 yrs.

Orozco, Jose-Luis (Selector-arranger) (Trans. Jose-Luis Orozco). 1994. *De Colores: And Other Latin-American Folk Songs for Children.* Illus. Elisa Kleven. New York: Dutton. 6–10 yrs.

Pena, Sylvia Cavazos (Ed.). 1985. *Tun-Ta-Ca-Tun: More Stories and Poems in English and Spanish for Children.* Houston: Arte Publico. 10–13 yrs.

———. (Ed.). 1989. *KiKiRiKi: Stories and Poems in English and Spanish for Children.* Illus. Narciso Pena. Houston: Arte Publico. 5–11 yrs.

Pomerantz, Charlotte. 1980. *The Tamarindo Puppy and Other Poems.* Illus. Byron Barton. New York: Greenwillow. 5–9 yrs.

Soto, G. 1995. *Canto Familiar.* Illus. Annika Nelson. San Diego, Calif.: Harcourt Brace. 10–13 yrs.

Soto, Gary. 1990. *A Fire in My Hands: A Book of Poems.* New York: Scholastic. 11–16 yrs.

———. 1990. *Baseball in April, and Other Stories.* San Diego: Harcourt Brace Jovanovich. 12–16 yrs.

———. 1992. *Neighborhood Odes.* Illus. David Diaz. San Diego: Harcourt Brace Jovanovich. 11–16 yrs.

———. 1993. *Local News.* San Diego: Harcourt Brace. 10–14 yrs.

Sullivan, Charles. 1994. *Here Is My Kingdom: Hispanic-American Literature and Art for Young People.* New York: Abrams. 10–14 yrs.

Tashlik, Phyllis. 1994. *Hispanic, Female and Young: An Anthology.* Houston, Tex.: Pinata. 12–15 yrs.

Westridge Young Writers Workshop. Kids Explore America's Hispanic Heritage. 1992. Sante Fe, N.M.: Muir Publications. 9–12 yrs.

TEACHER RESOURCES

Faces. The June 1990 issue is devoted to ancient Mexico and includes a recipe for quesadillas, directions for playing patolli, instructions for making a tree of life, and an illustrated glossary of ancient gods.

Lopez, Tiffany, Ana. 1993. *Growing Up Chicana/o: An Anthology.* New York: Morrow.

Parke, Marilyn & Sharon Panik. 1992. *A Quetzalcoatl: Tale of the Ball Game.* Illus. Lynn Castle. Columbus, Ohio: Fearon Teacher Aids. Spanish edition & teacher's guide. (See also: *A Quetzalcoatl: Tale of Corn.*)

Shalant, Phyllis. 1992. *Look What We've Brought You from Mexico.* Morristown, N.J.: Silver Burdett/Messner.

———. *Stencils: Ancient Mexico.* Five easy-to-do art projects with punchout stencils are available along with basic information about the country and its myths and games. Glenview, Ill.: Good Year Books/Scott, Foresman.

Vigil, Angel. 1994. *The Corn Woman: Stories and Legends of the Hispanic Southwest/La mujer del maiz: Cuentos y leyendes del sudoeste hispano.* Englewood, Colo.: Libraries Unlimited.

VIDEOS

Always Roses. 1991. 29 min. Direct Cinema Video. 10–15 yrs.

Children of Mexico. 1989. Producer Disney Educational Productions. 26 min. Coronet/MIT. Video and teacher's guide. 10–13 yrs.

Diego. 1992. 10 min. Videocassette. SRA School Group, P.O. Box 543, Blacklick, OH 43004. Gr. 2–5.

The Hispanic & Latin American Heritage Video Collection: Joan Baez, Simon Bolivar, Cesar Chavez, Roberto Clemente, Hernan Cortes, Ferdinand & Isabella, Pablo Neruda, Juan St Evita Peron, George Santayana, and Pancho Villa. 1995. Ten videocassettes, each 30 min. Producer Schlessinger Video. Library Video Company, P.O. Box 1110, Dept. B., Bala Cynwyd, PA 19004. Gr. 7–12.

Holidays for Children: Cinco de Mayo. 1994. 30 min. Producer Schlessinger Video. Library Video Company, P.O. Box 1110, Dept. B, Bala Cynwyd, PA 19004. Videocassette. 5–10 yrs.

Lyric Language Live Action Music Video: A Bilingual Music Program, Spanish/English, Series 1. 1992. 35 min. Penton Overseas, 2091

Las Palmas Dr., Ste. A, Carlsbad, CA 92009-1519. Videocassette. 9–16 yrs.

Mexico. 1988. 36 min. Gessler. Video. 6–12 yrs.

Multicultural Peoples of North America: Mexican Americans, Puerto Ricans, and Central Americans. 1993. Three videocassettes, each 30 min. Producer Schlessinger Video. Library Video Company. P.O. Box 1110 Dept. B, Bala Cynwyd, PA 19004. 9–16 yrs.

The No-Guitar Blues. 1991. 27 min. Director Gary Templeton. Phoenix Learning Group, 2349 Chaffee Dr., St. Louis MO 61346. Videocassette. 8–12 yrs.

The Pool Party. 1993. 29 min. Producers Cohn Kelly and Gary Soto. Director: Gary Soto. Gary Soto, 43 The Crescent, Berkeley CA 94708. Videocassette (close captioned). 9–12 yrs.

Sides Explore Mexico. 1989. Volume 1. Producer Children's International Network. 40 min. Encounter Video. Video and teacher's guide. 9–12 yrs. Where in the World series.

Suemi's Story: My Modern Mayan Home. 1991. Producer Little Fort Media. 25 min. United Learning. Video and teacher's guide. 12–14 yrs.

Victor. 1989. 26 min. Barr Films. 16mm film and teacher's guide. 6–12 yrs.

NATIVE AMERICAN LITERATURE

BOOKS WITH PICTURES: REALISTIC

Family

Joosse, Barbara M. 1991. *Mama, Do You Love Me?* Illus. Barbara Lavallee. San Francisco: Chronicle. 4–6 yrs.

Lemieux, Margo. 1994. *Full Worm Moon.* Illus. Robert Andrew Parker. New York: Tambourine. 5–8 yrs.

Luenn, Nancy. 1994. *Nessa's Story.* Illus. Neil Waldman. New York: Atheneum. 5–8 yrs.

Scott, Ann Herbert. 1992. *On Mother's Lap.* Illus. Glo Coalson. New York: Clarion. 5–7 yrs.

———. 1996. *Brave as a Mountain Lion.* Illus. Glo Coalson. New York: Clarion. 5–8 yrs.

Grandparents

Bruchac, Joseph. 1993. *Fox Song.* Illus. Paul Morin. New York: Philomel. 6–9 yrs.

Edmiston, Jim. 1993. *Little Eagle Lots of Owls.* Illus. Jane Ross. Boston: Houghton Mifflin. 6–9 yrs.

Garaway, Margaret K. 1989. *Ashkii and His Grandfather.* Tucson: Treasure Chest. 7–10 yrs.

Miller, M. 1987. *My Grandmother's Cookie Jar.* Los Angeles: Price Stern Sloan. 6–9 yrs.

Petersen, Palle. 1993. *Inunguak: The Little Greenlander.* Illus. Jens Rosing. New York: Lothrop, Lee & Shepard. 7–9 yrs.

Stroud, Virginia A. 1995. *A Walk to the Great Mystery.* New York: Dial. 6–9 yrs.

Weisman, Joan. 1993. *The Storyteller.* Illus. David P. Bradley. New York: Rizzoli. 6–9 yrs.

Contemporary Setting

Lyon, George Ella. 1993. *Dreamplace.* Illus. Peter Catalanotto. New York: Orchard/Jackson. 7–9 yrs.

Scott, A. 1996. *Brave as a Mountain Lion.* Illus. Glo Coalson. New York: Clarion. 6–9 yrs.

Sheldon, Dyan. 1994. *Under the Moon.* Illus. Gary Blythe. New York: Dial. 7–9 yrs.

Celebration

Conway, Diana Cohen. 1994. *Northern Lights: A Hanukkah Story.* Illus. Shelly O. Haas. Rockville, Md.: Kar-Ben. 6–8 yrs.

Winslow, Barbara. 1995. *Dance on a Sealskin.* Illus. Teri Sloat. Alaska. 6–9 yrs.

Animals

Lasky, Kathryn. 1994. *Cloud Eyes.* Illus. Barry Moser. San Diego: Harcourt Brace. 7–10 yrs.

Lowell, Susan 1992. *The Three Little Javelinas.* Illus. Jim Harris. Northland. 5–8 yrs.

Nature

Abrams, Marietta & Peter Brill. 1994. *Ravita and the Land of Unknown Shadows.* Illus. Laurie Smollett Kutscera. New York: Universe. 6–8 yrs.

Bandes, Hanna. 1993. *Sleepy River.* Illus. Jeanette Winter. New York: Philomel. 4–6 yrs.

Baylor, Byrd. 1975. *The Desert Is Theirs.* Illus. Peter Parnall. New York: Atheneum. 6–10 yrs.

———. 1976. *Hawk, I'm Your Brother.* Illus. Peter Parnall. New York: Scribners. 6–10 yrs.

Casler, Leigh. 1994. *The Boy Who Dreamed of an Acorn.* Illus. Shonto Begay. New York: Philomel. 6–9 yrs.

Franklin, Kristine L. 1994. *The Shepherd Boy.* Illus. Jill Kastner. New York: Atheneum. 5–7 yrs.

Jacobs, Shannon K. 1993. *The Boy Who Loved Morning.* Illus. Michael Hays. Boston: Little, Brown. 9–12 yrs.

Jeffers, Susan. 1991. *Brother Eagle, Sister Sky: A Message from Chief Seattle.* New York: Dial. 10–16 yrs.

Lemieux, M. 1995. *Paul and the Wolf.* Columbus, Ohio: Silver. 6–9 yrs.

Shaw-MacKinnon, M. 1996. *Tiktala.* Illus. Laszlo Gal. New York: Holiday. 6–9 yrs.

Strete, C. K. 1996. *They Thought They Saw Him.* Illus. Jose Aruego & Ariane Dewey. New York: Greenwillow. 6–9 yrs.

Whitethorne, Baje. 1994. *Sunpainters: Eclipse of the Navajo Sun.* Flagstaff, Ariz.: Northland. 7–10 yrs.

Wisniewski, David. 1994. *The Wave of the Sea-Wolf.* New York: Clarion. 7–9 yrs.

Survival

James, Betsy. 1994. *The Mud Family.* Illus. Paul Morin. New York: Putnam. 6–9 yrs.

Kroll, Virginia. 1994. *The Seasons and Someone.* Illus. Tatsuro Kiuchi. San Diego: Harcourt Brace. 5–7 yrs.

Strete, C. K. & M. N. Chacon. 1996. *How the Indians Bought the Farm.* Illus. Francisco X. Mora. New York: Greenwillow. 6–9 yrs.

Miscellaneous

Norman, Howard. 1987. *Who Paddled-Backward-with-Trout.* Boston: Little, Brown.

Informational Storybook

Carrier, L. 1996. *A Tree's Tale.* New York: Dial. 6–9 yrs.

Mitchell, B. 1996. *Red Bird.* Illus. Todd L. W. Doney. New York: Lothrop, Lee & Shepard. 6–9 yrs.

FOLK LITERATURE

Alta, Te (Adapter Lynn Moroney). 1989. *Baby Rattlesnake.* Illus.Veg Reisberg. Emeryville, Calif.: Children's Book Press. 5–9 yrs.

Bear, G. 1991. *Two Little Girls Lost in the Bush: A Cree Story for Children.* Saskatoon: Fifth House. 6–9 yrs.

Begay, Shonto. 1992. *Ma'ii and Cousin Horned Toad: A Traditional Navajo Story.* Illus. S. Begay. New York: Scholastic. 6–9 yrs.

Belting, Natalia M. 1992. *Moon Was Tired of Walking on Air.* Illus. Will Hillenbrand. Boston: Houghton Mifflin. 7–12 yrs.

Bernhard, Emery. 1993. *How Snowshoe Hare Rescued the Sun: A Tale from the Arctic.* Illus. Durga Bernhard. New York: Holiday. 6–9 yrs.

Bierhorst, John. 1971. *In the Trail of the Wind: American Indian Poems and Ritual Orations.* New York: Farrar, Straus & Giroux. 11–14 yrs.

———. 1984. *The Hungry Woman: Myths and Legends of the Aztecs.* New York: Morrow. 12–14 yrs.

———. 1984. *The Whistling Skeleton: American Indian Tales of the Supernatural.* New York: Four Winds. 10–14 yrs.

———. 1985. *The Mythology of North America.* New York: Morrow. 12–14 yrs.

———. 1987. *Doctor Coyote: A Native American Aesop's Fables.* New York: Macmillan. 5–9 yrs.

———. 1987. *The Naked Bear: Folktales of the Iroquois.* New York: Morrow. 11–14 yrs.

———. 1988. *The Mythology of South America.* New York: Morrow. 12–14 yrs.

———. 1990. *Spirit Child: A Story of the Nativity.* Illus. Barbara Cooney. New York: Morrow. 5–7 yrs.

———. (Ed.). 1992. *Lightning inside You, and Other Native American Riddles.* Illus. Louise Brierley. New York: Morrow. 8–12 yrs.

———. 1993. *The Woman Who Fell from the Sky: The Iroquois Story of Creation.* Illus. Robert Andrew Parker. New York: Morrow. 7–11 yrs.

———. 1995. *The White Deer: And Other Stories Told by the Lenape.* New York: Morrow. 12–16 yrs.

Browne, V. 1991. *Monster Slayer: A Navajo Folktale.* Flagstaff, Ariz.: Northland. 6–9 yrs.

———. 1993. *Monster Birds: A Navajo Folktale.* Illus. Baje Whitethorne. Flagstaff, Ariz.: Northland. 6–9 yrs.

Bruchac, Joseph. 1989. *Return of the Sun: Native American Tales from the Northeast Woodlands.* Illus. Gary Carpenter. Crossing Press. 12–16 yrs.

———. 1991. *Native American Stories.* Illus. John Kahiones Fadden. Golden, Colo.: Fulcrum. 10–14 yrs.

———. 1993. *The First Strawberries: A Cherokee Story.* Illus. Anna Vojtech. New York: Dial. 7–11 yrs.

———. 1994. *The Great Ball Game: A Muskogee Story.* Illus. Susan L. Roth. New York: Dial. 6–9 yrs.

———. 1995. *The Boy Who Lived with the Bears: And Other Iroquois Stories.* Illus. Murv Jacob. New York: HarperCollins. 9–13 yrs.

———. 1995. *Dog People: Native Dog Stories.* Golden, Colo.: Fulcrum. 9–13 yrs.

———. 1995. *Gluskabe and the Four Wishes.* Illus. Christine Nyburg Shrader. New York: Cobblehill. 5–9 yrs.

———. 1996. *Between Earth and Sky: Legends of Native American Sacred Places.* Illus. Thomas Locker. San Diego, Calif.: Harcourt Brace. 7–10 yrs.

Bruchac, Joseph & Gayle Ross. 1994. *The Girl Who Married the Moon: Tales from Native North America.* Mahwah, N.J.: BridgeWater. 10–13 yrs.

———. 1995. *The Story of the Milky Way: A Cherokee Tale.* Illus. Virginia A. Stroud. New York: Dial. 5–8 yrs.

Burland, Cottie. 1985. *North American Indian Mythology.* 12–14 yrs. New York: Bedrick. The Library of the World's Myths and Legends.

Carey, Valerie Scho (Adapter). 1990. *Quail Song: A Pueblo Indian Tale.* Illus. Ivan Barnett. New York: Putnam/Whitebird. 5–9 yrs.

Cohen, Caron Lee. 1988. *The Mud Pony.* Illus. Shonto Begay. New York: Scholastic. 5–9 yrs.

Cox, Christine (Illus.). 1995. *The Girl Who Swam with the Fish: An Athabascan Legend.* Illus. Christine Cox. Seattle, Wash.: Alaska. 6–9 yrs.

Crespo, George. 1995. *How Iwariwa the Cayman Learned to Share: A Yanomamo Myth.* New York: Clarion. 5–9 yrs.

DeArmond, Dale (Reteller). 1990. *The Boy Who Found the Light: Eskimo Folktales.* Illus. D. DeArmand. San Francisco: Sierra Club Books/Little, Brown. 9–12 yrs.

de Paola, Tomie. 1983. *The Legend of the Bluebonnet: An Old Tale of Texas.* New York: Putnam. 5–9 yrs.

———. 1988. *The Legend of the Indian Paintbrush.* New York: Putnam. 5–9 yrs. Sandcastle Series.

Dixon, Ann (Reteller). 1992. *How Raven Brought Light to People.* Illus. Jim Watts. New York: McElderry. 7–10 yrs.

———. 1994. *The Sleeping Lady.* Illus. Elizabeth Johns. Seattle, Wash.: Alaska. 7–10 yrs.

Duncan, L. 1996. *The Magic of Spider Woman.* Illus. Shonto Begay. New York: Scholastic. 5–9 yrs.

Erdoes, Richard & Alfonso Oritz (Eds.). 1985. *American Myths and Legends.* New York: Pantheon. 12–16 yrs.

Esbensen, Barbara Juster. 1994. *The Great Buffalo Race: How the Buffalo Got Its Hump: A Seneca Tale.* Illus. Helen K. Davie. Boston: Little, Brown. 7–10 yrs.

Feather Earring, Monica. 1978. *Prairie Legends.* Billings, Mont.: Council for Indian Education. 10–14 yrs. The Library of the World's Myths and Legends.

Flora. 1989. *Feathers like a Rainbow: An Amazon Indian Tale.* Illus. Flora. New York: Harper & Row. 6–10 yrs.

Galdone, Paul. 1979. *The Monkey and the Crocodile.* Boston; MA: Houghton Mifflin. 7–10 yrs.

Gifford, Douglas. 1987. *Warriors, Gods and Spirits from Central and South American Mythology.* Schocken. 10–14 yrs. World Mythologies Series.

Goble, Paul. 1978. *The Girl Who Loved Wild Horses.* New York: Bradbury. 7–10 yrs.

———. 1980. *The Gift of the Sacred Dog.* New York: Macmillan. 6–10 yrs.

———. 1984. *Buffalo Woman.* New York: Bradbury. 9–12 yrs.

———. 1985. *The Great Race of the Birds and Animals.* New York: Bradbury. 5–7 yrs.

———. 1988. *Iktomi and the Boulder: A Plains Indian Story.* New York: Orchard. 5–9 yrs.

———. 1988. *Her Seven Brothers.* New York: Bradbury. 9–11 yrs.

———. 1989. *Iktomi and the Berries: A Plains Indian Story.* New York: Orchard/Jackson. 6–10 yrs.

———. 1991. *Iktomi and the Buffalo Skull: A Plains Indian Story.* New York: Orchard Books/Richard Jackson. 6–9 yrs.

———. 1992. *Crow Chief: A Plains Indian Story.* New York: Orchard. 5–11 yrs.

———. 1992. *Love Flute.* New York: Bradbury. 8–11 yrs.

———. 1993. *The Lost Children: The Boys Who Were Neglected.* New York: Bradbury. 7–11 yrs.

———. 1994. *Iktomi and the Buzzard: A Plains Indian Story.* New York: Orchard/Jackson. 6–10 yrs.

———. 1996. *The Return of the Buffaloes: A Plains Indian Story about Famine and Renewal of the Earth.* Washington, D.C.: National. 7–11 yrs.

Greene, Ellin. 1993. *The Legend of the Cranberry: A Paleo-Indian Tale.* Illus. Brad Sneed. New York: Simon & Schuster. 7–11 yrs.

Gregg, Andy. 1993. *Great Rabbit and the Long-Tailed Wildcat.* Illus. Cat Bowman Smith. Morton Grove, Ill.: Whitman. 6–9 yrs.

Guard, Jean & Ray A. Williamson. 1987. *They Dance in the Sky: Native American Star Myths.* Boston: Houghton Mifflin. 10–14 yrs.

Haley, G. E. (Adapter). 1996. *Two Bad Boys: A Very Old Cherokee Tale.* New York: Dutton. 5–9 yrs.

Harrell, Beatrice Orcutt. 1995. *How Thunder and Lightning Came to Be: A Choctaw Legend.* Illus. Susan L. Roth. New York: Dial. 5–10 yrs.

Hausman, Gerald. 1995. *Coyote Walks on Two Legs: A Book of Navajo Myths and Legends.* Illus. Floyd Cooper. New York: Philomel. 5–10 yrs.

Hausman, Gerald. 1995. *How Chipmunk Got Tiny Feet: Native American Animal Origin Stories.* Illus. Ashley Wolff. New York: HarperCollins. 5–10 yrs.

———. 1996. *Eagle Boy: A Traditional Navajo Legend.* Illus. Cara and Barry Moser. New York: HarperCollins. 6–9 yrs.

Highwater, Jamake. 1981. *Moonsong Lullaby.* New York: Lothrop, Lee & Shepard. 9–12 yrs.

Hoffman, Mrs. Albert & Dorra Torres. 1977. *Cheyenne Short Stories: A Collection of Ten Traditional Stories of the Cheyenne.* Billings, Mont.: Council for Indian Education. 10–14 yrs.

Jackson, E. (Adapter). 1996. *The Precious Gift: A Navaho Creation Myth.* Illus. Woodleigh Marx Hubbard. New York: Simon & Schuster. 5–9 yrs.

Jessell, Tim. 1994. *Amorak.* Mankato, Minn.: Creative. 9–12 yrs.

Jones, Jennifer Berry. 1995. *Heetunka's Harvest: A Tale of the Plains Indians.* Illus. Shannon Keegan. Niwot, Colo.: Roberts. 5–10 yrs.

Keams, G. 1995. *Grandmother Spider Brings the Sun: A Cherokee Story.* Illus. James Bernardin. Flagstaff, Ariz.: Northland. 6–9 yrs.

Lacapa, Michael (Reteller). 1990. *The Flute Player: An Apache Folktale.* Illus. M. Lacapa. Flagstaff, Ariz.: Northland. 8–11 yrs.

Larry, Charles. 1993. *Peboan and Seegwun.* New York: Farrar, Straus & Giroux. 7–10 yrs.

London, Jonathan & Lanny Pinola. 1993. *Fire Race: A Karuk Coyote Tale about How Fire Came to the People.* Illus. Sylvia Long. San Francisco: Chronicle. 7–10 yrs.

MacGill-Callahan, Sheila. 1991. *And Still the Turtle Watched.* Illus. Barry Moser. New York: Dial. 7–12 yrs.

Marsh, Jessie. 1978. *Indian Folk Tales from Coast to Coast.* Billings, Mont.: Council for Indian Education, 10–14 yrs. Indian Culture Series.

Martin, Rafe. 1992. *The Rough-Face Girl.* Illus. David Shannon. New York: Putnam. 7–10 yrs.

———. 1993. *The Boy Who Lived with the Seals.* Illus. David Shannon. New York: Putnam. 7–11 yrs.

Mayo, Gretchen. 1994. *Big Trouble for Tricky Rabbit!* New York: Walker. 6–9 yrs. Native American Trickster Tales series.

———. 1994. *Here Comes Tricky Rabbit!* New York: Walker. 6–9 yrs. Native American Trickster Tales series.

McDermott, Beverly. 1975. *Sedna, An Eskimo Myth.* New York: Viking. 7–10 yrs.

McDermott, Gerald. 1974. *Arrow to the Sun: A Pueblo Indian Tale.* New York: Viking. 5–9 yrs.

———. 1993. *Raven: A Trickster Tale from the Pacific Northwest.* San Diego: Harcourt Brace. 7–10 yrs

———. 1994. *Coyote: A Trickster Tale from the American Southwest.* San Diego: Harcourt Brace. 7–10 yrs.

Melzack, R. 1967. *The Day Tuk Became a Hunter and Other Eskimo Stories.* New York: Dodd, Mead. 7–10 yrs.

Morgan, Pierr. 1995. *Supper for Crow: A Northwest Coast Indian Tale.* New York: Crown. 5–10 yrs.

Oliviero, J. 1995. *The Day Sun Was Stolen.* Illus. Sharon Hitchcock. New York: Hyperion. 6–9 yrs.

Osofsky, Audrey. 1992. *Dreamcatcher.* Illus. Ed Young. New York: Orchard. 4–9 yrs.

Oughton, Jerrie. 1992. *How the Stars Fell into the Sky: A Navajo Legend.* Illus. Lisa Desimini. Boston: Houghton Mifflin. 7–12 yrs.

_____. 1994. *The Magic Weaver of Rugs: A Tale of the Navajo.* Illus. Lisa Desimini. Boston: Houghton Mifflin. 7–10 yrs.

Pohrt, Tom (Adapter). 1995. *Coyte Goes Walking.* Illus. T. Pohrt. New York: Farrar, Straus & Giroux. 7–10 yrs.

Pollock, P. 1996. *The Turkey Girl: A Zuni Cinderella Story.* Illus. Ed Young. Boston: Little, Brown. 6–9 yrs.

Rodanas, Kristina (Reteller). 1991. *Dragonfly's Tale.* Illus. Kristina Rodanas. New York: Clarion. 7–12 yrs.

_____. 1994. *Dance of the Sacred Circle: A Native American Tale.* Boston: Little, Brown. 7–10 yrs.

_____. 1995. *The Eagle's Song: A Tale from the Pacific Northwest.* Boston: Little, Brown. 6–9 yrs.

Rosen, Michael. 1995. *Crow and Hawk: A Traditional Pueblo Indian Story.* Illus. John Clementson. San Diego: Harcourt Brace. 5–10 yrs.

Ross, Gayle. 1995. *How Turtle's Back Was Cracked: A Traditional Cherokee Tale.* Illus. Murv Jacob. New York: Dial. 5–10 yrs.

_____. (Adapter). 1996. *The Legend of the Windigo: A Tale from Native North America.* Illus. Murv Jacob. New York: Dial. 5–8 yrs.

Roth, Susan L. 1990. *The Story of Light.* Illus. Susan L. Roth. New York: Morrow. 7–10 yrs.

Rubalcaba, J. 1995. *Uncegila's Seventh Spot: A Lakota Legend.* Illus. Irving Toddy. New York: Clarion. 6–9 yrs.

Ruoff, A. L. & F. W. Porter (Eds.). 1991. *Literatures of the American Indians.* New York: Chelsea House. 12–16 yrs.

Sage, Jim. 1995. *Coyote Makes Man.* Illus. Britta Teckentrup. New York: Simon & Schuster. 5–10 yrs.

Shetterly, Susan Hand (Reteller). 1991. *Raven's Light: A Myth from the People of the Northwest Coast.* Illus. Robert Shetterly. New York: Atheneum. 7–10 yrs.

Sloat, Teri (Reteller). 1990. *The Eye of the Needle.* Illus. Teri Sloat. New York: Dutton.

_____. 1993. *The Hungry Giant of the Tundra.* Illus. Robert & Teri Sloat. New York: Dutton. 7–11 yrs.

Stevens, Janet. 1993. *Coyote Steals the Blanket: A Ute Tale.* New York: Holiday. 6–10 yrs.

_____. 1996. *Old Bag of Bones: A Coyote Tale.* Illus. J. Stevens. New York: Holiday. 5–7 yrs. (Shoshone tale.)

Strete, C. K. & M. N. Chacon. 1996. *How the Indians Bought the Farm.* Illus. Francisco X. Mora. New York: Greenwillow. 5–8 yrs.

Taylor, C. J. 1993. *The Secret of the White Buffalo: An Oglala Legend.* Plattsburgh, N.Y.: Tundra. 10–13 yrs.

Tall Bull, Henry & Tom Weist. 1971. *The Rolling Head: Cheyenne Tales.* Billings, Mont.: Council for Indian Education. 10–14 yrs. Indian Culture Series.

_____. 1972. *Cheyenne Legends of Creation.* Billings, Mont.: Council for Indian Education. 10–14 yrs. Indian Culture Series.

Taylor, C. J. 1993. *How We Saw the World: Nine Native Stories of the Way Things Began.* Plattsburgh, N.Y.: Tundra. 6–10 yrs.

Taylor, Harriet Peck. 1995. *Coyote and the Laughing Butterflies.* New York: Macmillan. 5–10 yrs.

Van Laan, Nancy. 1989. *Rainbow Crow: A Lenape Tale.* Illus. Beatriz Vidal. New York: Knopf/Borzoi. 6–11 yrs.

_____. 1993. *Buffalo Dance: A Blackfoot Legend.* Illus. Beatriz Vidal. Boston: Little, Brown. 7–10 yrs.

Villoldo, A. 1995. *Skeleton Woman.* Illus. Yoshi. New York: Simon & Schuster. 6–9 yrs. (Inuit.)

Wood, D. (Adapter). 1996. *The Windigo's Return: A North Woods Story.* Illus. Greg Couch. New York: Simon & Schuster. 5–8 yrs.

Wood, Marion. 1987. *Spirits, Heroes and Hunters from North American Indian Mythology.* Schocken. 10–16 yrs. World Mythologies Series.

Young, Ed. 1993. *Moon Mother: A Native American Creation Tale.* New York: HarperCollins/ Perlman. 7–10 yrs.

Young, Richard & Judy Dockrey. 1994. *Young Race with Buffalo: And Other Native American Stories for Young Readers.* Little Rock, Ark.: August. 12–16 yrs.

Literary Folk Tale

Goble, Paul. 1990. *Dream Wolf.* Illus. P. Goble. New York: Bradbury. 6–11 yrs.

REALISTIC NOVELS

History

Burks, B. 1995. *Runs with Horses.* San Diego, Calif.: Harcourt Brace. 11–16 yrs.

Family

Hamilton, Virginia. 1976. *Arilla Sun Down.* New York: Greenwillow. 11–16 yrs.

Irwin, Hadley. 1994. *Jim-Dandy.* New York: McElderry. 10–13 yrs.

Contemporary Life

Dorris, Michael. 1987. *A Yellow Raft in Blue Water.* New York: Holt. 12–16 yrs.

Hillerman, Tony. 1990. *Coyote Waits.* New York: HarperCollins. 12–16 yrs.

Lipsyte, Robert 1993. *The Chief.* New York: HarperCollins. 12–17 yrs.

Rostkowski, Margaret. 1995. *Moon Dancer.* San Diego: Harcourt Brace/Browndeer. 12–16 yrs.

Cultural Lifestyles & Identity

Bruchac, J. 1996. *Children of the Longhouse.* New York: Dial. 9–12 yrs.

Davis, Deborah. 1989. *The Secret of the Seal.* Illus. Jody Labrasca. New York: Crown. 9–12 yrs.

Highwater, Jamake. 1977. *ANPAO: An American Indian Odyssey.* Philadelphia: Lippincott. New York: Harper and Row, 1983. 12–16 yrs.

_____. 1985. *The Ceremony of Innocence.* New York: HarperCollins. 11–16 yrs.

Hobbs, Will. 1989. *Bearstone.* New York: Atheneum. 11–16 yrs.

Hudson, Jan. 1989. *Sweetgrass.* New York: Philomel Books. 8–12 yrs.

Pitts, Paul. 1988. *Racing the Sun.* New York: Avon. 11–16 yrs.

Roop, Peter & Connie Roop. 1992. *Ahyoka and the Talking Leaves.* Illus. Yoshi Miyake. New York: Lothrop, Lee & Shepard. 7–12 yrs.

Worcester, Donald. 1956. *Lone Hunter's Gray Pony.* New York: Oxford Univ. Press. Illus. Paige Pauley. 1985. 11–16 yrs.

Living in Two Worlds

Cannon, A. E. 1990. *The Shadow Brothers.* New York: Delacorte. 11–16 yrs.

Davis, Russell G. & Brent K. Ashabranner. 1994. *The Choctaw Code.* North Haven, Conn.: Linnet. 12–16 yrs.

George, Jean Craighead. 1972. *Julie of the Wolves.* Illus. John Schoenherr. New York: HarperCollins. 11–16 yrs.

_____. 1994. *Julie.* Illus. Wendell Minor. New York: HarperCollins. 10–13 yrs.

Girion, Barbara. 1990. *Indian Summer.* New York: Scholastic. 10–12 yrs.

Houston, James. 1992. *Drifting Snow: An Arctic Search.* New York: McElderry. 10–14 yrs.

Meyer, Carolyn. 1992. *Where the Broken Heart Still Beats: The Story of Cynthia Ann Parker.* San Diego: Harcourt Brace Jovanovich/ Gulliver Books. 8–12 yrs.

O'Dell, Scott. 1988. *Black Star, Bright Dawn.* Boston: Houghton Mifflin. 10–16 yrs.

Oughton, Jerrie. 1995. *Music from a Place Called Half Moon.* Boston: Houghton Mifflin. 10–13 yrs.

Robinson, Margaret A. 1990. *A Woman of Her Tribe.* New York: Scribners. 12–16 yrs.

Sneve, Virginia Driving Hawk. 1972. *Jimmy Yellow Hawk.* New York: Holiday. 10–16 yrs.

Wallin, Luke. 1987. *Ceremony of the Panther.* New York: Bradbury. 12–16 yrs.

Watkins, Sherrin. 1994. *White Bead Ceremony.* Illus. Kim Doner. Tulsa, Okla.: Council Oak Books. 6–10 yrs.

Wosmek, Frances. 1986. *A Brown Bird Singing.* Illus. Ted Lewin. New York: Lothrop, Lee & Shepard. 10–14 yrs.

Government-Indian Relations

DeFelice, Cynthia. 1990. *Weasel.* New York: Macmillan. 9–12 yrs.

Kudlinski, Kathleen V. 1993. *Night Bird: A Story of the Seminole Indians.* Illus. James Watling. New York: Viking. 9–12 yrs. Once upon America series.

Mattaei, Gary & Jewel Grutman. 1994. *The Ledgerbook of Thomas Blue Eagle.* Illus. Adam Cvijanovich. Charlottesville, Vir.: Thomasson. 10–13 yrs.

O'Dell, Scott & Elizabeth Hall. 1992. *Thunder Rolling in the Mountains.* Boston: Houghton Mifflin. 12–14 yrs.

Stewart, Elisabeth J. 1994. *On the Long Trail Home.* New York: Clarion. 10–13 yrs.

Oppression

Blair, David Nelson. 1992. *Fear the Condor.* New York: Lodestar. 10–15 yrs.

Johnson, Dolores. 1994. *Seminole Diary: Remembrances of a Slave.* Illus. D. Johnson. New York: Macmillan. 10–14 yrs.

Keehn, Sally M. 1991. *I Am Regina.* New York: Philomel. 10–16 yrs.

Russell, Sharman Apt. 1994. *The Humpbacked Fluteplayer.* New York: Knopf. 10–13 yrs.

Adventure

Gregory, Kristiana. 1994. *Jimmy Spoon and the Pony Express.* New York: Scholastic. 10–13 yrs.

Hobbs, Will. 1992. *The Big Wander.* New York: Atheneum. 10–13 yrs.

_____. 1993. *Beardance.* New York: Atheneum. 10–13 yrs.

Hudson, Jan. 1990. *Dawn Rider.* New York: Philomel. 10–16 yrs.

O'Dell, Scott. 1986. *Streams to the River, River to the Sea: A Novel of Sacagawea.* Boston: Houghton Mifflin. 10–15 yrs.

Sneve, V. D. H. 1995. *High Elk's Treasure.* Illus. Oren Lyons. New York: Holiday. 10–14 yrs.

Whelan, Gloria. 1993. *Night of the Full Moon.* Illus. Leslie Bowman. New York: Knopf. 9–11 yrs.

Wunderli, Stephen. 1992. *The Blue between the Clouds.* New York: Holt. 10–12 yrs.

Quest

Bennett, James. 1994. *Dakota Dream.* New York: Scholastic. 12–16 yrs.

Dorris, Michael. 1994. *Guests.* New York: Hyperion. 10–13 yrs.

George, Jean Craighead. 1983. *The Talking Earth.* New York: HarperCollins. 9–12 yrs.

Vick, Helen Hughes. 1993. *Walker of Time.* Tucson, Ariz.: Harbinger. 12–16 yrs.

Wangerin, Walter, Jr. 1994. *The Crying for a Vision.* New York: Simon & Schuster. 12–16 yrs.

Survival

Carter, Forrest. 1976. *The Education of Little Tree.* New York: Delacorte. 11–16 yrs.

Finley, Mary Peace. 1993. *Soaring Eagle.* New York: Simon & Schuster. 10–13 yrs.

Highwater, Jamake. 1984. *Legend Days.* New York: HarperCollins. 11–16 yrs.

Hill, Kirkpatrick. 1990. *Toughboy and Sister.* New York: McElderry. 9–12 yrs.

———. 1993. *Winter Camp.* New York: McElderry. 10–13 yrs.

Luhrmann, Winifred Bruce. 1989. *Only Brave Tomorrows.* Boston: Houghton Mifflin. 10–14 yrs.

Mazzio, Joann. 1993. *Leaving Eldorado.* Boston: Houghton Mifflin. 12–16 yrs.

O'Dell, Scott. 1960. *Island of the Blue Dolphins.* Boston: Houghton Mifflin 10–16 yrs.

Paulsen, Gary. 1994. *Mr. Tucket.* New York: Delacorte. 12–16 yrs.

Speare, Elizabeth George. 1983. *The Sign of the Beaver.* Boston: Houghton Mifflin. 10–16 yrs.

Williams, Jeanne. 1994. *New Medicine.* Dallas, Tex.: Hendrick. 12–16 yrs.

BIOGRAPHIES

Averill, Esther. 1993. *King Philip: The Indian Chief.* Illus. Vera Belsky. North Haven, Conn.: Linnet. 10–13 yrs.

Black, Sheila. *Sitting Bull and the Battle of the Little Bighorn.* 1989. Illus. L. L. Cundiff, Ed Lee, T. Lewis, Frank Riccio, Elm Sisco, & Robert L. Smith. Morristown, N.J.: Silver Burdett Press. 10–13 yrs. Alvin Josephy's Biography Series of American Indians.

Bland, Celia. 1994. *Osceola: Seminole Rebel.* New York: Chelsea. 10–13. North American Indians of Achievement series.

———. 1995. *Peter MacDonald: Former Chairman of the Navajo Nation.* Photos. New York: Chelsea. 10–13 yrs. North American Indians of Achievement series.

Bonvillain, Nancy. 1994. *Black Hawk: Sac Rebel.* B & W photos. New York: Chelsea. 10–13 yrs. North American Indians of Achievement series.

Bruchac, Joseph. 1995. *A Boy Called Slow: The True Story of Sitting Bull.* Illus. Rocco Baviera. New York: Philomel. 8–11 yrs.

Buerge, D. 1992. *Chief Seattle.* Seattle: Sasquatch. 8–11 yrs.

Christian, Mary Blount. 1993. *Who'd Believe John Colter?* Illus. Laszlo Kubinyi. New York: Macmillan. 10–13 yrs. Fictionalized Biography.

Cwiklik, Robert. 1989. *Sequoia Series: Alvin Josephy's History of the Native Americans.* Morristown, N.J.: Silver Burdett. 9–12 yrs.

———. 1989. *King Philip and the War with the Colonists; Sequoyah and the Cherokee Alphabet.* Illus. L. L. Cundiff, Ed Lee, T. Lewis, Frank Riccio, Elm Sisco, & Robert L. Smith. Morristown, N.J.: Silver Burdett Press. 10–13 yrs.

———. 1993. *Tecumseh: Shawnee Rebel.* B & W photos & drawings. New York: Chelsea. 12–16 yrs. North American Indians of Achievement series.

Ekoomiak, Normee. 1990. *Arctic Memories.* Illus. Normee Ekoomiak. New York: Holt. 8–12 yrs.

Fradin, Dennis Brindell. 1992. *Hiawatha: Messenger of Peace.* New York: Margaret K. McElderry. 11–14 yrs.

Freedman, R. 1996. *The Life and Death of Crazy Horse.* Illus. Amos Bad Heart Bull. New York: Holiday. 9–12 yrs.

George, Chief Dan. 1989. *My Heart Soars.* Vancouver: Hancock House. 10–16 yrs.

Gonzales, Catherine Troy. 1987. *Quanah Parker: Great Chief of the Comanches.* Illus. Mark Mitchell. Austin, Tex.: Eakin Press. 9–12 yrs.

Guttmacher, Peter. 1994. *Crazy Horse: Sioux War Chief.* New York: Chelsea. 10–13. North American Indians of Achievement series.

Henry, Christopher. 1994. *Ben Nighthorse Campbell: Cheyenne Chief and U.S. Senator.* New York: Chelsea. 10–13. North American Indians of Achievement series.

Johnson, Dolores. 1994. *Seminole Diary: Remembrances of a Slave.* Illus. D. Johnson. New York: Macmillan. 10–14 yrs.

Keegan, Marcia. 1991. *Pueblo Boy: Growing Up in Two Worlds.* Photos. New York: Cobblehill. 6–12 yrs.

Klausner, Janet. 1993. *Sequoyah's Gift: A Portrait of the Cherokee Leader.* New York: HarperCollins. 10–12 yrs.

Kroeber, Theodora. 1976. *Ishi in Two Worlds: A Biography of the Last Wild Indian in North America.* Photos. Berkeley: Univ. of Calif. Press. 12–16.

Lawlor, Laurie. 1994. *Shadow Catcher: The Life and Work of Edward S. Curtis.* New York: Walker. 10–13 yrs.

Lazar, Jerry. 1995. *Red Cloud: Sioux War Chief.* B & W photos. New York: Chelsea. 10–13 yrs. North American Indians of Achievement series.

Lazo, Caroline. 1995. *Wilma Mankiller.* B & W photos. Morristown, N.J.: Dillon. 10–13 yrs. Peacemakers series.

Lipsyte, Robert. 1993. *Jim Thorpe: Twentieth-Century Jock.* B & W photos. New York: HarperCollins. 10–13 yrs. Superstar Lineup series.

Littlechild, George. 1993. *This Land Is My Land.* Danbury, Conn.: Children's Press. 5–9 yrs.

Marrin, Albert. 1996. *Plains Warrior: Chief Quanah Parker and the Comanches.* Photos & map. New York: Atheneum. 12–15 yrs.

McClard, Megan, & George Ypsilantis. 1989. *Hiawatha and the Iroquois League.* Illus. L. L. Cundiff, Ed Lee, T. Lewis, Frank Riccio, Elm Sisco, & Robert L. Smith. Morristown, N.J.: Silver Burdett Press. 10–13 yrs. Alvin Josephy's Biography Series of American Indians.

New Mexico People and Energy Collective. 1991. *Red Ribbons for Emma.* Photos. Berkeley, Calif.: New Seed Press. 10–14 yrs.

Raphael, Elaine & Don Bolognese. 1994. *Sacajawea: The Journey West.* New York: Cartwheel. 6–9 yrs. Drawing America series.

Fictionalized Biography

Rowland, Della. 1989. *The Story of Sacajawea, Guide to Lewis and Clark.* Illus. Richard Leonard. New York: Dell/Yearling Books. 11–13 yrs.

Shorto, Russell. 1989. *Geronimo and the Struggle for Apache Freedom; Tecumseh and the Dream of an American Indian Nation.* Illus. L. L. Cundiff, Ed Lee, T. Lewis, Frank Riccio, Elm Sisco, & Robert L. Smith. Morristown, N.J.: Silver Burdett Press. 10–13 yrs.

Shumate, Jane. 1993. *Sequoyah: Inventor of the Cherokee Alphabet.* B & W photos. New York: Chelsea. 12–16 yrs. North American Indians of Achievement series.

Sonnebortt, Liz. 1993. *Will Rogers: Cherokee Entertainer.* B & W photos. New York: Chelsea. 12–16 yrs. North American Indians of Achievement series.

St. George, Judith. 1994. *Crazy Horse.* New York: Putnam. 10–13 yrs.

Supree, Burton (Ed.). 1989. *Bear's Heart: Scenes from the Life of a Cheyenne Artist of One Hundred Years Ago.* Illus. Bear's Heart. New York: HarperCollins. 12–16 yrs.

Taylor, Marlan W. 1993. *Chief Joseph: Nez Perce Leader.* B & W photos & drawings. New York: Chelsea. 12–16 yrs. North American Indians of Achievement series.

Williams, Neva (Recorder). 1994. *Patrick Des Jarlait: Conversations with a Native American Artist.* Paintings & photos P. Des Jarlait. Minneapolis, Minn.: Lerner/Runestone. 10–14 yrs.

Biographical Collections

Freedman, Russell. 1987. *Indian Chiefs.* Photos. New York: Holiday. 11–16 yrs.

Golston, S. E. 1996. *Changing Woman of the Apache: Women's Lives in Past and Present.* Photos. New York: Watts. 12–15 yrs. American Indian Experience series.

Moore, Reavis. 1993. *Native Artists of North America.* Santa Fe, N.M.: John Muir. 10–14 yrs.

St. George, J. 1996. *To See with the Heart: The Life of Sitting Bull.* New York: Putnam. 10–13 yrs.

INFORMATION BOOKS

Tribal History, Traditional Lifestyles, Customs

Andryszewski, Tricia. 1995. *The Seminoles: People of the Southeast.* Photos. Brookfield, Conn.: Millbrook. 10–13 yrs. Native Americans series.

Ayer, Eleanor H. 1993. *The Anasazi.* B & W photos. New York: Walker. 10–13 yrs.

Bleeker, Sonia. 1952. *The Cherokee Indians of the Mountains.* New York: Morrow. 11–16 yrs.

Bonvillain, Nancy. 1994. *The Haidas: People of the Northwest Coast.* B & W photos. Brookfield, Conn.: Millbrook. 10–13 yrs. Native Americans series.

———. 1994. *The Teton Sioux.* Color photos. New York: Chelsea. 12–16 yrs. Indians of North America series.

———. 1995. *The Navajos: People of the Southwest.* Photos. Brookfield, Conn.: Millbrook. 10–13 yrs. Native Americans series.

———. 1995. *The Sac and Fox.* New York: Chelsea. 12–16 yrs. Indians of North America series.

Carter, Alden R. 1989. *The Apaches and Navajos; The Iroquois.* Danbury, Conn.: Watts. 9–11 yrs. First Books series about Native Americans.

———. 1989. *The Shoshoni.* Danbury, Conn.: Watts. 9–12 yrs. First Books Series.

Cory, S. 1996. *Pueblo Indian.* Illus. Richard Erickson. Minneapolis, Minn.: Lerner. 9–12 yrs. American Pastfinder series.

Crosher, Judith. 1977. *The Aztecs. Peoples of the Past Series.* Morristown, N.J.: Silver Burdett. 10–14 yrs.

Dewey, J. O. 1996. *Stories on Stone: Rock Art: Images from the Ancient Ones.* Primitive drawings. Boston: Little, Brown. 6–9 yrs.

Fichter, George S. 1980. *How the Plains Indians Lived.* New York: McKay. 10–14 yrs.

Fleischner, Jennifer. 1994. *The Apaches: People of the Southwest.* B & W photos. Brookfield, Conn.: Millbrook. 10–13 yrs. Native Americans series.

Fradin, Dennis. 1988. *The Pawnee. A New True Book.* Chicago: Children's Press. 9–12 yrs.

Haluska, Vicki. 1993. *The Arapaho Indians.* B & W & color photos. New York: Chelsea. 10–12 yrs. Junior Library of American Indians series.

Hoig, Stan. 1992. *People of the Sacred Arrows: The Southern Cheyenne Today.* New York: Cobblehill. 10–14 yrs.

———. 1996. *Night of the Cruel Moon: Cherokee Removal and the Trail of Tears.* Photos. New York: Facts on File. 12–16 yrs. Library of American Indian History series.

Hughs, Jill. 1986. *Aztecs*. Danbury, Conn.: Watts/Gloucester Press, 10–16 yrs.

Hubbard-Brown, Janet. 1995. *The Shawnee*. New York: Chelsea. 12–16 yrs. Indians of North America series.

The Indian Texans. 1982. San Antonio: Univ. of Texas Institute of Texan Cultures. 10–14 yrs.

Jensen, V. 1996. *Carving a Totem Pole*. Photos. New York: Holt. 7–10 yrs.

Katz, J. B. 1995. *We Rode the Wind: Recollections of Native American Life*. Minneapolis, Minn.: Runestone. 9–12 yrs.

Katz, William Loren. 1986. *Black Indians: A Hidden Heritage*. Photos. New York: Atheneum. 12–16 yrs.

Lacey, Theresa Jensen. 1995. *The Blackfeet*. New York: Chelsea. 12–16 yrs. Indians of North America series.

Landau, Elaine. 1989. *The Sioux*. Danbury, Conn.: Watts. 9–12 yrs. First Books Series.

Lepthien, Emilie U. 1985. *The Seminole*. Danbury, Conn.: Children's Press. 9–11 yrs. A New True Book.

———. 1987. *The Choctaw*. Danbury, Conn.: Children's Press. 9–11 yrs. A New True Book.

Lucas, Eileen. 1993. *The Cherokees: People of the Southeast*. Brookfield, Conn.: Millbrook. 9–11 yrs.

———. 1994. *The Ojibwas: People of the Northern Forests*. Color, B & W photos. Brookfield, Conn.: Millbrook. 10–13 yrs. Native Americans series.

May, Robin. 1987. *Plains Indians of North America*. Vero Beach, Fla.: Rourke. 10–13 yrs. Original People Series.

McIntyre, Loren. 1975. *The Incredible Incas and Their Timeless Land*. Washington, D.C.: National Geographic Society. 10–16 yrs.

McKissack, Patricia. 1984. *The Apache*. Danbury, Conn.: Children's Press. 9–12 yrs. A New True Book.

———. 1985. *Aztec Indians*. Danbury, Conn.: Children's Press. 9–12 yrs. New True Books.

Meyer, C. 1996. *In a Different Light: Growing Up in a Yuptik Eskimo Village in Alaska*. Photos John McDonald. New York: McElderry. 9–12 yrs.

Morrison, Marion. 1987. *Indians of the Andes*. Vero Beach, Fla.: Rourke. 9–12 yrs. Original People Series.

Mott, E. C. 1996. *Dancing Rainbows: A Pueblo Boy's Story*. Color photos. New York: Cobblehill. 6–9 yrs.

Murdoch, David. 1995. *North American Indian*. Photos Lynton Gardiner. New York: Knopf. 9–12 yrs. Eyewitness series.

Osinski, Alice. 1984. *The Sioux*. Danbury, Conn.: Children's Press. 9–12 yrs. New True Books.

———. 1988. *The Nez Perce*. Danbury, Conn.: Children's Press. 9–12 yrs. New True Books.

Porter, Frank W. 1987. *The Nanticoke*. New York: Chelsea. 10–14 yrs. Indians of North America Series.

Presilla, M. E. & G. Soto. 1996. *Life around the Lake: Embroideries by the Women of Lake Patzcuaro*. New York: Holt. 6–9 yrs.

Sewall, Marcia. 1990. *People of the Breaking Day*. Illus. M. Sewall. New York: Atheneum. 8–12 yrs.

Sherrow, Victoria. 1993. *The Hopis: Pueblo People of the Southwest*. Color, B & W photos; paintings. Brookfield, Conn.: Millbrook. 10–13 yrs. Native Americans series.

———. 1994. *The Nez Perces: People of the Far West*. Color, B & W photos. Brookfield, Conn.: Millbrook. 10–13 yrs. Native Americans series.

Siy, Alexandra. 1993. *The Eeyou: People of Eastern James Bay*. Photos A. Siy. Morristown, N.J.: Dillon. 12–16 yrs.

Smith, J. H. 1987. *Eskimos: The Inuit of the Arctic*. Vero Beach, Fla.: Rourke. 10–14 yrs. Original People Series.

Sneve, Virginia Driving Hawk. 1993. *The Navajos: A First Americans Book*. Illus. Ronald Himler. New York: Holiday. 9–12 yrs.

———. 1993. *The Sioux: A First Americans Book*. Illus. Ronald Himler. New York: Holiday. 9–12 yrs.

———. 1994. *The Nez Perce: A First Americans Book*. Illus. Ronald Himler. New York: Holiday. 9–12 yrs. First Americans series.

———. 1994. *The Seminole*. Illus. Ronald Himler. New York: Holiday. 9–12 yrs. First Americans series.

———. 1995. *The Iroquois*. Illus. Ronald Himler. New York: Holiday. 9–12 yrs. First Americans series.

———. 1996. *The Cherokees*. Illus. Virginia Driving Hawk Sneve. New York: Holiday. 9–12 yrs. First Americans Series.

Stuart, Gene S. (Crump, Donald J., ed.). 1981. *The Mighty Aztecs*. Special Publications Series 16: No. 2. Washington, D.C.: National Geographic Society. 12–14 yrs.

Waters, Kate. 1996. *Tapenum's Day: A Wampanoag Indian Boy in Pilgrim Times*. Photos Russ Kendall. New York: Scholastic. 7–9 yrs.

Wolfson, Evelyn. 1993. *The Iroquois: People of the Northeast*. Archival illustrations. Brookfield, Conn.: Millbrook. 10–13 yrs. Native Americans series.

Wolfson, Evelyn. 1993. *The Teton Sioux: People of the Plains*. Archival illustrations. Brookfield, Conn.: Millbrook. 10–13 yrs. Native Americans series.

Wood, Leigh Hope. 1993. *The Crow Indians*. B & W & color photos. New York: Chelsea. 10–13 yrs. Junior Library of American Indians series.

Wunder, John R. 1989. *The Kiowa*. Photos & drawings. New York: Chelsea. 12–16 yrs. Indians of North America Series.

History

Aaseng, Nathan. 1992. *Navajo Code Talkers*. New York: Walker. 10–14 yrs.

Arnold, Caroline. 1992. *The Ancient Cliff Dwellers of Mesa Verde*. Photos Richard Hewett. New York: Clarion. 10–14 yrs.

Beater, A. W. 1996. *Only the Names Remain: The Cherokees and the Trail of Tears*. Illus. Kristina Rodanas. Boston: Little, Brown. 9–12 yrs.

Brown, Dee (Adapter Amy Ehrlich). 1975. *Wounded Knee: An Indian History of the American West*. Photos. New York: Dell. 12–16 yrs.

Deloria, Vine, Jr. 1980. *Custer Died for Your Sins: An Indian Manifesto*. Norman: Univ. of Oklahoma Press. 12–16 yrs.

Dunn, John M. 1994. *The Relocation of the North American Indian*. B & W photos. San Diego: Lucent. 12–16 yrs. World History series.

Echo-Hawk, Roger C. & Walter R. Echo-Hawk. 1994. *Battlefields and Burial Grounds: The Indian Struggle to Protect Ancestral Graves in the United States*. Minneapolis, Minn.: Lerner. 12–16 yrs.

Freedman, Russell. 1988. *Buffalo Hunt*. New York: Holiday. 10–14 yrs.

———. 1992. *An Indian Winter*. Illus. Karl Bodmer. New York: Holiday. 10–15 yrs.

Fremon, David K. 1994. *The Trail of Tears*. B & W photos & reproductions. New York: New Discovery. 12–16 yrs. American Events series.

Griffin-Pierce, Trudy. 1995. *The Encyclopedia of Native America*. B & W & color photos & art. New York: Viking. 12–16 yrs.

La Pierre, Yvette. 1994. *Native American Rock Art: Messages from the Past*. Illus. Lois Sloan. Charlottesville, Vir.: Thomasson. 10–13 yrs.

Merton, Thom. 1976. *Ishi Means Man: Essays on Native Americans*. Illus. Rita Corbin. Morris Plains, N.J.: Unicorn. 12–16 yrs.

Monroe, Jean Guard & Ray A. Williamson. 1993. *First Houses: Native American Homes and Sacred Structures*. Illus. Susan Johnston Carlson. Boston: Houghton Mifflin. 12–16 yrs.

Ortiz, Simon. 1988. *The People Shall Continue*. San Francisco: Children's Book Press. 7–10 yrs.

Sattler, Helen Roney. 1993. *The Earliest Americans*. Illus. Jean Day Zallinger. New York: Clarion. 12–16 yrs.

Shernie, Bonnie. 1993. *Mounds of Earth and Shell: Native Sites: The Southeast*. B & W & color photos. Plattsburgh, N.Y.: Tundra. 10–13 yrs. Native Dwellings series.

Thornton, Russell. 1987. *American Indian Holocaust and Survival: A Population History Since 1492*. Photos & maps. Norman: Univ. of Oklahoma Press. 12–16 yrs.

Trimble, Stephen. 1990. *The Village of Blue Stone*. Illus. Jennifer Owings Dewey & Deborah Reade. New York: Macmillan. 10–14 yrs.

Waters, K. 1996. *Tapenum's Day: A Wampanoag Indian Boy in Pilgrim Times*. Photos Russ Kendall. New York: Scholastic. 5–9 yrs.

Weiss, Harvey. 1988. *Shelters: From Tepee to Igloo*. New York: Crowell. 10–14 yrs.

Wittstock, Laura Waterman. 1993. *Ininatig's Gift of Sugar: Traditional Native Sugarmaking*. Photos Dale Kakkak. Minneapolis, Minn.: Lerner. 10–14 yrs.

Wolfson, Evelyn. 1993. *From the Earth to Beyond the Sky*. Illus. Jennifer Hewitson. Boston: Houghton Mifflin. 10–16 yrs.

Ceremonies & Celebrations

Ancona, George. 1993. *Powwow*. Photos. San Diego: Harcourt Brace. 10–14 yrs.

Behrens, June. 1983. *Powwow: Festivals and Holidays*. Danbury, Conn.: Children's Press. 5–12 yrs. Ethnic and Traditional Holidays Series.

King, Sandra Shannon. 1993. *An Ojibway Dancer*. Photos Catherine Whipple. Minneapolis, Minn.: Lerner. 11–14 yrs. We Are Still Here: Native Americans Today.

Roessel, Monty. 1993. *Kinaalda: A Navajo Girl Grows Up*. Photos M. Roessel. Minneapolis, Minn.: Lerner. 9–13 yrs. We Are Still Here: Native Americans Today.

Seymour, Trynge Van Ness. 1993. *The Gift of Changing Woman*. Folk art. New York: Holt. 6–9 yrs.

Wood, Ted (with Wanbli Numpa Afraid of Hawk). 1992. *A Boy Becomes a Man at Wounded Knee*. New York: Walker. 8–11 yrs.

Contemporary Children

Hoyt-Goldsmith, Diane. 1990. *Totem Pole*. Photos Lawrence Migdale. New York: Holiday. 8–12 yrs.

———. 1991. *Pueblo Storyteller*. Photos Lawrence Migdale. New York: Holiday. 8–12 yrs.

———. 1992. *Arctic Hunter*. Photos Lawrence Migdale. New York: Holiday. 8–12 yrs.

———. 1993. *Cherokee Summer*. Color photos Lawrence Migdale. New York: Holiday. 10–13 yrs.

———. 1995. *Apache Rodeo*. Photos Lawrence Migdale. New York: Holiday. 9–13 yrs.

Keegan, Marcia. 1991. *Pueblo Boy: Growing Up in Two Worlds*. Photos. M. Keegan. New York: Cobblehill. 7–10 yrs.

Kendall, Russ. 1992. *Eskimo Boy: Life in an Inupiaq Eskimo Village*. Photos R. Kendall. New York: Scholastic. 6–9 yrs.

Mangurian, David. 1979. *Children of the Incas.* New York: Four Winds. 10–13 yrs.

Peters, Russell M. 1992. *Clambake: A Wampanoag Tradition.* Photos. John Madama. Minneapolis, Minn.: Lerner. 8–11 yrs. We Are Still Here series.

Swentzell, Rina. 1992. *Children of Clay: A Family of Pueblo Potters.* Photos Bill Steen. Minneapolis, Minn.: Lerner. 8–10 yrs. We Are Still Here series.

Thornson, Peggy. 1995. *Kaffe Henio: Navajo Sheepherder.* Photos Paul Conklin. New York: Cobblehill. 10–12 yrs.

Living in Two Worlds

Ashabranner, Brent. 1984. *To Live in Two Worlds: American Indian Youth Today.* Photos Paul Conklin. New York: Dodd Mead. 12–16 yrs.

Erdrich, Louise. 1988. *Tracks.* New York: Holt. 12–16 yrs.

Krull, Kathleen. 1995. *One Nation, Many Tribes: How Kids Live in Milwaukee's Indian Community.* Photos David Hautzig. New York: Lodestar. World of Our Own series.

Contemporary Issues

Dorris, Michael. 1989. *The Broken Cord: A Family's Ongoing Struggle with Fetal Alcohol Syndrome.* New York: HarperCollins. 12–16 yrs.

Hanlan, Judith. 1987. *American Indians Today: Issues and Conflicts.* Danbury, Conn.: Watts. 10–14 yrs.

Nabokov, Peter (Ed.). 1978. *Native American Testimony: An Anthology of Indian and White Relations. First Encounter to Dispossession.* New York: Crowell. 12–16 yrs.

Science & Respect for Nature

Aliki. 1976. *Corn Is Maize: The Gift of the Indians.* New York: Crowell. 5–9 yrs. A Let's-Read-and-Find-Out Science Book.

Ashabranner, Brent. 1982. *Morning Star, Black Sun: The Northern Cheyenne Indians and America's Energy Crisis.* Photos Paul Conklin. New York: Putnam. 12–16 yrs.

Bierhorst, John. 1994. *The Way of the Earth: Native America and the Environment.* New York: Morrow. 12–16 yrs.

Stonehouse, Bernard. 1993. *Snow, Ice, and Cold.* Photos. New York: New Discovery. 10–13 yrs. Repairing the Damage series.

Swanson, D. 1996. *Buffalo Sunrise: The Story of a North American Giant.* Photos. San Francisco, Calif.: Sierra. 10–12 yrs.

Tannenbaum, Beulah & Harold E. Tannenbaum. 1988. *Science of the Early American Indians.* Danbury, Conn.: Watts. 10–14 yrs.

The Arts, Dance, Crafts, Music

Bernstein, Bonnie. 1982. *Native American Crafts Workshop.* Columbus, Ohio: Fearon Teacher Aids. 9–12 yrs.

Bierhorst, John. 1979. *A Cry from the Earth: Music of the North American Indians.* New York: Four Winds. 9–12 yrs.

Crum, Robert. 1994. *Eagle Drum: On the Powwow Trail with a Young Grass Dancer.* New York: Four Winds. 10–13 yrs.

Gates, Frieda. 1982. *North American Indian Masks: Craft and Legend.* New York: Walker. 9–12 yrs.

Glubok, Shirley. 1971. *The Art of the Southwest Indians.* New York: Macmillan. 9–12 yrs.

Haslam, Andrew, & Alexandra Parsons. 1995. *North American Indians.* New York: Thomson Learning. 10–13 yrs. Make It Work! series.

Highwater, Jamake. 1978. *Many Smokes, Many Moons: A Chronology of American Indian History through Indian Art.* New York: HarperCollins. 11–16 yrs.

Wolfson, Evelyn. 1981. *American Indian Tools and Ornaments: How to Make Implements and Jewelry with Bone and Shell.* Photos, drawings, & diagrams. New York: Random House/McKay. 11–16 yrs.

General Information: Lifestyles, Clothing, Traditions.

Boy Scouts of America. 1959. *Indian Lore.* New Brunswick, N.J.: The Scouts. 10–14 yrs.

Hirschfelder, Arlene. 1986. *Happily May I Walk: American Indians and Alaska Natives Today.* New York: Scribners. 12–16 yrs.

Hofsinde, Robert [Gray Wolf]. 1956. *Indian Sign Language.* New York: Morrow. 10–16 yrs.

———. 1968. *Indian Costumes.* New York: Morrow. 10–16 yrs.

Penner, Lucille Recht. 1994. *A Native American Feast.* New York: Macmillan. 10–13 yrs.

Regguinti, Gordon. 1992. *The Sacred Harvest: Ojibway Wild Rice Gathering.* Photos. Dale Kakkak. Minneapolis, Minn.: Lerner. 8–11 yrs. We Are Still Here series.

POETRY, STORIES, SONGS, ESSAYS

Bierhorst, John. 1994. *On the Road of Stars: Native American Night Poems and Sleep Charms.* Illus. Judy Pedersen. New York: Macmillan. 6–10 yrs.

Bruchac, J. 1996. *Four Ancestors: Stories, Songs, and Poems from Native North America.* Illus. S. S. Burrus, Jeffrey Chapman, Murv Jacob, & Duke Sine. Mahwah, N.J.: BridgeWater. 10–13 yrs.

Bruchac, Joseph & Jonathan London. 1992. *Thirteen Moons on Turtle's Back: A Native American Year of Moons.* Illus. Thomas Locker. New York: Philomel. 5–8 yrs.

Carlstrom, Nancy White. 1992. *Northern Lullaby.* Illus. Leo & Diane Dillon. New York: Philomel. 4–8 yrs.

Hirschfelder, Arlene B. & Beverly R. Singer (Compilers). 1992. *Rising Voices: Writings of Young Native Americans.* New York: Scribners. 12–16 yrs.

Gilford, Barry (Ed.). 1976. *Selected Writings of Edward D. Curtis.* 3rd ed. Photos Edward D. Curtis. Berkeley, Calif.: Creative Arts. 12–16 yrs.

London, J. 1996. *Fireflies, Fireflies, Light My Way.* Illus. Linda Messier. New York: Viking. 6–9 yrs. (Lullaby)

McLerran, A. 1995. *The Ghost Dance.* Illus. Paul Morin. New York: Clarion. 7–10 yrs.

Orie, Sandra. 1995. *Did You Hear Wind Sing Your Name?: An Oneida Song of Spring.* Illus. Christopher Canyon. New York: Walker. 6–10 yrs.

Siegen-Smith, N. 1996. *Songs for Survival: Songs and Chants from Tribal Peoples Around the World.* Illus. Bernard Lodge. New York: Dutton. 9–12 yrs.

Sneve, Virginia Driving Hawk (Ed.). 1978. *Dancing Teepees: Poems of American Indian Youth.* Illus. Stephen Gammell. New York: Holiday. 11–16 yrs.

Whipple, Laura. 1994. *Celebrating America: A Collection of Poems and Images of the American Spirit.* Paintings & photos. New York: Philomel. 10–13 yrs.

Wood, D. 1996. *Northwoods Cradle Song: From a Menominee Lullaby.* Illus. Lisa Desimini. New York: Simon & Schuster. 4–7 yrs.

ADULT RESOURCES

Caduto, Michael I. & Joseph Bruchac. 1988. *Keepers of the Earth: Native American Stories and Environmental Activities for Children.* Illus. John Kahionhes Fadden & Carol Wood. Golden, Colo.: Fulcrum. Tales & instructional activities.

———. 1991. *Keepers of the Animals: Native American Stories and Wildlife Activities for Children.* Illus. John Kahionhes Fadden. Golden, Colo.: Fulcrum. Folk Literature & instructional activities.

Earthmakers Lodge: Native American Folklore, Activities, and Foods. Available from Cobblestone, 7 School St., Peterborough, NH 03458. Collected stories & activities.

Rose, Cynthia & Duane Champagne. *Native North American Almanac.* Two volumes. Available from UXL Gale Research, 835 Penobscot Bldg., Detroit, MI 48226.

TEACHER REFERENCES FOR ALL PARALLEL CULTURES

Hayden, Carla D. (Ed.). 1992. *Venture into Cultures: A Resource Book of Multicultural Materials and Programs.* Chicago: American Library Association.

Heltshe, Mary Ann & Audrey Burie Kirchmer. 1991. *Multicultural Explorations.* Englewood, Colo.: Libraries Unlimited.

Tiedt, Pamela L. & Iris M. Tiedt. 1990. *Multicultural Teaching: A Handbook of Activities, Information, and Resources.* 3rd ed. Needham Heights, Mass.: Allyn & Bacon.

CHAPTER 10

CHILDREN'S BOOKS MENTIONED IN THE CHAPTER

Ahlberg, A. 1996. *The Better Brown Stories.* Illus. Fritz Wegner. New York: Viking. 9–12 yrs.

Aliki. 1996. *Wild and Woolly Mammoths.* New York: HarperCollins. 5–8 yrs.

Alter, J. 1989. *Growing Up in the Old West.* New York: Watts/First Books. 8–12 yrs.

Anderson, J. 1996. *Cowboys: Roundup on an American Ranch.* Photos George Ancona. New York: Scholastic. 9–12 yrs.

Babbitt, N. 1975. *Tuck Everlasting.* New York: Farrar, Straus & Giroux. 9–12 yrs.

Blake, Q. 1996. *Clown.* New York: Holt. 5–8 yrs.

Blume, J. 1990. *Fudge-a-Mania.* New York: Dell. 9–11 yrs.

Bruchac, J. 1996. *Four Ancestors: Stories, Songs, and Poems from Native North America.* Illus. S. S. Burrus, J. Chapman, M. Jacob, & D. Sine. Mahwah, N.J.: BridgeWater. 10–13 yrs.

Burdett, F. H. 1962. *The Secret Garden.* Illus. Tasha Tudor. New York: Lippincott. 10–14 yrs.

Byars, B. 1977. *The Pinball.* New York: HarperCollins. 11–14 yrs.

Carle, E. 1969. *The Very Hungry Caterpillar.* New York: Philomel. 4–7 yrs.

Christian, P. 1995. *The Bookstore Mouse.* Illus. Gary Lippincott. San Diego, Calif.: Harcourt Brace. 9–12 yrs.

Cleary, B. 1991. *Strider.* Illus. P. O. Zelinsky. New York: Morrow. 10–13 yrs.

Cooney, B. 1982. *Miss Rumphius.* New York: Viking. 7–11 yrs.

Cox, C. 1993. *The Forgotten Heroes: The Story of the Buffalo Soldiers.* Prints & photos. New York: Scholastic. 10–16 yrs.

Cullinan, B. E. 1995. *A Jar of Tiny Stars: Poems by NCTE Award-Winning Poets.* Illus. Andi MacLeod & Marc Nadel. Honesdale, Penn.: Wordsong. 9–12 yrs.

Dahl, R. 1961. *James and the Giant Peach.* Illus. Nancy Ekholm Burket. New York: Knopf. 8–12 yrs.

DeSpain, P. 1994. *Eleven Turtle Tales: Adventure Tales from Around the World.* Illus. Joe Shlichta. Little Rock, Ark.: August. 10–15 yrs.

Dr. Seuss. [T. S. Geisel] 1961. *Sneetches and Other Stories.* New York: Random House. 5–9 yrs.

Duffey, B. 1996. *Hey, New Kid!* Illus. Ellen Thompson. New York: Viking. 9–12 yrs.

Fleischman, P. 1988. *Joyful Noise: Poems for Two Voices.* Illus. Eric Beddows. New York: HarperCollins. 9–13 yrs.

Fleischman, S. 1986. *The Whipping Boy.* Illus. Peter Sis. New York: Greenwillow. 9–12 yrs.

Fox, P. 1995. *The Little Swineherd and Other Tales.* Illus. Robert Byrd. New York: Dutton. 7–12 yrs.

Hahn, M. D. 1996. *The Gentleman Outlaw and Me-Eli: A Story of the Old West.* New York: Clarion. 9–12 yrs.

Hamilton, V. 1996. *When Birds Could Talk and Bats Could Sing: The Adventures of Bruh Sparrow, Sis Wren, and Their Friends.* Illus. Barry Moser. New York: Blue Sky. 5–10 yrs.

Harris, J. C. 1883. *Nights with Uncle Remus.* Illus. A. B. Frost. Boston: Houghton Mifflin. 9–12 yrs.

Ketteman, H. 1995. *Luck With Potatoes.* Illus. Brian Floca. New York: Orchard/Jackson. 7–10 yrs.

Lear, E. 1996. *The Owl and the Pussy-Cat: And Other Nonsense Poems.* Illus. Michael Hauge. New York: North-South. 7–10 yrs.

Lenski, L. 1943. *Bayou Suzette.* Illus. L. Lenski. New York: Stokes. 9–13 yrs.

Lewis, C. S. 1961. *The Lion, the Witch, the Wardrobe.* Illus. P. Baynes. New York: Macmillan. 9–12 yrs.

London, J. 1995. *Master Elk and the Mountain Lion.* Illus. Wayne McLoughlin. New York: Crown. 7–12 yrs.

MacLachlan, P. 1985. *Sarah, Plain and Tall.* New York: HarperCollins. 9–12 yrs.

Mahy, M. 1996. *Tingleberries, Tuckertugs, and Telephones: A Tale of Love and Ice Cream.* Illus. Robert Staermose. New York: Viking. 9–12 yrs.

Martin, B. 1992. *Brown Bear, Brown Bear, What Do You See?* Illus. Eric Carle. New York: Henry Holt. 4–8 yrs.

McCaughrean, G. 1996. *The Golden Hoard: Myths and Legends of the World.* Illus. Bee Wiley. New York: McElderry. 9–12 yrs.

Milne, A. A. 1926. *Winnie the Pooh.* Illus. E. H. Shepard. New York: Dutton. 8–12 yrs.

Paterson, K. 1976. *The Bridge to Terabithia.* Illus. Donna Diamond. New York: HarperCollins. 9–12 yrs.

Paulsen, G. 1995. *Escape from Fire Mountain.* New York: Dell. 10–14 yrs.

Philip, N. (Comp). 1996. *American Fairy Tales: From Rip Van Winkle to the Rootabaga Stories.* Illus. Michael McCurdy. New York: Hyperion. 11–16 yrs.

Purdy, C. 1985. *Iva Dunnit and the Big Wind.* Illus. Steven Kellog. New York: Dial. 6–10 yrs.

Raskin, E. 1978. *The Westing Game.* New York: Dutton. 11–15 yrs.

Sachar, L. 1987. *There's a Boy in the Girl's Bathroom.* New York: Knopf. 9–11 yrs.

Scieszka, J. 1989. *The True Story of the Three Little Pigs.* Illus. Lane Smith. New York: Viking. 7–10 yrs.

Sendak, M. 1963. *Where the Wild Things Are.* New York: HarperCollins. 6–9 yrs.

Shakespeare, W. (Ann Keay Beeduce, Reteller). 1996. *The Tempest.* Illus. Gennady Spirin. New York: Philomel. 9–12 yrs.

Sherman, C. W. 1996. *Eli and the Swamp Man.* Illus. James Ransome. New York: HarperCollins. 9–12 yrs.

Sleator, W. 1995. *Interstellar Pig.* New York: Dutton. 9–12 yrs.

Siegelson, K. 1996. *The Terrible, Wonderful Tellin' at Hog Hammock.* Illus. Eric Velasquez. New York: HarperCollins. 9–12 yrs.

Steptoe, J. 1987. *Mufaro's Beautiful Daughters: An African Tale.* New York: Lothrop, Lee & Shepard. 8–12 yrs.

Tafuri, N. 1990. *Follow Me!* New York: Greenwillow. 4–9 yrs.

Taylor, M. 1976. *Roll of Thunder Hear My Cry.* New York: Viking. 10–14 yrs.

Turner, G. W. 1989. *Take a Walk in Their Shoes.* Illus. Elton C. Fax. New York: Puffin. 8–12 yrs.

Waddell, M. 1992. *Owl Babies.* Illus. Patrick Benson. Bergenfield, N.J.: Candlewick. 4–9 yrs.

Waters, K. 1996. *Tapenum's Day: A Wampanoag Indian Boy in Pilgrim Times.* Photos Russ Kendall. New York: Scholastic. 5–9 yrs.

Waugh, S. 1994. *The Mennyms.* New York: Greenwillow. 10–13 yrs.

White, E. B. 1952. *Charlotte's Web.* Illus. Garth Williams. New York: HarperCollins. 7–12 yrs.

Yep, L. 1991. *The Lost Garden.* New York: Messner. 10–14 yrs.

Yolen, J. 1987. *Owl Moon.* Illus. John Schoenherr. New York: Putnam. 5–10 yrs.

OUTSTANDING NEW BOOKS TO READ ALOUD

BOOKS WITH PICTURES FOR PRESCHOOL THROUGH PRIMARY FANTASY

Auch, M. J. 1995. *Hen Lake.* New York: Holiday. 5–9 yrs.

Buehner, C. 1996. *Fanny's Dream.* Illus. Mark Buehner. New York: Dial. 6–9 yrs.

Cottringer, A. 1996. *Ella and the Naughty Lion.* Illus. Russell Ayto. Boston: Lorraine/Houghton Mifflin. 3–5 yrs.

Egielski, R. 1995. *Buz.* New York: HarperCollins/Geringer. 6–9 yrs.

Hunter, A. 1996. *Possum's Harvest Moon.* Illus. Anne Hunter. Boston: Houghton Mifflin. 4–7 yrs.

MacDonald, A. 1996. *Cousin Ruth's Tooth.* Illus. Marjorie Priceman. Boston: Houghton Mifflin. 4–7 yrs.

McNaughton, C. 1995. *Here Come the Aliens!* Cambridge, Mass.: Candlewick. 4–7 yrs.

Pinkwater, D. 1995. *Mush, a Dog from Space.* New York: Atheneum. 6–9 yrs.

San Souci, R. D. (Adapter). 1996. *Pedro and the Monkey.* Illus. Michael Hays. New York: Morrow. 4–7 yrs.

Soto, G. 1996. *The Old Man and His Door.* Illus. Joe Cepeda. New York: Putnam. 4–6 yrs.

Stevenson, J. 1996. *The Oldest Elf.* Illus. J. Stevenson. New York: Greenwillow. 5–8 yrs.

Stoeke, J. M. 1996. *Minertoa Louise at School.* New York: Dutton. 3–6 yrs.

Yaccarino, D. 1996. *If I Had a Robot.* New York: Viking. 5–8 yrs.

Yep, L. 1995. *The City of Dragons.* Illus. Jean Tseng & Mou-Sien Tseng. New York: Scholastic. (Literary fairy tale.)

Walsh, E. S. 1996. *Samantha.* San Diego, Calif.: Harcourt Brace. 4–6 yrs.

CONTEMPORARY REALISTIC FICTION

Anderson, L. H. 1996. *Turkey Pox.* Illus. Dorothy Donohue. Morton Grove, Ill.: Whitman. 5–8 yrs.

Appelt, K. 1996. *Watermelon Day.* Illus. Dale Gottlieb. New York: Holt. 5–8 yrs.

Blumenthal, D. 1996. *The Chocolate-Covered-Cookie Tantrum.* Illus. Harvey Stevenson. New York: Clarion. 3–6 yrs.

Cowley, J. 1996. *Gracias: The Thanksgiving Turkey.* Illus. Joe Cepeda. New York: Scholastic. 5–8 yrs.

Dorros, A. 1995. *Isla.* Illus. Elisa Kleven. New York: Dutton. 6–9 yrs.

Ericsson, J. A. 1996. *The Most Beautiful Kid in the World.* Illus. Susan Meddaugh. New York: Tambourine. 4–8 yrs.

Ferguson, A. 1996. *Tumbleweed Christmas.* Illus. Tom Sully. New York: Simon & Schuster. 5–8 yrs.

Gaffney, T. R. 1996. *Grandpa Takes Me to the Moon.* Illus. Barry Root. New York: Tambourine. 5–8 yrs.

Henkes, K. 1996. *Lilly's Purple Plastic Purse.* Illus. K. Henkes. New York: Greenwillow. 5–8 yrs.

Hest, A. 1996. *Jamaica Louise James.* Illus. Sheila White Samton. Cambridge, Mass.: Candlewick. 4–7 yrs.

McNeal, T. & L. McNeal. 1996. *The Dog Who Lost His Boy.* Illus. John Sandford. Morton Grove, Ill.: Whitman. 5–8 yrs.

Wolf, J. 1996. *Daddy, Could I Have an Elephant?* Illus. Marylin Hafner. New York: Greenwillow. 4–7 yrs.

INFORMATION BOOKS

Brenner, B. & J. Takaya. 1996. *Chibi: A True Story from Japan.* Illus. June Otani. New York: Clarion. 6–10 yrs. (Read with R. McCloskey's *Make Way for Ducklings.* 1941. New York: Viking. 6–9 yrs.)

Brown, C. 1995. *Tractor.* New York: Greenwillow. 4–8 yrs.

Cole, J. 1995. *The Magic School Bus Inside a Hurricane.* Illus. Bruce Degen. New York: Scholastic. 7–10 yrs.

———. 1996. *The Magic School Bus Inside a Beehive.* Illus. Bruce Degen. New York: Scholastic. 7–10 yrs.

Facklam, M. 1996. *Creepy, Crawly Caterpillars.* Illus. Paul Facklam. Boston: Little, Brown. 5–9 yrs.

Hoban, T. 1996. *Just Look.* Photos. New York: Greenwillow. 3–6 yrs.

Johnson, S. A. 1995. *Raptor Rescue!: An Eagle Flies Free.* Color photos Ron Winch. New York: Dutton. 5–8 yrs.

Klinting, L. 1996. *Bruno the Carpenter.* Illus. Lars Klinting. New York: Holt. 5–8 yrs.

London, J. 1996. *Red Wolf Country.* Illus. Daniel San Souci. New York: Dutton. 3–6 yrs.

Matthews, D. 1995. *Arctic Foxes.* Color photos Dan Guravich & Nikita Ovsyanikov. New York: Simon & Schuster. 5–9 yrs.

Rotner, S. 1995. *Wheels Around.* Color photos. Boston: Houghton Mifflin. 3–8 yrs.

Simon, S. 1995. *Sharks.* Color photos. New York: HarperCollins. 5–8 yrs.

LITERATURE TO READ ALOUD TO ELEMENTARY AGE STUDENTS

Folk Literature

Adler, N. (Adapter). 1996. *The Dial Book of Animal Tales from Around the World.* Illus. Amanda Hall. New York: Dial. 9–12 yrs.

Duncan, L. 1996. *The Magic of Spider Woman.* Illus. Shonto Begay. New York: Scholastic. 5–9 yrs.

Froese, D. (Adapter). 1996. *The Wise Washerman: A Folktale from Burma.* Illus. Wang Kui. New York: Hyperion. 9–12 yrs.

Kimmel, E. A. (Adapter). 1996. *Billy Lazroe and the King of the Sea: A Tale of the Northwest.* Illus. Michael Steirnagle. San Diego, Calif.: Browndeer/Harcourt Brace. 10–13 yrs.

Mother Goose, Humpty Dumpty and Other Nursery Rhymes; Jack and Jill and Other Nursery Rhymes. 1996. Illus. Lucy Cousins. New York: Dutton. 1–4 yrs.

Philip, N. (Adapter). 1996. *Odin's Family: Myths of the Vikings.* Illus. Maryclare Foa. New York: Orchard. 10–13 yrs.

Pushkin, A. (Trans. Pauline Hehl). 1996. *The Tale of Tsar Saltan.* Illus. Gennady Spirin. New York: Dial. 12–16 yrs.

Souhami, J. 1996. *The Leopard's Drum: An Asante Tale from West Africa.* Boston: Little, Brown. 6–9 yrs. (Fable.)

Vande Velde, V. 1995. *Tales from the Brothers Grimm and the Sisters Weird.* San Diego, Calif.: Harcourt/Yolen. 7–10 yrs.

Wood, Audrey. 1996. *The Bunyans.* Illlus. David Shannon. New York: Scholastic. 6–12 yrs.

Fantasy

Avi. 1995. *Poppy.* Illus. Brian Floca. New York: Orchard/Jackson. 7–10 yrs.

Fleischman, S. *The 13th Floor: A Ghost Story.* Illus. Peter Sis. New York: Greenwillow. 9–12 yrs. (Time-slip fantasy.)

Gray, L. 1995. *Falcon's Egg.* Boston: Houghton Mifflin. 7–10 yrs.

King-Smith, D. 1995. *The School Mouse.* Illus. Cynthia Fisher. New York: Hyperion. 8–12 yrs.

Kipling, R. 1995. *The Jungle Book: The Mowgli Stories.* Illus. Jerry Pinkney. New York: Morrow. 8–12 yrs. Books of Wonder series.

Mazer, A. 1996. *A Sliver of Glass and Other Uncommon Tales.* New York: Hyperion. 12–16 yrs.

Morpurgo, M. 1996. *The Wreck of the Zanzibar.* Illus. Francois Place. New York: Viking. 9–12 yrs.

Moses, W. (Reteller). 1995. *The Legend of Sleepy Hollow.* New York: Philomel. 7–10 yrs.

Parish, P. 1995. *Come Back, Amelia Bedelia.* Illus. Wallace Tripp. New York: HarperCollins. 6–9 yrs.

Philip, N. (Collector & trans.) 1995. *Fairy Tales of Hans Christian Andersen.* Illus. Isabelle Brent. New York: Viking. 8–12 yrs.

Ryland, C. 1996. *Gooseberry Park.* Illus. A. Howard. San Diego, Calif.: Harcourt Brace. 7–10 yrs.

Rubinstein, G. 1995. *Galax-Arena: A Novel.* New York: Simon & Schuster. 12–16 yrs.

Strete, C. K. & M. N. Chacon. 1996. *How the Indians Bought the Baron.* Illus. Francisco X. Mora. New York: Greenwillow. 5–8 yrs. (Original trickster tale.)

Supraner, R. 1996. *Sam Sunday and the Mystery at the Ocean Beach Hotel.* Illus. Will Hillenbrand. New York: Viking. 5–8 yrs.

Turner, M. W. 1995. *Instead of Three Wishes.* New York: Greenwillow. 12–16 yrs.

Waite, M. P. 1996. *Jojofu.* Illus. Yoriko Ito. New York: Lothrop, Lee & Shepard. 5–8 yrs.

Waugh, S. 1996. *Mennyms Alone.* New York: Greenwillow. 11–14 yrs.

Yolen, J. 1996. *Passager.* San Diego, Calif.: Harcourt Brace. 9–12 yrs. Young Merlin Trilogy.

Yolen, J. & M. H. Greenberg. 1995. *The Haunted House: A Collection of Original Stories.* Illus. Doron Ben-Ami. New York: HarperCollins. 10–13 yrs.

Historical Fiction

Armstrong, J. 1996. *The Dreams of Mairhe Mehan.* New York: Knopf. 12–16 yrs.

Dexter, C. 1996. *Safe Return.* Cambridge, Mass.: Candlewick. 9–12 yrs.

Hermes, P. 1995. *On Winter's Wind: A Novel.* Boston: Little, Brown. 9–12 yrs.

Howard, E. 1996. *The Log Cabin Quilt.* Illus. Ronald Himler. New York: Holiday House. 6–8 yrs.

San Souci, R. D. 1995. *Kate Shelley: Bound for Legend.* Illus. Max Ginsburg. New York: Dial. 6–9 yrs.

Contemporary Realistic Fiction

Byars, B. 1995. *Tarot Says Beware.* New York: Viking. 9–12 yrs. Herculeah Jones Mystery.

———. 1996. *Tornado.* Illus. Doron Ben-Ami. New York: HarperCollins. 7–10 yrs.

Cameron, A. 1995. *The Stories Huey Tells.* Illus. Roberta Smith. New York: Knopf. 7–10 yrs.

Christopher, M. 1996. *Olympic Dream.* Illus. Karen Meyer. Boston, Mass.: Little, Brown. 9–12 yrs.

Clements, A. 1996. *Frindle.* Illus. Brian Selznick. New York: Simon & Schuster. 9–12 yrs.

Dickinson, P. 1996. *Chuck and Danielle.* Illus. Kees de Kiefte. New York: Delacorte. 9–12 yrs.

Doyle, B. 1996. *Spud in Winter.* Toronto, Canada: Groundwood. 12–15 yrs.

———. 1996. *Spud Sweetgrass.* Toronto, Canada: Groundwood. 12–15 yrs.

Flournoy, V. 1995. *Tanya's Reunion.* Illus. Jerry Pinkney. New York: Dial. 7–10 yrs.

Frieden, S. 1996. *The Care and Feeding of Fish.* Illus. Sarajo Frieden. Boston: Houghton Mifflin. 6–9 yrs.

Giff, P. R. 1996. *Good Luck, Ronald Morgan!* Illus. Susanna Natti. New York: Viking. 6–9 yrs.

Gutman, D. 1996. *The Kid Who Ran for President.* New York: Scholastic. 9–13 yrs.

Kimmel, E. A. 1996. *The Magic Dreidels: A Hanukkah Story.* Illus. Katya Krenina. New York: Holiday House. 5–9 yrs.

Levin, B. 1995. *Fire in the Wind.* New York: Greenwillow. 9–12 yrs.

Lowry, L. 1996. *See You Around, Sam.* Illus. Diane de Groat. Boston: Lorraine/Houghton Mifflin. 9–12 yrs.

McKay, H. 1995. *Dog Friday.* New York: McElderry. 9–12 yrs.

Mills, C. 1996. *Dinah Forever.* New York: Farrar, Straus & Giroux. 9–12 yrs.

Rahaman, V. 1996. *O Christmas Tree.* Illus. Frane Lessac. Honesdale, Penn.: Boyds Mills. 6–9 yrs.

Rosselson, L. 1996. *Rosa and Her Singing Grandfather.* Illus. Marcia Sewall. New York: Philomel. 9–12 yrs.

Say, A. 1996. *Emma's Rug.* Boston: Lorraine/ Houghton Mifflin. 6–8 yrs.

Small, D. 1996. *Fenwick's Suit.* Illus. D. Small. New York: Farrar, Straus & Giroux. 6–9 yrs.

Stevenson, J. 1996. *Yard Sale.* New York: Greenwillow. 6–9 yrs.

Wood, A. 1996. *The Red Racer.* Illus. A. Wood. New York: Simon & Schuster. 6–9 yrs.

Biography

Fritz, J. 1995. *You Want Women to Vote, Lizzie Stanton?* Illus. DyAnne DiSalvo-Ryan. New York: Putnam. 9–12 yrs.

Fleischman, S. 1996. *The Abracadabra Kid.* Photos. New York: Greenwillow. 11–16 yrs. (Autobiography.)

George, J. C. 1996. *The Tarantula in My Purse and 172 Other Wild Pets.* Illus. J. C. George. New York: HarperCollins. 9–12 yrs.

Kehret, P. 1996. *Small Steps: The Year I Got Polio.* Photos. Morton Grove, Ill.: Whitman. 9–12 yrs.

Lyons, M. E. 1996. *Painting Dreams: Minnie Evans, Visionary Artist.* Photos. Boston: Houghton Mifflin. 9–12 yrs.

Murphy, J. 1996. *A Young Patriot: The American Revolution as Experienced by One Boy.* Photos. New York: Clarion. 11–16 yrs.

Murphy, V. R. (Karen Zeinert, ed.). 1996. *Across the Plains in the Donner Party. With Letters by James Reed.* Photos. North Haven, Conn.: Linnet. 11–16 yrs.

Pinkney, A. D. 1996. *Bill Pickett: Rodeo-Ridin' Cowboy.* Illus. Brian Pinkney. San Diego, Calif.: Gulliver/Harcourt Brace. 7–10 yrs.

Stanley, D. 1996. *The True Adventure of Daniel Hall.* Illus. D. Stanley. New York: Dial. 9–12 yrs.

———. 1996. *Leonardo da Vinci.* Illus. D. Stanley. New York: Morrow. 9–12 yrs.

Switzer, E. 1995. *The Magic of Mozart: Mozart, the Magic Flute, and the Salzburg Marionettes.* Photos Costas. New York: Atheneum/Karl. 9–13 yrs.

Tingum, J. 1995. *E. B. White: The Elements of a Writer.* B & W illustrations. Minneapolis, Minn.: Lerner. 9–12 yrs.

Wallner, A. 1995. *Beatrix Potter.* New York: Holiday. 5–9 yrs.

Wilson, J. 1996. *The Ingenious Mr. Peale: Painter, Patriot and Man of Science.* Photos. New York: Atheneum. 11–14 yrs.

Winter, J. 1996. *Josefina.* Illus. J. Winter. San Diego, Calif.: Harcourt Brace. 4–8 yrs. (Fictionalized.)

Information Books

Jones, C. F. 1996. *Accidents May Happen: Fifty Inventions Discovered by Mistake.* Illus. John O'Brien. New York: Delacorte. 9–12 yrs.

Krensky, S. 1996. *Striking It Rich: The Story of the California Gold Rush.* Illus. Anna Di Vito. New York: Simon & Schuster. 7–10 yrs.

Lauber, P. 1996. *Hurricanes: Earth's Mightiest Storms.* Photos. New York: Scholastic. 9–12 yrs.

Lavender, D. 1996. *Snowbound: The Tragic Story of the Donner Party.* Photos. New York: Holiday. 10–15 yrs.

Lincoln, A. 1995. *The Gettysburg Address.* Illus. Michael McCurdy. Boston: Houghton Mifflin. 7–11 yrs.

Markle, S. 1995. *Measuring Up!: Experiments, Puzzles, and Games Exploring Measurement.* Color photos & graphics. New York: Atheneum. 8–12 yrs.

Nirgiotis, N. 1996. *Volcanoes: Mountains That Blow Their Tops.* Illus. Michael Radencich. New York: Grosset & Dunlap. 6–9 yrs.

Perl, L. & Marion Blumenthal Lazan. 1996. *Four Perfect Pebbles: A Holocaust Story.* Photos. New York: Greenwillow. 11–15 yrs.

Sneve, V. D. H. 1996. *The Cherokees.* Illus. Ronald Himler. New York: Holiday. 9–13 yrs.

Walker, B. M. 1995. *The Little House Cookbook: Frontier Foods from Laura Ingalls Wilder's Classic Stories.* Illus. Garth Williams. New York: HarperCollins. 9–12 yrs.

Warren, A. 1996. *Orphan Train Rider: One Boy's True Story.* Photos. Boston: Houghton Mifflin. 9–14 yrs.

Wexler, J. 1995. *Everyday Mysteries.* Color photos. New York: Dutton. 5–9 yrs.

Poetry

Child, L. M. 1996. *Over the River and Through the Wood.* Illus. David Catrow. New York: Holt. 5–8 yrs.

Dyer, J. 1996. *Animal Crackers: A Delectable Collection of Pictures, Poems, and Lullabies for the Very Young.* Boston, Mass.: Little, Brown. 4–9 yrs. (Traditional poems and lullabies.)

Hopkins, L. B. 1996. *Opening Days: Sports Poems.* Illus. Scott Medlock. San Diego, Calif.: Harcourt Brace. 9–12 yrs.

Kellogg, S. 1996. *Yankee Doodle.* Boston, Mass.: Simon & Schuster. 6–10 yrs. (Traditional ballad.)

Lewis, J. P. 1996. *Riddle-icious*. Illus. Debbie Tilley. New York: Knopf. 6–9 yrs. (Short poems.)
Prelutsky, J. 1996. *A Pizza the Size of the Sun*. Illus. James Stevenson. New York: Greenwillow. 8–13 yrs. (Poetry collection.)
Silverstein, S. 1996. *Falling Up*. Illus. S. Silverstein. New York: HarperCollins. 5–11 yrs. (Poetry collection.)
Singer, M. 1996. *All We Needed to Say: Poems about School from Tanya and Sophie*. Photos Lorna Clark. New York: Atheneum. 9–12 yrs. (Narrative poems.)
Thomas, J. C. 1995. *Gingerbread Days*. Illus. Floyd Cooper. New York: HarperCollins/Cotler. 5–9 yrs. (Poems.)

General Literature

Cole, J. & S. Calmenson. 1995. *Ready . . . Set . . . Read — and Laugh! A Funny Treasury for Beginning Readers*. New York: Doubleday. 6–9 yrs.

Hamanaka, S. 1995. *On the Wings of Peace*. Various artists. New York: Clarion. 9–12 yrs.
Pellowski, A. 1995. *The Storytelling Handbook: A Young People's Collection of Unusual Tales and Helpful Hints on How to Tell Them*. Illus. Martha Stoberock. New York: Simon & Schuster. 9–12 yrs.
Wynne-Jones, T. 1995. *The Book of Changes*. New York: Orchard/Kroupa. 9–12 yrs.

CHAPTER 11

CHILDREN'S BOOKS MENTIONED IN THE CHAPTER

Adler, D. 1981. *Cam Jansen & the Mystery of the Dinosaur Bones*. New York: Viking. 6–9 yrs.

———. 1996. *A Picture Book of Davy Crockett*. Illus. John & Alexandra Wallner. New York: Holiday. 5–9 yrs. Picture Book Biographies series.

Babbitt, N. 1975. *Tuck Everlasting*. New York: Farrar, Straus & Giroux. 10–13 yrs.
Brown, M. 1996. *Arthur Goes to School*. New York: Random House. 3–5 yrs.
Bruchac, J. 1996. *Children of the Longhouse*. New York: Dial. 9–12 yrs.
Burch, R. 1980. *Ida Early Comes Over the Mountain*. New York: Viking. 10–12 yrs.
Burton, V. 1939. *Mike Mulligan and His Steam Shovel*. Boston: Houghton Mifflin. 4–7 yrs.
Byars, B. 1996. *The Joy Boys*. Illus. Frank Remkiewixa. New York: Bantam. 5–8 yrs. *First Choice Chapter Book series*.
Cameron, A. 1981. *Stories Julian Tells*. New York: Pantheon. 6–9 yrs.
Carlstrom, N. W. 1993. *How Does the Wind Walk?* Illus. Deborah Kogan Ray. New York: Macmillan. 6–9 yrs.
Cauley, L. B. 1992. *Clap Your Hands*. New York: Putnam. 3–6 yrs.
Cole, J. 1996. *Riding Silver Star*. Color photos Margaret Miller. New York: Morrow. 5–9 yrs.
Cole, J. & S. Calmenson. 1996. *Give a Dog a Bone: Stories, Poems, Jokes, and Riddles about Dogs*. Illus. John Speirs and others. New York: Scholastic. 5–10 yrs.
Cullinan, B. 1995. *A Jar of Tiny Stars: Poems by NCTE Award-Winning Poets*. Illus. Andi MacLeod & Marc Nadel. Honesdale, Penn.: Wordsong. 6–12 yrs.
Dr. Seuss. [T. Geisel]. 1938. *The 500 Hats of Bartholomew Cubbins*. New York: Vanguard. 4–7 yrs.
Esbensen, B. J. 1996. *Echoes for the Eye: Poems to Celebrate Patterns in Nature*. Illus. Helen K. Davie. New York: HarperCollins. 10–12 yrs.
Freedman, R. 1987. *Indian Chiefs*. Photos. New York: Holiday. 10–16 yrs.

———. 1989. *Lincoln: A Photobiography*. New York: Clarion. 9–12 yrs.
Fine, A. 1996. *Step by Wicked Step*. Boston, Mass.: Little, Brown. 9–12 yrs.
Forian, D. 1996. *On the Wing*. San Diego, Calif.: Harcourt Brace. 5–9 yrs.
Gag, W. 1977. *Millions of Cats*. New York: Putnam. 4–8 yrs.
Gardiner, J. 1980. *Stone Fox*. Illus. Marcia Sewell. New York: Crowell. 9–12 yrs.
George, J. 1989. *Shark Beneath the Reef*. New York: HarperCollins. 9–12 yrs.
Gordon, J. 1991. *Six Sleepy Sheep*. Illus. John O'Brien. Lanham, Md.: Caroline. 2–6 yrs.

Grahame, K. 1908. *Wind in the Willows*. New York: Scribners. 9–12 yrs.
Grover, M. 1996. *Circles & Squares Everywhere*. San Diego, Calif.: Browndeer/Harcourt Brace. 4–8 yrs.
Hamilton, V. 1967. *Zeely*. Illus. Symeon Shimin. New York: Macmillan. 9–12 yrs.
Heller, R. 1990. *Merry-Go-Round: A Book About Nouns*. New York: Grosset & Dunlap. 5–12 yrs.
Hesse, K. 1992. *Letter from Rifka*. New York: Holt. 10–14 yrs.
Hoff, S. 1996. *Danny and the Dinosaur Go to Camp*. New York: HarperCollins. 5–8 yrs. I Can Read Book series.
Hoffman, M. 1995. *Boundless Grace*. New York: Dial. 6–9 yrs.
Howe, D. & J. Howe. 1982. *Hawiday Inn*. Illus. L. Munsinger. New York: Atheneum. 8–11 yrs.
Hurwitz, J. 1990. *Class President*. Illus. Sheila Hamanaka. New York: Morrow. 8–11 yrs.
King-Smith, D. 1996. *Sophie's Lucky*. Illus. Davi Parkins. Cambridge, Mass.: Candlewick. 6–9 yrs.
Lauber, P. 1996. *You're Aboard Spaceship Earth*. Illus. Holly Keller. New York: HarperCollins. 5–8 yrs. Let's-Read-and-Find-Out Science series.
Levinson, R. 1986. *I Go with My Family to Grandma's*. Illus. D. Goode. New York: Dutton. 4–7 yrs.
Lewis, J. P. 1996. *Riddle-icious*. Illus. Debbie Tiley. New York: Knopf. 5–9 yrs.
Lobel, A. 1970. *Frog and Toad Are Friends*. New York: HarperCollins. 5–8 yrs.
London, J. 1994. *Call of the Wild*. Illus. Barry Moser. New York: Macmillan. 10–14 yrs.
Lowery, L. 1993. *The Giver*. Boston, Mass.: Houghton Mifflin. 11–14 yrs.
Martin, B. 1996. *"Fire! Fire!" Said Mrs. McGuire*. Illus. Richard Egielski. San Diego, Calif.: Harcourt Brace. 3–6 yrs.
Mahy, M. 1996. *Tingleberries, Tuckertubs, and Telephones: A Tale of Love and Ice Cream*. Illus. Robert Staermose. New York: Viking. 9–12 yrs.
McCaughrean, G. 1996. *The Golden Hoard: Myths and Legends of the World*. Illus. Bee Wiley. New York: McElderry. 9–12 yrs.
McSwigan, M. 1942. *Snow Treasure*. Illus. M. Reardon. New York: Dutton. 9–12 yrs.
Medearis, A. S. 1991. *Dancing with the Indians*. Illus. Samuel Byrd. New York: Holiday. 7–9 yrs.
Millen. C. M. 1996. A Symphony for the Sheep. Illus. Mary Azarian. Boston: Houghton. 4–6 yrs.
Milne, A. A. 1926. *Winnie the Pooh*. Illus. E. H. Shepard. New York: Dutton.
Nash, O. 1996. *Custard the Dragon and the Wicked Knight*. Illus. Lynn Munsinger. Boston: Little, Brown. 6–10 yrs.
O'Dell, S. 1960. *Island of the Blue Dolphin*. Boston, Mass.: Houghton Mifflin. 10–13 yrs.

Parish, H. 1995. *Good Driving, Amelia Bedelia*. Illus. Lynn Sweat. New York: Greenwillow. 6–9 yrs.
Paulsen, G. 1990. *Woodsong*. New York: Puffin. 9–12 yrs.
Peck, R. N. 1974. *Soup*. New York: Knopf. 6–9 yrs.
Potter, B. 1902. *The Tale of Peter Rabbit*. New York: Warne. 4–8 yrs.
Ring, E. 1994. *Sled Dogs: Arctic Athletes*. Brookfield, Conn.: Millbrook. 5–9 yrs. Good Dogs! Series.
Sendak, M. 1963. *Where the Wild Things Are*. New York: HarperCollins. 5–9 yrs.
Sierra, J. 1996. *Good Night, Dinosaurs*. Illus. Victoria Chees. New York: Clarion. 5–9 yrs.
Simon, S. 1996. *Wildfires*. Color photos. New York: Morrow. 5–9 yrs.
Sobol, D. 1971. *Encyclopedia Brown Tracks Them Down*. Illus. Leonard Shortall. New York: Crowell. 7–10 yrs.
Speare, E. G. 1983. *The Sign of the Beaver*. New York: Yearling. 9–13 yrs.
Wadsworth, G. 1994. *Susan Butcher: Sled Dog Racer*. Minneapolis, Minn.: Lerner. 10–13 yrs. Achievers series.
Walsh, M. 1996. *Do Pigs Have Stripes?* Boston: Houghton Mifflin. 3–6 yrs.
Wetterer, M. & C. Wetterer. 1996. *The Snow Walker*. Illus. Mary O'Keefe Young. Minneapolis, Minn.: Carolrhoda. 6–9 yrs. On My Own Books series.
Whelan, G. 1988. *Silver*. Illus. Stephen Marchesi. New York: Random House. 7–10 yrs. A Stepping Stone Book.
White, E. B. 1952. *Charlotte's Web*. Illus. Garth Williams. New York: HarperCollins. 7–12 yrs.
Williams, M. 1922. *The Velveteen Rabbit*. Illus. William Nicholson. New York: Doubleday. 7–12 yrs.
Williams, S. 1996. *I Went Walking*. Illus. Julie Vivas. San Diego, Calif.: Red Wagon. 2–5 yrs.

REPRESENTATIVE BOOKS FOR BEGINNING LEARNERS

PARTICIPATION BOOKS

Arnold, T. 1995. *No More Water in the Tub?* New York: Dial. 4–8 yrs. Ridiculous events, cumulative rhymes.
Buller, J. & S. Schade. 1988. *I Love You, Good Night*. New York: Simon & Schuster. 2–5 yrs. Patterned text.
Cauley, L. B. 1992. *Clap Your Hands*. New York: Putnam. 3–6 yrs. Physical movement.
Christelow, E. 1969. *Five Little Monkeys Jumping on the Bed*. New York: Clarion. 3–6 yrs. Patterned text.
Engerle, J. R. & S. G. Tessler. 1996. *Nell Nugget and the Cow Caper*. Illus. Paul Yalowitz. New York: Simon & Schuster. 5–8 yrs. Making sounds.

Falwell, C. 1991. *Clowning Around.* New York: Orchard. 3–6 yrs. Rearranging letters.

Faulkner, K. 1996. *The Wide-Mouthed Frog: A Pop-Up Book.* Illus. Jonathan Lambert. New York: Dial. 4–7 yrs. Toy book.

Godwin, S. 1996. *Where's Caterpillar? A Hide-and-Seek Peephole Book.* Illus. Louise Batchelor. Hauppauge, N.Y.: Barron's. 3–7 yrs. Toy book.

Hawkins, C. & J. Hawkins. 1987. *I Know an Old Lady Who Swallowed a Fly.* New York: Putnam. 5–9 yrs. Dramatics, patterned text.

Hill, E. 1980. *Where's Spot?* New York: Putnam. 3–6 yrs. Hidden objects.

Langstaff, J. 1984. *Oh, A-Hunting We Will Go.* New York: Atheneum. 5–9 yrs. Song.

London, J. 1996. *Fireflies, Fireflies, Light My Way.* Illus. Linda Messier. New York: Viking. 6–9 yrs. Lullaby, repetitive text.

MacKinnon, D. *What Am I?* Photos Anthea Sieveking. New York: Dial. 4–7 yrs. Guess the occupation.

Newcome, Z. 1996. *Toddlerobics.* Cambridge, Mass.: Candlewick. 2–4 yrs. Bouncy rhymes.

Pelham, D. 1996. *Crawlies Creep.* New York: Dutton. 3–5 yrs. Rhyming words, toy book.

Raffi. 1989. *Tingalayo.* New York: Crown. Song.

Rosen, M. 1989. *We're Going on a Bear Hunt.* Illus. Helen Oxenbury. New York: McElderry. 3–8 yrs. Physical movement.

Souhami, J. 1996. *Old MacDonald.* Designer Paul McAlinden. New York: Orchard. 3–6 yrs. Toy book.

Stevenson, J. 1990. *Quick! Turn the Page!* New York: Greenwillow. 4–7 yrs. Turn the page.

West, C. 1996. *"I Don't Care!" Said the Bear.* Cambridge, Mass.: Candlewick. 6–9 yrs. Recite with oral reader.

Yoshi. 1987. *Who's Hiding Here?* Saxonville, Mass.: Picture Book Studio. 4–7 yrs. Hidden objects.

PATTERNED TEXT

Akass, S. 1995. *Swim, Number Nine Duckling.* Illus. Alex Ayliffe. Honesdale, Penn.: Boyds Mills. 3–6 yrs. Predictable text.

Brown, M. W. 1947. *Goodnight Moon.* New York: HarperCollins. 2–5 yrs. Predictable text.

Capucilli, A. S. 1995. *Inside a Barn in the Country: A Rebus Read-Along Story.* Illus. Tedd Arnold. New York: Cartwheel. 2–5 yrs. Cumulative rhymes.

Carle, E. 1989. *The Very Busy Spider.* New York: Philomel. 4–7 yrs. Predictable text.

———. 1990. *The Very Quiet Cricket.* New York: Philomel. 4–8 yrs. Predictable text.

Cowen-Fletcher, J. *Baby Angels.* Cambridge, Mass.: Candlewick. 4–8 yrs. Repetitive text.

de Vries, A. 1996. *My Elephant Can Do Almost Anything.* Illus. Ilja Walraven. Arden, N.C.: Front. 4–7. Predictable text.

Duffy, D. D. 1996. *Forest Tracks.* Illus. Janet Marshall. Honesdale, Penn.: Boyds Mills. 4–6 yrs. Repetitive text, information.

Emberley, B. 1967. *Drummer Hoff.* Illus. E. Emberley. Englewood Cliffs, N.J.: Prentice-Hall. 5–8 yrs. Patterned text.

Fox, M. *Shoes from Grandpa.* Illus. Patricia Mullins. New York: Orchard. 3–6 yrs. Cumulative text.

Hubbard, P. 1996. *My Crayons Talk.* Illus. G. Brian Karas. New York: Martin/Holt. 3–6 yrs. Repetitive phrases, scribbly drawings.

Janovitz, M. 1996. *Can I Help?* New York: North-South. 4–6 yrs. Cumulative, rhyming dialogue.

Kitchen, B. 1992. *Somewhere Today.* Cambridge, Mass.: Candlewick. 5–9 yrs. Repetitive phrase; information.

Lewison, W. 1992. *Buzz Said the Bee.* New York: Scholastic. 4–6 yrs. Predictable rhymes.

Martin, B. 1967. *Brown Bear, Brown Bear, What Do You See?* Illus. Eric Carle. New York: Henry Holt. 4–6 yrs. Repetitive, predictable, rhyming text.

Melmed, L. K. 1996. *The Marvelous Market on Mermaid.* Illus. Maryann Kovalski. New York: Lothrop, Lee & Shepard. 6–9 yrs. Cumulative text.

Numeroff, L. J. 1985. *If You Give a Mouse a Cookie.* Illus. Felicia Bond. New York: HarperCollins. 4–7 yrs. Repetitive text.

Paul, A. 1995. *The Tiger Who Lost His Stripes.* Illus. Michael Foreman. San Diego, Calif.: Harcourt Brace. 6–9 yrs. Cumulative text.

Perry, S. 1995. *If . . .* Santa Monica, Calif.: Getty/Children's Library Press. Oral descriptions.

Rockwell, A. 1995. *NO! NO! NO!* New York: Macmillan. 3–6 yrs. Predictable text.

Slobodkina, E. 1947. *Caps for Sale.* Reading, Mass.: Addison-Wesley. 5–9 yrs. Predictable text.

Viorst, J. 1995. *Alexander Who Is Not (Do You Hear Me?) Going (I Mean It) to Move.* Illus. Robin Glasser. New York: Atheneum. 6–10 yrs. Predictable, repetitive text.

Walter, V. 1995. *"Hi, Pizza Man!"* Illus. Ponder Goembel. New York: Orchard/Jackson. 5–9 yrs. Repetitive, language play.

Wood, A. 1996. *The Napping House.* Illus. Don Wood. San Diego, Calif.: Red Wagon. 5–8 yrs. Cumulative rhyme.

Yektai, N. 1989. *What's Silly?* Illus. Susannah Ryan. New York: Clarion. 2–8 yrs. Predictable text, word play.

BOOKS WITH LANGUAGE PLAY

Baer, G. 1989. *Thump, Thump, Rat-a-Tat-Tat.* Illus. Lois Ehlert. New York: Harper & Row/Zolotow. 2–7 yrs. Onomatopoeia, rhythmic text.

Brown, M. W. 1993. *Four Fur Feet.* New York: Doubleday. 4–6 yrs. Alliteration.

Browne, P. 1996. *A Gaggle of Geese: The Collective Names of the Animal Kingdom.* New York: Atheneum. 6–9 yrs. Mnemonic, rhymed text.

Carle, E. 1974. *All About Arthur (An Absolutely Absurd Ape).* New York: Watts. 4–6 yrs. Alliteration, patterned text.

Carlstrom, N. W. 1992. *Baby-O.* Illus. Sucie Stevenson. Boston: Little, Brown. 3–6 yrs. Onomatopoeic refrains.

Catalanotto, P. 1990. *Mr. Mumble.* New York: Orchard/Jackson. 4–7 yrs. Play with words.

Cazet, D. 1994. *Nothing at All.* New York: Orchard/Jackson. 4–6 yrs. Repetitive phrase, silly words.

Degan, B. 1996. *Sailaway Home.* New York: Scholastic. 3–6 yrs. Rhythmic repetition of words.

Denim, S. 1996. *Make Way for Dumb Bunnies.* Illus. Dav Pilkey. New York: Blue Sky 6–9 yrs. Gags, puns, foolishness.

de Regniers, B., E. Moore, M. White, & J. Carr. 1988. *Sing a Song of Popcorn.* Illus. Caldecott artists. New York: Scholastic. 5–12 yrs. Many rhymes focus on sounds, patterns.

Enderle, J. R. & S. G. Tessler. 1996. *Nell Nugget and the Cow Caper.* Illus. Paul Yalowitz. New York: Simon & Schuster. 5–8 yrs. Predictable text, sounds.

Geraghty, P. 1992. *Stop That Noise!* New York: Crown. 3–6 yrs. Sounds.

Gordon, J. R. 1991. *Six Sleepy Sheep.* Illus. John O'Brien. Lanham, Md.: Caroline. 2–6 yrs. Alliterative prose, counting.

Hall, K. & L. Eisenberg. 1996. *Sheepish Riddles.* Illus. R. W. Alley. New York: Dial. 5–9 yrs.

Heller, R. 1995. *Behind the Mask: A Book about Prepositions.* New York: Grosset & Dunlap. 6–9 yrs. Parts of speech. See also other books by the author: *A Cache of Jewels and Other Collective Nouns; Kites Sail High, A Book About Verbs;* and *Many Luscious Lollipops: A Book About Adjectives.*

Hilton, N. 1990. *Prince Lachlan.* Illus. Ann James. New York: Orchard. 3–6 yrs. Repetitive phrases and onomatopoeia.

Knutson, K. *Ska-tat!* New York: Macmillan. 5–7 yrs. Onomatopoeia.

Kuskin, K. 1990. *Roar and More.* New York: HarperTrophy. 4–9 yrs. Onomatopoeia rhymes.

Linscott, J. 1991. *Once Upon A to Z: An Alphabet Odyssey.* Illus. Claudia Porges Holland. New York: Doubleday. 4–8 yrs. Alliterative stories.

MacCarthy, P. 1991. *Herds of Words.* New York: Dial. 3–6 yrs. Collective nouns.

Martin, B., Jr., & J. Archambault. 1989. *Chicka Chicka Boom Boom.* Illus. Lois Ehlert. New York: Simon & Schuster. Rhythm, alphabet, & sounds.

———. 1994. *The Maestro Plays.* Illus. Vladimir Radunsky. New York: Holt. 4–6 yrs. Rhyming adverbs, instruments in an orchestra.

Merriam, E. 1992. *Fighting Words.* Illus. David Small. New York: Morrow. 5–8 yrs. Using words.

Millen, C. M. 1996. *A Symphony for the Sheep.* Illus. Mary Azarian. Boston, Mass.: Houghton Mifflin. 4–6 yrs. Wordplay.

Murphy, S. J. 1996. *The Best Bug Parade.* Illus. Holly Keller. New York: HarperCollins. 6–9 yrs. MathStart series. Adjectives, comparison, information.

Parish, P. 1992. *Amelia Bedelia.* Illus. Fritz Siebel. New York: HarperCollins. 6–9 yrs. I Can Read series. Literal interpretation of words.

Powell, P. 1996. *Just Dessert.* San Diego, Calif.: Harcourt Brace. 6–9 yrs. Alliteration.

Showers, P. 1991. *The Listening Walk.* New York: HarperTrophy. 4–6 yrs. Sounds.

Sturges, P. 1996. *What's That Sound, Wooly Bear?* Illus. Joan Paley. Boston, Mass.: Little, Brown. 6–9 yrs. Sound and visual information.

Ziefert, H. 1996. *What Rhymes with Eel?* Illus. Rick Brown. New York: Viking. 4–6 yrs. Word families; toy book.

REPRESENTATIVE LITERATURE FOR TRANSITIONAL LEARNERS

EARLY READERS

Allen, L. J. 1992. *Rollo and Tweedy and the Ghost at Dougal Castle.* New York: HarperCollins. 5–8 yrs. I Can Read series.

Boland, J. 1996. *A Dog Named Sam.* Illus. G. Brian Karas. New York: Dial. 5–8 yrs.

Bonsall, C. 1992. *The Case of the Hungry Stranger.* New York: HarperCollins. 6–8 yrs. I Can Read series.

———. 1996. *Mine's the Best.* New York: HarperCollins. 6–9 yrs. My First I Can Read series.

Brown, M. 1996. *Arthur's Reading Race.* New York: Random House. 4–7 yrs. Step Into Reading Sticker Books series.

Buck, N. 1996. *Sid and Sam.* Illus. G. Brian Karas. New York: HarperCollins. 6–9 yrs. My First I Can Read Book Series.

Byars, B. 1996. *My Brother, Ant.* Illus. Marc Simont. New York: Viking. 6–8 yrs.

Calmenson, S. 1994. *Marigold and Grandma on the Town.* Illus. Mary Chalmers. New York: HarperCollins. 6–9 yrs. I Can Read series.

Capucilli, A. S. 1996. *Biscuit.* Illus. Pat Schories. New York: HarperCollins. 4–7 yrs. I Can Read Book Series.

Champion, J. 1995. *Emily and Alice Again.* Illus. Sucie Stevenson. San Diego, Calif.: Gulliver. 6–9 yrs.

Coerr, E. 1992. *The Big Balloon Race.* Illus. Carolyn Croll. New York: HarperCollins. 6–9 yrs. I Can Read series.

_____. 1995. *Buffalo Bill and the Pony Express.* Illus. Don Bolognese. New York: HarperCollins. 7–10 yrs. I Can Read Series.

Fox, M. 1994. *Tough Boris.* Illus. Kathryn Brown. San Diego, Calif.: Harcourt Brace. 6–9 yrs.

Griffith, H. V. 1995. *Grandaddy's Stars.* Illus. James Stevenson. New York: Greenwillow. 6–9 yrs.

Hall, D. 1994. *The Farm Summer 1942.* Illus. Barry Moser. New York: Dial. 8–10 yrs.

Hest, A. 1994. *Nannies for Hire.* Illus. Irene Trivas. New York: Morrow. 7–10 yrs.

Isaacson, P. M. 1995. *Round Buildings, Square Buildings, and Buildings That Wiggle Like a Fish.* Color photos. New York: Knopf. 9–12 yrs.

Jewell, N. 1996. *Silly Times with Two Silly Trolls.* Illus. Lisa Thiesing. New York: HarperCollins. 6–9 yrs. I Can Read Book series.

Kalan, R. 1996. *Moving Day.* Illus. Yossi Abolafia. New York: Greenwillow. 4–7 yrs.

Krensky, S. 1992. *Lionel and Louise.* Illus. Susanna Natti. New York: Dial. 6–8 yrs. Easy-to-Read series.

_____. 1994. *Lionel in the Winter.* Illus. Susanna Natti. New York: Dial. 6–8 yrs. Easy-to-Read series.

Levinson, N. S. 1992. *Snowshoe Thompson.* Illus. Joan Sandin. New York: HarperCollins. 6–9 yrs. I Can Read series.

McCully, E. A. 1993. *Grandmas at Bat.* New York: HarperCollins. 6–8 yrs. I Can Read series.

McLlerran, A. 1996. *The Year of the Ranch.* Illus. Kimberly Bulcken Root. New York: Viking. 6–9 yrs.

Novak, M. 1996. *Newt.* New York: HarperCollins. 6–8 yrs.

Parish, P. 1996. *Play Ball, Amelia Bedelia.* Illus. Wallace Tripp. New York: HarperCollins. 5–8 yrs. I Can Read Book series.

_____. 1996. *Granny and the Desperadoes.* Illus. Steven Kellogg. New York: Simon & Schuster. 6–9 yrs. Ready-to-Read Series.

Platt, K. 1992. *Big Max.* Illus. Robert Lopshire. New York: HarperCollins. 6–9 yrs. I Can Read Series.

Rylant, C. 1994. *Mr. Puffer and Tabby Bake the Cake.* Illus. Arthur Howard. San Diego, Calif.: Harcourt Brace. 6–8 yrs.

_____. 1994. *Mr. Putter and Tabby Pour the Tea.* Illus. Arthur Howard. San Diego, Calif.: Harcourt Brace. 6–8 yrs.

_____. 1994. *Mr. Putter and Tabby Walk the Dog.* Illus. Arthur Howard. San Diego, Calif.: Harcourt Brace. 6–8 yrs.

_____. 1995. *Henry and Mudge and the Best Day of All: The Fourteenth Book of Their Adventures.* Illus. Sucie Stevenson. New York: Macmillan. 5–9 yrs.

Sharmat, M. W. 1996. *Mitchell Is Moving.* Illus. Jose Aruego & Ariane Dewey. New York: Simon & Schuster. 6–9 yrs. Ready-to-Read Series.

Skofield, J. 1996. *Detective Dinosaur.* Illus. R. W. Alley. New York: HarperCollins. 6–9 yrs. I Can Read Book series.

Van Leeuwen, J. 1992. *Oliver and Amanda's Halloween.* Illus. Ann Schweninger. New York: Dial. 6–8 yrs. Easy-to-Read series.

TRANSITIONAL READERS

Ackerman, K. 1995. *Bingleman's Midway.* Illus. Barry Moser. Honesdale, Penn.: Boyds Mills. 6–9 yrs.

Alphin, E. M. 1996. *A Bear for Miguel.* Illus. Joan Sandin. New York: HarperCollins. 6–9 yrs. I Can Read Book series.

Armstrong, J. 1996. *Patrick Doyle Is Full of Blarney.* Illus. Krista Brauckmann-Towns. New York: Random House. 6–9 yrs. Stepping Stone Book series.

Arnosky, J. 1995. *I See Animals Hiding.* New York: Scholastic. 5–9 yrs.

Bauer, M. D. 1996. *Alison's Wings.* Illus. Roger Roth. New York: Hyperion. 7–9 yrs.

Blos, J. W. 1996. *Nellie Bly's Monkey: His Remarkable Story in His Own Words.* Illus. Catherine Stock. New York: Morrow. 7–10 yrs.

Buehner, C. 1995. *It's a Spoon, Not a Shovel.* Illus. Mark Buehner. New York: Dial. 5–9 yrs.

Byars, B. 1994. *The Golly Sisters Ride Again.* Illus. Sue Truesdell. New York: HarperCollins. 7–9 yrs. I Can Read series.

Carmichael, C. 1996. *Bear at the Beach.* New York: North-South. 5–8 yrs.

Caseley, J. 1994. *Harry and Arney.* New York: Greenwillow. 7–9 yrs.

Cech, J. 1996. *The Southermost Cat.* Illus. Kathy Osborn. New York: Simon & Schuster. 7–9 yrs.

Champion, J. 1995. *Emily and Alice Again.* Illus. Sucie Stevenson. San Diego, Calif.: Gulliver. 6–9 yrs.

Doherty, B. 1994. *Willa and Old Miss Annie.* Illus. Kim Lewis. Cambridge, Mass.: Candlewick. 7–9 yrs.

Ehlert, L. 1996. *Under My Nose.* Photos Carlo Ontal. Katonah, N.Y.: Owen. 5–9 yrs. Meet the Author series. Also see other books in the series.

Greene, S. 1996. *Owen Foote, Second Grade Strongman.* Illus. Dee DeRosa. New York: Clarion. 6–9 yrs.

Griffith, H. V. 1995. *Grandaddy's Stars.* Illus. James Stevenson. New York: Greenwillow. 6–9 yrs.

Hall, D. 1996. *When Willard Met Babe Ruth.* Illus. Barry Moser. New York: Browndeer. 6–9 yrs.

Hass, J. 1996. *Clean House.* Illus. Yossi Abolafia. New York: Greenwillow. 6–9 yrs.

Heller, R. 1996. *Fine Lines.* Photos Michael Emery. Katonah, N.Y.: Owen. 5–9 yrs. Meet the Author series.

Hesse, K. 1994. *Sable.* Illus. Marcia Sewall. New York: Holt. 7–9 yrs. Redfeather series.

Howe, J. 1996. *Pinky and Rex and the Bully.* Illus. Melissa Sweet. New York: Atheneum. 7–9 yrs. Ready-to-Read series.

Hurwitz, J. 1995. *Elisa in the Middle.* Illus. Lillian Hoban. New York: Morrow. 6–9 yrs.

Lauber, P. 1995. *Who Eats What?: Food Chains and Food Webs.* Illus. Holly Keller. New York: HarperCollins. 5–9 yrs. Let's-Read-and-Find-Out Science series.

Lyon, G. E. 1996. *A Wordful Child.* Photos Ann W. Olson. Katonah, N.Y.: Owen. 5–9 yrs. Meet the Author series.

Markle, S. 1995. *Outside and Inside Snakes.* Color photos. New York: Macmillan. 5–9 yrs.

_____. 1996. *Outside and Inside Sharks.* Color photos. New York: Atheneum. 5–9 yrs.

Marshall, J. 1993. *Rats on the Range and Other Stories.* New York: Dial. 6–9 yrs.

_____. 1993. *Fox on Stage.* New York: Dial. 6–8 yrs. Easy-to-Read series.

Martin, J. B. 1996. *Grandmother Bryant's Pocket.* Illus. Petra Mathers. Boston: Houghton Mifflin. 6–9 yrs.

Matthews, M. 1996. *Magid Fasts for Ramadan.* Illus. E. B. Lewis. New York: Clarion. 6–9 yrs.

McCaulay, D. 1995. *Shortcut.* Boston: Houghton Mifflin. 7–10 yrs.

Nerlove, M. 1996. *Flowers on the Wall.* New York: McElderry. 6–9 yrs.

Novak, M. 1996. *Newt.* New York: HarperCollins. 6–8 yrs.

Patent, D. H. 1995. *Why Mammals Have Fur.* Photos William Muhoz. New York: Cobblehill. 5–9 yrs.

Pfeffer, S. B. 1996. *The Trouble with Wishes.* Illus. Jennifer Plecas. New York: Holt. 7–10 yrs. Redfeather Book series.

Pfeffer, W. 1996. *What's It Like to Be a Fish?* Illus. Holly Keller. New York: HarperCollins. 5–9 yrs. Let's-Read-and-Find-Out Science series.

Sanfield, S. 1996. *The Great Turtle Drive.* Illus. Dirk Zimmer. New York: Knopf. 7–10 yrs.

Schroeder, A. 1996. *Minty: A Story of Young Harriet Tubman.* Illus. Jerry Pinkney. New York: Dial. 6–9 yrs.

Schur, M. R. 1996. *When I Left My Village.* Illus. Brian Pinkney. New York: Dial. 6–9 yrs.

Spinelli, J. 1995. *Tooter Pepperday.* Illus. Donna Nelson. New York: Random House. 7–9 yrs. First Stepping Stone Series.

Stevenson, J. 1994. *Mud Flat Olympics.* New York: Greenwillow. 7–9 yrs.

_____. 1995. *A Village Full of Valentines.* New York: Greenwillow. 7–9 yrs.

_____. 1996. *Yard Sale.* New York: Greenwillow. 6–9 yrs.

Sweeney, J. 1996. *Me on the Map.* Illus. Annette Cable; photos. New York: Crown. 5–9 yrs.

Taberski, S. 1996. *Morning, Noon, and Night: Poems to Fill Your Day.* Illus. Nancy Doniger. Greenvale, N.Y.: Mondo. 5–9 yrs.

Van Leeuwen, J. 1994. *Two Girls in Sister Dresses.* Illus. Linda Benson. New York: Dial. 6–8 yrs.

Waggoner, K. 1995. *Partners.* Illus. Cat Bowman Smith. New York: Simon & Schuster. 7–10 yrs.

Willner-Pardo, G. 1996. *Hunting Grandma's Treasures.* Illus. Walter Lyon Krudop. New York: Clarion. 6–9 yrs.

York, C. B. 1994. *The Key to the Playhouse.* Illus. John Speirs. New York: Scholastic. 7–10 yrs.

SERIES FOR TRANSITION READERS

All Aboard Reading Series
Bank Street Ready-to-Read Series
Break-of-Day Series
Dino Easy Reader Series
Easy-to-Read Series
Hello Reading! Series
I Can Read Series
Step into Reading Series

INDIVIDUAL SERIES POPULAR WITH TRANSITIONAL READERS

David Adler, Cam Jansen (a mystery series)
Russell Hoban, Frances, the Badger (low fantasy, animal series)
Arnold Lobel, Toad and Frog Series (low fantasy, animal series)
Peggy & Herman Parrish, Amelia Bedelia Series (humorous literal interpretation of the language)
Kim Platt, Big Max Series (a detective series)
Cynthia Rylant, Henry and Mudge Series (a child and dog)
Marjorie Weinman Sharmat, Nate the Great (a detective series)
Dr. Seuss, Cat in the Hat Series (humorous language play)

REPRESENTATIVE LITERATURE FOR MATURING LEARNERS

Anaya, R. 1995. *The Farolitos of Christmas.* Illus. Edward Gonzales. New York: Hyperion. 6–9 yrs.

Anderson, J. 1996. *Batboy: An Inside Look at Spring Training.* Photos Matthew Cavanaugh. New York: Lodestar. 9–12 yrs.

Blegvad, L. 1996. *A Sound of Leaves.* New York: McElderry. 9–12 yrs.

Brandenburg, J. (Joann Bren Guernsey, Ed.). 1995. *An American Safari: Adventures on the*

North American Prairie. Color photos. New York: Walker. 9–12.

Brennan, H. 1995. *The Mystery Machine.* New York: McElderry. 9–12 yrs.

Christopher, M. 1996. *Olympic Dream.* Illus. Karen Meyer. Boston, Mass.: Little, Brown. 9–12 yrs.

Cole, J. & S. Wendy. 1996. *On the Bus with Joanna Cole: A Creative Autobiography.* Portsmouth, N.H.: Heinemann. 9–12 yrs. Creative Sparks series.

Cutler, J. 1996. *Rats!* Illus. Tracey Campbell Pearson. New York: Farrar, Straus & Giroux. 9–12 yrs.

Danziger, P. 1995. *Amber Brown Goes Fourth.* Illus. Tony Ross. New York: Putnam. 7–10 yrs.

———. 1995. *You Can't Eat Your Chicken Pox, Amber Brown.* Illus. Tony Ross. New York: Putnam. 7–10 yrs.

Demi. 1996. *Buddha.* New York: Holt. 6–10 yrs.

Duffey, B. 1995. *Utterly Yours, Booker Jones.* New York: Viking. 9–12 yrs.

———. 1996. *Hey, New Kid!* Illus. Ellen Thompson. New York: Viking. 9–12 yrs.

Hopkins, L. B. 1996. *Opening Days: Sport Poems.* Illus. Scott Medlock. San Diego, Calif.: Harcourt Brace. 9–12 yrs.

Hurwitz, J. 1995. *Ozzie on His Own.* Illus. Eileen McKeating. New York: Morrow. 9–12 yrs.

Kalman, E. 1995. *Tchaikovsky Discovers America.* Illus. Laura Fernandez & Rick Jacobson. New York: Orchard. 7–10 yrs.

Kamen, G. 1996. *Hidden Music: The Life of Fanny Mendelssohn.* New York: Atheneum. 9–12 yrs.

Kroll, S. 1996. *Pony Express!* Illus. Dan Andreasen. New York: Scholastic. 6–10 yrs.

Leverich, K. 1995. *Best Enemies Forever.* Illus. Walter Lorraine. New York: Greenwillow. 7–10 yrs.

Lowry, L. 1995. *Anastasia, Absolutely.* Boston: Houghton Mifflin. 9–12 yrs.

MacLachlan, P. 1986. *Sarah, Plain and Tall.* New York: HarperCollins. 9–12 yrs.

McPhail, D. 1996. *In Flight with David McPhail: A Creative Autobiography.* Portsmouth, N.H.: Heinemann. 9–12 yrs. Creative Sparks series.

Meyer, C. 1996. *In a Different Light: Growing Up in a Yuptik Eskimo Village in Alaska.* Photos John McDonald. New York: McElderry. 9–12 yrs.

Morpurgo, M. 1996. *The Wreck of the Zanzibar.* Illus. François Place. New York: Viking. 9–12 yrs.

Murphy, J. 1996. *A Young Patriot: The American Revolution as Experienced by One Boy.* Reproductions. New York: Clarion. 9–12 yrs.

Naylor, P. R. 1996. *Alice in Lace.* New York: Atheneum/Karl. 9–12 yrs.

Quinlan, S. E. 1995. *The Case of the Mummified Pigs: And Other Mysteries in Nature.* Illus. Jennifer Owings Dewey. Honesdale, Penn.: Boyds Mills. 9–12 yrs.

Rounds, G. 1995. *Sod Houses on the Great Plain.* New York: Holiday. 6–9 yrs.

Sawyer, R. 1995. *Roller Skates.* Illus. Valenti Angelo. New York: Viking. 9–11 yrs.

Shakespeare, W. (Ann Keay Beneduce, reteller). 1996. *The Tempest.* Illus. Gennady Spirin. New York: Philomel. 9–12 yrs.

Sneve, V. D. H. 1996. *The Cherokees.* Illus. Ronald Himler. New York: Holiday. 9–12 yrs. First Americans Book series.

Spinelli, E. 1995. *Lizzie Logan Wears Purple Sunglasses.* Illus. Melanie Hope Greenberg. New York: Simon & Schuster. 7–10 yrs.

Spinelli, J. 1996. *Crash.* New York: Knopf. 9–12 yrs.

Stanley, J. 1996. *Big Annie of Calumet: A True Story of the Industrial Revolution.* New York: Crown. 9–12 yrs.

Stefoff, R. 1996. *Children of the Westward Trail.* Archival photos & drawings. Brookfield, Conn.: Millbrook. 9–12 yrs.

Thurber, J. 1994. *Great Quillow.* Illus. Steven Kellogg. San Diego, Calif.: Harcourt Brace. 9–12 yrs. Contemporary Classic series.

Vail, R. 1996. *Daring to Be Abigail.* New York: Orchard/Jackson. 10–13 yrs.

Venezia, M. 1996. *Ludwig van Beethoven.* Paintings, engravings, color cartoons. Chicago, Ill.: Children's Press. 5–9 yrs. Getting to Know the World's Greatest Composers series.

Wells, R. (Reteller). 1995. *Lassie Come Home.* Illus. Susan Jeffers. New York: Holt. 7–10 yrs.

Wexler, J. 1995. *Sundew Stranglers: Plants That Eat Insects.* Color photos. New York: Dutton. 9–12 yrs.

Wilson, J. 1996. *The Ingenious Mr. Peale: Painter, Patriot and Man of Science.* Illus. Charles Wilson Peale. New York: Atheneum. 9–12 yrs.

Wright, B. R. 1996. *Haunted Summer.* New York: Scholastic. 9–12 yrs.

Yolen, J. 1996. *Passager.* San Diego, Calif.: Harcourt Brace. 9–12 yrs. Young Merlin Trilogy.

CHAPTER 12

CHILDREN'S BOOKS MENTIONED IN THE CHAPTER

Aylesworth, J. 1992. *Old Black Fly.* Illus. Stephen Gammell. New York: Holt. 5–8 yrs.

Babbitt, N. 1975. *Tuck Everlasting.* New York: Farrar, Straus & Giroux. 9–12 yrs.

Beatty, P. 1987. *Charley Skedaddle.* New York: Morrow. 9–12 yrs.

Belton, S. 1996. *Ernestine & Amanda.* New York: Simon & Schuster. 9–12 yrs.

Brown, M. 1996. *Arthur Goes to School.* New York: Random House. 3–5 yrs.

Byars, B. 1970. *Summer of the Swans.* New York: Viking. 10–13 yrs.

Duggleby, J. 1996. *Artist in Overalls: The Life of Grant Wood.* San Francisco, Calif.: Chronicle. 8–12 yrs.

Foley, M. 1996. *Fundamental Hockey.* Photos Andy King. Minneapolis, Minn.: Lerner. 9–12 yrs.

Freedman, R. 1989. *Lincoln: A Photobiography.* New York: Clarion. 9–14 yrs.

Gardiner, J. *Stone Fox.* 1980. Illus. Marcia Sewall. New York: HarperTrophy. 9–12 yrs.

George, G. C. 1972. *Julie and the Wolves.* Illus. J. Schoenheer. New York: HarperCollins. 10–14 yrs.

Gray, L. 1995. *My Mama Had a Dancing Heart.* Illus. Raul Colon. New York: Orchard. 7–10 yrs.

Lauber, P. 1995. *Who Eats What?: Food Chains and Food Webs.* Photos. New York: Scholastic. 9–12 yrs.

Lewis, P. O. 1995. *Storm Boy.* Hillsboro, Ore.: Beyond Words. 7–10 yrs.

McSwaig, M. 1942. *Snow Treasure.* New York: Scholastic. 10–13 yrs.

Numeroff, L. J. 1985. *If You Give a Mouse a Cookie.* Illus. Felicia Bond. New York: Harper. 4–7 yrs.

Reeder, C. 1989. *Shades of Gray.* New York: Macmillan. 9–12 yrs.

Stanley, D. 1992. *Bard of Avon: The Story of William Shakespeare.* New York: Morrow. 9–12 yrs.

———. 1993. *Charles Dickens: The Man Who Had Great Expectations.* New York: Morrow. 9–12 yrs.

———. 1996. *Leonardo da Vinci.* New York: Morrow. 9–12 yrs.

Taylor, M. 1990. *Mississippi Bridge.* Illus. Max Ginsburg. New York: Dial. 8–12 yrs.

Waddell, M. 1992. *The Pig in the Pond.* Illus. Jill Barton. Cambridge, Mass.: Candlewick. 5–8 yrs.

Wood, T. 1996. *Iditarod Dream: Dusty and His Sled Dogs Compete in Alaska's Jr. Iditarod.* Photos. New York: Walker. 9–12 yrs.

Van Allsburg, C. 1995. *Bad Day at Riverbend.* Boston: Houghton Mifflin. 4–8 yrs.

Yolen, J. 1987. *Owl Moon.* Illus. John Schoenherr. New York: Philomel. 5–10 yrs.

———. 1996. *Passager.* San Diego, Calif.: Harcourt Brace. 9–12 yrs.

Credits

Chapter 1

5: Art from *Swamp Angel* by Anne Isaacs, illustrated by Paul O. Zelinsky. Illustrations copyright © 1994 by Paul O. Zelinsky. Used by permission of Dutton Children's Books, a division of Penguin Books USA Inc. **10:** Photo Tony Freeman/ PhotoEdit. **13:** Art from *The Midnight Farm* by Reeve Lindbergh, illustrated by Susan Jeffers. Illustrations copyright © 1987 by Susan Jeffers. Used by permission of Dial Books for Young Readers, a division of Penguin Books USA Inc. **14:** Photo Myrleen Ferguson Cate/PhotoEdit. **16:** Photo Richard Hutchings/PhotoEdit. **17:** Art from Laura Ingalls Wilder, *Little House in the Big Woods*. Pictures copyright 1953 by Garth Williams. Renewed 1981 by Garth Williams. "Little House"® is a registered trademark of HarperCollins Publishers, Inc. Used by permission of HarperCollins Publishers.

Chapter 2

32: Art by John Schoenherr, used by permission of Philomel Books from *Owl Moon* by Jane Yolen; illustrations copyright © 1994 by John Schoenherr. **34:** Photo David Young-Wolff/PhotoEdit. **36:** Photo Frank Siteman/PhotoEdit. **39:** Photo Tony Freeman/PhotoEdit. **40:** Photo David Young-Wolff/PhotoEdit. **45:** Art from *Rondo in C* by Paul Fleischman, illustrated by Janet Wentworth, 1988. Published by Harper & Row Publishers, Inc. Used by permission of the illustrator. **46:** Art from *April's Kittens* published by Harper & Row. Copyright © 1940 by Claire Turlay Newberry. Used by permission of McIntosh & Otis, Inc. **53:** Photo Nancy Sheehan/PhotoEdit.

Chapter 3

69: Art by Leo & Diane Dillon from *Her Stories: African American Folktales, Fairy Tales, and True Tales* by Virginia Hamilton. Illustrations copyright © by Leo & Diane Dillon. Used by permission of Scholastic Inc. **70:** Photo courtesy of Diane & Leo Dillon. **78:** Art The Granger Collection, New York. **83:** Art from *William Tell* by Leonard Everett Fisher. Copyright © 1996 by Leonard Everett Fisher. Used by permission of Farrar, Straus & Giroux, Inc. **85:** Art from *American Tall Tales* by Mary Pope Osborne, illustrated by Michael McCurdy. Illustrations copyright © 1991 by Michael McCurdy. Used by permission of Alfred A. Knopf, Inc. **87:** Photo The Granger Collection, New York. **88:** Art from pp. 21–22 of *Mufaro's Beautiful Daughters* by John Steptoe. Copyright © 1987 by John Steptoe. Used by permission of Lothrop, Lee & Shepard Books, a division of William Morrow & Company, Inc. with the approval of the John Steptoe Literary Trust. **90:** Art The Granger Collection, New York. **91:** Art by Floyd Cooper, used by permission of Philomel Books from *The Girl Who Loved Caterpillars*, adapted by Jean Merril. Illustrations copyright © 1992 by Floyd Cooper. **93:** Art from *Rapunzel* by Alix Berenzy. Copyright © 1995 by Alix Berenzy. Used by permission of Henry Holt and Co., Inc. **98:** Art from *Zomo the Rabbit: A Trickster Tale from West Africa*, Copyright © 1992 by Gerald McDermott, reproduced by permission of Harcourt Brace & Company. **99:** Art from *Aesop's Fables* illustrated by Lisbeth Zerger. Copyright © 1989 Neugebauer Press, Salzburg, Austria. Used by permission of Simon & Schuster Books for Young Readers, an imprint of Simon & Schuster Children's Publishing Division.

Chapter 4

106: Art The Granger Collection, New York. **107:** Art from Maurice Sendak, *Where the Wild Things Are*. Copyright © 1963 by Maurice Sendak. Used by permission of HarperCollins Publishers. This selection may not be re-illustrated. **110:** Art from *The Spider Who Created the World* by Amy MacDonald, illustrated by G. Brian Karas. Illustration copyright by G. Brian Karas. Reproduced by permission of Orchard Books, New York. **112:** Photo The Granger Collection, New York. **115:** Art from *Tooth Fairy* by Peter Collington. Copyright © 1995 by Peter Collington. Used by permission of Alfred A. Knopf, Inc. **116:** Art from *Angela's Wings* by Eric Jon Nones. Copyright © 1995 by Eric Jon Nones. Used by permission of Farrar, Straus & Giroux, Inc. **117:** Photo Penguin USA/Vanessa Hamilton. **121:** Art from *Saint George and the Dragon* by Margaret Hodges. Text Copyright © 1984 by Margaret Hodges; illustrations copyright © 1984 by Trina Schart Hyman. Used by permission of Little, Brown and Company. **123:** Art The Granger Collection, New York. **130:** Art from *The Grey Lady and the Strawberry Snatcher* by Molly Bang. Copyright © 1980 Molly Bang. Used by permission of Simon & Schuster Books for Young Readers, an imprint of Simon & Schuster Children's Publishing Division. **133:** Art from *Night of the Gargoyles* by Eve Bunting. Illustrations copyright © 1994 by David Wiesner. Used by permission of Clarion Books/ Houghton Mifflin Company. All rights reserved.

Chapter 5

141: Photo Penguin USA/Andrea Cruise. **142:** Art by Tomie dePaola, used by permission of G. P. Putnam's Sons from *The Baby Sister*, copyright © 1996 by Tomie dePaola. **143:** Art from *Encounter* by Jane Yolen, illustrations copyright © 1992 by David Shannon, reproduced by permission of Harcourt Brace & Co. **144:** Art from *The Year of the Perfect Christmas Tree* by Gloria Houston, illustrated by Barbara Cooney. Illustrations copyright © 1988 by Barbara Cooney. Used by permission of Dial Books for Young Readers, a division of Penguin Books USA Inc. **146:** Art from *Peppe the Lamplighter* by Elisa Bartone, pp. 8–9. Illustrated by Ted Lewin. Illustration copyright © by Ted Lewin. Used by permission of Lothrop, Lee & Shepard Books, a division of William Morrow & Company, Inc. **148:** Art from *The Eleventh Hour* by Graeme Base, published by Penguin Australia Ltd. Used by permission of the publisher. **152:** Art (left and right) The Granger Collection, New York. **153:** Photo Simon & Schuster Children's Publishing Division/Rebecca Grose. **154:** Art from Alexander, *Who's Not (Do You Hear Me? I Mean It!) Going to Move* by Judith Viorst, illustrated by Robin Preiss Glasser in the style of Ray Cruz. Illustrations copyright © 1995 by Robin Preiss Glasser. Used by permission of Atheneum Books for Young Readers, an imprint of Simon & Schuster Children's Publishing Division. Photo Robin L. Sachs/PhotoEdit. **159:** Art from *Wagons West!* by Roy Gerrard. Copyright © 1996 by Roy Gerrard. Used by permission of Farrar, Straus & Giroux, Inc.

Chapter 6

169: Art used by permission of The Walters Art Gallery, Baltimore. **171:** Art from *Gandhi* by Leonard Everett Fisher. Copyright © 1995 Leonard Everett Fisher. Used by permission of Atheneum Books for Young Readers, an imprint of Simon & Schuster Children's Publishing Division. **172:** Art from *Grandfather's Journeys*. Copyright © 1993 by Allen Say. Used by permission of Houghton Mifflin Company. All rights reserved. **175:** Photo courtesy of Russell Freedman. **176:** Art from *My Fellow Americans: A Family Album*, copyright © 1995 by Alice Provensen, reproduced by permission of Harcourt Brace & Company. **181:** Art from *Cleopatra* by Diane Stanley and Peter Vennema. Illustration Copyright © 1994 by Diane Stanley Vennema. Used by permission of Morrow Junior Books, a division of William Morrow & Company, Inc. **184:** Art from *Stephen Biesty's Incredible Cross-Sections* by Stephen Biesty. Copyright © 1992 by Dorling Kindersley Limited. Used by permission of Alfred A. Knopf, Inc. **185:** Photo Harcourt Brace & Co./Kent Ancliffe. **187:** Art from *Where Once There Was a Wood* by Denise Fleming. Copyright © 1996 by Denise Fleming. Used by permission of Henry Holt and Co., Inc. **192:** Art from *Alphabet City* by Stephen T. Johnson. Copyright © 1995 by Stephen T. Johnson. Used by permission of Viking Kenstrel, a division of Penguin Books USA Inc. **193:** Photograph from *My New Kitten* by Joanna Cole. Photograph by Margaret Miller. Photographs © 1995 by Margaret Miller. Used by permission of Morrow Junior Books, a division of William Morrow & Co., Inc. **196:** Art from *Zin! Zin! A Violin* by Lloyd Moss, illustrated by Marjorie Priceman. Illustrations copyright © 1995 Marjorie Priceman. Used by permission of Simon & Schuster Books for Young Readers. **197:** Art from author John Amos Comenius, *Orbis Sensualium Pictus*, London 1700, p. 20, Flowers, KC1700, The Rare Books and Manuscript Division, The New York Public Library, Astor, Lenox, and Tilden Foundations. Used by permission of the New York Public Library.

Chapter 7

207: "Go With the Poem," Lilian Moore. Copyright © 1975 Lilian Moore. Used by permission of Marian Reiner for the author. **208:** "Poetry," Eleanor Farjeon. Used by permission of Harold Obe Associates, Inc. Copyright © 1938 by Eleanor Farjeon. Copyright renewed 1966 by Gervase Farjeon. **209:** Art from *Animal Cracker* by Jane Dyer. Copyright © 1996 by Jane Dyer. Used by permission of Little, Brown and Company. "Poems" by Bobbi Katz from *Inner Chimes, Poems on Poetry* selected by Bobbye S. Goldstein, copyright © 1992. Published by Wordsong/Boyds Mills Press, Inc. Used by permission of Boyds Mills Press, Inc. "Mummy Slept Late and Daddy Fixed Breakfast" from *You Read to Me, I'll Read to You* by John Ciardi. Copyright © 1962 by John Ciardi. Used by permission of HarperCollins Publishers. This selection may not be re-illustrated. **210:** "This Is My Rock" from *One at a Time* by David McCord. Copyright 1929 by David McCord. First appeared in the *Saturday Review*. Used by permission of Little, Brown and Company. "Keziah" from *Bronzeville Boys and Girls* by Gwendolyn Brooks. Copyright © 1956 by Gwendolyn Brooks Blakely. Used by permission of HarperCollins Publishers. **212:** "Feelings About Words" from *WORDS WORDS WORDS* by Mary O'Neill. Copyright © 1966 Mary O'Neill. © renewed 1993 Abigail Hagler and Erin Baroni. Used by permission of Marian Reiner. "Woodpecker" by Jane Yolen used by permission of Philomel Books from *Bird Watch*, text copyright © 1990 by Jane Yolen. **214:** Art from *If You're Not from the Prairie . . .* by David Bouchard, images by Henry Ripplinger. Illustrations copyright © 1995 Henry Ripplinger. Used by permission of Atheneum Books for Young Readers, an imprint of Simon & Schuster Children's Publishing Division. "Snow" from *Dogs & Dragons, Trees & Dreams* by Karla Kuskin. Copyright © by Karla Kuskin. Used by permission of HarperCollins Publishers. **215:** "The Other Side of the Door" from *The Other Side of the Door* by Jeff Moss. Copyright © 1991 by Jeff Moss. Used by permission of Bantam Books, a division of Bantam Doubleday Dell Publishing Group, Inc. "There Was an Old Man of Dundee" by Edward Lear from *A Book of Nonsense*, © 1992. Used by permission of Garland Publishing. **216:** "We Have Our Moments" from *Sports Pages* by Arnold Adoff. Text copyright © 1986 by Arnold Adoff. Used by permission of HarperCollins Publishers. This selection may not be re-illustrated.

Name & Title Index

Subject Index